Walking *by* the Spirit

Walking *by* the Spirit

Walking by the Spirit is presented as a class, with each chapter building on the truths of previous chapters. The first time through it is best studied systematically, in order, to get the most from it.

First published 2016

George Maciver

This work is published to the public domain under a Creative Commons Attribution – Non Commercial – No Derivatives international Licence. This work may be reproduced in any form, by photocopying or by any electronic or mechanical means, including information storage and retrieval systems, and distributed or translated in any format, printed or digital, provided this work is credited, it is not done for profit, and absolutely no changes of any kind are made to the text.

Walking by the Spirit

1. Why Read the Bible?	7
2. The Way of Life	15
3. Spiritual Integrity	20
4. The Law of Believing	36
5. Spiritual Integrity part 2	49
6. Dealing with Fear	62
7. Agapē: The Love of God	68
8. The Parting of the Red Sea	81
9. God is Faithful	88
10. God is our Protection	100
11. Angels	110
12. Smashed and Trashed	125
13. The Fall of Man	139
14. The god of this World	155
15. How we got the Bible	163
16. The Renewed Mind	175
17. Homosexuality: The Way of Life	189
18. Homosexuality: The Way of Death	198
19. Climate Change	208
20. Health and Nutrition	222
21. What Cost Priceless?	245
22. The Family	252
23. Military Intelligence	272
24. Weishaupt and the Illuminati	300
25. The Jesuits	310
26. Jesus Christ is not God	317
27. Where Are the Dead?	328
28. Predestination	345
29. The Course of this World	356
30. Christ and Christmas	370
31. The Wise Men and the Star	374
32. The Birth of Jesus Christ	385
33. Christmas and the Way of Life	395
34. God's Masterpiece	401
35. A Free Gift	410
36. God-Given Rights	418

37. Get Over It!	436
38. The Voice of God	457
39. Manifesting the Power of God	467
40. Filled to Overflowing	475
41. The Ages of Spirit	485
42. The Mystery	504
43. In Spirit and in Truth	511
44. Temples made with Hands	528
45. The Church in the Home	540
46. Self Governing	553
47. Self Propagating	566
48. Self Supporting	596
49. The More Abundant Life	627
50. Demonstrating God's Power	641
51. God's Delivering Nature	663
52. Living Victoriously	693
53. Jonah	703
54. At Thy Word	714
55. God is not Jesus Christ	730
56. Five Crucified	743
57. The Hope	754
58. The Revelation Administration	765
59. Money	776
60. Walking tongues	787
61. A Titanic Crime	796
62. Symptoms of Religion	806
63. 1 Corinthians 12	830
64. The Council of Acts 15	861
65. The Higher Powers	879
66. How to do Biblical Research	892
67. Peter, a very Human Man	900
68. The British Olympic Opening Ceremony	924
69. The Making of a Patriarch	926
70. Christ in You, the Hope of Glory	935
71. Distinctions	954
72. The Manifestation of Believing	970
73. 1 Corinthians 14	990
74. The Revelation Manifestations	1008
75. Miracles	1027
76. Healing	1040
77. The Way of Life Today	1068
Appendix – Uses of Pneuma	1093

1. Why Read the Bible?

Just as we learn anything in life, so it is with the spiritual – we must first learn about it and then practice it. Yes, we can walk by the spirit and have cosy, family fellowship with God, it is available, but first we have to learn about the gift of holy spirit, how to receive it, and how to energise it so that we can enjoy fellowship with him.

Learning anything in life requires effort and commitment. The spiritual knowledge of how to have fellowship with God can only be found in his word, so if you want fellowship with him you must first learn how to read the bible.

I think we all want to live a life which is more abundant. We all want to live powerful lives, victorious lives, with each day an adventure in living. That kind of life is available. It says so in John 10:10.

> John 10:10
> The thief cometh not, but for to steal, and to kill, and to destroy: I am come that they might have life, and that they might have *it* more abundantly.

Jesus Christ came so we could have an amazing life, but unfortunately there's a thief who comes only to steal, and to kill, and to destroy and that's why at times life can be anything but fun. This more abundant life then, isn't about strolling through some illusory paradise on earth, the proverbial bed of roses, it is about having the power to face up to the challenges of life and soundly defeat them. It is available to live this way, this is not make believe.

> Romans 8:37
> Nay, in all these things we are more than conquerors through him that loved us.

This verse doesn't say we are more than conquerors by our own muscles or brain power, or by the amazing solutions we figure out all by ourselves, it says we are more than conquerors through him that loved us. This concurs with John where it said that the more abundant life was made available by Jesus Christ. Both of these verses are in harmony with Philippians.

> Philippians 4:13
> I can do all things through Christ which strengtheneth me.

This verse does not say I can do all things, full stop, it says I can do all things through Christ which strengthens me. This agrees with Romans and John. The more abundant life, therefore, is not something we make available, it is something God makes available through Jesus Christ. Note that the verse does not say God is going to do it all for us either. It says, I can do all things through Christ which strengthens me. In other words, this is not automatic. We have a part to play in this.

God through Jesus Christ makes an amazing life available, but we definitely have something to do with getting there as it is not automatic. This isn't so hard to understand. God went to a lot of trouble through the centuries to have the bible written for us, he made it available, but reading our bibles is something we do, not something he does for us.

How then does Christ strengthen us? If God made this available, but isn't going to do this for us, how then does Christ strengthen us so we can do all things? We gain a clue in Ephesians.

> Ephesians 3:20
> Now unto him that is able to do exceeding abundantly above all that we ask or think, according to the power [Greek - dunamis] that worketh [energeō] in us,

God is able to do exceeding abundantly above all that we ask or think. That is without question, but is that the end of the verse? No, it isn't. God is able to do exceeding abundantly above all that we ask or think *according to* the power, the dunamis, the inherent power that works in us. Dunamis is potential power, latent power. We get words like *dynamo* and *dynamic* from this Greek word *dunamis*.

Worketh is the Greek word *energeō*, from which we get the words *energy* and *energise*. God is able to do exceeding abundantly above all that we ask or think according to the potential power, the inherent power that is energised in us. This power, this dunamis, this inherent power, this potential power that we energise is the source of our power for abundant living.

What is this power and how is it energised? We read the bible to find out. The bible is the manual on how to energise this power and learn how to live the abundant life Jesus Christ came to make available. This power is what is referred to in Philippians 4:13 when it says I can do all things through Christ which strengthens me. When this power is energised, it opens the door to God doing exceeding abundantly above all that we ask or think. Of course, if this power is not energised it will do nothing, it will achieve nothing, even though it is there.

Power accomplishes nothing unless it is energised. Having electricity in your house does nothing until you turn it on. The bible teaches us how to turn on the power. What is this power? Where does it come from? How do we get it? How do we energise it? These are good questions, and they are all answered in the bible. If you want answers, you have to learn how to read the bible and this class will teach you how to do just that.

> Romans 12:2
> And be not conformed to this world: but be ye transformed [metamorphoō] by the renewing of your mind, that ye may prove what *is* that good, and acceptable, and perfect, will of God.

Transformed is *metamorphoō* in the Greek, from which we derive the word *metamorphosis*, describing the change from a caterpillar to a butterfly. As we read the bible and renew our minds, we change into beautiful butterflies which spread life by pollinating everywhere we go. We read our bibles and renew our minds to prove God's good, acceptable, and perfect will. God's will is good, acceptable, and perfect. That's true whether we renew our minds or not. God's will is always good, acceptable, and perfect, regardless of anything we do. The promise here is that we can prove it. This is a promise to us, it is something we get to do if we renew our minds. We can prove that God's will is good, acceptable, and perfect. What is God's will in a situation? If we renew our minds we get to see it, that's the promise.

John 10:10
The thief cometh not, but for to steal, and to kill, and to destroy: I am come that they might have life, and that they might have *it* more abundantly.

What is God's good, acceptable, and perfect will here? That we have life, and that we have it more abundantly. That is God's good, acceptable, and perfect will. But this doesn't happen automatically. The promise in Romans 12 is that if we renew our minds we get the opportunity to prove God's good, acceptable, and perfect will and enjoy a life which is more abundant. If we don't renew our minds and we don't realise this more abundant life, it is still God's will that we have it. It is always God's will for us to have an abundant life, and it will always be God's will that we have an abundant life. An abundant life will always be available. It is available right now. So how do you get it? The renewed mind is the key, and you renew your mind by reading the bible. In other words, if you read the bible and apply the principles, you get to enjoy an abundant life.

The thief referred to in John is the devil, the god of this world, and he pumps filth into the world through television, movies, newspapers, magazines, computer games, the internet, and a thousand other ways so he can steal, kill and destroy. He pumps a continuous diet of poisoned filth into the world that makes us mentally sick, that strips our souls of vitality and passion. We are to put it off by renewing our minds. We change our mental diet. Instead of the world's filth, we feed our minds with a healthy, clean, vital, nutritious diet of God's word.

The world spews its poisons into homes, schools and universities, into politics and business, in hundreds of languages and dialects, in every country on the face of the planet, every minute of every day of the year. The world may have a fat slobbery mouth, but no one forces you to turn on your television instead of reading your bible, do they? Does the world march in, twist your arm, chuck your bible into a closet, and force you to watch TV? No, it is a decision you make. If you want mental health and the power of God in your life, change your mental diet.

2 Timothy 1:7
For God hath not given us the spirit of fear; but of power, and of love, and of a sound mind.

This isn't about not having fun either. I enjoy Star Trek, especially the latest movies with their brilliant special effects. I enjoy the characters, the stories, the sets, the alien worlds, the battles, the drama, and the adventures. I really do enjoy it, but I'm not poisoned by the subversive propaganda laced through practically every episode. I'm not taken in with the Federation and its United Nations bullshit programming us for one world governance. I don't fall for their cowardly garbage regarding what they call the prime directive. I enjoy Star Trek, but I'm not poisoned by it. Why? I have a healthy daily diet of God's word, so my mind is strong and isn't poisoned by the world. Do you see it? This isn't about cutting off the world and having no fun, it is about having a healthy, sane mind so you can enjoy life. A healthy daily diet of the word brings deliverance and strength.

> Nehemiah 8:8,12
> So they read in the book in the law of God distinctly, and gave the sense, and caused *them* to understand the reading.
>
> And all the people went their way to eat, and to drink, and to send portions, and to make great mirth, because they had understood the words that were declared unto them.

Reading and understanding the bible isn't drudgery and boredom, it is refreshing and invigorating. Understanding the word gives us life in all of its abundance. A healthy daily diet of God's word is the way of life for us today, just as it always has been. So if you want life, if you want strength to be more than a conqueror every day, make a decision to stuff your face with a healthy diet of God's word.

The reason we can talk about reading and studying the bible in terms of physical food is because God uses that figure of speech in the bible.

> Jeremiah 15:16
> Thy words were found, and I did eat them; and thy word was unto me the joy and rejoicing of mine heart: for I am called by thy name, O LORD God of hosts.

Did Jeremiah eat scrolls? No, this is a figure of speech emphasising that Jeremiah did more than just snack at the word a couple of times a week.

He ate it, he digested it, it provided the mental strength he needed to do his spiritual job, which was to walk by the spirit in his day and time.

Regarding figures of speech, Is there a figure of speech God employs to illustrate this power we can energise? Let's see.

> John 20:22
> And when he had said this, he [Jesus Christ] breathed on [in] ~~them~~, and saith unto them, Receive ye the Holy Ghost [holy spirit]:

Jesus Christ was instructing his disciples on how to energise the power when it arrived. The word *them* is in italics and it should be deleted. This is an important key to understanding the bible when you read it. Whenever and wherever the King James translators added English words that were not in the Greek text, they left those words in italics so we would know they had been added. In other words, if you scratched out every italicised word in the King James bible, you would not touch God's word because those italicised words were not in the Greek text from which the King James was translated. Many times these italicised words are helpful to our understanding, but often they mislead or are just wrong. Always be wary of italicised words, and never use them as doctrine unless you're sure they were correctly supplied by the translators. This is why I recommend the King James version which has the italicised words. No other English translation has them so you don't know what's been added to their texts.

In this verse, *them* is misleading. Why would Jesus Christ breathe on his apostles? To see if his breath was clean? Breathing on people is rude and most folks don't like it. The italicised word *them* should be deleted. The word *on* is the Greek word *en* and should have been translated *in*. Jesus Christ breathed in, and said, receive holy spirit. He took a deep breath, and told them that was how they were to receive the holy spirit when it eventually came. And that's exactly what the apostles did.

> Acts 2:1,2
> And when the day of Pentecost was fully come, they were all with one accord in one place.

And suddenly there came a sound from heaven as of a rushing mighty wind [a heavy breathing], and it filled all the house where they were sitting.

The words *as of a rushing mighty wind* are *as of a heavy breathing* in the text. The twelve apostles did what they had been instructed to do, and they all took deep breaths to receive the gift of holy spirit. The heavy sound of their deep breathing filled the temple because of the superb acoustics. Those old temples didn't have state of the art sound systems, but they did have state of the art acoustics to ensure anyone sitting anywhere in the temple heard what was being said on the main stage. The heavy breathing of these twelve men filled the temple.

> Acts 2:3,4
> And there appeared unto them cloven tongues like as of fire, and it sat upon each of them.
>
> And they were all filled with the Holy Ghost [holy spirit], and began to speak with other tongues, as the Spirit gave them utterance.

So breathing is again used to illustrate the receiving and manifesting of the power in the gift of holy spirit. Look at Timothy.

> 2 Timothy 3:16
> All scripture *is* **given by inspiration of God** [theopneustos], and *is* profitable for doctrine, for reproof, for correction, for instruction in righteousness:

The five English words *given by inspiration of God* are translated from one word, *theopneustos*. *Theos* is *God* while *pneustos* is *breathed*. All scripture is *God-breathed*, which is a reference to how we got the word, which was as holy men of God spoke as they were moved by the holy spirit, which was by revelation.

> 2 Peter 1:21
> For the prophecy came not in old time by the will of man: but holy men of God spake *as they were* moved by the Holy Ghost.

Walking *by* the Spirit

> Galatians 1:11,12
> But I certify you, brethren, that the gospel which was preached of me is not after man.
>
> For I neither received it of man, neither was I taught *it*, but by the revelation of Jesus Christ.

Here, the God-breathed word is a figurative reference to revelation, which is how we got the word. God breathed his word into existence, and that is why it is the word of life, the God-breathed word. This is another figurative reference to breathing in relation to energising supernatural power. Think of your study of God's word, your renewing of your mind as your mental diet, and walking by the spirit as your spiritual breath, your spiritual breathing. As we breathe spiritually, as we walk by the spirit, we have supernatural life.

Who gave us our physical bodies? God did. Who is responsible to look after them, to feed them, to keep them healthy with proper diet and exercise? God? No, we are. God gave them, but what we do with them is our responsibility. God supplies our food, but he isn't going to cook it for us and spoon it down our throats. Who gave us our soul, our character, our mind? Who made us who we are? God did. Who is responsible to look after our mental diet and keep ourselves healthy and strong? God? No, we are. God gave it, but what we do with our minds is up to us. God does not possess us. Who gave us eternal life, the power from on high, the gift of holy spirit? God did. Who is responsible to energise it, to ensure we grow and mature so we walk by the spirit and not by the senses? God? No, we are. God gave it, but what we do with that spirit is our business.

The more abundant life is here. The power is available. God is able to do exceeding abundantly above all that we ask or think, but only according to the power that is energised in us. We really can do all things through Christ which strengthens us. No matter what the world does, we can be more than conquerors through him that loved us. If you want this more abundant life, get your bibles open and read.

2. The Way of Life

You may have noticed that the world can be anything but enjoyable at times. Some folks blame God for the state of the world, but whose fault is it? Why is the world the way it is? Look at this promise in psalms.

> Psalm 33:12
> Blessed *is* the nation whose God *is* the LORD; *and* the people *whom* he hath chosen for his own inheritance.

This is an unbelievably short and concise verse which is easy to overlook. Blessed is the nation whose God is the Lord. That's only nine words. In just nine words God promises to bless entire nations who choose him as their God. Think about that. Does it not then follow that any nation that is having serious economical and social problems must have chosen another god? To start setting the tone for where we're going with this thing, note that Psalm 33:12 does not say blessed is the nation whose god is the government.

How does God bless entire nations? What happens to nations whose God is not the Lord? These are good questions and Moses addressed this very issue.

> Deuteronomy 30:19
> I call heaven and earth to record this day against you, *that* I have set before you life and death, blessing and cursing: therefore choose life, that both thou and thy seed may live:

Moses set the way of life and the way of death before God's people. It was a choice the people were to make. That choice is still available today. We get to choose which way we will walk. Life and blessing is the right choice, as Deuteronomy goes on to tell us.

Deuteronomy 28:1-14
And it shall come to pass, if thou shalt hearken diligently unto the voice of the LORD [Jehovah] thy God, to observe *and* to do all his commandments which I command thee this day, that the LORD thy God will set thee on high above all nations of the earth:

And all these blessings shall come on thee, and overtake thee, if thou shalt hearken unto the voice of the LORD thy God.

Blessed *shalt* thou *be* in the city, and blessed *shalt* thou *be* in the field.

Blessed *shall be* the fruit of thy body, and the fruit of thy ground, and the fruit of thy cattle, the increase of thy kine, and the flocks of thy sheep.

Blessed *shall be* thy basket and thy store.

Blessed *shalt* thou *be* when thou comest in, and blessed *shalt* thou *be* when thou goest out.

The LORD shall cause thine enemies that rise up against thee to be smitten before thy face: they shall come out against thee one way, and flee before thee seven ways.

The LORD shall command the blessing upon thee in thy storehouses, and in all that thou settest thine hand unto; and he shall bless thee in the land which the LORD thy God giveth thee.

The LORD shall establish thee an holy people unto himself, as he hath sworn unto thee, if thou shalt keep the commandments of the LORD thy God, and walk in his ways.

And all people of the earth shall see that thou art called by the name of the LORD; and they shall be afraid of thee.

And the LORD shall make thee plenteous in goods, in the fruit of thy body, and in the fruit of thy cattle, and in the fruit of thy ground, in the land which the LORD sware unto thy fathers to give thee.

> The LORD shall open unto thee his good treasure, the heaven to give the rain unto thy land in his season, and to bless all the work of thine hand: and thou shalt lend unto many nations, and thou shalt not borrow.
>
> And the LORD shall make thee the head, and not the tail; and thou shalt be above only, and thou shalt not be beneath; if that thou hearken unto the commandments of the LORD thy God, which I command thee this day, to observe and to do *them*:
>
> And thou shalt not go aside from any of the words which I command thee this day, *to* the right hand, or *to* the left, to go after other gods to serve them.

The word is clear here. Nothing is hazy, ethereal or nebulous about the promises in these verses. God categorically states, in black and white, that if we live by his word we will be blessed, even as entire nations. We will enjoy prosperity, long life, strong loving family relationships, and prosperous businesses – in fact abundance in every conceivable category of life. Not only does God promise all this, but it is his will, his desire, his driving passion for our lives. He wants us to have this.

> 3 John 2
> Beloved, I wish above all things that thou mayest prosper and be in health, even as thy soul prospereth.

Health and prosperity are available if we hearken diligently to the voice of the Lord our God. The voice of the Lord our God is his word, so to hearken diligently to God's voice is to hearken diligently to his word which is the bible.

Moses was clear on the blessings available for choosing to live life God's way, but he also clearly laid out before God's people what would happen to them if they walked away.

> Deuteronomy 28:15-19
> But it shall come to pass, if thou wilt not hearken unto the voice of the LORD thy God, to observe to do all his commandments and

his statutes which I command thee this day; that all these curses shall come upon thee, and overtake thee:

Cursed shalt thou be in the city, and cursed shalt thou be in the field.

Cursed shall be thy basket and thy store.

Cursed shall be the fruit of thy body, and the fruit of thy land, the increase of thy kine, and the flocks of thy sheep.

Cursed shalt thou be when thou comest in, and cursed shalt thou be when thou goest out.

Deuteronomy 28:33
The fruit of thy land, and all thy labours, shall a nation which thou knowest not eat up; and thou shalt be only oppressed and crushed alway:

Deuteronomy 28:51
And he shall eat the fruit of thy cattle, and the fruit of thy land, until thou be destroyed: which *also* shall not leave thee *either* corn, wine, or oil, *or* the increase of thy kine, or flocks of thy sheep, until he have destroyed thee.

Deuteronomy 30:19
I call heaven and earth to record this day against you, *that* I have set before you life and death, blessing and cursing: therefore choose life, that both thou and thy seed may live:

According to Moses, living God's way brings blessings while turning our backs on God brings consequences. If this is true, then perhaps we should sit up and take note because peoples of all nations are coming to our countries and getting a free life at our expense. They will eat everything we have until there is nothing left.

If we want a good life and prosperity, we can have it, it is freely available. If you're not happy with your life, you can change it. God wants you to have life and prosperity, he wants you to have a full life. It's your choice. You can have it if you want it.

In this class I'm going to take that which Moses wrote all those centuries ago and lay out in modern language the mechanics involved in how entire nations and individuals are blessed, and how entire nations and individuals have their prosperity, their health and their peace stolen from them. It isn't magic and it isn't luck. This class is going to explain the mechanics behind what actually happens to make it so.

3. Spiritual Integrity

The book of Job was the first book of the bible ever written. Although not placed first in the bible, and rightfully so, Job was the first book written. We know that the first revelation written with the finger of God was given to Moses, so it is safe to assume that he wrote the book of Job. Whenever God uses a word or a phrase in the bible for the first time, that first usage always embodies important information. Checking first usage of something illuminates truth we may never otherwise see. Job being the first written scriptural revelation from God to man, it holds truth of supreme importance.

This is easy to understand. For example, the first time parents teach their young children to cross the road they pay particular attention to the instruction they are giving. They teach their children that a green light at a pedestrian crossing means it is safe to cross, while a red light means it is not. They teach them to look both ways to check for traffic before stepping out into the road. These basic precepts are impressed on them with special emphasis because it is their introduction to road traffic safety and their lives depend on it. To all intents and purposes, Job is our introduction to spiritual road traffic safety.

So, what particular emphasis do we find in the book of Job? What is it that is so important about it? What are the first lessons God wanted man to know? Well, to begin with, Job is the only book that contrasts the goodness of God with the evil of the devil. It is the only book in the bible that does this. The book of Job also shows us how to live in fellowship with God for a lifetime and clearly reveals the primary weapons the devil uses against us to prevent that.

To revisit our example of teaching children to cross roads for a moment, consider that the lesson on green and red traffic lights never changes after that, regardless of how much further teaching we may receive. When we learn to drive as adults, those foundational truths regarding green and red traffic lights has not changed. Our perspective as responsible drivers as opposed to children being taught road traffic safety for the first time may have changed, but the foundational truths regarding red and green lights has not.

Despite the importance of traffic lights and their colours, when I sat my driving test I don't recall my driving instructor asking me if I knew what red and green traffic lights meant. It was not one of the questions required to pass my driving test. In fact, I don't think I would have appreciated my test instructor asking me if I knew the difference between red and green traffic lights. Have you ever seen parents take their adult children by the hand to the roadside to check if they still know what red and green traffic lights mean? How insulting and patronising would that be?

Similarly with the truths set in the first book of the bible ever written, the book of Job. The foundational truths regarding spiritual red and green traffic lights are set here, and God does not patronise us by repeating them all through his word. He expects us to remember these truths when we read the rest of the bible.

Here is a question for you – do you want to have the strength and commitment to stand for the true God for the rest of your life, regardless of anything the world may throw at you? If so, then pay attention, because the book of Job shows us how to do just that.

> Job 1:1
> There was a man in the land of Uz, whose name *was* Job; and that man was perfect and upright, and one that feared God, and eschewed evil.

This guy Job (pronounced Joab) was perfect and upright, someone who feared God – meaning he had tremendous awe, reverence, and respect for God – and he eschewed evil, it was distasteful to him. The word *fear* in 1611, when the King James bible was first translated, had more than one meaning, just as our modern word *bank* has more than one meaning. The context in which the word *bank* is used determines its meaning. In 1611 the word *fear* meant awe, reverence, and respect, as well as its more commonly understood meaning today, and the context within which it is employed determines its meaning.

Job was a faithful believer, a disciple. That is God's testimony of Job. This is important to remember as it is crucial to our understanding of what follows.

> Job 1:2
> And there were born unto him seven sons and three daughters.

Job had a big family, so he obviously got on well with his wife. How do I know? Well, women do not generally enjoy such productive sex lives with their husbands unless they are deeply in love with them. Job was a good husband. He was also a good father and family man.

> Job 1:3
> His substance also was seven thousand sheep, and three thousand camels, and five hundred yoke of oxen, and five hundred she asses, and a very great household; so that this man was the greatest of all the men of the east.

Not only was he a successful family man, Job was an amazingly successful businessman. It makes you wonder where folks get the idea that God wants his people to be poor. For the record, God invented commerce, not the devil, and true prosperity comes by applying biblical principles which are a little different to the world's standards. It is okay with God to have money. There is nothing wrong with wealth. Job was the richest man in the world in his day, and God was quite happy with that. It is our attitude to money that is the key, but more on that later.

God's testimony of Job is that he was perfect and upright, someone who found evil distasteful, unpalatable.

> Job 1:4,5
> And his sons went and feasted *in their* houses, every one his day; and sent and called for their three sisters to eat and to drink with them.
>
> And it was so, when the days of *their* feasting were gone about, that Job sent and sanctified them, and rose up early in the morning, and offered burnt offerings *according* to the number of them all: for Job said, It may be that my sons have sinned, and cursed God in their hearts. Thus did Job continually.

Here is our first clue that all is not well. Job was concerned that his children had broken fellowship with God, and perhaps had even cursed him in their hearts. So he did sacrifices for them, just in case. If he had these worries, why did he not deal with them? Why did he not sort this out with his family? Had his sons done or said things that may have caused him to worry about this? The word does not tell us, so we don't know. Whatever the reasons, Job had concerns that carried over into his actions by way of the sacrifices he made for his children. This is an important clue in understanding what happened next.

> Job 1:6,7
> Now there was a day when the sons of God came to present themselves before the LORD, and Satan came also among them.
>
> And the LORD said unto Satan, Whence comest thou? Then Satan answered the LORD, and said, From going to and fro in the earth, and from walking up and down in it.

There are some intriguing truths here. For example, the devil can only be in one place at one time. God is everywhere present, omni-present, but the devil is not. The all-seeing eye is not as all-seeing as he would have us believe.

> Job 1:8
> And the LORD said unto Satan, Hast thou considered my servant Job, that *there is* none like him in the earth, a perfect and an upright man, one that feareth God, and escheweth evil?

God repeats that Job is perfect and upright. The point is, Job has done nothing wrong. Remember this, because some who read Job ignore this fact or forget it very quickly.

> Job 1:9,10
> Then Satan answered the LORD, and said, Doth Job fear God for nought?
>
> Hast not thou made an hedge about him, and about his house, and about all that he hath on every side? thou hast blessed the work of his hands, and his substance is increased in the land.

Here is proof that God wants his people to have abundance. Even the devil himself informs us that it was God who blessed Job with everything.

> Job 1:11
> But put forth thine hand now, and touch all that he hath, and he will curse thee to thy face.

Remember the phrase *curse God to his face* because we will be dealing with it shortly. Suffice to mention that if the devil was trying to get Job to *curse God to his face*, whatever it is, it isn't something we should be doing.

> Job 1:12
> And the LORD said unto Satan, Behold, all that he hath *is* in thy power; only upon himself put not forth thine hand. So Satan went forth from the presence of the LORD.

It is interesting to note that the devil now had access into Job's life, but only because God had to allow it. This is fundamental. The devil can only get to us if we walk outside of God's protection, if we make a hole in the hedge for him to get in, so to speak.

God's protection can be likened to an umbrella in the rain – if we stay under the protective canopy we remain dry, but if we wander outside we become wet. If we stay within God's boundaries, within his hedge of protection, we remain safe. It is when we walk away from God's protection that the devil gains access.

> Job 1:13-19
> And there was a day when his sons and his daughters *were* eating and drinking wine in their eldest brother's house:
>
> And there came a messenger unto Job, and said, The oxen were plowing, and the asses feeding beside them:
>
> And the Sabeans fell *upon them*, and took them away; yea, they have slain the servants with the edge of the sword; and I only am escaped alone to tell thee.

While he *was* yet speaking, there came also another, and said, The fire of God is fallen from heaven, and hath burned up the sheep, and the servants, and consumed them; and I only am escaped alone to tell thee.

While he *was* yet speaking, there came also another, and said, The Chaldeans made out three bands, and fell upon the camels, and have carried them away, yea, and slain the servants with the edge of the sword; and I only am escaped alone to tell thee.

While he *was* yet speaking, there came also another, and said, Thy sons and thy daughters *were* eating and drinking wine in their eldest brother's house:

And, behold, there came a great wind from the wilderness, and smote the four corners of the house, and it fell upon the young men, and they are dead; and I only am escaped alone to tell thee.

In the space of just a few hours, Job's business empire lay in ruins and his children were dead. No longer the wealthiest man in the world, he was now one of its poorest. Job lost his entire business empire and his family through 'natural' catastrophes and invasion from enemies. And wasn't it nice of the devil to leave one man alive in each case to make sure Job heard the news as quickly as possible. There is nothing the devil enjoys more than ensuring folks hear the details of what he has been up to quickly so they will talk about him. He likes to brag about what he's been doing while events are still current and fresh. We will be handling newspapers and the media later.

Now it's time to stop and think. Who did all this to Job? Was it God or was it the devil? Well, it is clear, it was the devil. Being the first book of the bible ever written, these fundamental truths contrasting the goodness of God with the badness of the devil are set and established. Green lights mean go and red lights mean stop. God is good, and the devil is evil. This truth is set here, and it never changes again throughout the entire word of God.

Job 1:20-22
Then Job arose, and rent his mantle, and shaved his head, and fell down upon the ground, and worshipped,

And said, Naked came I out of my mother's womb, and naked shall I return thither: the LORD gave, and the LORD hath taken away; blessed be the name of the LORD.

In all this Job sinned not, nor charged God foolishly.

We know from verse 12 that it was the devil who did this to Job. That is very clear. There can be no mistaking who did this to Job. Yet look at what Job said: *the LORD gave, and the LORD hath taken away; blessed be the name of the LORD.*

Job seems to contradict what we have just learned, and appears to state that God did this to him. However, the word clearly teaches that it was satan, the devil, who did this to him. So what is the answer? Well, it is an idiom. An idiom is a figure of speech that is unique to a particular culture, where words are employed to mean something other than what they literally say. For example, in our culture a hotdog is not a roasted cocker spaniel, it is a sausage in a roll. To us that is so clear it needs no explanation. However, to a foreigner perhaps visiting our culture for the first time they might find it a little strange being offered a hotdog for lunch. Might they not picture a dog roasting on a spit? Job was using an idiom here, that which we refer to as the idiom of permission. Job was not stupid, he knew where the attacks were coming from. Look at what the word says:

Job 1:22
In all this Job sinned not, nor charged God foolishly.

Job did not charge God with having done all this to him, he did not blame God. If the police charge you, they charge you with a crime. Job did not charge God with these crimes.

The culture behind this idiom of permission is intriguing. Back in Job's day, folks detested the devil so much that they absolutely refused to give him any credence or credit for his works. They simply refused to talk about him, or acknowledge his power and influence. In other words, they did not read newspapers, they switched off their televisions when the news came on, and they certainly didn't spend their day discussing what he was up to. When things went wrong, as they did then just as they do today, instead of giving glory to the devil by discussing all his bad news, they understood things in light of God having granted permission to allow things to happen because they had messed up somewhere.

Another important aspect of this idiom of permission to understand is that God gave a specific commandment in the old testament to not even mention other gods.

> Exodus 23:13
> And in all *things* that I have said unto you be circumspect: and make no mention of the name of other gods, neither let it be heard out of thy mouth.

If they were not to make mention of the devil out of their mouths, then Job was doing what the word said in not making mention of the devil when he spoke.

Another way to understand this idiom of permission is to think of it in light of gravity. God designed gravity to bless man and enrich our lives. Can you imagine a world without gravity? Would we even be able to live without it? Now if someone is silly enough to fall off a cliff and badly injure himself, is that God's fault because he designed gravity and built it into the physics of life? Sure, you can blame your injuries on God because he made gravity, but the truth is your injuries are your fault. Somewhere along the way you messed up, you missed something, you didn't do your job.

Just as God is not responsible for injuries caused by gravity, even though he invented it, he is not responsible for what happened to Job. Satan attacked Job, but we have to understand that God gave him the permission to do it because he had no other choice. This is the first book of the bible ever written and this is the very first chapter of the first book of the bible ever written. God is good and the devil is bad. The devil did all this nasty stuff to Job, not God. God is always good, and that truth carries throughout the entire bible.

> 1 John 1:5
> This then is the message which we have heard of him, and declare unto you, that God is light, and in him is no darkness at all.

There is no darkness in God, none at all. God never did a mean thing to anyone in his life. Therefore, every time you read in the bible that God did something nasty you have to understand it in light of this idiom of permission. The devil only gets through because God is forced to allow it. That is this idiom of permission.

Now, why would this be the subject of the first chapter of the first book of the bible ever written? Simple, because it is probably the most fundamental spiritual lesson you will ever learn regarding spiritual road traffic safety. Green lights mean go, red lights mean stop. God is good, the devil is bad. This fundamental truth is set here and never changes again. Do not forget it. Your spiritual road safety will depend on it.

Job was perfect and upright. How do we know? God said so, twice so far. Job had a wonderful family life, and he was the richest man in the world. That wealth did not just pop in through his letterbox in the form of a lottery cheque either. He worked hard and was successful in business. Then the devil got in, destroyed his business empire and killed his children. However, that is not the end of the story. The devil is not finished with Job quite yet.

> Job 2:1-3
> Again there was a day when the sons of God came to present themselves before the LORD, and Satan came also among them to present himself before the LORD.
>
> And the LORD said unto Satan, From whence comest thou? And Satan answered the LORD, and said, From going to and fro in the earth, and from walking up and down in it.
>
> And the LORD said unto Satan, Hast thou considered my servant Job, that *there is* none like him in the earth, a perfect and an upright man, one that feareth God, and escheweth evil? and still he holdeth fast his integrity, although thou movedst me against him, to destroy him without cause.

What does God say about Job in verse 3? He says he is *perfect* and *upright*. That's the third time God's said this. Do you think he is making a point? All this nasty stuff did not happen to Job because he was evil then, did it? Why? Because he wasn't evil, he was perfect and upright. This is important. Some churches and ministers teach that God makes people sick and does nasty things to them because they are sinners, and they often quote Job as their example. Job was not a sinner, he had committed no crimes, he was perfect and upright. And just for the record, even if people are attacked, it is the devil attacking them, not God.

Job 2:4-8
And Satan answered the LORD, and said, Skin for skin, yea, all that a man hath will he give for his life.

But put forth thine hand now, and touch his bone and his flesh, and he will curse thee to thy face.

And the LORD said unto Satan, Behold, he *is* in thine hand; but save his life.

So went Satan forth from the presence of the LORD, and smote Job with sore boils from the sole of his foot unto his crown.

And he took him a potsherd to scrape himself withal; and he sat down among the ashes.

Who smote Job with sickness and disease? Was it God? No, it was not. It is clear that it was the devil. There can be no misunderstandings or misconceptions about who did this to Job. Read it again.

Job 2:7
So went Satan forth from the presence of the LORD, and smote Job with sore boils from the sole of his foot unto his crown.

It was satan, the devil, who smote Job. Was Job evil? Had Job committed any crimes? No, he was perfect and upright. Some teach that Job suffered these things because he was a sinner, but what they teach is religious horseshit that contradicts the bible. Job was perfect and upright. These things happened to him *without cause*. That is the testimony of the word and the word is true.

God's will for man is a wonderful family life with abundance, prosperity, and happiness. In contrast, we have seen the devil's will for man, which is poverty, sickness, and death. The two contrast starkly and this sets the tone and mood for the entire bible. God is good and the devil is evil.

> John 10:10
> The thief cometh not, but for to steal, and to kill, and to destroy: I am come that they might have life, and that they might have *it* more abundantly.

The thief here is a figurative reference to the devil. All he comes to do is to steal, to kill, and to destroy. That's it, nothing else. That is what he lives for. He is good at what he does too, and don't expect anything else from him. Everything he does is in the categories of stealing, killing, and destroying, even to those who worship him.

Job had an amazing life, but he lost everything. He lost his children, his business, and his health. He was so sick, he was at the point of death. His skin was suppurating with poisonous sores. He was disgustingly sick and diseased. Did he deserve it? No, he was perfect and upright. God has told us that three times. Look back at verse 3.

> Job 2:3
> And the LORD said unto Satan, Hast thou considered my servant Job, that *there is* none like him in the earth, a perfect and an upright man, one that feareth God, and escheweth evil? and still he holdeth fast his integrity, although thou movedst me against him, to destroy him without cause.

Do you see that word *integrity?* We are now going to find out what integrity is, what the bible says integrity is. Job retained his integrity despite the attacks on his life. It was Job's integrity the devil was after. Therefore, whatever integrity is, it must be hugely important that we hold it fast like Job did. These attacks on Job's life had a purpose other than just to make him miserable. They had design and purpose, they were an attempt to break his integrity.

Note also, that both times the devil asked for permission to attack Job, he bragged that he would get Job to *curse God to his face*.

Job 1:11
But put forth thine hand now, and touch all that he hath, and he will curse thee to thy face.

Job 2:5
But put forth thine hand now, and touch his bone and his flesh, and he will curse thee to thy face.

Is it possible, therefore, that integrity and cursing God to his face could somehow be linked? It is axiomatic, but we will take the time to explore this. Look at the last verse of chapter one.

Job 1:22
In all this Job sinned not, nor charged God foolishly.

This is the main point of the chapter. Even though the devil attacked Job so viciously, Job did not turn on God and waggle accusatory fingers at him. He knew where the attacks were coming from, and he did not blame God for the evil, he did not charge him with the crimes. Think about this in the context of Moses teaching this to the bitching and complaining Israelites escaping from Egypt.

Job still had his integrity intact. How do we know? God said so. Again, this destruction in his life was *without cause*, meaning he had not sinned, that he was perfect and upright, that he had not done anything to deserve this stuff. Now look at verse 9 of chapter 2 where we see *integrity* and *cursing God* woven tightly together.

Job 2:9
Then said his wife unto him, Dost thou still retain thine integrity? curse God, and die.

My goodness, after all Job had been through, his own wife turned on him. Before you write her off, think of what she's been through. All her children are dead. She must have loved them. Her husband's business is in tatters, he is stinking with suppurating sores, dripping with pus, at the point of death. Her sorrow and hurt, coupled with her public humiliation and shame must have been horrendous. How do you think she felt? Sure, she was wrong, but don't be so hard on her. How would you hold up under the same circumstances? Now look at Job's response. It is absolutely staggering. He didn't tell her to fuck off, he gently reproved her with the word.

> Job 2:10
> But he said unto her, Thou speakest as one of the foolish women speaketh. What? shall we receive good at the hand of God, and shall we not receive evil? In all this did not Job sin with his lips.

Lovingly and kindly, he brought her back to the word. Even though he was in such a mess, he still loved his wife enough to teach her the word. No wonder God called Job perfect and upright three times. God was impressed with this dude, and with good cause.

> Job 2:9
> Then said his wife unto him, Dost thou still retain thine integrity? curse God, and die.

The issue of his wife aside, here we see integrity, the biblical definition of integrity, contrasted with what it is not, which is to curse God. The implication here is that if you curse God, you break your integrity. To have integrity, therefore, is not to curse God. Look again at verse 5 and verse 3 very closely.

> Job 2:5
> But put forth thine hand now, and touch his bone and his flesh, and he will curse thee to thy face.

> Job 2:3
> And the LORD said unto Satan, Hast thou considered my servant Job, that *there is* none like him in the earth, a perfect and an upright man, one that feareth God, and escheweth evil? and still he holdeth fast his integrity, although thou movedst me against him, to destroy him without cause.

The devil tried to get Job to curse God to his face. He failed because Job held fast to his integrity. Do you see the connection? The devil even used Job's wife to try to coerce him into cursing God to his face. Whatever it is to curse God, it is serious in terms of spiritual consequences.

The devil was doing all this to Job for a reason, to get Job to curse God to his face. What was it that Job refused to do?

> Job 1:22
> In all this Job sinned not, nor charged God foolishly.

> Job 2:10
> But he said unto her, Thou speakest as one of the foolish women speaketh. What? shall we receive good at the hand of God, and shall we not receive evil? In all this did not Job sin with his lips.

Job did not blame God for what happened to him. That was the temptation, but he held onto his integrity. Even his wife said to him, *Dost thou still retain thine integrity? Curse God, and die.* To curse God was what the devil was trying to get him to do. Remember, this is the first lesson ever written in the bible, so this is rather important. Again, consider this in the context of Moses teaching this stuff to the Israelites coming out of Egypt. They obviously didn't listen to Moses because most of them wound up dead in the wilderness for blaming God for all their problems. James adds further light.

> James 1:12
> Blessed *is* the man that endureth temptation: for when he is tried, he shall receive the crown of life, which the Lord hath promised to them that love him.

Whatever *enduring temptation* is, it is definitely something we want to do. It is important and God even gives out a special reward for those who do it – they receive a crown of life, a special reward given in the future. Now don't go guessing about what the temptation is here, the next verses tell us.

> James 1:13-14
> Let no man say when he is tempted, I am tempted of God: for God cannot be tempted with evil, neither tempteth he any man:
>
> But every man is tempted, when he is drawn away of his own lust, and enticed.

What did Job's wife say? She said, *curse God and die*. To curse God, and to accuse God of tempting you with evil is actually the same thing. The devil tried to get Job to blame God for all the evil he had done to him. If Job had done so, that would have broken his integrity because it would have been cursing God to his face.

When the devil attacks us, we are not to blame God for it. We are to recognise that God is good and not hurl accusations in his face. We are not to charge God foolishly. If we are under attack, like Job was, and we accuse God for it, we have just cursed God to his face, we have just driven through a spiritual red light. That was what the devil was trying to get Job to do.

The temptation is to say your problems come from God. If you do, you compromise your spiritual integrity, you curse God to his face. Under pressure, we must always recognise that the nasty stuff in life comes from the devil and not from God. We must never blame God, ever, for anything. This is the first spiritual lesson God committed to writing in what we know today as the bible. If we accuse God of evil we have driven through a spiritual red light, and that's extremely dangerous.

> James 1:13
> Let no man say when he is tempted, I am tempted of God: for God cannot be tempted with evil, neither tempteth he any man:

God is always good. The devil is always bad. Nothing bad ever comes from God, it always comes from the devil. Like Job, the devil attempts to get us to blame God for all the nasty stuff in life. In Insurance, for example, they call earthquakes, tsunamis, and other disasters acts of God. If you believe that God deliberately causes earthquakes so he can murder people and destroy property, your spiritual integrity is under attack. If you think tsunamis come from God, your spiritual integrity is under attack. If you think illness comes from God, that God makes people sick and that he kills them, you have fallen for the devil's lies and your spiritual integrity is under attack. You are cursing God to his face. If your church teaches you that God makes people sick, you need to get out of that shithole before you start charging God with such crimes.

Ask yourself, if God makes people sick then what right did Jesus Christ have to go around healing them? If God makes people sick, then Jesus Christ contradicted God's will by healing them. If God wanted us sick, and Jesus Christ always did God's will, then why didn't Jesus Christ go around making people sick? The devil makes people sick. Jesus Christ went around healing them because that was God's will.

Acts 10:38
How God anointed Jesus of Nazareth with the Holy Ghost and with power: who went about doing good, and healing all that were oppressed of the devil; for God was with him.

1 John 3:8b
For this purpose the Son of God was manifested, that he might destroy the works of the devil.

Oh today, people blame God for everything. If their businesses fail, they blame God, if their marriages fail, they blame God, if their health fails, they blame God. Don't blame God for your problems. Don't throw your hands up in the air and make excuses by blaming it all on God. Take responsibility for your life, get back to the word, and God will help you sort out your messes.

If you think everything evil that happens comes from God, you are deceived. If you think God makes people sick, you are deceived. If you believe God orchestrates failed marriages, you are deceived. If your business failed and you think God made it happen, you are deceived. Quit making excuses for your failures and quit blaming them on God. It's time to quit driving through spiritual red lights.

So what happened to Job then? If he was perfect and upright, how did the devil get in? If Job wasn't evil, if he had done nothing wrong, had committed no crimes, then how did the devil breach that hedge of protection around him? We don't have to guess, because Job tells us himself in his own words, and we will cover that in the next chapter.

4. The Law of Believing

After all Job had been through, the devil was still not done with him. So far, despite killing his children, destroying his business empire, and making him so sick he was at the point of death, he had failed to break Job's integrity. It was time to try another approach.

> Job 2:11,12
> Now when Job's three friends heard of all this evil that was come upon him, they came every one from his own place; Eliphaz the Temanite, and Bildad the Shuhite, and Zophar the Naamathite: for they had made an appointment together to come to mourn with him and to comfort him.
>
> And when they lifted up their eyes afar off, and knew him not, they lifted up their voice, and wept; and they rent every one his mantle, and sprinkled dust upon their heads toward heaven.

Job was so sick and diseased, that his closest friends did not even recognise him. He must have been a mess.

> Job 2:13
> So they sat down with him upon the ground seven days and seven nights, and none spake a word unto him: for they saw that *his* grief was very great.

They sat there with him and didn't say a word for a whole week. Now it becomes even more important to remember that Job had done nothing to deserve what happened to him. God has told us three times that Job was perfect and upright, and added that all these events happened to him *without a cause*. Therefore, Job was perfect and upright, and had not done anything to deserve all this evil. After a week of silence, Job had a little moan to his three mates.

> Job 3:1,3
> After this opened Job his mouth, and cursed his day.

Let the day perish wherein I was born, and the night *in which* it was said, There is a man child conceived.

And so it goes to verse 24, but then we read something intriguing which begins to unlock the mystery as to how the devil broke through the hedge of protection around Job.

> Job 3:25
> For the thing which I greatly feared is come upon me, and that which I was afraid of is come unto me.

Could it be any plainer? Not only is it written plainly, but it is written twice so we cannot miss it. Job clearly states that what happened to him he had been afraid of all along. Everything was just too good to be true, and in his heart he feared he was going to lose the lot. A clue to this fear manifested itself earlier in the sacrifices he made continually for his children.

If fear is so powerful it can destroy your life like this, what is it? We had better now take some time to learn about fear and, more importantly, how to get rid of it if we have it.

Before moving on, let's visit the majestic courts of Pharaoh, the most powerful ruler on earth who had just dreamed two dreams. Pharaoh then summoned Joseph from prison to interpret them for him.

> Genesis 41:25,32
> And Joseph said unto Pharaoh, The dream of Pharaoh *is* one: God hath shewed Pharaoh what he *is* about to do.
>
> And for that the dream was doubled unto Pharaoh twice; *it is* because the thing *is* established by God, and God will shortly bring it to pass.

Here is a biblical truth that stands throughout the entire bible – when God says something twice it is established.

Job 3:25
For the thing which I greatly feared is come upon me, and that which I was afraid of is come unto me.

God records in the first book of the bible ever written why all this stuff happened to Job, and he recorded it twice, encapsulating it in a figure of speech so we couldn't miss it. It was fear that allowed the devil into Job's life. Job was afraid all this was going to happen to him. That is why it happened. That is how the devil got in, and this brings us to perhaps the most important law in life – the law of believing, that what you believe is what you will receive. Believing has two sides, a positive and a negative. The negative side of believing is called fear. What you believe in your heart is what you are going to bring into reality in your life. It's a law embroidered into the fabric of life that's just as real as gravity.

Mark 11:23
For verily I say unto you, That whosoever shall say unto this mountain, Be thou removed, and be thou cast into the sea; and shall not doubt in his heart, but shall believe that those things which he saith shall come to pass; he shall have whatsoever he saith.

Mark 11:23 is just as true as any other part of the bible. In Mark 5, Jairus, a ruler of the synagogue, asked Jesus to come and heal his young daughter who was at the point of death. Jesus agreed, and off they went. While they were on the way a woman pushed through the jostling crowds and touched the hem of his garment.

Mark 5:25-29
And a certain woman, which had an issue of blood twelve years,

And had suffered many things of many physicians, and had spent all that she had, and was nothing bettered, but rather grew worse,

When she had heard of Jesus, came in the press behind, and touched his garment.

For she said, If I may touch but his clothes, I shall be whole.

And straightway the fountain of her blood was dried up; and she felt in *her* body that she was healed of that plague.

She believed that if she but touched the hem of Jesus' robe she would be healed. She believed that. Note that Jesus did not heal this woman. He didn't do a thing. He was simply walking along the road chatting to Jairus, when this woman pushed through the crowds and stole the healing if you like.

Mark 5:30-34
And Jesus, immediately knowing in himself that virtue had gone out of him, turned him about in the press, and said, Who touched my clothes?

And his disciples said unto him, Thou seest the multitude thronging thee, and sayest thou, Who touched me?

And he looked round about to see her that had done this thing.

But the woman fearing and trembling, knowing what was done in her, came and fell down before him, and told him all the truth.

And he said unto her, Daughter, thy faith (Greek – pistis – believing) hath made thee whole; go in peace, and be whole of thy plague.

The word *faith* is the word *pistis* and should be translated believing here. It was her own believing that made her whole. How do we know? Jesus Christ said so. Jesus Christ didn't minister to her, he didn't lay hands on her, he did absolutely nothing. She was healed because of her own believing. Job lost everything because of his own fear. That is how the law of believing works, positively and negatively. Fear is negative believing. Fear is our enemy.

Jairus, whose daughter needed the healing, then received some bad news.

Mark 5:35
While he yet spake, there came from the ruler of the synagogue's *house certain* which said, Thy daughter is dead: why troublest thou the Master any further?

Being told his daughter was dead was an opportunity for Jairus to fear. We cannot allow negatives to make us afraid. We have to hold our minds to the truth and not be afraid.

> Mark 5:36
> As soon as Jesus heard the word that was spoken, he saith unto the ruler of the synagogue, Be not afraid, only believe.

Read that until you burn it into your mind permanently – be not afraid, only believe... be not afraid, only believe... be not afraid, only believe. God's will is for us to live fearlessly, full of believing. Fear will defeat us while believing will ensure we live powerful, abundant lives. It is up to us which way we live. If we have fear in our lives, we must get rid of it.

In Mark chapter 9, we see an astonishing record that clearly illustrates the law of believing. Jesus had just come down from a mountain with Peter, James, and John and he was approaching a crowd milling about his disciples. He could see something was going on.

> Mark 9:14,15
> And when he came to *his* disciples, he saw a great multitude about them, and the scribes questioning with them.
>
> And straightway all the people, when they beheld him, were greatly amazed, and running to *him* saluted him.

Jesus immediately took control of the situation.

> Mark 9:16
> And he asked the scribes, What question ye with them?

This father then stepped out of the crowd and explained that his son was possessed. He had taken him to Jesus' disciples to have the devil spirit taken out of him, but they had not been able to do it.

> Mark 9:17,18
> And one of the multitude answered and said, Master, I have brought unto thee my son, which hath a dumb spirit;

And wheresoever he [it – the devil spirit] taketh him, he teareth him: and he foameth, and gnasheth with his teeth, and pineth away: and I spake to thy disciples that they should cast him out; and they could not.

Pineth away means *wasted away*, like anorexia, just skin and bone. The boy was also an epileptic. The father took his boy to the disciples to be delivered and was blaming them for the failure.

From what we have just learned about fear and believing, whose job was it to believe for the boy's deliverance? The bleeding woman got deliverance because she believed. This guy didn't get his boy healed, and he blamed the disciples. Who was responsible to believe here? The problem lay with the father, not with the disciples. Jesus Christ became a little frustrated at this. Watch this develop.

Mark 9:19-21
He answereth him, and saith, O faithless [unbelieving] generation, how long shall I be with you? how long shall I suffer [endure] you? bring him unto me.

And they brought him unto him: and when he saw him, straightway the spirit tare him; and he fell on the ground, and wallowed foaming.

And he asked his father, How long is it ago since this came unto him? And he said, Of a child.

The boy had an epileptic fit right there in front of Jesus Christ. So there he was, foaming and jerking on the ground, but instead of ministering to the boy, Jesus turned to the father. Jesus did not immediately minister to the boy. Why not? Simple, because he knew it would be a waste of time. Instead, Jesus asked questions, working with the father. He knew what the problem was, and searched for a solution. The problem lay not with his disciples, he knew that. The father was responsible to believe for his boy's deliverance. The father continued.

Mark 9:22
And ofttimes it hath cast him into the fire, and into the waters, to destroy him: but if thou canst do any thing, have compassion on us, and help us.

It is remarkable this boy was still alive. The devil spirit had tried many times to drown him by making him jump into deep water, and to burn him to death by throwing him into fires. The father was obviously doing his best, that's for sure. Remember, the bleeding woman was healed because she believed, not because Jesus Christ waved a magic wand. There is no magic in this. Healing is available today, just as it was then, but it requires believing. Without believing, Jesus Christ knew he could do nothing. Jesus Christ could not heal people unless they believed. He was not some wizard who went around casting magic spells. Magic is for the lazy and the gullible.

Mark 9:23
Jesus said unto him, If thou canst believe, all things *are* possible to him that believeth.

If *thou* canst believe, he said, jabbing his figurative finger on the man's chest, all things are possible to him that believeth. He pointed at the father and told him straight – this is up to you.

Mark 9:24
And straightway the father of the child cried out, and said with tears, Lord, I believe; help thou mine unbelief.

Jesus Christ nailed the problem. When he was happy the man was believing, he then ministered to the boy, not before.

Mark 9:25,26
When Jesus saw that the people came running together, he rebuked the foul spirit, saying unto him, *Thou* dumb and deaf spirit, I charge thee, come out of him, and enter no more into him.

And *the spirit* cried, and rent him sore, and came out of him: and he was as one dead; insomuch that many said, He is dead.

'You've really done it now Jesus,' some of them muttered behind his back, 'you've killed the boy.'

> Mark 9:27
> But Jesus took him by the hand, and lifted him up; and he arose.

It was believing that was required, just as with the bleeding woman. A record in the gospel of John should help to establish this truth for us.

> John 5:2,3
> Now there is at Jerusalem by the sheep *market* a pool, which is called in the Hebrew tongue Bethesda, having five porches.
>
> In these lay a great multitude of impotent folk, of blind, halt, withered, waiting for the moving of the water.

How many is a great multitude? We don't know. The word does not tell us, and if the word does not tell us, then we do not know. However, a multitude is many people, we know that much. There were many sick, lame, and blind people lying around this pool.

> John 5:5,6
> And a certain man was there, which had an infirmity thirty and eight years.
>
> When Jesus saw him lie, and knew that he had been now a long time *in that case*, he saith unto him, Wilt thou be made whole?

Jesus Christ asked the guy the question to find out if he was believing. When he was sure the man was believing, he ministered to him.

> John 5:8,9
> Jesus saith unto him, Rise, take up thy bed, and walk.
>
> And immediately the man was made whole, and took up his bed, and walked: and on the same day was the sabbath.

More remarkable perhaps than this healing is that no one else around that pool was healed. Why didn't Jesus just heal everyone else down there? Why didn't he wave his magic wand and magic their problems away? Obviously, no one else down there was believing to be healed. It's that simple. Without believing, nothing happens. If we believe, we get the results. This is again illustrated in Acts 3.

> Acts 3:1,2
> Now Peter and John went up together into the temple at the hour of prayer, *being* the ninth *hour.*
>
> And a certain man lame from his mother's womb was carried, whom they laid daily at the gate of the temple which is called Beautiful, to ask alms of them that entered into the temple;

This man was laid at the gate of the temple every day. Chapter 4 even tells us how old he was.

> Acts 4:22
> For the man was above forty years old, on whom this miracle of healing was shewed.

How many times do you think Jesus went into the temple during his life? Hundreds of times? Thousands? The point is, how many times do you think Jesus Christ walked past this guy and didn't heal him? Why did Jesus not heal him? Well, now you know why. The man obviously had not believed to be healed. However, I will bet Jesus stopped and taught him the word on a number of occasions to help him build his believing, and I will also bet that's why the man was now believing at this point, and that was why the door opened for Peter and John to heal him. How do we build our believing then?

> Romans 10:17
> So then faith [believing] *cometh* by hearing, and hearing by the word of God.

So there was the lame man, believing to be healed. What happened?

> Act 3:3-8
> Who seeing Peter and John about to go into the temple asked an alms.

And Peter, fastening his eyes upon him with John, said, Look on us

And he gave heed unto them, expecting to receive something of them [he was believing].

Then Peter said, Silver and gold have I none; but such as I have give I thee: In the name of Jesus Christ of Nazareth rise up and walk.

And he took him by the right hand, and lifted *him* up: and immediately his feet and ankle bones received strength.

And he leaping up stood, and walked, and entered with them into the temple, walking, and leaping, and praising God.

There is no magic in believing or in healing. Believing comes by hearing, and hearing by the word of God, as it says in Romans 10:17. If you need healing but need to build your believing, get your head into God's word. Healing is available if you believe for it, and I don't care what the problem is. God can take care of anything if we believe. God can even make blind people see.

Mark 10:46,47
And they came to Jericho: and as he [Jesus] went out of Jericho with his disciples and a great number of people, blind Bartimaeus, the son of Timaeus, sat by the highway side begging.

And when he heard that it was Jesus of Nazareth, he began to cry out, and say, Jesus, *thou* Son of David, have mercy on me.

As Jesus wandered around Jericho, this blind guy at the side of the road heard the commotion and asked what was going on. When he heard it was Jesus, he started bawling for him to come heal him.

Mark 10:48
And many charged him that he should hold his peace: but he cried the more a great deal, *Thou* Son of David, have mercy on me.

Look at these people. What was their response? S*hut it mate, you're making a noise.* Bartimaeus ignored them, and bawled even louder.

Mark 10:49,50
And Jesus stood still, and commanded him to be called. And they call the blind man, saying unto him, Be of good comfort, rise; he calleth thee.

And he, casting away his garment, rose, and came to Jesus.

So Barty chucked away his robe and stumbled forward, helped no doubt by a few who were telling him to shut up moments earlier. We must not allow popular opinion and the fleeting social fads of the day to squelch our believing.

Mark 10:51,52
And Jesus answered and said unto him, What wilt thou that I should do unto thee? The blind man said unto him, Lord, that I might receive my sight.

And Jesus said unto him, Go thy way; thy faith [believing] hath made thee whole. And immediately he received his sight, and followed Jesus in the way.

Jesus did not wave a magic wand here either. The guy was believing, and that's why he got his sight back. The word is simple and beautiful. Look at this record of Paul healing a cripple in the book of Acts.

Acts 14:8-10
And there sat a certain man at Lystra, impotent in his feet, being a cripple from his mother's womb, who never had walked:

The same heard Paul speak: who stedfastly beholding him, and perceiving that he had faith [believing] to be healed,

Said with a loud voice, Stand upright on thy feet. And he leaped and walked.

Paul was able to heal him because he was believing. Perhaps you think your illness or incapacity is too big for God to sort out. Well, there is a record in the bible where a man who had no hand received a hand. God gave him a hand when he didn't even have one. God can do anything if we believe.

Mark 3:1-5
And he entered again into the synagogue; and there was a man there which had a withered hand.

And they [the church leaders] watched him, whether he would heal him on the sabbath day; that they might accuse him.

And he saith unto the man which had the withered hand, Stand forth.

And he saith unto them [the church leaders], Is it lawful to do good on the sabbath days, or to do evil? to save life, or to kill? But they held their peace.

And when he had looked round about on them with anger, being grieved for the hardness of their hearts, he saith unto the man, Stretch forth thine hand. And he stretched *it* out: and his hand was restored whole as the other.

Back to Job.

Job 3:25,26
For the thing which I greatly feared is come upon me, and that which I was afraid of is come unto me.

I was not in safety, neither had I rest, neither was I quiet; yet trouble came.

Job was afraid he was going to lose his business. He was afraid he was going to lose his children. He was afraid he was going to lose his health. Life was just too good, and in his heart he was afraid he was going to lose the lot. It happened just as he believed for it to happen. That was the break in the hedge that allowed the devil in. What we believe today is where we will be tomorrow. We will be tomorrow where our believing will take us. The law of believing is an integral part of life just like gravity. If you're afraid, God's word can replace that fear with believing. Put your fear building televisions away, pick up a bible and read it.

Proverbs 29:25
The fear of man bringeth a snare: but whoso putteth his trust in the LORD shall be safe.

Job was perfect and upright, yes, but he was afraid. Now that we understand why all this happened to him, it is time to go back and catch up with our friend Job.

5. Spiritual Integrity part 2

Before moving on, let's recall what God thinks of Job. You may think I'm labouring the point, but I have good reason.

> Job 1:1
> There was a man in the land of Uz, whose name *was* Job; and that man was perfect and upright, and one that feared God, and eschewed evil.

> Job 1:8
> And the LORD said unto Satan, Hast thou considered my servant Job, that *there is* none like him in the earth, a perfect and an upright man, one that feareth God, and escheweth evil?

> Job 2:3
> And the LORD said unto Satan, Hast thou considered my servant Job, that *there is* none like him in the earth, a perfect and an upright man, one that feareth God, and escheweth evil? and still he holdeth fast his integrity, although thou movedst me against him, to destroy him without cause.

God tells us three times Job was perfect and upright. That has not changed. We have also been told that all this happened to him *without cause*, he didn't do anything to deserve it. Now let's meet Eliphaz the Temanite, Bildad the Shuhite and Zophar the Naamathite. After a week of silence, Job's mate Eliphaz answered him with a sympathetic voice, intimating that he appreciated all the wonderful things Job had ever done.

> Job 4:1-7
> Then Eliphaz the Temanite answered and said,
>
> *If* we assay to commune with thee, wilt thou be grieved? but who can withhold himself from speaking?

> Behold, thou hast instructed many, and thou hast strengthened the weak hands.
>
> Thy words have upholden him that was falling, and thou hast strengthened the feeble knees.
>
> But now it is come upon thee, and thou faintest; it toucheth thee, and thou art troubled.
>
> *Is* not *this* thy fear, thy confidence, thy hope, and the uprightness of thy ways?
>
> Remember, I pray thee, who *ever* perished, being innocent? or where were the righteous cut off?

Wait a minute, what is this dude saying? God has told us three times that Job was perfect and upright; now Eliphaz tells him he must have done something terribly wrong in his life to deserve all this evil.

> Job 4:8
> Even as I have seen, they that plow iniquity, and sow wickedness, reap the same.

My goodness, Eliphaz told Job he reaped what he sowed, he got what he deserved. Job had just lost all his kids, and his mate told him he deserved it. Then Eliphaz told him, with a religiously sympathetic voice no doubt, that God did all this to him because he was evil. Here is the devil trying to make Job blame God for the evil, and this time he's doing it through his religious friends.

> Job 4:9
> By the blast of God they perish, and by the breath of his nostrils are they consumed.

You know something, Job did not need to be lectured here, he needed the word, he needed to be loved. Yet there was his religious mate waggling accusatory fingers at him when he was down. Isn't that just like religion, condemning people, making them feel guilty and worthless.

Job was in desperate need of love, comfort, and support, not religious lectures. Eliphaz continued.

> Job 5:2-4,17
> For wrath killeth the foolish man, and envy slayeth the silly one.
>
> I have seen the foolish taking root: but suddenly I cursed his habitation.
>
> His children are far from safety, and they are crushed in the gate, neither *is there* any to deliver *them*.
>
> Behold, happy *is* the man whom God correcteth: therefore despise not thou the chastening of the Almighty:

The devil did all the evil to Job, not God, but according to Eliphaz, God did all this to Job, and that Job was to accept it as punishment and be happy about it. You can hear this very same horseshit taught in churches and religions all around the world today. Nothing much has changed in a few thousand years, hey? Job was perfect and upright, so this dude, despite his sincerity and impressive religious education, was wrong. Oh, he thought he was right, he thought he was speaking for God, he thought he knew his bible, he was sincere and religious and sympathetic, but he was full of horseshit.

> Job 5:18
> For he maketh sore, and bindeth up: he woundeth, and his hands make whole.

Yes, the wicked and evil are going to suffer consequences for what they do, but Job was not wicked or evil was he? He was perfect and upright, remember? This stuff happened to him *without a cause*. The devil persistently whispers in our ears about how worthless we are, and how much we fall short. More often than not we hear this stuff through our closest friends and family, just like Job. It really makes no difference to the devil who speaks his words to us just so long as they are spoken.

> Job 5:27
> Lo this, we have searched it, so it *is*; hear it, and know thou *it* for thy good.

Eliphaz ended by telling Job to clean his life up, get back in fellowship with God, and everything would be fine again. What a patronising religious asshole.

Job had a little think about this, realised his friend was full of horseshit, pushed his extreme hurt to one side, and decided to reach out to him with the word to try to help him. Job loved Eliphaz enough to tell him honestly that he was handling the word of God deceitfully. Despite his pain, sorrow, and physical sickness, Job loved big enough to teach the truth to those who needed it.

> Job 6:15
> My brethren have dealt deceitfully as a brook, *and* as the stream of brooks they pass away;

Take a moment to consider Job's physical condition. Despite his circumstances, he was still ministering the word. No wonder God called him perfect and upright. Would we love people big enough to teach God's word if we were as sick and hurt as Job? Sometimes I don't feel like teaching when I have a stupid little cold or a headache. Think that through sometime. In addition, consider that these are the first lessons God ever had written in his word, selah.

> Job 6:25,28
> How forcible are right words! but what doth your arguing reprove?
>
> Now therefore be content, look upon me; for *it is* evident unto you if I lie.

The word has power, but the words spoken to Job were empty words. Job implores them to consider things because if he were a liar, it would be evident. Bildad's turn. Let's see if he was more spiritually alert than Eliphaz.

> Job 8:1,2
> Then answered Bildad the Shuhite, and said,
>
> How long wilt thou speak these *things*? and *how long shall* the words of thy mouth *be like* a strong wind?

Bildad started by telling Job he was full of wind. He then went on to lecture him a little more.

> Job 8:3
> Doth God pervert judgment? or doth the Almighty pervert justice?

Now we are getting to the point. Remember what the devil was up to here? He was trying to get Job to blame God for all his problems and thus break his integrity. Here was Bildad continuing with this same line of attack. Breaking Job's spiritual integrity had been the whole point of these attacks from the start. Bildad told Job that God did not pervert judgement, that if Job were perfect and upright, God would not have allowed all this to happen to him. He even went so far as to imply that Job, because he claimed he was righteous, was actually accusing God of perverting justice, which was accusing God of evil. Job's friends were convinced God did all this to him because Job had committed some serious crime or other.

> Job 8:6,13,20
> If thou *wert* pure and upright; surely now he would awake for thee, and make the habitation of thy righteousness prosperous.
>
> So *are* the paths of all that forget God; and the hypocrite's hope shall perish:
>
> Behold, God will not cast away a perfect *man*, neither will he help the evil doers:

Bildad closed by calling Job a hypocrite, explaining that God would not allow such calamities to happen to good men.

Job had another little think about all this, again pushed his personal hurt, his misery, sickness, and pain to one side, and decided to continue ministering the word to these guys. I think I would have told them to fuck off. I guess I have a bit of growing to do in the love category. Not Job, he was perfect and upright, he taught them the word. This guy was a disciple. This is what it takes to be perfect and upright, even in the face of such austere circumstances. Look at the strength in the man. Job continued:

Job 10:7
Thou [God] knowest that I am not wicked; and *there is* none that can deliver out of thine hand.

He talked aloud here, and he declared that God knew he was telling the truth. Then it was Zophar's turn.

Job 11:1-3
Then answered Zophar the Naamathite, and said,

Should not the multitude of words be answered? and should a man full of talk be justified?

Should thy lies make men hold their peace? and when thou mockest, shall no man make thee ashamed?

A man full of talk? A man full of wind? A hypocrite? A *liar?* What kind of friends are these? Oh, churches these days are full of friends like these, just as they were back then.

Job 11:4
For thou hast said, My doctrine *is* pure, and I am clean in thine eyes.

Job had said just that. He was still holding onto his integrity, refusing to blame God for what had happened to him. That is what the devil was trying to break in his mind. Job did not break when he lost everything. He did not break when his children were killed. He did not break when he became diseased. He did not break when his wife told him to curse God and die. The devil was still attacking, this time through his friends, still trying to break his integrity, still trying to get him to blame God for doing all the evil to him. His friends thought they were speaking the truth, while all the time they were speaking the devil's lies. If there is anything to learn from this in our day and time, it is to avoid those in religious robes with expensive religious educations. Churches to this day still teach that God makes people sick because they are sinners. Churches have learned nothing since the days of Job.

Job 11:5,6
But oh that God would speak, and open his lips against thee;

And that he would shew thee the secrets of wisdom, that *they are* double to that which is! Know therefore that God exacteth of thee *less* than thine iniquity *deserveth*.

Zophar reckoned Job got less than he deserved. What exactly did Job have left? Only his life. Barely. His mate told him he was so evil that God has been merciful to him in keeping him alive when he should have been dead.

Job 11:14,20
If iniquity *be* in thine hand, put it far away, and let not wickedness dwell in thy tabernacles.

But the eyes of the wicked shall fail, and they shall not escape, and their hope *shall be as* the giving up of the ghost.

Job had another little think about all this, and answered with some heavy sarcasm.

Job 12:2,3
No doubt but ye *are* the people, and wisdom shall die with you.

But I have understanding as well as you; I *am* not inferior to you: yea, who knoweth not such things as these?

Job 13:2,4,5
What ye know, *the same* do I know also: I *am* not inferior unto you.

But ye *are* forgers of lies, ye *are* all physicians of no value.

O that ye would altogether hold your peace! and it should be your wisdom.

Look at the power in these words. Forgers of lies. Physicians of no value. Then he told them the wisest thing they could do would be to shut up. And so it continues back and forth through the book of Job. Here are a few more instances where Job was accused of being evil, yet maintained his innocence and fought for his integrity. He absolutely refused to listen to their arguments that God had done this to him. He refused to succumb to their logic. He refused to blame God for making him sick, killing his children and destroying his business. That's holding fast your integrity.

> Job 15:1,2
> Then answered Eliphaz the Temanite, and said,
>
> Should a wise man utter vain knowledge, and fill his belly with the east wind?
>
> Job 16:1,2,16,17,19
> Then Job answered and said,
>
> I have heard many such things: miserable comforters *are* ye all.
>
> My face is foul with weeping, and on my eyelids *is* the shadow of death;
>
> Not for *any* injustice in mine hands: also my prayer *is* pure.
>
> Also now, behold, my witness *is* in heaven, and my record *is* on high.
>
> Job 18:1,21
> Then answered Bildad the Shuhite, and said,
>
> Surely such *are* the dwellings of the wicked, and this *is* the place *of him that* knoweth not God.
>
> Job 19:1,2,22-24
> Then Job answered and said,
>
> How long will ye vex my soul, and break me in pieces with words?
>
> Why do ye persecute me as God, and are not satisfied with my flesh?

Oh that my words were now written! oh that they were printed in a book!

That they were graven with an iron pen and lead in the rock for ever!

Job 20:1,3-5,29
Then answered Zophar the Naamathite, and said,

I have heard the check of my reproach, and the spirit of my understanding causeth me to answer.

Knowest thou *not* this of old, since man was placed upon earth,

That the triumphing of the wicked *is* short, and the joy of the hypocrite *but* for a moment?

This *is* the portion of a wicked man from God, and the heritage appointed unto him by God.

Job 22:1,5,10
Then Eliphaz the Temanite answered and said,

Is not thy wickedness great? and thine iniquities infinite?

Therefore snares *are* round about thee, and sudden fear troubleth thee;

Job 23:1,10-12
Then Job answered and said,

But he [God] knoweth the way that I take: *when* he hath tried me, I shall come forth as gold.

My foot hath held his steps, his way have I kept, and not declined.

Neither have I gone back from the commandment of his lips; I have esteemed the words of his mouth more than my necessary *food*.

Job 25:1,4,6
Then answered Bildad the Shuhite, and said,

How then can man be justified with God? or how can he be clean *that is* born of a woman?

How much less man, *that is* a worm? and the son of man, *which is* a worm? [author's note - you speak for yourself Bildad, wanker].

Job 26:1; Job 27:3-6
But Job answered and said,

All the while my breath *is* in me, and the spirit of God is in my nostrils;

My lips shall not speak wickedness, nor my tongue utter deceit.

God forbid that I should justify you: till I die I will not remove mine integrity from me.

My righteousness I hold fast, and will not let it go: my heart shall not reproach *me* so long as I live.

Here's a man taking a stand for his life, fighting for his integrity by refusing to blame God for his problems. This is what it takes to hold fast to your integrity. Learn this lesson well. God is good always. Learn to stop at this spiritual red traffic light. Do not ever accuse God of evil.

Job 31:39,40
If I have eaten the fruits thereof without money, or have caused the owners thereof to lose their life:

Let thistles grow instead of wheat, and cockle instead of barley. The words of Job are ended.

Job 32:1
So these three men ceased to answer Job, because he *was* righteous in his own eyes.

Spiritual integrity is important, so important that it is the main subject of the entire first book of the bible ever written. In the book of Job we clearly see the importance of holding fast to our integrity, refusing to blame God for evil. We also clearly see the effort the devil is willing to expend to break our integrity. When someone dies that is near and dear to us, do we hold our minds to the truth, or do we run the way of the world and in our sorrow and hurt blame God? If you really must blame someone for death, blame the devil, he is, after all, the author of it. God is not the author of death. He is light and in him is no darkness at all.

> 1 John 1:5
> This then is the message which we have heard of him, and declare unto you, that God is light, and in him is no darkness at all.

That is what the word says. Does this verse come to your mind when you are under attack and tempted to think evil about God? I have never blamed God for problems that have come up in my life, ever, or accused him of doing criminal, evil things to me. My integrity I hold fast and will not let it go, my heart shall not reproach me so long as I live.

It's interesting to be aware of the background to the book of Job, as it helps us understand why God had it written first. Look at what Moses had to deal with leading God's people out of slavery in Egypt. Those complaining, bitching Israelites accused God of taking them and their children into the wilderness to murder them with hunger, or murder them with their enemies swords, or murder them with thirst. No wonder these were the first lessons Moses wrote in what we know today as the bible. If you want the bible to make sense for you, and you want to see the power of God in your life, then start here and don't ever accuse God of evil. James has a verse worth memorising in this regards.

> James 4:7
> Submit yourselves therefore to God. Resist the devil, and he will flee from you.

I doubt any man that has ever lived has had to fight as hard as Job to retain his integrity. Did the devil flee? Oh yes, Job resisted and James 4:7 is the truth. If you hold the word and do not break, the devil will be defeated. God promises that and, unlike the devil, God is not a liar.

Job 42:7,8
And it was *so*, that after the LORD had spoken these words unto Job, the LORD said to Eliphaz the Temanite, My wrath is kindled against thee, and against thy two friends: for ye have not spoken of me *the thing that is* right, as my servant Job *hath*.

Therefore take unto you now seven bullocks and seven rams, and go to my servant Job, and offer up for yourselves a burnt offering; and my servant Job shall pray for you: for him will I accept: lest I deal with you *after your* folly, in that ye have not spoken of me *the thing which is* right, like my servant Job.

God took those three religious idiots into his office for a stern talking to. See, they were wrong all along and Job was right. Never accuse God of doing evil. Learn a few scriptures like 1 John 1:5 above and hold them in your mind so the next time you're tempted to think evil of God and hurl accusations in his face you can fight back with the word. Do not allow the devil to break your integrity.

Job 42:9,10
So Eliphaz the Temanite and Bildad the Shuhite *and* Zophar the Naamathite went, and did according as the LORD commanded them: the LORD also accepted Job.

And the LORD turned the captivity of Job, when he prayed for his friends: also the LORD gave Job twice as much as he had before.

Job had been the richest man in the world, and now he was twice as rich. That is deliverance. If you are under attack and want deliverance, blaming God for your problems is not the way to go. Rather, God has the answers and he is more than willing to help you. Just do not blame him for your problems.

Job 42:12-17
So the LORD blessed the latter end of Job more than his beginning: for he had fourteen thousand sheep, and six thousand camels, and a thousand yoke of oxen, and a thousand she asses.

He had also seven sons and three daughters.

And he called the name of the first, Jemima; and the name of the second, Kezia; and the name of the third, Kerenhappuch.

And in all the land were no women found *so* fair as the daughters of Job: and their father gave them inheritance among their brethren.

After this lived Job an hundred and forty years, and saw his sons, and his sons' sons, *even* four generations.

So Job died, *being* old and full of days.

Having us blame God for our problems, thereby breaking our spiritual integrity is perhaps the most effective weapon in the devil's arsenal. In the book of Job we see what it takes to withstand his attacks and be victorious. This is what it takes to stand for the true God for a lifetime. Do not ever break on this point. It is no wonder the book of Job was the first book of the bible ever written.

6. Dealing with Fear

It is time now to deal with fear. Anyone who has lived in fear doesn't have to be told it's a terrible place to be. Job didn't enjoy the consequences of fear, and we won't enjoy them either. I've been afraid, and I know from personal experience that fear encases and defeats you. Can fear be overcome? Can we live without fear? Is such a thing possible? According to God's word, yes it is, very much so.

> 2 Timothy 1:7
> For God hath not given us the spirit of fear; but of power, and of love, and of a sound mind.

Fear here is contrasted with power, love, and a sound mind. By biblical definition then, being afraid is not living with power, it is not living with love, and it is not having a sound mind. One of the benefits to having power, love and a sound mind is living without fear, and that's a wonderful place to be.

> 1 John 4:18
> There is no fear in love; but perfect love casteth out fear: because fear hath torment. He that feareth is not made perfect in love.

Here again, fear is contrasted with love. In other words, fear and love cannot mix. Contrary to common christian belief and teaching, someone cannot be full of love and full of fear at the same time. Like an antidote to snake poison, love is the antidote to fear. Love is, therefore, more powerful than fear. That's right, there is something more powerful in life than fear, and you can have it if you want it. David lived without fear, even when he was still a teenager looking after the family sheep.

> Psalm 23:4
> Yea, though I walk through the valley of the shadow of death, I will fear no evil: for thou art with me; thy rod and thy staff they comfort me.

It wasn't paradise for David living out in the wild countryside. The wilds had their challenges, and not just from the weather – there were dangerous animals, robbers, rustlers, and invading enemies to be concerned about. David lived in the wilds for much of his teenage life, day and night, in all weathers. He enjoyed his life and enjoyed sweet sleep, even while living rough in the country alone with his sheep.

> Proverbs 3:24
> When thou liest down, thou shalt not be afraid: yea, thou shalt lie down, and thy sleep shall be sweet.

David wasn't afraid of anything. Remember Goliath? David was only a teenager when he faced him. Even children can be fearless.

So does God want us to be afraid? No, because God didn't give us the spirit of fear. God gives us a spirit of power, and of love and of a sound mind. That's what God gives, therefore he does not want us to be afraid. If we have fear, we are not made perfect in love, because there is no fear in love. When the children of Israel were camped on the shores of the Red Sea and pharaoh's armies were marching after them, God told his people by way of his prophet Moses to fear not.

> Exodus 14:13
> And Moses said unto the people, Fear ye not, stand still, and see the salvation of the LORD, which he will shew to you to day: for the Egyptians whom ye have seen to day, ye shall see them again no more for ever.

When Moses was dead and Joshua was charged with leading God's people into the promised land, God told him to fear not.

Joshua 1:9
Have not I commanded thee? Be strong and of a good courage; be not afraid, neither be thou dismayed: for the LORD thy God *is* with thee whithersoever thou goest.

While Ahab was scouring the world for Elijah during a famine, God sent Elijah to Zidon to meet up with a widow who was preparing a last meal for her and her son. Elijah told her to fear not.

1 Kings 17:13,14
And Elijah said unto her, Fear not; go *and* do as thou hast said: but make me thereof a little cake first, and bring *it* unto me, and after make for thee and for thy son.

For thus saith the LORD God of Israel, The barrel of meal shall not waste, neither shall the cruse of oil fail, until the day *that* the LORD sendeth rain upon the earth.

When the king of Syria sent his special forces to take Elisha, and Elisha's servant looked over the city walls and saw the army, the word to him was fear not.

2 Kings 6:16
And he [Elisha] answered, Fear not: for they that *be* with us *are* more than they that *be* with them.

When Jairus had come to Jesus to ask for healing for his daughter, and his servants came and told him his daughter was dead, Jesus Christ immediately confronted his fear, and then went and healed his daughter anyway, despite her being dead.

Luke 8:50
But when Jesus heard *it*, he answered him, saying, Fear not: believe only, and she shall be made whole.

Time and again, throughout the bible, the exhortation is to fear not, to not be afraid, to be courageous, to be without fear.

Proverbs 3:25,26
Be not afraid of sudden fear, neither of the desolation of the wicked, when it cometh.

For the LORD shall be thy confidence, and shall keep thy foot from being taken.

Matthew 14:26,27
And when the disciples saw him walking on the sea, they were troubled, saying, It is a spirit; and they cried out for fear.

But straightway Jesus spake unto them, saying, Be of good cheer; it is I; be not afraid.

It is clear that fear and love cannot co-exist. They cannot survive together, they are not mutually compatible, they do not enjoy any kind of symbiosis. If you have love, you have no fear. If you're afraid, you are not made perfect in love. Love is the antidote, the cure, the fix, the solution, the way to escape from fear.

We now need to define our terms so that we can see clearly and think soundly regarding both love and fear. We need to know what they are. These are not nebulous concepts or ethereal myths, they are as real as gravity. They exist and they both affect our lives, so we need to understand exactly what they are. First, we will deal with fear. Here is a dictionary definition:

1. A distressing emotion aroused by impending danger, or evil, whether the threat is real or imagined; the feeling or condition of being afraid
2. A specific instance of or propensity for such a feeling, like an abnormal fear of heights.
3. Concern or anxiety; a fear for personal safety.
4. Reverential awe, especially toward God, used in the bible as the fear of God.
5. Something that causes feelings of dread or apprehension; something a person is afraid of, such as being in a road accident.

There are a number of points here. Firstly, fear has a few different meanings. Similar to our English word *bank*, which can be a river bank, a sand bank, an aircraft banking to port or starboard, or a bank where we stash our money, fear also has different meanings, and only from the context of where the word is set can we determine which meaning it carries.

Anxiety, for example, is a normal human emotion, and although technically it can be classified as fear, it can actually keep you safe. If you are driving too fast and you begin to feel anxious, it's probably because you are putting your life at risk. If you slow down, the anxiety fades and the danger passes. Feeling anxious isn't wrong. Without anxiety, life would be dangerous. I parachuted a few times out of a Hercules C130 aircraft, and I can assure you I know what anxiety feels like. But when a hand slapped my shoulder and someone shouted *Go*, I jumped. If I'd had fear, they would have weeded me out on the Trainasium during P Company at Aldershot. I wasn't afraid to jump out of an aircraft, but it sure made me anxious as hell waiting for that green light to come on. Anxiety is a normal human emotion which God built into the fabric of life to help keep us safe. Like any emotion, it can be controlled, so don't confuse anxiety with fear.

Anxiety if not controlled however, can lead to fear, that's the distinction. Like all emotions, it is only when anxiety gets out of control that we have problems. That's what happened with Job. Anxiety, like any emotion, if not controlled can become dangerous. Human love is great, but if not controlled it can quickly grow into lust, where you commit evil acts to satiate your own selfish desires, such as homosexuality, rape, bestiality, and paedophilia. It is how we deal with our emotions that determines whether we control them or they control us. If anxiety is not dealt with, it can grow into something particularly dangerous, as the book of Job teaches.

> Job 1:5
> And it was so, when the days of *their* feasting were gone about, that Job sent and sanctified them, and rose up early in the morning, and offered burnt offerings *according* to the number of them all: for Job said, It may be that my sons have sinned, and cursed God in their hearts. Thus did Job continually.

Job had anxiety. He was concerned that his sons were neglecting God and perhaps even cursing him silently in their hearts. Instead of dealing with it by confronting his sons and sorting it out, he offered burnt offerings for them every morning. What was it that made him think his children were cursing God in their hearts? Did he see things in their lives that caused him concern? Whatever the reasons, Job did not deal with his anxiety and allowed it to grow into dangerous fears. As the word teaches, fear is believing, and what we believe for is what we are going to see in our lives. Job learned this lesson the hard way. God had his life recorded so we could learn from him and avoid the consequences of fear. Job was a great man though. He pulled himself together and God turned his life around so that he had twice as much as before. He even had another family. He never again permitted fear into his life after that either.

Next, we need to look at love to ensure we know exactly what we're talking about here. You see the word *love* in 2 Timothy 1:7 and 1 John 4:18 isn't talking about human love, it is the Greek word *agapē* which is the love of God, and we will deal with that in the next chapter.

7. Agapē: The Love of God

Before we delve into agapē, I'll first point out that in over 35 years of biblical research and teaching, I have never taught on the love of God before now. Not once. Ever. Why? Simply, because in my heart I knew I didn't understand it. Oh, don't get me wrong, I've listened to hundreds of teachings on the subject, and I've pondered over it and scratched my head about it, but I've just never felt comfortable teaching it. You see 1 Corinthians 13 is set within the context of chapters 12 and 14, yet in all the hundreds of teachings on the love of God I've heard from 1 Corinthians 13, not one of them has ever set agapē, the love of God, within the context of the proper operation of the manifestations of holy spirit, which is what chapters 12 and 14 deal with. But let's not get ahead of ourselves.

Agapē, the love of God, often translated *charity* in the bible, has been defined as the love of God in the renewed mind in manifestation. This is a good definition, but unfortunately, as it is couched in rather scholarly language, it lends itself easily to misinterpretation. At the moment we're still defining our terms so we understand what fear is and what love is.

First, let's look at what love isn't. Often, a good way to see what something is in the bible is to look at what it is not. Ask yourself a question. Did Peter, Stephen, Paul, and Jesus Christ manifest the love of God? Without question, of course they did. Here are a few records then, where Peter, Stephen, Paul, and Jesus Christ manifested the love of God.

> Acts 5:1-11
> But a certain man named Ananias, with Sapphira his wife, sold a possession,
>
> And kept back *part* of the price, his wife also being privy *to it*, and brought a certain part, and laid *it* at the apostles' feet.

But Peter said, Ananias, why hath Satan filled thine heart to lie to the Holy Ghost, and to keep back *part* of the price of the land?

Whiles it remained, was it not thine own? and after it was sold, was it not in thine own power? why hast thou conceived this thing in thine heart? thou hast not lied unto men, but unto God.

And Ananias hearing these words fell down, and gave up the ghost [he died]: and great fear came on all them that heard these things.

And the young men arose, wound him up, and carried *him* out, and buried *him*.

And it was about the space of three hours after, when his wife, not knowing what was done, came in.

And Peter answered unto her, Tell me whether ye sold the land for so much? And she said, Yea, for so much.

Then Peter said unto her, How is it that ye have agreed together to tempt the Spirit of the Lord? behold, the feet of them which have buried thy husband *are* at the door, and shall carry thee out.

Then fell she down straightway at his feet, and yielded up the ghost: and the young men came in, and found her dead, and, carrying *her* forth, buried *her* by her husband.

And great fear came upon all the church, and upon as many as heard these things.

Did Peter walk with agapē, the love of God in the renewed mind in manifestation here? Certainly, that is without question. Peter was walking with the love of God in the renewed mind in manifestation when he confronted Ananias and Sapphira and they dropped dead right there in front of him. Peter didn't kill them, but he did confront them so publicly and so directly that their own shame and guilt killed them.

To understand this record, we need to look at a few details. Ananias and Sapphira were not *required* to sell this property. This was a surplus property they didn't need, and they decided to sell it and use the money to help move the word. Nothing wrong so far. When it was sold, they were not *required* to give any of that money to Peter. The problem here had nothing whatsoever to do with the money. The problem was that they lied about the amount they sold the house for. They lied, that was the issue, not the money. Rather than simply give honestly about the amount, which would have been wonderful with God and Peter, they lied about the amount the property was sold for, kept back part of the price, and lied to Peter when they gave the rest of the money, claiming it was the total proceeds of the sale. Their giving wasn't the issue, it was their lying that was the issue. Peter didn't confront their giving, he confronted their lying. Peter told Ananias he had not lied unto men but unto God.

Peter handled the situation with the love of God. If you have a problem understanding this in the context of love, then your understanding of agapē, the love of God in the renewed mind in manifestation, is misconstrued. What about Stephen? Did he walk with the love of God in the renewed mind in manifestation when he confronted the Sanhedrin?

> Acts 7:51-58
> Ye stiffnecked and uncircumcised in heart and ears, ye do always resist the Holy Ghost: as your fathers *did*, so *do* ye.
>
> Which of the prophets have not your fathers persecuted? and they have slain them which shewed before of the coming of the Just One; of whom ye have been now the betrayers and murderers:
>
> Who have received the law by the disposition of angels, and have not kept *it*.
>
> When they heard these things, they were cut to the heart, and they gnashed on him with *their* teeth.
>
> But he, being full of the Holy Ghost, looked up stedfastly into heaven, and saw the glory of God, and Jesus standing on the right hand of God,
>
> And said, Behold, I see the heavens opened, and the Son of man standing on the right hand of God.

Then they cried out with a loud voice, and stopped their ears, and ran upon him with one accord,

And cast *him* out of the city, and stoned *him*: and the witnesses laid down their clothes at a young man's feet, whose name was Saul.

Stephen had been illegally arrested and was on trial accused of breaking God's laws. False witnesses, liars had been paid by the Sanhedrin to commit perjury so they could prosecute Stephen. The council had set him up. Instead of grovelling before them, making excuses, and compromising so he could wriggle out of their slimy net, Stephen confronted them to their faces with their hypocrisy and lies. Stephen told the Sanhedrin to their faces in a court of law that they were uncircumcised in heart and ears. He insulted them publicly in the most vehement language he possessed and they stoned him to death for it.

Did Stephen walk with agapē, the love of God in the renewed mind in manifestation here? Certainly, without question. Stephen was walking with the love of God in the renewed mind in manifestation when he confronted those religious bastards. If you don't understand this record in the context of the love of God, then your perceptions of agapē are faulty. What about Paul? Did he walk with the love of God?

> Acts 13:6-12
> And when they had gone through the isle unto Paphos, they found a certain sorcerer, a false prophet, a Jew [Judean], whose name *was* Barjesus:
>
> Which was with the deputy of the country, Sergius Paulus, a prudent man; who called for Barnabas and Saul, and desired to hear the word of God.
>
> But Elymas the sorcerer (for so is his name by interpretation) withstood them, seeking to turn away the deputy from the faith.
>
> Then Saul, (who also *is called* Paul,) filled with the Holy Ghost [holy spirit], set his eyes on him,

And said, O full of all subtilty and all mischief, *thou* child of the devil, *thou* enemy of all righteousness, wilt thou not cease to pervert the right ways of the Lord?

And now, behold, the hand of the Lord *is* upon thee, and thou shalt be blind, not seeing the sun for a season. And immediately there fell on him a mist and a darkness; and he went about seeking some to lead him by the hand.

Then the deputy, when he saw what was done, believed, being astonished at the doctrine of the Lord.

Paul didn't mess about with Barjesus. He manifested the power of God and that religious sorcerer, that wizard became blind.

That sorcerer had been appointed to the political leader of Cyprus. These religious sorcerers are still around today by the way, only now we call them jesuits. You will find jesuits behind all our political leaders and all the top freemasons, manipulating them from behind the scenes just as in Paul's day. There is nothing new under the sun.

Did Paul walk with agapē, the love of God in the renewed mind in manifestation here? Certainly, without question. Paul was walking with the love of God in the renewed mind in manifestation when he confronted Barjesus. If you have a problem with this record in the context of the love of God, then your understanding of agapē needs adjusting. What about Jesus Christ? Did he walk with the love of God on the countless occasions he confronted the religious leaders and insulted them in public?

> Matthew 23:27,28
> Woe unto you, scribes and Pharisees, hypocrites! for ye are like unto whited sepulchres, which indeed appear beautiful outward, but are within full of dead *men's* bones, and of all uncleanness.
>
> Even so ye also outwardly appear righteous unto men, but within ye are full of hypocrisy and iniquity.

When Judeans touched a dead body they became unclean. Same with tombs and graves. Jesus Christ told these pharisees they were whited sepulchres, disguised graves that attracted the innocent and the unwitting, and when people approached them they approached death and were made unclean. Just as in Jesus' day, going to church in our day and time will make us unclean. Jesus Christ had a habit of talking to the church leaders in this fashion.

> Matthew 15:7-9,12
> *Ye* hypocrites, well did Esaias prophesy of you, saying,
>
> This people draweth nigh unto me with their mouth, and honoureth me with *their* lips; but their heart is far from me.
>
> But in vain they do worship me, teaching *for* doctrines the commandments of men.
>
> Then came his disciples, and said unto him, Knowest thou that the Pharisees were offended, after they heard this saying?

Jesus Christ regularly offended people. When it came to the word, he had no friends. For him, it was the word, the word, and nothing but the word.

> Matthew 21:12,13
> And Jesus went into the temple of God, and cast out all them that sold and bought in the temple, and overthrew the tables of the moneychangers, and the seats of them that sold doves,
>
> And said unto them, It is written, My house shall be called the house of prayer; but ye have made it a den of thieves.

I'm sure these merchants and vendors thought themselves honest traders, much like many businessmen today who also charge top dollar for garbage merchandise. Jesus Christ kicked their tables over, drove their animals out, and called them thieves to their faces. Quite right too, and that's what our businessmen and women are today for the most part, thieves and robbers overcharging for second rate trash. Commerce isn't about ripping people off and selling them garbage to line your greedy pockets, it's about producing your best products and providing honest services at a fair rate. Jesus Christ confronted those thieves publicly. He made greedy people so mad they eventually had him murdered by the Romans.

Did Jesus Christ walk with agapē, the love of God in the renewed mind in manifestation? Certainly, without question. If you have a problem understanding these records in the context of the love of God, then your perceptions of agapē are simply wrong.

Now yes, it isn't always about annoying people, there are plenty of records where these men healed folks and brought deliverance, and they were walking with the love of God in the renewed mind in manifestation in those situations as well. Multitudes of people often followed Jesus Christ to hear him teach and you don't attract large followings of people like that if you're an asshole.

So what's the answer? It all comes down to understanding the difference between the word *God* and the word *people*. Huh? Yes, that's right. Agapē is defined as the love of *God* in the renewed mind in manifestation, it is not defined as the love of *people* in the renewed mind in manifestation. What's the difference?

There is another love mentioned in the bible, which is phileō. Phileō is human love. Phileō is the love a woman has for her newborn baby. Phileō is the love a married couple share. Phileō is the love people can have for each other. However, it is human love, and it is not agapē love, the love of God. It is by confusing these two very different forms of love that the devil destroys energised ministries and mutates them into nasty little churches. If the devil can trick folks into thinking that learning to love each other with human love is walking with the love of God in the renewed mind in manifestation, they become just another dead church.

The bible has much to say about both phileō love and agapē love. Strong's compares the two thus:

Phileō; to be a friend to, fond of [an *individual or an object*], *that is have affection* for denoting *personal attachment, as a matter of sentiment or feeling; while agapē is wider, embracing especially the judgment and the deliberate assent of the will as a matter of principle, duty and propriety.*

This is a pretty decent comparison. Human love is very much a human thing, an emotional thing, while the love of God very much embodies making deliberate decisions and judgements based on God's word as a matter of principle and duty. There are some similarities, which is why the devil is so adept at confusing them. However, agapē love supersedes phileō love, and on no account must agapē love ever be compromised by preference for phileō love.

Additionally, agapē love is only available to those who have a knowledge of God's word and who manifest the gift of holy spirit. This is important to our understanding of 1 Corinthians 13, which deals with agapē within the context of the operation of the gift of holy spirit. Agapē is a spiritual quality, not a human quality. If you've not heard about the gift of holy spirit or the manifestations of holy spirit, don't worry about it, we will be getting there shortly. For now just hold the thought that agapē is a spiritual quality and not part of human nature.

You cannot take 1 Corinthians 13 out of the context of chapters 12 and 14 or your bible simply falls to pieces. Chapter 13 is a parenthesis sandwiched between chapters 12 and 14 which give instruction on spiritual matters including the proper operation of the manifestations of holy spirit. As a parenthesis, chapter 13 is a figure of speech giving it emphasis, but only within the context of spiritual matters and the correct and proper operation of the manifestations of holy spirit. You cannot take chapter 13 out of the context of the proper operation of the gift of holy spirit and rightly divide God's word.

Let's take this a step further. Only those who properly operate the gift of holy spirit, those who energise manifestations of holy spirit accurately and properly have any potential to walk with agapē, the love of God in the renewed mind in manifestation. That is the context of 1 Corinthians 13. If you take 1 Corinthians 13 out of that context, what you have is private interpretation. Agapē, the love of God in the renewed mind in manifestation, cannot be lived by anyone who does not first walk by the spirit. This is precisely the opposite of what most people think when they read this chapter.

> 1 Corinthians 13:1
> Though I speak with the tongues of men and of angels, and have not charity [agapē], I am become *as* sounding brass, or a tinkling cymbal.

Does this verse say that speaking in tongues is just making a noise like brass instruments and cymbals? No, it does not. It says those who do not walk with agapē, the love of God in the renewed mind in manifestation, are just making noise when they speak in tongues. Those who put phileō love before agapē love can speak in tongues all they want, but it is of no profit to them, they are just making religious noise. They would be as well joining a monastery and sitting in a dark room chanting all day. If you don't speak in tongues yet, that's okay, don't worry about it, we'll get there in the class. At this stage, we're only looking to understand the antidote to fear. If we're to live without fear, we are to walk with the love of God.

> 1 John 4:18
> There is no fear in love [agapē]; but perfect love [agapē] casteth out fear: because fear hath torment. He that feareth is not made perfect in love [agapē].

In other words, we're not going to cast out fear with any of our human abilities or talent or brains, it's going to take something spiritual, the love of God to get the job done. In this class we're going to find out how we can live with the love of God.

In the records we've seen, Peter, Stephen, Paul, and Jesus Christ all put God and his word first before their love of people. In other words, they spoke up when God wanted them to speak up. They refused to put their love for people before their love for God. They walked by the spirit, and they didn't care how many folks they offended in the process. If folks do not speak God's word because they are afraid of hurting people's feelings, or because they don't want to upset anyone, or because they feel it is unloving to confront people and annoy them when God is working in their hearts to speak up (and that's the key to this whole thing), then the truths of 1 Corinthians 13 apply to them. We are to help people, and if we don't help people then speaking in tongues profits us nothing.

If we don't listen to God when he is working within us to speak up or deal with something, and we compromise because we feel our phileō love for people is more important, or we're simply afraid, then we are not walking with the love of God in the renewed mind in manifestation, we still have fear in our life. Manifestations of holy spirit are only profitable to those who walk by the spirit, to those who love God more than they love people, to those who love God more than they love temples made with hands otherwise known as their local church or ministry, to those who want to help others.

Sure, they take scriptures like 1 Corinthians 10:32 and 2 Corinthians 6:3 out of context to justify their religious weakness, but their lives will not defeat the devil in any spiritual category. They are whited sepulchres full of dead men's bones and if you go to them you will be made unclean. God refuses to have anything to do with temples made by men and so should you. If you go to church, God won't be there.

If you want your life to be spiritually meaningful, to have spiritual value, you will have to love God first before people, which means you speak up when he wants you to speak up, and you act when he is working within you to will and to do of his good pleasure. This is the walk of anyone who wants to be a disciple, and it is axiomatic that we must first learn to operate the gift of holy spirit properly and accurately for that is the immediate context of this chapter.

> 1 Corinthians 13:2
> And though I have *the gift of* prophecy, and understand all mysteries, and all knowledge; and though I have all faith, so that I could remove mountains, and have not charity, I am nothing.

Listen, I know you're wonderful and you have a heart for God and want to know his word and do something for him, but really, anyone can run away from confrontation. That takes no ability or courage at all. If we're going to walk with the love of God we will have to deal with situations when God is working in our hearts to do so and that takes courage. That is walking with the love of God in the renewed mind in manifestation. This isn't about being nice to everyone and smiling inanely at them. Jesus Christ wasn't nice to everyone. Do you see how this fits within the context of 1 Corinthians 12 and 14? Unless we're walking by the spirit, properly operating the manifestations of holy spirit, chapter 13 is a world away from where we are, and all our talk about love is just noise.

The love of God is not an *alternative* way to walking by the spirit, it isn't an excuse to not walk by the spirit. The truth is, the only way to learn to walk with the love of God is to first learn to properly operate the manifestations and learn to walk by the spirit. That's the context. One builds upon the other. This is further corroborated in Galatians, where agapē is listed as a fruit of the spirit.

> Galatians 5:22,23
> But the fruit of the Spirit is love [agapē], joy, peace, longsuffering, gentleness, goodness, faith,
>
> Meekness, temperance: against such there is no law.

Fruit of the spirit is not fruit of the good works of man. You can't produce spiritual fruit by doing anything in the senses realm, which includes manifesting human phileō love. You can manifest phileō all you want, you can be the most phileō loving person on earth, but it will never produce fruit of the spirit. You can only produce spiritual fruit by manifesting the gift of holy spirit. This fits perfectly within the context of 1 Corinthians chapters 12-14. Agapē is only attainable by first manifesting the gift of holy spirit accurately and faithfully according to the instructions given in 1 Corinthians chapters 12 and 14.

If we lose this truth and attempt to manifest human love to everyone, we are walking by the senses and not by the spirit. We are attempting to perfect the flesh. Once these truths are lost regarding walking by the spirit, we have lost the meaning of the resurrection and the whole point of the Grace Administration.

> Philippians 3:3
> For we are the circumcision, which worship God in the spirit, and rejoice in Christ Jesus, and have no confidence in the flesh.

Now yes, once we're walking by the spirit, and we recognise God's still, small voice and we decide to be courageous, get involved and deal with situations when God works within us, it doesn't mean losing our temper and shouting at everyone. Sure, God wants us to deal with situations kindly, with love. Walking with the love of God isn't being horrible to everyone all the time, it's being courageous by doing God's will. Every situation is different and that is why we must first be walking by the spirit before we can be effectual ministers walking with the love of God.

1 Corinthians 13:4,5
Charity [agapē] suffereth long, *and* is kind; charity envieth not; charity vaunteth not itself, is not puffed up,

Doth not behave itself unseemly, seeketh not her own, is not easily provoked, thinketh no evil;

Was Jesus Christ long suffering and kind? Sure he was. He was long suffering and kind even when he was pissing off the religious leaders by calling them whited sepulchres and vipers. That's what the religious leaders were in Jesus Christ's day and they're no different today for the most part.

Matthew 12:34
O generation of vipers, how can ye, being evil, speak good things? for out of the abundance of the heart the mouth speaketh.

Jesus Christ took the religious leaders on so he could be kind and long suffering to God's people. Is that so hard to figure out? Are fathers loving and kind when they fight to protect their wives and children? Sure, they are. Love is not weak. Not even human love is that weak. Not even animal love is that weak! It takes strength, courage, and a sense of duty to live with this kind of love. Religious love isn't love at all, it's a disease.

1 Corinthians 13:13
And now abideth faith, hope, charity, these three; but the greatest of these *is* charity [agapē – the love of God].

Was I walking with the love of God putting this teaching together? Is it loving of me to confront those who wrongly interpret God's word and teach their nonsense on this most important subject? If you have a problem understanding this teaching in the context of the love of God, then your perceptions of agapē are still clouded by religious nonsense. I love people with the love of God, I love people enough to confront them with God's word to give them a chance to change. It's the only way to help people.

I mentioned in the previous chapter that love is more powerful than fear. This is true, but it's not talking about human love, it's talking about the love of God. Agapē love is more powerful than fear, but phileō love is not, and that is why perfect agapē love can cast out, or displace fear. Perfect love must necessarily be more powerful than fear otherwise it wouldn't be able to cast it out. God didn't give us a spirit of fear, he gave us a spirit of power, agapē love, and a sound mind.

This love God gave us isn't phileō love, human love – we were born with that – it is agapē love, the love of God in the renewed mind in manifestation. If you think smiling nicely at your fears with a religious phileō plastic smile is going to back off the challenges of life, you have no concept of the spiritual realities around you. If you want to confront and defeat fear it is going to take the strength, courage, and determination that comes only from knowing God's word, walking by the spirit, and living with the love of God in the renewed mind in manifestation.

That will do for now, but we will be back to the love of God later in the class.

8. The Parting of the Red Sea

The parting of the Red Sea so the Israelites could escape from Egypt, and the drowning of Pharaoh's army remains one of the most dramatic demonstrations of God's power in the history of the world. It stands as a testament to God being able and willing to rescue his people from anyone or anything at anytime when they put their trust in him. When the children of Israel were camped on the shores of the Red Sea and Pharaoh's armies marched after them, God told his people by way of his prophet Moses to fear not.

> Exodus 14:13
> And Moses said unto the people, Fear ye not, stand still, and see the salvation of the LORD, which he will shew to you to day: for the Egyptians whom ye have seen to day, ye shall see them again no more for ever.

In recent times, fossilised bones and chariot wheels encrusted with coral have been recovered from the bottom of the Gulf of Aqaba off the coast at Nuweiba. The Gulf of Aqaba is over a mile deep in places, with steep gradients to the bottom that would make it impossible to get down with children and animals. However, there is an underwater land bridge leading across the Gulf from Nuweiba to Saudi Arabia which lies not far under the surface, and it is here that chariot wheels and fossilised human and horse bones have been discovered by divers.

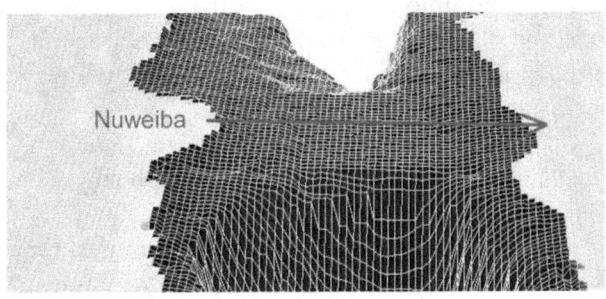

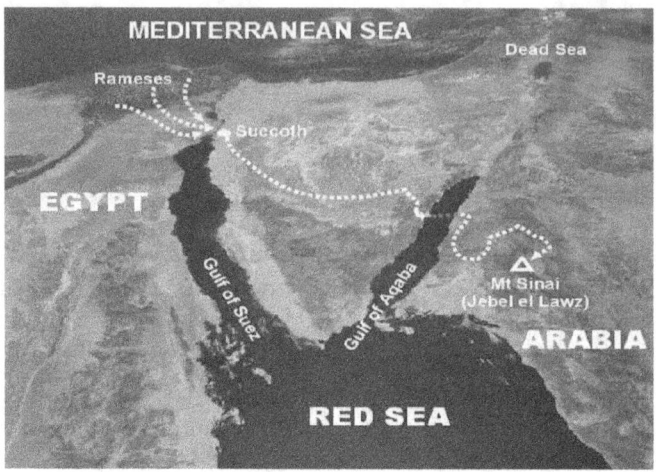

An ancient column was also found lying in the water at Nuweiba in 1978 by Ron Wyatt, but unfortunately the inscriptions had long been removed. Then a second pillar was discovered on the Saudi coastline opposite with the inscriptions still legible, containing the words Mizraim (Egypt), Solomon, Edom, death, Pharaoh, Moses, and God, indicating that King Solomon had set up these columns to mark the spot where the Israelites had crossed.

The Red Sea was divided at Nuweiba, the Israelites walked across on dry ground, Pharaoh and his army drowned, and all his chariots were wrecked. Archaeology can only confirm the biblical account. Let's now read Exodus and see if we can make sense of what happened. Read the details carefully, for they are important.

> Exodus 14:13-30
> And Moses said unto the people, Fear ye not, stand still, and see the salvation of the LORD, which he will shew to you to day: for the Egyptians whom ye have seen to day, ye shall see them again no more for ever.

> The LORD shall fight for you, and ye shall hold your peace.

> And the LORD said unto Moses, Wherefore criest thou unto me? speak unto the children of Israel, that they go forward:

But lift thou up thy rod, and stretch out thine hand over the sea, and divide it: and the children of Israel shall go on dry *ground* through the midst of the sea.

And I, behold, I will harden the hearts of the Egyptians, and they shall follow them: and I will get me honour upon Pharaoh, and upon all his host, upon his chariots, and upon his horsemen.

And the Egyptians shall know that I *am* the LORD, when I have gotten me honour upon Pharaoh, upon his chariots, and upon his horsemen.

And the angel of God, which went before the camp of Israel, removed and went behind them; and the pillar of the cloud went from before their face, and stood behind them:

And it came between the camp of the Egyptians and the camp of Israel; and it was a cloud and darkness *to them*, but it gave light by night *to these*: so that the one came not near the other all the night.

And Moses stretched out his hand over the sea; and the LORD caused the sea to go *back* by a strong east wind all that night, and made the sea dry *land*, and the waters were divided.

And the children of Israel went into the midst of the sea upon the dry *ground*: and the waters *were* a wall unto them on their right hand, and on their left.

And the Egyptians pursued, and went in after them to the midst of the sea, *even* all Pharaoh's horses, his chariots, and his horsemen.

And it came to pass, that in the morning watch the LORD looked unto the host of the Egyptians through the pillar of fire and of the cloud, and troubled the host of the Egyptians,

And took off their chariot wheels, that they drave them heavily: so that the Egyptians said, Let us flee from the face of Israel; for the LORD fighteth for them against the Egyptians.

And the LORD said unto Moses, Stretch out thine hand over the sea, that the waters may come again upon the Egyptians, upon their chariots, and upon their horsemen.

And Moses stretched forth his hand over the sea, and the sea returned to his strength when the morning appeared; and the Egyptians fled against it; and the LORD overthrew the Egyptians in the midst of the sea.

And the waters returned, and covered the chariots, and the horsemen, *and* all the host of Pharaoh that came into the sea after them; there remained not so much as one of them.

But the children of Israel walked upon dry *land* in the midst of the sea; and the waters *were* a wall unto them on their right hand, and on their left.

Thus the LORD saved Israel that day out of the hand of the Egyptians; and Israel saw the Egyptians dead upon the sea shore.

For years, I've had three issues with this record. First of all, how could a column of fire keep Pharaoh and his army from the Israelites all night? Why couldn't they just go around it? Then I saw photos from Nuweiba and it all made sense. There is only one narrow wadi leading through the mountains to Nuweiba, so a single column of fire would have been sufficient. Nuweiba is short for Nuwayba al Muzayyinah which means Waters of Moses Opening.

The narrow wadi leading to Nuweiba

The second issue I had was with the walls of water towering over the Israelites. We've all seen the pictures, right?

These depictions are ridiculous. If the wind was this strong, how come the Israelites didn't get blown away? This is religious nonsense. So what happened? The bible states that Moses held up his hands, there was a strong east wind, and God made the sea go back all that night. The easterly wind blew in one direction, it was strong, and it blew all night. All night in the middle east can be 10 hours or more. The sea going back means the sea level lowered like a tide going out. If God had simply parted the ocean without lowering the sea level, what would have been the point of the wind blowing all night?

Tidal motion is powerful. During high tides harbour walls can overflow, while during exceptionally low tides, boats can ground on the bottom. Every day there are naturally occurring tides where the sea level will drop 40ft or more. Water is also highly susceptible to wind motion. Have you ever blown water in a saucer? What happens? The water moves away from your mouth to the other side of the saucer. As this strong wind blew down the Gulf of Aqaba, the waters were blown down the Red Sea. This strong wind wouldn't have been in just one place, it would have blown from the top of the Gulf of Aqaba right down to the Indian Ocean. Waves 5ft high or more marched down the Red Sea all night, effectively skimming layers from the surface and lowering the sea level. Helped by a strong ebbing tide, the waters receded until the shallow land bridge broke the surface.

Once the land bridge appeared, there would have been water on each side of it, so the waters would have been divided. The children of Israel then marched down the gentle incline, their armed warriors bringing up the rear to ward off the advancing Egyptians, and they crossed on dry ground. As it's only 10 miles from Nuweiba to Saudi Arabia, they would have crossed in 3 hours or less. They'd just walked all the way from Egypt, so they would have been fit enough for a speedy crossing. If they'd begun walking while the tide was still an hour from it's lowest ebb, that would have given them enough time to cross before the waters returned. Nothing God did that day on the shores of the Gulf of Aqaba contradicted nature.

My third issue was in verse 22 where it states that *the waters were a wall unto them on their right hand, and on their left*. How could this be? This no doubt is the scripture which conjures up the images above in artists' minds. Concerning David and his men, a few shepherds had this to say about them:

> 1 Samuel 25:16
> They were a wall unto us both by night and day, all the while we were with them keeping the sheep.

Were David and his men walls? No, they were no more walls to those shepherds than the waters of the Red Sea were walls to Israel. The word *wall* was often used as a figurative reference to mean protection, that's all. Walls was used figuratively in Exodus to mean protection. It isn't difficult to see how this idiom became a part of their language.

City walls in the middle east

People lived in walled towns and cities. Walls kept them safe. Walls protected them, so walls were commonly used figuratively to simply mean protection. Just as David and his men were walls to those shepherds, so the waters of the Red Sea were walls of protection to Israel while they crossed in that Pharaoh and his army couldn't flank them to attack their vulnerable sides.

Once the Israelite people had crossed, the sea returned to its strength, meaning the tidal flow going down the gulf returned in a flood that destroyed the Egyptian army. It may even have hit the land bridge like a tsunami. Good riddance, that stupid pharaoh deserved all he got. He was given 10 opportunities to allow God's people to leave peaceably and he refused. Neither did he have to chase after them with his army. God was only protecting his people, which he will do if they are attacked and they believe for deliverance.

If I were diving for Egyptian chariots and fossilised human and horse bone, I'd be searching the northern reaches of that underwater land bridge at Nuweiba over towards the Saudi coastline.

9. God is Faithful

The love of God, *agapē* love, is so powerful that when we refuse to fear and instead believe God, he can even part oceans if that's what it takes to make a way for us to escape. So how do we get to the place where we can believe God to see such things? One aspect of the word that will inspire us to live without fear is to know that God will never leave us or forsake us. He didn't leave or forsake Moses and the children of Israel on the shores of the Red Sea, and he promises to never leave us or forsake us either. Look what he said to Joshua after Moses' death.

> Joshua 1:5
> There shall not any man be able to stand before thee all the days of thy life: as I was with Moses, *so* I will be with thee: I will not fail thee, nor forsake thee.

Just as he was always there for Moses and Joshua, he will always be there for us. I've proven this time and time again. God has always been there for me. He is always there when I need him. He always has the answers. He's amazing. The more I see his faithfulness, the more I learn to trust him. The more I learn to trust him, the more I see his faithfulness in my life. It's a beautiful cycle.

> Deuteronomy 7:9
> Know therefore that the LORD thy God, he *is* God, the faithful God, which keepeth covenant and mercy with them that love him and keep his commandments to a thousand generations;

A few synonyms for faithful are loyal, true, constant, and trustworthy. Our God is loyal, he's true, he's constant, and he's trustworthy.

Numbers 23:19
God *is* not a man, that he should lie; neither the son of man, that he should repent: hath he said, and shall he not do *it*? or hath he spoken, and shall he not make it good?

So what does God's faithfulness mean to us today? Are there any benefits to this? Well, here's one.

1 Corinthians 10:13
There hath no temptation taken you but such as is common to man: but God *is* faithful, who will not suffer [allow] you to be tempted above that ye are able; but will with the temptation also make a way to escape, that ye may be able to bear *it*.

With the temptation can be understood as *in close proximity with the temptation*. What this means is that along with every challenge in life, God will provide a way to escape that will not be far away. When the children of Israel looked for a way to escape pharaoh's army on the shores of the Red Sea, their escape route was right beside their feet. If we believe God and look for the ways to escape when we need them, they will be there. It doesn't matter if there is an ocean in the way. God can even part the sea if that's what it takes.

However, if people don't know there is a way to escape they won't look for it, and so the god of this world steals, kills, and destroys despite the ways to escape being there. That's one reason the devil buries the word under flashy layers of television, computer games, magazines, and movies, keeping folks mesmerised and away from the true light that would expose him.

Hosea 4:6a
My people are destroyed for lack of knowledge:

If we neglect God and his word, we will not see the ways he makes for us to escape. If we know God's word and look for his deliverance, it will always be there. You can trust that, because God is faithful, he is trustworthy. Look at this promise.

Walking *by* the Spirit

Psalm 46:1
God *is* our refuge and strength, a very present help in trouble.

Storms in life take many forms, such as health, finances, relationships, and business, but in all these things God is our refuge. When we look to him, when we trust in him, he will deliver us; the way to escape will be there.

I've lost count of how many times I've proven God's faithfulness in my life. I was in the Castle grounds in Stornoway, in the Outer Hebrides, with a couple of men from the sawmill. Our job that morning was to cut down a pine tree overhanging a single track road which was becoming a menace to drivers. We closed off the road and one of the guys surveyed the tree. It had grown out of a steep bank at an angle, then curved sharply upwards, a bit like a banana, only it had heavy branches jutting out everywhere. It wasn't a small tree either, with a trunk perhaps 4ft thick. I stood up on the grassy bank behind the tree, where I thought it was safe.

The chainsaw roared into life, and woodchips and dust filled the air. With two large wedges sliced out of the trunk, the tree showed no signs of going anywhere. After a short discussion, the chainsaw bit into the bark again. Suddenly there was a loud crack. We had all expected the tree to just fall down on the road. But it didn't. Instead, the banana shaped trunk rolled on the bank, the trunk swung up into the air, and the whole tree rolled over towards me. The guys shouted and jumped for cover. Life went into slow motion and I instinctively jumped backwards. The trunk crunched into the bank, the tree rolled down the grassy slope to the road, branches cracking like fireworks, and then everything went very quiet.

The guys stared at me in shock. They thought my legs had been crushed. I could see it in their eyes. When I got to my feet and brushed myself down, their shock turned to astonishment. With much head scratching, they paced out where I'd been standing and where I'd been lying when the tree hit the bank, and it was around 10 feet. No one can jump 10ft backwards from a standing position. I must admit, I had felt like I'd been floating through the air when life had gone into slow motion. God is faithful to his word, and when we apply the principles he will always be there for us.

> Romans 8:31
> What shall we then say to these things? If God *be* for us, who *can be* against us?

It was the late 70s, and I was in London. The two guys I'd been renting a flat with had left and gone home, leaving me a note filled with excuses, as well as all the bills. The rent was due the following day. The landlord was sympathetic, but wanted me out if I couldn't afford the whole rent. So, I paid him my share, paid what I could of the bills, and he used our rent deposit to cover the rest. There I was, homeless on the streets of London in december, a day before the holidays.

I had a huge suitcase which was too heavy to carry far. When I got home from work the following day, I packed, and without knowing where I was going, headed down the road towards the underground. I didn't make it. The suitcase was too heavy. As I sat on it by the side of the road watching traffic rumble by, I wondered what I was going to do. It was already getting dark, and I didn't have any money left after paying the rent and bills. How could God get me out of this?

There was a gate into a hostel of some kind behind me. It occurred to me to go in and ask them for help. The place was quiet and dark, but someone answered the door when I rang. I explained my situation, and the guy listened. Everyone staying in the hostel had just left for the christmas holidays, and the place was empty for two weeks. I could have a room until the new year, but I had to be out before the students returned. Soon, I was relaxing in a comfortable room that cost me nothing, and I had two weeks to sort things out. Can God meet all our need? Oh yes, it's not hard for him at all.

> Philippians 4:19
> But my God shall supply all your need according to his riches in glory by Christ Jesus.

Lorraine and I were driving from Aberdeen to Inverness. Conditions were good, and there wasn't much traffic. We were cruising comfortably, when a line of traffic approached. Without warning, a car suddenly pulled out to overtake and sped towards us. We were just yards apart, an instant away from a head on high speed smash.

It all happened so fast that my foot never even left the accelerator. I yanked the steering wheel left, then right, and we were back on the main road, the suicide car behind us. Lorraine had been reading a book and hadn't seen what had happened. She looked up at me curiously, with questions in her eyes. The overtaking car pulled in and sped off. Suicide? Death wish? I don't know.

Now don't get me wrong here, this was a narrow road, and there wasn't room for three cars. There was no verge, and there was a high bank on each side of the road. I hadn't even noticed the lay-by, but I could see it now in the mirror. My wheels must have clipped the verges of the lay-by going in and coming out again. It was just long enough to avoid that head on smash, and was perfectly placed so I could swerve in and out. A way to escape? Decades earlier, when that road had been built, God had worked in a road planning department to build a lay-by there, just for me, knowing I was going to need it years later. Don't ask me how he does it, I just know he does. Is anything too hard for God?

> Jeremiah 32:27
> Behold, I *am* the LORD, the God of all flesh: is there any thing too hard for me?

I'm unloading lorries at Makro in Bristol. These huge articulated trucks reverse up to the loading bays behind the warehouse, and then it's in with the forklifts to get them unloaded. One of my jobs was to guide the lorry drivers back by beckoning with an arm from the loading bay. I knew something was wrong because I was feeling sick inside. I'm hanging out the bay, keeping an eye on the driver in his mirror, letting him know there was still a couple of feet to go.

I don't know what happened next. Perhaps his foot slipped off the clutch or something, I'm not a lorry driver, but the lorry suddenly leapt backwards and clattered into the loading bay walls.

I stood there a little bewildered. A moment earlier, I'd been hanging out the loading bay doors, giving hand signals to the driver in his mirror. Then the lorry had smacked the walls of the warehouse where my head had been, and I was mysteriously standing back from the loading bay doors. A few of the lads looked over curiously, wondering what the noise was. Had I not been snatched back out of harm's way, my head would have been crushed like an egg. Can God keep us safe?

> Proverbs 3:25,26
> Be not afraid of sudden fear, neither of the desolation of the wicked, when it cometh.
>
> For the LORD shall be thy confidence, and shall keep thy foot from being taken.

We were on a deserted runway at night. It was winter, it was dark, it was freezing, and it was raining. British airways had simply dumped all our army kit out the back door of the aircraft onto the tarmac and pissed off. The dark mound of bergens seemed like a mountain. I glanced over at the warm coaches and my heart sank. How was I going to find my bergen among that lot? I'd be soaked and frozen long before I got on the coaches.

A pile of bodies leapt onto the mountain and started hauling bergens off in a frenzied attempt to find their kit and get onto the warm coaches out of the freezing rain. Something dark and heavy thudded at my feet. No, it couldn't be. It was impossible. I didn't even look down to check. Curiosity got the better of me. It was my bergen and it was sitting on my toes. I was one of the first guys onto the buses. Does God make a difference in life?

> 2 Corinthians 9:8
> And God *is* able to make all grace abound toward you; that ye, always having all sufficiency in all *things*, may abound to every good work:

It was dark. So dark, you would think it was the jungle. You hear folks talk about dark, but this was dark. I passed my hand in front of my face and saw nothing. We were Scottish paras returning from a military exercise, and were trying to find our camp in the forest. The only way to move was to hold onto the bergen of the guy in front and feel your way forward with your feet. I'd never experienced darkness like that before.

The guy in front of me started climbing. Not gentle climbing, like going up stairs, but steep climbing, like searching for something to hold onto to pull yourself up. I couldn't recall such a steep climb leaving camp. Then he disappeared. I felt all around but he was gone, and so were the guys behind me. I found the slim trunk of a small tree off to my right and held onto it while I pondered my situation. I could hear sounds below me. I was about to use the tree to pull myself up, when suddenly a torch flicked on below me, just for a moment, and then it went pitch dark again.

This might not sound like a world shattering event, but I can assure you that soldiers on exercise at night, especially well trained soldiers like the airborne, do not shine torches at night. Light at night can get you killed. However, in that split second, a light came on and I saw my situation. That tree I was holding onto was growing out of the top of a small cliff face. If I'd hauled myself over it, I would have gone straight down 20ft onto the rocks at the bottom. Can God give you light in darkness?

> Psalm 119:105
> Thy word *is* a lamp to my feet, and a light to my path.

I'd been testing what I thought would be the final run through of a custom Tomb Raider game I'd been designing and building called Jurassic Park, when random textures suddenly started stretching across the screen. Over the next few days I tried everything I knew to fix it. On one test, I reached the final area and thought the problem was gone when it showed itself again. I was getting tired. I'd done my best and didn't know what else to try.

Then I recalled the power of God. Okay, let's see if this works on computer games. I removed one small item from the map, asked God to heal my level in the name of Jesus Christ, and spoke in tongues. Next time I tested the level, it worked flawlessly. The texture stretching problem was gone and never returned. Can we use the power of God to heal Tomb Raider games? Absolutely.

> Philippians 4:13
> I can do all things through Christ which strengtheneth me.

We were gold panning in the Highlands, and I was working around and under a huge lump of bedrock sticking out of the riverbank. After a while, Tina moved downstream. The only reason I'd been working around that bedrock was so she could get into a hole I thought would be easier and more productive for her. She seemed happy enough in her new spot, and I felt an urge to move my kit downstream and work that original hole. So I did.

Not long afterwards, there was a huge splash and heavy crunching as that lump of bedrock dislodged from the bank and fell into the river. My goodness, it had been a huge boulder. If I'd been working under it when it fell in, I'd have been crushed and drowned. My mate was okay too. It had fallen just inches from him and nudged his toe as it settled on the bottom. Does God watch our backs?

> Joshua 1:9
> Have not I commanded thee? Be strong and of a good courage; be not afraid, neither be thou dismayed: for the LORD thy God *is* with thee whithersoever thou goest.

I always take care to ensure no pieces of egg shell ever get into dad's fried eggs. The two eggs cracked into the pan, and after close inspection they looked just fine. I was about to go do something else when it occurred to me that the eggs were too close to each other and I should take another look.

The first egg was already turning white, but the second egg was still fresh and runny. I figured it would only take a second to tilt the frying pan and separate them. Well, well, there were three pieces of eggshell tucked under the white of the first egg.

I find stuff like this really hard to comprehend sometimes. I mean, isn't the Creator of the heavens and earth too busy with things like keeping the universe in order to be concerned with silly little things like fried eggs? Obviously not, he enjoys being part of our lives.

> Matthew 6:26
> Behold the fowls of the air: for they sow not, neither do they reap, nor gather into barns; yet your heavenly Father feedeth them. Are ye not much better than they?

I was out testing a new 70-200mm f/2.8 camera lens that had just arrived in the post, and took a walk along the coast. I knew I should have taken a scarf and a hat, but the weather looked okay so I didn't bother. I was excited about the new lens and didn't take care to wear appropriate clothing.

Geez, it was cold. A biting wind cut through me from the sea. An hour later, I felt my body temperature drop alarmingly and I started shivering. I had to get home. I'd been too wrapped up in my new lens to notice I was going down. Totally out of the blue, the phone rang. It was my mate. Told him I was on the way up to his and to put the kettle on. He jumped in the car and came and picked me up a few minutes later because he wanted to see the new lens. Can God take care of us even when we're stupid enough to do silly things?

> Psalm 103:13
> Like as a father pitieth [cares for] *his* children, *so* the LORD pitieth [cares for] them that fear [love and respect] him.

Back in the winter of 2012, Tina and I were driving home in the dark from Dingwall. On the Tain bypass, a car suddenly stopped in the middle of the road and flashed its lights. I checked my lights, but they were fine. The car whacked on its hazard lights and flashed again. It wasn't until we braked hard and pulled into the verge that I noticed the woman lying by the side of the road.

First thought was to get Tina to phone for an ambulance, and then I went to check on the woman. Her mobile phone lay a couple of feet away. She must have tried to phone for help. The first thing I did was check for a pulse. There wasn't one. I checked her arm, checked her wrist, checked her elbow, checked her neck, there was no pulse. As I knelt there, it came to me that she was dead. What do you do? Well, I prayed for her in the name of Jesus Christ.

At that moment I felt a faint click in my finger tips. A pulse, cool. It was slow and barely discernable, but it was there. Tina got a paramedic on the phone and she began relaying instructions. I was to lay the woman on her back. That was not what I'd been taught, and I questioned it. Tina insisted. The authority in her voice was unmistakable, so I turned her on her back. Then I was to put a hand on her forehead and tilt her head back with my other hand. *What?* I'd been taught coma position and clear airways, but again the instruction was authoritative.

As soon as I tilted her head back, her whole body convulsed three or four times, just like you see in the movies when people are given electric shocks. As she convulsed, I kept a good hold on her head, and then I saw she was breathing. Checked her pulse, and it was beating away like a bass drum. She sat up just as the police arrived.

Then the world did what it usually does when the power of God is manifested, and carried on as if nothing had happened. The police took the woman home, and Tina and I drove off into the night. I didn't even know who she was. I can only assume she must have prayed before she passed out. Did God make a way for her to escape? Oh yes, he is faithful to his word. Can God still raise the dead? Absolutely.

> Acts 9:36-41
> Now there was at Joppa a certain disciple named Tabitha, which by interpretation is called Dorcas: this woman was full of good works and almsdeeds which she did.
>
> And it came to pass in those days, that she was sick, and died: whom when they had washed, they laid *her* in an upper chamber.
>
> And forasmuch as Lydda was nigh to Joppa, and the disciples had heard that Peter was there, they sent unto him two men, desiring *him* that he would not delay to come to them.
>
> Then Peter arose and went with them. When he was come, they brought him into the upper chamber: and all the widows stood by him weeping, and shewing the coats and garments which Dorcas made, while she was with them.
>
> But Peter put them all forth, and kneeled down, and prayed; and turning *him* to the body said, Tabitha, arise. And she opened her eyes: and when she saw Peter, she sat up.
>
> And he gave her *his* hand, and lifted her up, and when he had called the saints and widows, presented her alive.

Tina and I were off on a photo shoot to Golspie. It was early, around 8.30am or so, and I planned to head to the harbour first, and then work our way along the shore and perhaps shoot the waterfall later in the day when it was a bit brighter. It's always dark in the gorge by the waterfall.

However, on my way to pick up Tina, it was on my heart to head to the waterfall first. I even mentioned it to Tina that Father was working in me to head to the waterfall first. As we wandered up towards the falls, about half way there, it was on my heart to get there quickly. So that's what we did.

Well, well, it was a perfect combination of time of year and time of day. The leaves were just budding so the sun could peek through the dense lattice of trees towering over the gorge without being blocked by leaves, and the sun was just high enough and in just the right position to poke a few rays down into the gloom. As I walked around the rock face, the sun shone down into the gorge with soft light for just a few moments and lit up the waterfall. Talk about timing. Can God help you with your business?

> Job 1:9,10
> Then Satan answered the LORD, and said, Doth Job fear God for nought?
>
> Hast not thou made an hedge about him, and about his house, and about all that he hath on every side? thou hast blessed the work of his hands, and his substance is increased in the land.

Look, there is nothing too hard for God. There is no problem so big, no challenge so insurmountable, no obstacle so impenetrable that it is too big for God. With him as our helper, we can be more than victorious, more than conquerors in every situation.

> Romans 8:37
> Nay, in all these things we are more than conquerors through him that loved us.

I could fill books with stories like these. Just this morning while writing this chapter God helped me with a problem. I'd been upgrading my forums to the latest IP Board. I'd uploaded all the files and was running the upgrader, but for some reason I was getting an error message. No matter what I tried, the upgrader refused to run. After an hour or so trying everything I could think of, I asked God to show me what the problem was in the name of Jesus Christ.

I tried the upgrader again, but this time noticed I had an older version of PHP. So I went to my webhost, updated my PHP to version 5.4, and the next time I ran the upgrader I got a different error message – a file couldn't be read because my host had not installed Zend Optimiser. I had no idea what Zend Optimiser was. I'd never even heard of it. Okay, checked with my webhost and discovered that PHP would work fine with Ion Cube files rather than Zend. It would? Cool, off I went to Invision and discovered to my surprise that there was an Ion Cube version of my board software. Uploaded the files, and the upgrader performed flawlessly.

Now, what were the chances of me figuring that out by myself? God showed me how to fix the problem. He talks to me like this all the time. He is real, he exists, he *did* create the heavens and the earth, he *is* trustworthy, and he *is* faithful. I've proved God's word works over and over and over again. I know God is faithful, I know God is trustworthy, and I know he will be just as faithful and trustworthy for you if you dare to believe him. Stick with this class and I will show you how.

10. God is our Protection

It would be simple to read the final word in Isaiah 58:8 as re-reward, but to do so would be to miss a fabulous truth.

> Isaiah 58:8
> Then shall thy light break forth as the morning, and thine health shall spring forth speedily: and thy righteousness shall go before thee; the glory of the LORD shall be thy rereward.

Yes, God rewards believers, again and again, and that is a great truth in and of itself, but to limit this verse in such a way really misses the point. Understanding what God is actually saying here helps us to live without fear. As children, our earthly fathers bought us ice creams from time to time, and we always enjoyed them I'm sure, but rewards isn't what this verse is talking about. To begin to understand this, let's look at a few other places this word is used.

> Numbers 10:25
> And the standard of the camp of the children of Dan set forward, *which was* the rereward of all the camps throughout their hosts: and over his host *was* Ahiezer the son of Ammishaddai.

Here, the usage of rereward is very clear. The children of Dan were the rear-ward, the rearguard, to protect them from attack from enemies who would have been probing their defences for weaknesses. The word is used in a military sense.

> Joshua 6:9
> And the armed men went before the priests that blew with the trumpets, and the rereward came after the ark, *the priests* going on, and blowing with the trumpets.

Joshua 6:13
And seven priests bearing seven trumpets of rams' horns before the ark of the LORD went on continually, and blew with the trumpets: and the armed men went before them; but the rereward came after the ark of the LORD, *the priests* going on, and blowing with the trumpets.

Here is that same truth again. The priests bearing the ark had their backs protected by an armed military rearguard.

Isaiah 52:12
For ye shall not go out with haste, nor go by flight: for the LORD will go before you; and the God of Israel *will be* your rereward.

Now we begin to get a feel for this word. Going into battle is a serious business. In war, you have to be more committed than your enemy, and strategy and tactics definitely come into play. For example, when Joshua took Ai, after the ambush had set the city on fire, Joshua and the children of Israel had no problem defeating the men of Ai. Once the city fell, the men of Ai had no rearguard to protect their backs, and they were easily defeated.

Joshua 8:21,22
And when Joshua and all Israel saw that the ambush had taken the city, and that the smoke of the city ascended, then they turned again, and slew the men of Ai.

And the other issued out of the city against them; so they were in the midst of Israel, some on this side, and some on that side: and they smote them, so that they let none of them remain or escape.

You can see this truth in every field in life – from football teams looking to exploit weaknesses in their opponent's game plan, to businessmen looking for a bigger market share among their competitors – and war is no different. Your enemies will search for weaknesses to exploit. With God watching your back, you're protected.

In athletics, if a sprinter looks over his shoulder before he reaches the finish line to see what the others are doing, he loses forward momentum and it's likely others will pass him. Paul refers to this very truth in Philippians:

> Philippians 3:13,14
> Brethren, I count not myself to have apprehended: but *this* one thing *I do*, forgetting those things which are behind, and reaching forth unto those things which are before,
>
> I press toward the mark for the prize of the high calling of God in Christ Jesus.

When you sprint for the finish line you don't look over your shoulder, instead you focus your entire being on the finish line. Note that Paul says he does one thing and then lists three things. This isn't a contradiction as some claim, rather, forgetting what's behind, reaching forth to those things which are before and pressing toward the mark is all one action. It's referring to a sprinter expending his last ounce of strength to reach the finish line. What's behind is of no importance to him, he's reaching forward with his entire being, pushing his chest out to reach the tape, expending everything he has to be first to reach that finish line. It's one action of the renewed mind.

Just as in athletic competition, this truth holds true in the spiritual competition. We just don't have time to look back. If we look back at the past, man, we can get beat in no time. We have a formidable opponent, and the devil is good at what he does. Stealing, killing and destroying is the air he breathes. It is what sustains him, nourishes him, it is his reason for being. Job describes him briefly:

> Job 41:27-34
> He esteemeth iron as straw, *and* brass as rotten wood.
>
> The arrow cannot make him flee: slingstones are turned with him into stubble.
>
> Darts are counted as stubble: he laugheth at the shaking of a spear.
>
> Sharp stones *are* under him: he spreadeth sharp pointed things upon the mire.

He maketh the deep to boil like a pot: he maketh the sea like a pot of ointment.

He maketh a path to shine after him; *one* would think the deep *to be* hoary.

Upon earth there is not his like, who is made without fear.

He beholdeth all high *things*: he *is* a king over all the children of pride.

How could we possibly win against such an opponent? Not on our own abilities, that's for sure. No one is going to pick a fight with the devil and beat him. Not even Michael the Archangel would be foolish enough to try something so stupid.

Jude 1:9
Yet Michael the archangel, when contending with the devil he disputed about the body of Moses, durst not bring against him a railing accusation, but said, The Lord rebuke thee.

Look at the top respect Michael the archangel gave to the devil. We have a formidable adversary and we need to have top respect for him as the god of this world. If we're going to win in the spiritual competition and live a life which is more than abundant, it can only be accomplished by putting our entire trust in God, like Michael the Archangel. What a good example to follow. Although we may not be able to stand against the devil and beat him by our own abilities, God can. And guess who is watching our backs!

Isaiah 58:8
Then shall thy light break forth as the morning, and thine health shall spring forth speedily: and thy righteousness shall go before thee; the glory of the LORD shall be thy rereward.

God is our rereward, he watches our backs. With protection like that, that's why we can always win. As we forget the past, reach forth and press toward the mark, God watches our backs. He is our protection. That's why we can move forward without fear.

There is no way we could possibly know what ambushes the devil puts in our way, but God knows and he protects our backs by keeping us informed. As long as we are listening we are protected, because God keeps us wise. When we are living the word, God protects our backs by passing information to us.

> 2 Kings 6:8-12
> Then the king of Syria warred against Israel, and took counsel with his servants, saying, In such and such a place *shall be* my camp.
>
> And the man of God sent unto the king of Israel, saying, Beware that thou pass not such a place; for thither the Syrians are come down.
>
> And the king of Israel sent to the place which the man of God told him and warned him of, and saved himself there, not once nor twice.
>
> Therefore the heart of the king of Syria was sore troubled for this thing; and he called his servants, and said unto them, Will ye not shew me which of us *is* for the king of Israel?
>
> And one of his servants said, None, my lord, O king: but Elisha, the prophet that *is* in Israel, telleth the king of Israel the words that thou speakest in thy bedchamber.

Of course, the king of Israel could have scoffed at the man of God, as many do today. Could God still have protected the king if that were his attitude? What if the king had ignored the warnings, could God have protected him? Nope. Sure, God covers our backs, but only if we're listening. If we're not listening, don't be surprised if we're walking into every ambush going. God watches our backs by giving us information. What we do with that information is entirely up to us. If we ignore it and get beat, don't blame God. Look, walking through a minefield without a mine detector is dangerous. It's much more fun to avoid the mines and live abundantly.

Did God protect Paul in the book of Acts? Absolutely. How did God protect Paul? By waving a magic wand? No, he gave him information. Let's look at this while Paul was on his way to Jerusalem.

Walking *by* the Spirit

> Acts 20:22,23
> And now, behold, I go bound in the spirit unto Jerusalem, not knowing the things that shall befall me there:
>
> Save [except] that the Holy Ghost [holy spirit] witnesseth in every city, saying that bonds and afflictions abide me [await me].

Here's the background. Paul had been moving the word and teaching the Gentiles, which was what he was supposed to be doing. Then he decided to go to Jerusalem. However, God told him not to go to Jerusalem, but to stay with the Gentiles. How did God give Paul this information? Well, he was bound in the spirit for a start. To be bound means to be tied up, trussed up, chained up. Paul was in knots inside. God always tells you first and God told Paul not to go to Jerusalem. Paul also received information that imprisonment and worse awaited him at Jerusalem if he went. That information was given through holy spirit which witnessed to him in every city. Everywhere he went, God told Paul through believers walking by the spirit not to go to Jerusalem.

> Acts 20:24
> But none of these things move me, neither count I my life dear unto myself, so that I might finish my course with joy, and the ministry, which I have received of the Lord Jesus, to testify the gospel of the grace of God.

Was Paul sincere? Yes. Did that make him right? No. When God tells us not to do something, we would do well to listen. God can only be our protection if we act on the information he gives us. In this case, Paul didn't listen and continued with his journey to Jerusalem.

> Acts 21:1-4
> And it came to pass, that after we were gotten from them, and had launched, we came with a straight course unto Coos, and the *day* following unto Rhodes, and from thence unto Patara:
>
> And finding a ship sailing over unto Phenicia, we went aboard, and set forth.

> Now when we had discovered Cyprus, we left it on the left hand, and sailed into Syria, and landed at Tyre: for there the ship was to unlade her burden.
>
> And finding disciples, we tarried there seven days: who said to Paul through the Spirit, that he should not go up to Jerusalem.

Again, Paul is expressly told by the believers through the spirit by revelation that he should not go to Jerusalem. So what was the will of God? Obviously, not to go to Jerusalem. Who was determined to go to Jerusalem? Paul was. God was trying to stop him, but Paul's mind was made up. God can only protect us if we do what he says.

> Acts 21:10-12
> And as we tarried *there* many days, there came down from Judaea a certain prophet, named Agabus.
>
> And when he was come unto us, he took Paul's girdle, and bound his own hands and feet, and said, Thus saith the Holy Ghost, So shall the Jews [Judeans] at Jerusalem bind the man that owneth this girdle, and shall deliver *him* into the hands of the Gentiles.
>
> And when we heard these things, both we, and they of that place, besought him not to go up to Jerusalem.

As a last resort, God sent a prophet out of Jerusalem to intercept Paul to stop him from going there. Did Paul listen?

> Acts 21:13
> Then Paul answered, What mean ye to weep and to break mine heart? for I am ready not to be bound only, but also to die at Jerusalem for the name of the Lord Jesus.

No, he didn't, but look at the measures God took to try to keep Paul out of trouble. God is our protection, our rear ward, yes, but only if we act on the intelligence he passes our way. If we ignore God and his word, we have no protection.

Acts 21:14
And when he would not be persuaded, we ceased, saying, The will of the Lord be done.

Now this is an interesting verse. First of all, what was the will of God? Clearly, it was for Paul not to go to Jerusalem. Yet this verse seems to contradict that. From the context we see that if the will of the Lord was done, Paul would not have gone to Jerusalem. Paul refused to listen and adamantly continued on his way to Jerusalem. In the end the believers threw their arms up in the air in exasperation and said, okay, the will of the Lord be done. That makes no sense at all.

So why does this verse seem to contradict what is so clearly evident? The answer is in punctuation. In the original Aramaic and Greek texts there was no punctuation, and this is another key to unlocking the word's interpretation. If a verse seems to contradict the rest of the bible, one thing to check is punctuation. Every single comma, full stop and capital letter in the bible was added by translators. Is it accurate? Not always, and in this case it is clearly very wrong. Take out the comma after the word *ceased* and read the verse again.

Acts 21:14
And when he would not be persuaded, we ceased saying, The will of the Lord be done.

Now the word makes sense. See how one little comma can turn the bible into nonsense? By the way Paul did go to Jerusalem and he was almost beaten to death by a mob before being thrown in prison and carted off to Rome in chains. We would do well to learn to listen to God. He has our best interests at heart and when we listen to him we remain protected and stay out of trouble.

You often hear people blame God when terrible things happen, like young children being shot and stabbed in schools. Why are you blaming God? If we would listen to God and do what his word says, we would avoid these issues. If we refuse to listen to God, for example by abolishing the death penalty, disarming civilians, making it illegal to carry concealed weapons, and allow the bastards who do these things to live among us, don't be surprised when these things happen. If you want protection, get your head out of the world and back into God's word. Since armed air marshals were deployed on aircraft, hijacks are a thing of the past. Guns keep us protected. Mass murder with firearms only happens in gun-free zones. If you think the world is telling you the truth about guns, you watch too much television. More on this later.

I learned this truth about God being my protection in a very real way while walking to work one morning. The wind was blowing a gale and I could feel tension in the air. Police lights flashed up ahead. The traffic was backed right up and roads were blocked off. Police were everywhere. As I approached the scene, the police had begun taking down barriers and were reopening the roads. Whatever had happened, it was over.

Curious, I strolled on through the barriers, keeping my eyes open. However, God suggested I go another way. I looked down the road he was suggesting, shrugged and carried on. My curiosity, you see, was more important than listening. God was watching my back, but I wasn't listening. He does his job. The question is, are we listening?

There was sand on the road. Lots of sand. There had been a serious accident, and sand had been shovelled everywhere to soak up petrol and oil. As I approached the scene, the blustery gales whipped up sand from the road straight into my eyes! My eyes were burning and I couldn't see.

What makes this so real for me, is that this happened while I was in the middle of researching this teaching. Talk about bringing the word to life! At that moment, I realised the truth of this whole subject and made a promise to God that I would learn to listen. I washed out my eyes when I got to work and the lesson was learned. No harm had been done and God covered me despite my stupidity. He's good that way, but it's better to learn to listen and avoid the problems. Here is Derby's translation of Isaiah 58:8.

> Isaiah 58:8
> Then shall thy light break forth as the dawn, and thy health shall spring forth speedily; and thy righteousness shall go before thee, the glory of Jehovah shall be thy rearguard.

Rereward is translated rearguard here, and that's exactly what this word means in this context. Our backs are protected. Webster translates it this way.

> Isaiah 58:8
> Then shall thy light break forth as the morning, and thy health shall spring forth speedily: and thy righteousness shall go before thee; the glory of the LORD shall be thy rear-ward.

If we listen to God and his word, he will keep us protected. Much better than ice creams, don't you think? But don't worry, God hands out plenty of ice creams too. It's all part of living without fear, and enjoying life.

> Romans 8:31
> What shall we then say to these things? If God *be* for us, who *can be* against us?

11. Angels

There is a way of life and there's a way of death. However, this is nothing of which to be afraid. Quite the contrary, God's way, the way of life, is plainly marked and easily accessible. Anyone can get onto the way of life at any time.

> Isaiah 35:8
> And an highway shall be there, and a way, and it shall be called The way of holiness; the unclean shall not pass over it; but it *shall be* for those: the wayfaring men, though fools, shall not err *therein*.

Highways refer to the roads in those days, which were raised above the surrounding swamps and bogs so people could travel safely. God's highway is a safe road raised above the swamps and bogs of the world. Anyone is welcome to enjoy walking God's highway, but we have to climb out of the swamps and bogs to do so.

So where did this way of death come from in the first place, and how did we land in it? Why is there a need to search for the way of life and get onto it? Who is the devil? What are angels and what are devil spirits? Let's go to the word and find out.

When God created angels, they were under three heads – Gabriel, Michael, and Lucifer, and each had one third of the angels under their command.

Lucifer was the angel of light, the illuminated one, second in command in heaven. Underestimate him at your peril. The bible calls him the god of this world with good reason. He is a god. Look at what the word says about him before he became the devil.

Ezekiel 28:12
Son of man, take up a lamentation upon the king of Tyrus, and say unto him, Thus saith the Lord GOD; Thou sealest up the sum, full of wisdom, and perfect in beauty.

Although this appears to be addressed to a man, it is addressing Lucifer, the devil, who was the power behind the man.

Ezekiel 28:13
Thou hast been in Eden the garden of God; every precious stone was thy covering, the sardius, topaz, and the diamond, the beryl, the onyx, and the jasper, the sapphire, the emerald, and the carbuncle, and gold: the workmanship of thy tabrets and of thy pipes was prepared in thee in the day that thou wast created.

When Lucifer was created he was stunning, the greatest and the most powerful of the angels. The word also tells us he was full of wisdom and perfect in beauty.

Ezekiel 28:14,15
Thou art the anointed cherub that covereth; and I have set thee so: thou wast upon the holy mountain of God; thou hast walked up and down in the midst of the stones of fire.

Thou wast perfect in thy ways from the day that thou wast created, till iniquity was found in thee.

At one time the devil was perfect in all his ways. When he was the angel of light in heaven he was perfect, and I would have dearly loved to have known him then. Ah, but it all went horribly wrong. His heart was filled with pride and he wanted more. What more could he have than the throne of God himself?

Ezekiel 28:16-18
By the multitude of thy merchandise they have filled the midst of thee with violence, and thou hast sinned: therefore I will cast thee as profane out of the mountain of God: and I will destroy thee, O covering cherub, from the midst of the stones of fire.

Thine heart was lifted up because of thy beauty, thou hast corrupted thy wisdom by reason of thy brightness: I will cast thee to the ground, I will lay thee before kings, that they may behold thee.

Thou hast defiled thy sanctuaries by the multitude of thine iniquities, by the iniquity of thy traffick; therefore will I bring forth a fire from the midst of thee, it shall devour thee, and I will bring thee to ashes upon the earth in the sight of all them that behold thee.

Revelation 12:7-9
And there was war in heaven: Michael and his angels fought against the dragon; and the dragon fought and his angels,

And prevailed not; neither was their place found any more in heaven.

And the great dragon was cast out, that old serpent, called the Devil, and Satan, which deceiveth the whole world: he was cast out into the earth, and his angels were cast out with him.

Lucifer may have been cast out of heaven, but he is still Lucifer, and he still has all his power, beauty, and wisdom. Never underestimate the devil and always hold him in respect. His angels were cast out with him and it is those angels that make up the devil spirit realm. The only reason we can have life in this world is because God is our protection and we live under his shadow, we have his hedge of protection around us. Never, ever forget that.

Psalm 91:1-4
He that dwelleth in the secret place of the most High shall abide under the shadow of the Almighty.

I will say of the LORD, *He is* my refuge and my fortress: my God; in him will I trust.

Surely he shall deliver thee from the snare of the fowler, *and* from the noisome pestilence.

He shall cover thee with his feathers, and under his wings shalt thou trust: his truth *shall be thy* shield and buckler.

Gabriel is God's messenger angel, and his job is to deliver messages. Communication is an important part of all life, including the spiritual.

> Luke 1:19
> And the angel answering said unto him, I am Gabriel, that stand in the presence of God; and am sent to speak unto thee, and to shew thee these glad tidings.

This is a good job description of what Gabriel does. This is his job, his responsibility in the spiritual realm.

> Luke 1:26-28
> And in the sixth month the angel Gabriel was sent from God unto a city of Galilee, named Nazareth,
>
> To a virgin espoused to a man whose name was Joseph, of the house of David; and the virgin's name *was* Mary.
>
> And the angel came in unto her, and said, Hail, *thou that art* highly favoured, the Lord is with thee: blessed *art* thou among women.

Gabriel told Mary about her coming pregnancy. That's Gabriel's job, to deliver messages.

Michael, another of God's three archangels, has a job too. However, he is not a messenger, but a warrior, and he also has one third of the angels under his command. His job is to fight God's wars for him, and to protect God's people.

> Daniel 10:13
> But the prince of the kingdom of Persia withstood me one and twenty days: but, lo, Michael, one of the chief princes, came to help me; and I remained there with the kings of Persia
>
> Daniel 12:1
> And at that time shall Michael stand up, the great prince which standeth for the children of thy people: and there shall be a time of trouble, such as never was since there was a nation *even* to that

same time: and at that time thy people shall be delivered, every one that shall be found written in the book.

Not only is Michael a warrior, but he just so happens to be a rather good one. No one, but no one, messes with Michael.

> Revelation 12:7-9
> And there was war in heaven: Michael and his angels fought against the dragon; and the dragon fought and his angels,
>
> And prevailed not; neither was their place found any more in heaven.
>
> And the great dragon was cast out, that old serpent, called the Devil, and Satan, which deceiveth the whole world: he was cast out into the earth, and his angels were cast out with him.

It was Michael and his angels who kicked the devil and his angels out of heaven. Michael and his angels are God's spiritual Special Forces, his spiritual SAS, his spiritual Navy Seals. We can see this in 2 Kings.

> 2 Kings 6:8,9
> Then the king of Syria warred against Israel, and took counsel with his servants, saying, In such and such a place *shall be* my camp.
>
> And the man of God sent unto the king of Israel, saying, Beware that thou pass not such a place; for thither the Syrians are come down.

God was protecting his people by giving revelation to the man of God, who then warned the king about where the enemy were laying ambushes.

> 2 Kings 6:10
> And the king of Israel sent to the place which the man of God told him and warned him of, and saved himself there, not once nor twice.

This passing of intelligence to the king of Israel troubled the king of Syria, who began to suspect he had a traitor among his commanders.

> 2 Kings 6:11,12
> Therefore the heart of the king of Syria was sore troubled for this thing; and he called his servants, and said unto them, Will ye not shew me which of us *is* for the king of Israel?
>
> And one of his servants said, None, my lord, O king: but Elisha, the prophet that *is* in Israel, telleth the king of Israel the words that thou speakest in thy bedchamber.

When he discovered that Elisha was the intelligence leak, he sent his best men behind enemy lines to locate him.

> 2 Kings 6:13,14
> And he said, Go and spy where he *is*, that I may send and fetch him. And it was told him, saying, Behold, *he is* in Dothan.
>
> Therefore sent he thither horses, and chariots, and a great host: and they came by night, and compassed the city about.

Elisha awoke to find himself surrounded by enemy troops looking for him. The reality of this situation perhaps doesn't communicate immediately. How would you feel if you opened your front door and discovered a gang of Hells Angels standing outside patting baseball bats in the palms of their hands? Might you be tempted to twitch a little? Not Elisha, and this was no small motorcycle gang, this was an army.

> 2 Kings 6:15
> And when the servant of the man of God was risen early, and gone forth, behold, an host compassed the city both with horses and chariots. And his servant said unto him, Alas, my master! how shall we do?

His servant was terrified. I can't say I blame him. What was Elisha's response?

> 2 Kings 6:16
> And he answered, Fear not: for they that *be* with us *are* more than they that *be* with them.

Fear not! How many times do we read that in the word? Fear is our greatest enemy. There is nothing to fear, not even when an entire army of enemy soldiers surrounds us.

> Romans 8:31
> What shall we then say to these things? If God *be* for us, who *can be* against us?

Guess what, Romans 8:31 is true. Elisha's servant looked at the situation with his eyes, and to his mind the situation was impossible. He was afraid for his life. Elisha, however, looked at things from a different point of view, a different perspective, and he told his servant that there were more on their side than on the enemy's side. Okay, where were they?

> 2 Kings 6:17
> And Elisha prayed, and said, LORD, I pray thee, open his eyes, that he may see. And the LORD opened the eyes of the young man; and he saw: and, behold, the mountain *was* full of horses and chariots of fire round about Elisha.

From what we have learned so far about angels, who do you think was leading the spiritual forces lining the mountains? Michael, of course. That is what he does. Whenever the devil stacks the odds against us, we have nothing to fear. Even in war, we have nothing to fear, because we have God's protection.

What else can we learn from the word regarding angels? Oh lots, and while we're here we might as well dispel a few myths about them.

> Judges 13:2-4
> And there was a certain man of Zorah, of the family of the Danites, whose name *was* Manoah; and his wife *was* barren, and bare not.
>
> And the angel of the LORD appeared unto the woman, and said unto her, Behold now, thou *art* barren, and bearest not: but thou shalt conceive, and bear a son.
>
> Now therefore beware, I pray thee, and drink not wine nor strong drink, and eat not any unclean *thing*:

The angel gave this woman explicit instructions, which it was expected she would carry out. This is an important key. It is only when we do the word in the details that we get the results.

> Judges 13:5,6
> For, lo, thou shalt conceive, and bear a son; and no razor shall come on his head: for the child shall be a Nazarite unto God from the womb: and he shall begin to deliver Israel out of the hand of the Philistines.
>
> Then the woman came and told her husband, saying, A man of God came unto me, and his countenance *was* like the countenance of an angel of God, very terrible: but I asked him not whence he *was*, neither told he me his name:

This is interesting. She did not tell her husband she had spoken to an angel, she told him she had spoken to a man of God who reminded her of an angel. This is intriguing, because according to the bible, it really was an angel.

> Judges 13:7,8
> But he said unto me, Behold, thou shalt conceive, and bear a son; and now drink no wine nor strong drink, neither eat any unclean *thing*: for the child shall be a Nazarite to God from the womb to the day of his death.
>
> Then Manoah intreated the LORD, and said, O my Lord, let the man of God which thou didst send come again unto us, and teach us what we shall do unto the child that shall be born.

Her husband prayed that God would send back the man of God. Note that he didn't pray for God to send back an angel. He didn't know it was an angel.

> Judges 13:9,10
> And God hearkened to the voice of Manoah; and the angel of God came again unto the woman as she sat in the field: but Manoah her husband *was* not with her.

> And the woman made haste, and ran, and shewed her husband, and said unto him, Behold, the man [man, not angel] hath appeared unto me, that came unto me the *other* day.

Did she say that the angel who had previously appeared to her had returned? No, she said the man. Why did she not say angel? If you do not understand this yet, it is because your perception of angels, the picture you carry of them in your mind is wrong.

> Judges 13:11
> And Manoah arose, and went after his wife, and came to the man [not angel], and said unto him, *Art* thou the man that spakest unto the woman? And he said, I *am*.

They were talking face to face with an angel, yet they both thought he was a man. Why? Simple, because he looked like a man. In other words, angels do not have wings, they do not play harps, they do not have halos, and they do not float around in white robes chanting stupid religious ditties. They did not know he was an angel because he looked just like any other human being. Angels take human form when they appear. For the most part, they stand on the ground, they wear normal clothes, and they speak with normal voices. All the other rubbish you hear about them is just brown smelly religious horseshit. And I don't care if my language annoys you, the only thing I care about is the accuracy of God's word. If you want to live the more abundant life and manifest the power of God, shut up and listen. I'm teaching you the truth.

> Judges 13:12,13
> And Manoah said, Now let thy words come to pass. How shall we order the child, and *how* shall we do unto him?
>
> And the angel of the LORD said unto Manoah, Of all that I said unto the woman let her beware.

See, he was an angel. The word says so. It's just that Manoah and his wife didn't recognise him as such. This is an amazing truth.

Judges 13:14,15
She may not eat of any *thing* that cometh of the vine, neither let her drink wine or strong drink, nor eat any unclean *thing*: all that I commanded her let her observe.

And Manoah said unto the angel of the LORD, I pray thee, let us detain thee, until we shall have made ready a kid for thee.

Manoah still thinks the angel is a man.

Judges 13:16
And the angel of the LORD said unto Manoah, Though thou detain me, I will not eat of thy bread: and if thou wilt offer a burnt offering, thou must offer it unto the LORD. For Manoah knew not that he *was* an angel of the LORD.

That pretty much spells it out. Manoah and his wife thought he was a man, because they simply could not know he was an angel by looking at him. There was nothing about his appearance that would have remotely suggested he was anything other than a human being.

Judges 13:17-21
And Manoah said unto the angel of the LORD, What *is* thy name, that when thy sayings come to pass we may do thee honour?

And the angel of the LORD said unto him, Why askest thou thus after my name, seeing it *is* secret?

So Manoah took a kid with a meat offering, and offered *it* upon a rock unto the LORD: and *the angel* did wondrously; and Manoah and his wife looked on.

For it came to pass, when the flame went up toward heaven from off the altar, that the angel of the LORD ascended in the flame of the altar. And Manoah and his wife looked on *it*, and fell on their faces to the ground.

But the angel of the LORD did no more appear to Manoah and to his wife. Then Manoah knew that he *was* an angel of the LORD.

After Manoah lit a fire and made his offering, the angel went up into the sky in the smoke and vanished. I suppose that would have made an impact.

> Judges 13:22,23
> And Manoah said unto his wife, We shall surely die, because we have seen God.
>
> But his wife said unto him, If the LORD were pleased to kill us, he would not have received a burnt offering and a meat offering at our hands, neither would he have shewed us all these *things*, nor would as at this time have told us *such things* as these.

Good job Manoah had a sensible wife who could think.

> Judges 13:24
> And the woman bare a son, and called his name Samson: and the child grew, and the LORD blessed him.

Just look who this child was. These were Samson's parents. Hebrews gives more information on angels.

> Hebrews 13:2
> Be not forgetful to entertain strangers: for thereby some have entertained angels unawares.

The truth is, if you met an angel, you would not know it unless they wanted you to. They appear in human form, and look, talk, and dress like us. Sure, they can do all that fancy floating and disappearing stuff too, but primarily they come to do a job, not to show off. We can see these same truths regarding angels in Judges.

> Judges 6:1
> And the children of Israel did evil in the sight of the LORD: and the LORD delivered them into the hand of Midian seven years.

Here we go again, another turn your back on God and suffer the consequences scenario. God delivering them into the hand of Midian simply means God was forced to allow it to happen – it's the idiom of permission. It isn't that God is mean, it's that we walk away from him and his protection and so there's nothing he can do.

> Judges 6:2-5
> And the hand of Midian prevailed against Israel: *and* because of the Midianites the children of Israel made them the dens which *are* in the mountains, and caves, and strong holds.
>
> And *so* it was, when Israel had sown, that the Midianites came up, and the Amalekites, and the children of the east, even they came up against them;
>
> And they encamped against them, and destroyed the increase of the earth, till thou come unto Gaza, and left no sustenance for Israel, neither sheep, nor ox, nor ass.
>
> For they came up with their cattle and their tents, and they came as grasshoppers for multitude; *for* both they and their camels were without number: and they entered into the land to destroy it.

Whenever and wherever a nation turns away from God, catastrophe is inevitable. The devil exists only to steal, to kill, and to destroy. Whenever and wherever we walk away from God, we walk right back into the devil's world. Whenever and wherever people come back to God, he is always there to sort out their messes for them, individually or as entire nations. He is amazing.

> Judges 6:6-10
> And Israel was greatly impoverished because of the Midianites; and the children of Israel cried unto the LORD.
>
> And it came to pass, when the children of Israel cried unto the LORD because of the Midianites,
>
> That the LORD sent a prophet unto the children of Israel, which said unto them, Thus saith the LORD God of Israel, I brought you up from Egypt, and brought you forth out of the house of bondage;

> And I delivered you out of the hand of the Egyptians, and out of the hand of all that oppressed you, and drave them out from before you, and gave you their land;
>
> And I said unto you, I *am* the LORD your God; fear not the gods of the Amorites, in whose land ye dwell: but ye have not obeyed my voice.

God confronts them and tells them exactly why they are in this situation. They, by the freedom of their wills, turned away from him so he could no longer protect them. God did not go anywhere, they did. He is not condemning them though, he is explaining what happened, giving them a chance to change and showing them how to get back onto the way of life.

> Judges 6:11
> And there came an angel of the LORD, and sat under an oak which *was* in Ophrah, that *pertained* unto Joash the Abiezrite: and his son Gideon threshed wheat by the winepress, to hide it from the Midianites.

Here comes another angel. If we bear in mind what we learned earlier, that angels appear in human form, this record will make more sense.

> Judges 6:12-14
> And the angel of the LORD appeared unto him, and said unto him, The LORD *is* with thee, thou mighty man of valour.
>
> And Gideon said unto him, Oh my Lord, if the LORD be with us, why then is all this befallen us? and where *be* all his miracles which our fathers told us of, saying, Did not the LORD bring us up from Egypt? but now the LORD hath forsaken us, and delivered us into the hands of the Midianites.
>
> And the LORD looked upon him, and said, Go in this thy might, and thou shalt save Israel from the hand of the Midianites: have not I sent thee?

The children of Israel were not to sit around all day crying about their problems, they were to deal with them. Sitting around crying and complaining accomplishes nothing. When you have stopped crying and complaining, the problems are still there and you still have to deal with them. Notice that God doesn't just wave a magic wand and magic all their problems away either. Gideon was to lead Israel to war. War is hard dangerous work. Getting out of our problems can be extremely hard work, but if we listen and obey we sort our lives out. If we do not, we stay in the mess. It is really up to us. God's word works.

> Judges 6:15,16,21,22
> And he said unto him, Oh my Lord, wherewith shall I save Israel? behold, my family *is* poor in Manasseh, and I *am* the least in my father's house.
>
> And the LORD said unto him, Surely I will be with thee, and thou shalt smite the Midianites as one man
>
> Then the angel of the LORD put forth the end of the staff that *was* in his hand, and touched the flesh and the unleavened cakes; and there rose up fire out of the rock, and consumed the flesh and the unleavened cakes. Then the angel of the LORD departed out of his sight.
>
> And when Gideon perceived that he *was* an angel of the LORD, Gideon said, Alas, O Lord GOD! for because I have seen an angel of the LORD face to face.

Up until this point, Gideon thought he was talking to a man. He had no idea this was an angel until it did another vanishing act.

What we have just learned should clear up some of the religious fog shrouding this whole subject of angels. Angels are spirits, they are not physical beings. Devil spirits are also angels, spirit beings. You cannot see spirit, hear spirit, smell spirit, taste spirit, or touch spirit.

Devil spirits and angels are intelligent lifeforms that live in a different dimension, the spiritual. They are supernatural alien life, though I can assure you that neither Captains Kirk nor Picard are ever likely to encounter them on any planet anywhere because they are not physical beings.

Angels can take human form and appear to us. Devil spirits can also manifest themselves in the senses realm. Separating truth from error in this field takes an in-depth spiritual perception and awareness, which only comes from knowing and living the word.

Do angels come around today? If God sends them, yes. Here is how it works. You do your job, and if God thinks you need an angel he will send one. Just get on with what you are supposed to be doing. Don't go praying for them, and don't go looking for them. If God thinks you need one, he will send one. There is nothing in the bible anywhere that says you can pray to angels either, so don't do it. The spiritual realm is a dangerous place, and only when we walk by the revealed word and will of God will we remain safe.

Okay, it's time to head off into Genesis and find out what happened when man fell.

12. Smashed and Trashed

We now need to understand a few truths from Genesis.

> Genesis 1:1,2
> In the beginning God created the heaven and the earth.
>
> And the earth was without form, and void; and darkness *was* upon the face of the deep. And the Spirit of God moved upon the face of the waters.

The first word in the bible when it was originally written was the word *God*. God in the beginning created the heaven and the earth.

> Genesis 1:2
> And the earth was without form and void.

We will consider these words for there is much below the surface. When we perceive their depth, our perceptions of the world will never quite be the same again.

To begin, let us consider the words *form and void* which are *tohu va bohu* in the Hebrew. *Tohu va bohu* could literally be translated *without form and void*, but without understanding an important figure of speech at work we completely miss the whole point. The words *tohu va bohu* rhyme and this is intentional. It is the figure of speech **paronomasia** – rhyming words. To see the power in this figure of speech, consider the following:

> *He was extremely fit.*

This is a literal sentence, which means exactly what it says – he was extremely fit. There is no figure of speech employed, and the sentence is a basic statement of rather bland fact. There is no real power to the words. However, if we were to say:

He was lean and mean.

All of a sudden, the sentence resonates with power. We have images of the extreme fitness of this guy, and even his mental attitude. We can *feel* his fitness. That is what a figure of speech does – it brings words to life, emphasising them in a very special way, giving them power and resonance.

> Genesis 1:2
> And the earth was without form and void.

This is a poor translation of *tohu va bohu*, despite it being technically accurate. This is because the translators did not employ the figure of speech, and what we have is a rather bland statement of fact. Worse, this particular translation is misleading. If we were to translate these words employing the figure of speech that was intended, the verse develops a power that is almost overwhelming. Here is an attempt to translate the verse, employing the figure of speech *paronomasia*.

And the earth was smashed and trashed.

My goodness, sit down and consider those words. The earth was smashed and trashed? You mean it was not created that way? What happened? God created the heavens and the earth, and then it was smashed and trashed? Yes, that is precisely what the word is saying here. Whatever happened in Genesis 1:2 was so cataclysmic, the earth was totally without form and void, it could not support any form of life whatsoever, it was utterly smashed and trashed.

> Genesis 1:2
> And the earth was smashed and trashed; and darkness *was* upon the face of the deep. And the Spirit of God moved upon the face of the waters.

To understand what happened to the earth back in Genesis 1:2, it is necessary to look at a few other scriptures to build some background.

The bible talks of three heavens and three earths, and it is important to note that there is no overlapping of time between them, nor are they spheres within spheres, or levels within levels, as is often taught by spiritualists and sorcerers. These are three distinctly different heavens and earths in three completely different periods of time.

> 2 Peter 3:5-7
> For this they willingly are ignorant of, that by the word of God the heavens were of old, and the earth standing out of the water and in the water:
>
> Whereby the world that then was, being overflowed with water, perished:
>
> But the heavens and the earth, which are now, by the same word are kept in store, reserved unto fire against the day of judgment and perdition of ungodly men.

Peter talks of the first heavens and earth, and the present heavens and earth. He also gives us information. Water destroyed the first heaven and earth, but this is not referring to the flood of Noah's day for that flood did not smash and trash the earth. When the earth was smashed and trashed in Genesis 1:2, there was no life for it could not support life. Peter also talks of a third heavens and earth coming in the future:

> 2 Peter 3:13
> Nevertheless we, according to his promise, look for new heavens and a new earth, wherein dwelleth righteousness.

God put the first heavens and earth together. That earth was smashed and trashed. God put it back together again, and this is the second heavens and earth in which we now live. However, Adam and Eve messed things up and sometime in the future there will be a new heavens and earth where everything will be put right again.

So how was the first earth smashed and trashed? We gain clues from around the word, some of which we've seen before.

> Revelation 12:7-9
> And there was war in heaven: Michael and his angels fought against the dragon; and the dragon fought and his angels,

And prevailed not; neither was their place found any more in heaven.

And the great dragon was cast out, that old serpent, called the Devil, and Satan, which deceiveth the whole world: he was cast out into the earth, and his angels were cast out with him.

First of all, is this talking about a past event or a future event? The period of revelation, called the wrath in the bible, is still future, but there are references to past events throughout the book. For example, verses 1 and 2 inform us that both the sun and moon were visible in Virgo when Jesus Christ was born. This is clearly a reference to a past event. Some claim this war in heaven is still a future event and that the devil still resides in heaven, but consider these verses from Job and Peter which clearly teach that the devil is earthbound right now.

Job 1:7
And the LORD said unto Satan, Whence comest thou? Then Satan answered the LORD, and said, From going to and fro in the earth, and from walking up and down in it.

1 Peter 5:8
Be sober, be vigilant; because your adversary the devil, as a roaring lion, walketh about, seeking whom he may devour:

If the devil is earthbound, then clearly the prophecy in Revelation refers to a past event. No one can possibly deny that by the time Adam and Eve came along the devil had already rebelled. He was clearly already God's enemy before the foundations of this second heavens and earth. It was this spiritual war in the heavens that is the most likely cause of the smashed and trashed heavens and earth in Genesis. Isaiah substantiates this. Just look at *I Wills* in the following verses.

Isaiah 14:12-15
How art thou fallen from heaven, O Lucifer, son of the morning! *how* art thou cut down to the ground, which didst weaken the nations!

For thou hast said in thine heart, I will ascend into heaven, I will exalt my throne above the stars of God [the star, God]: I will sit also upon the mount of the congregation, in the sides of the north:

I will ascend above the heights of the clouds; I will be like the most High.

Yet thou shalt be brought down to hell, to the sides of the pit.

Lucifer, from Latin, means light bearer or brilliant one, illuminated one. Lucifer was second in command in heaven next to God. Each archangel had one third of the angels under their command. The angels, as we do, have freewill. Lucifer decided he wanted to be worshipped as God and committed treason by trying to usurp God and take his worship which started the war. Obviously God did not smash and trash his own earth, so we can safely conclude it was the devil who did it. Lucifer must be quite something if he felt he could take on God. Never underestimate him. We put our trust in God as our protection from him.

As an aside, here is another morsel of truth that enhances and adds light to the truth of the smashed and trashed earth of Genesis 1:2. After the flood of Noah's day, when the ark grounded and Noah and his family stepped back onto dry ground, God spoke to them:

Genesis 9:1
And God blessed Noah and his sons, and said unto them, Be fruitful, and multiply, and replenish the earth.

God told them to be fruitful and multiply and REPLENISH the earth. What does the word *replenish* mean? Here is a dictionary definition:

replenish
—*verb (used with object)*
to make full or complete again, as by supplying what is lacking, used up, etc.: *to replenish one's stock of food.*

In the case of Noah, this makes perfect sense. They were to replenish the earth because they were the only ones left. The earth had been populated, everyone apart from Noah and his family had drowned, and they were to repopulate, replenish the earth. Now look back at Genesis 1 when God spoke to Adam and Eve.

Genesis 1:27,28a
So God created man in his *own* image, in the image of God created he him; male and female created he them.

And God blessed them, and God said unto them, Be fruitful, and multiply, and REPLENISH the earth, and subdue it . . .

God told Adam and Eve to replenish the earth just as he told Noah. Intriguing stuff. See, the earth had been populated before Adam and Eve, before it was smashed and trashed in Genesis 1:2. Further, we can assume that it was the devil who did the smashing and trashing.

So, we have a smashed and trashed earth, there is no life, everything is cold and dark. That makes sense, because cold and dark implies an absence of light and heat. The devil's realm is not hot as some believe, it is extremely cold.

Genesis 1:3-5
And God said, Let there be light: and there was light.

And God saw the light, that *it was* good: and God divided the light from the darkness.

And God called the light Day, and the darkness he called Night. And the evening and the morning were the first day.

Darkness can only exist in the absence of light. Turn on the light and there is no darkness.

Genesis 1:6-8
And God said, Let there be a firmament [Hebrew - raqia] in the midst of the waters, and let it divide the waters from the waters.

And God made the firmament [raqia], and divided the waters which *were* under the firmament [raqia] from the waters which *were* above the firmament [raqia]: and it was so.

And God called the firmament [raqia] Heaven. And the evening and the morning were the second day.

What is the firmament? Verse 8 tells us the firmament is heaven, or the universe. The word translated *firmament* here is *raqia* in Hebrew, which is more accurately translated *expansion*, and it refers to the universe. The firmament is the universe so read these verses again employing universe instead of firmament.

> Genesis 1:6-8
> And God said, Let there be a universe in the midst of the waters, and let it divide the waters from the waters.
>
> And God made the universe, and divided the waters which *were* under the universe from the waters which *were* above the universe: and it was so.
>
> And God called the universe Heaven. And the evening and the morning were the second day.

Heaven is the universe, which is anywhere above earth. Biblically, if you want to go to heaven, jump up and down or fly in a plane. Every time you leave earth, you are in heaven. In Peter, we saw that the first earth was destroyed because it overflowed with water.

> 2 Peter 3:6
> Whereby the world that then was, being overflowed with water, perished:

This is fascinating. By putting the second heavens and earth back into order, God divided the waters into two distinct bodies. The waters under the universe refer to the waters on the smashed and trashed earth. These waters were separated from the waters above the universe. What is this saying? When the first heavens and earth were smashed and trashed, the entire planet earth was covered in water. These waters were then divided, separated, so that there was a universe between the waters on the earth and the waters above it. In other words, the universe does not go on forever, it is totally encased in water. You can picture it like a bubble in a sea, albeit a rather large bubble.

Some basic physics wouldn't go amiss here. God introduced light. Without light, and therefore heat, in what state is water? It is frozen.

Incidentally, so is oxygen, nitrogen, and all other normally gaseous material. The water that smashed and trashed the first heavens and earth was, therefore, frozen. The atmosphere would have liquefied and frozen. In this regards, isn't it amazing to note then that all scientists and geologists agree that the last Ice Age ended less than 10,000 years ago, the same time the bible says Adam and Eve were formed, made and created. Now consider this verse from Job:

> Job 38:30
> The waters are hid [hardened] as *with* a stone, and the face of the deep is frozen.

The word *hid* is the word *hardened*, and you can delete the italicised word *with*. These waters referred to in Job are hard like stone. Why? Because they are frozen. Total darkness is the absence of light and heat. Any guesses where the frozen face of the deep is? Yes, the frozen face of the deep refers to the waters above the universe. These waters are called in the bible, the deep, and its face is frozen.

> Genesis 1:2
> And the earth was without form, and void; and darkness *was* upon the face of the deep. And the Spirit of God moved upon the face of the waters.

What about this first heaven and earth then? Well, we know it was around for a long time from the rocks and fossils we can study. T Rex? Stick him in the first heaven and earth, for that is when he lived and breathed. Stick all your dinosaurs in there. See how beautifully the rightly divided word fits with true science?

Scientists today search for a link between what they call prehistoric man and modern man – the missing link – but they cannot find it. The reason is simple, there isn't one. The world was smashed and trashed. The men that lived in the first heaven and earth did not survive or evolve into this second heaven and earth. The oldest bones of modern man date to less than 10,000 years ago, the same time the last ice age ended. There is no conflict with true science and the bible. Science can only corroborate and substantiate the truths recorded in the word. By the way, this truth negates the theory of evolution. Man and all the animals on earth today are less than 10,000 years old. All the older fossils belong to life in the first heaven and earth.

Any idea what keeps the frozen face of the deep from freezing the earth today? Ever wondered what the stars are up there for? Sure, for signs and seasons, and they look pretty, but they also have a job to do, they keep us protected from all that cold up there. On day one, God introduced light to the smashed and trashed heavens and earth. On day two, he separated the waters with the universe. Now we are into day three.

> Genesis 1:9-13
> And God said, Let the waters under the heaven be gathered together unto one place, and let the dry *land* appear: and it was so.
>
> And God called the dry *land* Earth; and the gathering together of the waters called he Seas: and God saw that *it was* good.
>
> And God said, Let the earth bring forth grass, the herb yielding seed, *and* the fruit tree yielding fruit after his kind, whose seed *is* in itself, upon the earth: and it was so.
>
> And the earth brought forth grass, *and* herb yielding seed after his kind, and the tree yielding fruit, whose seed *was* in itself, after his kind: and God saw that *it was* good.
>
> And the evening and the morning were the third day.

Note that God did not create anything here, and nor did he create anything on day one or day two. The earth already existed, and because it already existed, God did not have to create it. To create, biblically, means *to bring into existence something that does not exist*. Hence, there is no creating going on here. The heavens and the earth existed, so God just had to put it back together again after it was smashed and trashed.

On day three, dry land appeared and the seas were gathered into one place, a reference to there being one large land mass surrounded by one ocean. At this stage of earth's development, there were no islands or continents. There is no problem getting science to fit any of this. Any child can look at a globe of the world and see how South America fits into Africa, and how all the continents could be pushed together like a giant jigsaw puzzle. Scientists and geologists have named this supercontinent Pangaea. The world has this to say about Pangaea.

Pangaea was a supercontinent that existed during the late Palaeozoic and early Mesozoic eras, forming approximately 300 million years ago. It began to break apart around 200 million years ago.

This is a monstrous lie. Pangaea broke up less than 10,000 years ago, and it happened suddenly, overnight, not over millions of years. The reason the world lies about when Pangaea broke apart is because they have no facts to substantiate their truths. It took a massive head on smash of continents to force the Himalayan Mountains into the sky. Perhaps honest scientists and geologists can put some stuff together now that makes sense.

Day three also sees plant life built back into the earth. The smashing and trashing of the first earth was so severe, no plant life or their seeds survived. The smashing and trashing was absolute, as emphasised by the figure of speech paronomasia. The earth was totally and utterly devoid of any form of life whatsoever because it was smashed and trashed. Now day four.

Genesis 1:14-19
And God said, Let there be lights in the firmament of the heaven [the universe] to divide the day from the night; and let them be for signs, and for seasons, and for days, and years:

And let them be for lights in the firmament of the heaven to give light upon the earth: and it was so.

And God made two great lights; the greater light to rule the day, and the lesser light to rule the night: *he made* the stars also.

And God set them in the firmament of the heaven to give light upon the earth,

And to rule over the day and over the night, and to divide the light from the darkness: and God saw that *it was* good.

And the evening and the morning were the fourth day.

There are some amazing truths here. God made light on day one, didn't he? Sure he did.

> Genesis 1:5
> And God called the light Day, and the darkness he called Night. And the evening and the morning were the first day.

Despite light being in existence since day one, the sun and the stars were not made until the fourth day. Light therefore does not originate from the sun or any of the stars. The sun and stars are merely transformers, power cells that convert light into useable energy that supports life on earth. The sun is not a source of light, because light existed before the sun was fired up. There is much below the surface here, but we cannot take the time in this work to delve into quantum physics. Suffice to mention that the same way you can use a microscope to look down into a completely new world at the cellular level, and then continue down into the atomic universe, you can zoom into God's word to find completely new dimensions of truth below the surface. There are vast astronomic and deep microscopic universes of perfection within God's word. Onto day five.

> Genesis 1:20-23
> And God said, Let the waters bring forth abundantly the moving creature [Hebrew: nephesh – soul] that hath life, and fowl *that* may fly above the earth in the open firmament of heaven.
>
> And God created great whales, and every living creature [nephesh – soul] that moveth, which the waters brought forth abundantly, after their kind, and every winged fowl after his kind: and God saw that *it was* good.
>
> And God blessed them, saying, Be fruitful, and multiply, and fill the waters in the seas, and let fowl multiply in the earth.
>
> And the evening and the morning were the fifth day.

In verse 20, the word *creature* is translated from a Hebrew word with which we will become familiar. It is the word *nephesh*, which means *soul*. Let the waters bring forth abundantly living souls. In verse 21, the word *creature* is again the word *nephesh* and it should have been translated soul.

Note also the correct usage of the word create. This is only the second time this word has been used so far in Genesis. Soul life did not exist at this point, which is why God had to create it. He brought into existence something that did not exist in any form anywhere. Soul life is breath life. If something breathes, it has soul. Whales, birds, fish, dogs and cats have souls. Anything that breathes has a soul. This is when soul life was created, and once something has been created, it does not require creating again because it already exists. Remember that when we come to man.

> Genesis 1:24-26
> And God said, Let the earth bring forth the living creature [nephesh] after his kind, cattle, and creeping thing, and beast of the earth after his kind: and it was so.
>
> And God made the beast of the earth after his kind, and cattle after their kind, and every thing that creepeth upon the earth after his kind: and God saw that *it was* good.
>
> And God said, Let us make man in our image, after our likeness: and let them have dominion over the fish of the sea, and over the fowl of the air, and over the cattle, and over all the earth, and over every creeping thing that creepeth upon the earth.

The animal and plant kingdoms were in place before man was formed, made, and created. However, man had something very special which no animal, fish or bird had, and that was spirit.

> Genesis 1:27
> So God created man in his *own* image, in the image of God created he him; male and female created he them.

The image of God is spirit, so when he created man in his own image, it means he created spirit within man. It was this spirit that set man above everything else, that was what made him special, that was what set him above the animal kingdom.

> Genesis 1:28-30
> And God blessed them, and God said unto them, Be fruitful, and multiply, and replenish the earth, and subdue it: and have dominion

over the fish of the sea, and over the fowl of the air, and over every living thing that moveth upon the earth.

And God said, Behold, I have given you every herb bearing seed, which *is* upon the face of all the earth, and every tree, in the which *is* the fruit of a tree yielding seed; to you it shall be for meat.

And to every beast of the earth, and to every fowl of the air, and to every thing that creepeth upon the earth, wherein *there is* life, *I have given* every green herb for meat: and it was so.

Man had dominion and authority over the earth and everything in it. Man was the earth's CEO if you like, he was the boss, the Lord of the earth, and it was God who gave him that job, that responsibility.

To finish off chapter one, notice that God states six times that what he had done was good, and then crowns it with a seventh usage of *very* good.

> Genesis 1:4,10,12,18,21,25,31
> And God saw the light, that *it was* **good**: and God divided the light from the darkness.
>
> And God called the dry *land* Earth; and the gathering together of the waters called he Seas: and God saw that *it was* **good**.
>
> And the earth brought forth grass, *and* herb yielding seed after his kind, and the tree yielding fruit, whose seed *was* in itself, after his kind: and God saw that *it was* **good**.
>
> And to rule over the day and over the night, and to divide the light from the darkness: and God saw that *it was* **good**.
>
> And God created great whales, and every living creature that moveth, which the waters brought forth abundantly, after their kind, and every winged fowl after his kind: and God saw that *it was* **good**.

And God made the beast of the earth after his kind, and cattle after their kind, and every thing that creepeth upon the earth after his kind: and God saw that *it was* **good**.

And God saw every thing that he had made, and, behold, *it was* **very good**. And the evening and the morning were the sixth day.

When God calls something good six times and then crowns it with a seventh usage of *very* good, be assured that the earth was in good shape. The balance of nature was perfect, the ocean environment was perfect, the plant kingdom was perfect, the animal kingdom was perfect, the climate was perfect, and our human bodies and souls were perfect. Everything was in perfect balance and perfect harmony.

Even today, God's perfection can still be seen everywhere. How many birds are there in the world? Yet they are all distinct, not just in colour and appearance, but in voice and behaviour. Look at the artistry in their plumage. Listen to their voices. Does God understand flight? Look how beautifully suited birds are to their environments. Not only can birds fly, some of them swim, and some of them dive under water. This was all by design, not chance. There is incredible intelligence behind creation, not chaos. Every sunset and sunrise is a witness to the love and heart that God has for us. He made all this for us. Look around you, look within you, and *feel* the love he has for you.

Ah, but if God made such a beautiful world, then why is it all such a mess today? We will pursue that in the next chapter.

13. The Fall of Man

So, we have a smashed and trashed heavens and earth, God puts it all back together again, and everything is wonderful. Adam and Eve are living in paradise, it is all sunshine and laughter, birds twittering away and happy days. Okay, what happened? Without understanding the differences between body, soul, and spirit, nothing in the bible will make much sense so we will look at that now. Thessalonians weaves these three parts together, and tells us they make up the whole man.

> 1 Thessalonians 5:23
> And the very God of peace sanctify you wholly; and *I pray God* your whole spirit and soul and body be preserved blameless unto the coming of our Lord Jesus Christ.

If something is whole, then there is nothing missing. If something is missing, then it is not whole. Body, soul and spirit make up a whole man. If man were missing any of these three parts, he would not be whole. Now, are body, soul and spirit synonymous? Do they mean the same thing? No, they do not. Apples are not oranges, monkeys are not cows, bodies are not souls. Easy to understand? Of course it is. Now use that same logic regarding soul and spirit – they are not the same thing. Consider this from Isaiah:

> Isaiah 43:7
> *Even* every one that is called by my name: for I have created him for my glory, I have formed him; yea, I have made him.

With reference to man, God says in Isaiah that he created man, he formed him, and he made him. Formed, made, and created are all translated from distinctly different Hebrew words. Are these words synonymous? No, they can't be, not if language has any rules. These words do not mean the same thing. God uses these words in Isaiah with accuracy and precision.

Formed is translated from the Hebrew word **yatsar,** which means *to fashion*. This word is used in the bible to describe how a potter fashions or forms a pot from a lump of clay.

Made is the Hebrew word **asah,** which is a very general term for *to do* or *to make*. You *make* dinner, you *do* your work, you *make* a noise – that's this very general word, asah, to do or to make something.

Created is translated from the Hebrew word **barah,** which means to bring into existence something that does not exist in any state or form. Contrary to most dictionaries, man has never created anything. Man can invent, fashion, produce, and manufacture all sorts of things, but only God can create, only God can bring into existence something that does not exist in any state or form.

Everyone can easily understand that body is not soul, but spirit is not soul either, and it is this confusion regarding soul and spirit which has muddied the clarity of God's word in the holy spirit field. Which part of man was formed? Which part of man was made? Which part of man was created? Let's deal with the easy option first:

> Genesis 2:7
> And the LORD God formed [yatsar] man *of* the dust of the ground...

Formed is our Hebrew word *yatsar*. Which part of man did God form? The body, obviously. The dust of the earth refers to everything in our bodies. We all developed from ingredients that originated from the earth, the dust of the ground. Our bodies do not just magic out of nothing, they come from the earth.

The same is true of the plant kingdom. If you plant a tree in a bucket of earth, when the tree is grown the bucket still has the same amount of earth in it. So where did the tree come from? It came from water in the ground and carbon in the atmosphere. Water and carbon dioxide are broken down through photosynthesis into oxygen and carbohydrates. It all comes from the earth. When we were developing in the womb, what did our bodies grow from? They grew from the food our mothers ate which came from the earth. Therefore, biblically, we can tie *formed* and *body* together. Now what about soul?

Genesis 2:7
And the LORD God formed man *of* the dust of the ground, and breathed into his nostrils the breath of life; and man became [asah – was made] a living soul.

Living soul in Hebrew is *nephesh chai*, *nephesh* being the word for *soul*, *chai* the word for *life*. It was in breathing that man became, or was made, *asah*, a living soul.

Our soul is who we are – our character, our emotions, our heart, our ambitions, our inner being, that which is housed within our bodies, that which gives life to our bodies. Again, this isn't so hard to understand. It is in breathing that we have soul, and it is in breathing, in having soul, that our bodies have life. When we eat, nutrients are transported around our bodies in our blood streams to the cells where they are needed. As we breathe, our blood circulates and gives life to our bodies. It's beautiful how they work together. Without breath, we have no life, no soul. Now, what about spirit?

Genesis 1:27
So God created man in his *own* image, in the image of God created he him; male and female created he them.

Created is the Hebrew word *barah*, to bring into existence something which does not exist in any state or form. To see the astonishing accuracy of God's word regarding these words, check out the usage of create in verse 21 regarding soul.

Genesis 1:21
And God created [barah] great whales, and every living creature [soul] that moveth, which the waters brought forth abundantly, after their kind, and every winged fowl after his kind: and God saw that *it was* good.

It says God *created* every living creature [nephesh – soul] in the seas, like whales and dolphins. Why did the translators not translate nephesh as soul here instead of creature? I don't know, but the point is, soul life did not exist anywhere in the universe at this time, so God had to create it out of nothing. If it existed, God would not have had to create it. Therefore, we can safely conclude that at the time of Adam and Eve, just a few thousand years ago, there was no breath life anywhere in the universe. In other words, less than 10,000 years ago there were no breathing aliens on any planets, in any solar system, in any galaxy anywhere. Soul life, breath life, just did not exist. If it did, God would not have had to create it in Genesis.

When God breathed soul life into man, soul life already existed in animals, which is why he did not have to create it again. Soul life already existed, so he just had to make it, to do it, and that is what he did and man became or was made, *asah*, a living soul, *nephesh chai*. The bible is astonishingly accurate and precise in its usage of words.

> Genesis 1:27
> So God created man in his *own* image, in the image of God created he him; male and female created he them.

What is God's image? Well, he does not have a body and soul like us, that's for sure. And another thing, we don't have to guess either, God's word tells us.

> John 4:24
> God *is* a Spirit: and they that worship him must worship *him* in spirit and in truth.

God is spirit. That is what he is, that is his image. So what part of man did God create? Body? No, that was formed. Soul? No, that was made. Spirit? Yes, God's image is spirit, and man was created in God's image. God has neither body nor soul, so it was spirit that God created. Man was now a three part being of body, soul, and spirit, he was a whole man. This basic understanding of what man was made of is rather important, as we shall see.

God formed, made, and created Adam, he was a three-part being of body, soul, and spirit. He lived in perfect harmony with God in a perfect world. Man was given dominion over the earth. Man was Lord of the earth as God intended him to be.

Genesis 1:28
And God blessed them, and God said unto them, Be fruitful, and multiply, and replenish the earth, and subdue it: and have dominion over the fish of the sea, and over the fowl of the air, and over every living thing that moveth upon the earth.

Although man was the Lord of the Earth, a position bestowed on him by God, there were conditions to his continuing in that position of authority.

Genesis 2:16,17
And the LORD God commanded the man, saying, Of every tree of the garden thou mayest freely eat:

But of the tree of the knowledge of good and evil, thou shalt not eat of it: for in the day that thou eatest thereof thou shalt surely die.

The knowledge of good and evil here is better understood from the Greek word translated *knowledge* from the Septuagint, the Greek translation of the old testament. It is from the Greek word *ginōskō*, which means *to know experientially, to know by experience*. Man had no *experiential* knowledge of the difference between good and evil. However, that does not mean man was ignorant of evil. Quite the contrary, Adam and Eve were fully instructed on what was good and what was evil. Genesis 2 clearly documents that God instructed Adam and his wife not to eat of the tree of the knowledge of good and evil. They were educated in what was right and what was wrong. They were also fully conscious of the consequences for disobedience. They knew the word, they were fully educated in that category of life.

To eat of the fruit of the knowledge of good and evil, in this context, was to *do* evil, to *experience* it. It is one thing to know what evil is because you have been taught about it, and quite another to know what it is because you have done it. At this point, Adam and Eve had not done anything wrong, they had not committed any evil, and, therefore, had no concept of guilt or any of the other consequences that result from it. To them, evil was something on the other side of the fence, something they knew existed, but it was not something they had ever experienced. That was all about to change.

Genesis 3:1
Now the serpent was more subtle than any beast of the field which the LORD God had made. And he said unto the woman, Yea, hath God said, Ye shall not eat of every tree of the garden?

The serpent is a figurative reference to the devil, who has many names and titles, such as satan and the god of this world. Why has he many names and titles? Well, I also have many names and titles. For example, I have my family name. To my parents I am a son. I am also an author, song writer, and photographer. These names and titles describe specific aspects of my life. I may be a son, but I am not a son to anyone but my parents. That particular title describes a specific relationship between my parents and me, no one else. Similarly, all the names and titles of the devil describe differing aspects and functions in how he operates and relates to others.

Here in Genesis, the devil is referred to as the serpent, which is a term emphasising his extraordinary craftiness and seductive slyness. Note that the word also tells us that he was more subtle than any beast of the field which God had made. That includes Gabriel, Michael and the rest of the angels. The only way we can live safe from the devil is to put all our trust in God. Adam and Eve were taught the word and they knew the consequences for disobedience. Once we know the word, we are to live it if we are to live lives which are more than abundant with God's hedge of protection around us.

The serpent uses cunning and stealth to lure us away from God's protection, hiding his devices within that which looks appealing, like hooks within bait. Bait is real food. The devil offers real food, but it has hooks stuck in it designed to take your life. For example, emotions make excellent bait. There is nothing wrong with emotion, but the devil can certainly stick hooks in them to catch you.

The way of life, the way of holiness, God's way on earth, can be likened to a river.

Psalm 46:4,5
There is a river, the streams whereof shall make glad the city of God, the holy *place* of the tabernacles of the most High.

God *is* in the midst of her; she shall not be moved: God shall help her, *and that* right early.

Psalm 36:7,8
How excellent *is* thy lovingkindness, O God! therefore the children of men put their trust under the shadow of thy wings.

They shall be abundantly satisfied with the fatness of thy house; and thou shalt make them drink of the river of thy pleasures.

Psalm 65:9
Thou visitest the earth, and waterest it: thou greatly enrichest it with the river of God, *which* is full of water: thou preparest them corn, when thou hast so provided for it.

The river of God teems with abundance, and is fresh and alive. However, it flows through the spiritual wilderness of the world, and the devil stalks its banks armed with a dazzling array of baits and lures, seeking whom he may catch and devour. The word makes us wise, and teaches us how to recognise the devil's methods. Adam and Eve had been taught all this, very clearly and succinctly. They were taught the word.

Genesis 3:1
Now the serpent was more subtil than any beast of the field which the LORD God had made. And he said unto the woman, Yea, hath God said, Ye shall not eat of every tree of the garden?

The devil first approached Eve with a question. This is remarkable and gives us information on how the enemy operates. Any general in any army knows how valuable good intelligence is. The devil instils questions and doubts regarding the word we have been taught. Fascinating stuff. The devil knew Eve had been taught the word, and he approached her with what appeared to be an appealing question regarding it. He probed her defences. If we are not clear on the word, these approaches soon grow into far more serious problems.

Genesis 3:2
And the woman said unto the serpent, We may eat of the fruit of the trees of the garden:

Wait a minute! Is that what God said?

> Genesis 2:16
> And the LORD God commanded the man, saying, Of every tree of the garden thou mayest freely eat:

Eve quoted her scripture retemory, but unfortunately she wasn't accurate. She omitted the word *freely*. If we omit a word from the word, do we have the word left? No, we do not. What we have is private interpretation. Eve thought she knew the word, but she was wrong. When it comes to rightly dividing God's word, it is imperative that we take great care with every word or we will have nothing but problems. Eve continued:

> Genesis 3:3
> But of the fruit of the tree which *is* in the midst of the garden, God hath said, Ye shall not eat of it, neither shall ye touch it, lest ye die.

Wait a minute! Is that what God said?

> Genesis 2:17
> But of the tree of the knowledge of good and evil, thou shalt not eat of it: for in the day that thou eatest thereof thou shalt surely die.

God said nothing about not touching the tree. Quite the contrary:

> Genesis 2:15
> And the LORD God took the man, and put him into the garden of Eden to dress it and to keep it.

God told man to dress and to keep the garden, and you cannot dress and keep gardens unless you touch the things growing in them. Not only did Eve omit a word from the word, now she has added words to the word. Eve thinks she knows the word, but she is hazy on the details. What we think the word says is of little value unless we are accurate on the details.

Eve finished with *lest ye die*. God said *thou shalt surely die*. Eve turned an absolute into a possibility. She omitted a word, added words, and finally changed the word. Eve was sincere, but sincerity is no guarantee of anything. Now watch what happens.

> Genesis 3:4
> And the serpent said unto the woman, Ye shall not surely die:

The devil lied and contradicted God's word. That is his very nature. He is the antithesis of everything the true God is. God is light, the devil is darkness. God tells us the truth through his word, the devil is a liar. God provides a more abundant life, the devil steals, kills, and destroys.

God told Adam and Eve they would surely die, while the devil told Eve she would not surely die. Whose words are you going to believe? The words of God or the words of the devil? If Eve had the slightest inkling of what was in the devil's heart, she would not have been having that conversation. She was seduced by the approach, the gentle, appealing nature of the words, and the manner in which they were presented. The devil has an extensive library of seductive arguments. Just look at this one.

> Genesis 3:5
> For God doth know that in the day ye eat thereof, then your eyes shall be opened, and ye shall be as gods, knowing good and evil.

To be as gods? Knowing what the gods know? Secret knowledge from the gods? That's some bait. Eve swallowed it, and her husband went right along with her.

> Genesis 3:6
> And when the woman saw that the tree *was* good for food, and that it *was* pleasant to the eyes, and a tree to be desired to make *one* wise, she took of the fruit thereof, and did eat, and gave also unto her husband with her; and he did eat.

The consequences for man's disobedience were catastrophic. Man died, that very day, just as God had warned them. At first glance, Genesis 5:5 would appear to contradict this, but this is entirely due to misunderstanding body, soul, and spirit.

> Genesis 5:5
> And all the days that Adam lived were nine hundred and thirty years: and he died.

God said that on the day, that *very* day, they would surely die.

> Genesis 2:17
> But of the tree of the knowledge of good and evil, thou shalt not eat of it: for in the day that thou eatest thereof thou shalt surely die.

Why did Adam live so long then? Is this a contradiction? Some say so, but there is no contradiction. Man was a three part being of body, soul, and spirit. Which part of man died that day? Not his body or soul, that's for sure. So which part died? Man died spiritually, he lost his spirit, he lost his connection with God. With only body and soul, man became no better than an animal. He was no longer whole. That wasn't the only consequence either. Man lost his job, and the earth found itself under new management, under a new lord. It was at this point that the devil became the god of this world.

Interestingly, there are only two records in the bible where the devil confronted human beings personally face to face. Eve was one, Jesus Christ was the other. We've seen how Eve was taken down because she didn't keep the word clear in her mind. Let's see how Jesus Christ fared.

> Luke 4:1-3
> And Jesus being full of the Holy Ghost returned from Jordan, and was led by the Spirit into the wilderness,
>
> Being forty days tempted of the devil. And in those days he did eat nothing: and when they were ended, he afterward hungered.
>
> And the devil said unto him, If thou be the Son of God, command this stone that it be made bread.

Do you remember how the devil first approached Eve? That's right, he tried to instil a doubt in her mind regarding what the word said. Here he goes again, using the same tactic thousands of years later, only this time he is trying it with Jesus Christ. *If* thou be the Son of God.

Luke 4:3
And the devil said unto him, If thou be the Son of God, command this stone that it be made bread.

His approach was designed to instil questions regarding the word and who Jesus Christ was as the son of God. In that regards it mirrored the approach made to Eve. Jesus Christ *was* the son of God. The devil approached with an arrogant *if* you're the son of God. However, unlike Eve, Jesus Christ had a clear, precise, and accurate understanding of the scriptures. He knew who he was.

There is a pattern here and much we can learn from it. If the devil feels this method of attack so effective that he would employ it with both Eve and Jesus Christ, do you think he might perhaps try it on us? Of course he does. For example, do we always feel worthy to stand before God? If not, why not? The word says we are holy and without blame before him in love, and that we are lovely and acceptable. That is what the word says. Do we hold onto that when the world attempts to make us feel less than worthy? Or do we cave in to the seductive sweet empty words of the world? The word in our minds is constantly under attack from the world. Jesus Christ wasn't fooled though.

Luke 4:4
And Jesus answered him, saying, It is written, That man shall not live by bread alone, but by every word of God.

Jesus Christ responded by quoting a short scripture, which isn't a particularly difficult scripture to memorise. In fact, it would only take a few seconds to learn by heart. However, consider that Jesus Christ did not know beforehand how the devil was going to approach him. He could have been approached in any one of a thousand different ways, so his having the right scripture memorised for that particular attack implies that his depth of knowledge of the scriptures was astonishing. That he had the right scripture in his mind, and could use it to counter the attack without having to run home for his bible and his concordance is testament to the fact that he studied the scriptures and memorised them to the point he had made the word his own. The more we understand this, the more we will understand the importance of the renewed mind, and the more we will comprehend what it takes to stand against the spiritual darkness of this world and prevail.

Also note Jesus Christ's respect for Lucifer. He didn't bad mouth him, he didn't tell him to fuck off, he didn't strut around him beating his chest and bragging about who he was as God's son. Jesus Christ knew who the devil was and held him in utmost respect, putting all his trust in God to keep him protected. That's a good example to follow. We must never get too big for our boots when dealing with devil spirits. We always put our trust in God and his word.

> Luke 4:5-8
> And the devil, taking him up into an high mountain, shewed unto him all the kingdoms of the world in a moment of time.
>
> And the devil said unto him, All this power will I give thee, and the glory of them: for that is delivered unto me; and to whomsoever I will I give it.
>
> If thou therefore wilt worship me, all shall be thine.
>
> And Jesus answered and said unto him, Get thee behind me, Satan: for it is written, Thou shalt worship the Lord thy God, and him only shalt thou serve.

Jesus Christ again had the right scripture at the right time to defeat this second attack, and again it is one short scripture that is easy to memorise. Look at the depth of his knowledge to be able to have in his mind the right scripture at the point of attack so he could use it. Unlike Eve, he did not add words, omit words, or change words, he quoted scripture accurately and precisely. The spoken word is powerful. Eve's retemory verses were not very difficult. She could have kept the word in her mind if she had wanted to. She had become hazy on the details because she obviously did not keep her head in the word. Whenever man loses the word, he loses everything.

By the way, you would not believe how much pertinent and relevant modern day truth is documented here. The devil offered Jesus Christ the glory of the world with all its power. In other words he offered him the presidency of a one world government. The devil was the power behind the governments and kingdoms of Christ's time, and to whomsoever he willed, he gave it. Do you think then that perhaps it is feasible that the powers behind one world governance in our day and time could be from the same source?

You know, Jesus Christ's response is amazing. He did not scoff at the devil or laugh at his claim. He knew the devil was telling the truth – he does have control of the political systems of the world. Jesus Christ did not argue the point. In Genesis, Adam and Eve were given dominion of the earth.

> Genesis 1:27,28
> So God created man in his *own* image, in the image of God created he him; male and female created he them.
>
> And God blessed them, and God said unto them, Be fruitful, and multiply, and replenish the earth, and subdue it: and have dominion over the fish of the sea, and over the fowl of the air, and over every living thing that moveth upon the earth.

Here in Luke, the devil told Jesus that all that authority, that dominion over the earth had been delivered, or handed to him. That's exactly what happened back in Genesis when man fell.

> Luke 4:6
> And the devil said unto him, All this power will I give thee, and the glory of them: for that is delivered unto me; and to whomsoever I will I give it.

The devil tricked Adam and Eve out of what was theirs and stole it from them. Adam and Eve gave that authority to the devil when they disobeyed God. In Genesis, man had the authority and dominion of the world – he was Lord of the earth – but when man fell, that authority was transferred to the devil. In this regards it is interesting to note that the bible talks of two gods – the true God, the Creator, and another god, the god of this world.

2 Corinthians 4:3,4
But if our gospel be hid, it is hid to them that are lost:

In whom the god of this world hath blinded the minds of them which believe not, lest the light of the glorious gospel of Christ, who is the image of God, should shine unto them.

Any guesses who the god of this world is? That's right, the devil. He became the god of this world when man fell, when the world was delivered to him. Man had been the Lord of the earth, and when man lost everything, the devil took control. That is who runs the world today, that is who the god of this world is.

Jesus Christ recognised this, but he was not seduced by it. Stop and think about that. It isn't everyday you are offered the presidency of a one world government. Rather than dream about palaces, fleets of Mercedes chariots, and pretty girls pandering to his every whim as be pranced around the world as its leader, Jesus Christ went to the scriptures and rejected that paltry bribe. Jesus Christ turned down the same bribe that turns men like Al Gore, Tony Blair, and Bill Clinton into traitors, men who sell out their own countries for promises of power and authority in the new world order. Men like them see themselves as that president of a one world government, and they sell us out in their lust for it. Thankfully, Jesus Christ turned it down. The devil was not quite finished yet though.

Luke 4:9-11
And he brought him to Jerusalem, and set him on a pinnacle of the temple, and said unto him, If thou be the Son of God, cast thyself down from hence:

For it is written, He shall give his angels charge over thee, to keep thee:

And in *their* hands they shall bear thee up, lest at any time thou dash thy foot against a stone.

Will you just look at that. The devil quoted scripture at Jesus Christ. Accurate scripture too. It's from Psalms.

Psalm 91:11,12
For he shall give his angels charge over thee, to keep thee in all thy ways.

They shall bear thee up in *their* hands, lest thou dash thy foot against a stone.

The devil knows the bible inside out. He has the whole thing memorised from start to finish. Every word. The only problem is, when he quotes it, he quotes it out of context, and he uses it to steal, to kill, and to destroy. Oh yes, the bible can be used to steal from people, kill them, and destroy them. Happens in churches all the time. Jesus Christ wasn't taken in by this deception. The bible does indeed say that God will protect our backs, that he is our protection, that is true.

Mark 16:18
They shall take up serpents; and if they drink any deadly thing, it shall not hurt them; they shall lay hands on the sick, and they shall recover.

There is a record in the book of Acts that illustrates this point, when a deadly snake bit the apostle Paul.

Acts 28:3-6
And when Paul had gathered a bundle of sticks, and laid *them* on the fire, there came a viper out of the heat, and fastened on his hand.

And when the barbarians saw the *venomous* beast hang on his hand, they said among themselves, No doubt this man is a murderer, whom, though he hath escaped the sea, yet vengeance suffereth not to live.

And he shook off the beast into the fire, and felt no harm.

Howbeit they looked when he should have swollen, or fallen down dead suddenly: but after they had looked a great while, and saw no harm come to him, they changed their minds, and said that he was a god.

Psalm 91 and Mark 16:18 are true. However, the key to understanding the subtle slyness and seductive nature of this temptation is the word *if*. Mark 16:18 uses *if* in the context of if it is accidental. We don't dash our feet against stones deliberately, do we? Paul did not see the snake coming, did he? He didn't stick his hand out there and deliberately let the snake bite him just to see if the word was true, did he? That would be like jumping off a cliff, or the pinnacle of a temple to see if God will protect you when you hit the bottom. No, he will not. If you're going to be that stupid, you're not going to live for very long. If you accidentally stumble, yes, God can be there for you, but not if you are going to deliberately harm yourself just to see if he is going to save you. That would be tempting God. Again, Jesus Christ was not deceived, and he had the right scripture to counter the attack.

> Luke 4:12,13
> And Jesus answering said unto him, It is said, Thou shalt not tempt the Lord thy God.
>
> And when the devil had ended all the temptation, he departed from him for a season.

During this intense face-to-face confrontation, three short memorised scriptures were sufficient for Jesus Christ to defeat the devil. The word really is that powerful. The only thing that can defeat the devil is the power of God through his word. If we have the word and apply it, we will live powerful and abundant lives. Eve went down and man lost everything because she did not keep the word clear in her mind. Consequently, man fell and the devil became the god of this world. Thankfully, that is not the end of the story.

14. The god of this World

After the fall of man, the devil became the god of this world. It was man who bestowed this office on him, and it is an office he continues to hold to this day. We can see this in Genesis when God confronted the devil immediately following the fall of man.

> Genesis 3:14
> And the LORD God said unto the serpent, Because thou hast done this, thou *art* cursed above all cattle, and above every beast of the field; upon thy belly shalt thou go, and dust shalt thou eat all the days of thy life:

Dust refers to the dust of the earth, and it is a figurative reference to the senses realm, the physical realm, the realm of the five senses. You eat to be nourished. Dust, referring to the senses realm, nourishes and sustains the devil. This makes sense because as the god of this world he controls the authority and dominion of the world. It is his meat, it is what sustains him. Here in Genesis, God is acknowledging the devil's new position as the god of this world. However, God was not particularly happy with this change in leadership over his earth, and he came up with a plan to sort things out.

> Genesis 3:15
> And I will put enmity between thee and the woman, and between thy seed and her seed; it shall bruise thy head, and thou shalt bruise his heel.

Here God promised a redeemer, the seed of the woman, who would bruise the devil's head, or crush his skull as the original scripture implies. This was realised when God raised Jesus Christ from the dead and sat him at his own right hand, accomplishing man's redemption. Since that time, the devil's existence has been drawing to a close. Jesus Christ dealt a mortal blow to his skull, and at some point in the future he will be destroyed permanently. In the meantime, however, he is still the god of this world and we had better respect that because he has the right to exert all his worldly influence, authority, power, and dominion to further his agendas. So who is this god? It was the life and ministry of the Lord Jesus Christ that fully exposed him. Look at how emphatically his will is expressed here:

> John 10:10
> The thief cometh not, but for to steal, and to kill, and to destroy: I am come that they might have life, and that they might have *it* more abundantly.

As the god of this world, the devil is passionately committed to hiding God's word by distracting people with the things of the world. He does not like being out in the open where we can see him so he conceals himself behind the senses realm. It is only the word that reveals who he is, so he designs the world to choke light from people's lives so they remain without knowledge of the truth. The devil is good at what he does too. He was once the archangel of light, second in command in heaven, full of wisdom and beauty, perfect in all his ways, so don't underestimate him. Don't underestimate those who work for him either, for they can be startlingly committed to their god.

> 2 Corinthians 11:13-15
> For such *are* false apostles, deceitful workers, transforming themselves into the apostles of Christ.
>
> And no marvel; for Satan himself is transformed into an angel of light.
>
> Therefore *it is* no great thing if his ministers also be transformed as the ministers of righteousness; whose end shall be according to their works.

Being so evil, the devil can't expose his true nature or no one would worship him, not even his *illuminated* ones. God protects us from the devil when we know his word and live accordingly. Why do you think God had his word written in the first place? Because he was bored? No, it was for us, it was so we could understand spiritual matters.

1 Corinthians 12:1
Now concerning spiritual *gifts*, [pneumatikos – spiritual matters] brethren, I would not have you ignorant.

If God's word exposes the devil, how then does the devil hide himself? How does he conceal his true nature from those who unwittingly, and not so unwittingly work for him? Through the world of which he is god, that's how. Clues to the nature of who runs the courses of the world are all over the word. It isn't as if God wants us ignorant of these things.

1 John 2:15
Love not the world, neither the things *that are* in the world. If any man love the world, the love of the Father is not in him.

Philippians 2:14,15
Do all things without murmurings and disputings:

That ye may be blameless and harmless, the sons of God, without rebuke, in the midst of a crooked and perverse nation, among whom ye shine as lights in the world;

Is the world crooked and perverse? Oh, yes. Jesus Christ frequently taught his disciples about the nature of the world.

John 15:19
If ye were of the world, the world would love his own: but because ye are not of the world, but I have chosen you out of the world, therefore the world hateth you.

Those who stand for the true God find themselves very much in direct opposition to the world. If God's people do not know the word, they are not going to get very far in life.

1 John 2:16
For all that *is* in the world, the lust of the flesh, and the lust of the eyes, and the pride of life, is not of the Father, but is of the world.

The term *world* here obviously doesn't refer to the physical earth, it represents its words, its concepts, its ideals, its fashions, its political systems, and its religious systems. In 1 John 2:15 and 16, the word *world* is used five times. Two of those uses clearly document that the things of the world are not of the true God. This obviously is not referring to beautiful plants and animals, but rather to the political, religious, and social agendas being promoted behind the scenes, such as the love of money, the lust for possessions, churches, religions and other distasteful things. These worldly pursuits are designed to choke the light of God's word from people, and they are very effective.

> 2 Corinthians 4:3,4
> But if our gospel be hid, it is hid to them that are lost:
>
> In whom the god of this world hath blinded the minds of them which believe not, lest the light of the glorious gospel of Christ, who is the image of God, should shine unto them.

We live in a world of darkness and confusion, a world unable to find its way. Those of us who know the truth have the privilege to bring light to the world so people can see. The devil, the god of this world, does not want people to see that light, so he does his best to snuff it out. He does this through the systems, the courses of the world.

The world is accustomed to living in shadows. The world has no understanding of what is going on behind the scenes. The god of this world does this by conditioning people with illusions and lies from the time they are born. Perhaps his greatest deception has been to convince mankind that he does not exist. This is the work of a master illusionist, a master magician, a master sorcerer.

Have you ever been to a magician's show? It's quite a spectacle. The magician comes out in his cape, waves his little magic wand and his show dazzles the crowds. His aim is to distract the audience with glitter and movement to keep them from seeing his sleight of hand, what he is really doing behind the scenes. People are awestruck by what looks convincing, but is in fact an illusion. The devil does the same with the things of the world. He is a master magician, a master illusionist. He keeps the world distracted with glitter and movement, and herein lies the power behind words and concepts.

Without a true standard of truth, the devil has access to people's minds and hearts through the words and concepts of his world. The world's media churns out his words and concepts relentlessly so that they are widely accepted as truth. These words and concepts often seem appealing because many of those who teach, endorse, and promote them are extremely passionate about what they do. However, when accepted and practiced, these words and ideals of the god of this world do nothing but fulfil his agendas of steal, kill, and destroy.

> Isaiah 14:12-17
> How art thou fallen from heaven, O Lucifer, son of the morning! *how* art thou cut down to the ground, which didst weaken the nations!
>
> For thou hast said in thine heart, I will ascend into heaven, I will exalt my throne above the stars of God [above *the* star, God]: I will sit also upon the mount of the congregation, in the sides of the north:
>
> I will ascend above the heights of the clouds; I will be like the most High.
>
> Yet thou shalt be brought down to hell, to the sides of the pit.
>
> They that see thee shall narrowly look upon thee, *and* consider thee, *saying, Is* this the man that made the earth to tremble, that did shake kingdoms;
>
> *That* made the world as a wilderness, and destroyed the cities thereof; *that* opened not the house of his prisoners?

These verses refer to a certain king who lived during those times, but the deeper reference is directed towards the god he worshipped, the power behind the man. It is the devil who made this world a spiritual wilderness, and he does it through men who do his bidding. The book of Job contains a vivid description of the devil.

> Job 41:1,2
> Canst thou draw out leviathan with an hook? or his tongue with a cord *which* thou lettest down?

Canst thou put an hook into his nose? or bore his jaw through with a thorn?

Man may have walked on the moon, but he is never going to cast a fishing lure into the Deep and catch the devil.

Job 41:7
Canst thou fill his skin with barbed irons? or his head with fish spears?

Job 41:15-22
His scales *are his* pride, shut up together *as with* a close seal.

One is so near to another, that no air can come between them.

They are joined one to another, they stick together, that they cannot be sundered.

By his neesings a light doth shine, and his eyes are like the eyelids of the morning.

Out of his mouth go burning lamps, *and* sparks of fire leap out.

Out of his nostrils goeth smoke, as *out* of a seething pot or caldron.

His breath kindleth coals, and a flame goeth out of his mouth.

In his neck remaineth strength, and sorrow is turned into joy before him.

Here is the dragon, the devil, the god of this world for those with eyes to see. What gives him joy? Our sorrow. The more pain, sorrow, misery, suffering, and death he can inflict on us, the more joy he has. That is his meat, that is what sustains him. This is the god of this world.

Job 41:33,34
Upon earth there is not his like, who is made without fear.

He beholdeth all high *things*: he *is* a king over all the children of pride.

Walking *by* the Spirit

It is difficult to begin to comprehend the heart of the devil.

Revelation 12:3-9
And there appeared another wonder in heaven; and behold a great red dragon, having seven heads and ten horns, and seven crowns upon his heads.

And his tail drew the third part of the stars of heaven, and did cast them to the earth: and the dragon stood before the woman which was ready to be delivered, for to devour her child as soon as it was born.

And she brought forth a man child, who was to rule all nations with a rod of iron: and her child was caught up unto God, and *to* his throne.

And the woman fled into the wilderness, where she hath a place prepared of God, that they should feed her there a thousand two hundred *and* threescore days.

And there was war in heaven: Michael and his angels fought against the dragon; and the dragon fought and his angels,

And prevailed not; neither was their place found any more in heaven.

And the great dragon was cast out, that old serpent, called the Devil, and Satan, which deceiveth the whole world: he was cast out into the earth, and his angels were cast out with him.

Revelation 12:13-17
And when the dragon saw that he was cast unto the earth, he persecuted the woman which brought forth the man *child*.

And to the woman were given two wings of a great eagle, that she might fly into the wilderness, into her place, where she is nourished for a time, and times, and half a time, from the face of the serpent.

And the serpent cast out of his mouth water as a flood after the woman, that he might cause her to be carried away of the flood.

And the earth helped the woman, and the earth opened her mouth, and swallowed up the flood which the dragon cast out of his mouth.

And the dragon was wroth with the woman, and went to make war with the remnant of her seed, which keep the commandments of God, and have the testimony of Jesus Christ.

In Acts, Paul recalled the purpose of his ministry in carrying out the works of Jesus Christ.

Acts 26:18
To open their eyes, *and* to turn *them* from darkness to light, and *from* the power of Satan unto God, that they may receive forgiveness of sins, and inheritance among them which are sanctified by faith that is in me.

It says here *to open their eyes*. Figuratively, eyes represent people's understanding. People's eyes are closed due to the influences of the dragon, the god of this world. The world promotes the opposite of what the word teaches. The world tirelessly advertises social, political, economic, religious, and environmental agendas that blind men's minds to spiritual realities. These agendas blur perceptions and break down the very morals and ethics that would keep us protected. As the god of this world, the devil pushes his agendas of stealing, killing, and destroying from behind the scenes through the world's media, as well as environmental, religious and political movements. Make no mistake, the world is under bad management.

15. How we got the Bible

Language is simply a means by which thought is transferred from one person to another. No matter the method employed, so long as thought is conveyed, it is language.

Semaphore is a method of communicating with flags. Morse code, which can be flashes of light or blips of sound, is another way we can talk to each other. Language is not constrained just by sight or sound either, and people who are deaf or blind have sign language and braille. Hieroglyphics and runes use pictures to communicate.

Understanding that language is not exclusively restricted to written or spoken words helps us to understand that God originally wrote his word in the stars, centuries before it was ever written down in the languages of men. God originally taught man how to read the stars so we could understand what he was saying.

> Psalm 19:1
> The heavens declare the glory of God; and the firmament [raqia] sheweth his handywork.

The word *declare* is the Hebrew word *caphor*, which means *to score with a mark as a tally or record; to inscribe, to celebrate in full communion fellowship; to rehearse.* Firmament is *raqia*, the word we saw in Genesis which means the universe. The stars in the universe record the glory of God. God inscribed his word in the stars.

> Psalm 19:2
> Day unto day uttereth speech, and night unto night sheweth knowledge.

This means exactly what it says. The knowledge of God's word is all around us in the sky, and we can see it every time we look up.

Psalm 19:3,4
There is no speech nor language, *where* their voice is not heard.

Their line is gone out through all the earth, and their words to the end of the world. In them hath he set a tabernacle for the sun,

The tabernacle for the sun refers to the twelve signs of the zodiac, the twelve constellations which the sun travels through every year. Verse four is quoted in Romans. The word of God has been declared all over the earth, to every generation since Genesis, since God first wrote his word in the stars and taught man how to read them.

Romans 10:18
But I say, Have they not heard? Yes verily, their sound went into all the earth, and their words unto the ends of the world.

Back in Genesis, these stars were set in the universe on the fourth day, before man was formed, made and created. Therefore, the stars were set in the heavens before the fall of man.

Genesis 1:14,19
And God said, Let there be lights in the firmament of the heaven to divide the day from the night; and let them be for signs, and for seasons, and for days, and years:

And the evening and the morning were the fourth day.

If the word of God was inscribed in the stars, and the stars were put in the sky before man was formed, made and created, does this mean then that Adam and Eve knew they would fall and need a redeemer before these events actually occurred? No, that would be ridiculous. Such logic elevates God to tyrant status and places man on earth merely as puppets with no control over their own destiny. Yes, God has foreknowledge, but Adam and Eve did not have to fall. Man could have continued in the original paradise administration without the need of ever requiring a messiah, thus making any plan of salvation written in the stars unnecessary. However, God knew man would fall and made provision ahead of time, but he did not programme the fall to take place regardless of anything Adam and Eve would or would not have done.

Adam could not have been taught the word of God written in the stars regarding the coming redeemer before the fall of man, because at that time man did not require a redeemer. Think of it this way – would God have taught Adam that he was going to fall and that the dominion of the world would be transferred to the devil and that a Christ would be required to redeem man before any of these events had taken place? No matter from which angle you view this, you can never make this fit. God is good always. If you lose that truth, your spiritual integrity has been compromised.

God knew man would fall, and he made provision ahead of time, but Adam and Eve could not possibly have known about the Christ before Genesis 3:15 when the promise of his coming was first spoken or your bible falls to pieces. Therefore, the word written in the stars could not have been known to Adam and Eve before that time because that word had not yet been written, it only existed in God's foreknowledge. And it only existed in God's foreknowledge because he knew it was going to happen. God did not *make* it happen.

That the stars were there in Genesis on the fourth day, before man was formed, made, and created, is without question. That the word of God regarding the fall of man and the coming redeemer is written in the stars, is also without question. That man would not have been taught the truths regarding the coming redeemer before Genesis 3:15, which is the first reference in the bible to Jesus Christ, is also without question. So how can we make sense of this?

Well, there is one fact about stars which provides an answer. The stars are set in the heavens at astronomically large distances from the Earth. Light from some stars takes hundreds of years to reach us. Does it not then logically follow that on the fourth day of creation, although all the stars were up there and doing their job, they would not yet have been visible on earth? Aside from our sun, the stars were not visible on earth at the time God put them in the heavens on the fourth day in Genesis. Consider these words, selah, for this is new light to the world.

Let's take this further. As the stars are set at differing distances from earth, which star then would have been the first star to appear in the heavens? What would have been the first star to twinkle in the night sky? Obviously, the closest star, Alpha Centauri, a binary star system whose light takes just over four years to reach us.

Consider this regarding Alpha Centauri:

> ***Alpha Centauri:*** *A binary star, white and yellowish, on the toe of the right front hoof of the centaur, Centaurus.*
>
> *It bears the proper name* **Rigil Kentaurus** *(often shortened to* **Rigil Kent***) derived from the Arabic phrase Al Rijl al Kentaurus, meaning 'foot of the centaur,' but is nonetheless usually referred to by its Bayer's designation Alpha Centauri. Another alternative name is* **Toliman** *from a Hebrew word meaning 'the heretofore and the hereafter'. It is also sometimes known as* **Bungula***, possibly from the Latin word ungula meaning 'hoof'.*
>
> ***From Witness of the Stars by EW Bullinger:*** *The brightest star (in the horse's fore-foot), has come down to us with the ancient name of Toliman, which means the heretofore and hereafter, marking him as the one which is, and which was, and which is to come.*

The one which was to come is a reference to the coming redeemer, Jesus Christ. Regarding the constellation as a whole, Bullinger states:

> *It (Centaurus) is one of the lowest constellations, ie, the farthest south from the northern centre. It is situated immediately over the Cross, which bespeaks his own death; he is seen in the act of destroying the enemy.*

Does any of this remind us of a verse in Genesis?

> Genesis 3:15
> And I will put enmity between thee and the woman, and between thy seed and her seed; it shall bruise thy head, and thou shalt bruise his heel.

This is the first revelation given in the bible concerning the coming of the promised seed, Jesus Christ. It foretells that he would redeem man, that he would die, and that he would crush the head of the devil. The first star that appeared in the night sky carries *precisely* this meaning.

Here in Genesis 3:15 is the first occurrence of the word being written in the stars and taught to man. It is most probable that Alpha Centauri first appeared in the night sky at the very moment this prophecy was spoken. Adam and Eve were probably looking up at the first and only star shining in the night sky when God spoke Genesis 3:15 to them, thus associating this truth to that star.

It is without question that the first spoken revelation regarding Jesus Christ would have also been the first written reference to Jesus Christ in the stars. Later, as other stars appeared, God would have continued to teach his word to Adam and Eve until they had the entire word written in the stars taught to them. Adam and Eve then taught their children, and that's how the word in the stars was passed down from generation to generation. That was how we got the word written in the stars.

Centuries later, the knowledge of how to read God's word in the stars was lost, and so God gave Moses revelation to begin writing the written word, that which we know today as the bible. How did God's people in those days lose the word in the stars? Abraham knew it, but by the time Moses went into Egypt to lead God's people out of slavery a few hundred years later, it was all gone. What we do know is that the word was to be taught by parents to their children to keep the word alive from generation to generation. Parents, therefore, were not doing their job, they were not teaching their children God's word. This isn't conjecture, that is what happened. That is the only way the word could have been lost, and that was most likely *why* God's people were enslaved in Egypt.

Look, God could have taught his word in the stars to Moses, and Moses could have taught it again to the children of Israel. However, God knew that parents would not teach their children and the word would just be lost again, so he had it written down so it could continue from generation to generation. It is not the government's responsibility to teach your children, it is yours. It is not any church or ministry's responsibility to teach your children, it is yours. If you ignore your responsibility to teach your children the word of God and instead allow television, the government, or some church or ministry to educate them, your children will never know God's word.

Hosea 4:6
My people are destroyed for lack of knowledge: because thou hast rejected knowledge, I will also reject thee, that thou shalt be no priest to me: seeing thou hast forgotten the law of thy God, I will also forget thy children.

This is not a threat, this is a loving statement of fact. God went to a lot of trouble to get his word to us so we could understand spiritual matters. If we do not teach God's word to our children, they won't know him, and the world will steal from them, kill them, and destroy them. Bibles are readily available, so there are no excuses. Whenever and wherever people lose the word, they are enslaved. Moses knew this, which is why he pointedly commanded the parents in his day to teach their children, and warned them of the consequences if they did not.

Deuteronomy 6:6-12
And these words, which I command thee this day, shall be in thine heart:

And thou shalt teach them diligently unto thy children, and shalt talk of them when thou sittest in thine house, and when thou walkest by the way, and when thou liest down, and when thou risest up.

And thou shalt bind them for a sign upon thine hand, and they shall be as frontlets between thine eyes.

And thou shalt write them upon the posts of thy house, and on thy gates.

And it shall be, when the LORD thy God shall have brought thee into the land which he sware unto thy fathers, to Abraham, to Isaac, and to Jacob, to give thee great and goodly cities, which thou buildedst not,

And houses full of all good *things*, which thou filledst not, and wells digged, which thou diggedst not, vineyards and olive trees, which thou plantedst not; when thou shalt have eaten and be full;

Then beware lest thou forget the LORD, which brought thee forth out of the land of Egypt, from the house of bondage.

The best way to teach your family is to run a church in your home so you all enjoy a healthy, balanced, regular diet of God's word. Teach your children at bedtime, teach your family during the day as you're living life and opportunities present themselves. Without teaching, we lose the word. You may know it and enjoy the benefits of it, but if you don't teach it, then the word you know is lost when you die. We have to teach. If you don't know God's word, don't worry about it as this class will teach you how to read the bible so you can understand it well enough to teach it.

2 Timothy 2:2
And the things that thou hast heard of me among many witnesses, the same commit thou to faithful men, who shall be able to teach others also.

Regarding the written word, the bible, which was given to Moses and the other prophets, God has this to say:

2 Timothy 3:16
All scripture *is* **given by inspiration of God** [theopneustos], and *is* profitable for doctrine, for reproof, for correction, for instruction in righteousness:

All scripture means all scripture without exception, from Genesis 1:1 to Revelation 22:21. All scripture was given by inspiration of God. The five English words, *given by inspiration of God*, are translated from one Greek word, *theopneustos* – a compound word derived from *theos*, God, and *pneustos*, breathed. Literally this verse says that all scripture is God-breathed. That means all of it without exception from Genesis to Revelation is God-breathed. God is the author of the bible.

2 Peter 1:20
Knowing this first, that no prophecy of the scripture is of any private [idios - one's own] interpretation.

The word *private* in verse 20 is the Greek word *idios*, which means *his own* or *one's own*. No prophecy of the scripture, none of it, from Genesis to Revelation, is of any private, personal, one's own interpretation. Why? Because it is God-breathed. God gave the sense and the meaning to his words, and we are to understand them in light of what God intended, not according to what we think they mean.

> 2 Peter 1:21
> For the prophecy came not in old time by the will of man: but holy men of God spake *as they were* moved by the Holy Ghost.

This is how we got the God-breathed word. Holy men of God spoke as they were moved by the Holy Spirit, God. What does this mean?

> Galatians 1:11,12
> But I certify you, brethren, that the gospel which was preached of me [Paul] is not after man.
>
> For I neither received it of man, neither was I taught *it*, but by the revelation of Jesus Christ.

There is a law stating that things equal to the same thing are equal to each other. As all these scriptures refer to the same thing, how we got the word, it is axiomatic then that *God-breathed* equals *moved by the Holy Spirit* equals *revelation*. That is how we got the word of God – by revelation.

Moses did not sit down one day under a tree with his iPad and decide to write Genesis. That is not how we got the bible. We saw in Genesis 3:15 that it was God who wrote his word in the stars and taught it to Adam and Eve. Similarly, God told Moses to get his pen, sit down and start writing, and Moses did what he was told and wrote down what he was told to write down. The word was given by spiritual dictation, if you please. The first occurrence of God giving written revelation to man tells us just that.

> Exodus 31:18
> And he gave unto Moses, when he had made an end of communing with him upon mount Sinai, two tables of testimony, tables of stone, written with the finger of God.

Being first occurrence of the written word mentioned in the bible, this verse holds special meaning and importance. The truth that the word was written with the finger of God holds true for every single word in the original texts which comprised the original God-breathed word, that which we know today as the bible. Every word in the original bible was God-breathed, which means every word was written with the finger of God.

There is an account in the old testament of God dictating his word to a man by revelation, who with the help of a scribe wrote it down. However, God's word didn't particularly please the politicians of that day and they attempted to destroy that original scroll by chucking it in a fire.

> Jeremiah 36:1-3
> And it came to pass in the fourth year of Jehoiakim the son of Josiah king of Judah, *that* this word came unto Jeremiah from the LORD, saying,
>
> Take thee a roll of a book, and write therein all the words that I have spoken unto thee against Israel, and against Judah, and against all the nations, from the day I spake unto thee, from the days of Josiah, even unto this day.
>
> It may be that the house of Judah will hear all the evil which I purpose to do unto them; that they may return every man from his evil way; that I may forgive their iniquity and their sin.

God's intent, the heart behind his words is clearly indicated here. As we learn in the book of Job, the first book of the bible ever written, God is always good. He was confronting people with their evil so they could turn back to him and once again enjoy protection from the god of this world who was on the verge of destroying them. God did not want these people destroyed, so he was giving them yet another chance to change. If God had wanted these people destroyed, he would not have sent a prophet to them to try to help them.

> Jeremiah 36:4
> Then Jeremiah called Baruch the son of Neriah: and Baruch wrote from the mouth of Jeremiah all the words of the LORD, which he had spoken unto him, upon a roll of a book.

God spoke to Jeremiah, and Jeremiah spoke to Baruch who wrote it all down. God is the author of his word. When news of this revelation reached the ears of the politicians, they called for Baruch to hear what God had to say.

Jeremiah 36:14-18
Therefore all the princes sent Jehudi the son of Nethaniah, the son of Shelemiah, the son of Cushi, unto Baruch, saying, Take in thine hand the roll wherein thou hast read in the ears of the people, and come. So Baruch the son of Neriah took the roll in his hand, and came unto them.

And they said unto him, Sit down now, and read it in our ears. So Baruch read *it* in their ears.

Now it came to pass, when they had heard all the words, they were afraid both one and other, and said unto Baruch, We will surely tell the king of all these words.

And they asked Baruch, saying, Tell us now, How didst thou write all these words at his mouth?

Then Baruch answered them, He pronounced all these words unto me with his mouth, and I wrote *them* with ink in the book.

See, God spoke to Jeremiah, and Jeremiah spoke to Baruch, and Baruch wrote down the word of God in a scroll. That is how we got the word of God, the original bible.

Jeremiah 36:19-24
Then said the princes unto Baruch, Go, hide thee, thou and Jeremiah; and let no man know where ye be.

And they went in to the king into the court, but they laid up the roll in the chamber of Elishama the scribe, and told all the words in the ears of the king.

So the king sent Jehudi to fetch the roll: and he took it out of Elishama the scribe's chamber. And Jehudi read it in the ears of the king, and in the ears of all the princes which stood beside the king.

Now the king sat in the winterhouse in the ninth month: and *there was a fire* on the hearth burning before him.

And it came to pass, *that* when Jehudi had read three or four leaves, he cut it with the penknife, and cast *it* into the fire that *was* on the hearth, until all the roll was consumed in the fire that *was* on the hearth.

Yet they were not afraid, nor rent their garments, *neither* the king, nor any of his servants that heard all these words.

That king did not have much respect for God and his word. Did he destroy God's word by chucking it in the fire? Perhaps he thought so, but he was wrong. God simply had his word rewritten, only this time he included a few extra words regarding that king.

Jeremiah 36:27-32
Then the word of the LORD came to Jeremiah, after that the king had burned the roll, and the words which Baruch wrote at the mouth of Jeremiah, saying,

Take thee again another roll, and write in it all the former words that were in the first roll, which Jehoiakim the king of Judah hath burned.

And thou shalt say to Jehoiakim king of Judah, Thus saith the LORD; Thou hast burned this roll, saying, Why hast thou written therein, saying, The king of Babylon shall certainly come and destroy this land, and shall cause to cease from thence man and beast?

Therefore thus saith the LORD of Jehoiakim king of Judah; He shall have none to sit upon the throne of David: and his dead body shall be cast out in the day to the heat, and in the night to the frost.

And I will punish him and his seed and his servants for their iniquity; and I will bring upon them, and upon the inhabitants of Jerusalem, and upon the men of Judah, all the evil that I have pronounced against them; but they hearkened not.

Then took Jeremiah another roll, and gave it to Baruch the scribe, the son of Neriah; who wrote therein from the mouth of Jeremiah all the words of the book which Jehoiakim king of Judah had burned in the fire: and there were added besides unto them many like words.

Did God punish the king? No, God simply proclaimed by revelation what was going to happen to him for walking away from his protection. The protection was there, it was available, but the king walked away into the darkness. It was his choice, his decision.

Understanding how we got the bible helps us to have confidence in it. Knowing that it is God's word, not the words of men, helps us to trust those words and live by them knowing that we will enjoy the benefits guaranteed therein.

What about today then? Is there any more bible to be written? Do we need new bibles given by revelation? Do we need new books written, like the book of Mormon? Good question, and the bible answers it.

Colossians 1:25
Whereof I am made a minister, according to the dispensation of God which is given to me for you, to fulfil the word of God;

All the revelation given to Paul fulfilled the word of God. This word *fulfilled* is from the Greek word *pleroō*, which means *to fill to capacity*. To emphasise the point, God employs a rare fourth conjugation here. In Aramaic and Hebrew there are four conjugations to intensify a verb. In our English language there are only three. In this case, the verb *fulfilled* is what we could call an extra-extensive form of the verb. A good translation of Colossians 1:25 would be:

Colossians 1:25
Whereof I am made a minister, according to the dispensation of God which is given to me for you, to completely, utterly, absolutely fill to capacity the word of God.

Rest assured, the bible, the God-breathed word written with the finger of God, is entire, complete and fulfilled.

16. The Renewed Mind

It is clear then, that defeating fear by building a strong believing mind and putting our trust in God requires a new way of thinking. Instead of understanding fear from a purely human point of view, we must learn to evaluate it from a spiritual perspective and believe that God is bigger than any problems we may face. This change of mind, this change of believing, this change of perspective comes about by understanding that the bible is God's word. As we read the bible with this understanding and apply the principles we learn, we go through a process called the renewed mind.

> Romans 12:2
> And be not conformed [*suschēmatizo*] to this world: but be ye transformed by the renewing of your mind, that ye may prove what *is* that good, and acceptable, and perfect, will of God.

Conformed is the Greek word *suschēmatizō*, a derivative of *schēma*, and means *to conform to the same pattern, to conform to, to fashion yourself according to*. Our English word *schematic* comes from this word. We are not to fashion ourselves, model ourselves, or conform ourselves to the schematics of the world. Movies, newspapers, magazines, literature, television, education and everything else in the world fashions and conforms us to this world. We are not to be conformed, fashioned or modelled according to the schematics and purposes of this world.

Easy enough to say, but what does that mean? We live in the world, so we can't just ignore it. This isn't about finding a quiet island in the middle of the ocean and opting out of life. Jesus Christ didn't ignore life. This doesn't mean we ignore education and can't watch movies. That isn't what it means. The devil is the god of this world, a position he has held since Genesis chapter 3 when man fell from the position God had given him. Since then, everything in the world conforms to the god of this world's agendas and purposes. Religion, education, the traditions of men, media – everything in the world contrives to conform men's minds to the political, religious, ethical, moral and spiritualist systems of this world. We are not to be moulded into this filth.

We can't avoid the world, so what do we do? What steps can we take to ensure we are not conformed to this world? We don't have to guess, just carry on reading because the verse tells us.

> Romans 12:2
> And be not conformed to this world: but be ye transformed [*metamorphoō*] *by* the renewing of your mind, that ye may prove what *is* that good, and acceptable, and perfect, will of God.

In contrast to being fashioned to the world, we are to be transformed by the renewing of our mind. *Transformed* is the word *metamorphoō*, from which we get our word *metamorphosis*, describing the change in form from a caterpillar to a butterfly. To be transformed then implies a complete change in our thoughts, a process by which our thoughts actually change form.

Caterpillars are regarded by many as pests because all they do is eat. Some species even have two mouths so they can devour more. After metamorphosis, however, caterpillars change from being devouring pests to butterflies that pollinate and spread life everywhere they go. This is the figure of speech God employed to illustrate the change we can enjoy if we renew our minds.

> Ephesians 4:22-24
> That ye put off concerning the former conversation the old man, which is corrupt according to the deceitful lusts;
>
> And be renewed in the spirit of your mind;
>
> And that ye put on [*enduō*] the new man, which after God is created in righteousness and true holiness.

Conversation in verse 22 means *behaviour*. Our former conversation or behaviour refers to our manner of life before we were born again, when we were just body and soul, without spirit, dead in the devil's world, without God and without hope. That is what the bible refers to as our old man, our old ways. To *put on* is *enduō* in the Greek, which means *to clothe*. This is something we do. We put it on, we renew our minds, it is something we do, not something God does for us.

Briefly then, to renew the mind is to develop a totally new way of thinking. Now, why would we want to do this?

> Proverbs 4:23
> Keep thy heart with all diligence; for out of it *are* the issues of life.

Heart refers to the innermost part of your being, that from which all believing and fear emanates. Our believing or our fear determines what we manifest in life, and believing and fear come from the heart. Here is an excellent translation of Proverbs 4:23.

Above all that heart must be guarded, for out of it are the sources of all outflow of all life.

How we build our heart and our believing is with our thoughts. We can be anything we want in life simply by believing. The god of this world knows this, so he does all he can to feed us fear so we will be afraid. No one can go beyond what they are taught, so if all we know is the fear the world breeds, that is all we will manifest. If all we watch is television and all we read are newspapers, magazines, and the world's literature, then that is all we will think, that is all that will be in our heads and in our hearts. We will have been fashioned and conformed to this world. However, we can choose to put different thoughts into our minds, the thoughts of the bible. If we do, instead of being conformed to the world, we will be transformed as we renew our minds and learn to believe God and thereby prove his good, acceptable, and perfect will.

> John 10:10
> The thief cometh not, but for to steal, and to kill, and to destroy: I am come that they might have life, and that they might have *it* more abundantly.

The devil, the thief, comes only to steal, to kill, and to destroy. Jesus Christ came that we might have life and have it more abundantly. Which life do you want? One is the way of death, the other is the way of life. One is the course of this world, the other is the way of God. It's our choice, it is up to us which life we live. Both are available, and we can have either. If we are fashioned and conformed to the world, we will live a life that's really not worth living, regardless of how much money we make. Life with God isn't about making money, it's about having all your need met. If we renew our minds, we experience God's good, acceptable, and perfect will by enjoying a more abundant life. If this sounds good, then get your mind out of the world and renew your mind with God's thoughts. Yes, that's right, learning to think the bible is learning to think like God, because the bible consists entirely of his thoughts.

Isaiah 55:7-13
Let the wicked forsake his way, and the unrighteous man his thoughts: and let him return unto the LORD, and he will have mercy upon him; and to our God, for he will abundantly pardon.

For my thoughts *are* not your thoughts, neither *are* your ways my ways, saith the LORD.

For *as* the heavens are higher than the earth, so are my ways higher than your ways, and my thoughts than your thoughts.

For as the rain cometh down, and the snow from heaven, and returneth not thither, but watereth the earth, and maketh it bring forth and bud, that it may give seed to the sower, and bread to the eater:

So shall my word be that goeth forth out of my mouth: it shall not return unto me void, but it shall accomplish that which I please, and it shall prosper *in the thing* whereto I sent it.

For ye shall go out with joy, and be led forth with peace: the mountains and the hills shall break forth before you into singing, and all the trees of the field shall clap *their* hands.

Instead of the thorn shall come up the fir tree, and instead of the brier shall come up the myrtle tree: and it shall be to the LORD for a name, for an everlasting sign *that* shall not be cut off.

How you forsake your thoughts is to quit being conformed to this world. How you return to God is by reading and studying his word and thinking his thoughts instead. If we take this action, God promises to forgive us for everything we've ever done, regardless of how terrible we were, and we will go out with joy, be led forth with peace, and the mountains and the hills will break forth before us into singing.

Here is a simple example of how we can renew our minds. According to God's word we are blameless and we have been made lovely and acceptable.

> Ephesians 1:4
> According as he hath chosen us in him before the foundation of the world, that we should be holy and without blame before him in love:

> Ephesians 1:6
> To the praise of the glory of his grace, wherein he hath made us accepted [lovely and acceptable] in the beloved.

God tells us we are blameless and that he thinks of us as lovely and acceptable. God doesn't say we are faultless, but rather that despite our faults we are blameless. According to God, we are blameless and lovely and acceptable. Now, is that how you think of yourself? Is that how the world thinks of you? Is that what television tells you? Is that what you read in newspapers? Are you taught this in school or at university? Do you read this in books? Do you hear this at the movies? I think you get the idea.

So what do we do when we feel less than lovely, when we feel guilty, when we feel garbage about ourselves? We have a choice to make. We can put aside our old thoughts and decide to think God's thoughts. How we do that is by memorising Ephesians 1:4 and 6 and quoting them to ourselves until we start believing God's word rather than what the world teaches us about ourselves. That's how you renew your mind.

Let's now consider another aspect of this. As there is obviously work involved, is renewing the mind painful? Does renewing the mind cause warts to grow on your head? Does replacing your old thoughts with new ones make your ears bleed? Not at all, quite the opposite, if you think

God's word day and night your life will be like a tree planted by rivers of water and you will enjoy a fruitful life.

> Psalm 1:1-3
> Blessed *is* the man that walketh not in the counsel of the ungodly, nor standeth in the way of sinners, nor sitteth in the seat of the scornful.
>
> But his delight *is* in the law of the LORD; and in his law doth he meditate day and night.
>
> And he shall be like a tree planted by the rivers of water, that bringeth forth his fruit in his season; his leaf also shall not wither; and whatsoever he doeth shall prosper.

If this is what you want, it is time to put your televisions, newspapers, magazines and computer games aside, and pick up a bible and start reading. To give us more of a feel for what it means to renew our minds, to see its simplicity and its benefits, let's look at a record where Jesus Christ renewed his mind in an extremely challenging situation.

As far as we know, only two humans have ever faced the devil in a direct face to face confrontation – Eve and Jesus Christ. Eve was seduced, man fell, and the devil became the god of this world. Jesus Christ, however, defeated the devil and reconciled man back to God. Why did Eve get taken down, and what was it that allowed Jesus Christ to prevail? The renewed mind is the simple answer. Eve thought she knew her bible, but she was wrong. She omitted a word from God's word, she added words, and finally she changed the word. Let's briefly compare her knowledge of scripture with what God actually said.

> Genesis 2:16,17
> And the LORD God commanded the man, saying, Of every tree of the garden thou mayest freely eat:
>
> But of the tree of the knowledge of good and evil, thou shalt not eat of it: for in the day that thou eatest thereof thou shalt surely die.

How long would it take to memorise these two short verses? A few seconds? Two minutes? There really isn't too much work involved in memorising these scriptures. Of every tree of the garden you may freely eat, but of the tree of the knowledge of good and evil, you shall not eat of it: for in the day that you eat thereof you shall surely die. How difficult is that to memorise? It's not difficult. However, look at Eve's response to the serpent.

> Genesis 3:2,3
> And the woman said unto the serpent, We may eat of the fruit of the trees of the garden:
>
> But of the fruit of the tree which *is* in the midst of the garden, God hath said, Ye shall not eat of it, neither shall ye touch it, lest ye die.

Eve omitted the word *freely*, she added the words *neither shall ye touch it*, and she changed the word from *thou shalt surely die* to *lest ye die*. Eve thought she knew her bible. Eve was religious, but she did not retain God's word clearly in her mind. Perhaps she watched too much television, I don't know, but for some reason she did not keep her mind in God's word and she became hazy on the details. She neglected the word and when she needed it, it was not there.

Eve did not know God's word, she only thought she did. Consequently the devil tricked her out of what was hers. Man died spiritually, and that death still affects us all to this day. That's why man needs a redeemer, someone to pay the price to purchase us back from the god of this world. In his face to face confrontation, Jesus Christ defeated the devil with three simple and easy to memorise scriptures.

> Luke 4:3,4
> And the devil said unto him, If thou be the Son of God, command this stone that it be made bread.
>
> And Jesus answered him, saying, It is written, That man shall not live by bread alone, but by every word of God.
>
> Luke 4:5-8
> And the devil, taking him up into an high mountain, shewed unto him all the kingdoms of the world in a moment of time.

And the devil said unto him, All this power will I give thee, and the glory of them: for that is delivered unto me; and to whomsoever I will I give it.

If thou therefore wilt worship me, all shall be thine.

And Jesus answered and said unto him, Get thee behind me, Satan: for it is written, Thou shalt worship the Lord thy God, and him only shalt thou serve.

Luke 4:9-12
And he brought him to Jerusalem, and set him on a pinnacle of the temple, and said unto him, If thou be the Son of God, cast thyself down from hence:

For it is written, He shall give his angels charge over thee, to keep thee:

And in *their* hands they shall bear thee up, lest at any time thou dash thy foot against a stone.

And Jesus answering said unto him, It is said, Thou shalt not tempt the Lord thy God.

Unlike Eve, Jesus Christ knew the word, and those easy to memorise scriptures were powerful enough to defeat the devil in a face to face confrontation. Think about that. Want some power in your life? The renewed mind is the key to power.

To sum up, God taught his word to Eve. The devil contradicted God's word and attempted to get Eve to doubt it. As she had become hazy on the details, she was easily seduced and defeated. Jesus Christ was taught God's word. As he was clear on the scriptures, he was not seduced and he was victorious. So how does all this relate to us today? Can we learn anything from this in a practical sense that we can apply in our lives? Well, let's look at a few real life examples.

Philippians 3:2
Beware of dogs [backbiters], beware of evil workers, beware of the concision.

It is pretty clear that backbiting – bitching about someone behind their back – is something God says we should not do. However, the world promotes backbiting. Politicians, for example, do it all the time. Every soap opera on TV teaches you how to backbite and bitch about people. It's practically impossible in our day and time to live a week without being drawn into bitching about someone behind their back. What do we do about it? Cry? Shout at those who do it? Write long emails? Ignore it? No, we go to the word.

Proverbs 25:23
The north wind driveth away rain: so *doth* an angry countenance a backbiting tongue.

The antidote to being drawn into backbiting and bitching is an angry face. If someone bitches to you about someone behind their back, you don't have to say or do anything, just pull an angry face and that will shut them up. That's what the word says. Now, are you going to believe it? Are you prepared to be courageous and believe God and do what his word says? If you want power in your life, learn, memorise, and apply God's word. When you are drawn into backbiting, for example, quote Proverbs 25:23 to yourself and put on an angry face. There is no need to send emails, quote scriptures, or confront people, just put on an angry face and that will deal with the problem. Try it and see.

How long does it take to memorise Proverbs 25:23? A few seconds? A minute? If you know this scripture, then you know how to deal with backbiting. If you find yourself in a backbiting situation, you can run Proverbs 25:23 through your mind and make a conscious decision to put on an angry face. That's renewing the mind in action. What other people do is up to them, but if they bitch to you, put your angry face on. If someone has a problem with someone else, they should go and sort it out with them in private, not go bitching behind their back.

Jesus Christ taught us how to deal with such matters as believers in our home churches. If someone needs sorting out the first thing you do is go and bitch about them behind their back, right? No, the first thing you do is go and have a quiet discussion, just the two of you in private and get it sorted out. If that doesn't get their attention, you publicly bitch about them all over Facebook, right? No, you confront them with one or two trusted witnesses, again in private. If that doesn't sort the situation, you take it further and go see your home church leader who will then become responsible to sort it out. At no time does backbiting ever come into it.

> Matthew 18:15-17
> Moreover if thy brother shall trespass against thee, go and tell him his fault between thee and him alone: if he shall hear thee, thou hast gained thy brother.
>
> But if he will not hear *thee, then* take with thee one or two more, that in the mouth of two or three witnesses every word may be established.
>
> And if he shall neglect to hear them, tell *it* unto the church: but if he neglect to hear the church, let him be unto thee as an heathen man and a publican.

There are rules to life. Fire is lovely stuff, but if you don't control it, it will burn you or damage your property. If that happens, it's not God's fault, it's yours for not controlling it properly. If fire burns you, God isn't punishing you, it's your fault. You missed the mark somewhere, and that's what sin means, to miss the mark. Sin comes from a word meaning to miss the mark, as an archer missing his target. Bitching and complaining is missing the mark. Bitching and complaining carry consequences, not because God is punishing you, but because you missed the mark.

> Psalms 77:3
> I remembered God, and was troubled: I complained, and my spirit was overwhelmed. Selah.

The psalmist described what happened when he complained and bitched. His spirit, his soul, his entire being was overwhelmed. That's what happens when you bitch and complain. That's just the nature of life, that's why God warns us about it in his word. What are we supposed to do instead of bitching and complaining?

1 Thessalonians 5:18
In every thing give thanks: for this is the will of God in Christ Jesus concerning you.

Rather than bitch and complain, we should be thankful, we should give thanks, we should keep our minds thankful. That's hitting the mark, not missing it.

Philippians 4:8
Finally, brethren, whatsoever things are true, whatsoever things *are* honest, whatsoever things *are* just, whatsoever things *are* pure, whatsoever things *are* lovely, whatsoever things *are* of good report; if *there be* any virtue, and if *there be* any praise, think on these things.

If we think wonderful things, we will have plenty to be thankful for, the trees will clap their hands and the mountains will break forth before us into singing. If we break God's word and go the world's way of bitching and complaining, well, we will be troubled and our souls will be overwhelmed. Jesus Christ resisted with the truth of God's word and he was victorious. We can do the same. That's renewing the mind.

James 4:7
Submit yourselves therefore to God. Resist the devil, and he will flee from you.

How you submit to God is to submit to his word, which is to renew your mind. If you renew your mind and apply the word, you will defeat the devil. If you want the garbage out of your life, if you want power in your life, if you want to be more than a conqueror in every situation, learn the word and do what it says. Let's look at another example.

Ephesians 4:25
Wherefore putting away lying, speak every man truth with his neighbour: for we are members one of another.

I think we all know that lying is wrong, that it is missing the mark. Would we lie to our children? Of course not. Oh? What about santa claus then? What about the tooth fairy? What about the easter bunny? The word says to put away lying. Are the traditions of men more important to you than doing God's word? Do you think it's okay with God to lie to your children? You can choose to renew your mind and enjoy the more abundant life, or you can be conformed to this world and lie to your children because santa claus, the tooth fairy and the easter bunny are more important to you. Are the traditions of men more important to you than the truth? See how this works? Renewing the mind isn't difficult, but it does require moving away from the courses of this world. What do you think God meant when he commanded us to not be conformed to this world?

Let's clarify something here regarding the renewed mind. Renewing the mind is not a destination. You cannot learn so much of God's word that you no longer need to renew your mind anymore. It isn't like climbing a mountain, or studying for a degree, or walking from John O'Groats to Lands End. There is no finish line. Renewing the mind is not a place where you can put your feet up and relax because you have arrived. Think of it in terms of daily food. You will need to eat as long as you live. If you quit renewing your mind, if you neglect God's word like Eve and go back to your television, you will slump back into your old man ways, most likely without even realising it.

Each and every day we have to continue to walk by the revealed word and will of God, the bible, and to do that we must learn it, we must renew our minds. This may be a continual process, but it isn't tedious, laborious or wearisome. Is enjoying a good meal every day wearisome? Not at all, good food is a joy, and so it is with God's word. It's a joy to renew the mind, it's a joy to have the strength to defeat anything that comes at you in life, to be more than a conqueror in every situation. Let's look at another example.

> Romans 13:8
> Owe no man any thing, but to love one another: for he that loveth another hath fulfilled the law.
>
> Philippians 4:19
> But my God shall supply all your need according to his riches in glory by Christ Jesus.

The world sells debt to us with glittering smiles, as if that's the only way we can get the things we need. God says he will supply all our need. So who is your god going to be from now on? The true God, who will supply all your need, or your credit card? Living a debt-free life with all your need met is very much a part of the more abundant life. The thief wants to steal that life from you, and is quite happy to dangle new cars, new computers and new clothes in front of you to get you into debt. If God supplies all your need, you don't have to go into debt then, do you?

Have you any idea how much misery is in the world because folks go into debt? It's missing the mark and it carries consequences. Someone once wrote: *There are two ways to conquer and enslave a country. One is by the sword. The other is by debt.* Have you any idea who it is lending you all that money so you will be in their debt? If you knew, you wouldn't touch it.

Next time you're tempted to spend money you don't have, quote Romans 13:8 to yourself and Philippians 4:19. They don't take very long to memorise. Next time you need something, will you trust God to meet your need, or will you put your trust in a piece of plastic? That's renewing the mind. Now yes, if you're in debt, God can part the oceans and lead you out of that slavery, but you're going to have to renew your mind and learn how to manage your money according to his word if you want his help. Let's look at one more example.

> Ephesians 4:28
> Let him that stole steal no more: but rather let him labour, working with *his* hands the thing which is good, that he may have to give to him that needeth.

We wouldn't steal anything, would we? Of course not. What about taking things home from work that don't belong to you? What about tampering with your electricity meter? What about buying goods you know have been stolen? What about salmon poaching? What about pirated movies, music and software? What about fare dodging? The world has an endless supply of things you can steal and an endless supply of reasons as to why you should do it. The masons know all about stealing.

You freemasons, do you think it is okay to steal all the best jobs and dish them out to other masons, putting everyone else out of work even though they would make better employees? Do you think it is okay with God to secretly break companies up and deliberately put them out of business so fellow masons with companies in communist China will benefit? Do you think it is okay with God to lie in court to keep guilty masons out of jail? You masons in politics, do you think it is okay with God to implement policies that poison and tax to death the very people who voted you into office and pay your wages?

I don't care what the jesuits tell you, or what the communist manifesto says, I'm telling you what God's word says, and if you don't change your lying stealing ways, you will pay for it. The communist manifesto may say it's okay to steal, the jesuits may tell you it's okay to steal, that the end justifies the means, but if you steal from life it will steal from you. That's just the way life is because what you sow in the ground is what you will get out of it.

Change, apologise to God, and do things his way, and you will be forgiven and everything God has will be made available to you. I don't care who you are or what you've done, or how big a player you are in the criminal and terrorist underworld, you can change your course at anytime. If you do, God will honour your believing and he will be there for you.

You may think you will be looked after in the new world order, but you are deceived. One world governance will not bring peace on earth, it will not bring an end to poverty, it will only bring the horrors described in the book of Revelation. You are betraying your own people for political ideals conjured up by the devil. You are being corrupted into traitors, liars and thieves for nothing more noble than a fistful of bribes. If you change, God will be there for you.

> Ezekiel 33:11
> Say unto them, *As* I live, saith the Lord GOD, I have no pleasure in the death of the wicked; but that the wicked turn from his way and live: turn ye, turn ye from your evil ways; for why will ye die, O house of Israel?

To renew the mind then, requires study of God's word, memorising scripture, and then living it. Anyone can do it, it isn't difficult or painful, and the benefits are out of this world.

17. Homosexuality: The Way of Life

God warns us there are men in the world who promote evil as good and good as evil, who replace light with darkness, and who substitute sweet for bitter.

> Isaiah 5:20
> Woe unto them that call evil good, and good evil; that put darkness for light, and light for darkness; that put bitter for sweet, and sweet for bitter!

Obviously this is going on in the world otherwise God would not have felt the need to warn us about it. Furthermore, it is being done with intent, with deliberate systematic execution. Conditioning us to believe that evil is good and good is evil is the world's modus operandi, the way it works. The devil is the god of this world, so this makes sense.

Now, this is where we need to start dealing with a few things, and for the next few chapters we are going to be comparing the word with the world, comparing what is good with what is evil.

We know that in order to live protected from the devil we need to believe God's word and live it. However, there may be things in God's word that we don't agree with and we may find shocking or even disturbing. This is where we need to stop and take a breath and think about things. We were all brought up in the world and we have been conditioned to think of evil as good and good as evil. Remember, Lucifer is the god of this world. The word says that he was the angel of light at one time, full of wisdom and beauty, and that he was perfect in all his ways. As the god of this world, he knows how to replace good with evil and evil with good.

If we find our thoughts don't line up with God's word on any particular subject we have to make a decision. Are we going to renew our minds to God's word or not? Often it's easy to change, sometimes it's not. We have to make up our minds on the word. Is it the truth or not?

When I first got into the word I was a drunk, I smoked dope, I was a thief, a salmon poacher, and I had quite a few other little and not so little problems that didn't line up with God's word. I had decisions to make. I quit drinking, smoking dope, and stealing. It took a while longer to get my head around salmon poaching, but I gave that up as well. The more I lived the word, the better my life became. It didn't happen overnight, in fact it took a couple of years to clean my life up, and even then I still made mistakes. The question is, do we want to walk by the spirit or not? Do we want fellowship with God? Do we want God's hedge of protection around us? Do we want to be able to help people with God's word or not? If so, then we renew our minds to the word and change where we need to change so our thoughts and our lives line up with the word.

As an example to clarify and illustrate what I'm talking about, let us look at homosexuality and compare viewpoints – God's and the world's. If you're a homosexual or a lesbian and you honestly want to know God and live his word, this section is probably going to be traumatic and disturbing. However hold yourself together, because God loves you just as much as anyone else. He sent his son to die for everyone, and that includes you as well as it did me.

> John 3:16
> For God so loved the world, that he gave his only begotten Son, that whosoever believeth in him should not perish, but have everlasting life.

If you want eternal life, just make the decision to change. The apostle Paul changed from a murdering religious dragon and God was there for him like he was there for me and he will be there for you too. The more abundant life is for everyone. All you have to do is renew your mind, clean up your life, and God will be there for you. Okay, let's deal with some stuff.

> Leviticus 20:13
> If a man also lie with mankind, as he lieth with a woman, both of them have committed an abomination: they shall surely be put to death; their blood *shall be* upon them.

Can it be any clearer? In the old testament, homosexuals were to be executed. *Executed?* That's right, homosexuals were to be stoned to death. That is a harsh penalty. If God commanded his people to stone homosexuals to death, does that mean then that perhaps they are not just enjoying an alternative lifestyle as the world advocates? Well, God certainly doesn't think so. That is the old testament, what about the new testament?

> Romans 1:26-28,32
> For this cause God gave them up unto vile [repulsive, repugnant, disgusting, putrid] affections: for even their women did change the natural use into that which is against nature [lesbians]:
>
> And likewise also the men, leaving the natural use of the woman, burned in their lust one toward another; men with men working that which is unseemly [homosexuality], and receiving in themselves that recompence of their error which was meet.
>
> And even as they did not like to retain God in *their* knowledge, God gave them over to a reprobate mind [an insane mind – to commit homosexual and lesbian acts is criminally insane], to do those things which are not convenient;
>
> Who knowing the judgment of God, that they which commit such things are worthy of death, not only do the same, but have pleasure in them that do them.

Verse 32 clearly states that homosexuals and lesbians are worthy of death. That is explicit and clear. What about Jesus Christ then? What did he think? He was all love, right? In Matthew, Jesus addressed the people regarding John the Baptist.

> Matthew 11:8,9
> But what went ye out for to see? A man clothed in soft raiment? behold, they that wear soft *clothing* are in kings' houses.
>
> But what went ye out for to see? A prophet? yea, I say unto you, and more than a prophet.

The word *soft* in verse 8 is better translated *effeminate*. Men who wear effeminate clothing in this context are homosexuals. What is Jesus Christ saying here?

> *What went you out to see? A homo? Behold, you will find the homos infesting royalty and your politicians. No, John the Baptist was no homo, he was a man of God, a prophet, yes, and more than a prophet.*

Now, this may come as a bit of shock if you have grown up conditioned by the world regarding homosexuality. If this is the case, it is likely your mind may have a great deal of difficulty grasping the enormity of just how serious a crime homosexuality is. According to God's word, homosexuality warrants the death penalty. It doesn't get much more serious than that. Homosexuals are not just consenting adults enjoying sex, not if God's word is right. This isn't about consent, this is about what is right and what is wrong, what is good and what is evil, what is light and what is darkness.

> John 10:10
> The thief cometh not, but for to steal, and to kill, and to destroy: I am come that they might have life, and that they might have *it* more abundantly.

If we want an abundant life, we must come back to the word of God and walk in the way of life. To further our understanding of this, let's consider a record from the old testament.

> Genesis 19:1
> And there came two angels to Sodom at even; and Lot sat in the gate of Sodom: and Lot seeing *them* rose up to meet them; and he bowed himself with his face toward the ground;

It was customary in that day for the residents of a community to lodge and entertain travellers. There were no newspapers, televisions, or Internet in those days, and as travellers brought the latest news from around the country, this was a mutually beneficial arrangement. This was their bed and breakfast system – news in exchange for lodgings. Lot had room in his house, and he was doing what was customary by offering hospitality. On this particular evening however, unknown to him, he met two angels.

Genesis 19:2-5
And he said, Behold now, my lords, turn in, I pray you, into your servant's house, and tarry all night, and wash your feet, and ye shall rise up early, and go on your ways. And they said, Nay; but we will abide in the street all night.

And he pressed upon them greatly; and they turned in unto him, and entered into his house; and he made them a feast, and did bake unleavened bread, and they did eat.

But before they lay down, the men of the city, *even* the men of Sodom, compassed the house round, both old and young, all the people from every quarter:

And they called unto Lot, and said unto him, Where *are* the men which came in to thee this night? bring them out unto us, that we may know them.

It says the men of the city, both young and old, from every occupation and lifestyle surrounded Lot's house and demanded that he hand over the two men that they may *know them*, or have homosexual relations with them. What is this, but unrestrained homosexual gang rape. Does it sound familiar? It's happening all around us in our day and time. How do cultures become infested with vicious predatory homos like this? The promotion of human rights and tolerance, of course. Look, this is God's word. This is the way of life. Look around you, the way of death is everywhere.

Genesis 19:6-10
And Lot went out at the door unto them, and shut the door after him,

And said, I pray you, brethren, do not so wickedly.

Behold now, I have two daughters which have not known man; let me, I pray you, bring them out unto you, and do ye to them as *is* good in your eyes: only unto these men do nothing; for therefore came they under the shadow of my roof.

And they said, Stand back. And they said *again*, This one *fellow* came in to sojourn, and he will needs be a judge: now will we deal worse with thee, than with them. And they pressed sore upon the man, *even* Lot, and came near to break the door.

But the men put forth their hand, and pulled Lot into the house to them, and shut to the door.

The homos of Sodom were going to gang rape Lot for daring to confront them. If homosexuality is not dealt with according to God's word, this is where it always leads, to gang rape, violence, and murder.

There is another record in the old testament where a man, his wife, and his servant were travelling through Israel. As night fell, they entered Gibeah, a city of Israel, to seek lodgings.

Judges 19:15
And they turned aside thither, to go in *and* to lodge in Gibeah: and when he went in, he sat him down in a street of the city: for *there was* no man that took them into his house to lodging.

To understand why he sat in the street, we have to understand that it was their culture to look after the needs of travellers. All the bed and breakfasts were closed even though there were vacancies. That man was observing the correct cultural protocols in seeking lodgings for the night. However, no one took them in.

Judges 19:16-21
And, behold, there came an old man from his work out of the field at even, which *was* also of mount Ephraim; and he sojourned in Gibeah: but the men of the place *were* Benjamites.

And when he had lifted up his eyes, he saw a wayfaring man in the street of the city: and the old man said, Whither goest thou? and whence comest thou?

And he said unto him, We *are* passing from Bethlehemjudah toward the side of mount Ephraim; from thence *am* I: and I went to

Bethlehemjudah, but I *am now* going to the house of the LORD; and there *is* no man that receiveth me to house.

Yet there is both straw and provender for our asses; and there is bread and wine also for me, and for thy handmaid, and for the young man *which is* with thy servants: *there is* no want of any thing.

And the old man said, Peace *be* with thee; howsoever *let* all thy wants *lie* upon me; only lodge not in the street.

So he brought him into his house, and gave provender unto the asses: and they washed their feet, and did eat and drink.

Finally, one old man of this city extended kindness and courtesy to the man. This traveller was not poor because he was sitting in the street, quite the contrary, there was no want of anything. He was simply looking for bed and breakfast in the customary manner.

Judges 19:22
Now as they were making their hearts merry, behold, the men of the city, certain sons of Belial, beset the house round about, *and* beat at the door, and spake to the master of the house, the old man, saying, Bring forth the man that came into thine house, that we may know him.

Here we go again, unrestrained homosexual gang rape and violence. No wonder all the bed and breakfasts were closed – no one wanted the homos breaking down their door during the night to gang rape their guests.

Judges 19:23-29
And the man, the master of the house, went out unto them, and said unto them, Nay, my brethren, *nay*, I pray you, do not *so* wickedly; seeing that this man is come into mine house, do not this folly.

Behold, *here is* my daughter a maiden, and his concubine; them I will bring out now, and humble ye them, and do with them what seemeth good unto you: but unto this man do not so vile a thing.

But the men would not hearken to him: so the man took his concubine, and brought her forth unto them; and they knew her, and abused her all the night until the morning: and when the day began to spring, they let her go.

Then came the woman in the dawning of the day, and fell down at the door of the man's house where her lord *was*, till it was light.

And her lord rose up in the morning, and opened the doors of the house, and went out to go his way: and, behold, the woman his concubine was fallen down *at* the door of the house, and her hands *were* upon the threshold.

And he said unto her, Up, and let us be going. But none answered [she died]. Then the man took her *up* upon an ass, and the man rose up, and gat him unto his place.

And when he was come into his house, he took a knife, and laid hold on his concubine, and divided her, *together* with her bones, into twelve pieces, and sent her into all the coasts of Israel.

These last few decades have seen an increase in sexual violence around the world that is staggering. It is due entirely to the legalising of homosexuality – granting homosexuals and lesbians protection by law – and censoring news reports so as not to expose their brutal sexual predations. In the old testament, God's people were to stone them to death. They were not to be tolerated, they were not to be given jobs as politicians, they were not to be ordained as ministers and priests, they were to be stoned to death. Not only did God advocate the death penalty for homosexuality in the old testament, he had Paul warning us about it in the very first chapter of the book of Romans.

Just for the record, the bible does not advocate or condone lynching, public riots, or civil unrest, it advocates administering justice through existing judicial systems. Those in government are responsible for how they govern the countries to which they were elected to serve. If you are in government and care about the people you serve, then perhaps this would be a good place to start when you next sit down to discuss policy.

The world may change our laws and call homosexuality normal healthy behaviour, while at the same time criminalising those who dare to stand against them, but the word of God stands.

> Isaiah 5:20
> Woe unto them that call evil good, and good evil; that put darkness for light, and light for darkness; that put bitter for sweet, and sweet for bitter!

Promoting homosexuality is calling evil good, while prosecuting those who stand against them is calling good, evil. Promoting homosexuality is putting darkness for light, and bitter for sweet. This is the way of life in this category. Choose wisely your way.

18. Homosexuality: The Way of Death

Like the true God, the devil is spirit, and just as the true God needs men and women to teach and minister to bring light to people's minds, so the devil requires men and women to move his darkness. Note Jesus Christ's words to his disciples:

> John 15:19
> If ye were of the world, the world would love his own: but because ye are not of the world, but I have chosen you out of the world, therefore the world hateth you.

Again, *world* doesn't refer to God's creation, it refers to the authority and dominion that the devil, the god of this world has over it.

> Ephesians 2:2
> Wherein in time past ye walked according to the course of this world, according to the prince of the power of the air, the spirit that now worketh in the children of disobedience:

The prince of the power of the air, the god of this world, determines the course of this world. The devil promotes his agendas through the world by way of those who work for him. Without men and women working for him, the devil would have no power or influence in the physical realm. Adam and Eve handed this authority and power to the devil when they fell, and it is this authority and power that the devil uses to mobilise his forces. Always remember though, that our fight is not against people.

> Ephesians 6:12
> For we wrestle not against flesh and blood, but against principalities, against powers, against the rulers of the darkness of this world, against spiritual wickedness in high *places*.

Principalities, powers, the rulers of the darkness of this world, and spiritual wickedness from on high are all clues as to how the devil manipulates things through the senses world. Spiritual wickedness that steals from us, kills us, and destroys us has a source from which it emanates. Evil is not something ethereal and nebulous, it is intelligent, it is systematic, it is bold, it is powerful, and it has a rich purse. The word consistently warns us about the nature of this world.

> Philippians 2:15
> That ye may be blameless and harmless, the sons of God, without rebuke, in the midst of a crooked and perverse nation, among whom ye shine as lights in the world;

> 1 John 2:15
> Love not the world, neither the things *that are* in the world. If any man love the world, the love of the Father is not in him.

Do you love the political systems of the world? Do you love the power, dominion, and authority of the world? Do you love freemasonry, communism and one world governance? If so, you lack understanding of the spiritual nature of life.

According to the word of God, homosexuality warrants the death penalty. Just a few decades ago, homosexuality was a criminal offence both in the United States and in the United Kingdom. What happened to those excellent laws that kept us protected from them? Who dismantled them?

In the past few decades homosexuality has been promoted in our newspapers, on television, in the movies we watch, in the books we read, the art we enjoy, the music we listen to, and in every other form of art and entertainment imaginable. It is even being taught in our schools to our children. We kiss our children on the cheek in the morning and send them off to spend their day being groomed for homosexuality in our State run schools. This is an example of the truth of Isaiah 5:20.

> Isaiah 5:20
> Woe unto them that call evil good, and good evil; that put darkness for light, and light for darkness; that put bitter for sweet, and sweet for bitter!

Most folks today think those who oppose homosexuality are narrow minded and intolerant. In fact it is a criminal offence in some countries to stand against homosexuals and their perversions. How did this troubling change come about?

Let's look at one example, the press. Our newspapers have become the most influential power within our civilisations, more powerful than our politicians and our judiciary who seem to enjoy bending over for news editors. National newspaper coverage is now powerful enough to elect scurrilous presidents and prime ministers whose only agenda is to destroy the countries they were elected to serve.

To whom are newspapers responsible? Most of us are unaware that all UK newspapers are controlled by one central organisation that dictates to all news editors what to print. Our newspapers are told which stories to print and what not to print. In reality, our newspapers are not free to print anything other than that which they are told to print. What is this central body that controls our newspapers? Who are the men sitting in these powerful positions without our knowledge, who dictate which stories we read and which stories we will not read? Don't you find it ironic that they call this freedom of speech?

Freedom of speech is not freedom at all, it is primarily a weapon. Through freedom of speech, our national secrets are stolen and those guilty are not prosecuted. Regarding freedom of speech, is it enjoyed by those who condemn homosexuality? Freedom of speech and freedom of the press are among the biggest lies and deceptions of the last two centuries.

The same is true of publishing houses and television stations. Every major publishing house in the United Kingdom submits manuscripts they are considering publishing to an outside source before making any decisions. If their source recommends they do not publish any particular book, they do not publish it. They do this without question. Televisions are told what stories to air on their news programmes, and what stories not to air. Who are these people working behind the scenes determining and controlling our mental diet?

In the last two decades, international homo and lesbian associations have spread like weeds, with authority to promote and foster what the world terms fair and accurate coverage of homosexual and lesbian issues and to oppose media bias against them. In America, perhaps the most effective pressure group working within the media is the National Lesbian and Gay Journalists Association. In the year 2000, the NLGJA's president worked at the Dallas Morning News, while one vice president worked at CNN and another at Newsday. The treasurer of the NLGJA worked at the New York Times and the secretary worked for USA Today.

This is systematic and organisational manipulation at work behind the scenes. This is the course of the world at work. Who founded these international homosexual organisations? Who funds them? Who put these homosexuals into such prominent and powerful positions within the media? Why did the media companies simply open their mouths and swallow them? Why did the media never report anything about this on the news? Well, that was a bit of a silly question, wasn't it.

So successful has this psychological propaganda been that today to stand on the word of God and proclaim that homosexuality is a crime could land you in court in violation of human rights laws. Instead of executing homosexuals and lesbians, we now allow them to adopt young children so they can gang rape them in the privacy of their own homes without fear of prosecution.

Homosexuals brutally rape and murder young boys and we stand back and do nothing, afraid of infringing their human rights. Perhaps the most spiritually nauseating perversion of all is seeing homosexuals being ordained in churches who profess to teach the bible.

Why is it that we never read in newspapers or hear in television news reports about how homosexual men infected with AIDS gang rape four-year-old boys in their own homes? Why is it that we never read or hear about homosexual partners binding and gagging ten-year-old boys and repeatedly sodomising them in ritualistic rape murders? Why is it that we never read about how homosexuals have tried to infect our blood banks with HIV? All this is happening in real life but we never hear about it in the media. Why not? Here is a quote by Robert Schwab, former president of the Texas Human Rights Foundation in the Dallas Gay News, May 20, 1983.

There has come the idea that if research money (for AIDS) is not forthcoming at a certain level by a certain date, all gay males should give blood ... Whatever action is required to get national attention is valid. If that includes blood terrorism, so be it.

Did you know that wilfully injecting a fatal disease into someone knowing that it will kill them is murder? That is what homosexual men do to each other. They murder each other to satiate their lusts, and they call it love. Well, God has a different viewpoint.

Violent sex is on the rise. Ejaculating into ten-year-old boys while they quiver and die is a fantasy amongst hard-core homosexuals. The newspapers and televisions will not tell you that. The word of God does though. God sounded the alarm about them thousands of years ago. Who are you going to believe? You are having set before you the way of life and the way of death. The word of God is the truth and the world stands in direct opposition to that truth. However, that's hardly surprising when you understand who the god of this world is.

Our modern stance on homosexuality and lesbianism is largely due to the influence of such men as Alfred C Kinsey. Kinsey's research into sexual matters can be summarised in his findings that while Americans pretended to be virtuous, virginal, monogamous and faithfully heterosexual, they were in reality hypocritical, promiscuous, closeted homosexuals. That is what Kinsey claimed. In truth, Kinsey was a sadistic bisexual monster who seduced his male students and coerced his wife, his staff and their wives to perform in illegal pornographic films made in the family attic.

Kinsey solicited and paid paedophiles to sexually violate between 300 to 2000 infants and children for his experiments into child sexuality. These experiments included oral and anal sodomy, genital intercourse, and manual abuse. That these crimes were committed is proven in his own graphs and charts. Table 34 on page 181 of Kinsey's Male volume claims to be a scientific record of multiple orgasms in pre-adolescent males. Infants as young as five months were timed with a stopwatch for orgasm by Kinsey's aides, with one four year-old being tested 24-hours around the clock for an alleged 26 orgasms.

Kinsey defined children screaming, writhing in pain, fainting and convulsing as having orgasms. And this in infants too young to speak. The data collected from Kinsey's experiments is commonly quoted today by sex educators and their advocates to prove children's needs for homosexual, heterosexual and bisexual relationships. It was this *research* that opened the door to legalised paedophilia.

How could Kinsey's scientific report be hyped globally to bestseller status and yet draw no questions from news reporters as to where infants for human sexual experiments came from, or indeed, how children could be fed to such depraved men in the name of science? Of course, Kinsey's critics were largely ignored or slandered in the media as sexually repressed, ignorantly religious, mean spirited, unscientific, and backward.

The word of God clearly educates us about the horrendous evils of homosexuality, so how then does the god of this world promote such naturally abhorrent and perverted acts to our minds to the point we think it natural? Toby Morotta, a Harvard homosexual PhD writes in his work, The Politics of Homosexuality (1981), of how the media and establishment politicians were used to build gay power.

Like the NIH, professional journals have commonly assigned GAU [Gay Academic Union] *and other homosexual peer reviewers to research touching on homosexuality, generally resulting in a quick death to possible unfavorable findings.*

Researchers and academics who stand against homosexuality often find their careers come to an abrupt end. Not only have our universities become a haven for communist extremists, they now actively seek and prefer homosexual lecturers. In reality, communists and homosexuals are often indistinguishable. This has mostly come about because of the recent tsunami of International laws spewing from the United Nations.

Human rights opened the doors for homosexuals to be given positions of power in every conceivable position of authority within our western cultures. They infest our schools, our media, our medical profession, our legal profession, our businesses, our political systems, our universities, our law enforcement agencies, our military, and every other part of British and American social life.

The National Association for Research and Therapy of Homosexuality has this to say about homosexuality.

With the sharing of knowledge, NARTH serves as an antidote to the misinformation disseminated by the media, as well as the misinformation of some of our own psychological and psychiatric professional organizations. The homosexual, his or her family, and the public have a right of access to scientific information. We believe this is true even when this information runs counter to the ideas of socio-political activists... During the last twenty years, powerful political pressures have done much to erode scientific exploration and study of this disorder.

Many researchers have been intimidated into trading truth for silence... Homosexuality distorts the natural bond of friendship that would normally unite persons of the same sex. It works against society's essential male/female design and family unit. Yet today children from kindergarten and beyond are being taught in public school that homosexuality is nothing but a normal, healthy option.... Our task is to discuss issues misrepresented by social-activist groups, who have portrayed sexual deviancy as a normal way of life.

Homosexuality is not normal behaviour, it's a moral and social disease. It is abhorrent and those who become so depraved they indulge in such practices, according to the word of God, should be executed. Homosexuals are not born, they are recruited. It is not genetic.

Kinsey's paedophile data proving infants and children were capable and deserving of orgasm from birth, and that homosexuality and sodomy were normal has resulted in our children being influenced as soon as they are old enough to go to school. Indeed, television has been pushing homosexuality on our children since Noddy and Big Ears slept in the same bed. If you didn't know Noddy and Big Ears were homosexuals, then perhaps you also didn't know that Bill and Ben, Andy Pandy, the Tellytubbies, and a host of other children's television characters are homosexuals. If you did not know, then perhaps it is time you began to think about dragging your children away from homo infested television land and read them the bible instead.

An FBI report, Lanning and Burgess (1984), said this regarding child pornography and sex rings:

Clinical data are increasingly suggesting that boys may be at equal risk for sexual victimization since they are the preferred target of habitual pedophiles and victims of child sex rings.

Look, hardcore homosexuals are not nice men. They will quite happily rape and murder your boys to satisfy their lusts, and then go on their way laughing and joking while looking for their next victim. They can and do brutally rape and sodomise babies and children. They enjoy orgasm while the child is dying and convulsing. They like to put small animals up their backsides and orgasm as these animals suffocate and die. They even murder each other by knowingly infecting each other with fatal diseases. If you think this is normal, healthy behaviour, you are insane and you are worthy of death, as it states in Romans.

Let us reacquaint ourselves with our old friend Leviticus just in case we have forgotten what God thinks of homosexuality.

> Leviticus 20:13
> If a man also lie with mankind, as he lieth with a woman, both of them have committed an abomination: they shall surely be put to death; their blood *shall be* upon them.

Why does God take such an extreme stance against homosexuality? There must be a good reason. A quick recap of what occurred in the cities of Sodom and Gomorrah should suffice to sound the alarm.

> Genesis 19:1-5
> And there came two angels to Sodom at even; and Lot sat in the gate of Sodom: and Lot seeing *them* rose up to meet them; and he bowed himself with his face toward the ground;
>
> And he said, Behold now, my lords, turn in, I pray you, into your servant's house, and tarry all night, and wash your feet, and ye shall rise up early, and go on your ways. And they said, Nay; but we will abide in the street all night.
>
> And he pressed upon them greatly; and they turned in unto him, and entered into his house; and he made them a feast, and did bake unleavened bread, and they did eat.

> But before they lay down, the men of the city, *even* the men of Sodom, compassed the house round, both old and young, all the people from every quarter:
>
> And they called unto Lot, and said unto him, Where *are* the men which came in to thee this night? bring them out unto us, that we may know them.
>
> Genesis 19:24,25
> Then the LORD rained upon Sodom and upon Gomorrah brimstone and fire from the LORD out of heaven;
>
> And he overthrew those cities, and all the plain, and all the inhabitants of the cities, and that which grew upon the ground.

Sodom and Gomorrah were destroyed because of homosexuality. It is a cancer that will destroy any civilisation that becomes infected with it. The devil knows this and that is why he is promoting homosexuality within your civilisations. If you do not come back to the word of God, you will suffer terrible consequences.

The way of life and the way of death regarding homosexuality is set before you. It is up to you which way you will choose. Are the perverted and twisted words of the United Nations your bible? Then change what you are putting into your mind. If you call yourself a christian and you think homosexuality is normal, you need to get your head back into the bible because you stand in direct opposition to the God you claim to serve.

I have heard it said that the test of good literature is how long it remains in circulation. Many of the old classics, for example, are still widely read. The word of God has been around for thousands of years, and it is still the most widely read book on earth. Newspapers are in our trash the day they are published, a fitting tribute to their value.

Does God hate homosexuals? Not at all. If homosexuals wish to clean up their lives, it's available. Jesus Christ died for them as much as anyone else, and they can have deliverance if they want it.

John 3:16
For God so loved the world, that he gave his only begotten Son, that whosoever believeth in him should not perish, but have everlasting life.

Whosoever means whosoever, and that must include homos. Repent biblically, (translated from the Greek word *metanoeō)* simply means to change your mind. Instead of thinking homosexuality is good, you line your thoughts up with God's word and think of it as evil. As you change your thoughts, your habits will change. That's what repentance means. If homosexuals want deliverance, it's available, they can come to God's word and get it.

Is the world contradictory to the word of God regarding homosexuality? Unquestionably. What are you going to believe? It is a choice. One is the way of life, the other is the way of death. The world promotes homosexuality, the word of God categorically states they are worthy of death. The devil's sole purpose is to steal from us, kill us, and destroy us, God wants us to have life and have it more abundantly. Those are your two choices. And how ironic that it is under banners of human rights and tolerance with which the god of this world shafts you up the backside with his filth.

If we do not get serious about removing the homos and lesbians from our civilisations, we may well be destroyed as peoples.

19. Climate Change

Every generation it seems is subjected to an endless stream of terrifying prophesies of catastrophes that will destroy the earth. If a comet doesn't get us, an ice age will, if an ice age doesn't get us, a hole in the ozone layer will, if the ozone layer doesn't get us, global warming will. It goes on generation after generation, ad nauseum. This media powered merry-go-round of earth doom is promoted primarily through newspapers, television, Hollywood, music, literature, art, and school classrooms. A recent hot topic has been climate change.

It isn't that long since it was prophecies of an impending ice age we were shivering over. Does anyone remember the ozone layer breaking down? Where did all the front page news reports and scientific studies on that disappear to? How does all this earth doom stuff stand up to the word of God anyway?

The devil is the god of this world for the time being, that is true and undisputed. However, there is a rather important distinction to be made here – he does not *own* the earth. Ownership of the earth is still with the true God. The title deeds of the earth were never transferred to Adam and Eve so man never owned the earth – he was simply its caretaker, its manager, its CEO, its Lord. The devil could not take the title deeds of the earth from Adam and Eve because they did not have them.

The earth belonged to God before the fall of man, the earth belonged to God after the fall of man, and the earth still belongs to God today. All the devil took was the manager's job and the benefits that went with it. The earth is not the devil's property, he is merely in charge of how it is governed. If the god of this world owned the earth, there would be no life because God would not be able to protect us environmentally. God is still very much the earth's owner, so he is very much in control of how it operates despite the current management.

Psalm 47:9
The princes of the people are gathered together, *even* the people of the God of Abraham: for the shields of the earth *belong* unto God: he is greatly exalted.

The shields of the earth mentioned in Psalm 47 refer to the defences of the earth. A shield is a defence. Warriors of old used shields to deflect arrow, sword, axe, and lance strikes. The shields of the earth refer to the earth's defences, which deflect anything that would harm it. God put the shields of the earth, the defences of the earth in place, and his word assures us that these shields are more than adequate for the job for which they were designed. In other words, there is nothing in the universe that is going to penetrate the earth's defences and render the planet dysfunctional. The shields of the earth are impregnable.

Psalm 93:1
The LORD reigneth, he is clothed with majesty; the LORD is clothed with strength, *wherewith* he hath girded himself: the world also is stablished, that it cannot be moved.

For example, it is a well known astronomical phenomenon that the gravitational pull of the planet Jupiter deflects comets and space debris that may be on a collision course for earth and draws them safely into orbit around the sun. Indeed, such is the power of Jupiter's gravitational pull that comets have been observed in recent times to strike the planet itself. Earth is in no danger from comet strikes because Jupiter makes sure of that, while our own atmosphere burns up any little stuff Jupiter doesn't take care of. God put the shields of the earth in place. That is it, end of story. The earth is not in any danger from *anything*. That is the testimony of God's word.

After the flood of Noah's time God made a promise.

Genesis 8:21,22
And the LORD smelled a sweet savour; and the LORD said in his heart, I will not again curse the ground any more for man's sake; for the imagination of man's heart *is* evil from his youth; neither will I again smite any more every thing living, as I have done.

> While the earth remaineth, seedtime and harvest, and cold and heat, and summer and winter, and day and night shall not cease.

Although these verses attribute the flood to God, we must remember what we learned in the book of Job regarding the idiom of permission. Just as the meanings of green and red traffic lights have not changed since we read Job, the truth that God is good and the devil is evil hasn't changed either. Compare these verses from Revelation.

> Revelation 12:13-17
> And when the dragon saw that he was cast unto the earth, he persecuted the woman which brought forth the man *child*.
>
> And to the woman were given two wings of a great eagle, that she might fly into the wilderness, into her place, where she is nourished for a time, and times, and half a time, from the face of the serpent.
>
> And the serpent cast out of his mouth water as a flood after the woman, that he might cause her to be carried away of the flood.
>
> And the earth helped the woman, and the earth opened her mouth, and swallowed up the flood which the dragon cast out of his mouth.
>
> And the dragon was wroth with the woman, and went to make war with the remnant of her seed, which keep the commandments of God, and have the testimony of Jesus Christ.

The dragon is a figurative reference to the devil, the god of this world. According to Revelation, who flooded the earth? The devil did. So when we read in Genesis that God did it, we have to understand it in light of the idiom of permission. This truth never changes throughout the entire word of God.

Back in Noah's day, the devil almost succeeded in destroying man from the face of the earth, thereby destroying the Christ line and preventing Jesus Christ from ever being born. Those who work for the god of this world think their god has their best interests at heart, but they are sadly deceived. His aim is the destruction of the human race, which includes those who work for him and worship him, as he almost succeeded in doing back in Noah's day. The true God can be trusted and wants to bless you with abundance in every category of life.

After the flood, God promised that earth would never again become uninhabitable for man. It is not going to happen. God is faithful to his word and he keeps his promises. God even gave us a visible sign to remind us of this promise.

> Genesis 9:11-17
> And I will establish my covenant with you; neither shall all flesh be cut off any more by the waters of a flood; neither shall there any more be a flood to destroy the earth.
>
> And God said, This *is* the token of the covenant which I make between me and you and every living creature that *is* with you, for perpetual generations:
>
> I do set my bow in the cloud, [the rainbow] and it shall be for a token of a covenant between me and the earth.
>
> And it shall come to pass, when I bring a cloud over the earth, that the bow shall be seen in the cloud:
>
> And I will remember my covenant, which *is* between me and you and every living creature of all flesh; and the waters shall no more become a flood to destroy all flesh.
>
> And the bow shall be in the cloud; and I will look upon it, that I may remember the everlasting covenant between God and every living creature of all flesh that *is* upon the earth.
>
> And God said unto Noah, This *is* the token of the covenant, which I have established between me and all flesh that *is* upon the earth.

The rainbow is a visible token of the promise God made to man back in Noah's time. Rest assured, God is faithful to keep his promises and the earth is not in any danger. The shields of the earth belong to God and nothing is going to get through them. That is the testimony of God's word.

Colossians 1:16,17
For by him were all things created, that are in heaven, and that are in earth, visible and invisible, whether *they be* thrones, or dominions, or principalities, or powers: all things were created by him, and for him:

And he is before all things, and by him all things consist.

The word *consist* would be better translated *cohere*. Cohere means to stick or to hold together. This planet we live on is stuck together, held together by God. The shields of the earth belong to God. In other words, God has put in place an ecosystem with built in air conditioning that he has guaranteed will continue to function correctly regardless of anything man thinks he can do to mess it up. Of course, I'm not advocating irresponsibility here, not at all, the point I'm making is, even if we do abuse the environment and do our best to mess it up, the earth is still going to continue to function correctly. There is nothing man can do that will mess up the earth to the point it becomes non-functional. Hiroshima is prospering and doing just fine these days, ever noticed?

So, if the earth is not in any danger from anything, then what is really behind climate change and environmentalism? First of all, either God's word is true or the devil's words are true. If you believe the world, you are deceived. The question is, why would the devil take so much trouble to convince us that we are destroying the earth when the earth isn't in danger from anything? So what is climate change about then? Whatever it is, it has nothing whatsoever to do with saving the earth.

A brief summary of the hype surrounding climate change may give us some clues. To encapsulate, human beings are supposedly causing global warming because we release carbon dioxide into the atmosphere. This carbon dioxide is a gas which is causing the earth to warm up. Earth's icecaps will melt, polar bears will die, and entire cities will disappear under water. To prevent these disasters, radical changes are required to reduce the amount of man-made carbon dioxide that is being released. These radical changes include government control of carbon dioxide output enforced by International legislation and treaties to reduce what has been termed our carbon footprint. The situation is deemed so serious that individual nations are being urged to pass strict laws controlling carbon dioxide emissions. International treaties are to be signed and ratified hurriedly to ensure we reduce our carbon dioxide emissions to safeguard our futures.

Hey, hang on a minute. Then why is communist China, an illegally occupied country, who forced the legitimate Chinese government into exile in Taiwan when the bastards took the country and murdered over 20 million Chinese, refusing to take any part in any measures to curb so-called global warming? Incidentally, so do a few other illegally occupied communist countries, like North Korea. If global warming is such a problem, then why isn't the United Nations lecturing them about it? Do the communists stand to gain anything from all this? Keep that thought in mind because we will be back to it shortly.

Let's now take a quick look at the science behind global warming. For a start there is no such thing as a determinable, measureable, precise, world mean temperature. No one knows the exact mean temperature of the earth. In fact, it is impossible to determine the mean temperature of the entire earth and, therefore, to calculate whether it is rising or falling globally.

Secondly, it is impossible to determine how much carbon dioxide is in the atmosphere, or how much of it is produced by man's activity. Carbon emissions cannot be stopped anyway, because every living thing on earth breathes out carbon dioxide. Surprisingly, no doubt to some, this carbon dioxide is *required* by plant life in order to grow and flourish. Through photosynthesis, plants convert carbon dioxide and water into carbohydrates and oxygen. Without carbon dioxide in the atmosphere, all life on earth would die.

In 2009, the key players were in place in Washington and in state government across America to officially label carbon dioxide as a pollutant and enact laws to tax Americans for their carbon footprints. However, carbon dioxide is not a pollutant. Carbon dioxide is a precious gaseous element that is very much needed in the atmosphere to sustain life. Without it, we would all die. It is beautiful stuff.

Thirdly, the global warming models and forecasts touted by the proponents of global warming are based entirely on mathematical models and scenarios that did not include such things as solar activity. Climate models can at best be useful only for explaining climate changes after the fact. Global warming and, indeed, global cooling are natural phenomena over which we have no control.

Not surprisingly therefore, there was an enormous surge of dissent among scientists worldwide regarding global warming. At a UN global warming conference in Poland in 2009 there were over 650 dissenting scientists from all parts of the world who criticized the climate claims made by the UN Intergovernmental Panel on Climate Change, the UN IPCC. Many of these scientists were current and former UN IPCC scientists. That is over twelve times the number of UN scientists who authored the media hyped IPCC 2007 Summary for Policymakers. Indeed, a few prominent scientists have warned that global warming is the most outrageous scientific scam the world has ever seen. Not a word of this was uttered on television, in our school classrooms, or in our newspapers.

Genuine science thrives on the quality of its data, as well as the replication and sharing of that data. In 2009, computer hackers obtained around 160 megabytes of emails from the Climate Research Unit at the University of East Anglia in England. These emails, which were soon confirmed as authentic, brazenly discussed the destruction and hiding of data that did not support global warming claims. Digital technology uncovered a secretive group of scientists who suppressed data, froze others out of the debate, flouted freedom-of-information laws, and boasted about how they had suppressed hard questions about that data. The scientists and academics involved had all, not surprisingly, worked closely with the UN IPCC.

Climategate, as the affair came to be known, even affected Russia. The Russian Institute of Economic Analysis (IEA) issued a report soon after these revelations claiming that the Hadley Centre for Climate Change based at the headquarters of the British Meteorological Office in Exeter *had probably tampered with Russian-climate data. The IEA believes that Russian meteorological-station data did not substantiate the anthropogenic global-warming theory.* Analysts say Russian meteorological stations cover most of the country's territory, and that the Hadley Centre had used data submitted by only 25% of such stations in its reports.

Over 40% of Russian territory was not included in global temperature calculations made by the UN IPCC.

In 2007, the most comprehensive report to date on global warming, issued by the United Nations IPCC, made a shocking claim – the Himalayan glaciers could melt and disappear by the year 2035. These glaciers provide the headwaters for Asia's largest rivers and provide lifelines for millions upon millions of people who live downstream. Melting ice and snow would create mass flooding, followed by mass drought. The glacier story was reported around the world. A spokesman for the World Wildlife Fund, an environmental group of activists and social terrorists, stated, *The deal reached at Copenhagen would have huge ramifications for the lives of hundreds of millions of people who are already highly vulnerable due to widespread poverty.*

It turned out that this report was based solely on a pamphlet published by the WWF itself, which was based on no science at all. When its background became known on the eve of Copenhagen, Rajendra Pachauri, the head of the IPCC, shrugged it off. And this, the guy who in 2007 on behalf of the IPCC picked up the Nobel Peace Prize jointly with Al Gore, and stated that the decision to award the prize to the IPCC was *a clarion call for the protection of the earth as it faces the widespread impacts of climate change*, and who later described the genuine science that contradicted the myth of global warming as *voodoo science.*

Other IPCC claims have turned out to be just as illusory. For example, the IPCC warned that large tracts of the Amazon rain forest might be wiped out by global warming because they are extremely susceptible to even modest decreases in rainfall. The sole source for that claim, reported The Sunday Times of London, was a magazine article written by a pair of climate activists, one of whom worked for the WWF. Worse still, the Times discovered that Mr Pachauri's own Energy and Resources Unit, based in New Delhi, had collected millions in grants to study the effects of glacial melting – all on the strength of a fabricated glacier claim which was endorsed by the same scientist who now runs the unit that got the money.

As Christopher Booker wrote in the London Telegraph, a Canadian analyst identified more than 20 passages in the IPCC report that cited

WWF or Greenpeace reports as their authority. Similarly, the Times of London reported that the claim that global warming could endanger *up to 40 percent* of the Amazon rainforest came from an anti-smoking activist and had no scientific basis whatsoever.

In another global warming episode, hurricane Katrina had hardly finished devastating New Orleans before a 'hurricane war' broke out among climate scientists. The proponents of global warming warned that Katrina was only the beginning, and that we would soon see superstorms of unprecedented fury. There was so little science to corroborate this outrageous theory that a furious Chris Landsea, a meteorologist with the National Hurricane Centre in Miami, withdrew from his participation in the IPCC. Studies have since been published that finally disprove the supposed link between hurricanes and global warming. At first, the fear of monster storms seemed easily justified. Scientists conjectured that as the oceans became warmer, hurricanes would accumulate more energy. However, it is a known scientific fact that wind shear can destroy a hurricane at an early stage and the likelihood of wind shear increases in a warmer climate. For this reason, many computer models now point to a decline in hurricane activity should the earth actually become warmer. This was not reported on television or in our newspapers, and no apologies for terrifying us with nonsense were ever issued.

Funnily enough, despite the whole global warming scam having been exposed, and the lies and treachery from within the UN and the IPCC fully documented, a few world leaders still flew to Copenhagen to attend the UN sponsored Copenhagen Climate summit in support of legislation curbing carbon dioxide emissions. That they attended this charade, which was nothing more than a UN press release, is a clear indication that those who think they control our lives know more about what's going on behind the scenes than they would have us believe.

Robert F. Kennedy Jr. publicly stated that climate change scepticism was treason and that we should treat sceptics as traitors. In 2007, the Weather Channel's Heidi Cullen stated that meteorologists who were sceptical of manmade global warming should be decertified. The emails from the University of East Anglia's Climate Research Unit prove rather that everyone behind the global warming scam are either grossly deceived or are indeed themselves traitors.

Incidentally, on the day the Copenhagen Climate Summit opened, the US Environmental Protection Agency (EPA) claimed jurisdiction over the regulation of carbon emissions by declaring them a danger to human health. Since we operate in an overwhelmingly carbon based economy, such jurisdiction would give the EPA regulatory control over practically everything – building complexes, hospitals, plants, schools, and businesses. Not since the creation of government tax departments have agencies been given such intrusive powers into every aspect of economic life.

So what is the EPA and who controls it? President Obama appointed Lisa Heinzerling to be senior policy counsel on climate change at the EPA, a position that does not require confirmation. Heinzerling has argued that since global warming kills people, a failure to address it is tantamount to somebody not acting on prior knowledge that a homicide is going to take place.

Knowledge that death and suffering will result from our actions leads uncontroversially to a moral obligation to change our behavior, Heinzerling wrote in a 2008 article for the Georgetown Law Journal. *In the United States, knowing killing is condemned in the criminal laws of all 50 states, in modern regulatory laws at the federal level, and in civil jury awards in tort cases. These laws embody a moral commitment against knowing killing that, in traditional criminal contexts, is uncontroversial. It should be no more controversial when it occurs on a global scale.*

Subsequently the Obama administration took steps towards imposing federal limits on what they call climate changing pollution from cars, power plants, and factories, declaring there was compelling scientific evidence that global warming from manmade greenhouse gases endangered Americans' health. In reality, the only thing endangering Americans' health are the pollutants issuing from the lying mouths of those who promote global warming. Perhaps Heinzerling should instead argue against homosexuals who indeed knowingly inject lethal diseases into their partners.

Moreover, it isn't just America that is under attack. One of the ways the European Union plans to combat global warming is by switching food crops to bio fuels. Even the experts within the European Commission admit that in order to meet the EU's bio fuel targets they would eventually need almost all the food producing land in Europe to do so. Global warming is being used as a pretext to engineer famine as we speak.

Here is a scientific fact: greenhouse gasses keep the Earth 30°C warmer than it would be without them. Instead of the average surface temperature being −15°C it is +15°C. Of those gases, carbon dioxide contributes about 10% of the effect, so that equates to around 3°. The pre-industrial level of carbon dioxide in the atmosphere was 280 ppm. So if the heating effect was a linear relationship, each 100 ppm contributes 1°C. With the atmospheric concentration rising by 2 ppm annually, it would go up by 100 ppm every 50 years and we would all fry as per the IPCC predictions, if their science was correct.

However, the heating relationship isn't linear, it is logarithmic. What's the difference? As an example, human hearing is better measured on a logarithmic scale than a linear scale. As sound gets louder, we don't hear it in direct proportion to the volume. On a linear scale, a change between two values is perceived based on the difference between the values. A change from 1 to 2 would be perceived as the same amount of increase from 4 to 5. On a logarithmic scale, a change between two values is perceived based on the *ratio* of the two values. A change from 1 to 2 would be perceived as the same amount as from 4 to 8.

Now here is the scary thing for those with eyes to see and ears to hear. Plant growth shuts down at 150 ppm of carbon dioxide in the atmosphere. During the Dark Ages, the human race was within 30 ppm of extinction. Terrestrial life during the Dark Ages came close to being wiped out due to a *lack* of CO_2 in the atmosphere. If plants were doing climate science instead of the UN IPCC, they would have an entirely different opinion about what constitutes a dangerous carbon dioxide level.

Global warming is scientific nonsense. Hurricanes were predicted to run rampant, they haven't, polar bears were all going to die, they are doing just fine, no cities are sinking beneath the oceans, none of the gloom and doom prophesied has taken place. This is an example of how the shields of the earth belong unto God. Nothing the devil or the United Nations on his behalf can do is going to get through those shields.

Now we must ask the question, why would the god of this world go to such lengths to create a scientific lie of such epic proportions? What is he really up to? Remember China? According to reams of independent surveys on the effects of the legislation to be introduced to tackle global warming, America's economic competitiveness would be severely damaged internationally and at home, principally by raising the cost of doing business to exorbitant levels relative to other countries that had no mandatory carbon emission policies. In effect, if all the carbon reduction legislation drawn up was put into place in America, American businesses and jobs would move oversees to China. This economic avalanche would tip the global economic balance in favour of China and other communist enemies of the United States, leaving America impoverished and vulnerable. This legislation, were it to be ratified and enforced, would mean the total restructuring of western industrial society, a venture that would cost trillions of dollars, while costing China nothing as she continued to *increase* her industrial output of CO_2.

In 1997, the American Senate voted favourably 95-0 on the Byrd-Hagel resolution, which stated amongst other things, that the United States should not sign any international climate change treaty that would mandate greenhouse gas reductions without also requiring specific commitments from developing countries over the same compliance period that would result in serious economic harm to the United States. And isn't it interesting to note that China had the arrogance to publicly criticize some of the policies being pushed through the American political system regarding curbing global warming as being *too weak*. Interestingly, the accords failed at Kyoto and Copenhagen, primarily because the biggest growth in carbon dioxide production is from China.

If the earth isn't in any danger from anything, and global warming is a fabricated lie, and countries like China refuse to have anything to do with it, and as the communists stand to gain as America topples into an abyss of poverty and recession over it, then isn't it conceivable that global warming is in fact a weapon? The communists know they cannot take America militarily, so isn't it conceivable they would try other means to cripple and destroy her? Do we have enemies that hate us so much that they would assemble and detonate economic weapons of mass destruction among us? If you do not think so, then you have no concept of evil.

Consider this deeply – without question, one of the greatest security threats of an international climate treaty would be to degrade the economies of the United States and its allies to such an extent they would be deprived of the capability to defend themselves militarily. Our military forces are the largest consumers of fossil fuels in the world. Without fossil fuels, our military forces could not operate. Who stands to benefit from that? War is not waged exclusively on military battlefields.

The alarm over climate change is nothing more than an instrument of social control, a pretext for major business and political battle. The sweeping energy and global warming counter measures touted, including the so-called cap-and-trade bills, are nothing more than invented energy taxes designed to impose wide scale economic destruction through devastating energy price increases and consequent job losses. These bills contain regulations on everything from light bulb standards to the specifications of hot tubs, and they would completely reshape our western economies and impoverish us, turning us into third world countries while our communist enemies would flourish at our expense. The proponents of global warming argue that cap-and-trade is necessary to save the world, but they are liars and traitors because the world has never been in any danger from anything.

The same is true regarding the entire environmental and green movements. The earth is not in any danger from anything, so environmentalism is founded on lies and deception. The god of this world has only stealing, killing, and destroying in his heart when he moves his agendas. Wind farms mean no nuclear reactors. No nuclear reactors means no enriching of uranium. No enriched uranium means no nuclear weapons. It is our defences that are being systematically dismantled.

Environmentalism has nothing whatsoever to do with saving the planet, it has everything to do with destroying us. The more green legislation that is passed through our parliaments and senates, the more costly it is for us to do business, the higher our fuel bills rise, the more we destroy our economies, the more we cannot afford our military, the more of our businesses move to China, the closer we come to ruin. We are on the brink.

Like global warming, environmentalism is an economic weapon of mass destruction. Check the money that founded and finances the worldwide environmental movement, and you will uncover not philanthropists who love you, but men with hatreds so passionate they seek only your destruction.

To sum up, there is no scientific data to prove that the earth is becoming warmer. The science we have been fed was manipulated and forged. UN scientists lied and the papers published their lies around the world. Global warming is entirely fabricated. Indeed, the most prominent proponent of global warming, Al Gore, isn't even a scientist. His scurrilous television documentary was banned from being shown in British schools due to a lack of any scientific validity whatsoever. Would we go to a double glazing salesman for advice on a serious medical condition? Yet we allow pop stars, politicians and news editors to educate us on world affairs, military strategy and science?

Global warming is an economic nuclear weapon that was assembled to destroy us by swinging the balance of economic and military might to our enemies.

This is war.

20. Health and Nutrition

If, as suggested in the previous chapter, there are those who would devise, design, construct, and detonate economic weapons of mass destruction in our midst, might there not be other targets within our civilisations that would interest them? If our enemies are so weak militarily, that to consider deploying military forces against us is not an option, isn't it conceivable that they would attack us in other ways? Do you really think the god of this world cares how he steals, kills, and destroys?

What other ways are there? What about our food and water? Wouldn't the same people who invented the lie of global warming to fabricate a pretext to campaign for destructive economic laws to destroy us also attempt to dismantle our trade laws so they could poison our food?

I'll be frank here, this chapter should be a book in its own right. However I am not here to write an encyclopaedia on how the god of this world operates, I am more concerned in this class with showing people how to walk by the spirit. To write a dissertation on the entire food processing industry is something I will not even contemplate. I am simply going to rustle up a few delicacies to give you a taste for how the god of this world steals, kills, and destroys.

Here is an appetiser – since the early 1970s an entire stratum of British middle class food retailers has all but been wiped out. They no longer exist. Think about that. An entire stratum of British middle class has disappeared in just a few decades. Our butchers, greengrocers, bakers, fishmongers, and other middle class food producers and retailers are almost extinct. Where did they go? Who devoured them?

Other stratums of British middle class such as family owned shoe shops, clothes shops, and a whole host of other middle class family businesses have also disappeared. These middle class businesses were excellent employers who provided homely places to work, paid good wages, and often rewarded their staff with shares of the profits they made. They are all gone. Does this remind us of anything we have read in the word recently?

> Deuteronomy 28:1-4
> And it shall come to pass, if thou shalt hearken diligently unto the voice of the LORD thy God, to observe *and* to do all his commandments which I command thee this day, that the LORD thy God will set thee on high above all nations of the earth:
>
> And all these blessings shall come on thee, and overtake thee, if thou shalt hearken unto the voice of the LORD thy God.
>
> Blessed *shalt* thou *be* in the city, and blessed *shalt* thou *be* in the field.
>
> Blessed *shall be* the fruit of thy body, and the fruit of thy ground, and the fruit of thy cattle, the increase of thy kine, and the flocks of thy sheep.
>
> Deuteronomy 28:15-18,33
> But it shall come to pass, if thou wilt not hearken unto the voice of the LORD thy God, to observe to do all his commandments and his statutes which I command thee this day; that all these curses shall come upon thee, and overtake thee:
>
> Cursed *shalt* thou *be* in the city, and cursed *shalt* thou *be* in the field.
>
> Cursed *shall be* thy basket and thy store.
>
> Cursed *shall be* the fruit of thy body, and the fruit of thy land, the increase of thy kine, and the flocks of thy sheep.
>
> The fruit of thy land, and all thy labours, shall a nation which thou knowest not eat up; and thou shalt be only oppressed and crushed alway:

Whenever and wherever we live according to the principles of God's word, our lives are blessed abundantly. Whenever and wherever we turn away from God, we lose everything. Today our food is indeed cursed, and others are devouring the fruit of our land and the fruits of our labours. How does the devil accomplish this? What mechanics are involved?

The British Merchant Navy was once the pride of the seven seas, their sleek hulls gracing exotic horizons as they hauled cargoes to all parts of the world. The shipyards that built and supported this navy were once the proud flagship of British industry. The British Merchant Navy barely still exists, and the shipyards are gone. What happened? Many things. Back in the 1970s, Russia, an illegally occupied communist country, undercut British shipping freight charges by up to 70%. The communists subsidised the Russian merchant navy to put us out of business. At the same time trade unions appeared like a rash all over Britain and seduced our workers out onto the streets to protest against imagined grievances that didn't exist. The British ship building industry became uneconomical and collapsed, and the workers were all out of jobs.

In other words, the destruction of the British merchant navy and the supporting shipyards was planned and ruthlessly executed. The destruction of our industries and wealth is still the intent of communism and trade unionism, and they do so under the pretext of fighting for the rights of the working man. Health and Safety also puts us out of business by crippling us with expensive trade laws that make us uncompetitive. There are many other economic weapons deployed which are destroying us, like litigation, taking our employers to court to see what we can get out of them. If that isn't biting the hand that feeds you, what is?

China on the other hand isn't shackled and restrained by a mountain of insane litigation and Health and Safety laws. Suing the businesses that employ you is insane. Put all your employers out of business and who are you going to turn to for jobs? The trade unions? China? Do you think the communists are going to send you a welfare cheque every week when your country caves in? They have the gas chambers of the new world order lined up for you.

Moses knew what would happen to people if they ever walked away from God, and that's why he warned us about it thousands of years ago.

Deuteronomy 28:33
The fruit of thy land, and all thy labours, shall a nation which thou knowest not eat up; and thou shalt be only oppressed and crushed alway:

When it comes to food and drink, there are many issues to consider. For example, growing food in soil that is fertile is the way God intended food to grow. Wholesome food is nourishing, gives us strength, and keeps us healthy. If the necessary nutrients and vitamins we need for good health are not in the ground to begin with, they will not be in the food produced from it. There is no magic involved in growing food.

When I was young, I used to love to go fishing. One of my favourite places to dig for worms was alongside a stone dyke bordering a small plot of waste ground behind the local school. One day I noticed someone had ploughed this piece of ground and planted potatoes. Undaunted, off I went with my spade to dig around the edges of the ploughed ground. As I started to dig, I got the fright of my young life. All the worms were soggy and dead, dissolved by fertilizers. I remember going home feeling very uneasy. Let's get one thing clear, the soil, the ground in which food grows, is supposed to be full of worms, bugs, beetles, and small mammals. They have jobs to do. God put them in there for a reason. Pesticides and fertilizers do not protect us and make our food healthier, they poison the ground and the food we eat.

Root vegetables absorb herbicides, pesticides, and fungicides that we put in the soil. In the case of potatoes – the nation's most popular vegetable – they are treated with fungicides during the growing season and then sprayed with herbicides to kill off the fibrous vines before harvesting. Washing is not enough to remove the chemicals that have been absorbed into the flesh. One expert who talked with potato growers made the remarkable discovery that for the most part they never ate the potatoes they sold but had separate plots where they grew potatoes for themselves without all the chemicals.

Traditional food processing makes food more digestible and preserves it so we can store it. Foods like sausage and haggis can be kept for longer periods than say fresh meat. Other processed foods include cheese, pickles, and wine, amongst many others. In the past, farmers, bakers, cheese makers, and other artisans provided us with delicious foods from a hard working and honest middle class. This traditional food processing increased the nutritional value of food, made it more digestible, and we all enjoyed healthier lives.

Then along came industrial food processing. No longer were we served fresh wholesome delicious foods produced in our communities by people we would know by name. Instead we were sold foods processed in faceless factories using processes which destroy the nutrients in food making it more difficult to digest, and which rely on harmful products for their processes, such as sugar, bleached flour, processed and hydrogenated oils, and artificial additives.

Consider this, in days past, if a butcher or a baker produced substandard food, word got around the communities quickly, folks would take their custom elsewhere and the bad guys went out of business. Is that not how it should be? Do we really need politicians and bureaucrats, foreign ones at that, legislating what we eat, who can produce it, and where we can buy it? There is plenty of good food around; we just do not get it. Healthy eggs from healthy chickens, fresh local meat reared on proper grass, home grown vegetables, fresh full cream milk from the local dairy, fresh fish from local boats, cheese, fresh bread without chemicals that make your ass itch, and other wholesome foods are available. Rather than take the time to source them, off we go to the supermarkets and fill our trolleys with God knows what from who knows where.

Finding this difficult to digest? Okay, let's start our day with breakfast. In the past, we enjoyed hearty breakfasts of wholesome foods produced by local farmers and bakers. Now we buy mass produced breakfast cereals that are produced by a process called extrusion. Slurry is produced from the grain and then extruded through a little hole at high pressure and high temperature. The shapes are formed depending on the shape of the hole, and these shapes are then sprayed with a coating of oil to give them crunch. All dry cereals that come in boxes are made this way. Just how nutritious is this stuff?

There have been a number of experiments conducted with rats fed breakfast cereals. In one experiment, four groups of rats were given special diets. One group received plain whole wheat, water, and synthetic vitamins and minerals, a second group received a breakfast cereal, water, and the same nutrient solution, a third group was given only water, and the fourth group was given nothing but water and chemical nutrients. The rats that received the whole wheat lived for over a year. The rats that got nothing but water and vitamins lived about two months. The rats that lived on water alone died after about a month. Amazingly, the rats given the vitamins, water, and breakfast cereal died within two weeks. That's right, the rats fed breakfast cereal died before the rats that got no food at all. Oh, and it was nothing to do with malnutrition, autopsy revealed dysfunction of the pancreas, liver, and kidneys, and degeneration of the nerves of the spine, which are all signs of insulin shock.

Yet another experiment was conducted in the 1960s. Researchers at Ann Arbor University were given a number of rats that they divided into three groups. One group received corn flakes and water, a second group was given the cardboard box that the corn flakes came in and water, and the third group received rat food and water. The rats in the third group remained in good health throughout the experiment. The rats eating the cardboard cereal box became lethargic and eventually died of malnutrition. However, the rats fed corn flakes and water died before the rats fed the cardboard box. Not only that, but before death, the corn flake rats developed schizophrenic behaviour, threw fits, bit each other, and finally went into convulsions. Fact: there is more nourishment in the cardboard box most breakfast cereals are packaged in than in the actual cereals they contain. Even cereals sold in health food shops are made the same way.

Although I have a Certificate of Natural Sciences awarded by the Open University, I am not a scientist, and I do not claim to know how to evaluate this information scientifically. However, I do know my bible and I've learned a thing or two about the world in my time. If you look around you won't find any scientific studies on breakfast cereals and their effects on human life readily available to the public. They did exist at one time, but they have all mysteriously disappeared, just like the data on the research into global warming.

The god of this world goes to extraordinary lengths to destroy our food and make us sick. A whole chapter could be written on the poisoning of our cattle, for example, starting with food fed to them they were not designed to eat. Cattle were designed to eat grass, but some farmers today are more concerned with fattening up their animals faster for slaughter and making more money. More money for cattle farmers may mean lower prices at the grocery store, but it also means a lot less nutrition for us. A recent comprehensive study conducted by the USDA and researchers from Clemson University found that compared with corn-fed beef, grass-fed beef is higher in beta-carotene, vitamin E, omega-3s, conjugated linoleic acid (CLA), calcium, magnesium, and potassium; lower in inflammatory omega-6s; and lower in saturated fats that have been linked to heart disease. One expert in the field remarked: *we need to respect the fact that cows are herbivores, and that does not mean feeding them corn mixed with chicken manure.* Now here's the thing – a lot of farmers only do this because the supermarkets would not buy their products otherwise and they would be forced out of business. A strong middle class of food retailers like butchers wouldn't buy such animals, which would mean farmers would raise their cattle properly, which would be good for us. Do you begin to see how this works? A strong middle class is essential to a healthy country.

Cows are supposed to eat grass, not industrial waste products like chicken shit. That is what they are feeding you in the supermarkets. Cows fed this filth produce watery milk that is very low in fat. In fact, most of the milk products that make it to our supermarket shelves should not even be called milk because it is no longer milk. This sterile pasteurised industrial waste is sometimes so dead that bugs will not even eat it. Milk is supposed to go sour, but supermarkets would not be able to sell it if it did so they destroy it to lengthen its shelf life and fatten their profits.

Do I even need to mention skimmed milk? Where did that stuff come from anyway? Is it really healthy and good for us? Its history is quite illuminating. It is an industrial waste by-product of milk that once cost money to dispose of. Then someone came up with the idea of sticking it in plastic bottles, shoving it on supermarket shelves (there are the supermarkets again), and calling it fat-free and healthy. It is not healthy, it is of no nutritional value whatsoever. It is industrial waste that once cost money to dispose of and which now turns them a profit.

What about babies and mother's milk? Every farmer knows how important it is to ensure new born baby animals get mother's milk immediately to stand the best chances for survival and to enjoy a healthy life. Breast-feeding babies is the best for baby and mother. Depriving babies and mothers of that personal human touch, and instead feeding infants on chemical powders must have the god of this world creased over in laughter. Only in dire health situations that put the mother and child at risk should powdered milk be considered. It should only be used as a last resort because of health issues.

Margarine anyone? After all, it's much healthier than butter isn't it? Is it? Margarine was discovered in 1869 by Hippolyte Mège Mouriès, a French food research chemist, in response to Napoleon III's request for a cheap alternative to butter to supply to the French army. In a laboratory, Mège Mouriès solidified purified fat, after which the resulting substance was pressed in a thin cloth, which process formed stearine and discharged oil. This oil formed the basis of what he termed margaric acid.

Food manufacturers cannot use liquid oils in baked goods or for frying, and they are not spreadable. This does not make them money so liquid vegetable oils are hardened to make margarine. Unfortunately, all the vitamins and anti-oxidants are removed in the process, but the solvents and the pesticides remain. The stinking grey cottage cheese filth that's produced is mixed with emulsifiers, steam cleaned to get rid of the smell, and then bleached to get rid of the colour before being turned into margarine by adding artificial flavours and synthetic vitamins and being packaged in colourful plastic tubs.

Margarine is often advertised as being derived from polyunsaturated oils. However, manufacturers surprisingly neglect to mention that the oil is changed into margarine by hydrogenation, a process by which the oil is saturated with hydrogen so it solidifies from a liquid. Once a vegetable oil is hydrogenised, a new fat has been created. Such artificially manufactured hydrogenated vegetable fats are a very recent addition to the human diet and our bodies have no experience with them. Margarine is entirely fabricated, artificial, and synthetic. It is not a food, it is a manmade chemical which is just a molecule or two away from being a plastic.

Elaborate statistical analysis of the incidence of heart disease and the consumption of hydrogenated fats in England has shown a dramatic and detailed correlation between the two. Where margarine and solid vegetable shortenings are used in significant quantities, the rate of heart attack is always higher than where they are not. And here comes television again – the advertising campaign launched by margarine manufacturers was once termed as a most unprincipled food promotion, with television commercials described as noisy, ubiquitous, and shameless. Lacking real scientific information about how the hydrogenation process affects human health and the hazards of too much processed polyunsaturated fat in our bodies, we began switching from butter to margarine and from animal fats to vegetable oils.

Hydrogenated fats have a higher melting point than fats that are liquid at room temperature, and as such they do not circulate in blood properly or move through tissues as liquids. They may even prevent the normal transport of nutrients in and out of cells. Hydrogenated fats produce a deficiency of essential fatty acids by destroying them, or producing abnormal toxic fatty acids. Deficiency of essential fatty acids is a contributory cause in neurological diseases, heart disease, arteriosclerosis, skin disease, various degenerative conditions such as cataract and arthritis, and cancer. They also prevent the proper formation of bile in the liver from cholesterol, and therefore can elevate blood cholesterol. Margarine most likely raises cholesterol and yet it is promoted as reducing it.

Trans fatty acids are the type of fat molecules produced by the process referred to as partial hydrogenation, which rearranges hydrogen atoms to produce a fat that is solid at room temperature. Natural saturated fatty acids have molecules that pack together easily so they tend to be solid at room temperature. In a saturated fatty acid each carbon atom is joined to two hydrogen atoms arranged in pairs. This molecular structure is essential to our cell membranes for chemical reactions to occur.

During partial hydrogenation, one of the hydrogen atoms in a pair is moved to the other side of the molecule, forming a trans fatty acid, such as elaidic acid. This causes the molecules to straighten out so that they pack together easily and form a solid fat at room temperature. However, when these trans fatty acids are incorporated into the cell membrane they are missing the hydrogen pairs needed for chemical reactions to occur. The result is damaging at the cellular level. Interestingly, all margarines and spreads contain trans fats as well as many other artificial ingredients. Virtually all packaged or processed foods contain trans fatty acids. Most desserts sold today are nothing more than sugar, partially hydrogenated oils, and a long list of artificial ingredients.

Butter is a natural product and is made with real cream, making it a far healthier food than margarine. There is no scientific evidence to the contrary. Butter has been in the diet for thousands of years so you can have confidence in it. Butter is no more fattening than margarine. It is the advertising of margarine by the world that has convinced us otherwise. The fat content of butter and margarine are identical but the fats in butter are important to a well-balanced diet while the fats in margarine are probably killing us. A study reported in the prestigious journal Atherosclerosis reported that neither milk, cream, cheese, nor butter have any consistent effect upon blood cholesterol.

The last few decades have seen a huge increase in the consumption of processed vegetable oils, while at the same time we have seen a proportional decline in the consumption of animal fats. These processed oils look clean and bright on the grocer's shelves, but even a cursory glance at how these oils are produced is enough to show us what they really are.

The processing of these oils begins with extraction from seeds, a process that requires high temperatures and pressures and often involves solvents. The oils go through stages of development and refinement that involve caustic refining, bleaching, and deodorizing. Most of these steps involve heat, and produce toxic breakdown products known as free radicals, which, incidentally, can cause cancer. These vegetable oils look clean, but they are completely unnatural and carcinogenic. Of course, these oils are also loaded with residual pesticides from the original seeds.

Many diseases have been associated with trans fatty acids, such as heart disease, cancer, digestive disorders, and degeneration of joints and tendons, which is just one reason why we have so many hip replacements today. Trans fats are associated with autoimmune disease, skin problems, growth problems in children, and learning disabilities.

It goes without saying that these artificial products are obviously priced to sell. The supermarkets make fortunes while our middle class food producers go out of business. Our middle class goes out of business because we do not buy their foods. They cannot afford to produce them any cheaper to compete with the supermarkets so they go out of business. That is how the communists destroyed the UK's Merchant Navy, and that is how they are destroying our food producing middle class. Once the middle class competition is gone, prices skyrocket. This is how economic warfare is waged. Have you ever wondered who actually owns the supermarkets?

Don't think turning to other mass produced 'healthy' foods, like orange juice, is the answer either. Oranges are a heavily sprayed crop grown in ground that is basically dead. If what we need is not in the ground to begin with, it will not be in the fruit. The sprays used are cholinesterase inhibitors, which are neurotoxins. When they put the oranges in vats and squeeze them, all these pesticides go into the juice. The left over citrus peels are then used as cattle feed and, funnily enough, it is these processed cakes (another industrial waste), loaded with cholinesterase and organophosphates which studies have shown are probably responsible for Bovine Spongiform Encephalitis or BSE (mad cow disease). If cows were fed grass grown in fertile healthy ground, we would not have these problems. Why are cows not fed grass? More to the point, why are we buying poisoned food and stuffing our faces with it?

Monosodium glutamate (MSG) is worthy of mention. It is an artificial flavouring that breaks down the nervous system. We have known about the problems caused by monosodium glutamate since 1957 when scientists found that mice became blind and obese when administered the drug by feeding tube. Monosodium glutamate is a neurotoxic substance that causes a wide range of reactions, from temporary headaches to permanent brain damage, and can be attributed to a huge increase in Alzheimer's, brain cancer, seizures, multiple sclerosis, and diseases of the nervous system, as well as being associated with violent behaviour and causing obesity. Interestingly, most processed foods contain monosodium glutamate, and in the late 1950s, it was even added to baby food. It is now more commonly known as hydrolyzed protein. Monosodium glutamate is in nearly all processed foods. The world sold it to us as a flavour enhancer.

A chapter could be written on the drug caffeine. Yes, caffeine is a registered drug on which we can become dependent, and which will induce withdrawal symptoms if we do not keep up with our daily fixes. Headaches, migraines, and nausea are all associated withdrawal symptoms. Did you ever stop to consider why you crave chocolate all the time? It is a drug. Well, the god of this world had to come up with something pretty tasty to wean us off fruit, didn't he?

We have not even touched on alcohol and tobacco. Need we? Alcoholics do not need to be told they have a problem, they know. People who smoke do not need to be told it is killing them, they know. Perhaps understanding the world and how it works and who is supplying them with their alcohol and tobacco while stealing all their money from them may give them the motivation to quit their habits and get back to healthy living. How many guinness drinkers suffer from piles? They don't mention that in their glossy television adverts, do they? No, only real men get drunk, according to our televisions.

Ever noticed how seductive alcohol advertisements are? The god of this world knows how to seduce, but what amazes me is how folks do not seem to be able to recognise that the problems they have stem many times from things like alcohol. I once read a book by a soldier who was always depressed, who was violent, who believed he was going insane, and who eventually committed suicide. He blamed the army, yet the root of his problem was very evident – he was an alcoholic. If he'd quit drinking, his problems would have disappeared.

While we are here, alcohol provides a good working illustration of how the god of this world operates. Many folks think being drunk is cool and fun (probably because they watch those seductive adverts on television we just mentioned), but the consequences are anything but fun. If folks had any idea how much misery drink has caused, how many lives it has ruined, how many marriages it has wrecked, how many businesses it has destroyed, how many deaths it has been responsible for, they would not get drunk. The word is clear on drunkenness. There can be no mistaking what it is saying.

> Proverbs 20:1
> Wine *is* a mocker, strong drink *is* raging: and whosoever is deceived thereby is not wise.

Isaiah 5:11,12
Woe unto them that rise up early in the morning, *that* they may follow strong drink; that continue until night, *till* wine inflame them!

And the harp, and the viol, the tabret, and pipe, and wine, are in their feasts: but they regard not the work of the LORD, neither consider the operation of his hands.

Note that the bible does not say we shouldn't drink alcohol, but that we shouldn't get drunk. Alcohol can actually be quite good for you. Good quality wines, for example, can be therapeutic and encourage good health.

1 Timothy 5:23
Drink no longer water, but use a little wine for thy stomach's sake and thine often infirmities.

I think most of us know the difference between having a social drink and being a drunk, but just in case you don't see it, try this:

Proverbs 23:29-35
Who hath woe? who hath sorrow? who hath contentions? who hath babbling? who hath wounds without cause? who hath redness of eyes?

They that tarry long at the wine; they that go to seek mixed wine.

Look not thou upon the wine when it is red, when it giveth his colour in the cup, *when* it moveth itself aright.

At the last it biteth like a serpent, and stingeth like an adder.

Thine eyes shall behold strange women, and thine heart shall utter perverse things.

Yea, thou shalt be as he that lieth down in the midst of the sea, or as he that lieth upon the top of a mast.

They have stricken me, *shalt thou say, and* I was not sick; they have beaten me, *and* I felt *it* not: when shall I awake? I will seek it yet again.

Don't waggle your tongue at me either and say I don't know what I'm talking about. I can personally testify from experience that every single point God makes in this section of scripture is entirely true. I've been beaten and felt it not, my eyes have beheld strange women, my heart has uttered perverse things, and I've felt the sting of the serpent's bite. I've woken early in the morning with red eyes and reached for a can of beer. If you are sick of your life and want a new one, try doing things God's way. This is your chance to change. You can have another life if you want it. I was once a drunk and I got out of it and so can you if you want to. By the way, it is no coincidence that strong drinks are called *spirits*.

I've touched on quite a number of foods, but not nearly enough. You can look at the production and processing of any food and soon realise that what we are being fed is not only not good for us, but it makes us sick. Even fresh wholesome food like salmon is now raised artificially, the young salmon fed filthy industrial waste products which is then fed to us. God did not intend for salmon to be crammed into pens and fed soy, chicken shit, and hydrolyzed chicken feathers. Farmed salmon is lower in vitamin D and higher in contaminants, including carcinogens, PCBs, brominated flame-retardants, and pesticides such as dioxin and DDT. There is also concern about the high levels of antibiotics and pesticides used to treat these fish. When you eat farmed salmon, you are dosed with the same drugs and chemicals that were administered to them.

As we've touched on industrial waste, we might as well look into it as it comes up a lot in food processing. Turning industrial waste into lucrative money spinning industries is not something new. In 1997, the Seattle Times wrote an investigative article that revealed that industrial wastes such as lead, arsenic, and even radioactive material were being turned into fertilizers for farms and gardens. Did you know that harmful industrial waste is now put into paints, soaps, cosmetics and many other everyday products? Look, the devil wants us sick and dead, and everything he does is geared towards that goal.

Do you remember the foot and mouth epidemic that put a third of British livestock farmers out of business? That particular strain of foot and mouth was developed in a British research laboratory. Why did the British Labour government attack the farmers? The farmers stood against the government on fuel prices by organising the nationwide blockades at petrol stations and refineries at the time. The foot and mouth epidemic was a deliberate offensive action by the British Labour government against our farmers for daring to stand against them. Did you know that months before the outbreak of the epidemic, the British government had stockpiled mountains of old railway sleepers with which to burn the corpses of diseased animals? They knew the epidemic was coming. Did you also know that foot and mouth antidotes were available, but they were never offered to our farmers because the United Nations forbade the British government to help them.

Have you any idea how many billions of dollars cold and flu remedies bring in every year? Has it ever crossed your mind that the drug companies who make so much money from misery could perhaps be deliberately infecting us every year with new strains of colds and flu's? All those laboratories in the Far East researching cold and flu bugs are not doing it for your good, but to make money out of you. They develop new strains of flu, blame it on chickens and swine, infect a few aircraft flying to international destinations, and truckloads of your cash chinks into their bank accounts. If you don't think this is going on, you have no concept of the god who runs your world and the greedy cunts who work for him.

Do you suffer from coughing, runny noses, wheezing and skin complaints? Does your doctor tell you it might be due to the faeces of dust mites infesting your pillows, mattresses and duvets, or do they simply prescribe you drugs to alleviate the symptoms? Dust mite proof bedding is readily available, but does your doctor tell you that? Or do they just type your symptoms into a computer and give you prescriptions at tax payer's expense that make drug companies billions in revenue?

Finding all this a bit hard to swallow? I have not even started. Ever heard of fluoride? Everyone has heard of fluoride. It is promoted on billboards everywhere by smiling folks with cosmetic white teeth holding up toothbrushes laden with a good dollop of the stuff.

Fluoride is a nuclear waste derived from the production of uranium, as well as pesticides, fertilizers, aluminium, iron, steel, copper, lead, brick, cement, and glass. That's right, fluoride is another industrial waste. Can you see a pattern emerging here regarding industrial waste? A few grams of the stuff is enough to kill you. It is more poisonous than lead and just slightly less poisonous than arsenic. Fluoride is widely used as rat poison. A family-sized tube of fluoride toothpaste contains enough rat poison to kill a child. Fluoride has been linked to pains in bones and joints, sensations of burning, prickling and tingling in the limbs, muscle weakness, chronic fatigue, gastrointestinal disorders, backache, osteoarthritis, and cancer. Fluoride gradually builds up in the bones and causes adverse changes to bone structure. Quite a few studies have shown that fluoridation leads to increases in hip fractures and that the tensile strength of the hip is destroyed over time by fluoride ingestion. Studies have also pointed to fluoride as a cause for infertility among women. The most astonishing fact of all is that fluoride does absolutely nothing for your teeth.

Fluoride compounds added to our water, toothpaste, and supplement tablets (including some vitamins) were never tested for safety before approval. Recent independent research by scientists not associated with dental trade organisations has shown that fluoride is neurotoxic and lowers IQ. A scientific paper published shows that fluoride builds up in the brains of animals when exposed to moderate levels, resulting in brain damage and adverse behavioural patterns. The toxic effect of fluoride on the nervous system has subsequently been confirmed.

A study published in Brain Research showed that rats given fluoride in their water to drink developed lesions in their brains similar to Alzheimer's disease, and dementia. In addition, evidence pointed to possible damage to the blood brain barrier from extended fluoride exposure.

One Department of Health in America found that bone cancer in male children was between two and seven times greater in areas where water was fluoridated. A recent study has linked fluoridation of water to uterine cancer deaths. Several studies have shown that fluoridated water often causes gastrointestinal symptoms, stomatitis, joint pains, polydipsia, headaches, visual disturbances, muscular weakness, and extreme tiredness. Fluoride can cause severe skeletal fluorosis at high levels.

Decades of ingestion of fluoride can be expected to cause these symptoms in large numbers of people because fluoride builds up in the body over a period of years. A clinical study in New Zealand showed that fluoride ingestion might be a contributing factor in the development of Repetitive Strain Injury since such ingestion may encourage the development of apatite crystal formation. Surprisingly, an increasing number of children are experiencing dental fluorosis, which is a permanent adverse structural change to the teeth due to fluoride ingestion. As fluoride builds up in different parts of the body, it can disrupt the actions of many key enzymes. This fact has been known for decades. Many non-organic juices also have large amounts of fluoride in them from pesticide residues. Fluoride is not good for you. It is rat poison.

Of what we have touched on so far, could all this be related to the love of money being the root of all evil? Yes, it can. As early as 1930, companies and organisations used the promotion of fluoridation as a way to avoid lawsuits due to dumping toxic wastes. Fluoride once cost vast sums of money to dispose of. Not only did these business gurus find a way to avoid these costs, they conjured up new markets, making themselves fortunes in the process. Now they sell their toxic industrial wastes to us for profit and we ingest their poisons into our bodies and smile as we get sick and die.

If fluoride is so bad, you would think that mountains of scientific reports and studies into the effects of decades of this medication use would be readily available, but they are not. Any genuine scientific research on this subject is quietly ushered to the bottom drawers of dusty filing cabinets, no doubt along with all the global warming and breakfast cereal scientific reports. Moreover, just like the global warming camp, with all their official organisations and government and United Nations departments, all the prominent health associations assure us fluoride is lovely tasty stuff that is good for you. No government or United Nations health department will tell you that fluoride is bad for you. Instead, they close ranks and alleviate our fears with quiet words and disarming smiles. We are being hysterical, they soothe, claiming that internet research into fluoride is merely scaremongering. Really? So why has fluoride been used as rat poison for nearly a century? The god of this world is a liar and a murderer, as clearly stated by Jesus Christ when confronting the robed religious fruitcakes of his day.

John 8:44
Ye are of *your* father the devil, and the lusts of your father ye will do. He was a murderer from the beginning, and abode not in the truth, because there is no truth in him. When he speaketh a lie, he speaketh of his own: for he is a liar, and the father of it.

You know, we do not have to use fluoride toothpastes. In fact, there is one brand readily available with none in it. Yet off we go to the supermarket and pick up the little coloured boxes adorned with smiling white teeth and drop them into our shopping trolleys, trusting everything we see and hear on television. You have to admire the god of this world because he is brilliant at what he does.

Interestingly, concerned that too many young children were swallowing toothpaste, the Food and Drug Administration in America did require the following warning to appear on tubes of fluoridated toothpaste: *Use only a pea sized amount and supervise child's brushing and rinsing (to minimize swallowing).* Parents were warned to *keep the toothpaste out of the reach of children under 6* and to *seek professional help or contact a poison centre immediately* if more than what was used for brushing was accidentally swallowed.

In 1999, a union of 1,200 scientists, doctors, and lawyers announced their opposition to water fluoridation because of a growing body of evidence that indicated a causal link between it and cancer, genetic damage, neurological impairment and bone pathology. The American Dental Association for its part stated that *the overwhelming weight of scientific evidence indicates that fluoridation of community water supplies is both safe and effective.* The Washington State Dental Association calls fluoridation *one of the most significant public health success stories of the century.* Who controls the American Dental Association? Who is making the decisions for us in the State Dental Associations? If fluoride is but one of a number of significant health stories, what else are they up to?

Dr. John Colquhoun, a dental officer in New Zealand wrote a paper entitled *Why I changed my mind about water fluoridation*. Colquhoun had become concerned by the apparent link between fluoridation and weakened bones. *Common sense*, he wrote, *tells us that if a poison circulating in a child's body can damage the tooth-forming cells, then other harm also is likely*. In 1984, Colquhoun warned the Auckland Regional Authority that some of the children with dental fluorosis could also suffer damage to their bones. He was scorned and derided for challenging the dental establishment.

In 1990, the first study suggesting a link between fluoridated water and hip fractures in the elderly was published. The report contained this interesting comment – *hip fracture rates have increased dramatically, independently of the increasing age of populations.*

Colquhoun also wrote: *clinical trials have demonstrated that when fluoride is used in an attempt to treat osteoporosis (in the belief it strengthened bones), it actually caused more hip fractures. That is, when fluoride accumulates in bones, it weakens them.*

In the 1980s, studies in Finland revealed that osteoporosis sufferers had extremely high levels of fluoride in their bones. Finland immediately banned fluoridation because of the study. Holland banned fluoridation of water supplies after studies revealed that it caused reversible neuromuscular and gastrointestinal harm.

The first public proposal that the United States should fluoridate its water supplies was made not by a doctor or a dentist, but by Gerald J Cox, an industry scientist working for the Aluminium Company of America (Alcoa). Industries worldwide feared a coming rush of lawsuits by fluoride damage claims and public outcry that could force new government regulations and cost billions in pollution control. In 1939, Cox proposed that fluoride be used to reduce cavities in children. After fluoridating lab rats, he concluded that fluoride reduced cavities and declared, *The case should be regarded as proved.*

This was, of course, a brilliant piece of public relations. Fluoride was introduced as a health enhancing substance and quickly added to the environment for the sake of our children. Anyone who stood against having rat poison put in their water and in their toothpaste was publicly ridiculed as a quack or a lunatic. According to Dr Yiamouyiannis who received his BS in Biochemistry from the University of Chicago and his PhD from the University of Rhode Island, fluoridation is responsible for the chronic poisoning of over 130 million Americans.

Fluoride is known to cause skin eruptions such as atopic dermatitis, eczema, or urticaria, gastric distress, headache, weakness, pains in joints and muscles, dental fluorosis, bone damage, genetic damage, infertility, cancer, and weakened immune systems. Fluoride is used as treatments at dentist's offices, is put in our toothpaste and mouth rinse products, and it is in food that has been prepared with fluoridated water. Fluoride is rat poison.

By the way, none of this is news to the medical world. The Journal of the American Medical Association and the New England Journal of Medicine have both reported greater incidence of hip fractures in fluoridated areas. The National Institute of Environmental and Health Services has linked fluoridation with cancer. A book by Dr. John Yiamouyiannis, titled Fluoride, The Aging Factor, shows that the drug causes a premature aging process. He notes that in areas where fluoride is consumed in the drinking water, there are higher rates of bone disorders (skeletal fluorosis, osteoporosis, and arthritic pain), and people suffer from brown decaying teeth.

Yet even with all this concern from so many knowledgeable men and women, fluoride is still put in our toothpaste and into our drinking water. Why? Isn't it perhaps time we started questioning what the world tells us? Isn't it perhaps time we took a second look at our televisions and began to question what is coming out of them and where it is coming from? Almost all the beverages we drink, such as beer, fizzy drinks, and juice, are made with fluoridated water. Fish and other foods contain fluoride, and the vegetables we eat are often grown with fertilizers that contain fluoride. We cook most of our foods in fluoridated water. And isn't it incredible how in just the last few decades since fluoridation of our water and the introduction of fluoride into our toothpaste that the incidence of hip replacements and cancer, as well as female infertility and a host of other medical conditions, has exploded in our societies. Do you think this is coincidence?

You have to ask the question – if fluoride is such an effective rat poison, why are some people today pushing fluoridation more than ever? Who are these people? Is there perhaps a common thread tying them all together? Could the very same people behind the systematic poisoning of entire civilisations be the same people who are pushing global warming?

Could there be intelligence, design, and a global unifying motivation behind all this? If you think genocide is something that only occurs in backward African countries, you had better open your eyes.

Did you know the Nazis used fluoride to pacify prisoners in concentration camps before gassing them? Folks often wonder why the Jews walked placidly to their deaths like herded cattle, without so much as a raised voice. It is because they were drugged. The same thing is happening today all over Europe and America, only on a much grander scale.

One often hears the media laughing at obese Americans, but is it really their fault? Rather than Americans being gluttons, as is often portrayed in the media, could it instead be due to the processed foods they are being fed? In case you didn't know it, there are drugs in our foods that make us fat. Food producers want us to eat more food because it makes them more profit. Just four decades ago, fat kids in classrooms were a rarity, but now almost all kids in classrooms are overweight. And don't blame it on computers, it is the drugs in the food they are being fed. Drugs help sell billions of extra revenue in food sales you would never crave otherwise.

It isn't that long ago that one cat food manufacturer was exposed for putting drugs in their cat food. Do you really think cats frantically scratching the kitchen cupboard to get at their food is due to their being hungry? Designer drugs such as High Fructose Corn Syrup (HFCS, or isoglucose as it is called in Europe) is in practically every processed food you buy now. What is HFCS? Didn't you know you were being drugged? They won't tell you that on television will they? No, they smile, hold up their dogshit and tell you it's good for you.

HFCS is a make-you-fat drug that has been superciliously put into our food to produce more profit. Biting into a supersized burger makes you hungrier than before, even though it technically fills you up. Why can't you help yourself when you are suddenly overcome with cravings? Sure, some people may lack self-control and need more exercise, but mere over indulgence can't explain this international pandemic that is destroying entire generations of kids, many of whom already have adult diabetes.

High Fructose Corn Syrup is an addictive designer chemical. It is not refined sugar. The ordinary sugar that used to be in these foods has increasingly been replaced by High Fructose Corn Syrup, which we have been told is natural and healthier than refined sugar (sucrose). But HFCS is neither natural nor healthy. It is manufactured from cornstarch in vats of murky fermenting liquid, fungus, genetically modified enzymes, ion exchange, and lots of chemical tweaking, which all takes place in chemical plants. It works in exactly the opposite way to diet pills, raising your levels of the very same make-you-fat hormones that diet pills are engineered to block.

Unlike table sugar, HFCS does not trigger the release of leptin, the substance that makes you feel full and stop eating, nor does it suppress the release of ghrelin, the substance that makes you hungry. That's why folks are always hungry and why they can't stop eating. At the time of writing, the average American now eats an astonishing 41.5 lbs of High Fructose Corn Syrup per year. American subsidies and tariffs have resulted in corn being a much more economical sweetener than sugar. Now that high fructose corn syrup is being added to an increasing variety of foods (breads, cereals, soft drinks, and condiments), isn't it time we had some real scientific research done on its effects and some legislation passed to ban it?

Recent studies have reported that rats, which normally live for a good two years, died after just five weeks when put on a high-fructose, low copper diet. One of the few human studies of low-copper, high-fructose diets was abruptly stopped when four of the twenty-four subjects developed heart-related abnormalities. High fructose diets have also been implicated in the development of adult-onset diabetes. Fructose, especially when combined with other sugars, reduces stores of chromium, a mineral essential for maintaining balanced insulin levels.

The Department of Agriculture in America directly links HFCS to sky-rocketing diabetes and obesity. So why is it now in our food and drink? Well, it extends the shelf life of processed foods, and it is cheaper than sugar. In other words, it makes more profit.

> 1 Timothy 6:10a
> For the love of money is the root of all evil:

The word says that the love of money is the root of all evil. When you understand that there are men and women in the world who will make decisions that ultimately put profit before people, then the truth of 1 Timothy 6:10 begins to make sense.

We know from animal studies that if you continue a deficient diet for three generations, reproduction ceases. Today, about 25% of our couples are infertile. Is the big picture beginning to come into focus here? If not, it will before you finish this class. If we would simply get back to eating proper homemade, nourishing food, in a good balanced diet, we would be amazed at how many of our health problems would simply vanish, and how much more enjoyable our lives would be. Perhaps it's time to start growing our own food again.

Personally, I do not see the need for anyone to mandate what I eat and to put rat poison in my toothpaste under the pretext of caring for my teeth. You are not responsible for what I eat and nor are you responsible for my teeth. I do not want your cancers or your broken hips, but more on that later, once we have learned a little more about you, who you are and why you do what you do.

21. What Cost Priceless?

We've had a brief and sobering glimpse into how much the devil values us, which isn't very much. Now, what about God? How much does God value us? Just as it is difficult to comprehend the evil of the devil, it is equally difficult to comprehend the goodness of God and just how much we mean to him. When man fell in Genesis and became just body and soul, spiritually dead in the devil's new world order, God did not leave man there. He could have, but he didn't. Rather, he loved us so much he came up with a plan to get us out of the mess we had made for ourselves. That plan was Jesus Christ, a man who put his hand up and volunteered to die in our place.

> Romans 3:21-24
> But now [since the day of Pentecost] the righteousness of God without the law is manifested, being witnessed by the law and the prophets;
>
> Even the righteousness of God *which is* by faith of Jesus Christ unto all and upon all them that believe: for there is no difference:
>
> For all have sinned, and come short of the glory of God;
>
> Being justified freely by his grace through the redemption that is in Christ Jesus:

It is through the redemption that is in Christ Jesus that we are justified freely by God's grace. Redemption refers to the price that was paid to buy us back from the devil. Here is a dictionary definition of *redeem*.

> *To recover ownership of by paying a specified sum.*

Man at one time belonged to God, but when man fell, man became the devil's subjects, we were citizens in the world of which he was its god.

To get us back, God had to redeem us, a price had to be paid. That price was paid in blood.

> Ephesians 1:7
> In whom we have redemption through his blood, the forgiveness of sins, according to the riches of his grace;

We lost the spirit when man fell back in Genesis and became just body and soul. Jesus Christ was the price that was paid to redeem us, to buy us back from that state of death. God paid for us with his own son. He gave his only son to the devil, to die the most horrendous death ever experienced by any human being in the history of the world so that we could be redeemed. That was the price that had to be paid, and God paid it.

> Romans 5:6-8
> For when we were yet without strength, in due time Christ died for the ungodly.
>
> For scarcely for a righteous man will one die: yet peradventure for a good man some would even dare to die.
>
> But God commendeth his love toward us, in that, while we were yet sinners, Christ died for us.

God paid a price beyond anything we could imagine or comprehend. Does that give us value? Very much so. How much are we worth to God? He paid a very high price for us. That price was his son Jesus Christ, who died in our place. Man was a three-part being back in Genesis, but as a consequence of his disobedience man lost his spirit and became just body and soul. Since the day of Pentecost, because of the work Jesus Christ accomplished, because of the price that was paid, it is once again available for man to be a three part being of body, soul, and spirit.

Now, how do we determine value? What gives something worth? What makes something valuable? One thing that determines value is cost, how much you would be willing to pay for something.

For example, what is a camera worth, or a car, or a new outfit, or a computer, or a new washing machine? When looking for any of these things, you have to count the cost and weigh up how much you're willing to spend. You also have to consider what you need it for and for how long before making any decisions. A camera may cost from £50 to £5000 or more, so determining which model is best for your needs is important before making a decision. If all you need is a pocket camera to take snapshots to share on the internet, you do not need a £5000 camera. However, regardless of which camera you eventually opt for, there is no way you would pay more than its current market value for it. If the camera you decide on is selling for £300 new in the shops, you would not spend £600 to purchase it second hand from the internet. Its value is £300, and you would not spend any more than that to acquire it. More than likely, you would shop around to find it a bit cheaper to try and save some money. Its value is £300, at most, that's all.

So cameras and other material things in the world have price tags, which are pretty much the same no matter where you look, and that's how much they are worth, that's their market value. So value can be determined by how much you spend on something. The more you spend on something, the more valuable you would consider it to be. The more it costs to make and produce something would affect its market value and make it more expensive to buy, therefore making it more valuable.

What else can have value? Material things can actually be worth more than their market value. Take Scottish panned gold for example. In pure monetary terms, Scottish gold is worth no more than the market price of gold bullion. However, Scottish jewellers pay high premiums for Scottish panned gold because it is scarce and in demand for Scottish jewellery, particularly Scottish wedding rings. So value isn't just determined by market value, some things can be worth more than their market value depending on demand and supply.

What else can be valuable? What else constitutes worth? What about a book? How valuable is it? It took me 18 years to research and write this biblical research work and bring it to publication. What is it worth to you and what is it worth to me? What would you expect to earn for 18 years work? £180k? £250k? £500k? More? Would I sell the copyright for this book if I were offered £250,000 for it? No, I wouldn't. The point is, to one person a work may be worth just a few bucks, but to another that same work could be worth millions. So value can fluctuate greatly between people depending on rights.

Is there anything else that could help us to understand value? I have a signed piece of card which I've had for over 35 years. It is worth absolutely nothing, it has no value whatsoever. It is just a piece of card. So why have I held onto it for over 35 years? Why do I still take it out and look at it sometimes? It is signed by Dr Wierwille, the man who taught me how to read and understand the bible, so this is something very special and I would miss it should I lose it. This is what we would term sentimental value. It has great value, but it is worth nothing in monetary terms.

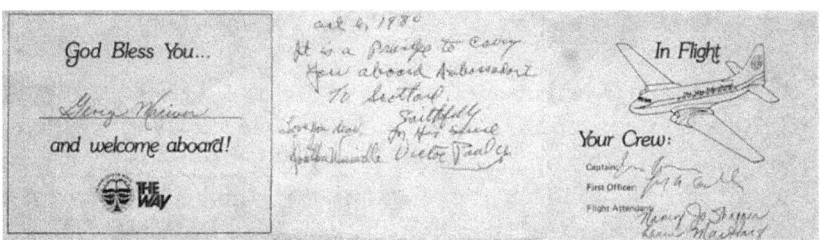

What else has value? What about children? Are children valuable? Oh yes, but can you put a price on them? Is there a price tag you can stick on children? Would we sell our children? Would we sell them for a million bucks? 10 million? 100 million? What about for the world? Of course not. Some things in life are beyond value, beyond price, you cannot buy them, they are not for sale. Children are priceless.

Value, then, varies greatly, but generally speaking, how much you'd be willing to spend on something would determine its value. If you cannot put a price on something, if it is beyond value, it is priceless. So, how valuable are we? Not very much to the devil, but what about God?

> 1 Corinthians 6:20
> For ye are bought with a price: therefore glorify God in your body, and in your spirit, which are God's.

We were bought with a price. What price? What price did God pay for us? How much did God pay to redeem us from the god of this world? How much does he value us? God took the one thing he had that was priceless, beyond value, his son, and that was the price he paid for us. If how much we are willing to pay for something determines its value, how much then are we worth? If you're not sure how much you're worth, take a look at the price tag on you.

God paid for us with his own son. He gave his only child to the devil to die the most horrendous and tortuous death ever experienced by any human being in the history of the world so that we could be raised from the dead and have eternal life.

Are we valuable? How valuable are your children to you? To God, we are priceless. Of all God has, we are his most valuable possessions.

> Romans 8:37-39
> Nay, in all these things we are more than conquerors through him that loved us.
>
> For I am persuaded, that neither death, nor life, nor angels, nor principalities, nor powers, nor things present, nor things to come,
>
> Nor height, nor depth, nor any other creature, shall be able to separate us from the love of God, which is in Christ Jesus our Lord.

Do you think there is anything that can take us away from God? Do you think there is a price God would sell us for? We are priceless, beyond value, beyond cost. There is no price that can separate us from this love of God. There is nothing the devil can do to take us away from God.

Knowing all this, we now have choices to make here. Are we going to believe the world's opinion of our value, or God's? See, that depends on us. If we spend our whole time watching television, playing computer games, watching movies, and reading newspapers and magazines, our perceptions of our own worth are going to reflect the god of this world's opinion of our worth, which isn't very much. However, if we keep our hearts and minds in God's word, our perceptions of our own worth will reflect our true value.

The world looks out at the universe, shows us how big it is, and tells us we amount to nothing. The bible looks out at the universe, shows us how big it is, and tells us that we are the only reason it is there. One viewpoint is a lie, while the other is the truth. What we look at is what we will believe and become.

> 2 Corinthians 3:18
> But we all, with open face beholding as in a glass the glory of the Lord, are changed into the same image from glory to glory, *even* as by the Spirit of the Lord.

A glass is a mirror. As we look into the bible, we see the glory of God reflected from its pages and if we keep our focus there, we will be changed into that same image. If we hold our minds in the world, then that's what we will reflect in our hearts and lives. Where we keep our thoughts is up to us. It's a choice we make.

God paid a high price for us. Jesus Christ was the price that was paid to redeem us from death so we could freely enjoy eternal life. Do you know what eternal life really is? It is being born again of God's seed and becoming his child.

> 1 Peter 1:23
> Being born again, not of corruptible seed, but of incorruptible, by the word of God, which liveth and abideth for ever.

This isn't make believe, this isn't Aesop's fables, this isn't a myth, this isn't a fairy tale, this is the truth – we literally are born of God's seed, incorruptible seed. We *are* his children, he *did* pay that price for us, and he *did* redeem us from the devil and death.

> Galatians 4:6,7
> And because ye are sons, God hath sent forth the Spirit of his Son into your hearts, crying, Abba, Father.
>
> Wherefore thou art no more a servant, but a son; and if a son, then an heir of God through Christ.

Now, to give you a little more sense of your worth, here's a thought that once saved my life. Before the day of Pentecost, from Genesis to the day of Pentecost, God had no guarantee that anyone would believe his word and be born again. Sure, he has foreknowledge and he knew we would, but he had no guarantee of that. What if God knew in his foreknowledge that you would be the only person to ever be born again, that you would be the only one to ever believe his word? Would God have still paid that price just for you? He paid the price without any guarantee of anything, before anyone was ever born again, so yes, you really are that precious to God, that priceless. He paid that price just for you.

God paid a price so high for us that it's beyond human comprehension. Eternal life may be free to us, but trust me, it cost God everything. To the god of this world we are worthless, but to God we are priceless. Which God are you going to serve?

22. The Family

Have you ever wondered why God set up the family the way he did? Have you ever wondered why the god of this world goes to such extraordinary lengths to destroy the family? This is worth exploring.

> Ephesians 2:4,5
> But God, who is rich in mercy, for his great love wherewith he loved us,
>
> Even when we were dead in sins, hath quickened us [made us alive] together with Christ, (by grace ye are saved;) [sōzō - made whole]

Sōzō in the Greek means *to be made whole*. To be saved is generally not understood today. We are born into this world just body and soul, without spirit, and when we are born again, when we are saved, made whole, we receive God's gift of holy spirit. It is this gift of holy spirit that makes us whole, having three parts again instead of two. That is what it means to be saved, *sōzō*, made whole.

Dead in sins in verse 5 is simply a reference to man being just body and soul, without spirit. *Quickened* is Old English language meaning *to be made alive*. When we receive this spirit and become whole again, we are made alive and, therefore, we are no longer dead. We are saved, made whole, by grace. By grace means it isn't something we work for or earn. Someone else paid the price so that we could have it for free. It costs us nothing. It cost God everything.

> Ephesians 2:6-8
> And hath raised *us* up together, and made *us* sit together in heavenly *places* in Christ Jesus:
>
> That in the ages to come he might shew the exceeding riches of his grace in *his* kindness toward us through Christ Jesus.

For by grace are ye saved (sōzō – made whole) through faith [believing]; and that not of yourselves: *it is* the gift of God:

How do we get this gift of spirit? How are we made whole? It couldn't be easier.

Romans 10:9
That if thou shalt confess with thy mouth the Lord Jesus, and shalt believe in thine heart that God hath raised him from the dead, thou shalt be saved [sōzō – made whole].

Eternal life is a gift from God, and it's a gift he freely gave. After the fall of man back in Genesis, man was in such a mess that there was literally nothing he could do to get himself out of that mess. It took God coming up with a plan to get the job done. Jesus Christ was the fulfilment of that plan, and on the day of Pentecost it became available once again for man to be made whole, to be a three-part being of body, soul, and spirit. Who is welcome to receive this gift of holy spirit? Well, anyone. Jesus Christ paid the price for everyone.

John 3:16
For God so loved the world, that he gave his only begotten Son, that whosoever believeth in him should not perish, but have everlasting life.

When you were born the first time, a seed from your father impregnated an egg in your mother. The seed was fertilised and a few months later you were born into the world, body and soul, but because you had no spirit you had a big empty hole inside you. I remember that big empty hole while I was growing up. Sometimes I felt so empty that life didn't feel worth living. That hole has been filled with the gift of holy spirit. There is nothing missing inside me now, I've been made whole.

When we're born again, seed is also involved, only this time it is God's seed, which is incorruptible, and it is that seed, that holy spirit born in us that fills that hole.

1 Peter 1:23
Being born again, not of corruptible seed, but of incorruptible, by the word of God, which liveth and abideth for ever.

This seed born within you, this holy spirit that makes you whole, is seed from God. Just as seed from your earthly father made you your father's child, so the seed from God makes you his child.

> Romans 8:16
> The Spirit itself beareth witness with our spirit, that we are the children of God:

> 1 John 3:2
> Beloved, now are we the sons of God, and it doth not yet appear what we shall be: but we know that, when he shall appear, we shall be like him; for we shall see him as he is.

As God's seed is involved, that makes this a family thing. Christianity therefore is not about candles and alters, meaningless ceremonies and mindless rituals, it is the way of a Father with his children, it is a family thing. That's why God set up families, so we could learn about him being our Father as we grew up. Children find it easy to relate to God as their Father when they grow up in strong loving families.

It is available to have strong marriages in loving relationships that last a lifetime. This is not make believe, this is not a fairytale, this is not science fiction, this is the truth. The bible also explains in detail how to achieve it. As an example, here are a few keys to a successful marriage and family life. Obviously, this is not an exhaustive biblical study, nor is it intended as such, but it will serve to contrast a few differences between God's way of doing things and the world's.

> Ephesians 5:22
> Wives, submit [hupotassō] yourselves unto your own husbands, as unto the Lord.

The word *hupotassō* means *loving obedience by proper arrangement and deliberate decision*. Wives, by their choice, by their freedom of will, are to submit to their husbands. That's part of God's plan for a successful, loving, strong marriage relationship that lasts a lifetime.

Ephesians 5:23,24
For the husband is the head of the wife, even as Christ is the head of the church: and he is the saviour of the body.

Therefore as the church is subject unto Christ, so *let* the wives *be* to their own husbands in every thing.

God is the head of Christ, Christ is the head of the husband, and in the marriage relationship, the husband is the head of the wife. Just as God promoted Christ to be the head of the church, he also promoted the husband to be the head, the leader in the marriage relationship. The wife is to be a companion for the man, as well as his helper and assistant. That is a woman's job description in the marriage relationship. Husbands' and wives' responsibilities in marriage are equal in importance, but not in authority. Men are to lead, that is how God designed marriage.

For anything to be successful in life, someone must lead. Without leadership, businesses fail. Without leadership, military forces are destroyed on the battlefield. Nothing in life works without leadership, and the same is true in marriage. Ladies, the relationships you long for are only available in this context. Men, take charge, be the leader, grow a pair of balls and do your job.

Ladies, if all this seems rather alien to you, consider that if the man is the head then he is responsible before God for the marriage, not you. Men, don't throw your responsibilities back in God's face and dump your job on your wife. It is your job, your duty to keep your family safe and protected, cared for and loved. A woman is inspired to submit to a husband who takes care of her, not just physically, but who takes care of her heart, encourages her and loves her as Jesus Christ loved the church.

Ephesians 5:25-27
Husbands, love your wives, even as Christ also loved the church, and gave himself for it;

That he might sanctify and cleanse it with the washing of water by the word,

That he might present it to himself a glorious church, not having spot, or wrinkle, or any such thing; but that it should be holy and without blemish.

These verses compare the love that Jesus Christ had for the church with the love that a husband is to have for his wife. Jesus Christ gave his life for his church and make no mistake men, marriage may require a sacrificial love. Are you willing to put yourself in harm's way if necessary to protect your wife and family?

In the family of God we are all children and God is our father. We are to care for each other and look after each other as brothers and sisters with God as our father. As we live life here on earth, we are to live as a family, caring for each other as children of the living God. When new people are born again, we are to look after them as babies in Christ. If we can learn to love each other with this kind of love, life will be sweet and the family will grow.

Now, all this should give us a clue then as to why the god of this world goes to such extremes to destroy the family. If people grow up with no concepts of true family values, it is almost impossible for them to relate to God as a father. Additionally, if people in any culture or civilisation cease to have families, birth rates will fall, and that culture or civilisation will go into decline. Astonishingly, the world markets this particular brand of genocide as *birth control*.

So in this context, what resources are available to the god of this world to help destroy the marriage relationship, lower birth rates, and edge our civilisations into decline? Homosexuality serves his purposes very well. The more semen ejaculated up the backsides of men, the fewer eggs are fertilised in women and the fewer children are born. How the god of this world must laugh when he sees a nation's semen stolen from the wombs of its women and pumped up the backsides of the male populace. How God must vomit when he sees christians ordaining homosexual ministers and lobbying for homosexual marriages. As it is written, the dog is turned to his own vomit again, and the sow that was washed to her wallowing in the mire.

Much of what we call the western world will effectively disappear within our lifetimes if we do not wake up and reverse our direction. If a nation does not produce X number of babies per capita, that nation will go into decline, and if the trend is not reversed that nation will eventually become extinct. Government funded birth control is in reality a taxpayer funded form of genocide. You know, we pay for it. The government steals our money through illegal taxes, and then uses it to exterminate us.

In Europe, the indigenous peoples of France, Germany, Spain, Italy, and Great Britain will most likely not exist within a few decades. Europe is on the verge of civilisation change. Europe and America are awash with resources and abundance, but what use is that if we are running out of people? The one truly indispensible resource without which no culture or civilisation can possibly survive is children. Unless we change, there is no future for us as peoples. What can we do about it? Well, God is still there, he hasn't gone anywhere. The promises in his word are still available to anyone who believes them.

We just do not understand how far down the way of death we have gone in our so-called developed world. In its reliance on immigration, as well as its promotion of homosexuality, Europe is financing its own extinction. America will not be far behind either unless they change their course.

Here is some current hard data on birth rates from around the world and the news is sobering. By the time you read this, these figures will probably be worse. We are running out of babies much faster than we are of oil. The replacement fertility rate, the number of babies you need for a stable population, is 2.1 babies per woman. Some countries are well above that. The global fertility leader, Niger, is 7.60 babies per woman, Uganda 6.69, Mali 6.44, and Somalia 6.35.

So, the Muslims are doing just fine. What about the rest of us? Scroll down to number 123 and you will eventually find the United States, with a replacement birth rate of 2.06 births per woman. Ireland is further down, at 2.02, the United Kingdom 1.91, Norway 1.77, Canada 1.58, and Germany 1.41.

Interestingly, as fertility shrivels, societies get older. Japan and much of Europe are set to grow older than any functioning societies have ever been at any time in recorded history. And we all know what comes after old age, don't we? Unless we can find the will to change our ways, we will cease to exist as peoples.

There was and is no population explosion in the developed world. It was a media lie. Birth rates are declining all over the western world. In 1968 we should have realised that Paul Ehrlich's so-called population explosion was in reality a massive population readjustment. Of the increase in global population between 1970 and 2000, the developed world accounted for less than 9 percent of it, while the Muslims accounted for 26 percent of the increase. Between 1970 and 2000, the developed world declined from just under 30 percent of the world's population to just over 20 percent. We are dying.

Can these trends continue for another few decades without having serious consequences? The grand buildings of Europe may still be standing in years to come but the peoples who built them may well be gone. We are living through a remarkable period of self-extinction, suicide if you like. A society that has no children has no future. I'll put it another way – homosexuality is a terminal disease. It used to be a criminal offence to be a homosexual. Who changed those laws? Who promotes homosexuality in our schools? Who threatens anyone who stands against homosexuals with prosecution for violating their human rights? If we can spotlight those responsible, could we perhaps then unveil what is really going on around us?

Our enemies love birth control. Warren Buffet, Bill Gates, and Ted Turner, for example, have donated billions to spreading the gospel of contraception, abortion, and feminism using the United Nations and US Aid. Rockefeller funded the invention of the pill and the IUD and also owns the rights to the abortion drug RU-486. In the last 50 years, billions of public dollars in America have been spent on family planning that is designed to limit population. Of course it is, why else would we spend so heavily on so-called family planning if it were not to control birth rates? But it isn't about family planning, it's about genocide, it's about a war against populations.

In July 2003, speaking to the United States Congress, Tony Blair remarked: *As Britain knows, all predominant power seems for a time invincible but, in fact, it is transient. The question is: What do you leave behind?* Tony Blair knows Europe is on the verge of caving in. He should do, he was a big part of our continuing demise. Instead of hanging traitors, we now make them prime ministers and presidents and pay them huge sums of money from the public purse so they can change laws that protect us and introduce laws that steal our prosperity, destroy our families, and make us sick. Trade laws and immigration laws were put in place to protect us. Someone once went to a great deal of effort to put them there. The ones who benefit from them being dismantled are our enemies.

As I said earlier, genocide comes in many different guises. Take the condom for instance. A few decades ago, the media screamed safe sex at us while condom factories sprang up everywhere. Well, I have some news for you. Condoms were not designed to keep you safe, they were designed to stop you having babies. They are a part of the devil's genocidal plan for the western world. It's been working too. Care to read the birth rate statistics I've listed above one more time? Of course, condoms are big business. Any idea who built the factories that produce them and who profits from them? Do some research and you may be surprised to see whose pockets are being lined at our expense. All roads lead to Rome, as we were once fond of saying.

So, what else can the god of this world do to break down the family unit? The strength of any nation is a strong middle class. How you build a strong middle class is by having strong families – men and women who marry, remain devoted and true to each other their whole lives, and who raise strong children. The god of this world knows this and has consequently declared war on middle class families. Ever noticed all the homosexuals living together, both working, both driving the latest fancy cars, wearing all the latest fashions, infesting night clubs and cruise ships, enjoying one long party, while your average working man with a wife and family can't afford to take his wife to the local restaurant for a meal at the weekend?

That isn't the way God set life up but it is the way the god of this world manipulates things through government, social security, and illegal taxes. Women leave their husbands because the government offers them free housing, free money, free furnishings, free everything. How does a working man compete with that? In case you didn't realise it, the government has no money of its own, what they have they steal from us. Ladies, do you really trust the government to look after you? What are you going to do when the government runs out of stolen taxes and has no more money to give you? Do you think your men will have you back?

The god of this world has other powerful weapons with which to attack the family. Let's look at another – disciplining children. God has plenty to say on this subject.

> Proverbs 22:15
> Foolishness *is* bound in the heart of a child; *but* the rod of correction shall drive it far from him.

Foolishness is bound, packed into the heart of a child. That is what the word says. The only way to get that foolishness out of the child is with the rod of correction (the rod being a figurative usage for discipline). The rod of correction could be a small wooden spoon lightly tapped on the back of a child's leg or hand. In the case of teenagers, it could be curtailed privileges. Whatever works, we are to discipline our children to get the foolishness out of them. That is how children grow up able to handle life responsibly so they can deal maturely with the challenges that will come their way.

The world, however, maintains that spanking teaches violence. No, it does not. That is the opposite of what the word teaches, therefore, it is a lie. Using the rod of correction properly teaches consequences. The world also maintains that if you discipline your children you do not love them. Here is what the word says.

> Proverbs 13:24
> He that spareth his rod hateth his son: but he that loveth him chasteneth him betimes.

Contrary to the world's depraved standards, the word is clear – if you do not discipline your children responsibly, you do not love them. That is the truth. Any parent who loves their children will discipline them so they will grow up strong and able to handle life, with the foolishness that was in their hearts removed. Parents who do not discipline their children, hate their children. That is what the bible says.

The United Nations hates children. They are passing laws through the International Courts to make it illegal to discipline children. The United Nations hates your children with a passion you just do not understand. Undisciplined children lead unproductive lives and contribute nothing to themselves or the places they live in. The United Nations knows this. Everyone can see the fruits of the United Nation's stand against disciplining children, which they push through the courts in the guise of protecting their human rights. It does not protect them at all, it destroys them. Undisciplined children have no self-respect, no respect for their parents, and absolutely no concept of consequences, because the foolishness they were born with is still packed into their hearts.

> Proverbs 19:18
> Chasten thy son while there is hope, and let not thy soul spare for his crying.

There is no such thing as ODD (Oppositional Defiant Disorder), a term the world uses to label unruly children. That is just smelly brown dribbly stuff from the rear end of male cows. If you want to call it something, call it CSUNB, Consequences for Swallowing United Nations Bullshit. If children are fools, don't listen to their parents, and have no respect for authority, it is because they were not raised properly. In other words, it is the parents' fault, not the child's. And don't go blaming God either. If you listened to him and did things his way you wouldn't have the problems.

Now, let's put spanking into perspective here, it certainly does not involve harming children. A light tap on the back of a hand or the leg with a wooden spoon, coupled with the word 'no' is sufficient to get a young child's attention. Don't use your hands as they are supposed to be a safe, loving refuge for a child to go to when they need comfort and love. If they associate a wooden spoon with disobedience and a little smack, often just the brandishing of the spoon will get their attention and will be sufficient to drive the foolishness from their hearts. That is loving children. If you don't do this, you do not love your children. Thus saith God, and he knows what's best for us. He loves us and cares about us, which is why he teaches us how to live life and raise families. The god of this world comes only to steal, to kill and to destroy. Who are you going to believe?

Proverbs 13:24
He that spareth his rod hateth his son: but he that loveth him chasteneth him betimes.

The UN tries to convince us that disciplining children is child abuse. No, it is not. The world may take some horrific child murder and twist the facts to enforce legislation that removes the rights of parents to discipline their children, but that's just how the devil works. The god of this world is quite happy to send some possessed bastard to murder a few kids so the United Nations can force legislation through the international courts to remove our rights to love our children and discipline them. The United Nations are child abusers of the most vicious kind. It is the United Nations we should be taking to court for child abuse, not loving parents who love their children enough to discipline them responsibly. Actually, If we really understood the United Nations, we would confiscate their property, freeze their assets, and kick them out of our countries at the point of a gun.

Responsible adults respect consequences. Responsible adults understand that the more severe the mistakes they make in life, the more severe the consequences will be. Why is it that the UN does not want our children to learn about consequences? What chance do children stand in this world without ever learning that? Teaching a young child that fire burns and that they must stay away from the cooker while mom is cooking is not abusing a child's human rights, it is protecting them from possible serious harm. That is what parents are supposed to do, it is their duty as parents. If a child ignores the warnings and insists on trying to climb up on the cooker while mom is cooking, it is time to brandish the wooden spoon, not listen to the UN, stand back and watch our children spill boiling water over their heads.

The UN exhorts us not to break our children by disciplining them. Yeah right. Disciplining children does not break them, it protects them. Allowing children to grow up the UN way, as savages, will break them. Children need love and affection, yes, but they also require structure, boundaries, and effective discipline. They need to understand that there are consequences for every wrong action. How else could anyone possibly grow up to be successful in life?

While we are on the subject of the family, let's handle another weapon in the devil's arsenal that is clearly directed at the breakdown of the family unit – feminism. Feminism teaches women to hate men, practice witchcraft, and become lesbians. And I don't care if I make you mad. I have the word of God backing me up. I'm telling you the truth. What do you have backing you up? The United Nations? The homos? The BBC? Hollywood? Fine, if that is what you want to believe, go ahead, walk the world's ways and see where it takes you.

The god of this world is the real power behind sexual and homosexual *liberation*. Through media control, we are conditioned to regard sex as merely casual recreational activity rather than as an expression of love resulting in children. Feminism pretends to be about giving women equal opportunities, especially in the workplace, when in fact it was primarily devised to foment hatred for men, promote lesbianism, and break down families. The social stigma now attached to motherhood is so repulsive to some that being a homemaker has been compared to being an inmate in a Nazi concentration camp. This is psychological warfare of the most vicious kind.

Feminists also like to spotlight things such as the statistical pay gap between men and women, and scream about oppression and tyranny. In America, reports state that for every dollar a man earns, a woman earns 77 cents and that women coming out of college earn less than men do. This is true, but what the feminists do not tell you is why this is so. Most of this gap is due entirely to factors that are a matter of the choices that women make about their work. For example, women overwhelmingly choose to work in such jobs as social work, teaching, government, non-profits, and humanities, rather than in higher paying technical jobs in engineering and business. The jobs they choose offer plenty of personal rewards, but on a strictly statistical basis, they lower the baseline income that is factored in for all working women.

Additionally, women tend to choose part-time work over full-time work (resulting in lower overall job experience and resulting pay), they leave work earlier in life to spend time with family, and spend more time away from work during their careers for things such as having babies. All these factors weighed together give women a lower average pay than men statistically. Add it all together, and the gap in pay can be directly attributed to the freewill choices women make and has nothing whatsoever to do with employers being tyrannical and oppressive towards women. The difference is not part of some diabolical scheme to undermine women by short-changing them in their salaries, rather, the feminists are the ones devising diabolical schemes by twisting statistical data to further the god of this world's agendas.

In the last four decades, we have experienced an unprecedented breakdown in the family. It is well known that most of our social problems such as crime, educational underachievement, alcohol and drug abuse, depression and suicide, are symptoms of the breakup of the family. Instead of seeking rest and fulfilment in marriage and raising children, more and more of our best women are wasting their lives in jobs that can never give them the fulfilment and joy that a strong family life could. In our day and time, women have never been so liberated and women have never been so miserable. The world only offers women money, a shit life, and then death. Come back to God ladies, it's where the abundance is.

Are there any other weapons stocking the devil's anti-family arsenal? Oh yes, plenty. Take adultery for example. The problem is endemic and yet it is considered by most as normal social behaviour.

It doesn't take much to expose adultery for what it is. Did you know that adulterers were stoned to death in the old testament? That's right. Adultery is a crime. It may not be a crime in our societies and may not carry legal consequences, but it is a crime and it does carry consequences in life. God told Moses to have adulterers stoned to death. There must have been a good reason for that. Today it is promoted on television, in movies, newspapers, magazines, and music, but is that really so surprising?

Look, adultery is not just a little problem, it is a big problem. Married couples wonder why their lives are miserable and threadbare, yet they lie and cheat on their partners, betraying the oaths they made when they married? I am sorry if this is news to you and you have been caught up in this, but now is your opportunity to change, this is your opportunity to get off the way of death and get onto the way of life where you can live in true abundance and with true power. Make the decision to change and you will be forgiven. Here is what Job said about adultery.

Job 31:9-12
If mine heart have been deceived by a woman, or *if* I have laid wait at my neighbour's door;

Then let my wife grind unto another, and let others bow down upon her.

For this *is* an heinous crime; yea, it *is* an iniquity *to be punished by* the judges.

For it *is* a fire *that* consumeth to destruction, and would root out all mine increase [adultery will make you poor].

Adultery is not open to debate. If you saw it for the monster it really is, you would run as far away from it as fast as your little legs could carry you. I understand that emotions can be very powerful here, particularly if your marriage is in ruins. If that is the case, don't lie, don't cheat, talk to each other, and if there is no future in your relationship, divorce and then you will be free to start over. If you want your marriage to work, then make it work. Adultery is not an option either way. Adultery is the coward's way out and it will ruin you and you will lose everything. God does not want folks lives ruined by the devil, which is why he took the time to warn us about this in his word.

Proverbs 6:32-35
But whoso committeth adultery with a woman lacketh understanding: he *that* doeth it destroyeth his own soul.

A wound and dishonour shall he get; and his reproach shall not be wiped away.

For jealousy *is* the rage of a man: therefore he will not spare in the day of vengeance.

He will not regard any ransom; neither will he rest content, though thou givest many gifts.

Don't think you can use grace as an excuse to sleep around with other men's wives either. If you think grace allows you to sleep around and it's okay with God, then why don't you tell your children and your wife what you're doing, and tell the children of your partner and her husband what you're doing? The word says to put away lying and speak every man truth with his neighbour. Don't use grace as an excuse to sin or you will pay dearly because the devil will have direct access into your life through a break in the hedge of protection around you. Learn to control your emotions and keep them in subjection.

> Romans 6:15
> What then? shall we sin, because we are not under the law, but under grace? God forbid.

I am not teaching this to make anyone feel bad or to make anyone feel guilty, I am teaching this so anyone caught up in this can get back onto the way of life and enjoy God's abundance. No matter what you have done in the past, no matter where you have been, you can get onto the way of life at any time. The devil wants us miserable, sick, and dead, and he does everything within his power to lead us away from God's protection. God wishes above all things that we prosper and be in health, that we enjoy abundant and prosperous lives in every category.

God does not care about your past. Jesus Christ, who always did God's will, even cared about those who had committed adultery. So do I, which is why I'm teaching this stuff. I care about people enough to want to help them.

> John 8:3-5
> And the scribes and Pharisees brought unto him [Jesus] a woman taken in adultery; and when they had set her in the midst,
>
> They say unto him, Master, this woman was taken in adultery, in the very act.
>
> Now Moses in the law commanded us, that such should be stoned: but what sayest thou?

First of all, Jesus did not know ahead of time this was going to happen. Those religious bastards burst into his meeting dragging that woman with them, and confronted him in public, looking to incriminate him in his words. They didn't care about the woman, but Jesus Christ did.

> John 8:6
> This they said, tempting him, that they might have to accuse him. But Jesus stooped down, and with *his* finger wrote on the ground, *as though he heard them not.*

Look at these religious leaders' attitudes. They did not do this to help the woman, or to do anything for God, or because they loved people, they did it to tempt Jesus Christ. That was their motive, that's what was in their hearts. This thing was done out of jealousy and hatred for Jesus Christ. They were looking for an excuse to accuse him so they could prosecute him.

Jesus Christ's response, however, was to sit down and doodle in the dust on the ground with his finger. More than likely he was thinking and running scriptures through his mind, pondering how best to deal with the situation while waiting for God to let him know what to do.

Another very interesting point is that these religious leaders were technically right. Moses does state in the old testament law that such women were to be stoned. Those scribes and pharisees were quoting accurate scripture and it was in context. Jesus knew that and he knew that to contradict them would be to contradict the bible. That's what those religious leaders were hoping he would do. However, let's look at this from another point of view. The word is a heart thing. We have to learn to look on the heart.

> 1 Samuel 16:7
> But the LORD said unto Samuel, Look not on his countenance, or on the height of his stature; because I have refused him: for *the LORD seeth* not as man seeth; for man looketh on the outward appearance, but the LORD looketh on the heart.

Forgiveness has always been available. Even Adam and Eve were forgiven and went on to enjoy prosperous lives in fellowship with God. Forgiveness was available to people who broke old testament law. David was forgiven after his affair with Bathsheba. Forgiveness has always been available, it is available today, and it will continue to remain available. The word must be understood in this light. It does not matter to God where a person has been, or even what they did yesterday, he is only interested in where they are now and where they want to be tomorrow.

These religious leaders, although they were right, were wrong because of their attitude of heart. Whose side do you think God was on? The religious leaders? Or that poor woman? If God were on side with the religious leaders, Jesus Christ himself would have agreed with them, picked up a stone and been the first to throw it at her.

Think about the woman too. Put yourself in her sandals. What must she have been going through? Caught in the very act of adultery. More than likely, they set her up. She had been literally dragged out of bed by those bastards, hauled to the temple, and paraded in public. She was facing death by stoning. The public humiliation and the threat of death must have left her feeling pretty wretched. Did God still love her? Let's find out.

The scribes and the pharisees pestered him until he eventually stood up and turned in their direction. Note that he didn't hit them with his more usual response, *it is written*, and then quote scriptures. He didn't have any scriptures on this occasion because there were none. Instead, he went for their consciences.

> John 8:7-9
> So when they continued asking him, he lifted up himself, and said unto them, He that is without sin among you, let him first cast a stone at her.
>
> And again he stooped down, and wrote on the ground.
>
> And they which heard *it*, being convicted by *their own* conscience, went out one by one, beginning at the eldest, *even* unto the last: and Jesus was left alone, and the woman standing in the midst.

They left, one by one, until they were all gone. Jesus didn't tell them they were wrong, he didn't quote scriptures at them, he didn't lecture them, he simply told them that whoever among them was guiltless should be the first to stone her. I'm not so sure that is what the woman would have wanted to hear, and at that point she probably expected rocks to begin splintering her bones. However, they all left, one by one, until Jesus and the woman were left alone in the midst of the people. I'll bet you could have heard the proverbial pin drop in the temple that morning.

> John 8:10,11
> When Jesus had lifted up himself, and saw none but the woman, he said unto her, Woman, where are those thine accusers? hath no man condemned thee?
>
> She said, No man, Lord. And Jesus said unto her, Neither do I condemn thee: go, and sin no more.

See, God does not care about your past, he only cares about where you are now and where you want to be. This woman obviously wanted to change. She wasn't hardhearted and calloused. She didn't have an attitude. She didn't strut around the temple screaming at Jesus, or calling God names. She was genuinely sorry. I'll bet she was praying to God silently the whole time, telling God what a wonderful believer she was going to be from then on. Here you can see God's love, forgiveness, and mercy. God understands us, he's on our side, and he's there for us when we come back to him regardless of anything we've done.

> Psalm 103:14
> For he knoweth our frame; he remembereth that we *are* dust.

We are all human. God knows that. We all sin, which simply means to miss the mark. No one is perfect. We all get it wrong at some point. Jesus Christ took care of everything we've done wrong in the past, everything we may do wrong today, and everything we will ever do wrong in the future. The key is our heart. Are we willing to change? Jesus Christ dealt with the root cause of the sin problem, and once we come back to God, all those old sins of ours no longer exist. They are gone, forever.

> Psalm 103:12
> As far as the east is from the west, *so* far hath he removed our transgressions from us.

This verse says *east and west*, not *north and south*. If you go far enough north and cross the pole, you will start going south. Unlike north and south, east and west never meet. Either you are going east or you are going west. If you are going east, you are travelling away from west. If you stop and go west, you are now heading away from east. There is infinity between them. It isn't that God is simply hiding his eyes from our sins, pretending not to see them, they really do not exist anymore. Jesus Christ did a thorough job of getting rid of them.

> Hebrews 10:12,17
> But this man, [Jesus Christ] after he had offered one sacrifice for sins for ever, sat down on the right hand of God;
>
> And their sins and iniquities will I remember no more.

God will remember our sins no more because they no longer exist, and when God forgives, he also forgets. When God has forgiven you he will never bring it up again. Why? Because our sins no longer exist. They were dealt with. They are gone. There is nothing to deal with because they are not there. They are as far away as the east is from the west. There is nothing to remember because they don't exist.

> Colossians 2:13,14
> And you, being dead in your sins and the uncircumcision of your flesh, hath he quickened together with him, having forgiven you all trespasses;
>
> Blotting out the handwriting of ordinances that was against us, which was contrary to us, and took it out of the way, nailing it to his cross;

Whether you believe in God or not, whether you are a christian or not, God's forgiveness is available. The question is, do you want it? God isn't the issue here. If you want it, make your peace with God and change. It's a new day. You can have a new life starting right now, and it will cost you nothing. As soon as you make the decision to change, you are forgiven. It is as easy as children apologising to their parents. How can it be so easy? How can it cost us nothing? Well, it cost God a great deal. How much did it cost him? Only his son, and he willingly paid that price for you.

Want a new life? Want abundance and power in your life? Want to put the past behind you and move on? Every day can be a new day, just like it was a new day for that woman in the temple. It can even be a new day for you homos and lesbians, if you want it. Yes, God will even forgive you if you change. Which life do you want? One is the way of life and the other is the way of death. The choices are clear. Take your pick.

23. Military Intelligence

King David, the word records, was a man after God's own heart.

> Acts 13:22
> And when he had removed him, [Saul] he raised up unto them David to be their king; to whom also he gave testimony, and said, I have found David the *son* of Jesse, a man after mine own heart, which shall fulfil all my will.

This verse could not be any clearer, any more plainly written – David was a man after God's own heart, who would fulfil all God's will. With this in mind we will take a brief look at David's military life. As David was a warrior and a man after God's own heart, we should therefore be able to see a little of what God thinks regarding military intelligence.

> 1 Samuel 17:1-3
> Now the Philistines gathered together their armies to battle, and were gathered together at Shochoh, which *belongeth* to Judah, and pitched between Shochoh and Azekah, in Ephesdammim.
>
> And Saul and the men of Israel were gathered together, and pitched by the valley of Elah, and set the battle in array against the Philistines.
>
> And the Philistines stood on a mountain on the one side, and Israel stood on a mountain on the other side: and *there was* a valley between them.

Israel was under attack from the Philistines. Saul and the men of Israel gathered their armies and headed out to take them on in battle. This was God's people going out to battle, therefore, we can conclude that the right to self-defence is an inalienable human right built into the fabric of life. If God did not want his people going out to fight the

Philistines here, he would have said so. If you want human rights, then start here, with the God-given right to self-defence. Israel went to war to protect themselves.

> 1 Samuel 17:4-10
> And there went out a champion out of the camp of the Philistines, named Goliath, of Gath, whose height *was* six cubits and a span.
>
> And *he had* an helmet of brass upon his head, and he *was* armed with a coat of mail; and the weight of the coat *was* five thousand shekels of brass.
>
> And *he had* greaves of brass upon his legs, and a target of brass between his shoulders.
>
> And the staff of his spear *was* like a weaver's beam; and his spear's head *weighed* six hundred shekels of iron: and one bearing a shield went before him.
>
> And he stood and cried unto the armies of Israel, and said unto them, Why are ye come out to set *your* battle in array? *am* not I a Philistine, and ye servants to Saul? choose you a man for you, and let him come down to me.
>
> If he be able to fight with me, and to kill me, then will we be your servants: but if I prevail against him, and kill him, then shall ye be our servants, and serve us.
>
> And the Philistine said, I defy the armies of Israel this day; give me a man, that we may fight together.

Goliath was so well trained in the art of war and hand-to-hand combat, and so well equipped with the latest weaponry and body armour, that he had the confidence to stand in front of an entire army and shout his fat mouth off at God's people.

> 1 Samuel 17:11
> When Saul and all Israel heard those words of the Philistine, they were dismayed, and greatly afraid.

Fear is our greatest enemy, not the Goliaths of the world, as we shall see.

1 Samuel 17:12-25
Now David *was* the son of that Ephrathite of Bethlehemjudah, whose name *was* Jesse; and he had eight sons: and the man went among men *for* an old man in the days of Saul.

And the three eldest sons of Jesse went *and* followed Saul to the battle: and the names of his three sons that went to the battle *were* Eliab the firstborn, and next unto him Abinadab, and the third Shammah.

And David *was* the youngest: and the three eldest followed Saul.

But David went and returned from Saul to feed his father's sheep at Bethlehem.

And the Philistine drew near morning and evening, and presented himself forty days.

And Jesse said unto David his son, Take now for thy brethren an ephah of this parched *corn*, and these ten loaves, and run to the camp to thy brethren;

And carry these ten cheeses unto the captain of *their* thousand, and look how thy brethren fare, and take their pledge.

Now Saul, and they, and all the men of Israel, *were* in the valley of Elah, fighting with the Philistines.

And David rose up early in the morning, and left the sheep with a keeper, and took, and went, as Jesse had commanded him; and he came to the trench, as the host was going forth to the fight, and shouted for the battle.

For Israel and the Philistines had put the battle in array, army against army.

> And David left his carriage in the hand of the keeper of the carriage, and ran into the army, and came and saluted his brethren.
>
> And as he talked with them, behold, there came up the champion, the Philistine of Gath, Goliath by name, out of the armies of the Philistines, and spake according to the same words: and David heard *them*.
>
> And all the men of Israel, when they saw the man, fled from him, and were sore afraid.
>
> And the men of Israel said, Have ye seen this man that is come up? surely to defy Israel is he come up: and it shall be, *that* the man who killeth him, the king will enrich him with great riches, and will give him his daughter, and make his father's house free in Israel.

At this point in his life, David was a teenager, probably around sixteen or seventeen years old. His father had sent him to see how his brothers were doing and to deliver mail and gifts from the family. While he was there, he witnessed Goliath's ultimatum. After watching with dismay Israel's fearful response, his blood boiled.

> 1 Samuel 17:26
> And David spake to the men that stood by him, saying, What shall be done to the man that killeth this Philistine, and taketh away the reproach from Israel? for who *is* this uncircumcised Philistine, that he should defy the armies of the living God?

Calling Goliath an uncircumcised Philistine was the most terrible and vehement curse David could have uttered. Nothing in our culture even comes close to the disdain, contempt, and anger he felt for that man.

> 1 Samuel 17:31-37
> And when the words were heard which David spake, they rehearsed *them* before Saul: and he sent for him.
>
> And David said to Saul, Let no man's heart fail because of him; thy servant will go and fight with this Philistine.

And Saul said to David, Thou art not able to go against this Philistine to fight with him: for thou *art but* a youth, and he a man of war from his youth.

And David said unto Saul, Thy servant kept his father's sheep, and there came a lion, and a bear, and took a lamb out of the flock:

And I went out after him, and smote him, and delivered *it* out of his mouth: and when he arose against me, I caught *him* by his beard, and smote him, and slew him.

Thy servant slew both the lion and the bear: and this uncircumcised Philistine shall be as one of them, seeing he hath defied the armies of the living God.

David said moreover, The LORD that delivered me out of the paw of the lion, and out of the paw of the bear, he will deliver me out of the hand of this Philistine. And Saul said unto David, Go, and the LORD be with thee.

David may have been a teenager, but make no mistake, he was already a warrior. Years spent looking after his father's sheep in the wild countryside protecting them from savage animals had taught him a few skills in hand-to-hand combat, including being master of the sling, a deadly weapon at close range. He knew his weapon and he knew how to use it. He had seen Goliath, and he knew he could take him down. It was not recklessness or stupidity, he knew he had the hand-to-hand combat training and experience to take the guy down, and he knew that God was with him. That's what you call an unbeatable mindset.

1 Samuel 17:38,39
And Saul armed David with his armour, and he put an helmet of brass upon his head; also he armed him with a coat of mail.

And David girded his sword upon his armour, and he assayed [hesitated] to go; for he had not proved *it*. And David said unto Saul, I cannot go with these; for I have not proved *them*. And David put them off him.

These two verses simply state that David was uncomfortable with the latest body armour and weaponry because he'd had no training with them. They would slow him down and hinder him. We hear that many times today from our Special Forces, who rightly maintain that weighing themselves down with the latest heavy body armour could jeopardise operations where stealth and agility are of paramount importance. David knew he needed to be agile and fleet of foot to do the job so he put the ungainly and cumbersome armour and weapons from him. Instead, he took his staff, his sling, and selected five smooth stones from a nearby brook as ammunition.

> 1 Samuel 17:40-44
> And he took his staff in his hand, and chose him five smooth stones out of the brook, and put them in a shepherd's bag which he had, even in a scrip; and his sling *was* in his hand: and he drew near to the Philistine.
>
> And the Philistine came on and drew near unto David; and the man that bare the shield *went* before him.
>
> And when the Philistine looked about, and saw David, he disdained him: for he was *but* a youth, and ruddy, and of a fair countenance.
>
> And the Philistine said unto David, *Am* I a dog, that thou comest to me with staves? And the Philistine cursed David by his gods.
>
> And the Philistine said to David, Come to me, and I will give thy flesh unto the fowls of the air, and to the beasts of the field.

Goliath was visibly shocked. He recognised the staff in David's hand as a shepherd's stick used to fend off wild dogs, which explains his comment, *am I a dog that you come to me with a stick?* Goliath was also publicly humiliated in front of both armies. There he was, defying the armies of Israel, and a teenager had come out to fight him with a stick. He was so angered and humiliated, he swore to tear David limb from limb with his bare hands and feed him to the animals. David, however, was not afraid. His blood was boiling.

1 Samuel 17:45-47
Then said David to the Philistine, Thou comest to me with a sword, and with a spear, and with a shield: but I come to thee in the name of the LORD of hosts, the God of the armies of Israel, whom thou hast defied.

This day will the LORD deliver thee into mine hand; and I will smite thee, and take thine head from thee; and I will give the carcases of the host of the Philistines this day unto the fowls of the air, and to the wild beasts of the earth; that all the earth may know that there is a God in Israel.

And all this assembly shall know that the LORD saveth not with sword and spear: for the battle *is* the LORD'S, and he will give you into our hands.

Hand-to-hand combat takes courage, strength, ability, training, and prowess. That kind of strength doesn't come from sitting all week in front of televisions swallowing subversive propaganda about getting rid of your guns and dismantling your national defences. Why do you think the god of this world wants to take your guns and defences away from you anyway? Because he loves you and cares for you? Yeah right.

Remember, God didn't hate those Philistines, and he certainly didn't hate Goliath. The Israelites were not the bullies here. If the Philistines had left God's people alone and stayed home, they would have been quite safe. Now they will suffer the consequences for their arrogance in attacking God's people.

It is difficult to comprehend the strength in the boy David, but that is the strength that comes from knowing God's word and living it. If this is the kind of strength you want, I recommend less television, opening your bibles and reading them.

1 Samuel 17:48-52
And it came to pass, when the Philistine arose, and came and drew nigh to meet David, that David hasted, and ran toward the army to meet the Philistine.

And David put his hand in his bag, and took thence a stone, and slang *it*, and smote the Philistine in his forehead, that the stone sunk into his forehead; and he fell upon his face to the earth.

So David prevailed over the Philistine with a sling and with a stone, and smote the Philistine, and slew him; but *there was* no sword in the hand of David.

Therefore David ran, and stood upon the Philistine, and took his sword, and drew it out of the sheath thereof, and slew him, and cut off his head therewith. And when the Philistines saw their champion was dead, they fled.

And the men of Israel and of Judah arose, and shouted, and pursued the Philistines, until thou come to the valley, and to the gates of Ekron. And the wounded of the Philistines fell down by the way to Shaaraim, even unto Gath, and unto Ekron.

1 Samuel 17:57
And as David returned from the slaughter of the Philistine, Abner took him, and brought him before Saul with the head of the Philistine in his hand.

It is interesting to look at what David *didn't* do here. He didn't try to talk to Goliath to broker a peace deal. He killed him, cut off his head and held it up to the Philistines. The Philistines for their part shit their pants and ran.

Note that the Israelites didn't just stand there and let the Philistines go either, they chased after them and killed as many of the bastards as they could. They didn't offer them social programmes or send them foreign aid, they killed them.

You soldiers out there, many of you retired, beating yourselves up every week because you've killed men in battle. Why? How many cases of PTSD are entirely due to being stressed out over how many people you've shot and killed? God isn't mad at you, you did your job, he's proud of you. Killing men in battle isn't murder, it's what you're supposed to do when you're attacked. If a wild dog attacks your children and you kill it, are you going to stress yourself out over the dog? I don't think so. Killing enemy troops is no reason to be distressed. Get over it and be proud of your service. God is proud of you, and you should be proud you served your country.

This, of course, doesn't apply to cowards who run around city streets murdering unarmed civilians. Any asshole can run around gunning down unarmed civilians who don't shoot back. You religious nuts, why don't you read this class and get yourself born again? God will forgive you, and you can take his word to your people and do some good with your life.

Perhaps if our governments hadn't stolen all our guns and stripped us of our defences by making it illegal to carry them, these things wouldn't happen.

This principle of self-defence applies to not just military warfare, but to any form of attack from any quarter, be it military or economic (think climate change). God's people have a duty to fight for the freedoms God has given them and to kill as many of their enemies as is needed to be left alone in peace.

> 1 Samuel 18:6
> And it came to pass as they came, when David was returned from the slaughter of the Philistine, that the women came out of all cities of Israel, singing and dancing, to meet king Saul, with tabrets, with joy, and with instruments of musick.

God's people came out with joy, singing, and dancing after winning against their enemies. Thousands of Philistines had been slaughtered on the battlefields, run through with swords, their heads caved in with axes, their bodies pierced with arrows, and there was joy, singing, and dancing among God's people. This is a little different to what is portrayed in the world's media today regarding war, wouldn't you say?

No doubt in David's day, the Daily Philistine Newspapers would have been filled with jubilant front page stories of Goliath standing for his human rights against the nasty Israelites, with pictures of him rattling his sword against his shield and the flames of war burning in his eyes.

I doubt the same newspapers would have published a picture of his headless corpse the next day though. More than likely they were publishing stories of Israeli atrocities and running off to the International courts with ridiculous stories of terrible Israeli war crimes. Not much has changed in a few thousand years. What are you going to read and believe? The daily newspapers or God's word?

You would be stunned if you knew just how powerful an image can be. Take this picture of Che Guevara for example, a murdering communist terrorist asshole which has been admired by just about everyone on the planet, and then compare it with the second photo of him taken just after he had been shot dead. The world's media only show us the first image and not the second because they are owned and controlled by the enemy.

 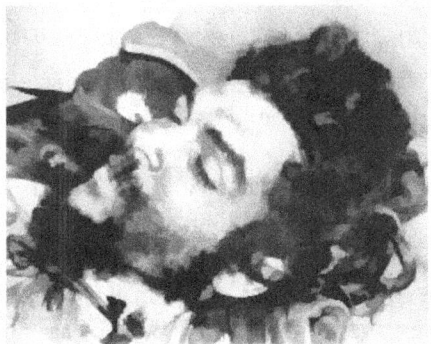

This record of David and Goliath isn't unique in the word either. Abraham, Moses, Joshua, Ehud, Barak, Gideon, Samson, Hezekiah, and others took on their enemies and soundly defeated them. The god of this world does not have our best interests at heart. He may couch his devices in pleasant sounding glib phrases like *human rights, solidarity*, and *tolerance*, but dispel the smoke screens and you will recoil in horror at what you see slavering before you. National disarmament is insane. Taking guns away from citizens is insane. If we want to live in peace and safety in this world we are going to have to have weapons and know how to use them.

There is a track record throughout the old testament of God blessing his people militarily and helping them to defeat their enemies.

> 2 Chronicles 17:1-5
> And Jehoshaphat his son [a godly king of Judah] reigned in his stead, and strengthened himself against Israel [the northern tribes who were not very godly at that time].
>
> And he placed forces in all the fenced cities of Judah, and set garrisons in the land of Judah, and in the cities of Ephraim, which Asa his father had taken.
>
> And the LORD was with Jehoshaphat, because he walked in the first ways of his father David, and sought not unto Baalim;
>
> But sought to the *LORD* God of his father, and walked in his commandments, and not after the doings of Israel.
>
> Therefore the LORD stablished the kingdom in his hand; and all Judah brought to Jehoshaphat presents; and he had riches and honour in abundance.

Jehoshaphat had riches and honour in abundance because he did the will of God by building his military, defeating his enemies in battle, and putting garrisons in places that could not be trusted. Read the word and see it for yourself. When Israel left Egypt under the command of Moses, the word says they went out as an army.

> Exodus 12:51
> And it came to pass the selfsame day, *that* the LORD did bring the children of Israel out of the land of Egypt by their armies.

You are not an army unless you have weapons, and an army that doesn't have men who know how to kill the enemy isn't an army either. When Israel left Egypt, they were an army. They had lances, swords, bows, and any other weapons that were available. Israel was armed, they were trained, and they were ready to fight and kill. Any free nation today that wishes to remain free requires men who are trained and committed to fight. However, more and more, through the influence of the United Nations and generations of traitors, we are cutting our best men out of the military and replacing them with homos.

Do you still think God is wrong about homos? There is a record of an incident that occurred during the Falklands war. One of the British warships sailing to the islands had all its main deck guns put out of action in one night and the ship had to return to the UK. The culprit was found and, yes, he was a homo, a coward who had no stomach to do his duty. That wasn't reported on the news, was it?

Our military men and women are the cream of society, and they should be paid more than anyone else, including politicians. Civilians should take their hats off and show top respect to our military, and any civilian who does not, in my opinion, has no right to the free air they breathe that was paid for with the blood of better men than they.

Any nation that desires to remain free has to be willing to protect itself. It is ridiculous to disarm and think everyone else is going to disarm too. They will not. As soon as they think they are stronger than you are, they will take what is yours from you and more than likely put you to death. We should be spending more money on national defence instead of squandering it through social services on bums and deadbeats. You cannot protect domestic tranquillity by disarming the military and disarming private citizens. Military strength, being stronger than those who would attack us, is an essential component to living in free countries.

Now, the god of this world is not stupid. He knows all this. He knows what the word says, and he knows any country that upholds biblical principles will be strong. Therefore, he puts unbelievable reserves of energy and effort through the courses of the world into disarming us. Now is the time to strengthen ourselves and repair the damage that has been done by generations of traitors.

Didn't Obama sign a nuclear arms treaty with Russia that agreed to reduce America's operational nuclear weapons while the awfully nice Russians agreed to reduce theirs to twice as many as America? And that's not taking into account China. Didn't Obama also unilaterally announce that any nation that attacked the United States with biological or chemical weapons wouldn't be attacked back with nuclear weapons? On whose side do you think he is?

These traitors will dismantle your military, take your weapons from you, dismantle your space programmes, give all your money to bums and deadbeats, destroy your economy, move your businesses to China, put you all on welfare, and then laugh as your country caves in. That is their intent and they know what they are doing. They hate you with a passion you do not understand and as long as you keep your heads immersed in their television instead of in God's word, you will never see it.

Being armed and knowing how to use weapons, while having the strength and character of mind to be willing to use them, is godly and right. In fact, it is our duty. Was Samson, one of the greatest men of God of all time, afraid of a fight?

> Judges 15:14-16
> *And* when he came unto Lehi, the Philistines shouted against him: and the Spirit of the LORD came mightily upon him, and the cords that *were* upon his arms became as flax that was burnt with fire, and his bands loosed from off his hands.
>
> And he found a new jawbone of an ass, and put forth his hand, and took it, and slew a thousand men therewith.
>
> And Samson said, With the jawbone of an ass, heaps upon heaps, with the jaw of an ass have I slain a thousand men.

Samson killed one thousand men in hand-to-hand combat with a shard of animal skull. Anyone reading this want to argue that Samson wasn't a man of God? Go on then, make a fool of yourself. Whenever and wherever God's people are strong, no one dare mess with them. Whenever and wherever God's people are weak, they lose everything, including their lives. That is the nature of this world, because it is the devil's world.

The devil has murdered hundreds of millions of God's people through the centuries because they allowed their weapons to be taken from them. God's people have a right to defend themselves, their property, and their countries. The UN is committed to removing those rights from you.

From even a cursory reading of the bible, it can be seen that whenever Israel were strong militarily, they were strong as a nation, and whenever Israel were weak militarily, they were weak as a nation. For God's people, military strength is required to live in prosperity and peace.

By the way, sending our soldiers to be mercenaries for the United Nations is not what I'm talking about here. Our soldiers in Afghanistan are nothing more than mercenaries for the United Nations and its drug running operations. We are sending our men and women over there to fight and die for drug running criminals, that's all. It would take just a few hours to destroy all the opium crops in Afghanistan. Instead opium production has exploded over 900% since we ousted the nasty Taliban. We're not over there to destroy opium or to keep the peace, we're there to protect the opium and protect the United Nations gangsters who make trillions of dollars from it.

When America took Afghanistan, America should not have handed the country over to the United Nations. America should have kept the country, policed the country, administered the country, and made it America. The same goes with Iraq. Taking countries and then handing them over to the United Nations is no different to going to war for the communists, spilling your blood for them at your expense, and then handing the country over to them free of charge so they can rape and plunder it.

Okay, so that's the biblical perspective; what about the world's perspective? Well, we can begin from the premise that the devil will do everything he can to disarm God's people. That is exactly what the devil does through the United Nations. But don't just take my word for it, here is what Adolf Hitler had to say about gun control:

The most foolish mistake we could possibly make would be to allow the subject races to possess arms. History shows that all conquerors who have allowed their subject races to carry arms have prepared their own downfall by doing so.

Gun control is the work of our enemies, those who lust after our countries. If you think having your guns taken from you reduces crime and makes your communities safer to live in, you watch too much television. God wants to protect his people, but if God's people are so stupid as to allow the devil to take their guns away from them, whose fault is that?

It is a documented fact that gun control does not reduce violent crime, it increases it. That's right, unrestricted access to firearms for everyone results in a safer and more civilised place to live. In highly populated cities where the right to own firearms is rigidly restricted, crime flourishes. Where gun ownership is not restricted, crime falls – often dramatically. That is a documented fact. Your televisions and newspapers lie about this. How surprising.

Statistical proof confirms what has been evident for years. As a case in point, the women of Orlando, Florida, began to flock to gun stores to protect themselves after a spate of rapes over a nine-month period. The police offered firearms safety courses and women carried guns. Everybody in Orlando knew this, and in the following nine months there were only three rapes. Violent crime in general declined dramatically. Orlando, Florida, was the only US city with a population of over 100,000 that had a reduction in violent crime that year.

Opponents of Florida's right-to-carry legislation had claimed their state would become known as the *Gunshine State*. They were wrong and this is where most people don't see the forest for the trees. The opponents of right-to-carry legislation are not misguided for the most part, they know they are lying and they know what they are doing. They know gun control increases crime and still they advocate it and push legislation through government. Check their backgrounds, educations, political and religious persuasions, as well as affiliations with secret societies and you will begin to see a pattern emerging.

As to statistics, well, you can manipulate statistics to say anything you like. In Caithness in the Highlands of Scotland where the Dounreay Nuclear reactor was built, a news report in the media in the 1980s claimed there was a substantial increase in the likelihood of contracting leukaemia if you lived near the reactor. The statistics were sound. However, what the media didn't tell you was that these statistics were based on there being three cases of leukaemia over a period covering many decades when the national average should have been two. That's right, three cases instead of two. That isn't statistics, that is manipulation of information, propaganda, psychological warfare, and domestic terrorism. And it's related to gun control. Dounreay was involved in the production of nuclear weapons.

One has only to glimpse what happened to the christians in Rwanda between April and July of 1994 to imagine what lies in store for Europeans and Americans. The genocide was planned, not by the Hutus or the Tutsis, but by the United Nations who disarmed them prior to the murders. After the people had been disarmed by governmental decree in the early 1990s, military forces began to systematically massacre them. Using machetes rather than bullets to save money, a state of abject fear and terror was instilled as they butchered hundreds of thousands. Estimates of the death toll have ranged between 500,000 and 1,000,000, or as much as 20% of the total population.

Nor is this an isolated case. In 1929, the Soviet Union established gun control. From 1929 to 1953, about 20 million Russian *dissidents*, unable to defend themselves, were rounded up and exterminated. In 1911, Turkey established gun control. From 1915 to 1917, around 1.5 million Armenians, unable to defend themselves, were rounded up and exterminated. In 1938, Hitler established gun control in Germany, and from 1939 to 1945, over 13 million people, unable to defend themselves, were rounded up and exterminated. In 1935, China established gun control. From 1948 to 1952, over 20 million political *dissidents*, unable to defend themselves, were murdered, many of them drowned by having their heads pushed into barrels of human excrement. In 1964, Guatemala established gun control. From 1964 to 1981, around 100,000 Mayan Indians, unable to defend themselves were rounded up and murdered. Uganda established gun control before murdering over 300,000 christians. Cambodia established gun control prior to exterminating over one million people who were unable to defend themselves. Whenever and wherever a government disarms its citizens, murder is in its heart.

Currently, restrictive gun control laws are in force throughout Europe, with the exception of Switzerland where the devil hoards his money. Every home in Switzerland is armed with automatic rifles given to them by the government. Why isn't this ever mentioned on television? American gun control laws are under siege. Australian statistics since the government enforced new gun control laws there show that in the following 12 month period murders were up 3.2 percent, assaults 8.6 percent, and armed robberies 44 percent. Australian politicians claim to be at a loss to explain how public safety has decreased after such monumental effort and expense was expended in successfully ridding their society of guns. The Australian experience and other historical facts prove it. As Janet Reno publicly stated regarding gun control in America: *Waiting periods are only a step. Registration is only a step. The prohibition of private firearms is the goal.* Gun control is not about protecting you, it is about dismantling your defences. Gun control isn't about guns, it is about control.

Unfortunately, a large number of religious authorities back gun control, stating that the bible says we should not kill. How they can arrive at such a conclusion from scripture is criminal. How anyone can swallow such perverting of scripture is unbelievable. When God told Joshua to take the Promised Land, one wonders how Joshua was going to do it without killing anyone. What, he was going to negotiate terms with them? If your minister advocates a policy of disarmament, get out of his shithole church. More than likely, he's a homo anyway.

The original word used in the commandment *thou shalt not kill* means thou shalt not murder. There are plenty of records in the bible where God told people to kill. Take the death penalty as an example. God *commanded* us to carry out the death penalty in certain cases. How can you execute someone without killing them? It is misinterpretation and criminal misrepresentation of the bible to use the scripture *thou shalt not kill* as a means to remove our weapons of self-defence.

If guns cause crime, then cameras cause pornography. Know guns, know peace, know safety – no guns, no peace, no safety. Assault is a type of behaviour, not a type of hardware. Firearm safety is a matter of education, not legislation. Honest citizens don't carry guns to kill people, they carry guns to keep from being killed. They don't carry guns because they are evil but because they have lived long enough to see the evil in the world. They don't carry guns because they're angry but so they don't spend the rest of their lives living with the consequences of failing to be prepared to deal with criminals. They only carry guns because they want to die of old age, not by a roadside somewhere tomorrow. Men don't carry guns to make them feel like men, they carry guns because real men know how to take care of those they love.

By the way, it isn't the police's responsibility to protect you and your family, it's yours. Gun control survives as an ideology because most believe that the police are there to protect us and, therefore, we don't need guns. If you don't know why that belief is founded on myth, then you cannot destroy gun control. Antigun lobbyists get away with proposing to completely disarm us only because most of us assume the police will protect us. That assumption is false. The police owe no legal duty to protect individuals from crime. The police in most places do not even have to come when you call.

Gun prohibitionist lobbyists, human rights groups, the United Nations, and the media have sold us the lie of police protection. Picking up the phone is not self-protection. Trusting in a phone number for your own safety and the safety of those you love won't work. Many people have died as a result of violent crime because the police did not or could not help them. You cannot defend yourself by picking up a phone, only by picking up a weapon and knowing how to use it. God expects us to know how to use weapons and protect ourselves. The world is not telling us the truth about guns.

Do you think there are no solutions to the world's problems? An Australian SAS soldier went to Colombia in 2006 to work as a private bodyguard. His method was to follow at a distance behind his clients' cars on a motorbike, then ride up and shoot criminals in the act of kidnapping. He was so successful that kidnappings in Colombia decreased over 80%. That is a verifiable fact. One man reduced violent kidnappings in an entire country single-handedly by over 80%. Rest in peace Sooki, we need more like you.

While on the subject, let's look at the concept of peacekeeping and peacemaking, the military wing of the United Nations. Bear in mind, of course, that soldiers merely carry out orders and do what they believe to be their duty. They are men who are willing to put themselves in harm's way for their countrymen, and who feel the freedoms we enjoy worth the sacrifice they pay. The UN misuses them. As an example, here are a few excerpts from an article written by an Australian soldier who was sent to Rwanda as part of a UN peacekeeping force.

There is a section of 2/4 RAR riflemen and an RMO and some medics at the RAP. The RAP is located to the right on a small knoll with an old mission nearby us. We are forced to stay within the UN rules of engagement and that is not to discharge our weapons unless directly fired at.

The Tutsi soldiers are continually firing into the women and children in the hope of hitting the men who are using them as shields. There are many dead and dying in front of us, but we can only help a few when they drop close to us.

One man in his 20's makes a break from the crowd and runs toward us for shelter. He is hit about 20 metres from our location. He is wounded in the upper thigh and judging by the amount of dark blood coming from the wound the bullet has obviously hit a major artery. We call for him to crawl to us as we are not allowed to collect him. It is against the UN rules. He is crying for us to help. But we cant. It would be breaking the rules.

After about 2 hours, he managed to crawl close enough for me and a mate to dart out and haul him into the RAP. But he is too far gone. The RMO bandages the wound and gives him a dose of morphine. But he won't survive.

The Tutsi are still firing into the crowds and the dead and wounded are everywhere. The young man with the leg wound dies and I'm thankful I no longer have to look into his eyes. I will never forget those eyes.

We are angry, but there is nothing we can do but watch the massacre. The Tutsi have a Quad .50 cal set up on a truck with the barrels pointed at the RAP. The gunners stand nearby. Whenever we look like moving forward to pick up someone, the gunners jump onto the truck and point the .50 cal at us. There is nothing we can do but watch.

The Tutsi commander finally gives us permission to put the wounded women and children into the old mission and treat them. We collect about 200 people and begin to help and treat them as best we can. But it was a trick. We are ordered out of the mission and sent back to the RAP. This isn't good. Again, there is nothing we can do.

Walking *by* the Spirit

We move back to the RAP and watch as the Tutsi close up the doors to the mission, leaving the women and children inside. They set fire to the mission. We can hear the gunshots and screams. It is sickening. And so it goes on.

We stood among the dead and wounded with our symbols of world peace on our blue helmets and our representation of humanity on our shoulders. We looked and tried to comprehend what we saw before us. My boots were covered in human faeces and everywhere I looked, babies lay next to dead mothers who had been murdered the night before.

Through the smell and the stench came a young girl, no older than seven. On her back was her baby brother and in her arms was her baby sister. She had walked over many bodies to speak to these saviours with the UN helmets on their tired and unshaven heads. As she looked up at me with tears in her eyes and with an empty water bottle in her hand, I had to tell her to return to where she came from for I had no water.

I do not understand what I am doing here or how the world can know and yet we can or will do nothing. This uniform means nothing to me now, for I have watched a man as he was shot three times, not twenty metres in front of me and I could do nothing. Why?

The murderers who committed this atrocity stand free next to me and laugh as I treat a three year old with machete wounds. I am angry and cannot comprehend.

If you were to ask me how it feels to come home after helping these people in the name of humanity and world peace, I am sorry but I don't have an answer. I only have unanswered questions and tragic memories of something which in its madness will someday happen again.

If this is your idea of world peace, you can shove it up your ass.

It is evident that winning is not news in our western countries. All we ever hear about is when we lose. Our soldiers can win fifty battles and lose one and we would never hear about the fifty victorious battles, all we would see on our televisions would be weeks of reports on the one battle we lost. I guess our media would call this freedom of speech. Quite how the world gets away with such blatant propaganda is testament to the power of the media when the bible is neglected.

Recently, the Australian SAS acting on intelligence regarding Taliban leadership, stormed a compound in Afghanistan and killed the bad guys. No civilians were injured during the operation, which was carried out in hazardous conditions. The mission was a complete success. If just one civilian had been injured, it would have been front page news all over the world the following day, yet not one word of this operation was breathed in the Australian or the world's media for weeks. When the story was finally released the headline read – Four Australian Solders injured in Afghanistan.

Fortunately, one of the Australian soldiers had worn a helmet camera and filmed the operation. On reading the news report, the footage was released on YouTube and disseminated around the world through Facebook.

The Australian Ministry of Defence, after weeks of demands to know why the story had been deliberately suppressed and the facts twisted, eventually made a press release to the effect that to release information could jeopardise ongoing operations. Really? Then how come if one civilian had been injured or killed full details of the entire operation would have been front page news all over the world the following day? Someone somewhere is lying. The question is, who and why?

Another common pattern, which is easy to see in any conflict in which the United Nations is involved, is that when the terrorists are winning, the United Nations stands by and does nothing. Whenever a government dares to take a stand against terrorism and fights back, the UN brokers a peace deal. In reality, all the United Nations does is act as bodyguards for terrorists. Once the terrorists recover sufficiently, the UN pulls out and it's back to business as usual. When terrorists are winning, the UN does nothing.

Look, the UN are liars, gangsters, paedophiles, and murderers, whose only interest is stealing the world for their god. As long as legitimate governments are weakened, the UN does nothing. Whenever terrorists, rebels, freedom fighters, call them what you will, are attacked by government forces, the UN steps in to protect them. When the UN feels the danger to the terrorists is over and they have had sufficient time to regroup and rearm, the UN pulls out and the government finds itself once more in the position it was in before any UN intervention.

One must ask, how does such blatant and obvious support for terror by the United Nations and the International Red Cross go unnoticed and unchallenged? Good question. Did you know the same men who use Al Jazeera to spew their subversive propaganda out through the loudspeakers of the entire Arab and Muslim world are the same men spewing poison into your brain every time you switch on the news or pick up your daily paper? Haven't you ever noticed that in any armed conflict, the United Nations and the International Red Cross always work on the side of terrorists against governments? Unless, of course, it's China, Russia or North Korea. Why is that?

In Vietnam, the communist terrorists required *enormous* supplies of food and arms to be able to keep fighting. The logistics were staggering. The Ho Chi Minh trail was the lifeline through the jungle that supplied them from communist China. It moved like an army of ants, 24hrs a day, back and forth, in all weathers, transporting food and arms to the front lines. Amazingly, America knew where it was and had it watched but were forbidden by the UN to attack it, so they didn't. Try to find that fact in any of your school history books.

World terrorism today requires a much larger 'Ho Chi Minh' trail to keep the world's terrorist armies in ammunition, food, and medical supplies. The International Red Cross is the modern Ho Chi Minh trail that keeps international terrorism thriving on every continent in the world, transporting colossal loads around the world in aircraft and by ship labelled as humanitarian aid.

Where do you think all the money that is raised in charity drives on television to feed the world's poor goes? Do you think it goes to help people? What's left after the funds have been plundered by the greedy bastards who own the charities goes to feed, house, train, and arm terrorists across the globe. Every penny you send to the United Nations and the International Red Cross through their fund drives and humanitarian aid drives goes straight into the terrorist purse. If you give money to them you are funding world terrorism, you are funding your own extinction. The next time these beggars interrupt your dinner with heartrending pleas on television to send money to them, tell them to fuck off.

Everything the United Nations does helps the terrorist cause. The UN banned the SAS from using sawn off shotguns in the jungles of Malaya. Why? Because the SAS were killing too many terrorists, that's why. Sawn off shotguns were too effective, so the UN banned them for being 'inhumane', to give the terrorists more of a chance. We should give the SAS back their sawn off shotguns, and while we are at it, we should pay them big bonuses for every terrorist head they bring back in a plastic bag.

Of course, Hollywood – and by the way, magic wands are made from holly wood – plays a big part in keeping the world sympathetic to the terrorist cause. What do you think of Robin Hood? A dashing young man putting the world to rights, helping oppressed people by sorting out the nasty government? Robin Hood was a terrorist who robbed and murdered honest people to fund his campaign to overthrow the government. And here perhaps, we find our first clue to what is really going on in the world. You see Robin Hood's spiritual advisor was a Roman Catholic 'holy' man sent by the vatican whose only intent was the overthrow of the throne in Great Britain and the installation of a Roman Catholic king. I have no idea why some Muslims are mad at America for the crusades, it was the vatican who ordered their extermination. America was not even around at the time.

Wars are engineered. All of them. They don't just happen. War is being engineered right now between the west and the Muslims. Why is America and Britain on side with terrorists, fighting to overthrow Arab and Muslim countries for the UN? Why are the Russians and the Chinese not directly involved? If the UN wants these Muslim countries democratised, why don't they send in the Russian and Chinese military? Why are we now fighting for world communism? Why is America being seen as the enemy of the Muslim world when it is the UN giving the orders? Why are the Arabs and Muslims not getting mad at the United Nations? Who is feeding, housing, arming, and paying the wages of all these so-called rebels anyway? Who is supplying their medical needs? Everyone today is mad at the Muslims, and the Muslims are mad at us. Why instead are we not both getting mad at those who are stirring things up between us?

So, who engineers wars and for what purpose? Let's look at the Falklands as an example, as it's happening again right now, in 2015. In 1964, Argentina and the United Nations discussed Argentina's right to sovereignty over the Falklands and immediately drew Britain to the negotiating table. In 1964, Lord Caradon declared that the interests of the inhabitants of the territories were paramount after the Falkland islanders conveyed to the UN General Assembly that under all circumstances they wished to remain a British dependency. Argentina then played the imperialist card, no doubt at the prompting of the UN.

Costa Mendes, the Argentinean foreign minister at the time – a UN crony educated in Internationalism at Oxford – saw the pursuit of Argentina's claim as a means of strengthening the nation's identity. In July 1966, a series of secret meetings were held in London between Henry Hohler of the Foreign Office and Juan Carlos Beltramino. As a result of these meetings, a group of armed terrorists hijacked a Dakota over Patagonia and flew to Port Stanley where they 'arrested' two British officials. Instead of executing those terrorists, we returned them to Argentina at the tax payer's expense.

In 1967, meetings continued between the UN, Argentina, and Britain, Costa Mendes now meeting with his new British counterpart, George Brown. This secret initiative was only discovered by Parliament in 1968. When it was discovered that secret negotiations over sovereignty of the Falklands was being discussed, uproar resulted in Britain and George Brown was forced to resign.

On three occasions, in 1968, 1977, and 1981, British governments could have suspended talks on the grounds that the principle of self-determination represented an impossible obstacle to progress. A few of our politicians however, deliberately kept the process open. The damage was done and the nation was on a course for war. The United Nations engineered the Falklands War.

The Middle East is another good example. The KGB founded the PLO. That's right, Arafat and the PLO were founded and financed by the communists, and it was the UN through the Oslo peace accords that put Arafat and the PLO into power. Arafat was a hard core Communist. Even the Muslims know that. Paradoxically, it was also the UN behind the founding of present day Israel and therein lays the key to the current Middle East conflict. This whole political mess was engineered, conjured up out of nothing, and the Palestinians and the Israelis are paying the price. The UN does not want peace in the Middle East, rather they are responsible for it and actively encourage it.

Look, the bad guys want us dead, and, funnily enough, they also want the Muslims dead. They want our countries, they want our lands, our properties, everything. If the west and the Muslims go to war and destroy each other, the United Nations and the communists get their one world government because there will be no one left to oppose them.

The United Nations is a terror organisation, as is the International Red Cross. They both work in conjunction through their worldwide network of human rights groups to subvert legitimate governments in furtherance of one world governance so they can bring us what they call peace on earth. The only problem is, we have to go so they can have their world. How they get rid of us isn't important, just so long as they get their world.

Disarmament is a synonym for extinction. We need our military now more than at any time before in earth's history. So, either we get real about what is happening in the world, or we're marched to the gas chambers of the new world order.

Before closing, let's consider *who* we are at war with. If we face Chinese troops on the battlefield, does that mean we are at war with the Chinese? Not at all. China is an illegally occupied country and has been for nearly a century. Their military men and women simply do what they believe to be their duty. I have no quarrel with the Chinese. I was brought up in Hong Kong and learned to love the Chinese at a very young age. Their art is unparalleled in passion and heart. They are a wonderful people.

So is communism our enemy then? Communism is but a political device. To say we are at war with communism is to say we are at war with dreams. Go to war with such concepts and you will be fighting shadows. Folks should think of communism less as an army of boogie men and more as a disease. The belief that one world governance is the answer to all the world's ills is a virus that can infect the man next to you in your workplace. Communism transcends race, gender, skin colour, and religion, turning men into traitors, men who consider the destruction of their own country and their own fellow countrymen worth the price of a new world order. This they call selfless. In truth, they are corrupted by moral disease, they are traitors, and they are worthy of death.

Before you can defeat your enemy, you must be able to see him. Who controls communism? Where did communism come from? Do we have communist traitors among us?

Roosevelt, who gave Poland to the communists and who was the first western leader to grant communist Russia diplomatic recognition, was a member of the Council on Foreign Relations (the CFR). He referred to Stalin as Uncle Joe and ensured the Russians were the first to reach Berlin by holding back the Allied Forces.

Following the victories in Europe and the Far East, the Truman administration continued with this policy of aiding communists by permitting huge amounts of Japanese armaments to fall into the hands of Mao Tse Tung's forces in China. When the Chinese leader Chiang Kai Shek refused Truman's orders to admit communists into his government, Truman cut off all aid to him. The communists took China in 1949 and the legitimate Chinese government fled to Taiwan. China is an illegally occupied country whose legitimate government is still in Taiwan. In 1950, America went to war in Korea under Truman. Truman was a member of the CFR.

Clinton granted full diplomatic recognition to communist Vietnam. He granted favoured nation status to communist China, and he did nothing to prevent the Panama Canal from falling under the control of the Chinese military. Clinton dismantled the American military to the point that it was almost ineffectual. He binned Star Wars leaving America and its Allies defenceless to missile attack. Clinton was a member of the CFR.

Dulles was senior United States adviser at the San Francisco conference at which the United Nations came into being. Dulles was a member of the CFR.

Alger Hiss was a communist spy. Alger Hiss was one of the American delegates at the forming of the United Nations. Alger Hiss was in the CFR.

President Woodrow Wilson who signed into law two planks of the Communist Manifesto but who failed in his bid to institute a one world government through the League of Nations, was in the CFR.

Paul Warburg, who with other International bankers staged the secret meetings and the sinking of the Titanic which paved the way for the creation of the American Federal Reserve system, effectively giving financial control of America to International bankers, was in the CFR.

The CFR is known as The Establishment, or the invisible government. At least forty-seven CFR members were among the American delegates to the founding of the United Nations in San Francisco in 1945. Members of the CFR group included Harold Stassen, John J McCloy, Owen Lattimore, Alger Hiss, Nelson Rockefeller, John Foster Dulles, John Vincent Carter, and Dean Acheson.

So completely has the CFR dominated the State Department over the past few decades that every Secretary of State except Cordell Hull, James Byrnes, and William Rogers has been a member of the CFR.

Among the communications corporations represented in the CFR are National, Columbia, Time, Life, Fortune, Look, Newsweek, the New York Times, the Washington Post, the Los Angeles Times, the New York Post, Simon and Schuster, Harper Bros, Random House, Little Brown and Co, Macmillan, Viking, Business Week, etc, ad nauseum.

David Rockefeller himself, in his own words, wrote:

We are grateful to the Washington Post, the New York Times, Time magazine and other great publications whose directors have attended our meetings and respected their promises of discretion for almost forty years. It would have been impossible for us to develop our plan for the world if we had been subjected to the lights of publicity during those years. But, the world is now more sophisticated and prepared to march towards a world government. The super national sovereignty of an intellectual elite and world bankers is surely preferable to the national auto determination practiced in past centuries.

To conclude, here are three excerpts from the writings of those who would destroy us. These men exist. They are intelligent, they are educated, they are powerful, they are rich, and they are committed. Note the tie in here with climate change, the current economic nuclear weapon aimed at America with the power to destroy it.

It is indispensable for our purpose that wars, so far as possible, should not result in territorial gains: war will thus be brought on to the economic ground, where the nations will not fail to perceive in the assistance we give the strength of our predominance, and this state of things will put both sides at the mercy of our international agentur; which possesses millions of eyes ever on the watch and unhampered by any limitations whatsoever. Our international rights will then wipe out national rights, in the proper sense of right, and will rule the nations precisely as the civil law of States rules the relations of their subjects among themselves.

Remember the French Revolution, to which it was we who gave the name of 'Great': the secrets of its preparations are well known to us for it was wholly the work of our hands.

Should anyone of a liberal mind say that such reflections as the above are immoral, I would put the following questions: If every State has two foes and if in regard to the external foe it is allowed and not considered immoral to use every manner and art of conflict, as for example to keep the enemy in ignorance of plans of attack and defense, to attack him by night or in superior numbers, then in what way can the same means in regard to a worse foe, the destroyer of the structure of society and the commonweal, be called immoral and not permissible?

The same men who engineered the French Revolution, for engineered it was – planned and systematically implemented – are the same men, in an organisational sense, who planned the communist takeovers of Russia and China. Who wrote those words? We shall soon see.

24. Weishaupt and the Illuminati

I think we are beginning to get the idea that Lucifer, the devil, the god of this world, satan, the prince of the power of the air, call him what you will, does not like us. Is that really so surprising? Man gave the Lordship of the earth to the devil way back in Genesis. We got ourselves into this mess, so don't go blaming God for the state of the world. Instead, be thankful God didn't leave us in this mess, but came up with a plan to get us out of it. Let's reacquaint ourselves with an old friend from the gospel of John.

> John 10:10
> The thief cometh not, but for to steal, and to kill, and to destroy: I am come that they might have life, and that they might have *it* more abundantly.

The god of this world paints evil with a colourful brush, while at the same time painting christianity with a drab brush. How he colours the senses realm in this manner is quite illuminating to observe.

For example, alcohol is promoted socially and advertised through the media as fun and entertaining, something to look forward to at the weekend, something worth spending all our money on. The bible on the other hand warns us that drunkenness is an open door to major problems. Did you know that most homos and lesbians are recruited when they are drunk? If they had not been drunk, that door would not have opened and they would not have been corrupted.

Drunkenness, however, isn't forced on us, it is something we open our minds to by our own freedom of will, it is something that we allow into our lives through the influences of the world and social pressure. God warns people not to get drunk, not because he wants us to have no fun, but because he wants us to enjoy life and avoid the serious problems that drunkenness brings. Refusing to get drunk is something we can choose to do.

Who floods our streets with alcohol and drugs? Who grooms our children for them when they are young? Follow the money to the top of the pyramid and you will find not philanthropists who love you, but greedy men who love money.

If people understood Lucifer, the god of this world, no one would do anything for him. He knows this, so he hides from view. From behind the scenes he entices, seduces, and bribes those within his grasp to do his bidding. Fortunately, quite unlike the true God, the devil is not all-knowing, nor is he all-powerful, nor is he everywhere present. He can only be in one place at one time.

> Job 1:7
> And the LORD said unto Satan, Whence comest thou? Then Satan answered the LORD, and said, From going to and fro in the earth, and from walking up and down in it.

> 1 Peter 5:8
> Be sober, be vigilant; because your adversary the devil, as a roaring lion, walketh about, seeking whom he may devour:

From what we've read and understood so far in this work, it follows then that because Lucifer isn't all knowing and isn't everywhere present, he must have some kind of worldwide intelligence network in place in the world through which he remains informed. The god of this world doesn't depict himself as an all seeing eye for no reason. Obviously, these earthly operational networks are shrouded in secrecy and mystery to keep them concealed. Indeed, we even refer to them as secret societies.

Secret societies have been around since Nimrod, back in the book of Genesis. There have been so many of them, and they are so veiled in mystery and intrigue, that it is almost impossible to track them and to know what is going on within them. Even their own members have no idea what is going on in the circles above them. To begin to break into these circles we have to start somewhere, so let's begin with the Illuminati.

The Founder of the Illuminati, Adam Weishaupt, was born and raised in Ingolstadt, Bavaria, Germany. On May 1, 1776, he founded a secret society that he called the Order of Perfectibilists, which later became the Order of Illuminati. Within this order, he adopted the name of Brother Spartacus.

Amazingly, history books and encyclopaedias are astonishingly silent on the subject of both Weishaupt and the Illuminati. A cursory glance through available schoolbooks and university textbooks will reveal nothing, and you could be fooled into thinking neither existed. This isn't surprising because secret societies, as the term implies, like to remain secret, hidden from view. Whenever and wherever we inadvertently catch fleeting glimpses of them through the lenses of the world's media, they quickly waggle their tongues at anyone sounding the alarm, dismissing them as lunatic conspiracy theorists while hastily covering their tracks through an organised public relations exercise of misinformation, lies, and deception.

To put this into a modern day perspective, when I first Googled the word *Illuminati* around 1998, only six results were returned. Five of those links led to spoof sites. One led to a religious site through which I had to sift with care and thoroughness in order to find sufficient information to begin a meaningful search. If you Google Illuminati now you will be drowned in an ocean of millions of search results, making finding the few morsels of truth available even more difficult than when there were no results at all. Most of this misinformation and deception has been disseminated by secret societies themselves to cover their tracks. Weishaupt himself wrote:

The great strength of our Order lies in its concealment; let it never appear in any place in its own name, but always covered by another name, and another occupation... Of all the means I know to lead men, the most effectual is a concealed mystery. The hankering of the mind is irresistible.

According to the vast majority of the information now available regarding Weishaupt and the Illuminati, he was ineffectual, he denounced the Illuminati before he died, the Illuminati was destroyed in Bavaria, and there is nothing to worry about. If you believe that, you need to change your source of education and replace the Internet, along with your televisions and newspapers, with a source a little more reliable, like the word of God. Just because the devil conceals himself from view does not mean he does not exist.

So who was Weishaupt and what happened to the Illuminati? Adam Weishaupt was a professor of law. On May 1st, 1766, Weishaupt, on orders from his superiors, founded the Illuminati. Their aim was the formation of a one world government and to that end they devised a new concept in political thinking – communism. Weishaupt was the brains, Rothschild (the Vatican banker) the money, behind the masonic Jacobin clubs that sprang up all over France just prior to, and which fomented and were responsible for, the French revolution.

Incidentally, May 1st is universally recognised as the birth date of communism, and it is rather sad to observe it is now being celebrated in free countries every year on what we call May Day. This holiday should be struck from our calendars. It is no cause for celebration.

In 1785, lightning struck and killed one of Weishaupt's men, and important documents fell into the hands of the Bavarian government. They immediately ordered the police to raid the headquarters of the Illuminati in Germany. Weishaupt fled for his life and the Illuminati went underground.

Sometime later, they changed their name to the League of the Just and had a notable man join them – Karl Marx. In 1842, Marx was commissioned to update the writings of Weishaupt. The Communist Manifesto appeared in 1843 and the Illuminati again changed their name, this time to the League of Communists. In the 1890s, a certain Vladimir Ulyanov joined them and travelled to Russia on an American passport. The British police tried to stop him, but the Illuminati in the States, under the influence of Albert Pike, had grown strong. Ulyanov later changed his name to Lenin. Using the same principles they had learned in France, the Illuminati overthrew the tsar and founded the first Communist superpower.

After the First World War and their success in Russia, the Illuminati again changed their name, this time to the League of Nations, with its headquarters in Geneva. Believing that a war-ravaged earth would be easy prey they made an attempt to form a one world government. However, the American President at the time, Woodrow Wilson, who was one of the Illuminati, failed to get the two-thirds majority he needed to ratify the treaty. Undaunted, the Illuminati acquired a prime site along the East River in New York – donated to them incidentally by John D Rockefeller – built their new headquarters on it and changed their name yet again, this time to the United Nations.

The United Nations is the modern day Illuminati. Their aim is one world governance. The power and money behind the United Nations is the same power and money that was behind the Illuminati when they first formed, and it is the same power and money that was behind the French, Russian, and Chinese revolutions. It is the same power and money behind the so-called democratisation of the Muslim and Arab world today. It is the same power and money behind every human rights organisation on earth, all struggling together for the same *cause*, marching beneath trite banners of world peace and an end to poverty. The hidden truth behind their banners however, is somewhat more terrifying.

You could write entire books on the United Nations, many have, but in this work they are having but a mention as I do not deem them worth any more of my time. However, I will highlight a couple of aspects of the United Nations, such as their stance on justice and human rights.

The United Nations has declared that every human being has a right to life. Chapter and verse please. That statement, though couched in fancy religious robes, is not scriptural. Does the United Nations really believe that homosexual monsters that rape and murder little boys should be protected from justice and not executed for their horrific crimes? Obviously, they do. Everyone has a right to life, they say, and they go out of their way to stop us from executing the bastards.

What about the human rights of all the sodomised and murdered young boys we keep hearing about? They are even raping and murdering babies now. Does the United Nations care more about protecting monsters from justice than in protecting our children from them? Obviously they do, but why? That is the question we should be asking about the United Nations. Why does the United Nations protect such criminals and do nothing to provide justice for our murdered children? Could it be that their leaders indulge in such practices? Well, who is running the world?

The United Nations stands in direct opposition to the bible on justice. God's word is clear on the use of the death penalty. So, we have a choice to make. Are we going to put our trust in God and his word, or in the United Nations and its words?

What the bible says about homosexuality is what God thinks about homosexuality. God instituted the death penalty for homosexuality, not me. I am merely telling you what the bible says. If our courts are protecting homosexuals and our schools are promoting it as a healthy lifestyle to our children, then something is seriously wrong. So the next time some young boy gets raped and murdered by homo paedophiles, don't go blaming God, blame the United Nations because they are responsible. They are the ones who have dismantled the laws that God told us to put in place to protect us and our children from such foul creatures.

I have the right to choose what I believe. I choose to believe God's word rather than the words of the United Nations. I choose to think of homosexuality as the depraved, disgusting perversion worthy of death that God's word says it is. Some will say I hate homosexuals or that I am homophobic. No, I don't hate homosexuals, I love them enough to tell them the truth and give them an opportunity to change. Nor am I homophobic, I'm not afraid of them in the slightest, which is what a phobia is. It is time to warn our children against homosexuality and prevent the world from grooming them for it.

The United Nations won't like my stance? The International Red Cross is going to be upset? Greenpeace will be horrified? Amnesty International will issue proclamations decrying me for being anti-human rights? The UCLA is going to take God to court? If they have a problem with God and his word, I suggest they take their grievances up with him. You make up your own mind. The world stands in active opposition to God's word because the devil is the god of this world.

The United Nations and the legions of human rights and environmental organisations it has spawned over the last few decades claim they are fighting for freedom and peace. However, when you take a closer look behind the slogans they march through our media you will soon realise that all the so-called human rights they champion are being doled out to criminals, while honest people are being stripped of their rights to protection from them.

It was the UN that put Mugabe in power and destroyed Rhodesia with their promises of freedom, peace, and solidarity for all. If you want to see what is really behind the United Nations, look at Rhodesia and see what human rights did to it. The United Nations turned a food exporting country into a poverty ridden criminal cesspit run by a tyrant in just a few years. That is what the United Nations does through its promotion of human rights, but let's not lose sight of the purpose of this chapter.

The Illuminati has been socially revered out of all proportion to their position within the circles of secret societies. They are not the top echelon, they are but another circle further down the pyramid of secret societies. The foundation of this pyramid, the foundation upon which all secret societies are supported, is freemasonry. As you ascend through their degrees of deception and concealment, you will eventually move through higher and higher circles, such as the Knights of Malta, Opus Dei, Skull and Bones, and the Illuminati, until you reach the top of the pyramid.

Each circle has a job to perform. Take the round table for example. Between the ages of twenty-four and twenty-six Cecil Rhodes made a number of wills. The first established a secret society that became the round table, while the last established Rhodes scholarships. By the beginning of World War 1 there were round table groups established in seven countries – The United States, The UK, South Africa, Canada, Australia, New Zealand, and India. After the Paris Peace Conference in March 1919, these round table groups were formally established as the Institutes of International Affairs at a meeting held at the Majestic Hotel in Paris. However, in 1920, because of anti-British feelings in America caused by the war, the American group adopted the rather cryptic name, The Council on Foreign Relations.

The CFR runs the State Department and the CIA. They work together to deceive and misinform the president into acting in the best interests of the CFR and not the American people. The CFR members that surround the president are known as 'the Secret Team'. They help carry out psycho-political operations scripted by CFR members in the State Department and the Intelligence Organisations. A group of CFR members called the Special Group, which evolved from the Psychological Strategy Board (PSB), coordinates these psychopolitical operations. CFR members Gordon Gray and Henry Kissinger ran the PSB. However, the American people became wary of the PSB, so Eisenhower issued an executive order changing its name to the Operations Coordination Board. The OCB was bigger and more powerful, and Gray and Kissinger ran that too. John F Kennedy abolished the OCB. After Kennedy's assassination, which no doubt served as a warning to future Presidents, the OCB became an ad hoc committee called the Special Group, which exists today, and it always has CFR members running and sitting on it. These are unelected men who continue from administration to administration, regardless of any elections or their outcomes. Democracy, mob rule, no longer exists.

The overriding aim of the CFR is the same as the communists, the formation of a one world government, and like their illegitimate brethren, the Institutes of International Affairs, they are committed to destroying sovereignty in the countries in which they operate.

Secret society members control the world. They hold all the top positions and all answer to the same people at the top of the pyramid of secret societies. The World Bank, The United Nations, The Royal Institute of International Affairs (Chatham House), The Trilateral Commission, The Council on Foreign Relations, The Department for International Development, The World Health Organisation, The International Red Cross, Greenpeace, CND, Amnesty International, the World Council of Churches, the RSPB – to name but a few – are all controlled by the same men and all work together towards the same goal – the dismantling of all sovereignty worldwide and the institution of a single world government. Did you know that at the time of writing there were 1500 newspapers, 100 magazines, 9000 radio stations, 1500 TV stations, and 2400 publishers worldwide owned by just 3 companies? That is how the god of this world controls what you think.

Each degree within the masons only has real knowledge of those in the immediate degrees above them. They have no idea what is going on over their heads. This keeps the top masons protected, as even their own members don't know who they are. Even thirty-third degree freemasons are but lowly subordinates to those in other secret societies. Unlike the true God, the god of this world is not all knowing so he requires this world network to stay informed and through which to channel his orders.

All the world's top terrorist and criminal organisations are secret societies. The top men of the IRA, PIRA, ETA, and the Mafia are all high-ranking members of secret societies. They are masons who all take their orders from the same men and they will even work together from time to time. It was the IRA who sent men over to South America to train PIRA terrorists in bomb making. All the world's tyrants were spawned in secret societies. Arafat, Pol Pot, Hitler, Lenin, Marx, Mao Tse Tung, Mugabe, Clinton and Blair were all recruited from within the masonic sperm pool. However, these men were and are merely puppets on the world stage, their strings pulled by others.

The more you look at the world through the filter of secret societies, the more your understanding of the world will flow together. Lowly masons, for the most part, are good men who really believe they are helping to save the world. However, as they are initiated into ever higher circles within their orders, they are gradually corrupted. It starts with little lies, small thefts, little deceits, but quickly grows into far more serious problems. The end justifies the means is the doctrine to which they succumb as they are bribed and coerced into doing the will of the god of this world. Those most easily corrupted are quickly promoted, which is why shit always floats to the top of the masonic sewer. This hand signal represents the horns of Lucifer, whom these men worship.

You masons, your first and foremost responsibility is not to your order. The secret knowledge with which you are bewitched is the same secret knowledge that seduced Eve. Yes, it is knowledge from the gods, and Lucifer is powerful, but the magic and sorcery you seek will destroy you. Only by coming back to the true God and his word will you ever realise the fulfilment of true spiritual power. You may think you are saving the world, but your lives are nothing more than traitorous puppets for the devil. Remain on your present course and your hearts will be broken on the rocks of despair and sorrow.

> 1 Timothy 6:10
> For the love of money is the root of all evil: which while some coveted after, they have erred from the faith, and pierced themselves through with many sorrows.

So who is at the top of the pyramid then? Who is big enough and powerful enough to control the Mafia? Who is big enough and ruthless enough to control the IRA? Who is big enough and powerful enough to control ETA and PIRA? Who is big enough and powerful enough to control the United Nations, the International Red Cross, Greenpeace, the World Bank, CND, the RSPB and the host of other criminal and terrorist organisations choking the life out of the planet? Who is big enough and powerful enough to keep them all in step, working towards the same idealistic goal of a single world government? Perhaps we can get another clue from our old pal Weishaupt. You see, Weishaupt was a jesuit priest.

25. The Jesuits

I didn't understand evil until I began to understand the jesuits. Have you ever wondered what a jesuit goes through when he is accepted into the order? When a jesuit takes his final oaths, the superior first speaks:

My son, heretofore you have been taught to act the dissembler: among Roman Catholics to be a Roman Catholic, and to be a spy even among your own brethren; to believe no man, to trust no man. Among the Reformers, to be a Reformer; among the Huguenots, to be a Huguenot; among the Calvinists, to be a Calvinist; among other Protestants, generally to be a Protestant; and obtaining their confidence, to seek even to preach from their pulpits, and to denounce with all the vehemence in your nature our Holy Religion and the Pope; and even to descend so low as to become a Jew among Jews, that you might be enabled to gather together all information for the benefit of your Order as a faithful soldier of the Pope. You have been taught to plant insidiously the seeds of jealousy and hatred between communities, provinces, states that were at peace, and to incite them to deeds of blood, involving them in war with each other, and to create revolutions and civil wars in countries that were independent and pros-perous, cultivating the arts and the sciences and enjoying the blessings of peace; to take sides with the combatants and to act secretly with your brother Jesuit, who might be engaged on the other side, but openly opposed to that with which you might be connected, only that the Church might be the gainer in the end, in the conditions fixed in the treaties for peace and that the end justifies the means.

You have been taught your duty as a spy, to gather all statistics, facts and information in your power from every source; to ingratiate yourself into the confidence of the family circle of Protestants and heretics of every class and character, as well as that of the merchant, the banker, the lawyer, among the schools and universities, in parliaments and legislatures, and the judiciaries and councils of state, and to be all things to all men, for the Pope's sake, whose servants we are unto death. You have received all your instructions heretofore as a novice, a neophyte, and have served as co-adjurer, confessor and priest, but you have not yet been invested with all that is necessary to command in the Army of Loyola in the service of the Pope. You must serve the proper time as the instrument and executioner as directed by your superiors; for none can command here who has not consecrated his labours with the blood of the heretic; for 'without the shedding of blood no man can be saved'. Therefore, to fit yourself for your work and make your own salvation sure, you will, in addition to your former oath of obedience to your order and allegiance to the Pope, repeat after me:

These words are then spoken by the new initiate into their order:

I *insert name*, now in the presence of Almighty God, the blessed Virgin Mary, the blessed St. John the Baptist, the Holy Apostles, St. Peter and St. Paul, and all the saints, sacred host of Heaven, and to you, my Ghostly Father, the superior general of the Society of Jesus, founded by St. Ignatius Loyola, in the pontification of *insert name of pope*, and continued to the present, do by the womb of the Virgin, the matrix of God, and the rod of Jesus Christ, declare and swear that His Holiness, the Pope, is Christ's Vice-Regent and is the true and only head of the Catholic or Universal Church throughout the earth; and that by the virtue of the keys of binding and loosing given to His Holiness by my Saviour, Jesus Christ, he hath power to depose heretical Kings, Princes, States, Commonwealths, and Governments, and they may be safely destroyed.

Therefore to the utmost of my power I will defend this doctrine and His Holiness's right and custom against all usurpers of the heretical or Protestant authority whatever, especially the Lutheran Church of Germany, Holland, Denmark, Sweden and Norway, and the now pretended authority and Churches of England and Scotland, and the branches of same now established in Ireland and on the continent of America and elsewhere and all adherents in regard that they may be usurped and heretical, opposing the sacred Mother Church of Rome.

I do now denounce and disown any allegiance as due to any heretical king, prince or State, named Protestant or Liberal, or obedience to any of their laws, magistrates or officers. I do further declare the doctrine of the Churches of England and Scotland of the Calvinists, Huguenots, and others of the name of Protestants to be damnable, and they themselves to be damned who will not forsake the same. I do further declare that I will help, assist, and advise all or any of His Holiness's agents, in any place where I should be, in Switzerland, Germany, Holland, Ireland or America, or in any other kingdom or territory I shall come to, and do my utmost to extirpate the heretical Protestant doctrines and to destroy all their pretended powers, legal or otherwise. I do further promise and declare that, notwithstanding, I am dispensed with to assume any religion heretical for the propagation of the Mother Church's interest; to keep secret and private all her agents' counsels from time to time, as they entrust me, and not to divulge, directly or indirectly, by word, writing or circumstances whatever; but to execute all that should be proposed, given in charge, or discovered unto me by you, my Ghostly Father, or any of this sacred order. I do further promise and declare that I will have no opinion or will of my own or any mental reservation whatever, even as a corpse or cadaver (perinde ac cadaver), but will unhesitatingly obey each and every command that I may receive from my superiors in the militia of the Pope and of Jesus Christ.

That I will go to any part of the world whithersoever I may be sent, to the frozen regions north, jungles of India, to the centres of civilisation of Europe, or to the wild haunts of the barbarous savages of America without murmuring or repining, and will be submissive in all things, whatsoever is communicated to me. I do further promise and declare that I will, when opportunity presents, make and wage relentless war, secretly and openly, against all heretics and Protestants, as I am directed to do, to extirpate them from the face of the whole earth; and that I will spare neither age, sex nor condition, and that I will hang, burn, waste, boil, flay, strangle, and bury alive these infamous heretics; rip up the stomachs and wombs of their women, and crush their infants' heads against the walls in order to annihilate their execrable race. That when the same cannot be done openly I will secretly use the poisonous cup, the strangulation cord, the steel of the poniard, or the leaden bullet, regardless of the honour, rank, dignity or authority of the persons, whatever may be their condition in life, either public or private, as I at any time may be directed so to do by any agents of the Pope or Superior of the Brotherhood of the Holy Father of the Society of Jesus.

In confirmation of which I hereby dedicate my life, soul, and all corporal powers, and with the dagger which I now receive I will subscribe my name written in my blood in testimony thereof; and should I prove false, or weaken in my determination, may my brethren and fellow soldiers of the militia of the Pope cut off my hands and feet and my throat from ear to ear, my belly be opened and sulphur burned therein with all the punishment that can be in-

flicted upon me on earth, and my soul shall be tortured by demons in eternal hell forever. That I will in voting always vote for a Knight of Columbus in preference to a Protestant, and that I will leave my party so to do; that if two Catholics are on the ticket I will satisfy myself which is the better supporter of Mother Church and vote accordingly. That I will not deal with or employ a Protestant if in my power to deal with or employ a Catholic. That I will place Catholic girls in Protestant families that a weekly report may be made of the inner movements of the heretics. That I will provide myself with arms and ammunition that I may be in readiness when the word is passed, or I am commanded to defend the Church either as an individual or with the militia of the Pope. All of which I, *insert name*, do swear by the blessed Trinity and blessed sacrament which I am now to receive to perform and on part to keep this my oath. In testimony hereof, I take this most holy and blessed sacrament of the Eucharist and witness the same further with my name written with the point of this dagger dipped in my own blood and seal in the face of this holy sacrament.*

The vatican is committed to exterminating anyone who is not a catholic. You will not change them. The jesuits are terrorists, trained to willingly and gladly commit murder to further the vatican's goals. Indeed, they believe that without the shedding of blood (the murder of non catholics), you cannot command within the jesuit hierarchy. It follows them that the jesuit order is run by men who have committed murder. The current pope is the jesuit general, so it logically follows that the pope has committed murder.

The god of this world has set up the jesuits, and secret societies in general, to gradually and quietly corrupt those they recruit. If you allow the jesuits to take control in politics, in law, in education, in media, and in other facets of social life, you are walking to the gas chambers of the new world order. The jesuits will do everything in their power to exterminate you. You will not change them.

Do you think I am wrong? Don't take my word for it; here are a couple of excerpts from the Roman Catholic Encyclopaedia.

We declare, say, define, and pronounce that every being should be subject to the Roman Pontiff.
The Catholic Encyclopedia, Vol. XV, p. 126.

Heretics may be not only excommunicated, but also justly put to death. The Catholic Encyclopaedia, Vol. XIV, p. 768.

It isn't the Jews behind one world governance. It isn't the Muslims. It isn't America. It is the vatican. The jesuits control the United Nations and the communists. Sure, the Jews and the Muslims have their traitors, just like the rest of us, like George Soros and Arafat, but blow away the smoke screens and you will see the vatican and their control of world masonry, communism, and international terrorism behind their religious and patriotic veils. As you can see from their oaths, they are committed to shedding our blood and stealing what is ours to further the goals of their god Lucifer.

Jesuits educated Joseph Stalin in Georgia, a country south of Russia, to which the Emperor's banning of the jesuits, his Ukase, did not reach. After training Stalin, they brought him in after the revolution and made him secretary of the communist party in 1922. The jesuits were behind the communist takeover of Russia and the murder of over 20 million Russians.

The Germans never started World War I. The vatican started WW1 by ordering France, Russia, and England to destroy Germany because they had expelled the jesuits. During that war, the Germans requested an armistice to stop the communist revolution within Germany. Who lead the revolution? The German freemasons. According to the Kaiser, in his memoirs, it was German freemasonry that got him off his throne and deposed him. The jesuits control world masonry. Like the communist manifesto, jesuits penned the protocols of Zion, not Jews. Weishaupt was a jesuit. While we're here, Jesuit Staempfle wrote mein kampf for Hitler. I believe Hitler may have been a jesuit. He was certainly taking his orders from them.

According to some sources, there were over two thousand jesuits in various US government positions prior to 1980. If this is true, and all indications appear that it is, there is no telling how many there are now and how much power they wield in Washington and state government. They control the CIA, the FBI, the Council on Foreign Relations, everything. The CIA wasn't founded to protect the American people, it was founded so that the vatican and the jesuits could spy on them so they could destroy them.

President Lincoln, who was assassinated by the jesuits, put it rather succinctly:

If the Protestants of the North and the South could learn what the priests, nuns, and monks, who daily land on our shores, under the pretext of preaching their religion, were doing in our schools and hospitals, as emissaries of the Pope and the other despots of Europe, to undermine our institutions and alienate the hearts of our people from our Constitution and our laws, and prepare a reign of anarchy here, as they have done in Ireland, Mexico, Spain, and wherever there are people that wish to be free, they would unite in taking power out of their hands.

The jesuit order is an absolute monarchy. Their general, otherwise known as the black pope, rules for life. The pattern of their own order has shaped their thinking about all other political structures.

Jesuits are sleeping terror cells embedded within our cultures, and they will give their lives if necessary to further the aims of the vatican (though they prefer others to give their lives on their behalf if at all possible). Perhaps now we can understand why men like Edward John Smith, the captain of the Titanic, would deliberately sink his ship to murder all the men on board to ensure the creation of the federal reserve, perhaps the most evil financial institution on earth. Edward John Smith was a jesuit or he was trained by them and acting on their orders. Rasputin, the mysterious holy man who corrupted the tsars and subsequently paved the way for the communist takeover of Russia was most likely a jesuit. Guy Fawkes, who attempted to blow up the Houses of Parliament in a vatican attempt to take power, was either a jesuit or was acting on their orders.

The vatican supplies terrorist organisations worldwide with vehicles, food, and weapons through the United Nations and the International Red Cross in the guise of humanitarian aid. Monies donated to Charities that claim to be feeding the world are actually going to arm, train, and feed terrorists the world over. Yes, Bob Geldof is a communist and a big freemason who wants you dead, and begs you to help pay for it. Every penny you give to charities claiming to feed the world is being used to help train communist terrorists worldwide so you can be exterminated. If you give money to them, you are financing your own extinction.

The United Nations is also active in Muslim countries and even in Israel. The Muslims and the Jews both have their traitors working for the United Nations, just as we do, and it is the jesuits and the vatican controlling the UN. And isn't it ironic that it was the vatican who ordered the extermination of Muslims worldwide during the Crusades, that it was the vatican behind Hitler and the Nazis, and it is the vatican that has us all fooled into thinking Jews, Muslims or Americans are the enemy. The truth is, Muslims, Jews, and we in the West all share a common enemy. The Great Satan resides in Vatican City. If you're looking for the anti-Christ, that would be a good place to settle your gaze.

Have you ever noticed that the Millennium Bridge in London leads directly to St Paul's Cathedral? All roads lead to Rome. The Millennium Bridge stands as a monument to the subversive powers at work within the UK. It would appear our queen has caved in under pressure from the pagan gods of Rome. Only by coming back to God and his word will things change for the better. Perhaps it's time our queen took back the power that was stolen from her by the jesuits, and started doing her job again. Elizabeth, if you want answers, they are available. What about a new political party called the Royal Party, and when elected into power you dissolve parliament and restore Great Britain to a kingdom governed by a king or queen? Elizabeth the First banished the jesuits from her Empire. If any jesuits were caught within the borders of the British Empire they were to be drawn and quartered. I believe that law could still be in force. It's time to sink the Spanish Armada again or watch your country go down.

If we do not get serious about bringing back the death penalty and enforcing it according to the standards set in God's word there is no future for us.

26. Jesus Christ is not God

Let's assume for a moment that perhaps the vatican really is onto something here, that they really do have a grasp on what is right for the world, and that they really are doing God's will. Let's assume briefly that communism isn't a political disease, that it really is the answer to all the world's ills. I mean, perhaps the world *would* be a better place if everyone was of the same religion and we only had one government. Perhaps that really would put an end to wars and poverty. One can readily see how such an argument could be persuasive. Perhaps murdering billions of people all over the planet and forcing everyone at the point of a gun to live under the rule of one god and one government is the way to go.

I'm sure most catholics have absolutely no idea that the pope worships Lucifer. I'm also sure that most masons and communists believe that murdering everyone on the planet will somehow save it.

Before delving further into this, I'll state for the record that I don't hate Catholics. Quite the contrary, I love them. They are the shakers and movers in the world today. We also have Martin Luther and the Catholics of his day to thank for The Reformation. The Inquisition burned, hanged, tortured, and murdered hundreds of thousands of Catholics across Europe in an attempt to stamp out what they called the heretical teachings of Luther. I believe we owe a great debt to the Catholic men and women who gave their blood during the Reformation so we could have the freedoms we enjoy today. Don't ever bad mouth Catholics to my face. Protestants today make me sick with their self righteous horseshit. They think they know everything because they go to church once a week and sit through a shit religious ceremony. I know very few of them who even read their bibles. If the word of God ever moves and lives again, I believe it could very well come from within the Roman Catholic people.

So, to satisfy ourselves regarding the jesuit's claims to the world, we must compare their doctrine with God's word. How accurate is the vatican when it comes to scripture? Let's see if the jesuits and the pope really do know their stuff.

First, we need to be clear in our minds about who Jesus Christ was and who he was not. The bible uses the phrase, Son of God, 50 times. Consider these verses.

> John 20:30,31
> And many other signs truly did Jesus in the presence of his disciples, which are not written in this book:
>
> But these are written, that ye might believe that Jesus is the Christ, the Son of God; and that believing ye might have life through his name.
>
> Mark 1:1
> The beginning of the gospel of Jesus Christ, the Son of God;
>
> Mark 1:11
> And there came a voice from heaven, *saying*, Thou art my beloved Son, in whom I am well pleased.
>
> Mark 9:7
> And there was a cloud that overshadowed them: and a voice came out of the cloud, saying, This is my beloved Son: hear him.

Even devil spirits called Jesus Christ the Son of God.

> Matthew 8:28,29
> And when he was come to the other side into the country of the Gergesenes, there met him two possessed with devils, coming out of the tombs, exceeding fierce, so that no man might pass by that way.
>
> And, behold, they cried out, saying, What have we to do with thee, Jesus, thou Son of God? art thou come hither to torment us before the time?

These verses are extremely clear – Jesus Christ is the son of God. In this context, it is quite astonishing to learn that there is not one single verse anywhere in the entire bible that says that Jesus is God the Son. The phrase *God the son* does not exist in scripture. Fifty times Jesus Christ is called the son of God and not once is he called God the son. Take that to any court of law in any country in the world and you would find it conclusive evidence as to the identity of Jesus Christ. However, let's explore further. Can God be tempted with evil? This is rhetoric, of course.

> James 1:13
> Let no man say when he is tempted, I am tempted of God: for God cannot be tempted with evil, neither tempteth he any man:

Pretty clear? God cannot be tempted with evil. It is just not possible, end of story. Now compare that with these verses:

> Luke 4:1,2
> And Jesus being full of the Holy Ghost returned from Jordan, and was led by the Spirit into the wilderness,
>
> Being forty days tempted of the devil. And in those days he did eat nothing: and when they were ended, he afterward hungered.

> Hebrews 4:15
> For we have not an high priest [referring to Jesus Christ] which cannot be touched with the feeling of our infirmities; but was in all points tempted like as *we are, yet* without sin.

> Hebrews 2:18
> For in that he himself hath suffered being tempted, he is able to succour them that are tempted.

Jesus Christ endured temptation. In fact, he was tempted in all things just as we are. If it is impossible for God to be tempted with evil, and Jesus Christ was tempted with evil, then how could Jesus Christ be God? Another difference between them is their distinct and separate wills.

Matthew 26:39,42
And he went a little further, and fell on his face, and prayed, saying, O my Father, if it be possible, let this cup pass from me: nevertheless not as I will, but as thou *wilt*.

He went away again the second time, and prayed, saying, O my Father, if this cup may not pass away from me, except I drink it, thy will be done.

If Jesus Christ is God, then to whom was he praying? Himself? Jesus Christ clearly had his own will, which was distinctly his own and completely separate from God. Two distinct and separate wills clearly indicates two distinct and separate beings.

John 4:34
Jesus saith unto them, My meat is to do the will of him that sent me, and to finish his work.

John 5:19
Then answered Jesus and said unto them, Verily, verily, I say unto you, The Son can do nothing of himself, but what he seeth the Father do: for what things soever he doeth, these also doeth the Son likewise.

John 5:30
I can of mine own self do nothing: as I hear, I judge: and my judgment is just; because I seek not mine own will, but the will of the Father which hath sent me.

John 6:38
For I came down from heaven, not to do mine own will, but the will of him that sent me.

Jesus Christ could not even nominate who sat on his right hand and on his left hand in his Father's kingdom. No disrespect, but he was hardly all-powerful then, was he?

Matthew 20:23
And he saith unto them, Ye shall drink indeed of my cup, and be baptized with the baptism that I am baptized with: but to sit on my

right hand, and on my left, is not mine to give, but *it shall be given to them* for whom it is prepared of my Father.

Jesus Christ was obedient and did his Father's will, not his own will. If Jesus Christ was God, these scriptures are absurd. Yet another problem arises when we consider the following two verses.

John 1:18
No man hath seen God at any time; the only begotten Son, which is in the bosom of the Father, he hath declared *him*.

1 John 4:12
No man hath seen God at any time. If we love one another, God dwelleth in us, and his love is perfected in us.

No man means no man. The scripture is clear. No man, no one, no human being has ever seen God. Did anyone ever see Jesus Christ? Yes, quite a few million during his lifetime I would guess. If Jesus Christ is God, then words have no meaning.

The doctrine of Jesus Christ being God becomes even more ridiculous when we read this verse in John.

John 14:12
Verily, verily, I say unto you, He that believeth on me, the works that I do shall he do also; and greater *works* than these shall he do; because I go unto my Father.

We can do greater works than Jesus Christ did. That is what this verse says and that is what this verse means. Since the day of Pentecost, it has been available to do greater works than Jesus Christ did while he was here on earth. If Jesus Christ is God, then according to this verse we can do greater works than God, which is absolute nonsense. The doctrine that Jesus Christ is God is easily exposed as religious horseshit when illuminated with rightly divided scripture.

In the following verse, Jesus Christ himself obviously knew that he was not God otherwise he would have said something like, 'thanks for calling me good because I am God.'

Matthew 19:17
And he [Jesus Christ] said unto him, Why callest thou me good? *there is* none good but one, *that is*, God: but if thou wilt enter into life, keep the commandments.

Here is another interesting verse.

Matthew 1:18
Now the birth [gennēsis] of Jesus Christ was on this wise: When as his mother Mary was espoused to Joseph, before they came together, she was found with child of the Holy Ghost.

The word *birth* is the word *gennēsis*, from which we get our English word *genesis*. Genesis means beginning. There can be no doubt as to the meaning of the word genesis. Its meaning is not open to debate. Jesus Christ had a beginning and it was right here in Matthew when he was born. Jesus Christ was not around before this point in time. His birth was his beginning, his genesis.

So, where does the doctrine that Jesus Christ is God come from? It is interesting to note that most, if not all of the ancient religions had a trinity. The Hindu trinity was Brahma, Vishnu, and Shiva. The Greek trinity was Zeus, Athena, and Apollo. The Roman trinity was Jupiter, Mercury, and Venus. The Sumerian trinity was Anu, Enlill and Ea. The Egyptians had quite a few trinities, including Osiris, Isis and Horus.

We can track trinities through pagan religions back to the dawn of time. The heathen belief that gods visit the earth in human form is nothing new.

Acts 14:8-11
And there sat a certain man at Lystra, impotent in his feet, being a cripple from his mother's womb, who never had walked:

The same heard Paul speak: who stedfastly beholding him, and perceiving that he had faith [believing] to be healed,

Said with a loud voice, Stand upright on thy feet. And he leaped and walked.

And when the people saw what Paul had done, they lifted up their voices, saying in the speech of Lycaonia, The gods are come down to us in the likeness of men.

This pagan belief that gods visit the earth in human form has been rife among those with no understanding since prehistoric times. The belief that Jesus Christ is God who visited earth in human form has its roots in heathen paganism, not the bible.

Perhaps we should now consider a few of the manipulated and twisted scriptures used to teach that Jesus Christ is God. Here is perhaps the most abused scripture in this regards:

John 10:30
I and *my* Father are one.

Okay, for the sake of argument, let's assume that this verse does indeed teach that Jesus Christ is God. Let's forget about all the previous verses we've looked at, let's forget about the fact that there are fifty verses that clearly state that Jesus Christ is the Son of God, and that there are no scriptures anywhere in the bible that say he is God the Son. Let's ignore all the scriptures we've seen that highlight the differences between Jesus Christ and God, and let's pull this one verse totally out of the context of the rest of the bible and use it to teach that Jesus Christ is God. Okay, now that we've done that, check out these verses a few chapters later, where Jesus Christ is praying.

John 17:20-22
Neither pray I for these alone, but for them also which shall believe on me through their word;

That they all may be one; as thou, Father, *art* in me, and I in thee, that they also may be one in us: that the world may believe that thou hast sent me.

And the glory which thou gavest me I have given them; that they may be one, even as we are one:

Okay then, if John 10:30 teaches that Jesus Christ is God, then John 17:20-22 teaches that I am God too and so are you. The trinity is religious horseshit. To gain an understanding of what John 10:30 is talking about, we must read the immediate context.

> John10:27-30
> My sheep hear my voice, and I know them, and they follow me:
>
> And I give unto them eternal life; and they shall never perish, neither shall any *man* pluck them out of my hand.
>
> My Father, which gave *them* me, is greater than all; and no *man* is able to pluck *them* out of my Father's hand.
>
> I and *my* Father are one.

Verse 28 declares that no man shall pluck the sheep out of Jesus Christ's hand, while verse 29 declares that no man is able to pluck the sheep out of his Father's hand either. Then verse 30 follows when Jesus Christ states that he and his Father are one. One in what? In that no man is able to pluck sheep out of their hands. Is reading the context so difficult? The word translated *one* here is the Greek word *hen*, which is in the neuter gender, and means *one in purpose*. One and the same person would be the Greek word *heis* – the masculine gender. Consider this following use of *hen*:

> 1 Corinthians 3:6-8
> I have planted, Apollos watered; but God gave the increase.
>
> So then neither is he that planteth any thing, neither he that watereth; but God that giveth the increase.
>
> Now he that planteth and he that watereth are one [hen]: and every man shall receive his own reward according to his own labour.

When it says that Paul and Apollos were one, does this mean they were one and the same person? How ridiculous! Paul and Apollos were not the same person any more than God and Jesus Christ were the same person. They were one in purpose, they were likeminded. This logic can also be applied to the following verses.

John 1:1,2,14
In the beginning was the Word, and the Word was with God, and the Word was God.

The same was in the beginning with God.

And the Word was made flesh, and dwelt among us, (and we beheld his glory, the glory as of the only begotten of the Father,) full of grace and truth.

Do these verses say that Jesus Christ was God? Not if language has rules. It says the *word* was there in the beginning with God, not Jesus Christ, and that the word was *later* made flesh in the form of Jesus Christ. Nevertheless, assume for the sake of argument that John 1 does indeed teach that Jesus Christ was God and that he was there in the beginning with him. Okay, now compare these verses.

Ephesians 1:4
According as he hath chosen us in him before the foundation of the world, that we should be holy and without blame before him in love:

2 Thessalonians 2:13
But we are bound to give thanks alway to God for you, brethren beloved of the Lord, because God hath from the beginning chosen you to salvation through sanctification of the Spirit and belief of the truth:

According to Ephesians and Thessalonians, God also knew about us back in the beginning before the foundation of the world. So does that mean we were actually there? Yes, we were there in the beginning with God, just like Jesus Christ. This is true. However, these verses are referring to God's foreknowledge. We were not literally there with him back in Genesis, no more so than Jesus Christ was literally there. Jesus Christ had his beginning, his *genesis*, when he was born, just as we did. So what are these verses in John saying?

John 1:1,2,14
In the beginning was the Word, and the Word was with God, and the Word was God.

The same was in the beginning with God.

And the Word was made flesh, and dwelt among us, (and we beheld his glory, the glory as of the only begotten of the Father,) full of grace and truth.

What these verses say is that Jesus Christ epitomised the word during his life by being a living example of it. It was the word that was there in the beginning and Jesus Christ later lived it to such a standard during his life that we could see the living word in him as a breathing reality. We could look at Jesus Christ and see God's word living in someone. We too can live the word to such a degree that we are living epistles, and that doesn't make us God anymore than Jesus Christ.

2 Corinthians 3:2
Ye are our epistle written in our hearts, known and read of all men:

When the word says we are epistles, known and read of all men, does that mean that we are God? No, it simply means we bring the word to life by living it, so that others can see the word in our lives. To teach Jesus Christ was God because he lived the word is just as ridiculous as saying we are God because we live the word.

This is not an exhaustive work on the subject. Most of the other scriptures used to teach that Jesus Christ is God are forgeries, but I don't have the time to write a book on this, that's already been done. It's time to move on, but suffice to say that we have shed a little light into what is perhaps the darkest regions of religion possible. Why do I say that? Because to worship anything or anyone other than the true God is idolatry, and worshipping Jesus Christ as God is exactly that – idolatry. Jesus Christ was not God, he was a man, a human being.

Romans 5:15
But not as the offence, so also *is* the free gift. For if through the offence of one many be dead, much more the grace of God, and the gift by grace, *which is* by one man, Jesus Christ, hath abounded unto many.

1 Timothy 2:5
For *there is* one God, and one mediator between God and men, the man Christ Jesus;

This, of course, entrenches the doctrine of the trinity clearly within the framework of idolatry. To worship a man as God is idolatry. Therefore idolatry is the foundation stone on which Roman Catholicism and vatican doctrine is built. If you didn't know this, apologise to God, move on and put that cult behind you.

27. Where Are the Dead?

We've established that the doctrine of the trinity has its roots in prehistoric paganism and that worshipping a man as God is idolatry. If the pope and the jesuits are idolaters who worship a man as God, do they perhaps know their bible then when it comes to what happens when you die? I mean, the vatican has made fortunes taking money from grieving families to spring dead souls from purgatory, so surely they must know their bible in this field.

Just about every religion on earth teaches that when you die you go to some kind of paradise, or some kind of hell, or somewhere in between, but is that what happens? The word is clear on this subject.

> Psalm 6:5
> For in death *there is* no remembrance of thee: in the grave who shall give thee thanks?

It says that there is no remembrance of anyone who has died. This verse is talking about the remembrance, the memories, the thoughts and consciousness of those who have died. After someone has died they cannot remember God, and nor can they thank him for anything.

My grandfather died many years ago and I still remember him. I still remember how he took his false teeth out, pulled funny faces and made me laugh. *He* doesn't remember *me*. It is his thoughts, his remembrance, his consciousness that has died, and it went the moment he took his last breath.

> Psalm 146:4
> His breath goeth forth, he returneth to his earth; in that very day his thoughts perish.

When you take your last breath, your life has gone and at that moment your thoughts are no more. You have no more consciousness, which means absolutely no thoughts or emotions. That is logical because you are dead, and dead, by definition, means dead, it does not mean alive.

> Ecclesiastes 9:5,6,10
> For the living know that they shall die: but the dead know not any thing, neither have they any more a reward; for the memory of them is forgotten [their memory, their thoughts are gone].
>
> Also their love, and their hatred, and their envy, is now perished; neither have they any more a portion for ever in any *thing* that is done under the sun.
>
> Whatsoever thy hand findeth to do, do *it* with thy might; for *there is* no work, nor device, nor knowledge, nor wisdom, in the grave, whither thou goest.

This supports the truth of Psalm 146:4 – there is absolutely nothing awaiting anyone in the grave other than death, a state of nothingness.

> Psalm 30:9
> What profit *is there* in my blood, when I go down to the pit? Shall the dust praise thee? shall it declare thy truth?

Forget about being with God and enjoying a party in heaven when you die. The dead go into the grave, they do not party in heaven.

> Psalm 115:17
> The dead praise not the LORD, neither any that go down into silence.

People who believe they live immediately after they die, or go to be with Jesus, or get showered with virgins, or go to some feasting hall for warriors, have been deceived. Those who teach that when you die you go to heaven, to hell, or to purgatory, either have no understanding of the scriptures or they are liars. If you go to a church or a religion that teaches this stuff, you are being taught nonsense.

> Isaiah 38:18
> For the grave cannot praise thee, death can *not* celebrate thee: they that go down into the pit cannot hope for thy truth.

So what happens to all these dead people? Is there any point to life other than just living it while it lasts? Job gives us a clue.

> Job 14:10-12
> But man dieth, and wasteth away: yea, man giveth up the ghost, and where *is* he?
>
> *As* the waters fail from the sea, and the flood decayeth and drieth up:
>
> So man lieth down, and riseth not: till the heavens *be* no more, they shall not awake, nor be raised out of their sleep.

Until the heavens be no more is a reference to a point in time which is still future, when the dead shall be raised from what the word often refers to euphemistically as sleep. David also knew of a day coming in the future when he would be raised from death.

> Psalm 16:9-11
> Therefore my heart is glad, and my glory rejoiceth: my flesh also shall rest in hope.
>
> For thou wilt not leave my soul in hell [in the grave]; neither wilt thou suffer thine Holy One to see corruption.
>
> Thou wilt shew me the path of life: in thy presence *is* fulness of joy; at thy right hand *there are* pleasures for evermore.

Curiously, the word translated hell in the bible is from the Greek word *hades*, which simply refers to the state of death. Everyone who dies goes to hades, to hell. Hell is nothing more than the continuing state of death. Everyone who dies goes to hell, whether christian or not. David knew he was going to hell when he died. Hell is not a place where bad people go to be tormented in another life, it is where all people go when they die. Even Jesus Christ went to hell when he died.

The word is clear that the dead being raised from death is an event that happens in the future. In the meantime, everyone who has died is dead and will remain so until that point in the future when they will be raised.

1 Thessalonians 4:14
For if we believe that Jesus died and rose again, even so them also which sleep in Jesus will God bring with him.

This is referring to a future event when Jesus Christ returns to gather the church of God. The word *sleep* is a euphemism referring to death, a figure of speech employed to soften the harsh reality of death. The word calls death an enemy, and also tells us that the last enemy that shall be destroyed is death.

1 Corinthians 15:26
The last enemy *that* shall be destroyed *is* death.

So when do those who have died with holy spirit rise from the dead? Keep reading!

1 Thessalonians 4:15
For this we say unto you by the word of the Lord, that we which are alive *and* remain unto the coming of the Lord shall not prevent [precede] them which are asleep.

What does it mean when it says those of us who are alive and remain shall not *prevent* them which are asleep? That makes no sense. If we understand this verse in light of our modern understanding of the word *prevent* we can come to all kinds of silly conclusions. Why on earth would we want to stop our brothers and sisters in Christ who have died from getting into heaven in the first place? Why would God tell us we can't prevent that? Makes no sense.

The word *prevent* is an archaic usage of our modern word *precede*, and this brings us to a very important key to the bible's interpretation – a word or words must be understood in light of their biblical usage (what the words meant when they were written). In 1611 when this was translated the word *prevent* meant *to precede, to go before*. Here is a dictionary definition.

Main Entry: **pre·vent**
Pronunciation: \pri-vent\
Function: verb

Etymology: Middle English, to anticipate, from Latin praeventus, past participle of praevenire to come before, anticipate, forestall, from prae- + venire to come.
Date: 15th century
Archaic a: to be in readiness for (as an occasion) b: to meet or satisfy in advance c: to act ahead of d: to go or arrive before.

Now the verse makes sense. The word *prevent* means *precede*, to go ahead of, to arrive before. Its meaning has changed since 1611, but we must understand the word according to its biblical usage, not what it means now. Other scriptures will now make more sense too. Look at this usage from psalm 119.

> Psalm 119:147
> I prevented the dawning of the morning, and cried: I hoped in thy word.

Are we to imagine that David prevented the sun from coming up? How ridiculous. David *preceded* the sun coming up – in other words he got up very early while it was yet dark so he could get into the bible. He loved the word of God so much, he set his alarm clock an hour or two earlier just so he could get up and study the bible before getting into his day. Back to Thessalonians.

We that are alive and remain when Jesus Christ comes back will not precede those who have died. In other words, the dead in Christ will be raised from the dead before those of us who are still alive are changed. That is *precisely* what the bible says in the next two verses.

> 1 Thessalonians 4:16,17
> For the Lord himself shall descend from heaven with a shout, with the voice of the archangel, and with the trump of God: and the dead in Christ shall rise first:
>
> Then we which are alive *and* remain shall be caught up together with them in the clouds, to meet the Lord in the air: and so shall we ever be with the Lord.

Now ask yourself, if when you die you go to heaven, why would Jesus Christ have to come back to earth for you? If you are already alive, how could God raise you from the dead? If you were alive, there would be no need to raise you from the dead because you would already be alive. The teaching that when you die you don't really die has no scriptural basis. In this context, it is intriguing to recall the first lie ever recorded in the bible, way back in Genesis.

> Genesis 3:1-4
> Now the serpent was more subtil than any beast of the field which the LORD God had made. And he said unto the woman, Yea, hath God said, Ye shall not eat of every tree of the garden?
>
> And the woman said unto the serpent, We may eat of the fruit of the trees of the garden:
>
> But of the fruit of the tree which *is* in the midst of the garden, God hath said, Ye shall not eat of it, neither shall ye touch it, lest ye die.
>
> And the serpent said unto the woman, Ye shall not surely die:

There you go – the first lie in the bible is that when you die you don't really die. God said they would die, the devil told Eve she would not die. This is still the biggest lie in the world today. All religions teach that when you die you go to some place called heaven, or you go to some burning hell, or to some place in between called limbo or purgatory. It is all lies. When people die, they are dead, they do not go anywhere except into a grave. Anyone who teaches otherwise has no knowledge of scripture or they are liars.

This means, of course, that you cannot buy anyone out of purgatory and get them into heaven, because there is no such place as purgatory and everyone who has died is dead. The Roman Catholic church, therefore, is engaged in serious criminal fraud when it offers to release souls from purgatory in exchange for sums of money.

In the context of swindling grieving families and widows, consider these extracts from secret instructions issued to jesuits.

Chapter VI: Of proper methods for inducing rich widows to be liberal to our Society.

I. For the managing of this affair, let such members only be chosen as are advanced in age, of a lively complexion and agreeable conversation; let these frequently visit such widows, and the minute they begin to show any affection towards our order, then is the time to lay before them the good works and merits of the society. If they seem kindly to give ear to this, and begin to visit our churches, we must by all means take care to provide them confessors by whom they may be well admonished, especially to a constant perseverance in their state of widowhood, and this, by enumerating and praising the advantages and felicity of a single life: and let them pawn their faiths, and themselves too, as a security that a firm continuance in such a pious resolution will infallibly purchase an eternal merit, and prove a most effectual means of escaping the otherwise certain pains of purgatory.

IV. Care must be taken to remove such servants particularly as do not keep a good understanding with the Society; but let this be done by little and little; and when we have managed to work them out, let such be recommended as already are, or willingly would become our creatures; thus shall we dive into every secret, and have a finger in every affair transacted in the family.

Chapter VII: How such widows are to be secured, and in what manner their effects are to be disposed of.

I. They are perpetually to be pressed to a perseverance in their devotion and good works, in such manner, that no week pass in which they do not, of their own accord, lay somewhat apart out of their abundance for the honour of Christ, the blessed Virgin, or their patron saint; and let them dispose of it in relief of the poor, or in beautifying of churches, till they are entirely stripped of their superfluous stores and unnecessary riches.

XIII. Let the confessors take diligent care to prevent such widows as are their penitents, from visiting ecclesiastics of other orders, or entering into familiarity with them, under any pretence whatsoever; for which end, let them, at proper opportunities, cry up the Society as infinitely superior to all other orders; of the greatest service in the church of God, and of greater authority with the Pope, and all princes; and that it is the most perfect in itself, in that it discards all persons offensive or unqualified, from its community, and therefore is purified from that scum and dregs with which these monks are infected, who, generally speaking, are a set of men unlearned, stupid, and slothful, negligent of their duty, and slaves to their bellies.

XIV. Let the confessors propose to them, and endeavour to persuade them to pay small pensions and contributions towards the yearly support of colleges and professed houses, but especially of the professed house at Rome; not let them forget the ornaments of churches, tapers, wine, and things necessary in the celebration of the sacrifice of mass.

XV. If any widow does in her life-time make over her whole estate to the Society; whenever opportunity offers, but especially when she is seized with sickness, or in danger of life, let some take care to represent to her the poverty of the greatest number of our colleges, whereof many just erected have hardly as yet any foundation; engage her, by a winning behaviour and inducing arguments, to such a liberality as (you must persuade her) will lay a certain foundation for her eternal happiness.

XVI. The same art must be used with princes and other benefactors; for they must be wrought up to a belief, that these are the only acts which will perpetuate their memories in this world, and secure them eternal glory in the next.

This practice of mercilessly robbing widows was prevalent in Jesus Christ's time and he warned the people of his day about it, just as I'm doing today.

> Matthew 23:14
> Woe unto you, scribes and Pharisees, hypocrites! for ye devour widows' houses, and for a pretence make long prayer: therefore ye shall receive the greater damnation.

Look, when you die, you are dead and you remain dead until some point in the future when Jesus Christ comes back either to gather the church or at the resurrections of the just and the unjust. Those who are born again in this administration are part of the church of God and will be gathered when Jesus Christ returns, those who are not will be part of the resurrections of the just and the unjust at a later date. We will deal with this in much more detail later in the class. Regarding the gathering of the church, the word has this to say:

1 Thessalonians 4:16,17
For the Lord himself shall descend from heaven with a shout, with the voice of the archangel, and with the trump of God: and the dead in Christ shall rise first:

Then we which are alive *and* remain shall be caught up together with them in the clouds, to meet the Lord in the air: and so shall we ever be with the Lord.

The return of Christ for the church will happen. We do not know when, but it will happen. It could be today, it could be tomorrow, it could be next century, we don't know. Until then, everyone who has died will remain dead, without consciousness, thought, memory, emotion or anything.

1 Corinthians 15:51-54
Behold, I shew you a mystery; We shall not all sleep, but we shall all be changed,

In a moment, in the twinkling of an eye, at the last trump: for the trumpet shall sound, and the dead shall be raised incorruptible, and we shall be changed.

For this corruptible must put on incorruption, and this mortal *must* put on immortality.

So when this corruptible shall have put on incorruption, and this mortal shall have put on immortality, then shall be brought to pass the saying that is written, Death is swallowed up in victory.

If this is news to you, your immediate reaction may be one of sorrow on realising loved ones you thought were in heaven are actually dead. Folks often claim that believing their dead husbands and wives and fathers and mothers and children are alive gives them comfort. I know people who have conversations with dead people, convinced they are listening.

I'm sorry the world has lied to you, but either the word is true or it isn't.

Thessalonians shows that genuine comfort in death is knowing you and your loved ones will be raised at some point in the future, and that you will spend eternity together. When a person who is born again dies, someone who has body, soul and spirit, their next waking thought will be the return of Jesus Christ as documented in Thessalonians. Centuries may pass, but because they were dead it will seem to them as but a moment, as if awakening from sleep, with no concept of the time that has passed. When we take our last breath, the next moment for us, in a real sense, will be the return. If I live for another twenty years, then for me the return of the Lord Jesus Christ is no longer than twenty years away. He may return sooner, of course, but the time I have remaining on earth is all the time I have to wait until the return. When I take my last breath and die, the very next moment for me will be the return, even though I may have been dead for centuries. The same is true for you if you have holy spirit. I find it very comforting to know I'll be together with everyone I love at the return of Jesus Christ. This is our hope and this is what protects us from sorrow.

> 1 Thessalonians 4:13,16-18
> But I would not have you to be ignorant, brethren, concerning them which are asleep, that ye sorrow not, even as others which have no hope.
>
> For the Lord himself shall descend from heaven with a shout, with the voice of the archangel, and with the trump of God: and the dead in Christ shall rise first:
>
> Then we which are alive *and* remain shall be caught up together with them in the clouds, to meet the Lord in the air: and so shall we ever be with the Lord.
>
> Wherefore comfort one another with these words.

Now, about this first lie recorded in Genesis chapter 3:

> Genesis 3:4
> And the serpent said unto the woman, Ye shall not surely die:

The first usage of a word or phrase or usage of words in the bible has special meaning. First usage holds significant and foundational truth. This is the first lie recorded in the bible and its importance cannot be overstated. Without understanding this lie and its implications, life is an extremely dangerous place.

For example, the vatican has literally hundreds and hundreds of saints in heaven to which you can pray. God is too busy to answer everyone's prayers they tell you, so these saints are there to take your prayers to God. For a start, the true God is all-knowing, all-powerful, and everywhere present. He is quite capable of hearing your prayers without the need of some rotten dead corpse to help him out. If your god is too busy to hear your prayers, perhaps it's time to find yourself another one. If the dead are dead, as the bible teaches, then these so-called saints are not up there anyway. Check this out regarding saints:

Ephesians 1:1,2
Paul, an apostle of Jesus Christ by the will of God, to the saints which are at Ephesus, and to the faithful in Christ Jesus:

Grace *be* to you, and peace, from God our Father, and *from* the Lord Jesus Christ.

These verses are indeed addressed to saints, but these saints were *alive* at the time Ephesians was written. Biblically, saints are alive people, not dead people. No dead people are alive apart from the Lord Jesus Christ whom God raised from the dead three days and three nights after his crucifixion and murder. Everyone else who has died is dead and will remain so until Jesus Christ comes back. Therefore, the vatican and the jesuits are lying when they say the dead are alive now and are up there in heaven watching over you and you can pray to them. It is all fairy tales.

It should come as no surprise then, that just as with the doctrine of the trinity, there are a number of scriptures in the bible that are twisted to teach that the dead are alive. We will take a little time to look at a few of them.

Psalm 116 contains a verse that is often recited at funerals to teach that God is overjoyed because he has killed someone and now has another dead person in heaven with him.

> Psalm 116:15
> Precious in the sight of the LORD *is* the death of his saints.

If God killed people and it was God's will for people to die, then why did Jesus Christ not go around killing people? Jesus Christ always did God's will, right? So if it was God's will for people to be sick and die, wouldn't Jesus Christ have carried out that will and gone around making people sick so they would die? If God *wanted* sick people and God *wanted* dead people, then who did Jesus Christ think he was going around healing them? Jesus Christ always did his Father's will, so healing people must be God's will. The teaching that God kills people and makes them sick is so unscriptural it is astounding that people can be so blind as to believe it. If God kills people and makes them sick, then why bring the devil into it? What is he doing if God does all the nasty things in life? Quite the contrary, it is the devil who kills people and makes them sick.

> Acts 10:38
> How God anointed Jesus of Nazareth with the Holy Ghost and with power: who went about doing good, and healing all that were oppressed of the devil; for God was with him.

So how do we explain Psalm 116:15? There is nothing to explain. If something is precious, it is valuable, it is costly. A rare diamond is precious because it is extremely costly. Precious in the sight of the Lord is the death of his saints, means costly in the sight of the Lord is the death of his saints. It costs God when his people die. Our deaths cost him dearly.

There is no good side to the god of this world. At one time Lucifer was full of beauty and wisdom, and was perfect in all his ways, but that has all changed. He has no mercy. He has no compassion. Deceiving folks into believing that God is doing all the nasty things to them when it is the devil himself doing them keeps him hidden and happy. One can readily see why God had the book of Job written first so we would know it was the devil doing all the nasty stuff in life. If we do not know this and believe God makes us sick and kills us, our spiritual integrity is at great risk. The lie that the dead are not dead is pivotal to the god of this world's deceptions. Without this lie, his power to steal, kill, and destroy is greatly diminished.

Another scripture misused in this regards is the translation of Enoch.

> Hebrews 11:5
> By faith [believing] Enoch was translated that he should not see death; and was not found, because God had translated him: for before his translation he had this testimony, that he pleased God.

Without getting into a lengthy debate, very simply, this verse does not say Enoch did not die, it says he never saw death. Had God meant Enoch did not die, the verse would read: *By faith Enoch was translated that he should not die.* The word *see* in the Greek, is *eidon*, which means *to look at with actual perception with one's eyes.* Enoch never saw death, he never saw anyone die. However, he himself died. How do I know? The word says so a few verses later.

> Hebrews 11:13
> These all died in faith [including Enoch], not having received the promises, but having seen them afar off, and were persuaded of *them*, and embraced *them*, and confessed that they were strangers and pilgrims on the earth.

There are a few other scriptures used to teach that the dead are alive and there is a place called purgatory, such as the parable of the rich man and Lazarus. A parable is a story, a fiction, a make believe fable to illustrate a point, that's all. There never was any dead rich man in real life living in some burning hell begging for some dude called Lazarus to come quench his thirst. They were merely fictional characters in a parable, a story Jesus Christ made up. Does that require any further explanation? Look, just because Captain Kirk visited some alien world and met Klingons does not mean that Klingons exist. They are make believe, fictional characters that live in a make believe world. Parables were merely stories Jesus Christ made up to illustrate a specific truth. You cannot make a literal doctrine out of a fiction. Well, the vatican does so it can defraud grieving families and swindle them out of their money, but you can't blame God for that.

If the bible is right then the dead people mediums and spiritualists call up in their séances and meetings are not what they purport to be. In real life, folks do actually hear voices of dead people at these séances, and they recognise these voices, so what's the answer?

Jane Fletcher has lost her husband and she is grieving. She is missing him terribly. Someone tells her he's really alive and she could talk to him at a spiritualist's meeting, at a séance. Along she goes and she hears his voice and he tells her things, little secret things it would be impossible for anyone else to know. She rejoices because in her heart she knows her husband is alive and enjoying the afterlife. It brings her comfort and hope for the future. Or so the spiritualists would have us believe. If the dead are dead, who or what was this woman talking to, and how did it know the little intimate secrets she and her husband shared?

The discerning of spirits field is without doubt the largest field of human understanding imaginable. The devil spirit kingdom is breathtakingly immense and diverse, stunningly powerful and unbelievably deceptive. To have any chance of understanding the spiritual depth to life we must take the word of God as our standard for truth and work every-thing else from that premise. The dead are dead, it is that simple. Whoever or whatever it was that talked to Jane Fletcher, it was not her husband. So what was it?

Devil spirits have jobs to do and the bible teaches us much about it. Some devil spirits work well in politics and power. Some are good at depressing and oppressing folks, driving them to despair and suicide. Others are adept at working in religious circles, deceiving those who seek to know the truth, deafening their ears so they neglect the word, blinding them and leading them into ditches.

Another job spirits have is to watch people. The bible refers to these particular devil spirits as familiar spirits. Their job is to watch people, to become familiar with them. They watch people all their lives from the moment they are born until the moment they die. Then they move onto another person. They do this century after century, building vast archives of knowledge about people. They are familiar with people, which is why they are called in the bible familiar spirits. Incidentally, these are the same devil spirits behind the lie of reincarnation.

Jane Fletcher goes to the spiritualist meeting. The medium asks a few questions. The devil spirits possessing the medium get information. They then find the spirit that is familiar with her dead husband and it is summoned. Jane has a chat with this devil spirit, which is capable of impersonating her dead husband's voice through the medium, and it tells her all the little secrets they shared. These spirits can mimic the actual voices of dead people while they speak out through the men and women they possess. It's a puerile trick, but it's effective.

The record of Saul and the witch of Endor is another scriptural record used to teach that the dead are alive. However, the bible doesn't teach that the dead are alive, it teaches that the dead are dead. So who was Saul talking to at that séance with the witch of Endor? The bible doesn't say it was Samuel, the bible says that Saul *perceived* it to be Samuel. Just because Saul thought it was Samuel doesn't make it so.

> 1 Samuel 28:7,12-14
> Then said Saul unto his servants, Seek me a woman that hath a familiar spirit, that I may go to her, and enquire of her. And his servants said to him, Behold, *there is* a woman that hath a familiar spirit at Endor.
>
> And when the woman saw Samuel, she cried with a loud voice: and the woman spake to Saul, saying, Why hast thou deceived me? for thou *art* Saul.
>
> And the king said unto her, Be not afraid: for what sawest thou? And the woman said unto Saul, I saw gods ascending out of the earth.
>
> And he said unto her, What form *is* he of? And she said, An old man cometh up; and he *is* covered with a mantle. And Saul perceived that it *was* Samuel, and he stooped with *his* face to the ground, and bowed himself.

It wasn't Samuel because Samuel was dead, it was a devil spirit impersonating him. Unlike David, Saul obviously didn't rise early every morning to study his bible or he would have known this. Consequently he had a head full of religious horseshit which led to his death.

The whole realm of witchcraft and spiritualism is built upon the lie that the dead are not dead, that they are alive. But why? Why would devils go to such lengths? Whatever their motives are, it is to steal, to kill, and to destroy. Was this lie effective against Eve? Oh yes, do not underestimate its power.

To further illustrate, two women once explained how they went to a spiritualist meeting in the Philippines which over 70 people attended. The medium's particular emphasis that day was faith healing. Everyone was there to get healing. However, the medium refused to minister to these two women. Everyone else was ministered to and they were all healed. The two women left, without being healed. Later, they learned about spiritualism from the biblical perspective. Out of curiosity, they tracked down every person who had been ministered to at that meeting in the Philippines and were stunned to discover that every single one of them was dead. This is a true story. Little children, keep yourselves from idols, keep yourselves from tarot cards, fortune tellers, hypnosis, magic, horoscopes, psychics, witchcraft and all the rest of the devil's horseshit for it will take your life.

The word of God , the bible, has to be our only standard for truth if we are to live powerful, abundant lives. Once we are redeemed from the power of Lucifer who is the god of this world, the devil, he no longer has jurisdiction over us. We can learn to walk in power and deliver people from his deceptions and cruelty.

> 1 John 4:4
> Ye are of God, little children, and have overcome them: because greater is he that is in you, than he that is in the world.

Just as with the trinity, the teaching that the dead are alive entrenches vatican doctrine, as well as all other religions, clearly within the realms of paganism and witchcraft. Their doctrine is unscriptural, their beliefs pagan. The jesuits may cloak themselves in religious robes and claim they know what is best for the world, but in truth, they serve their god Lucifer. Rather than bringing us peace on earth, they are destroying it on behalf of their god. The end justifies the means only when it is the god of this world issuing the orders. So the next time you hear the pope praying for *world peace*, smile warmly as you realise that what he is really praying for is your extermination.

If this all seems a little overpowering, remember that light dispels darkness. Switch on light and there is no darkness. Darkness cannot exist in light. It is that easy to dispel darkness. How you turn on spiritual light in your life begins with opening your bible and reading. Or are movies, newspapers, magazines, television programmes and the internet more important to you? Whether you live in darkness or whether you live in light is a choice you make.

28. Predestination

Predestination is a word that breezes comfortably through our minds and flows easily from our tongues. However, if we were to see that word for what the world has made of it, we would rather chew nettles than speak it. Spiritually, it's one of the filthiest words in language, with the power to overthrow entire cultures and civilisations. How this can be is staggering to grasp.

Understanding how the devil manipulates language is fundamental to our understanding of this study, so we will take a brief look into it. The manipulation of language is one of the most devious activities engaged in worldwide. For example, through the devil's control of media, words from scripture are twisted and given horrendous undertones, while his filthy words are bottle fed to us as infants so we grow up comfortable with them. One of the most effective methods employed against the word of God is the perverting of the meanings of words. For example:

> Exodus 21:2,5,6
> If thou buy an Hebrew servant, six years he shall serve: and in the seventh he shall go out free for nothing.
>
> And if the servant shall plainly say, I love my master, my wife, and my children; I will not go out free:
>
> Then his master shall bring him unto the judges; he shall also bring him to the door, or unto the door post; and his master shall bore his ear through with an aul; and he shall serve him for ever.

To understand these verses we must understand the culture. Back then there was no social security, no welfare, no free money handouts from government. So what happened to someone whose business failed? What happened to someone who perhaps had a wife and kids to feed but who was without income? God knew these things would happen and he made provision for them.

Rather than a government welfare system, God's people implemented a system whereby if you became unemployed and ran out of money you could work as a servant for a businessman or farmer for a period of time. In return, your master would take care of your every need, including clothing, food, and housing. At the end of six years your period of service would expire and the master of the house was then required to give you your freedom and pay you a lump sum that would be enough to start your own business again. Not a bad deal!

However, if the servant had built up such a relationship with his master that he loved his job so much that he didn't want to leave, there was an option for him to remain as a servant within the master's household for the rest of his life. If a servant chose this option, he would have his ear pierced so all would know he was a servant for life in the service of his master.

This lifetime of service was a highly venerated and revered position that carried high social honour and prestige. After all, the servant had the option of leaving and setting up his own business, but instead had chosen, by his own freewill, to remain within his master's household and serve him for the rest of his life. Such servants were greatly honoured and highly valued, and they usually held high office within the master's household. In the Greek, such a servant is called a *doulos*, a slave. *A slave?*

A few centuries ago, evil men made vast sums of money from kidnapping black Africans, transporting them around the world in horrendous conditions, and selling them as property. Those poor men and women came to be known as slaves. However, they were not slaves according to the biblical definition of that word. Why did the devil use this wonderful term from the bible that describes perhaps the most revered and honoured relationship possible between an employer and an employee and apply it to the criminal trafficking of human beings? Why do you think?

Most of us today would rather die than be slaves, wouldn't we? How do people feel when they first hear this term used in the bible in reference to us being a doulos, a slave for the Lord Jesus Christ? This is how the world conditions people to think by manipulating language so that God's word sounds revolting rather than attractive. In Romans, Paul refers to himself as a slave.

> Romans 1:1
> Paul, a servant [doulos] of Jesus Christ, called *to be* an apostle, separated unto the gospel of God,

Paul was a slave, but he wasn't some ill-treated piece of property that had been kidnapped and sold against his will to work in the employ of a tyrant. Rather, this is the highest position in life to which any human being can aspire, a position that carries tremendous prestige, honour, and responsibility. This is but one example of how the devil twists language to destroy the word.

The same is true in reverse. Words that should make us shudder with revulsion have been sprinkled with chocolate and cream and tarted up to make them appealing and desirable. Words like homosexuality. I'm going to remove the chocolate and cream from *predestination*, as it is currently understood, and let you see that word for the pile of dogshit it really is.

> Ephesians 1:3-5
> Blessed *be* the God and Father of our Lord Jesus Christ, who hath blessed us with all spiritual blessings in heavenly *places* in Christ:
>
> According as he hath chosen us in him before the foundation of the world, that we should be holy and without blame before him in love:
>
> Having predestinated us unto the adoption of children by Jesus Christ to himself, according to the good pleasure of his will,

God *chose* us from before the foundation of the world, and we were *predestinated* according to God's good pleasure. Does this mean that no matter what we would have done with our lives, we had absolutely no say whatsoever in whether or not we would become God's children? Is everything that happens to us totally beyond our control? I think you can begin to smell the stink already.

Matthew 22:14
For many are called, but few *are* chosen.

This must be one of the most misused scriptures in the whole bible. It is usually quoted to make people feel bad about themselves when they make mistakes. It also paints God in a terrible light, as if he is poking around with a stick looking for someone worth keeping. When people make mistakes and fall short, as we all do, this scripture is often used against them as a weapon, to make them feel guilty and unworthy.

There are a number of important keys to the word's interpretation, and one of them is that a scripture must be in harmony with all the other scriptures relating to the same subject. If we have many clear verses on a subject and one apparently contradictory verse, do we ignore the many clear verses and focus solely on the unclear verse? Not if we are interested in an honest handling of the word of God, we don't. Here are a few scriptures that clearly teach that God is no respecter of persons.

Romans 2:11
For there is no respect of persons with God.

Ephesians 6:9b
...neither is there respect of persons with him.

1 Timothy 2:3,4
For this *is* good and acceptable in the sight of God our Saviour;

Who will have all men to be saved, and to come unto the knowledge of the truth.

John 3:16
For God so loved the world, that he gave his only begotten Son, that whosoever believeth in him should not perish, but have everlasting life.

Without labouring the point, God isn't fussy about whom he chooses. Therefore, if Matthew 22:14 teaches that God is choosy about people, it contradicts the rest of the bible.

Another key to the interpretation of the word is that all scripture interprets itself in the verse, in its context, or where it has been used before. The immediate context of Matthew 22:14 happens to be a parable. A parable is a figure of speech, in this case, an extended simile. A simile is the simplest figure of speech in language and as such makes only one point of comparison. For example, if we say a person runs like a cheetah, the only point we are making is that the person is a fast runner. We are not implying that the person has four legs, a spotty fur coat, and likes to eat monkeys. That would be absurd. The only comparison made is regarding the person's speed as a runner. Similarly, this parable being an extended simile makes only one point of comparison and one point only. You cannot spiritualise every single point in this parable as if it were an allegory.

Jesus Christ used this parable, a simile, to paint a picture in the minds of his listeners. He used their culture and language to illustrate one point regarding the kingdom of God – *many are called, but few are chosen*. Therefore, if we can understand the meaning of the parable, we will understand the meaning behind those words. The entire parable illustrates this one spiritual truth, nothing else.

> Matthew 22:1,2
> And Jesus answered and spake unto them again by parables, and said,
>
> The kingdom of heaven is like unto a certain king, which made a marriage for his son,

The words *like unto* tell us this is the figure of speech simile.

> Matthew 22:3-7
> And sent forth his servants to call them that were bidden to the wedding: and they would not come.
>
> Again, he sent forth other servants, saying, Tell them which are bidden, Behold, I have prepared my dinner: my oxen and *my* fatlings *are* killed, and all things *are* ready: come unto the marriage.
>
> But they made light of *it*, and went their ways, one to his farm, another to his merchandise:

And the remnant took his servants, and entreated *them* spitefully, and slew *them*.

But when the king heard *thereof*, he was wroth: and he sent forth his armies, and destroyed those murderers, and burned up their city.

Remember, this is a parable with only one point of comparison. It is not an allegory. You cannot take each aspect and spiritualise it, as it only makes one point of comparison. There is nothing to learn *spiritually* from the parable so far as it is merely part of an illustration from their culture that Jesus is using to paint a picture for those listening. It is a fiction, a made up story, not a real life event. This has never happened. He is merely building a mind picture for them using words they understood so that at the end he could make a single spiritual truth live for them in a very real, unique, and special way. If you were to try to say this is referring to Israel in the old testament then are you also saying that it was God who did all this killing and burning? This was simply just a story he made up that they would understand so he could illustrate a single point regarding the kingdom of God, that many are called but few are chosen.

Matthew 22:8-14
Then saith he to his servants, The wedding is ready, but they which are bidden were not worthy,

Go ye therefore into the highways, and as many as ye shall find, bid to the marriage.

So those servants went out into the highways, and gathered together all as many as they found, both bad and good: and the wedding was furnished with guests.

And when the king came in to see the guests, he saw there a man which had not on a wedding garment:

And he said unto him, Friend, how camest thou in hither not having a wedding garment? And he was speechless.

Then said the king to the servants, Bind him hand and foot, and take him away, and cast *him* into outer darkness; there shall be weeping and gnashing of teeth.

For many are called, but few *are* chosen.

Now we need to check another key to the word's interpretation – all scripture must be understood according to the culture and mannerisms of the time. The bible is an eastern book filled with eastern customs and we often need to understand these orientalisms to get to the truth behind the words. Understanding eastern culture is important to understanding this parable and the truth it illustrates.

In Jesus' day in his culture, guests did not wear their own clothes to a royal wedding. The king personally sent out wedding clothes to everyone on the guest list. It was the king's responsibility to provide tux and tails for the gentlemen and dresses for the ladies. That was their culture. Of course, everyone Jesus Christ was talking to here would have known that. They would have also known that to turn up at a royal wedding in your own clothes, having deliberately refused to wear the clothes provided by the king, would have been an unpardonable breach of etiquette. It would be a bit like turning up for dinner with the queen at a State banquet dressed in tatty jeans and a rude t-shirt, only much worse. Refusing to wear the royal wedding garment would have been an unpardonable act of disrespect, like spitting in the king's face in public.

When this person was confronted, he was speechless. What could he say? He had been freely given a royal wedding garment and had knowingly and willingly refused to wear it, showing public disrespect for the king, and breaking every cultural protocol imaginable. It was his choice to do so because he had freedom of will.

Matthew 8:14
For many are called, but few are chosen.

Whether we choose to clothe ourselves with what God has made freely available is *our* choice. *We* decide whether or not we are one of the chosen few. It is our choice, our decision. We can decide to clothe ourselves with what God has made freely available, or we can choose to ignore the invitation. If people want to march into God's presence and tell him that what he has made available isn't good enough for them, that's fine, let them be among the many who are called but not chosen. It's their choice. Let's look again at those verses in Ephesians.

> Ephesians 1:3-5
> Blessed *be* the God and Father of our Lord Jesus Christ, who hath blessed us with all spiritual blessings in heavenly *places* in Christ:
>
> According as he hath chosen us in him before the foundation of the world, that we should be holy and without blame before him in love:
>
> Having predestinated us unto the adoption of children by Jesus Christ to himself, according to the good pleasure of his will,

Is eternal life available to all? Yes, it is. Who decides whether or not we are one of the chosen? We do. It is our choice. By the freedom of our will, we decide to become one of God's chosen. God in his foreknowledge knew we would believe before the foundation of the world and, therefore, he *foreordained* us to the adoption of children. He knew we would believe, but it was we ourselves by our freedom of will who made the choice to become God's child. How did we do that?

> Romans 10:9,10
> That if thou shalt confess with thy mouth the Lord Jesus, and shalt believe in thine heart that God hath raised him from the dead, thou shalt be saved [sōzō].
>
> For with the heart man believeth unto righteousness; and with the mouth confession is made unto salvation.

Confessing with our mouths and believing in our hearts are actions and decisions we make. Without believing and confessing as stated in Romans 10:9, we would not receive the gift of holy spirit, we would not be clothed with power from on high. The receiving of the gift of holy spirit is entirely conditional on us carrying out the instruction given in Romans. When we confess with our mouths Jesus as Lord and believe in our hearts that God raised him from the dead, we are saved, sōzō, made whole, referring to once again being complete, being whole, with body, soul and spirit.

Does God force us to believe? No, God never forces anyone to do anything. He gave us freedom of will and it is up to us whether we choose to believe God and his word or not. Therefore, predestination here is simply a reference to God's foreknowledge. He knew way back in the beginning that we would believe, and so we were predestined, foreordained to become sons and daughters of God.

The twisting of the meaning of the word *predestination* was something that even affected Jesus Christ's closest disciples.

> John 9:1,2
> And as *Jesus* passed by, he saw a man which was blind from *his* birth.
>
> And his disciples asked him, saying, Master, who did sin, this man, or his parents, that he was born blind?

To understand this you have to ask the question, how could this man have been born blind because of his own sin? Can babies sin in the womb before they are born? No, that's ridiculous. The disciples indicated that they believed it was possible for a person to be born blind because of his own sin. They asked this because predestination, and how it ties in with reincarnation, had been engrained into their thinking through religion and culture. They believed the man might have sinned in a previous life and consequently been *predestined* to be born blind because of his previous sins. They got this nonsense from the religious teachings in their synagogues, which wasn't much different to the horseshit taught in churches today. Predestination, where everything in life is beyond our control, which includes reincarnation, is unscriptural. Note Jesus Christ's response.

> John 9:3,4
> Jesus answered, Neither hath this man sinned, nor his parents [full stop, period]: but that the works of God should be made manifest in him [comma].
>
> I must work the works of him that sent me, while it is day: the night cometh, when no man can work.

Be careful with punctuation as the original texts had none. Every full stop and comma has been added by the translators and they are entirely devoid of any authority whatsoever. No punctuation is God-breathed, therefore all punctuation has to fit within the context of the bible. The comma after the word *parents* is clearly wrong as the verse then depicts them as puppets whose son God made blind just so Jesus could do a miracle. This man wasn't born blind because of anyone's sins. He was not *predestined* by God or anyone else to be reincarnated into a blind body. Look at how prevalent and insidious this doctrine of predestination can really be. People can only believe such horseshit if they believe that when you die you don't really die. Do you begin to see the power in that original lie with which the serpent seduced Eve? Jesus Christ had to deal with this even among his own disciples.

The following verse from Isaiah is a prophecy regarding the physical beatings the Lord Jesus Christ endured prior to his death.

> Isaiah 52:14
> As many were astonied at thee; his visage was so marred more than any man, and his form more than the sons of men:

What this verse prophecies is that the Lord Jesus Christ would be beaten so badly during the two days he was tortured before his crucifixion, that his form, his physical body would be disfigured more than any man in human history. His physical body was pulped during the forty hours he was beaten, whipped, and tortured. Jesus Christ was so badly beaten, he was unrecognisable as a human being as he was dragged to his crucifixion.

This was prophesied of hundreds of years before it actually happened. So does that mean that those who beat Jesus Christ to a pulp did not have freedom of will? Were they simply puppets and robots doing what God made them do just so God could bring his word to pass? Maybe now you can begin to smell the stink behind this word *predestination* as it is widely understood today. Even though we see old testament prophesies coming to pass in the new testament, all those involved in the brutal beatings of the Lord Jesus Christ, all of them, exercised their own freedom of will. God may have known in his foreknowledge what would happen and had it recorded centuries earlier, but that does not mean that those involved were not exercising freewill.

Jesus Christ decided by his freedom of will to be the passover lamb that year for all mankind, and he laid down his life. He gave it, it was not taken from him. The religious leaders of his time, the church hierarchy, those who worked for the god of this world just as they do today, also made freewill decisions. God in his foreknowledge knew what would happen and recorded it, but he did not force anyone to do anything just to make sure his word came to pass. This is true of all scripture prophesying of future events.

In short, predestination as it is understood today destroys people. It gives people excuses for their failures. Instead of taking responsibility for their failed marriages, businesses, families, health, and everything else in their lives, they come up with all sorts of excuses and blame it all on God. It was *predestined* and they had nothing to do with it. Folks are taught they have no control, that everything is *meant to be*. So they blame their failed marriages and failed businesses on God, they blame their failed health on God, because it was all *meant to be*. Put your noses into this dogshit of predestination and take a good sniff. It is a stinking lie. Sure, God will light our path so we can see where we are going, but we have control of our own lives and over which paths we walk. The decisions we make determine where we go in life, as well as our successes and our failures. If we fail, it's not God's fault, it's ours. God never made a failure.

When the devil attacks, he likes nothing more than to watch people lie down and die. That is why he weakens us with such lies. He doesn't like it when people stand up and fight back, it defeats his purposes. If he can get us to just accept defeat because we think it was *meant to be*, then he wins and we lose. This lie has the power to destroy entire races and civilisations.

Your life is yours to live so be careful with what you think was *meant to be*. We all grow up in the devil's world and grow up exposed to his filthy language, but that's no excuse for your thoughts to be contrary to the bible. Put your televisions and newspapers and religious horseshit aside, open your bibles again and put your hearts into the word. Be watchful, because predestination is the language of extinction.

29. The Course of this World

Now it's time to look a little more closely at how the devil conducts his business. Ephesians 2:2 talks about the course of this world.

> Ephesians 2:2
> Wherein in time past ye walked according to the course of this world, according to the prince of the power of the air, the spirit that now worketh in the children of disobedience:

If we can understand how the devil moves within the framework of the five senses, which is the course of this world, things will become clearer for us when it comes to making decisions that affect our lives and the lives of others. While going through this, always remember that our fight is not against flesh and blood.

> Ephesians 6:12
> For we wrestle not against flesh and blood, but against principalities, against powers, against the rulers of the darkness of this world, against spiritual wickedness in high *places*.

Flesh and blood is a figurative reference to the senses realm. Our fight isn't against the senses realm, but against the spiritual powers working through people from behind the scenes. With that in mind, we can now dispel a few smoke screens so we can see more clearly what is going on around us. We have already gained many clues and it is time to put things together.

We'll begin by studying the arrest, the illegal trials, and the crucifixion of the Lord Jesus Christ. Between his arrest and his execution, Jesus Christ endured unparalleled evil and brutality. Remember, he did this willingly. He went through this for you and me. He laid down his life freely by his choice, it was not taken from him against his will.

From his arrest until his death was a period of about forty hours, during which time he was beaten to a pulp as prophesied in Isaiah. What makes this so poignant is that Jesus Christ knew it was coming throughout his ministry. He would have known this verse in Isaiah by heart, and he would have known it referred to him.

> Isaiah 52:14
> As many were astonied at thee; his visage was so marred more than any man, and his form more than the sons of men:

His visage, his form, his physical body was marred more than any other human being that has ever lived. He *knew* all through his ministry that he was going to be beaten more than any man in the history of the world, before or since and yet he still loved people and ministered. He was beaten so badly, his physical body no longer resembled that of a human being. How did the devil orchestrate this? It was men who did this to Jesus Christ, but how did the god of this world orchestrate it?

At the time of the crucifixion, there was no sovereign nation of Israel. Palestine, which included Judea, had been occupied and governed by the Romans since 63 BC. As an occupying force, the Romans permitted the Judeans to practice their religion and law under the direction of the Sanhedrin, the ruling body of Judaism. Thus there were two sophisticated legal systems in operation during Jesus Christ's ministry, one Judean and one Roman. The devil used the existing governmental and religious systems in place at the time by working through those with the political and religious power to execute this heinous crime.

> John 18:12,13
> Then the band and the captain and officers of the Jews [Judeans] took Jesus, and bound him,
>
> And led him away to Annas first; for he was father in law to Caiaphas, which was the high priest that same year.

Annas and Caiaphas were both most likely members of the Sanhedrin. Even though the Romans had deposed Annas, the Judeans considered him high priest for life. His influence with the Romans was evident by their appointment of his son-in-law Caiaphas to replace him as high priest. The Judeans revered Annas much as Roman Catholics revere the pope today.

In his book The Life and Times of Jesus the Messiah, Alfred Edershiem states that the Annas family derived their chief source of income from selling sacrifices in the temple, the very practice Jesus had condemned three days earlier when he drove the merchants and their animals out. This was obviously a big part of what stirred such dark emotional hatreds within Annas and Caiaphas. Jesus Christ taught the truth and that affected their income. The love of money is the root of all evil, and pity help anyone who messes with the income of evil men. Paul encountered a similar problem at Ephesus from the silversmiths who made money by selling shrines dedicated to Diana.

> Acts 19:23-32
> And the same time there arose no small stir about that way.
>
> For a certain *man* named Demetrius, a silversmith, which made silver shrines for Diana, brought no small gain unto the craftsmen;
>
> Whom he called together with the workmen of like occupation, and said, Sirs, ye know that by this craft we have our wealth.
>
> Moreover ye see and hear, that not alone at Ephesus, but almost throughout all Asia, this Paul hath persuaded and turned away much people, saying that they be no gods, which are made with hands:
>
> So that not only this our craft is in danger to be set at nought; but also that the temple of the great goddess Diana should be despised, and her magnificence should be destroyed, whom all Asia and the world worshippeth.
>
> And when they heard *these sayings*, they were full of wrath, and cried out, saying, Great *is* Diana of the Ephesians.
>
> And the whole city was filled with confusion: and having caught Gaius and Aristarchus, men of Macedonia, Paul's companions in travel, they rushed with one accord into the theatre.

And when Paul would have entered in unto the people, the disciples suffered him not.

And certain of the chief of Asia, which were his friends, sent unto him, desiring *him* that he would not adventure himself into the theatre.

Some therefore cried one thing, and some another: for the assembly was confused; and the more part knew not wherefore they were come together.

Men stirred up this riot, men who loved money more than truth. We can safely deduce then that the god of this world ensures that men who love money are promoted to high political and religious office.

A man with no accurate understanding of God's word generally views his life according to whatever material possessions he has acquired. The more stuff he owns, the more complete he feels his life is. Expensive villas, fast cars, and good suits make him feel successful and fulfilled. They represent what he has made of himself. Those who don't have as much as others feel somehow inferior, and so they are lured onto the devil's treadmill to try to accumulate some stuff of their own. As born again believers, do our lives consist of what we own? Jesus Christ answered that very question.

> Luke 12:15
> And he said unto them, Take heed, and beware of covetousness: for a man's life consisteth not in the abundance of the things which he possesseth.

Our lives do not consist of the abundance of things that we own. When man views his life according to what he owns, he is on the devil's treadmill, or what is commonly referred to as the rat race.

> 1 Timothy 6:6
> But godliness with contentment is great gain.

The secret to living in Godly contentment, is to be content with having all our need met, which God promises to supply.

> 1 Timothy 6:7,8
> For we brought nothing into *this* world, *and it is* certain we can carry nothing out.
>
> And having food and raiment let us be therewith content.
>
> Philippians 4:19
> But my God shall supply all your need according to his riches in glory by Christ Jesus.

Food and raiment would obviously include somewhere comfortable to live. In other words, with plenty to eat, nice clothes to wear, and somewhere comfortable to live, we should be content.

This isn't to say that being rich is necessarily evil, not at all, Job was the richest man in the world in his day. Solomon was rich beyond imagination. It is our attitude that is important. Do we love money more than we love God? Do we allow our ethics and morals to be corrupted in the pursuit of money, and the property, power, and worldly prestige that brings? If we're not living in godly contentment, we have been seduced by the world, like Annas and Caiaphas, who were willing to commit murder to protect their criminal money making rackets. Annas and Caiaphas loved money more than anything else in life, and when the source of their income was threatened by Jesus Christ, the hatreds that burned within them drove them to murder.

> John 18:14
> Now Caiaphas was he, which gave counsel to the Jews [Judeans], that it was expedient that one man should die for the people.

Although the Romans had given Caiaphas the power and legal authority, Annas still wielded the influence. Both are referred to as high priests in the gospel records. After his arrest, Jesus appeared first before Annas.

> John 18:19-23
> The high priest then asked Jesus of his disciples, and of his doctrine.

Jesus answered him, I spake openly to the world; I ever taught in the synagogue, and in the temple, whither the Jews [Judeans] always resort; and in secret have I said nothing.

Why askest thou me? ask them which heard me, what I have said unto them: behold, they know what I said.

And when he had thus spoken, one of the officers which stood by struck Jesus with the palm of his hand, saying, Answerest thou the high priest so?

Jesus answered him, If I have spoken evil, bear witness of the evil: but if well, why smitest thou me?

The words *struck with the palm of his hand* can mean *to beat repeatedly with a heavy wooden rod*. The word *smitest* means to skin, to flay, or scourge, and scourge means to flog. This was a brutal and illegal act perpetrated by the religious authorities of the time. Things have not changed much in the last 2000 years.

After this trial, they took Jesus to Caiaphas for a more formal trial. It was late at night.

Matthew 26:57,59-63
And they that had laid hold on Jesus led *him* away to Caiaphas the high priest, where the scribes and the elders were assembled.

Now the chief priests, and elders, and all the council, sought false witness against Jesus, to put him to death;

But found none: yea, though many false witnesses came, *yet* found they none. At the last came two false witnesses,

And said, This *fellow* said, I am able to destroy the temple of God, and to build it in three days.

And the high priest arose, and said unto him, Answerest thou nothing? what *is it which* these witness against thee?

But Jesus held his peace. And the high priest answered and said unto him, I adjure thee by the living God, that thou tell us whether thou be the Christ, the Son of God.

Conducting legal proceedings at night was illegal. Intentionally seeking false witnesses was illegal. Those men were comfortable committing criminal acts. This is another clue in our search.

Matthew 26:65-67
Then the high priest rent his clothes, saying, He hath spoken blasphemy; what further need have we of witnesses? behold, now ye have heard his blasphemy.

What think ye? They answered and said, He is guilty of death.

Then did they spit in his face, and buffeted him; and others smote *him* with the palms of their hands,

Under Judean law, blasphemy was indeed punishable by death. Bullinger's Lexicon and Concordance defines the word *smote* in verse 67 as *to rap or strike with a stick or to beat with rods or to scourge*. They hit Jesus repeatedly on the head with thin, flexible whip like canes which would wrap around his face, cutting the flesh. The hatred that burned within these men is indescribable. Remember, these are the top religious men, the church leaders perpetrating these crimes.

Not one person at the trial voiced surprise or concern that laws were being broken. This was well-oiled criminal machinery at work, and the top gangsters, for gangsters they were, involved in all sorts of illegal and immoral money making rackets, were wearing religious robes.

The following morning, they brought Jesus to trial a third time and asked the same questions. This third trial was a pretence, a spectacle merely to keep the Romans happy, giving his trials a façade of legality. Even so, the religious leaders managed to break yet another law because they convicted Jesus on his own testimony, which was illegal. After this third and final illegal Judean trial, they dragged him before the Romans.

Luke 23:1
And the whole multitude of them arose, and led him unto Pilate.

John 18:29
Pilate then went out unto them, and said, What accusation bring ye against this man?

Annas would have been instrumental in devising the plans to have Jesus crucified, including the crimes laid against him. He also knew Pilate as a Roman would refuse to accept blasphemy as a legitimate criminal charge, so the next verse lists the actual charges they brought against him.

Luke 23:2
And they began to accuse him, saying, We found this *fellow* perverting the nation, and forbidding to give tribute to Caesar, saying that he himself is Christ a King.

The first charge, perverting the nation, is sedition, treason under Roman law. Forbidding to give tribute to Caesar is tax evasion. The third charge was claiming to be Christ, a king. Pilate knew that the first two charges were related to the third, that all were entirely religious in nature, and didn't want to get involved. Notice there is no mention of blasphemy in the charges.

Luke 23:4
Then said Pilate to the chief priests and *to* the people, I find no fault in this man.

The Roman governor found no crime worthy of death had been committed, and set his heart on freeing the man. Pilate appealed several times to the Judeans to allow him to let Jesus go. He even went so far as to make the Judeans choose between him and Barabbas, a terrorist and murderer. The religious hierarchy incited the people to choose Barabbas.

Matthew 27:20
But the chief priests and elders persuaded the multitude that they should ask Barabbas, and destroy Jesus.

Here is yet another clue to how the devil works within the courses of the world to bring his devices to pass. It says the chief priests and the elders persuaded the multitude. Annas and Caiaphas didn't go down into the crowd themselves and do this, they organised it, they orchestrated it. Annas and Caiaphas were obviously powerful and influential. There is organisation at work here behind the scenes. This is how the devil moves the courses of the world.

So what was this organisation that Annas and Caiaphas controlled? It was a secret society, an organisation that worked behind the scenes, out of the glare of the public eye. In modern day language, they were big freemasons. Their subordinates infiltrated the crowd and swayed opinion towards Barabbas by shouting down those who put their hands up for Jesus. Threats of retaliation and other forms of domestic terrorism would no doubt have been levelled at anyone daring to stand against the will of Annas and Caiaphas. Fear of reprisals and violence would have silenced the crowd, leaving the loud-mouthed minority to shout for Barabbas and sway the multitude.

> Matthew 27:26-28
> When Pilate saw that he could prevail nothing, but *that* rather a tumult was made, he took water, and washed *his* hands before the multitude, saying, I am innocent of the blood of this just person: see ye *to it*.
>
> Then answered all the people, and said, His blood *be* on us, and on our children.
>
> Then released he Barabbas unto them: and when he had scourged Jesus, he delivered *him* to be crucified.

More events are recorded in God's word about what happened in Jerusalem on the 13th of Nisan, 28 AD, than any other day in history, and there is much we can learn, not only about the actual events, but also of the powers working behind the scenes that orchestrated this most heinous of all crimes.

This is still how riots are fomented to this day. Hard core groups of free masons, communists, call them what you like, those doing the bidding of the jesuits and who serve their god, infiltrate demonstrations and incite protesters to riot. Demonstrations are in fact usually organised solely for the intent of starting riots. When demonstrations turn into riots, government resolve crumbles and breaks. Terrorism works, and the jesuits know that. The threat of violence and rioting keeps our politicians afraid. More than likely, Barabbas was a member of the same masonic order headed by Annas and Caiaphas. More than likely they supported Barabbas and financed him behind the scenes in his murderous terror campaigns.

The primary motivating force behind the murder of Jesus Christ was the love of money. Obviously, the devil didn't give a damn about the money Annas and Caiaphas were making, but he used their *love* of money to push them emotionally to orchestrate the murder of Jesus Christ. The love of money is still the motivating force that drives world terrorism and social unrest today. You can call them Maoists or freedom fighters or whatever you like, but communism and terrorism, including so-called Muslim terrorism, are political weapons wielded by the vatican. It isn't Muslims behind Arab terrorism, it is the vatican. The Muslims have their traitors just like the rest of us. Arafat was in the employ of the vatican. Arafat was a communist and it was the KGB who founded the PLO.

Only organisations as sophisticated and powerful as freemasonry, which includes the Knights of Malta, have the power to enact religious and political acts of the magnitude of the murder of the Lord Jesus Christ. Annas and Caiaphas would have been the jesuits of their day controlling the 33rd degree masons if you please, and it was that authority that allowed them to foment and orchestrate this crime through the political and religious systems of that day. This is still how the devil moves the courses of the world in our time.

One day king Ahab decided he wanted a new vineyard. Only it was not for sale.

> 1 Kings 21:1-3
> And it came to pass after these things, *that* Naboth the Jezreelite had a vineyard, which *was* in Jezreel, hard by the palace of Ahab king of Samaria.

> And Ahab spake unto Naboth, saying, Give me thy vineyard, that I may have it for a garden of herbs, because it is near unto my house: and I will give thee for it a better vineyard than it; *or*, if it seem good to thee, I will give thee the worth of it in money.
>
> And Naboth said to Ahab, The LORD forbid it me, that I should give the inheritance of my fathers unto thee.

Naboth lived by the old testament law, in which it was forbidden to sell the land God had blessed him with. Naboth was a believer, a disciple, one who put God's word before money. This gives us a clue then as to why the devil would want him dead. Ahab loved money more than he loved God, in this case a valuable property. It was his love of money that was the means with which the devil would move the courses of the world to get his bidding done. The love of money is a spiritual lever.

> 1 Kings 21:4
> And Ahab came into his house heavy and displeased because of the word which Naboth the Jezreelite had spoken to him: for he had said, I will not give thee the inheritance of my fathers. And he laid him down upon his bed, and turned away his face, and would eat no bread.

One can only imagine the emotional darkness swirling through Ahab here. He was not living in godly contentment, and the devil was at work through his dark emotions. Then just at the right time, Jezebel his wife, one of the slimiest bitches of all time, crept in.

> 1 Kings 21:5-7
> But Jezebel his wife came to him, and said unto him, Why is thy spirit so sad, that thou eatest no bread?
>
> And he said unto her, Because I spake unto Naboth the Jezreelite, and said unto him, Give me thy vineyard for money; or else, if it please thee, I will give thee *another* vineyard for it: and he answered, I will not give thee my vineyard.
>
> And Jezebel his wife said unto him, Dost thou now govern the kingdom of Israel? arise, *and* eat bread, and let thine heart be merry: I will give thee the vineyard of Naboth the Jezreelite.

The god of this world now goes to work fomenting emotions in Jezebel. You are seeing here firsthand how the courses of this world operate. This is how the devil gets things done. He wants Naboth dead, and the love of money is how he is orchestrating the systems of the world to get the deed done.

1 Kings 21:8
So she wrote letters in Ahab's name, and sealed *them* with his seal, and sent the letters unto the elders and to the nobles that *were* in his city, dwelling with Naboth.

Now wait just a minute here. Obviously, Jezebel wasn't sending these letters through regular channels or regular post. If she had sent any of these letters to the wrong men, Naboth would have been warned, and she would have been at risk of criminal proceedings. She put something into operation behind the scenes. There was some secret and criminal organisation at work within the political framework. Masonry goes back a very long way.

1 Kings 21:9-16
And she wrote in the letters, saying, Proclaim a fast, and set Naboth on high among the people:

And set two men, sons of Belial, before him, to bear witness against him, saying, Thou didst blaspheme God and the king. And *then* carry him out, and stone him, that he may die.

And the men of his city, *even* the elders and the nobles who were the inhabitants in his city, did as Jezebel had sent unto them, *and* as it *was* written in the letters which she had sent unto them.

They proclaimed a fast, and set Naboth on high among the people.

And there came in two men, children of Belial, and sat before him: and the men of Belial witnessed against him, *even* against Naboth, in the presence of the people, saying, Naboth did blaspheme God and the king. Then they carried him forth out of the city, and stoned him with stones, that he died.

Then they sent to Jezebel, saying, Naboth is stoned, and is dead.

And it came to pass, when Jezebel heard that Naboth was stoned, and was dead, that Jezebel said to Ahab, Arise, take possession of the vineyard of Naboth the Jezreelite, which he refused to give thee for money: for Naboth is not alive, but dead.

And it came to pass, when Ahab heard that Naboth was dead, that Ahab rose up to go down to the vineyard of Naboth the Jezreelite, to take possession of it.

As with the murder of the Lord Jesus Christ, the murder of Naboth was the work of the god of this world. Ahab may have got his vineyard, but the god of this world got what he wanted done, and that was the whole point. Not in vain does the word say that the love of money is the root of all evil. Note also that Jezebel and Ahab were very much leaders in the church of Baal at that time.

1 Kings 18:19
Now therefore send, *and* gather to me all Israel unto mount Carmel, and the prophets of Baal four hundred and fifty, and the prophets of the groves four hundred, which eat at Jezebel's table.

It is no different today than it was in Jesus' day, and it is no different to how it was back in the days of Ahab. Are people today wrongly convicted in court and sent to prison because prosecutors lie? Happens all the time. Our soldiers are sent to prison for killing our enemies. The enemy is among us and they protect their own at our expense. The more the jesuits and the masons take control, the more treacherous our politicians, our judiciary, and our other civil leaders become.

It was no different in the days of Ezekiel either. God showed Ezekiel by revelation what was going on inside the temple.

Ezekiel 8:8-12;16
Then said he unto me, Son of man, dig now in the wall: and when I had digged in the wall, behold a door.

And he said unto me, Go in, and behold the wicked abominations that they do here.

So I went in and saw; and behold every form of creeping things, and abominable beasts, and all the idols of the house of Israel, pourtrayed upon the wall round about.

And there stood before them seventy men of the ancients of the house of Israel, and in the midst of them stood Jaazaniah the son of Shaphan, with every man his censer in his hand; and a thick cloud of incense went up.

Then said he unto me, Son of man, hast thou seen what the ancients of the house of Israel do in the dark, every man in the chambers of his imagery? for they say, The LORD seeth us not; the LORD hath forsaken the earth.

And he brought me into the inner court of the LORD'S house, and, behold, at the door of the temple of the LORD, between the porch and the altar, *were* about five and twenty men, with their backs toward the temple of the LORD, and their faces toward the east; and they worshipped the sun toward the east.

Hooded robes and chanting? Incense and religious ritual? What is this but a masonic meeting of religious nuts? The jesuits are the god of this world's hierarchy today. From them, the devil's agendas are filtered down behind the scenes through secret societies and freemasonry until it is manifested through the political and religious systems of the world.

The god of this world is formidable. However, when God raised his son the Lord Jesus Christ from the dead, the devil was defeated.

30. Christ and Christmas

We've been hearing quite a bit about this Jesus Christ dude, but what do we really know about him? We know that he was a man and that he redeemed us from the god of this world, but not much else. Now it's time to take a closer look at his life. However, before we do that, let's dispel a few myths about him. For example, was he really born on december 25th? Before we delve into this, let's first look at some of the history behind christmas.

A good place to begin a meaningful search is with the Romans. Within their empire they observed the yearly holiday of Saturnalia, a week long period of lawlessness culminating on december 25th. The civil courts were not only closed, but the law dictated that no one could be prosecuted for damaging property or even for injuring anyone during the holidays. Ancient writers noted that daylight began to increase after december 22nd. Thus they believed that the sun god had died and risen from the dead three days later, which they concluded to be the reason for increasing daylight. It was deemed a good enough reason for wild celebration, drunkenness, feasting, and giving of gifts.

One ancient Greek historian mentioned that there was much drunkenness, going from house to house singing while naked, widespread rape, and eating human-shaped biscuits. The celebration also involved selecting one person from each community, force feeding them royal dainties, subjecting them to sexual rituals, and finally murdering them as sacrifices on december 25th to signify destroying the forces of darkness.

Going back even further to the druids of prehistoric times, this yearly practice of the worship of the sun god takes on even darker tones, where human sacrifice, the hanging of human body parts on evergreen trees, and cannibalism was part of their rituals. Just as it was a principle in the Mosaic law that the priests ate of whatever was offered as sin offerings, so it was with the heathen priests of Nimrod and Baal, who were required to eat of their human sacrifices. Thus it has come to pass that cahna-Bal, the Priest of Baal, is the established word in our own tongue for someone who eats human flesh. Here then we glimpse our first clues that human sacrifice and the eating of human flesh were behind the ancient origins of our modern christmas.

The evergreen tree has since time immemorial been seen as a symbol of life and worshipped as a phallic fertility symbol. Witches and other pagans regarded the red holly as a symbol of the menstrual blood of the queen of heaven, also known as Diana, while the white mistletoe berries were believed to be droplets of semen from the sun god. Both holly and mistletoe were hung in doorways of temples and homes to invoke powers of fertility in those who kissed beneath them by inviting the spirits of the gods and goddesses [devil spirits] to enter them.

In Norse mythology, the god Balder was killed using a mistletoe arrow by his rival god Hoder while fighting for the female Nanna. Druid rituals used mistletoe to poison their human sacrificial victims. The christian custom of kissing under the mistletoe is an evolvement from the sexual license of Saturnalia with the Druidic sacrificial rituals. Holly wood is used by witches and sorcerers to make magic wands. Makes you wonder where our present day Hollywood, the centre of the world's movie industry derived its name.

Without labouring the point, the roots of our modern christmas celebration has its roots in witchcraft, human ritualistic murder, and the eating of human flesh. Think on that the next time you're tempted to eat one of those cute little chocolate body parts hanging on a tree.

As to santa claus, Saint Nicholas was born in Parara, Turkey in 270 AD and was only named a saint in the 19th century. Nicholas was one of the bishops at the Council of Nicaea in 325 AD, where the teaching of the trinity was formally established as the cornerstone of vatican doctrine. In 1087 AD a group of sailors moved his bones from Turkey to a sanctuary in Italy, where he supplanted a female deity who filled children's stockings with gifts. The unfortunate goddess was evicted from her shrine and it became the centre of the Nicholas cult.

The cult spread until it was adopted by German and Celtic pagans who worshipped many gods led by Woden, who was depicted as having a long white beard, and who rode a horse through the heavens one night each year. In its bid for pagan adherents in Europe, the vatican adopted the Nicholas cult along with all their traditions.

In 1809, the novelist Washington Irving wrote a Dutch satire entitled Knickerbocker History, which refers several times to a white bearded Santa Claus (Saint Nicholas' Dutch name) riding a flying horse. Dr Clement Moore, a professor at Union Seminary, read Knickerbocker History and in 1822 published a poem portraying a santa who descended chimneys and rode a sleigh across the sky pulled by eight reindeer.

From 1862 to 1886, the Bavarian illustrator Thomas Nast drew more than 2,200 cartoons of santa for Harper's Weekly, portraying him in green clothing, with a home at the North Pole which had a workshop filled with elves, and who had a list of all the good and bad children in the world. In 1931, Coca Cola commissioned the Swedish artist Haddon Sundblom to create a new Santa, insisting he wear a fur-trimmed suit of bright red rather than green, and that he should be portrayed drinking a bottle of coke. That's the history of santa claus.

What has any of this to do with Jesus Christ or the bible? Obviously, absolutely nothing. The Reverend Increase Mather of Boston observed in 1687 that:

The early Christians who first observed the Nativity on December 25 did not do so thinking that Christ was born in that Month, but because the Heathens' Saturnalia was at that time kept in Rome, and they were willing to have those Pagan Holidays metamorphosed into Christianity.

Many of the most popular christmas customs – christmas trees, mistletoe, gifts, drunkenness, and santa claus – are modern incarnations of the most depraved witchcraft rituals ever practiced on earth.

The word *christmas* itself reveals who was responsible for introducing this horseshit into christianity. It is a derivative of the words *Christ* and *mass*. The word *mass* means *death* and the ritual of the mass involves the death of Christ and the distribution of the host, a word taken from the Latin word *hostiall* meaning *victim*. The vatican simply welcomed the pagan beliefs and customs surrounding the festival of Saturnalia into their doctrines, changed the focus from the birth of the sun god to the birth of the son of god and blithely handed us christmas.

Jesus Christ was not born on december 25th, in fact he was not even born in december. Regardless of the controversy and debate this stirs up, everyone knows Jesus Christ was not born in december. So why do churches all over the world knowingly and willingly contradict the bible in their teachings? Who is this sun god, and why do churches all over the world celebrate his birthday on December 25th? Before going deeper into this, let's first consider the biblical account of the events surrounding the birth of Jesus Christ.

31. The Wise Men and the Star

There are quite a number of significant events recorded regarding the birth of Jesus Christ. In this study we won't be covering every detail as that would necessarily be the work of many books. Instead, we will just touch on a few highlights, particularly his star and the main events surrounding his birth.

> Matthew 2:1-3
> Now when Jesus was born in Bethlehem of Judaea in the days of Herod the king, behold, there came wise men from the east to Jerusalem,
>
> Saying, Where is he that is born King of the Jews [Judeans]? for we have seen his star in the east, and are come to worship him.
>
> When Herod the king had heard *these things*, he was troubled, and all Jerusalem with him.

A number of interesting points arise here. Who were these wise men? What was this star they saw? How come these wise men knew about the birth of Jesus Christ while no one in Jerusalem knew anything about it? Why was Jerusalem troubled at the news instead of rejoicing?

We have to start somewhere, so first of all does it say there were three wise men? No, it doesn't. Nor does the word ever hint at such a number. Just because there were three gifts does not mean there were only three wise men. In fact, there were far more than three of them, as we shall see.

Was Herod overjoyed at the news? No, he was troubled. *Troubled* in the Greek is the word *tarassō* which means *mental pressure*. He was greatly distressed mentally by this news. It caused him severe headaches and put him under immense pressure. This reaction to hearing about the birth of the Christ tells us a great deal about his heart and what kind of a man he was.

> Mathew 2:4
> And when he had gathered all the chief priests and scribes of the people together, he demanded of them where Christ should be born.

Herod gathered all the biblical scholars and religious leaders together and *demanded* to know where this Christ was born.

> Matthew 2:5,6
> And they said unto him, In Bethlehem of Judaea: for thus it is written by the prophet,
>
> And thou Bethlehem, *in* the land of Juda, art not the least among the princes of Juda: for out of thee shall come a Governor, that shall rule my people Israel.

They found this scripture in Malachi and told him it was in Bethlehem. It's amazing and intriguing that these wise men knew about Jesus Christ's birth, yet no one in Israel knew anything about it. How could this be? How could these foreigners from a distant land know about this event while not one person in Jerusalem knew anything about it? Let's find out.

The Greek word translated *wise men* is *Magi* or *magoi* (it's the same word). Now for some interesting history. The Magi were priests from Persia. The earliest Magi lived in Media and Persia before the time of Zoroaster (ca 600 BC) who was the founder and prophet of the Zoroastrian religion. Before Zoroaster, it is thought the Magi were nature worshippers. When Zoroastrianism became the prominent religion of Persia, many of the Magi adopted it. After the death of Zoroaster, the magian sect splintered into two. Some of the Magi remained true to the teachings of Zoroaster while others returned to their nature worship.

During Christ's time, many of these nature worshipping magian priests had left Persia and settled in the Roman Empire where they further developed their magical arts of astrology and sorcery. The words *magic* and *magician* come directly from these magian spiritualists and sorcerers. Simon the sorcerer in Acts 8:9 was one of these spiritualist magian priests.

> Acts 8:9
> But there was a certain man, called Simon, which beforetime in the same city used sorcery [mageuō], and bewitched the people of Samaria, giving out that himself was some great one:

The eastern Magi back in Persia remained faithful to the teachings of Zoroaster, and further developed their religion. It is these Magi who are referred to in verse 1. The epithet *from the east* is probably a reference to their reputation (distinguishing them from the western Magi spiritualists infesting the Roman Empire), as well as to their geographic location. It was these eastern Magi from Persia who travelled to Jerusalem to see Herod.

> Matthew 2:1
> Now when [after] Jesus was born in Bethlehem of Judaea in the days of Herod the king, behold, there came wise men [Magi] from the east to Jerusalem.

These were noted and highly respected astronomers and scholars with an International reputation. These eastern Magi were not spiritualists and mediums like their counterparts in the Roman Empire, they were brilliant men, astronomers and scholars.

Another thing, these Magi were part of a royal entourage sent from the king of Persia. Magi held high office in Persia and had the king's ear. They were the king's personal advisors. The king of Persia would have known about the birth of the young Judean king and would have sent the customary royal gifts along with the Magi to present to him. These gifts would have been highly valuable. There is no way just three men would have carried such wealth hundreds of miles through dangerous country and risk being robbed. This was, in fact, a royal caravan with gifts for the new Judean king from the king of Persia. I'm sure most of the magian priests in Persia would have wanted to make this pilgrimage so this was not just three men on camels. With such treasure, and travelling such great distances through country infested with robbers and wild animals, security would have been essential. The caravan would have had a formidable military escort. There could have been *hundreds* of people in that caravan.

Unbelievable that no one in Judea was expecting them and no one in Judea knew anything about the birth of the Christ. The first they knew of it was when this royal Persian caravan of magian priests turned up with their military escort. Herod was taken completely by surprise. He knew nothing about any Christ or king being born. No wonder he was pissed off. He was the king, and suddenly he heard there was another one? And how come none of his religious advisors had told him anything about it? Herod wanted answers! That's why he barked at the religious leaders and *demanded* of them where the Christ should be born. He was troubled, for sure, and all Jerusalem was troubled with him. He had murder in his heart.

So just how did these Persian Magi know about the birth of the Christ anyway? If these guys knew about it, you would think God's so-called people would have known. How did these Persians know?

A few hundred years earlier, Nebuchadnezzar invaded Israel and Judaea, and carried away many captives to Babylon, the capital of the Persian Empire. Among them were Daniel, Shadrach, Meshach and Abednego. After interpreting a dream for Nebuchadnezzar, Daniel was promoted.

> Daniel 2:48
> Then the king made Daniel a great man, and gave him many great gifts, and made him ruler over the whole province of Babylon, and chief of the governors over all the wise *men* of Babylon.

Daniel was a disciple, and he was promoted to the top spiritual job, as well as presiding over all the political advisors and scholars in the Persian empire.

> Daniel 5:11
> There is a man in thy kingdom, in whom *is* the spirit of the holy gods; and in the days of thy father light and understanding and wisdom, like the wisdom of the gods, was found in him; whom the king Nebuchadnezzar thy father, the king, *I say*, thy father, made

master of the magicians, astrologers, Chaldeans, *and* soothsayers [mgushe].

Daniel was the master of the magicians, astrologers, Chaldeans and soothsayers. That means he was their master. The Aramaic word for *soothsayers* is *mgushe*, the Old Testament equivalent of the Greek word *Magi*. Daniel was promoted to master of the Magi in the Persian Empire five to six hundred years before Christ was born. As their master, Daniel would have taught them about the stars. Hundreds of years later, that knowledge was still being taught, which is why the Magi who arrived in Jerusalem were knowledgeable about his star.

> Matthew 2:2
> Saying, Where is he that is born King of the Jews [Judeans]? for we have seen his star in the east, and are come to worship him.

An interesting sideline here is that Daniel and Zoroaster could very well have been one and the same person. I'm not going to research this, but if you check dates and the history of Zoroastrianism, Daniel and Zoroaster may very well have been alive in the same country at the same time, making it plausible they were one and the same.

The Magi saw his star *in the east* or *in the sun rising* as it should be translated. These guys were astronomers. The birth of Christ had been announced in the night skies and it was Daniel hundreds of years earlier who had taught them how to read the stars. That's how they knew what to look for. The knowledge of how to read the stars had been lost in Israel, which is why no one knew anything about it. That knowledge is still in the stars today, it's just that no one knows how to read it. Only those Magi who knew how to read the stars saw the celestial events announcing the birth of the Christ.

God's word is written in the stars. Before there was a written bible, that was how folks learned the word. It's still all up there, but we've lost its meaning. It was because we lost the meaning of the word in the stars that God was forced to have the bible written in the languages of men. To understand what his star was, we need to look into God's word to see what we can learn about stars.

In the word, Jesus Christ is referred to as the bright and morning star. He's also referred to as the evening star. Both of these uses refer to the planet Venus. Venus is much closer to the sun than Earth, so it always appears close to the sun in the sky. Of course, during the day you can't see Venus because the sun is too bright. Late at night you can't see it either because it sets with the sun. Depending on its orbit, we see it in the morning at dawn as the sun rises, or in the evening at dusk when the sun sets. That's why it's called the bright and morning star and the evening star. In addition to Venus, Jupiter also represents Jesus Christ, and is referred to as the king planet. Any celestial announcements regarding the birth of Jesus Christ would necessarily therefore have to include both Jupiter and Venus. This is a very basic example of how the word is written in the stars.

Now yes, we know today that Jupiter and Venus are planets, but back then they were called stars, wandering stars in fact, because they wandered around the heavens.

We don't have time here to go into any detail on this, but the stars and planets all represent spiritual matters and have spiritual meanings. For example, Mercury represents Gabriel, while Mars represents Michael, God's Warrior Archangel. Even today, Mars is still recognised as a planet representing war. There is a war going on in the heavens and Michael leads God's spiritual warriors against the devil and his spirits. Saturn represents satan, the devil, which is intriguing in the context of christmas being a modern incarnation of the feast of Saturnalia.

As their master and teacher, Daniel would have taught all this to the Magi in his day. Hundreds of years later, that teaching was still being observed, which was why those Persian Magi recognised something in the heavens announcing the birth of the Lord Jesus Christ. What was it they saw? Astronomy is a precise science, so it's easy to look at the sky at any time in history. If we know what to look for we can again see what it was the Magi saw. Any good planetarium can re-run the events taking place in the night skies at any time, even thousands of years ago. That's how exact and precise the movements of the stars and planets are. That's how beautiful and accurate and precise the word is in the stars too. That knowledge is still all up there. Let's observe a few more details.

The word makes clear in Matthew 2 and Luke 1 that Herod the Great was alive and ruling Judaea when Jesus Christ was born and that he died shortly before Passover. This helps to narrow down the time frame as we can check that information historically. Once we know what history tells us about Herod the Great, we can then check the astronomical records and piece it all together with the biblical records.

Josephus, a Roman historian, also chronicled that Herod died shortly after an eclipse of the moon. Since lunar eclipses can be calculated with mathematical exactness and scientific precision, we can check out all the eclipses visible in Palestine, select the one that matches the biblical records, and then study astronomical candidates for his star prior to that eclipse.

To cut a long story short, all scholars agree that Herod died sometime between 7 BC and 1 BC. During that time there were four lunar eclipses visible in Palestine - a total eclipse on march 23, 5 BC, a total eclipse on september 15, 5 BC, a partial eclipse on march 13, 4 BC, and a total eclipse on january 9, 1 BC.

Josephus also noted that a number of events took place between the eclipse and passover the year Herod died. Two high priests were executed by Herod, his illness became worse so he travelled to Callirrhoe to seek relief in hot baths. He returned to Jericho and sent messengers throughout Judea to bring every principal man from every town and village to Jericho where he confined them to the hippodrome so he could execute them when he died. Envoys from Rome then arrived giving Herod permission to execute or banish his son, Antipater, and Herod had him executed immediately. Herod died five days later. Herod's other son Archelaus became king in his stead and released the prisoners from the Hippodrome. A lavish funeral followed during which the funeral procession marched from Jericho to the Herodian, a fortified mountain near Jerusalem, which scholars estimate would have taken at least twenty five days. Archelaus returned to Jerusalem and mourned for a further seven days before preparing to leave for Rome to have his reign confirmed by Caesar. Before he left, a serious riot broke out in Jerusalem and Archelaus had to send in the Roman Army. Adding all this together gives us a time period of approximately two to three months.

Bearing all this in mind, the lunar eclipse of march 23, 5 BC cannot be the one mentioned by Josephus as march 23 was the actual date of Passover that year. The eclipse on march 13, 4 BC cannot be the eclipse either as there is simply not enough time between then and the passover on april 11 for all the events recorded by Josephus to have taken place. A few scholars have proposed the eclipse of september 15, 5 BC as the one mentioned by Josephus as that eclipse gives us a six month period between Herod's death and passover the following year. However, the eclipse on january 9, 1 BC most perfectly fits the timeline, giving us three months between the eclipse and passover on April 8 of that year. Most scholars now also agree that Jesus Christ was born in 3 BC, not 4 BC as previously thought, so we have our eclipse and a timeline in which to search for candidates for the astronomical events announcing the birth of Jesus Christ.

Armed with this information, let's now take a look at the biblical records and look at one of the prophesies in the bible regarding the coming of the Lord Jesus Christ. It is well known that Jesus Christ was a Judean. What does God's word say regarding the tribe of Judah in reference to the stars?

> Genesis 49:8-10
> Judah, thou *art he* whom thy brethren shall praise: thy hand *shall be* in the neck of thine enemies; thy father's children shall bow down before thee.
>
> Judah *is* a lion's whelp: from the prey, my son, thou art gone up: he stooped down, he couched as a lion, and as an old lion; who shall rouse him up?
>
> The sceptre shall not depart from Judah, nor a lawgiver from between his feet, until Shiloh come; and unto him *shall* the gathering of the people *be*.

What the heck is this talking about? Judah is a lions whelp? Which constellation in the night sky depicts a lion? The constellation Leo. Okay, so the constellation of Leo represents the tribe of Judah. Now, as Jesus Christ was a Judean, which constellation do you think might have been involved in the astronomical announcement that he had been born? Scorpio? No, Leo, from which tribe came Jesus Christ. So without question, the constellation Leo would have had to play a prominent role in any announcements regarding his birth, and we can also expect the planets Jupiter and Venus to be in there as well.

Leo has long been known as the constellation representing the tribe of Judah, out of which tribe would come the messiah, the Lord Jesus Christ. In verse 10 of Genesis 49, *lawgiver* is the Hebrew word *regel*, from which we get our English word *regal*. The Arabic *regel* means *foot* and is identical in meaning to the Aramaic *regla* and the Hebrew *regel*.

> Genesis 49:10
> The sceptre shall not depart from Judah, nor a lawgiver [regel] from between his feet, until Shiloh come; and unto him *shall* the gathering of the people *be*.

Guess which star is the brightest in Leo? That's right, Regulus. This prophecy in Genesis is referring to the star Regulus in Leo. Thus the brightest star in Leo, Regulus, has the biblical connotation of the foot, tying in with from *between his feet*. These words form the basis of our English word *regal*, the basis of a king, that upon which a king stands. So we can now add Regulus to our list of stars that would have had to have been part of the celestial announcement of the birth of Christ.

To sum up, Regulus is regarded as the king star and it is appropriately placed in the constellation of Leo. In addition, Jupiter is regarded as the king planet. Venus, as the bright and morning star and the evening star, again refers to the Lord Jesus Christ. So it follows that any celestial announcements regarding the birth of Jesus Christ must have been in the constellation Leo and would have included Regulus, Venus and Jupiter.

Meanwhile, back in Persia, our astronomer Magi pals were staying up late, looking up at the night skies, sipping hot drinks and scoffing sandwiches, as they had been doing for hundreds of years. They were looking for a sign in the heavens announcing the birth of the Christ. Daniel had taught them what to look for, and hundreds of years later they were still looking, their gaze fixed on the constellation Leo.

At this juncture, we also need to understand a few astronomical terms, like *conjunction*, which is when two planets or a planet and a star are very close together and are lined up with the north pole. Sometimes they can even merge. That's a conjunction. Another term we need to understand is *retrograde motion*. It is a difficult concept to explain in few words, so do some of your own research.

Essentially, because the planets all travel at different speeds, and because of earth's orbit around the sun, planets can appear to stop in the night sky and then go backwards. As the earth then ducks round behind the sun, these planets can then appear to stop and carry on forwards again. This phenomenon is called retrograde motion. To an astronomer, retrograde motion is a celestial fireworks display. To literally see a planet stop in the night sky, go backwards, stop and then go forwards again is an event which greatly excites astronomers.

Before beginning to examine the celestial events, I think we can safely assume that the constellation Leo, the star Regulus, and the planets Jupiter and Venus would have been involved, and we could expect Mars and Mercury to be in there somewhere as well, but certainly not Saturn. Cutting a long story short, by examining astronomical records within the time period we researched earlier, we come up with this.

- August 12, 3 BC Jupiter and Venus in conjunction in Leo.
- September 14, 3 BC Jupiter and Regulus in conjunction in Leo.

Jupiter then went into retrograde motion, it stopped and went backwards in the sky.

- February 17, 2 BC Jupiter and Regulus in conjunction in Leo.

Jupiter then stopped and went forwards again.

- May 8, 2 BC Jupiter and Regulus in conjunction in Leo for a third time.
- June 17, 2 BC Jupiter and Venus in conjunction in Leo for a second time.

You've heard of a once in a lifetime event? Well, astronomically, this was a once in the history of the world event. And no one in Israel even noticed. No one. God announced it to the whole world yet no one but those Magi in Persia saw it. Amazingly, that wasn't all. After this once in a history of the world celestial fireworks display, there was a final starburst that shook the heavens – the massing of the planets Jupiter, Venus, Mercury and Mars in the constellation Leo.

- August 27, 2 BC Jupiter, Mars, Mercury, and Venus all mass in Leo, with Jupiter and Mars in conjunction.

A triple conjunction is a celestial fireworks display to an astronomer. It is such an event, that today they still cause ripples of excitement in astronomical circles. Jupiter being the prime mover is obviously the best candidate for his star as noted by the Magi. Sometime prior to Jesus Christ's birth, because of retrograde motion, Jupiter appeared to stop and go backwards and then stop and go forwards again, thus completing three distinct and separate conjunctions with the star Regulus. This triple conjunction sandwiched between a double conjunction of Jupiter and Venus, and all within the constellation of Leo, would have set their hearts fluttering.

Finally, the massing of the planets Jupiter, Venus, Mercury and Mars in the constellation Leo had them running to saddle up their camels. They knew the Messiah had been born and off they headed to Jerusalem with their gifts in search of the new born Judean king.

32. The Birth of Jesus Christ

We've followed the Magi to Jerusalem, where they presented themselves to Herod and enquired about the Judean king. Now let's look at the actual birth of the Lord Jesus Christ.

> Luke 2:1,2
> And it came to pass in those days, that there went out a decree from Caesar Augustus, that all the world should be taxed.
>
> (*And* this taxing was first made when Cyrenius was governor of Syria.)

The word *taxed* is the word *enrolled* – this was a nationwide census, and for this particular census everyone had to return to their home towns and villages. Remember, there were no such things as computers back then, so the census had to be conducted with the resources the Roman government had at its disposal.

> Luke 2:3-6
> And all went to be taxed [enrolled], every one into his own city.
>
> And Joseph also went up from Galilee, out of the city of Nazareth, into Judaea, unto the city of David, which is called Bethlehem; (because he was of the house and lineage of David:)
>
> To be taxed [enrolled] with Mary his espoused wife, being great with child.
>
> And so it was, that, while they were there, the days were accomplished that she should be delivered.

Being from Bethlehem, that's where Joseph took his family. Mary was heavily pregnant during that trip down from Galilee, and not long after they arrived, she gave birth.

Now we need to stop and think for a few moments. The world teaches that Jesus Christ was born on december 25th. If that were true, then we have some major problems, and not just with biblical accuracy, but with astronomy and common sense. This is Israel we're talking about, and it gets cold there in winter. It snows in Israel in winter. There was no public transport. As well as the risk of blizzards, the mountains were infested with armed bandits and wild animals. Would the Romans have demanded old folks, pregnant women and children travel in winter?

I've done a little hill walking in Scotland in winter. The weather can be extremely unpredictable, and getting caught out on the hills at night can kill you. The Romans calling for such nationwide travel in Israel in winter would have been madness. Even common sense tells you something isn't right with the logic that this is december. If the weather closed in and winter storms hit, the people would have been without shelter. No one in their right mind would organise such a census in the middle of winter, and had the Romans done so there would have been riots. Bear this in mind, because we'll come back to it. Anyway, Mary made it to Bethlehem where she had her baby.

> Luke 2:7
> And she brought forth her firstborn son, and wrapped him in swaddling clothes, and laid him in a manger; because there was no room for them in the inn.

The word tells us that there was no room at the Inn. One thing to note here is what the word does *not* say. It does not say Joseph and Mary were poor and couldn't afford a room. It says there were no vacancies. The whole country was on the move. All the bed and breakfasts and all the hotels were full, that's all. There was no room. That's what it says, that's what it means. All we have to do is read what's written.

Another thing, this wasn't a smelly old barn full of cows and sheep with cold wind rattling through the stalls. It wasn't winter. The horses, cattle and sheep would have been out grazing in the fields. These stables would have been comfortable, warm, clean and dry. Joseph and Mary were simply camping out for a night or two until a room became available. What a wonderful family thing to do. They would have rolled out their blankets in a warm and dry part of the stables, and enjoyed quiet family time together.

So there they are, camped down in Bethlehem, and Mary gives birth to her son. This wasn't a palace, it was a stable. And yet this is where God's Son, the Lord Jesus Christ, the king of the Judeans, the redeemer of all mankind was born. That speaks volumes to those with ears to hear.

> Luke 2:8
> And there were in the same country shepherds abiding in the field, keeping watch over their flock by night.

If this was winter, the shepherds wouldn't have been out in the country with their sheep. It's too cold and dangerous for shepherds to be out in the country with their sheep during the winter, especially at night. One doesn't have to be intelligent to understand this, but one does have to not be religious. This isn't winter, this is autumn. The weather is warm, and the conditions for travelling and camping outdoors are perfect. This is not december.

> Luke 2:9-12
> And, lo, the angel of the Lord came upon them, and the glory of the Lord shone round about them: and they were sore afraid.
>
> And the angel said unto them, Fear not: for, behold, I bring you good tidings of great joy, which shall be to all people.
>
> For unto you is born this day in the city of David a Saviour, which is Christ the Lord.
>
> And this *shall be* a sign unto you; Ye shall find the babe wrapped in swaddling clothes, lying in a manger.

That must have woken the shepherds up.

> Luke 2:13,14
> And suddenly there was with the angel a multitude of the heavenly host praising God, and saying,
>
> Glory to God in the highest, and on earth peace, good will toward men.

Interesting point here. Does it say the angels were singing? No, it does not. It says they were saying. Saying and singing something are two totally different things. It's intriguing to note that there is not one record in the bible that records angels singing. Nothing against singing, but let's keep things accurate in our minds.

> Luke 2:15-20
> And it came to pass, as the angels were gone away from them into heaven, the shepherds said one to another, Let us now go even unto Bethlehem, and see this thing which is come to pass, which the Lord hath made known unto us.
>
> And they came with haste, and found Mary, and Joseph, and the babe lying in a manger.
>
> And when they had seen *it*, they made known abroad the saying which was told them concerning this child.
>
> And all they that heard *it* wondered at those things which were told them by the shepherds.
>
> But Mary kept all these things, and pondered *them* in her heart.
>
> And the shepherds returned, glorifying and praising God for all the things that they had heard and seen, as it was told unto them.

To quickly recap, Joseph and Mary were camped in the stables behind the Inn because all the rooms were full. Mary gave birth and a short time later the shepherds showed up. Can you see any wise men here? Any cows lowing? Drummer boys? Fat men in sleighs handing out presents? Reindeer? And why no mention of the wise men, the Magi? Simple, they hadn't arrived yet. They were still in Persia watching the stars. How do we know this? Check the following in Matthew carefully.

> Matthew 2:7
> Then Herod, when he had privily called the wise men [the Magi], enquired of them diligently what time the star appeared.

When Herod heard this news about a new king, he sat down with the Magi and *enquired diligently* when the star appeared. The Magi would have gone into great detail. They would have told Herod all about the triple conjunction of Jupiter and Regulus sandwiched between the two conjunctions of Jupiter and Venus in Leo, as well as the timings of the conjunctions. After hearing them, Herod was convinced the Christ had been born and set about making plans to have him murdered.

No one else on earth saw anything unusual in the night skies. Most folks today can't even tell the difference between a star and a planet. How many people today know which star is Regulus and which of those shiny thingies are the planets Jupiter and Venus? What chance would anyone today have of noticing a triple conjunction in a constellation? No one in Jerusalem had seen his announcement in the stars because they didn't know how to read them. So his star wasn't a blazing comet streaking across the sky and zooming down to Bethlehem then, was it? I mean, everyone would have seen that, right? What a load of religious horseshit that is.

> Matthew 2:8-10
> And he sent them to Bethlehem, and said, Go and search diligently for the young child; and when ye have found *him*, bring me word again, that I may come and worship him also.
>
> When they had heard the king, they departed; and, lo, the star, which they saw in the east, went before them, till it came and stood over where the young child was.
>
> When they saw the star, they rejoiced with exceeding great joy.

These are amazing verses. First of all, in the bible planets are called stars not planets, and are often referred to as wandering stars because of the way they seem to wander around the night skies among the other stars. The prime mover in the heavens the Magi had been watching was Jupiter. There was a conjunction between Jupiter and Venus, then the triple conjunction of Jupiter and Regulus, then the second conjunction of Jupiter and Venus, and finally the massing of the planets Jupiter, Venus, Mars and Mercury, and all in the constellation Leo. So Jupiter has to be the main contender for the star in Matthew 2:9.

The words *stood over* are interesting in this regards too. The sun rises in the east and sets in the west. At midday the sun reaches its zenith, its highest point in the sky before starting to go down again. It goes up in the morning, reaches the highest point at midday and then goes down towards the west where it sets. Well, so do stars and planets. They all do this because of the spin of the earth. This *standing* refers to this highest point on the meridian that Jupiter reached that night, its zenith, before it began to set towards the west.

Understanding that, you are going to love this next bit. In the northern hemisphere, the sun is south at its highest point. In the southern hemisphere, the sun is north at its highest point. It is only directly on the equator that the sun is directly over your head at midday. On that particular night, Jupiter was due south of the Magi when it reached the highest point on the meridian. Any ideas where Bethlehem is from Jerusalem? It is about six miles due south. That night the Magi were travelling exactly due south from Jerusalem on the way to Bethlehem when Jupiter, the star they'd been watching for years, rose from the east until it reached its highest point on the meridian directly above Bethlehem just as they were arriving. It rose in the night sky until it reached its zenith and stood directly above Bethlehem. How is that for breathtaking biblical accuracy? Can you imagine how the Magi must have felt that night, sitting on their camels on the hills surrounding Bethlehem with Jupiter right there above the town, knowing the Christ was down there somewhere?

And what must the neighbours have thought when this royal Persian caravan arrived? Can you imagine the neighbours?

'Hey JOHN! Get your ass out of bed! *Come and see this!*'
'What is it hun?'
slowly peeks through the curtains
'Who are they?'
'Dunno, but they have the SAS surrounding the village.'
'They look like Persian Magi. Hey, they're knocking at Joseph and Mary's door!'
'I always knew that family would come to no good.'
'Holy shit, is that a chest of gold?'
'LOOK! The Magi are bowing to Mary's boy!'

'Quick! *Phone the Smiths!*'

> Matthew 2:11
> And when they were come into the **house**, they saw the **young child** with Mary his mother, and fell down, and worshipped him: and when they had opened their treasures, they presented unto him gifts; gold, and frankincense, and myrrh.

These were fabulous gifts from the Persian king to the baby Judean king. Can you imagine how much wealth was there? This money set Joseph and Mary up for life. Where do we get the idea from that Joseph and Mary were poor? Joseph was not a poor carpenter, he was a wealthy one. Joseph and Mary were most likely millionaires.

There are three very important words to notice here – the words *house* and *young child*. House means just that, a house, a place where folks live, a dwelling place. This is a house, not a stable, that's the point. Young child is also accurate. It says young child, not baby. This is a young child and they were in a house. Got that? Good. This is not a stable and this is not a baby. The Greek word for *baby* is a totally different word to the one used here for a young child. And another thing, can you see any shepherds here? Nope. Any cows mooing? Nope. Not surprising really, as you don't usually find cows in folk's homes.

> Matthew 2:12
> And being warned of God in a dream that they should not return to Herod, they departed into their own country another way.

God, by revelation, told the Magi not to go back to Jerusalem. Herod was waiting to hear from them, remember? God gave them other directions and they obeyed. The Magi were not afraid of Herod and they were not running away. They were being courageous by obeying God. It takes courage to believe the word.

> Matthew 2:13
> And when they were departed, behold, the angel of the Lord appeareth to Joseph in a dream, saying, Arise, and take the young child and his mother, and flee into Egypt, and be thou there until I bring thee word: for Herod will seek the young child to destroy him.

Herod had already made up his mind to have the child murdered so it's a good job Joseph didn't argue with God. And by the way, Joseph fleeing to Egypt wasn't a reaction to fear either. He was doing what God told him to do, just like the Magi did. If God had told Joseph to go to Jerusalem and present the child to Herod, that is what he would have done. Obeying God has nothing to do with being afraid, it has everything to do with having the courage to do what is right.

> Matthew 2:14
> When he arose, he took the young child and his mother by night, and departed into Egypt:

He didn't hang around either. He left that night – packed the suitcases, slung them over the mules and off they went down the road to Egypt. When God says move, you move.

> Matthew 2:16
> Then Herod, when he saw that he was mocked of the wise men, was exceeding wroth, and sent forth, and slew all the children that were in Bethlehem, and in all the coasts thereof, from two years old and under, according to the time which he had diligently enquired of the wise men.

Herod was severely pissed off when he found out the Magi had legged it back to Persia. Do you remember he had asked the Magi diligently about the star and the timings? He knew *precisely* what times the conjunctions had occurred. If Jesus Christ had just been born that night, why did Herod murder all the children two years old and under? Why not just kill all the babies? Jesus wasn't a baby, that's why. He was a young child. In fact, he was over a year old. He was a toddler and would have been speaking his first words. It makes sense now that Herod murdered all the toddlers. He gave himself a few months though, just to be on the safe side.

One other point while we're here. You often hear the question, why did God not protect all the other children in Bethlehem? The reason the other parents didn't hear God is because they weren't listening. God would have been quite happy to see all the toddlers saved, but if people aren't listening, there isn't anything he can do. This visit by the Magi was most likely in late december, so folks were probably too busy singing stupid religious carols around their christmas trees to hear anything from God.

Incidentally, we can answer a question here that perhaps you hadn't thought to ask. How did the wise men find the right house when they arrived in Bethlehem? Remember the shepherds a year earlier?

> Luke 2:17,18
> And when they [the shepherds] had seen *it*, they made known abroad the saying which was told them concerning this child.

And all they that heard *it* wondered at those things which were told them by the shepherds.

What had the angel told them? That the Christ had been born. The shepherds visited the family in the stable and then told everyone about it. Gossip travelled fast in those days just as it does today. So when the Magi caravan turned up asking where the Christ had been born everyone knew which house to point at.

One final thing we will consider regarding Jesus Christ's birth was his actual birth date. First, let's summarise the astronomical events occurring in the night skies over Israel around the time of Christ's birth.

- August 12, 3 BC Jupiter and Venus in conjunction in Leo.
- September 14, 3 BC Jupiter and Regulus in conjunction in Leo.
- February 17, 2 BC Jupiter and Regulus in conjunction in Leo.
- May 8, 2 BC Jupiter and Regulus in conjunction in Leo.
- June 17, 2 BC Jupiter and Venus in conjunction in Leo.
- August 27, 2 BC Jupiter, Mars, Mercury, and Venus all mass in Leo, with Jupiter and Mars in conjunction.

Remember all that? Good, now let's go to the book of Revelation.

> Revelation 12:1,2
> And there appeared a great wonder in heaven; a woman clothed with the sun, and the moon under her feet, and upon her head a crown of twelve stars:

And she being with child cried, travailing in birth, and pained to be delivered.

There is much more to this than we have time to get into right now so I'm just going to touch on the highlights. The *woman* refers to the constellation Virgo, so this particular astronomical event appeared in Virgo. *Clothed with the sun* simply means that the sun was in the constellation of Virgo. The sun goes through all twelve constellations once per year, so it is only in Virgo for approximately one month every year. And guess what? It isn't december.

You can't see stars when the sun has risen, so stars are only visible together with the sun for a very short period of time, either early in the morning at dawn, or late in the evening at dusk. This event would only have been visible at either daybreak or nightfall, and it occurred during the time the sun was in Virgo in 3 BC.

Revelation also gives us further information. It tells us that the moon was visible *under her feet*. This phenomenon of the sun being visible in the stars of Virgo with the moon under her feet only occurred once in 3 BC in Palestine. Using astronomical data we can narrow down the time of the birth of the Lord Jesus Christ to September 11th 3BC, between sunset at 6.18pm and moonset at 7.39pm Palestine time. Jesus Christ was born between 6.18pm and 7.39pm on September 11th 3BC.

33. Christmas and the Way of Life

Now that we've clarified that the customs and traditions surrounding christmas are entirely pagan in origin, having spawned from demonic witchcraft practices of human sacrifice to celebrate the birth of the sun god, and that Christ and the biblical records do not support any of the current teachings regarding Christ having been born in december, let's ask the question, does it matter? One hears that question most frequently from christians who know christmas is not biblical, who know Christ was not born in december, and yet still celebrate it.

Does it matter? Well, yes it does. In fact, we can handle christmas with one verse.

> Ephesians 4:25
> Wherefore putting away lying, speak every man truth with his neighbour: for we are members one of another.

Do you think it is okay to lie to young children? Do you think it is okay with God to tell lies to young children? If you do, your head is full of the spirit of christmas. Lying is simply wrong. Yet, this is what people do every christmas. They choose to ignore God's word and instead lie to their children, filling their heads with witchcraft rituals that originate and culminate in human sacrifice, usually that of young children.

> Colossians 3:9
> Lie not one to another, seeing that ye have put off the old man with his deeds;

Look, I don't care about all your reasons and excuses, lying to children breaks the word. I don't care how much you wrap it up in tinsel or how flashy the lights are on your tree, lying is lying, and parents lying to their children is against the will of God. You do it for the kids?

What exactly is it you do for the kids? You wrap up presents for them, put them under a tree, and enjoy a good family day together with an excellent meal. Why can't you do that without lying? Why not bin the tree and put the presents around the fireplace instead? Why not open the presents and have your family day on December 24th? If your children question what you're doing, tell them the truth. Tell them only heathen people celebrate the birth of the sun god on December 25th, and santa clause doesn't exist, he's a lie. Tell them their presents represent the gifts the Magi gave to Jesus Christ when he was a toddler in Bethlehem. Teach your children the truth, don't lie to them. They will still enjoy unwrapping their presents. They will still enjoy the family time and their dinner. Do it for the kids.

Still think God thinks it is okay if you celebrate christmas and lie to your children? Try this then.

> Jeremiah 10:2-4
> Thus saith the LORD, Learn not the way of the heathen, and be not dismayed at the signs of heaven; for the heathen are dismayed at them.
>
> For the customs of the people *are* vain: for *one* cutteth a tree out of the forest, the work of the hands of the workman, with the axe.
>
> They deck it with silver and with gold; they fasten it with nails and with hammers, that it move not.

God in his word very clearly states that we are not to learn the ways of the heathen. That God had to confront this practice hundreds of years before Christ certainly confirms that decorating trees was a well practiced heathen tradition even then. If you lie to your children, you are in direct opposition to God and his word. And don't waggle your tongue at me and tell me this is the age of grace. Grace is not to be used as an excuse to sin, and lying is sin.

Still think it doesn't matter? Saul thought it didn't matter to disobey God as long as it was for a *good cause*.

> 1 Samuel 15:22,23
> And Samuel said, Hath the LORD *as great* delight in burnt offerings and sacrifices, as in obeying the voice of the LORD?

Behold, to obey *is* better than sacrifice, *and* to hearken than the fat of rams.

For rebellion *is as* the sin of witchcraft, and stubbornness *is as* iniquity and idolatry. Because thou hast rejected the word of the LORD, he hath also rejected thee from *being* king.

Still think it doesn't matter? Jesus Christ had much to say about the traditions of men, confronting those who chose to put the traditions of men above the word of God. Christmas is very much a tradition of men that is contrary to the word of God and which is fuelled by the love of money, so Jesus Christ's confrontation is still relevant.

Mark 7:9
And he said unto them, Full well ye reject the commandment of God, that ye may keep your own tradition.

If you reject the word of God and lie to children, you are rejecting the commandment of God. Lying to young children is not acceptable under any circumstances. Forget trees and presents and family time, lying is the issue here. If you hold the traditions of men in higher esteem than God's word and lie to your children, you are rejecting the commandment of God. Am I killing santa claus? I certainly hope so.

Here are a few more points for you to consider. The feast of Saturnalia is the worship of the birth of the sun god, another name for the devil, and it is a feast which was consummated in ritualistic human murder. The devil became the god of this world, the sun god, when man fell back in Genesis 3, so this may very well have occurred on december 25th. Human sacrifices are most likely spiritual representations of the fall of man, when Adam and Eve died spiritually on the very day that they disobeyed God and handed their dominion of the world to Lucifer. The celebration of the birth of the sun god on december 25th is a celebration of the fall of man and the inauguration of the devil as the god of this world. And you want to celebrate that?

If you still think it doesn't matter, try this.

Isaiah 5:20
Woe unto them that call evil good, and good evil; that put darkness for light, and light for darkness; that put bitter for sweet, and sweet for bitter!

Living God's way is a decision, it's a choice we make. You cannot use grace as an excuse to lie to children. The word says to put away lying, and that must include lying to children about fat bastards like santa claus.

In this administration, we are told in Colossians that we are not to allow any man to judge us in respect of holy days, and this is the verse folks use to justify their celebrating christmas. They read this and then say it's okay to celebrate christmas and no one has a right to judge them.

Colossians 2:16
Let no man therefore judge you in meat, or in drink, or in respect of an holyday, or of the new moon, or of the sabbath *days*:

Now yes, we know this is the age of Grace and that there's nothing unclean of itself, and that a tree is just a piece of wood and having one in your home is neither good nor evil in and of itself, but Colossians can't contradict Galatians, can it? Try this then.

Galatians 4:9-11
But now, after that ye have known God, or rather are known of God, how turn ye again to the weak and beggarly elements, whereunto ye desire again to be in bondage?

Ye observe days, and months, and times, and years.

I am afraid of you, lest I have bestowed upon you labour in vain.

Whatever Colossians is saying, it can't contradict the rest of the bible, can it? So what is Colossians actually saying then? It is not saying that it's okay to celebrate days, months, times and years and we are not to allow other christians to judge us for it, for that would contradict Galatians and a hundred other scriptures. According to Galatians, if you celebrate christmas, labour has been bestowed upon you in vain, teaching you the word has been a waste of fucking time. So Colossians means the opposite of what most dumb christians think. It is saying that we don't allow UNBELIEVERS to judge us for *abstaining* from observing their stupid traditions like christmas, and for *abstaining* from their meats and drunkenness. This is further corroborated by Peter.

> 1 Peter 4:3,4
> For the time past of *our* life may suffice us to have wrought the will of the Gentiles, when we walked in lasciviousness, lusts, excess of wine, revellings, banquetings, and abominable idolatries:
>
> Wherein they think it strange that ye run not with *them* to the same excess of riot, speaking evil of *you*:

What Colossians is saying is that we don't stand for unbelievers judging us for not sticking our noses in their horseshit. If you give up christmas the world is going to speak evil of you, I can assure you, because the world is greedy and it will hurt their income. What's more important to you, God or the traditions of greedy men?

In return for celebrating christmas, the world offers a few days of pretty decent family time, albeit at high cost in gifts and debt, and which was first observed to celebrate the fall of man and the devil becoming the god of this world. With God, you can have pretty decent family time all year round, for free, with no ulterior motives. It's your choice. If you choose the wrong way and put the traditions of men above the word, don't go blaming God when life turns and bites you.

> Deuteronomy 30:19
> I call heaven and earth to record this day against you, *that* I have set before you life and death, blessing and cursing: therefore choose life, that both thou and thy seed may live:

There are many benefits to enjoy going God's way.

> Psalm 1:1-3
> Blessed *is* the man that walketh not in the counsel of the ungodly, nor standeth in the way of sinners, nor sitteth in the seat of the scornful.

But his delight *is* in the law of the LORD; and in his law doth he meditate day and night.

And he shall be like a tree planted by the rivers of water, that bringeth forth his fruit in his season; his leaf also shall not wither; and whatsoever he doeth shall prosper.

As for me and my house, I will serve God, and I don't give a fuck about that freemason prick Dickens and his fanciful stories depicting me as a scrooge. He served his god and I shall serve mine.

34. God's Masterpiece

Now that we understand a little about spiritual matters, about how the world works, and what renewing the mind is – that it is something we do, and that it is the key to power – it is time to start looking at the power itself. Putting off the old man, our old ways, our old behaviours is renewing the mind, it is the key to power, but it is not the power itself. Renewing the mind is not our power for abundant living, it is not our supernatural life, it is simply replacing our old worldly thoughts with the thoughts in the bible. Think of the renewed mind as a key to a car. There is no power in the key, none whatsoever, but you can't start the car without it. The renewed mind is the *key* to power. Renewing the mind in and of itself is a waste of time unless we use it to energise the power that comes from God. If we do not learn to walk by the spirit and demonstrate the power of God, renewing our minds is just another work of the flesh. It is worshipping a key, worshipping a work of the flesh rather than worshipping God in spirit and in truth.

Just prior to the ascension, Jesus Christ gave instructions to the apostles on what they were to do while waiting for the power to come. They were to remain in Jerusalem.

> Luke 24:49
> And, behold, I send the promise of my Father upon you: but tarry ye in the city of Jerusalem, until ye be endued with power [dunamis – inherent power] from on high.

Was it available for the apostles to renew their minds while they were waiting for the power to arrive? Yes, of course, the renewed mind is very much a part of the senses, a work of the flesh, something man does with his body and soul abilities. The power from on high is spiritual power that comes from God. The receiving of this power from God is what we call the new birth, it is our supernatural life. The renewed mind is the key to energising that power resident within the gift of holy spirit that comes with the new birth.

The new birth has been trodden under centuries of religious horseshit so we need to take the time to dig it out of the pages of the bible and explore it. We've all heard the expressions *born again* and *born dead in sins* but do we know what they mean? With our deeper understanding of body, soul and spirit, we are now ready to embark on an adventure into the holy spirit field and learn how to walk by the spirit.

Man was a three-part being back in Genesis, but as a consequence of his disobedience, he lost his spirit and became just body and soul. With this understanding, many scriptures will now make sense.

> Ephesians 2:1
> And you hath he quickened [made alive], who were dead in trespasses and sins;

To be made alive is a reference to the receiving of the gift of holy spirit, which is to be born again. To be born dead in trespasses and sins is a reference to our physical birth into this world. It has absolutely nothing to do with sex being evil, as some teach, it is merely a reference to us being born body and soul with no spirit. Man is born without spirit, so he is dead at birth. I don't care how religious and nice and good some people think they are, if they have no spirit, they are dead.

Man died back in Genesis when he lost his spirit, and it is this lack of spirit which is referred to here. Being dead in trespasses and sins is simply a reference to man being born without spirit. Without spirit, man is dead, so when man is born into the world without spirit he is dead in trespasses and sins. It is merely a reference to the fall of man and its consequences.

Back in Genesis, man was body, soul, and spirit. Man died, he lost his spirit and became an animal of just body and soul. Jesus Christ paid for man's redemption and reconciled man back to God so he could be whole again, with body, soul, and spirit. It is the receiving of the gift of holy spirit that is the new birth, and it is that spirit that is our power for abundant living.

Ephesians 5:14
Wherefore he saith, Awake thou that sleepest, and arise from the dead, and Christ shall give thee light.

God is light and the gift of holy spirit is light. When we are born again, we are raised from the dead and become children of light.

1 Thessalonians 5:5
Ye are all the children of light, and the children of the day: we are not of the night, nor of darkness.

This being raised from death, this receiving of spiritual light, is what is referred to in the bible as being *saved*. Being saved is a beautiful term, but unfortunately it has been smeared with centuries of religious horseshit. It's time to hose it down and see what it really means.

Ephesians 2:4,5
But God, who is rich in mercy, for his great love wherewith he loved us,

Even when we were dead in sins, hath quickened us [made us alive] together with Christ, (by grace ye are saved [sōzō – made whole];)

Sōzō in the Greek simply means *to be made whole*. We are born into this world without spirit and when we are born again and receive God's gift of holy spirit, we are saved, made whole, having three parts again instead of two. That is what it means to be saved, *sōzō*, made whole.

Dead in sins is a reference to being born without spirit. *Quickened* is old language meaning *to be made alive*. When we receive this spirit and become whole again, we are made alive and, therefore, we are no longer dead. We are born into a new life.

The receiving of the gift of holy spirit, the new birth, first became available on the day of Pentecost when man could once again be made whole by receiving spirit. So what do we have to do to receive it? What mechanics are involved? Romans gives us the details.

Romans 10:9
That if thou shalt confess with thy mouth the Lord Jesus, and shalt believe in thine heart that God hath raised him from the dead, thou shalt be saved [sōzō – made whole].

Whenever and wherever a man, woman, or child confesses Jesus as Lord and believes in their heart that God raised him from the dead, that person receives the gift of holy spirit. In that very instant, they are born again, raised from the dead, saved, made whole – they receive spirit. That spirit is a new creation, something that has never existed before.

2 Corinthians 5:17
Therefore if any man *be* in Christ, *he is* a new creature [creation]: old things are passed away; behold, all things are become new.

Jesus Christ taught these truths to Nicodemus, a Pharisee and one of the rulers of the Judeans, a member of the Sanhedrin, and it would be worthwhile looking at the record.

John 3:1,2
There was a man of the Pharisees, named Nicodemus, a ruler of the Jews [Judeans]:

The same came to Jesus by night, and said unto him, Rabbi, we know that thou art a teacher come from God: for no man can do these miracles that thou doest, except God be with him.

Most times it would be prudent to avoid religious leaders like Nicodemus. For example, I would avoid jesuits like I would avoid someone with a contagious disease. Their minds are rotted by moral disease and they infect the world with their poisons through freemasonry and religion. It isn't that they can't get help, the question is do they want it? Only God can answer that, so it is *imperative* that we walk by the spirit when approached by such men.

Here, Jesus Christ was approached by a member of the Sanhedrin, a Pharisee. Many times the Pharisees sought to incriminate and kill him, so Jesus Christ had to be walking by the spirit to know how to handle this situation. He pursued the conversation, but ignored the flattery and immediately confronted Nicodemus on spiritual matters.

> John 3:3,4
> Jesus answered and said unto him, Verily, verily, I say unto thee, Except a man be born again [anothēn – from above], he cannot see the kingdom of God.
>
> Nicodemus saith unto him, How can a man be born when he is old? can he enter the second time into his mother's womb, and be born?

Here is the first reference in the bible to being born again, or born from above, as that is what the Greek word *anothēn* means. At that time it wasn't available to be born from above, which is intriguing, because it means Jesus Christ knew about the supernatural spiritual birth that was coming before it was available. Judging by his response, Nicodemus obviously had no concept of such a thing. The notion was totally alien to him.

> John 3:5-7
> Jesus answered, Verily, verily, I say unto thee, Except a man be born of water and *of* the Spirit, he cannot enter into the kingdom of God.
>
> That which is born of the flesh is flesh; and that which is born of the Spirit is spirit.
>
> Marvel not that I said unto thee, Ye must be born again [anothēn – from above].

To be born of water is a reference to the first physical birth, when the amniotic sac surrounding a baby breaks and the waters burst. To be born of the spirit is the second birth, the supernatural birth. Without being born again, no one can enter into the kingdom of God. Why? Because a person of just body and soul is dead, they have no spirit, they have no connection with God, they have no supernatural power, they have no life. Peter gives us additional information.

> 1 Peter 1:23-25
> Being born again, not of corruptible seed, but of incorruptible, by the word of God, which liveth and abideth for ever.

For all flesh *is* as grass, and all the glory of man as the flower of grass. The grass withereth, and the flower thereof falleth away:

But the word of the Lord endureth for ever. And this is the word which by the gospel is preached unto you.

Corruptible seed is again a reference to the first physical birth. The life that we were born with was corrupted back in Genesis when man lost his spirit and died. Everyone who is born into this world since then is born of corruptible seed, seed that will corrupt and die, but those of us who are born again are born of incorruptible seed, seed from God, spiritual seed that is born within us. Incorruptible seed is seed that will live forever, it is eternal life.

Romans 6:23
For the wages of sin *is* death; but the gift of God *is* eternal life through Jesus Christ our Lord.

Man's wages for his original sin, his original missing of the mark back in Genesis was death. Don't blame God for that. God gave man freewill and he never possesses us, he will never force us to do anything. Instead of blaming God for death and all our problems, try thanking him for being so kind as to come up with a way to redeem us back from the power of death. That way was Jesus Christ.

1 Corinthians 15:50-57
Now this I say, brethren, that flesh and blood [a reference to body and soul] cannot inherit the kingdom of God; neither doth corruption inherit incorruption.

Behold, I shew you a mystery; We shall not all sleep, but we shall all be changed,

In a moment, in the twinkling of an eye, at the last trump: for the trumpet shall sound, and the dead shall be raised incorruptible, and we shall be changed.

For this corruptible must put on incorruption, and this mortal *must* put on immortality.

So when this corruptible shall have put on incorruption, and this mortal shall have put on immortality, then shall be brought to pass the saying that is written, Death is swallowed up in victory.

O death, where *is* thy sting? O grave, where *is* thy victory?

The sting of death *is* sin; and the strength of sin *is* the law.

But thanks *be* to God, which giveth us the victory through our Lord Jesus Christ.

When you're born the first time into this world, you are the child of your parents. The seed within you came from your father, and for as long as you live you will always be his child. That can't be changed. When we are born again of God's incorruptible seed, from that moment we are his child with eternal life because we have his seed born within us.

1 John 3:1,2
Behold, what manner of love the Father hath bestowed upon us, that we should be called the sons of God: therefore the world knoweth us not, because it knew him not.

Beloved, now are we the sons of God, and it doth not yet appear what we shall be: but we know that, when he shall appear, we shall be like him; for we shall see him as he is.

God bestowed this sonship on us, which means he gave it to us. When we carry out the specific instruction given in Romans on how to be made whole – confess Jesus as Lord and believe God raised him from the dead – we are born again, we are born into the family of God, we have his seed born in us and we become his child. From that moment, we have eternal life and we are in God's family.

Romans 8:14-16
For as many as are led by the Spirit of God, they are the sons of God.

For ye have not received the spirit of bondage again to fear; but ye have received the Spirit of adoption [huiothesia – sonship], whereby we cry, Abba, Father.

The Spirit itself beareth witness with our spirit, that we are the children of God:

The Greek word *huiothesia* means *to make or place as a son*, and yes, adoption is one way we can be made or placed as sons. However, there is another way, to be born. God does not adopt us, like he did in the old testament with Israel, rather we are impregnated with his seed, we are literally born into his spiritual family. *Abba* could be more properly translated as *daddy*. Jesus Christ is no longer the only son of God. He was the firstborn, and there is now a much bigger family.

Romans 8:29
For whom he did foreknow, he also did predestinate *to be* conformed to the image of his Son, that he might be the firstborn among many brethren.

This gift from God is referred to in many different ways throughout Acts and the epistles. In Colossians it is referred to as *Christ in you*.

Colossians 1:26,27
Even the mystery which hath been hid from ages and from generations, but now is made manifest to his saints:

To whom God would make known what *is* the riches of the glory of this mystery among the Gentiles; which is Christ in you, the hope of glory:

It is this Christ in us which is our power to walk by the spirit, and of all God's works, it is his greatest. Until now we've been taught that the greatest of all God's works was the written word. The scripture we've been taught this from has been Psalm 138:2.

Psalm 138:2
I will worship toward thy holy temple, and praise thy name for thy lovingkindness and for thy truth: for thou hast magnified thy word above all thy name.

In all of God's creation, nothing comes close to the magnificence of his word. However, it is not his greatest work. That makes sense, because the written word is merely a means to an end, not an end in itself.

A person's greatest work is more usually referred to as their masterpiece. Psalm 138:2 does not tell us that the word is God's masterpiece, it says he magnified it above all his name. We have to go to Ephesians to find his masterpiece, and that makes sense too, because Ephesians is the greatest revelation ever given to man.

> Ephesians 2:10
> For we are his workmanship [masterpiece], created in Christ Jesus unto good works, which God hath before ordained that we should walk in them.

The word *workmanship* is the word *masterpiece*. There you go, very clearly we can see that the greatest of all God's works is not his word, it is the Christ in us that each of us receives at the time of the new birth. It is time we elevated the Christ within us, the gift of holy spirit created within us at the time of the new birth to its rightful position as the greatest of all God's works. We are God's masterpiece.

35. A Free Gift

Amazingly, the gift of holy spirit, the Christ in us, eternal life, our spiritual life, is a free gift which anyone can receive and enjoy.

> John 3:16
> For God so loved the world, that he gave his only begotten Son, that whosoever believeth in him should not perish, but have everlasting life.

Whosoever means whosoever. As we were all born without spirit and there was nothing we could do to redeem ourselves from that state of death, it took God coming up with a plan to help us. The fulfilment of that plan was Jesus Christ, and now anyone can have eternal life as a free gift from God.

> Acts 2:38
> Then Peter said unto them, Repent, and be baptized every one of you in the name of Jesus Christ for the remission of sins, and ye shall receive the gift of the Holy Ghost.

> Romans 5:21
> That as sin hath reigned unto death, even so might grace reign through righteousness unto eternal life by Jesus Christ our Lord.

> Romans 6:23
> For the wages of sin *is* death; but the gift of God *is* eternal life through Jesus Christ our Lord.

Why is it free? Nothing in life is free. A gift may be free to you and me, but don't ever underestimate its cost to someone else. We were all born dead into this world. We may have had body and soul, but we had no spiritual life. Since the day of Pentecost, because of the work Jesus

Christ accomplished, spiritual life is now freely available. Jesus Christ paid the full legal price to free us from the power of death.

> Colossians 2:13,14
> And you, being dead in your sins and the uncircumcision of your flesh, hath he quickened together with him, having forgiven you all trespasses;
>
> Blotting out the handwriting of ordinances that was against us, which was contrary to us, and took it out of the way, nailing it to his cross;

Despite what your church or religion teaches, being good will not get you anything from God. Neither will counting beads, lighting candles, kneeling at alters, burning incense, blowing yourself up, chanting, going to church, bowing, holding up holy hands, repeating mindless prayers, giving all your money away, hanging crosses around your neck, becoming a nun, capitalising pronouns referring to God or smiling inanely at everyone. There is *nothing* you or I or anyone else can do in the body and soul categories of life to make ourselves righteous before God. God made us righteous, we didn't. Being a nice person has nothing to do with this. How many times do you think the word *nice* is used in the bible anyway? I've looked, and I can't find it, not once, not anywhere in the entire bible. Forget about trying to earn your own righteousness. This is about accepting God's righteousness despite how terrible we've been.

> Romans 10:1-3
> Brethren, my heart's desire and prayer to God for Israel is, that they might be saved [sōtēria – rescued].
>
> For I bear them record that they have a zeal of God, but not according to knowledge.
>
> For they being ignorant of God's righteousness, and going about to establish their own righteousness, have not submitted themselves unto the righteousness of God.

When Paul wrote this, folks just didn't understand the depth of the new birth. Those Israelites had no idea what had been accomplished for them. They were still zealous for law and were trying to establish their own righteousness. No one can be righteous by their own works, it is impossible. There is nothing a dead body can do to raise itself from the dead. God can do it, and it's freely available, but it is something he does, it isn't something we do. The righteousness of God comes with the new birth. We receive that righteousness when we are born again, born from above, and receive the gift of holy spirit, the Christ in us.

You don't agree? You think the price God paid was not high enough for you? You think the price Jesus Christ paid for your redemption is not good enough for you? You want to do it yourself? Wake up dude.

> Romans 10:4
> For Christ *is* the end of the law for righteousness to every one that believeth.

What does it mean when it says Christ is the end of the law? Exactly what it says. The law is over with, it's done, it is no longer relevant, it is not something we have to observe and keep and do anymore. The Law Administration is over.

> Galatians 3:11
> But that no man is justified by the law in the sight of God, *it is* evident: for, The just shall live by faith [pistis – believing].

No man, means no man. No one is justified by the law. No man can justify himself by his own works. Not even the pope, he's just as dead as everyone else. No human being can do anything to make himself justified. Why? Because we were all born dead into this world, without life, and there is nothing a corpse can do to raise itself from death.

Before moving on, it's time to handle faith. Without understanding what faith is, its meaning is easily manipulated. Take the phrase *blind faith* for example, which can't be found anywhere in the bible. It's an entirely fictitious myth used by ignorant church leaders who have no answers. *Blind faith* is simply a device that fools people into accepting religious horseshit that makes no sense. There is no such thing as *blind faith*. If your church teaches you *blind faith*, you are being led by the blind. God does not want us ignorant and certainly does not expect us to take anything by *blind faith*. God even states this fact seven times in the epistles, and he states it in the negative to emphasise the greatness of this truth. He does not want us ignorant.

God does not want us ignorant of the benefits of the gift ministries (Romans 1:13), the mystery (Romans 11:25), the consequences of unbelief and idolatry (1 Corinthians 10:1-11), manifestations of holy spirit and the gift ministries (1 Corinthians 12:1), how he delivers us in times of pressure (2 Corinthians 1:8), satan's devices (2 Corinthians 2:11), and our hope, when Christ comes back for us (1 Thessalonians 4:13). I think that just about covers everything. So where does *blind faith* come into it? It doesn't. God does not want us stupid and ignorant. Anyone who teaches blind faith is just that, blind, and those who follow them are going to fall into the ditch with them.

So why do churches and religions keep their people ignorant? Folks, you need to get out of the world's churches and religions. God does not dwell in temples made with hands and neither should you.

So what is faith? It's translated from the word *pistis* which means to believe. To have faith simply means to believe, as that's what *pistis* means, to believe. Anyone can believe, indeed, everyone does believe something, whether they are followers of the Lord Jesus Christ or not. By the way, a follower of the way is a follower of the Lord Jesus Christ who is the way, it is someone who walks by the spirit with Christ as his head, not some follower of a church constructed by men which calls itself the way.

Everything in life comes by believing, positive or negative, regardless of political or religious persuasions. There is even a record in Luke where Jesus Christ declared a Roman centurion, a gentile, to have had greater believing than anyone he had ever encountered in Israel among God's people.

> Luke 7:9
> When Jesus heard these things, he marvelled at him, and turned him about, and said unto the people that followed him, I say unto you, I have not found so great faith [pistis – believing], no, not in Israel.

So faith in most cases should be translated believing. Regular normal human believing is not a spiritual thing, it is very much a part of our human abilities. To help illustrate this, how many times do you think the word *faith* is used in the old testament from Genesis to Malachi? Have a guess. Hundreds? Thousands? Nope, just two times, and in both cases it is a wrong translation from words meaning established, trusty, firmness, and moral fidelity. The word faith is not used anywhere in the old testament, not once. Don't believe me? Go and look. Switch off your tellavision and go search the scriptures, see if these things are so.

Although pistis could always be translated as believing, in order to differentiate between Jesus Christ's believing, which was perfect, and our believing, which is far from perfect, his believing is referred to as faith. We can think of the faith of Jesus Christ simply as the perfect believing of Jesus Christ. The more we renew our minds and replace our old worldly thoughts with the thoughts of God's word, the more we can believe like Jesus Christ did. The more of the word we hold in our minds and apply, the more our believing grows. We renew our minds, but it is the word we put into our minds that does the job.

> Romans 10:17
> So then faith [pistis – believing] *cometh* by hearing, and hearing by the word of God.

Believing is something anyone can do. Renewing the mind is something everyone can do. However, if you spend all your time watching television you won't have much in the way of godly believing manifesting itself in your life. If you want spiritual power, get your head into the bible and read. God will do his part if you do yours.

When I first asked God for his help I was aboard a cargo ship steaming up a moonlit Gulf of Aqaba in the Red Sea. I was a teenager and my life was a mess. I was a drunk, took drugs, was violent, and had become suicidal. When I'd left home to join that ship, I'd grabbed a bible from a shelf inside the front door and shoved it in my suitcase. I hadn't read it, but there it was, sitting on a small shelf under the porthole in my cabin.

And there I was, staring into a mirror, digging my nails into my cheeks until the blood was running down my face, and pulling my hair out by the roots in handfuls. I saw moonlight reflecting on the surface of the Red Sea and I knew it was time to end it. As I got to my feet, I asked God for his help. I needed to know if there was any point to life because I just couldn't go on. At that moment, the ship hit what must have been a freak wave, for the ship juddered violently. The bible fell off the porthole, bounced on my bunk and fell open just as a tiny shaft of light slanted in the porthole and lit up a short passage of scripture on one of the pages. God talked to me, and his words were like fire in me as I read.

> Proverbs 2:1-5
> My son, if thou wilt receive my words, and hide my commandments with thee;
>
> So that thou incline thine ear unto wisdom, *and* apply thine heart to understanding;
>
> Yea, if thou criest after knowledge, *and* liftest up thy voice for understanding;
>
> If thou seekest her as silver, and searchest for her as *for* hid treasures;
>
> Then shalt thou understand the fear of the LORD, and find the knowledge of God.

God saved my life that night, and since then I've studied my ass off. I inclined my ear to wisdom, my heart to understanding, and I have found the knowledge of God. God has taught me and now I am teaching you. Incidentally, I learned recently that when God talked to me that moonlit night in the Gulf of Aqaba, we were at the very place where God parted the Red Sea for Moses. If you want to find the knowledge of God, you are going to have to do some work. I'll teach you, but you're going to have to study the word for yourself and make it your own.

Regarding the faith of Jesus Christ, the believing of Jesus Christ, there is much we can learn. There is a verse in Galatians that uses *pistis* twice, once in the context of the perfect believing of Jesus Christ and once as regular human believing.

Galatians 3:22
But the scripture hath concluded all under sin, that the promise by faith of Jesus Christ [pistis – believing of Jesus Christ] might be given to them that believe [pisteuō – verb form – believing in action].

Although man is born dead, without spirit, the promise of eternal life which came by way of the faith of Jesus Christ, the perfect believing of Jesus Christ, is given as a gift to those who believe according to the instructions given in Romans 10:9. Anyone who confesses Jesus as Lord and who believes in their heart that God raised him from the dead receives the gift of holy spirit which was made available by the perfect believing of Jesus Christ. See how simple it is to understand this?

Galatians 3:23
But before faith came, we were kept under the law, shut up unto the faith which should afterwards be revealed.

There was a time when there was no faith, no perfect believing of Jesus Christ, a time when man could not be born again of God's spirit. Therefore, this faith talked about in Galatians 3:23 cannot be referring to regular believing, because that's been available since Genesis. It must therefore be referring to the faith of Jesus Christ, the perfect believing of Jesus Christ. See how this all fits so beautifully?

Galatians 3:24
Wherefore the law was our schoolmaster ~~to bring us~~ unto Christ, that we might be justified by faith [pistis – believing].

Here is an excellent example of italicised words that were added to the text by the translators being absolutely wrong. This verse states with the italicised words included that law was our schoolmaster to bring us to Christ. Churches use this to teach that we must keep the law or we can't get to Christ. This is obviously a forgery because it contradicts other scriptures on the same subject, such as Romans 10:4.

Romans 10:4
For Christ *is* the end of the law for righteousness to every one that believeth.

Remove the italicised words, and the word fits.

> Galatians 3:24
> Wherefore the law was our schoolmaster ~~to bring us~~ unto [until] Christ, that we might be justified by faith.

The law was our schoolmaster up until Christ. Christ was the end of the law for righteousness to everyone that believes. Until Christ came, God's people were kept under the law, but after he accomplished man's redemption, the law was done away with, and that's exactly what the next verse tells us.

> Galatians 3:25,26
> But after that faith is come [the faith of Jesus Christ], we are no longer under a schoolmaster.
>
> For ye are all the children of God by faith [pistis – believing] in Christ Jesus.

> Galatians 3:13,14
> Christ hath redeemed us from the curse of the law, being made a curse for us: for it is written, Cursed *is* every one that hangeth on a tree:
>
> That the blessing of Abraham might come on the Gentiles through Jesus Christ; that we might receive the promise of the Spirit through faith [pistis – believing].

> Galatians 5:1
> Stand fast therefore in the liberty wherewith Christ hath made us free, and be not entangled again with the yoke of bondage.

Now that the perfect believing of Jesus Christ is here, we are freed from the law, the yoke of bondage. If you want freedom from religious horse-shit and want to learn how to believe, it's here.

36. God-Given Rights

Every single person on earth was born without spirit as a consequence for man's disobedience back in Genesis and will die because of it. There is nothing anyone can do to raise themselves from this condition of death. No one can beat his chest, march up to God and demand eternal life because they are so *nice* to everyone. The only way out of death is to be born again and accept what God has made available.

> Ephesians 1:3
> Blessed *be* the God and Father of our Lord Jesus Christ, who hath blessed us with all spiritual blessings in heavenly *places* in Christ:

God blessed us with all spiritual blessings. These blessings come with the new birth. When we are born again, these blessings come as part of the Christ in us. With sonship comes all spiritual blessings. With sonship comes rights. For example, when we are born again, from that moment we are holy and without blame.

> Ephesians 1:4
> According as he hath chosen us in him before the foundation of the world, that we should be holy and without blame before him in love:

Why are we holy and without blame? We've all done terrible things, yet we're holy and without blame? Yes, that's what the word says. It's not what the world tells you, but it is what the word says. Who are you going to believe? The devil is a liar, God tells the truth.

The gift of holy spirit, the Christ in us, is perfect. It is incorruptible seed and it is eternal life, which means it lives forever. If it is incorruptible, it is not corruptible. There is nothing you can do to corrupt that eternal life within you. Regardless of anything you have done or ever will do, that Christ in you cannot be corrupted. That's why we are holy and without blame. We have been raised from the dead, we have Christ in us the hope of glory, and it is that spirit that is holy and without blame. If you're born again you could choose to ignore the word and live like the devil, but that wouldn't mess up your holy spirit, it would only mess up your life.

Incidentally, it is our spirit that is holy and without blame, so trying to make our bodies and souls holy and without blame as well is a waste of time. That's what religion does, and that's why religious people are so sickly nice all the time. The bible does not teach us to transform the old man into something nice, it teaches us to put the stinky thing off.

> Ephesians 4:22-24
> That ye put off concerning the former conversation the old man, which is corrupt according to the deceitful lusts;
>
> And be renewed in the spirit of your mind;
>
> And that ye put on the new man, which after God is created in righteousness and true holiness.

The point is, we are holy and without blame because of the price that was paid, and because of the Christ in us we received at the time of the new birth, not because of anything we have done or ever will do with our body and soul abilities. We have been raised from death into a new life.

> 2 Corinthians 5:17
> Therefore if any man *be* in Christ, *he is* a new creature [creation]: old things are passed away; behold, all things are become new.

This is something God did for us, not something we did for ourselves. Jesus Christ was the fulfilment of God's plan for us, so we could have eternal life. God wanted a family, he wanted children, and that's us. Children have nothing to do with whether or not they are born the first time into natural life, and they have nothing to do with their being raised from the dead into the new supernatural life either. We simply confess Jesus as Lord and believe in our hearts that God raised him from the dead, and suddenly we're born into a new life.

When we are born again we are holy and without blame because one of the rights that comes with the gift of holy spirit is righteousness. No one can earn righteousness by their own works. The righteousness of God comes with the new birth. We receive that righteousness when we are born again. It's encoded in the nature of the Christ in us. Before we were born again, our nature was children of wrath.

> Ephesians 2:3
> Among whom also we all had our conversation [behaviour] in times past in the lusts of our flesh, fulfilling the desires of the flesh and of the mind; and were by nature the children of wrath, even as others.

Once we receive that incorruptible seed from God, we become his children with a new divine, supernatural nature.

> 2 Peter 1:4
> Whereby are given unto us exceeding great and precious promises: that by these ye might be partakers of the divine nature, having escaped the corruption that is in the world through lust.

The corruption in the world is death. If we've escaped it, we've what? Escaped it. The seed born within us came from God so it carries his nature, his genetic coding, and as we develop that spirit within us the more his nature grows within us, the more like God we become. It is our new nature, it is our new genetic coding, our new spiritual DNA, it is the new man. That's why God asks us to follow him, to be imitators of him. We do that by putting off the old man and putting on the new. Putting off the old man is renewing our minds, while putting on the new man is learning to walk by the spirit.

> Ephesians 5:1,2
> Be ye therefore followers [mimētēs – imitators, mimics] of God, as dear children;
>
> And walk in love, as Christ also hath loved us, and hath given himself for us an offering and a sacrifice to God for a sweetsmelling savour.

As we renew our minds and put on the new man – which is to learn to think the word while at the same time developing that spirit within us – our spiritual nature will develop and flourish and produce fruit.

> Galatians 5:22,23
> But the fruit of the Spirit is love [agapē], joy, peace, longsuffering, gentleness, goodness, faith,
>
> Meekness, temperance: against such there is no law.

Fruit of the spirit is not fruit of the good works of man. Developing love, for example, this love of God, this agapē love, is not learning to love people with human phileō love. It is not a human ability that can be taught and developed. This is spiritual fruit, something that grows from the Christ in you, and it can only be produced from the Christ in you, the gift of holy spirit. Smiling inanely and being nice to everyone is not fruit of the spirit, it is the putrid fruit of religion.

Fruit isn't developed, it grows, so it isn't something you practice to get good at, like learning to play the piano. It isn't a human ability or talent. If you want to cultivate genuine fruit of the spirit, you need to learn how to manifest that Christ in you. As you do, the more you will grow spiritually, the more the nature of God will grow within you, and the more like God you will become.

This new life we grow into has nothing to do with our old man. Yes, we renew our minds and put off the old man, which is to replace the thoughts of the world with God's thoughts revealed in the bible (and that is a human ability), but that is not our power for abundant living. Renewing the mind is simply the key to power. Don't ever forget that.

Renewing the mind is profitless without learning to walk by the spirit. Without energising the spirit, renewing the mind is simply another work of the flesh. You can memorise the entire bible from Genesis to Revelation, but without energising that spirit all you have is a bloated head that's of no value to anyone. Don't believe me? Look at the apostle Paul's life before he was born again and walked by the spirit. I doubt anyone on earth besides the Lord Jesus Christ has ever had a knowledge of the bible like he did. What good was it to anyone? What good was it to God? His knowledge of scripture served only to transform him into a murdering religious monster, much like the jesuits today. It was not until Paul was born again and energised the gift of holy spirit that his knowledge of scripture served any worthwhile purpose. How did he energise that gift and start walking by the spirit? Let me give you a clue, in his own words.

> 1 Corinthians 14:18
> I thank my God, I speak with tongues more than ye all:

Paul's religious life, his worldly education, his responsibilities in the Sanhedrin, his family background, his upbringing, in fact his entire life before he was born again he counted but dung in comparison to the excellence of the knowledge of Christ Jesus his lord. Walking by the spirit was all that mattered to him.

> Philippians 3:3
> For we are the circumcision, which worship God in the spirit, and rejoice in Christ Jesus, and have no confidence in the flesh.

Who are the circumcision? Who are the true worshippers? Those who worship God in spirit and in truth, that's who.

> John 4:23,24
> But the hour cometh, and now is, when the true worshippers shall worship the Father in spirit and in truth: for the Father seeketh such to worship him.
>
> God *is* a Spirit: and they that worship him must worship *him* in spirit and in truth.

If you want to worship God, you're not going to do it with anything in the senses realm. You can go to church, give all your money away, smile and be nice to everyone your whole life, and you will not even come close to being a true worshipper. There is nothing you can do in the body and soul categories of life that will worship God. Candles don't do it, incense doesn't do it, going to mass or attending any other religious meeting won't do it, crying your eyes out doesn't do it, kneeling at alters won't do it, capitalising pronouns referring to God doesn't do it, and praying on your knees for hours on end certainly doesn't do it. That is all religious horseshit. There is only one way you can truly worship God, and that is in spirit and in truth, truly by way of the spirit. What is worshipping God in spirit? It is speaking in tongues.

> Acts 2:4,11
> And they were all filled with the Holy Ghost [pneuma hagion – holy spirit], and began to speak with other tongues, as the Spirit gave them utterance.
>
> Cretes and Arabians, we do hear them speak in our tongues the wonderful works of God.
>
> Acts 10:45,46a
> And they of the circumcision which believed were astonished, as many as came with Peter, because that on the Gentiles also was poured out the gift of the Holy Ghost [pneuma hagion – holy spirit].
>
> For they heard them speak with tongues, and magnify God.
>
> 1 Corinthians 14:2
> For he that speaketh in an *unknown* tongue speaketh not unto men, but unto God: for no man understandeth *him*; howbeit in the spirit he speaketh mysteries [divine secrets].

Speaking in tongues is one of nine ways you can energise the gift of holy spirit, and we will be learning much more about this. Suffice to say that a relationship with God has nothing to do with religious ceremony or ritual. Quite the contrary, it has everything to do with energising the gift of holy spirit. Anything else is a work of the flesh. Back to Paul in Philippians.

> Philippians 3:4-6
> Though I might also have confidence in the flesh. If any other man thinketh that he hath whereof he might trust in the flesh, I more:
>
> Circumcised the eighth day, of the stock of Israel, *of* the tribe of Benjamin, an Hebrew of the Hebrews; as touching the law, a Pharisee;

> Concerning zeal, persecuting the church; touching the righteousness which is in the law, blameless.

Paul had an expensive education, an impeccable background, a formidable intelligence, and he was influential in government and affairs of state. Compared with the knowledge of what Christ had accomplished for him however, he didn't consider his past life worth very much at all.

> Philippians 3:7-9
> But what things were gain to me, those I counted loss for Christ.
>
> Yea doubtless, and I count all things *but* loss for the excellency of the knowledge of Christ Jesus my Lord: for whom I have suffered the loss of all things, and do count them *but* dung, that I may win Christ,
>
> And be found in him, not having mine own righteousness, which is of the law, but that which is through the faith of Christ, the righteousness which is of God by faith [pistis – believing]:

Folks, there is nothing you can do to make yourselves righteous before God. Not a damn thing. Righteousness comes with the new birth. If you are born again you are righteous now, you are holy and without blame without ever having to do anything. Attempting to make yourself righteous is not worth the effort because you can't do it. If you try you will fail. It's a waste of time.

> Romans 3:20
> Therefore by the deeds of the law there shall no flesh be justified in his sight: for by the law *is* the knowledge of sin.

The deeds of the law refers to the old testament Mosaic law, of which there were over 900. I suspect most christians think the old testament law only refers to the 10 commandments. Well, I'll tell you something about the 10 commandments. It was rather sad that God had to tell his people to quit stealing from each other, quit murdering each other, quit shagging other men's wives, and quit telling lies about each other. That's how low God's people had sunk during their captivity in Egypt, and God had no choice but to tell Moses to tell his people to stop doing those things. Jesus Christ understood that, which is why he summarised the hundreds and hundreds of old testament laws into just two.

> Matthew 22:37-40
> Jesus said unto him, Thou shalt love the Lord thy God with all thy heart, and with all thy soul, and with all thy mind.
>
> This is the first and great commandment.
>
> And the second *is* like unto it, Thou shalt love thy neighbour as thyself.
>
> On these two commandments hang all the law and the prophets.

What did he mean when he said on these two commandments hang all the law and the prophets? Simple, if you love someone you don't need to be told not to steal from them because you wouldn't do it. You don't need to be told to quit murdering your brothers and sisters in Christ. You don't need to be told to stop shagging other men's wives. You don't need to be told to stop lying about people in court to have them wrongly convicted. If you love people, you just don't do these things. The Mosaic law was basically a last ditch effort by God to keep his people salvageable until Christ came and the new birth could be made available. So don't go worshipping the old testament law and think it was so great. Christ was the end of the law for righteousness to everyone that believes and good riddance to it. Who wants to live under that horseshit?

Now, you have to ask the question: how did God's people sink so low in the first place that God had to tell them to quit stealing, lying, committing adultery, and murdering? How did the god of this world corrupt them to such an extent? He did it the same way he does today, through secret societies. You can track secret societies right back to Genesis. For example, masons are taught they are special and have the right to steal from non-masons. This is what the god of this world teaches them. This is how the world corrupts them. It starts with simple things, like promoting fellow masons in the workplace. Perfectly good employees are passed over for promotion as masons promote wives, daughters, girlfriends and concubines into the best paying jobs, whether they're good employees or not. This, of course, means lying to non-masons and stealing their jobs. As it's all done behind people's backs, in secret, it breeds distrust and discontent, and soon grows into far more serious problems.

Did you know that all the world's worst criminals are masons? They never mention that in the news, do they? Mass murderers all happen to be masons. The worst paedophiles are masons. All the Brink's Mat robbers were masons. All the world's most vicious terrorists and gangsters are masons. The Mafia, the IRA, PIRA, FARC and all the other terrorists are run by masons. Hitler, Pol Pot, Lenin and Mao Tse Tung were all masons. Manipulating and controlling world masonry from the top of the pyramid are the most cruel and heartless bastards on earth, the jesuits. This is the world's way, this is the underworld.

Why do they do it? Freemasons do it for money because they love it. Jesuits do it for their god Lucifer, whom they worship. They infect masonry with poisonous doctrines that corrupt them, such as it is okay to do evil so long as it results in good, that the end justifies the means, that it doesn't matter how they accomplish one world governance just so long as they achieve that goal. It starts with lying at interviews and giving the best jobs to masons. As soon as you join the masons, the bribery and corruption begins. That is how the god of this world corrupts the earth. Those who are willingly corrupted soon find themselves being promoted, which is why those who are most easily corrupted find themselves quickly advancing through the ranks. That's why the world is run by criminals.

We live above their standards and do what is right according to God's word, not according to the dictates of the communist manifesto which was penned by the jesuits. Masonry is a social and spiritual disease, and when a country is sufficiently weakened, the jesuits take power through social unrest and revolution, as they did in France, Russia, and China. When the jesuits take power, which they will once you let them in, they will steal your country and enslave you. You masons, you can change. You're not *special*, you're not knights in the service of the true God, you're traitors, liars, and thieves in the employ of the devil. The spiritual witchcrafts with which you have been enchanted are not from God, it is devil spirit power. You can change. You can have the righteousness of God. You can have a fresh start if you want it.

Same for you jesuits. You don't have to serve Lucifer. I know he's beautiful, and I know he's powerful. The word says he was full of all wisdom and beauty, and that he was perfect in all his ways. As the angel of light he was the most powerful angel in the spiritual realm next to God himself. I really would have loved to have known him back then, but pride filled his heart and he fell. However beautiful he was, you still have a choice, you can change Gods and have eternal life instead of death awaiting you. Paul changed and God was there for him. You can change too and God will be there for you as well. We are all born dead in sins, without spirit. Dead is dead, regardless of how much or how little evil we've done, and you can be raised from that death and have eternal life just like anyone else if you want it. There is no joy in using sorcery to turn the skies black and flood folks out of their homes. Sure, you can use your sorceries to whip up tornadoes that destroy property and kill people, but that just makes you murderers. If that's all your life amounts to, you don't have much going for you. I believe this prophecy in Revelation foretells the future of Vatican City. The merchants of the earth refers to the masons who make their money from peddling evil.

Revelation 18:1-11
And after these things I saw another angel come down from heaven, having great power; and the earth was lightened with his glory.

And he cried mightily with a strong voice, saying, Babylon the great is fallen, is fallen, and is become the habitation of devils, and the hold of every foul spirit, and a cage of every unclean and hateful bird.

For all nations have drunk of the wine of the wrath of her fornication, and the kings of the earth have committed fornication with her, and the merchants of the earth are waxed rich through the abundance of her delicacies.

And I heard another voice from heaven, saying, Come out of her, my people, that ye be not partakers of her sins, and that ye receive not of her plagues.

For her sins have reached unto heaven, and God hath remembered her iniquities.

Reward her even as she rewarded you, and double unto her double according to her works: in the cup which she hath filled fill to her double.

How much she hath glorified herself, and lived deliciously, so much torment and sorrow give her: for she saith in her heart, I sit a queen, and am no widow, and shall see no sorrow.

Therefore shall her plagues come in one day, death, and mourning, and famine; and she shall be utterly burned with fire: for strong is the Lord God who judgeth her.

And the kings of the earth, who have committed fornication and lived deliciously with her, shall bewail her, and lament for her, when they shall see the smoke of her burning,

Standing afar off for the fear of her torment, saying, Alas, alas, that great city Babylon, that mighty city! for in one hour is thy judgment come.

And the merchants of the earth shall weep and mourn over her; for no man buyeth their merchandise any more:

I believe one day this prophecy will be fulfilled when someone presses a button that destroys Vatican City with a hail of nuclear bombs. One day someone is going to nuke Vatican City, for what you sow is what you will reap. I'd love to see some of you jesuits come out of that cult. We need another Paul, another Martin Luther. We need another reformation, and I believe it may just come from within your own ranks. Like Paul, you would be more than welcome in God's family. Now let's get back on topic.

The righteousness of God comes wrapped up in the gift of holy spirit. Whenever and wherever a man or woman is born again, they have the righteousness of God, despite anything they may have done or ever will do during their life.

Romans 3:22,23
Even the righteousness of God *which is* by faith of Jesus Christ unto all and upon all them that believe: for there is no difference:

For all have sinned, and come short of the glory of God;

The faith of Jesus Christ should be understood as the perfect believing of Jesus Christ. His believing was perfect, and the translators decided to call it faith to try to distinguish it from the imperfect believing of man. The word faith should always be understood as believing.

Romans 3:24
Being justified freely by his grace through the redemption that is in Christ Jesus:

Justification is the legal side to righteousness. It is part of the God-given rights that come with the new birth.

Romans 3:28
Therefore we conclude that a man is justified by faith [by believing] without the deeds of the law.

We receive the righteousness of God at the time of the new birth, and that righteousness of God justifies us by our believing. We are justified without having to do any of the old testament law. Christ was the end of the law. Everything we do in the senses realm is a work of the flesh. The righteousness of God that comes with the new birth is something God made available through Jesus Christ. We are made righteous not by our own works, but by the work of Jesus Christ. And do you know something? It was God's good pleasure to do this for us.

Ephesians 1:5
Having predestinated us unto the adoption [huiothesia – sonship] of children by Jesus Christ to himself, according to the good pleasure of his will,

God *enjoyed* raising us from death. It wasn't done out of obligation, it wasn't done out of guilt or necessity, and he certainly wasn't coerced into it. God did this for us because he wanted to, it was his good pleasure. What parent doesn't want children they can love?

This gift from God is a gift of grace. God was not *required* to give it. He was under no obligations to make it available. He was not under any legal constraints that forced him into helping us. Man by his own freewill disobeyed God and marched willingly to his death. God could have thrown his hands up and walked away and been quite within his rights to do so. Man threw away everything God had given him and handed the lordship of the earth to his enemy, the devil. Man committed treason, which is a crime punishable by death. People tend to blame God for all their problems, but the truth is, all our problems are of our own doing. It was God's good pleasure to help us. It was something he wanted to do, out of grace and mercy.

> Ephesians 2:1-3
> And you *hath he quickened* [made alive], who were dead in trespasses and sins;
>
> Wherein in time past ye walked according to the course of this world, according to the prince of the power of the air, the spirit that now worketh in the children of disobedience:
>
> Among whom also we all had our conversation [behaviour] in times past in the lusts of our flesh, fulfilling the desires of the flesh and of the mind; and were by nature the children of wrath, even as others.

When we were born, we were born dead into a world whose god is the devil. What worse scenario can you imagine? By his own choice, man willingly walked into this mess. God, by his grace, figured out a way to get us out of the mess we made for ourselves. Why are you waggling fingers at God and accusing him of evil? The devil is the author of sickness and death, and he it was who stole the world from us. You have to admire Lucifer, because he is good at what he does.

Deliverance from death is available and eternal life as a free gift is part of the deal. It is all by God's grace and there is nothing we can do to earn it. Eternal life is a gift from God.

> Ephesians 2:4-8
> But God, who is rich in mercy, for his great love wherewith he loved us,

> Even when we were dead in sins, hath quickened us [made us alive] together with Christ, (by grace ye are saved;)
>
> And hath raised *us* up together, and made *us* sit together in heavenly *places* in Christ Jesus:
>
> That in the ages to come he might shew the exceeding riches of his grace in *his* kindness toward us through Christ Jesus.
>
> For by grace are ye saved [sōzō – made whole] through faith [believing]; and that not of yourselves: *it is* the gift of God:

Here this truth that we are made whole by grace is stated twice, establishing it for us. It is a gift from God. If I give you something as a gift, it isn't wages, you didn't do anything to earn it, it is something I gave you. It costs me something, but it costs you nothing. It took God coming up with a plan to get the job done. Jesus Christ was the fulfilment of that plan, and after his death and resurrection our redemption was secured. The gift of holy spirit isn't a reward for being good, nor is it wages for labour, it is a gift.

If you have a problem accepting this, and still believe you need to do something to make yourself acceptable to God, think of it this way: did you have any say in Adam and Eve's original sin? Were you there, were you part of their decision to walk away from God and hand the world to the devil? No, you were not, yet you still enjoy the consequences of their actions and have to face death. Just as it was a man who got us into this mess, without any input from us, it took a man to get us out of it, without any input from us. The consequences of Adam and Eve's disobedience is something we inherited at birth.

> Romans 5:12,13
> Wherefore, as by one man sin entered into the world, and death by sin; and so death passed upon all men, for that all have sinned:
>
> (For until the law sin was in the world: but sin is not imputed when there is no law.

The law refers to the law of Moses. Before the law of Moses, sin was not imputed because there was no law and, therefore, there were no legal consequences. If there is no law, you can't break it so you can't be charged with anything. However, there were still practical consequences in life. For example, if you drove your chariot too fast around a corner you could go off the road and crash. You would damage your chariot, and possibly even injure or kill yourself. You would suffer practical consequences for breaking the laws of physics God built into life. However, because there were no speeding laws in place, you would face no legal consequences. If there were speeding laws in place, you could also be charged for breaking those laws. So as well as the practical consequences, you could also be taken to court. Once the law of Moses was given, there were legal consequences as well as the practical consequences for folk's actions.

> Romans 5:14
> Nevertheless death reigned from Adam to Moses, even over them that had not sinned after the similitude of Adam's transgression, who is the figure of him that was to come.

Despite there being no law, the practical consequences of Adam's sin was still very evident in that every man was born with death built into him from birth. Just as death is something we inherit because of Adam, eternal life is something we inherit because of Jesus Christ.

> Romans 5:15
> But not as the offence, so also *is* the free gift. For if through the offence of one many be dead, much more the grace of God, and the gift by grace, *which is* by one man, Jesus Christ, hath abounded unto many.

The free gift refers to the gift of holy spirit, the Christ in you, the incorruptible seed that was born within us at the time of the new birth. Just as we suffer death because of one man, Adam, we now enjoy life because of one man, Jesus Christ.

> Romans 5:16-18
> And not as *it was* by one that sinned, *so is* the gift: for the judgment *was* by one to condemnation, but the free gift *is* of many offences unto justification.

For if by one man's offence death reigned by one; much more they which receive abundance of grace and of the gift of righteousness shall reign in life by one, Jesus Christ.)

Therefore as by the offence of one *judgment came* upon all men to condemnation; even so by the righteousness of one *the free gift came* upon all men unto justification of life.

Justification is the legal side to righteousness. The Christ in us is incorruptible, it cannot sin, it cannot miss the mark. There is nothing anyone can do to make their spirit sin. It is impossible to corrupt it with sin. That is why it is eternal life When we are born again, God takes his gavel, slams it down and declares us not guilty, not because of our body and souls, not because of our old man, but because of the gift of holy spirit that is born within us. It is the spirit that makes us righteous. Righteousness and justification come wrapped up with the new birth. They are God-given rights that come with the Christ in us.

Romans 5:19
For as by one man's disobedience many were made sinners, so by the obedience of one shall many be made righteous.

Adam's disobedience made us all guilty of death, and so death was the penalty we all had to pay. That's why we were all born dead into this world with no spiritual life. God didn't do that to us, the devil did. Man committed a sin so vile, it warranted the death penalty. Man died and the devil became the god of this world. Thankfully, God came up with a way to spring us from death, and that way was Jesus Christ, who died in our place to accomplish our redemption.

Romans 5:20,21
Moreover the law entered, that the offence might abound. But where sin abounded, grace did much more abound:

That as sin hath reigned unto death, even so might grace reign through righteousness unto eternal life by Jesus Christ our Lord.

Just as Adam's sin introduced death for us, Jesus Christ's death and resurrection introduced eternal life for us. The consequence of Adam's sin was death. Jesus Christ carried that legal burden and it was nailed to the tree where he gave his life in our place. As the legal consequences for man's sin are now paid for, we are free from the consequences of that sin.

> Galatians 4:4-7
> But when the fulness of the time was come, God sent forth his Son, made of a woman, made under the law,
>
> To redeem them that were under the law, that we might receive the adoption of sons [huiothesia – sonship].
>
> And because ye are sons, God hath sent forth the Spirit of his Son into your hearts, crying, Abba, Father.
>
> Wherefore thou art no more a servant, but a son; and if a son, then an heir of God through Christ.

Jesus Christ redeemed us from death. To redeem means *to recover ownership of by paying a specified sum.* Jesus Christ paid the full price required to buy us back from death. That redemption carries with it the legal justification and the righteousness that sets us apart for eternal life. When we are born again, we are literally raised from the dead. At that very moment, ownership of us changes. The god of this world no longer has any rights over us because the required legal price was paid for our redemption and we were bought back from him.

> 1 Corinthians 6:19
> What? know ye not that your body is the temple of the Holy Ghost [pneuma hagion – holy spirit] *which is* in you, which ye have of God, and ye are not your own?

The holy ghost refers to the gift of holy spirit within us. Ghost is a poor translation and carries spiritually filthy undertones in modern language. Always translate ghost as spirit in your mind when reading the bible. Our bodies house the gift of holy spirit, which we received from God, and it isn't a devil spirit, a ghost.

1 Corinthians 6:20
For ye are bought with a price: therefore glorify God in your body, and in your spirit, which are God's.

It is because we were redeemed that we were justified, made righteous, and sanctified, which means to be set apart. This all occurs when we are raised from the dead at the time of the new birth. From that moment on, we are God's sons and daughters, his children with supernatural eternal life. It isn't our bodies that are going to live forever, it is the gift of holy spirit within us that is our eternal life. We have been born into a new life.

Romans 6:23
For the wages of sin *is* death; but the gift of God *is* eternal life through Jesus Christ our Lord.

37. Get Over It!

Jesus Christ took care of everything we've ever done wrong in the past, and most folks are okay with that once they realise how much it cost God and how much it cost Jesus Christ to accomplish it. However, folks often struggle to comprehend that Jesus Christ not only paid for the sins we've done in the past, but he also paid for all the sins we've not even committed yet.

> Colossians 2:13,14
> And you, being dead in your sins and the uncircumcision of your flesh, hath he quickened together with him, having forgiven you all trespasses;
>
> Blotting out the handwriting of ordinances that was against us, which was contrary to us, and took it out of the way, nailing it to his cross;

Jesus Christ died for us, and we are righteous because of what he did, not because of anything we've ever done or ever will do. We didn't earn the gift of holy spirit, it was something God wanted us to have and it was his good pleasure to give it. The price he paid was his only son.

This was all done by God's mercy and grace, because he loved us and it was his good pleasure to do it for us. Does it follow then that he did it so he could beat us up all the time and make us sick? That garbage is certainly spouted from pulpits all over the world, but it is not the truth. God may not go to church or hang out in any religion, but devil spirits surely do.

We are righteous and we are justified, there is nothing of which we are guilty. God took all my sins, placed them on Jesus Christ, and he took them to the grave with him. He died in my place. If all my sins were put on Jesus Christ and died with him, are they any longer on me? No, they are not, and that's why I have the righteousness of God.

Romans 3:22
Even the righteousness of God *which is* by faith of Jesus Christ unto all and upon all them that believe: for there is no difference:

At the moment we are born again, everything stacked against us, all the sins we've ever done are washed away. God didn't just take those old sins of ours and lock them away in a closet, or brush them under the carpet out of view, they no longer exist. All of our sins literally died with Jesus Christ and they are gone forever. That is why God isn't looking for fault. This is illustrated succinctly in Psalm 103.

Psalm 103:8-10
The LORD *is* merciful and gracious, slow to anger, and plenteous in mercy.

He will not always chide: neither will he keep *his anger* for ever.

He hath not dealt with us after our sins; nor rewarded us according to our iniquities.

Listen to how kind the language is here. The point is, God isn't mad at us. Verse 10 employs a figure of speech in which two sentences say exactly the same thing in two different ways. God said the same thing twice to emphasise and to establish the point that he does not deal with us after our sins nor reward us according to our iniquities. So he can't be watching us with a critical eye so he can whack us over the head then, can he?

The god who looks for any reason to whack us is better known as the devil, the god of this world, Lucifer, and it is he who controls all world religion. A temple is a place where men go to worship. If God doesn't dwell in temples made with hands, who then are folks worshipping when they go to church if it isn't God? Any religion, church, organisation, or ministry that is controlled by central governing bodies of men is a temple made with hands, it is a broken cistern constructed by men. Psalm 103 continues.

Psalm 103:11
For as the heaven is high above the earth, *so* great is his mercy toward them that fear [respect, reverence] him.

How high is the heaven above the earth? How high is the universe? Have you ever tried to fathom the universe? The distances involved are staggering beyond human comprehension. That's how great God's mercy is to us. It is staggering, beyond human comprehension. Mercy is the withholding of merited judgement. In other words, we deserved punishment but God withheld it. See, God does not want to beat us up for our sins. His mercy is staggering, beyond human comprehension.

> Psalm 103:12
> As far as the east is from the west, *so* far hath he removed our transgressions from us.

Interesting that this verse says *east and west* and not *north and south*. If you go far enough north and cross the pole, you will start going south. If you continue south and cross the other pole, you will go north again. North and south meet, but east and west don't. It is a physical impossibility for east and west to meet. You are either going east or you are going west. If you are going east, you are travelling away from west. If you stop and go west, you are now heading away from east. There is infinity between them. That is how far we have been removed from all the sin, all the mistakes and bad things we've ever done. You see, it isn't that God simply hides his eyes from our sins and pretends not to see them, they really do not exist anymore. Jesus Christ was the price it cost to get rid of them for us. We have been freed from sin and the power of death. Yes, that even includes you if you're a jesuit and you read this class and get born again. God's mercy is staggering.

To clarify this, let's look at how God dealt with sin in the old testament. One way was with animal sacrifices. The animals were sacrificed and their blood made atonement for Israel. Before we go any further, let's make it clear that animal sacrifice was not God's idea, it was man's.

> Jeremiah 7:22
> For I spake not unto your fathers, nor commanded them in the day that I brought them out of the land of Egypt, concerning burnt offerings or sacrifices:

See, God commanded nothing regarding killing animals as sacrifices. It wasn't in his heart, it wasn't something he wanted. He spoke nothing about sacrificing animals. The next verse tells us what God wanted.

> Jeremiah 7:23
> But this thing commanded I them, saying, Obey my voice, and I will be your God, and ye shall be my people: and walk ye in all the ways that I have commanded you, that it may be well unto you.

Rather than animal sacrifices, God wanted his people to simply live in fellowship with him and enjoy a good life.

> Jeremiah 7:24
> But they hearkened not, nor inclined their ear, but walked in the counsels *and* in the imagination of their evil heart, and went backward, and not forward.

Rather than obey God, the Israelites wanted animal sacrifices, just like all the devil worshipping heathen around them. They wanted to stick knives in animals and spurt blood everywhere, just like the pagans and druids they lived among. They wanted to be just like everybody else. God therefore had no choice but to put up with their garbage, and because they insisted on killing animals he was forced to give them a few guidelines on how best to go about it. Listen to Samuel's words when he confronted Saul.

> 1 Samuel 15:22
> And Samuel said, Hath the LORD *as great* delight in burnt offerings and sacrifices, as in obeying the voice of the LORD? Behold, to obey *is* better than sacrifice, *and* to hearken than the fat of rams.

Solomon put animal sacrifice into its proper context in Proverbs.

> Proverbs 21:2,3
> Every way of a man *is* right in his own eyes: but the LORD pondereth the hearts.
>
> To do justice and judgment *is* more acceptable to the LORD than sacrifice.

Sacrificing animals wasn't God's idea, it was a symbolic gesture as he endured man's stubborn ways. Talk about patience and mercy?

You can see this same demand for horseshit when Israel demanded Samuel find them a king. They wanted a king like all the other nations, so they bitched about not having one and told Samuel to sort it out. The Jones syndrome goes back a long way.

> 1 Samuel 8:4-9,22
> Then all the elders of Israel gathered themselves together, and came to Samuel unto Ramah,
>
> And said unto him, Behold, thou art old, and thy sons walk not in thy ways: now make us a king to judge us like all the nations.
>
> But the thing displeased Samuel, when they said, Give us a king to judge us. And Samuel prayed unto the LORD.
>
> And the LORD said unto Samuel, Hearken unto the voice of the people in all that they say unto thee: for they have not rejected thee, but they have rejected me, that I should not reign over them.
>
> According to all the works which they have done since the day that I brought them up out of Egypt even unto this day, wherewith they have forsaken me, and served other gods, so do they also unto thee.
>
> Now therefore hearken unto their voice: howbeit yet protest solemnly unto them, and shew them the manner of the king that shall reign over them.
>
> And the LORD said to Samuel, Hearken unto their voice, and make them a king. And Samuel said unto the men of Israel, Go ye every man unto his city.

Was it God's idea to give them a king? No, it wasn't. Whose idea was it? It was man's idea. God warned them about the nature of their king, but they refused to listen and demanded God give them a king. So God gave them one.

Was it God's idea to have animal sacrifices in the old testament? No, it wasn't. Whose idea was it? It was man's idea. Man wanted to stick knives in animals to ease his guilt, and demanded God accept these sacrifices. That's why animal sacrifices became a way of life in the old testament. It wasn't because God wanted it, but because we wanted it. God then later used these sacrifices as illustrations to teach us about the Lord Jesus Christ, who was sacrificed to redeem us from death.

> Hebrews 9:11,12
> But Christ being come an high priest of good things to come, by a greater and more perfect tabernacle, not made with hands, that is to say, not of this building;
>
> Neither by the blood of goats and calves, but by his own blood he entered in once into the holy place, having obtained eternal redemption *for us*.

Our redemption wasn't bought by the blood of animals. It was Jesus Christ's own blood that paid the price. He died in our place and it was his death that paid for the sin problem for all men. The problem has now been dealt with and there is no longer a sin problem. It's dealt with. We are righteous now, we have the righteousness of God.

> Hebrews 9:13,14
> For if the blood of bulls and of goats, and the ashes of an heifer sprinkling the unclean, sanctifieth to the purifying of the flesh:
>
> How much more shall the blood of Christ, who through the eternal Spirit offered himself without spot to God, purge your conscience from dead works to serve the living God?

In the old testament, animals dealt with Israel's sin problem, but it was only symbolic, a stop gap measure that only temporarily put a lid on the garbage bin. What Hebrews says is that if a few animal sacrifices can symbolically deal with sin, what about the sacrifice of the Lord Jesus Christ? How much greater a sacrifice was he compared to an animal? How much better a job did he do?

Hebrews 9:25
Nor yet that he should offer himself often, as the high priest entereth into the holy place every year with blood of others;

In the old testament they had to sacrifice animals every year. They sinned, they sacrificed animals, they were clean again, they sinned, they sacrificed animals, they were clean again – it went on and on and on. The point is, sacrificing animals was not a permanent solution to the sin problem. However, Jesus Christ was. See the difference here? Jesus Christ didn't keep offering himself periodically as a sacrifice, over and over and over again, he did it once, and that obtained eternal redemption for us.

Hebrews 9:26
For then must he often have suffered since the foundation of the world: but now once in the end of the world hath he appeared to put away sin by the sacrifice of himself.

His sacrifice took care of the sin problem once and for all.

Hebrews 9:27,28
And as it is appointed unto men once to die, but after this the judgment:

So Christ was once offered to bear the sins of many; and unto them that look for him shall he appear the second time without sin unto salvation.

His sacrifice took care of the sin problem because he was a perfect sacrifice. That's why we are righteous now. We are righteous not by our own works but because of what was done on our behalf. The blood of animals was just a temporary measure, a symbolic gesture God was forced to endure because man demanded it.

Now that Jesus Christ has dealt with sin permanently, there is no more need for sacrifices. The problem has been dealt with.

Hebrews 10:1
For the law having a shadow of good things to come, *and* not the very image of the things, can never with those sacrifices which

they offered year by year continually make the comers thereunto perfect.

The law and the sacrifices could not make people perfect. They simply could not take care of the sin and death problem that Adam and Eve's disobedience introduced.

> Hebrews 10:2
> For then would they not have ceased to be offered? because that the worshippers once purged should have had no more conscience of sins.

If old testament sacrifices of animals made people perfect, wouldn't they then have stopped sacrificing because it was no longer required? See the logic here? But animal sacrifices didn't make people perfect, which is why they kept sacrificing more animals to alleviate their guilt.

> Hebrews 10:3,4
> But in those *sacrifices there is* a remembrance again made of sins every year.
>
> For *it is* not possible that the blood of bulls and of goats should take away sins.

It wasn't possible to deal with the sin problem by killing animals. It was a man who caused the problem in the first place and it took a man to solve it. Someone had to pay the price for Adam's disobedience, and that someone was Jesus Christ. However, in contrast to the death of animals, Jesus Christ's death did a perfect job.

> Hebrews 10:12,14-17
> But this man, after he had offered one sacrifice for sins for ever, sat down on the right hand of God;
>
> For by one offering he hath perfected for ever them that are sanctified.
>
> *Whereof* the Holy Ghost [pneuma hagion – holy spirit] also is a witness to us: for after that he had said before,

> This *is* the covenant that I will make with them after those days, saith the Lord, I will put my laws into their hearts, and in their minds will I write them;
>
> And their sins and iniquities will I remember no more.

God will remember our iniquities no more because they no longer exist. That's why when God forgives, he forgets and never brings it up again. There is nothing to remember because there is nothing there. It's as far away as the east is from the west.

> Hebrews 10:18
> Now where remission [aphesis] of these *is, there is* no more offering for sin.

Remission and *forgiveness* are from compound words meaning simply to send away. *Aphesis* is from *apōtheomai*, *apo*, away from, and *ōtheō* or *ōthō*, to *shove*. So *apōtheomai* means to *push off*, figuratively to *reject:* to *cast away*, to *put away from*, to *thrust away from*. This is the background to *aphesis* and another closely related word which is also translated forgiveness at times, *aphiēmi*. Now that sin has been sent away, dismissed, thrust away, there is no more need for sacrifices as there is no longer a problem. We are righteous because of the sacrifice of Jesus Christ.

> Hebrews 10:19
> Having therefore, brethren, boldness to enter into the holiest by the blood of Jesus,

The holiest refers to the inner sanctuary of the temple, the holy of holies as it was called. That was where God dwelt, where he lived among his people before the day of Pentecost. God no longer dwells, he no longer lives, he no longer resides in temples made with hands, or any place of worship which is constructed, governed and controlled by men. Since the day of Pentecost we now have direct access to God through the gift of holy spirit. We can go directly to God anytime we wish and request an audience. Not only that, but he will grant us that audience every time. Our father has time for his children.

> Hebrews 10:20-22
> By a new and living way, which he hath consecrated for us, through the veil, that is to say, his flesh;
>
> And *having* an high priest over the house of God;
>
> Let us draw near with a true heart in full assurance of faith [pistis – believing], having our hearts sprinkled from an evil conscience, and our bodies washed with pure water.

The sin problem no longer exists. We are sanctified, set apart because we are redeemed, because we are justified, and because we are righteous. God has forgiven us and there is nothing of which we are guilty. We are holy and without blame before him in love.

So how come my mind doesn't always agree with this? How come my mind continually reminds me of all the terrible things I've done? How come my heart seems to enjoy making me feel guilty? This is the guts of the whole thing, it's called the renewed mind. We have to train our minds to think what the word says, and that's damned hard work at times. We have to decide between our feelings or what the word says. It's a choice we make to believe one way or the other.

Accepting forgiveness when we don't deserve it seems to be difficult for us earthlings. God understands this and so did Jesus Christ. In fact, Jesus Christ once told a story to help us understand forgiveness. It's wrongly known as the parable of the prodigal son because the point of the parable isn't the son, but the forgiveness of his father.

> Luke 15:1
> Then drew near unto him all the publicans and sinners for to hear him.

Jesus Christ did not have a problem with people. He was quite happy teaching the word to publicans and sinners, so God must have been quite happy with that too as Jesus Christ always did his Father's will. Unfortunately, the religious church leaders didn't approve of this. Much the same today isn't it? Why aren't the jesuits out lovingly preaching their gospel to publicans and sinners instead of continually coming up with new ways to exterminate them?

> Luke 15:2
> And the Pharisees and scribes murmured, saying, This man receiveth sinners, and eateth with them.

Oh, how awful, Jesus ate with *bad* people. Notice that these religious pricks didn't take it up with Jesus either, but muttered behind his back.

> Luke 15:3
> And he spake this parable unto them, saying,

Remember, Jesus had been accused of eating with sinners as if it was a crime, so the people he was eating with would have been hurt by these unjust and cruel words from the mouths of the jesuits of that day. Those people were there to hear God's word, and the devil used those religious creatures to try to prevent the word from being taught. Jesus Christ had to deal with it, so the parable although spoken to the scribes and Pharisees was not for their benefit, but for the people with him. He told this story to illustrate that God didn't have a problem forgiving people, regardless of their past. He told this story to counteract the cruel words of the religious leaders who did not want God's people to hear the truth. You will not find God in temples made with hands.

> Luke 15:11,12
> And he said, A certain man had two sons:

And the younger of them said to *his* father, Father, give me the portion of goods that falleth *to me*. And he divided unto them *his* living.

The son asked for his share of the inheritance which was legally and rightfully his. The parable also says that the father divided unto *them* his living. In other words, he gave both his sons their inheritance.

> Luke 15:13
> And not many days after the younger son gathered all together, and took his journey into a far country, and there wasted his substance with riotous living.

Most of us know what riotous living is. I wasted quite a few years of my life in riotous living, so this parable computes for me.

> Luke 15:14
> And when he had spent all, there arose a mighty famine in that land; and he began to be in want.

His money ran out, as it does when you live riotously. If you've never been hungry, this probably won't hit your heart as poignantly as someone who has been in great need. Unless people come back to God's word again, they're going to find out what great need is pretty soon.

> Luke 15:15
> And he went and joined himself to a citizen of that country; and he sent him into his fields to feed swine.

The worst job in the world to an Israelite was feeding pigs. Swineherds were not paid, and they had to eat the swill fed to the pigs to keep themselves alive. This son's situation had changed somewhat.

> Luke 15:16
> And he would fain have filled his belly with the husks that the swine did eat: and no man gave unto him.

Makes you wonder where all his friends went, doesn't it? Where were all the friends who helped him drink away his inheritance? Where were all his mates now that he was eating swill with the pigs? Probably going to church every week to listen to the pharisees spouting their horseshit about sinners, or going to masonic meetings to discuss how best to package pig swill and put it on supermarket shelves to make more money. I'm not cynical, this is how the world works.

> Luke 15:17
> And when he came to himself, he said, How many hired servants of my father's have bread enough and to spare, and I perish with hunger!

The pig swill wasn't even sufficient to keep him alive.

Luke 15:18,19
I will arise and go to my father, and will say unto him, Father, I have sinned against heaven, and before thee,

And am no more worthy to be called thy son: make me as one of thy hired servants.

So he made the decision to go home. Not sure what he might have expected, but he had nowhere else to go except to face death.

Luke 15:20-22
And he arose, and came to his father. But when he was yet a great way off, his father saw him, and had compassion, and ran, and fell on his neck, and kissed him.

And the son said unto him, Father, I have sinned against heaven, and in thy sight, and am no more worthy to be called thy son.

But the father said to his servants, Bring forth the best robe, and put *it* on him; and put a ring on his hand, and shoes on *his* feet:

Signet rings were used to stamp wax seals. The ring meant he could buy stuff and use the signet ring like we use a credit card. Did his father tell him to fuck off? No, God isn't mad at us for what we've done in the past, that's the point of this parable. God's mercy is staggering.

Luke 15:23,24
And bring hither the fatted calf, and kill *it;* and let us eat, and be merry:

For this my son was dead, and is alive again; he was lost, and is found. And they began to be merry.

When we are born again and receive the gift of holy spirit, our past life is dealt with. Everything we've done wrong is gone – we have a clean sheet, a fresh start in life because we receive the righteousness of God. Jesus Christ paid the price so we could have the righteousness of God. God does not have a problem with anyone's past, regardless of what they've done.

Okay, we've pretty much established that we are righteous when we receive the gift of holy spirit, but what about all the sins we do after that point? Sure, I've been forgiven for my past, I'm born again, I have the righteousness of God, so I go out and get drunk. What now? Understanding this difference is to understand the difference between our standing and our state.

Our standing in the household of God is one of a son or daughter, as children, and that never fluctuates or changes. We have eternal life. Always remember, you cannot corrupt the gift of holy spirit. You can sure mess up your life in the body and soul category, but you can't corrupt the gift of holy spirit. It is eternal life, and even if you get drunk, that spirit is still incorruptible, you still have the righteousness of God. That's why we must renew our minds. What use is it having the righteousness of God if we're out getting drunk all the time? Unless we renew our minds and live the word, we won't ever be able to enjoy the benefits of the gift of holy spirit because the renewed mind is the key to power. However, regardless of whether or not we renew our minds, we still have the righteousness of God, we still have the gift of holy spirit, we are still God's children.

Our state, however, is dependent on our fellowship with God. Although we are his children, it doesn't necessarily follow that we are going to walk by the spirit and enjoy his fellowship. Jesus Christ redeemed us, yes, and when we confess Jesus as lord and believe in our hearts that God raised him from the dead, from that moment on we have eternal life, but what if we don't renew our minds? What if we just continue living riotously? What if we ignore the bible and keep our minds in the world's television? Will your life benefit from the promises in God's word? No, your life will not change at all because you will still be grunting in the world's pig swill. Why? It's not God's fault. It's up to you to renew your mind and turn on the power. God made the gift of holy spirit available, and he gave us his word to teach us how to manifest it. Now it's up to us to learn that word, renew our minds and use it to turn on the spiritual power. That's what makes the difference in life. It isn't religious ceremony or ritual, it isn't going to church every week, it isn't about how much money you give to charities, it isn't about how wide your inane smiles are, it's about turning on the power.

Now let's take this a step further. Let's assume we *are* renewing our minds, that we *are* learning God's word, and that we *are* doing our best to live it. Guess what, you're still going to mess up from time to time. You're still going to make mistakes on a regular basis. When our children grow up, are they perfect? No, of course now, every parent knows that, but do parents expect their children to be perfect? Hardly. Well, God is a parent, and just like any parent, he knows his children are going to break his word from time to time. That's just life. Jesus Christ was perfect, that's why he was the perfect sacrifice, that's why he was able to redeem us, but we're not perfect. We're perfect spiritually, yes, but we still have an old man to contend with that we must put off. This is a process, not a one time event. Just as parents love their children despite all their mistakes, so God loves his children, despite all their mistakes.

> Psalm 103:8,10,13
> The LORD *is* merciful and gracious, slow to anger, and plenteous in mercy.
>
> He hath not dealt with us after our sins; nor rewarded us according to our iniquities.
>
> Like as a father pitieth *his* children, *so* the LORD pitieth them that fear him.

This word *pity* as used in the King James is one of those words that means something different today than it did in 1611 when it was first written. Fathers today don't pity their children, they care for them and love them, understanding their frailties. That's what the word meant when it was written all those centuries ago. A similar fact is relevant with the word *fear*. In 1611, the word *fear* in this context meant awe, reverence and respect.

Forgiveness has always been available. Even Adam and Eve were forgiven and lived productive lives, albeit without the spirit that had been created within them. Forgiveness has always been available, and the word must be understood in that light. It doesn't matter to God where a person has been, or what they've done in the past, he's only interested in where they are now and where they want to be tomorrow. Religious people, like those pharisees and scribes, are cold, hard, self seeking and self righteous, turning people away from the truth. They are vipers and scorpions, whited sepulchres full of dead men's bones. Do not expect to find God in churches run by those creatures.

Eternal life is a free gift, but continuing in fellowship with God after that point is dependant on our walk. How we live determines our state. Our standing as children will never change, but our state, our fellowship with God can fluctuate greatly. Regardless of our state, we will always have the righteousness of God.

The key to power is the renewed mind. If I don't know I'm righteous, and I mess up, feel guilty and run out and get drunk, I'm going to suffer consequences because I'm missing the mark. I'm still righteous, but I won't enjoy the benefits of that righteousness, and my fellowship with God will suffer dramatically. However, if instead of running out to get drunk when I mess up, I go to God's word, read about my sonship rights, read about how Jesus Christ paid for that mistake I just made, and decide to renew my mind and get over it and move on in life, now I'm starting to get somewhere spiritually. That's why the renewed mind is the key to power.

This is not about being faultless, it is about keeping God's word in our minds despite our old man nature. It isn't about how few times we fall down, it's about how quickly we get up again after we fall. A faithful man isn't someone who only falls down once a year but stays down for weeks in condemnation, it's someone who falls down many times but who jumps right back up again and carries on knowing he has the righteousness of God. We put off the old by renewing our minds, and put on the new by energising the power in the gift of holy spirit.

> Psalm 103:14
> For he knoweth our frame; he remembereth that we *are* dust.

Sonship is our standing as children of God, but fellowship is our state, our personal relationship with him. We can be children of God, but not be in fellowship with him. That doesn't mean God doesn't love us, it means we're out swilling it with the pigs. To get back in fellowship, we have to decide to leave the world's troughs and return to God. The devil doesn't want that, which is why he uses religion and freemasonry to dress up his pig swill in such attractive packaging. They get truckloads of our money out of it while we suffer.

> 2 Corinthians 4:4
> In whom the god of this world hath blinded the minds of them which believe not, lest the light of the glorious gospel of Christ, who is the image of God, should shine unto them.

> 1 John 2:15-17
> Love not the world, neither the things *that are* in the world. If any man love the world, the love of the Father is not in him.
>
> For all that *is* in the world, the lust of the flesh, and the lust of the eyes, and the pride of life, is not of the Father, but is of the world.
>
> And the world passeth away, and the lust thereof: but he that doeth the will of God abideth for ever.

> Revelation 12:9
> And the great dragon was cast out, that old serpent, called the Devil, and Satan, which deceiveth the whole world: he was cast out into the earth, and his angels were cast out with him.

Although we're perfect spiritually, God doesn't expect us to be perfect physically. He knows our human capabilities and shortcomings. What parent doesn't understand that their children are not perfect? We're all human. God knows that and he made provision for it.

> 1 John 1:3,4
> That which we have seen and heard declare we unto you, that ye also may have fellowship with us: and truly our fellowship *is* with the Father, and with his Son Jesus Christ.
>
> And these things write we unto you, that your joy may be full.

What is the context here? What is this section of scripture talking about? Fellowship! What God is revealing here by revelation is how we can enjoy fellowship with him, and with his son Jesus Christ, that our joy may be full. This isn't talking about being saved, being born again, it's talking about fellowship after we're born again. This isn't dealing with our standing as sons of God, it's dealing with our state.

1 John 1:5
This then is the message which we have heard of him, and declare unto you, that God is light, and in him is no darkness at all.

God is light and in him is no darkness at all. None. Not a bit. Not even a little shadow. Have you ever seen darkness inside light? Darkness can't exist where there is light.

1 John 1:6
If we say that we have fellowship with him, and walk in darkness, we lie, and do not the truth:

If we're out swilling it with pigs, it's our own fault. That drunkard son was not forced into a life of riotous living, and nor are we. We have the freedom of will to choose which life we're going to live, the way of life or the way of death. Regardless of which life we choose, we are still righteous if we are born again, but what about our standing, what about our fellowship, what about the quality of our lives?

1 John 1:7
But if we walk in the light, as he is in the light, we have fellowship one with another, and the blood of Jesus Christ his Son cleanseth us from all sin.

When we walk according to the word, we're in fellowship with God, and that's where the beauty and richness in life resides.

1 John 1:8,9
If we say that we have no sin, we deceive ourselves, and the truth is not in us.

If we confess our sins, he is faithful and just to forgive us *our* sins, and to cleanse us from all unrighteousness.

This section of scripture isn't talking about getting born again, being made whole, receiving eternal life, this is talking about fellowship. The context is fellowship. Confessing sins is not how you get born again, it's how to get back into fellowship *after* you've been born again and messed up. See the difference? You can't have fellowship with God if you're not born again and don't have the gift of holy spirit, can you? You have to have spirit before you can have fellowship. How can a child have fellowship with a parent if they've not even been born? So we get born again, we receive the spirit, we become children of God and then we can begin to develop our fellowship with our father.

This verse says we need to confess our sins, but remember this is not talking about getting born again. This is so important to recognise. If you are forty years old when you are born again, how the heck are you going to remember all the sins you've ever done in your life? That's impossible. But I can sure remember the one I did this morning. When we are born again, all our past sins are taken care of, so this confession of sins isn't about being born again, it's about maintaining fellowship. This isn't talking about our sonship, it's talking about our state, our fellowship.

Forgiveness, or remission of sin is what we receive when we are born again, when we receive the gift of holy spirit. That takes care of every single thing we've done in the past. At the time of the new birth we receive the righteousness of God and that will never change. However, although we are righteous and have eternal life, our fellowship with God may be less than satisfactory. We are sons, but we can sure still live riotously and swill it with the pigs down on animal farm. Every time we come back to God, he is willing and just to forgive us our sins, and to cleanse us from all unrighteousness. We return to God by leaving the world's pig swill and renewing our minds.

It's not difficult to figure this out. For example, let's say our mind, or some religious dickhead, or even one of our friends or family brings up something from the past we'd rather forget and we're tempted to run out and get drunk. Okay, we have some work to do. Either we listen to the world and what it thinks of us and run out and get drunk, or we listen to the word and believe what God thinks of us. This is all part of the renewed mind.

Romans 12:2
And be not conformed to this world: but be ye transformed by the renewing of your mind, that ye may prove what is that good, and acceptable, and perfect, will of God.

The renewed mind is the key to this whole thing. We have to retrain our minds to think a new way. God says we're his children, but our friends and families may tell us otherwise and point out our shortcomings. We have to train our minds until we think of ourselves as the word says despite our mistakes. We are God's children. That's the truth, but sometimes when we mess up we won't feel like it. Does it matter what we feel like? No, the word is true, not what we feel like. If we fall short and think less of ourselves than what the word says, we replace those thoughts with the word. We apologise to God, replace our thoughts with the word, and move on.

1 John 1:9
If we confess our sins, he is faithful and just to forgive us *our* sins, and to cleanse us from all unrighteousness.

Ephesians 1:4
According as he hath chosen us in him before the foundation of the world, that we should be holy and without blame before him in love:

Jesus Christ redeemed me, and I received remission of sin. I have the righteousness of God and I don't really care what anyone thinks to the contrary. When it comes to the word, I don't have any friends unless they are helping me to think and live the word. God declares me not guilty, despite all my failings and that's why I have peace with him.

Romans 5:1
Therefore being justified by faith [pistis – believing], we have peace with God through our Lord Jesus Christ:

The same is true for you. God isn't mad at us, we have peace with him. He's not upset with us, he's not pissed off with all the garbage in our lives. Our garbage was paid for and dumped as far away as the east from the west. We've been declared not guilty, and now we have peace with

God. He isn't mad at us for anything, and he will never be mad at us for anything in the future. When we make mistakes, we simply recognise the error (confess our sins), rectify the problem so it doesn't happen again, and move on in perfect fellowship with our father who is always faithful and just to forgive us.

So, to sum up, get over it!

38. The Voice of God

People often think that if they could only spend a little personal time with Jesus Christ and watch him do a few healings and miracles, that it would be easy for them to believe. In my experience, I've found that folks who think this way cave in easily under pressure. Why? Well, Jesus Christ isn't here, so there is nothing in that kind of thinking that is of any value in a crisis. Nowhere in the bible does it state that when you are under pressure you are to wish you had been with Jesus. That kind of thinking invites failure. Besides, we have something far better than *being with Jesus* could ever be. Let's take a look at this in more detail.

When Jesus was arrested in the Garden of Gethsemane, do you know what his apostles and closest disciples did?

> Mark 14:50
> And they all forsook him, and fled.

That's right, they all ran away. Do you still think being with Jesus is the answer to all your problems? These guys had been with Jesus Christ for months. Some of them had seen Lazarus raised from the dead. Peter had walked on water and had heard the voice of God out of a cloud on the mount of transfiguration. They'd seen blind men, lepers, and lame people healed. Yet they all ran away. And where were these same disciples just a few days later?

> John 20:19
> Then the same day at evening, being the first *day* of the week, when the doors were shut where the disciples were assembled for fear of the Jews [Judeans], came Jesus and stood in the midst, and saith unto them, Peace *be* unto you.

Where were they? Cowering in fear behind closed doors. If you still think being with Jesus would be the answer to all your problems, you had better think again.

However, Peter and the other disciples changed. Less than fifty days later, on the day of Pentecost, instead of cowering behind closed doors for fear of the Judeans, Peter and the other apostles confronted them to their faces in public.

> Acts 2:14
> But Peter, standing up with the eleven, lifted up his voice, and said unto them, Ye men of Judaea, and all *ye* that dwell at Jerusalem, be this known unto you, and hearken to my words:

Where did his fear go? This was in the temple, by the way, where the very same religious criminals would have been who'd had the Romans murder Jesus Christ. This was the same Peter who had run away from them earlier. What changed Peter? What changed the other apostles? Being with Jesus hadn't done it. Jesus wasn't even around anymore.

Some folks are also tempted to think that if only Moses was here, or one of the other great men of God, they would find it easy to believe. Really? Okay, let's imagine you're with Moses and you're in Egypt during the time of the Exodus. Moses has just led you and the Israeli people out of the slavery of Egypt, and you've witnessed the plagues that happened to Pharaoh and his people. Now you would find it easy to believe God and trust in him, right? Okay, let's see what happened when the Israelites were on the shores of the Red Sea and Pharaoh and his army were coming after them.

> Exodus 14:10-12
> And when Pharaoh drew nigh, the children of Israel lifted up their eyes, and, behold, the Egyptians marched after them; and they were sore afraid: and the children of Israel cried out unto the LORD.
>
> And they said unto Moses, Because *there were* no graves in Egypt, hast thou taken us away to die in the wilderness? wherefore hast thou dealt thus with us, to carry us forth out of Egypt?

> *Is* not this the word that we did tell thee in Egypt, saying, Let us alone, that we may serve the Egyptians? For *it had been* better for us to serve the Egyptians, than that we should die in the wilderness.

Not only did the people not trust in God, they actually accused Moses of taking them out into the wilderness to kill them. God, however, being merciful and long suffering, provided a way for them to escape. He literally parted the waters of the Red Sea and the Israelites walked to the other side on dry ground. When Pharaoh and his army came after them, they were drowned by the returning waters.

> Exodus 14:30,31
> Thus the LORD saved Israel that day out of the hand of the Egyptians; and Israel saw the Egyptians dead upon the sea shore.
>
> And Israel saw that great work which the LORD did upon the Egyptians: and the people feared the LORD, and believed the LORD, and his servant Moses.

God's people saw all this with their own eyes. If you were there, you would have been beating your chest and finding it easy to believe God, right? Let's continue reading.

> Exodus 16:1-3
> And they took their journey from Elim, and all the congregation of the children of Israel came unto the wilderness of Sin, which *is* between Elim and Sinai, on the fifteenth day of the second month after their departing out of the land of Egypt.
>
> And the whole congregation of the children of Israel murmured against Moses and Aaron in the wilderness:
>
> And the children of Israel said unto them, Would to God we had died by the hand of the LORD in the land of Egypt, when we sat by the flesh pots, *and* when we did eat bread to the full; for ye have brought us forth into this wilderness, to kill this whole assembly with hunger.

A few days later they're bitching about the food and accusing Moses of dragging them into the wilderness to kill them with starvation. They had already forgotten what God had done for them at the Red Sea. However, God being merciful and long suffering provided them with manna to eat. He fed over two million people in a barren desert with manna, bread from heaven. Surely now they will believe?

Exodus 17:1-4
And all the congregation of the children of Israel journeyed from the wilderness of Sin, after their journeys, according to the commandment of the LORD, and pitched in Rephidim: and *there was* no water for the people to drink.

Wherefore the people did chide with Moses, and said, Give us water that we may drink. And Moses said unto them, Why chide ye with me? wherefore do ye tempt the LORD?

And the people thirsted there for water; and the people murmured against Moses, and said, Wherefore *is* this *that* thou hast brought us up out of Egypt, to kill us and our children and our cattle with thirst?

And Moses cried unto the LORD, saying, What shall I do unto this people? they be almost ready to stone me.

A few days later they're bitching again, this time about water. They've forgotten everything God did for them in Egypt, they've forgotten all about the Red Sea, and they're already taking for granted the manna they're eating. All they can see is there is no water, and they accused Moses of leading them into the wilderness to murder them with thirst. They were so pissed off, they were on the verge of stoning him. Again, God is merciful and long suffering, and provides them with water. Surely now they will believe God will take care of them? Some time later, God summoned Moses for a little chat and off he went up a mountain.

Exodus 32:1-4
And when the people saw that Moses delayed to come down out of the mount, the people gathered themselves together unto Aaron, and said unto him, Up, make us gods, which shall go before us; for *as for* this Moses, the man that brought us up out of the land of Egypt, we wot not what is become of him.

And Aaron said unto them, Break off the golden earrings, which *are* in the ears of your wives, of your sons, and of your daughters, and bring *them* unto me.

And all the people brake off the golden earrings which *were* in their ears, and brought *them* unto Aaron.

And he received *them* at their hand, and fashioned it with a graving tool, after he had made it a molten calf: and they said, These *be* thy gods, O Israel, which brought thee up out of the land of Egypt.

Forty days was all it took for these people to forget everything God had done for them and return to the idolatry of Egypt. Whining, bitching, and accusing is all they seem to know how to do. That's what idolatry does to people. Do you still think being with Moses is the answer to all your problems?

Once again, God being merciful and long suffering sorted it out, and had Moses lead them to the borders of the promised land. There it was, spread before them, a land of milk and honey, and all they had to do was walk in and take it. Their response?

Numbers 14:2-4
And all the children of Israel murmured against Moses and against Aaron: and the whole congregation said unto them, Would God that we had died in the land of Egypt! or would God we had died in this wilderness!

And wherefore hath the LORD brought us unto this land, to fall by the sword, that our wives and our children should be a prey? were it not better for us to return into Egypt?

And they said one to another, Let us make a captain, and let us return into Egypt.

They took one look at the land and started bitching and complaining, even going so far as to accuse God of leading them there to murder them with war. You may think seeing miracles like the parting of the Red Sea and being with Moses or Jesus would be the answer to all your problems, but if you do, you're deluded. You are making excuses for your unbelief.

Jesus Christ handled this kind of thinking in his day and time. He was right there, doing miracle after miracle, and people refused to believe. They told him that if only he would raise someone from the dead, they would believe, so he told them a little parable to confront their anaemic thinking.

> Luke 16:19-24
> There was a certain rich man, which was clothed in purple and fine linen, and fared sumptuously every day:
>
> And there was a certain beggar named Lazarus, which was laid at his gate, full of sores,
>
> And desiring to be fed with the crumbs which fell from the rich man's table: moreover the dogs came and licked his sores.
>
> And it came to pass, that the beggar died, and was carried by the angels into Abraham's bosom: the rich man also died, and was buried;
>
> And in hell he lift up his eyes, being in torments, and seeth Abraham afar off, and Lazarus in his bosom.
>
> And he cried and said, Father Abraham, have mercy on me, and send Lazarus, that he may dip the tip of his finger in water, and cool my tongue; for I am tormented in this flame.

Remember, this parable is just a story, a fiction, which he knew those listening would understand. If I told a parable about good and evil to Star Trek fans that involved the Borg and the Federation, that wouldn't mean I believed there were starships warping around the universe and that an invasion by aliens was imminent. Jesus Christ knew that the dead were dead. This parable isn't a true story, it's merely a fictional illustration to make a point to the science fiction fans of his day.

Luke 16:25-31
But Abraham said, Son, remember that thou in thy lifetime receivedst thy good things, and likewise Lazarus evil things: but now he is comforted, and thou art tormented.

And beside all this, between us and you there is a great gulf fixed: so that they which would pass from hence to you cannot; neither can they pass to us, that *would come* from thence.

Then he said, I pray thee therefore, father, that thou wouldest send him to my father's house:

For I have five brethren; that he may testify unto them, lest they also come into this place of torment.

Abraham saith unto him, They have Moses and the prophets; let them hear them.

And he said, Nay, father Abraham: but if one went unto them from the dead, they will repent.

And he said unto him, If they hear not Moses and the prophets, neither will they be persuaded, though one rose from the dead.

I used to have a problem with this parable, in that I couldn't understand how actually witnessing someone being raised from the dead wouldn't make people believe. I guess I doubted the truth Jesus Christ taught here. Well, I recently raised someone from the dead. She was lying by the side of the road, in winter, and it was late at night and very dark. I was the first on the scene, and she had no pulse. I had someone call the emergency services, I prayed, carried out a few instructions, and she sat up just as the police arrived.

I am in absolutely no doubt whatsoever that if I had not been there that night, she would now be buried in a cemetery somewhere. I told this story the following week to a group of christians. I could see they weren't interested in anything I had to say, but I told the story anyway, believing it would get a response. When I was done, they said nothing, looked away and went back to watching something more important on television. My words had no impact. At that very moment, I thought of this parable in Luke and the truth of it hit me like a brick on the head.

Jesus Christ illustrated the truth in this parable. If people will not hear the word, whether it be from Jesus, Moses, one of the prophets or from me, they will not hear the word even though someone was raised from the dead right before them. I now know this by experience. Believing God is simple. It's a choice people make. If you are a christian and television is more important to you than the word of God, then TV is your god, and I don't give a fuck how religious and nice you think you are. As a christian you are supposed to be an example, a living epistle, not a mouthpiece for the world.

So what changed Peter? Simply being with Jesus obviously hadn't done it. Hearing the voice of God out of a cloud hadn't done it. Walking on water hadn't done it. Seeing Lazarus raised from the dead hadn't done it. Peter himself gives us a clue in his own epistle.

> 2 Peter 1:16-19
> For we have not followed cunningly devised fables, when we made known unto you the power and coming of our Lord Jesus Christ, but were eyewitnesses of his majesty.
>
> For he received from God the Father honour and glory, when there came such a voice to him from the excellent glory, This is my beloved Son, in whom I am well pleased.
>
> And this voice which came from heaven we heard, when we were with him in the holy mount.
>
> We have also a more sure word of prophecy; whereunto ye do well that ye take heed, as unto a light that shineth in a dark place, until the day dawn, and the day star arise in your hearts:

According to Peter, there is a *more sure word of prophecy*, something more sure, more reliable, more dependable than hearing the audible voice of God. What on earth is Peter talking about? What could be more sure than hearing the voice of God booming out of a cloud?

As we've seen with the Israelites following Moses, what we see with our eyes and hear with our ears isn't sufficient to fuel our believing for the long term. Time has a habit of dulling our memories. What we saw yesterday doesn't have the same impact on our hearts and minds as it does today, and it will have even less impact tomorrow. We are human and we forget. The Israelites had been with Moses and seen miracle after miracle, yet it wasn't enough to keep them thankful and believing. Peter had been with Jesus, and yet he had run away when it mattered. Simply being with Jesus had not been enough to overcome his fear. Even after Jesus Christ had been raised from the dead, his apostles still refused to believe.

> Mark 16:9-11
> Now when *Jesus* was risen early the first *day* of the week, he appeared first to Mary Magdalene, out of whom he had cast seven devils.
>
> *And* she went and told them that had been with him, as they mourned and wept.
>
> And they, when they had heard that he was alive, and had been seen of her, believed not.
>
> Luke 24:10,11
> It was Mary Magdalene, and Joanna, and Mary *the mother* of James, and other *women that were* with them, which told these things unto the apostles.
>
> And their words seemed to them as idle tales, and they believed them not.

Do you still think being with Jesus Christ would solve all your believing problems? Jesus Christ was a man, as was Moses, as am I. The truth is, if you won't hear the word from me, you wouldn't hear it from Jesus Christ or Moses either. They were not magicians any more than I am. There is no magic in this. Either you decide to believe the word or you don't. If you want to be a believer, I suggest you get your head out of television world and into the bible. How much do you want it?

Romans 10:17
So then faith [pistis – believing] *cometh* by hearing, and hearing by the word of God.

The renewed mind is the key to power, but it certainly isn't the power itself. Peter knew the word, but it takes more than that. He even fell asleep in the Garden of Gethsemane when Jesus Christ needed his support. He denied Jesus when he was accused of being one of his followers. He was human. Yet, just fifty days later he went through a remarkable transformation on the day of Pentecost when he stood up in the temple and publicly confronted the Judeans. Do these sound like the words of a man full of fear?

Acts 2:36
Therefore let all the house of Israel know assuredly, that God hath made that same Jesus, whom ye have crucified, both Lord and Christ.

Any idea what changed Peter? Any idea what the more sure word of prophecy is? What changed Peter is what happened that morning in Jerusalem.

Acts 2:4
And they were all filled with the Holy Ghost [pneuma hagion – holy spirit], and began to speak with other tongues, as the Spirit gave them utterance.

It is speaking in tongues that Peter referred to as being a more sure word of prophecy than hearing the audible voice of God from a cloud. Right now, we have something far more reliable and dependable to fuel our believing than simply seeing a few miracles done by Jesus or Moses. Memories dim and we forget, but we can speak in tongues and hear the voice of God at any time we choose. That spirit within us is supernatural power just waiting to be energised and overflow out of us. It was the energising of this power that changed Peter. When Peter spoke in tongues and energised the spirit, it changed him and it will change you too. We can hear the voice of God every moment of every day out of our own mouths.

39. Manifesting the Power of God

When Peter stood up in the temple and confronted the Judeans, he had just that morning received the gift of holy spirit and energised its power by speaking in tongues. Speaking in tongues is spiritual power and we can manifest it at anytime. That's why it is a more sure word of prophecy than hearing a one off audible voice of God from a cloud. Amazingly, it is only one of nine manifestations of the gift of holy spirit at our disposal. They are listed in Corinthians.

> 1 Corinthians 12:7-10
> But the manifestation of the Spirit [pneuma - spirit] is given to every man to profit withal.
>
> For to one is given by the Spirit the word of wisdom; to another the word of knowledge by the same Spirit;
>
> To another faith [pistis – believing] by the same Spirit; to another the gifts of healing by the same Spirit;
>
> To another the working of miracles; to another prophecy; to another discerning of spirits; to another ~~divers~~ kinds of tongues; to another the interpretation of tongues:

According to 1 Corinthians 12, speaking in tongues is a manifestation of the gift of holy spirit. First of all, what is a manifestation? What does the word manifestation mean? Let's take a look at it. The word manifest can be used as an adjective, a verb, or a noun. As an adjective, it means readily perceived by the eye or by the understanding, it means that something is evident, obvious, apparent and plain to see or understand. As a verb, it means to make evident, obvious, apparent and plain to see or understand. As a verb, it also means to prove, to put beyond question or doubt. As a noun, it is used of a ship's cargo manifest, which is the inventory of the cargo the ship carries in its holds, a document detailing the cargo inside a ship.

Speaking in tongues is a manifestation of holy spirit. By definition then, speaking in tongues is the evidence that makes holy spirit obvious, apparent and plain to see or understand, it puts the existence of holy spirit beyond question or doubt, it is the document that details the holy spirit we have within. Now let's look at this section of scripture in more detail.

> 1 Corinthians 12:7
> But the manifestation of the Spirit [pneuma - spirit] is given to every man to profit withal.

The manifestation of the spirit is given to every man, to every born again believer. That is what it says and that is what it means. Does this verse say that the manifestation of the spirit is only given to a few select special people? No, it does not. It clearly states that the manifestation of the spirit is given to *every* man to profit withal. Every person who has the gift of holy spirit can manifest it and profit from it. Is a manifestation a gift? Let's read the verse again.

> 1 Corinthians 12:7
> But the manifestation of the Spirit [pneuma - spirit] is given to every man to profit withal.

It doesn't say gift, it says manifestation. A manifestation is not a gift, any more than an apple is a monkey. A gift is a gift and a manifestation is a manifestation. They are different words with different meanings and cannot be used synonymously. The manifestation of speaking in tongues is not a gift, it is a manifestation.

This seems elementary, yet most christians have the idea that speaking in tongues is a gift. Where do they get such nonsense? They must get it from those horseshit churches they go to that God doesn't attend. The word gift is mentioned in verse 1, but it is in italics, which tells us that it was added by the translators. Scratch it out because it should not be there.

1 Corinthians 12:1
Now concerning spiritual ~~gifts~~, brethren, I would not have you ignorant.

Verse 1 sets the context for the coming verses and we must delete the word gifts, for God did not put that word in his bible, man did. The King James translators left the word *gifts* in italics so we would know this. There is absolutely no excuse for anyone to leave the word *gifts* in the text here and teach that manifestations of holy spirit are gifts. The Greek word for *spiritual* is *pneumatikos*, which could be translated as *spiritual matters*, *things of the spirit*, or simply *spirituality*. The context is spiritual matters.

1 Corinthians 12:7
But the manifestation of the Spirit [pneuma] is given to every man to profit withal.

The manifestation of holy spirit is not a gift. You cannot insert the word *gift* into the text here, and I really don't care if you have a problem with that. I'm teaching you the truth, and if you read these manifestations as gifts, you are not rightly dividing God's word, you are wrong. Yes, the word *gifts* is used in verse 4, but there have been subject changes since then and here in verse 7 we're talking about the manifestation of the spirit, not gifts of the spirit. The context is spiritual matters, of which gifts and manifestations are a part. Gifts are spiritual matters and manifestations are spiritual matters.

Well, what gifts did God give us? If you don't know, don't guess. You do not have the right to make up your own ideas on what God's gifts are. No prophecy of the scripture is of any private [idios – one's own] interpretation. If you want to know what gifts God gave, they are listed in his word. Here's one.

Romans 6:23
For the wages of sin *is* death; but the gift of God *is* eternal life through Jesus Christ our Lord.

Ephesians 2:8
For by grace are ye saved [sōzō – made whole] through faith [believing]; and that not of yourselves: *it is* the gift of God:

Eternal life, the Christ in us, the holy spirit we received at the time of the new birth is a gift. How do we know? The bible tells us. There is no guesswork in this. There is no private interpretation in this. The bible interprets itself. Are there any other gifts?

> Ephesians 4:8,11
> Wherefore he saith, When he ascended up on high, he led captivity captive, and gave gifts unto men.
>
> And he gave some, apostles; and some, prophets; and some, evangelists; and some, pastors and teachers;

These are the five special gift ministries God gave, apostles, prophets, evangelists, pastors and teachers, and their purposes are listed in the next verse.

> Ephesians 4:12
> For the perfecting of the saints, for the work of the ministry, for the edifying of the body of Christ:

From God's word we know that holy spirit is a gift, and that God also gave five gift ministries. Are there any other specific gifts mentioned? Yes, actually the word *gifts* is used of one of the manifestations of holy spirit.

> 1 Corinthians 12:9
> To another faith [believing] by the same Spirit; to another the gifts of healing by the same Spirit;

In this case, the word gifts is not in italics. God did have the word *gifts* placed here when he had Paul write this. However, this is not saying that the manifestation of healing is a gift, it is saying that when someone is healed by the manifestation of holy spirit, the healing is a gift to the person receiving the healing.

Are there any other places gifts is used? What about this one in the next chapter?

> 1 Corinthians 13:2a
> And though I have *the gift of* prophecy,

Is the manifestation of prophecy a gift? No, it isn't, it is a manifestation of the gift of holy spirit. The word *gift* is in italics, so we know it was added by the translators. Delete it for it is wrong, it should not be there.

> 1 Corinthians 13:2a
> And though I have ~~the gift of~~ prophecy,

In case someone thinks it's okay to add words to the bible to promote their particular brand of religious horseshit, try these two scriptures on for size.

> Revelation 22:18,19
> For I testify unto every man that heareth the words of the prophecy of this book, If any man shall add unto these things, God shall add unto him the plagues that are written in this book:
>
> And if any man shall take away from the words of the book of this prophecy, God shall take away his part out of the book of life, and out of the holy city, and *from* the things which are written in this book.

Back to Corinthians, where we have established that we are talking about the *manifestation* of the *gift* of holy spirit. God gave us holy spirit as a gift, and with that spirit comes the ability to manifest it. See the distinction here? This isn't difficult to understand. If someone gives me a camera, or a computer, or a pen as a gift, I can then use that gift for what it was intended. The use of the gift itself is not a gift, it is simply using the gift you were given.

Moving on. Most read verse 7 and then interpret what follows in verses 8-10 as *to one person is given the gift* of word of wisdom, *to another person is given the gift* of word of knowledge, *to another person is given the gift* of speaking tongues, and so on.

> 1 Corinthians 12:7,8
> But the manifestation of the Spirit is given to every man to profit withal.
>
> For to one is given by the Spirit the word of wisdom; to another the word of knowledge by the same Spirit;

First of all, these manifestations are not gifts. Further, verse 7 tells us that the manifestation of the spirit is given to *every* man, not individual men, so verses 8-10 cannot possibly contradict that. Verse 7 also tells us the manifestation of the spirit is given to every man to *profit* withal. Now let's tie this all together.

The word *one* in verse 8 is a pronoun, which relates itself back to its closest associated noun. For example, here are two short sentences:

John had a ball. He kicked the ball into the goal.

In the second sentence, the pronoun *he* refers back to John, not the ball. The ball obviously didn't kick itself into the goal, did it? *He* is a pronoun and we track the context back until we find which noun it is associated with, in this case, John. Now consider these two sentences:

John had a ball. John kicked it into the goal.

In this case, the pronoun *it* refers back to the ball, which John kicked into the goal. It is fundamentally important to track the pronouns in God's word. So which noun do the pronouns *one* and *another* relate back to in 1 Corinthians 12:8-10?

> 1 Corinthians 12:8
> For to one [to one what?] is given by the Spirit the word of wisdom; to another [to another what?] the word of knowledge by the same Spirit;

To find out, we simply check the context. Is it the noun *man* in verse 7?

> 1 Corinthians 12:7
> But the manifestation of the Spirit is given to every man to profit withal.

Verse 7 talks about the manifestation of the spirit being given to every man for *profit*. The point here isn't men, but the *profit* of the manifestation of the spirit *to* men. The word *profit* is a noun. It is this noun the pronoun *one* in verse 8 relates back to. Verses 8 to 10 are a parenthesis emphasising that each manifestation of the gift of holy spirit has a distinct and separate profit. Let's read verses 7 through 10 with this understanding.

> 1 Corinthians 12:7-10
> But the manifestation of the Spirit is given to every man to profit withal.
>
> For to one [profit] is given by the Spirit the word of wisdom; to another [profit] the word of knowledge by the same Spirit;
>
> To another [profit] faith by the same Spirit; to another [profit] the gifts of healing by the same Spirit;
>
> To another [profit] the working of miracles; to another [profit] prophecy; to another [profit] discerning of spirits; to another [profit] ~~divers~~ kinds of tongues; to another [profit] the interpretation of tongues:

This all fits perfectly and precisely. The word teaches that the manifestation of the spirit is given to *every* man for *profit*. Each manifestation has a different and distinct profit. Anyone who has the gift of holy spirit can learn to manifest it for spiritual and physical profit.

> 1 Corinthians 12:11
> But all these worketh [energeō – energises] that one and the selfsame Spirit, dividing to every man severally [idios – his own] as he [the man] will.

The word *severally* here is a forgery, a deliberate criminal tampering with God's word. It is translated from the Greek word *idios*, which is used 112 times in the new testament. It is translated *his own* or *one's own* 76 times, *private* or *privately* 9 times, a few other ways, and severally just once. Here are two places where *idios* has been properly translated.

> Acts 2:6
> Now when this was noised abroad, the multitude came together, and were confounded, because that every man heard them speak in **his own** [idios] language.

Acts 2:8
And how hear we every man in **our own** [idios] tongue, wherein we were born?

The meaning of the Greek word *idios* isn't open to debate. It means *one's own*. To translate it as *severally* is nothing more than a criminal forgery to attempt to substantiate erroneous religious horseshit.

The manifestation of the spirit – which consists of nine different energisings or operations all with their own distinct profit – is given to *every* man. It is up to us to believe to manifest them. We have to will, to determine, to believe to speak in tongues, interpret tongues, and prophesy, receive word of knowledge, word of wisdom, and discerning of spirits, and bring into manifestation believing (the manifestation of believing is different from regular believing), miracles, and healing. It isn't up to God whether or not we manifest the gift of holy spirit, it is up to us.

Oh, the world is full of people manifesting devilish spiritual abilities. People get possessed and predict the future, move things without touching them, spontaneously combust, make things disappear and reappear, walk on burning coals in their bare feet, kiss poisonous snakes, and turn sunny days into stormy weather. Magic is for the lazy and gullible. Any idiot can open their minds to devil spirit possession through drugs, witchcraft, or religious instruction. We don't open our minds to possession and allow a devil spirit in so it can operate its power through us. We are not channels or mediums for God, and the gift of holy spirit does not possess us. It is something we control at all times. We have to believe to operate the power we have been given, it does not control us.

God gave us the gift of holy spirit and he gave us his word to teach us about it. Now it is up to us to believe and manifest it. God isn't going to *make* anyone manifest *anything*. It is as *we* will. When we believe to operate the gift of holy spirit then God energises within us and his power is manifested. This is true spiritual power.

40. Filled to Overflowing

On the day of Pentecost the gift of holy spirit was first given, and the first manifestation, the first evidence, the initial energising of that gift was speaking in tongues.

> Acts 2:4
> And they were all filled with the Holy Ghost [pneuma hagion – holy spirit], and began to speak with other tongues, as the Spirit gave them utterance.

First of all, let's determine who they were. The word *they* is a pronoun, so we must go back through the context to find its closest associated noun. Verse 3 tells us cloven tongues like as of fire sat upon each of them. Who is them? We still don't know. Verse 2 talks about the house where *they* were sitting. Verse 1 says *they* were all with one accord in one place. We still don't know who *they* were so we must continue tracking back through the context. We find our answer in the last verse of chapter 1.

> Acts 1:26
> And they gave forth their lots; and the lot fell upon Matthias; and he was numbered with the eleven apostles.

Grammatically, the pronouns *they* and *them* in Acts 2:1-4 relate back to Matthias and the other eleven apostles. The pronouns in Acts 2:1-4 refer to 12 men who were in the temple, not 120 people in an upper room. This isn't open to debate, this is simply how language works. This is an excellent example of how the bible interprets itself.

> Acts 2:4
> And they [the eleven apostles and Matthias] were all filled with the Holy Ghost [pneuma hagion – holy spirit], and began to speak with other tongues, as the Spirit gave them utterance.

It is important to note who did the speaking here – they did. The bible clearly states that the twelve apostles did the speaking. It does not say God spoke through them. God did not possess them and manipulate their mouths for them. That's what devil spirits do when they possess mediums at séances. They, the twelve apostles, did the speaking in tongues. They moved their own mouths and formed the words themselves by their own freedom of will. The distinction here is that what they spoke was as the spirit gave them utterance.

When we speak in a tongue, we do the speaking, and as we speak God energises the spirit within us with the words that we speak. The renewed mind is the key to power. When we renew our minds and step out with believing we can speak in tongues, and as we speak the power within us is energised. That's why the renewed mind is the key to power. They, the apostles, did the speaking, but it was God who gave them the words that they spoke. To understand this distinction is important. God never possesses anyone, ever. Only devil spirits do that. If you pray for God to make you speak in tongues, or make you do anything for that matter, you are asking God to possess you. Do you really think he is going to answer prayers like that? No, he won't, but a devil spirit will. Where do people learn to open their minds to stuff like that anyway? Where else, but at those spiritually filthy churches and ministries they insist on going to every week that God does not attend.

> Acts 2:4
> And they were all filled with the Holy Ghost, [pneuma hagion – holy spirit] and began to speak with other tongues, as the Spirit [pneuma] gave them utterance.

If someone wants to become a guitarist or a pianist, not only must they acquire an instrument, but they must also learn how to play it. No one becomes a musician by simply owning an instrument. Similarly with spiritual matters. No one walks by the spirit and develops a relationship with God simply by being born again and having the gift of holy spirit. We must learn to energise the gift of holy spirit if we want to walk by the spirit.

Without a plan, no one achieves anything in life. To learn to play an instrument can be as simple as attending a class for an hour each week and doing half an hour's practice every day. That is a plan. If someone is faithful to that plan, they will become a musician. The longer they stick with their plan, the better musician they will be. If we are to become spiritual men and women, we must have a plan, which can be as simple as attending a church in someone's home where the accurate word of God is taught and believed, studying for half an hour every day, and speaking in tongues much. It doesn't have to take forever either, an aspiring guitarist or pianist can play beautiful songs by learning just three chords.

Now, before moving any further into the holy spirit field, we need to understand a few simple things.

> Acts 2:4
> And they were all filled with the Holy Ghost, [pneuma hagion – holy spirit] and began to speak with other tongues, as the Spirit [pneuma] gave them utterance.

In the bible, regardless of which version you have, the Greek words *pneuma hagion* are arbitrarily capitalised, and often with deliberate intent to deceive. There is a big difference between Holy Spirit, God, and the gift he gave, holy spirit, which we receive at the time of the new birth. Consequently, there is much confusion between God, who is Holy Spirit, and his gift, which is holy spirit.

Ancient Greek texts did not have upper and lower cases to differentiate between proper nouns. The sense of most nouns are not affected whether or not they are capitalised, but this is not true of pneuma and pneuma hagion. There is a universe of difference between Holy Spirit and holy spirit. Here is an excellent example where the two have been properly translated and the difference is clear.

> John 3:6
> That which is born of the flesh is flesh; and that which is born of the Spirit is spirit.

This is accurate capitalisation of pneuma, highlighting the difference between God and his gift. It is important that we recognise and understand this difference when reading the bible. In the Stephens Greek text, from which our KJV was translated, the word *pneuma* is used 385 times. It is translated Spirit – 133 times, spirit – 153 times, spiritual – 1, ghost – 2, life – 1, wind – 1, and spiritually – 1. With *hagion*, it is used as Holy Spirit 4 times and Holy Ghost 89 times.

A further challenge arises with the understanding of *pneuma* and *hagion* because the article *the* has been added and deleted by the KJV translators whenever they felt like it. In the Aramaic language – which most scholars believe was the original language of the written bible while Greek a translation from it – there was no article *the* at all. There is a big difference between pneuma hagion and *the* pneuma hagion. Here is an example.

> Luke 11:11-13
> If a son shall ask bread of any of you that is a father, will he give him a stone? or if *he ask* a fish, will he for a fish give him a serpent?
>
> Or if he shall ask an egg, will he offer him a scorpion?
>
> If ye then, being evil, know how to give good gifts unto your children: how much more shall *your* heavenly Father give ~~the~~ Holy Spirit [holy spirit] to them that ask him?

God would hardly give himself to those who ask him, so this must be referring to the gift of holy spirit. Jesus Christ was teaching about the coming gift of holy spirit, which was not yet available. He knew it was coming and he was preparing people to receive it. However, people were afraid they might receive something harmful like a devil spirit, so he was dealing with it.

To our minds, these verses don't carry the intended impact because we don't understand the culture. When we think of bread, for example, we think of packaged sliced loaves, but to understand the truths in these verses we need to think in terms of the customs prevalent in Jesus Christ's day. They didn't have supermarkets providing all their food for them back then, so they made their own bread. Considering the garbage the supermarkets are poisoning and drugging us with today, perhaps going back to making our own bread isn't such a bad idea. Anyway, back to the point, they made round flat bread on small round flat stones heated on open fires. After a while with constant use, these stones would actually start to look like the bread itself. If you bit into one, however, you would break your teeth. The point is, if we wouldn't make the mistake of handing one of these stones that looked like bread to our children to eat, would God make the mistake of accidentally giving us a devil spirit when we carry out the instructions on how to receive holy spirit in Romans 10:9?

> Romans 10:9
> That if thou shalt confess with thy mouth the Lord Jesus, and shalt believe in thine heart that God hath raised him from the dead, thou shalt be saved [sozō – made whole].

How on earth can you mistake a fish for a serpent? Again, we have to understand the orientalism. This is talking about two fish which are similar in appearance, but one of which is poisonous. Regarding the egg and the scorpion, there is a species of scorpion in the middle east which actually resembles an egg when it curls up. If we can distinguish between poisonous and non poisonous fish, and between eggs and scorpions, and protect our children by giving them good food to eat rather than something that might kill them, surely God is capable of making sure we don't receive a nasty devil spirit by mistake at the time of the new birth.

The context is clearly talking about God giving his gift. God doesn't give himself to them that ask him, he gives his gift of holy spirit, so this is a clear example of an erroneous capitalisation of pneuma hagion accompanied by an insertion of the article *the* which was not in the Greek texts. The article *the* should be deleted. God, who is Holy Spirit, gives his gift of holy spirit to those who ask him.

Here is another obvious example of manipulation of scripture by capitalising pneuma hagion.

> Acts 19:1-3
> And it came to pass, that, while Apollos was at Corinth, Paul having passed through the upper coasts came to Ephesus: and finding certain disciples,

> He said unto them, Have ye received ~~the~~ Holy Ghost [holy spirit] since ye believed? And they said unto him, We have not so much as heard whether there be any Holy Ghost [holy spirit].
>
> And he said unto them, Unto what then were ye baptized? And they said, Unto John's baptism.

Paul found disciples. A disciple, by definition, would obviously have heard of God. I mean, everyone has heard of God, right? Paul didn't ask them if they'd received God, he asked them if they had received his gift. They didn't reply they'd never heard of God, but that they'd not heard anything about his gift. They had no idea God had given them a gift. They had no idea about the new birth and the power they had. All they knew was water baptism.

> Acts 19:4-6
> Then said Paul, John verily baptized with the baptism of repentance, saying unto the people, that they should believe on him which should come after him, that is, on Christ Jesus.
>
> When they heard *this*, they were baptized in the name of the Lord Jesus.
>
> And when Paul had laid *his* hands upon them, the Holy Ghost [holy spirit] came on them; and they spake with tongues, and prophesied.

If we want to get to know God, then it is imperative that when we read his word we understand it. We need to know when the bible is talking about the gift of holy spirit and when it is talking about God, who is *the* Holy Spirit. See Appendix 1 for a full list of every use of *pneuma* in the new testament and how it's used. In Acts chapter 2, we can delete the article *the* and ditch the capitalisation of holy spirit.

> Acts 2:4
> And they were all filled [plethō] with ~~the~~ Holy Ghost [holy spirit], and began to speak with other tongues, as the Spirit gave them utterance.

There are a number of Greek words translated *fill* in the bible, and in this study we will look at two – *pleroō* and *plethō*. *Pleroō* means filled to capacity, *Plethō* means filled to overflowing. *Pleroō* can be seen in verse 2, where the house was filled [pleroō – filled to capacity] where they were sitting.

> Acts 2:2
> And suddenly there came a sound from heaven as of a rushing mighty wind, and it filled [pleroō] all the house where they were sitting.

This sound filled the house, the temple area where they were sitting. This makes sense, because sound fills all the available space. If you are playing music, you will be able to hear it all around the room in which it is playing. You won't find a little space floating around somewhere in the middle of the room where you can't hear any music. Sound fills space to capacity, hence *pleroō*, which is also used in John of an odour, a scent, a smell.

> John 12:3
> Then took Mary a pound of ointment of spikenard, very costly, and anointed the feet of Jesus, and wiped his feet with her hair: and the house was filled [pleroō] with the odour of the ointment.

An odour is a gas, and a gas by nature expands to fill all the available space as well. So the entire house was filled to capacity with the smell. Now let's compare pleroō with plethō.

> Matthew 27:48
> And straightway one of them ran, and took a spunge, and filled [plethō] *it* with vinegar, and put *it* on a reed, and gave him to drink.

The imagery here very clearly sets the distinction. Ever sat in the bath with a sponge? Hold it under the surface and it fills with water, pleroō, but what happens when you lift it out of the bath? It is so full it overflows. This sponge offered to Jesus while he was nailed to the cross was literally dripping with drink. That's *plethō*, filled to overflowing. Our English word *plethora*, an oversupply or excess, comes directly from this Greek word *plethō*.

When *plethō* is used regarding the gift of holy spirit, it describes what happens whenever someone speaks in tongues or energises one of the other manifestations – the spirit overflows out of them.

> Acts 13:9-11
> Then Saul, (who also is called Paul) filled [plethō] with ~~the~~ Holy Ghost [holy spirit], set his eyes on him,
>
> And said, O full of all subtilty and all mischief, *thou* child of the devil, *thou* enemy of all righteousness, wilt thou not cease to pervert the right ways of the Lord?
>
> And now, behold, the hand of the Lord *is* upon thee, and thou shalt be blind, not seeing the sun for a season. And immediately there fell on him a mist and a darkness; and he went about seeking some to lead him by the hand.

Paul was filled to overflowing with holy spirit when he confronted this spiritualist sorcerer. In other words, the gift of holy spirit with which he was filled to capacity [pleroō], was energised and overflowed out of him [plethō] into the senses realm. The manifestation of holy spirit is an overflowing of supernatural power from the spiritual realm out into the senses realm. It isn't sorcery, but it is supernatural.

When someone is filled to overflowing with holy spirit, a manifestation is the result. When we were born again we were filled to capacity with holy spirit, completely filled, and when we manifest the gift by speaking in tongues, that spirit is energised and the result is an overflowing from the spiritual realm into the senses realm. That is what a manifestation is, an overflowing of spiritual power into the physical realm.

Regarding being filled to overflowing, check out this usage of *plethō*.

> Acts 13:45
> But when the Jews [Judeans] saw the multitudes, they were filled [plethō] with envy, and spake against those things which were spoken by Paul, contradicting and blaspheming.

Here come the church people again. You would think religious people who claim to worship the true God would be delighted that multitudes were applying the power of God for themselves. Quite the contrary, they overflowed with envy. There was a lot of spiritual filth overflowing out of the churches in Christ's day, just as there is a lot of spiritual filth spewing out of the churches in our day. Why do you think God refuses to dwell in temples made with hands? More to the point, why do people still go to those horseshit places? Those religious leaders were filled to overflowing with envy, and it manifested itself by overflowing out of their filthy mouths and into their actions. Back to Acts 2.

> Acts 2:4
> And they were all filled [plethō] with ~~the~~ Holy Ghost [holy spirit], and began to speak with other tongues, as the Spirit [God] gave them utterance.

As the apostles believed, the holy spirit they had just been filled to capacity with [pleroō], poured out of them and overflowed into the senses realm as they energised that spirit by speaking in tongues. As they believed and spoke in tongues, God gave them the words that they spoke. Jesus Christ had prophesied of this outpouring of the gift of holy spirit during his earthly ministry.

> John 7:38
> He that believeth on me, as the scripture hath said, out of his belly shall flow rivers of living water.

Jesus Christ was referring to the coming of the gift of holy spirit. This overflowing of the spirit, this *plethō*, this manifestation of the gift, is what he figuratively prophesied of when he referred to rivers of living water flowing out of people. Living waters is obviously a figure of speech as people don't literally have water flow out of them when they speak in tongues. In Jeremiah, God is also referred to as living water.

> Jeremiah 2:13
> For my people have committed two evils; they have forsaken me the fountain of living waters, *and* hewed them out cisterns, broken cisterns, that can hold no water.

God is a fountain of living spiritual waters. Figuratively then, this living water Jesus Christ mentioned is a reference to spiritual power which flows out of us. As we speak in tongues, spiritual power overflows out of us into the world. This is the living water Jesus Christ was talking about. I think we've all had quite enough of that broken cistern church shit hey.

Speaking in tongues is not being filled with God, nor is it a religious outpouring of some emotion. It is the manifestation of the holy spirit within us. This gift of holy spirit which we freely received at the time of the new birth is ours to energise at any time. It is up to us whether or not we speak in tongues. We do the speaking by our choice, it is something we choose to do, something we believe to do, and we are in control of it at all times.

41. The Ages of Spirit

Although we have looked at Acts 2:4 in some detail, there is still much to uncover. You just can't exhaust God's word.

> Acts 2:4
> And they were all filled with ~~the~~ Holy Ghost [pneuma hagion – holy spirit], and began to speak with other tongues, as the Spirit gave them utterance.

When a word or phrase is first used in the bible, God always gives us special information that carries through to every other usage of that word or phrase. To illustrate this truth, consider this record of Joseph, who had just been summoned from the Egyptian dungeons to interpret two dreams for Pharaoh.

> Genesis 41:14-16,28,32
> Then Pharaoh sent and called Joseph, and they brought him hastily out of the dungeon: and he shaved *himself*, and changed his raiment, and came in unto Pharaoh.
>
> And Pharaoh said unto Joseph, I have dreamed a dream, and *there is* none that can interpret it: and I have heard say of thee, *that* thou canst understand a dream to interpret it.
>
> And Joseph answered Pharaoh, saying, *It is* not in me: God shall give Pharaoh an answer of peace.
>
> This *is* the thing which I have spoken unto Pharaoh: What God *is* about to do he sheweth unto Pharaoh.
>
> And for that the dream was doubled unto Pharaoh twice; *it is* because the thing *is* established by God, and God will shortly bring it to pass.

This is the first occurrence of revelation being given twice, and Joseph told Pharaoh it was because the revelation was established. In other words, there was no way to avoid this famine, it could not be averted. From this we learn that revelation from the true God given twice is established and will come to pass. From this point on, whenever God says something twice, rest assured the revelation will not change. For example, consider this in Psalms.

> Psalm 103:10
> He hath not dealt with us after our sins; nor rewarded us according to our iniquities.

Here, God states the same thing twice, in two different ways. This is a figure of speech that establishes the truth that God will not deal with us according to our sins. Regardless of anything we have ever done, God has not and will not reward us according to our sins. You can see this beginning with Adam and Eve. God did not reward them for what they did. Instead, he came up with a plan of redemption to get them out of the mess they had made for themselves, and helped them deal with the consequences of their actions. This truth is established and has never changed because God stated it twice. God never deals with us according to our deeds. He will even help us with the consequences of our actions when we mess up. I doesn't matter what it is your guilt is destroying you with, God does not deal with you according to anything you've ever done. Yes, there are consequences for our actions when we do things wrong, but that's just life, that's not God punishing us.

We also learn from this that revelation given just once may change if the circumstances change. Consider Isaiah and Hezekiah.

> Isaiah 38:1-5
> In those days was Hezekiah sick unto death. And Isaiah the prophet the son of Amoz came unto him, and said unto him, Thus saith the LORD, Set thine house in order: for thou shalt die, and not live.
>
> Then Hezekiah turned his face toward the wall, and prayed unto the LORD,

And said, Remember now, O LORD, I beseech thee, how I have walked before thee in truth and with a perfect heart, and have done *that which is* good in thy sight. And Hezekiah wept sore.

Then came the word of the LORD to Isaiah, saying,

Go, and say to Hezekiah, Thus saith the LORD, the God of David thy father, I have heard thy prayer, I have seen thy tears: behold, I will add unto thy days fifteen years.

God told Isaiah to tell Hezekiah he was going to die, and to set his house in order. This wasn't mean of God as Hezekiah was the king and was responsible for God's people. God simply wanted to ensure Hezekiah took care of business before his death so the kingdom would enjoy a stable political transition to a new king. However, the revelation prompted Hezekiah to change his believing and so the revelation to Isaiah changed.

Here, in a real life situation, we see that revelation given once may change if circumstances change. Revelation given twice, however, is established. This is an important key to walking by the spirit. We learn all this from that first usage in Genesis.

Regarding the first occurrence of the new birth in Acts 2, the initial outpouring of the gift of holy spirit, the first manifestations of the Christ in us, is there anything important recorded? First occurrence always gives us important information. For a start, we can summarise what we learned in the previous session. Speaking in tongues is an overflowing of supernatural power from the spiritual realm into the physical realm. The holy spirit is ours to energise at will and it is something we control at all times. These truths are set here and never change. These truths still apply today and they will continue to apply until Jesus Christ returns to usher in the next administration.

Is there anything else we can learn? How about the fact that *all* the apostles spoke in tongues? This is important. They spoke in tongues, all of them, not just some of them, and this sets the standard for this administration, the Age of Grace. Everyone who receives the gift of holy spirit in this administration can and should speak in tongues.

I keep mentioning administrations so I guess this would be a good time to handle the seven administrations, the seven ages, the seven distinct and different time periods in the bible. The Age of Grace, the age in which we now live, is but one of them.

Every country in the world, every nation, every culture, and every civilisation since the dawn of time has gone through changes. Britain has seen changes from prehistory through the Saxons, Normans, Picts, Romans, Celts, Vikings, and others, each bringing with them a different way of life and changes in civilisation. Different peoples have differing laws and customs, and whenever civilisation changes occur, there are changes in culture, law, and life. Even unimportant things like political elections bring changes to law and life. For example, if a king or queen, or other head of state introduce laws granting human rights to homosexuals, and promote that lifestyle to our children by way of education and the media, that nation is headed towards extinction like Sodom and Gomorrah. However, if another king or queen, or another head of state decided to believe God instead of bending over for the jesuits and the United Nations, and would bring back the death penalty for homosexuality and carry it through, life for them and their people would change for the better. The point is, when there are changes in administrations, there are changes to life.

Similarly with changes of administration in the bible. Paul's epistles for example often contradict scriptures in the old testament. To illustrate this, recall that God told Abraham to circumcise himself and all the males in his family.

> Genesis 17:10,11
> This *is* my covenant, which ye shall keep, between me and you and thy seed after thee; Every man child among you shall be circumcised.
>
> And ye shall circumcise the flesh of your foreskin; and it shall be a token of the covenant betwixt me and you.

Paul contradicts this revelation given to Abraham in quite a few places.

Galatians 5:2-6
Behold, I Paul say unto you, that if ye be circumcised, Christ shall profit you nothing.

For I testify again to every man that is circumcised, that he is a debtor to do the whole law.

Christ is become of no effect unto you, whosoever of you are justified by the law; ye are fallen from grace.

For we through the Spirit wait for the hope of righteousness by faith.

For in Jesus Christ neither circumcision availeth any thing, nor uncircumcision; but faith [believing] which worketh [energeō – is energised] by love.

Why do Paul's epistles contradict the old testament? Does this mean the bible is full of contradictions, as many claim? No, it doesn't. Look, both Moses and Paul wrote by revelation what God told them to write, and God doesn't contradict himself. There had been administrational changes and of necessity there were changes in how certain things were done. When trying to make sense of the bible, we must recognise the administrations in which scriptures were written and apply them accordingly.

When Adam and Eve fell and the devil became the god of this world, there was a civilisation change which brought massive changes to life. Instead of being the lords of the earth, having dominion, authority, and power over everything, man lost his job and the devil was elected into power. The consequences were catastrophic.

Genesis 3:17-19
And unto Adam he said, Because thou hast hearkened unto the voice of thy wife, and hast eaten of the tree, of which I commanded thee, saying, Thou shalt not eat of it: cursed *is* the ground for thy sake; in sorrow shalt thou eat *of* it all the days of thy life;

Thorns also and thistles shall it bring forth to thee; and thou shalt eat the herb of the field;

In the sweat of thy face shalt thou eat bread, till thou return unto the ground; for out of it wast thou taken: for dust thou *art*, and unto dust shalt thou return.

Luke 4:6
And the devil said unto him, All this power will I give thee, and the glory of them: for that is delivered unto me; and to whomsoever I will I give it.

See, there was a change of administration from man being the Lord of the earth to the devil becoming the Lord of the earth. There were different rules before and after the fall of man. This is the first administrational change in the bible, from the Original Paradise to what we call the Patriarchal Administration. There was a change from paradise to an overthrown world, in which man suffered the consequences of death and the devil had the authority to rule the world as he pleased. This is a clear change in administration, with obvious changes to life.

The Patriarchal Administration was set up to keep man safe from the world's new Lord, the devil. Man had died spiritually, he had no spirit, so God could no longer communicate, no longer talk with him. Therefore, God had his word written in the stars so man could know and learn of him. This word in the stars included the plan of redemption about a coming messiah who would defeat the devil and deliver God's people from death. The devil then went to war with man to prevent this redeemer from ever being born.

Revelation 12:4,15-17
And his tail drew the third part of the stars of heaven, and did cast them to the earth: and the dragon stood before the woman which was ready to be delivered, for to devour her child as soon as it was born.

And the serpent cast out of his mouth water as a flood after the woman, that he might cause her to be carried away of the flood.

And the earth helped the woman, and the earth opened her mouth, and swallowed up the flood which the dragon cast out of his mouth.

And the dragon was wroth with the woman, and went to make war with the remnant of her seed, which keep the commandments of God, and have the testimony of Jesus Christ.

Make no mistake we are in a spiritual competition. We have a very real adversary who comes not but for to steal, to kill, and to destroy. As we walk according to the revealed word and will of God, we are protected from him, we have God's hedge of protection around us.

In the Patriarchal Administration, God set things up to keep his people protected, and this required communication. As man had died spiritually, this presented enormous communication challenges as all man had left with which to receive information was his five senses. He had no spirit, so he could no longer talk with God. Man was separated from God, cut off from him, so God had to come up with a way to get through, and the only way he could get through was to use primitive methods of communication, like writing his word in the stars, burning bushes and dreams. Spiritually, these archaic methods can be likened to using Morse code, semaphore, or sign language. It was a bit like banging pipes to pass messages between cells in the devil's new world prison order.

When God first spoke to Moses, it was out of a burning bush. Moses saw a burning bush with his eyes and heard an audible voice with his ears. God talked to Moses by way of primitive phenomenal manifestations because Moses had no spirit and could not talk with God.

Exodus 3:1-4
Now Moses kept the flock of Jethro his father in law, the priest of Midian: and he led the flock to the backside of the desert, and came to the mountain of God, *even* to Horeb.

And the angel of the LORD appeared unto him in a flame of fire out of the midst of a bush: and he looked, and, behold, the bush burned with fire, and the bush *was* not consumed.

And Moses said, I will now turn aside, and see this great sight, why the bush is not burnt.

And when the LORD saw that he turned aside to see, God called unto him out of the midst of the bush, and said, Moses, Moses. And he said, Here *am* I.

Later on, once Moses had learned a thing or two, God was able to give him spirit. Other men, like Noah, Abraham, Isaac, Jacob, Joseph, Joshua, Samuel, David, Isaiah, Jeremiah, and many others are also recorded as having had spirit. So, we know there was some kind of holy spirit available in the old testament after the fall of man. However, there are some striking differences between the spirit which was available in the old testament, and the gift of holy spirit we have today.

One major difference between the two spirits is that in the old testament only a handful of people were given spirit, whereas today in the Grace Administration *every* born again believer is given spirit. This is remarkable. Another major difference, is that old testament spirit was tailor made and custom built for specific jobs. Joshua, for example, was tasked by Moses to lead God's people into the promised land. To do that, he would need to know how to do it. There were no university courses available at the time on how to take promised lands, so he was stepping into the unknown. He had absolutely no idea what challenges lay ahead of him, or how he would deal with them. Before his death, God instructed Moses to lay his hands on Joshua, and from that time on, Joshua was filled with the spirit of wisdom. This is tremendous to understand.

> Deuteronomy 34:8,9
> And the children of Israel wept for Moses in the plains of Moab thirty days: so the days of weeping *and* mourning for Moses were ended.
>
> And Joshua the son of Nun was full of the spirit of wisdom; for Moses had laid his hands upon him: and the children of Israel hearkened unto him, and did as the LORD commanded Moses.

Another difference is that there were only seven manifestations available with the old testament spirit, not nine as there are today. Which manifestations do you think Joshua needed? Joshua didn't need word of knowledge, as he already knew what he was supposed to do – take the promised land. Word of knowledge would have been of no value to him or the children of Israel. He needed to know *how* to take the promised land, so God gave him word of wisdom. The spirit of wisdom, or word of wisdom, is a revelation manifestation which gives you information on what to do in certain situations when you can't know what to do by your five senses. See, old testament spirit was tailor made and custom built for specific jobs so men and women could carry out their spiritual responsibilities.

Another major difference between old testament spirit and the holy spirit we have today is that you could lose old testament spirit. Saul found that out to his cost when he refused to obey God and David was anointed king in his place.

> 1 Samuel 15:22,23
> And Samuel said [to Saul], Hath the LORD *as great* delight in burnt offerings and sacrifices, as in obeying the voice of the LORD? Behold, to obey *is* better than sacrifice, *and* to hearken than the fat of rams.
>
> For rebellion *is as* the sin of witchcraft, and stubbornness *is as* iniquity and idolatry. Because thou hast rejected the word of the LORD, he hath also rejected thee from *being* king.
>
> 1 Samuel 16:13,14
> Then Samuel took the horn of oil, and anointed him [David] in the midst of his brethren: and the Spirit of the LORD came upon David from that day forward. So Samuel rose up, and went to Ramah.
>
> But the Spirit of the LORD departed from Saul, and an evil spirit from the LORD troubled him.

Saul lost the spirit God had given him because he was rebellious, disobedient, arrogant, and stubborn. Whose fault was that? God's? Nope.

Saul could have changed and not lost the spirit he was given. We can see that in David's life. David later had Uriah the Hittite, one of his best men deliberately placed into a dangerous situation during a war where he would be killed. David did that so he could marry Uriah's wife who was pregnant with his child. Just as God had sent Samuel the prophet to confront Saul, God sent Nathan the prophet to confront David. However, unlike Saul, David realised what he had done and humbled himself. He even wrote a psalm about this after Nathan had confronted him. Note how David prays that God wouldn't take his spirit away.

> Psalm 51:1,2,11
> Have mercy upon me, O God, according to thy lovingkindness: according unto the multitude of thy tender mercies blot out my transgressions.
>
> Wash me throughly from mine iniquity, and cleanse me from my sin.
>
> Cast me not away from thy presence; and take not thy holy spirit from me.

David asked God to allow him to keep his holy spirit and not take it away. There you go, right from the scriptures, we can see clearly that old testament spirit was conditional and you could lose it. The holy spirit we are given today is unconditional, and once we have it, once we are born again of God's spirit, we are his children for eternity. The holy spirit we have today in the Grace Administration is unconditional.

As an exciting sideline here, verse 11 of Psalm 51 is that figure of speech when the same thing is stated twice in two different ways. For God to cast David away from his presence would have been to take away the spirit from him. It's the same thing. Without spirit, we cannot enter into God's presence. David knew that, which is why he begged God to allow him to keep his spirit. In this Administration of Grace, it is *impossible* for God to cast us away from his presence, because the seed with which he impregnated us at the time of the new birth is eternal life. We have a permanent spirit born within us which those in the old testament did not. God can no more take his seed out of us than our earthly father's could take theirs.

Another major difference between old testament spirit and the Christ in us, the gift of holy spirit, is that old testament spirit was measured out, or dished out in varying proportions or amounts.

> 2 Kings 2:9,10
> And it came to pass, when they were gone over, that Elijah said unto Elisha, Ask what I shall do for thee, before I be taken away from thee. And Elisha said, I pray thee, let a double portion of thy spirit be upon me.
>
> And he said, Thou hast asked a hard thing: *nevertheless*, if thou see me *when I am* taken from thee, it shall be so unto thee; but if not, it shall not be *so*.

Elisha did see Elijah go, and he did receive twice as much spirit as Elijah had, a double portion. If you count the miracles recorded in the bible that these two men of God performed, Elisha did exactly twice as many as Elijah.

The old testament spirit was tailor made and custom built for specific jobs, it was measured out in differing proportions, and it was conditional. The only man to ever have a full measure of the old testament spirit was Jesus Christ.

> John 3:34
> For he whom God hath sent speaketh the words of God: for God giveth not the Spirit by measure *unto him*.

John the Baptist by revelation recorded that Jesus Christ was the only human being to ever receive the full measure of the spirit that was available in the old testament. In this Administration of Grace, there are no differing amounts. No one gets any more, and no one gets any less. We all get the same measure of the spirit, the gift of Christ in us, and we all get everything that's available. We are all blessed with all spiritual blessings. All of us. None of us misses anything.

> Ephesians 1:3
> Blessed *be* the God and Father of our Lord Jesus Christ, who hath blessed us with all spiritual blessings in heavenly *places* in Christ:

Ephesians 4:7
But unto every one of us is given grace according to the measure of the gift of Christ.

Another major difference between old testament spirit and what we have today is that each time someone is born again of the gift of holy spirit it is an entirely new creation, something which has never existed before. Old testament spirit was not. Each one of us in this Age of Grace has something created within us at the time of the new birth which never existed before. It is a new creation, which means every single person who has the gift of holy spirit has something completely and absolutely unique, entirely different from anyone else's holy spirit.

2 Corinthians 5:17
Therefore if any man *be* in Christ, *he is* a new creature [creation]: old things [former things] are passed away; behold, all things are become new.

We all get the same measure, we can all manifest it the same way, but like earthly children, we are all different. Each one of us is inimitably and distinctively different and special to our father, God. We really are his children, and we're not clones.

So, the gift of holy spirit which we have today is remarkably different from the holy spirit which was available in the old testament. Even the holy spirit Jesus Christ had was different from the holy spirit we have today. It took Jesus Christ's death and resurrection to make the gift of holy spirit available. Without his death and resurrection there would have been no gift of holy spirit and no Grace Administration.

Now we understand old testament spirit a little better, let's return to the Patriarchal Administration, where things were set up to keep man protected from the world's new Lord. God wrote his word in the stars for them, and he also gave old testament spirit to the patriarchs so he could talk to them. A patriarch is a man who rules an entire family, a clan, or tribe. During the Patriarchal Administration, God set things up so his people could get information from him by reading his word written in the stars, as well as from the patriarchs who had spirit.

Incidentally, Jacob passed his patriarchal responsibilities and his inheritance to his son Joseph, which is why Joseph had spirit upon him and why the devil energised through his brothers to hate him so much they plotted to murder him. When God's people followed the direction of the patriarchs, that kept them protected because God could keep his people informed and wise as to what the devil was up to by talking to the patriarch who had spirit. If the devil had succeeded in having Joseph murdered, God's people would have been without protection because they would have had no patriarch with spirit. God protected his people during that time by passing information to the patriarchs who had spirit.

Eventually, however, God's people grew into a multitude so large the Patriarchal system could no longer do the job for which it was designed and a change was necessary. God's people had also lost the knowledge of how to read the word in the stars because parents were not teaching it to their children. So major changes were needed. We can see this in Moses' life. After he had led the children of Israel out of slavery in Egypt, we see him up from morning until night judging God's people. He was doing 12 hour shifts every day being the link between God and his people.

> Exodus 18:13-16
> And it came to pass on the morrow, that Moses sat to judge the people: and the people stood by Moses from the morning unto the evening.
>
> And when Moses' father in law saw all that he did to the people, he said, What *is* this thing that thou doest to the people? why sittest thou thyself alone, and all the people stand by thee from morning unto even?
>
> And Moses said unto his father in law, Because the people come unto me to enquire of God:
>
> When they have a matter, they come unto me; and I judge between one and another, and I do make *them* know the statutes of God, and his laws.

Clearly, the Patriarchal system was no longer adequate and a change was necessary. As God's people had also lost the knowledge of how to read his word in the stars, God had Moses begin writing the bible as we know it today. With Moses there was a change of Administration, from the Patriarchal to what we know as the Law Administration. From that time on, God's people were to follow the law, which was written in the old testament scriptures. God no longer honoured the patriarchal system, and being a patriarch was not an entitlement to any kind of spirit. During the Law Administration, spirit was given where it was needed, whether men were patriarchs or not. God's people had the written word in scripture, which they could refer to for guidance on spiritual matters, and if something came up that was not covered by scripture, they could then go and find a man or woman of God with spirit who would go to God on their behalf for their answers.

Samuel, for example, was not a patriarch, but he was a man of God, a prophet. In his day, Saul was searching for some missing animals, and there is nothing in the bible about that. How to find missing animals is not covered in scripture. Saul and his servant searched for them for days and couldn't find them, so additional information was needed.

> 1 Samuel 9:3-6
> And the asses of Kish Saul's father were lost. And Kish said to Saul his son, Take now one of the servants with thee, and arise, go seek the asses.
>
> And he passed through mount Ephraim, and passed through the land of Shalisha, but they found *them* not: then they passed through the land of Shalim, and *there they were* not: and he passed through the land of the Benjamites, but they found *them* not.
>
> *And* when they were come to the land of Zuph, Saul said to his servant that *was* with him, Come, and let us return; lest my father leave *caring* for the asses, and take thought for us.
>
> And he said unto him, Behold now, *there is* in this city a man of God, and *he is* an honourable man; all that he saith cometh surely to pass: now let us go thither; peradventure he can shew us our way that we should go.

Throughout the Law Administration, men and women had spirit upon them to whom God's people could go for spiritual guidance - men and women like Samuel, Nathan, Deborah, Isaiah, Jeremiah, Ezekiel, Elijah, Elisha, and many others. Often there were a few of them at one time, all available with spirit upon them for people to get answers from God. How long did the Law Administration last? We don't have to guess, the bible tells us. There is no private interpretation in this.

> Matthew 11:13
> For all the prophets and the law prophesied until John.

> Luke 16:16a
> The law and the prophets *were* until John:

The Law ended with John the Baptist. Why? Jesus Christ was around, that's why. John the Baptist was the last prophet of that Administration. At that time there was another change in administration, from the Law to the Christ Administration.

The Christ Administration, however, ended abruptly as the Judeans had the Romans brutally murder their messiah. After Christ's resurrection from the dead and his ascension, a new Administration was quietly ushered in, the Administration of Grace, the Administration of the Mystery, the age in which we now live.

This Administration of Grace will end with the return of Jesus Christ, as recorded in 1 Thessalonians 4, which event will usher in the Revelation Administration, the time of the wrath, as recorded in the book of Revelation. At that time, the devil will have his one world government and the earth will not be a pleasant world in which to live. Following the Revelation Administration, the final administration will begin, the final Paradise Administration, when everything is put right again and the devil and his spirits are introduced to the lake of fire.

Here are the seven Administrations listed in the bible.

The Original Paradise.
The Patriarchal.
The Law.

The Christ Administration.
The Age of Grace (the Administration of the Mystery).
Revelation.
The Final Paradise.

It is important to realise that with each change of administration, there were changes to life. That is why some things in one administration in the bible contradict things in other administrations. When interpreting the bible, we must interpret it with the understanding that with changes in administrations, there were changes in the bible too. For example, in the Law Administration there were over 900 laws. In the Administration of Grace we are not obligated to keep all those laws, and that's why Paul gave us different revelation regarding circumcision. It no longer applies. It isn't a contradiction, it was simply a change in life due to a change in administration.

> Galatians 5:2
> Behold, I Paul say unto you, that if ye be circumcised, Christ shall profit you nothing.

Perhaps the biggest change through all these administrations until the present day, is how God spoke with and fellowshipped with man. In the Original Paradise, man had spirit and could talk with God freely. After the fall man had no spirit, so God did his best to give spirit when and where he could to keep communication lines open while his plan of redemption was steadily working towards its fulfilment on the day of Pentecost. The patriarchs kept God's people informed, and when God's people listened to and obeyed the patriarchs, they were protected. Eventually, God's people grew into a multitude so large, the patriarchal system was no longer adequate and there was another change in administration. The Law was not a patriarchal system, and there were men and women of God with spirit upon them available as necessary.

When Jesus Christ was alive during his earthly ministry, God stepped things up another notch and we got to see his word actually living in someone who had the full measure of old testament holy spirit. All these changes had been gearing towards the Age of Grace, which began on the day of Pentecost. In this Age of Grace, everyone who is born again has the full measure of the gift of holy spirit and can talk to God directly themselves.

We all have direct and personal access to God every moment of every day. We no longer require patriarchs – or matriarchs for that matter – as Christ is our head, and any information we need that is not covered in the bible we can go directly to God ourselves for. Men and women with holy spirit today are not to go to God on our behalf and run our lives for us, their job is to minister and teach us how to energise and operate the gift of holy spirit for ourselves. They are not there to go to God on our behalf to get us our answers, and God will not energise in broken cisterns that attempt to run things as they were run in the Patriarchal and Law administrations.

The Age of Grace is absolutely not another patriarchal system. That is why God no longer dwells, no longer resides, no longer frequents temples made with hands. We must learn to walk by the spirit for ourselves. As soon as you have councils of men, like a board of directors running an outfit, you are in a temple made with hands and Christ is not your head. These man-made systems trick you into thinking that God works with them on your behalf. That is a lie because this is not a patriarchal system, and we are no longer in the Law or Christ Administrations either when that would have been true. God will no longer honour such a system, which is why he told Paul to tell us he no longer lives in temples made with hands.

Since the day of Pentecost, with the dawn of the Grace Administration, things have changed. In this Administration, because of what Jesus Christ accomplished, the gift of holy spirit has become available to everyone. There is no longer a need to go looking for someone who has spirit in order to get answers from God. We all have spirit and, therefore, we all have direct access to God. If we wish an audience with God, we have access directly to him at any time of day or night, wherever we may be.

> Romans 5:1,2
> Therefore being justified by faith, we have peace with God through our Lord Jesus Christ:

By whom also we have access [prosagogē] by faith [by believing] into this grace wherein we stand, and rejoice in hope of the glory of God.

We all have spirit born within us and it is that spirit that gives each and every one of us direct access to God. Access is the Greek word *prosagogē*, which means a leading to or bringing to the presence of someone, freedom of access, an introduction. Jesus Christ led us into the presence of God and we now have that introduction and freedom of access. We all have immediate and intimate access directly to God, our Father, by way of the holy spirit within us.

Hebrews 4:16
Let us therefore come boldly unto the throne of grace, that we may obtain mercy, and find grace to help in time of need.

Are we to run off to men to obtain mercy and find grace to help in time of need? That's not what the bible teaches in this Administration. That was what men and women in the Patriarchal, Law, and Christ Administrations did, but it is absolutely not what we do in this Age of Grace. My job as a minister is not to run your life for you, it is to teach you how to go to God yourself and take responsibility for your own life. I don't want to run your life for you and I thank God I don't have to. If you're wise, you'll tell those who want to control you in temples made with hands to fuck off. I teach you the word, you take responsibility for your own life, you get your life together with God, you learn to walk by the spirit for yourself, and then you teach others how to do the same.

One last thing, people today often yearn for those old testament signs and wonders they read about, like burning bushes, dreams, and voices from heaven. They were primitive methods of communication that God was forced to employ because man no longer had spirit and couldn't hear him. Man was spiritually deaf. A burning bush was like God using a torch to send Morse code signals to the earth in the hope someone would see.

In our day, would God work with a primitive Morse code system when there is a state-of-the-art holy spirit communications system in place?

The simple answer is, no, except in dire situations of ignorance when there simply wouldn't be any other way to get through. Talking bushes is not one of the manifestations of holy spirit.

Would a modern business rely on carrier pigeons to convey messages rather than use the telephones? Not if they want to remain in business they don't. Burning bushes and other old testament phenomena are gone, replaced by the gift of holy spirit. It is up to us to learn what it is we have and how to use it properly.

42. The Mystery

So what is this Age of Grace, this Administration of the Mystery, this time in which we live? What is so special about it? What sets it apart from all the others? Corinthians has some intriguing information.

> 1 Corinthians 2:6
> Howbeit we speak wisdom among them that are perfect [mature]: yet not the wisdom of this world, nor of the princes of this world, that come to nought:

The princes of this world refers to the god of this world and his devil spirits. We don't speak their horseshit, like climate change and homo is okay, because the wisdom of this world comes to nothing.

> 1 Corinthians 2:7
> But we speak the wisdom of God in a mystery, ~~even~~ the hidden ~~wisdom~~, which God ordained before the world unto our glory:

Here we find a reference to the mystery, often referred to as the great mystery or the hidden. A mystery is something that is hidden. If something is hidden, we don't know about its existence. From this we also learn that the mystery was ordained by God for our glory, it was for our benefit.

> 1 Corinthians 2:8
> Which none of the princes of this world knew: for had they known *it* they would not have crucified the Lord of glory.

Had the god of this world and his devil spirits known the mystery, they would not have murdered Jesus Christ. They didn't know anything about it because it was hidden. God kept the mystery a secret. No one knew anything about it, not even the god of this world. No one knew anything about it until God revealed the mystery to the apostle Paul.

Romans 16:25,26
Now to him that is of power to stablish you according to my gospel, and the preaching of Jesus Christ, according to the revelation of the mystery, which was kept secret since the world began,

But now is made manifest, and by the scriptures of the prophets, according to the commandment of the everlasting God, made known to all nations for the obedience of faith:

Peter refers to the Administration of the Mystery, the age of Grace in one of his epistles.

1 Peter 1:10,11
Of which salvation the prophets have enquired and **searched** [exereunaō] diligently, who prophesied of the grace *that should come* unto you:

Searching what, or what manner of time the Spirit of Christ which was in them did signify, when it testified beforehand the sufferings of Christ, and the glory that should follow.

This word exereunaō is only used once in the bible. Thayer defines it as to search out diligently, while Bullinger defines it as to explore, to search diligently. As it is only used once in the bible, we really need to look at ancient Greek literature to get a taste for the word, and there we find it used in reference to dogs sniffing out game. Dogs are used to flush out birds such as grouse and pheasant. The dogs sniff around and follow scent until they flush the birds out. That's exereunaō.

Old testament prophets, such as Moses, Elijah, Jeremiah and Isaiah, sniffed through the scriptures on the scent of this hidden mystery. They searched the scriptures diligently and prophesied of it, knowing there was something between the sufferings of Christ and the glory that should follow. They knew something was missing and they searched diligently through the old testament scriptures to try to flush it out. They didn't find it because it was hidden. Peter tells us that in addition to searching they also enquired about it, they asked God about it. Here's the record of Moses doing just that.

Exodus 33:18,21-23
And he [Moses] said, I beseech thee [God], shew me thy glory.

And the LORD said, Behold, *there is* a place by me, and thou shalt stand upon a rock:

And it shall come to pass, while my glory passeth by, that I will put thee in a clift of the rock, and will cover thee with my hand while I pass by:

And I will take away mine hand, and thou shalt see my back parts: but my face shall not be seen.

The back parts of God refers to the understanding of the old testament scriptures, while his face refers to the hidden time period of the grace administration which Moses knew was between the sufferings of Christ and the glory that should follow. Moses knew there was something hidden and asked God to reveal it to him. God told him that knowledge was not available. In the context of the mystery being hidden, look what Corinthians says about it.

1 Corinthians 2:8,9
Which none of the princes of this world knew: for had they known *it*, they would not have crucified the Lord of glory.

But as it is written, Eye hath not seen, nor ear heard, neither have entered into the heart of man, the things which God hath prepared for them that love him.

The knowledge of the mystery was not seen by any eye, nor heard of by any ear; it never even entered into the wildest imaginations of man's heart. The revelation of the mystery, the revealing of what it actually is, was something Jesus Christ discussed with his disciples.

John 16:12,13
I have yet many things to say unto you, but ye cannot bear them now.

Howbeit when he [it], the Spirit of truth, is come, he will guide you into all truth: for he shall not speak of himself; but whatsoever he shall hear, *that* shall he speak: and he will shew you things to come.

Jesus Christ told his disciples that the spirit of truth was coming and that when it came, it would guide them into the all truth. The spirit of truth is a reference to the gift of holy spirit which came on the day of Pentecost. This prophecy regarding the all truth was fulfilled when God revealed the mystery to the apostle Paul. Before God revealed it to Paul, it was not available to know about it because it was a mystery, it was hidden. Even angels wanted to look into it.

1 Peter 1:12
Unto whom it was revealed [the mystery] ... which things the angels desire to look into.

So what is the mystery? We know that if the devil and his ruling spirits had known about it, they would not have murdered Jesus Christ. So whatever it is, it must be something astonishing. As the mystery has now been revealed in the all truth given by revelation to the apostle Paul, let's discover what it is. Moses and all the other old testament prophets couldn't find it, but it's there for us to discover.

Ephesians 3:2-4
If ye have heard of the dispensation [oikonomia – administration] of the grace of God which is given me to you-ward:

How that by revelation he made known unto me the mystery; (as I wrote afore in few words,

Whereby, when ye read, ye may understand my knowledge [sunesis] in the mystery of Christ)

The revelation of the administration of the grace of God was given to Paul, which he mentioned previously in few words back in Romans 16 which we've already looked at. It is only by reading Paul's epistles that the understanding of the mystery comes. You can read the old testament scriptures exhaustively and you will never find the mystery in them. Why? Because it was hidden from old testament eyes. God had to keep it secret so the devil wouldn't know his plans. If he'd had even the slightest suspicions regarding what it was about, the devil would not have crucified Jesus Christ.

This word *knowledge*, sunesis in the Greek, is defined by Thayer as a running together, a flowing together with, and it was used in Greek literature of the confluence of two rivers, the place where two rivers joined and flowed together. As we read Paul's epistles with a background understanding of the old testament scriptures, knowledge will flow together in our minds as the two meet.

> Ephesians 3:5
> Which in other ages was not made known unto the sons of men, as it is now revealed unto his holy apostles and prophets by the Spirit;

The knowledge of the mystery was not made known to anyone before this administration. The old testament prophets searched diligently for it, but it was hidden, it was a secret, it was a mystery. God revealed it to Paul and here it is written in Ephesians.

> Ephesians 3:6
> That the Gentiles should be fellowheirs, and of the same body, and partakers of his promise in Christ by the gospel:

This is what the mystery is, a concise definition of it, but it embodies everything within the gift of holy spirit and what it means to us. To be fellowheirs with Christ, of the same body, and partakers of the promise encompasses being born again, having the seed of God born within us, having the gift of holy spirit, having eternal life. It is everything being God's child means. It is the ability to walk by the spirit with Christ as our head. In this administration it is available to become a new creation, a child of the creator with his spiritual incorruptible seed born inside us. And it is not just exclusively available to Judeans, it is also available to Gentiles, to anyone anywhere on earth regardless of ethnic, cultural, religious, or educational background.

> Ephesians 3:7,8
> Whereof I was made a minister, according to the gift of the grace of God given unto me by the effectual working of his power.

> Unto me, who am less than the least of all saints, is this grace given, that I should preach among the Gentiles the unsearchable [untraceable] riches of Christ;

The mystery was unsearchable, untraceable, untrackable through the old testament, but it was revealed to Paul, and he revealed that information to us in his epistles which make up the all truth prophesied of by Jesus Christ.

> Colossians 1:25-27
> Whereof I am made a minister, according to the dispensation [administration] of God which is given to me for you, to fulfil the word of God;
>
> *Even* the mystery which hath been hid from ages and from generations, but now is made manifest to his saints:
>
> To whom God would make known what *is* the riches of the glory of this mystery among the Gentiles; which is Christ in you, the hope of glory:

It is the Christ in you, the Christ in me that was hidden, and of which the devil suspected nothing. In the old testament, men and women had no spirit, they were dead. In this administration, men and women can be raised from the dead with power to operate the gift of holy spirit, walk with Christ as their head, and raise more people from the dead.

> Ephesians 5:14
> Wherefore he saith, Awake thou that sleepest, and arise from the dead, and Christ shall give thee light.

Every time we get someone born again, we raise them from the dead. These are the greater works that Jesus Christ referred to back in John 14:12. We really can do greater works than he did. Jesus Christ could not raise anyone from the dead and give them eternal life. We can.

When the devil and his spirits orchestrated the murder of Jesus Christ they had no idea what was coming. If they'd had even an inkling, they would not have crucified him. When Jesus Christ was alive and had the full measure of the spirit that was available then, he could only be in one place at one time. Now, in this Age of Grace, the Administration of the Mystery, everyone who is born again has Christ in them. The god of this world would rather have had Jesus Christ the son of God on earth by himself than have you and me walking around raising people from the dead. Man, the power and authority we have if we only knew it.

43. In Spirit and in Truth

Ephesians is set up in balance. On one side you have chapters 1, 2, and 3, which is the doctrinal section of Ephesians, while on the other side you have chapters 4, 5, and 6, which is the practical section of Ephesians, how to live the doctrine of chapters 1, 2, and 3. God wants us to live in balance. Not only does he want us to know the doctrine, he also wants us to live it. He says so in the first verse of the practical section of Ephesians.

> Ephesians 4:1
> I therefore, the prisoner of the Lord, beseech you that ye walk worthy [axios] of the vocation wherewith ye are called,

Worthy is *axios*, which means *appropriately* and implies *balance*. Our English word *axle* comes from it. So to kick off the practical section of Ephesians here, God beseeches us, God lovingly implores us, God begs us to walk in balance, knowing the doctrine and also living it in practice. Those who know the word but don't live it are not walking appropriately, they are not walking in balance. If someone does not walk by the spirit, they are walking by the senses, which is off balance and inappropriate. It is no surprise then to find that churches made with hands don't teach their people how to walk by the spirit, but rather teach doctrines aimed at improving a persons senses abilities, such as being nice to everyone and smiling inanely. Such an unbalanced lifestyle can only end in guilt, condemnation, and defeat for we are not to walk by the senses. This isn't about polishing up the old man, it's about putting the smelly thing off and walking by the spirit despite him.

> Romans 8:1,4
> *There is* therefore now no condemnation to them which are in Christ Jesus, who walk not after the flesh, but after the Spirit.

That the righteousness of the law might be fulfilled in us, who walk not after the flesh, but after the Spirit.

Those who walk after the flesh, who walk by the senses, who attempt to improve their old man, thinking that's how you move the word and please God, will only experience either condemnation and defeat, or they will become religious assholes. Attempting to improve the old man is the way of the broken cisterns of religion.

Walking by the spirit isn't about acquiring education, mastering musical instruments, learning languages, becoming cultured, developing social and administrational skills, or anything else related to our five senses abilities, it is about developing the Christ in you and learning to walk by the spirit. Demonstrating God's power is what this is about, not trying to impress the world with your human abilities. Paul put it quite aptly in Corinthians.

1 Corinthians 2:4,5
And my speech and my preaching *was* not with enticing words of man's wisdom, but in demonstration of the Spirit and of power:

That your faith [believing] should not stand in the wisdom of men, but in the power of God.

Amos was a man of God, but he was a swineherd, a man who fed pigs and who survived by eating figs, a socially demeaning fruit reserved for the poorest and lowliest of people. Amos had absolutely no social status whatsoever, but he was a man of God who walked by the spirit and God was quite happy with him. God loves us for who we are.

Amos 7:12-15
Also Amaziah said unto Amos, O thou seer, go, flee thee away into the land of Judah, and there eat bread, and prophesy there:

But prophesy not again any more at Bethel: for it *is* the king's chapel, and it *is* the king's court.

Then answered Amos, and said to Amaziah, I *was* no prophet, neither *was* I a prophet's son; but I *was* an herdman, and a gatherer of sycomore fruit:

And the LORD took me as I followed the flock, and the LORD said unto me, Go, prophesy unto my people Israel.

Never mind trying to impress anyone with your worldly abilities, what are you doing with the power of God? If you're walking by the spirit, then yes, perhaps an ability to play the guitar or sing might be useful to help you move the word, but without walking by the spirit the guitar and singing is of no value whatsoever, get it?

I never went to university, and I don't have a degree. Does that make me unworthy to teach the word? Be careful with your answer, because there is sufficient research and work in this class for 3 PhDs. God is only interested in seeing people walk by the spirit no matter who they are, and you don't need any old man abilities for that. Being able to read is basically the only qualification you need to learn to walk by the spirit.

If you don't think you're up to it, or don't think you're good enough to walk by the spirit, or perhaps think you just don't have what it takes, you need to change your thinking. You can't look at this from a senses evaluation, you have to learn to look at the Christ in you. Paul had no more spirit than any of us. We all have *exactly* the same amount of spirit he did, and we can all learn to energise it and demonstrate God's power like he did. Look at Ephesians again.

> Ephesians 4:1
> I therefore, the prisoner of the Lord, beseech you that ye walk worthy [axios] of the vocation wherewith ye are called,

Now be honest here. Do you think God would beseech us to do something that we were not able to do? Do you think God would implore us to do something of which we were incapable? Do you think God would beg us to do something that was beyond our power? No, of course not. Would you expect a one year old child to go out and get a job so he could pay rent? God isn't like that. He implores us to walk worthy, to walk in balance because it's something we can do. Even swineherds can do this thing. No one needs to be intelligent, or educated, or have a degree, or speak well, or have talent or good looks or money to live for God. Nothing wrong with that stuff, but that's not what it takes to move the word.

God gave us the ability to walk worthy, to walk in balance, all we have to do is use what he gave us.

> Ephesians 4:7
> But unto every one of us is given grace according to the measure of the gift of Christ.

When we are born again, we receive a gift, and the gift here in verse 7 is a gift to each one of us as individuals. It doesn't say *but unto us is given grace according to the measure of the gift of Christ*; it says *unto every one of us is given grace according to the measure of the gift of Christ*. What's the difference? If I give a gift to a group, it would be a gift for all of them together, one gift they all shared. But if I give a gift to each person in that group, they all get a gift that is distinct from everybody else's gift. If each gift is measured with the same measure, no one gets any more than anyone else and no one gets any less than anyone else. Furthermore, a gift isn't earned, it is given freely. We each receive this gift, this measure of the gift of Christ by grace.

> Ephesians 2:4-9
> But God, who is rich in mercy, for his great love wherewith he loved us,
>
> Even when we were dead in sins, hath quickened us together with Christ, (by grace ye are saved;)
>
> And hath raised *us* up together, and made *us* sit together in heavenly *places* in Christ Jesus:
>
> That in the ages to come he might shew the exceeding riches of his grace in *his* kindness toward us through Christ Jesus.
>
> For by grace are ye saved through faith [believing]; and that not of yourselves: *it is* the gift of God:
>
> Not of works, lest any man should boast.

We have all been given grace according to the measure of the gift of Christ. So, did you get any more spirit than me? No, you did not. So why do some people think they know better than I do how I should live my life? You live your own life and quit sticking your snotty nose into mine unless I need reproof or correction. In this administration we all have spirit and we don't need patriarchs and overseers running our lives for us.

> Ephesians 4:7
> But unto every one of us is given grace according to the measure of the gift of Christ.

Did I get anymore spirit than you? No, I did not. We all got the same amount, we each were given grace according to the measure of the gift of Christ, which is the gift of holy spirit, that Christ in us. No one gets any more spirit than anyone else and no one gets any less spirit than anyone else. There is only one measure of the gift of Christ, and we all get the same measure, the same amount. You have spirit just as I do, so what right then do I have to try to be a patriarch and run your life for you? I have no right whatsoever. I have no interest whatsoever in running your life for you. You take responsibility for your own life, I'm not going to do it for you. The Age of Grace is not a patriarchal administration. We all have the spirit in full measure, and so we all have a responsibility to learn to walk by that spirit.

Trying to run a religious organisation, where a handful of men and women make all the decisions for everyone else is spiritual horseshit in this administration. God no longer dwells in temples made with hands. God knows everything, you don't, and I don't care how intelligent and educated and right you think you are. You cannot do God's job for him. What makes you think you can handle spiritual matters 4000 miles away by telephone? You don't know the first thing about what's going on in that area, but the home church leaders over there do. You think God is going to give you all the revelation for everyone? Horseshit, you err greatly not knowing the scriptures nor the power of God. Our job as ministers in this administration is to teach people to take responsibility for their own lives, to teach them to walk by the spirit and go to God for their answers. That's the only way Christ can be head over all things to the church.

Churches, religious organisations, ministries and groups controlled and administered by councils of men are really something. We know from scripture that they have no more spirit than we do, that we have the same measure of the gift of Christ that they do, so what makes them think they know what's best for us? Why are they not instead teaching their people how to walk by the spirit with Christ as their head? I'll tell you why, it's because they love their comfortable lifestyles, the tithe money people send them, the power that comes with the job, and the glory they get from men. What they should be doing if they want to serve God is run a church in their homes and teach people how to walk by the spirit. They should get back out into life and start moving the word instead. We need home church leaders teaching the word and ministering, men and women with a heart to walk by the spirit, not a queue of aspiring patriarchs falling over themselves for the highest positions in man-made temples. Run a church in your home and do something worthwhile with your life. The church in the home is very much God's plan for this administration of Grace.

Now we need to define our terms. The word *church* has come to mean a lot of things to a lot of people, but no modern understanding of this word comes close to its original biblical meaning. In order to understand the church in the home, we need to understand what the word *church* means. Remember, the bible is of no private interpretation, it is of no man's personal interpretation, and we are to understand it in light of what God intended when he wrote it. So the word *church* must be understood with the same sense, the same meaning as when God first used it in his word. To find out what God meant when he used the word *church* we must do a little study so we can rightly divide the bible here. Study is good!

> 2 Timothy 2:15
> Study to shew thyself approved unto God, a workman that needeth not to be ashamed, rightly dividing [orthotomeō] the word of truth.

Rightly dividing is the Greek word *orthotomeō*, a compound word derived from *orthos*, right or straight, and *temnō*, to cut. Literally, it means to cut rightly. This word is used in ancient Greek literature with reference to diamond cutters.

A raw diamond is just a lump of rock and looks unremarkable. It has a dull, battered external surface often covered by a gummy, opaque skin.

Cutting and polishing a diamond brings out its hidden beauty in dramatic fashion. The refractive index of a diamond is responsible for its brilliance, which is the amount of light reflected back out of the stone. A diamond's dispersive power is its ability to split white light into its component spectral colours. A diamond's fire is determined by how it's cut. When properly cut, a diamond acts as a prism and reflects light out in a brilliant flash of exquisite light. These flashes of spectral colour known as fire are only apparent after an *orthotomeō* right cutting of a diamond.

The word is like that. If you take the time to rightly divide the word – put in the effort to cut and polish it accurately and precisely – its light will fill your heart with a dazzling display of spiritual fire.

If we are going to enjoy a healthy spiritual lifestyle and manifest the power that God has freely given to us, we are going to have to study God's word in a planned, systematic fashion. Each of us is different and our daily schedules vary considerably. However, just as we wouldn't go without food for any length of time, we must ensure we keep our minds consistently well fed on proper mental food from the word. A healthy daily consistent diet is what we are after.

By the way, you don't need to spend years and years locked away in an attic, poring over scrolls and dusty text books before you start getting anywhere spiritually. This is not a scholarly thing, this is a dietary thing. So relax, you're not going to become some reclusive scribe studying ancient texts for the rest of your life. Quite the opposite, your existing life is going to blossom with vibrancy and adventure.

Rather than think *scholar* when you read the word *study*, think in terms of scheduling an hour into your day when you're going to sit down and munch on God's word. What would constitute a good diet? Perhaps breakfast, a snack at lunch time, and a decent evening meal would make for a reasonably healthy lifestyle. Fifteen minutes in the morning, fifteen minutes at lunch time, and half an hour in the evening should provide sufficient daily sustenance. Everyone is different, even with our eating habits, so figure out what works for you. What we are after is a healthy diet, so whatever works for you is right.

I think most would agree that a decent breakfast is a good way to start your day. So it is with God's word. First thing every morning you could read three chapters of the bible, starting from Genesis, and working all the way through. Start your day with God's word. It only takes a few minutes to read three chapters. You don't have to read fifty chapters, or study a whole scholarly text book, simply sit down and read three chapters of the bible for your breakfast. It might not sound like much, but I've read through the entire bible, cover to cover, over twenty times now just at breakfast time. You see, this isn't about stuffing all the knowledge of the whole bible into your head in a week, it's about diet – healthy, consistent, faithful daily diet. That's the key. And that's something anyone can do, something anyone can start right now.

> Acts 17:10,11
> And the brethren immediately sent away Paul and Silas by night unto Berea: who coming *thither* went into the synagogue of the Jews [Judeans].
>
> These were more noble than those in Thessalonica, in that they received the word with all readiness of mind, and searched the scriptures daily, whether those things were so.

Like the believers in Berea, we simply search the scriptures daily, we read the scriptures every day to see whether these things are so. Those people in Berea had lives, they had jobs to go to, they had children to raise, they had social events to attend, leisure pursuits, they probably enjoyed going fishing, hill walking, playing music, and many other things. Real people have real lives, and as with our food, we simply build a systematic, steady diet of God's word into our daily routine. Are we ever too busy to eat? If we are so busy that we can't eat properly and regularly, we will become ill. And so with the word of God. If we're too busy to build a daily diet of God's word into our lives, we will become ill with mental diseases like doubt, worry, anxiety, fear, frustration and other nasty stuff. If we enjoy a healthy daily diet of God's word, we will be healthy mentally, with a sound mind, prepared to take on any challenge in life that may present itself and defeat it.

Diet starts with breakfast, putting God first in your life. When you wake up, train your thoughts to go to God and thank him for your day, then grab your bible and have your breakfast. Lunch could be memorising a scripture. No, you don't have to memorise the whole bible, remember this is simply a dietary thing, a growing thing. If you maintain a healthy diet, you will eventually have scriptures like 2 Timothy 1:7 memorised, which can be a real help when you are tempted to fear.

> 2 Timothy 1:7
> For God hath not given us the spirit of fear; but of power, and of love, and of a sound mind.

How long would it take to memorise this verse? A few seconds? I think many of us unconsciously feel that simply memorising one scripture is a waste of time, and that if we were going to start we should really memorise hundreds of them. That is just not so. That kind of thinking will keep you where you are and you will never get anywhere. Think diet. You don't need to eat a hundred pies in one meal to be full, one will do just fine.

That's the great thing about this! It's something *anyone* can do. Just start the diet. Sure, after a few years you may have dozens of scriptures memorised, but you won't have any if you don't get your diet sorted out. Memorising one scripture a week is over 50 scriptures a year, which is over 500 scriptures in ten years. Memorise a scripture to start your week, and then spend the rest of the week running it over and over in your mind until it's burned in there permanently. A journey is taken one step at a time.

An evening meal is important. A good meal from God's word each day is important. You may have to schedule in half an hour, perhaps just after dinner, or before you go to bed. Perhaps study a session of this class every day until you know it so well you could teach it, or go to a home church where the word is rightly divided and taught accurately, where people teach you how to walk by the spirit. Back to 2 Timothy.

> 2 Timothy 2:15
> Study [spoudazō] to shew thyself approved unto God, a workman that needeth not to be ashamed, rightly dividing the word of truth.

Timothy is addressed to those with responsibility to take care of the church of God, so these truths are specifically written to leadership. New believers, babes in the word, wouldn't be required to spend so much time in study. This makes sense, because home church leaders have a responsibility to ensure that what they teach is accurate, timely, and nourishing. It is the parent's job to provide for the children. All enjoy the benefits of good food, but the cook is responsible to prepare the meals so they are as nourishing and tasty as possible. The home church leaders, those who teach God's word, are to study to rightly divide God's word so they can serve rightly divided truth that is tasty and nutritious. By the way, that does not mean digesting a DVD or cassette tape every week and then spoon feeding that garbage to the people God has entrusted to *your* care. You are to walk by the spirit, so do your job. God knows what is going on in your area spiritually and knows what needs to be taught, so learn to walk by the spirit and teach what God stirs in your heart. That is part of making Christ your head. That is how you move the word in your area.

The word *study* in Timothy is the Greek word *spoudazō*, which means to put some effort and some urgency into it. Here is another place *spoudazō* is used, only this time it isn't translated *study*, it is translated *diligence*:

> 2 Timothy 4:21
> Do thy diligence [spoudazō] to come before winter. Eubulus greeteth thee, and Pudens, and Linus, and Claudia, and all the brethren.

Travel in winter in the Middle East in those days was not something folks contemplated. Even travel in summer was dangerous as they had to travel on foot through country infested by robbers and wild animals. In winter, the dangers were compounded by the risk of blizzards and storms. In this verse, we can see then that to *spoudazō* to travel before winter would require haste and diligence to arrive before the bad weather hit. This is the urgency with which home church leaders are to expend energy in their study of God's word.

Now let's move into the subject of the church and enjoy some quality study time in God's word. What did the word *church* mean when it was written? If we know that, then we know what God meant when he used the word *church*. I can assure you, it meant something very different to what we understand by the word today.

The word *church* is translated from the Greek word *ekklēsia*, a compound word derived from *ek*, a primary preposition meaning *out from, out from among*, and *kaleō*, meaning *to call, to bid, to call forth*. Therefore, a literal translation of *ekklēsia* could be a calling out from among, or simply, a calling out, a calling forth.

There are three intriguing uses of *ekklēsia* in Acts 19. Paul was in Ephesus where the great temple of Diana stood, long before it was drowned in a swamp and became the habitation of frogs. Back in bible times, the local jewellers made fortunes selling little silver shrines to Diana, but Paul was threatening their comfortable incomes by teaching the truth that God didn't dwell in temples made with hands. One of the silversmiths got a bit pissed off with this and called a union meeting.

> Acts 19:23-29
> And the same time there arose no small stir about that way.
>
> For a certain *man* named Demetrius, a silversmith, which made silver shrines for Diana, brought no small gain unto the craftsmen;
>
> Whom he called together with the workmen of like occupation, and said, Sirs, ye know that by this craft we have our wealth.
>
> Moreover ye see and hear, that not alone at Ephesus, but almost throughout all Asia, this Paul hath persuaded and turned away much people, saying that they be no gods, which are made with hands:
>
> So that not only this our craft is in danger to be set at nought; but also that the temple of the great goddess Diana should be despised, and her magnificence should be destroyed, whom all Asia and the world worshippeth.
>
> And when they heard *these sayings*, they were full of wrath, and cried out, saying, Great *is* Diana of the Ephesians.

> And the whole city was filled with confusion: and having caught Gaius and Aristarchus, men of Macedonia, Paul's companions in travel, they rushed with one accord into the theatre.

The whole city rushed into the amphitheatre, the centre of Ephesian social, judicial, and political life, dragging two of Paul's companions with them.

> Acts 19:30-32
> And when Paul would have entered in unto the people, the disciples suffered [allowed] him not.
>
> And certain of the chief of Asia, which were his friends, sent unto him, desiring *him* that he would not adventure himself into the theatre.
>
> Some therefore cried one thing, and some another: for the **assembly** [ekklēsia - the church] was confused; and the more part knew not wherefore they were come together.

Now isn't that something? Here a rioting mob is called a church, an *ekklēsia*. In the new testament, *ekklēsia* is used 116 times, where it is translated church or churches 113 times. Yet here in Acts 19, *ekklēsia* is translated three times as assembly, with two of those translations in reference to a mob. Why didn't the translators render *ekklēsia* here as church? I don't know, but I suspect it was because it didn't fit with their stupid theology. This mob, this stadium full of rioters, is called an *ekklēsia*, a church. This fits well with the original meaning and intent of the word in that this mob was called out to a specific place for a specific purpose. This illustrates the correct biblical meaning of the Greek word *ekklēsia*. So when God used this word *ekklēsia* in the bible, this is what he meant, a group of people called out for a specific purpose. This meaning embodies any group of people called together for any purpose, including a riot. Next time you see riots on television, with folks setting fires to cars and smashing shop windows, you are looking at a church, a group of people called out for a specific purpose.

Acts 19:33-41
And they drew Alexander out of the multitude, the Jews [Judeans] putting him forward. And Alexander beckoned with the hand, and would have made his defence unto the people.

But when they knew that he was a Jew [Judean], all with one voice about the space of two hours cried out, Great is Diana of the Ephesians.

And when the townclerk had appeased the people, he said, *Ye* men of Ephesus, what man is there that knoweth not how that the city of the Ephesians is a worshipper of the great goddess Diana, and of the *image* which fell down from Jupiter?

Seeing then that these things cannot be spoken against, ye ought to be quiet, and to do nothing rashly.

For ye have brought hither these men, which are neither robbers of churches, nor yet blasphemers of your goddess.

Wherefore if Demetrius, and the craftsmen which are with him, have a matter against any man, the law is open, and there are deputies: let them implead one another.

But if ye enquire any thing concerning other matters, it shall be determined in a lawful **assembly** [ekklēsia].

For we are in danger to be called in question for this day's uproar, there being no cause whereby we may give an account of this concourse.

And when he had thus spoken, he dismissed the **assembly** [ekklēsia - church].

As we can clearly see, the word *ekklēsia* encompasses any group of people called out for any common purpose. A lawful assembly, a lawful court, a group of legal representatives called together to sort out a legal complaint is called an *ekklēsia*, a church. In verse 41, a confused and unstable mob is called an *ekklēsia*, a church. In studying the word *church* in the bible, it is of great importance that we remember that the proper meaning of *ekklēsia* is a calling together of a group of people for any purpose, and that it is used exclusively in reference to PEOPLE. It cannot be used to mean a church building, a religion, a ministry, or any ecclesiastical structure of any kind. No church or ministry can claim to be the church of God, the household of God, because ekklēsia cannot be used in that context. To do so is deceptive and manipulative as it is a wrong dividing of God's word.

The Roman Catholic church is not the church of God. The people within may be part of the church of God if they are born again, but the Roman Catholic church itself is just another temple made with hands. The Mormons, the Jehovahs, the Anglicans, the Baptists, and all the thousands of other *churches* around the world are not the church of God. The people within may be part of that church if they are born again, but those religions are all just temples made with hands. The Way International is not the church of God. The people within may be part of that church, but the ministry itself is just another temple made with hands, and God dwelleth not in temples made with hands. Back to Ephesians and walking in balance.

> Ephesians 4:1
> I therefore, the prisoner of the Lord, beseech you that ye walk worthy [axios] of the vocation wherewith ye are called,

So this walking in balance, this walking worthy has nothing whatsoever to do with walking by the senses, it has everything to do with walking by the spirit, which is what the practical section of Ephesians is all about.

Here in the practical section we are exhorted to endeavour to keep the unity of the spirit in the bond of peace, not to endeavour to keep the unity of the ministry in the bond of peace.

> Ephesians 4:3
> Endeavouring to keep the unity of the Spirit in the bond of peace.

A ministry or religious group is not the spirit, and to claim this verse teaches us that we are to build a unified ministry or group, claiming it is the church of God is a wrong dividing of the bible. No religious organisation can claim to be the church of God or the body of Christ. The body of Christ comprises disciples who walk by the spirit with Christ as their head, not any patriarchal system or any temple made with hands. Quite the contrary, endeavouring to keep the unity of the spirit necessarily includes staying well clear of temples made with hands.

Ephesians teaches that we are to put off the old man and put on the new, that we are to walk in light, and that we are to walk circumspectly. It teaches that we are not to be drunk with wine but be filled with the spirit, that we are to sing spiritual songs, which is to sing in the spirit by singing in tongues, making melody in our hearts. It teaches us that we are to put on all the resources of God, having our loins girt about with truth, that we are to pray always with all prayer and supplication *in the spirit*. Ephesians, the greatest revelation ever given to man is all about disciples, the faithful in Christ *walking by the spirit*.

Walking by the spirit begins with speaking in tongues. The first occurrence of the outpouring of the gift of holy spirit on the day of Pentecost makes this abundantly clear.

> Acts 2:4
> And they were all filled with ~~the~~ Holy Ghost [pneuma hagion – holy spirit], and began to speak with other tongues, as the Spirit gave them utterance.

They all spoke in tongues, not some of them, and it was the first thing they all did as soon as they were born again. That sets the standard for this administration, the Age of Grace. Everyone who receives the gift of holy spirit in this administration should speak in tongues right away. Speaking in tongues is the foundation to walking by the spirit. It is our spiritual breath. The first time Gentiles were born again, the first thing they did was speak in tongues.

> Acts 10:45,46
> And they of the circumcision which believed were astonished, as many as came with Peter, because that on the Gentiles also was poured out the gift of the Holy Ghost.
>
> For they heard them speak with tongues, and magnify God.

When Paul arrived in Ephesus, he found believers who had not been taught about the gift of holy spirit. He taught them the word, and they all spoke in tongues. Not some of them, all of them, and they did it right away.

> Acts 19:1-7
> And it came to pass, that, while Apollos was at Corinth, Paul having passed through the upper coasts came to Ephesus: and finding certain disciples,
>
> He said unto them, Have ye received the Holy Ghost [pneuma hagion – holy spirit] since ye believed? And they said unto him, We have not so much as heard whether there be any Holy Ghost [pneuma hagion – holy spirit].
>
> And he said unto them, Unto what then were ye baptized? And they said, Unto John's baptism.
>
> Then said Paul, John verily baptized with the baptism of repentance, saying unto the people, that they should believe on him which should come after him, that is, on Christ Jesus.
>
> When they heard *this*, they were baptized in the name of the Lord Jesus.
>
> And when Paul had laid *his* hands upon them, the Holy Ghost [pneuma hagion – holy spirit] came on them; and they spake with tongues, and prophesied.
>
> And all the men were about twelve.

Speaking in tongues is speaking the wonderful works of God.

> Acts 2:11
> Cretes and Arabians, we do hear them speak in our tongues the wonderful works of God.

Speaking in tongues is magnifying God, and it is your spirit speaking.

Acts 10:46
For they heard them speak with tongues, and magnify God.

1 Corinthians 14:14
For if I pray in an ~~unknown~~ tongue, my spirit prayeth, but my understanding is unfruitful.

Speaking in tongues, therefore, is worshipping God in spirit and in truth, and that's what God wants.

John 4:24
God *is* a Spirit: and they that worship him must worship ~~him~~ in spirit and in truth.

If you want to worship God, you must speak in tongues. There is no other way to do it. God isn't interested in our education, family lineage, how well spoken we are, or whether or not we use a napkin before taking a sip of water at the dinner table, only in true worshippers who worship him in spirit and in truth. The Pharisees and all the rest of the religious leaders were the ones obsessed with education, etiquette, and social advancement.

God's way and the world's religions are two very different ways. Take your pick, but choose wisely. God dwelleth not in temples made with hands, but devil spirits surely do. Never forget, it was the religious church leaders in Christ's day who had him murdered by the Romans. Stay away from patriarchs, and stay out of their filthy churches. Put your trust in God and learn to walk by the spirit instead.

Paul was probably the most cultured and educated man on the planet, a man who had been brought up with kings. Amos had been a swineherd, a man who fed pigs. I think that just about covers it for everyone, including you. It doesn't matter who you are or where you've come from, once you start walking by the spirit everything else in your life will fall into place and God's spiritual abundance will become yours.

44. Temples made with Hands

You won't find God in any religious organisations constructed by men because he does not frequent those places, he does not hang around in them, he does not attend them, he has nothing to do with them.

> Acts 7:48,49
> Howbeit the most High dwelleth not in temples made with hands; as saith the prophet,
>
> Heaven *is* my throne, and earth *is* my footstool: what house will ye build me? saith the Lord: or what *is* the place of my rest?
>
> Acts 17:24,25
> God that made the world and all things therein, seeing that he is Lord of heaven and earth, dwelleth not in temples made with hands;
>
> Neither is worshipped with men's hands, as though he needed any thing, seeing he giveth to all life, and breath, and all things;

A temple is any religious structure built by the work of men's hands. In addition to churches and cathedrals, religious organisations are man-made structures built by the work of men's hands. Is a religion a work of men's hands? Certainly. Is a church, or group, or denomination a work of men's hands? Unquestionably. They have all been built by men. Does God dwell in temples made with hands? Certainly not, and that includes the Roman Catholic church, the Muslim religion, the Way International, the Hindu religion, the Salvation Army, and every other denomination, ministry and religion. They have all been built by men.

Jesus Christ's biggest challenges came from the organised churches in his day, and it was the religious leaders who had him murdered by the Romans. You cannot and will not defeat the devil by constructing and maintaining churches made with hands. You will not find God in any church, organised religion, denomination or ministry, because God dwelleth not in temples made with hands.

So where does God dwell today then? If it isn't in religions, groups, ministries, churches, temples or other works of men's hands, where is it? The woman at Jacob's well asked Jesus Christ this very question. Let's go and meet this woman.

> John 4:5,6
> Then cometh he [Jesus Christ] to a city of Samaria, which is called Sychar, near to the parcel of ground that Jacob gave to his son Joseph.
>
> Now Jacob's well was there. Jesus therefore, being wearied with *his* journey, sat thus on the well: *and* it was about the sixth hour.

This is what you call living life. Jesus Christ had been travelling and he was tired, so he sat himself down for a rest. The disciples had gone into a nearby town to get some lunch, so he was on his own, enjoying the day. One interesting point here is that Jesus Christ was tired. Does God ever get tired? Nope, so Jesus Christ wasn't God then, was he? Then along came one of the women from the nearby town.

> John 4:7-9
> There cometh a woman of Samaria to draw water: Jesus saith unto her, Give me to drink.
>
> (For his disciples were gone away unto the city to buy meat.)
>
> Then saith the woman of Samaria unto him, How is it that thou, being a Jew, [Judean] askest drink of me, which am a woman of Samaria? for the Jews [Judeans] have no dealings with the Samaritans.

The woman was surprised. She was accustomed to Judeans ignoring her because they considered Samaritans half breeds. She had grown up with this Judean attitude, and yet here was this Judean man speaking to her.

John 4:10
Jesus answered and said unto her, If thou knewest the gift of God, and who it is that saith to thee, Give me to drink; thou wouldest have asked of him, and he would have given thee living water.

Jesus Christ obviously enjoyed talking to people, even if they were half breeds. He had no hang ups about people, no prejudices, no bigotry. He even spoke to Samaritans.

John 4:11-15
The woman saith unto him, Sir, thou hast nothing to draw with, and the well is deep: from whence then hast thou that living water?

Art thou greater than our father Jacob, which gave us the well, and drank thereof himself, and his children, and his cattle?

Jesus answered and said unto her, Whosoever drinketh of this water shall thirst again:

But whosoever drinketh of the water that I shall give him shall never thirst; but the water that I shall give him shall be in him a well of water springing up into everlasting life.

The woman saith unto him, Sir, give me this water, that I thirst not, neither come hither to draw.

The woman wanted this living water Jesus Christ was offering. Living water is mentioned in Jeremiah, and this is worth exploring.

Jeremiah 2:13
For my people have committed two evils; they have forsaken me the fountain of living waters, *and* hewed them out cisterns, broken cisterns, that can hold no water.

The living waters in Jeremiah refer to God, who is the fountain of living waters, therefore the living waters Jesus Christ referred to was a reference to something spiritual. In Jeremiah's time, people had forsaken the fountain of living waters and hewed them out man-made cisterns. A cistern is something man makes to hold water. If our supply is God, a living fountain, there is no requirement for a cistern, as a fountain has an endless supply. Men hew out cisterns because they do not believe God will supply all their need. Consequently, they turn their backs on the fountain and hew out for themselves cisterns, they build churches, ministries, religions and organisations to contain their religion. They put their trust in the work of their own hands rather than in the living God.

Not only are cisterns limited in their supply, man-made spiritual cisterns are broken, they are not capable of holding any living water, any spiritual power. Religions, churches, denominations and organisational ministries are all cisterns, man-made cisterns, broken cisterns that can hold no living water. Any flowing of living waters, any manifestations of holy spirit they once energised will eventually leak out until all that is left is dry religious ceremony. That is why God dwelleth not in temples made with hands. You will not find God in any religion, church, ministry, or religious organisation for they are all broken cisterns. If you want to find the unlimited supply of living waters, forget about cisterns, all of them, for they are broken and they leak.

Jesus Christ made another reference to living water in the gospel of John, where he was clearly referring to manifestations of holy spirit.

> John 7:38,39
> He that believeth on me, as the scripture hath said, out of his belly shall flow rivers of living water.
>
> (But this spake he of the Spirit [spirit], which they that believe on him should receive: for the Holy Ghost [holy spirit] was not yet *given*; because that Jesus was not yet glorified.)

This fits with what Jesus Christ was teaching the woman at the well. He offered her living water, which he knew he had come to make available, and it was a reference to the future gift of holy spirit which we now know came on Pentecost. Jesus then changed the subject.

> John 4:16-19
> Jesus saith unto her, Go, call thy husband, and come hither.

The woman answered and said, I have no husband. Jesus said unto her, Thou hast well said, I have no husband:

For thou hast had five husbands; and he whom thou now hast is not thy husband: in that saidst thou truly.

The woman saith unto him, Sir, I perceive that thou art a prophet.

Now that Jesus Christ had her attention, she asked him the one question that was burning in her heart.

John 4:20
Our fathers worshipped in this mountain; and ye say, that in Jerusalem is the place where men ought to worship.

The woman wanted to know where she could worship God, to know where she could have a personal relationship with him. The Judeans taught her that you found God in their temple at Jerusalem. Her people taught her that she had to go up to the pagan temples on the tops of the mountains. Doesn't this sound just like religion today? Join this group, join that group, join this religion, join that religion, join this ministry, join that ministry, right? It's all bullshit. You don't have to join any ministry or church to find God. You can find him anywhere, yet miss him everywhere. He's right where you are now, and you will discover and learn of him in the pages of the bible. You don't have to go to any church or group or ministry or religion to find God, just learn to read your bible.

John 4:21-24
Jesus saith unto her, Woman, believe me, the hour cometh, when ye shall neither in this mountain, nor yet at Jerusalem, worship the Father.

Ye worship ye know not what: we know what we worship: for salvation is of the Jews [Judeans].

But the hour cometh, and now is, when the true worshippers shall worship the Father in spirit and in truth: for the Father seeketh such to worship him.

God *is* a Spirit: and they that worship him must worship *him* in spirit and in truth.

The woman wanted to find God and wondered if going to the temple in Jerusalem rather than up to the temples built on the hilltops was the place to go. Jesus Christ told her to forget both because the Father desired people who would worship him in spirit and in truth, which was a reference to manifestations of holy spirit. This same truth is relevant today. If you want to find God, forget about churches, organisations, ministries, religions and temples. God dwelleth not in temples made with hands. If you want to worship God, you can only worship him in spirit and in truth, truthfully by way of spirit, and that does not involve performing weekly ceremonies inside religious buildings or ministries. Stay away from churches and groups and religions and ministries, no matter how much *truth* they claim to have, for God is not in them.

If any church, ministry, organisation, religion or group offers to teach you how to worship God in spirit and in truth only on condition you join them and give them your money, it is a bribe. Both God and Jesus Christ gave the word unconditionally, without charge. Folks gave their money to support Jesus, yes, but it was not conditional on getting the word in return, it was a thankful response to being taught the word free of charge.

In answer to the woman's question, Jesus Christ told her to forget about churches, all of them, because God was looking for people to worship him in spirit and in truth. What does that mean? Well obviously you cannot worship God by attending religious meetings, going to church, performing ceremonies, singing songs, going to prayer meetings, lighting candles, or reading bible verses. If you want to worship God, you must worship him in spirit and in truth, you must learn to walk by the spirit and that is not something that comes by going to church, joining ministries or groups, or leaving one religion to join another. I don't care what religion you are, or what group or ministry you are a part of, you can speak in tongues and learn to walk by the spirit right now right where you are. God dwelleth not in temples made with hands. He used to, but not anymore.

Back in the old testament, God instructed Moses to build the tabernacle, a tent in which he could live among his people. Looking back it is easy to see that the tabernacle was a temporary home for God, a temporary residence.

> Exodus 29:44-46
> And I will sanctify the tabernacle of the congregation, and the altar: I will sanctify also both Aaron and his sons, to minister to me in the priest's office.
>
> And I will dwell among the children of Israel, and will be their God.
>
> And they shall know that I *am* the LORD their God, that brought them forth out of the land of Egypt, that I may dwell among them: I *am* the LORD their God.

After the tabernacle was built, God moved in.

> Exodus 40:34,35
> Then a cloud covered the tent of the congregation, and the glory of the LORD filled the tabernacle.
>
> And Moses was not able to enter into the tent of the congregation, because the cloud abode thereon, and the glory of the LORD filled the tabernacle.

God has always desired with great longing to live among his people. His heart bursts to be with us, to have fellowship with us, and the tabernacle was a first step towards that reality. Later, Solomon built the temple, and with the coming of the greater, the lesser was no longer necessary. After the building of the temple, God moved home, he moved out of the tabernacle and into the temple, and that became his new home among his people.

> 1 Kings 8:2-11
> And all the men of Israel assembled themselves unto king Solomon at the feast in the month Ethanim, which *is* the seventh month.
>
> And all the elders of Israel came, and the priests took up the ark.

And they brought up the ark of the LORD, and the tabernacle of the congregation, and all the holy vessels that *were* in the tabernacle, even those did the priests and the Levites bring up.

And king Solomon, and all the congregation of Israel, that were assembled unto him, *were* with him before the ark, sacrificing sheep and oxen, that could not be told nor numbered for multitude.

And the priests brought in the ark of the covenant of the LORD unto his place, into the oracle of the house, to the most holy *place, even* under the wings of the cherubims.

For the cherubims spread forth *their* two wings over the place of the ark, and the cherubims covered the ark and the staves thereof above.

And they drew out the staves, that the ends of the staves were seen out in the holy *place* before the oracle, and they were not seen without: and there they are unto this day.

There was nothing in the ark save the two tables of stone, which Moses put there at Horeb, when the LORD made *a covenant* with the children of Israel, when they came out of the land of Egypt.

And it came to pass, when the priests were come out of the holy *place*, that the cloud filled the house of the LORD,

So that the priests could not stand to minister because of the cloud: for the glory of the LORD had filled the house of the LORD.

This is where God moved into his new home. However, Solomon's temple was also temporary housing, it was not God's permanent home among his people. In this Administration of Grace, since the day of Pentecost, God no longer dwells, God no longer lives, God no longer resides in temples made with hands. On the day of Pentecost, God moved house. Neither the tabernacle nor the temple sufficed to contain him, neither afforded the home comforts, the companionship and love he desired. They were provisional arrangements, temporary housing until a permanent home became available.

A basic understanding of the overall structure of the temple affords us a few clues in our search for God's dwelling place. The temple was basically divided into three separate areas. There was the court of the Gentiles, which was where Jesus Christ turned over the tables of the crooked merchants and drove out their animals. Another part consisted of the sacred courts for Judeans only, which Gentiles were not permitted to enter. The third part was the Holy of Holies, where God resided, and into which only the High Priest entered once a year. These three separate areas were divided off with walls and veils. Ephesians teaches us what Jesus Christ accomplished regarding these divisions between the Gentiles, the Judeans, and God.

> Ephesians 2:13
> But now in Christ Jesus ye who sometimes were far off are made nigh by the blood of Christ.

Those who were far off refers to the Gentiles mentioned in verses 11 and 12, who were aliens from the commonwealth of Israel, strangers from the covenants of promise, and who were without hope and without God in the world. The blood of Jesus Christ brought the Gentiles nigh, close, next of kin to God.

> Ephesians 2:14
> For he is our peace, who hath made both one, and hath broken down the middle wall of partition *between us;*

The middle wall of partition refers to the wall separating the court of the Gentiles from the sacred courts of the Judeans in the temple. As well as figuratively, at his death there was an earthquake which literally destroyed this wall separating the Gentiles from the Judeans. Jesus Christ broke that wall down. That's why he is our peace.

> Ephesians 2:15
> Having abolished in his flesh the enmity, *even* the law of commandments *contained* in ordinances; for to make in himself of twain one new man, *so* making peace;

Jesus Christ made of two one new man, the two being the Gentiles and the Judeans. Of these two, Jesus Christ made one new man, and that's how he made peace between us. He abolished that enmity between Judeans and Gentiles in his flesh, referring to the price he paid in giving his life.

> Ephesians 2:16
> And that he might reconcile both unto God in one body by the cross, having slain the enmity thereby:

The price Jesus Christ paid reconciled both Judeans and Gentiles to God in that one body, that new man he had made of the two. The enmity was slain, destroyed, it no longer existed.

At the same time as the wall of separation between the Gentiles and the Judeans was broken down, the veil separating all of us from God in the Holy of Holies was torn from the top to the bottom.

> Mark 15:38
> And the veil of the temple was rent in twain from the top to the bottom.

As well as breaking down the walls of separation, the earthquake also tore the veil, signifying that the way back to God was now open to all men, whether Judean or Gentile. What man had lost in Adam back in Genesis had been regained by Jesus Christ. Man had been reconciled back to God.

> Ephesians 2:17,18
> And came and preached peace to you which were afar off, and to them that were nigh.
>
> For through him we both have access by one Spirit unto the Father.

Through Jesus Christ, both Judeans and Gentiles have access by one spirit unto the Father, our heavenly Father, God.

> Ephesians 2:19-21
> Now therefore ye are no more strangers and foreigners, but fellowcitizens with the saints, and of the household of God;

> And are built upon the foundation of the apostles and prophets, Jesus Christ himself being the chief corner *stone*;
>
> In whom all the building fitly framed together groweth unto an holy temple in the Lord:

In contrast to Solomon's temple, which was made of stone, we are now built together as people into a holy temple, a permanent home for God through the spirit. It is the spirit, that gift of holy spirit we receive at the time of the new birth, that is our eternal life. God now lives in us through the gift of holy spirit. We are God's permanent home. God no longer dwells in temples made with hands, he lives within those of us who have his spirit and together we make up the true temple.

There is only one building God lives in now, and it isn't a temple made with hands, it is not any ministry, group, or religion, it is within those of us who are born again of his spirit, those of us who are his children. We make up the household of God. The household of God is not a ministry or a church building, because God dwelleth not in temples made with hands, and they are all the work of men's hands. We, his children, are the temple, the house, the home of the living God, and we are not temporary accommodation, we are his for eternity.

> 1 Corinthians 3:16
> Know ye not that ye are the temple of God, and *that* the Spirit of God dwelleth in you?
>
> 1 Corinthians 6:19
> What? know ye not that your body is the temple of the Holy Ghost *which is* in you, which ye have of God, and ye are not your own?
>
> 2 Corinthians 6:16
> And what agreement hath the temple of God with idols? for ye are the temple of the living God; as God hath said, I will dwell in them, and walk in *them*; and I will be their God, and they shall be my people.

Ephesians 2:22
In whom ye also are builded together for an habitation of God through the Spirit.

It is an interesting phenomenon that most folks in religions around the world think they are right, that they are in what they believe to be the true household of God. Quite how the devil instils this insipid lie into people is really brilliant. The vatican believes it is the only true church on earth, and the pope and the jesuits are committed to exterminating everyone on earth who is not one of them. All other christians regard themselves as right. Muslims believe they are the only true followers of God on earth. Buddhists believe they have found the true way to God. Jehovah's witnesses, a particularly insipid brand of religion, believe they are the only true way to God. Mormons believe they are the only true church on earth. The Way International believes it is the only true household of God and instils that lie into its followers. Folks, God dwelleth not in temples made with hands, they are all broken cisterns, they all leak. If God does not live in them, how can they be a source of living waters?

The good news is, God does not want you to leave one religion or church and join another. What he wants you to do is enjoy his endless supply of living waters. Forget ceremonies and rituals, forget going to church and making a fool of yourself. God isn't there anyway, so going to them is a waste of time. Constructing churches over the graves of once energised ministers is how the devil destroys the word they stood for.

God does not live in the vatican. God does not live in the Muslim religion. God does not live in the jehovah's witnesses. God does not live in the mormon church. God does not live in the Hindu religion. God does not live in the way international. These religions may teach they are the only true way on earth, but they are liars, for God in his word teaches that he does not dwell in temples made with hands. Regardless of which religion you were raised in, whether you've never been to church in your entire life, or even if you're a freemason or a jesuit, you can have fellowship with the true God right now right where you are and worship him in spirit and in truth.

45. The Church in the Home

Now that we've defined our terms and know what the word *ekklēsia* means, it's time to look at the church of God in this administration of Grace. In the old testament, God lived among his people first in the tabernacle and later in the temple, but God no longer dwells in temples made with hands.

> Acts 17:24
> God that made the world and all things therein, seeing that he is Lord of heaven and earth, dwelleth not in temples made with hands;

It is clear in scripture that God did at one time live in temples made with hands, but it is also abundantly clear in scripture that God moved home on the day of Pentecost when the age of Grace was ushered in. Where is his home now? Where does God live now?

> 1 Corinthians 3:16
> Know ye not that ye are the temple of God, and *that* the Spirit of God dwelleth in you?

We need to take a look at this. Here in Corinthians, these believers are referred to as the temple of God. We know that God dwelleth not in temples made with hands, so we can assuredly and categorically state that this temple referred to here is not any temple made with hands. This temple is most definitely not any ecclesiastical structure, ministry, church, religion or organisation which has been built by men. The spirit of God no longer lives in temples made with hands, so no ministry, church, religion or organisation can claim to be the temple of God, the church of God, or the household of God.

When we are born again and receive the gift of holy spirit, God moves into us. That's right, God now lives inside you and me. God now lives in people, not in temples made with hands. This is quite something.

In old English language, the pronoun *ye* was a plural pronoun, referring to everyone in a group, while the pronoun *thou* was a singular pronoun referring to individuals within a group. Modern English no longer has this distinction, but it is there in the King James. Take Romans 10:9 for example, where *thou* is used.

> Romans 10:9
> That if thou shalt confess with thy mouth the Lord Jesus, and shalt believe in thine heart that God hath raised him from the dead, thou shalt be saved [sōzō – made whole].

This is addressed to every person as an individual as this is something everyone has to make a decision to either accept or reject for themselves. If you confess Jesus as Lord and believe in your heart that God raised him from the dead, you will be made whole with body, soul, and spirit, and at that moment God will move in and make his home with you. Being born again isn't something that we within the church of God as a whole group are responsible to do together, this is something we as individuals do to get into that group. That's why *thou* is used here. Now look at this example.

> Romans 15:10,11
> And again he saith, Rejoice, ye Gentiles, with his people.
>
> And again, Praise the Lord, all ye Gentiles; and laud him, all ye people.

Here the word Gentiles obviously refers to all Gentiles, everyone within that group, so *ye* is used addressing all of them together. Back to Corinthians.

> 1 Corinthians 3:16
> Know ye not that ye are the temple of God, and *that* the Spirit of God dwelleth in you?

Here, a group of people is collectively called the temple of God. What group is this? Who are these people? Who is this addressed to? This is a good question, because it brings us to another extremely important key to the bible's interpretation. The bible interprets itself, yes, but we must apply keys to unlock that interpretation. We already know that we must understand the administrations in the bible so we can properly apply scripture written during each administration, as well as a few other keys, but we must also know to whom certain books of the bible are addressed. Not everything in the bible is addressed to everyone. If you read the bible thinking it is all addressed to you, major problems in understanding await to assail you. For example, take these verses in Romans.

> Romans 8:38,39
> For I am persuaded, that neither death, nor life, nor angels, nor principalities, nor powers, nor things present, nor things to come,
>
> Nor height, nor depth, nor any other creature [creation], shall be able to separate us from the love of God, which is in Christ Jesus our Lord.
>
> Romans 11:22
> Behold therefore the goodness and severity of God: on them which fell, severity; but toward thee, goodness, if thou continue in *his* goodness: otherwise thou also shalt be cut off.

According to Romans 8, nothing can separate us from the love of God which is in Christ Jesus our lord, not even death, yet three chapters later Romans states that if I'm not careful I'm going to be cut off. Most waggle their fingers at this and call the bible contradictory, but is it?

Men have different classifications for men and divide humanity into many groups, like nationality and culture, race and religion, but God only divides men into three general categories.

> 1 Corinthians 10:32
> Give none offence, neither to the Jews [Judeans], nor to the Gentiles, nor to the church of God:

Here Corinthians succinctly places all men into just three categories. According to God, every single human being on the planet is either a Judean, a Gentile, or part of the church of God. That's it. That is God's classification of men. Either we are Judeans, Gentiles, or church of God. According to Ephesians, the church of God is made up of both Judeans and Gentiles who have received the gift of holy spirit. This definition clearly and unquestionably exposes any ministry or group or religion that claims to be *the church of God* as liars. The church of God, by definition, comprises men and women called out from both Judeans and Gentiles who have been born again and who have received power from on high, the gift of holy spirit. Anyone who has Christ in them is part of the church of God, the *ekklēsia*, the called out of God. And I don't care what the Way International or the vatican claim to the contrary. By definition and by scripture, ecclesiastical and religious structures built by men which claim to be the church of God are liars. God dwelleth not in temples made with hands.

Okay, so if God classifies all men as either Judean, Gentile, or church of God, does it follow then that everything in the bible is addressed to either Judeans, Gentiles, or to the church of God? Yes, it does. Everything in the bible is addressed to either Judeans, Gentiles, or to the church of God, and to make it easy for us, all scripture in the bible is clearly addressed so there can be no mistakes. For example, who is the book of Isaiah addressed to? It tells us in the very first verse of chapter 1.

> Isaiah 1:1
> The vision of Isaiah the son of Amoz, which he saw concerning Judah and Jerusalem in the days of Uzziah, Jotham, Ahaz, *and* Hezekiah, kings of Judah.

The revelation of Isaiah was written specifically to Judeans. There is no guesswork in this. The bible is of no private interpretation. So is Isaiah addressed to the church of God? No, it isn't, it is addressed to Judeans who lived during the Law Administration. So when you read all the nasty prophetic stuff Isaiah confronted the Judeans with back in the Law Administration, you can relax because it doesn't apply to you personally in this Age of Grace. The same goes with everything in the old testament. Nothing in the old testament, including the so called gospels of Matthew, Mark, Luke and John is addressed to the church of God. Not one iota, not one jot or tittle.

Does this mean then that we can simply ignore the old testament? No, of course not. Without the old testament, nothing in Paul's epistles would make much sense. Without an understanding of the temple and how it related to God's people during the Law, the church of God being called the temple of God in this administration would mean nothing to us. The more we understand the old, the more we'll understand the new. Romans tells us just that.

> Romans 15:4
> For whatsoever things were written aforetime were written for our learning, that we through patience and comfort of the scriptures might have hope.

The whatsoever things written aforetime refers to the scriptures of the old testament, which are not addressed specifically *to* the church of God. I like to think of this in terms of an electricity bill a neighbour just received through the post. Could I learn anything from that bill? Yes, I could see how much units of electricity cost and check my own usage and budget accordingly. Would that be profitable? Oh yes, having the money put aside to pay your bills before they actually arrive is living the more abundant life. If my budget didn't match my electricity usage, I would be heading for financial problems. So if I could sit down, study my neighbour's bill and work out my own electricity usage, I could then budget properly to ensure my electricity bill would be covered when it arrived. I could learn tremendous stuff from that bill addressed to my neighbour. But would I take my neighbour's bill to the electricity shop or to the Post Office to pay it? No, that would be ridiculous. The bill isn't addressed to me so I don't have to pay it, he does. Although we can learn much from the old testament, we do not have to live under Patriarchal or Law systems of authority and governance.

The books of the bible addressed to the church of God are Romans, 1 and 2 Corinthians, Galatians, Ephesians, Philippians, Colossians, and Thessalonians. Timothy, Titus and Philemon are addressed to leadership within the church of God. You can't go wrong here, because each epistle from Romans through Thessalonians has to whom it is addressed clearly marked.

Romans 1:1,7
Paul, a servant of Jesus Christ, called ~~to be~~ an apostle, separated unto the gospel of God,

To all that be in Rome, beloved of God, called ~~to be~~ saints: Grace to you and peace from God our Father, and the Lord Jesus Christ.

1 Corinthians 1:1,2
Paul, called *to be* an apostle of Jesus Christ through the will of God, and Sosthenes *our* brother,

Unto the church of God which is at Corinth, to them that are sanctified in Christ Jesus, called *to be* saints, with all that in every place call upon the name of Jesus Christ our Lord, both theirs and ours:

2 Corinthians 1:1
Paul, an apostle of Jesus Christ by the will of God, and Timothy *our* brother, unto the church of God which is at Corinth, with all the saints which are in all Achaia:

Galatians 1:1,2
Paul, an apostle, (not of men, neither by man, but by Jesus Christ, and God the Father, who raised him from the dead;)

And all the brethren which are with me, unto the churches of Galatia:

Ephesians 1:1
Paul, an apostle of Jesus Christ by the will of God, to the saints which are at Ephesus, and to the faithful in Christ Jesus:

Philippians 1:1
Paul and Timotheus, the servants of Jesus Christ, to all the saints in Christ Jesus which are at Philippi, with the bishops and deacons:

Colossians 1:1,2
Paul, an apostle of Jesus Christ by the will of God, and Timotheus *our* brother,

To the saints and faithful brethren in Christ which are at Colosse: Grace *be* unto you, and peace, from God our Father and the Lord Jesus Christ.

1 Thessalonians 1:1
Paul, and Silvanus, and Timotheus, unto the church of the Thessalonians *which is* in God the Father and *in* the Lord Jesus Christ: Grace *be* unto you, and peace, from God our Father, and the Lord Jesus Christ.

2 Thessalonians 1:1
Paul, and Silvanus, and Timotheus, unto the church of the Thessalonians in God our Father and the Lord Jesus Christ:

The saints, the beloved of God, and the faithful in Christ Jesus all refer to those in the church of God. Which books of the bible are addressed to those of us in the Age of Grace who are born again and have the seed of Christ in us? Romans through Thessalonians. These are the books addressed to us in the church which contain specific doctrine which God expects us to apply and live. So am I expected to keep all the old testament laws, like circumcision, or live under a patriarchal system? No, those scriptures are not addressed to me. God even tells his church to avoid being entangled with the old testament law, which he refers to as a yoke of bondage.

Galatians 5:1-4
Stand fast therefore in the liberty wherewith Christ hath made us free, and be not entangled again with the yoke of bondage.

Behold, I Paul say unto you, that if ye be circumcised, Christ shall profit you nothing.

For I testify again to every man that is circumcised, that he is a debtor to do the whole law.

Christ is become of no effect unto you, whosoever of you are justified by the law; ye are fallen from grace.

Being entangled in law or even in a patriarchal religious ministry made with hands is something God commands us to avoid. Again, just to further clarify the point that God does not dwell in temples made with hands, these books, Romans through Thessalonians, are addressed to the church of God, not any ministry or religious organisation. In other words, anyone in any country in any part of the world, regardless of affiliations with any group or religious organisation can apply the truths of Romans through Thessalonians and immediately enjoy the benefits.

Anyone anywhere on the planet, for example, can speak in tongues and learn to walk by the spirit right now. You don't have to join the Way International and take their classes, join the Roman Catholics and become a homo priest, or join the Muslims and blow your guts out all over infidels, all you have to do is read the bible and apply the principles addressed specifically to you. This is something anyone can do anywhere in the world at any time. If you can learn to read the bible and allow it to interpret itself, you can learn to walk by the spirit and be an effective minister without joining anything. Joining religious groups is not something God commands us to do in this administration, in fact it is something he commands us to avoid.

So what about those apparently contradictory verses in Romans? Let's look at them again and see if we can make them fit now.

> Romans 8:38,39
> For I am persuaded, that neither death, nor life, nor angels, nor principalities, nor powers, nor things present, nor things to come,
>
> Nor height, nor depth, nor any other creature, shall be able to separate us from the love of God, which is in Christ Jesus our Lord.
>
> Romans 11:22
> Behold therefore the goodness and severity of God: on them which fell, severity; but toward thee, goodness, if thou continue in *his* goodness: otherwise thou also shalt be cut off.

We know Romans is addressed to the beloved of God, the saints, which is us. If you follow the context of Romans, you will find that the truths of Romans 8 are addressed to the beloved of God, the saints, those of us who have the gift of holy spirit and are part of the church of God. However, in chapter 9 there is a change of address.

> Romans 9:3,4
> For I could wish that myself were accursed from Christ for my brethren, my kinsmen according to the flesh:
>
> Who are Israelites; to whom *pertaineth* the adoption, and the glory, and the covenants, and the giving of the law, and the service *of God,* and the promises;

Who is Paul addressing here? He's talking specifically to his kinsmen according to the flesh, the Judeans. He is talking to the Israelites to whom pertained the adoption, the glory, the covenants, the law, the service and the promises. There has been a change of address. This is remarkable to see and understand, because the revelation on how to get born again, how to be made whole, how to receive the gift of holy spirit and become a saint in the church of God is given in a section of scripture within Romans that isn't specifically addressed to the church of God.

> Romans 10:1
> Brethren, my heart's desire and prayer to God for Israel is, that they might be saved [sōzō - made whole].

Think about that. Why would God have to tell you how to get born again if you're already born again? He wouldn't, would he? Romans 10 is addressed to those who are *not* born again, showing them *how* to be born again. Although Romans was initially addressed to the church of God, the beloved of God, the saints, there is a change of address in chapter 9. There is another change of address in chapter 11.

> Romans 11:13
> For I speak to you Gentiles, inasmuch as I am the apostle of the Gentiles, I magnify mine office:

Who is Paul addressing here? The church of God? No, the Gentiles. Look, this isn't difficult. The bible is easy to read and understand. You just need to know a few simple keys to unlock its interpretation for yourself and this is one of them. So the apparently contradictory verse we read earlier from Romans 11 is addressed to the Gentiles, not the church of God.

> Romans 11:22
> Behold therefore the goodness and severity of God: on them which fell, severity; but toward thee, goodness, if thou continue in *his* goodness: otherwise thou also shalt be cut off.

Yes, Gentiles had better watch out because if they don't get born again, they're going to die without spirit which will permanently cut them off from God. However, everyone in the church of God has that spirit and, therefore, cannot be separated from the love of God. Not even death can separate us from the love of God because we have eternal life. The Gentiles and the Judeans do not. If they do what it says in Romans 10:9, they will receive holy spirit and immediately become part of the church of God and these truths in Romans 8 will then apply to them.

> Romans 8:38,39
> For I am persuaded, that neither death, nor life, nor angels, nor principalities, nor powers, nor things present, nor things to come,
>
> Nor height, nor depth, nor any other creature, shall be able to separate us from the love of God, which is in Christ Jesus our Lord.

The bible does not contradict itself. It fits from Genesis to Revelation with a grammatical flawlessness that is breathtaking. You cannot break God's word. Back to Corinthians.

> 1 Corinthians 3:16
> Know ye not that ye are the temple of God, and *that* the Spirit of God dwelleth in you?

Here, the church comprising those who are born again and have the gift of holy spirit is referred to as the temple of God. Elsewhere in the epistles, individuals are occasionally referred to as tabernacles.

2 Corinthians 5:4
For we that are in *this* tabernacle do groan, being burdened: not for that we would be unclothed, but clothed upon, that mortality might be swallowed up of life.

Now stay with me here, because this is important. We know that the Greek word *ekklēsia* is only ever used in the bible in reference to a called out group of people, and that it cannot be applied to any man-made religious ministry or organisation such as the Roman Catholic church or the Way International. This is beyond dispute. So what is the temple of God? Well, it certainly isn't the Roman Catholic church or the Way International. It most certainly isn't the Jehovah's witnesses who don't understand the bible. It isn't the Presbyterians. It isn't the Baptists. It isn't the Lutherans. It isn't the Mormons. It isn't the Muslims. It isn't the Buddhists. It isn't the Free church, whatever that's supposed to mean. It isn't the Anglican church, the Hindus, or the Church of Scotland. It isn't any of them, because they are all temples constructed by men.

The temple of God comprises those who are born again, those who have the gift of holy spirit, those with Christ in them, called out from among both Judeans and Gentiles. If someone who is a Roman Catholic has the gift of holy spirit, or someone who is a follower of the Way International has holy spirit, or someone who is a Muslim gets born again, they are part of the church of God and therefore part of the temple of God, but the man-made religious temples they waste their lives attending are not.

Today you don't need any ministry running your life for you, just start a church in your home. Read your bible, speak in tongues much and learn to walk by the spirit with Christ as your head. Don't be afraid, for you can do all things through Christ who strengthens you. That strength doesn't come by following a board of directors, a council of men, or a pope, it comes from the Christ in you.

Yes, I know it's hard to leave a church, something you've been brought up in all your life, but just because you were born a Muslim, or a catholic, or a follower of the Way International doesn't mean you are where God wants you to be. They all say they're right, but the bible says God doesn't dwell in any of them. Leaving a church, ministry, or religion you've given much of your life to is difficult. I know that from experience. It can leave you feeling guilty, as if you've walked away from God. You can feel as if God no longer loves you or cares for you, or that you've walked away from his protection. Nothing could be further from the truth. When you walk away from a man-made temple and their patriarchal systems, you're not walking away from God, you're escaping from a religious dungeon.

God now lives in each of us. We all have the spirit of God living within us, and together we make up the church of God, the *ekklēsia* of God. The church is not to construct any more temples made with hands, it is to meet in people's homes. In this administration of Grace, God wants his people meeting in home churches, well away from temples made with hands. This is made remarkably clear in Romans through Thessalonians, the scriptures addressed to the church of God.

> Romans 16:5
> Likewise *greet* the church that is in their house. Salute my wellbeloved Epaenetus, who is the firstfruits of Achaia unto Christ.
>
> 1 Corinthians 16:19
> The churches of Asia salute you. Aquila and Priscilla salute you much in the Lord, with the church that is in their house.
>
> Colossians 4:15
> Salute the brethren which are in Laodicea, and Nymphas, and the church which is in his house.
>
> Philemon 1:2
> And to *our* beloved Apphia, and Archippus our fellowsoldier, and to the church in thy house:
>
> Acts 9:31
> Then had the churches rest throughout all Judaea and Galilee and Samaria, and were edified; and walking in the fear of the Lord, and in the comfort of the Holy Ghost [pistis – holy spirit], were multiplied.
>
> Acts 15:41
> And he went through Syria and Cilicia, confirming the churches.

God wants to hang out with us, fellowship with us, enjoy our company with us in our homes. The centre of outreach in the 1st Century was not some centralised ministry headquarters where everyone sent all their money to support a patriarchal hierarchy, it was in folk's homes. God lives in us, we are his church making up the temple of God, and he wants us to teach and minister in our homes well away from suffocating patriarchal temples of men. Get away from them for they do not walk by the spirit, but by worldly senses wisdom they seek through councils of men. Find a home church where people speak in tongues, walk by the spirit, and operate the power of God.

If there isn't one, start one. It isn't difficult. You and your family can get together two or three times a week, read a section of God's word, perhaps read a chapter from this class together, pray together, and learn to speak in tongues together. That's a basic start for a home church. That's where God wants to be, in your home with you, enjoying your fellowship. For the word to live it has to be moved out of temples made with hands and into people's homes, into home churches free from the restraints and control of central governing bodies of men.

46. Self Governing

Churches in the home should be self governing, self propagating, and self supporting. We learn this from the work of Dr Wierwille and Henry Venn, primary shapers and movers of recent outreach movements who taught God's word in meetings at their homes. God's plan in the Age of Grace is to teach and minister in our homes. To be successful, each home church is to be self governing, self propagating, and self supporting. Let's look at each of these, beginning with self governing.

First of all, what Dr Wierwille and Henry Venn meant by self governing was that each home church was to conduct its affairs from within, not allow itself to be governed by outside councils of men. Self governing, by definition, requires breaking away from the restraints and control of central governing councils of men.

Self governing, by definition, implies that home church leaders govern their churches, and they can only do that effectively if they walk by the spirit with Christ as their head instead of men. Following the direction of a council of men which teaches that God is giving them all the revelation regarding how the word is to move within the entire body of Christ is deceptive, manipulative, and contrary to God's word. We are not to follow councils of men, we are to follow men and women who lead by example, and we can only do that if those leaders are actually part of our everyday lives. This can only be realised in home churches. We don't need patriarchs stuck away in ivory towers, we need real people to follow in real life so we can learn to walk by the spirit for ourselves. That's how you edify and build up the body of Christ.

> *I'd rather see a sermon than hear one any day;*
> *I'd rather one should walk with me than merely tell the way.*
> *The eye's a better pupil and more willing than the ear,*
> *Fine counsel is confusing, but example's always clear;*

And the best of all the preachers are the men who live their creeds,
For to see good put in action is what everybody needs.
I soon can learn to do it if you'll let me see it done;
I can watch your hands in action, but your tongue too fast may run.

And the lecture you deliver may be very wise and true,
But I'd rather get my lessons by observing what you do;
For I might misunderstand you and the high advice you give,
But there's no misunderstanding how you act and how you live.

When I see a deed of kindness, I am eager to be kind.
When a weaker brother stumbles and a strong man stays behind
Just to see if he can help him, then the wish grows strong in me
To become as big and thoughtful as I know that friend to be.

And all travellers can witness that the best of guides today
Is not the one who tells them, but the one who shows the way.
One good man teaches many, men believe what they behold;
One deed of kindness noticed is worth forty that are told.

Who stands with men of honour learns to hold his honour dear,
For right living speaks a language which to every one is clear.
Though an able speaker charms me with his eloquence, I say,
I'd rather see a sermon than hear one, any day. - Edgar Guest

Now, where did Henry Venn and Dr Wierwille get this stuff about every home church being self governing, self propagating, and self supporting? From the word, obviously. From what we know about the Age of Grace and the word specifically addressed to the church of God, we must look at Paul's epistles to see it, as well as the book of Acts which documents the rise and expansion of the church in the 1st Century.

At the very start of this administration on the day of Pentecost, there were just twelve men who had the gift of holy spirit, the apostles. They didn't know the Mystery because it hadn't yet been revealed. They didn't know much about the Christ in them, because the details of the Mystery had not yet been given. That day about three thousand souls were added to the church. Those people also knew nothing of the Mystery and had their heads full of Law. Therefore, it's understandable that the

1st Century church continued to apply Law Administration standards for a time into the Grace Administration until God was able to gradually reveal the details of the new Administration. The book of Acts records this transition.

As an example, remember that although it was God's plan for the Gentiles to be a part of the body of Christ immediately, it wasn't until Acts 10, some 15 to 25 years after the day of Pentecost, that God was able to get through to Peter to take the word to them. The book of Acts records this transition from Law to Grace, and we have to understand that it took time for the 1st Century church to change and to adapt to the principles of the Grace Administration. Therefore, it is of no surprise to see patriarchal aspirations and leadership struggles within the book of Acts during this administrational transition.

The point is, you can't look at these leadership struggles and teach that God supports a patriarchal system controlled by a central governing body of men. Paul very clearly taught that God does not dwell in temples made with hands. It's just a pity that he ran off to Jerusalem in Acts 21 to try to save the 'ministry' when God had tried so hard to stop him from going. Just as Peter had not seen the depth of the truth regarding the Gentiles, Paul simply had not seen the depth of the truth that God no longer lived in temples made with hands.

God wanted Paul to stay with the Gentiles, but he ran off to Jerusalem to try to save a ministry that was under construction. There is no future in man-made temples. There is no future in the vatican, there is no future in Protestantism, there is no future in the Way International, in fact there is no future in any religion. God does not want us wasting our time with man-made temples anymore than he wanted Paul to go to Jerusalem. Stay with the people in your home church, show them how to walk by the spirit and teach them that God does not dwell in temples made with hands. God's people now and in future generations must be taught to avoid going to churches constructed by men.

Anyway, back to the twelve apostles on the day of Pentecost. This was the start of the rise and expansion of God's church in this Administration of Grace, so it's understandable that in the beginning these twelve men were looked up to as a leadership system by the people. As the numbers of believers grew and multiplied, it wasn't long before the word was spilling out of Jerusalem into Judea and Samaria and to the uttermost parts of the world. With this rise and expansion came squabbling and bickering over who would be the patriarch, the big boss their president. When Paul came along, the revelation of the Mystery was given and the details of the Grace Administration were taught. One of the things Paul confronted was patriarchal thinking in the minds of the church.

> 1 Corinthians 1:11,12
> For it hath been declared unto me of you, my brethren, by them *which are of the house* of Chloe, that there are contentions among you.
>
> Now this I say, that every one of you saith, I am of Paul; and I of Apollos; and I of Cephas; and I of Christ.

Isn't this remarkable? The 1st Century believers bickered over who was the president of their ministry. Look, the way is not a temple made with hands run by a patriarch, Jesus Christ is the way. That's what Paul was confronting. I don't follow Martindale, or the dalai lama, or Muhammad, or the pope, in fact, from now on I will never follow any man ever again unless he is my home church leader. Is this starting to make sense yet? Do you really think God gives other people, people you have never even met, people thousands of miles away, all the revelation regarding what you should teach as a home church leader in your area? Better wake up dude.

According to God's word, who and what is the way? Jesus Christ is the way, the truth, and the life. Is the way then some religious man-made temple over in America? No, it is not. Am I the way? No, I am not. Jesus Christ is the way. Am I setting up another temple made with hands here? No, I am not, I am showing God's people how to establish churches in their homes, move the word, and how to walk by the spirit with Christ as their head instead of men. The Lord Jesus Christ is the way, and a follower of the way is a follower of the Lord Jesus Christ, it is someone who walks by the spirit with Christ as their head and not men. If you think otherwise, you are not rightly dividing God's word. In the book of Acts, the believers were referred to as followers of the way.

Acts 9:2
And [Saul – later the apostle Paul] desired of him letters to Damascus to the synagogues, that if he found any of **this way** [the way], whether they were men or women, he might bring them bound unto Jerusalem.

Acts 19:9
But when divers [many] were hardened, and believed not, but spake evil of **that way** [the way] before the multitude, he [Paul] departed from them, and separated the disciples, disputing daily in the school of one Tyrannus.

Acts 19:23
And the same time there arose no small stir about **that way** [the way].

Acts 22:4
And I [Paul] persecuted **this way** [the way] unto the death, binding and delivering into prisons both men and women.

Acts 24:14
But this I [Paul] confess unto thee, that after **the way** which they call heresy, so worship I the God of my fathers, believing all things which are written in the law and in the prophets:

Acts 24:22
And when Felix heard these things, having more perfect knowledge of ***that* way** [the way], he deferred them, and said, When Lysias the chief captain shall come down, I will know the uttermost of your matter.

The believers in the 1st Century were known as followers of the way. This is beyond dispute. What is questionable is what is the way today? Is it a temple made with hands? No it isn't, not any more than it was then. A follower of the way is someone who follows the Lord Jesus Christ. How you follow the Lord Jesus Christ is by energising the Christ in you and walking by the spirit, not joining some dead religious temple constructed and maintained by men. Come on people, wake up! If you think the way is a religious ministry with its headquarters in America, you are deceived. If you want to walk with Christ as your head, get out of the world's man-made temples, and learn to walk by the spirit. Paul concluded his reproof in Corinthians with this.

> 1 Corinthians 1:30,31
> But of him are ye in Christ Jesus, who of God is made unto us wisdom, and righteousness, and sanctification, and redemption:
>
> That, according as it is written, He that glorieth, let him glory in the Lord.

How are we in Christ Jesus? It's referring to the Christ in us, the gift of holy spirit. Christ is you is what you receive at the time of the new birth. You in Christ is you learning to energise that spirit and walk with Christ as your head.

> Colossians 1:27
> To whom God would make known what *is* the riches of the glory of this mystery among the Gentiles; which is Christ in you, the hope of glory:

The riches of the glory of the mystery is Christ in you the hope of glory. It's Christ in you. When we are born again and receive the gift of holy spirit, we receive Christ in us, the hope of glory. We can do all things through this Christ in us, through this gift of holy spirit.

> Philippians 4:13
> I can do all things through Christ which strengtheneth [endunamoō – enables, empowers] me.

Who strengthens us? Christ strengthens us. How does Christ strengthen us? Does Jesus Christ personally come down to earth, knock on your door and hand you a magic pill? No, it's a reference to the Christ in you, the gift of holy spirit which we all have.

Endunamoō means to *empower*. How does Christ empower us? How does Christ enable us? By following councils of men and attending temples made with hands? No, a thousand times no. If you want power, you are going to have to energise that Christ in you, and that starts with speaking in tongues. You are to make Christ your head, so get out of those damnable ministries and religions, energise that Christ in you and walk with power in your life. So who then is our big leader? Who is our head? The bible says it is Christ, that Christ is our head.

> Ephesians 1:22
> And hath put all *things* under his feet, and gave him [Christ] *to be* the head over all *things* to the church,

God made Christ our head and he is the head over all things to the church, not men. When I am born again, I become part of the church, the called out of God, and Christ becomes my head. Christ is the head over all things to the church. Now ask yourself, does God give all the revelation for the church to just one person at the head of a ministry, or to a council of men? No, God never made councils of men to be head over his church, he made Christ to be head over all things to the church. We all have Christ in us, and how we make Christ our head is by learning to walk by the spirit of God born within us, that Christ in us.

> 1 Corinthians 11:3
> But I would have you know, that the head of every man is Christ; and the head of the woman *is* the man; and the head of Christ *is* God.

The head of every man, not some men, all men (which is an inclusive noun and includes women) is Christ. When a woman marries, her husband then becomes her head. This does not mean she doesn't walk by the spirit, it means that God gives specific revelation regarding that marriage and how it should move to the husband, not the wife.

Obviously, the head of Christ is God. So when we walk by the spirit, by that Christ in us, we are walking with Christ as our head. So for me to make a man (or woman) my head would be to contradict God's word. We are not to follow the direction of a board of directors any more than a married woman is to follow the direction of men who are not her husband. The way tree is God to Christ to you, not God to Christ to a patriarch to a board of directors to a limb coordinator to a branch coordinator to a home church leader and then to you. There you go, I've just documented the way tree from the scriptures addressed to us in the

Walking *by* the Spirit

church, and if you don't like it I don't give a fuck. Go and quote your old testament garbage at God and argue with him all you like. God no longer honours old wineskins and he will not work with them. God no longer dwells in temples made with hands.

Colossians 1:18
And he [Christ] is the head of the body, the church: who is the beginning, the firstborn from the dead; that in all *things* he might have the preeminence.

Christ is the head of the body, the church. The church, the body of Christ is made up of PEOPLE, men and women from among both Judeans and Gentiles who are born again. It is absolutely not any religious organisation or ministry constructed by men. Anyone who has Christ in them is part of the church of God. Ministries or religious organisations constructed by men which claim to be the body of Christ are liars.

Colossians 2:18,19
Let no man beguile you of your reward in a voluntary humility and worshipping of angels, intruding into those things which he hath not seen, vainly puffed up by his fleshly mind,

And not holding the Head, from which all the body by joints and bands having nourishment ministered, and knit together, increaseth with the increase of God.

To be vainly puffed up by your fleshly mind would be to walk by the senses, not by the spirit. Seeking wisdom from councils of men is seeking senses fleshly wisdom, not walking by the spirit. Sure, we all need each other and the body of Christ works together, but that does not negate your responsibility to walk by the spirit. Picking up a telephone to seek wisdom from men thinking that God gives them revelation for you is not how God set up revelation in this administration to work. You are to make Christ your head and learn to walk by the spirit for yourself.

The manifestation of the gift of holy spirit is your operation of the abilities God gave you, starting with speaking in tongues. Instead of thinking telephone when you need help, think God and energise that Christ in you. Why do you think God gave it to you anyway? So you could run to a telephone for help? If a telephone has become your very present help in time of trouble, then you're no different to someone who has made the government their god and relies on the government to supply their need. If you put men first before God, you are walking by the senses. God gave us the ministry of reconciliation, committed to us the word of reconciliation, and made us more than conquerors through the Christ in us, so do your job and energise that gift of holy spirit.

Now yes, when people are taking their first spiritual breaths having just been born again, they are going to need looking after. Think of this in terms of a family. When you teach and minister the word, you are responsible to look after the people God entrusts to you by teaching them and showing them how to walk by the spirit for themselves. They don't know the word and they don't know anything about spiritual matters, so they are going to continue to walk by their senses for a while. It's your job to look after them, teach them the word, and show them how to walk by the spirit. That doesn't mean you're a patriarch and you're going to run their lives for them, it means you look after them until they grow up and learn to walk by the spirit for themselves. God is their father, their parent, but you are to look after them and care for them until they are spiritually mature and can look after themselves.

Children eventually grow up and become responsible for their own lives, but when do you know when God's children grow up spiritually? This is a family thing. Parents just know when their children are mature enough to live their own lives. This isn't difficult to figure out. There comes a time when children grow up into adults and become responsible to live their own lives. The same is true spiritually. Once someone can walk by the spirit on their own, they are to make Christ their head and take responsibility for their own lives and then help others do the same. It isn't difficult to know when someone is walking by the spirit.

Can there be any doubt that the church of God is not any man-made religious organisation or ministry? No, this is indisputable. I really don't care how right you think you are or how right you think your ministry or church is. Whether you are a catholic, a Muslim, a follower of the Way International, a Buddhist, a protestant or any other brand of religion, if you think the man-made church you belong to is the church of God, you are wrong and you are teaching other people to be wrong. You are the blind leading the blind and you're both in the ditch. The church of God, the called out of God, the ekklēsia of God comprises both Judeans and Gentiles who have received the gift of holy spirit and have Christ in them. Being part of the church of God absolutely does not involve anyone joining a church, ministry or religion, understand?

Okay, now keeping this most basic understanding of the church in mind, that it is made up of those from among both the Judeans and the Gentiles who have received the gift of holy spirit, and that it is not made up of members of any particular brand of religion, let's head on over to Corinthians and take a closer look at the body of Christ.

> 1 Corinthians 12:13
> For by one Spirit are we all baptized into one body, whether *we be* Jews [Judeans] or Gentiles, whether *we be* bond or free; and have been all made to drink into one Spirit.

This one body is made up of Judeans and Gentiles, and refers to the church of God. The church of God, by definition, includes everyone who has the gift of holy spirit and does not refer to members of any religious structure built by men. If you are born again, you are part of the church of God and, therefore, part of the body of Christ. It is the devil, not God, who has built all the world's religions, and he did it with the sole purpose of blinding the eyes of the church and rendering it ineffective and useless. As long as you are giving your life and resources to any religious ministry, group or church controlled by men, you are wasting the life God gave you.

> 1 Corinthians 12:14
> For the body is not one member, but many.

The body of Christ comprises everyone in the church of God. We have all been made to drink into one spirit. We all have that spirit. This is not a patriarchal administration. Christ is our head, not any man or woman. Christ is to lead his church, not any board of directors. How Christ leads his church is by everyone in the body of Christ walking by the spirit. God gives revelation where it is needed, to his people on the ground moving the word, not to some exclusive club at the head of a religious organisation which thinks God is talking to them on behalf of everyone. No, he isn't. If that's how you think, your wisdom is earthly, sensual and devilish, sought from councils of men and not from the spirit of God. You are walking by your senses and using scripture from the old testament to justify your error.

It is the word that stands, not what we think. Do you really want to build a ministry based on old testament principles implemented during a time when God's people did not have spirit, a time when God's people needed leadership to go to God on their behalf? The epistles have much to say regarding that. You think there's safety in a multitude of councillors? I see nothing in the epistles about seeking wisdom from councils of men. However, I do see Paul obeying wisdom he received from the leadership in Jerusalem at that time and it almost cost him his life. Doing what councils of men have told me to do through the years has almost cost me my life more than once. You are destroying God's people because you are not teaching them how to walk by the spirit, you are teaching them to walk by the counsel of men.

1 Corinthians 12:27
Now ye are the body of Christ, and members in particular.

The 1st Century church had problems keeping Christ as their head, and were forever making men their head. That's why Paul confronted them about who their head was. Our head is Christ, not men. How we make Christ our head is not by following men in temples made with hands, but by walking by the spirit and energising the Christ in us. We do what God wants, not what we feel like doing, and certainly not what men tell us to do. God will *always* talk to you first. It's only when you're not listening that he tells someone else to get involved. God certainly talked to Paul first before sending Agabus the prophet to try to stop him from going to Jerusalem. God tried everything to stop Paul from going to Jerusalem, and he is still trying everything he can to keep his people out of temples made with hands.

Colossians 2:18
Let no man beguile you of your reward in a voluntary humility and worshipping of angels, intruding into those things which he hath not seen, vainly puffed up by his fleshly mind,

It is men who beguile us, who seduce us out of our reward. People are vainly puffed up by their fleshly minds because they follow counsels of men instead of walking by the spirit.

> Colossians 2:19
> And not holding the Head, from which all the body by joints and bands having nourishment ministered, and knit together, increaseth with the increase of God.

Our head is Christ, and it is through the Christ in us, energising that gift of holy spirit and walking by the spirit that the body of Christ is nourished and knit together and increases. If we follow men, we will be vainly puffed up by senses garbage, which includes building and maintaining temples made with hands.

> Colossians 3:1,2
> If ye then be risen with Christ, seek those things which are above, where Christ sitteth on the right hand of God.
>
> Set your affection [your thoughts] on things above, not on things on the earth.

In this Age of Grace, we are to seek things above, and how you seek things above is by energising the gift of holy spirit and learning to walk by the spirit. When you walk by the spirit, God will be there. As you learn to recognise his voice, and learn to walk with him, you will be helping to nourish and build up the body of Christ. That is setting your thoughts, your affections on things above, on spiritual matters. If you set your thoughts and affections on things of the earth, like constructing and maintaining temples made with hands, you will be turned into a blithering interfering religious idiot who thinks he knows how to run everyone's lives for them.

God needs people to rise up to oversee churches in their homes and be responsible for the people he entrusts to them. A home church leader is to be responsible for the church in their home, no one else. If any man or ministry tries to interfere and steal those people from you, tell them to fuck off. The love of money is the root of all evil and all they're after is the tithe money those people represent to help them support their garbage man-made temples.

If you run a church in your home, and you are faithful to teach and minister the rightly divided word, God will give you increase, God will entrust you with people to oversee. The home church leader is the one who makes the decisions regarding what is taught, when it is taught, and how it is taught. These decisions are not to be made by councils of men hundreds or thousands of miles away. The home church leaders are the ones God will work with both to will and to do of his good pleasure to give direction on how to move the word in that area.

If you run a home church, you are not responsible to anyone but God. Think of your home church as a small family where God's children can be nurtured from the nursery until they become responsible spiritual adults. God entrusts you with his children because he knows you are the right person for that job. Don't allow greedy men to steal them from you so they can get their sweaty little hands on their money.

This is the Age of Grace, we all have spirit, we all have direct access to God by way of that spirit, and we all have a responsibility to learn to walk by that spirit for ourselves. This is not open to debate. Thus saith God. This is the Way of the 21st Century.

47. Self Propagating

God's plan for his people in this Age of Grace is to use their homes for outreach. This is because we're a family and we're to treat each other as family. We're all children of God, we're all brothers and sisters together in the church of God. Just as families grow together in the world and new brothers and sisters are born into them, so it is with the family of God.

This of course can only happen if each home church is the centre of outreach for the move of the word in its area, not some headquarters of temples made with hands. Just as each family in the world is headed by the parents without any interference from without, so each home church is to be headed by the home church leaders without any interference from without. The worldwide network of families meeting together as the church in people's homes make up the body of Christ.

Understanding this, it's easy to see why God wants home churches to be self governing. To put it in plain language, each home church is to be the headquarters for the movement of God's word in that area.

The very term self propagating, by definition, implies that each home church has a responsibility to teach and minister the word in their area without any interference from without. For a home church to be self propagating, by definition, demands that home churches grow from within by way of their own efforts as a family. Only then can the church of God function with Christ as its head without any meddling or interference from patriarchs and councils of men. This, of course, does not mean help from without may not be sought and given, we're simply talking authority and control here. This is a family thing, not a patriarchal thing. Just as parents know best how to raise their children and it's no one else's business, so it is with raising God's children. We run churches in our homes and raise disciples in a family setting. As we walk with Christ as our head, God energises in us to will and to do of his good pleasure so we know how best to care for his children.

Regarding increase, we know that it is God who gives it, but without us doing some planting and watering, there is none.

> 1 Corinthians 3:6,7
> I have planted, Apollos watered; but God gave the increase.
>
> So then neither is he that planteth any thing, neither he that watereth; but God that giveth the increase.

Any home church that faithfully lives the word will see increase, growth from within. It is axiomatic then, that if a home church is not producing increase, it is not God's fault. Sure, go ahead, blame the world, blame the economic situations, blame the environmental situations, blame the politicians, blame everything and everyone, but the truth is, if you are doing things the word's way the increase will be there.

> 1 Corinthians 3:8,9
> Now he that planteth and he that watereth are one: and every man shall receive his own [idios] reward according to his own [idios] labour.
>
> For we are labourers together with God: ye are God's husbandry, *ye are* God's building.

Just as we need to plant and water to grow flowers, we need to plant and water to grow disciples. God gives increase as we labour together with him. As people grow and mature spiritually, they learn how to labour together with God for themselves, and so increase continues from generation to generation.

How the devil suffocates spiritual growth is by having men construct temples made with hands and installing patriarchs and councils of men to run them. Having a religious organisation take control of people is how the devil suffocates outreach.

Paul states very clearly in Corinthians that every man shall receive his own reward according to his own labour. I could teach a whole class on every man receiving his own reward according to his own labour, but I don't have time. I'm just going to spell it out and you can do what you like with it. Paul put it this way in Galatians.

> Galatians 6:4
> But let every man prove his own [idios] work, and then shall he have rejoicing in himself alone, and not in another.

Here's how it works. A man walks by the spirit, lives the word, teaches the word and ministers in his area. God gives increase and a home church family is born. Together they live the word, teach and minister, and God's children grow and mature. The home church leader is an example and walks by the spirit. God is a lamp to his feet and a light to his path, and he teaches the people God had entrusted to him how to walk by the spirit for themselves. Christ is his head because he operates the gift of holy spirit and God teaches him how to move the word in his area, keeping him wise as to what's going on spiritually so he can be an effective minister. The home church leader labours together with God, he walks by the spirit with Christ as his head.

Regarding daily fellowship and its relationship to outreach, the word is clear.

> Acts 2:42-47
> And they continued stedfastly in the apostles' doctrine and fellowship, and in breaking of bread, and in prayers.
>
> And fear [awe and respect] came upon every soul: and many wonders and signs were done by the apostles.
>
> And all that believed were together, and had all things common;
>
> And sold their possessions and goods, and parted them to all *men*, as every man had need.
>
> And they, continuing daily with one accord in the temple, and breaking bread from house to house, did eat their meat with gladness and singleness of heart,
>
> Praising God, and having favour with all the people. And the Lord added to the church daily such as should be saved [sozō – made whole by receiving the gift of holy spirit].

Walking *by* the Spirit

The book of Acts is God's blueprint, God's plan, God's manual on how to conduct home church families and move the word in outreach. This first section of the Book of Acts explains the foundations upon which home church families are to be built. In other words, without living the principles set here, outreach will never happen because there is no family foundation.

These principles for running home church families and raising disciples are continuing daily in one accord (with one mind, with one passion), eating together from house to house, praying together, and praising God, which is a reference to speaking in tongues. Just as life begins with breathing, so spiritual life begins with speaking in tongues, praising God by worshipping him in spirit and in truth. I mean, really, if you've read my class this far and still think praising God means singing stupid congregational songs in church, it's time you got out of the ditch.

In Acts, each home church lived life together every day as a family. They went shopping together, went to the amphitheatre together, went into town together, enjoyed meals together, went out into the countryside together, enjoyed sports together, and they lived this way every day. If we live this way as families, God will give increase.

It does say they met in the temple, but remember Paul wasn't around yet and the revelation of the Mystery, part of which was that God no longer dwelled in temples made with hands had not yet been revealed. Later on in Acts, you won't find any believers meeting up in the temple or going to the synagogues unless they were looking for an open door to speak the word.

When new people come to our home churches and get born again, we are to welcome them into the family of God. We are responsible to take care of them and look after them as they learn the word and grow. We are to invite them to our homes for meals, we are to meet up with them and do things together with them, when we watch a movie, we are to invite them round. I mean, what's your interpretation of a family? Would you leave a baby unattended for a few days? Folks, we have to learn to love people and start taking care of them if the word is to live.

We know from the scriptures that it is God that brings about increase, we don't, so if there is no increase it is not God at fault. God is the one who causes flowers to grow, but if we don't plant and water there will be nothing but weeds, get it? There are conditions to be met in order to grow flowers, and when we meet those requirements by planting and watering, God gives us flowers to enjoy. We don't make the flowers grow, God does. When we live life as they did in the first Century, we will have the joy of watching disciples grow. Just as flowers will only grow when we plant and water, God can only entrust us with people if we apply these basic principles for outreach outlined in Acts 2:46 and 47. That's why God wrote the bible in the first place, so we could know how to do this thing. These principles work.

Each home church is to live life together as a family every day. That is God's plan for this administration. This is a family thing. Successful families live life together every day. Living life as a family is how you raise children, and living life as a family is how you raise disciples. If you don't live this way, there will be no outreach. You just want to live your life all by yourself and never meet up with your brothers and sisters in Christ? Fine, you will never see the word live and you will never experience the joy of raising disciples in a home church family. You will also never experience the joy of meeting people at the Return of Christ who you got born again and taught the word to. Have you any idea how thankful they will be to the person who got them born again? You have no idea how much joy you're missing out on if you don't live the word. Home church families is where all the joy in life is.

> Philippians 4:1
> Therefore, my brethren dearly beloved and longed for, my joy and crown, so stand fast in the Lord, my dearly beloved.

> 1 Thessalonians 2:19
> For what is our hope, or joy, or crown of rejoicing? Are not even ye in the presence of our Lord Jesus Christ at his coming?

The home church leaders who walk by the spirit with Christ as their head set the spiritual pace for the home church family, just as a father should set the pace for any earthly family. A father leads by example, and gives his life for his family. As God adds to a home church family, the home church leaders are responsible to raise them as disciples. Each person in a home church is to care for everyone else as a family, standing in the spiritual competition together as a family, submitting themselves to their home church leadership.

What parent would leave their young children unsupervised for a few hours, let alone a few days or weeks? We have to love God's children as we would love our own children. God needs good men and women to look after his kids, so if you want to run a home church, you need to learn how to be a good brother or sister to them so you can protect them in the spiritual competition, while teaching them and showing them how to be disciples by being an example.

Here's a question for you, how can home church leaders raise families if a council of men sends someone with a flashy nametag to take over the running of their home church? That is not how families work, not in the physical realm and certainly not in the spiritual. Those you father in the word are your responsibility, and it's your duty to look after those people until they can take care of themselves. God gave those people to you, and as you assume that responsibility God will work within you both to will and to do of his good pleasure to keep his children protected. That's why it is imperative that we learn to walk by the spirit with Christ as our head and not men.

Now, of course, this doesn't mean we have to be perfect, any more than successful parents in the world are perfect. We have Christ in us so we are sufficient to do everything that God asks of us, and we are still holy and without blame before him in love regardless of how many times we fall short in that duty. Faithfulness isn't measured by how few times we fall, it is measured by how quickly we pick ourselves up and get back into the spiritual competition after we fall. A man who falls down half a dozen times a day, but who picks himself right back up and moves forward again is more faithful than a man who falls down once a year and drowns in self pity, guilt and condemnation for weeks. This isn't about striving to become perfect because spiritually we already are.

The words of the bible with which we plant and water are just words on paper, but they change lives. Why? Because God breathed life into these words. These words, according to Timothy, are *theopneustos*, they are God-breathed words.

> 2 Timothy 3:16
> All scripture *is* **given by inspiration of God** [theopneustos], and *is* profitable for doctrine, for reproof, for correction, for instruction in righteousness:

The five English words *given by inspiration of God* are translated from the one Greek word *theopneustos*, God-breathed. All scripture is God-breathed. God breathed life, spiritual life into his word, just as he breathed physical life into man back in Genesis.

> Genesis 2:7
> And the LORD God formed man *of* the dust of the ground, and breathed into his nostrils the breath of life; and man became a living soul.

God breathed life into the bible, that's why these words give us life. When we speak these words to people, we speak God-breathed life to them and if they hear, they receive spiritual life.

> Acts 5:20
> Go, stand and speak in the temple to the people all the words of this life.

There is life in these words, that's why this is the word of life. That life is spiritual and you receive that life when you receive the gift of holy spirit. You manifest that life, you begin your spiritual breathing when you energise that gift of holy spirit and speak in tongues. As we live life together with our brothers and sisters in Christ as families, then the word will move.

> Philippians 2:16
> Holding forth the word of life; that I may rejoice in the day of Christ, that I have not run in vain, neither laboured in vain.

We speak these words of life so that others also can have life. As we speak life, people are raised from the dead and are made whole by receiving spirit. Every time we speak the word and someone is born again, we literally raise them from the dead. We really can do greater works than Jesus Christ did.

> John 14:12
> Verily, verily, I say unto you, He that believeth on me, the works that I do shall he do also; and greater *works* than these shall he do; because I go unto my Father.

> Ephesians 5:14
> Wherefore he saith, Awake thou that sleepest, and arise from the dead, and Christ shall give thee light.

The light is the Christ in us, the gift of holy spirit. When we energise holy spirit we shine spiritual light into this dark world. We speak these words of life so others can receive the gift of holy spirit and learn how to energise that life and learn to walk by the spirit for themselves.

> Philippians 2:15
> That ye may be blameless and harmless, the sons of God, without rebuke, in the midst of a crooked and perverse nation, among whom ye shine as lights in the world;

Going around knocking doors, chattering out scriptures and annoying people isn't shining as a light. That isn't moving the word. When salesmen constantly knock on your door to try to sell you stuff, do you enjoy the experience? Oh, you might argue that knocking on doors sells double glazing. Sure it might sell a few windows for that company for a while, but it is counter productive in the long run. How you sell double glazing successfully in the long term is by providing excellent windows, having craftsmen fit them, providing excellent after sales service, and caring for your customers. Word of mouth will do the rest.

Think I'm wrong? I was a branch manager for quite a number of double glazing companies so I know what I'm talking about. Those who employ large canvassing teams to knock doors and annoy people never last. I've seen hundreds of double glazing companies go broke and I know door knocking is counter productive. Pissing people off in their homes is not how you move the word. There may be exceptions to the rule in specific cases, but that is up to each believer who walks by the spirit to decide, not for a council of men to mandate.

Regarding how we approach unbelievers and speak the word to them, Peter sums it up very nicely.

> 1 Peter 3:15
> But sanctify the Lord God in your hearts: and *be* ready always to *give* an answer to every man that asketh you a reason of the hope that is in you with meekness and fear [respect]:

Paul also gives us a clue as to how we approach the world and speak these words of life.

> 2 Corinthians 3:2
> Ye are our epistle written in our hearts, known and read of all men:

We are to be ready to speak when people approach us with questions. This is the key to planting and watering which brings about increase. Knocking on doors without an invitation is not moving the word, it is annoying people and giving God a bad name. The quality of your life should open doors. If it isn't, then take another look at your life. The quality of life enjoyed by the believers in the 1st Century was their epistle, their witness which was known and read of all men. They lived life as families and that was what attracted people to them, which in turn opened doors to speak.

As Peter says, sanctify God in your hearts, walk by the spirit, and be ready to speak the word as you live life and people approach you. It is God who gives the increase and he *will* open doors for you to speak if you are living the more abundant life. A light in darkness is attractive without it having to do anything. You don't have to knock doors or annoy strangers in the street to move the word. If that's what you think outreach is, you're an embarrassment to the God who gave you the ministry of reconciliation. This isn't difficult, just do what it says in Acts 2:46 and 47, live life as families, and enjoy the more abundant life. Get that Christ in you energised and shine.

Paul is an excellent example of moving the word. Did he go around annoying people in their homes? Show it to me in the bible. I don't see it. From the very moment he began his ministry, he only spoke where he was invited to speak, where he had an open door. When Paul went to the synagogue he knew he would have open doors. He didn't just march in there and arrogantly push the local synagogue leaders aside. Had he done that he would have been thrown out into the street. This isn't about forcing doors open where there are none, this is about being alert and being ready to speak when one opens.

> Acts 9:19,20
> And when he had received meat, he was strengthened. Then was Saul certain days with the disciples which were at Damascus.
>
> And straightway he preached Christ in the synagogues, that he is the Son of God.

When Paul and Barnabas went off together to move the word, they started in the synagogues where they had open doors. They knew that if they went to the synagogues they would be invited to speak because it was a Judean custom to invite visitors to speak. If you go to a church today you will not be invited to speak to their people, so this would not work in our culture. Paul and Barnabas only spoke where they had open doors. When Paul and Barnabas began the work in Antioch in Pisidia, it was because they were invited to speak.

> Acts 13:14-16
> But when they departed from Perga, they came to Antioch in Pisidia, and went into the synagogue on the sabbath day, and sat down.
>
> And after the reading of the law and the prophets the rulers of the synagogue sent unto them, saying, *Ye* men *and* brethren, if ye have any word of exhortation for the people, say on.
>
> Then Paul stood up, and beckoning with *his* hand said, Men of Israel, and ye that fear God, give audience.

Paul and Barnabas were invited by Sergius Paulus to come and see him because he wanted to hear the word. They didn't knock on his door and annoy him. If you want to speak to people in their homes, then find ways to get yourself invited in and stop annoying people.

> Acts 13:5-7
> And when they were at Salamis, they preached the word of God in the synagogues of the Jews [Judeans]: and they had also John to *their* minister.
>
> And when they had gone through the isle unto Paphos, they found a certain sorcerer, a false prophet, a Jew [Judean], whose name *was* Barjesus:
>
> Which was with the deputy of the country, Sergius Paulus, a prudent man; who called for Barnabas and Saul, and desired to hear the word of God.

Let me put this another way, you require an open door to speak the word or you are not labouring together with God. If you're trying to force doors open, you're walking by the senses and doing things your way, not God's way. If your idea of outreach is cold calling by knocking on doors, you need to step back and take a good look at what you're being taught because you're not walking by the spirit with Christ as your head. If your home church leader is walking by the spirit and God inspires him to go out knocking doors, fine, follow his lead and you will enjoy the experience. However, if he is getting his instructions from a council of men at the head of some religious temple made with hands, more than likely you're just going to make a fool of yourself in public and head home feeling guilty and used. And don't tell me I don't know what I'm talking about because I've knocked more doors and annoyed more people than anyone reading this class.

Yes, Philip did approach a total stranger in Acts 8, but guess what, he was walking by the spirit when he did it.

> Acts 8:26-31
> And the angel of the Lord spake unto Philip, saying, Arise, and go toward the south unto the way that goeth down from Jerusalem unto Gaza, which is desert.

And he arose and went: and, behold, a man of Ethiopia, an eunuch of great authority under Candace queen of the Ethiopians, who had the charge of all her treasure, and had come to Jerusalem for to worship,

Was returning, and sitting in his chariot read Esaias the prophet.

Then the Spirit said unto Philip, Go near, and join thyself to this chariot.

And Philip ran thither to *him,* and heard him read the prophet Esaias, and said, Understandest thou what thou readest?

And he said, How can I, except some man should guide me? And he desired Philip that he would come up and sit with him.

Occasionally, God may inspire you to approach a stranger or knock a particular door, but these are isolated and specific cases. This is not something any council of men or any patriarch can pass legislation on. The key is to walk by the spirit with Christ as your head and labour together with God. That's walking circumspectly and not as a fool.

Paul didn't just chatter out scriptures everywhere he went to everyone he met. You have to walk with wisdom, you have to walk circumspectly when you're dealing with people. Many times Paul didn't speak a word to anyone.

Acts 16:6-10
Now when they had gone throughout Phrygia and the region of Galatia, and were forbidden of the Holy Ghost [pneuma hagion – holy spirit] to preach the word in Asia,

After they were come to Mysia, they assayed to go into Bithynia: but the Spirit suffered [allowed] them not.

And they passing by Mysia came down to Troas.

And a vision appeared to Paul in the night; There stood a man of Macedonia, and prayed him, saying, Come over into Macedonia, and help us.

And after he had seen the vision, immediately we endeavoured to go into Macedonia, assuredly gathering that the Lord had called us for to preach the gospel unto them.

See, Paul walked by the spirit, not by his senses, and that's what we are supposed to do. If you don't walk by the spirit with this thing, you are not walking circumspectly with spiritual accuracy and precision, you're walking by the senses and making a religious fool of yourself. Paul didn't just chatter out scriptures everywhere he went, he looked for open doors and only spoke when he had them. Well, we are to be followers of Paul, remember?

> 1 Corinthians 4:16
> Wherefore I beseech you, be ye followers [mimētēs - imitators] of me [Paul].

> 1 Corinthians 11:1
> Be ye followers [mimētēs - imitators] of me [Paul], even as I also *am* of Christ.

Paul followed Christ. Christ wasn't literally there, so this is a reference to the Christ in him, the gift of holy spirit. Paul walked by the spirit with Christ as his head, and that's what we are supposed to do as well. We are to imitate Paul's example of walking by the spirit with Christ as his head. Most religious dungeons use these verses to teach the opposite of what they actually say, to teach patriarchal principles that manipulate people into blindly following some egotistical wanker at the top of their temple as if he was getting all the revelation for everyone. Well, I think you know where that's coming from by now.

Walking by the direction and council of men is a garbage way of life. Get out of those damnable churches, those crappy temples made with hands, those imprisoning ministries and cults, and start moving the word and have some fun in life again. Living in constant fear of leadership watching everything you do so they can pick on you for every little mistake is not the more abundant life. That's not the freedom Christ came to make available. When I was involved in man-made ministries I was constantly afraid of reproof for not checking everything I was doing through my leadership. All the eyes watching me made me afraid to walk by the spirit. Fear is the devil's language. Fear is a dungeon, and I don't care how much of the word you think you're being taught. Christ came to make us free and we can only truly be free if we disentangle ourselves from temples made with hands and walk with Christ as our head.

> Galatians 5:1
> Stand fast therefore in the liberty wherewith Christ hath made us free, and be not entangled again with the yoke of bondage.

Being entangled again in the yoke of bondage isn't just a reference to obeying the old testament law, it's also a reference to being entangled in old testament principles such as being a part of temples made with hands. Folks, God wants you free and he wants you living a more abundant life. It's your choice. I've been entangled and now I'm free and I can assure you my life is far more abundant living with Christ as my head than it ever was when men were my head. I wouldn't change my life for anything. Walking by the spirit is the way to go.

Paul sure enjoyed a more abundant life. It wasn't a life of great riches or a life without challenges, but he was more than a conqueror in every situation because he walked by the spirit. If we follow his example and walk by the spirit, we will enjoy a victorious life.

> Psalm 37:25
> I have been young, and *now* am old; yet have I not seen the righteous forsaken, nor his seed begging bread.

When Paul was in Athens, as well as the open doors of utterance he had in the synagogue, he also went to the market every day, but note that he only spoke with those who met with him, those who *wanted* to hear what he had to say. He didn't just go around the marketplace annoying people, poking his nose in where it wasn't welcome.

> Acts 17:16,17
> Now while Paul waited for them at Athens, his spirit was stirred in him, when he saw the city wholly given to idolatry.

Therefore disputed he in the synagogue with the Jews [Judeans], and with the devout persons, and in the market daily with them that met with him.

Paul didn't always have it his own way in the synagogues. At Ephesus, spiritual adversity forced him to move from the synagogue and teach in a local school. So we have to be adaptable. That's why we are the new dynamic church, ever changing and adapting how we do things.

Acts 19:8-10
And he went into the synagogue, and spake boldly for the space of three months, disputing and persuading the things concerning the kingdom of God.

But when divers [many] were hardened, and believed not, but spake evil of that way [the way] before the multitude, he departed from them, and separated the disciples, disputing daily in the school of one Tyrannus.

And this continued by the space of two years; so that all they which dwelt in Asia heard the word of the Lord Jesus, both Jews [Judeans] and Greeks.

The key to outreach is to be living epistles, known and read of all men, shining as lights by energising the gift of holy spirit, and speaking all the words of this life as we have open doors to speak.

So how do we move the word today? We have to be around people, that's the key. The devil has everyone stuck in crappy jobs they hate all day, and hunkered around televisions watching his garbage all night, so how can you reach them? Knock their door? Any brainless idiot can knock a door and annoy people, that takes no talent and it certainly requires no walking by the spirit. Getting yourself invited into someone's home is going to take some labouring together with God, some walking by the spirit with Christ as your head.

Regarding the winning of neighbours, a Korean man of God once told a story of one woman living in an apartment in a block of flats who he appointed as a home church leader and told her to get the neighbours involved. The woman prayed and asked God for ideas, because she did not know how to reach the people living in the other flats as she never saw any of them. God asked her how people in flats reached their homes. She replied by way of the elevator, so God told her to ride the elevator for a while everyday and that's what she did. From that day on she would ride up and down in the elevator for an hour or two just to meet people. She didn't annoy them by chattering scriptures at them, instead she would offer to help carry a small child home or help older folks carry their groceries. Eventually, she got to know most of the people living in the flats and they began to invite her into their homes. That's walking by the spirit and working together with God to get some doors open.

This is about people, so spend time where there are people. If you're into running, join a running club. Share their passion and make some friends. If you make a few friends, don't be surprised when you're invited around to their homes. Whatever you do, don't just go there to annoy everyone by being a religious asshole and quoting scriptures at them. Be human and enjoy life. If doors open, be ready to speak, that's all. If no doors open, great, enjoy your running with them. By now you should no longer be part of any ministries made with hands, so you no longer have to worry about phoning some ministry leader to tell them how many people you spoke the word to and annoyed today. What a load of horseshit that is.

If you're into hill walking, join a hill walking club. If you're into canoeing, join a canoeing club. If you're into sports, get along to your local sports club. If you love rock climbing, go join your local rock climbing group. If birding is your thing, or you would like to get into birding, go join your local bird group. If photography excites you, get along to your local photography group. Whatever your passion is in life, go and spend time with like minded people who share that passion. Be the best you can be in your field, enjoy your time there, and get to know the others who share your passion. Get yourself out into life and enjoy it, and just be ready to speak when folks ask honest questions. As home churches live this way, doors will open, and you will have the chance to plant and water.

As home churches grow, spiritual specialities and long suits will emerge and develop among the believers, and people will soon learn who to go to for help in specific categories. Some people will be strong in believing, so when folks need help with believing, they will know who to go to. Some people will be good at ministering healing, so when folks need ministering to for health issues, they will know who to see to get the help they need. Some people will excel at working heartily, living within their means, and staying out of debt, so those within that home church or just added to it who need help with money will quickly learn who to go to for help in getting out of debt. As home churches live this way, God adds to his church daily such as should be saved, made whole, those who are being born again, those who are given the gift of holy spirit and have eternal life.

In contrast, this is not how it works. A man walks by the spirit, lives the word, teaches the word and ministers in his area. God gives increase and a home church is born. He joins a temple made with hands and they send someone to take over his work, a man to whom God has given no increase, a man who walks by his senses, a man who bitches and gossips about people behind their backs, complains about everything, thinks evil continually, and refuses to hear reproof and correction when it's given by a man of God who walks by the spirit.

Selecting a home church leader must not be determined by how many bible classes someone has or hasn't taken. That's how the Pharisees appraised people and how religious people today still appraise people. That is not how this thing works. Just because someone is a graduate of some crappy advanced bible class and struts about sporting a flashy nametag is no qualification for leadership positions. The word clearly states that every man is to prove his own work. This does not mean you look at how many bible classes someone has taken, you look at their life. If you can't see past a person's nametag and perceive whether or not they're walking by the spirit, you're blind and groping around in a ditch.

The word is clear on being able to know if someone is living the word by their life and by their believing. If a home church lives the word, the increase will be there. If they don't live the word, there will be no increase. God gives the increase, so if there is no increase, there has been no labouring together with God. There may have been plenty of labouring together with other men to build and maintain a religious organisation, but that is not labouring together with God because he does not live in temples made with hands. Argue with the bible all you like, but if you have no fruit to show for your labours, then your labours are in vain. It's time to stop labouring in man-made temples and get back out into the world and labour with God to move the word. That is what terrifies devil spirits and that is what they fight so hard to prevent.

Regarding gift ministries, God sets them in the church as it pleases him. The church of God, as we know, is not some temple made with hands, it is everyone who is called out from among both Judeans and Gentiles. Everyone who is born again is in the church of God, regardless of any religious affiliations. The body of Christ, however, is made up of those who walk by the spirit with Christ as their head, and you are not going to be able to do that if you're a practicing catholic doing what the pope tells you or you're a follower of the Way International doing what their board of directors tell you.

See how this works? When someone in the church of God learns to walk by the spirit with Christ as their head, they become part of the body of Christ. You don't become part of the body of Christ by joining some church or ministry and taking all their classes, you become part of the body of Christ when you learn to walk by the spirit with Christ as your head. You can know the whole bible and memorise it, but if you don't energise the gift of holy spirit and walk with Christ as your head, all that bible is of no profit to you. Paul didn't care how much bible someone knew, he looked for people who energised spiritual power.

> 1 Corinthians 4:19,20
> But I will come to you shortly, if the Lord will, and will know, not the speech of them which are puffed up, but the power [dunamis].
>
> For the kingdom of God *is* not in word, but in power [dunamis].

Dunamis is one of a number of Greek words translated power, and it means inherent power, implying that we all have the power source but that it's up to us whether or not we energise that power. Our English words *dynamo* and *dynamic* come directly from *dunamis*. We all have this potential power resident within the gift of holy spirit, but we must energise it. Paul wasn't interested in how many bible classes someone had taken, only in how much spiritual power they were manifesting. Knowledge without power is all you will find in temples made with hands, and that knowledge will be corrupted because they twist scriptures to prop up their particular creaky brand of religious horseshit.

> 1 Corinthians 2:4,5
> And my speech and my preaching *was* not with enticing words of man's wisdom, but in demonstration of the Spirit and of power [dunamis]:
>
> That your faith [believing] should not stand in the wisdom of men, but in the power [dunamis] of God.

The functioning, energised body of disciples who walk by the spirit with Christ as their head, those who demonstrate the power of God make up the body of Christ, regardless of any organisational affiliations. The body of Christ is *absolutely not* any man-made temple, it is comprised of the church of God, those called out from among both Judeans and Gentiles, who energise the gift of holy spirit by speaking in tongues and who learn to walk by the spirit with Christ as their head.

As a home church lives this way, there will be increase, and God then places gift ministries where they're needed. These ministries are for the perfecting of the saints, ensuring they are fully equipped and in good repair with all they need to be successful. The gift ministries are also for the work of the ministry (the ministry of reconciliation which is moving the word at the home church level), and they are for the building up of the body of Christ, not for the construction and maintenance of yet more man-made temples.

> Ephesians 4:11,12
> And he gave some, apostles; and some, prophets; and some, evangelists; and some, pastors and teachers;
>
> For the perfecting [katartismos] of the saints, for the work of the ministry, for the edifying of the body of Christ:

This word *perfecting* is quite something. It is the Greek word *katartismos* which is derived from *katartizō*, a compound word made up from *kata* + *artios*. Thayer defines *katartismos* as a complete furnishing, a complete equipping, and *katartizō* as to mend what has been broken, to repair; to fit out, to furnish, to equip; and to strengthen, to complete, to make one what he ought to be. Katartizō can be seen in Mark.

> Mark 1:19
> And when he had gone a little further thence, he saw James the *son* of Zebedee, and John his brother, who also were in the ship mending [katartizō] their nets.

What use is a broken net? It won't catch fish. Fishermen keep their nets in good repair. The gift ministries are there to keep the believers in good repair. Artios can be seen in 2 Timothy.

> 2 Timothy 3:16,17
> All scripture *is* given by inspiration of God, and *is* profitable for doctrine, for reproof, for correction, for instruction in righteousness:
>
> That the man of God may be perfect [artios], throughly furnished [exartizō] unto all good works.

Thayer defines *exartizō* as to complete, to furnish or equip perfectly. An excellent way to get a good feel for what a word means is to check other uses of it in the bible. Anyone can pick up a concordance, look up an English word to find its Greek equivalent and then track that Greek word through the new testament to see how it is used. However, if a particular word is not used very often, a good way to get a feel for it is to look at literature written at the same time. Greek writers used *exartizō* to describe a ship fully equipped for a long voyage. Before a ship sets sail, it has everything stashed aboard it will ever need for that voyage. All God-breathed scripture is given that the man of God may be fully equipped, fully furnished with everything he will ever need to voyage through life.

> 2 Peter 1:3
> According as his divine power hath given unto us all things that *pertain* unto life and godliness, through the knowledge of him that hath called us to glory and virtue:

However important the word is, it is the Christ in us, the holy spirit that makes us complete.

Colossians 2:10
And ye are complete in him, which is the head of all principality and power:

This word *complete* is a rare fourth conjugation of the Greek verb *pleroō*, and could be translated as totally, utterly, absolutely filled to capacity. In whom are we totally, utterly, absolutely filled to capacity? We are complete in him, Christ, a reference to the gift of holy spirit, the Christ in us. We are fully complete, equipped with absolutely everything we could possibly need to voyage through this thing called life. We have the word and we have the power of God, and as if that wasn't enough, God even gives gift ministries where they are needed to keep us in good repair. What more could God do? There is no more he can do. He has done everything. Now it's our turn. We have to switch on the power and manifest this more abundant life.

Now, how these gift ministries help people to become disciples is by living real life with them every day. That was how Jesus Christ moved the word. Jesus Christ didn't lock himself away behind a desk inside a temple constructed by men and grow fat on the tithes and offerings of the people, he moved out in real life and demonstrated God's power in real everyday life, bringing deliverance to God's people. The gift ministries are to be out there in real life, where they can be energised and put to God's work, preaching the word, healing the broken hearted, preaching deliverance to the captives, recovering the sight of the blind, and setting at liberty them that are bruised.

If your idea of being an effective minister of the Lord Jesus Christ is locking yourself away from the world at the headquarters of some religious organisation and sending out magazines, tapes and DVDs to subscribers, you really have no concept of the spiritual competition. Stealing energised gift ministries from God's people and putting them to work maintaining the headquarters of churches and ministries strips God's people of the very help they need to grow as disciples. Those gift ministries are given by God to ensure his people are in a constant state of good preparedness and repair in the spiritual competition, not to labour away in administrative roles stuck away in offices at the headquarters of temples made with hands.

By the way, gift ministries are given by God, they are not doled out by councils of men just because someone attended some stupid seminary or biblical college. If you think God only gives gift ministries to people at the head of temples constructed and maintained by men, who follow the direction of councils of men rather than walk by the spirit, you really are blind. I don't see anyone anywhere in the bible calling anyone reverend. If that's what you think gift ministries are, well, I don't know what to say. Get out of the ditch.

While we're here, it's time to set a few things straight regarding gift ministries. There are five of them. Pastors is only one of them. Everyone loves a pastor hey, because they're so personable and sociable, great to be around, kind and gentle, good at binding up hurts and making people feel good. Sure they are, that's their job, but there are also prophets listed among the gift ministries, and they are just as important as pastors. The problem is, prophets aren't as personable and sociable as pastors, so people don't tend to like them very much, and often regard them as trouble makers. Samuel was a prophet and the people in Bethlehem trembled at his coming.

> 1 Samuel 16:4
> And Samuel did that which the LORD spake, and came to Bethlehem. And the elders of the town trembled at his coming, and said, Comest thou peaceably?

They were right to tremble. Prophets are the men who face up against the attacks of the devil to protect God's people. Devil spirits energise and operate through people, so it is no surprise then that prophets are in your face if you're not walking by the spirit. As prophets constantly deal with stuff like arrogance, pride, hard heartedness, stubbornness, laziness, and a few other nasty little attitudes, this tends to make people who have those attitudes afraid of them. Prophets don't tend to have many friends.

Conversely, when things are going well and people are living the word, prophets tend to blend into the background, and often you wouldn't even know they were there. They can even seem recluse, watching everything from a distance. They are not generally social men, and often prefer their own company. This is actually a good thing, but to understand it, you have to understand the nature and depth of the spiritual competition.

Consider the white blood cells in the human body. Observing them in a healthy body, one would consider them sluggish, ineffective, lethargic, and useless at patrolling territory much less repelling attacks. That is, until an attack occurs. White blood cells are actually the body's military special forces.

When the body is punctured, muscle cells contract around the damage preventing loss of blood. Clotting agents also halt the flow of blood at the skin surface. Scavenger cells then appear to clean up debris. Fibril blasts, the body's reweaving cells gather around the injury site to begin repairs. However impressive this all is, by far the most dramatic event involves the listless white blood cells. As soon as the human body is punctured, they parachute in from all directions. Using their unique shape changing qualities they can ooze between overlapping cells of capillary walls and even pass through actual tissue in their haste to reach the war zone. When they arrive the battle begins in earnest. White cells contain granules of chemical explosives and as soon as any bacteria are absorbed, the chemicals detonate and destroy the germs. Within a minute, the only cells remaining on the battlefield are the white blood cells.

Strip the human body of the white blood cells and that body is going down at the first attack because it has no defences. Stripping home churches of its prophets, getting rid of them because you don't like them is the devil's work. Just because they are in your face when you walk away from the word doesn't mean they're trouble makers. Like white blood cells, their job is to protect the body of Christ and they will smash through walls to take on spiritual attack. Without them, there would be no body of Christ because it would be destroyed by every germ going. Prophets keep the germs out of your home churches. Put all your trust in pastors because they're so *nice* to everyone and you're going down hard. You prophets out there, you need to understand this stuff too. You are a spiritual warrior and you have a duty to perform, regardless of social acceptance.

William J Bennet stated in a lecture to the US Naval Academy:

Honor never grows old, and honor rejoices the heart of age. It does so because honor is, finally, about defending those noble and worthy things that deserve defending, even if it comes at a high cost. In our time, that may mean social disapproval, public scorn, hardship, persecution, or as always, even death itself. The question remains: What is worth defending? What is worth dying for? What is worth living for?

A Vietnam veteran, a retired colonel once said:

Most of the people in our society are sheep. They are kind, gentle, productive creatures who can only hurt one another by accident. Then there are the wolves, and the wolves feed on the sheep without mercy. There are evil men in this world and they are capable of evil deeds. The moment you forget that or pretend it is not so, you become a sheep. There is no safety in denial. Then there are sheepdogs, and I'm a sheepdog. I live to protect the flock and confront the wolf.

Lt Col Dave Grossman wrote in his book, On Combat:

If you have no capacity for violence then you are a healthy productive citizen: a sheep. If you have a capacity for violence and no empathy for your fellow citizens, then you have defined an aggressive sociopath--a wolf. But what if you have a capacity for violence, and a deep love for your fellow citizens? Then you are a sheepdog, a warrior, someone who is walking the hero's path. Someone who can walk into the heart of darkness, into the universal human phobia, and walk out unscathed.

We know that the sheep live in denial; that is what makes them sheep. They do not want to believe that there is evil in the world. They can accept the fact that fires can happen, which is why they want fire extinguishers, fire sprinklers, fire alarms and fire exits throughout their kids' schools. But many of them are outraged at the idea of putting an armed police officer in their kid's school. Our children are dozens of times more likely to be killed, and thousands of times more likely to be seriously injured, by school violence than by school fires, but the sheep's only response to the possibility of violence is denial. The idea of someone coming to kill or harm their children is just too hard, so they choose the path of denial.

The sheep generally do not like the sheepdog. He looks a lot like the wolf. He has fangs and the capacity for violence. The difference, though, is that the sheepdog must not, cannot and will not ever harm the sheep.

Still, the sheepdog disturbs the sheep. He is a constant reminder that there are wolves in the land. They would prefer that he didn't stand at the ready in our airports in camouflage fatigues holding an M-16. The sheep would much rather have the sheepdog cash in his fangs, spray paint himself white, and go, 'Baa'.

Until the wolf shows up.

The sheepdog is always sniffing around out on the perimeter, checking the breeze, barking at things that go bump in the night, and yearning for a righteous battle. That is, the young sheepdogs yearn for a righteous battle. The old sheepdogs are a little older and wiser, but they move to the sound of the guns when needed right along with the young ones.

The sheep pretend the wolf will never come, but the sheepdog lives for that day. After the attacks on September 11, 2001, most of the sheep, that is, most citizens in America said, 'Thank God I wasn't on one of those planes.' The sheepdogs, the warriors, said, 'Dear God, I wish I could have been on one of those planes. Maybe I could have made a difference.'

Okay, we know we're not referred to as sheep in the bible in the Age of Grace, but it gets the point across. People were referred to as sheep in the old testament because they had no spirit and needed a shepherd with spirit upon them to look after them. In this administration everyone has spirit, so we are no longer sheep in need of a shepherd, but we do need the gift ministries to keep us in good repair.

You prophets out there are to confront spiritual attacks on the body of Christ, so do your job and don't be afraid of social suspicion, distrust and even revulsion among God's people. Do your fucking job and kick butt when butt needs kicked. You believers out there who claim you love God, when a prophet is in your face you had better learn to shut up and listen. You home church leaders, if you have a prophet in your church, you'd better learn to respect him instead of looking for ways to get rid of him because you think he's a trouble maker.

Are you listening? Try this then – telephones are not God's plan for ministering. Telephones serve only to keep God's people who have not been taught how to walk by the spirit enslaved in man-made temples. Going to a man or woman with spirit upon them to get help from God was how they did things in the old testament. It is not how God energises in the Age of Grace. If you want answers, go directly to God yourself. You have holy spirit, you are more than a conqueror in every situation, you can do all things through Christ who strengthens you, so what do you need a telephone for? Rather than put your trust in God, you'd rather put your trust in a man who is too lazy to get out of bed and come round and see you when you need help? Geez, no wonder the word died.

As a home church leader practices the principles of the book of Acts, God will give increase and eventually he or she will need help to minister and teach effectively. How big does a home church need to be before it branches out? Well, how much work can you handle? Is everyone in your home church having all their need met? If not, it might be time to start thinking about establishing another home church. If you are walking by the spirit, you will already have an able assistant trained up and ready to handle the responsibility.

How do you know who to select as a home church leader? Well, if you can't see any increase in their lives, it isn't them, that's for sure, and I don't care how many bible classes they've taken, how personable they are, or how many flashy nametags they have. If you are walking by the spirit it is easy to know if someone else is walking by the spirit. If you're not walking by the spirit, you're one of those blind leaders of the blind Jesus Christ warned us about.

Each one win one should be our goal for moving the word. Each one win one, that is the word's way. If a church consists of two people, and they each win one, you have four. Once those two new people have learned to walk by the spirit and each one wins one again, there are now eight believers. Each one wins one again, and you have sixteen believers. Each one wins one again, and before you know it there are thirty two people walking by the spirit in that area and that home church should be thinking about splitting into two.

The man or woman who began the work there still has a responsibility to oversee the move of the word in that area, but he or she is going to need some help. God gives gift ministries to help with the work of the ministry. So if you are a home church leader, give your people room to move and grow. Don't stifle them by trying to be the big patriarch, recognise that each of them has God in Christ in them and that God is energising in them to will and to do of his good pleasure. Your job is to oversee things, not control everything. Give people room to grow and learn to perceive when God is energising in people to will and to do of his good pleasure.

The point is, what you have built up is your responsibility, but you will need some help, you can't do it all yourself. Believers are going to be hurt, so there needs to be a pastor around to take care of them. The devil is going to attack, so there needs to be a prophet around. See how it works? Don't be a patriarch and stifle the spirit in everyone, thinking you are the only one God gives revelation to. Let people grow and encourage them to walk by the spirit for themselves. In this Age of Grace we're not playing follow the leader, we have to learn to make Christ our head and quit trying to be the head ourselves or making other men our head. We need to get our minds out of the gutter of the temple rut and think more in terms of the Christ in every one of us.

Who did God give the ministry of reconciliation to? The Pope? The Way International? The Muslims? The jehovah's witnesses? No, he gave the ministry to you. The ministry is not some man-made temple, it is something God gave to everyone born into the church of God. It is one of our sonship rights.

> 2 Corinthians 5:18
> And all things *are* of God, who hath reconciled us to himself by Jesus Christ, and hath given to us the ministry of reconciliation;

Another thing, I don't see anywhere in the bible in this Administration of Grace where people were forced to join some organisation in return for being taught the word. Forcing people to join your particular brand of religion and prove their allegiance to you before giving them the word is bribery. Holding back the word until people have become entrenched in your man-made temple system before giving them the depth of the word is worse than bribery. You are no better than the vatican who have locked away the word in their catacombs and would read the bible in Latin if they could get away with it.

God gave to us the ministry of reconciliation. That means it's *our* job to do the work of the ministry. The ministry is not any man-made temple. Each of us is to take responsibility for those God has entrusted to our care. Every man is to prove his own work. That's how this thing moves. We all have Christ in us, so we all have the ability to do this. God even committed to us his word, so we can move this ministry and learn to walk with Christ as our head.

> 2 Corinthians 5:19
> To wit, that God was in Christ, reconciling the world unto himself, not imputing their trespasses unto them; and hath committed unto us the word of reconciliation.

To whom did God commit his word? Us, collectively, we who are part of the church of God, which is who Corinthians is addressed to. Whose responsibility then is the ministry? God's? Jesus Christ's? The angels? No, it's ours. God gave that responsibility to us. God isn't going to do it, nor is Jesus Christ, and nor are the angels. This is our thing. This is what makes us ambassadors for Christ.

> 2 Corinthians 5:20
> Now then we are ambassadors for Christ, as though God did beseech *you* by us: we pray *you* in Christ's stead, be ye reconciled to God.

When the Ethiopian eunuch needed someone to teach him, God didn't send an angel to do the ministry of reconciliation, he sent an angel who told Philip to go and see him.

> Acts 8:26,29
> And the angel of the Lord spake unto Philip, saying, Arise, and go toward the south unto the way that goeth down from Jerusalem unto Gaza, which is desert.

Then the Spirit said unto Philip, Go near, and join thyself to this chariot.

When Jesus Christ confronted Saul at the gates of Damascus, he didn't teach him the word or minister to him, that job was given to a disciple called Ananias.

Acts 9:6
And he [Saul] trembling and astonished said, Lord, what wilt thou have me to do? And the Lord [Jesus Christ] *said* unto him, Arise, and go into the city, and it shall be told thee what thou must do.

Acts 9:10-12
And there was a certain disciple at Damascus, named Ananias; and to him said the Lord in a vision, Ananias. And he said, Behold, I *am here* Lord.

And the Lord *said* unto him, Arise, and go into the street which is called Straight, and enquire in the house of Judas for *one* called Saul, of Tarsus: for, behold, he prayeth,

And hath seen in a vision a man named Ananias coming in, and putting *his* hand on him, that he might receive his sight.

Jesus Christ does not have the ministry of reconciliation, neither does God, and neither do the angels, that's why Ananias was sent to see Paul. The ministry of reconciliation is our job, our responsibility. When the angel appeared to the Gentile Cornelius, the angel didn't teach him anything, it simply told him to send for Peter because the ministry of reconciliation was Peter's job not the angel's job.

Acts 10:4-6
And when he [Cornelius] looked on him [the angel], he was afraid, and said, What is it, Lord? And he said unto him, Thy prayers and thine alms are come up for a memorial before God.

And now send men to Joppa, and call for *one* Simon, whose surname is Peter:

He lodgeth with one Simon a tanner, whose house is by the sea side: he shall tell thee what thou oughtest to do.

You see, the ministry of reconciliation was not given to anyone else but us. That's why the angel told Cornelius to send for Peter. If we don't do this thing, it won't get done.

There is a time for all things. It is time to leave the world's temples, establish home churches, do the work of the ministry and build up the body of Christ. The world has never been in such need and it is up to us to do it. We have absolutely everything we will ever need to do that job in the gift of holy spirit. We can do all things through Christ who strengthens us. We are totally, utterly, absolutely filled to capacity with the gift of holy spirit, the Christ in us, and God has committed to us his word. When we live life as families, energise the power we have and speak all the words of this life as we have opportunity, then we truly are ambassadors for Christ and the word will live.

48. Self Supporting

If God does not dwell in temples made with hands, would he therefore want you to give your money to them? Think about it. If God does not live in, if God does not frequent, if God does not attend man-made ministries, religions or churches, would he want you to give money to them? Do I really need to answer that? I guess I do, so let's go back to grass roots.

> 1 Timothy 6:10a
> For the love of money is the root of all evil:

As the love of money is the root of all evil, the proper understanding of how we are to use it is, therefore, of paramount importance. All evil, all of it, has its roots in the love of money. Trees grow from the roots up, so all evil grows from the love of money. Strong's defines this word *all* as *all, any, every, the whole*. That means all evil has its roots in the love of money, not just some of it, but all of it.

Why am I labouring this point? Well, I thought for decades that this *all evil* simply referred to people who commit crimes in order to acquire money. You know, from defrauding electricity companies by fixing their meters, to selling government stocks of gold bullion when gold prices are low so communist mason gangsters reap vast profits from it when gold prices go up. However, this verse has no such distinction, it clearly says all evil, so that must include evil that would take believers away from God's word. Therefore, if any person walks away from God and his word, or any ministry or church constructed by men leads people away from the truth of God's word in any category, the love of money is at the root of it. Argue with God all you like, but that's what his word says. We will come back to this shortly.

Please keep the distinction in your mind that money itself is not the root of all evil, it is the *love* of money that is the root of all evil. There is nothing wrong with money in and of itself. Some of the greatest men of God in the bible were rich, like David, Solomon, Joseph and many others. Job was the richest man on earth in his day. It isn't money, but the love of it that is the root of all evil. This is the truth, so we need to take the time to study this, and what better place to begin than back in Genesis, with Cain and Abel.

> Genesis 4:1-5
> And Adam knew Eve his wife; and she conceived, and bare Cain, and said, I have gotten a man from the LORD.
>
> And she again bare his brother Abel. And Abel was a keeper of sheep, but Cain was a tiller of the ground.
>
> And in process of time it came to pass, that Cain brought of the fruit of the ground an offering unto the LORD.
>
> And Abel, he also brought of the firstlings of his flock and of the fat thereof. And the LORD had respect unto Abel and to his offering:
>
> But unto Cain and to his offering he had not respect. And Cain was very wroth, and his countenance [his face] fell.

Before venturing further, let's set the stage. The earth has a new lord, the devil, who has just seduced man into giving him that position. As a consequence of his actions, man has just died spiritually, he no longer has spirit. God has put into motion the plan of redemption and driven man from the garden. Genesis 4 then is the very beginnings, the first faltering steps of man into the Patriarchal administration, his first tentative steps into the devil's new world order.

The enormity of the moment is incomprehensible. God has confronted Adam and Eve and promised them the messiah, a man who would redeem them from their state of spiritual death. For his part, the devil was feverishly putting together his plans to systematise evil to keep the world under his control. And isn't it remarkable that the very first thing that comes up in the new administration was financial gain and our attitude towards it. Pay attention, because this is the first thing God brings up in the Patriarchal administration after the fall of man.

Adam and Eve had two boys who grew up and began work as farmers, Cain growing crops and Abel tending livestock. They both gave of their increase, their income to God. God enjoyed Abel's offering, but not Cain's. Why not? We know that God is no respecter of persons, so this wasn't God playing favourites, there must have been something wrong with Cain's offering.

> Hebrews 11:4
> By faith [believing] Abel offered unto God a more excellent sacrifice than Cain, by which he obtained witness that he was righteous, God testifying of his gifts: and by it he being dead yet speaketh.

Hebrews informs us that Abel's offering was a witness to his righteousness, so axiomatically, Cain's offering, whatever it was, indicated that he was less than righteous, otherwise God would have accepted his offering as well. That's just common sense.

To begin to understand this, we have to take a look around the bible to get a taste for what went on back in Genesis. Regarding our attitude towards giving, we can learn much from Jacob who fathered the twelve tribes of Israel. He had served Laban with good quality work for years, and during that time Laban had rewarded him by cutting his wages ten times. However, Jacob did not allow this treatment to corrupt him and he remained righteous in his attitude towards income and money. When Jacob left him, Laban pursued after him and accused him of theft.

> Genesis 31:36-42
> And Jacob was wroth, and chode with Laban: and Jacob answered and said to Laban, What *is* my trespass? what *is* my sin, that thou hast so hotly pursued after me?
>
> Whereas thou hast searched all my stuff, what hast thou found of all thy household stuff? set *it* here before my brethren and thy brethren, that they may judge betwixt us both.
>
> This twenty years *have* I *been* with thee; thy ewes and thy she goats have not cast their young, and the rams of thy flock have I not eaten.

> That which was torn *of beasts* I brought not unto thee; I bare the loss of it; of my hand didst thou require it, *whether* stolen by day, or stolen by night.
>
> *Thus* I was; in the day the drought consumed me, and the frost by night; and my sleep departed from mine eyes.
>
> Thus have I been twenty years in thy house; I served thee fourteen years for thy two daughters, and six years for thy cattle: and thou hast changed my wages ten times.
>
> Except the God of my father, the God of Abraham, and the fear of Isaac, had been with me, surely thou hadst sent me away now empty. God hath seen mine affliction and the labour of my hands, and rebuked *thee* yesternight.

God made sure Jacob was well taken care of despite Laban's greed and treachery. Here we begin to see the proper attitudes we should have regarding money and financial gain. We are never to love money more than we love God.

> Romans 12:17
> Recompense to no man evil for evil. Provide things honest in the sight of all men.

Laban was evil in his financial dealings, but Jacob did not recompense him that evil with evil. Jacob provided things honest in the sight of all men, despite the evil that was being done to him. Yes, there is a devil in the world, yes, the world is evil, and yes, the world will try to steal from us what is rightfully ours. We are still to provide things honest in the sight of all men. Our business transactions are to be conducted honestly, regardless of what the world is doing. That's God's word. Of course, this does not mean we just let scum bags like Laban steal everything from us, it just means we don't lower ourselves to their standards. Jacob didn't let Laban get away with his evil and meekly put up with it, did he? Not at all, he went to God and God ensured he was a wealthy man when he left him. If we do things God's way, we will be taken care of.

Regarding attitudes towards giving, consider the following:

> Malachi 1:13
> Ye said also, Behold, what a weariness *is it!* and ye have snuffed at it, saith the LORD of hosts; and ye brought *that which was* torn, and the lame, and the sick; thus ye brought an offering: should I accept this of your hand? saith the LORD.

In the Law Administration, the Levites were to be ministers and priests to God's people, and the Israelites were to support them with their tithes and offerings. God doesn't need money, but his ministers do in order to get things done in this world. God confronted his people in Malachi because they were grudging God his tithe. Instead of bringing good produce with a willing heart, they were grudgingly offering dead, lame and sick animals which were of no value to anyone. Our attitude towards giving is more important than the giving itself.

> 2 Corinthians 9:6-8
> But this *I say*, He which soweth sparingly shall reap also sparingly; and he which soweth bountifully shall reap also bountifully.
>
> Every man according as he purposeth in his heart, *so let him give;* not grudgingly, or of necessity: for God loveth a cheerful giver.
>
> And God *is* able to make all grace abound toward you; that ye, always having all sufficiency in all *things,* may abound to every good work:

Let's head back to Cain and Abel and put this all together.

> Genesis 4:6,7
> And the LORD said unto Cain, Why art thou wroth? and why is thy countenance fallen?
>
> If thou doest well, shalt thou not be accepted? and if thou doest not well, sin lieth at the door. And unto thee *shall be* his desire, and thou shalt rule over him.

The immediate context is giving offerings to God, so these verses refer specifically to giving of income, which in our day and time relates to giving money to God. Cain's attitude to giving was obviously faulty. The word doesn't tell us as much, but we can safely assume from other records in the bible that he was offering sub-standard goods with a grudging heart. God confronted him and gave him an opportunity to change. Look at the confrontation, look at what God told him – if you don't keep your attitudes about money in order, sin lies at your door.

This is mind bending stuff, because the love of money is the root of all evil. If we love money more than God, sin lies at our door. The devil uses the love of money to corrupt men so he can grow his evil. If we are corrupted in our attitudes towards money, the evil that lies at our door will move in and make itself at home. Did Cain respond to the reproof and change his ways?

> Genesis 4:8
> And Cain talked with Abel his brother: and it came to pass, when they were in the field, that Cain rose up against Abel his brother, and slew [murdered] him.

This should get your attention. The love of money is the root of all evil. Cain's murderous ways were rooted in the love of money. He didn't want to give any of his money to God because he loved his money more than he loved God.

Now we need to ask the question, why would God want money from us in the first place? He's God, right? So why would he need money? He doesn't, however, those of us who work for God here on earth do. Nothing in life moves without money. The devil certainly knows this, and he ensures his people have plenty of it so they can grow his evil. For evil to be an effective and powerful force, it requires great deals of money. Have you any idea how much it costs the United Nations every year to sponsor world terrorism? Where does the United Nations get that money? We give most of it to them through taxes, world charities, and foreign aid. So, we give money to the devil to grow his evil, yet we grudge the true God a little money to help him move his word?

It's time to put money and our giving of it to God into context here. Who put the world together? Who put all the stuff into the earth for us? Who put all the vast treasures like oil, gold, gems and minerals into the earth? Who makes crops to grow? Who makes animals multiply? Who put the atmosphere here which we breathe? Who gave us our bodies so we can walk around and enjoy life? Who put all the prosperity and increase into the earth so we can work heartily and enjoy reaping the goodness of life?

Let me put this another way, we did absolutely nothing for the body we live in. It was given to us for nothing. We have no title deed to our body. This might come as a bit of a shock, but your body is not yours. You did nothing for it, and one day you will leave it. You do not own it, it is not your property. You may be fooled by the devil into thinking all your increase has come from your own efforts, but God gave you that body for nothing and all that increase was put there by God in the first place. If you raise animals, it is God who put the animals here and who makes grass grow to feed them. As you produce more animals, that increase is still God's, not yours. When you sell those animals for profit, that money you raise has come from God. This is true of any field in life. All increase comes from the earth and that increase was put there by God. When you make a profit, that profit has come from the earth in one form or another and it was put there by God for us to enjoy. If God had not put it there, you could not have it. So all your clothes, all your furnishings, your house, your car, everything you own has come from God. Nothing in life belongs to anyone, we simply enjoy what God has made available.

> Psalm 50:10
> For every beast of the forest *is* mine, *and* the cattle upon a thousand hills.

You think all your stuff is yours? Okay, come back with it in 100 years and perhaps I'll listen to you. Or do you plan on taking it all with you when you take your last breath? Nothing on this earth is ours. There is nothing on this earth we can stand up before God and claim as our property, not even the body we live in.

> 1 Timothy 6:7
> For we brought nothing into *this* world, *and it is* certain we can carry nothing out.

You see, our attitude shouldn't be about how much *stuff* we can get our greedy hands on, it should be one of thankfulness to God for freely giving us everything so we can enjoy life. If we become greedy and start loving money, then the evil that lies at our doors will march into our lives and make itself at home. That is how the god of this world grows his evil. He sets life up to revolve around the love of money, and when people start lusting after the things of the world and grudging God his money, evil is at their door. This is the very first lesson in the Patriarchal Administration after the fall of man.

Everything we have comes from God. We are not our own sufficiency, it is God who makes all sufficiency abound towards us in all things that we may abound to every good work. If we start thinking of ourselves as our own sufficiency, which is what the world promotes, then we are deceived.

Let's now track the tithe through the bible and see what we can learn. When Moses led the children of Israel from the slavery of Egypt and divided up the promised land, the Levites were given no inheritance. Instead, they were to be full time ministers to the other eleven tribes. The other tribes were to tithe of their income and that tithe was to be given to the Levites to support them as they ministered to God's people and taught the word.

> Numbers 18:24
> But the tithes of the children of Israel, which they offer *as* an heave offering unto the LORD, I have given to the Levites to inherit: therefore I have said unto them, Among the children of Israel they shall have no inheritance.

> Nehemiah 10:37
> And *that* we should bring the firstfruits of our dough, and our offerings, and the fruit of all manner of trees, of wine and of oil, unto the priests, to the chambers of the house of our God; and the tithes of our ground unto the Levites, that the same Levites might have the tithes in all the cities of our tillage.

God certainly doesn't need money, but those who do his work on earth can't function without it. In the Law Administration, the tithe was given to support the Levites who worked full time maintaining the tabernacle and the temple, and teaching and ministering. God's people who tithed benefitted from the arrangement by always having ministers around who could teach them the word. There are other benefits to tithing as well.

> Proverbs 3:9,10
> Honour the LORD with thy substance, and with the firstfruits of all thine increase:
>
> So shall thy barns be filled with plenty, and thy presses shall burst out with new wine.

Do you want barns filled with plenty and your presses bursting out with new wine? Tithing is the way to go. Tithing is 10% of your income. You think 10% is extortionate? You think God asking you for 10% of your income is mean? How much does your government steal from you in taxes? Add up income tax, VAT, duty on petrol and other goods, national insurances, road taxes, and all the other taxes robbing you of the prosperity God wants you to have, and you will find that well over 60% of your income is stolen from you by the government in one form or another. And what does your government do for you in return other than stick their dick up your ass? God asks for 10%, promises barns filled with plenty, and you turn your nose up at God and wonder why your life is shit?

> Malachi 3:8
> Will a man rob God? Yet ye have robbed me. But ye say, Wherein have we robbed thee? In tithes and offerings.

Refusing to tithe is robbing God. The tithe is not your money. It's God's rent for living on his earth. If you're not tithing, you're not paying God his rent for living here. You're a squatter.

> Malachi 3:9
> Ye *are* cursed with a curse: for ye have robbed me, *even* this whole nation.

Is your life shit? If you don't tithe, it's no wonder. This isn't just talking about being rich either – most of the devil's greedy men are filthy rich – this is talking about life in all its abundance, all your need met, good health, wonderful loving family lives, good jobs to go to, great places to live, enjoying peace, and living without worry, fear and frustration. If you think this is just about being rich and having tons of *stuff*, then you have no idea what true abundance is. Of course, there is nothing wrong with money and having lots of it, just keep your attitudes in alignment with God and his word.

> 1 Timothy 6:17-19
> Charge them that are rich in this world, that they be not highminded, nor trust in uncertain riches, but in the living God, who giveth us richly all things to enjoy;
>
> That they do good, that they be rich in good works, ready to distribute, willing to communicate;
>
> Laying up in store for themselves a good foundation against the time to come, that they may lay hold on eternal life.

See, nothing wrong with being rich, just keep your attitudes about it out of the gutter. Your money is not your sufficiency, God is. The warnings about falling in love with money are clear.

> 1 Timothy 6:9,10
> But they that will be rich fall into temptation and a snare, and *into* many foolish and hurtful lusts, which drown men in destruction and perdition.
>
> For the love of money is the root of all evil: which while some coveted after, they have erred from the faith, and pierced themselves through with many sorrows.

If you don't want to be pierced through with many sorrows, don't ever fall in love with money. History is littered with the corpses of rich and famous suicide victims who were pierced through with many sorrows because they loved money. Back to the tithe.

> Malachi 3:10
> Bring ye all the tithes into the storehouse, that there may be meat in mine house, and prove me now herewith, saith the LORD of

hosts, if I will not open you the windows of heaven, and pour you out a blessing, that *there shall* not *be room* enough *to receive it.*

Want the windows of heaven opened and pouring out blessings for you? Tithing is the way to go. Cursed with a curse for robbing God is the alternative. If you're tired of the gangsters running your government stealing all your money from you and poisoning your food to get rid of you, try coming back to God and doing things his way. God isn't afraid of a challenge. Prove him by tithing, and see if he doesn't open the windows of heaven for you.

Malachi 3:11
And I will rebuke the devourer for your sakes, and he shall not destroy the fruits of your ground; neither shall your vine cast her fruit before the time in the field, saith the LORD of hosts.

Want the devourer rebuked? Want protection for your stuff? Want income and prosperity to enjoy? Want to experience the goodness of life for a change? The tithe does more than just pay your rent, it also comes with a spiritual life insurance policy built in. Not death insurance that only pays out on death, but a life insurance policy that guarantees the devourer is rebuked and kept out of your life. All for 10%? Seems like a good deal to me. The Philippians certainly proved that tithing worked.

Philippians 4:15,16,19
Now ye Philippians know also, that in the beginning of the gospel, when I departed from Macedonia, no church communicated with me as concerning giving and receiving, but ye only.

For even in Thessalonica ye sent once and again unto my necessity.

But my God shall supply all your need according to his riches in glory by Christ Jesus.

This promise in Philippians 4:19 is set in the context of giving money. In other words, you can't claim the promise of Philippians 4:19 *unless* you give of your money to God. And this transitions very nicely into *who* we are to give our money to in this Age of Grace. Notice that Paul did not get this money from some patriarch doling it out at the ministry headquarters of some temple made with hands where everyone sent all their money to, it was sent to him from the home churches in Philippi. God's money was kept and used at the home church level and decisions regarding how it was spent were made by the home church leaders. This is what home churches being self supporting means. This is extraordinarily powerful new light with the potential to really destroy the works of the devil.

Our home churches are to be self governing, self propagating, and self supporting, the tithes and abundant sharing being used to move the word in our areas. How can a home church be self supporting if it sends all God's money away to the headquarters of a temple made with hands? God's money is to be used to move his word in your home church area, so keep it and use it properly.

Let's now track money through the Grace Administration to see what else we can learn, and what better place to start than at the end of the first section of the book of Acts? If we live these principles, the word will move again.

> Acts 2:44-47
> And all that believed were together, and had all things common;
>
> And sold their possessions and goods, and parted them to all *men*, as every man had need.
>
> And they, continuing daily with one accord in the temple, and breaking bread from house to house, did eat their meat with gladness and singleness of heart,
>
> Praising God, and having favour with all the people. And the Lord added to the church daily such as should be saved.

These people didn't sell all they had, they simply sold what they didn't need. You can see this in the use of the plural nouns *possessions* and *goods*.

> Acts 4:34,35
> Neither was there any among them that lacked: for as many as were possessors of lands or houses sold them, and brought the prices of the things that were sold,

And laid *them* down at the apostles' feet: and distribution was made unto every man according as he had need.

Again, the use of the plural nouns *lands* and *houses* is important. The believers didn't sell everything they had, just what they didn't need. To illustrate this, compare the following verses from Acts 4.

Acts 4:36,37
And Joses, who by the apostles was surnamed Barnabas, (which is, being interpreted, The son of consolation,) a Levite, *and* of the country of Cyprus,

Having land, sold *it*, and brought the money, and laid *it* at the apostles' feet.

Here the noun *land* is singular. This isn't a typo, this is the accuracy of God's word. Barnabas was a Levite, and in the old testament Levites were not given land as an inheritance. Instead, they were paid from the tithes as we saw earlier. Therefore, this singular property was plurality because he was paid from Israel's tithe money and all his need was met from that. This money was indeed given to the apostles, but remember, this is the very beginnings of the Administration of the Mystery, this Age of Grace, so the apostles would have been the very first home church leaders. This money was being used at the home church level.

These believers used their plurality to support each other. Isn't that what a family is supposed to do? If you have children, do you do all you can from the money you have coming in to keep them clothed and fed with a roof over their heads? Yes, God supplies all our need, but God doesn't have any money to hand out, he works within people who walk by the spirit to will and to do of his good pleasure to ensure his people are well cared for.

If the home churches have no money because they send it all away to the headquarters of temples made with hands, how can the word move? It can't, which is why the devil establishes churches and ministries run by patriarchs and councils of men so they can steal all God's tithe money from you so you have no money to move the word in your area. Home churches are to be self supporting, and God's money is to be kept at the home church level to be used to move the word.

This brings us back to our attitudes towards money. Money is the root of all evil, right? I mentioned we would be back to this, so let's delve into it a little more in Timothy.

> 1 Timothy 6:5-8
> Perverse disputings of men of corrupt minds, and destitute of the truth, supposing that gain is godliness: from such withdraw thyself.
>
> But godliness with contentment is great gain.
>
> For we brought nothing into *this* world, *and it is* certain we can carry nothing out.
>
> And having food and raiment let us be therewith content.

There are some who believe that gain is godliness, that if they are prosperous financially (have lots of money in their bank accounts) that they are somehow godly people and that God is blessing them. The word says that we are to withdraw from such. However, we need to make a distinction here because there is nothing wrong with having money in our bank accounts. The distinction we need to keep clear is that money isn't the root of all evil, it is the *love* of money that's the root of all evil.

This isn't just talking about people who commit crimes to make money, although that is a big part of it. Masons, jesuits, communists, and other greedy bastards in government and corporations make decisions to poison our food so it lasts longer on supermarket shelves so it makes them more money. That's a crime and it's a clear example of the love of money being the root of all evil.

Taking industrial waste like fluoride, a rat poison, and putting it in toothpaste so they don't have to pay to dispose of it and instead make profit from it is a crime and is a clear example of the love of money being the root of all evil. These evil men love money, so they commit crimes that ultimately does the will of their god. Developing new strains of cold and flu viruses and deliberately infecting us with them to make billions from cold and flu remedies is a crime and it's an example of the love of money being the root of all evil. These are obvious examples, but it goes much deeper than this, and it can be far more insidious among God's people.

Let's look at an example. I got together enough people here in the Highlands of Scotland to run a bible class for The Way International. After the class, the Way International sent a man and his wife here to run my area. I did all the work, they came and took over that work. They then moved the work from my village and two of us then had to drive every week for an hour to attend this new home meeting. We would leave after breakfast and get home sometime in the afternoon. Not only did this cost us a considerable amount of our petrol budget every month, it was also effectively a day out of our lives every week. At the time, we didn't mind paying the petrol or giving the time as we believed we were doing God's will.

The funny thing about this is that the so-called home fellowship leader was hardly ever there himself as he was too busy working at being a bus driver to attend. We would perhaps see him once, occasionally twice a month. He was responsible to run a home fellowship meeting every week, but he was off driving buses instead. His income was more important to him than doing the work of the ministry and carrying out his spiritual responsibilities.

The most vivid recollection of that time we spent travelling to that home fellowship meeting was how cold the house was. Not only was the house cold, but we were compelled to take our shoes off at the front door and walk on freezing wooden floors. They not only left the heating off, there were usually windows open too, even in winter. It was so cold at times, my toes would sting. At the time I thought they were perhaps struggling with money and couldn't afford to heat the house, so I put up with it.

A few months later, that home fellowship leader bragged to me one day about how he had saved up £5000 in his first year working as a bus driver. Really? So while the two of us had spent over £1000 in travelling expenses to freeze every week in meetings that he didn't even attend himself, that bastard had saved up £5000? He put his savings before heating his house so we could be warm? It was around that time that I began to see the depth of the truth that God dwells not in temples made with hands. That couple were quite happy having us freeze to death in their home, because they loved their wallet and their purse more than they loved God and the people they were supposed to be caring for.

That's an excellent example of how the love of money is the root of all evil, even among God's people.

Well, I suppose he supposed that gain is godliness. I have no doubt he thought himself a really godly person. The word says we are to withdraw from such. Despite numerous correspondence to both him, his leadership and the Way International headquarters leadership, that man was not reprimanded, he did not change his ways, and at the time of writing he still ran a home fellowship meeting on behalf of The Way. They stole my work and stole the people God entrusted to my care, and I can only assume they did it for the tithe money it would generate. I now consider The Way International as mark and avoid. If you have ever been a part of Dr Wierwille's ministry and still have a heart for God, establish a church in your home and use God's money to move the word.

The Way International expected me to submit myself to that man because they considered him my leadership even though I had done all the work and God had given me the increase, and for a time I did to my extreme detriment. Regarding carrying out instructions given by councils of men in temples made with hands, Paul went to Jerusalem in Acts 21 and did just that.

> Acts 21:23,24
> Do therefore this that we say to thee: We have four men which have a vow on them;
>
> Them take, and purify thyself with them, and be at charges with them, that they may shave *their* heads: and all may know that those things, whereof they were informed concerning thee, are nothing; but *that* thou thyself also walkest orderly, and keepest the law.

The instruction was clear, and Paul carried it out to the letter. So, let's see what happens when you do the will of councils of men

> Acts 21:26-31
> Then Paul took the men, and the next day purifying himself with them entered into the temple, to signify the accomplishment of the days of purification, until that an offering should be offered for every one of them.

And when the seven days were almost ended, the Jews [Judeans] which were of Asia, when they saw him in the temple, stirred up all the people, and laid hands on him,

Crying out, Men of Israel, help: This is the man, that teacheth all *men* every where against the people, and the law, and this place: and further brought Greeks also into the temple, and hath polluted this holy place.

(For they had seen before with him in the city Trophimus an Ephesian, whom they supposed that Paul had brought into the temple.)

And all the city was moved, and the people ran together: and they took Paul, and drew him out of the temple: and forthwith the doors were shut.

And as they went about to kill him, tidings came unto the chief captain of the band, that all Jerusalem was in an uproar.

Doing the will of men almost killed Paul, and he wound up in prison for it. Doing the will of councils of men will not lead you to a life which is more than abundant, it will only lead you into freezing, backbiting, bitching, religious prisons run by greedy little cunts. We are to love each other as a family, and look after and care for each other, and use our money to care for people and move the word. That's what they did in the book of Acts and that's why the word moved. Let's see what else we can turn up regarding money.

We've already looked at the record of Ananias and Sapphira in an earlier session, but it might be profitable to have another quick look at it in light of the love of money being the root of all evil. This is something that can affect any disciple if we don't keep our thoughts in the word. It isn't difficult to see the love of money being the root of all evil here.

Acts 5:1-4
But a certain man named Ananias, with Sapphira his wife, sold a possession,

And kept back *part* of the price, his wife also being privy *to it*, and brought a certain part, and laid *it* at the apostles' feet.

But Peter said, Ananias, why hath Satan filled thine heart to lie to the Holy Ghost, and to keep back *part* of the price of the land?

Whiles it remained, was it not thine own? and after it was sold, was it not in thine own power? why hast thou conceived this thing in thine heart? thou hast not lied unto men, but unto God.

Money is again handled in Acts 6.

Acts 6:1-3
And in those days, when the number of the disciples was multiplied, there arose a murmuring of the Grecians against the Hebrews, because their widows were neglected in the daily ministration.

Then the twelve called the multitude of the disciples *unto them*, and said, It is not reason that we should leave the word of God, and serve tables.

Wherefore, brethren, look ye out among you seven men of honest report, full of the Holy Ghost [pneuma hagion – holy spirit] and wisdom [adept in the manifestation of word of wisdom], whom we may appoint over this business.

We're looking at this from a different perspective, so read it again and consider what it's saying. First of all, this is *not* saying all the disciples were sending all their money to some headquarters of a structured man-made ministry run by the apostles. These verses clearly imply that the twelve had no control over the money and what was being done with it. They didn't want it either. The problem was that the home church leadership who were responsible for what was done with the money were neglecting the widows, so the twelve told the disciples over there to appoint seven men to take care of things. In other words, the money, God's money was being kept and used at the home church level. Peter was not a patriarch, the twelve were not a council of men running the whole ministry, and the disciples did not send all their money to them. God's money was used at the home church level. That is what self supporting means. What else can we learn?

Walking *by* the Spirit

Acts 11:27-30
And in these days came prophets from Jerusalem unto Antioch.

And there stood up one of them named Agabus, and signified by the Spirit that there should be great dearth throughout all the world: which came to pass in the days of Claudius Caesar.

Then the disciples, every man according to his ability, determined to send relief unto the brethren which dwelt in Judaea:

Which also they did, and sent it to the elders by the hands of Barnabas and Saul.

In this record, who made the decisions regarding what was done with this relief money? The disciples in Antioch did. It wasn't decided by a council of men at the head of a temple made with hands. The home church leaders got together with their people, and they made the decisions regarding how much of God's money within the churches in that area they would send. Note that there is no mention of Paul and Barnabas dipping into any headquarters funds. That's because no one in the 1st Century sent money to any headquarters to support a hierarchical leadership council. Paul and Barnabas took this money from disciples in one area and transported it to disciples in another area. Can we learn anything else? Oh yes.

Acts 18:1-3
After these things Paul departed from Athens, and came to Corinth;

And found a certain Jew [Judean] named Aquila, born in Pontus, lately come from Italy, with his wife Priscilla; (because that Claudius had commanded all Jews [Judeans] to depart from Rome:) and came unto them.

And because he was of the same craft, he abode with them, and wrought: for by their occupation they were tentmakers.

Paul by this time was recognised as one of the top leaders, if not *the* leader of the 1st Century church. So how come he had to work for a living? Why didn't he work full time with the ministry and take his pay from God's money? I'll tell you why, it was because there was no manmade structured ministry headquarters to which everyone sent all their money, and there was no centralised depository from which he could draw funds The headquarters of the ministry was each home church.

The highest positions in the body of Christ are the home church leadership. There is no higher position available in the body of Christ. If you want to be a leader, then set your sights on learning to walk by the spirit and running a church in your home with Christ as your head. Remember Paul's words to the leadership at Ephesus while he was on his way to Jerusalem?

> Acts 20:32-34
> And now, brethren, I commend you to God, and to the word of his grace, which is able to build you up, and to give you an inheritance among all them which are sanctified.
>
> I have coveted no man's silver, or gold, or apparel.
>
> Yea, ye yourselves know, that these hands have ministered unto my necessities, and to them that were with me.

See, no one sent God's money to Paul, he worked for a living. God's money is to be kept at the home church level, and decisions regarding its use are to be determined by the home church leaders who, if they are walking by the spirit, will use it as God directs them. It is to be used at the home church level to move the word there.

> Romans 12:13
> Distributing to the necessity of saints; given to hospitality.

Paul is addressing the believers here, not the leadership of some temple made with hands. Paul was instructing the believers to be ready to use their money to help support each other, so that implies that God's money was being kept at the home church level. I've seen a home church leader dishing out God's money to his daughter to pay her electricity bill because she was too lazy to budget her money properly. This is not what this is talking about. The necessity of saints includes the word first and foremost, so God's money is to be used to move the word. That could mean hiring a local hall for a special teaching series. It could mean hiring a hotel somewhere to hold a special weekend for all the believers in your area. If there are three or four home churches, they could get together and agree how much each would put towards a special teaching event. Catering, hotel rooms, transport could all be paid for from God's money within each home church to bless the believers who gave that money in the first place. The key is to walk by the spirit and use God's money as he wants it spent.

Now yes, God may want to use some of his money to help a specific believer in that home church, but that's something the home church leader decides because he's walking by the spirit and God has energised in him to will and to do of his good pleasure. A few things home church leaders could use God's money for would be perhaps petrol money when God wants someone to drive somewhere to minister and teach. It could be putting on an event in your home, or help with heating and electricity costs to keep your home warm and cosy during home church meetings so it's a blessing for the believers to be there. In fact, anything that helps move the word is a good way to spend God's money. If you are a home church leader responsible for God's money, and you're walking by the spirit with Christ as your head, God *will* work within you both to will and to do of his good pleasure to let you know how and when to spend it.

You see, this isn't about sending all your money away to a man-made temple and getting a crappy magazine and a ton of guilt in return, this is about walking by the spirit with Christ as your head, being fellow labourers together with God, and using God's money to move the word. It is the devil who wants you to send all God's money away so God has none. Tell the vatican, the presbyterians, the baptists, the mormons, the jehovah's, the salvation army, the way international and all the other man-made temples out there to fuck off and don't send them anymore of God's money. Start a home church and use it to move the word instead. It's God's money so don't let the devil steal anymore of it. Here's an interesting section of scripture in this light.

> Romans 13:1
> Let every soul be subject unto the higher powers. For there is no power but of God: the powers that be are ordained of God.

This is perhaps one of the most misused scriptures in the bible, used by all sorts of criminals, patriarchs, councils of men, and religious nuts to demand allegiance from those they control under threat of all sorts of recriminations from God if they don't. First of all, Paul did *not* say, let every soul be subject unto *me*. If Paul was the higher power back then, surely he would have said let every soul be subject unto *me*, but that's not what he said, is it? So Paul was clearly no patriarch at the head of some ministry then, was he?

So who do you think these higher powers are? The leadership of the Way International? The pope? The dalai lama? Barack Obama? The united nations? Until now we've been taught that these higher powers are our ministry leadership, you know, those who hold leadership positions within man-made temples. It just can't be. The higher powers also can't be referring simply to someone who manifests holy spirit for we can all do that. The higher powers are the gift ministries, and this is handled in much more depth later in the class. Look at who we support with God's money in this context.

> Romans 13:6,7
> For for this cause pay ye tribute also: for they are God's ministers, attending continually upon this very thing.
>
> Render therefore to all their dues: tribute to whom tribute *is due;* custom to whom custom; fear to whom fear; honour to whom honour.

We give God's money to our home church leaders, and from that they are to support the energised gift ministries. Now isn't it good to know that the money you give to God is to be used by your home church leaders to help you move the word in your area. God wants *you* to enjoy the immediate benefits of the money you give to him as he works together with your home church leadership to move the word. Here's a good section of scripture to consider in this light.

> 2 Corinthians 9:1-5
> For as touching the ministering to the saints, it is superfluous for me to write to you:

> For I know the forwardness of your mind, for which I boast of you to them of Macedonia, that Achaia was ready a year ago; and your zeal hath provoked very many.
>
> Yet have I sent the brethren, lest our boasting of you should be in vain in this behalf; that, as I said, ye may be ready:
>
> Lest haply if they of Macedonia come with me, and find you unprepared, we (that we say not, ye) should be ashamed in this same confident boasting.
>
> Therefore I thought it necessary to exhort the brethren, that they would go before unto you, and make up beforehand your bounty, whereof ye had notice before, that the same might be ready, as *a matter of* bounty, and not as *of* covetousness.

For decades I read into these verses what isn't written there. It does not state or even imply that everyone was to gather in their money so Paul could take it away with him to some ministry headquarters. Yet that is what churches read into these verses and teach you, so you will give your money to them. It isn't there. There is nothing in these verses that implies we give God's money to anyone but our home church leaders who are to use it to minister to the saints. Notice also that God's money is referred to here as bounty. In this administration of Grace we are not under the law so it is inappropriate to refer to God's money as tithe money. Paul called it bounty, I call it God's money, but it makes no difference what we call it. We give as we purpose in our hearts that which we can comfortably afford and are happy to give, but it is obviously subject to a minimum of ten percent. We don't give of our need, only our plurality, that which we don't need.

> 2 Corinthians 9:6-8
> But this *I say*, He which soweth sparingly shall reap also sparingly; and he which soweth bountifully shall reap also bountifully.
>
> Every man according as he purposeth in his heart, *so let him give;* not grudgingly, or of necessity: for God loveth a cheerful giver.

And God *is* able to make all grace abound toward you; that ye, always having all sufficiency in all *things,* may abound to every good work:

This reaping sparingly isn't a threat, it is simply God teaching us that what we put into the ground is what we will get out of it. Every farmer knows this without having to be told. If a farmer sows seed sparingly, he will reap sparingly because you can only get out of the ground what you put into it. That's how God set life up. If you want bumper crops weighed down with increase, you must sow bountifully. As you give in life, so you receive. What you put into life is what you get out of it, and this is worth exploring a little deeper.

Proverbs 11:24
There is that scattereth, and yet increaseth; and *there is* that withholdeth more than is meet, but *it tendeth* to poverty.

This truth that what you sow you reap isn't just a money thing, it is a life thing. You only get out of life what you put into it. Social security isn't social security at all. Once a government stops rewarding those who put their life into their country and instead steals from them and hands out their increase to bums and deadbeats, that civilisation is on the road to extinction. Darwin's theory of Natural Selection very much applies to man, as well as to the animal kingdom. A country that steals from the strong to support the weak, produces weaker people, and over time that will destroy a country. Keeping drunks, drug addicts, bums, deadbeats and lazy bastards alive by handing them free money stolen from working people is the politics of extinction. No species on earth can survive with such insane politics. You don't even need the bible to understand this, just go read Darwin.

2 Thessalonians 3:10
For even when we were with you, this we commanded you, that if any would [thelō] not work, neither should he eat.

Thayer defines *thelō* as *to will, to have in mind, to be resolved or determined, to purpose, to desire, to wish, to love, to like to do a thing, to be fond of doing, to take delight in, to have pleasure in.* In other words, if someone does not want to work, does not have it in his mind to work for a living, is not resolved, determined, and purposed to work, does not desire or wish to work, they should not eat. Any individual with this attitude towards work should be left to starve to death. That's God's word, take it or leave it. The more you refuse to listen to God, the closer you march to extermination and extinction.

Look, if you're a farmer and you don't sow any seed, you're not going to grow any crops, it's that simple. If you're that lazy and stupid, I don't fucking care if you starve to death. Yet some politicians think they're so smart by stealing another farmer's crops under threat of prosecution and jail and hand it to the lazy. That is insane, and that's the politics of social security. If you're a bum or a deadbeat, sure, you can change. Go and get a job or start your own business. Go clean windows, mow people's grass, clean their cars, do their gardens, just go to work. God says he will supply all your need, but he isn't going to support you if you refuse to work.

Now, if there's a farmer who for some reason can't sow any seed due to ill health or other reasons, but who *wants* to sow seed, then now it's time for the church to pull together and help that farmer get his fields sown, understand? This doesn't apply to honest men and women who want to work, and are looking for work. This is where home churches being self supporting comes to the fore. If you have honest men and women struggling financially who have a heart to work, then help them. God may even work with the home church leader to use his money to help with things like travel expenses to job interviews. In situations like these, the home church believers are to pull together and look after each other and ensure everyone has all their needs met. Would I buy a week's groceries for a brother or sister in my home church if they were not working and were running out of money? Of course I would.

> 1 John 3:16-18
> Hereby perceive we the love *of God*, because he laid down his life for us: and we ought to lay down *our* lives for the brethren.
>
> But whoso hath this world's good, and seeth his brother have need, and shutteth up his bowels *of compassion* from him, how dwelleth the love of God in him?

My little children, let us not love in word, neither in tongue; but in deed and in truth.

The key to understanding these verses is understanding the shutting up of the bowels. You see, compassion that wells up inside us is often how God energises in us to help someone.

If you're walking by the spirit and God wells that compassion up inside you to help, and you do nothing, how dwells the love of God in you? When Jesus Christ fed the multitudes with fish and loaves, he did it because he walked by the spirit and God moved him with compassion.

Mark 8:2
I have compassion on the multitude, because they have now been with me three days, and have nothing to eat:

Conversely, it isn't always just a case of chucking cash or food at every problem. Jesus Christ didn't feed everyone everywhere he went, those were two isolated cases. Sometimes someone may just need a good kick in the arse to get out there and get a job, and that may be how God energises you to move. The key is to walk by the spirit.

If we don't give in life, we are not going to receive anything from life, and there's another side to this, if we steal from life, life will steal from us. I've seen this thousands of times. I've seen people fiddle their electricity meters and then seen their houses broken into and all their stuff stolen. I've seen men defraud others and then go out of business. If you are stealing, then life is going to steal from you, for what you sow is what you will reap.

Hosea 8:7a
For they have sown the wind, and they shall reap the whirlwind:

If people are sowing the wind they can have no complaints when they reap the whirlwind, the tornado, the monsoon, and the hurricane. I'm not saying this to scare you, I'm just telling you the truth. This is the way life is. If you don't like tornadoes destroying your life then change your lying stealing ways. If that means resigning from the freemasons, then do it.

Romans 12:17
Recompense to no man evil for evil. Provide things honest in the sight of all men.

Why did God write this in his word? So we would be miserable and have no fun? No, it's because what you put in the ground is what you will get out of it. If someone rips you off by selling you a dodgy car they knew needed work, they will reap what they sow. They will not get away with it. Life is like that, but we *never* lower our ethics and morals because of hurt or anger and start ripping off other people in return. Jacob did not do it with Laban and we are not to do it either. We are to trust in God to keep us protected and if we give of our plurality we can claim that promise. Keep yourselves out of crime. You don't remove out of date stickers on food items in your shops, you don't overcharge for crappy goods, you don't sell dodgy cars that need work, you don't rip off insurance companies, you don't shoplift, you don't pirate software or music, you don't feed dog food to humans. If people don't listen and change their ways, the whirlwind is coming.

Luke 6:38
Give, and it shall be given unto you; good measure, pressed down, and shaken together, and running over, shall men give into your bosom. For with the same measure that ye mete withal it shall be measured to you again.

These merchants would shake their baskets to settle the grain so they could get more in. Not like the world's greedy merchants today hey? If you want your life overflowing, then this is the way to go. What you sow is what you will reap. It applies to all life. If you don't enjoy what life is dealing out to you, change what you're putting into it.

2 Corinthians 9:6,7
But this *I say*, He which soweth sparingly shall reap also sparingly; and he which soweth bountifully shall reap also bountifully.

Every man according as he purposeth in his heart, *so let him give;* not grudgingly, or of necessity: for God loveth a cheerful giver.

It doesn't specifically state any percentages here, does it? It does not state ten percent. However, if you think this gives you a licence to be greedy and hold back God's money because you're only cheerful to give one percent of your income, don't expect the windows of heaven to open for you. What you sow is what you will reap. The tithe is the bottom line. Anything over the tithe falls into the *every man according as he purposes* category. We've already looked at Philippians in this context, but there's another angle we can consider here.

> Philippians 4:15,16
> Now ye Philippians know also, that in the beginning of the gospel, when I departed from Macedonia, no church communicated with me as concerning giving and receiving, but ye only.
>
> For even in Thessalonica ye sent once and again unto my necessity.

When Paul was at Thessalonica, the Philippians sent him money to take care of his needs. Why did the home churches in Thessalonica not take care of his needs? We don't know, because the word doesn't tell us. Perhaps it was a new work and the believers hadn't got their heads around giving money yet. To guess is private interpretation, and it doesn't really matter anyway. The point is, God's money was kept at the home church level and decisions regarding its use was made by the home church leaders. God obviously worked in the church leaders at Philippi to send money to Paul when he was in Thessalonica. The workman is worthy of his hire, Paul was labouring together with God to move the word, God promises to meet all our need, so he had the churches in Philippi send him money. Again, walking by the spirit is the key to understanding this.

Look, God doesn't meet our needs by showering us with bank notes that flutter down out of the sky, he energises the gift of holy spirit in believers who walk with Christ as their head to spend money where he wants it spent. If you send all God's money away to a temple made with hands to keep a council of men in comfortable lifestyles at your expense, how can the word move in your area? Another thing, if God's money is kept at the home church level, it could be used to invite men and women of God with gift ministries to visit the church in your home by paying for their travel expenses. That's another way the money you give can benefit you directly. Paul was certainly thankful for the money that came from the home churches in Philippi to help him move the word. You can see the same thing when Paul was in Corinth.

> 2 Corinthians 11:8,9
> I robbed other churches, taking wages of them, to do you service.
>
> And when I was present with you, and wanted, I was chargeable to no man: for that which was lacking to me the brethren which came from Macedonia supplied: and in all things I have kept myself from being burdensome unto you, and so will I keep myself.

Look at this! Paul took money from other home churches while he was ministering to the Corinthians. When he was actually there present in Corinth and had needs, it was supplied by God's money that came from the Macedonian home churches. There can be no doubt that God wants home churches to be self governing, self propagating, and self supporting.

If you are a home church leader and your home church splits because you've grown too big, all the money from the believers in the new home church is to stay there for them to use to move the word. This is the only way to keep evil men who love money out of the body of Christ. Paul started hundreds and hundreds of home churches and not one of them sent him all their money, they merely supported him as and when God energised within the home church leaders to do so.

Debt we've already handled. To owe no man anything, means you don't owe anyone anything.

> Romans 13:8
> Owe no man any thing, but to love one another: for he that loveth another hath fulfilled the law.

If you're in debt, get out of it. Your outgoings have to be less than your income, simple. If you spend more than you earn, you are going into debt. God supplies all your need, so if your income does not cover your expenses, it isn't God at fault, you are out of control with your spending habits. If you drive a new car you bought on credit, sell it, pay off the loan and buy a second hand car that you can afford to run. If it would cost less money to pay off the remaining debt and keep the car, then apologise to God and promise him you won't be so stupid in future. If two people own a car each, could you sell one, split the money and share the costs to run the other one between you? If you rent a 3 bedroom house, could you rent a 2 bedroom instead? If you're in debt and get serious about paying it off, God will help you get there.

Get out of debt. Controlling your budget and making your expenses fit your income is *your* responsibility. Spending money you don't have and going into debt is insane. Nothing in life will ever be your property anyway, so why go into debt for it? Do a weekly or monthly budget, make your income fit your living needs, cut your expenses if you have to and get in control of your money.

Budgeting isn't difficult. If a new computer costs £500 and you need to upgrade every four years, then you need to save £10 a month. If you do that, every four years you will have enough to buy a new computer. If you like new clothes, put £30 a month into a saving fund and every year you will have £360 to go on a shopping spree. That is budgeting, that is believing, and that is how you control your money. Get your budget sorted out and make your money fit that budget. Whatever it takes, you do it. It is the love of money that is the root of all evil, so stop loving money and get yourself out of the evil of debt. If you can't make your budget fit your expenses, sit down and find a way to make it work. If your car's total running costs work out at £4000 a year all in, sell it and buy a car that costs you £2000 a year. Whatever it takes, make your expenses fit your budget and stay out of debt.

To close this session, let's consider a few scriptures and make a decision to use our money not in cars we don't need, clothes we hardly ever wear, and other worldly garbage, but in looking after our brothers and sisters in Christ who want to walk by the spirit and in showing and teaching them how to live abundantly for themselves.

> 1 Thessalonians 4:11,12
> And that ye study to be quiet, and to do your own business, and to work with your own hands, as we commanded you;
>
> That ye may walk honestly toward them that are without, and *that* ye may have lack of nothing.

Proverbs 30:8
Remove far from me vanity and lies: give me neither poverty nor riches; feed me with food convenient for me:

Luke 12:15
And he [Jesus Christ] said unto them, Take heed, and beware of covetousness: for a man's life consisteth not in the abundance of the things which he possesseth.

1 Timothy 6:6-8
But godliness with contentment is great gain.

For we brought nothing into *this* world, *and it is* certain we can carry nothing out.

And having food and raiment let us be therewith content.

49. The More Abundant Life

Just as living life requires a certain lifestyle in order to be successful at it, so too living a more abundant spiritual life requires a certain lifestyle in order to be successful at it. For example, a successful life requires personal grooming, good diet, exercise, paying the bills, keeping your home comfortable, and leisure pursuits to keep your days interesting and fulfilling. There is no one thing that does it all. Cleaning your teeth every morning doesn't do it by itself. Cleaning your teeth is just a part of what makes up a successful lifestyle.

Let's break down an average morning so we can get a handle on this. First, we have to wake up early enough that we can rise and get ready for the day. We either set an alarm, or have someone wake us, then we do our daily grooming, get clothed, have breakfast, then it's off to work, get the kids ready for school or something else. If we drive a car, then we have to ensure it is roadworthy, and it has water, oil and petrol in it so it's functional and will get us to work. Every week we have to shop so we have sufficient food in the house so there is something on the table for breakfast, and that requires planning, budgeting and going shopping. We have to keep our clothes clean and in good repair so we can look our best when we're out and about. The point is, to live life requires believing, which involves planning coupled with action. If we can't get out of bed, we never clean our clothes or take care with our personal grooming, never exercise, and eat chocolate and drink coffee all day, our lives are not going to be very successful. In fact, we will most likely be ill, overweight, have no money and smell. The same is true spiritually.

Just as children must develop life skills as they grow to maturity, we also must learn and develop spiritual skills as we grow. This spiritually minded lifestyle is referred to in Ephesians as walking circumspectly.

> Ephesians 5:15
> See then that ye walk circumspectly, not as fools, but as wise,

When this was written, Paul was under house arrest in Rome chained to a Roman guard. Paul did not walk by the spirit when he went to Jerusalem in Acts 21. He walked by his senses and unwisely followed the direction of a council of men at the ministry headquarters there. Consequently, he nearly lost his life and he wound up imprisoned in Rome. Paul wrote Ephesians *after* he had disobeyed God by going to Jerusalem when he knew he should have remained with the Gentiles. Did Paul walk circumspectly by going to Jerusalem? No, however, he didn't allow his past to prevent him from teaching the Ephesians to walk circumspectly. Did condemnation stop him from teaching about walking circumspectly when he hadn't? Did Paul feel unworthy to teach the Ephesians about walking circumspectly because he'd messed up and everyone in Ephesus knew he'd messed up? Not at all. Paul was a master at putting the past behind him.

> Philippians 3:13,14
> Brethren, I count not myself to have apprehended: but *this* one thing *I do*, forgetting those things which are behind, and reaching forth unto those things which are before,
>
> I press toward the mark for the prize of the high calling of God in Christ Jesus.

So if Paul could put his past behind him and go on to receive the revelation to write the book of Ephesians, can we also walk circumspectly today, despite what we did yesterday? Yes, we can pick ourselves up at any time, start walking again and God will be there. No matter what we have done or how badly we've messed up, we can still speak in tongues and get back into fellowship at any time and live the more abundant life. Now isn't that nice to know? Living a more abundant life therefore, isn't conditional on our being perfect, it's conditional on our being faithful despite our mistakes.

God didn't hide what Paul did by going to Jerusalem, did he? God told Luke to record what happened when he wrote the book of Acts. Why? To embarrass Paul? So we could waggle our fingers at him? No, so we could learn from him. Paul walked circumspectly again after going to Jerusalem and went on to receive the greatest revelation ever given to men, the book of Ephesians. So no matter what we've done in the past, or what mistakes we made yesterday, we can walk circumspectly today.

That's one of the great things about this Grace Administration – every day is a new day. Can you still speak in tongues? Of course you can. We can live the word today, regardless of yesterday, because we are holy and without blame before God in love.

> Ephesians 1:4
> According as he hath chosen us in him before the foundation of the world, that we should be holy and without blame before him in love:

So, what does it mean to walk circumspectly? In the KJV the word translated *circumspectly* is the Greek word *akribos*, and it is translated *diligently – 2 times, circumspectly – 1 time, perfect – 4 times, and perfectly – 2 times*. Bible dictionaries define it as *exactly, accurately*, and *diligently*.

The Darby Bible translates Ephesians 5:15:

> Ephesians 5:15
> See therefore how ye walk carefully, not as unwise but as wise,

The Murdock Bible says it this way:

> Ephesians 5:15
> See therefore, that ye walk circumspectly; not like the simple,

The Lexham English Bible states it:

> Ephesians 5:15
> Therefore, consider carefully how you live, not as unwise but as wise,

With this background, let's explore the word *akribos* in the bible.

> Acts 18:24-26
> And a certain Jew [Judean] named Apollos, born at Alexandria, an eloquent man, *and* mighty in the scriptures, came to Ephesus.
>
> This man was instructed in the way of the Lord; and being fervent in the spirit, he spake and taught diligently [akribos] the things of the Lord, knowing only the baptism of John.

And he began to speak boldly in the synagogue: whom when Aquila and Priscilla had heard, they took him unto *them*, and expounded unto him the way of God more perfectly [akribos].

Apollos taught diligently (*akribos*) the things of the Lord, knowing only the water baptism of John. Aquila and Priscilla then taught him the way of God more perfectly (more *akribos*). For Aquila and Priscilla to be able to teach more *akribos* than Apollos, they must have known the word in greater depth than Apollos. So who had taught them the word? Well, they had lived and worked with Paul at Corinth. Later they had sailed with Paul to Ephesus and decided to live there, and it was in Ephesus they met Apollos.

God had taught Paul, Paul had taught them, and that was how they were able to teach the way of the Lord more perfectly, more *akribos*, to Apollos who knew only water baptism. By the way, water baptism was part of the old testament and isn't part of the Grace Administration. Washing in water was simply a symbolic old testament ceremony to illustrate what was coming, which was baptism in the holy spirit. With the coming of the greater, the lesser was no longer necessary. That is what Aquila and Priscilla taught Apollos. That's how the word moves. We have to teach.

There are further usages of *akribos* in Matthew, in the record of Herod and the Magi from Persia.

> Matthew 2:1-16
> Now when Jesus was born in Bethlehem of Judaea in the days of Herod the king, behold, there came wise men [Magos] from the east to Jerusalem,
>
> Saying, Where is he that is born King of the Jews [Judeans]? for we have seen his star in the east, and are come to worship him.
>
> When Herod the king had heard *these things*, he was troubled, and all Jerusalem with him.
>
> And when he had gathered all the chief priests and scribes of the people together, he demanded of them where Christ should be born.

And they said unto him, In Bethlehem of Judaea: for thus it is written by the prophet,

And thou Bethlehem, *in* the land of Juda, art not the least among the princes of Juda: for out of thee shall come a Governor, that shall rule my people Israel.

Then Herod, when he had privily called the wise men, **enquired** of them **diligently** [akriboō] what time the star appeared.

And he sent them to Bethlehem, and said, Go and search **diligently** [akribos] for the young child; and when ye have found *him*, bring me word again, that I may come and worship him also.

When they had heard the king, they departed; and, lo, the star, which they saw in the east, went before them, till it came and stood over where the young child was.

When they saw the star, they rejoiced with exceeding great joy.

And when they were come into the house, they saw the young child with Mary his mother, and fell down, and worshipped him: and when they had opened their treasures, they presented unto him gifts; gold, and frankincense, and myrrh.

And being warned of God in a dream that they should not return to Herod, they departed into their own country another way.

And when they were departed, behold, the angel of the Lord appeareth to Joseph in a dream, saying, Arise, and take the young child and his mother, and flee into Egypt, and be thou there until I bring thee word: for Herod will seek the young child to destroy him

When he arose, he took the young child and his mother by night, and departed into Egypt:

And was there until the death of Herod: that it might be fulfilled which was spoken of the Lord by the prophet, saying, Out of Egypt have I called my son.

Then Herod, when he saw that he was mocked of the wise men, was exceeding wroth, and sent forth, and slew all the children that were in Bethlehem, and in all the coasts thereof, from two years old and under, according to the time which he had **diligently enquired** [akriboō] of the wise men.

When Herod heard this news about a new king, he sat down with the Magi and *enquired diligently* (akribos) when the star appeared. The Magi would have gone into great detail and explained everything. They would have told Herod all about the triple conjunction of Jupiter and Regulus in Leo sandwiched between a double conjunction of Jupiter and Venus, as well as the massing of the planets Jupiter, Venus, Mars and Mercury in Leo. By the end of the session, Herod himself was convinced the Christ had been born and set about making plans to have him murdered.

When the Magi legged it back to Persia and Herod found out, he was extremely pissed off. Do you remember he asked the Magi diligently about the star? He knew *precisely* what times the conjunctions had occurred, and he knew Jesus Christ would already have been a young child, a toddler, which was why he murdered all the children two years old and under.

So this adds to our understanding of *akribos* and helps us understand what it is to walk circumspectly, but we can learn more. Many times in the bible, Greek words are employed that do not appear very often, as is the case with *akribos*. In fact, some words are used only once, so gaining a taste for the flavour of a word often requires seeing how words were used in secular literature at the same time the bible was written. Bullinger's Critical Greek Lexicon and Concordance states of *akribos*:

Going up to the top or summit; and as this requires great pains, care, and diligence, it means accurate, exact, precise.

Bullinger learned this from how *akribos* was employed in other writings at the time where it illustrated a mountaineer's ascent to a summit. Climbing a mountain requires exactness and precision, as well as good levels of fitness. It requires you know what you are doing, that you have the right equipment, and that you're conditioned and fit for the climb.

For years, this definition subconsciously added concern into my thinking. I mean mountain climbing is dangerous. One slip and you can fall over a cliff. Deep down inside, I wasn't sure I wanted to be a part of all that walking circumspectly stuff because I wasn't sure my life would ever be so perfect I could live it in safety.

The good news is that this unconscious stratum of doubt I had about the circumspect walk isn't accurate. Mountaineering is a sport. People do it for enjoyment and sport. To enjoy climbing mountains, you just need the right gear, the right levels of health and fitness, and to know what you're doing. It's something to look forward to with anticipation and excitement. Sports such as mountaineering are enjoyable. When you experience walking circumspectly, it is something you will love. I've climbed a few Scottish mountains and it can be exhilarating.

However, it is a mature walk. What does that mean? Well, driving a car provides a good working analogy. Driving cars can be dangerous if you don't know what you're doing. Would you throw the car keys to a ten year old boy and tell him to go and have some fun on the roads? No. Why not? Driving is enjoyable, it's fun, it's exhilarating, it's great, but it's not for ten year old children is it? Just as you wouldn't give the car keys to a child, nor would you take them mountaineering with you in winter. The walk circumspectly isn't for children, it's for the mature, the faithful in Christ Jesus, which is who Ephesians is addressed to. However, it *is* something children should look forward to! Growing into the walk circumspectly is a bit like passing your driving test and getting the keys to your first car. Remember how exciting that was?

Just as parents wouldn't give the car keys to their ten year old children, neither will God put his children into positions where they could be harmed in the spiritual competition until they can handle it. Certain responsibilities in the body of Christ are only given to those who know something about the spiritual competition. It wouldn't be loving or right to put new born believers into positions of spiritual responsibility where they would come under direct attack from the spirit realm. We need to protect God's children until they mature into the Ephesians walk and learn how to walk circumspectly for themselves. Once people are mature enough to drive safely, the walk circumspectly is a lot of fun.

How can we apply this to our lives? One aspect that helps illustrate the practical side of this circumspect walk is finances. The immature walk is to buy on impulse. Children have to have everything right now, hey? To strip that nonsense, foolishness and immaturity out of them, we have to teach them how to budget, save up, shop around properly, and not buy things they don't need. Children don't understand money and have to learn about it. Our children are not sinful, that's just life. Those of us who know the truth have a responsibility to help the younger believers get strong with their finances and learn to walk circumspectly in that area of life. Part of the more abundant life is dependent on how we deal with our money.

The walk circumspectly in finances, therefore, would be learning how to handle money maturely, which precludes impulse buying and using credit cards to buy stuff with money we don't have. We learn to budget and we learn to enjoy living out of debt. Every month we sit down with our finances and work our budget. When we're happy with it, we stick with it. As we grow in our understanding of finances, buying on impulse becomes something we are no longer even tempted with. When we have a need, we save up and then shop around. When we're sure we've done our homework and the money is available, we make an informed decision and make the purchase.

Now listen, this isn't drudgery, walking circumspectly in the financial realm is a heck of a lot more fun than spending money you don't have and going into debt. Having control of your finances and having all your need met, all the time, in every situation, is far better than being in debt and someone else getting rich at your expense. The circumspect walk is where all the fun in life is. This is something we really *do* want to grow up into and anticipate with great desire and make great diligent effort (akribos) to achieve.

The same is true in every part of life. The more of the word we know, the more we can enjoy life. However, this does not mean that a more abundant life is only available to mature disciples. Just as life in all its abundance is available to babies as soon as they are born, all God's abundance is available to his children as soon as they are born into his family. The more abundant life is immediately available to everyone in God's family. The distinction is that with maturity comes greater responsibility which God expects us to live up to.

So what is involved in a healthy spiritual lifestyle that will allow us to live the more abundant life Jesus Christ came to make available? Well, as we've seen, it changes with maturity. More is expected of teenagers than of children, and more is expected of adults than of teenagers. So of someone who has just been born again, very little is expected simply because they know nothing regarding spiritual matters, and all God's abundance is immediately available to them. However, from that moment on they have a responsibility to develop themselves spiritually so they grow and mature into the Ephesians lifestyle, which is the lifestyle of a disciple, someone who is faithful in Christ Jesus, someone who walks by the spirit. The newest baby born into the church of God requires daily sustenance, so we have to feed them the word and baby them until they are reading and studying the word every day for themselves.

Now just as in life there are many things that make up a successful lifestyle, so it is with the more abundant life. Little is expected of children, but if adults sit around all day expecting everything to be handed to them the word says they should not eat. There are no excuses for mature believers to neglect the word by not reading, studying and memorising it every day. There are no excuses for mature believers to not speak in tongues and walk by the spirit. There are no excuses for mature believers to refuse to give God his share of their money. This mature walk isn't tough, that's for sure, but it does require faithfulness.

> Matthew 11:28-30
> Come unto me, all *ye* that labour and are heavy laden, and I will give you rest.
>
> Take my yoke upon you, and learn of me; for I am meek and lowly in heart: and ye shall find rest unto your souls.
>
> For my yoke *is* easy, and my burden is light.
>
> It's really simple to live the more abundant life, and it brings rest to our souls. Religion is burdensome and oppressive, but not discipleship.

There are three parts to every member of the church of God – body, soul, and spirit – and they all require daily attention and maintenance. Fundamentally then, an abundant prosperous life requires healthy diet and exercise in all three categories, as well as living according to the standards of God's word.

Most people know what constitutes a good life in the physical – we must eat and drink properly, exercise adequately, and look after ourselves. Similarly we require a healthy mental diet if we are to enjoy being who we are and enjoy quality of life. A systematic study of God's word to renew our minds is the basis for this. At the same time we learn to walk by the spirit and build ourselves up by way of speaking in tongues. Without developing the Christ in us, having a healthy body and a sound mind is of little value. If you neglect the Christ in you and don't learn to walk by the spirit, eventually you will either walk away from God or become a religious arsehole.

Just as we build good daily habits into our lives, such as enjoying breakfast, lunch and dinner, we must build good habits like reading, studying, and memorising God's word so we think the word rather than the world's thoughts. Couple that with energising the gift of holy spirit by speaking in tongues much throughout your day, and you are well on your way to maturing into the Ephesians lifestyle and having God throw you the keys to the car.

Money and our attitudes towards it we handled in the previous session, and money and our attitudes towards it plays a big part in the more abundant life. Giving God his share of your money is your rent for living on his earth and paying your rent ensures you enjoy open windows from heaven through which God pours out all the goodness of life for you. This isn't simply referring to having loads of *stuff*, but refers to much more, like always having the answers you need so you can be more than a conqueror in every situation.

Regarding speaking God's word, we are simply to be living epistles living life together as a family, our lifestyles being our preaching. Who we are and the quality of life we enjoy opens doors for us to show others how they too can escape the world's garbage and live this more abundant life.

And that's basically it. From these foundations, you can learn to walk by the spirit. Be warned though, just as in the world there are things that will detract from your quality of life, like drink, drugs and bad food, so there are things in the world that will detract from your spiritual quality of life. Here are a couple of examples.

> Ephesians 4:25
> Wherefore putting away lying, speak every man truth with his neighbour: for we are members one of another.

> Ephesians 4:28
> Let him that stole steal no more: but rather let him labour, working with *his* hands the thing which is good, that he may have to give to him that needeth.

If we steal from life, life will steal from us, for what we sow we will reap. This is regardless of whether we tithe as the tithe does not supersede the laws of life. If we deliberately jump off a cliff, gravity will take us down and we will either be seriously injured or killed when we hit the bottom. Tithing does not negate gravity any more than it negates the ground only producing what goes into it.

Consider the tithe as providing the hedge of protection around us that Job also enjoyed, but that breaking principles in life will poke holes through that protection. Without the tithe there is no hedge, but we must also live the word. So as we learn the word we renew our minds and change our thinking to line up with it.

Homosexuality, for example, is not an alternative healthy lifestyle, it is a reprehensible criminal act worthy of death. If you partake of that filth, God will not be able to protect you despite your tithe. If you're a homo or a slimy lesbian, and you're happy with that, keep your scabby tithe and stay there. If you want to clean up your life, God will be there for you and all his abundance will be made available to you. But don't think you can do both. As we learn God's word, we have to change our thinking to line up with God's thinking. That's how we develop a sound mind.

> 2 Timothy 1:7
> For God hath not given us the spirit of fear; but of power, and of love, and of a sound mind.

No, you can't just continue living in your old man life, refuse to change, and expect God to open the windows of heaven for you. If you want God's abundance, you do things God's way. God isn't going to change the laws of life just for you and I don't care how mad that makes you. No renewing of the mind and no living the word equals no abundant life for you. You may have lots of money, but what's that worth at the end of the day? If you want abundance, you do things God's way.

When I first got into the word, I was accustomed to stealing stuff. I stole all the time, it was a way of life for me. While in the merchant navy I would steal cargo from the holds. When I got born again, I was involved in a ring of sailors who did this all the time. Getting out of that criminal ring proved intimidating. I was afraid of them and what they might do to me if I refused to break into anymore cargo holds. The pressure was intense and I feared for my safety. While deliberating over this, one evening God showed me a vision. I was sitting in the middle of a circle drawn on the ground and there was a lion walking around the outside of the circle. The lion wanted to bite me and every time it roared I huddled on the ground and froze in fear. After a while however, I realised that if I stayed inside the circle it couldn't bite me, all it could do was make a ferocious noise. I was safe inside the circle. The funny thing is, I didn't know this scripture in Peter at the time and had never read it.

> 1 Peter 5:8
> Be sober, be vigilant; because your adversary the devil, as a roaring lion, walketh about, seeking whom he may devour:

The point is, if we stay within God's protection, the devil can't bite us. I *knew* that if I just refused to steal any more cargo, I would be safe, and that's what I did. I renewed my mind and did the word. The lion roared to frighten me, but I did the word and those sailors left me alone. I've grown so much in this category I wouldn't even take a paper clip from an employer now if it didn't belong to me. God's protection is very real. I don't care how deeply entrenched you are in the world, or how big a mason or terrorist or gangster you are, or how afraid you are of your boss or the jesuits, if you make up your mind to do things God's way, the protection, the way to escape will be there.

James 4:7
Submit yourselves therefore to God. Resist the devil, and he will flee from you.

This is the truth and you can trust this truth. How we submit to God is by learning his word and renewing our minds. As we strengthen ourselves in the principles of the word and become unbreakable in them, the devil can no longer attack us.

I was also an alcoholic and smoked drugs when I first got born again. Getting out of alcoholism and drugs wasn't an easy road for me, but I did it. God is faithful to his word, even for men like me, so there are no excuses for anyone else. If I can do this thing, anyone can.

Paul imprisoned, tortured, and murdered believers before he was born again on the road to Damascus. How do you think he must have felt going to home churches and teaching to people he'd had beaten and imprisoned or worse? You see, this isn't about us and what we've been in the past, it's about the Christ in us, it's about what God did for us. When we are born again, we become a new creation, created in Christ Jesus.

2 Corinthians 5:17
Therefore if any man *be* in Christ, *he is* a new creature [creation]: old things are passed away; behold, all things are become new.

When we are born again, a new creation comes into being, something that has never existed before, a supernatural life, a spiritual being. We really are sons of God with his seed, his spirit born within us. That's the new man, that's the Christ in us, that's the grace we've been given.

This spiritual walk isn't about converting the old man, it isn't about purifying the flesh, it isn't about making your old man lovely and acceptable, it's about reckoning it dead and putting the damn thing off. Don't worry about the past, forget about it. If you are a homo, a criminal, a gangster, an alcoholic, a drug addict, or even a jesuit, and you want to know God, just get out of that lifestyle and God will be there for you, understand? He doesn't *care* about your past, just put it off and move on. This isn't about the old man, this is about the new man, so get the world out of your life and get the God-breathed word into your head and put it into your heart, get those manifestations of holy spirit into operation, speak in tongues like a house on fire, and demonstrate the power of God in your life.

50. Demonstrating God's Power

We will now look a little deeper into demonstrating God's power, which is what this whole walking by the spirit thing is all about.

> 1 Corinthians 2:4,5
> And my speech and my preaching *was* not with enticing words of man's wisdom, but in demonstration of the Spirit and of power:
>
> That your faith [believing] should not stand in the wisdom of men, but in the power of God.

Without demonstrating God's power there is no point in attempting to live a christian life. Once you strip the supernatural out of christianity all you have left is religion, man's attempts to worship God not in spirit and in truth, but with his five senses. Rather than walk by the spirit, man hews him out broken cisterns, man-made temples to contain his religion. Rather than accepting the righteousness of God that comes with the new birth, man chooses to seek his own righteousness by attempting to perfect the flesh.

> Romans 10:3
> For they being ignorant of God's righteousness, and going about to establish their own righteousness, have not submitted themselves unto the righteousness of God.

We are not to attempt to establish our own righteousness, we are simply to accept the righteousness that comes with the new birth and demonstrate God's power.

> Acts 2:4
> And they were all filled with the Holy Ghost [holy spirit], and began to speak with other tongues, as the Spirit gave them utterance.

Demonstrating God's power begins with speaking in tongues. So what benefits are there to speaking in tongues, and how do we do it? Let's start in 1 Corinthians.

> 1 Corinthians 14:2
> For he that speaketh in an *unknown* tongue speaketh not unto men, but unto God: for no man understandeth *him*; howbeit in the spirit he speaketh mysteries.

First, let's strip the errors from the verse. The word *unknown* is in italics. That tells us it's been added to the text. How can a tongue, a language be unknown? That's absurd. Someone somewhere has to be able to understand it or it wouldn't be a language. When we speak in tongues, *we* don't know what we're saying, but someone somewhere would or it wouldn't be a language. This is a good example of why you can't trust italics in the bible. God didn't write them, the translators added them. We study the word to get back to God's original intent, and a King James version which shows the italics is an excellent tool to help us in that regards. We can scratch out the word *unknown*.

While we're at it, let's scratch out the word *him* as well, because it is also an italicised word added by the translators and it is simply wrong. When the twelve spoke in tongues on the day of Pentecost, they didn't understand what they were saying but there were plenty who did.

> Acts 2:6-11
> Now when this was noised abroad, the multitude came together, and were confounded, because that every man heard them speak in his own language.
>
> And they were all amazed and marvelled, saying one to another, Behold, are not all these which speak Galilaeans?
>
> And how hear we every man in our own tongue, wherein we were born?
>
> Parthians, and Medes, and Elamites, and the dwellers in Mesopotamia, and in Judaea, and Cappadocia, in Pontus, and Asia,

Phrygia, and Pamphylia, in Egypt, and in the parts of Libya about Cyrene, and strangers of Rome, Jews [Judeans] and proselytes,

Cretes and Arabians, we do hear them speak in our tongues the wonderful works of God.

Did these men understand what the apostles were saying when they spoke in tongues? Yes, they did, because it says so in verses 6, 8 and 11. So scratch out the italicised words in 1 Corinthians 14:2 and read it again.

> 1 Corinthians 14:2
> For he that speaketh in an ~~unknown~~ tongue speaketh not unto men, but unto God: for no man understandeth ~~him~~; howbeit in the spirit he speaketh mysteries.

On the day of Pentecost Peter and the other eleven apostles were filled with the power of the holy spirit and the first thing they did was demonstrate that power by speaking in tongues. When Peter spoke in tongues, he had no idea what he was saying, but there were people there who did. Even though we don't understand what we're saying when we speak in tongues, it is a language, understand? If I happened to speak in tongues in Mandarin Chinese, even though I didn't understand a word of it, everyone else who speaks that language would be able to understand every word I said. That's what happened on the day of Pentecost. Speaking in tongues is speaking a language you do not know. It is a supernatural manifestation of the gift of holy spirit. Every time you speak in tongues, you demonstrate God's power.

Right, let's deal with some stuff here. There are some who say you shouldn't speak in tongues in public to unbelievers. Chapter and verse please! Whatever garbage privately interpreted bible version you're reading, Peter and the other eleven apostles obviously didn't. They spoke in tongues in public to a huge crowd gathered in the temple. So stick that in your dried out broken cistern. How do you expect the word to move if we don't demonstrate God's power to people?

The key to understanding when you should and when you shouldn't demonstrate God's power in public is to walk by the spirit, *not* by the direction of a council of men. Get out there and teach people about the power of God and show them how to speak in tongues, that's how you demonstrate God's power. Sure, you don't do it all the time to everyone you meet, just as you don't annoy people by chattering out scriptures everywhere you go either. Look for open doors, walk by the spirit and have some fun with this thing.

There are some who teach you should only speak in tongues in public at home church meetings when the interpretation should also be given. Chapter and verse please! Whatever garbage privately interpreted bible version you're reading, Peter and the other eleven apostles obviously didn't. There is no mention of Peter or the other eleven apostles interpreting anything on the day of Pentecost. Sure, interpretation of tongues and prophecy are for church meetings, but don't drag speaking in tongues into that context. All you're doing is making people afraid to demonstrate God's power with your stupid rules and doctrines of men, and we all know where fear comes from, don't we? This is the first occurrence of the outpouring of the gift of holy spirit, and first occurrence sets the standard for this administration. We are to demonstrate God's power in public when we have opportunity. Jesus Christ himself, in his resurrected body, *commanded* the apostles to demonstrate God's power to the world.

> Acts 1:8
> But ye shall receive [lambanō] power [dunamis], after that the Holy Ghost [pneuma hagion – holy spirit] is come upon you: and ye shall be witnesses unto me both in Jerusalem, and in all Judaea, and in Samaria, and unto the uttermost part of the earth.

From this we can clearly see that being a witness of the Lord Jesus Christ has absolutely nothing whatsoever to do with chattering out scriptures at people. Read the verse again. It's talking about receiving power on the day of Pentecost, which was still in the future at that time. Those men were *already* speaking the word to people and yet they were not witnesses and wouldn't be until the day of Pentecost, so being a witness of the Lord Jesus Christ has absolutely nothing to do with teaching the bible or preaching or any other five senses ability. This is talking exclusively about manifesting the supernatural power they would receive with the coming of the gift of holy spirit. In other words, if you're not speaking in tongues and demonstrating God's power to people, you're not a witness of the Lord Jesus Christ. If this goes against what you've been taught, get out of that broken cistern shithole church or ministry you've been going to, get over your fear and start demonstrating God's power to people.

The word *receive* is *lambanō* in the Greek, and carries tremendous truth when understood. There are many words translated *receive* in the bible, and we will look at two of them, *lambanō* and *dechomai*. There is a record in Acts where both of these Greek words are used.

> Acts 8:14-19
> Now when the apostles which were at Jerusalem heard that Samaria had received [dechomai] the word of God, they sent unto them Peter and John:
>
> Who, when they were come down, prayed for them, that they might receive [lambanō] the Holy Ghost [holy spirit]:
>
> (For as yet he was fallen upon none of them: only they were baptized in the name of the Lord Jesus.)
>
> Then laid they *their* hands on them, and they received [lambanō] the Holy Ghost [holy spirit].
>
> And when Simon saw that through laying on of the apostles' hands the Holy Ghost [holy spirit] was given, he offered them money,
>
> Saying, Give me also this power, that on whomsoever I lay hands, he may receive [lambanō] the Holy Ghost [pneuma hagion – holy spirit].

With just a cursory reading, it would appear as if these people were born again when Peter and John laid hands on them, but that isn't the case. First of all, the words *Holy Ghost* should not be capitalised here. This isn't talking about people receiving God, it's talking about people receiving the gift of holy spirit from God.

Now we have to ask the question – how can someone receive the word of God but not receive holy spirit? That doesn't make sense. As soon as someone does what it says in Romans 10:9, which is to confess Jesus as Lord and believe in their heart that God raised him from the dead, they are born again, they receive the gift of holy spirit. These folks were most definitely born again, so what's going on? To understand these verses, we need to know the difference between *lambanō* and *dechomai*.

Dechomai means to receive something subjectively, without using it for that which it was intended. *Lambanō* means to receive something objectively, through to using it for that which it was intended. This is remarkable! If I give you a pen and you put it in your pocket and never use it, you have received the pen [dechomai], but you have not received the pen through to actually using it. Once you take the pen out and write with it, you have then received it [lambanō] through to using it for that which it was intended. Now let's read the verses again with this understanding and put it together.

> Acts 8:14
> Now when the apostles which were at Jerusalem heard that Samaria had received [dechomai] the word of God, they sent unto them Peter and John:

The believers in Samaria had received, *dechomai*, the word of God but they had not received, *lambanō*, the gift of holy spirit. Simply put, these believers were born again and had holy spirit but had not manifested it. They had received the gift of holy spirit subjectively but had not yet put it into operation. The situation was deemed so serious, that Peter and John went down there to sort it out.

What can we learn from this? Well, as soon as people are born again we are to *immediately* lead them into speaking in tongues so they *lambanō* holy spirit. This should be done *immediately*. If people are born again and do not immediately speak in tongues, God considers this a serious problem which is to be resolved *immediately*. Okay then, so what about man-made temples which run bible classes and tell their new people to wait until they take a class before they are taught how to speak in tongues? I'll spell it out for you – they err greatly, not understanding the scriptures nor the power of God.

So what was the problem in Samaria? We know that these believers were born again, that they had received, *dechomai*, the word of God, so God wasn't the problem, he'd done his job. The problem was that they had not received, *lambanō*, the gift of holy spirit by manifesting it, which was *their* job. Why was there a problem? We gain clues from the immediate context.

> Acts 8:9-11
> But there was a certain man, called Simon, which beforetime in the same city used sorcery, and bewitched the people of Samaria, giving out that himself was some great one:
>
> To whom they all gave heed, from the least to the greatest, saying, This man is the great power of God.
>
> And to him they had regard, because that of long time he had bewitched them with sorceries.

Witchcraft was the problem. These people had been entrenched in spiritualism and witchcraft for a long time. Devil spirits were behind the problem. It took Peter and John walking by the spirit and operating the revelation and power manifestations to deal with it.

> Acts 8:15
> Who, when they were come down, prayed for them, that they might receive [lambanō] the Holy Ghost [pneuma hagion – holy spirit]:

First they prayed that God would help them deal with this situation so the believers could receive, *lambanō*, holy spirit. The next verse is a parenthesis that adds further light to the problem.

> Acts 8:16
> (For as yet he [it – the gift of holy spirit] was fallen upon [epipiptō epi] none of them: only they were baptized in the name of the Lord Jesus.)

In the Aramaic, there was no neuter gender. Therefore third person singular would be translated *he*. However, many times *he* should be translated *it*, as is the case here because holy spirit is neuter gender.

Fallen upon in the Greek is *epipiptō epi*. *Epi* = *upon*, and *piptō* = *to fall*. *Epipiptō* would be *to fall upon*. *Epipiptō epi*, therefore, would be *to fall upon from upon*. *Epi* is used in the dative case and indicates actual superposition, *at rest upon,* in other words to fall from a higher plane to a position at rest on a lower plane. *Fallen upon none of them* simply means that the holy spirit which they had received subjectively [dechomai] had not been manifested, it had not fallen from its higher spiritual position to a position at rest in the senses realm. There was no *plethō*, no filled to overflowing.

The gift of holy spirit is that which a person receives, *dechomai*, at the time of the new birth, which is to be baptized in the name of the Lord Jesus. When you manifest holy spirit, that's the lambanō.

> Romans 10:9
> That if thou shalt confess with thy mouth the Lord Jesus, and shalt believe in thine heart that God hath raised him from the dead, thou shalt be saved [sozō – made whole].

> Acts 2:38
> Then Peter said unto them, Repent [metanoeō – change your minds], and be baptized every one of you in the name of Jesus Christ for the remission of sins, and ye shall receive [lambanō] the gift of the Holy Ghost.

When you are born again, you receive, *dechomai*, the gift of holy spirit, and with this gift comes the ability or potential to operate nine manifestations. Receiving the gift, *dechomai*, makes you whole, with body, soul and spirit, but we are also to *lambanō* this gift of holy spirit by putting it into operation. The problem in Samaria was that the people had been born again – they had received, *dechomai*, the word of God – but they had not put it into operation, *lambanō*, they had not received it through to manifestation. After praying, God energised in Peter and John to will and to do of his good pleasure as they operated the revelation and power manifestations to resolve the problem.

> Acts 8:17
> Then laid they *their* hands on them, and they received [lambanō] the Holy Ghost [holy spirit].

The foundational manifestation is speaking in tongues. In every record in the book of Acts, starting with the apostles on the day of Pentecost,

Walking *by* the Spirit

the first thing new believers manifested when they were born again was speaking in tongues.

> Acts 2:4
> And they were all filled [plethō] with the Holy Ghost [holy spirit], and began to speak with other tongues, as the Spirit gave them utterance.

> Acts 10:45,46
> And they of the circumcision which believed were astonished, as many as came with Peter, because that on the Gentiles also was poured out the gift of the Holy Ghost [holy spirit].

For they heard them speak with tongues, and magnify God.

> Acts 19:6
> And when Paul had laid *his* hands upon them, the Holy Ghost [holy spirit] came on them; and they spake with tongues, and prophesied.

What Simon saw with his five senses back in Samaria was believers speaking in tongues.

> Acts 8:18,19
> And when Simon saw that through laying on of the apostles' hands the Holy Ghost [holy spirit] was given, he offered them money,
>
> Saying, Give me also this power, that on whomsoever I lay hands, he may receive [lambanō] the Holy Ghost [holy spirit].

The gift of holy spirit we receive at the time of the new birth is spiritual power, but it can remain dormant within us without being manifested. It's our spirit and it is up to us to believe to operate it. God isn't going to possess us and make us do it, we have to believe and speak. Now that we understand what *lambanō* means, look again at Acts 1:8.

> Acts 1:8
> But ye shall receive [lambanō] power [dunamis], after that the Holy Ghost [holy spirit] is come upon you: and ye shall be witnesses unto me both in Jerusalem, and in all Judaea, and in Samaria, and unto the uttermost part of the earth.

It is the manifestation of the gift of holy spirit in the senses realm that is the witness of the Lord Jesus Christ.

When Peter and the other apostles spoke in tongues on the day of Pentecost, they didn't know which languages they were speaking. However, as they all took turns to speak in different tongues, people among the crowd in the temple that day understood every word they were saying. The apostles took it in turns to speak in tongues, and they would have spoken in dozens, perhaps hundreds of different languages and dialects that day. What was it the people heard?

> Acts 2:9-11
> Parthians, and Medes, and Elamites, and the dwellers in Mesopotamia, and in Judaea, and Cappadocia, in Pontus, and Asia,
>
> Phrygia, and Pamphylia, in Egypt, and in the parts of Libya about Cyrene, and strangers of Rome, Jews [Judeans] and proselytes,
>
> Cretes and Arabians, we do hear them speak in our tongues the wonderful works of God.

They all heard the apostles speaking the wonderful works of God. So, from this we know that one of the benefits of speaking in tongues is that it is speaking the wonderful works of God. Speaking in tongues is worshipping God in spirit and in truth. This is established in Acts 10.

> Acts 10:46a
> For they heard them speak with tongues, and magnify God.

If you want to be a true worshipper, you must speak in tongues for there is no other way. God is looking for people to worship him in spirit and in truth.

> John 4:23,24
> But the hour cometh, and now is, when the true worshippers shall worship the Father in spirit and in truth: for the Father seeketh such to worship him.

God *is* a Spirit: and they that worship him must worship *him* in spirit and in truth.

Speaking in tongues is extremely versatile and has many benefits. Worshipping God in spirit and in truth is only one of them. Let's look at a few more.

> 1 Corinthians 14:2
> For he that speaketh in an ~~unknown~~ tongue speaketh not unto men, but unto God: for no man understandeth ~~him~~; howbeit in the spirit he speaketh mysteries.

Speaking in tongues is speaking mysteries, or divine secrets with God. If you want to talk to God, you are going to have to speak in tongues, because God is spirit and we can only directly communicate with him by way of the spirit we receive at the time of the new birth. Adam and Eve lost their spiritual connection, but Jesus Christ regained it for us. It is that *spirit* that is our connection to God, not our five senses old man abilities. You can't communicate with God using your five senses. If you could, there would have been no need for patriarchs in the Patriarchal Administration, no need for spirit upon men and women in the old testament, and no need for a gift of holy spirit. Sure, God knows what you're saying when you blabber on for hours in stupid long religious prayers, but you can't hear him, understand? Get that spirit energised if you want to hear from God.

Here's another benefit.

> 1 Corinthians 14:4
> He that speaketh in an ~~unknown~~ tongue edifieth himself; but he that prophesieth edifieth the church.

Scratch out the word *unknown* again, because it is nonsense. How can a language be unknown? If no one knew it, it wouldn't be a language. When we speak in tongues we are edified. To edify is to build up. A house or an office block is often referred to as an edifice because it was built. Now here's an important truth – things that are built are built one brick, one stone at a time. This edifying, this building up occurs when we speak in tongues. In other words, if we don't speak in tongues, there is no building up of our spirit. We build up our bodies with food and exercise, we build up our souls, our minds, with the word, but we build up our spirit by speaking in tongues.

> 1 Corinthians 14:14
> For if I pray in an *unknown* tongue, my spirit prayeth, but my understanding is unfruitful.

When you pray in tongues, your spirit prays but your understanding is unfruitful. In other words your mind gets nothing out of it. Praying in tongues and speaking in tongues does absolutely nothing for your mind. Your understanding is unfruitful, it furnishes nothing because you don't understand a word you're saying. Speaking in tongues edifies your spirit.

> Jude 1:20
> But ye, beloved, building up yourselves on your most holy faith, praying in the Holy Ghost [holy spirit],

This establishes it for us. Speaking in tongues, which is praying in the holy spirit, is how you build yourself up, how you edify yourself spiritually. Speaking in tongues is also giving thanks well.

> 1 Corinthians 14:15-17
> What is it then? I will pray with the spirit, and I will pray with the understanding also: I will sing with the spirit, and I will sing with the understanding also.
>
> Else when thou shalt bless with the spirit, how shall he that occupieth the room of the unlearned say Amen at thy giving of thanks, seeing he understandeth not what thou sayest?
>
> For thou verily givest thanks well, but the other is not edified.

Before venturing further, let's set the context of chapter 14, as some use this chapter as an excuse to not speak in tongues.

> 1 Corinthians 14:4,5
> He that speaketh in an *unknown* tongue edifieth himself; but he that prophesieth edifieth the church.

> I would that ye all spake with tongues, but rather that ye prophesied: for greater *is* he that prophesieth than he that speaketh with tongues, except he interpret, that the church may receive edifying.

Some christians think it's okay just to go to a meeting occasionally where they might sometimes speak in tongues, interpret tongues, and prophecy, yet never speak in tongues during their everyday lives. These are the verses they use to justify their lack of commitment. Some even use these verses to teach that speaking in tongues isn't important.

First of the all, the context of chapter 14 is *in the church*, in a believer's home church meeting, where believers gather together to fellowship, have manifestations, and learn the word together. Chapter 14 is addressing how *home church* meetings are to be conducted. Yes, in our home church meetings, prophesy is greater than speaking in tongues, because if someone just spoke in tongues no one else there would get anything out of it unless the tongue was interpreted. In other words, chapter 14 is teaching us how to conduct manifestations properly during home church meetings, not during our everyday lives. Now read verses 15-17 again in this light, and it will all make sense.

> 1 Corinthians 14:15-17
> What is it then? I will pray with the spirit, and I will pray with the understanding also: I will sing with the spirit, and I will sing with the understanding also.
>
> Else when thou shalt bless with the spirit, how shall he that occupieth the room of the unlearned say Amen at thy giving of thanks, seeing he understandeth not what thou sayest?
>
> For thou verily givest thanks well, but the other is not edified.

From this we know we should all pray with the spirit and with the understanding, and we should all sing with the spirit and with the understanding in our private lives, but when we get to a home church our priorities change from edifying ourselves to edifying others. Speaking in tongues is not unimportant, it's just of not much profit at a home church meeting unless it is interpreted that others may be edified.

In addition, we now know that speaking in tongues is spiritual prayer, and as such must be perfect because our spirit is perfect.

> Romans 8:26,27
> Likewise the Spirit also helpeth our infirmities: for we know not what we should pray for as we ought: but the Spirit itself maketh intercession for us with groanings which cannot be uttered.
>
> And he that searcheth the hearts knoweth what *is* the mind of the Spirit, because he maketh intercession for the saints according to *the will of* God.

The gift of holy spirit makes intercession for people when we pray in tongues, and as we pray in tongues we speak words which we don't understand therefore we can't utter them, but God is energising the words that we are speaking and that's why it's perfect prayer. There is no way we can possibly know all the time what to pray for, how to pray perfectly with our minds using our five senses abilities, but God knows and when we pray in tongues we are praying perfectly because the spirit is making intercession for people according to the will of God. How do you pray in tongues for people then? Easy, simply picture them in your mind and speak in tongues.

I Corinthians 14:17 told us that speaking in tongues is giving thanks well.

> 1 Corinthians 14:17
> For thou verily givest thanks well, but the other is not edified.

Want to thank God for something? Then you're going to have to speak in tongues, because that's how you thank God. This defines *how* we give thanks to God in this administration.

If I give you a pen today, will it be a pencil tomorrow? No, it won't, it will still be a pen. If I give you a pen today, would I call it a pencil tomorrow even if I knew it was still a pen? That's absurd, and yet this is how people handle God's word. God tells us in this Administration of Grace in the scriptures directly addressed to the church of God that speaking in tongues is giving thanks well. So, what will giving thanks well be tomorrow? Going to church and crying your eyes out for hours before an alter? See, that's absurd. Giving thanks well is speaking in tongues. It will *always* be speaking in tongues throughout this administration. What am I getting at? Okay, consider these verses.

> Ephesians 5:19,20
> Speaking to yourselves in psalms and hymns and spiritual songs, singing and making melody in your heart to the Lord;
>
> Giving thanks always for all things unto God and the Father in the name of our Lord Jesus Christ;

How do you give thanks to God always for all things? Well, what was called a pen yesterday will still be a pen today, not a pencil. Verse 19 even sets the context by telling us to sing spiritual songs, which is a reference to singing in tongues. Giving thanks to God according to 1 Corinthians 14 is to speak in tongues. So if giving thanks well in Corinthians is speaking in tongues, guess what is included in this giving of thanks in Ephesians? Yes, speaking in tongues.

Look, a spiritual song is not some congregational churchy garbage hymn sung by black people at gospel meetings in America, it is singing in tongues as we saw in Corinthians. Do you see now how temples made with hands do nothing but strip the supernatural out of christianity and turn it into religious horseshit? God is not the author of religion, the devil is, and it is men who construct his temples.

As a case in point, the Anglican Church was set up in England in the sixth century when pope Gregory sent Augustine to Britain to counter the Celtic Christian movement. Very little is known about the Scottish people in prehistoric times, as they did not write books and kept no historical records. What we do know is that the arrival of the Romans coincided with the emergence of the Picts in history. What the Picts were doing before the arrival of the Romans, or where they originally came from, no one knows.

That all changed with the arrival of the Romans. It is clear that the formation of a Pictish nation that united the Celtic peoples of Scotland was due to the arrival of the Romans. That the emergence of Scottish brochs on a national scale, massive stone defensive fortresses, is associated with the period of Roman influence in Scotland is also clearly no coincidence.

Most Highland brochs were built between 100 BC and 100 AD, a period of just 200 years that coincided with the arrival of the Romans, who first landed in England in 55 BC. By 47 AD, the Romans had conquered the whole of the south of England and declared Britain part of the Roman Empire. It was during this time that the Picts were constructing brochs all over the Highlands, so there can be no doubt that they were built with military defensive purpose.

By 79 AD, the whole of England had been conquered and Agricola attempted to conquer Scotland. After a number of failed military campaigns, which included the annihilation of the 9th Legion around 117 AD, the Romans retreated south and built Hadrian's wall for their own protection. In 142 AD, the Romans again tried to take Scotland, made some territorial gains and built Antonine's wall, a second defensive wall that stretched from the Firth of Clyde to the Firth of Forth. In 163 AD, the Romans retreated from Antonine's wall and cowered behind Hadrian's wall for the second time.

In 208 AD, the Romans marched again to conquer Scotland. In 212 AD, they left defeated. In 367 AD, the Picts with the help of the Irish invaded England and together they pushed the Romans back from their last defensive positions at Hadrian's wall. Not long after that, the Romans left Britain. It is plausible that the defeats suffered by the Romans at the hands of the Picts were instrumental in laying the groundwork for the collapse of the Roman empire.

Calach, or Calgacus as the Romans called him, was the Pictish king who united the peoples of Scotland against the tyranny of Rome. He is said to have described the Romans as *Robbers of the world, having by their universal plunder exhausted the land, they rifle the deep. If the enemy be rich, they are rapacious; if he be poor, they lust for dominion; neither the east nor the west has been able to satisfy them. Alone among men they covet with equal eagerness poverty and riches. To robbery, slaughter, plunder, they give the lying name of empire; they make a desolation and call it peace.*

Nothing much has changed regarding Rome in the last 2000 years. They still lust after the world and march with one step for the uniting of the nations under the same banners of world peace, while murdering hundreds of millions who refuse to bow to their gods.

What is not generally known however, is that one of Jesus Christ's disciples, Joseph of Arimathaea travelled to Scotland around the time of the Roman invasion of Britain and taught God's word to the Picts. It was the word living in Scotland that defeated the Romans, and that's why pope Gregory sent Augustine to Britain.

The devil destroys the work of God with religion. Religions are man-made broken cisterns that destroy God's people. Religion is Lucifer's counterfeit for the real thing. Now do you understand why it was the religious leaders in Christ's day who had him murdered by the Romans? Get away from them and stop giving them your money for they will use it to destroy you. Sincerity is no guarantee for truth. Praising God is speaking in tongues, magnifying God is speaking in tongues, giving thanks well is speaking in tongues. It's all part of worshipping God in spirit and in truth, and they will not teach you that at church.

Ephesians 1:15,16
Wherefore I also, after I heard of your faith in the Lord Jesus, and love unto all the saints,

Cease not to give thanks for you, making mention of you in my prayers;

How did Paul give thanks ceaselessly for these believers? By walking around all day saying, thank you God for these people, thank you God for these people, over and over and over again, like some mindless homo priest chanting out hail mary's and our fathers all day? No, Paul pictured these believers in his mind and spoke in tongues for them. If you really want to pray for people, picture them in your mind and speak in tongues for them. It's perfect prayer and it's giving thanks well for them. Praying with the senses, praying for things you need is fine, but the real power is in manifesting the gift of holy spirit. When someone else is praying with their understanding in a home church meeting, you can speak in tongues and picture whatever it is they are praying for.

I do this all the time. When I need good weather to enjoy being outdoors, I picture blue skies and sunshine and speak in tongues. As I'm faithful to hold that picture in my mind and speak in tongues, the rain stops and the sun comes through. The more faithful you are with your believing, the more sunshine you will enjoy in your life.

> Mark 11:23
> For verily I say unto you, That whosoever shall say unto this mountain, Be thou removed, and be thou cast into the sea; and shall not doubt in his heart, but shall believe that those things which he saith shall come to pass; he shall have whatsoever he saith.

Here's another benefit to speaking in tongues.

> Romans 8:16,17
> The Spirit itself beareth witness with our spirit, that we are the children of God:
>
> And if children, then heirs; heirs of God, and joint-heirs with Christ; if so be that we suffer [endure patiently] with *him*, that we may be also glorified together.

When we speak in tongues, we are bearing witness that we are God's children, born of his seed, with eternal life, and consequently we have an inheritance coming to us because we are joint heirs with Christ. How is this a benefit to me? Well, every time I don't feel like a son of God, or feel less than the word says about me, I can speak in tongues and that's my proof to me that I *am* God's son, and that I have eternal life. No amount of ridiculous religious chanting can give you that.

Try this one:

> Romans 8:11
> But if the Spirit [spirit] of him that raised up Jesus from the dead dwell in you, he that raised up Christ from the dead shall also quicken [make alive] your mortal bodies by his Spirit [spirit] that dwelleth in you.

Both of these uses of pneuma are in reference to the gift of holy spirit within us, so neither usage refers directly to God and therefore neither usage should be capitalised. So what is this saying? It's saying that as we energise the gift of holy spirit within us, which is to speak in tongues, it will actually affect our mortal bodies in a wonderful way. What does that mean? Well, as an example, I've experienced pain at times in my life. I've woken up at night in pain on a few occasions. What I did was speak in tongues for the pain to go away, and after a few minutes the pain has always gone away and I've gone happily back to sleep. Speaking in tongues has very real tangible benefits. The manifestation of the spirit is given to every man to *profit* withal.

As if all this wasn't enough, what about enjoying fruit of the spirit in your life?

> Galatians 5:22,23
> But the fruit of the Spirit is love, joy, peace, longsuffering, gentleness, goodness, faith [believing],
>
> Meekness, temperance: against such there is no law.

Spirit here is not referring to God, it is referring to the gift of holy spirit. This is not the fruit of God, nor is it the fruit of the good works of man, this is fruit that can only be produced by manifesting holy spirit. You can't produce this fruit by exercising your five senses abilities, talents or expertise, no matter how good you may be at it. It is religion that drives man to develop his five senses in an attempt to produce works that please God. No matter how much you develop your human abilities, they can never produce fruit of the spirit. There is no possible way to develop fruit of the spirit other than by manifesting the gift of holy spirit. Only by energising holy spirit can you produce fruit of the spirit, and that begins with speaking in tongues.

Would you like to be part of an exclusive group of special people? Then worship God in spirit and in truth, which is rejoicing in Christ Jesus and having no confidence in the flesh.

> Philippians 3:3
> For we are the circumcision, which worship God in the spirit, and rejoice in Christ Jesus, and have no confidence in the flesh.

So how do you speak in tongues? Well, it's easy. It's so easy, you don't even have to think about it. It's easier than speaking your own language. When speaking your own language you have to think about what you're saying, but with speaking in tongues you just speak. When the apostles spoke in tongues on the day of Pentecost, they did the speaking.

> Acts 2:4
> And they were all filled with the Holy Ghost [holy spirit], and began to speak with other tongues, as the Spirit gave them utterance.

They did the speaking, but what they spoke was as the spirit gave them utterance. In other words, precisely the same actions required to speak your own language are required to speak in tongues. The only difference is that you don't think about the words you are speaking, you simply speak the words out. You speak in tongues by articulating the words, just as you would articulate words in your own language.

Speak out loud in your own language and be conscious of how you form words. As you pronounce certain vowels and consonants, your lips, your mouth and your tongue all move together to form the sounds. It is exactly the same with speaking in tongues. You have to form the words using your lips, your mouth and your tongue to speak. The only difference between speaking in your own language and speaking in tongues is that you don't think about the words. As you speak, the words will be there. It's God's job to give us the words, but it's our job to speak.

No, you can't pray to God to make you speak in tongues because he would have to possess you to do that. The holy spirit born within you is yours to energise and operate. God will never possess you. The gift of holy spirit is always at our command and we have to believe to energise it. If we do not energise it, nothing will happen. When it comes to speaking in tongues, we simply speak. Try it, just speak, the words will be there.

Before his ascension, Jesus Christ taught his apostles how to receive into manifestation the gift of holy spirit which was coming on the day of Pentecost, and we can learn from the specific instruction he gave them.

> John 20:22
> And when he had said this, he breathed on [in] *them*, and saith unto them, Receive [lambanō] ye the Holy Ghost [holy spirit]:

This usage of *lambanō* clearly indicates that Jesus Christ was not just teaching them how to be born again, but how to manifest the gift of holy spirit once they were born again. He breathed in deeply, he took a deep breath, and told them that was how they were to receive the holy spirit and manifest it. Guess what, that's exactly what they did and they all spoke in tongues.

> Acts 2:1-4
> And when the day of Pentecost was fully come, they were all with one accord in one place.
>
> And suddenly there came a sound from heaven as of a rushing mighty wind [as of a heavy breathing], and it filled all the house where they were sitting.
>
> And there appeared unto them cloven tongues like as of fire, and it sat upon each of them.
>
> And they were all filled [plethō] with the Holy Ghost [holy spirit], and began to speak with other tongues, as the Spirit gave them utterance.

At the moment the gift of holy spirit first became available, the twelve all breathed in deeply, just as Jesus Christ had taught them, and the sound of their heavy breathing filled the temple where they were sitting. As they all breathed in deeply, they were all filled, plethō, filled to overflowing with holy spirit and they all spoke in tongues.

Just as new born babies into the world are to breathe as soon as they are born, so God's children are to spiritually breathe and speak in tongues as soon as they are born again. Speaking in tongues is a commandment in this administration. Paul says so in Corinthians.

> 1 Corinthians 14:5,18,37
> I would that ye all spake with tongues

I thank my God, I speak with tongues more than ye all:

If any man think himself to be a prophet, or spiritual, let him acknowledge that the things that I write unto you are the commandments of the Lord.

If you're born again and you don't speak in tongues, you need to get started *immediately*. Whether you speak in tongues or not is up to you. God has made everything available in Christ Jesus, now it's your job to believe and learn to walk by the spirit.

51. God's Delivering Nature

It is time to put together everything we've learned so far regarding how the god of this world moves the courses of the world and contrast that with how God moves to understand how we can walk by the spirit and be more than conquerors in real life situations.

Esther is the true story of how God delivered his people during an horrendous, unprovoked attack that threatened to wipe out their civilisation. God will rescue anyone from any situation, in any culture, in any country, at any time when they turn to him for his help and believe for deliverance. It doesn't matter how bleak or impossible things may look, God always has a way to escape.

> Esther 1:1
> Now it came to pass in the days of Ahasuerus, (this *is* Ahasuerus which reigned, from India even unto Ethiopia, *over* an hundred and seven and twenty provinces:)

India borders China in the north, and Ethiopia is well down into Africa. This king would have ruled everywhere in between too, including most of Europe and the Middle East. Powerful dude. One hundred and twenty seven provinces under his rule. One day he decided to hold a summit at the palace and invited all his top leadership from around the world to attend.

> Esther 1:2-4
> *That* in those days, when the king Ahasuerus sat on the throne of his kingdom, which *was* in Shushan the palace,
>
> In the third year of his reign, he made a feast unto all his princes and his servants; the power of Persia and Media, the nobles and princes of the provinces, *being* before him:

When he shewed the riches of his glorious kingdom and the honour of his excellent majesty many days, *even* an hundred and fourscore days.

Every dignitary in his government was invited, every ruler of every province. They all trundled in on their chariots and camels to fanfare and pomp, dressed in their finest robes, and flanked by their best soldiers. The crowds would have been lining the streets as these powerful world dignitaries arrived at the palace. Security would have been immense. This was a summit of world leaders who were coming at the behest of one of most powerful kings of all time, and they were arriving at probably the most lavish palace ever built. This wasn't just a weekend affair either, this was a State occasion that was to last six months.

In trying to comprehend the enormity of this event, consider that they didn't have television, radio, phones, computers, internet, or public transport. There was no way to communicate over long distances except by personal couriers on horseback. This event would have taken some planning. The invitations alone would have taken weeks just to post and deliver. Some of these dudes would have had to travel for weeks just to get there. Accommodation and food for these travelling dignitaries and their attendants would have required camel trains with formidable military escorts.

With his entire world leadership around him, the king would have wanted to use the opportunity to spend quality time with them. He would have held hundreds of councils, discussing everything from the security of the kingdom, to increasing its income, to stabilising trouble spots, to discussing future world affairs. The king would have wanted detailed reports on what was going on in every province. All the while, they were banqueting and being entertained. There is nothing in our modern world to compare to the magnificence of this occasion. Presidential State visits to the UK are afternoon tea and biscuits compared to this.

Esther 1:5,6
And when these days were expired, the king made a feast unto all the people that were present in Shushan the palace, both unto great and small, seven days, in the court of the garden of the king's palace;

Where were white, green, and blue, *hangings*, fastened with cords of fine linen and purple to silver rings and pillars of marble: the beds *were of* gold and silver, upon a pavement of red, and blue, and white, and black, marble.

To conclude this grand summit, the king arranged for a banquet in his gardens. People today talk about wealth, but really, we have no concept of wealth on this scale. These gardens were what we refer to today as the hanging gardens of Babylon, one of the seven wonders of the ancient world. Marble pillars on beds of gold. Jewelled tapestries laced with gold hanging everywhere.

Esther 1:7
And they gave *them* drink in vessels of gold, (the vessels being diverse one from another,) and royal wine in abundance, according to the state of the king.

Their goblets were made of gold, each one hand crafted and individually engraved, and there were *hundreds* of them. The king's dinner set alone was worth more than most modern politicians' entire estates. And while the men were having fun, the women were having some fun of their own.

Esther 1:8-11
And the drinking *was* according to the law; none did compel: for so the king had appointed to all the officers of his house, that they should do according to every man's pleasure.

Also Vashti the queen made a feast for the women *in* the royal house which *belonged* to king Ahasuerus.

On the seventh day, when the heart of the king was merry with wine, he commanded Mehuman, Biztha, Harbona, Bigtha, and Abagtha, Zethar, and Carcas, the seven chamberlains that served in the presence of Ahasuerus the king,

To bring Vashti the queen before the king with the crown royal, to shew the people and the princes her beauty: for she *was* fair to look on.

These chamberlains would have been top men in the kingdom, not just in authority but also in education and ability. As well as being top diplomats with the best education available, they would have been his personal bodyguard, warriors trained in combat and close quarter battle. The fact that God has actually named them individually is a glowing testament to their prowess and professionalism.

During the feast, the king decided to show off his wife because she was an amazing woman. He obviously loved her, and he wanted his entire world leadership to meet the girl. He was proud of her and wanted to show her off. What higher compliment could a woman have from her husband?

> Esther 1:12
> But the queen Vashti refused to come at the king's commandment by *his* chamberlains: therefore was the king very wroth, and his anger burned in him.

Oh dear, his lovely wife told him to beat it. Can you imagine the shock wave of whispers that would have hissed around the banquet? Can you imagine the king's humiliation and embarrassment in front of his entire world leadership? The most powerful man in the world, and his wife told him to beat it? This is serious stuff, and not only because of protocol but because of law. You see, the king's word was also the law, and to break the king's commandment was to break the law. This was much more than a domestic squabble between the king and his wife.

> Esther 1:13,14
> Then the king said to the wise men, which knew the times, (for so *was* the king's manner toward all that knew law and judgment:
>
> And the next unto him *was* Carshena, Shethar, Admatha, Tarshish, Meres, Marsena, *and* Memucan, the seven princes of Persia and Media, which saw the king's face, *and* which sat the first in the kingdom;)

Interesting to note that the king didn't knee jerk, he didn't react emotionally even though he was emotional. This was a legal matter, so he sat down with his top legal advisers and they discussed the issue.

Esther 1:15
What shall we do unto the queen Vashti according to law, because she hath not performed the commandment of the king Ahasuerus by the chamberlains?

His wife had broken the law. Who knows what her motives were? Who knows what emotions drove her to this? Pride? Arrogance? Perhaps wanting to make herself look like the *real* power behind the throne in front of all the world's top women? Perhaps it was in her horoscope? Who knows?

Esther 1:16-18
And Memucan answered before the king and the princes, Vashti the queen hath not done wrong to the king only, but also to all the princes, and to all the people that *are* in all the provinces of the king Ahasuerus.

For *this* deed of the queen shall come abroad unto all women, so that they shall despise their husbands in their eyes, when it shall be reported, The king Ahasuerus commanded Vashti the queen to be brought in before him, but she came not.

Likewise shall the ladies of Persia and Media say this day unto all the king's princes, which have heard of the deed of the queen. Thus *shall there arise* too much contempt and wrath.

They agreed that if they didn't deal with this issue, women all over the kingdom were going to hold their husbands in contempt. Pissed off husbands do not make good politicians, so this was a major problem that was going to affect the entire kingdom. Something had to be done.

Esther 1:19,20
If it please the king, let there go a royal commandment from him, and let it be written among the laws of the Persians and the Medes, that it be not altered, That Vashti come no more before king Ahasuerus; and let the king give her royal estate unto another that is better than she.

And when the king's decree which he shall make shall be published throughout all his empire, (for it is great,) all the wives shall give to their husbands honour, both to great and small.

After lengthy deliberations, the court ruled that the king should divorce her.

> Esther 1:21,22
> And the saying pleased the king and the princes; and the king did according to the word of Memucan:
>
> For he sent letters into all the king's provinces, into every province according to the writing thereof, and to every people after their language, that every man should bear rule in his own house, and that *it* should be published according to the language of every people.

Not only did he divorce her, but he also passed a new law demanding that wives respect the oversight and direction of their husbands, which is a godly principle, amazingly enough.

> Esther 2:1
> After these things, when the wrath of king Ahasuerus was appeased, he remembered Vashti, and what she had done, and what was decreed against her.

Aw poor king, he must have loved the girl. Once he calmed down, he missed her. Nevertheless, the law was the law and she was divorced. So it was decided to find him another wife. A beauty contest was organised, with the winner getting to marry the king and become queen.

> Esther 2:2,3
> Then said the king's servants that ministered unto him, Let there be fair young virgins sought for the king:
>
> And let the king appoint officers in all the provinces of his kingdom, that they may gather together all the fair young virgins unto Shushan the palace, to the house of the women, unto the custody of Hege the king's chamberlain, keeper of the women; and let their things for purification be given *them*:

Only the most beautiful, intelligent, educated, and cultured women were sought. It was going to take a special woman to take care of a man who governed the world.

Esther 2:4,5
And let the maiden which pleaseth the king be queen instead of Vashti. And the thing pleased the king; and he did so.

Now in Shushan the palace there was a certain Jew [Judean], whose name was Mordecai, the son of Jair, the son of Shimei, the son of Kish, a Benjamite;

The word Jew used here is misleading and manipulative. The word *Jew* did not appear in any bible until 1775. It's a forgery. The word *Jew* must always be understood as being the word *Judean* – those from the country of Judea, or those of the Judean religion.

Esther 2:6,7
Who had been carried away from Jerusalem with the captivity which had been carried away with Jeconiah king of Judah, whom Nebuchadnezzar the king of Babylon had carried away.

And he brought up Hadassah, that *is*, Esther, his uncle's daughter: for she had neither father nor mother, and the maid *was* fair and beautiful; whom Mordecai, when her father and mother were dead, took for his own daughter.

Mordecai and Esther had been taken captive by an invading army, and Mordecai had adopted his young niece and brought her up as his own daughter. God will even look after his people in war. Isn't that nice to know.

Esther 2:8
So it came to pass, when the king's commandment and his decree was heard, and when many maidens were gathered together unto Shushan the palace, to the custody of Hegai, that Esther was brought also unto the king's house, to the custody of Hegai, keeper of the women.

Young Esther was a bit of a babe, who had brains and education, so much so that she was selected for this beauty contest.

Esther 2:9
And the maiden pleased him, and she obtained kindness of him; and he speedily gave her her things for purification, with such

things as belonged to her, and seven maidens, *which were* meet to be given her, out of the king's house: and he preferred her and her maids unto the best *place* of the house of the women.

Esther impressed the heck out of Hegai, so she must have been really something. Not just sexy and educated, but warm, considerate, intelligent, courageous, a real lady, cultured, mannered – everything a king could possibly want. Mordecai had done a good job raising the girl.

Esther 2:10
Esther had not shewed her people nor her kindred: for Mordecai had charged her that she should not shew *it*.

Now sit up and pay attention! Why would Mordecai tell Esther not to tell anyone she was a Judean? Okay, here is a clue – Mordecai was a believer, a disciple. How is that a clue? Well, God must have been moving here. Something was brewing spiritually. We may not always know what the devil is up to, but God does. Being disciples, Mordecai obeyed God and Esther obeyed Mordecai. Here you see a man walking by the spirit. God is our protection, our rereward, yes, but only when we walk by the spirit. He gives us information and when we listen and obey we are more than conquerors. Young believers in a home church who are still figuring out how to walk by the spirit instead of by their senses are to subject themselves to their home church leadership who already walk by the spirit and that keeps them protected.

Look, we have to learn to quit arguing with God and learn to move and carry out his instructions when he works within us to will and to do of his good pleasure. This transition takes time, so don't worry about it when you get it wrong. Learn from it and get it right next time. I'm still learning in this category, but I'm far better than I was a few years ago. Walking by the spirit works in real life.

Esther 2:11-13
And Mordecai walked every day before the court of the women's house, to know how Esther did, and what should become of her.

Now when every maid's turn was come to go in to king Ahasuerus, after that she had been twelve months, according to the manner of the women, (for so were the days of their purifications accomplished, *to wit*, six months with oil of myrrh, and six months with sweet odours, and with *other* things for the purifying of the women

Then thus came *every* maiden unto the king; whatsoever she desired was given her to go with her out of the house of the women unto the king's house.

This competition was twelve months in preparation. In addition to personal grooming, there would have been education and training. The women would have had to be educated in how to be a queen – matters of state, matters of law, royal protocols, and diplomacy, in fact everything they would need to know to do the job properly.

Esther 2:14-17
In the evening she went, and on the morrow she returned into the second house of the women, to the custody of Shaashgaz, the king's chamberlain, which kept the concubines: she came in unto the king no more, except the king delighted in her, and that she were called by name.

Now when the turn of Esther, the daughter of Abihail the uncle of Mordecai, who had taken her for his daughter, was come to go in unto the king, she required nothing but what Hegai the king's chamberlain, the keeper of the women, appointed. And Esther obtained favour in the sight of all them that looked upon her.

So Esther was taken unto king Ahasuerus into his house royal in the tenth month, which *is* the month Tebeth, in the seventh year of his reign.

And the king loved Esther above all the women, and she obtained grace and favour in his sight more than all the virgins; so that he set the royal crown upon her head, and made her queen instead of Vashti.

God's daughters *should* be better than the women of the world. They should be the best educated, the warmest, the most considerate, loving, courageous, honest and sexy, and that doesn't imply being a doormat. It takes real strength to be that kind of a woman. A king, just like any man, needs a woman with a backbone to stand beside him, someone he can rely on and trust in a crisis. The word builds that kind of strength into a woman.

> Esther 2:18
> Then the king made a great feast unto all his princes and his servants, *even* Esther's feast; and he made a release to the provinces, and gave gifts, according to the state of the king.

So, he married her. No modern royal wedding could hold a candle to this marriage. This was the social event of the Millennium.

> Esther 2:19,20
> And when the virgins were gathered together the second time, then Mordecai sat in the king's gate.
>
> Esther had not *yet* shewed her kindred nor her people; as Mordecai had charged her: for Esther did the commandment of Mordecai, like as when she was brought up with him.

This is the second time the word tells us Esther kept her nationality to herself. Esther did not even tell the king she was a Judean. She did what Mordecai told her to do, without question. Was Mordecai controlling her? No, don't be ridiculous. Esther carried out his instruction because she knew you only get the blessings from God by obedience. You can't force people to do anything, that's for sure, but living the word is not being controlled. If you want to be controlled, go watch TV. Walking by the spirit is not being controlled by God. God absolutely never forces anyone to do anything, but he will help you if you want his help. If you're walking by the spirit and obey him you get the benefits.

So Esther is married and she's queen, the king is happy again, and things in the kingdom move on. No one knows she is a Judean. Intriguing. Don't argue with God, just trust him. He knows what he's doing.

> Esther 2:21,22
> In those days, while Mordecai sat in the king's gate, two of the king's chamberlains, Bigthan and Teresh, of those which

kept the door, were wroth, and sought to lay hands on the king Ahasuerus.

And the thing was known to Mordecai, who told *it* unto Esther the queen; and Esther certified the king *thereof* in Mordecai's name.

Here you are seeing the way of life and the way of death in operation. The devil moves his evil by stirring dark emotions in people who will do anything for money. God counters the devil's work by giving information to disciples who walk by the spirit. The god of this world moves his darkness through religion and freemasonry. Freemasonry is religion of a very dark kind. Any bets Bigthan and Teresh were members of secret societies? All the world's worst criminals from Jack the Ripper to Bill Clinton to Charles Manson to Hitler to Thomas Hamilton to Tony Blair to Anders Breivik and everyone in between, were and are masons. This isn't coincidence. God keeps us protected from evil as we learn his word and learn to walk by the spirit. Here in Esther, the devil stirred a plot in evil men to assassinate the king and God countered that by giving information to Mordecai who was walking by the spirit.

Psalm 119:105
Thy word is a lamp unto my feet, and a light unto my path.

God showed Mordecai that Esther's husband's life was at risk. Well, he is Esther's husband after all, so that makes him family. When Mordecai acted on that information, the god of this world was defeated. If you want light in your life, get on the way of life and walk by the spirit.

Esther 2:23
And when inquisition was made of the matter, it was found out; therefore they were both hanged on a tree: and it was written in the book of the chronicles before the king.

Interesting that the king didn't offer these two dudes social programmes at taxpayer's expense so as not to infringe their human rights. No, he executed them. It is only when we install jesuits as lawmakers that God's laws, which keep us protected from them, are dismantled.

Esther 3:1,2
After these things did king Ahasuerus promote Haman the son of Hammedatha the Agagite, and advanced him, and set his seat above all the princes that *were* with him.

And all the king's servants, that *were* in the king's gate, bowed, and reverenced Haman: for the king had so commanded concerning him. But Mordecai bowed not, nor did *him* reverence.

The king promoted Haman, and commanded that everyone reverence him. Of course, being the king's commandment meant it was also law. Mordecai therefore was breaking the law here. But why? Why would Mordecai break the law? We gain clues back in Genesis.

Joseph was a teenager sold into slavery in Egypt by his jealous brothers, and an Egyptian bought him as a piece of property. His master's wife came onto him, but he refused her sexual advances. The situation degenerated to the point the woman lied and accused him of attempted rape. Joseph was chucked in the dungeons and was there for over two years. Do you see how the devil used emotions to get his will done? Joseph was to be the next patriarch for God's people, yet through dark emotions, the devil succeeded in having him locked away in the dungeons of a foreign country.

One night, Pharaoh dreamed twice, and Joseph, who was known for being adept at interpreting dreams, was summoned from prison. Now we will see the way of life in operation.

Genesis 41:14
Then Pharaoh sent and called Joseph, and they brought him hastily out of the dungeon: and he shaved *himself*, and changed his raiment, and came in unto Pharaoh.

Now some background for you here. Culturally at that time, the only Egyptian man permitted by law to wear a beard was Pharaoh. All other Egyptian men had to shave. That was the culture and that was the law. Hebrew culture however, was different. All Hebrew men wore beards. It was a disgrace for a Hebrew man to be shaved. We can see that when king David sent men to Hanun to comfort him after his father's death.

2 Samuel 10:4
Wherefore Hanun took David's servants, and shaved off the one half of their beards, and cut off their garments in the middle, *even* to their buttocks, and sent them away.

This bastard shaved off half the men's beards and cut off their robes in the middle, like miniskirts. He made them look like homos and sent them back to David.

2 Samuel 10:5
When they told *it* unto David, he sent to meet them, because the men were greatly ashamed: and the king said, Tarry at Jericho until your beards be grown, and *then* return.

It was an absolute cultural disgrace for a Hebrew man to shave. Interestingly enough, treating David's men like homos was sufficient reason for him to go to war, but you can read that record for yourself. Back to Genesis.

Genesis 41:14
Then Pharaoh sent and called Joseph, and they brought him hastily out of the dungeon: and he shaved *himself*, and changed his raiment, and came in unto Pharaoh.

Joseph shaved himself. As a Hebrew man, he would have been entitled to wear his beard. Have you any idea what shaving would have meant to him? The only reason he did it was out of respect for Pharaoh. Look at the respect Joseph showed to that politician. He didn't arrogantly march in there unshaved and with an attitude. He showed top protocol and respect.

Okay, so why did Mordecai refuse to show respect to Haman? Intriguing question and a good one. Every truth must fit within the framework of the manifestations. Here's a clue – both Joseph and Mordecai had spirit upon them and they both walked by the spirit. How is that a clue? Read on.

Esther 3:3
Then the king's servants, which *were* in the king's gate, said unto Mordecai, Why transgressest thou the king's commandment?

The other officials around the palace noticed that Mordecai was not bowing to Haman. Now why would Joseph show top protocol to Pharaoh, and yet Mordecai showed none for Haman? You have to understand that both of these men walked by the spirit, not by their senses.

Esther 3:4
Now it came to pass, when they spake daily unto him, and he hearkened not unto them, that they told Haman, to see whether Mordecai's matters would stand: for he had told them that he *was* a Jew [Judean].

Mordecai told them he was a Judean! Now why would Mordecai tell Esther not to tell anyone she was a Judean, and yet he told them he was? Mordecai did what God told him to do by way of the manifestations of holy spirit. Understanding that makes these records come alive. This is the way of life in operation. Now contrast that with the way of death in the next two verses.

Esther 3:5,6
And when Haman saw that Mordecai bowed not, nor did him reverence, then was Haman full of wrath.

And he thought scorn to lay hands on Mordecai alone; for they had shewed him the people of Mordecai: wherefore Haman sought to destroy all the Jews [Judeans] that *were* throughout the whole kingdom of Ahasuerus, *even* the people of Mordecai.

Not only did Haman want Mordecai dead, he decided he was going to murder every single Judean on the face of the planet while he was at it. Genocide always has men like Haman behind it. The god of this world always wants God's people exterminated, and in this situation he was going to use Haman to try to get the job done. Haman is second in command over the entire kingdom, next to the king in authority and power, and he had the authority and the ability to do this thing. Any bets Haman was religious, a freemason, heavily into witchcraft, a man who loved money more than anything else, and that it was his freemason cronies who had contrived to have him promoted into this position? You don't have to bet, the next verse tells us about him.

Esther 3:7
In the first month, that *is*, the month Nisan, in the twelfth year of king Ahasuerus, they cast Pur, that *is*, the lot, before Haman from day to day, and from month to month, *to* the twelfth *month*, that *is*, the month Adar.

To cast the lot is to practice spiritualism and witchcraft. See, he was a spiritualist. Casting Pur is the same as going to fortune tellers, it is having your tarot cards read, it is reading palms and tea leaves. Haman was a spiritualist who went to mediums for guidance. He would have had his own personal psychic, just as most politicians do today. This is another way the devil spirit realm influences the decisions our politicians make. This is the way of death, the courses of this world in operation. Devil spirits gave Haman information, they told him how to put this plan to murder all God's people into motion from behind the scenes, through witchcraft. Notice also that having a single world government in place greatly assists devil spirits move such evil.

Look, the devil is always trying to murder God's people so he can destroy God's word from the planet. You can track this all through the bible, from when Cain murdered Abel to Herod murdering all the young boys in Bethlehem in an attempt to kill the Christ. For Mordecai and the Judean people, this is what you call a pressure situation.

Esther 3:8
And Haman said unto king Ahasuerus, There is a certain people scattered abroad and dispersed among the people in all the provinces of thy kingdom; and their laws *are* diverse from all people; neither keep they the king's laws: therefore it *is* not for the king's profit to suffer them.

Remember, Haman and the king do not know that the queen is a Judean. God knew what he was doing when he told Mordecai to tell Esther to keep her nationality a secret. Here is the way of life in operation. It takes obedience to the word, both written and that received when we walk by the spirit. Devil spirits give information to people through witchcraft, sorcery, freemasonry and spiritualism to get the devil's will done, God gives information to people who walk by the spirit to counter what the devil is up to.

God knows what the devil is up to, and he always keeps us protected when we are listening. Mordecai and Esther would not have known why God suggested she keep her nationality a secret. Many times, we don't know the reasons behind everything either. If you want prosperous lives, it is insane to bury your head in the world's televisions and ignore God.

This situation facing Mordecai and the Judeans is serious. We are not just talking about a few executions here, we are talking about the whole race – women, children, old folks, all of them. Forget human rights. Human rights is a weapon. Human rights protects evil people from justice while they plot your extermination, that's all. Human rights as defined by the United Nations is a weapon of mass destruction.

> Esther 3:9,10
> If it please the king, let it be written that they may be destroyed: and I will pay ten thousand talents of silver to the hands of those that have the charge of the business, to bring *it* into the king's treasuries.
>
> And the king took his ring from his hand, and gave it unto Haman the son of Hammedatha the Agagite, the Jews' [Judean's] enemy.

Haman here is called the Judean's enemy, and that is absolutely *illuminating* for anyone with eyes to see. It means he didn't just hate God's people, he hated God. Mordecai was right to show that bastard no respect. Haman was on the wrong side, the dark side, while the Pharaoh back in Joseph's time obviously wasn't. God had shown this to Mordecai, which is why Mordecai refused to reverence him. Esther is now queen and no one knows she is a Judean. Not even Haman knows the queen is a Judean.

> Esther 3:11,12
> And the king said unto Haman, The silver *is* given to thee, the people also, to do with them as it seemeth good to thee.
>
> Then were the king's scribes called on the thirteenth day of the first month, and there was written according to all that Haman had commanded unto the king's lieutenants, and to the governors that *were* over every province, and to the rulers of every people of

every province according to the writing thereof, and *to* every people after their language; in the name of king Ahasuerus was it written, and sealed with the king's ring.

The new law was passed and published in every province throughout the kingdom. All Judeans were to be executed. It was now International law. Isn't it International law today that is attempting to destroy America through the lie of global warming with cap and trade? The Hamans of our day and time hold high office at the United Nations and they are all high ranking freemasons who dabble in witchcraft.

Esther 3:13-15
And the letters were sent by posts into all the king's provinces, to destroy, to kill, and to cause to perish, all Jews [Judeans], both young and old, little children and women, in one day, *even* upon the thirteenth *day* of the twelfth month, which is the month Adar, and *to take* the spoil of them for a prey.

The copy of the writing for a commandment to be given in every province was published unto all people, that they should be ready against that day.

The posts went out, being hastened by the king's commandment, and the decree was given in Shushan the palace. And the king and Haman sat down to drink; but the city Shushan was perplexed.

It was all set up. The law was passed and the death penalty for being one of God's kids, for being a believer, for being a disciple, was instituted.

Esther 4:1,2
When Mordecai perceived all that was done, Mordecai rent his clothes, and put on sackcloth with ashes, and went out into the midst of the city, and cried with a loud and a bitter cry;

And came even before the king's gate: for none *might* enter into the king's gate clothed with sackcloth.

Here is a guy hurting inside. A law had just been passed sentencing him and all his people to death – women, children, old people, all of them.

You don't hurt much more than that. I suppose Mordecai could have thrown his hands up and blamed God for it. Isn't that what most people do when terrible things happen? Why don't people ever blame the devil for anything? Fortunately, Mordecai didn't charge God foolishly. He had obviously studied the book of Job. He held his mind together, and immediately set about believing God for a solution. He fought back. Instead of blaming God, he went to him for help.

God knew this situation was coming. He knows everything, including everything coming in the future. He saw it coming, which is why he told Mordecai to tell Esther not to tell anyone she was a Judean. See, our God already had a plan in place to rescue his people. He always has a plan. He always has a way to escape. He tells us that in his word.

> 1 Corinthians 10:13
> There hath no temptation taken you but such as is common to man: but God *is* faithful, who will not suffer you to be tempted above that ye are able; but will with the temptation also make a way to escape, that ye may be able to bear *it*.

America and Europe can escape the coming storms if they want to. God always has a way to escape. In America, for example, what is secession? You never hear about it in the media unless it is portrayed as something sinister which no person in their right mind would ever think of considering. Well, what do you *expect* the TV to tell you? The truth? That right is still there for Americans. Isn't it time to explore the options? The UK could be out of the insanity of the EU in no time, if they wanted to. Why don't the British people have the right to a referendum on this? Isn't democracy where the majority get their way? We don't live in democracies any longer; the Hamans at the UN make sure of that. They just call it democracy. The democratising of the Arab world is simply a power grab by the United Nations to try to draw America and the Muslims into a war that will destroy both of them.

God had the book of Esther written so we could learn from it, so we could learn how to walk by the spirit and be more than conquerors in every situation. If God can sort out a problem of this seriousness and this magnitude, can he sort out your life for you? Sure he can, but you are going to have to learn how to walk by the spirit. This isn't magic. In the book of Esther, God already had a plan in place to protect his people. The question isn't whether God can get us out of our problems or not, the question is are we listening?

> Esther 4:3
> And in every province, whithersoever the king's commandment and his decree came, *there was* great mourning among the Jews [Judeans], and fasting, and weeping, and wailing; and many lay in sackcloth and ashes.

The couriers went through the entire kingdom, bringing the news to every province. The Judeans were devastated. What had they done to deserve this? Death for being a believer? Is being a believer such a crime? The god of this world thinks so. The jesuits think so. The United Nations thinks so. The communists think so. The UCLA thinks so. And what must the parents have been feeling looking at their children, knowing that soldiers were coming to stick swords in them? No matter how terrible things look, we can't allow our minds to fear. Fear will kill us. We must believe God for answers. When God says move, we move. When he says jump, we jump. We don't ask how high, we just jump. He knows what he is doing. We get the deliverance if we follow his direction, and we can only hear him if we're walking by the spirit.

> Esther 4:4
> So Esther's maids and her chamberlains came and told *it* her. Then was the queen exceedingly grieved; and she sent raiment to clothe Mordecai, and to take away his sackcloth from him: but he received *it* not.

Esther heard that Mordecai was sitting in the streets clothed in sackcloth. She knew he was hurting, so she sent to find out what the problem was.

> Esther 4:5,6
> Then called Esther for Hatach, *one* of the king's chamberlains, whom he had appointed to attend upon her, and gave him a commandment to Mordecai, to know what it *was*, and why it *was*.
>
> So Hatach went forth to Mordecai unto the street of the city, which was before the king's gate.

Amazing how Esther still had not told anyone she was a Judean. She obviously knew how to control her tongue.

> Esther 4:7,8
> And Mordecai told him of all that had happened unto him, and of the sum of the money that Haman had promised to pay to the king's treasuries for the Jews [Judeans], to destroy them.
>
> Also he gave him the copy of the writing of the decree that was given at Shushan to destroy them, to shew *it* unto Esther, and to declare *it* unto her, and to charge her that she should go in unto the king, to make supplication unto him, and to make request before him for her people.

Mordecai made his move. Esther was to go and see the king and try to have the law reversed. Look at how God had Esther in a position of authority where she could be ready to handle this situation. God energises in those who know and believe his word. Just do your best at your job, walk by the spirit, and believe God.

> Esther 4:9-12
> And Hatach came and told Esther the words of Mordecai
>
> Again Esther spake unto Hatach, and gave him commandment unto Mordecai;
>
> All the king's servants, and the people of the king's provinces, do know, that whosoever, whether man or woman, shall come unto the king into the inner court, who is not called, *there is* one law of his to put *him* to death, except such to whom the king shall hold out the golden sceptre, that he may live: but I have not been called to come in unto the king these thirty days.
>
> And they told to Mordecai Esther's words.

Esther had a problem. There was another law, and one that carried the death penalty – no one, but no one entered the king's inner court unless summoned. Anyone who broke that law was executed unless the king held out his sceptre. That was the law. Look at the pressure these believers had to handle.

It is only the word we hold in our minds that holds us together when we are under pressure. We can decide to think our old crappy thoughts of doubt, worry, and fear, and bitch and complain about everything, or we can decide to think what the word says. The choice is ours. Whichever way we choose determines the outcome. Sure, Esther had a problem, but Mordecai confronted her fear and helped her overcome it.

> Esther 4:13,14
> Then Mordecai commanded to answer Esther, Think not with thyself that thou shalt escape in the king's house, more than all the Jews [Judeans].
>
> For if thou altogether holdest thy peace at this time, *then* shall there enlargement and deliverance arise to the Jews [Judeans] from another place; but thou and thy father's house shall be destroyed: and who knoweth whether thou art come to the kingdom for *such* a time as this?

He confronted her fear and told her straight that if she refused to act because of fear, God would find another way to save his people and she would be destroyed. Her fear would have killed her had Mordecai not confronted it. Fear is the only thing we have to fear. He confronted her fear. Was he controlling her? Don't be ridiculous, he was saving her life.

> Esther 4:15-17;5:1
> Then Esther bade *them* return Mordecai *this answer*,
>
> Go, gather together all the Jews [Judeans] that are present in Shushan, and fast ye for me, and neither eat nor drink three days, night or day: I also and my maidens will fast likewise; and so will I go in unto the king, which *is* not according to the law: and if I perish, I perish.
>
> So Mordecai went his way, and did according to all that Esther had commanded him.

> Now it came to pass on the third day, that Esther put on *her* royal *apparel*, and stood in the inner court of the king's house, over against the king's house: and the king sat upon his royal throne in the royal house, over against the gate of the house.

Esther dressed herself up, put on her makeup, took a deep breath, and walked to her execution. Only she wasn't walking to her execution, she was believing God, trusting his word. She obeyed the word and did it, despite the fact that she was facing the death penalty. Believing God can be quite scary at times and demand tremendous courage. Sometimes it can be incredibly tough to do the word, but if we do it we get the results. If we fear and cave in, we get beat.

> Esther 5:2
> And it was so, when the king saw Esther the queen standing in the court, *that* she obtained favour in his sight: and the king held out to Esther the golden sceptre that *was* in his hand. So Esther drew near, and touched the top of the sceptre.

See, when we believe and act on the word, we get the positive results promised. Of course, Esther wasn't being reckless here either. She didn't run in there every other day just because she thought she could get away with it.

> Esther 5:3,4
> Then said the king unto her, What wilt thou, queen Esther? and what *is* thy request? it shall be even given thee to the half of the kingdom.
>
> And Esther answered, If *it seem* good unto the king, let the king and Haman come this day unto the banquet that I have prepared for him.

A *banquet?* A private party with the king and queen? For *Haman?* What is going on here? Makes you wonder why Esther didn't just blurt it all out, hey? Why didn't she tell the king all about the problem, that she was a Judean and beg to save her people? I'll tell you why, because she was a disciple and she was walking by the spirit, doing what God told her to do. It was God who told her to invite Haman to a private banquet with just the three of them, and that's what she did. She didn't just make this up. You can only understand the word by understanding how manifestations energise. This is the way of life in operation. Walking by the spirit is the way to go.

> Esther 5:5,6
> Then the king said, Cause Haman to make haste, that he may do as Esther hath said. So the king and Haman came to the banquet that Esther had prepared.
>
> And the king said unto Esther at the banquet of wine, What *is* thy petition? and it shall be granted thee: and what *is* thy request? even to the half of the kingdom it shall be performed.

So there they are, enjoying good food, good wine, just the three of them, the king, the queen, and Haman. Esther had risked her life to ask for a private banquet with Haman. The king was intrigued, and she certainly had his attention. He knew there was a problem because she had risked death to come and see him. People don't do that unless there is a major problem. He was her husband, he cared about her, he wanted to know, he wanted to help.

> Esther 5:7,8
> Then answered Esther, and said, My petition and my request *is*;
>
> If I have found favour in the sight of the king, and if it please the king to grant my petition, and to perform my request, let the king and Haman come to the banquet that I shall prepare for them, and I will do to morrow as the king hath said.

She asked for *another* private banquet for just the three of them! Now look, be sensible here. I'll bet Esther was having quiet words with God about this. I'll bet this wasn't her idea of dealing with the problem. I'll bet inviting Haman to a private banquet wasn't easy for her. I'll bet Haman was the last person on earth she wanted to be around. I'll bet her emotions were in turmoil. However, she was a disciple. She went to God, was told what to do, and she did it. That's the way of life.

Esther 5:9
Then went Haman forth that day joyful and with a glad heart: but when Haman saw Mordecai in the king's gate, that he stood not up, nor moved for him, he was full of indignation against Mordecai.

Haman was joyful, and had a glad heart. Those emotions were real. Then he saw Mordecai and hatred bubbled up through his joy, overpowering him. That is how the way of death is energised. There is nothing wrong with emotions, we just can't allow them to get out of control like this. Haman was beyond belief. In fact, he was born of the seed of the serpent, which is referred to in the bible as the unforgiveable sin. That's why the bible tells us he was the enemy of God. People who are born of the seed of the serpent are literally the devil's children and have a permanent spiritual wedge driven into their minds which keeps them open to devil spirit possession. It is unforgiveable because it is seed, it is the devil's seed, and seed cannot be taken out of a person. In this context, look at what Jesus Christ said to a few of the religious leaders of his day.

John 8:44
Ye are of *your* father the devil, and the lusts of your father ye will do. He was a murderer from the beginning, and abode not in the truth, because there is no truth in him. When he speaketh a lie, he speaketh of his own: for he is a liar, and the father of it.

Those pharisees were born of the seed of the serpent, they were the devil's children and the devil was their father. Seed is permanent and that's why being born of the seed of the serpent is unforgiveable. Just as many jesuits today are born of the seed of the serpent, so was Haman. That's why hatred could bubble up through his joy instantaneously and drive him to murder. All this evil in Haman had grown from his love of money. It is those born of the seed of the serpent who control the world for their god.

Esther 5:10-13
Nevertheless Haman refrained himself: and when he came home, he sent and called for his friends, and Zeresh his wife.

And Haman told them of the glory of his riches, and the multitude of his children, and all *the things* wherein the king had promoted him, and how he had advanced him above the princes and servants of the king.

Haman said moreover, Yea, Esther the queen did let no man come in with the king unto the banquet that she had prepared but myself; and to morrow am I invited unto her also with the king.

Yet all this availeth me nothing, so long as I see Mordecai the Jew [Judean] sitting at the king's gate.

Even though he was the most powerful man in the world next to the king, wealthy beyond imagination, with power and family and influence, none of it mattered to him so much as seeing Mordecai dead. That was the driving passion of his life. Nothing else mattered. Our emotions are not to drive us. The more we fill our minds and hearts with God's word, the less our emotions dictate our lives for us. When we take control of our lives, then the god of this world can no longer get in. That is precisely what James says.

James 4:7
Submit yourselves therefore to God. Resist the devil, and he will flee from you.

We submit to God by learning his word, and by taking control of our thoughts and emotions. As we do that, we become strong in areas where we were once weak and the attacks stop. If we resist, the devil will be defeated.

Esther 5:14
Then said Zeresh his wife and all his friends unto him, Let a gallows be made of fifty cubits high, and to morrow speak thou unto the king that Mordecai may be hanged thereon: then go thou in merrily with the king unto the banquet. And the thing pleased Haman; and he caused the gallows to be made.

Haman's wife wasn't much better. She was in on his murderous ways too. Be very wary of the world's women that hold political power. Remember Jezebel?

Esther 6:1-3
On that night could not the king sleep, and he commanded to bring the book of records of the chronicles; and they were read before the king.

And it was found written, that Mordecai had told of Bigthana and Teresh, two of the king's chamberlains, the keepers of the door, who sought to lay hand on the king Ahasuerus.

And the king said, What honour and dignity hath been done to Mordecai for this? Then said the king's servants that ministered unto him, There is nothing done for him.

Old kingie boy couldn't sleep. His conscience was bothering him. Do you remember that God had showed Mordecai about that plot to murder the king? Well, guess what, the king forgot all about that little incident and no reward was ever given to Mordecai. Now he remembered. Any guesses who was at work here? God is amazing. Haman was planning to ask the king to have Mordecai murdered just as this came into the king's heart. Look at the timing of this thing. Look how God pricked this king's heart at the right moment. Can God turn any situation around? Yes, he can, he can sort out anything in your life because nothing is too hard for him.

Jeremiah 32:27
Behold, I am the LORD, the God of all flesh: is there any thing too hard for me?

Esther 6:4,5
And the king said, Who *is* in the court? Now Haman was come into the outward court of the king's house, to speak unto the king to hang Mordecai on the gallows that he had prepared for him.

And the king's servants said unto him, Behold, Haman standeth in the court.

The king was happy to see his top adviser, the second most powerful man in the kingdom, and decided to ask his advice about the situation with Mordecai.

Esther 6:6
So Haman came in. And the king said unto him, What shall be done unto the man whom the king delighteth to honour? Now Haman thought in his heart, To whom would the king delight to do honour more than to myself?

Look at the ego dripping out of that creature. All he can think about is himself. Esther did what God told her to do and Haman had attended a private banquet and been invited to another. So here, Haman just naturally assumed it was him. It didn't even occur to him that it might have been someone else. In essence, the two private banquets were a set up. God knew what he was doing. Another thing, Esther didn't complain and bitch about it either. She knew it was all part of God's plan and obeyed. This is the way of life in operation. This is how you walk by the spirit as more than a conqueror in every situation.

Watch Haman lay it on now. He told the king what to do to Mordecai, thinking the king was going to do it to him, and the only reason he went to see the king in the first place was to ask for permission to hang Mordecai.

Esther 6:7,8
And Haman answered the king, For the man whom the king delighteth to honour,

Let the royal apparel be brought which the king *useth* to wear, and the horse that the king rideth upon, and the crown royal which is set upon his head:

It is interesting to see what was in Haman's heart, as he obviously fancied himself as the next king. He reckoned he was second in line for the throne. It is that kind of lust for political power that twists such men into these foul creatures.

Esther 6:9
And let this apparel and horse be delivered to the hand of one of the king's most noble princes, that they may array the man *withal* whom the king delighteth to honour, and bring him on horseback through the street of the city, and proclaim before him, Thus shall it be done to the man whom the king delighteth to honour.

The king thought this a splendid idea.

> Esther 6:10,11
> Then the king said to Haman, Make haste, *and* take the apparel and the horse, as thou hast said, and do even so to Mordecai the Jew [Judean], that sitteth at the king's gate: let nothing fail of all that thou hast spoken.

Then took Haman the apparel and the horse, and arrayed Mordecai, and brought him on horseback through the street of the city, and proclaimed before him, Thus shall it be done unto the man whom the king delighteth to honour.

Haman himself was forced to personally be the man who did the proclaiming before Mordecai. Can you imagine what his twisted emotions must have been doing to him around that time? God knows how to deliver us when we believe him and trust him.

> Esther 6:12-14
> And Mordecai came again to the king's gate. But Haman hasted to his house mourning, and having his head covered.
>
> And Haman told Zeresh his wife and all his friends every *thing* that had befallen him. Then said his wise men and Zeresh his wife unto him, If Mordecai *be* of the seed of the Jews [Judeans], before whom thou hast begun to fall, thou shalt not prevail against him, but shalt surely fall before him.
>
> And while they *were* yet talking with him, came the king's chamberlains, and hasted to bring Haman unto the banquet that Esther had prepared.

Where would Mordecai have wound up if he had been afraid, or blamed God for all their problems? Dangling from the gallows, that's where. But he kept his heart and mind in the scriptures. He delighted himself in God and his word. God can deliver us from anything. It is up to us to believe his word, and we can't do that with our heads stuck in the world's televisions all day.

Esther 7:1
So the king and Haman came to banquet with Esther the queen.

By this time, the king must have been positively itching to know what Esther's problem was.

Esther 7:2
And the king said again unto Esther on the second day at the banquet of wine, What *is* thy petition, queen Esther? and it shall be granted thee: and what *is* thy request? and it shall be performed, *even* to the half of the kingdom.

God then gave her the green light to reveal her nationality. She didn't move until she had the green light, and then she went for Haman's throat. That woman was absolutely fearless. When we're walking by the spirit, we must never act until we have the green light, the go sign.

Esther 7:3-6
Then Esther the queen answered and said, If I have found favour in thy sight, O king, and if it please the king, let my life be given me at my petition, and my people at my request:

For we are sold, I and my people, to be destroyed, to be slain, and to perish. But if we had been sold for bondmen and bondwomen, I had held my tongue, although the enemy could not countervail the king's damage.

Then the king Ahasuerus answered and said unto Esther the queen, Who is he, and where is he, that durst presume in his heart to do so?

And Esther said, The adversary and enemy *is* this wicked Haman. Then Haman was afraid before the king and the queen.

She told the king she was a Judean. That must have knocked him on his back. I wonder what that did to Haman? His eyes must have bulged out of his head. That was one powerful moment in time. The emotions going on in that room at that moment must have been beyond words. Haman was afraid. Good, he deserved it. I hope he enjoyed what happened to him next.

Esther 7:7
And the king arising from the banquet of wine in his wrath *went* into the palace garden: and Haman stood up to make request for his life to Esther the queen; for he saw that there was evil determined against him by the king.

The king was so angry, he had to leave the room to gather his wits. His face must have been black, and Haman knew he was in trouble. The miserable creature then ran to the queen to try to save his skin. He was so terrified, he even got physical about it.

Esther 7:8-10
Then the king returned out of the palace garden into the place of the banquet of wine; and Haman was fallen upon the bed whereon Esther *was*. Then said the king, Will he force the queen also before me in the house? As the word went out of the king's mouth, they covered Haman's face.

And Harbonah, one of the chamberlains, said before the king, Behold also, the gallows fifty cubits high, which Haman had made for Mordecai, who had spoken good for the king, standeth in the house of Haman. Then the king said, Hang him thereon.

So they hanged Haman on the gallows that he had prepared for Mordecai. Then was the king's wrath pacified.

You have to ask yourself, if God can sort out problems on a scale like this, can he sort out your problems for you? Yes, he can, and I don't care what your problems are. God can sort out anything. If you read the rest of the book of Esther, you will see that God delivered his people. The law was reversed, the Judeans were saved, and they had the mastery over their enemies.

We too, with God's help, can overcome any problem, as individuals or as entire nations. God always has a way to escape, and he will provide the answers we need when we need them if we are listening and we obey his word. To be victorious in life, we must walk by the spirit.

52. Living Victoriously

Living a victorious life, a super conqueror lifestyle, the I can do lifestyle of Philippians has absolutely nothing to do with who we are, but rather is entirely dependent on how we think and what we do. The apostle Paul was one of the most educated, influential and well connected men on the planet while Amos had been a swineherd, yet both of them lived victorious lifestyles. Mordecai and Esther were not superhuman, yet they overcame every challenge that came their way. Our lives are certainly not without challenges either, and we can also be victorious in overcoming any and all challenges that come our way. Being a believer doesn't mean we never face challenges in life, it means we can overcome them and be victorious.

Everyone faces challenges in life, sometimes serious challenges. The more abundant life Jesus Christ made available is not a life without challenges, it is having the strength to be victorious despite the world we live in. To achieve it we simply have to raise our thinking to new elevations, to new heights and take appropriate action. By the end of this class you will understand what I'm talking about.

In this regards, Psalm 18 is fascinating. There may be one hundred and fifty psalms, but God marked this particular psalm in a very special way by having it written out in its entirety twice in his word to establish its importance. By having it written out in full twice, once in psalms and once in 2 Samuel 22, God expects us to sit up and take note. As if that wasn't enough reason to pay attention, it was written by David who the word declares was a man after God's own heart.

> Acts 13:22
> And when he had removed him, he raised up unto them David to be their king; to whom also he gave testimony, and said, I have found David the son of Jesse, a man after mine own heart, which shall fulfil all my will.

A psalm is a song. David wrote many of the psalms, including psalm 18, and they were all originally written to music. David was an accomplished musician, and his music and his words were powerful enough to cast out devil spirits.

> 1 Samuel 16:23
> And it came to pass, when the evil spirit from God was upon Saul, that David took an harp, and played with his hand: so Saul was refreshed, and was well, and the evil spirit departed from him.

If David's songs were powerful enough to cast out devil spirits, and God had psalm 18 written out twice in the bible, and David was a man after God's own heart, then open your ears and listen.

> Psalm 18:2,3
> The LORD is my rock, and my fortress, and my deliverer; my God, my strength, in whom I will trust; my buckler, and the horn of my salvation, and my high tower.
>
> I will call upon the LORD, who is worthy to be praised: so shall I be saved from mine enemies.

To give us a taste of where we're going with this, look at where the words are coming from. David wrote this song after he'd been delivered from Saul and all his enemies. He wrote this from a position of strength, from a position of victory, from a position of deliverance. David walked by the spirit and overcame many challenging situations in which he could have lost his life, and here he was singing from that position of deliverance and victory. Despite the many attempts on his life, he had been crowned king of Israel, had overcome every challenge and subdued all his enemies. He was singing his heart out from that position of strength and victory. Now compare his words with these words from a modern church hymn book.

> Tempted and tried, we're oft made to wonder
> Why it should be thus all the day long,
> While there are others living about us
> Never molested tho' in the wrong

Farther along we'll know all about it
Farther along we'll understand why
Cheer up, my brother, live in the sunshine
We'll understand it all by and by.

Look at the vantage point of these words and compare them to David's. Were they written from a position of strength and victory? No, they were not, they were written from a victim's point of view, from someone who had been beaten up by the world and who had no concept of what it is to be a super conqueror. Their answer to a shit life was to smile inanely at their problems and conjure up imaginary sunshine. That's what going to church does to people. Back to David. Savour these words, speak them out loud, taste them, digest them.

Psalm 18:4-17
The sorrows of death compassed me, and the floods of ungodly men made me afraid.

The sorrows of hell [the grave] compassed me about: the snares of death prevented [preceded] me.

In my distress I called upon the LORD, and cried unto my God: he heard my voice out of his temple, and my cry came before him, even into his ears.

Then the earth shook and trembled; the foundations also of the hills moved and were shaken, because he was wroth.

There went up a smoke out of his nostrils, and fire out of his mouth devoured: coals were kindled by it.

He bowed the heavens also, and came down: and darkness was under his feet.

And he rode upon a cherub, and did fly: yea, he did fly upon the wings of the wind.

He made darkness his secret place; his pavilion round about him were dark waters and thick clouds of the skies.

> At the brightness that was before him his thick clouds passed, hail stones and coals of fire.
>
> The LORD also thundered in the heavens, and the Highest gave his voice; hail stones and coals of fire.
>
> Yea, he sent out his arrows, and scattered them; and he shot out lightnings, and discomfited them.
>
> Then the channels of waters were seen, and the foundations of the world were discovered at thy rebuke, O LORD, at the blast of the breath of thy nostrils.
>
> He sent from above, he took me, he drew me out of many waters.
>
> He delivered me from my strong enemy, and from them which hated me: for they were too strong for me.

David had faced unbelievably challenging situations and God had fought for him and delivered him. David had defeated every enemy he'd faced and in this psalm he was singing from that position of deliverance and strength. Now compare his words with these from that same church hymn book. Don't savour these words, just skim over them quickly.

> Have you a heart that's weary
> Tending a load of care?
> Are you a soul that's seeking
> Rest from the burden you bear?
>
> Who knows your disappointments?
> Who hears each time you cry?
> Who understands your heartaches?
> Who dries the tears from your eyes?

Excuse my language, but what a load of fucking weak religious anaemic horseshit. Do these words give glory to God? Do they sing of God's deliverance and power? Do they come from a position of strength and victory? No, they were written by some weak idiot whose answer to all their problems was to cry their eyes out all day. That's what going to church does to people. Back to David.

> Psalm 18:32
> It is God that girdeth me with strength, and maketh my way perfect.

Will God gird us with strength today, as he did for David? Oh yes, look at this promise in Ephesians.

> Ephesians 3:16
> That he would grant you, according to the riches of his glory, to be strengthened with might by his Spirit in the inner man;

Have a look at these words from another well known church hymn.

> How long has it been
> Since you talked with the Lord
> And told him your heart's hidden secrets?
> How long since you prayed?
> How long since you stayed
> On your knees till the light shone through?
> How long has it been
> Since your mind felt at ease?
> How long since your heart knew no burden.
> Can you call him your friend?
> How long has it been?
> Since you knew that he cared for you?

Excuse me, I enjoy fellowship with God every day thanks very much, and I don't have any burdens. Oh and I don't pray on my knees either you religious numpty. Do you think it makes any difference to God if you pray on your knees? The only idiots I see in the bible getting down on their knees to pray are the worshippers of Baal. I talk to God all the time and he talks to me. The light shines for me every day. And just for the record, God isn't my friend either, he's my father. Back to David.

> Psalm 18:33
> He maketh my feet like hinds' feet, and setteth me upon my high places.

David didn't write this from the bottom of the mountains looking up with wishful thinking, he was standing on his high places looking down at the world below. He wrote this from a position of strength and deliverance. Isn't that where you would like to be? If so, then you had better not sing songs like this.

> Though the angry surges roll on my tempest driven soul,
> I am peaceful, for I know, wildly though the winds may blow,
> I've an anchor safe and sure, that can evermore endure.
>
> Troubles almost 'whelm my soul, griefs like billows o'er me roll,
> Tempters seek to lure astray, storms obscure the light of day,
> But in Christ I can be bold, I've an anchor that shall hold.

This writer was obviously living a life of grief, defeat and misery, where every day was one storm after another. A victorious life isn't a life trying to be peaceful while smiling inanely through all your problems, it's about dealing with stuff, kicking the shit out of your problems and being a super conqueror. That's how you get peace and enjoy a life worth living. This writer wasn't enjoying life on his high places, he was sitting in the gutter of defeat pretending everything was okay. Do you begin to see the difference now in viewpoints between what religion offers and what God offers? If you want a shit life go to church or join a ministry, for that's all they will give you. If you want a victorious life, come back to God and his word.

> Romans 8:31,37
> What shall we then say to these things? If God be for us, who can be against us?
>
> Nay, in all these things we are more than conquerors through him that loved us.

We are not to sit in defeat and put up with a shit life, we are to rise up and fight for a victorious life of abundance and power, as David did.

> Psalm18:39-42
> For thou hast girded me with strength unto the battle: thou hast subdued under me those that rose up against me.

> Thou hast also given me the necks of mine enemies; that I might destroy them that hate me.
>
> They cried, but there was none to save them: even unto the LORD, but he answered them not.
>
> Then did I beat them small as the dust before the wind: I did cast them out as the dirt in the streets.

David sang from the heart of a conqueror who had defeated every challenge and who enjoyed an incredible life. What do you think God meant when he told us that we can do all things through Christ who strengthens us? What do you think God meant when he told us we are more than conquerors through him that loved us? Do you think the people who wrote the hymns above understood what God meant?

I'll tell you something, churches and ministries that sing songs about putting up with burdens and trials and conjuring up make-believe sunshine can shove their anaemic religious garbage up their backsides. Do you think it's a glory to God to be a defeated miserable christian who never deals with anything and just takes all the shit from the world and puts up with it? Do you think it's a glory to God to be overcome by problems and deal with them by crying your eyes out all day? Back to David.

> Psalm 18:47-50
> It is God that avengeth me, and subdueth the people under me.
>
> He delivereth me from mine enemies: yea, thou liftest me up above those that rise up against me: thou hast delivered me from the violent man.
>
> Therefore will I give thanks unto thee, O LORD, among the heathen, and sing praises unto thy name.
>
> Great deliverance giveth he to his king; and sheweth mercy to his anointed, to David, and to his seed for evermore.

Psalm 18 is a song that gives glory to God, which was written by a man after God's own heart who knew what it took to stand against the wiles of the devil and defeat him. This abundant life Jesus Christ came to make available is a life of power, abundance, deliverance and victory, not a miserable servile pathetic existence of struggling through life burdened down with problems, like many church hymns portray.

Let me state this plainly. If you think God enjoys hearing his people sing songs about putting up with trials and burdens and not dealing with them and being victorious over them, you have no concept of his power, strength, and delivering nature. Get out of those damnable man-made ministries and churches sucking the energy out of you if you want to enjoy deliverance and power in your life. Look at these words of David's.

> Psalm 3:6
> I will not be afraid of ten thousands of people, that have set themselves against me round about.
>
> Psalm 23:4
> Yea, though I walk through the valley of the shadow of death, I will fear no evil: for thou art with me; thy rod and thy staff they comfort me.
>
> Psalm 27:1
> The LORD is my light and my salvation; whom shall I fear? the LORD is the strength of my life; of whom shall I be afraid?
>
> Psalm 29:11
> The LORD will give strength unto his people; the LORD will bless his people with peace.

David had problems just as we all do, make no mistake, but he dealt with them, defeated them, and lived victoriously. It wasn't only foreign armies he dealt with either, look at some of the personal problems he had to deal with.

> Psalm 41:5-11
> Mine enemies speak evil of me, When shall he die, and his name perish?

> And if he come to see me, he speaketh vanity: his heart gathereth iniquity to itself; when he goeth abroad, he telleth it.
>
> All that hate me whisper together against me: against me do they devise my hurt.
>
> An evil disease, say they, cleaveth fast unto him: and now that he lieth he shall rise up no more.
>
> Yea, mine own familiar friend, in whom I trusted, which did eat of my bread, hath lifted up his heel against me.
>
> But thou, O LORD, be merciful unto me, and raise me up, that I may requite them.
>
> By this I know that thou favourest me, because mine enemy doth not triumph over me.

David lived with this kind of garbage, but he didn't succumb to it. Sure he had challenges in life, just as we all do. When he was so sick he was on his deathbed, even his friends whispered behind his back and wished him dead. How did he deal with it? By crying his eyes out all day and feeling sorry for himself? No, he went to God and believed for deliverance. He trusted in God and he was victorious. He believed that God would deliver him and he fought for his life. Guess what, that's what we're supposed to do as well.

> Romans 8:31
> What shall we then say to these things? If God *be* for us, who *can be* against us?

Do you think it was an oversight on God's part having psalm 18 written twice to establish its truths? The old testament was written for our learning, and like David we are to fight for our lives and not put up with the world dumping its shit all over us. This kind of deliverance doesn't come by magic, or by wishful thinking, or by crying your eyes out all day, it comes by believing, by being fearless, by having the courage and strength to put your trust in God and walk by the spirit.

Hebrews 11:6
But without faith [believing] it is impossible to please him: for he that cometh to God must believe that he is, and that he is a rewarder of them that diligently seek him.

No believing, no results, that's how it works. David was a believer, the religious idiots who wrote all those hymns about suffering pathetically through all their burdens and problems were not. How do you learn to be a believer? Stay away from churches and ministries for a start, and get your head into the bible everyday.

Romans10:17
So then faith [believing] cometh by hearing, and hearing by the word of God.

What you believe is what you will receive. Confession of receipt yields receipt of confession. What you look at is what you will become. If you want to live the more abundant life Jesus Christ made available, then you had better stop attending churches and ministries that sing songs like those above for if you sing about being burdened and living in defeat your life will show it. If you want out of the gutter of unbelief, get your head out of the gutter of religion and back into God's word.

53. Jonah

When we were children and our parents told us not to stick our fingers into electrical sockets, were they being mean and simply trying to spoil our fun? No, they were protecting us from serious harm and looking out for our best interests because they loved us. So it is with God. When he suggests something, if we listen and obey we enjoy the benefits because he has our best interests at heart. The god of this world is ruthless and comes only to steal, to kill and to destroy. When we live according to God's word, we live abundantly and we have God's protection. When he tells us stuff it's not to spoil our fun, it's because he's protecting us and looking out for our best interests. The god of this world entices and seduces us away from the word so he can harm us. Arguing with God and refusing to listen to him is insane.

Now, the thing is, no one is perfect and we all get it wrong from time to time. Sometimes we even turn our noses up at God and stubbornly refuse to do things his way even when we know better. Such disobedience often leads to consequences in life that we would rather have avoided, not because God is punishing us but because we decided to disobey and stick our fingers into spiritual electrical sockets.

The good thing is that whenever and wherever we return to God he is always there to help us sort things out. There is no situation or problem that we get ourselves into that is too big for God to deal with. It may seem that way sometimes, but if we lift up our believing and focus on God and his word despite our disobedience and mistakes, the answers will always be there. The book of Jonah makes for interesting reading in this regards.

> Jonah 1:1,2
> Now the word of the LORD came unto Jonah the son of Amittai, saying,

> Arise, go to Nineveh, that great city, and cry against it; for their wickedness is come up before me.

Nineveh was a city of Northern Africa, the capital city of the Assyrians who were enemies of the Israelites. God told Jonah, who was a prophet, to go to Nineveh and confront them because of their evil ways. That's what prophets do. If you are off the word, don't be surprised to find a prophet in your face confronting you. Sure he'll make you mad, but once you calm down and get your head back into the word you may find yourself being grateful someone loved you big enough to get in there and help you. Confrontation is necessary to get people's attention when they are walking away from God. Here in Jonah, God gave the Assyrians an opportunity to change their ways by sending a prophet to confront them. Jonah unfortunately had a problem with his assignment.

> Jonah 1:3
> But Jonah rose up to flee unto Tarshish from the presence of the LORD, and went down to Joppa; and he found a ship going to Tarshish: so he paid the fare thereof, and went down into it, to go with them unto Tarshish from the presence of the LORD.

Tarshish is modern day Seville in Spain, which is a long way away from Nineveh. Jonah knew that if he confronted the Assyrians they could change their ways and escape their imminent destruction. He *wanted* the Assyrians destroyed because they were the enemies of his people. So he came up with a plan – he decided to disobey God and run as far away from Nineveh as possible so the Assyrians would be destroyed.

Jonah obviously loved people more than he loved God. He ran away not because he was afraid, but because he believed he was protecting his people. Often in life when you're in the spiritual competition the word can be difficult to carry out and the easy option is to run away. Using a credit card to buy something for which you don't have the money and going into debt is running away from God. It is the easy option for people who can't or won't believe God will supply their need. Jonah took the easy option and ran away. Doing the word is what's important, not doing what our feelings dictate. Do we follow our head or do we follow our heart? That's the choice the world gives us but they're both wrong. We follow God and his word despite anything either our heads or our hearts tell us.

Jonah 1:4
But the LORD sent out a great wind into the sea, and there was a mighty tempest in the sea, so that the ship was like to be broken.

So there was Jonah sailing away from Nineveh and a storm hit. Not just any old storm either, it was a massive typhoon, a hurricane. Now before we continue, let's have a spot quiz. Did anyone spot the idiom of permission? Think back to Job in the opening sessions of the class. Who did all the nasty things to Job? God or the devil? The devil, right? We know that it was the devil who killed his children, destroyed his business and stole his health. We understand the idiom by recognising that Job had fear in his life which allowed access to him by the devil. Do you see the same idiom of permission used here? The meaning of green and red traffic lights has not changed since you read the book of Job and neither has the truth that God is good and the devil is bad. It wasn't God who wanted Jonah dead, it was the devil. The difference between Job and Jonah though is different in that Job was afraid while Jonah was simply being disobedient.

Jonah 1:5
Then the mariners [sailors] were afraid, and cried every man unto his god, and cast forth the wares [the cargoes] that *were* in the ship into the sea, to lighten *it* of them. But Jonah was gone down into the sides of the ship; and he lay, and was fast asleep.

This is fascinating. That storm was so powerful that the crew dumped the cargo overboard because they were in fear of their lives, yet Jonah was fast asleep. How do you manage to sleep in the midst of a hurricane aboard a small wooden ship while everyone around you is terrified for their lives? Jonah was very comfortable with his decision to run away, so comfortable in fact that he was quite happy to die rather than do God's will. He thought he was giving his life for his people. Very noble but very wrong. The question is, do we love God more than we love people? If not, we are not walking with the love of God in the renewed mind in manifestation. Jonah loved people more than he loved God. Jonah was out of fellowship. The captain of the ship then got a bit pissed off with Jonah and kicked him out of his bunk.

Jonah 1:6
So the shipmaster came to him, and said unto him, What meanest thou, O sleeper? arise, call upon thy God, if so be that God will think upon us, that we perish not.

There was something about that storm that made those sailors suspicious. It was no ordinary storm and they had the feeling there was some spiritual force behind it. All bad weather basically has spirit power behind it. Tornadoes don't just happen.

Jonah 1:7-11
And they said every one to his fellow, Come, and let us cast lots, that we may know for whose cause this evil *is* upon us. So they cast lots, and the lot fell upon Jonah.

Then said they unto him, Tell us, we pray thee, for whose cause this evil *is* upon us; What *is* thine occupation? and whence comest thou? what *is* thy country? and of what people *art* thou?

And he said unto them, I *am* an Hebrew; and I fear the LORD, the God of heaven, which hath made the sea and the dry *land*.

Then were the men exceedingly afraid, and said unto him, Why hast thou done this? For the men knew that he fled from the presence of the LORD, because he had told them.

Then said they unto him, What shall we do unto thee, that the sea may be calm unto us? for the sea wrought, and was tempestuous.

Once the crew knew he was a man of God, a prophet, and a disobedient one at that, they asked Jonah what they needed to do to escape that storm and save their lives. Jonah knew he had run away from God and he was quite comfortable with that. If he died, the Assyrians wouldn't get the word and they would be destroyed. In his mind he was dying for his nation. The devil certainly didn't want Jonah around, so it was in his best interests to kill him as quickly as possible while he had the chance.

Jonah 1:12-16
And he said unto them, Take me up, and cast me forth into the sea; so shall the sea be calm unto you: for I know that for my sake this great tempest *is* upon you.

Nevertheless the men rowed hard to bring *it* to the land; but they could not: for the sea wrought, and was tempestuous against them.

Wherefore they cried unto the LORD, and said, We beseech thee, O LORD, we beseech thee, let us not perish for this man's life, and lay not upon us innocent blood: for thou, O LORD, hast done as it pleased thee.

So they took up Jonah, and cast him forth into the sea: and the sea ceased from her raging.

Then the men feared the LORD exceedingly, and offered a sacrifice unto the LORD, and made vows.

So Jonah was chucked overboard and the storm ceased.

Jonah 1:17
Now the LORD had prepared a great fish to swallow up Jonah. And Jonah was in the belly of the fish three days and three nights.

Chapter one ends with an intriguing truth. God had prepared a fish to eat Jonah and it was lurking at the bottom of the Mediterranean Sea. Note that it doesn't say a whale, it says a big fish. Also consider that God had prepared for this big fish to be there. This is remarkable. God in his word promises that he will always provide a way to escape for us out of any situation.

1 Corinthians 10:13
There hath no temptation taken you but such as is common to man: but God *is* faithful, who will not suffer you to be tempted above that ye are able; but will with the temptation also make a way to escape, that ye may be able to bear *it*.

God is also faithful to his word and he does not lie.

> Numbers 23:19
> God *is* not a man, that he should lie; neither the son of man, that he should repent: hath he said, and shall he not do *it?* or hath he spoken, and shall he not make it good?

The way to escape will always be there, even at the bottom of oceans. In Jonah's case, while he was sinking to the bottom of the sea something amazing happened. First of all, verses 2-9 of chapter 2 are a prayer and all the verbs are in the past tense. This tells us that Jonah spoke these words later, after he was out of the fish. Verse one even tells us just that.

> Jonah 2:1
> Then Jonah prayed unto the LORD his God out of the fish's belly,

It says *then*. Then when? Then, after Jonah was out of the fish's belly, which was three days and three nights later. Jonah prayed later, not when he was in the fish's belly but when he was out of it. That's what it says if you just read it. This prayer was prayed after Jonah was out of the fish's belly. That's why all the verbs in verses 2 to 9 are in the past tense. Jonah couldn't possibly have prayed this while he was still actually in the fish's belly, for Jonah was dead.

> Jonah 2:2,3
> And [Jonah] said, I cried by reason of mine affliction unto the LORD, and he heard me; out of the belly of hell [the grave] cried I, *and* thou heardest my voice.
>
> For thou hadst cast me into the deep, in the midst of the seas; and the floods compassed me about: all thy billows and thy waves passed over me.

Jonah used the idiom of permission here. Who chucked Jonah over the side of the ship? The crew or God? It wasn't God, it was the crew. See the idiom? This is the idiom of permission, the truth that was set in the book of Job which holds true throughout the entire bible. The meaning of red and green traffic lights has not changed.

This was quite a situation. Jonah was sinking to the bottom of the Mediterranean Sea after being chucked overboard from a ship during a monster storm. As he sank towards the sea bed he knew he didn't have much time left. All around him was dark ocean. The light of the sky would have been fading far above him. His lungs would have been bursting as he ran out of air. He was dying. Then a remarkable thing happened. Jonah decided to get himself back into fellowship with God.

Jonah 2:4
Then I said, I am cast out of thy sight; yet I will look again toward thy holy temple.

Looking towards God's holy temple was a scriptural reference to the prayer Solomon made when he dedicated the temple he'd just built.

1 Kings 8:22,44-50
And Solomon stood before the altar of the LORD in the presence of all the congregation of Israel, and spread forth his hands toward heaven:

If thy people go out to battle against their enemy, whithersoever thou shalt send them, and shall pray unto the LORD toward the city which thou hast chosen, and *toward* the house that I have built for thy name:

Then hear thou in heaven their prayer and their supplication, and maintain their cause.

If they sin against thee, (for *there is* no man that sinneth not,) and thou be angry with them, and deliver them to the enemy, so that they carry them away captives unto the land of the enemy, far or near;

Yet if they shall bethink themselves in the land whither they were carried captives, and repent, and make supplication unto thee in the land of them that carried them captives, saying, We have sinned, and have done perversely, we have committed wickedness;

And *so* return unto thee with all their heart, and with all their soul, in the land of their enemies, which led them away captive, and pray unto thee toward their land, which thou gavest unto their fathers, the city which thou hast chosen, and the house which I have built for thy name:

Then hear thou their prayer and their supplication in heaven thy dwelling place, and maintain their cause,

And forgive thy people that have sinned against thee, and all their transgressions wherein they have transgressed against thee...

So there was Jonah sinking to the bottom of the ocean and he got himself back into fellowship with God. Isn't that remarkable.

Jonah 2:5-7
The waters compassed me about, *even* to the soul: the depth closed me round about, the weeds were wrapped about my head.

I went down to the bottoms of the mountains; the earth with her bars *was* about me for ever: yet hast thou brought up my life from corruption, O LORD my God.

When my soul fainted within me I remembered the LORD: and my prayer came in unto thee, into thine holy temple.

Jonah sank to the bottom and the weeds closed around his head. Just as his soul fainted within him, at the very moment of his death, Jonah got himself back into fellowship with God. These were his last dying thoughts as he turned his heart back to God. When Jonah later prayed this prayer, he was back on dry land. When he was out of the fish and back on land, God raised him from the dead, God brought up his life from corruption.

God is always there, ready and willing to forgive and forget. He's great. God never turns his back on anyone. Whenever people come back to him he's right there with the answers. It doesn't matter if you're wrapped in seaweed at the bottom of the ocean or even if you're floating around at the edge of the universe far away in the vastness of space. God can rescue anyone from anywhere.

Deuteronomy 30:4
If any of thine be driven out unto the outmost parts of heaven, from thence will the LORD thy God gather thee, and from thence will he fetch thee:

To make sure we don't miss this truth, God had it written twice to establish it. This truth will never change, it is established.

Nehemiah 1:8,9
Remember, I beseech thee, the word that thou commandedst thy servant Moses, saying, *If* ye transgress, I will scatter you abroad among the nations:

But *if* ye turn unto me, and keep my commandments, and do them; though there were of you cast out unto the uttermost part of the heaven, *yet* will I gather them from thence, and will bring them unto the place that I have chosen to set my name there.

God is not a man that he should lie. If we were literally floating around somewhere in the universe in a distant galaxy hundreds of light years from earth, God would have a way to get us home. He can deliver anyone from anything at any time. Our believing is the key to seeing God's deliverance.

So just how does God rescue a drowning man from the bottom of the ocean? Was this situation beyond what even God could handle? Not really, all it took was a fish.

Jeremiah 32:27
Behold, I *am* the LORD, the God of all flesh: is there any thing too hard for me?

Look, if God always has a way to escape, even from the bottom of an ocean, then God is always going to have that way to escape prepared beforehand. It's there, you can trust that because God is not a man that he should lie. The way to escape will always be there if you believe and look for it.

So down at the bottom of the ocean just before Jonah died, he got himself back into fellowship with God and a big fish swallowed him whole.

He was in the belly of that fish for three days and three nights. Eventually the fish became a little nauseous about its indigestible cargo and vomited Jonah up onto the shore where God then raised him from the dead.

> Jonah 2:10
> And the LORD spake unto the fish, and it vomited out Jonah upon the dry *land*.

Jonah had been dead for three days and three nights. Jesus Christ later used this truth to teach that he would also be dead for three days and three nights.

> Matthew 12:38-40
> Then certain of the scribes and of the Pharisees answered, saying, Master, we would see a sign from thee.
>
> But he [Jesus] answered and said unto them, An evil and adulterous generation seeketh after a sign; and there shall no sign be given to it, but the sign of the prophet Jonas:
>
> For as Jonas was three days and three nights in the whale's belly; so shall the Son of man be three days and three nights in the heart of the earth.

Can you imagine how Jonah must have felt when he regained consciousness on the shore? Can you imagine how he must have felt when he stood up and looked out over the sea and realised what God had done? No wonder he prayed that prayer.

Look, if God can get Jonah from the bottom of the ocean back to dry land, can he sort out your problems for you? Are your problems as bad as Jonah's? Are you running out of air at the bottom of the ocean? It may feel like we're drowning in life at times, but God has the answers and he can sort out any messes we get ourselves into whenever and wherever we decide we're going to do things God's way and ask him for his help.

I don't care how much of a scoundrel you've been in the past, if you're drowning, and you turn your heart back to God he will be there for you. God isn't some mean nasty old devil spirit who is looking for ways to beat you up, not at all, he's wonderful, and he's looking for men and women with the courage and strength to believe in him and trust him so he can deliver them. The deliverance is there, the question is are you willing to do things God's way and put your trust in him? Jonah got himself back into fellowship, was delivered from the weeds at the bottom of the sea and went on to do his job as a prophet.

Jonah 3:1-3
And the word of the LORD came unto Jonah the second time, saying,

Arise, go unto Nineveh, that great city, and preach unto it the preaching that I bid thee.

So Jonah arose, and went unto Nineveh, according to the word of the LORD.

So what is it going to be? Are you going to cry your eyes out and bitch and complain about all your problems, or are you going to get your head into God's word, stand up, claim God's promises and live victoriously? It isn't up to God what kind of life you live, it is entirely up to you.

54. At Thy Word

When Elijah confronted the people of Israel on Mount Carmel, he made a remarkable statement.

1 Kings 18:36
And it came to pass at *the time of* the offering of the *evening* sacrifice, that Elijah the prophet came near, and said, LORD God of Abraham, Isaac, and of Israel, let it be known this day that thou *art* God in Israel, and *that* I *am* thy servant, and *that* I have done all these things at thy word.

Elijah clearly states that everything he did was done because God had told him to do it. Does God talk to men? Yes, he does. So just exactly how does God talk to men? Well, by the end of this class you will know. To begin our journey beyond speaking in tongues into the operation of the other manifestations of holy spirit, we will explore this record of Elijah to get an idea of what we can also accomplish when we walk by the spirit.

We already know that the bible was given by revelation. So the written word is revelation from God. Now let's make something very clear here. If you can't read and carry out the instruction God has already given by revelation in his word, you can forget about going any further spiritually. To progress further into the holy spirit field and learn how to walk with the power of God like Elijah, it is assumed that you are established in the foundational principles taught in the bible and that you are living them on a daily basis. If you want God to talk to you, first learn to hear what he's saying in the bible and carry out that instruction. The revelation manifestations begin where the bible ends. What you can know by your five senses from reading the bible God expects you to know.

For example, you do not need revelation from God to know that a hard core homosexual or lesbian is infested with devil spirits because that revelation is already clearly written in the bible. However, if you don't know if someone is a homo or lesbian, God may have to show you that by revelation if you need to know. God once showed me a picture in my mind of slimy green snakes all twisting and slithering together and that's the picture he shows me if I need to know there's a lesbian around. He might also have to show you by revelation how to deliver someone from that filth if they want deliverance. That information isn't written in the bible and as it will be different in every situation God may have to give you additional information so you can help them. See how this works? Now listen, if you have homo and lesbian friends and you call yourself a christian, you're no better than the fucking heathen and if you expect God to give you revelation when you can't even read his bible and believe that, you're full of religious horseshit. Now, let's go meet this dude Elijah.

> 1 Kings 17:1
> And Elijah the Tishbite, *who was* of the inhabitants of Gilead, said unto Ahab, *As* the LORD God of Israel liveth, before whom I stand, there shall not be dew nor rain these years, but according to my word.

Elijah was a prophet. Ahab was an evil king who ruled Israel. Elijah was dealing with some real issues here and by revelation he believed for no rain.

> James 5:17
> Elias [Elijah] was a man subject to like passions as we are, and he prayed earnestly that it might not rain: and it rained not on the earth [ground] by the space of three years and six months.

Okay, we have to stop and think here. God is light and in him is no darkness at all. Yet Elijah believed for no rain, and we know that he did it because everything in this record was done because God told him to do it. Does this make God evil then? Bear with me here and let's think back to when we were children. Good parents who are responsible adults understand that the more severe the mistakes they make in life, the more severe the consequences will be. They also know their children need to learn that so they will be successful in life.

Teaching a young child that fire burns and that they must stay away from the cooker while mom is preparing dinner is not abusing a child's human rights, it is protecting them from possible serious harm. That is what good loving parents are supposed to do. If a child ignores the warnings and insists on trying to climb up on the cooker while mom is cooking it is time to brandish the wooden spoon, not stand back and watch our children spill boiling water over their heads. Children may not enjoy the sting of a wooden spoon and they may cry, but I'm pretty sure they would prefer that to a pan of boiling water over their heads, wouldn't you agree?

In this record of Elijah and Ahab, God was trying his best to get his people's attention by brandishing a wooden spoon in an attempt to save them from far worse things that were coming. God was doing his best as a responsible and loving God to try to help his people avoid serious consequences for their evil ways. Incidentally, this dry spell did not destroy the country and kill millions of people with famine, and it did get his people's attention and turn their hearts back to him as we shall see. There was tremendous profit to this withholding of the rain. Learning to see spiritual profit is one way to distinguish between the genuine and the counterfeit.

> 1 Kings 17:2-6
> And the word of the LORD came unto him, saying,
>
> Get thee hence, and turn thee eastward, and hide thyself by the brook Cherith, that *is* before Jordan.
>
> And it shall be, *that* thou shalt drink of the brook; and I have commanded the ravens to feed thee there.
>
> So he went and did according unto the word of the LORD: for he went and dwelt by the brook Cherith, that *is* before Jordan.
>
> And the ravens brought him bread and flesh in the morning, and bread and flesh in the evening; and he drank of the brook.

Elijah had water and the birds dropped off breakfast and dinner for him every day. God knows how to look after his people. The question is, are we walking by the spirit and listening? What if Elijah had gone to another brook other than the Cherith? Well, he wouldn't have had food and water.

> 1 Kings 17:7-9
> And it came to pass after a while, that the brook dried up, because there had been no rain in the land.
>
> And the word of the LORD came unto him, saying,
>
> Arise, get thee to Zarephath, which *belongeth* to Zidon, and dwell there: behold, I have commanded a widow woman there to sustain thee.

For a second time, God told Elijah where to go and what to do. This passing of information from God to man, this communication with God is very real. It's available for anyone on earth right now to learn to talk to God and get this kind of spiritual communication going. This type of communication with God is what we know as revelation and three of the manifestations which any born again person can learn to energise are revelation manifestations.

The manifestations available to everyone in this Grace Administration who has the gift of holy spirit are listed in Corinthians.

> 1 Corinthians 12:7-10
> But the manifestation of the Spirit is given to every man to profit withal.
>
> For to one is given by the Spirit the word of wisdom; to another the word of knowledge by the same Spirit;
>
> To another faith [believing] by the same Spirit; to another the gifts of healing by the same Spirit;
>
> To another the working of miracles; to another prophecy; to another discerning of spirits; to another *divers* kinds of tongues; to another the interpretation of tongues:

These nine manifestations can be broken down into three groups. The manifestations of speaking in tongues, interpretation of tongues and prophecy is one group, the revelation manifestations of word of knowledge, word of wisdom and discerning of spirits is another group, and the power manifestations of believing, gifts of healing and working of miracles is the third group. They are all important and they all have different and distinct profit. Elijah was receiving information by way of the revelation manifestations built into the old testament spirit he had upon him.

When reading the bible we must understand it in light of the manifestations of holy spirit. Without an understanding of how manifestations energise, the bible will never make sense. Every truth must fit within the framework of the manifestations of holy spirit or you will never make sense of these records. Everything Elijah did, he did because God told him to do it.

> 1 Kings 18:36b
> ... let it be known this day that thou *art* God in Israel, and *that* I *am* thy servant, and *that* I have done all these things at thy word.

Done all these things at thy word is a reference to revelation. God gave Elijah information, and in this record we are seeing some of the specific information given to him. It is very much available in our day and time to receive revelation from God.

In the world there is tangible, intelligent evil at work. Not only must we recognise that, and where it comes from, more importantly we must recognise that God is our sufficiency, that greater is he that is in us than he that is in the world, and that we are more than conquerors in every situation when we walk by the spirit. That is how we prevail in life. The more abundant life has nothing whatsoever to do with living without challenges, it is about having the strength and wisdom to defeat them. That can only happen if we walk by the spirit and put our trust in God. Anyone can cave in and be beaten by life, that takes no brains, or talent or effort whatsoever. If you want to stand and prevail you will require the strength and commitment that comes only from knowing and believing God's word. It takes believing God and walking by the spirit to prevail in life.

Elijah was told to go to Zarephath and that's where he went. He didn't go to Jerusalem or stay where he was and cry about all his problems. He trusted God and went to Zarephath. He didn't argue with God, he moved when God told him to move. We don't argue with God. He knows best. If we listen, we prevail in life. If we argue, complain, cry and disobey, well, we're going to get beat. It's that simple. That's not because God is punishing us, it's because we don't listen.

1 Kings 17:10-16
So he arose and went to Zarephath. And when he came to the gate of the city, behold, the widow woman *was* there gathering of sticks: and he called to her, and said, Fetch me, I pray thee, a little water in a vessel, that I may drink.

And as she was going to fetch *it*, he called to her, and said, Bring me, I pray thee, a morsel of bread in thine hand.

And she said, *As* the LORD thy God liveth, I have not a cake, but an handful of meal in a barrel, and a little oil in a cruse: and, behold, I *am* gathering two sticks, that I may go in and dress it for me and my son, that we may eat it, and die.

And Elijah said unto her, Fear not; go *and* do as thou hast said: but make me thereof a little cake first, and bring *it* unto me, and after make for thee and for thy son.

For thus saith the LORD God of Israel, The barrel of meal shall not waste, neither shall the cruse of oil fail, until the day *that* the LORD sendeth rain upon the earth.

And she went and did according to the saying of Elijah: and she, and he, and her house, did eat *many* days.

And the barrel of meal wasted not, neither did the cruse of oil fail, according to the word of the LORD, which he spake by Elijah.

God pulled off something rather special for them in that the food never ran out. There was always enough left to make the next meal for the three of them. Amazing. But then the woman's son died. Life can be challenging, even for men of God like Elijah.

> 1 Kings 17:17,18
> And it came to pass after these things, *that* the son of the woman, the mistress of the house, fell sick; and his sickness was so sore, that there was no breath left in him.
>
> And she said unto Elijah, What have I to do with thee, O thou man of God? art thou come unto me to call my sin to remembrance, and to slay my son?

Walking by the spirit and living a more abundant life isn't about escaping life, it's about dealing with it, it's about walking by the spirit and believing God to bring deliverance. Let's see how Elijah handles this.

> 1 Kings 17:19-22
> And he said unto her, Give me thy son. And he took him out of her bosom, and carried him up into a loft, where he abode, and laid him upon his own bed.
>
> And he cried unto the LORD, and said, O LORD my God, hast thou also brought evil upon the widow with whom I sojourn, by slaying her son?
>
> And he stretched himself upon the child three times, and cried unto the LORD, and said, O LORD my God, I pray thee, let this child's soul come into him again.
>
> And the LORD heard the voice of Elijah; and the soul of the child came into him again, and he revived.

As an interesting sideline here, if God had killed this boy nothing Elijah could have done would have ever raised him from death. God didn't kill him, the devil did. God is good always. No matter how challenging life may be, we must always remember that God is light and in him is no darkness at all.

> 1 Kings 17:23,24
> And Elijah took the child, and brought him down out of the chamber into the house, and delivered him unto his mother: and Elijah said, See, thy son liveth.

> And the woman said to Elijah, Now by this I know that thou *art* a man of God, *and* that the word of the LORD in thy mouth *is* truth.
>
> 1 Kings 18:1,2
> And it came to pass *after* many days, that the word of the LORD came to Elijah in the third year, saying, Go, shew thyself unto Ahab; and I will send rain upon the earth.
>
> And Elijah went to shew himself unto Ahab. And *there was* a sore famine in Samaria.

God again spoke to Elijah and gave him information. Notice Elijah didn't move until God gave him revelation and a green light. First God told him to go to the brook Cherith by Jordan, and that's what he did. Then God told him to go to Zarephath and that's what he did. Then God told him to go see Ahab, and that's what he did. There are two important keys to walking by the spirit here which will be coming up time and time again. We never do any more or any less than the revelation God gives us, and we don't move until we get the go sign, the green light, the revelation to move. We never do anymore or any less than the specific instruction given to us. We carry out the revelation given to us to the letter, no more, no less, and we don't move until God says go.

> 1 Kings 18:3,4
> And Ahab called Obadiah, which *was* the governor of *his* house. (Now Obadiah feared the LORD greatly:
>
> For it was *so*, when Jezebel cut off the prophets of the LORD, that Obadiah took an hundred prophets, and hid them by fifty in a cave, and fed them with bread and water.)

Jezebel was Ahab's wife, and she had murdered as many men of God as she could find. Nice woman.

> 1 Kings 18:5-9
> And Ahab said unto Obadiah, Go into the land, unto all fountains of water, and unto all brooks: peradventure we may find grass to save the horses and mules alive, that we lose not all the beasts.

So they divided the land between them to pass throughout it: Ahab went one way by himself, and Obadiah went another way by himself.

And as Obadiah was in the way, behold, Elijah met him: and he knew him, and fell on his face, and said, *Art* thou that my lord Elijah?

And he answered him, I *am:* go, tell thy lord, Behold, Elijah *is here*.

And he said, What have I sinned, that thou wouldest deliver thy servant into the hand of Ahab, to slay me?

The instruction from Elijah gave Obadiah reason for pause. It's okay if you have a problem with something God asks you to do, just take it up with him from an honest heart and he will help you. That's what Obadiah was doing. He wasn't bitching and complaining, he just needed some reassurances because he knew his life was at great risk.

1 Kings 18:10
As the LORD thy God liveth, there is no nation or kingdom, whither my lord hath not sent to seek thee: and when they said, *He is* not *there;* he took an oath of the kingdom and nation, that they found thee not.

Ahab had sent his spies around the world to search out Elijah who had been right under his nose the whole time. As it was such a cultural taboo for a man of God to live with a widow, Ahab wouldn't even have thought of checking widow's houses for him. It wouldn't even have entered his head. See, God knows what he's doing. What if Elijah had argued with God and refused to live with that widow because he was concerned about his social standing? When we walk by the spirit we can't be conditioned by the cultures and traditions of men. God's word supersedes both.

1 Kings 18:11-15
And now thou sayest, Go, tell thy lord, Behold, Elijah *is here*.

And it shall come to pass, *as soon as* I am gone from thee, that the Spirit of the LORD shall carry thee whither I know not;

and *so* when I come and tell Ahab, and he cannot find thee, he shall slay me: but I thy servant fear the LORD from my youth.

Was it not told my lord what I did when Jezebel slew the prophets of the LORD, how I hid an hundred men of the LORD'S prophets by fifty in a cave, and fed them with bread and water?

And now thou sayest, Go, tell thy lord, Behold, Elijah *is here:* and he shall slay me.

And Elijah said, *As* the LORD of hosts liveth, before whom I stand, I will surely shew myself unto him to day.

Elijah dealt with Obadiah's concerns and settled his heart. Obadiah didn't try to hide his concern, he dealt with it. Elijah didn't ridicule him or shout at him either, he listened to him and gave him the reassurances he needed.

1 Kings 18:16,17
So Obadiah went to meet Ahab, and told him: and Ahab went to meet Elijah.

And it came to pass, when Ahab saw Elijah, that Ahab said unto him, *Art* thou he that troubleth Israel?

Well, well, look who Ahab blamed for all the country's troubles. Isn't that just like evil men. They always blame someone else, usually God and his men. Elijah countered his accusations with the truth.

1 Kings 18:18
And he answered, I have not troubled Israel; but thou, and thy father's house, in that ye have forsaken the commandments of the LORD, and thou hast followed Baalim.

The whole country was worshipping the devil in the form of Baalim. Fashion may change, but devil spirits don't. It is the same devil spirits energising through religion today that were around in Elijah's day. It is just the labels that have changed. These days you will find the same devil spirits Elijah had to deal with behind every religion on earth. Elijah ended this confrontation by challenging Baal's religious leaders to a spiritual duel. Remember, Elijah did all this *at thy word*.

> 1 Kings 18:19
> Now therefore send, *and* gather to me all Israel unto mount Carmel, and the prophets of Baal four hundred and fifty, and the prophets of the groves four hundred, which eat at Jezebel's table.

Jezebel was Ahab's wife, so as a family they were supporting the church of Baal. It's no different today. Our politicians and the UN serve the god of this world and steal our money through illegal taxes and give it to Baal. His top religious leaders these days aren't known as prophets, they're known as jesuits.

> 1 Kings 18:20,21
> So Ahab sent unto all the children of Israel, and gathered the prophets together unto mount Carmel.
>
> And Elijah came unto all the people, and said, How long halt ye between two opinions? if the LORD *be* God, follow him: but if Baal, *then* follow him. And the people answered him not a word.

Elijah publicly confronted the entire nation. To put this in perspective, I often find it difficult to confront one person in private. It's uncomfortable and unpleasant. Confrontation is never pleasant. Yet there was Elijah confronting the entire nation to their faces in public. Look at the strength in the man, look at his courage. Where do you think that strength came from? Watching telly? If this is the kind of strength you want in your life, then get your head out of the world's drivel and into God's word.

We can now also clearly see what the withholding of the rain was all about. Elijah had the attention of the entire country. The wooden spoon works. Now that he had their attention, Elijah set the rules for a little contest between God and Baal.

> 1 Kings 18:22-24
> Then said Elijah unto the people, I, *even* I only, remain a prophet of the LORD; but Baal's prophets *are* four hundred and fifty men.

> Let them therefore give us two bullocks; and let them choose one bullock for themselves, and cut it in pieces, and lay *it* on wood, and put no fire *under:* and I will dress the other bullock, and lay *it* on wood, and put no fire *under:*
>
> And call ye on the name of your gods, and I will call on the name of the LORD: and the God that answereth by fire, let him be God. And all the people answered and said, It is well spoken.

The rules were simple. One bullock each, the prophets of Baal called on their god, Elijah called on his and whoever answered with fire won.

> 1 Kings 18:25,26
> And Elijah said unto the prophets of Baal, Choose you one bullock for yourselves, and dress *it* first; for ye *are* many; and call on the name of your gods, but put no fire *under.*
>
> And they took the bullock which was given them, and they dressed *it,* and called on the name of Baal from morning even until noon, saying, O Baal, hear us. But *there was* no voice, nor any that answered. And they leaped upon the altar which was made.

From morning to noon is a few hours. That's a long religious ceremony by anyone's standards. Four hundred and fifty chanting religious hoodies called on Baal all morning and nothing happened. It must have looked impressive initially, in their fancy religious robes with all their incense, chanting, and religious ritual, but guess what? Religion has nothing of any value inside. Elijah then ridiculed them in public and drove them mad.

> 1 Kings 18:27-29
> And it came to pass at noon, that Elijah mocked them, and said, Cry aloud: for he *is* a god; either he is talking, or he is pursuing, or he is in a journey, *or* peradventure he sleepeth, and must be awaked.
>
> And they cried aloud, and cut themselves after their manner with knives and lancets, till the blood gushed out upon them.

> And it came to pass, when midday was past, and they prophesied until the *time* of the offering of the *evening* sacrifice, that *there was* neither voice, nor any to answer, nor any that regarded.

By the time evening came everyone was bored out of their skulls. Who wouldn't be? Religious ceremonies and rituals are mindless, designed to put you to sleep. That's all churches do, put people to sleep with the spirit of slumber with their mindless horseshit. There is no power in their meaningless ceremonies and rituals.

> 1 Kings 18:30-35
> And Elijah said unto all the people, Come near unto me. And all the people came near unto him. And he repaired the altar of the LORD *that was* broken down.
>
> And Elijah took twelve stones, according to the number of the tribes of the sons of Jacob, unto whom the word of the LORD came, saying, Israel shall be thy name:
>
> And with the stones he built an altar in the name of the LORD: and he made a trench about the altar, as great as would contain two measures of seed.
>
> And he put the wood in order, and cut the bullock in pieces, and laid *him* on the wood, and said, Fill four barrels with water, and pour *it* on the burnt sacrifice, and on the wood.
>
> And he said, Do *it* the second time. And they did *it* the second time. And he said, Do *it* the third time. And they did *it* the third time.
>
> And the water ran round about the altar; and he filled the trench also with water.

Now pay attention, we are about to witness one of the most powerful prayers in the entire bible. If you want to learn how to pray effectively, take a look at this one by Elijah.

1 Kings 18:36,37
And it came to pass at *the time of* the offering of the *evening* sacrifice, that Elijah the prophet came near, and said, LORD God of Abraham, Isaac, and of Israel, let it be known this day that thou *art* God in Israel, and *that* I *am* thy servant, and *that* I have done all these things at thy word.

Hear me, O LORD, hear me, that this people may know that thou *art* the LORD God, and *that* thou hast turned their heart back again.

This prayer is just two sentences long. Compare that to the prophets of Baal who had been praying all day. Did their prayers do any good? They had prayed and chanted and shouted and danced and leaped on their alter and cut themselves with knives for hours and hours and hours and nothing happened. Answer to prayer doesn't come by way of religious nonsense, it comes by enjoying a personal relationship with God. If you pray and nothing happens, it isn't God's fault.

James 4:2-8
Ye lust, and have not: ye kill, and desire to have, and cannot obtain: ye fight and war, yet ye have not, because ye ask not.

Ye ask, and receive not, because ye ask amiss, that ye may consume *it* upon your lusts.

Ye adulterers and adulteresses, know ye not that the friendship of the world is enmity with God? whosoever therefore will be a friend of the world is the enemy of God.

Do ye think that the scripture saith in vain, The spirit that dwelleth in us lusteth to envy?

But he giveth more grace. Wherefore he saith, God resisteth the proud, but giveth grace unto the humble.

Submit yourselves therefore to God. Resist the devil, and he will flee from you.

> Draw nigh to God, and he will draw nigh to you. Cleanse *your* hands, *ye* sinners; and purify *your* hearts, *ye* double minded.

Genuine prayer has nothing whatsoever to do with performing rituals. Prayer isn't a ceremony, it isn't a religious thing, it is a relationship with God that comes when you walk by the spirit. The religious prayers of the prophets of Baal had lasted all day and nothing happened. Elijah's prayer was only two sentences long. Now let's compare the results.

> 1 Kings 18:38,39
> Then the fire of the LORD fell, and consumed the burnt sacrifice, and the wood, and the stones, and the dust, and licked up the water that *was* in the trench.
>
> And when all the people saw *it,* they fell on their faces: and they said, The LORD, he *is* the God; the LORD, he *is* the God.

Look at the power in the life of Elijah. A ten second prayer and look at the power. The prophets of Baal prayed all day and nothing happened. The power behind Elijah's prayer came from God. Prayer isn't a ritual, it isn't a ceremony, it is a believing thing. Elijah didn't mindlessly repeat his prayer a thousand times, or chatter out a few hundred hail mary's, he walked by the spirit and enjoyed a personal relationship with God. Prayer without believing is just a ritual. How you tap into this power is by learning to walk by the spirit and doing things *at thy word.* Prayer isn't about begging and hoping, it's about believing.

Which power do you want in your life? Do you want robes and rituals and candles and alters and incense and ceremonies and no power, or do you want to enjoy a relationship with God like Elijah? It's a choice you make. You can go the world's way or you can go God's way, it's entirely up to you.

After God chucked the fire down, he had his people's attention and their hearts were turned back to him. Then God gave Elijah the green light revelation to believe for rain.

1 Kings 18:45
And it came to pass in the mean while, that the heaven was black with clouds and wind, and there was a great rain. And Ahab rode, and went to Jezreel.

So where does power like this come from today? How do we tap into it? How do we switch it on? In the book of Acts there is another record that mentions fire from heaven.

Acts 2:1-4
And when the day of Pentecost was fully come, they were all with one accord in one place.

And suddenly there came a sound from heaven as of a rushing mighty wind, and it filled all the house where they were sitting.

And there appeared unto them cloven tongues like as of fire, and it sat upon each of them.

And they were all filled with the Holy Ghost, and began to speak with other tongues, as the Spirit gave them utterance.

Elijah brought down fire from heaven and here in Acts the fire from heaven signified the giving of the gift of holy spirit. There is quite a parallel to draw here when considering the power of God. How did the apostles manifest this power? It all began with speaking in tongues. Walking by the spirit and energising manifestations is how the fire of God falls from heaven in this Administration of Grace.

55. God is not Jesus Christ

We already know that Jesus Christ is not God. Sure, Jesus Christ is not God, right? You couldn't be fooled into thinking Jesus Christ is God, could you? No, of course not. Well, who exactly is the Lord then? What am I talking about? Brace yourself, for there is some astonishing new light on the way.

First, we need to define our terms. We need to understand exactly and precisely what the word *lord* means in the bible. In the old testament, the word *lord* is translated from the Hebrew word *adon*, while in the new testament it is translated from the Greek word *kurios*.

The Hebrew word *adon* means one who has absolute control. It denotes a master, a ruler, a top boss, one who has supreme authority. The Greek word *kurios* is from *kuros* meaning supremacy. *Kurios* is the Greek equivalent of the Hebrew word *adon* and means one with authority, a master, a ruler. To give us a taste for what the word *lord* means in the bible, let's look at a few examples.

> Genesis 24:14
> And let it come to pass, that the damsel to whom I shall say, Let down thy pitcher, I pray thee, that I may drink; and she shall say, Drink, and I will give thy camels drink also: *let the same be* she *that* thou hast appointed for thy servant Isaac; and thereby shall I know that thou hast shewed kindness unto my master [adon - lord].

Abraham's servant referred to his master as lord because Abraham was his master, his ruler. There may have been many managers under Abraham within his household, but Abraham was the top manager, the chief ruler, the master over his household, the lord. In the following example, Joseph refers to himself as lord of Pharaoh's house.

Genesis 45:8
So now *it was* not you *that* sent me hither, but God: and he hath made me a father to Pharaoh, and lord [adon] of all his house, and a ruler throughout all the land of Egypt.

Joseph was not the lord of Egypt, he was only the lord of Pharaoh's house. In other words, he conducted all Pharaoh's personal and business affairs for him, and everyone in Pharaoh's household would have answered to him.

In both of these instances, men are called lords. Adon and kurios simply mean top boss, supreme ruler, chief master. Abraham was his servant's lord because Abraham was a patriarch, the head over all his household. Pharaoh made Joseph lord over all his house. Lord simply means top boss. If you work for a company, the top man at the head of the company is the lord, the top boss. There may be many managers under him, but the top man is the lord over all the employees of that company. There is even an example in Genesis of a married woman calling her husband her lord.

Genesis 18:12
Therefore Sarah laughed within herself, saying, After I am waxed old shall I have pleasure, my lord [adon] being old also?

From this we can see that the word *lord* does not mean God. It is a very human word as common in the bible as *boss* is in English. Lord simply refers to the most senior executive, manager or administrator in charge of anything. It is a human title given to men. Adon, lord, is also a very common name in the bible. Adonibezek for example simply means lord of bezek.

Judges 1:6,7
But Adonibezek fled; and they pursued after him, and caught him, and cut off his thumbs and his great toes.

And Adonibezek said, Threescore and ten kings, having their thumbs and their great toes cut off, gathered *their meat* under my table: as I have done, so God hath requited me. And they brought him to Jerusalem, and there he died.

Consider this record in Matthew, carefully noting the usage of the word lord, kurios.

> Matthew 18:23-35
> Therefore is the kingdom of heaven likened unto a certain king, which would take account of his servants.
>
> And when he had begun to reckon, one was brought unto him, which owed him ten thousand talents.
>
> But forasmuch as he had not to pay, his lord [kurios] commanded him to be sold, and his wife, and children, and all that he had, and payment to be made.
>
> The servant therefore fell down, and worshipped him, saying, Lord [kurios], have patience with me, and I will pay thee all.
>
> Then the lord [kurios] of that servant was moved with compassion, and loosed him, and forgave him the debt.
>
> But the same servant went out, and found one of his fellowservants, which owed him an hundred pence: and he laid hands on him, and took *him* by the throat, saying, Pay me that thou owest.
>
> And his fellowservant fell down at his feet, and besought him, saying, Have patience with me, and I will pay thee all.
>
> And he would not: but went and cast him into prison, till he should pay the debt.
>
> So when his fellowservants saw what was done, they were very sorry, and came and told unto their lord [kurios] all that was done.
>
> Then his lord [kurios], after that he had called him, said unto him, O thou wicked servant, I forgave thee all that debt, because thou desiredst me:
>
> Shouldest not thou also have had compassion on thy fellowservant, even as I had pity on thee?

> And his lord [kurios] was wroth, and delivered him to the tormentors, till he should pay all that was due unto him.
>
> So likewise shall my heavenly Father do also unto you, if ye from your hearts forgive not every one his brother their trespasses.

It is clear that the word *lord* in the bible does not mean God, it means boss. Calling God lord is simply calling him boss, that's all. Lord is a very human word meaning supreme master or ruler.

As an aside, note that this section of scripture implies that unless we forgive others God will not forgive us. This was true in the old testament, of which the four gospels are a part, but it is not true in this Administration of the Mystery, the Age of Grace. Our forgiveness is no longer dependent on anything we do, it is dependent on what Jesus Christ did for us.

> Ephesians 1:7
> In whom we have redemption through his blood, the forgiveness of sins, according to the riches of his grace;
>
> Colossians 2:13,14
> And you, being dead in your sins and the uncircumcision of your flesh, hath he quickened together with him, having forgiven you all trespasses;
>
> Blotting out the handwriting of ordinances that was against us, which was contrary to us, and took it out of the way, nailing it to his cross;

This is a good example of how important it is to recognise and interpret scripture according to whom it was written while understanding the differences between administrations. Now, although this doesn't apply directly to us today, can we learn anything from it? Sure, my forgiveness from God and my eternal life may not be dependent on my forgiveness of others, but it is a good way to live and enjoy fellowship with God and my brothers and sisters in Christ.

> Ephesians 4:31,32
> Let all bitterness, and wrath, and anger, and clamour, and evil speaking, be put away from you, with all malice:

And be ye kind one to another, tenderhearted, forgiving one another, even as God for Christ's sake hath forgiven you.

In this Administration of the Mystery we don't forgive in order to be forgiven by God, we forgive because God has already forgiven us.

So, we can safely assume that the word lord, adon in Hebrew and kurios in Greek, is not a specific name of God like elohim and Jehovah. Now, this is where things become a little more interesting. The phrase *Lord thy God* in the old testament is so common that we hardly notice it when reading the bible, like these two verses for example.

> Exodus 20:2
> I *am* the LORD [Jehovah] thy God, [elohim] which have brought thee out of the land of Egypt, out of the house of bondage.

> Deuteronomy 2:7
> For the LORD [Jehovah] thy God [elohim] hath blessed thee in all the works of thy hand: he knoweth thy walking through this great wilderness: these forty years the LORD [Jehovah] thy God [elohim] *hath been* with thee; thou hast lacked nothing.

The funny thing is, the word lord is not adon at all, it is the word Jehovah, God. Elohim, translated God would be more accurately understood as creator. Every time you see LORD in all capitals in the old testament of the King James version it is the word Jehovah, it is absolutely not the word adon. So why was Jehovah translated as lord and not God? Ladies and gentlemen, this is a forgery of breathtaking proportions.

Thankfully, the all capitals are still there in the old testament of the KJV so we can readily see this. Where the translators employed LORD it does not mean lord at all, it means God. Jehovah is God in relationship to his creation, while elohim is God as the creator. This is fundamentally important. The phrase *LORD thy God* would be better understood as *God thy creator*. Okay, now check with care this verse from Luke.

Luke 4:8
And Jesus answered and said unto him, Get thee behind me, Satan: for it is written, Thou shalt worship the Lord [kurios] thy God [theos], and him only shalt thou serve.

Here the Greek clearly uses the words *kurios* and *theos* for *Lord thy God*. This is actually a quote from the old testament, so let's compare them.

Deuteronomy 6:13a
Thou shalt fear [worship] the LORD [Jehovah] thy God [elohim], and serve him,

Now isn't this remarkable. The quote in Luke 4:8 contradicts the verse in the old testament from which it came. The old testament scripture states in the Hebrew thousands of years before Luke was written that we are to serve the LORD [Jehovah] our God [elohim]. So the word *kurios* in Luke is a forgery because adon is not there in the original scripture. The original texts read thou shalt worship the Jehovah thy elohim and him only shalt thou serve. Kurioser and kurioser, so how did kurios get into Luke? I don't know. Nor is this an isolated case. Check out these usages of *kurios* as *lord* in regards to angels.

Matthew 1:24
Then Joseph being raised from sleep did as the angel of the Lord [kurios] had bidden him, and took unto him his wife:

Matthew 2:19
But when Herod was dead, behold, an angel of the Lord [kurios] appeareth in a dream to Joseph in Egypt,

Luke 1:11
And there appeared unto him an angel of the Lord [kurios] standing on the right side of the altar of incense.

Acts 5:19
But the angel of the Lord [kurios] by night opened the prison doors, and brought them forth, and said,

These verses all clearly state that these were angels of the kurios, angels of the lord. Now compare the verses with a few from the old testament.

> Genesis 16:7
> And the angel of the LORD [Jehovah] found her by a fountain of water in the wilderness, by the fountain in the way to Shur.

> Genesis 22:11
> And the angel of the LORD [Jehovah] called unto him out of heaven, and said, Abraham, Abraham: and he said, Here *am* I.

> Numbers 22:25
> And when the ass saw the angel of the LORD [Jehovah], she thrust herself unto the wall, and crushed Balaam's foot against the wall: and he smote her again.

> Judges 2:1
> And an angel of the LORD [Jehovah] came up from Gilgal to Bochim, and said, I made you to go up out of Egypt, and have brought you unto the land which I sware unto your fathers; and I said, I will never break my covenant with you.

In the old testament, an angel is always called an angel of Jehovah, an angel of God, never an angel of adon, an angel of the lord. As the old testament scriptures predate those of the new by thousands of years in some cases, we must understand that the word *kurios* in the Greek when applied to angels is a forgery. Angels are angels of God, not angels of the lord. Translating Jehovah as LORD is a forgery. Jehovah means God. Let's consider a few other similar examples.

> John 12:38
> That the saying of Esaias the prophet might be fulfilled, which he spake, Lord [kurios], who hath believed our report? and to whom hath the arm of the Lord [kurios] been revealed?

John 12 quotes Isaiah and uses kurios twice. Let's look at the scripture in Isaiah and compare them.

> Isaiah 53:1
> Who hath believed our report? and to whom is the arm of the LORD [Jehovah] revealed?

Well, will you look at that? No sign of the Hebrew word *adon* at the start of the verse, and the word LORD is Jehovah. It would appear that both occurrences of the words lord in John 12 were simply not there in the original Hebrew texts of the old testament. To further corroborate this discovery, let's look at a prophecy from the book of Joel which is quoted in the book of Acts.

> Acts 2:20,21
> The sun shall be turned into darkness, and the moon into blood, before that great and notable day of the Lord [kurios] come:
>
> And it shall come to pass, *that* whosoever shall call on the name of the Lord [kurios] shall be saved.

Now compare them with the originals from Joel.

> Joel 2:31,32
> The sun shall be turned into darkness, and the moon into blood, before the great and the terrible day of the LORD [Jehovah] come.
>
> And it shall come to pass, *that* whosoever shall call on the name of the LORD [Jehovah] shall be delivered:

Although the Greek word *kurios* is employed in Acts, the original word when the bible was first written was Jehovah not adon. Simply put, the bible has been massively and criminally tampered with to fool us into thinking that God is our lord when he is no such thing. Let's compare a few more scriptures, just to satisfy ourselves that these are not a few isolated or coincidental occurrences.

> Acts 2:25
> For David speaketh concerning him, I foresaw the Lord [kurios] always before my face, for he is on my right hand, that I should not be moved:

Psalm 16:8
I have set the LORD [Jehovah] always before me: because *he is* at my right hand, I shall not be moved.

Acts 3:22
For Moses truly said unto the fathers, A prophet shall the Lord [kurios] your God raise up unto you of your brethren, like unto me; him shall ye hear in all things whatsoever he shall say unto you.

Deuteronomy 18:15
The LORD [Jehovah] thy God [elohim] will raise up unto thee a Prophet from the midst of thee, of thy brethren, like unto me; unto him ye shall hearken;

Acts 4:26
The kings of the earth stood up, and the rulers were gathered together against the Lord [kurios], and against his Christ.

Psalm 2:2
The kings of the earth set themselves, and the rulers take counsel together, against the LORD [Jehovah], and against his anointed,

Acts 7:31
When Moses saw *it*, he wondered at the sight: and as he drew near to behold *it*, the voice of the Lord [kurios] came unto him,

Exodus 3:4
And when the LORD [Jehovah] saw that he turned aside to see, God [elohim] called unto him out of the midst of the bush, and said, Moses, Moses. And he said, Here *am* I

It is abundantly clear that God was not called lord in the old testament, he was most commonly called God, Jehovah, and the creator, elohim. As if that wasn't enough, compare the following verse in Mark with the original scripture in Deuteronomy.

Mark 12:29,30
And Jesus answered him, The first of all the commandments *is*, Hear, O Israel; The Lord [kurios] our God is one Lord [kurios]:

And thou shalt love the Lord [kurios] thy God with all thy heart, and with all thy soul, and with all thy mind, and with all thy strength: this *is* the first commandment.

Deuteronomy 6:4,5
Hear, O Israel: The LORD [Jehovah] our God *is* one LORD [Jehovah]:

And thou shalt love the LORD [Jehovah] thy God [elohim] with all thine heart, and with all thy soul, and with all thy might.

Jesus Christ knew who God was and he would not have made the simple mistake of misquoting scripture. I do not believe Jesus Christ misquoted those scriptures, therefore these usages of kurios in Mark must be more recent forgeries. Is it any wonder the Vatican locks away the oldest manuscripts in its vaults so we can't see what they've been up to?

Before we move on, check this verse in Acts quoting Psalms which unbelievably capitalises *kurios*.

Acts 2:34
For David is not ascended into the heavens: but he saith himself, The LORD [kurios] said unto my Lord [kurios], Sit thou on my right hand,

Psalm 110:1
The LORD [Jehovah] said unto my Lord [adon], Sit thou at my right hand, until I make thine enemies thy footstool.

Amazingly the King James translators knew there was a problem with this verse and capitalised this usage of kurios knowing full well it should have been translated as God, not lord. This is remarkable and really quite shocking. Can you see just how deeply the devil has rooted this forgery into the thinking of God's people?

Now, what do you suppose the translators would have done had they came across *adon* and *Jehovah* in the same verse and both usages referred to God? Well, we can easily find out because there are a number of such verses. Here is one in Ezekiel.

Ezekiel 33:11
Say unto them, As I live, saith the Lord [adonai] GOD [Jehovah], I have no pleasure in the death of the wicked; but that the wicked turn from his way and live: turn ye, turn ye from your evil ways; for why will ye die, O house of Israel?

Isn't that something? Here they translated Jehovah correctly as God because they couldn't possibly get away with translating the verse as the Lord LORD.

I suppose most would say it doesn't matter. Well, the accuracy of the word does matter, it is the opinions of men that don't matter. God is not our lord. He is our God, he is our father, he is our creator, he is the almighty, he is many things, but he is not our lord. Nowhere in Paul's epistles is God specifically called our lord. Yet all over the world people pray to the lord, they bow to the lord, they worship the lord, they do everything to the lord, but God is not our lord. So who is our lord then? Let's go see.

Acts 2:36
Therefore let all the house of Israel know assuredly, that God hath made that same Jesus, whom ye have crucified, both Lord and Christ.

Romans 1:3
Concerning his Son Jesus Christ our Lord, which was made of the seed of David according to the flesh;

Romans 6:23
For the wages of sin *is* death; but the gift of God *is* eternal life through Jesus Christ our Lord.

Romans 10:9
That if thou shalt confess with thy mouth the Lord Jesus, and shalt believe in thine heart that God hath raised him from the dead, thou shalt be saved.

Romans 15:6
That ye may with one mind *and* one mouth glorify God, even the Father of our Lord Jesus Christ.

1 Corinthians 15:57
But thanks *be* to God, which giveth us the victory through our Lord Jesus Christ.

Ephesians 1:2
Grace *be* to you, and peace, from God our Father, and *from* the Lord Jesus Christ.

Ephesians 3:11
According to the eternal purpose which he purposed in Christ Jesus our Lord:

Ephesians 3:14
For this cause I bow my knees unto the Father of our Lord Jesus Christ,

Ephesians 5:20
Giving thanks always for all things unto God and the Father in the name of our Lord Jesus Christ;

Philippians 2:11
And *that* every tongue should confess that Jesus Christ *is* Lord, to the glory of God the Father.

Philippians 3:8
Yea doubtless, and I count all things *but* loss for the excellency of the knowledge of Christ Jesus my Lord: for whom I have suffered the loss of all things, and do count them *but* dung, that I may win Christ,

1 Thessalonians 5:9
For God hath not appointed us to wrath, but to obtain salvation by our Lord Jesus Christ,

2 Peter 3:18
But grow in grace, and *in* the knowledge of our Lord and Saviour Jesus Christ. To him *be* glory both now and for ever. Amen.

2 John 3
Grace be with you, mercy, *and* peace, from God the Father, and from the Lord Jesus Christ, the Son of the Father, in truth and love.

Revelation 19:16
And he hath on *his* vesture and on his thigh a name written, KING OF KINGS, AND LORD OF LORDS.

It is clear in scripture that Jesus Christ is not God. It is now also clear in scripture that God is not Jesus Christ either. If people all over the world have been conditioned to worship the lord, they have been conditioned to worship a man. This is rather important, as we shall soon see.

56. Five Crucified

As we move deeper into the holy spirit field, it will become increasingly more important to check and track the details in God's word. Life is in the details and it is no different with the bible. The best way I know to illustrate this is with the others crucified with Jesus Christ. Tradition teaches that there were two others, but what does the bible say?

There are four gospels, and there are four gospels for a reason. If every detail on every situation was written in all four gospels there would be no need for four, one would do. You cannot get all the available information from studying just one of the gospels, so you have to layer them over each other to see the bigger picture. This method of interpreting the bible is usually referred to as narrative development or scripture build-up. I call it layering as you have to overlay the records to see the full story.

When it comes to understanding the bible we can't afford to guess at what it is saying. There are four gospels, Matthew, Mark, Luke and John, and they are all necessary. They are not identical and they don't all give the same information. Why didn't God put everything about Jesus Christ's ministry into one book, one gospel? He could have if he'd wanted to, right? I mean, he's God and he can do anything. The reason is that each gospel highlights a different aspect of his life and views his ministry from a different perspective, from a different viewpoint.

In Matthew, Jesus Christ as the messiah is emphasised and illustrated, while in Mark his life as a servant is emphasised and illustrated. In Luke his life as a man is emphasised and illustrated, while in John his life as the son of God is emphasised and illustrated. By piecing information together from all four gospels and overlaying it we gain a fuller understanding of what God is saying. That's why they do not all give the same information and that's why four gospels were needed. You have to put the four records together, you have to overlay them, overlap them if you like, to get the full story.

To see how this works, let's look at the others crucified with Jesus Christ. Can the traditions of men be trusted? Let's compare tradition (which teaches there were three crucified) with the word and see what we can discover.

> Luke 23:32-38
> And there were also two other, malefactors [kakourgoi], led with him to be put to death.
>
> And when they were come to the place, which is called Calvary, there they crucified him, and the malefactors, one on the right hand, and the other on the left.
>
> Then said Jesus, Father, forgive them; for they know not what they do. And they parted his raiment, and cast lots.
>
> And the people stood beholding. And the rulers also with them derided *him*, saying, He saved others; let him save himself, if he be Christ, the chosen of God.
>
> And the soldiers also mocked him, coming to him, and offering him vinegar,
>
> And saying, If thou be the king of the Jews [Judeans], save thyself.
>
> And a superscription also was written over him in letters of Greek, and Latin, and Hebrew, THIS IS THE KING OF THE JEWS [Judeans].

We can see that a number of events took place here over a period of time. How long did it take to get to the place of crucifixion? How long did it take to nail the three men to their stakes and raise them into position? How long did it take for the soldiers to gamble for his garments? How long did it take to set up his superscription over his head? We don't know exactly, but we do know it all took some time.

The Greek word for *malefactors* is *kakourgoi* which means *evildoers or criminals*. The word does not tell us what their crime was, all we know is that it warranted the death penalty under Roman law. Let's see what else we can learn from Luke.

> Luke 23:39-43
> And one of the malefactors [kakourgoi] which were hanged railed on him, saying, If thou be Christ, save thyself and us.
>
> But the other [heteros] answering rebuked him, saying, Dost not thou fear God, seeing thou art in the same condemnation?
>
> And we indeed justly; for we receive the due reward of our deeds: but this man hath done nothing amiss.
>
> And he said unto Jesus, Lord, remember me when thou comest into thy kingdom.
>
> And Jesus said unto him, Verily I say unto thee, To day shalt thou be with me in paradise.

The record in Luke is clear when it says that only one of the malefactors attacked Jesus with vicious words, while the other [heteros] stood with him. In return, Jesus promised him that he would be with him in paradise. *Heteros* is defined in Thayer's bible dictionary as the other of only two. Remember this as we will be back to it.

It is also interesting to note in this record how a wrongly placed comma can cause confusion. We already know that when you die you stay dead until Jesus Christ comes back for his church or until the resurrections of the just and the unjust, yet verse 43 seems to imply that Jesus told the malefactor he would be with him later that day in paradise. Well, for a start, Jesus didn't go to paradise that day, he died and was dead for three days and three nights until God raised him from the dead. So what's the answer? It's a wrongly placed comma, a forgery. Move the comma from before the word *today* to after it and read it again.

> Luke 23:43
> And Jesus said unto him, Verily I say unto thee To day, shalt thou be with me in paradise.

See, there are no contradictions in the bible, just errors and forgeries by translators. Always remember, there was no punctuation in the original texts so all punctuation is private interpretation inserted by men and it can't be trusted.

Let's quickly recap on what we've learned from Luke before moving on.

> ~ Jesus was led away to be crucified along with two malefactors (kakourgoi).
>
> ~ When they arrived at the place of crucifixion, Jesus was crucified with a malefactor on each side of him.
>
> ~ They parted his garments and cast lots.
>
> ~ The soldiers mocked him.
>
> ~ A superscription was set up over his head.
>
> ~ Only one of the malefactors attacked him with words while the other defended him.

Keeping all this in mind, let's now look at the information in Matthew.

> Matthew 27:31-38
> And after that they had mocked him, they took the robe off from him, and put his own raiment on him, and led him away to crucify *him*.
>
> And as they came out, they found a man of Cyrene, Simon by name: him they compelled to bear his cross.
>
> And when they were come unto a place called Golgotha, that is to say, a place of a skull,
>
> They gave him vinegar to drink mingled with gall: and when he had tasted *thereof,* he would not drink.
>
> And they crucified him, and parted his garments, casting lots: that it might be fulfilled which was spoken by the prophet, They

parted my garments among them, and upon my vesture did they cast lots.

And sitting down they watched him there;

And set up over his head his accusation written, THIS IS JESUS THE KING OF THE JEWS [Judeans].

Then [THEN] were there two thieves [duo lestai] crucified with him, one on the right hand, and another on the left.

Here is the sequence of events recorded in Matthew.

~ Jesus was led away to be crucified.

~ When they arrived at the place of crucifixion he refused painkilling drugs.

~ He was crucified.

~ They gambled for his garments.

~ They sat down and watched him.

~ They set up his accusation over his head.

~ THEN, after all this time, *then* two thieves were crucified with him.

How does this information compare with Luke?

~ Jesus was led away to be crucified along with two malefactors (kakourgoi).

~ When they arrived at the place of crucifixion, Jesus was crucified with a malefactor on each side of him.

~ They parted his garments and cast lots.

~ The soldiers mocked him.

~ A superscription was set up over his head.

In Luke, Jesus was led away with two malefactors and they were all crucified together before they parted his garments, before the soldiers mocked him and before they set up his accusation over his head. In Matthew, after all these events, two thieves were crucified with him, one on either side. The Greek words for thieves is *Duo Lestai – two robbers*. We know what these two did to warrant being executed, we are told their crime – they were robbers. A thief sneaks in quietly to steal stuff and such a crime wouldn't warrant the death penalty under Roman law, but a robber uses weapons and violence. What other information does Matthew give us?

Matthew 27:39-44
And they that passed by reviled him, wagging their heads,

And saying, Thou that destroyest the temple, and buildest *it* in three days, save thyself. If thou be the Son of God, come down from the cross.

Likewise also the chief priests mocking *him*, with the scribes and elders, said,

He saved others; himself he cannot save. If he be the King of Israel, let him now come down from the cross, and we will believe him.

He trusted in God; let him deliver him now, if he will have him: for he said, I am the Son of God.

The thieves [robbers] also, which were crucified with him, cast the same in his teeth.

Putting the two records together and overlapping them informs us that two malefactors were led away with Jesus and crucified with him, one on either side, a series of events took place and then two robbers were crucified with him, one on either side. Only one of the malefactors cast the same in his teeth while both robbers cast the same in his teeth. Despite traditional teaching that there were only two others crucified with Jesus, clearly the two robbers and the two malefactors cannot be the same men or words have no meaning and the bible cannot be trusted. However, the bible can be trusted and it is the traditions of men that have no meaning.

Mark adds nothing new to either record so we'll now look at John.

> John 19:16-18
> Then delivered he him therefore unto them to be crucified. And they took Jesus, and led *him* away.
>
> And he bearing his cross went forth into a place called *the place* of a skull, which is called in the Hebrew Golgotha:
>
> Where they crucified him, and two other with him, on either side one, and Jesus in the midst.

There are a number of things here and we will start with the word *midst* which is most revealing. Let's look at an example to see what we can learn.

> Matthew 18:1,2
> At the same time came the disciples unto Jesus, saying, Who is the greatest in the kingdom of heaven?
>
> And Jesus called a little child unto him, and set him in the midst of them,

Here we have a bunch of disciples and Jesus sets this child in their midst. Now compare this with the following record.

> Acts 12:6
> And when Herod would have brought him forth, the same night Peter was sleeping between two soldiers, bound with two chains: and the keepers before the door kept the prison.

Here Peter is sleeping between two soldiers. Why doesn't the word say Peter was sleeping in the midst of two soldiers? Well, simply it's because grammatically you can't be in the midst of two. To be in the midst of people you need three or more. If there had only been two others crucified with Jesus, he would have been between them, not in their midst. Grammatically, you cannot break the word. The accuracy and precision of the word is absolutely astonishing. There were two malefactors [kakourgoi] and two robbers [duo lestai] crucified with him and he was crucified in their midst.

That's not all either, there is more. Read this verse below and then compare it with the interlinear translation of the Stephen's Greek text from which the King James was translated.

John 19:18
Where they crucified him, and two other with him, on either side [one], and Jesus in the midst.

See the word *one* which I've bracketed? Notice that in the Greek interlinear Stephens text from which the KJV was translated that this word *one* is also in a parenthesis and that it has no corresponding Greek word above it.

What does this tell us? It tells us that there was no such word in the Greek texts. The translators of the King James bible left the word one in brackets to let us know they added it. In other words, the word *one* is not in the bible, it is another forgery. Now read the verse without the forgery and see what it says.

> John 19:18
> Where they crucified him, and two other with him on either side, and Jesus in the midst.

Now things are making sense and our bible is fitting together beautifully. But as if that's not enough, there's more!

> John 19:31-33
> The Jews therefore, because it was the preparation, that the bodies should not remain upon the cross on the sabbath day, (for that sabbath day was an high day,) besought Pilate that their legs might be broken, and *that* they might be taken away.
>
> Then came the soldiers, and brake the legs of the first, and of the other [allos] which was crucified with him.
>
> But when they came to Jesus, and saw that he was dead already, they brake not his legs:

Let's make one thing perfectly clear here. Read these verses carefully.

> Matthew 27:38
> Then were there two thieves [duo lestai] crucified with him, one on the right hand, and another on the left.

> Mark 15:27
> And with him they crucify two thieves [duo lestai]; the one on his right hand, and the other on his left.

> Luke 23:33
> And when they were come to the place, which is called Calvary, there they crucified him, and the malefactors [kakourgoi], one on the right hand, and the other on the left.

John 19:18
Where they crucified him, and two other with him on either side ~~one~~, and Jesus in the midst.

All four records state that Jesus Christ was crucified with the others on either side of him, on his right hand and on his left. Why does God make this point in all four gospels? God has made it very clear that the men were crucified in a *straight line*, that they were not crucified in a circle or in a haphazard fashion. All five of them were in a straight line. Now read the following verses in John 19 again.

John 19:32,33
Then came the soldiers, and brake the legs of the first, and of the other [another - allos] which was crucified with him.

But when they came to Jesus, and saw that he was dead already, they brake not his legs:

The soldiers started at one end of this straight line of men and broke the legs of the first criminal. Then they came to the second man and broke his legs. Then they came to Jesus, who was third in line on the centre cross and found he was dead already. There is no need to be stupid and religious and try to explain how the soldiers somehow didn't see Jesus and wandered past him with their eyes closed to get to a bloke on the other side of him. The accuracy of the word is simply stunning. You cannot break it.

Did you also notice that the word translated *other* here was not the word *heteros* that we saw earlier? Heteros is defined as the other of only two, however allos is defined as another, or other when more than two are involved. If there were only two others, the word *heteros* and not *allos* would have been used here in John 19:32.

Well, I think that covers it adequately. How many were crucified with Jesus? There were two malefactors and two robbers, making five men in total. This is a brilliant example of how the bible interprets itself when we layer similar records over each other to see the bigger picture.

Knowing that the word can be trusted in minute detail, that it cannot be broken, that it is grammatically flawless is fundamentally important to where we are going in this class. As to the traditions of men? They can't even count to five so stay out of their shithole churches. If you have an opportunity, tell them the truth, and if they don't like it walk away. When it comes to choosing between truth and error, we choose truth. If others choose error, we confront them with the truth when we have an opportunity. If they reject it, we walk away. We must learn to love God more than we love people.

57. The Hope

Before delving into this most important subject, let's define our terms, let's make sure we understand what the word hope means. Hope is translated from the Greek word *elpis* which is derived from the Greek word *elpo*, a primary word meaning to anticipate, usually with pleasure. *Elpis* means confident expectation, so to hope for something is to confidently expect it and wait for it patiently.

To hope for something therefore is not the same as believing for something. Very simply, you can believe for something which is available right now, but you can't believe for something which is not available right now. If something is not available right now but will be available at some point in the future, then we hope for it, we expectantly wait for it patiently. If something from God is available now, we can believe for it, but if something from God is not available now, no matter how much we believe for it we can't have it. If something is not available now but will be in the future, we hope for it, we confidently expect it and look forward to it.

Our hope is the return of the Lord Jesus Christ. We cannot believe for Jesus Christ to come back immediately because it is not available to believe for him to come back immediately. He will return when God is good and ready to send him. It is a future event to which we look forward with patience and great expectation. It is our hope.

> 1 Thessalonians 4:13
> But I would not have you to be ignorant, brethren, concerning them which are asleep, that ye sorrow not, even as others which have no hope.

Those who are not born again have no hope because they have no spirit. They are men of body and soul, without God and without hope. They have no hope because when Jesus Christ returns they will be left behind. We were all in that dire situation at one time.

Ephesians 2:11,12
Wherefore remember, that ye *being* in time past Gentiles in the flesh, who are called Uncircumcision by that which is called the Circumcision in the flesh made by hands;

That at that time ye were without Christ, being aliens from the commonwealth of Israel, and strangers from the covenants of promise, having no hope, and without God in the world:

When man confesses Jesus as Lord and believes in his heart that God raised him from the dead he is born again, he receives the gift of holy spirit and from that moment he has hope.

1 Thessalonians 4:14-18
For if we believe that Jesus died and rose again, even so them also which sleep in Jesus will God bring with him.

For this we say unto you by the word of the Lord, that we which are alive *and* remain unto the coming of the Lord shall not prevent [precede] them which are asleep.

For the Lord himself shall descend from heaven with a shout, with the voice of the archangel, and with the trump of God: and the dead in Christ shall rise first:

Then we which are alive *and* remain shall be caught up together with them in the clouds, to meet the Lord in the air: and so shall we ever be with the Lord.

Wherefore comfort one another with these words.

When Jesus Christ returns, not everyone who is born again will be dead. This is important to understand because it means the return is not technically a resurrection. To have a resurrection of a group of people everyone within that group must be dead. When Jesus Christ returns, not everyone who is born again will be dead so it is not a resurrection. Therefore the return documented in Thessalonians can't possibly be either the resurrection of the just or the unjust, it is the return. The resurrections of the just and the unjust occur at a later date.

At the return, those who were born again when they died will be raised from death, then after that event those of us who are still alive will be changed and we will all meet the Lord Jesus Christ in the air, somewhere up there in the sky, and so shall we ever be with him. A point to note here is that Jesus Christ does not return to earth during this event. We meet him in the air, not on earth. Jesus Christ's return to earth with his saints is a future event that occurs much later.

> 1 Corinthians 15:51
> Behold, I shew you a mystery; We shall not all sleep [die], but we shall all be changed,

At the return we shall not all be dead. Some of us are going to be alive when he comes back. If he came back right now, I would still be alive and so would you. After the dead are raised, then we which are alive and remain will be changed and meet him in the air. We will simply disappear off the face of the earth, leaving just a pile of clothes on the ground. All over the world the born again believers will disappear off the planet. This event will mark the end of the Administration of the Mystery, the Age of Grace and will usher in the next administration, the Revelation Administration.

> 1 Corinthians 15:52
> In a moment, in the twinkling of an eye, at the last trump: for the trumpet shall sound, and the dead shall be raised incorruptible, and we shall be changed.

At the time of this change we will receive a new body, an eternal spiritual body like Jesus Christ's resurrected body, and it will be ours for eternity.

> Philippians 3:20,21
> For our conversation [politeuma - citizenship] is in heaven; from whence also we look for the Saviour, the Lord Jesus Christ:
>
> Who shall change our vile body, that it may be fashioned like unto his glorious body, according to the working [energeia - energising] whereby he is able even to subdue all things unto himself.

1 John 3:1-3
Behold, what manner of love the Father hath bestowed upon us, that we should be called the sons of God: therefore the world knoweth us not, because it knew him not.

Beloved, now are we the sons of God, and it doth not yet appear what we shall be: but we know that, when he shall appear, we shall be like him; for we shall see him as he is.

And every man that hath this hope in him purifieth himself, even as he is pure.

When Jesus Christ was raised from the dead, he received a new spiritual body, and we will be getting one like his at the return. We don't know very much about this new spiritual body, but we can look at the records of Jesus Christ after his resurrection from the dead and get a few ideas. For example, he could suddenly appear in the middle of a room where his disciples were cowering in fear. He could eat. He could change his appearance. He could appear and disappear at will. At the return, those of us who are born again will receive a new spiritual body that will be like Jesus Christ's resurrected spiritual body. Now that's something to look forward to with patience and great expectation. That's our hope.

The return is the event that marks the end of this Administration of the Mystery and the beginnings of the Revelation Administration when the god of this world will have his one world government. It is then that all the horrors recorded in the book of Revelation will come to pass. It will be a time of evil like no other, a time so cruel and vicious that eventually every single human being on earth will die. However, we will not be here so we will not have to endure it, we will not have to go through it. The word tells us that.

Romans 5:9
Much more then, being now justified by his blood, we shall be saved from wrath through him.

1 Thessalonians 1:10
And to wait for his Son from heaven, whom he raised from the dead, *even* Jesus, which delivered us from the wrath to come.

Now isn't it nice to know that we will never have to go through the wrath, the time of the Revelation Administration. That age begins at the return of Jesus Christ for his church, so none of us who are born again will ever have to go through that. Oh, and don't listen to the jehovah's witnesses and their horseshit that we're going through the tribulation right now, tell them to fuck off. Don't let those people near you or your family. If you are a jehovah's witness and have a heart to walk by the spirit, get out of that shithole religion.

We have been delivered from the wrath to come. It's part of our hope. When Jesus Christ returns for us, we get a new body, we meet the Lord in the air and so shall we ever be with him. Our hope is part of the Mystery.

> Colossians 1:27
> To whom God would make known what *is* the riches of the glory of this mystery among the Gentiles; which is Christ in you, the hope of glory:

The hope of glory is part of the Mystery. It is something we look forward to with great expectation, patience and desire. One day Jesus Christ will come back for us and we will meet him face to face and be with him forever. It could be today. It isn't something we can believe to bring to pass, so we wait patiently for it, looking forward with expectation and excitement to what is going to be one amazing time.

> Romans 8:24,25
> For we are saved by hope: but hope that is seen is not hope: for what a man seeth, why doth he yet hope for?
>
> But if we hope for that we see not, *then* do we with patience wait for *it*.

> Titus 1:1,2
> Paul, a servant of God, and an apostle of Jesus Christ, according to the faith of God's elect, and the acknowledging of the truth which is after godliness;
>
> In hope of eternal life, which God, that cannot lie, promised before the world began;

> 1 Peter 1:3,4
> Blessed *be* the God and Father of our Lord Jesus Christ, which according to his abundant mercy hath begotten us again unto a lively hope by the resurrection of Jesus Christ from the dead,
>
> To an inheritance incorruptible, and undefiled, and that fadeth not away, reserved in heaven for you,

So that's us taken care of, but what about everyone else? What about Moses, David, Job, Elijah, Elisha and all the old testament believers who were not born again? What happens to them? What about all the dickheads and god rejecters and religious idiots, what about them? Are they going to get away with all the evil they're doing? Oh no, not on your life. No one is getting away with anything. If we're born again, we're forgiven, but those who are not will have to give an account for their lives at the resurrections of the just and the unjust.

In the book of Acts, Paul succinctly included the resurrections of the just and the unjust as part of man's hope.

> Acts 24:14,15
> But this I confess unto thee, that after the way which they call heresy, so worship I the God of my fathers, believing all things which are written in the law and in the prophets:
>
> And have hope toward God, which they themselves also allow, that there shall be a resurrection of the dead, both of the just and unjust.

The resurrections of the just and the unjust have nothing whatsoever to do with the return of Jesus Christ for his church when we meet him in the air, it has everything to do with everyone else, including the jesuits. They're not going to particularly enjoy that time either. This is also part of our hope too, because we will see justice done. We will look into their eyes when God confronts them and deals with them. We will be there and we will see justice done.

So we can clearly see that there are two separate and distinct phases to Christ's coming, his return for his church when we meet him in the air, and his return to earth at a later time. The next administration, the Revelation or Appearing Administration begins when this Age of Grace terminates. At that time the events of the book of Revelation will begin to unfold.

Regarding the transformation we enjoy at the return, the word has much to say.

> 1 Corinthians 15:35
> But some *man* will say, How are the dead raised up? and with what body do they come?

Sure, some will question the word. Eternal life and getting a new immortal body when Jesus Christ returns is going to stir up the minds of men. That's why Paul is taking the time here to address this.

> 1 Corinthians 15:36
> *Thou* fool, that which thou sowest is not quickened [made alive], except it die:

When you plant a seed in the ground, you do not get that same identical seed back at the top of the plant do you? No, it dies and new life sprouts from it. That's easy enough for anyone to understand. The seeds that you plant are not the fruits that you reap.

> 1 Corinthians 15:37
> And that which thou sowest, thou sowest not that body that shall be, but bare grain, it may chance of wheat, or of some other *grain*:

If you plant an apple seed, do you expect that seed to come out of the ground? No, you expect an apple tree to come out of the ground. The seed dies, but from it grows an apple tree. You don't plant a seed expecting to get that seed back, you plant a seed expecting to get new life sprouting from it. See Paul's logic here?

> 1 Corinthians 15:38,39
> But God giveth it a body as it hath pleased him, and to every seed his own body.

All flesh *is* not the same flesh: but *there is* one *kind of* flesh of men, another flesh of beasts, another of fishes, *and* another of birds.

Each seed in the world is different. Each seed produces a different type of life. Apple trees grow from apple seeds. Salmon grow from salmon eggs fertilised with salmon milt, salmon seed. Birds and animals all grow from seeds. You grew from a seed, your father's seed. Every seed produces a different form, a different flesh. The sperm that became you died when it fertilised the egg in your mother and that was necessary so you could be born into the life you now have.

1 Corinthians 15:40-43
There are also celestial bodies, and bodies terrestrial: but the glory of the celestial *is* one, and the *glory* of the terrestrial *is* another.

There is one glory of the sun, and another glory of the moon, and another glory of the stars: for *one* star differeth from *another* star in glory.

So also *is* the resurrection of the dead. It is sown in corruption; it is raised in incorruption:

It is sown in dishonour; it is raised in glory: it is sown in weakness; it is raised in power:

The seed of Christ in us will produce another body, a spiritual body, an incorruptible body. The bodies we are currently lumbered with will die one day, and if Jesus Christ returns before then they will be changed.

1 Corinthians 15:43
It is sown a natural body; it is raised a spiritual body. There is a natural body, and there is a spiritual body.

When Jesus Christ comes back to gather us and we meet him in the air we will be in our new spiritual bodies. We will not be taking these crappy earthly things with us. These natural bodies will be raised a spiritual body.

1 Corinthians 15:45-49
And so it is written, The first man Adam was made a living soul; the last Adam *was made* a quickening spirit.

Howbeit that *was* not first which is spiritual, but that which is natural; and afterward that which is spiritual.

The first man *is* of the earth, earthy: the second man *is* the Lord from heaven.

As *is* the earthy, such *are* they also that are earthy: and as *is* the heavenly, such *are* they also that are heavenly.

And as we have borne the image of the earthy, we shall also bear the image of the heavenly.

The last Adam is Jesus Christ. He was raised from death with a spiritual body, and when he comes back we will also be raised with a new spiritual body like his.

1 John 3:1-3
Behold, what manner of love the Father hath bestowed upon us, that we should be called the sons of God: therefore the world knoweth us not, because it knew him not.

Beloved, now are we the sons of God, and it doth not yet appear what we shall be: but we know that, when he shall appear, we shall be like him; for we shall see him as he is.

And every man that hath this hope in him purifieth himself, even as he is pure.

It doesn't yet appear what we shall be. It is impossible for us to comprehend what we are going to become. The sperm that impregnated the egg that became me had no comprehension of what it was giving birth to, nor would it have been possible to teach it. A sperm is simply not capable of understanding the life it gives birth to. Now listen, the change from the physical body to the spiritual body will be greater than the change from the sperm you once were to the person you are now.

1 Corinthians 15:50-54
Now this I say, brethren, that flesh and blood cannot inherit the kingdom of God; neither doth corruption inherit incorruption.

Behold, I shew you a mystery; We shall not all sleep [die], but we shall all be changed,

In a moment, in the twinkling of an eye, at the last trump: for the trumpet shall sound, and the dead shall be raised incorruptible, and we shall be changed.

For this corruptible must put on incorruption, and this mortal *must* put on immortality.

So when this corruptible shall have put on incorruption, and this mortal shall have put on immortality, then shall be brought to pass the saying that is written, Death is swallowed up in victory.

One day Jesus Christ is coming back to get us and we will leave earth to meet him in the air. Those who have died will be raised from death in their new spiritual body, and then those of us who are still alive will be changed and put on immortality.

1 Corinthians 15:55-58
O death, where *is* thy sting? O grave, where *is* thy victory?

The sting of death *is* sin; and the strength of sin *is* the law.

But thanks *be* to God, which giveth us the victory through our Lord Jesus Christ.

Therefore, my beloved brethren, be ye stedfast, unmoveable, always abounding in the work of the Lord, forasmuch as ye know that your labour is not in vain in the Lord.

Those of us who have the gift of holy spirit, that Christ in us which is our eternal life, those of us who are of the family of God, born again of his seed will be gathered when Jesus Christ returns in the clouds. Those who have died will remain dead until that time. At the return, which could be at any moment, those who have died with holy spirit will be raised from death, and then those of us who are still alive will be changed and put on immortality. We will all get a new spiritual body similar to the body Jesus Christ was raised with. When we leave to meet our Lord in the air, the Age of Grace, the Administration of the Mystery will end and the Revelation Administration will begin.

58. The Revelation Administration

Let me first make it clear that I am not an authority on the book of Revelation. I have not studied it much and hardly ever even read it, but I do know a thing or two about the world. Hopefully this short study will be sufficient to make us extremely thankful that we've been rescued from the wrath to come.

After the return of Jesus Christ to gather his church, as recorded in Thessalonians, things on earth will take a rather distinct turn for the worse. When we leave earth, the machinery that is already in place for one world governance will crank into operation. During the revelation administration, one world governance will be a reality.

> 2 Thessalonians 2:1-4
> Now we beseech you, brethren, by the coming of our Lord Jesus Christ, and *by* our gathering together unto him,
>
> That ye be not soon shaken in mind, or be troubled, neither by spirit, nor by word, nor by letter as from us, as that the day of Christ is at hand.
>
> Let no man deceive you by any means: for *that day shall not come,* except there come a falling away first [a departure, referring to the first return of Jesus Christ], and that man of sin be revealed, the son of perdition [referring to the antichrist];
>
> Who opposeth and exalteth himself above all that is called God, or that is worshipped; so that he as God sitteth in the temple of God, shewing himself that he is God.

The pope is the only man on earth who can possibly fit this description, and now that the jesuit general is the pope, it doesn't take too much intelligence to piece this together. Catholics worship the pope as the vicar of Christ with the keys to heaven and are already brainwashed into believing that Jesus Christ is God, so it is only a small step to promote the pope to God status. The world will worship a man as god.

> 2 Thessalonians 2:5-11
> Remember ye not, that, when I was yet with you, I told you these things?
>
> And now ye know what withholdeth that he might be revealed in his time.
>
> For the mystery of iniquity doth already work: only he who now letteth *will let*, until he be taken out of the way.
>
> And then [in the Revelation Administration] shall that Wicked be revealed, whom the Lord shall consume with the spirit of his mouth, and shall destroy with the brightness of his coming:
>
> *Even him,* whose coming is after the working of Satan with all power and signs and lying wonders,
>
> And with all deceivableness of unrighteousness in them that perish; because they received not the love of the truth, that they might be saved.
>
> And for this cause God shall send them strong delusion, that they should believe a lie:

At the return, the believers will simply disappear off the face of the earth. Whether we are driving cars, shopping, flying aircraft, operating machinery, welding, weeding the garden or whatever, we will all simply disappear. How many of us will be driving cars on motorways when Jesus Christ returns? I tell you, the next administration is going to start with a bang. The world will be so stunned, so shocked and terrified by so many people simply disappearing off the planet that the god of this world will have no difficulty mobilising his military forces through the United Nations to take it.

The word records a little of that time in many books and you can piece together much of it by scripture build-up and layering the records over each other. The record in Matthew of Jesus Christ teaching his disciples about future events was during the time he was here on earth, before the Grace Administration, before the Mystery had been revealed. As the hidden period of the Grace Administration had not yet been revealed and the Mystery was still a secret, these truths cannot possibly refer to anything during this Grace Administration. Rather, they foretell of events that are still future, events which will come to pass in the Revelation or Appearing Administration.

People are just as curious today about what's going to happen in the future as they were back in Jesus Christ's day, so let's now take a brief stroll through Big Brother Google's earth and let's see if one world governance really will bring us world peace.

> Matthew 24:1,2
> And Jesus went out, and departed from the temple: and his disciples came to *him* for to shew him the buildings of the temple.
>
> And Jesus said unto them, See ye not all these things? verily I say unto you, There shall not be left here one stone upon another, that shall not be thrown down.

Like Jesus' disciples, I often hear people today express astonishment and wonder at buildings constructed by men. They stand in awe of the Eiffel Tower for example, or at the Christ the Redeemer statue in Rio De Janeiro, or gasp in wonder when they step inside the Sistine Chapel. There is more wonder in a single dead leaf falling from a tree than in all the buildings man has ever constructed piled together.

Walking *by* the Spirit

You think the Eiffel Tower is amazing? Did you know that it is in fact a representation of a pyramid with an eye at the top? You think that statue in Rio De Janeiro depicts Jesus Christ? Jesus Christ was nothing like that faggot prick up on that hill. That monstrosity is a statue of the antichrist who will be revealed during the Revelation Administration. As for Michelangelo, he was a homo and David was his boy lover. The Sistine Chapel is nothing more than a homosexual brothel for paedophile priests. Of all these works of men there shall not be left one stone or one iron girder upon another that shall not be broken down.

> Matthew 24:3,4
> And as he sat upon the mount of Olives, the disciples came unto him privately, saying, Tell us, when shall these things be? and what *shall be* the sign of thy coming, and of the end of the world?
>
> And Jesus answered and said unto them, Take heed that no man deceive you.

Now remember, the Mystery had not yet been revealed, so this coming Jesus Christ talks about is absolutely not referring to his return to gather his church, he is talking about his return to earth in the future Revelation Administration when he comes to sort things out. All these prophesies will still be in the future after Christ's return for his church when we meet him in the air.

> Matthew 24:5-9
> For many shall come in my name, saying, I am Christ; and shall deceive many.
>
> And ye shall hear of wars and rumours of wars: see that ye be not troubled: for all *these things* must come to pass, but the end is not yet.
>
> For nation shall rise against nation, and kingdom against kingdom: and there shall be famines, and pestilences, and earthquakes, in divers [many] places.
>
> All these *are* the beginning of sorrows.
>
> Then shall they deliver you up to be afflicted, and shall kill you: and ye shall be hated of all nations for my name's sake.

The believers in the next administration are going to have to endure some stuff. This is where Google and Facebook and all the other spy agencies will come to the fore. Anyone who is found to read the bible or speak about it will be hunted down, imprisoned, tortured and executed. The believers will be hated of all nations most likely because of their stance against the homos who will be running the world. Why do you think the god of this world is installing CCTV everywhere? To keep you safe? Why do you think GPS is being installed in every camera and phone on the planet? So you can know where you are? You already know where you are, it's so *they* can know where you are. Why do you think the skies are being filled with armed drones? So they can take pictures? Why do you think the world is installing computers into every car? To prevent crime? It's expensive and cuts into their profits, and I can assure you it's not for your benefit. The technology to access car computers to make brakes fail, take control of the steering wheel, or simply pilot a driverless car right into you is already in place.

Wherever God's people will be, they will be hunted down. Social media like Google, Facebook, and Twitter will be monitored not to find terrorists, but to locate God's people who will be hated of all nations. You think Batman is just a vigilante comic book character saving the world from nasty criminals? Not at all, Batman is conditioning the world for a new breed of special forces operative trained exclusively to track down God's people. The believers in the next administration are going to be hated with a passion that is simply incomprehensible. It will be such a time of mistrust, fear, murder and terror that the believers will even turn on each other in desperation.

> Matthew 24:10-12
> And then shall many be offended, and shall betray one another, and shall hate one another.
>
> And many false prophets shall rise, and shall deceive many.
>
> And because iniquity shall abound, the love of many shall wax cold.

If you think the world is evil now, just wait until the next administration. When Jesus Christ returns to gather those of us who are born again and we all leave earth to meet him in the air, evil will explode all over the earth like vomit. So much for one world governance bringing us world peace.

> Matthew 24:13
> But he that shall endure unto the end, the same shall be saved.

In this Administration of Grace we are saved by believing, not by our own works but by the works of Jesus Christ. However, the next administration will be a return to law when the believers will once again be judged according to their works. The new birth will no longer be available so they will have to work for their salvation, and they will have to endure to death without breaking so as not to lose it.

> Matthew 24:21
> For then shall be great tribulation, such as was not since the beginning of the world to this time, no, nor ever shall be.

And why will the world be such a cruel place? Simply because it will be run by homosexual sorcerer priests doing the bidding of their god. Their hatred for the believers will be so passionate they will hunt them down relentlessly. You think Google glass is just a fun gimmick? The technology for a Big Brother spy world is already in place, only now we don't call it Big Brother, we call it Google earth.

Joel gives us a few more insights into those days. Again, Joel is in the old testament so this has nothing whatsoever to do with the Mystery and the Age of Grace in which we now live. This pouring out of spirit upon all flesh and all the other prophecies are references to truths that will come to pass during the Revelation Administration.

> Joel 2:28-31
> And it shall come to pass afterward, *that* I will pour out my spirit upon all flesh; and your sons and your daughters shall prophesy, your old men shall dream dreams, your young men shall see visions:
>
> And also upon the servants and upon the handmaids in those days will I pour out my spirit.
>
> And I will shew wonders in the heavens and in the earth, blood, and fire, and pillars of smoke.
>
> The sun shall be turned into darkness, and the moon into blood, before the great and the terrible day of the LORD come.

The sun being turned into darkness is a prophecy that one day the entire earth will be covered with a permanent cloud layer that the sun will not be able to penetrate. The entire planet will be dark and will not know sunshine. The world has been tampering with the weather systems for quite some time. Did you know all aircraft are fitted with spray systems that spray chemicals into the jet stream at high altitudes? Look out the windows next time you're flying and you will see the spray nozzles behind the wings.

The moon being turned into blood is a figure of speech. One day there will be war on the moon. So much blood will be shed that the word says the moon will be turned into blood. The figure of speech emphasises the amount of blood that will be shed. Who will be fighting and for what I have no idea, but there will be war on the moon.

Ezekiel establishes some of this for us, and adds a few more details.

> Ezekiel 32:6,7
> I will also water with thy blood the land wherein thou swimmest, *even* to the mountains; and the rivers shall be full of thee.
>
> And when I shall put thee out, I will cover the heaven, and make the stars thereof dark; I will cover the sun with a cloud, and the moon shall not give her light.

The Revelation Administration is going to be a time of unimaginable cruelty, wars on a scale never dreamed of, diseases, plagues and disasters such as have never been seen before and will never be seen again. The funny thing is, man is bringing this on himself. Every man who gives his life to one world governance, communism, world peace and an end to poverty is bringing this on themselves and everyone else on earth. And how ironic that they refer to themselves as philanthropists. Let's go to the book of Revelation and piece together a few more details.

> Revelation 2:10,11
> Fear none of those things which thou shalt suffer: behold, the devil shall cast *some* of you into prison, that ye may be tried; and ye shall have tribulation ten days: be thou faithful unto death, and I will give thee a crown of life.
>
> He that hath an ear, let him hear what the Spirit saith unto the churches; He that overcometh shall not be hurt of the second death.

In this Age of Grace, the mental pressures we endure are nothing compared to what the believers in the next administration will have to endure. My advice to you believers in the next administration who read this class is to be careful what you say in public, on the internet, and over the phone. They will even be watching you through your televisions, as fibre optics and digitisation gave them the technology to look into your living rooms and hear what you are saying. Walk by the spirit for your very lives will depend on it.

Revelation 8:7
The first angel sounded, and there followed hail and fire mingled with blood, and they were cast upon the earth: and the third part of trees was burnt up, and all green grass was burnt up.

A third of the world's trees will be destroyed by fire? Think about that. In the next administration hail and fire is going to destroy one third of all the world's trees. Have you any idea how many people are going to be killed and how much property is going to be destroyed during that firestorm?

Revelation 8:8,9
And the second angel sounded, and as it were a great mountain burning with fire was cast into the sea: and the third part of the sea became blood;

And the third part of the creatures which were in the sea, and had life, died; and the third part of the ships were destroyed.

This could be a huge meteor striking the earth, or a massive volcano I don't know for sure, but its impact is going to destroy one third of all life in the oceans and one third of all the world's shipping. Think about that. One third of all life in the sea and on it, from fish to crabs to dolphins to whales to men is going to die. There will be so much blood in the ocean that the bible says figuratively that the sea will become blood. The pyroclastic cloud that spews from this enormous event will be so massive that it will cover one third of the oceans and destroy everything.

Revelation 9:1-6,10
And the fifth angel sounded, and I saw a star fall from heaven unto the earth: and to him was given the key of the bottomless pit.

And he opened the bottomless pit; and there arose a smoke out of the pit, as the smoke of a great furnace; and the sun and the air were darkened by reason of the smoke of the pit.

And there came out of the smoke locusts upon the earth: and unto them was given power, as the scorpions of the earth have power.

> And it was commanded them that they should not hurt the grass of the earth, neither any green thing, neither any tree; but only those men which have not the seal of God in their foreheads.
>
> And to them it was given that they should not kill them, but that they should be tormented five months: and their torment *was* as the torment of a scorpion, when he striketh a man.
>
> And in those days shall men seek death, and shall not find it; and shall desire to die, and death shall flee from them.
>
> And they had tails like unto scorpions, and there were stings in their tails: and their power *was* to hurt men five months.

Armour plated locusts that feed on human flesh and sting like a scorpion? And the poison will be in your body for five months? The next time you curse midges or mosquitoes, just be thankful these little bastards aren't around yet. I'm not sure what a bottomless pit is, but the mention of a star means it could be a reference to a black hole. Remember, all these things will only happen because men will be so evil that God will be unable to protect them.

> Revelation 9:20,21
> And the rest of the men which were not killed by these plagues yet repented not of the works of their hands, that they should not worship devils, and idols of gold, and silver, and brass, and stone, and of wood: which neither can see, nor hear, nor walk:
>
> Neither repented they of their murders, nor of their sorceries, nor of their fornication, nor of their thefts.

And so it goes on. At some point during this next Administration Jesus Christ will return to earth with his saints, with those of us who are born again and who will have a new spiritual body, and we will begin the cleanup operation. Armageddon will be the final battle on earth when every remaining human being on the planet will be killed. At some point during that administration there will be the resurrection of the just and some time later the resurrection of the unjust. During that time, everything will be put right, the garbage will be disposed of in the lake of fire, and then the seventh and final Administration, the final Paradise Administration will begin.

The believers from the old testament and from the next administration will not receive new spiritual bodies like we do because they will never have had Christ in them. They will live forever in the final paradise here on a new earth. We, the believers in this administration who are born again will receive new spiritual bodies and will reign in the heavens with Jesus Christ as children of the living God.

Revelation 22:1-5
And he shewed me a pure river of water of life, clear as crystal, proceeding out of the throne of God and of the Lamb.

In the midst of the street of it, and on either side of the river, *was there* the tree of life, which bare twelve *manner of* fruits, *and* yielded her fruit every month: and the leaves of the tree *were* for the healing of the nations.

And there shall be no more curse: but the throne of God and of the Lamb shall be in it; and his servants shall serve him:

And they shall see his face; and his name *shall be* in their foreheads.

And there shall be no night there; and they need no candle, neither light of the sun; for the Lord God giveth them light: and they shall reign for ever and ever.

It is no wonder the god of this world would not have murdered Jesus Christ had he known the Mystery, had he known that we would have Christ in us and be children of the living God.

59. Money

The next administration is going to be terrible. As the love of money is the root of all evil, it follows then that the love of money will be the root cause of it. Money is a subject of such importance that we are now going to explore it again in even more depth. Let's kick off in the book of Revelation.

> Revelation 13:11-18
> And I beheld another beast coming up out of the earth; and he had two horns like a lamb, and he spake as a dragon.
>
> And he exerciseth all the power of the first beast before him, and causeth the earth and them which dwell therein to worship the first beast, whose deadly wound was healed.
>
> And he doeth great wonders, so that he maketh fire come down from heaven on the earth in the sight of men,
>
> And deceiveth them that dwell on the earth by *the means of* those miracles which he had power to do in the sight of the beast; saying to them that dwell on the earth, that they should make an image to the beast, which had the wound by a sword, and did live.
>
> And he had power to give life unto the image of the beast, that the image of the beast should both speak, and cause that as many as would not worship the image of the beast should be killed.
>
> And he causeth all, both small and great, rich and poor, free and bond, to receive a mark in their right hand, or in their foreheads:
>
> And that no man might buy or sell, save he that had the mark, or the name of the beast, or the number of his name.

Here is wisdom. Let him that hath understanding count the number of the beast: for it is the number of a man; and his number *is* Six hundred threescore *and* six.

Here we can clearly see the unifying single minded purpose behind one world governance. It is not to bring peace on earth, it is not to bring an end to poverty, it is to establish a world religion that worships the beast. In the next administration it will be international law that every person on earth will worship this beast or be executed. It logically follows then that an international criminal court will need to be in place so as to be able to enforce this law in every country on earth. I've said it before, but any god who demands worship at the point of a gun really doesn't have a lot going for him.

Actually, this is nothing new. Back in Daniel's day, Nebuchadnezzar instituted a one world religion and demanded all men worship his golden penis or be thrown in a burning fiery furnace.

> Daniel 3:1-6
> Nebuchadnezzar the king made an image of gold, whose height *was* threescore cubits, *and* the breadth thereof six cubits: he set it up in the plain of Dura, in the province of Babylon.
>
> Then Nebuchadnezzar the king sent to gather together the princes, the governors, and the captains, the judges, the treasurers, the counsellors, the sheriffs, and all the rulers of the provinces, to come to the dedication of the image which Nebuchadnezzar the king had set up.
>
> Then the princes, the governors, and captains, the judges, the treasurers, the counsellors, the sheriffs, and all the rulers of the provinces, were gathered together unto the dedication of the image that Nebuchadnezzar the king had set up; and they stood before the image that Nebuchadnezzar had set up.
>
> Then an herald cried aloud, To you it is commanded, O people, nations, and languages,

That at what time ye hear the sound of the cornet, flute, harp, sackbut, psaltery, dulcimer, and all kinds of musick, ye fall down and worship the golden image that Nebuchadnezzar the king hath set up:

And whoso falleth not down and worshippeth shall the same hour be cast into the midst of a burning fiery furnace.

The god of this world, Lucifer, lusts for, desires and demands worship. He wants men to bow to him. He was the angel of light, full of wisdom and beauty, perfect in all his ways, but pride lifted his heart, and his lust for worship was the motivation behind his rebellion, as we see in Isaiah.

Isaiah 14:12-14
How art thou fallen from heaven, O Lucifer, son of the morning! *How* art thou cut down to the ground, which didst weaken the nations!

For thou hast said in thine heart, I will ascend into heaven, I will exalt my throne above the stars of God: I will sit also upon the mount of the congregation, in the sides of the north:

I will ascend above the heights of the clouds; I will be like the most High.

The god of this world is not the true God, he is not all powerful, he is not all knowing, he is not everywhere present. He is a god consumed by hatred, jealousy, arrogance and pride. He is the author of death and all sickness and disease. He only became the god of this world because he stole from man what wasn't his and took the world from him. He is a liar, a thief and a murderer. He has also been defeated and he will be destroyed in the lake of fire. Back to Revelation.

It is important to note that this one world government with its one world religion worshipping the beast will only be possible because they will control the world's money. That's why the world is conditioning you through television and Hollywood with such propaganda as Star Trek and a world where no one needs any money and there are no wars or poverty because it's controlled by a single world government called the

Federation. If you believe the world's horseshit, you really should stop watching television for a while. Let's look again at three verses we've just read.

> Revelation 13:16-18
> And he causeth all, both small and great, rich and poor, free and bond, to receive a mark in their right hand, or in their foreheads:
>
> And that no man might buy or sell, save he that had the mark, or the name of the beast, or the number of his name.
>
> Here is wisdom. Let him that hath understanding count the number of the beast: for it is the number of a man; and his number *is* Six hundred threescore *and* six.

This might come as a shock to some, but this technology is already in place and we are already comfortable using it. What am I talking about? Here's a clue.

This is a barcode, a device which every product in the world will one day carry and without which no one on earth will be able to sell anything. It is an interesting feature of barcodes in that they all carry a defining mark. At the beginning, in the middle and at the end of every barcode you will see two parallel lines with no corresponding number. These two parallel lines are the number 6. Every barcode is integrated within the number 666. Next time you pick up a product, check the barcode and you will see this in every one of them.

The reference in Revelation to marks in the right hand or in the forehead are prophecies regarding credit card chips being implanted under the human skin in every person on earth. They will do this under the pretext of preventing credit card fraud. When you check out at the supermarket, your hand or your forehead will be scanned for your credit card details. This technology is already in widespread use around the world, ostensibly to keep track of old people and pets. These are in fact trials of the new technology so they can perfect it. Without these implants you will not be able to buy anything.

Of course, these chips will also mean every single person on earth can be tracked by computer so they will always know where you are. To those of you in the next administration, always remember, God is your sufficiency not the world. God is not constrained to meet your needs exclusively by the world's methods. Money is in fact an illusion.

In this banknote you can read the words *The Royal Bank of Scotland promise to pay the bearer on demand Twenty Pounds at their head office in Edinburgh*. You will read similar words on all British bank notes. What exactly does this mean? Well, this may come as another shock but a £20 note is not worth £20, it is in fact worthless. It is simply a piece of paper. The history of bank notes is quite illuminating.

In the 16th century, bankers gave receipts for gold coins deposited with them. These receipts were made out in the name of the depositor and

Walking *by* the Spirit

the bank promised to pay him his gold on demand. In 1694 the Bank of England was established to raise money for the war with France and immediately issued notes in return for gold deposits. These notes were a means of exchange and carried a promise to pay the bearer the sum of the note in gold on demand. This meant that the note could be redeemed at the bank for gold by anyone presenting it for payment.

In 1759, gold shortages caused by the Seven Years War forced the bank of England to issue a £10 note for the first time. A £5 note soon followed which remained the lowest denomination until 1797, when a series of runs on the bank drained its gold bullion reserves forcing them to issue £1 notes and stop paying out gold on demand. This was known as the Restriction Period and lasted until 1821 when gold sovereigns took the place of these £1 bank notes.

These early bank notes were hand written and it wasn't until 1853 that the first fully printed notes appeared. No longer did cashiers have to fill out notes with the name of the payee and sign each one individually. The practice of writing the name of the Chief Cashier as the payee on notes was halted in favour of the anonymous *I promise to pay the bearer on demand* which has remained unchanged to this day.

The First World War saw the link with gold broken once again as the government felt it prudent to preserve its gold stock, and so the bank refused to pay out gold for its notes. So much for governmental and bank promises, which have always been treacherously unreliable.

The gold standard was partially restored in 1925 and the Bank was once again obliged to exchange its notes for gold, but only in multiples of 400 ounces or more. Britain finally left the gold standard in 1931 and bank notes became what we have today, worthless shit backed by securities instead of gold. In other words, all the gold in Britain has been stolen from the people by the banks and replaced with pieces of paper.

I know this is difficult to comprehend, but you don't actually have anything of any value regardless of how much you have in the bank. Everything you had has been stolen from you. The banks have stolen all your gold and silver and issued you with worthless paper notes instead. To understand how this happened, we must go back in time to when there were no banks.

Before banks and governments were around, countries were ruled by kings supported by an aristocracy, and communities were basically self supporting and self sufficient consisting mostly of a huge middle class, where most folks had their own business. The strength of Great Britain was its middle class family businesses. For example, cows would have been in demand as tractors to pull ploughs, while horses would have been in demand as cars so folks could travel. Sheep would have been valuable for wool so folks could make warm clothes. Animal hides would have been in demand for leather to make shoes and jackets. Farmers would have grown fruit and vegetables and sold them in markets. Fishermen would have owned their own boats and sold their fish in markets. People would have milked cows to make cheese and butter, which would have been sold in the markets. Bakers would have produced wonderful home made bread and other foods which would have been sold in markets.

As the communities grew, people would have been too busy being farmers and fishermen to have had the time to make leather shoes for their families, so opportunities for cobblers would have opened and more thriving middle class businesses would have been established. Folks would have needed furniture so every community would have had a carpenter's shop. An ironmonger would have been in constant demand for shoeing horses and providing metal tools and equipment. Inns and stables would have been needed to look after travellers and their horses. Middle class tailors would have flourished. Transport companies would have been in demand, with horses and carts transporting goods. Cart makers would have placed orders with local ironmongers and carpenters for parts. In addition, all these middle class businesses would have had to employ villagers who would have been paid bonuses and shared in the profits they helped to earn.

President Calvin Coolidge (1872-1933) had this to say regarding business and commerce:

I want the people of America to be able to work less for the government and more for themselves. I want them to have the rewards of their own industry.

This is the chief meaning of freedom. Until we can re-establish a condition under which the earnings of the people can be kept by the people, we are bound to suffer a very severe and distinct curtailment of our liberty.

A strong middle class can only exist if we are using gold and silver as currency. Gold and silver would have circulated around the towns and villages, and as it went up in value people would have been more prosperous. The fisherman who was paid in gold would have bought his clothes, shoes, food, furniture, horse and other needs with that gold. Gold and silver would have been paid as wages to employees, who in turn would have used it to buy their own clothes, shoes, food and other needs. Travellers would have brought gold with them, adding to the prosperous middle class way of life. As gold continued to rise in value, people's savings would increase in value with it and there would have been business opportunities for luxury items and crafts. This is how God set life up to be lived. This is how you enjoy a strong, prosperous middle class.

Now, the devil looks at this and scratches his head. How is he going to steal all that gold and destroy the middle class so he can make everyone poor, sick and miserable? Easy, start a bank so everyone will put their gold into it for safe keeping. After all, no one wants to risk losing all their gold by having it stolen, hey? So it was the fear of losing their gold that made people run to the banks to let them look after it for them. Fear is believing and what you fear will become reality. A few hundred years later, all the gold is gone and so are the middle classes. There are no more cobblers, no more bakers, no more fruit and vegetable shops, no more tailors, no more middle class businesses because the banks gave all your gold to the fucking freemasons who used it to start up huge manufacturing plants during the industrial revolution which destroyed your middle class and turned you all into slaves working for them and being paid shit in return. And don't blame God, if we did things his way we wouldn't have these problems.

Deuteronomy 28:15,33
But it shall come to pass, if thou wilt not hearken unto the voice of the LORD thy God, to observe to do all his commandments and his statutes which I command thee this day; that all these curses shall come upon thee, and overtake thee:

> The fruit of thy land, and all thy labours, shall a nation which thou knowest not eat up; and thou shalt be only oppressed and crushed alway:

Gold and silver doesn't really go down in value for extended periods of time, it goes up, so where gold and silver is in circulation inflation would not be possible. Inflation is just a criminal's way of reducing the value of your savings which is no more ethical than breaking into your home and stealing your possessions. Greedy men never have enough. Once they have all your gold, they will get you into debt, creaming vast profits from your misery. When you have nothing left they will take your country and then the world. Even the world itself will not be enough for them. Trust me, get yourselves out of debt any way you can. Cut up your credit cards if you have to and tell them to fuck off. Get out of debt while there is still time. If you have savings, why not buy some gold?

It isn't as if God hasn't warned us about the world and greedy men. We would do well to keep Psalm 73 in mind.

> Psalm 73:1-3
> Truly God is good to Israel, *even* to such as are of a clean heart.
>
> But as for me, my feet were almost gone; my steps had well nigh slipped.
>
> For I was envious at the foolish, *when* I saw the prosperity of the wicked.

Truly, God is good to those of us who live by his word and live righteously, wherever we are, in whatever time we live. However, the temptation to love money is strong and seduces many, as happened to this believer back in the old testament. He looked at the world's rich and famous and was envious. He wanted lots of money too and it was nearly his downfall. The psalm then gives us a little inside information regarding greedy men who love money.

> Psalm 73:4-9
> For *there are* no bands in their death: but their strength *is* firm.

> They *are* not in trouble *as other* men; neither are they plagued like *other* men.
>
> Therefore pride compasseth them about as a chain; violence covereth them *as* a garment.
>
> Their eyes stand out with fatness: they have more than heart could wish.
>
> They are corrupt, and speak wickedly *concerning* oppression: they speak loftily.
>
> They set their mouth against the heavens, and their tongue walketh through the earth [their words are published all over the world].

Quite a revelation hey? Greedy men have wealth beyond imagination, and violence clothes them. The vatican, the mafia, the IRA and all the other criminal organisations are rich and they are clothed in violence. See the comparison? There is nothing new under the sun. Criminal organisations have existed in one form or another since prehistoric times. The are all simply secret societies run by greedy men who love money and who use violence to get it. That's why secret societies are secret. Criminals always work in the shadows behind your back. Once the freemasons infiltrate your governments, your police forces, your military, your judicial systems and every other part of social life, which they will if you cower before their bullying ways, they will eventually steal everything from you. Greed cannot be controlled. Greed is not good, it consumes everything. Greed never has enough. Don't underestimate greed because it can corrupt even God's people.

> Psalm 73:10
> Therefore his people [God's people] return hither: and waters of a full *cup* are wrung out to them.

God's people run off after greedy men because they are greedy themselves, and in return a few drips from full cups are wrung out for them. These words penned by jesuits establishes this truth God warned us of thousands of years ago.

What is it to the proletariat labourer, bowed double over his heavy toil, crushed by his lot in life, if talkers get the right to babble, if journalists get the right to scribble any nonsense side by side with good stuff, once the proletariat has no other profit out of the constitution save only those pitiful crumbs which we fling them from our table in return for their voting in favour of what we dictate, in favour of the men we place in power, the servants of our agentur.

God's people today work for crumbs for gangster freemason taskmasters who cream off all the profits from their labours and pay them shit in return. If we come back to God and do things his way again, we can have a strong, prosperous middle class lifestyle. It's not up to God what kind of life we live, it's up to us, it's a choice we make.

> Deuteronomy 28:1-4
> And it shall come to pass, if thou shalt hearken diligently unto the voice of the LORD thy God, to observe and to do all his commandments which I command thee this day, that the LORD thy God will set thee on high above all nations of the earth:
>
> And all these blessings shall come on thee, and overtake thee, if thou shalt hearken unto the voice of the LORD thy God.
>
> Blessed *shalt* thou *be* in the city, and blessed *shalt* thou *be* in the field.
>
> Blessed *shall be* the fruit of thy body, and the fruit of thy ground, and the fruit of thy cattle, the increase of thy kine, and the flocks of thy sheep.

If you think giving your gold to the banks to look after for you is wise, you're insane. If you think world bankers are nice men looking after your best interests, you had better wake up. If you think a single world government run by jesuits and bankers will bring us peace on earth, you had better get your head out of their televisions while you still have one.

This, of course, is just the tip of the iceberg that sank the Titanic, as we shall soon see.

60. Walking tongues

In the previous session we came across an intriguing verse of scripture that is really quite shocking when you first perceive its depth. Regarding evil men who love money, the word has this to say:

Psalm 73:9
They set [shathath] their mouth against the heavens, and their tongue walketh through the earth.

Evil men set their mouth against the heavens, meaning they set their word against God's word. Walking tongues is a figurative reference to their words being published all over the world. Understanding the depth of this is important to understanding how all our gold was stolen from us, so we must look deeper into the verse to uncover what God is saying. Digging into the word is how you uncover the treasures buried within it.

Proverbs 2:1-5
My son, if thou wilt receive my words, and hide my commandments with thee;

So that thou incline thine ear unto wisdom, *and* apply thine heart to understanding;

Yea, if thou criest after knowledge, *and* liftest up thy voice for understanding;

If thou seekest her as silver, and searchest for her as *for* hid treasures;

Then shalt thou understand the fear of the LORD, and find the knowledge of God.

In Psalm 33:9, the word *set* is the Hebrew word *shathath*, and it is also used in Psalm 49 where it is used in the context of death feeding on all men.

Psalm 49:14
Like sheep they are laid [shathath] in the grave; death shall feed on them; and the upright shall have dominion over them in the morning; and their beauty shall consume in the grave from their dwelling.

Evil men set their mouths, they lay their words in death against the heavens, against the true God. Their words are death, they are set against the heavens, and they are spoken all over the world. In other words, all that comes out of your television and all that comes out of Hollywood is death, words that speak against God so death can feed on you. If you want life, then change the words you feed on. For example, the words I teach in this class are not words of death, they are words of life.

John 6:63
It is the spirit that quickeneth; the flesh profiteth nothing: the words that I speak unto you, *they* are spirit, and *they* are life.

To begin to give us a real depth of understanding of Psalm 73, let's consider a 21st Century real life example. I love movies. I especially love good acting and special effects movies. A few weeks back, while deliberating over the direction this session of the class should take, I was watching a Robert De Niro movie called Cape Fear. I love De Niro because he produces mesmerising performances. He's right up there with Al Pacino. I think these two guys are among the best actors in the world. I have many other favourites, of course, but anyway, there I was enjoying Cape Fear. As the story developed, De Niro's character, Mark Cady, was clearly shown to be a dangerous man with violent rape and murder on his mind. No problems so far. Then Cady was revealed to have religious tattoos, to be educated in the bible, and enjoyed quoting scriptures. As the plot developed, Cady was shown to have conversations with God, and at the end of the movie he spoke in tongues as he disappeared under the water and drowned.

Well, although I was a little shocked I wasn't all that surprised. In the 70s and 80s, God's people moved the word in much the same way that Cady stalked his victims in Cape Fear. They would phone out of the blue just to say hello, visit folk's homes when they weren't expected, they got involved in people's everyday lives, they knew their bibles, they spoke to God and they spoke in tongues. Drawing a parallel between believers moving the word and Mark Cady as a murderous stalker was a masterstroke of worldly propaganda.

This 1991 remake of Cape Fear was a huge box office success making $182,291,969 on a $35 million budget, so it was watched by practically the entire western world where the word of God was being taught. I wonder how many people still subconsciously picture Cady in their minds when I tell them I speak in tongues? I certainly don't enjoy being portrayed as a murderous evil rapist stalker when all I want to do is help people. This is one way the god of this world blinds the minds of men to keep them from the light we teach.

> 2 Corinthians 4:3,4
> But if our gospel be hid, it is hid to them that are lost:
>
> In whom the god of this world hath blinded the minds of them which believe not, lest the light of the glorious gospel of Christ, who is the image of God, should shine unto them.

After sitting in silence for a few minutes after the movie, I suddenly knew the direction this session of the class would take and that I had some homework to do. By the way, this is an example of how God has been working within me to will and to do of his good pleasure the whole time I've been researching and writing this class. It's called walking by the spirit.

The first thing I did was order a copy of the original film which was made in 1962 and starred Robert Mitchum as Cady. In that version there was no bible, no quoting scriptures, no doing the will of God, no religious tattoos, and no speaking in tongues. In fact, there were no religious undertones to the Cady character whatsoever. Cady's religious background in the 1991 film was entirely fabricated out of nothing. It simply was not there in the original film. In other words, someone had taken the original movie and deliberately manipulated the plot to portray God's people who walk by the spirit and speak in tongues as evil rapist murdering cunts to be avoided at all costs. This is how the tongues of evil men walk through the earth.

So where did the religious side to Cady and his speaking in tongues come from? To find out, we need to dig a little more. It was certainly not there in the original film, but what about the book from which it came?

The Executioners by John D Macdonald is a dark psychological thriller published in 1957. The overall tone of the novel is not nearly as brutal as the 1991 film adaptation. Interestingly, Cape Fear itself was not featured anywhere in the book. In the novel, Cady was a soldier court-martialed for the brutal rape of a 14 year old girl. The censors stepped in, banned the use of the word *rape* and stated that depicting Cady as a soldier reflected adversely on US military personnel. The film's director, J Lee Thompson then changed the plot to keep the censors happy. Intriguing that back then the censors didn't allow Thompson to portray the US military in a bad light, but in 1991 they said nothing against portraying God's people in a much worse light. You need look no further than freemasonry and their commitment to promoting only other masons to prominent positions of authority and influence to understand how this happens. That aside, we still have no clues as to where the religious undertones to Cady in the 1991 version of the movie came from. We need to dig a little more.

The 1991 film was originally developed by Steven Spielberg, who decided it was too violent for his tastes and traded it with Martin Scorsese for Schindler's List. Scorsese then took the plot and added elements from a previous Robert Mitchum movie, The Night of the Hunter, which was a 1955 film adaptation of the 1953 novel of the same name by Davis Grubb. In Night of the Hunter, Mitchum plays the Reverend Harry Powell, a serial murderer with the words LOVE and HATE tattooed onto his knuckles.

Grubb took his inspiration for his novel from the real life story of Harry Powers, who lived in Quiet Dell, West Virginia. Powers lured widows to his home by way of lonely heart adverts in newspaper columns. He murdered several of them for their money and was subsequently hanged in 1932 at the state prison in Moundsville. Harry Powers was a serial killer but he was not a religious man, he didn't quote scriptures, he didn't have religious tattoos, and he didn't speak in tongues.

Walking *by* the Spirit

You can delve as deeply as you like into all the books and movies leading up to the 1991 version of Cape Fear and you will not find any basis for Cady being a religious man who spoke in tongues and read the bible. So where did it come from? To find our answers, we have to look at the life of Martin Scorsese himself.

Martin Scorsese was born in New York in 1942, of Sicilian parents. He spent his life in Roman Catholic schools, and in 1956 entered the priesthood and joined a seminary in New York run by the jesuits. The official line is that he is a failed priest who left the seminary and went on to become a successful movie director. Now this is where you have to look through the trees to see the forest. You see, there are literally thousands of *failed* priests in prominent positions around the world where they control everything we do and think. They were commissioned into these positions, and the official line of them being failed priests is simply a smoke screen to cover the tracks of the jesuits.

The plot for the 1991 film version of Cape Fear portraying Cady as a religious nut who spoke in tongues and talked to God came directly from the jesuits and its sole purpose was to hinder the move of God's word. Have you any idea how many jesuits are involved in the movie industry? Try doing a few background checks and you might be shocked by what you discover.

These days movies are filled with masonic symbols, pyramids with eyes, and actors who seem to think it's cool to flash masonic symbols during their performances. They are hardly underground any more. Scorsese himself once stated, *My whole life has been movies and religion. That's it. Nothing else.* In other words, movies are but a medium for him to walk the jesuit's evil tongues through the world.

Regarding Scorsese's upcoming movie, Silence, which tells the story of a jesuit commissioned to take the Roman Catholic doctrine to the Buddhists of Japan, he has reportedly sought guidance from James Martin, a prominent jesuit who writes for America Magazine. See, the jesuits are everywhere, dictating to the masses what they think.

Jesuits are behind just about everything we read and watch in the world, from newspapers, to magazines, to books, to television programmes, to movies, to university and school text books, to children's education, to political policies and everything in between, and it's all pro Roman Catholic, twisting history and perverting facts to promote their pagan religion. It isn't the Arabs behind the world's media, it isn't the Muslims, it isn't the Jews, it isn't the Americans, it is the jesuits. They are the wormtongues of Tolkien's Lord of the Rings.

To take walking tongues a slippery step further, consider that when I first began researching the Illuminati in the early 1990s just six results were returned by Google. Try a Google search now and you will be drowned in a murky ocean of search results. Just 20 years ago they were entirely hidden from view, but when I began to expose them they flooded the internet with a tidal wave of misinformation and deception to make it almost impossible to find the truth I teach about them.

The Order of the Illuminati was founded by Weishaupt, a jesuit priest. The current pope, Pope Francis, is the Jesuit General. It doesn't take much to realise who controls the Illuminati and all the other secret societies, such as Opus Dei. They do not want you to know this so their evil tongues walk through the earth blinding the minds of men.

As a further example, consider Robin Hood. He was not some hero saving the world from the nasty government, he was a Roman Catholic robbing murdering bastard led by a Roman Catholic priest we now know as Friar Tuck. Robin Hood's sole purpose was the overthrow of the government and the installation of a Roman Catholic king, Richard the Lyingheart who was off murdering Muslims on the orders of the pope. Legends and myths about him abound and stories vary, but one stark fact is embroidered through them all, that Robin Hood was a terrorist sponsored by the vatican to overthrow the government. Tuck was more than likely a Knights Templar or similar, the forerunners of the jesuits.

The Vatican did not persecute the Templars, they simply changed their name when they went out of public favour for losing the holy lands during the pope's Crusades. Hollywood portrays Robin Hood as some kind of folk hero, so no surprises there. Such propaganda merely serves to recruit gullible young men to the terrorist cause. Dark sorcerers always operate in the shadows behind the scenes in secret societies, but their words walk through the earth and are always in your face. These servants of the dark Lord have been around since the days of Nimrod back in the book of Genesis.

You can track the tongues of evil men through the media quite easily once you see through their disguises and smoke screens. I teach the truth about the world and how it is using its resources to find ways to make us sick so evil men can make money from us while they destroy us. For its part, Hollywood puts together movies like Contagion, which portrays me as an evil greedy internet scaremonger with nothing better to do than bad mouth the wonderful World Health Organisation which really has our best interests at heart. Yeah right. My standard for truth is the bible. The World Health Organisation's standard for truth is one world governance at any cost including the genocide of any country or people that will not bow to the gods of Rome.

Now, let's get one thing very clear here. Although the tongues of evil men walk through the earth against the true God, his will is not to see them die but to see them change and come back to him. He takes no pleasure from the death of evil men.

> Ezekiel 33:11
> Say unto them, *As* I live, saith the Lord GOD, I have no pleasure in the death of the wicked; but that the wicked turn from his way and live: turn ye, turn ye from your evil ways; for why will ye die, O house of Israel?

So, if God has no pleasure in the death of evil men and would rather they change their ways, how is that going to happen? Well, let me give you a clue.

> Romans 10:12-15
> For there is no difference between the Jew [Judean] and the Greek [Gentile]: for the same Lord over all is rich unto all that call upon him.
>
> For whosoever shall call upon the name of the Lord shall be saved [made whole].

> How then shall they call on him in whom they have not believed? and how shall they believe in him of whom they have not heard? and how shall they hear without a preacher?
>
> And how shall they preach, except they be sent? as it is written, How beautiful are the feet of them that preach the gospel of peace, and bring glad tidings of good things!

That's right, we have to open our mouths, and always remember that being a witness of the Lord Jesus Christ is to manifest the power of God, not chatter out scriptures mindlessly and annoy people everywhere we go. We have to show these dudes that there is a far superior spiritual power available, and that there is a better God available than the one they serve. That's our job as ambassadors for Christ. It was Paul who wrote those words we just read in Romans. He was an evil religious man who tortured and murdered God's people and he changed, so don't rule it out for the rest of them.

Can I live with the world portraying me as Mark Cady? Well, the word tells us many times that the world hates us and to expect nothing less from them. Even Jesus Christ was accused of being an evil possessed bastard operating devil spirits by the religious leaders of his day, so not much has changed in two thousand years.

> Matthew 9 33:34
> And when the devil was cast out, the dumb spake: and the multitudes marvelled, saying, It was never so seen in Israel.
>
> But the Pharisees said, He casteth out devils through the prince of the devils.

The same devil spirits that energised in the religious leaders of Jesus Christ's day are the very same devil spirits energising through the jesuits in our day. Don't allow the world to intimidate you with their walking tongues, just get out there and demonstrate God's power and show people how to speak in tongues and walk by the spirit.

> 1 John 3:13
> Marvel not, my brethren, if the world hate you.

John 16:33
These things I have spoken unto you, that in me ye might have peace. In the world ye shall have tribulation: but be of good cheer; I have overcome the world.

1 John 4:4
Ye are of God, little children, and have overcome them: because greater is he that is in you, than he that is in the world.

Understanding how the tongues of evil men walk through the earth and how they control the media is significantly important to understanding the machinery behind the creation of the Federal Reserve System, the means by which America's gold was stolen and replaced with worthless paper notes. That's where we're going next.

61. A Titanic Crime

Having all your gold deposited in banks was just the first step to stealing it entirely. To grasp how it was done, we have to understand political events in the past, we have to understand gold, and we have to understand greed. If you do not understand that there are greedy men in the world who will do *anything* for gold, you can never understand events such as the sinking of the Titanic. God has been warning us about greedy men for thousands of years.

> Proverbs 1:10-16
> My son, if sinners entice thee, consent thou not.
>
> If they say, Come with us, let us lay wait for blood, let us lurk privily for the innocent without cause:
>
> Let us swallow them up alive as the grave; and whole, as those that go down into the pit:
>
> We shall find all precious substance, we shall fill our houses with spoil:
>
> Cast in thy lot among us; let us all have one purse:
>
> My son, walk not thou in the way with them; refrain thy foot from their path:
>
> For their feet run to evil, and make haste to shed blood.

Such men exist. They breathe, they are real, and they spend their days scheming to murder people so they can fill their houses with spoil. Religious men tend to be the greediest.

Now, before you can steal a country's gold, you first have to have it all stashed somewhere so you can get your hands on it. To be able to steal a people's gold, you first have to take it away from them. To do that, you need a central bank.

Before 1913, America did not have a central bank like Great Britain so the creation of one was of great importance. Without a central bank, America's gold could not be stolen. Little is generally known today about the political face of America at that time, but we can be thankful to L Frank Baum who encapsulated what was actually going on during the 1890s in his brilliant allegorical children's story, The Wonderful Wizard of Oz. The story was later made into a movie in 1932, when it was updated to capture the background to the stock market crash of 1929 and the great depression that followed.

Just as you can read between the lines in newspapers on any given day and discover clues as to what's really going on behind the scenes, so too we can read between the lines of this classic children's tale regarding the robbery of America's gold. First of all, let's look at the original book and take a peek into the political and economic events of the 1890s, which was plagued by a depression almost as severe as the great depression of the 1930s.

In every presidential election between 1872 and 1896, a third national party organised by the farmers ran on a platform of financial reform. This party was a people's party, not one of the conventional parties that ran for office, and their primary political aim was banking and financial reform. The characters in the book The Wonderful Wizard of Oz represent the main players involved in the political and financial events of that day.

The Scarecrow represented the farmers, who lived like serfs on their own land because they were in debt to the bankers. They had mortgaged their farms and equipment in order to survive and had sometimes even taken out loans for the seeds they needed for planting.

The Tin Woodsman represented industrial workers in the cities, who were unemployed and rusty from a lack of currency to lubricate the wheels of industry.

The Cowardly Lion represented William Jennings Bryan, a powerful speaker whose roar was as mighty as a lion's, but who had been branded a coward by his opponents for refusing to back illegal wars in other countries.

Dorothy represented the average American, who although strong and basically good, was up against powers stronger than any one person. She represented Americans who needed to learn to work together in order to take advantage of their strength in numbers.

The Wizard of Oz himself represented the chief sorcerer behind the stealing of America's gold represented by the yellow brick road which you had to follow to find out where the gold went. All gold is measured in ounces, abbreviated as oz. Even tons of gold are recorded in ozs. The wizard of oz, the wizard of gold was a master of illusion who terrified Americans into blind obedience because they perceived him as frighteningly intelligent and mercilessly powerful through his control of the media and the legal system.

Almira Gulch was shown to own half of Kansas. Miss Gulch accused Dorothy's dog, Toto, of having bitten her and she came to the farm with an order from the Sheriff demanding Toto be taken into custody. When Dorothy refused to surrender Toto, Miss Gulch lashed out: 'If you don't hand over that dog I'll bring a damned suit that will take your whole farm!'

Miss Gulch represented the American legal system, which was the primary lever used to transfer all the wealth in America from the people to the government and then to the banks. The word Toto in legal language means *everything*. It was the legal system that was used by the wizard of oz to steal America's gold.

Around the time of the stock market crash of 1929 and the depression that followed, The Wizard of Oz was made into a movie, and to this day it serves as an allegory for the new state of affairs in America that came into being. The setting of the movie was Kansas in heartland America, which was filmed in black and white to illustrate the harshness of the times. The cyclone that uprooted the farm represented the financial storm of the stock market crash and the subsequent theft of America's gold by the Federal Reserve Bank, which they then shipped off to England and Germany. When bankruptcy was declared in 1933, Americans were required to turn in all gold coin, gold bullion, and gold certificates by May 1st, the birth date of Communism.

At this juncture we must now delve into the creation of the Federal Reserve System to find out exactly what it is and how it came into being so we can piece this all together.

In 1910, seven men met on Jekyll Island just off the coast of Georgia to establish an American central bank. They called it the Federal Reserve Bank. The men were Nelson Aldrich, Abram Piatt Andrew, Frank Vanderlip, Henry Davison, Charles Norton, Benjamin Strong, and Paul Warburg. Nelson Aldrich and Frank Vanderlip represented the Rockefeller empire. Henry Davison, Charles Norton, and Benjamin Strong represented J.P. Morgan. Paul Warburg represented the Rothschild banking dynasty. Piatt Andrew was the Assistant Secretary of the Treasury.

The Rothschilds are the banking agents for the vatican. They hold the keys to the wealth of the Roman Catholic Church. JP Morgan's London operations were saved from financial ruin in 1857 by the Bank of England over which the Rothschilds held great influence. From that time, JP Morgan appears to have served as a Rothschild financial agent, despite their charade to appear completely American.

These three financial families, the Rothschilds, the Morgans, and the Rockefellers are the backbone of all vatican financial matters and as such are completely controlled by the Jesuit Order who oversee every transaction and financial dealing they are involved with.

At the time, a number of men, including three of the richest and most powerful men in America, had made it publicly clear they would oppose the creation of the Federal Reserve System. These three powerful men were Benjamin Guggenheim, Isador Strauss, the head of Macy's Department Stores, and John Jacob Astor, probably the wealthiest man in the world. Their total wealth by today's standards would be in the region of almost eleven billion dollars.

The jesuits knew their Federal Reserve central American bank would never be born as long as these men were alive, so they devised a scheme to have them all murdered.

The building of the Titanic began in 1909 at a shipyard in Belfast, Northern Ireland. It was one of a fleet of ships owned by the White Star Line. The White Star Line was owned by JP Morgan. The Titanic was heralded worldwide in all the media as a modern wonder of the world, an unsinkable ship, the pinnacle of human engineering brilliance. Its maiden voyage was to be such an occasion that only the most elite and rich from around the world were invited to sail on her. Every man opposed to the creation of the Federal Reserve Bank, including Benjamin Guggenheim, Isador Strauss, and John Jacob Astor were invited to sail on the Titanic.

To cover their tracks, the jesuits shielded themselves from suspicion of involvement in what was coming by also inviting many Irish, French, and Italian Roman Catholic immigrants to sail on the new marvel ship. The jesuits have no qualms about murdering their own people if it serves their purpose. To them, people are expendable in their quest for the world. To further cover their tracks, Protestants from Belfast who wanted to emigrate to the United States were also invited aboard.

Edward Smith, the captain of the Titanic, had sailed the North Atlantic for twenty-six years and was perhaps the world's most experienced captain of the North Atlantic sailing routes. Previously, he had worked for JP Morgan.

Edward Smith was also a jesuit of what is known as the short robe. This might come as a surprise, but not all jesuits are priests. Those who are not priests serve the order through their profession, wherever they are commissioned and sent, be it the movie industry, politics, education, or sailing the oceans in preparation for a crime that would steal the entire gold reserves of America. Anyone can be a jesuit and their identity not known. Edward Smith, the captain of the Titanic, served the Jesuit Order.

When the Titanic sailed from England on April 10, 1912, Francis Browne, a jesuit priest, boarded the Titanic for words with Captain Edward Smith. Francis Browne was the most powerful jesuit in Ireland

and answered directly to the general of the Jesuit Order in Vatican City. Edward Smith was given an order by the jesuits to sink the Titanic and that is exactly what he did.

On the night the Titanic hit the iceberg, Edward Smith kept his ship at full speed ahead, twenty-two knots, on a moonless night through a terrible ice field. Despite eight telegrams warning him to slow down, and despite repeated warnings from other officers, he kept that ship at full speed ahead until it slammed into an iceberg and began to sink.

When the Titanic fired distress flares, they were not red, they were white. White flares to passing shipping was not a distress signal, it was a statement that everybody was having a party, a celebration which no doubt the jesuits were enjoying. This was obviously done deliberately before the ship sailed to ensure no one would come to their aid.

When the lifeboats were launched, Captain Smith prevented any men from entering the boats. When the lifeboats left the sinking ship, many of them were only half full with just women and children aboard. John Jacob Astor's wife was saved. John Jacob Astor himself, and every other American opposed to the creation of the Federal Reserve Bank perished in the freezing waters of the north Atlantic when the Titanic went to the bottom of the ocean.

In April 1912, all opposition to the Federal Reserve was eliminated, and in December 1913, the Federal Reserve Bank was born. America now had a central bank into which all America's gold could be deposited. It was not owned by the American government, it was owned and controlled by the jesuits through JP Morgan, the Rothschild banking dynasty, and the Rockefeller empire. When America was declared bankrupt in 1933, President Franklin Roosevelt declared gold hoarding illegal and forced Americans to sell off their gold to the Federal Reserve. Executive Order 6102 signed by the president on April 5, 1933 forbade the hoarding of gold coin, gold bullion, and gold certificates within the continental United States. The order criminalized the possession of monetary gold by any individual, partnership, association or corporation under threat of huge fines or prison terms of between 5 to 10 years.

Roosevelt was known to act on the advice of England's leading economist, John Maynard Keynes, a homosexual who was a member of the Illuminati. Maynard stated that deficit spending would be a shot in the arm for America's economy. Most of the American New Deal spending programs intended to fight the economic depression were based on his theories on deficit spending, and borrowing against future taxes.

Keynes later wrote: *Lenin was certainly right, there is no more positive, or subtler, no surer means of overturning the existing basis of society than to debauch the currency. The process engages all of the hidden forces of economic law on the side of destruction, and does it in a manner that not one man in a million is able to diagnose.*

That ladies and gentlemen was how America's gold was stolen. Since that time, international bankers controlled by the jesuits have owned America. That is how the god of this world steals, kills and destroys. The jesuits do the bidding of the god of this world, just as did the religious leaders in Jesus Christ's day.

> John 8:42-44
> Jesus said unto them [the religious leaders], If God were your Father, ye would love me: for I proceeded forth and came from God; neither came I of myself, but he sent me.
>
> Why do ye not understand my speech? *even* because ye cannot hear my word.
>
> Ye are of *your* father the devil, and the lusts of your father ye will do. He was a murderer from the beginning, and abode not in the truth, because there is no truth in him. When he speaketh a lie, he speaketh of his own: for he is a liar, and the father of it.

The jesuits are the ring wraiths of the dark lord, his most loyal and obedient servants. They are the masters of the criminal underworld. The jesuits serve Lucifer.

It wasn't muslim terrorists behind 9/11, it was a crime. Most of the gold that was stored in the vaults beneath the towers was stolen before the towers were demolished. It is estimated that over $1 billion worth of gold was in the vaults before the attack and yet only $230 million worth has since been accounted for. The missing gold was not in the vaults when the towers came down. The attack on America on 9/11 was a crime, just as the sinking of the Titanic was a crime.

My advice to anyone out there who has ears to hear would be to get yourselves out of debt as quickly as you can by any means while you can, and tell the banks and the loan sharks to fuck off. The banking business is built on you putting your money into their vaults so they can loan it back to you for profit and have you in their debt. Do you really want to borrow your own money from the jesuits so they can get rich at your expense? It isn't their money they're gambling on the stock markets, it's yours. Take it back from them.

Instead of putting your money into the banks so the vatican can keep it safe for you, why not put a little of your long term savings into gold and bolt a decent safe into your house to keep it in. If enough people in a country rise up and believe God's word again, God can and will fight for you and bring you the abundance only he can provide.

Look, the wizard of oz was not some all powerful all knowing god we need to be afraid of, he was just some weedy little man who was terrified of being discovered. The jesuits may portray themselves as Jedi knights and all powerful sorcerers through their control of Hollywood and such movies as Star Wars, but in reality they are only as powerful as the fear they breed in others. There is no good side and dark side to the 'force', it's all dark. Just as the power the apostle Paul and others manifested in the book of Acts was more powerful than the devil spirits operating through the religious systems in his day, so too the power of God is far superior to any devil spirit power in the world today. We just have to rise up and use the power we have been given and demonstrate it to the world.

> 1 John 4:4
> Ye are of God, little children, and have overcome them: because greater is he that is in you, than he that is in the world.

Light dispels darkness and there are ways back from the economic abyss into which we have been thrown. God always has a way to escape. You are not required to live under the dictates of Rome. The vaults of the Federal Reserve Bank have your stolen gold. It is yours, not theirs. Come back to God and his word and you can again live in prosperity and freedom. Only by living the word of God is it possible to enjoy any kind of abundant life.

> Deuteronomy 28:1,7,11,12
> And it shall come to pass, if thou shalt hearken diligently unto the voice of the LORD thy God, to observe *and* to do all his commandments which I command thee this day, that the LORD thy God will set thee on high above all nations of the earth:
>
> The LORD shall cause thine enemies that rise up against thee to be smitten before thy face: they shall come out against thee one way, and flee before thee seven ways.
>
> And the LORD shall make thee plenteous in goods, in the fruit of thy body, and in the fruit of thy cattle, and in the fruit of thy ground, in the land which the LORD sware unto thy fathers to give thee.
>
> The LORD shall open unto thee his good treasure, the heaven to give the rain unto thy land in his season, and to bless all the work of thine hand: and thou shalt lend unto many nations, and thou shalt not borrow.
>
> Psalm 33:12
> Blessed *is* the nation whose God *is* the LORD; *and* the people *whom* he hath chosen for his own inheritance.

Now listen up you jesuits and you freemasons. I know you believe you are doing god's will. I know what you've been through, but know this, God isn't mad at you. He wants you to be a part of everything he has. He does not wish evil for you. His heart's desire is for you to change gods, to quit serving Lucifer, the god of this world and come back to him. He offers so much more than anything the world can give you. Sure, the god of this world is powerful and intelligent beyond human comprehension, dazzling and beautiful, and he can enrich you beyond your wildest dreams, but all he offers is fleeting and illusory.

Ezekiel 18:21-23
But if the wicked will turn from all his sins that he hath committed, and keep all my statutes, and do that which is lawful and right, he shall surely live, he shall not die.

All his transgressions that he hath committed, they shall not be mentioned unto him: in his righteousness that he hath done he shall live.

Have I any pleasure at all that the wicked should die? saith the Lord GOD: and not that he should return from his ways, and live?

Leave Rome, change your god and the true God will be there for you. Come back to him and you will be forgiven. There is a new life available if you want it. God doesn't care what you've done or where you've been, he will be there for you. He needs capable men more than ever to help him move his word. Do something worthwhile with your life and learn to walk by the spirit so you can heal the hearts you've broken and give recovering of sight to those you have blinded. Light has so much more to offer than darkness.

62. Symptoms of Religion

Religion is quite something, and God has much to say about it in his word. It isn't as if God wants us ignorant. Quite the contrary, he wants us educated and wise.

> 1 Corinthians 12:1
> Now concerning spiritual [pneumatikos - spiritual matters] *gifts*, brethren, I would not have you ignorant.

God had his word written so that rather than being ignorant of spiritual matters we could understand them. It follows then that if we do not read the bible and understand it, we will be ignorant. We may know a heck of a lot about church administration, politics, spiritualism, religion, astrology, communism and freemasonry, but we will be ignorant. If we do not learn the bible and walk by the spirit, we will be in the dark. To be able to see, we must have our eyes open.

> Ephesians 1:17-19
> That the God of our Lord Jesus Christ, the Father of glory, may give unto you the spirit of wisdom and revelation in the knowledge of him:
>
> The eyes of your understanding being enlightened; that ye may know what is the hope of his calling, and what the riches of the glory of his inheritance in the saints,
>
> And what *is* the exceeding greatness of his power to us-ward who believe, according to the working of his mighty power,

Wisdom and knowledge come from an understanding of the bible. Knowing the hope of our calling comes from knowing the scriptures. Perceiving the exceeding greatness of God's power comes only from a knowledge of the word of God and manifesting that power. If we do not know the bible, we are ignorant. Someone may have a PhD, but without a knowledge of God's word they are uneducated, they have no understanding of spiritual matters. Don't take my word for it though, Paul was one of the most educated, influential and religious men on the planet and here's how he put it.

> Philippians 3:8
> Yea doubtless, and I count all things *but* loss for the excellency of the knowledge of Christ Jesus my Lord: for whom I have suffered the loss of all things, and do count them *but* dung, that I may win Christ,

The world educates about anything and everything except the truth of God's word, and does everything it can to prevent accurate teaching of the bible. The devil is a master at keeping people ignorant.

> 2 Corinthians 4:3,4
> But if our gospel be hid, it is hid to them that are lost:
>
> In whom the god of this world hath blinded the minds of them which believe not, lest the light of the glorious gospel of Christ, who is the image of God, should shine unto them.

Now, the devil isn't stupid. He is brilliant at what he does. He has been watching us for a long time and he knows us. He knows some of us will occasionally have a yearning for an understanding of spiritual matters and that we might go to the bible for help. To keep us blinded and to prevent us from ever coming to a knowledge of the truth and an understanding of spiritual matters, he invented religion. Religion is a disease that rots out the eyes and ears of anyone searching for an accurate knowledge of spiritual matters. Of course, the devil needs men to run these religions for him so it is no surprise to find sociable, personable, intelligent, educated men in control of the world's religions.

> 2 Corinthians 11:13-15
> For such *are* false apostles, deceitful workers, transforming themselves into the apostles of Christ.
>
> And no marvel; for Satan himself is transformed into an angel of light.

Therefore *it is* no great thing if his ministers also be transformed as the ministers of righteousness; whose end shall be according to their works.

As religion is a disease, it is only prudent that we learn to recognise the symptoms so we can treat ourselves if we become infected with it. To help us we will look at the life of Jeroboam, the first king of the northern tribes of Israel.

When Solomon turned his back on God's word by marrying unbelieving women, they turned his heart just as God had said they would.

> 1 Kings 11:1-13
> But king Solomon loved many strange women, together with the daughter of Pharaoh, women of the Moabites, Ammonites, Edomites, Zidonians, *and* Hittites;
>
> Of the nations *concerning* which the LORD said unto the children of Israel, Ye shall not go in to them, neither shall they come in unto you: *for* surely they will turn away your heart after their gods: Solomon clave unto these in love.
>
> And he had seven hundred wives, princesses, and three hundred concubines: and his wives turned away his heart.
>
> For it came to pass, when Solomon was old, *that* his wives turned away his heart after other gods: and his heart was not perfect with the LORD his God, as *was* the heart of David his father.
>
> For Solomon went after Ashtoreth the goddess of the Zidonians, and after Milcom the abomination of the Ammonites.
>
> And Solomon did evil in the sight of the LORD, and went not fully after the LORD, as *did* David his father.
>
> Then did Solomon build an high place for Chemosh, the abomination of Moab, in the hill that *is* before Jerusalem, and for Molech, the abomination of the children of Ammon.

And likewise did he for all his strange wives, which burnt incense and sacrificed unto their gods.

And the LORD was angry with Solomon, because his heart was turned from the LORD God of Israel, which had appeared unto him twice,

And had commanded him concerning this thing, that he should not go after other gods: but he kept not that which the LORD commanded.

Wherefore the LORD said unto Solomon, Forasmuch as this is done of thee, and thou hast not kept my covenant and my statutes, which I have commanded thee, I will surely rend the kingdom from thee, and will give it to thy servant.

Notwithstanding in thy days I will not do it for David thy father's sake: *but* I will rend it out of the hand of thy son.

Howbeit I will not rend away all the kingdom; *but* will give one tribe to thy son for David my servant's sake, and for Jerusalem's sake which I have chosen.

Whenever and wherever we turn our backs on God by ignoring his word, the thief has access to our lives. Solomon's love for women was more important to him than doing the word. He loved people more than he loved God. What is there in your life that is more important to you than doing the word? Is using your credit card to buy things for which you do not have the money more important than believing God to supply your need? Is having that brand new outfit or computer or latest gaming system by flashing your credit card more important to you than saving up for it and budgeting properly? You see, we have to discipline ourselves to do things God's way if we want to keep the thief out of our lives.

When Solomon turned his back on God, it was not a good situation for the children of Israel because Solomon was their king and it put their nation at great risk. God therefore took steps to try to protect his people by sending a prophet to speak to Jeroboam, a man who was a believer, a disciple, someone who loved God and had a heart to serve him and do what was right.

1 Kings 11:28-38
And the man Jeroboam *was* a mighty man of valour: and Solomon seeing the young man that he was industrious, he made him ruler over all the charge of the house of Joseph.

And it came to pass at that time when Jeroboam went out of Jerusalem, that the prophet Ahijah the Shilonite found him in the way; and he had clad himself with a new garment; and they two *were* alone in the field:

And Ahijah caught the new garment that *was* on him, and rent it *in* twelve pieces:

And he said to Jeroboam, Take thee ten pieces: for thus saith the LORD, the God of Israel, Behold, I will rend the kingdom out of the hand of Solomon, and will give ten tribes to thee:

(But he shall have one tribe for my servant David's sake, and for Jerusalem's sake, the city which I have chosen out of all the tribes of Israel:)

Because that they have forsaken me, and have worshipped Ashtoreth the goddess of the Zidonians, Chemosh the god of the Moabites, and Milcom the god of the children of Ammon, and have not walked in my ways, to do *that which is* right in mine eyes, and *to keep* my statutes and my judgments, as *did* David his father.

Howbeit I will not take the whole kingdom out of his hand: but I will make him prince all the days of his life for David my servant's sake, whom I chose, because he kept my commandments and my statutes:

But I will take the kingdom out of his son's hand, and will give it unto thee, *even* ten tribes.

And unto his son will I give one tribe, that David my servant may have a light alway before me in Jerusalem, the city which I have chosen me to put my name there.

And I will take thee, and thou shalt reign according to all that thy soul desireth, and shalt be king over Israel.

And it shall be, if thou wilt hearken unto all that I command thee, and wilt walk in my ways, and do *that is* right in my sight, to keep my statutes and my commandments, as David my servant did; that I will be with thee, and build thee a sure house, as I built for David, and will give Israel unto thee.

God always does his best for us. Whenever and wherever men and women put their trust in him and believe his word he is there to help them. God never goes anywhere because he is everywhere. God never walks away from people, it is always people who walk away from God. After Solomon's death the kingdom split, just as God had said. Solomon's son Rehoboam ruled Judea, and Jeroboam ruled northern Israel. God's word is trustworthy, you can rely on it, you can trust your life to it.

When Jeroboam had ruled for a while, for some reason he began to fear losing his position as king. He didn't deal with his fears either, he let them take root and grow. Perhaps he was too busy with his job to have time to keep himself in the word, like I've heard a thousand times from people in our day. Listen, if you love God, you love his word. If you don't have time for the word, you don't have time for God and all your talk about love is religious horseshit. If you neglect God's word because you're too busy with life, or too lazy to maintain a consistent faithful diet, or something else in life is more important to you, you are walking away from God. Is television more important to you than spending time in the word? Are computer games and magazines more important to you than spending time in the word? Are your hobbies and pursuits more important to you than spending time in the word? If so, change your direction. God isn't going anywhere, it's you that's walking away.

If we ever feel fear creeping into our lives in any category, we should be scrambling to get to the word. Look at what Jeroboam said in his heart, look at his fear.

1 Kings 12:25-27
Then Jeroboam built Shechem in mount Ephraim, and dwelt therein; and went out from thence, and built Penuel.

And Jeroboam said in his heart, Now shall the kingdom return to the house of David:

If this people go up to do sacrifice in the house of the LORD at Jerusalem, then shall the heart of this people turn again unto their lord, *even* unto Rehoboam king of Judah, and they shall kill me, and go again to Rehoboam king of Judah.

He was afraid of losing his job and consequently his life. Hey, wasn't it fear that almost destroyed Job? The book of Job existed during Jeroboam's day, so why didn't he keep his heart in the word? Look again at what God told him by way of a prophet.

1 Kings 11:30,31,37,38
And Ahijah caught the new garment that *was* on him, and rent it *in* twelve pieces:

And he said to Jeroboam, Take thee ten pieces: for thus saith the LORD, the God of Israel, Behold, I will rend the kingdom out of the hand of Solomon, and will give ten tribes to thee:

And I will take thee, and thou shalt reign according to all that thy soul desireth, and shalt be king over Israel.

And it shall be, if thou wilt hearken unto all that I command thee, and wilt walk in my ways, and do *that is* right in my sight, to keep my statutes and my commandments, as David my servant did; that I will be with thee, and build thee a sure house, as I built for David, and will give Israel unto thee.

Why didn't Jeroboam stay faithful to God's word by keeping it clear in his mind? Good question. Why don't people today believe God's word? It has everything to do with keeping ourselves in the bible and maintaining a faithful, daily diet of God's word. If we don't keep ourselves in the word, we will lose it. That's not a threat, that's just life. If you don't eat, your body will become weak and ill and you will eventually die. You don't have to eat, but if you don't, you're not going to enjoy much of a life because you will be dead. If you neglect the word, fears await you and what you fear will become reality in your life. If you don't believe me, go and spend some time in the book of Job, which is where Jeroboam should have gone. He was afraid of losing his job, he was afraid of losing his kingdom, he was afraid of losing the power and authority he had obviously developed a taste for, and he was afraid of losing his life.

1 Kings 12:27
If this people go up to do sacrifice in the house of the LORD at Jerusalem, then shall the heart of this people turn again unto their lord, *even* unto Rehoboam king of Judah, and they shall kill me, and go again to Rehoboam king of Judah.

Instead of going to God's word to deal with his fears, Jeroboam made a few plans of his own. Do we walk by the senses or do we walk by the revealed word and will of God? Jeroboam decided to do things his way.

1 Kings 12:28-33
Whereupon the king took counsel, and made two calves *of* gold, and said unto them, It is too much for you to go up to Jerusalem: behold thy gods, O Israel, which brought thee up out of the land of Egypt.

And he set the one in Bethel, and the other put he in Dan.

And this thing became a sin: for the people went *to worship* before the one, *even* unto Dan.

And he made an house of high places, and made priests of the lowest of the people, which were not of the sons of Levi.

And Jeroboam ordained a feast in the eighth month, on the fifteenth day of the month, like unto the feast that *is* in Judah, and he offered upon the altar. So did he in Bethel, sacrificing unto the calves that he had made: and he placed in Bethel the priests of the high places which he had made.

So he offered upon the altar which he had made in Bethel the fifteenth day of the eighth month, *even* in the month which he had devised of his own heart; and ordained a feast unto the children of Israel: and he offered upon the altar, and burnt incense.

Will you look at that. Jeroboam built a new religion. He turned his back on the fountain of living waters and hewed him out a broken cistern in which to house his fears.

Jeremiah 2:13
For my people have committed two evils; they have forsaken me the fountain of living waters, *and* hewed them out cisterns, broken cisterns, that can hold no water.

A church or ministry is something man makes in which to house his religion. Man just seems to feel the need to have some kind of organised structure complete with layers of leadership into which he can place his religion. Always remember, God does not dwell in temples made with hands. If you lose this truth, you will be blown about with every wind of doctrine by the sleight of men and the cunning craftiness whereby they lie in wait to deceive. Churches, ministries, and religions constructed by men are broken cisterns that can hold no water. Any flowing of living waters they once energised will eventually leak out of them until all that is left is dry religious ceremony.

Let's look at this new religion of Jeroboam's to see what we can learn. Remember, Jeroboam had been a disciple, a disciplined follower of God, a man who loved God and his word. He neglected the word, and in its place constructed a religion, complete with gods in the form of golden calves.

1 Kings 12:28
Whereupon the king took counsel, and made two calves *of* gold, and said unto them, It is too much for you to go up to Jerusalem: behold thy gods, O Israel, which brought thee up out of the land of Egypt.

The first thing he did was to replace the true God with alternative gods. People require something to worship, something they can call their god.

In this administration, golden calves wouldn't work, so the devil has to adapt. The intent is to strip the power of God out of people's lives and replace it with religious ceremony.

The living waters of Jeremiah refers to the energising of God's power, the manifestation of spiritual power, therefore replacing the manifestation of spiritual power with ceremony and ritual is an important stage in the development of a broken cistern. In modern day language, this would equate to turning people away from walking by the spirit to walking by the counsel of men. Instead of walking with Christ as their head, people are taught to walk within a structure of leadership who all report up the chain to a patriarch who feels responsible for the entire religious structure. That is walking by the senses because it is putting your trust in men. If you have Christ in you and you can walk by the spirit, what do you need a patriarchal system for? Either Christ is your head or men are your head. The only leadership anyone needs is whoever witnessed to them, the person who is responsible to look after them, teach them the word, and show them how to walk by the spirit for themselves. This is a family thing, a home church thing, not a monstrous patriarchal leadership man-made temple thing.

The next phase of Jeroboam's plan was to construct religious buildings in which to house his new gods. No doubt the temples he made for his golden calves would have had elaborate religious design intended to draw gasps of wonder from folks stepping inside. No doubt people would have talked in awe about the grandeur of those temples in Bethal and Dan and spread the word of the new religion.

Any religious organisation with a central headquarters whose staff support a patriarchal system of leadership that walks by counsels of men thinking there is safety in a multitude of counsellors is a temple made with hands. As there are thousands of such man-made temples around, with some brands having church buildings on practically every street corner, it's also a good idea to label them so people can choose which broken cistern they would feel comfortable supporting. After all, people like to brag about the broken cisterns they've dedicated their lives to despite God stating very clearly in this administration that he does not have anything to do with any of them.

Acts 7:48-50
Howbeit the most High dwelleth not in temples made with hands; as saith the prophet,

Heaven *is* my throne, and earth *is* my footstool: what house will ye build me? saith the Lord: or what *is* the place of my rest?

Hath not my hand made all these things?

The next thing Jeroboam did was construct an administrational system around his new religion and staff it with wonderfully sincere religious pricks, oh sorry, priests.

1 Kings 12:31
And he made an house of high places, and made priests of the lowest of the people, which were not of the sons of Levi.

The sons of Levi were God's leadership in the old testament. In this age of Grace, there is no priesthood. Instead, those of us with a knowledge of the word and who walk by the spirit are to establish churches in our homes and teach others how to do the same. To support this work, God gives gift ministries of apostles, prophets, evangelists, pastors and teachers. These gift ministries are for the perfecting of the saints (the mending, the caring of God's people), for the work of the ministry, and for the edifying of the body of Christ. These gift ministries are to be energised at the home church level for that is where they are needed. And another thing, God gives these ministries, not men. Who ordains leadership in broken cisterns? Men do. They also give them nice religious titles such as reverend, labels that you won't find anywhere in the bible. God gives gift ministries, and he absolutely does not do it through counsels of men. The worldwide network of energised believers who walk with Christ as their head make up the body of Christ, not some dead religious temple made with hands.

Ephesians 4:11,12
And he gave some, apostles; and some, prophets; and some, evangelists; and some, pastors and teachers;

For the perfecting of the saints, for the work of the ministry, for the edifying of the body of Christ:

I've never been in any church or ministry leadership programmes. I've never been to any religious educational institutions for further education, and I don't have any degrees or university qualifications. Do I have any gift ministries? Well, what does an apostle do? He brings new light to his generation, therefore how would you know if God had given someone the gift ministry of an apostle? By reading his name tag? I don't see reverend listed in the gift ministries, I see apostles, prophets, evangelists, pastors and teachers.

I don't see anyone calling Paul reverend, I see everyone referring to him as the apostle Paul. I don't see Reverend Philip in the bible, I see Philip the evangelist. I don't see Reverend Agabus in the bible, I see Agabus the prophet. Who gave these ministries to those men? God or a structure of leadership who took it on themselves to do it? People may call themselves reverend and enjoy the worship they get from men, but in truth they're nothing more than priests ordained by men to help prop up their particular brand of religious horseshit.

What about the gift ministry of a prophet? What qualities exemplify a prophet? A nametag with reverend on it? Prophets confront God's people and bring them back to the word. What about the gift ministry of an apostle? What qualities exemplify an apostle? A nametag with reverend on it? Apostles bring new light to God's people. It may be old light, but it's new to the generation to which he brings it. These definitions make it rather easy to see where gift ministries are in operation. Men do not give gift ministries, God gives gift ministries where it pleases him, and I can assure you that he has absolutely nothing whatsoever to do with patriarchs and counsels of men dishing out reverend titles in temples made with hands.

Next, Jeroboam instituted a religious calendar complete with special holy days, alters, incense, feasts, ceremonies and rituals. Which days top your religious calendar? Christmas? Easter? The anniversary of your broken cistern?

> 1 Kings 12:33
> So he [Jeroboam] offered upon the altar which he had made in Bethel the fifteenth day of the eighth month, *even* in the month which he had devised of his own heart; and ordained a feast unto the children of Israel: and he offered upon the altar, and burnt incense.

This doesn't sound much different to every other religion on earth today, does it? You just will not find God within any religious man-made ministries or organisations anywhere on earth. They are all broken cisterns. Every one of them without exception. Just because a church or ministry sings a few congregational songs every sunday followed by the reading of a script splattered with a few bible verses is no indication of anything.

So, Jeroboam constructed a new religion in which to house his fears. His fears were the motivation for turning his back on God and hewing out for himself a broken cistern. We know that fear is believing, so how did things turn out for the king?

> 1 Kings 15:29
> And it came to pass, when he [Baasha] reigned, *that* he smote all the house of Jeroboam; he left not to Jeroboam any that breathed, until he had destroyed him, according unto the saying of the LORD, which he spake by his servant Ahijah the Shilonite:

Oh dear, perhaps hewing out broken cisterns and decorating them with glittering religious trappings isn't the way to go. By the way, while we're here, religious trappings come in many forms, a few of which might surprise and shock you. For example, while Moses was leading the Israelites from Egypt to the promised land, at one point they had a major problem with the local wildlife.

> Numbers 21:5-9
> And the people spake against God, and against Moses, Wherefore have ye brought us up out of Egypt to die in the wilderness? For *there is* no bread, neither *is there any* water; and our soul loatheth this light bread.
>
> And the LORD sent fiery serpents among the people, and they bit the people; and much people of Israel died.

> Therefore the people came to Moses, and said, We have sinned, for we have spoken against the LORD, and against thee; pray unto the LORD, that he take away the serpents from us. And Moses prayed for the people.
>
> And the LORD said unto Moses, Make thee a fiery serpent, and set it upon a pole: and it shall come to pass, that every one that is bitten, when he looketh upon it, shall live.
>
> And Moses made a serpent of brass, and put it upon a pole, and it came to pass, that if a serpent had bitten any man, when he beheld the serpent of brass, he lived.

The Israelites still had not got their heads around the truths in the book of Job regarding not accusing God of doing criminal things to them. Once you start accusing God of doing criminal things to you, the doors are open to all sorts of problems. The devil tried to break Job's integrity by getting him to blame God for his problems. Job didn't break, but these Israelites just couldn't stop themselves. Here they go again, this time accusing God of taking them out into the wilderness so he could kill them with hunger. Go to any church in the world today and you will hear folks accusing God of making them sick and killing them. People, you had better wake up to the truth that God does not dwell in temples made with hands and stay well away from them.

As a consequence of their unbelief, God couldn't protect those people from fiery serpents, but when the people came back to God and apologised for accusing him of doing evil things to them, he made a way for them to escape, he provided a solution. Every time we come back to God, no matter how much we've neglected him or even how terrible we've been, he will always be there to help us sort out our problems. In this case, Moses was to make a brass image of the serpents that were biting them and if someone was bitten all they had to do was run to the brass serpent, look at it and they would be healed. Now listen, selah, God had Moses make that brass serpent for a particular job. Once the people were out of the danger area and into the promised land, did they need the brass serpent any longer? No, they didn't. It had served its purpose. However, hundreds of years later during the reign of Hezekiah, the Israelites were still worshipping that stupid thing.

2 Kings 18:1-4
Now it came to pass in the third year of Hoshea son of Elah king of Israel, *that* Hezekiah the son of Ahaz king of Judah began to reign.

Twenty and five years old was he when he began to reign; and he reigned twenty and nine years in Jerusalem. His mother's name also *was* Abi, the daughter of Zachariah.

And he did *that which was* right in the sight of the LORD, according to all that David his father did.

He removed the high places, and brake the images, and cut down the groves, and brake in pieces the brasen serpent that Moses had made: for unto those days the children of Israel did burn incense to it: and he called it Nehushtan [a piece of brass].

This is amazing. Can you see now how religion takes the things of God and turns them into mindless ceremony and ritual? Hundreds of years later, the Israelites were still worshipping that stupid piece of brass. Hezekiah took it out of its temple and broke it in pieces. If we want to live for God, we are going to have to take down any religious idols we may have and break them in pieces.

For example, what does the word say about water baptism? Was water baptism part of the patriarchal system? No, it wasn't. Was it part of the law administration? Moses wrote nothing about water baptism. Search and look, Moses wrote absolutely nothing regarding water baptism. In fact, there is nothing in the bible about it until John the baptist came along.

Matthew 3:1-6
In those days came John the Baptist, preaching in the wilderness of Judaea,

And saying, Repent ye: for the kingdom of heaven is at hand.

For this is he that was spoken of by the prophet Esaias, saying, The voice of one crying in the wilderness, Prepare ye the way of the Lord, make his paths straight.

And the same John had his raiment of camel's hair, and a leathern girdle about his loins; and his meat was locusts and wild honey.

Then went out to him Jerusalem, and all Judaea, and all the region round about Jordan,

And were baptized of him in Jordan, confessing their sins.

John the baptist was a prophet, a man of God, just like Moses, and God told John to get out into the wilderness and water baptize people in the River Jordan. Just as God had Moses set up that brass serpent to bless his people, God also had John institute water baptism to bless his people. However, look at what John said to Jesus Christ when he came to him to be baptised.

Matthew 3:13-15
Then cometh Jesus from Galilee to Jordan unto John, to be baptized of him.

But John forbad him, saying, I have need to be baptized of thee, and comest thou to me?

And Jesus answering said unto him, Suffer [allow] *it to be so* now: for thus it becometh us to fulfil all righteousness. Then he suffered [allowed] him.

Will you just look at that. It's almost unbelievable. John refused to water baptize Jesus Christ, the son of God. John told Jesus he wasn't going to do it, and then told him that he had need to be baptized of him with something better. John the baptist himself knew that something better than water baptism was coming and that Jesus Christ would make it available. John the baptist knew his water baptism was but a temporary symbolic gesture until that something greater came along. Look at what John said publicly in verse 11, before Jesus came to him.

Matthew 3:11
I indeed baptize you with water unto repentance: but he that cometh after me is mightier than I, whose shoes I am not worthy

to bear: he shall baptize you with the Holy Ghost [holy spirit], and *with* fire:

John knew that his water baptism was but a symbolic gesture preparing people for what was coming, something far greater, which was to be baptized with the holy spirit. His entire ministry was simply to prepare people for what was coming. Water baptism isn't worthy to bear the shoes of baptism with the holy spirit.

> Mark 1:8
> I indeed have baptized you with water: but he shall baptize you with the Holy Ghost [holy spirit].
>
> John 1:32,33
> And John bare record, saying, I saw the Spirit descending from heaven like a dove, and it abode upon him.
>
> And I knew him not: but he that sent me to baptize with water, the same said unto me, Upon whom thou shalt see the Spirit descending, and remaining on him, the same is he which baptizeth with the Holy Ghost [holy spirit].

God told John to water baptize people in Jordan as a symbolic illustration to prepare them for the baptism with the holy spirit which Jesus Christ had come to make available. John the baptist himself taught his followers that Jesus Christ was the true way to God. John knew his ministry of water baptism was temporary and that it would be replaced.

> John 3:25-30
> Then there arose a question between *some* of John's disciples and the Jews [Judeans] about purifying.
>
> And they came unto John, and said unto him, Rabbi, he that was with thee beyond Jordan, to whom thou barest witness, behold, the same baptizeth, and all *men* come to him.
>
> John answered and said, A man can receive nothing, except it be given him from heaven.

Ye yourselves bear me witness, that I said, I am not the Christ, but that I am sent before him.

He that hath the bride is the bridegroom: but the friend of the bridegroom, which standeth and heareth him, rejoiceth greatly because of the bridegroom's voice: this my joy therefore is fulfilled.

He must increase, but I *must* decrease.

Jesus Christ also knew that he would make a far better baptism than John's available. On the day of the ascension, he again brought up water baptism and told his apostles that John's water baptism would be replaced in a few days.

> Acts 1:4,5
> And, being assembled together with *them*, commanded them that they should not depart from Jerusalem, but wait for the promise of the Father, which, *saith he*, ye have heard of me.
>
> For John truly baptized with water; but ye shall be baptized with the Holy Ghost [holy spirit] not many days hence.

Jesus Christ came to make baptism with the holy spirit available, which was something far superior to water baptism, and it first came on the day of Pentecost.

> Acts 2:1-4
> And when the day of Pentecost was fully come, they were all with one accord in one place.
>
> And suddenly there came a sound from heaven as of a rushing mighty wind, and it filled all the house where they were sitting.
>
> And there appeared unto them cloven tongues like as of fire, and it sat upon each of them.
>
> And they were all filled with the Holy Ghost [holy spirit], and began to speak with other tongues, as the Spirit gave them utterance.

With the coming of the greater, the lesser was no longer needed. With the coming of the baptism of the holy spirit, water baptism was no longer necessary, it had served its purpose. Like Moses' brass serpent, water baptism was simply a temporary measure, and once baptism with the holy spirit became available it was no longer needed. Water baptism was a symbolic cleansing, a ceremony John instituted to illustrate what was coming, to prepare the way for Jesus Christ. The actual receiving of the gift of holy spirit, which is to be baptized in holy spirit, cleanses you within and washes you entirely, making you righteous before God. No amount of washing in water can do that for anyone.

So why then do churches today two thousand years later still perform water baptism ceremonies? They dunk people, sprinkle them, immerse them, and submerge them in rivers. Why? Same reason the people in Hezekiah's day still worshipped that stupid brass serpent. Look, getting wet will get you nothing from God. The only way we can get anything from God is to confess Jesus as Lord and believe in our hearts that God raised him from the dead. At that moment we are saved, sozō, made whole by receiving the gift of holy spirit which is to be baptized with the holy spirit. The receiving of that spirit washes us completely and gives us the righteousness of God. Water baptism is religious horseshit, a religious ceremony, a mindless ritual that accomplishes absolutely nothing other than making people wet.

What other religious trappings could we have in our lives? Well, anything that we do with our five senses, with our human abilities to try to please God falls into the category of religion. It is impossible for any man or any woman to do any works of any kind in order to be baptized with holy spirit. It is impossible to worship God except in spirit and in truth, which is to manifest the gift of holy spirit by speaking in tongues. Anything a person may do with their five senses abilities because they think it's how you please God falls into the category of religion.

Like wearing a cross around your neck. The cross symbolises torture and murder. If Jesus Christ had been run through with a sword, would you wear a sword around your neck? If Jesus Christ had been shot, would you wear a gun around your neck? If Jesus Christ has been beaten to death with an iron bar, would you wear an iron bar around your neck? If you think worshipping the very tool the devil used to murder Jesus Christ pleases God, you're insane. This isn't about his death, this is about his resurrection from the dead. Get those filthy icons of death out of your life. While you're at it, you can dump all your guardian angel garbage, as well as any pictures or statues of Jesus and Mary, or any other religious trash you have around. They cost you money? Getting money from you was the whole point.

What else? Well, what about your written words? Do you think God enjoys seeing you capitalise pronouns referring to Him and His Word? Do you think He appreciates what you consider He might want? He does not want you worshipping Him with works of the flesh so shove your capitalisation up Your religious broken cistern ass. All you do with that religious garbage is alienate yourselves from the world by making yourself look ridiculous. If someone insists you should do it, ask them for the chapter and verse.

What about saying *Amen* at the end of prayers? Do you even know what *amen* means? If you don't know what it means and you just repeat it mindlessly at the end of prayers, you're just performing a religious ceremony. We don't pray to God in the name of Amen, we pray to God in the name of Jesus Christ. I once read that a hindu woman with a red spot on her forehead was asked about it and she didn't have a clue what it meant. She replied that it was just their custom. Her mother did it, so she did it too. If that's all Amen means to you, shut the fuck up. Try speaking in tongues and worshipping God in spirit and in truth instead. It is perfect prayer, after all. Amen was a congregational response to a prayer which meant no more than *wot he said* in modern language. It is not some magic word that somehow opens the windows of heaven for you. Used mindlessly, it is just another piece of religious horseshit.

What about saying *God bless you* to people, or signing your letters and emails off with *God bless you?* It's nice to be nice, don't you think? Is it? I don't see God bless you in the book of Acts or anywhere in Paul's epistles. I see grace, mercy and peace to you from God our father and from the Lord Jesus Christ, but I don't see God bless you. Quite the contrary, I see that God has already blessed me with all spiritual blessings.

Ephesians 1:3
Blessed *be* the God and Father of our Lord Jesus Christ, who hath blessed us with all spiritual blessings in heavenly *places* in Christ:

Why do you say God bless you to people? If they're born again, God has already blessed them with all spiritual blessings. Are you implying that God didn't do a decent enough job and that he still has some blessings to give to that person? If so, you're contradicting the bible, because the word says that God has already blessed us, all of us who are born again, with all spiritual blessings. If you want to bless someone in this administration, Corinthians tells you how to do it.

1 Corinthians 14:16,17
Else when thou shalt bless with the spirit, how shall he that occupieth the room of the unlearned say Amen at thy giving of thanks, seeing he understandeth not what thou sayest?

For thou verily givest thanks well, but the other is not edified.

According to Corinthians, if you want to bless someone you're going to have to believe to operate tongues with interpretation and prophecy at a home church meeting.

God bless you? Where did you learn that anyway? From the bible or from a broken cistern? Why do you say *God bless you* to people? Because it's in the bible or because everyone else at your broken cistern shithole church says it? It's time to be honest people. Saying God bless you to people is religious horseshit. You're already blessed with all spiritual blessings, don't ever forget that.

The origin of saying *God bless you* is quite intriguing. The phrase *God bless you* is actually attributed to Pope Gregory who uttered it in the sixth century during the bubonic plague epidemic that killed over 25 million people. In other words, saying God bless you to someone originated in death. Every time you say God bless you to someone, you are thinking death of them. It originated with a fucking pope who claimed God was killing all those people with the black death to bless them.

The following few verses in Corinthians have been taught extensively regarding believers marrying unbelievers, and I'm sure that's a tiny part of it, however, read the verses again in light of what we've just learned regarding religion.

> 2 Corinthians 6:14-18
> Be ye not unequally yoked together with unbelievers: for what fellowship hath righteousness with unrighteousness? and what communion hath light with darkness?
>
> And what concord hath Christ with Belial? or what part hath he that believeth with an infidel?
>
> And what agreement hath the temple of God with idols? for ye are the temple of the living God; as God hath said, I will dwell in them, and walk in *them;* and I will be their God, and they shall be my people.
>
> Wherefore come out from among them, and be ye separate, saith the Lord, and touch not the unclean *thing;* and I will receive you,
>
> And will be a Father unto you, and ye shall be my sons and daughters, saith the Lord Almighty.

Are these verses simply addressing marriage? I don't think so! These verses address having fellowship with religious nuts in their temples made with hands. Come out from among them and be ye separate. Touch not the unclean thing, walk by the spirit instead because God is your father and he will not be found in temples made with hands.

What about putting your hands together when you pray? Do you really think it makes any difference to God what you do with your hands when you pray? Nowhere in the entire bible is anyone ever instructed by God to clasp their hands together when praying. So where does it come from? Haven't you ever stopped to wonder where that religious piece of shit comes from? I mean, just look at it. It doesn't take much imagination to realise that it's just making a penis in front of your face to pray to which is what the ancient pagans did. What a wonderful christian thing for parents to teach their young children hey?

Walking *by* the Spirit

I could go on forever on this subject, but I think I've made the point God wanted me to make. Yes, it is God who has been energising within me to will and to do of his good pleasure while I've been putting this class and this session together. And another thing, God is quite happy with my language. Do you think swearing means I'm not a man of God? The word says my speech should always be with grace, seasoned with salt so that I should know how to answer every man.

> Colossians 4:6
> Let your speech *be* alway with grace, seasoned with salt, that ye may know how ye ought to answer every man.

This verse mentions grace and salt, it says nothing about swearing. If you insert swearing into this verse, you're full of religious horseshit. Do you even know what grace is? This is the grace administration. I'm extending grace by teaching about God's grace. You will find grace all the way through my teachings. I teach grace, therefore my speech is always with grace. Salt is a reference to commitment. Does anyone out there doubt my commitment to what I do? If you think being holy and righteous means you don't swear, you're worshipping a brass serpent, attempting to establish your own holiness with works of the flesh. I worship God in spirit and in truth, do you? I walk by the spirit and not by counsels of men, do you?

While I was researching and writing this session, one morning I woke up without any idea where the class was going after Jeroboam. I was half way through and I didn't have a clue where it was going next. As I sat up and swung my legs over the side of the bed, at that moment I saw very clearly the direction I had to take. When I later finished writing up the first draft, God filled me with a deep peaceful feeling inside to let me know the job was done. All I had to do then was tidy it up and prepare it for publishing. I can assure you, God is quite happy with my language because it communicates. If he didn't like my language he would not have worked within me to do this thing and pull it all together. My righteousness I hold fast and will not let it go, my heart shall not reproach me so long as I live.

Look, I don't hate religious people and nor does God. Well, he loves them a lot more than I do, but I'm not simply out to annoy them just for the sake of it, I'm trying to get their attention. I'm confronting the world because I love enough to want to see the word live. Come out of those broken cisterns my brothers and sisters in Christ, energise that gift of holy spirit within you and establish churches in your homes that are self governing, self propagating and self supporting. Only then can you be truly free.

63. 1 Corinthians 12

Not only do we look into God's word to see what something is, we often look into the bible to see what something is not. Understanding what something is not helps us to understand what it is. It is always the word that is important, not what men say or do. We must never set our standards by men, rather, the word must always be our standard for truth.

In the last session we took an in-depth look into religion to understand what a home church is not to be. Now that we know what a home church is not, it's time to go to the word to see exactly what it is and how we should conduct church meetings in our homes.

As we know, the word *church*, the Greek word *ekklēsia* encompasses any group of people called out for any purpose. In Acts 19:32, a confused and unstable mob is called an *ekklēsia*, a church, while in verse 39, a lawful assembly, a group of legal representatives called together to sort out a legal complaint is called an *ekklēsia*, a church.

> Acts 19:32,39
> Some therefore cried one thing, and some another: for the assembly [ekklēsia] was confused; and the more part knew not wherefore they were come together.
>
> But if ye enquire any thing concerning other matters, it shall be determined in a lawful assembly [ekklēsia].

In studying the word *church* in the bible, it is of paramount importance that we remember that it always refers to people, without exception. This of course means that *ekklēsia* cannot be used to mean a church building, religion, ministry, or any ecclesiastical structure or religious organisation of any kind. It is absolutely impossible for anyone to go to church. Why? Because people are the church not that stupid stained glass shithole building they go to every week.

The same is true of home church meetings. A home church consists of the people that come to your home. It is not your living room understand? The church of God is people, not a collection of living rooms or any man-made ministry. Whenever and wherever we meet together for any reason, whether it's in someone's home or not, we are the church of God, not the building or ministry or religious organisation we may happen to be a part of. If we go to the movies together, we are the church of God at the movies. If we go for a walk in the countryside, we are the church of God in the countryside. If we have a meeting in someone's home, we are the church of God in that living room.

So how do we conduct church meetings in our homes? What mechanics are involved? If you think it is just about one person leading a meeting once or twice a week, singing a few congregational songs, having a 'season' of prayer, going through the motions of manifestations, then listening to someone read a boring bible script that's been prepared for weeks, you either have no experiential understanding of the power of God or you've forgotten what it's like to walk by the spirit. Consider this in Corinthians.

> 1 Corinthians 14:26
> How is it then, brethren? when ye come together, every one of you hath a psalm, hath a doctrine, hath a tongue, hath a revelation, hath an interpretation. Let all things be done unto edifying.

Paul is confronting the Corinthian believers here because the home church meetings were not edifying. The verse however does clearly indicate what they were doing in their home churches. For example, it is evident that these home church meetings were not led by a single person who controlled everything. If that were the case, then only those who had been asked to do anything would have prepared for the meetings and everyone else would have turned up, sat down, shut up and listened. So what can we learn from this? Well, home church meetings are not to be led by a single person who nominates who does what. If a church meeting, whether in the home, in a stained glass shithole building, or at the headquarters of some ministry constructed by men is led by a single person while everyone else sits and watches, it is nothing more than a religious horseshit ceremony.

Those believers in Corinth turned up at their home church meetings and everyone wanted to sing a song, play their musical instruments, manifest tongues with interpretation and prophecy, tell everyone what God was doing for them, and teach. They were all excited and everyone wanted to give. In other words, there was absolutely no preparation beforehand other than getting the house ready. Think about that, selah. No one had been selected by the home church leader to teach, no one had been asked beforehand to prepare songs or anything else. Their home church meetings were not ceremonies prepared in advance. The believers walked by the spirit and were going to their meetings bubbling over with real life stuff to share about how God was moving in their lives. They were living the present truth.

2 Peter 1:12
Wherefore I will not be negligent to put you always in remembrance of these things, though ye know *them*, and be established in the present truth.

Do you understand what the word *present* means? Here's a dictionary definition.

Present
The period of time that is happening now, not the past or the future.

If someone reads a script prepared months in advance as a teaching, by sheer definition how can it possibly be present truth? When Peter stood up on the day of Pentecost, did he have his teaching prepared beforehand? He probably didn't have a clue what he was going to teach until he stood up and God gave him his first scripture. And what a teaching! It was current, fresh and alive because Peter walked by the spirit and God energised in him to will and to do of his good pleasure.

When Peter taught in the temple in Acts 3 after healing the man born lame, did he pull out a teaching he'd prepared weeks earlier? How ridiculous, he couldn't possibly have known what was going to happen that morning when he went to the temple.

When Peter opened his mouth and taught the word to Cornelius and his household in Acts 10, did he pull out the notes on a teaching he'd been putting together for months? He couldn't possibly have known the gentiles were about to manifest the power of God by speaking in tongues, so his teaching was entirely inspirational, made up on the spur of the moment as he was going along, a bit like how this class is coming together. He walked by the spirit, just as I am doing with this class, and God was there energising within him as he does with me and will do with you if you walk by the spirit.

People, wake up, get the religious sleep out of your eyes, either we're walking by the spirit or we're walking by the senses, make up your mind. If you have a problem with this, take it up with God, I didn't write the bible.

> Mark 13:11
> But when they shall lead *you*, and deliver you up, take no thought beforehand what ye shall speak, neither do ye premeditate: but whatsoever shall be given you in that hour, that speak ye: for it is not ye that speak, but the Holy Ghost [holy spirit].

If we walk by the spirit, then we are living in the present truth. If we're following men and preparing teachings weeks and months and even years in advance, we're walking by the flesh, we're following men, it's that simple, and I don't give a fuck what the pope says to the contrary. He can worship Lucifer if he wants, that's his business, but we don't have to. People, it's time to come out of all those temples made with hands, all those religions, churches and ministries constructed by men. It's time to stop following men and make Christ our head. It's time to walk by the spirit and demonstrate the power of God.

Now of course, there are times when preparing a teaching in advance is appropriate and right. God may inspire you to teach on a subject you're not entirely comfortable or familiar with and you may need to sit down and study it. God may inspire you to teach a class over a period of days or weeks, so yes, you will have time to prepare. The point is, you're still walking by the spirit. God has given you the time to prepare because he knows you need it. And this brings us to a critically important key to walking by the spirit - God may only give revelation at the very moment you need it.

The world knows this principle. Everyone from military commanders to police chiefs to business executives to politicians only give information on a need to know basis. To the world, it's common sense. Well, what about God? He's smarter than anyone else on the planet surely? Haven't you ever noticed that more often than not you only get revelation at the last minute, on a need to know basis? I'd say that the majority of revelation I get is last minute stuff. Why is that? Why does God keep the majority of revelation information from us until the last minute? It's to keep us protected. If we don't know what he's about to do, then the devil doesn't know either so he doesn't have time to muster his forces and lay ambushes. It comes out of the blue at him. If I have no idea what the next session of this class is going to be about, then nor does any devil spirit. They don't know what's coming next because I don't and I'm writing the class.

Doesn't this make sense now you understand it? I used to wonder why God kept stuff from me until the very moment I needed it, but no longer, not now that I understand why. This, of course, means you need to be tuned in spiritually all the time so you don't miss stuff. Walking by the spirit isn't something you only turn on once or twice a week to try to impress people when you sit through a meeting.

If you're a home church leader and you're walking by the spirit and moving the word, very often God will show you what's going on in your area and inspire you to teach on a specific subject just hours before a home church meeting. Don't worry though, he always gives you enough time to prepare if you need it. It was back in 1998 that God first told me to buy a computer and start writing a book. I had to learn from scratch and teach myself how to write. I had absolutely no idea where it was all going then, but I understand it now.

Even if you've had time to prepare a teaching beforehand, God can and does interrupt you while you're actually teaching with scriptures and stuff that needs to be handled. Learn to listen and teach what God wants taught, and you can't do that if you're mindlessly reading a stupid script. Expect God to give you revelation while you're teaching and follow his lead because he knows what he's doing. It might only be a ten minute teaching, so what? Your home churches might be more fun if three or four people taught inspirational present truth for ten minutes each rather than one person droning on for forty minutes.

Back in Corinthians, we can clearly see that the believers were not preparing teachings for their home churches months in advance, in fact it's more than likely no one knew who would be teaching what until they all showed up.

> 1 Corinthians 14:26
> How is it then, brethren? when ye come together, every one of you hath a psalm, hath a doctrine, hath a tongue, hath a revelation, hath an interpretation. Let all things be done unto edifying.

Those whom God inspired sang songs, manifested, taught present truth, and shared what God had been revealing to them that week. The problem was they were all jumping up at the same time and clamouring to be heard. There's plenty of time folks, just enjoy your home church meetings and let everyone do their thing, by course, in order so it's edifying. That's when the word will be fresh and alive and the word will move. Who the fuck wants to sit through boring lifeless horseshit religious ceremonies?

I mean really, that is all churches and ministries offer today - boring religious ceremonies. How do I know? I've sat through thousands of the damn things, from Roman Catholic, Methodist, Free church and Hare Krishna services to home church meetings. If a home church leader is following a teaching curriculum prepared months in advance by counsels of men, they are not walking by the spirit, they are walking by the senses. Christ is not their head, their trust is in the flesh. This is not a patriarchal administration and God no longer has anything to do with temples made with hands.

When you think home church, don't think religious service, think family. How does a family work? Does mom sit there and tell each child when they can speak and when they can't? Home churches are not to be cold and religious, they are to be families, warm places where children can thrive and flourish. The home church leaders are not there to control everyone like some little dictator, they are there to oversee and be an example to God's kids as they learn to walk by the spirit for themselves.

> 1 Peter 5:2,3
> Feed the flock of God which is among you, taking the oversight *thereof,* not by constraint, but willingly; not for filthy lucre, but of a ready mind;
>
> Neither as being lords over *God's* heritage, but being ensamples to the flock.

We're examples over God's heritage like parents are with their children. This isn't about everyone going to a service and listening to some prick prattle on for hours about what he thinks we should be doing, this is about living life as a family with those God has given us to look after. What child isn't excited and comes running home to share the good news when something wonderful happens? Of course we should be running to our home churches with amazing stories of deliverance, and want to teach and manifest, sing songs and read poems. Yes, everything is to be done unto edifying, and that is the home church leader's responsibility, but the other extreme when no one gets to share anything and everyone sits in silence through a pre-arranged religious ceremony is far worse.

This verse we've been looking at in Corinthians is set within the context of running a home church and the proper operation of the manifestations of the gift of holy spirit, so we will now take the time to see how God wants home family church meetings to be conducted.

> 1 Corinthians 12:1
> Now concerning spiritual *gifts,* [pneumatikos - spiritual matters] brethren, I would not have you ignorant.

Concerning things of the spirit, spiritual matters, God does not want us ignorant. How simple is that to understand? I mean, if God wanted us stupid, all he had to do was tell Moses and all the others to shut up and not write the bible. It would have been quite easy for God to keep us ignorant, if that's what he wanted. God doesn't want us ignorant. He had the bible written so we could understand spiritual matters. All we have to do is read it and study it. We don't have to be ignorant of spiritual matters if we don't want to be. How wise we are spiritually is up to us, not God. He wants us wise. Whether you read and study the bible or not is entirely up to you.

Walking *by* the Spirit

1 Corinthians 12:2
Ye know that ye were Gentiles, carried away unto these dumb idols, even as ye were led.

No one goes beyond what they're taught. Did you know the Hare Krishnas grew pig tails because they were taught that God would take them to heaven by grabbing their hair and that if they didn't have a pig tail his hand might slip off their heads and they would be left behind. You can laugh, but really, religion turns people into idiots. Are your beliefs any better? Do you believe Jesus Christ is God? That's just as ridiculous as pig tails. So is believing that when you die you're not really dead you just go somewhere else. It's all pig tails.

Roman Catholics believe that Jesus Christ is God because that's what they are taught. Protestants walk around in fear wondering if God is going to make them sick or kill them because that's what they're taught. The world leads people to these dumb idols. Dumb idols include religious ceremonies conducted by people who walk by the senses and not by the spirit of God. Just because people pray, sing together, and teach from a bible means absolutely nothing. It's all pig tails and dumb idols if people are not walking by the spirit.

When I first started reading the bible, I was clueless. All I had was religious horseshit in my head that I'd picked up from the stupid churches my mother sent me to as a child. One day I was doing something and suddenly realised it was sunday. I thought God was going to kill me for breaking the sabbath and I skulked home cowering beneath the clouds waiting for a lightning bolt to hit me. That's what religion does to you. Christianity is not religion, it's about family, it's about the way of a father with his children. Do parents kill their children for making mistakes? God is my father and he isn't looking for excuses to kill me or make me sick. When I make mistakes, he just smiles, teaches me his word, and on we go again.

I learned later of course that the sabbath isn't sunday anyway, it's saturday, and that in this Administration of Grace we're freed from the law so working the sabbath is no longer an issue. As Jesus Christ taught, the sabbath was made for man, not man for the sabbath. Religion is horseshit that we must scrub from our minds if we're going to enjoy any kind of relationship with our heavenly father.

> 1 Corinthians 12:3
> Wherefore I give you to understand, that no man speaking by the Spirit of God calleth Jesus accursed: and *that* no man can [dunamai] say that Jesus is the Lord, but by the Holy Ghost [pneuma hagion].

God gives us to understand. God doesn't withhold understanding, he gives it, therefore if people have no understanding it isn't God's fault. People who do not read and study the bible have no understanding. That isn't God's fault. Bibles are readily available and anyone can pick one up and start reading it. If we don't, whose fault is that?

> Hosea 4:6a
> My people are destroyed for lack of knowledge:

God's people are destroyed because they walk away from him. It isn't God who walks away, it is people who walk away from him. We do that by rejecting the knowledge in the bible and walking by the senses instead. God gives us to understand, he wants us to be wise. One thing God does not want us ignorant of is that no man who speaks in tongues is cursing Jesus Christ. Paul brought this up by revelation because that was what was circulating through the home churches at that time. People were teaching that when you spoke in tongues you could be cursing Jesus Christ. The devil will try anything to stop people manifesting holy spirit.

> 1 Corinthians 12:3
> Wherefore I give you to understand, that no man speaking by the Spirit of God calleth Jesus accursed: and *that* no man can [dunamai] say that Jesus is the Lord, but by the Holy Ghost [pneuma hagion].

Not only is it impossible to curse Jesus Christ when you speak in tongues, Paul clearly states that it is in fact the ONLY way you can say that Jesus is the Lord. The word *can* is the Greek word *dunamai* from *dunamis*, which is inherent potential power. Holy Ghost should have been translated holy spirit, and it refers to the gift of holy spirit we receive at the time of the new birth. Without having holy spirit no one has the potential power to say that Jesus is their Lord.

Speaking in tongues is the only way to do it. If you want to say Jesus is your Lord, the only way to do it is by holy spirit, which is to speak in tongues. That's what the word says and that's what it means. So all the talk out there about how much people love Jesus is religious horseshit if they do not speak in tongues. The only way anyone can say that Jesus is their lord is by holy spirit.

> 1 Corinthians 12:4-6
> Now there are diversities [diairesis - differences, distinctions] of gifts [charismata], but the same Spirit.
>
> And there are differences [diairesis] of administrations [diakonia], but the same Lord.
>
> And there are diversities [diairesis] of operations [energēma], but it is the same God which worketh [energēo] all in all.

These verses seem quite complicated at first, but they're really quite easy to understand. The context is spiritual matters, pneumatikos, so these all refer to spiritual matters. The gifts of verse 4 is the Greek word *charisma* referring to gifts of God's grace. All the gifts we receive by God's grace are listed in scripture, and there are differences between them. The new birth is a gift and so are the five gift ministries, and clearly there are differences between them. However, there is only one God who gives these gifts.

The Greek word for *administrations* in verse 5 is *diakonia* not *oikonomia* and should be translated *ministries* or *services*. There are different ways we can serve and minister in the body of Christ, but we only have one Lord, the Lord Jesus Christ.

The Greek word for *operations* in verse 6 is *energēma* from which we get such English words as *energy* and *energise*. The operations of verse 6 are energisings of spiritual power within the body of Christ, of which there are many, such as speaking in tongues and healing people. There may be differences between the available energisings of holy spirit, but there is only one God who energises in all of us, as it clearly states in Philippians.

> Philippians 2:13
> For it is God which worketh [energēo - energises] in you both to will and to do of *his* good pleasure.

Paul is building the context here in preparation for teaching about the body of Christ before launching into how to conduct home church meetings, so sit up and pay attention. Follow the logic because it will help you to understand what's coming.

> 1 Corinthians 12:7-10
> But the manifestation of the Spirit is given to every man to profit withal.
>
> For to one is given by the Spirit the word of wisdom; to another the word of knowledge by the same Spirit;
>
> To another faith [believing] by the same Spirit; to another the gifts of healing by the same Spirit;
>
> To another the working of miracles; to another prophecy; to another discerning of spirits; to another *divers* kinds of tongues; to another the interpretation of tongues:

These verses we have already covered in some depth. Each of us has the potential to energise all nine of these manifestations as we choose to believe. Each manifestation has a unique and distinct profit. As we grow in our believing, we will energise more of these manifestations more frequently, and we will enjoy more of the benefits. Verse 11 again emphasises what verses 4-6 teach, that there is only one God who energises in each of us.

> 1 Corinthians 12:11
> But all these worketh [energēo - energises] that one and the selfsame Spirit, dividing to every man severally [idios - his own] as he [the man] will.

Now let's look at the body of Christ.

1 Corinthians 12:12
For as the body is one, and hath many members, and all the members of that one body, being many, are one body: so also *is* Christ.

This figure of speech regarding the body of Christ is a fabulous truth when you understand it. When Christ was here on earth, the bible refers to Israel as his bride. The bride of Christ is entirely different to the body of Christ. Those who confuse the two lack understanding. The bride of Christ is not the body of Christ and the body of Christ has nothing whatsoever to do with the bride of Christ. During the Christ administration while Jesus Christ was alive on earth, his entire ministry was to Israel who are referred to as the bride. However, Israel had Jesus Christ murdered by the Romans, so I guess that's reasonable grounds for divorce. Since the day of Pentecost, in this Administration of Grace, the church of God is no longer referred to as the bride of Christ, it is referred to as the body of Christ. What's the difference? Track with me here, because there is some sensational new light on the way.

I hear people today wish they'd been with Jesus while he was alive. Man, those people are ignorant. If folks understood the difference between the bride of Christ and the body of Christ they wouldn't wish for such things. If they were somehow granted their wish and went back in time, Jesus Christ would have had fuck all to do with them unless they were a Judean.

Matthew 15:22-28
And, behold, a woman of Canaan came out of the same coasts, and cried unto him, saying, Have mercy on me, O Lord, *thou* Son of David; my daughter is grievously vexed with a devil.

But he answered her not a word. And his disciples came and besought him, saying, Send her away; for she crieth after us.

But he answered and said, I am not sent but unto the lost sheep of the house of Israel.

Then came she and worshipped him, saying, Lord, help me.

But he answered and said, It is not meet to take the children's bread, and to cast *it* to dogs.

And she said, Truth, Lord: yet the dogs eat of the crumbs which fall from their masters' table.

Then Jesus answered and said unto her, O woman, great *is* thy faith [believing]: be it unto thee even as thou wilt. And her daughter was made whole from that very hour.

If you think this is horrible, you have no understanding of what the mystery really means to us in this Administration. Back in the old testament and during the gospels, us gentiles were dogs, and God's people would have nothing to do with us. We were animals to be avoided. Yes, you could become a proselyte if you gave up everything including your culture, your family, your friends, and your country, but it wasn't an easy thing to do. If you doubt me, go and read the book of Ruth. That woman became a proselyte and you can clearly see what it cost her. So don't waste your life wishing you'd been with Jesus, he would have had nothing to do with you and his disciples would have sent you away.

Romans 15:8
Now I say that Jesus Christ was a minister of [to] the circumcision for the truth of God, to confirm the promises *made* unto the fathers:

Perhaps now you might be a little more thankful for what God accomplished for us in Jesus Christ when he raised him from the dead.

Ephesians 2:11-15
Wherefore remember, that ye *being* in time past Gentiles in the flesh, who are called Uncircumcision by that which is called the Circumcision in the flesh made by hands;

That at that time ye were without Christ, being aliens from the commonwealth of Israel, and strangers from the covenants of promise, having no hope, and without God in the world:

But now in Christ Jesus ye who sometimes were far off are made nigh by the blood of Christ.

For he is our peace, who hath made both one, and hath broken down the middle wall of partition *between us;*

Having abolished in his flesh the enmity, *even* the law of commandments *contained* in ordinances; for to make in himself of twain one new man, *so* making peace;

When God raised Jesus Christ from the dead, us Gentiles were reconciled to God in one body with the Israelites. Christ is our peace who abolished the enmity between us and brought us into the presence of God. Since the day of Pentecost, even us Gentiles can be born again and be a part of the body of Christ. How amazing is that?

Before I started writing this session of the class, I became more than a little concerned because I saw I was going to have to handle this subject of the bride and the body of Christ. I was concerned because I didn't really understand the difference between the two figures of speech. I mean, a bride? All that figure of speech put in my head was a silly picture of Jesus walking around with a woman in a long white dress. A figure of speech is supposed to give us mind pictures to emphasise spiritual truths, but in my heart I knew that wasn't the picture God intended. This concerned me so much, I decided not to teach it. Then one morning while preparing for this session, I saw that there was no way to avoid it.

A couple of pages into this teaching, plodding towards the bride and the body with some reluctance, I found myself one afternoon listening to an old teaching by Dr Wierwille entitled The Bride and the Bridegroom. At first, I didn't realise how timely it was. I'd been working through all his old live audio teachings and this just happened to be the next one. A few minutes into the teaching, I suddenly realised where we were and my mind sat up and paid attention. Maybe, I thought, I'd learn something.

Now don't get me wrong. I've studied this topic hundreds of times and know as much about it as anyone else on the planet. I know all about the differences in administrations, Christ's ministry being to Israel, and about Christ in us the hope of glory. The thing I didn't understand was why God chose those two figures of speech depicting the church of Israel as a bride and the church of grace as a body. Why use a bride and a body? What has a woman in a white dress got to do with Christ? What was God talking about? I knew it had to be deeper than I understood it.

About half way through the teaching, God showed me a picture in a moment of time that cleared it all up. He showed me a blackboard with chalk drawings on it, just like in a classroom at school. On one side was a small chalk circle representing Christ with a line drawn to a big chalk circle filled with little chalk marks representing the people of Israel. On the other side of the blackboard was a small circle representing Christ with loads of small circles below him all with a single chalk mark within representing a single believer. This image shows you what God showed me.

This picture was only in my mind for a split second, but that was all it took to show me the difference between the bride of Christ and the body of Christ. Israel were all inside one big circle and Christ was their bridegroom - he married the whole bunch of them as one unit. We all have Christ in us and so he is joined to each one of us individually, and we are all joined to him in one body. We all make up the body of Christ as individuals, not as one huge group. By the way, this is an excellent example of how revelation manifestations energise within us.

The revelation manifestations are word of knowledge, word of wisdom, and discerning of spirits. God communicates with us by revelation. His word is revelation so we are expected to know that first. When you know the word, God can and will show you additional things by sight, by hearing, by smell, by taste, or by touch. He will communicate with you personally, and as you walk by the spirit and develop your abilities you will learn to recognise when God is telling you something. He regularly tells me things by revelation. While I'm writing these class sessions he always lets me know when the first draft is complete by filling me with a deep peaceful feeling inside. That's his way of letting me know the session is complete and it's time to knock it into shape and sort it out for publishing. That deep peaceful feeling inside is his way of telling me a job is done. When I'm ministering for example I keep going until I get that peace.

Another example of revelation is when I feel sick inside. It's God's way of letting me know something is wrong and I need to speak in tongues. I don't know what the problem is or what it is I'm praying for, but I speak in tongues and pray perfectly until the sick feeling goes away.

Another way he gives revelation is with compassion that wells up inside. That's often the green light to get involved in situations and help someone. Without that compassion welling up inside, I don't minister. Neither did Jesus Christ for that matter. When God welled up that compassion within him, he moved and he ministered. That was his green light to feed the five thousand and heal the leper. Without that green light he would not have moved, understand?

> Matthew 15:32
> Then Jesus called his disciples *unto him*, and said, I have compassion on the multitude, because they continue with me now three days, and have nothing to eat: and I will not send them away fasting, lest they faint in the way.

> Mark 1:40-42
> And there came a leper to him, beseeching him, and kneeling down to him, and saying unto him, If thou wilt, thou canst make me clean.

> And Jesus, moved with compassion, put forth *his* hand, and touched him, and saith unto him, I will; be thou clean.

> And as soon as he had spoken, immediately the leprosy departed from him, and he was cleansed.

Compassion, peace, and feeling sick inside are also normal human emotions. God doesn't work outside the framework of the senses realm, he works within it otherwise we wouldn't have a clue what he was saying. What we have to learn when we begin to walk by the spirit is to differentiate between our emotions and when God is giving us revelation. It isn't difficult, but it isn't automatic. We have to learn to walk by the spirit. We take the steps and as we stumble forwards we learn how to keep our balance and eventually we learn how to run the race with patience.

Hebrews 5:13,14
For every one that useth milk *is* unskilful in the word of righteousness: for he is a babe.

But strong meat belongeth to them that are of full age, *even* those who by reason of use have their senses exercised to discern both good and evil.

Hebrews 12:1
Wherefore seeing we also are compassed about with so great a cloud of witnesses, let us lay aside every weight, and the sin which doth so easily beset *us,* and let us run with patience the race that is set before us,

God will talk to you on your level and communicate with you in ways you will understand. Revelation is very personal, it's the way of a father with his children. Ah, and there's the peaceful feeling inside letting me know that's enough on revelation for the time being and it's time to move on. Now read the following verses in Corinthians regarding the body of Christ in this new light.

1 Corinthians 12:13-27
For by one Spirit are we all baptized into one body, whether *we be* Jews [Judeans] or Gentiles, whether *we be* bond or free; and have been all made to drink into one Spirit.

For the body is not one member, but many.

If the foot shall say, Because I am not the hand, I am not of the body; is it therefore not of the body?

And if the ear shall say, Because I am not the eye, I am not of the body; is it therefore not of the body?

If the whole body *were* an eye, where *were* the hearing? If the whole *were* hearing, where *were* the smelling?

But now hath God set the members every one of them in the body, as it hath pleased him.

And if they were all one member, where *were* the body?

But now *are they* many members, yet but one body.

And the eye cannot say unto the hand, I have no need of thee: nor again the head to the feet, I have no need of you.

Nay, much more those members of the body, which seem to be more feeble, are necessary:

And those *members* of the body, which we think to be less honourable, upon these we bestow more abundant honour; and our uncomely *parts* have more abundant comeliness.

For our comely *parts* have no need: but God hath tempered the body together, having given more abundant honour to that *part* which lacked:

That there should be no schism in the body; but *that* the members should have the same care one for another.

And whether one member suffer, all the members suffer with it; or one member be honoured, all the members rejoice with it.

Now ye are the body of Christ, and members in particular.

Remember, the body of Christ is not some man-made religious structure, so this is absolutely not referring to positions of administration or prominence within any organisation or ministry of any kind. According to verse 13, the body of Christ comprises individuals who have the gift of holy spirit and have been called out from among both Judeans and Gentiles, bond or free (a reference to Roman social class distinctions). The functioning body of Christ is those of us who walk by the spirit with Christ as our head, it is not some religious organisation run by men who walk by their senses.

If Christ is our head, then it does not matter if I don't know you and you don't know me as Christ knows both of us. You may live in Africa and I in Scotland, but as we both walk by the spirit with Christ as our head we are like minded, and we are edifying the body of Christ together, in one accord. We don't have to be part of some man-made ministry in order to be in one accord. Being like minded has nothing whatsoever to do with getting along with everyone in some crappy temple made with hands. Getting along with people is a senses ability and there is nothing spiritual about it. I don't get along with very many people at all. When you've spent the majority of your ministering life confronting God's people with the word because they're full of fucking religious horseshit, it doesn't tend to make you very popular and I'm extremely comfortable with that.

Bearing all this in mind, read the next verses very carefully, noting that the context now specifically deals with **in the church**.

> 1 Corinthians 12:28-31
> And God hath set some **in the church**, first apostles, secondarily prophets, thirdly teachers, after that miracles, then gifts of healings, helps, governments, diversities of tongues.
>
> *Are* all apostles? *are* all prophets? *are* all teachers? *are* all workers of miracles?
>
> Have all the gifts of healing? do all speak with tongues? do all interpret?
>
> But covet earnestly the best gifts: and yet shew I unto you a more excellent way.

As the context of the verses is clearly marked as **in the church**, they cannot be taken out of that context. In the church means exactly what it says, in the church. These verses are referring to church meetings. As the church of God comprises people who are born again, called out from among both Judeans and Gentiles and as such are part of the body of Christ, these verses exclusively deal with how we conduct church meetings. We are now dealing specifically with how to conduct church meetings in our homes.

No ministry or religion or organisation constructed by men can claim to be the church of God because ekklēsia cannot be used in that context. This means, of course, that the Roman Catholic church, the Way International, the Methodist church, the Baptist church, the Jehovah's Witnesses, the Anglicans, the Salvation Army and every other religious organisation on earth are not the church of God. When people who are born again go to these places they are not going to church, they are the church wasting their lives attending broken cisterns.

As an aside here, did you know that the founder of the Salvation Army, William Booth was a 33rd degree freemason who was financed by the Rothschilds? The Rothschilds are the vatican bankers. In essence, Booth was financed by the vatican to found and establish the Salvation Army in 1865. But why? Being a charity, the Salvation Army's income can't be tracked because on paper it's all voluntary contributions. The Salvation Army is a criminal front that was used to launder vatican drug money being landed in London by the East India Company. Drug money went in as charitable contributions and came out the other side laundered and clean. And stupid christians actually work for them and send money to the fuckers. Can you believe that?

> 1 Corinthians 12:18
> But now hath God set the members every one of them in the body, as it hath pleased him.

This verse simply can't be used by any organisation to teach that God places people in administrative roles within their ministry because they are the body of Christ. God has nothing whatsoever to do with placing people in jobs within any religious organisations. They advertise, they hold interviews, they read CVs, they conduct meetings, and then they select the people best suited for the available jobs. That is walking by the senses. Just because they pray and ask God for guidance doesn't turn walking by the senses into walking by the spirit. Sure, God can give you revelation regarding employing someone if you need it, but don't confuse walking by the senses with walking by the spirit.

No ministry anywhere on earth can claim to be the church of God or the body of Christ. To take these scriptures and teach that a church, religion or ministry constructed by men is the body of Christ and that everyone in their organisation is there because God placed them in the body where it pleased him is criminal misrepresentation of scripture. Come out from among them and be ye separate saith God, and touch not the unclean thing and I will receive you. God's arms are open. Come out of the world's religious dungeons my brothers and sisters in Christ and be free again, let living waters flow from you and walk as a son or daughter of God. Back to the church.

> 1 Corinthians 12:28
> And God hath set some **in the church**, first apostles, secondarily prophets, thirdly teachers, after that miracles [dunamis], then gifts of healings, helps, governments, diversities of tongues.

This verse has had me baffled for decades and it was only while working this session that I understood what it's talking about. I mean, how can apostles be more important than prophets, and prophets be more important than teachers? And why is there no mention of evangelists or pastors? This never made any sense to me until I finally realised the context, that we are *in the church*. We are dealing with how to conduct churches in our homes. This isn't God playing favourites because God is no respecter of persons and all the gift ministries are just as important as any others. So what's it talking about? This isn't about importance, it's about progression. This is the order in which we are to run our home church meetings.

An apostle is someone who has been given a gift ministry. It isn't a gift to the man, it is a gift to the body. As such, it is a spiritual gift which means that when an apostle is energised there is flowing of living waters from him. The context of the chapter was set in verse one as spiritual matters so we are still discussing spiritual matters. The energising of a gift ministry is a spiritual matter. Specifically though, the context has tuned in to home church meetings. We are concerning ourselves now with spiritual matters as they relate to the running of home churches.

So, what is the first thing we should be doing at our home church meetings? Praying? Manifestations? Singing? Announcements? We don't have to guess, the word tells us. The word says apostles who have new light teach first. This is how we open home church meetings. New light is taught first. Now, isn't it amazing and refreshing to realise that the teaching of the word is to be first in our churches, not last.

Now although apostles bring new light to their generation, this does not mean that it always has to be new light to the world. Remember, there were new believers turning up every week at those home churches in Corinth, so new light would have needed to be taught every week to them. It wouldn't have been new light to the disciples necessarily, but it would certainly have been new light to the new believers. What were they teaching? Scripts prepared months earlier at the headquarters of man-made temples? I don't think so. They taught what needed to be taught as God energised in them to will and to do of his good pleasure.

As new believers turned up every week, the needs would have been constantly changing. That's why we must be in the present truth and be walking by the spirit. When you have a counsel of men mandating what is to be taught for the next year throughout their entire ministry, you are not walking by the spirit and living in the present truth, you're walking by the senses and putting your trust in men. We teach what God wants taught and quite often you won't know what that is until it's time to teach, just as Peter didn't know what he was going to teach later that day when he got up early on Pentecost and was stuffing his face with breakfast. What we teach will obviously vary from home church to home church depending on the need. We move with God, not counsels of men.

Once any new light has been taught, then the prophets get their turn. If there is stuff that needs confronting and sorting out, that comes next. With new people constantly coming through the doors with all their bad habits and crappy thoughts, this is perhaps more important than you might at first think. Home churches were not there to cater to disciples who turned up every week full of shit that needed sorting out because they were too fucking lazy to keep themselves in the word. Disciples are to be strong in the Lord, ready to help new believers. If you want to be a disciple, get out of those horseshit temples you hold so dear, establish a church in your home, and teach and minister.

After the apostles and prophets have done their thing, then comes teaching. New believers would require much teaching. Remember, none of this has been prearranged by anyone. Christ is the head over all things to the church and it is God who energises all in all. Whoever God has inspired to teach, they take the floor next. In Corinth every home church began with a number of exciting, relevant teachings.

Why aren't evangelists mentioned? Well, evangelists don't go to a home church to evangelise, they do that out in the world. A home church meeting is not the place to witness to new people! See how beautifully this all fits together? Why are pastors not mentioned? Sit up and pay attention, because this is mind blowing. Pastors take care of disciples who have been beaten up in the spiritual competition. Figuratively speaking, they patch up hurt disciples and care for them until they're fit to get back out into the fight. So why are they not mentioned here? Well, brace yourself, it's because home church meetings are not the place for pastors to do their thing. Home church meetings are where the children learn the word and learn how to walk by the spirit.

Adults are to take care of their stuff away from the kids. If you're beat up and discouraged and feeling hurt because you've been taking the world on and it's dumped shit all over you, that's okay, it happens, we're human. God still loves you, go and find a pastor, someone who can help you, and get sorted out behind the scenes. Don't let the kids see you like that.

As parents and adults do we go to our kids with our problems and dump it on them? No, of course not, it wouldn't be profitable for them. See how this works? That's why pastors are not mentioned here. And one more thing, a home church meeting is not the place for fucked up disciples who are too lazy to keep themselves in the word. If that's all your life is, don't come to my home church or I'll kick you out the fucking door. If you're a disciple and come to my home church, you come prepared and ready to give, you come ready to help me look after the kids and help me teach them to walk by the spirit by being an example.

> 1 Corinthians 12:28
> And God hath set some in the church, first apostles, secondarily prophets, thirdly teachers, after that miracles [**dunamis**], then gifts of healings, helps, governments, diversities of tongues.

After the word had been taught, the churches moved into miracles and healings. Miracles is the Greek word *dunamis* which means power, inherent potential power. What is this talking about? It's talking about manifestations of holy spirit.

> Acts 1:8
> But ye shall receive **power [dunamis]**, after that the Holy Ghost [pneuma hagion] is come upon you: and ye shall be witnesses unto me both in Jerusalem, and in all Judaea, and in Samaria, and unto the uttermost part of the earth.

> Acts 10:38
> How God anointed Jesus of Nazareth with the Holy Ghost [pneuma hagion] and with **power [dunamis]**: who went about doing good, and healing all that were oppressed of the devil; for God was with him.

> Romans 15:19
> Through mighty signs and wonders, by the **power [dunamis]** of the Spirit of God; so that from Jerusalem, and round about unto Illyricum, I have fully preached the gospel of Christ.

This power obviously includes speaking in tongues with interpretation and prophecy. So, right after the teaching of the word you have manifestations. When I went to home churches in the past, I sometimes used to struggle to get myself into the right frame of mind to manifest. More often than not I simply was not in the right frame of mind and I had to work my mind beforehand so I was ready. The word was always last in those meetings. Now that it's first, I find that after hearing the word I'm fired up and ready by the time we get to manifestations. It is at this point in a home church meeting that the believers manifested tongues with interpretation and prophecy, and operated revelation and power manifestations to help people who needed it. This all followed the teaching of the word.

Why do you think God gave us nine manifestations? They are there so we can minister the power of God to those who need it. New people coming through the doors means problem after problem coming through the doors as people escape from the world. What are you going to do? Tell them to sign up for a fucking class and make them wait weeks or months thinking a stupid fucking class is going to help them? Get in there and minister, get that gift of holy spirit energised and go and have some fun in life. Let's get the word moving again.

Okay, people need ministering to, so who does the ministering? People nominated by the home church leader? Or those inspired by God? Is Christ our head or is our home church leader our head? We follow the direction of our home church leaders, yes, but they are not our head. When it comes to manifestations and walking by the spirit, Christ is our head, not men. We don't wait for our home church leaders to tell us what to do, we walk by the spirit with Christ as our head. If you're at a home church meeting and you see someone with a need and God moves compassion within you to help them, that's your green light. Fuck the home church leader, go and minister.

Who sent Ananias to go see Paul? His home church leader or Jesus Christ? Ananias would not even have checked with his home church leader before heading over to the street called Straight.

> Acts 9:10-12,17
> And there was a certain disciple at Damascus, named Ananias; and to him said the Lord in a vision, Ananias. And he said, Behold, I *am here*, Lord.
>
> And the Lord *said* unto him, Arise, and go into the street which is called Straight, and enquire in the house of Judas for *one* called Saul, of Tarsus: for, behold, he prayeth,
>
> And hath seen in a vision a man named Ananias coming in, and putting *his* hand on him, that he might receive his sight.
>
> And Ananias went his way, and entered into the house; and putting his hands on him said, Brother Saul, the Lord, *even* Jesus, that appeared unto thee in the way as thou camest, hath sent me, that thou mightest receive thy sight, and be filled with the Holy Ghost.

Do you think Ananias' home church leader would have been pissed off with him for not checking through him first before heading over to see

Paul? Had Ananias been so religious and stupid, I think Christ might have found someone else to send.

> 1 Corinthians 12:28
> And God hath set some in the church, first apostles, secondarily prophets, thirdly teachers, after that miracles, then gifts of healings, helps, governments, diversities of tongues.

Helps refers to support. This is where singing songs and reading poems would be beneficial. Have you ever noticed how a song sung on the lips of a believer can be healing? This is where folks can play their guitars and minister the healing power of God through music.

> 1 Samuel 16:23
> And it came to pass, when the *evil* spirit from God was upon Saul, that David took an harp, and played with his hand: so Saul was refreshed, and was well, and the evil spirit departed from him.

Support would also include taking care of any needs any disciples or new believers might have, like jobs and making sure everyone is taken care of. This is where the home church leader might use some of the tithe money to help someone through a difficult time. We have to learn to take care of people and have all things common or the word will never move. The home churches have to learn to look after each other so everyone always has all their need met.

> Acts 2:44-47
> And all that believed were together, and had all things common;
>
> And sold their possessions and goods, and parted them to all *men*, as every man had need.
>
> And they, continuing daily with one accord in the temple, and breaking bread from house to house, did eat their meat with gladness and singleness of heart,
>
> Praising God, and having favour with all the people. And the Lord added to the church daily such as should be saved.

This doesn't mean we carry lazy people, it means we walk by the spirit and every situation will be different. Only by walking by the spirit can this be accomplished. Walking by the senses will lead you into ditches filled with the blind. We're not here to start another welfare system. Compassion can help us to understand this.

> 1 John 3:17
> But whoso hath this world's good, and seeth his brother have need, and shutteth up his bowels *of compassion* from him, how dwelleth the love of God in him?

If God moves your bowels he is filling you with compassion to help someone. If you don't do it, how dwells the love of God in you? This isn't about being stupid and giving all your money away, it's about walking by the spirit. Manifesting the love of God isn't about being religious, sweet and sickly with everyone you meet, it's about walking by the spirit and doing what God wants done. This can only work if we all walk by the spirit with Christ as our head. One day God may fill you with compassion to buy a family a week's groceries. If you are filled with compassion, you have the money, you see the need but you decide to keep the money for yourself, how dwells the love of God in you? God wants you to help that family but you're so greedy you want to keep all your money to yourself? How dwells the love of God in you? However, if there is no compassion yet you give all your money away, you're just being religious and stupid.

Another time God may tell you to buy someone new clothes so they will be presentable at a job interview. Another time he may tell you to confront someone in the home church for lying and they might drop dead right there in front of you.

> Acts 5:8-11
> And Peter answered unto her, Tell me whether ye sold the land for so much? And she said, Yea, for so much.
>
> Then Peter said unto her, How is it that ye have agreed together to tempt the Spirit of the Lord? behold, the feet of them which have buried thy husband *are* at the door, and shall carry thee out.

Walking *by* the Spirit

> Then fell she down straightway at his feet, and yielded up the ghost: and the young men came in, and found her dead, and, carrying *her* forth, buried *her* by her husband.
>
> And great fear [awe and respect] came upon all the church, and upon as many as heard these things.

If we don't walk by the spirit, this whole church of the body thing simply will not work. Running a home church isn't something we can make rules about or they will turn into religious ceremonies filled with sweet plastic smiles. We must all walk by the spirit and learn to keep the grievous wolves who want to control everything away from us and our people.

Terminology has a great deal to do with this. For example, what is fellowship? This may seem like a silly question, but do you know what fellowship actually is? What comes into your mind when you hear the word fellowship spoken or see it written? What does the word convey to you? Is it a place where you go to get into the word with others? If so, your perceptions of the word are absolutely wrong. Not once anywhere in the church epistles or in the book of Acts is a home church referred to as a home fellowship. Home churches are home churches, they are not home fellowships. Why is this distinction important? Well, let's take a look at it.

> 1 John 1:3
> That which we have seen and heard declare we unto you, that ye also may have fellowship with us: and truly our fellowship *is* with the Father, and with his Son Jesus Christ.

Is fellowship somewhere you go twice a week? Is fellowship somewhere you go to congregate with other believers? Not according to the bible it isn't. Fellowship is our relationship with God our father and with his son Jesus Christ. Fellowship isn't somewhere you go to, it's something you live everyday with your father. If you are a disciple walking by the spirit you are in fellowship. We go to a home church not to have fellowship, but to help new believers learn how to have fellowship every day with their father just as we do. Our purpose in life isn't to go to a home *fellowship* twice a week and sit through a fucking ceremony, it is to have fellowship with God and his son Jesus Christ all day every day.

> Ecclesiastes 12:13
> Let us hear the conclusion of the whole matter: Fear God, and keep his commandments: for this *is* the whole *duty* of man.

> 2 Corinthians 10:5
> Casting down imaginations, and every high thing that exalteth itself against the knowledge of God, and bringing into captivity every thought to the obedience of Christ;

Bringing every thought captive to the obedience of Christ is walking by the spirit every moment of every day. It is having fellowship with God and with Jesus Christ. We don't go anywhere to have fellowship, it is a way of life. We have to start calling our home churches what the bible calls them and stop calling them fellowships. The church of God who walk by the spirit are in fellowship with God, they live in fellowship with God every day. Note also that not only do we have daily fellowship with God, but we also have daily fellowship with his son Jesus Christ. Keep this in mind, because it's going to be coming up later.

> 1 Corinthians 12:28
> And God hath set some in the church, first apostles, secondarily prophets, thirdly teachers, after that miracles, then gifts of healings, helps, governments, diversities of tongues.

Governments refers to leadership stuff, where the church leaders keep folks informed of what's going on in their area. You know, announcements. With so many believers coming and going, and so many new believers turning up every week, it was important for the churches in Corinth to keep everyone up to date with home church activities. If day trips were planned it would require planning and preparation so everyone knew where to meet up and at what time and had an idea of what to bring with them. If they were all going to meet up at the amphitheatre for a show, folks would need to know the details. If special teachings or classes were planned, venues and times would need to be sorted out so everyone was happy. It is at this juncture in a home church meeting that all this stuff is discussed.

To close the meetings, they had diversity of tongues. Why isn't interpretation mentioned? God didn't want it mentioned because this isn't talking about tongues with interpretation, it's talking about diversity of tongues. We've already had manifestations earlier in the meeting, remember? So what's this talking about? Remember all those new believers who had come to their first meeting and had just heard the most amazing word of God taught and had seen the power of God in manifestation? Well, now it was their turn. Leading new believers into speaking in tongues is to be a part of every home church meeting. Practice sessions to get them fluent with speaking in tongues is a big part of this. That's what diversities of tongues refers to here. People need to practice speaking in tongues together, and the home churches are the places to do it. When new believers come, we are to lead them into speaking in tongues before everyone leaves.

Reading these verses I get the impression that home church meetings were perhaps a little bigger than we're used to. Sure, in our living rooms perhaps we can only fit in up to a dozen people, but back in the middle east in the 1st Century a lot of homes surrounded a central courtyard, so it leads me to think that their home churches may have had in the region of 20-40 disciples or more, plus all their new believers. With new people turning up all the time, there would have been a great need to keep splitting home churches to keep things manageable. Again, walking by the spirit is the key but I think we should raise our sights and perhaps believe for bigger living rooms. This isn't about one person controlling everything, it's about God giving gift ministries where they are needed so the word will live. Perhaps it's time to buy a few stacks of comfortable chairs so we can pack people in and make a real joyful noise.

Now remember, none of this is to be religious or ceremonious in nature. Keeping religion out of a home church is the home church leader's responsibility. Keep things vibrant, fresh and alive and the word will live. And isn't it remarkable to note that churches all over the world today do things backwards and put the word last after all their ceremonial horseshit. I guess we have the vatican to thank for that, as usual.

> 1 Corinthians 12:29-31
> *Are* all apostles? *are* all prophets? *are* all teachers? *are* all workers of miracles?

Have all the gifts of healing? do all speak with tongues? do all interpret?

But covet earnestly the best gifts: and yet shew I unto you a more excellent way.

Not everyone is an apostle or a prophet, are they? In our home churches does every person there speak in tongues and interpret? If you had forty people there you'd be at it all night. No, not everyone speaks in tongues and interprets at a home church meeting even though everyone there who was instructed in the manifestations of holy spirit could, see it? Another thing, it's those who are inspired at the time who are given the opportunity to manifest, not a few picked out a day earlier by the home church leader when he was putting his little ceremony together. Christ is our head, not men, don't ever forget that.

64. The Council of Acts 15

I've heard quite a few teachings on the council of Acts 15, and listened to equally great men of God teach different perspectives and viewpoints often contradicting each other. This is the first time I've ever taught on the council of Acts 15 and I'm only doing so because I was given the green light as well as a little new light. Strap yourselves in because this is going to rattle some heads and change some hearts.

Until now all the arguments, discussions and teachings I've listened to regarding the council of Acts 15 have been from the perspective of leadership struggles within the church. Well, I'm going to teach it from a different perspective, the truth that God no longer dwells in temples made with hands. If we keep this in mind and recognise that God's church comprises people and not any building or church or religion or organisation or ministry, Acts 15 falls into place with a clarity so stunning it is shocking.

> Acts 15:1
> And certain men which came down from Judaea taught the brethren, *and said*, Except ye be circumcised after the manner of Moses, ye cannot be saved.

To set the stage, Paul and Barnabas had been moving the word while travelling around Asia during what some now refer to as Paul's first missionary journey. They began back in Antioch of Syria, sailed to Cyprus, where they taught the word to Sergius Paulus and confronted Elymas the sorcerer. Later, they sailed to Perga in Pamphylia, where John departed from them. Paul and Barnabas then travelled to Antioch in Pisidia, where the next sabbath day came almost the whole city together to hear the word of God. From there Paul and Barnabas travelled to Iconium, then onto Lystra and Derbe. While at Lystra, Paul healed a man who had been a cripple from birth. The people were astonished and declared that Paul and Barnabas were gods come down from heaven in the likeness of men. After some persecution, Paul was stoned and dragged out of the city and left for dead. Later he returned to Lystra, Iconium and Antioch in Pisidia, then passed through Pamphylia to Perga, took ship and sailed back to Antioch in Syria, where the word says Paul and Barnabas abode a long time with the disciples.

Then these men from Judea showed up, infiltrated the home churches and taught that unless the Gentiles were circumcised they could not be saved. Who were these men? Who sent them? Why were they there? On whose authority were they acting? What made them think they had the right to march in there and start teaching? What made them think they knew better than Paul? Were they walking by the spirit? If God didn't send them, who did? We must ask these questions because they are important.

> Acts 15:2
> When therefore Paul and Barnabas had no small dissension and disputation with them, they determined [tassō] that Paul and Barnabas, and certain other of them, should go up to Jerusalem unto the apostles and elders about this question.

No small dissension and disputation, means heated and lengthy arguments and debates. Voices were raised, eyes locked as Paul and Barnabas took those men on. They obviously weren't listening to Paul, were they? Why not? This is the question we must ask. Who was walking by the spirit here and who was walking by the direction and counsel of men?

With no resolution in sight, *they* determined that Paul and Barnabas and certain others of them should go up to Jerusalem. The word *they* is a pronoun so we must be clear on exactly who the pronoun *they* refers to. Does it refer to Paul? No, it does not. It says *they*, and if you track back through the verse you will see that *they* relates itself to the preceding word *them* which is a pronoun referring to the men which came down from Judea. If the pronoun referred back to Paul and Barnabas, the next closest nouns, and we insert their names into the verse it doesn't make sense. Look at it.

When therefore Paul and Barnabas had no small dissension and disputation with them, Paul and Barnabas determined that Paul and Barnabas, and certain other of them, should go up to Jerusalem unto the apostles and elders about this question.

See, that's nonsense. The pronoun refers back to the men from Judea.

When therefore Paul and Barnabas had no small dissension and disputation with them, the men from Judea, they, the men from Judea determined that Paul and Barnabas, and certain other of them, should go up to Jerusalem unto the apostles and elders about this question.

Now your bible makes sense. It was the men who came down from Judea who determined that Paul and Barnabas and certain others of them should go up to Jerusalem to see the apostles and elders. This decision by those men from Judea was absolutely not based on revelation. Those men were not walking by the spirit, because if they were, they would not have been arguing with Paul.

The word *determined* is the Greek word tassō, to arrange, to appoint, to determine. In other words, this was a senses decision based on senses reasoning. Those men from Judea had already substituted walking by the spirit with walking by the counsel of men. That is how energised ministries turn their backs on the fountain of living waters and hew them out broken cisterns that can hold no water. They substitute the energising of holy spirit with walking by the senses. Instead of Christ being their head, they make decisions determined by counsels of men. No doubt they quoted old testament scriptures at Paul and Barnabas, and lectured them from Proverbs.

> Proverbs 11:14
> Where no counsel *is*, the people fall: but in the multitude of counsellors *there is* safety.

In the old testament people did not have spirit generally available, they were as sheep without a shepherd, so they needed men and women around who had spirit upon them to be their shepherds, like Samuel, Moses, Isaiah, Huldah the prophetess and all the others. As they had no spirit of their own, the people held counsels where they would make the best decisions they could based on their knowledge of scripture. This of course required leadership structures with prominent men and women stepping in to make final decisions that affected everyone. When they couldn't find solutions, they would go to a man or woman of God who had spirit for their answers. That is absolutely not how things work in this administration. We all have spirit and we are all to walk by the spirit and not by the senses. When these men from Judea saw that Paul and Barnabas were not going to listen to them, they, the men from Judea told Paul and Barnabas to go to Jerusalem so the ministry leadership could sort them out. They were sending Paul and Barnabas to be disciplined by the ministry leadership for not submitting themselves and not heeding the reproof and correction they were given.

There is definitely a conflict here between believers who walked by the senses and believers who walked by the spirit. Now, we must understand that the book of Acts records the transition from law to grace and that it took time for the believers to adjust. On the day of Pentecost a new administration began and the rules changed. The believers didn't know about these changes as yet, so they continued in their old ways until the details of the new administration were gradually revealed. It all took time.

For example, Peter didn't take the word to the Gentiles until 15-25 years after the day of Pentecost, and it took revelation to get through to him to do so. Years after the day of Pentecost, not one of the believers was taking the word to the Gentiles even though it had been available since Pentecost. See, it took time to get the old administration out of their heads and get the new principles of the Grace Administration into their thinking and believing.

Even after Acts 10, Paul had to confront Peter to his face because his heart was still bogged down in Judean old testament horseshit regarding Gentiles.

> Galatians 2:11-13
> But when Peter was come to Antioch, I withstood him to the face, because he was to be blamed.
>
> For before that certain came from James, he did eat with the Gentiles: but when they were come, he withdrew and separated himself, fearing them which were of the circumcision.

> And the other Jews [Judeans] dissembled likewise with him; insomuch that Barnabas also was carried away with their dissimulation.

People need time to change, it doesn't happen overnight. Heck, it's taken me 35 years to finally see the truth that God does not dwell in temples made with hands. I've read that scripture thousands of times but it was only very recently I understood what it was saying. We can't read the book of Acts and make sense of it without understanding that people needed time to change. Understanding this helps us to make sense of the council of Acts 15, and why Peter and the other apostles were still wrapped up in this horseshit dribbling out of Jerusalem. We need to understand that they were still transitioning from law to grace and they still had old testament principles engrained in their thinking and believing. Those men from Judea were hanging onto the Law Administration principles of circumcision and walking by the counsel of men.

Acts 15 isn't showing us leadership struggles, it's showing us how the devil constructs temples made with hands over energised ministries and transforms them into religious horseshit. The church in Jerusalem had constructed layers of leadership within a man-made ministry which they expected God's church to submit to and obey. Those men from Judea were obviously quite high up in the ranks, and probably had real flashy nametags. Well, who is our head? The elders at Jerusalem? A board of Directors? Or is it Christ? Make up your mind.

If we put our trust in men and women who walk by their senses we will be disappointed in our expectations. Walking by the flesh is a guaranteed path of frustration and defeat. When we submit to men rather than to Christ, when we walk by what leadership structures of men direct rather than by the spirit, then we turn our backs on the fountain of living waters and hew out a broken cistern.

Paul, of course walked by the spirit and knew those men from Judea were full of horseshit. Now let's get one thing very clear here - Paul did not go up to Jerusalem because those men from Judea told him to, he went up by revelation. When all was said and done and those men from Judea told him to go to Jerusalem and get himself sorted out by his *leadership*, Paul went to God for guidance and God gave him the green light to go. Paul didn't go to Jerusalem because those men from Judea determined it, but because he walked by the spirit and God told him to go. Galatians refers to this record in Acts 15 and tells us exactly that.

> Galatians 2:1,2
> Then fourteen years after I went up again to Jerusalem with Barnabas, and took Titus with *me* also.
>
> And I went up by revelation, and communicated unto them that gospel which I preach among the Gentiles, but privately to them which were of reputation, lest by any means I should run, or had run, in vain.

This revelation was only given to Paul, it wasn't given to a counsel of men. When God gives revelation, does he give the same revelation to a bunch of people all at the same time? No, that's not how revelation works. That's why the pronoun *them* in Acts 15:2 cannot refer to Paul and Barnabas. Paul didn't go up to Jerusalem because a counsel of men determined it, but because he went to God and got revelation. Go and search the scriptures. God only gives revelation to individuals.

> Acts 8:29
> Then the Spirit said unto Philip, Go near, and join thyself to this chariot.

Did this revelation to go teach come from Philip's home church leader? Did it come from his branch coordinator? Did it come from his country coordinator? Did it come from the leadership at the ministry headquarters in Jerusalem? No, it came from the Christ in him. He walked by the spirit and Christ was his head. Did he report to his home church leader, branch coordinator, country coordinator or ministry leadership before doing what the spirit directed him to do? No, he did not. Well, what do you think God wants us to do in our day and time? Walk by the gift of holy spirit, the Christ in us, or by the direction and counsel of men?

> Acts 9:10-12
> And there was a certain disciple at Damascus, named Ananias; and to him said the Lord in a vision, Ananias. And he said, Behold, I *am here*, Lord.

And the Lord *said* unto him, Arise, and go into the street which is called Straight, and enquire in the house of Judas for *one* called Saul, of Tarsus: for, behold, he prayeth,

And hath seen in a vision a man named Ananias coming in, and putting *his* hand on him, that he might receive his sight.

Did this revelation to go minister to Paul come from Ananias' home church leader? Did it come from his branch coordinator? Did it come from his country coordinator? Did it come from the leadership at the ministry headquarters in Jerusalem? No, it came from the Christ in him. He walked by the spirit and the Christ in him was his head. Same with Peter.

Acts 10:19,20
While Peter thought on the vision, the Spirit said unto him, Behold, three men seek thee.

Arise therefore, and get thee down, and go with them, doubting nothing: for I have sent them.

Did this revelation to go witness to the Gentiles come from Peter's home church leader? Did it come from his branch coordinator? Did it come from his country coordinator? Did it come from the leadership at the ministry headquarters in Jerusalem? No, it came from the Christ in him. He walked by the spirit and Christ was his head.

Look, if God dwelled in temples made with hands, revelation would have to be given to the ministry leadership and then handed down the chain of command. Don't you see it? This is so important, I'm going to say it again. Make sure you read this and understand it, selah. If God dwelled in temples made with hands, revelation would have to be given to the ministry leadership and then handed down the chain of command. But God no longer dwells in temples made with hands, does he?

Acts 16:9
And a vision appeared to Paul in the night; There stood a man of Macedonia, and prayed him, saying, Come over into Macedonia, and help us.

This revelation to Paul about going to Macedonia was only given to him, it wasn't given to anyone else. Nowhere in the bible do I see God giving the same revelation to a bunch of people all at the same time. The same was true back in Acts 15 regarding his going to Jerusalem. Paul walked by the spirit and he got the green light to go up to Jerusalem. That revelation wasn't given to Barnabas and it certainly wasn't given to those fucking interfering religious pricks from Judea.

Now we have to ask the question, *why* did God give revelation to Paul in Acts 15 to go up to Jerusalem? Was it for the benefit of the religious pricks from Judea? No, it wasn't, it was for the benefit of the believers in Antioch. They were Paul's work. He had been their home church leader when the word first took root. He was responsible for them because he had taught them the word. That's why God gave him revelation on how best to protect his people in Antioch from those religious interfering fuckwits. God gave the revelation to Paul because his people were his responsibility. God most certainly did not give revelation regarding the move of the word in Antioch to anyone back at the headquarters of any ministry in Jerusalem.

What can we learn from this? Well, if you're a home church leader and God has given you people to work with, he will only work with you to help those people, he will not go over your head. Any revelation that's needed in your area to keep God's people safe will go to you, not to any ministry *leadership*. You are the one who has proven your own work, you are the one to whom God has given increase, and you are the one with the responsibility and authority to look after those people. You are the leadership God will work with for your home church. We need to keep interfering religious fuckwits like those men from Judea well away from our home churches and well away from our people. How do you like that for new light?

This thing about who exactly God gives revelation to is one of the most important keys to walking by the spirit you will ever learn. God gives revelation only to those with the responsibility to carry it out. Even if you're off the word God will always try to get through to you first. If you don't listen, it's only then God may give revelation to others to get involved to try and help you, like he did with Paul going to Jerusalem in Acts 21. Paul was told first though, wasn't he? Agabus and the others only got involved because Paul wasn't listening. Let's see some of these principles in scripture. Jeroboam, who we met earlier in the class, was burning incense by the alter he'd had made for his new religion and God wasn't exactly pleased with it.

> 1 Kings 13:1
> And, behold, there came a man of God [Elohim] out of Judah by the word of the LORD [Jehovah] unto Bethel: and Jeroboam stood by the altar to burn incense.

This man of God was sent to Jeroboam by revelation. God gave the prophet information on where to go, what to do, and what to say.

> 1 Kings 13:2,3
> And he cried against the altar in the word of the LORD [Jehovah], and said, O altar, altar, thus saith the LORD; Behold, a child shall be born unto the house of David, Josiah by name; and upon thee shall he offer the priests of the high places that burn incense upon thee, and men's bones shall be burnt upon thee.
>
> And he gave a sign the same day, saying, This *is* the sign which the LORD hath spoken; Behold, the altar shall be rent, and the ashes that *are* upon it shall be poured out.

The prophet did exactly what he was told and delivered precisely the message he was told to deliver. While we're here, it's time to start getting LORD out of our heads when it comes to God. The reasons will become more apparent later in the class. Jehovah should always be translated God. Elohim is God the creator. We're so conditioned to calling God the Lord that this is going to take some work. I'm still having difficulty with this but the more I force my mind to see the word God every place Jehovah is used, the easier it becomes. Elohim I read as elohim, understanding it as God the creator. Up to you on this one, just get Lord out of your head when it comes to God. God is absolutely not our lord. Jesus Christ is our Lord. I've made a few changes in the following verses to help you. Back to a rather pissed off Jeroboam.

> 1 Kings 13:4-6
> And it came to pass, when king Jeroboam heard the saying of the man of God [elohim], which had cried against the altar in Bethel,

Walking *by* the Spirit

that he put forth his hand from the altar, saying, Lay hold on him. And his hand, which he put forth against him, dried up, so that he could not pull it in again to him.

The altar also was rent, and the ashes poured out from the altar, according to the sign which the man of God [elohim] had given by the word of ~~the LORD~~ [God].

And the king answered and said unto the man of God [elohim], Intreat now the face of the LORD thy God [God thy elohim], and pray for me, that my hand may be restored me again. And the man of God [elohim] besought the LORD [God], and the king's hand was restored him again, and became as *it was* before.

I know this is going to take some retraining of our minds, and I appreciate that, but we must get lord out of our heads when it comes to God. This forgery will be a major lever in promoting the antichrist, a man, to God status. Jesus Christ is a man, he is our Lord, but he is not God. God is our creator, he is our God, but he is not our Lord. Let's see how this confrontation between the man of elohim and Jeroboam develops.

1 Kings 13:7-10
And the king said unto the man of God, Come home with me, and refresh thyself, and I will give thee a reward.

And the man of God said unto the king, If thou wilt give me half thine house, I will not go in with thee, neither will I eat bread nor drink water in this place:

For so was it charged me by the word of the LORD, saying, Eat no bread, nor drink water, nor turn again by the same way that thou camest.

So he went another way, and returned not by the way that he came to Bethel.

Here we must clarify the importance of exactly who God gives revelation to. God told his man that he was to eat nothing, drink nothing, and return home by a different route. Is any of that difficult to understand?

Walking *by* the Spirit

There is nothing ambiguous or complicated about the revelation. Most importantly, this revelation was given to the man of God, the man with the authority and responsibility to carry it out, not to anyone else. Now watch what happens.

> 1 Kings 13:11-18
> Now there dwelt an old prophet in Bethel; and his sons came and told him all the works that the man of God had done that day in Bethel: the words which he had spoken unto the king, them they told also to their father.
>
> And their father said unto them, What way went he? For his sons had seen what way the man of God went, which came from Judah.
>
> And he said unto his sons, Saddle me the ass. So they saddled him the ass: and he rode thereon,
>
> And went after the man of God, and found him sitting under an oak: and he said unto him, *Art* thou the man of God that camest from Judah? And he said, I *am*.
>
> Then he said unto him, Come home with me, and eat bread.
>
> And he said, I may not return with thee, nor go in with thee: neither will I eat bread nor drink water with thee in this place:
>
> For it was said to me by the word of the LORD, Thou shalt eat no bread nor drink water there, nor turn again to go by the way that thou camest.
>
> He said unto him, I *am* a prophet also as thou *art;* and an angel spake unto me by the word of the LORD, saying, Bring him back with thee into thine house, that he may eat bread and drink water. *But* he lied unto him.

This is one key to walking by the spirit you had better learn well. This old fucker lied about being given revelation for someone else. God will always tell you first. Always, without exception. God will never give revelation to others to give to you to carry out, ever, unless you're a new born believer and you're clueless about spiritual matters, in which case it would go to the person who taught you the word and who is responsible for you. If he's not around, then it might go to your home church leader or whoever else from your home church might be around. If you don't learn this, you are headed for major problems.

> 1 Kings 13:19-26
> So he went back with him, and did eat bread in his house, and drank water.
>
> And it came to pass, as they sat at the table, that the word of the LORD [God] came unto the prophet that brought him back:
>
> And he cried unto the man of God that came from Judah, saying, Thus saith the LORD, Forasmuch as thou hast disobeyed the mouth of the LORD, and hast not kept the commandment which the LORD thy God commanded thee,
>
> But camest back, and hast eaten bread and drunk water in the place, of the which *the LORD* did say to thee, Eat no bread, and drink no water; thy carcase shall not come unto the sepulchre of thy fathers.
>
> And it came to pass, after he had eaten bread, and after he had drunk, that he saddled for him the ass, *to wit,* for the prophet whom he had brought back.
>
> And when he was gone, a lion met him by the way, and slew him: and his carcase was cast in the way, and the ass stood by it, the lion also stood by the carcase.
>
> And, behold, men passed by, and saw the carcase cast in the way, and the lion standing by the carcase: and they came and told *it* in the city where the old prophet dwelt.
>
> And when the prophet that brought him back from the way heard *thereof,* he said, It *is* the man of God, who was disobedient unto the word of the LORD: therefore the LORD hath delivered him unto the lion, which hath torn him, and slain him, according to the word of the LORD, which he spake unto him.

Who killed the man of God? Was it a lion or was it God? Remember the idiom of permission. God is always good, the devil is always evil. The devil only gets in when we are disobedient to the word. That old prophet lied to the man of God about receiving revelation on his behalf, the man of God believed him and walked to his death. God did not kill that man. Had God wanted him dead, he wouldn't have given him the information on how to get home again safely. God basically gave him a map through a spiritual minefield. When he strayed from the map, he was killed. He obviously didn't understand this truth I'm now teaching you.

So, in this administration, does God give revelation to every Tom, Dick and Harry about you? No, he does not. He will work with you directly and personally, or if you're a new believer, with the person responsible for looking after you until you learn to walk by the spirit for yourself. We are a family, after all.

> Philippians 2:13
> For it is God which worketh [energises] in you both to will and to do of *his* good pleasure.

There are distinctions to this, of course. In the marriage relationship, all revelation regarding the direction of the marriage goes to the husband.

> Ephesians 5:22-24
> Wives, submit yourselves unto your own husbands, as unto the Lord.
>
> For the husband is the head of the wife, even as Christ is the head of the church: and he is the saviour of the body.
>
> Therefore as the church is subject unto Christ, so *let* the wives *be* to their own husbands in every thing.

Revelation regarding children goes to their parents, whoever God feels it best to give it to at the time. As the mother spends most of her time with the kids, the vast majority of revelation would logically therefore go to her.

Ephesians 6:1
Children, obey your parents in the Lord: for this is right.

See how this works? Home church leaders don't get revelation about everyone in their home churches, they only get revelation on how best to move the word and keep things spiritually clean. They won't get revelation on what job you should do or who you should marry, that's none of their business. It's your life, you live it. Don't be a religious idiot thinking God gives revelation to everyone else about what you should do with your life, get that spirit energised within you and walk on your own two feet. When Paul disobeyed God by going to Jerusalem in Acts 21 and was told what to do by the ministry leadership there, were they walking by the spirit? No, they were walking by their senses, and doing what James and the elders told him to do almost cost Paul his life. There was no safety there in a multitude of counsellors, was there? Walking by the counsel of men is walking by the senses, it is putting your trust in the flesh.

If you're a brand new believer, okay, perhaps you will need a little help, but that help will come from within your own home church, not from the leadership of some temple made with hands. That's why every home church is to be self supporting, self propagating and self governing. The home churches are to be the headquarters of the move of the word in their areas. All you have to do is think family rather than ministry. The churches in Antioch were fine until the ministry in Jerusalem stuck their snotty interfering religious noses in, see it?

Ministry is old testament, family is Grace Administration. Think family, think responsibility, think young children, think teenagers and think adults. Is this class, Walking by the Spirit for young children? No it isn't, it's geared towards maturing teenagers and adults. I don't expect brand new believers to walk by the spirit and understand this stuff, and yes, God does give me revelation on how best to look after new believers under my care. As they mature spiritually and learn how to walk by the spirit for themselves, God will energise more and more with them and less and less with me, understand? It's a family thing. Just as parents are spiritually responsible for their children until they mature, so we are spiritually responsible for those we witness to until they learn to walk by the spirit for themselves. The church of God in the Grace Administration simply cannot function unless it is done home church by home church as families, with each home church being self governing, self propagating and self supporting.

If we submit ourselves to structures of leadership within man-made ministries we will lose the word because God does not dwell in temples made with hands. We must all learn to walk by the spirit with Christ as our head or there is no flowing of living waters. Christ is our head, not men, and God will only give revelation in this administration to whoever has the responsibility and authority to carry it out. God will not give revelation to any man regarding a marriage other than to a woman's husband. I mean that is just so obvious, yet when it comes to running home churches why can't we see that it's just as obvious that God only gives revelation regarding how a home church is to operate and function to the home church leader, the person responsible for that home church? The person responsible is the person who began the work and built it up, not some religious prick from some man-made ministry who was sent there to take over your work. God gave your people to you so do your job and look after them. It's your job to keep the wolves from your people.

Once a man-made structure of leadership takes over responsibility for how home churches operate and function, the fountain of living waters is cut off because God will not honour any other system than that which he has set up for this administration.

Those men from Judea thought they were so right, hey? When Paul didn't listen to them, they threw their hands up and told him to go to Jerusalem so his leadership could sort him out. Paul walked by the spirit, went to God and got the green light to go to Jerusalem. If God had not given him the green light, he would not have gone despite those men from Judea determining that he should. The word was already being lost in the 1st Century church because the believers were being taught to submit themselves to an organised structure of leadership within a man-made ministry rather than to walk by the spirit with Christ as their head. Paul did go to Jerusalem, and he did sort things out for his believers back in Antioch, so there was tremendous profit to his going.

Acts 15:3-6
And being brought on their way by the church, they passed through Phenice and Samaria, declaring the conversion of the Gentiles: and they caused great joy unto all the brethren.

And when they were come to Jerusalem, they were received of the church, and *of* the apostles and elders, and they declared all things that God had done with them.

But there rose up certain of the sect of the Pharisees which believed, saying, That it was needful to circumcise them, and to command *them* to keep the law of Moses.

And the apostles and elders came together for to consider of this matter.

It's interesting to note that the apostles are mentioned here. Peter, John and all the others were still in Jerusalem at this time. It is also interesting to note that when Paul went to Jerusalem in Acts 21, when he disobeyed God by going, there is no mention of any apostles.

Acts 21:18
And the *day* following Paul went in with us unto James; and all the elders were present.

The point is, there was spiritual profit in Paul going to that developing man-made ministry headquarters in Jerusalem in Acts 15 because God still had some good men there with eyes to see and ears to hear. However, by the time Acts 21 came along, God screamed at Paul not to go. Paul however was quite willing to give his life in an attempt to try to save the ministry. Look, God doesn't give a fuck about man-made ministries, he only cares about people, his people, his church. God does not dwell in temples made with hands, but he did send Paul into one that was being constructed to try to reach the apostles and to protect his people back in Antioch. As we continue reading we see that Peter definitely responded. I wish people today would respond and get out of all those shithole man-made temples they waste their lives and money attending. Galatians adds more light regarding those pharisees who were into circumcision.

Galatians 2:3-5
But neither Titus, who was with me, being a Greek, was compelled to be circumcised:

And that because of false brethren unawares brought in, who came in privily to spy out our liberty which we have in Christ Jesus, that they might bring us into bondage:

To whom we gave place by subjection, no, not for an hour; that the truth of the gospel might continue with you.

How can false brethren be brought in without anyone knowing? I'll tell you why, it's because God will not support man-made temples by giving revelation to counsels of men who walk by their senses. Do you know how those religious cunts were spying out their liberty? They placed men in the public urinals to check the men's cocks as they were pissing to see if they were circumcised or not. I tell you, God has fuck all to do with man-made temples and all their layers of leadership who have turned their backs on the fountain of living waters and instead walk by the counsel and direction of men. Yes, this subject makes me angry, you can probably feel it. If you'd wasted twenty years of your life and tens of thousands of pounds of God's money being duped by wankers in a temple run by men, you'd be pissed off as well. Just be thankful you don't need to go through what I went through to get to this word I'm now teaching.

Acts 15:7-11
And when there had been much disputing, Peter rose up, and said unto them, Men *and* brethren, ye know how that a good while ago God made choice among us, that the Gentiles by my mouth should hear the word of the gospel, and believe.

And God, which knoweth the hearts, bare them witness, giving them the Holy Ghost [holy spirit], even as *he did* unto us;

And put no difference between us and them, purifying their hearts by faith [believing].

Now therefore why tempt ye God, to put a yoke upon the neck of the disciples, which neither our fathers nor we were able to bear?

But we believe that through the grace of the Lord Jesus Christ we shall be saved, even as they.

See, here's the profit. Paul reached Peter, and the believers in Antioch were protected from any further interference. We can safely assume Paul also reached the other apostles as well because by the time of Acts 21 there were no apostles in Jerusalem having anything to do with that monstrosity of a ministry.

Now you can read the record for yourself and make sense of it. This will also give you some good background to the record in Acts 21 and perhaps a little more understanding of why Paul went to Jerusalem despite God telling him not to go. He simply had not yet seen the depth of the truth that God does not dwell in temples made with hands. He tried to save the ministry. Folks, you cannot save or change a broken cistern. You just simply cannot put new wine into old wineskins without bursting the skins and losing the wine. Just get the fuck out of them. Wineskins were made from animal hides. When you put new wine into them, the wine fermented and stretched the skins. If you put new wine into an old skin, a skin which had already been stretched by fermentation, the skin would split and you'd lose both the wine and the skin.

Ministry is old testament, self governing, self supporting and self propagating home churches are Grace Administration. Ministry is broken cistern, home churches are where life is. Walking by the spirit with fountains of living waters flowing from you is a far more refreshing and invigorating way to live.

Wow, now that's what I call peace. This session is a done deal.

65. The Higher Powers

> Romans 13:1
> Let every soul be subject unto the higher powers. For there is no power but of God: the powers that be are ordained of God.

Until now we've been taught that these higher powers are our ministry leadership, those who hold leadership positions within religious structures, organisations, churches and ministries. If God doesn't dwell in temples made with hands, and he has nothing to do with man-made organisations or ministries, then these higher powers mentioned in Romans can't be the leadership of any ministry or church. Is someone who joins a ministry, takes their classes, gives their money to them, attends all their events, applies for a job in a leadership position, attends interviews, and gets promoted into a position of responsibility someone we must be subject to? Is going through all this required in order to become one of the higher powers referred to in Romans? If God does not dwell in temples made with hands, this just can't be.

Back in Acts 15, when those men from Judea turned up in Antioch and taught the believers they had to be circumcised, were they these higher powers? They had no doubts in their own minds that they were.

> Acts 15:1,2
> And certain men which came down from Judaea taught the brethren, *and said,* Except ye be circumcised after the manner of Moses, ye cannot be saved.

When therefore Paul and Barnabas had no small dissension and disputation with them, they determined that Paul and Barnabas, and certain other of them, should go up to Jerusalem unto the apostles and elders about this question.

Paul and Barnabas were the higher powers, we know that, but what is remarkable to note is that those men from Judea did not recognise them as the higher powers and certainly did not submit themselves to them. Those men were part of a ministry which was attempting to take control of God's people by teaching them that the church of God was to submit themselves to their structure of leadership. They expected Paul and Barnabas who were the higher powers to submit themselves to them. There was a broken cistern under construction in Jerusalem which had begun to cut off the fountain of living waters.

If we are to separate truth from error here so we can protect our home churches, we really must be clear on exactly who these higher powers are.

> Romans 13:1
> Let every soul be subject unto the higher powers [exousia]. For there is no power [exousia] but of God: the powers [exousia] that be are ordained [tassō] of God.

There are a number of Greek words translated power in the new testament, and we need to understand a few of them. The Greek word dunamis is translated as power, as well as a few other ways, and it can be tracked and marked in your bible using any good concordance or bible software programme that includes a concordance. It is a good idea to mark all these words in your bible so you can recognise them when you're reading and teaching.

> Acts 1:8
> But ye shall receive power [dunamis], after that the Holy Ghost [holy spirit] is come upon you: and ye shall be witnesses unto me both in Jerusalem, and in all Judaea, and in Samaria, and unto the uttermost part of the earth.

Dunamis is inherent, potential power. Our English words dynamo and dynamic come directly from dunamis. A dynamo converts potential power into kinetic energy which can be used. When you are born again, spiritual power is there within you. It is potential, latent, inherent dunamis power that comes with the gift of holy spirit.

Our next word is the Greek word energeō, from which our English words energy and energise come. We are born again with potential dunamis power, and we can energise that power. Every time we speak in tongues we energise the dunamis power that comes with the gift of holy spirit.

Our next word is the Greek word exousia, from which we derive our English word exercise. This is the word used in Romans. We exercise the dunamis power within us by energising it.

> Romans 13:1
> Let every soul be subject unto the higher powers [exousia]. For there is no power [exousia] but of God: the powers [exousia] that be are ordained [tassō] of God.

The last word we will consider is the Greek word kratos, which means power with an impact. Kratos is the effect power has on something, the effect produced. When we energise the gift of holy spirit, we exercise the potential dunamis power within us and the effect produced is the kratos, the impact of the energising of that dunamis power.

> Ephesians 3:16
> That he would grant you, according to the riches of his glory, to be strengthened [krataioō] with might [dunamis] by his Spirit in the inner man;

How are we strengthened with might? By energising the spirit. When we energise the gift of holy spirit, the dunamis power within us, the impact, the kratos is that we are strengthened in the inner man. If you want to walk by the spirit, read the following verses carefully.

> Ephesians 1:17-19
> That the God of our Lord Jesus Christ, the Father of glory, may give unto you the spirit of wisdom and revelation in the knowledge of him:
>
> The eyes of your understanding being enlightened; that ye may know what is the hope of his calling, and what the riches of the glory of his inheritance in the saints,

> And what *is* the exceeding greatness of his power [dunamis] to usward who believe, according to the working [energeia] of his mighty power [kratos],

The spirit of wisdom and revelation in the knowledge of him, could be understood as spiritual wisdom and revelation knowledge. This refers to the revelation manifestations. When we walk by the spirit, the eyes of our understanding are enlightened, and when our eyes are open we understand the riches of the glory of the inheritance which is awaiting us at the return. When we walk by the spirit and exercise the gift of holy spirit, we understand the exceeding greatness of that dunamis power because we believe by energising the gift of holy spirit which brings a kratos impact into the world.

So, who then are the higher powers of Romans?

> Romans 13:1
> Let every soul be subject unto the higher powers [exousia]. For there is no power [exousia] but of God: the powers [exousia] that be are ordained [tassō] of God.

Whoever they are, they are ordained of God. As we already know, tassō means to arrange, to appoint, to determine. God arranges, appoints and determines who these higher powers are, and we who make up God's church are to subject ourselves to them. Power is the Greek word exousia, exercised power, and it's obviously referring to the manifestation of energised spiritual power. God arranges, appoints and determines that certain individuals within his church are given spiritual power which they have the authority to exercise within the church and to whom we are to subject ourselves.

So who are these men and women? Leadership in a temple made with hands? A board of directors promoted into positions of responsibility in made-made churches and religious ministries? A structure of leadership that reports up through a chain of command to some dude heading up some patriarchal cult? No, a thousand times no. Don't think ministry constructed by men, think family - think self governing, self supporting and self propagating home churches.

Now stop and think for a minute. Are these higher powers referring to men and women who simply manifest the gift of holy spirit? No, that can't be because we all have the gift of holy spirit and we can all operate all nine manifestations. So these higher powers are not referring to men and women who are simply born again and manifest the gift of holy spirit because we can all do that.

Are these higher powers our home church leaders? I don't see God dishing out any special spiritual powers to home church leaders anywhere in the bible. We know it's a spiritual power given by God, and that it isn't the gift of holy spirit because we all have that, so what other spiritual power does God give? Let's not guess anymore, because the word tells us.

> Ephesians 4:8,11,12
> Wherefore he saith, When he ascended up on high, he led captivity captive, and gave gifts unto men.
>
> And he gave some, apostles; and some, prophets; and some, evangelists; and some, pastors and teachers;
>
> For the perfecting of the saints, for the work of the ministry, for the edifying of the body of Christ:

Here in Ephesians, who the gift ministries are given to and their purpose is clearly explained in language anyone can understand. These gift ministries are arranged, appointed and determined by God, and these are the higher exousia spiritual powers to which we, the church are to subject ourselves. There is nothing difficult about understanding the bible once we scrub the broken cistern horseshit from our heads.

The gift ministries are given to men and women within the church. God determines who gets them and where they are placed in the church. This giving and this determining is absolutely not done through any counsels of men. These gifts are in addition to the gift of holy spirit, they are special gifts given to the church, and they are spiritual gifts. Their purpose is explained in verse 12.

> Ephesians 4:12
> For the perfecting [katartizō - mending] of the saints, for the work of the ministry, for the edifying of the body of Christ:

These gift ministries are for the mending, the repairing of the saints, the work of the ministry, which is the worldwide network of self governing, self supporting and self propagating home churches, and it is for the edifying, the building up of the body of Christ. We all have Christ in us and together as the church of God we make up the body of Christ. To help us, God gives special spiritual gift ministries and it is them to whom we subject ourselves.

Back in Acts 15 then, who were the higher powers? Paul and Barnabas or those men from Judaea?

> Acts 15:1,2
> And certain men which came down from Judaea taught the brethren, *and said,* Except ye be circumcised after the manner of Moses, ye cannot be saved.
>
> When therefore Paul and Barnabas had no small dissension and disputation with them, they determined that Paul and Barnabas, and certain other of them, should go up to Jerusalem unto the apostles and elders about this question.

Let me give you a clue.

> Acts 13:1,2
> Now there were in the church that was at Antioch certain prophets and teachers; as Barnabas, and Simeon that was called Niger, and Lucius of Cyrene, and Manaen, which had been brought up with Herod the tetrarch, and Saul.
>
> As they ministered to the Lord, and fasted, the Holy Ghost said, Separate me Barnabas and Saul for the work whereunto I have called them.

> Romans 1:1
> Paul, a servant of Jesus Christ, called *to be* an apostle, separated unto the gospel of God,

Galatians 1:1
Paul, an apostle, (not of men, neither by man, but by Jesus Christ, and God the Father, who raised him from the dead;)

Ephesians 1:1
Paul, an apostle of Jesus Christ by the will of God, to the saints which are at Ephesus, and to the faithful in Christ Jesus:

Colossians 1:1
Paul, an apostle of Jesus Christ by the will of God, and Timotheus *our* brother,

God determined by his own counsel and will to give gift ministries to Paul and Barnabas. We know Barnabas was a prophet and a teacher, and we know Paul was also an apostle. God gave Paul the gift ministry of an apostle and placed him in a position within the church to which everyone was to subject themselves. It is these gift ministries which are the higher powers of Romans. They are higher spiritual powers because they are given in addition to the gift of holy spirit. Everyone in the church of God has the gift of holy spirit, but there are a few with gift ministries given by God and they are these higher powers.

So why then did those men who came down from Judea not subject themselves to Paul? Why did they expect him to subject himself to them? I'll tell you why, it was because they had been promoted within a man-made ministry which was under construction in Jerusalem. Those dudes from Judea were the forerunners of our modern day reverends which hold command in temples made with hands and who expect and demand that everyone submit themselves to them. Not me, not any more, they can fuck off. Christ is my head, not a bunch of religious wankers with impressive educations and fancy nametags. The gift ministries are apostles, prophets, evangelists, pastors and teachers, and I don't see reverends promoted by men listed among them.

The higher powers, the higher exercised powers we are to subject ourselves to are not reverends or leadership structures in temples made with hands, they are the apostles, prophets, evangelists, pastors and teachers energising their gift ministries within the home churches where God places them. In this light, let's now read Romans 13 and see if it makes sense.

Romans 13:1
Let every soul be subject unto the higher powers. For there is no power but of God: the powers that be are ordained of God.

The gift ministries are given by God as gifts to the church. They are for the repairing and mending of the saints. They are also given for the work of the ministry, which is the work being done at the home church level. They are also for the building up, the edifying of the body of Christ, which is the worldwide network of believers who walk by the spirit with Christ as their head. We are to be subject to the apostles, prophets, evangelists, pastors and teachers energising in our home churches, which is where God wants them and where he places them. Doesn't that just make perfect sense?

Think about it. If you were God, where would you want the gift ministries operating and energising? At some headquarters of a temple made with hands thousands of miles away, locked away from the world? Or would you want your best men and women out there in the home churches, on the front lines, looking after God's kids and leading the charge against the spiritual darkness of the world? There is no question in my mind where God wants his apostles, prophets, evangelists, pastors and teachers energised. Even a cursory reading of the book of Acts will clearly show you that the gift ministries energised at the home church level. What else does Romans tell us?

Romans 13:2
Whosoever therefore resisteth [opposes] the power [exousia], resisteth the ordinance [diatagē- arrangement] of God: and they that resist shall receive to themselves damnation [condemnation].

Can you see how simple this is to understand once you remove temples made with hands and all their religious horseshit from the equation? The higher powers are right there with you in your home churches. How do you know who they are? By reading their nametag? By checking to see how many stupid bible classes they've taken? What a load of fucking shite that is. Apostles, prophets, evangelists, pastors and teachers are easily recognisable to anyone with ears to hear and eyes to see. If you're off the word and someone gets in your face, taps the pages of the bible and shows you where you're missing the mark, chances are you're being confronted by a prophet. Oppose them at your peril, because God places them in the body where it pleases him and we are to subject ourselves to them. If God has given him a green light to confront you, you'd better shut up and listen because he is loving you big enough to try to mend you.

> Romans 13:3
> For rulers are not a terror to good works, but to the evil. Wilt thou then not be afraid of the power [exousia]? do that which is good, and thou shalt have praise of the same:

Now stop for a moment and think. It says rulers here, right? So who are these rulers? Your home church leader? Your branch leader? Your country coordinator? Some board of Directors? Not on your life. These rulers are the higher powers, the gift ministries which God gave to men for the perfecting of the saints, the work of the ministry and the edifying of the body of Christ. Our home church leaders are not the higher powers. Even home church leaders are to subject themselves to the gift ministries. How do you like that for new light?

Are you tired of being lectured to by some arrogant prick home church leader in a temple made with hands who thinks he knows everything, demands you submit to him and quotes Romans 13 at you? Tell him to fuck off. The higher powers are the energised gift ministries operating in the home churches. They are the ones God put there to look after the disciples. Disciples are only responsible for themselves and those God has given them to undershepherd. This is a family thing, not a ministry thing, understand?

> Romans 13:4-6
> For he is the minister of God to thee for good. But if thou do that which is evil, be afraid; for he beareth not the sword in vain: for he is the minister of God, a revenger to *execute* wrath upon him that doeth evil.
>
> Wherefore *ye* must needs be subject, not only for wrath, but also for conscience sake.

> For for this cause pay ye tribute also: for they are God's ministers, attending continually upon this very thing.

The gift ministries are only terrible to those who walk away from the word. It is the devil spirit realm their wrath is directed towards. And just look at who we are to pay tribute to. Temples made with hands use these verses to teach you to send all your money to them. That's not surprising because the love of money is the root of all evil. God's money is to be kept and used at the home church level and the gift ministries are to be supported from that money. If the gift ministries need money to move the word, the money held by the home church leaders is to be used to support them as they do God's work. That's another principle you can see throughout the book of Acts and Paul's epistles. The home churches financially supported the gift ministries. You home church leaders are responsible to walk by the spirit and support the gift ministries who are doing God's work. You don't send all God's money to them, you support them from God's money as God works within you to will and to do of his good pleasure. This is not difficult to understand, but to see it you will have to walk by the spirit with Christ as your head and not by the direction and counsel of men.

Knowing where the gift ministries are being energised isn't difficult. Apostles bring new light to their generation, so isn't it obvious that I'm an apostle? God is teaching me and I'm teaching you. It isn't something I brag about and I certainly don't have any nametags with Apostle George scrawled on them. If I did, I'd burn them. I don't ask to be called the Apostle George and I never will. It isn't a position I applied for, it isn't something I asked God for, and it certainly isn't anything I ever expected to be given. Unto me who am less than the least of all saints is this grace given that I might preach among the gentiles the clearly searchable riches of the truth that God does not dwell in temples made with hands. I understand only too well what Paul meant when he first spoke similar words.

You know, I've never once thought that I was gift ministry material. To me, the gift ministries were all those educated, intelligent, sociable, motivated, committed, disciplined, well dressed men in top leadership positions in temples made with hands that strutted around with fancy nametags. I wasn't as clever and smart as them and I knew I could never aspire to be anything like them. I kept my head in the word, studied the word, listened to thousands of teachings, and did a little research. I kept myself in the word on a daily basis. I may not have been as intelligent and educated as the rest of them, but I was faithful.

Then one day I was kicked out of the Way International. I guess I didn't measure up to the expectations of men who walked by their senses. Nothing new there. I never amounted to much in the world's eyes. It was around that time I returned to the Highlands of Scotland. I still studied the word every day, still listened to teachings, still studied my bible, and still taught the word when I had opportunity.

Then one day God told me he wanted to give me something. This would have been in the late 90s I guess. He didn't tell me what it was, just that he had something to give me. However, there was a catch. It was waiting for me at the summit of Ben Armine and I had to climb up there to get it. *Ben Armine?* That meant walking from Sciberscross in Strath Brora, roughly a 23 mile hike through the moors and hills of Sutherland. There was a land rover track to Ben Armine lodge, but it was rough going from there to the summit.

Inside I was more than a little intimidated with this and it took me a few weeks to steel my mind to get into training. There was something for me at the summit of Ben Armine and I wanted to know what it was. When I started training, it took me three months to prepare before I felt ready for the hike. One morning I set off very early and I did reach the summit of Ben Armine. I have no photographs from the day, only the memory that while I was walking back down from the summit I knew I had something I didn't have when I went up there. I didn't know what it was, but I knew I had something.

That walk back to the car will remain one of the most arduous walks of my entire life. I went through the Parachute Regiment training and passed P Company at Aldershot, but I tell you, nothing they put me through was as difficult as the last five miles of that walk back to the car. Father kept telling me that if I just kept going, I'd make it back to the car, and similarly, no matter what came up in my life, if I just kept going I'd always get there, the car would always be there.

Well, I did reach the car, and I can't describe what it was like to set my heavy bergen down and take my boots off. As I drove home, I asked God what he'd given me, but he didn't tell me. All I knew was that I was heading home with something I didn't have when I got up that morning. Since that day I often scratched my head and asked God repeatedly to tell me what it was he'd given me. I pestered him for years, but he never told me. I had no idea what it was he'd given me and he never told me.

It's only in the last couple of years that I've realised what it was God gave me that day up on the summit of Ben Armine. He gave me the gift ministry of an apostle. As I look back through the long years since Ben Armine, I can see clearly now how relevant it was what God taught me that day. I'll tell you something else about a gift ministry, it really isn't something you want. A gift ministry isn't an invitation to some kind of amazing life for special people at the headquarters of temples made with hands, it's an invitation to face up to the full force of evil and hatred the world has and put your life in harm's way for God's kids. Think I'm joking? I now understand in part where Paul was coming from when he wrote these words.

> 2 Corinthians 11:23-28
> Are they ministers of Christ? (I speak as a fool) I *am* more; in labours more abundant, in stripes above measure, in prisons more frequent, in deaths oft.
>
> Of the Jews [Judeans] five times received I forty *stripes* save one.
>
> Thrice was I beaten with rods, once was I stoned, thrice I suffered shipwreck, a night and a day I have been in the deep;
>
> *In* journeyings often, *in* perils of waters, *in* perils of robbers, *in* perils by *mine own* countrymen, *in* perils by the heathen, *in* perils in the city, *in* perils in the wilderness, *in* perils in the sea, *in* perils among false brethren;
>
> In weariness and painfulness, in watchings often, in hunger and thirst, in fastings often, in cold and nakedness.

> Beside those things that are without, that which cometh upon me daily, the care of all the churches.

So why did God give such a gift to me? Well, it wasn't for my benefit, I can assure you. It wasn't a special little gift or favour to me because I was so wonderful. It wasn't because I was the best, or the most intelligent, or the most disciplined, or the most educated, or the most sociable, or the most personable person on earth, God knows I'm none of those things. Do you know why he gave me the gift ministry of an apostle? It was for you. He knew I would go to the gates of hell to finally dig out the truth that God does not dwell in temples made with hands, and he knew I would be faithful to teach it. The question therefore, isn't about me, it's about you. Never mind me, what are you going to do with the word now that you have it?

66. How to do Biblical Research

We have been exploring quite a few Greek words on our travels, and to some I guess the thought of doing Greek research probably conjures up mind pictures of locking yourself away from the world and poring over dusty scrolls. Nothing could be further from the truth. When it comes to studying the word just think diet. All we're after is a healthy daily diet. In this session I'm going to show you how to do simple Greek research so you can begin to explore the hidden treasures below the surface of the pages of the bible.

The only tools you will need to get started is a decent Greek concordance and a bible dictionary, or good bible software that includes them. For this study I will be using Youngs Analytical Concordance and the amazing e-sword free bible software. So, without further ado, let's dive into this and see just how easy and how fun it can be. To get started, read through these first four verses of Luke.

> Luke 1:1-4
> Forasmuch as many have taken in hand to set forth in order a declaration of those things which are most surely believed among us,
>
> Even as they delivered them unto us, which from the beginning were eyewitnesses, and ministers of the word;
>
> It seemed good to me also, having had perfect understanding of all things from the very first, to write unto thee in order, most excellent Theophilus,
>
> That thou mightest know the certainty of those things, wherein thou hast been instructed.

According to Luke, in his own words, he claims to have had perfect understanding of all things from the very first. How can any man claim to have perfect understanding of all things from the very first? Only God has perfect understanding of all things from the very first. Luke obviously wasn't God, so we have a rather clumsy scripture here that doesn't make any sense. Read it again.

Luke 1:3
It seemed good to me also, having had perfect understanding of all things from the very first, to write unto thee in order, most excellent Theophilus,

To begin to unravel this little problem and get to the truth of what Luke was actually saying, we need to check the Greek. Here is what the verse looks like in e-sword which has a few free add-ins installed.

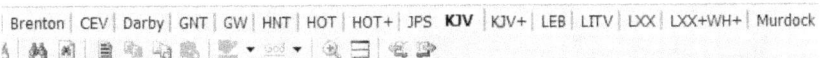

1:1 Forasmuch as many have taken in hand to set forth in order a declaration of those things wh
1:2 Even as they delivered them unto us, which from the beginning were eyewitnesses, and mini:
1:3 It seemed good to me also, having had perfect understanding of all things from the very first,

Along the top we can see all the resources listed on the tabs. KJV is the King James Version, while KJV+ is the King James with Strongs concordance markings. If you hover over the green numbers, the Greek words are revealed. In this case, hovering over G509 lets us see that *from the very first* is translated from the Greek word anōthen. Clicking on G509 gives us all sorts of information. We see that anōthen is translated above 6 times, again 3 times, top 3 times, beginning 1 time, and first 1 time.

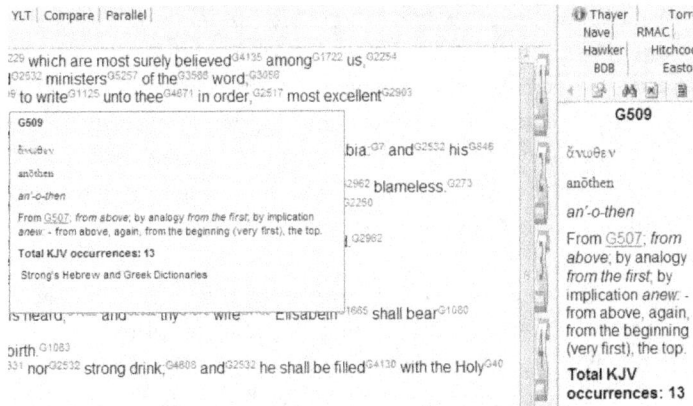

We can now click on the verses listed and go and see how anōthen is used in other places in the bible. With the word translated 6 times as *above* and only once as *first*, we can see that the translation in Luke 1:3 might be wrong. Here are a few other places anōthen is used.

John 3:31
He that cometh **from above** is above all: he that is of the earth is earthly, and speaketh of the earth: he that cometh from heaven is above all.

James 1:17
Every good gift and every perfect gift is **from above**, and cometh down from the Father of lights, with whom is no variableness, neither shadow of turning.

James 3:17
But the wisdom that is **from above** is first pure, then peaceable, gentle, *and* easy to be intreated, full of mercy and good fruits, without partiality, and without hypocrisy.

If anōthen is properly translated in Luke, the verse makes sense.

Luke 1:3
It seemed good to me also, having had perfect understanding of all things **from above**, to write unto thee in order, most excellent Theophilus,

Luke wasn't God then, was he? His perfect understanding of all things came from above, by revelation from God. Was that difficult to figure out? Did doing a little Greek research make your ears bleed? Digging into the word like this is exciting and fun, it's an adventure and it is extremely rewarding. Having all the scriptures listed where anōthen is used means you can also go through your bible and mark them so when you're reading and teaching you can see it.

Of course, with bible software programmes like e-sword, you have to learn how to use them and set them up so you're comfortable with them, and that involves a learning curve and work. So what? If you want to drive a car, there's a learning curve. Learning to play guitar involves a

Walking *by* the Spirit

learning curve and a lot of work. Even hobbies and computer games involve learning curves. Without learning curves and work, life would be no fun at all.

Do you know why God gave me the job of confronting the world with his word? Because I'm so intelligent? Because I'm so personable and such a nice guy? Hardly, it's because I am faithful. If you want to be a disciple and do something for God, you will have to put some time and work into his word to make it your own. Sure, you can pull a long face, but really, was passing your driving test and getting the keys to your first car really such a drag? If you love something, putting work into it is a joy. The only way to learn to love God's word is to be in it every day.

So how does this study thing work if you're not using software? I use Young's Analytical Concordance, other's prefer Strongs, and there are others to choose from. They all have their strengths and their weaknesses, but as I've always used Youngs, I'll show you how I use it to track Greek words through my bible. First, find the verse with the word you're interested in.

```
2. Foremost, first, πρῶτος prōtos.
    Matt 26. 17 Now the first (day) of the..unleavened
    Mark 14. 12 And the first day of unleavened bread
         16.  9 [risen early the first (day) of the week]
FIRST estate —
Beginning, principality, ἀρχή archē.
    Jude    6 angels which kept not their first estate
FIRST, from the very —
From above, from the first, ἄνωθεν anōthen.
    Luke 1.  3 understanding of all..from the very first
FIRST of all —
1. Among the foremost, ἐν πρώτοις en prōtois.
    1 Co. 15.  3 I delivered unto you first of all that which
2. First, πρῶτον prōton.
    Luke 12. 1 began to say unto his disciples first of a.
    1 Co. 11. 18 For first of all, when ye come together
FIRST begotten —
First born, πρωτότοκος prōtotokos.
    Heb.  1.  6 when He bringeth in the first begotten
    Rev.  1.  5 Jesus Christ..the first begotten of the d.
```

In Young's, when you locate the word it gives the Greek word above. From Young's we learn that anōthen is translated as the phrase **from the very first**. The reason I've crossed out a few words in my concordance is to let me know they've already been marked in my bible. Now we have to turn to the Lexicon at the back and find anōthen.

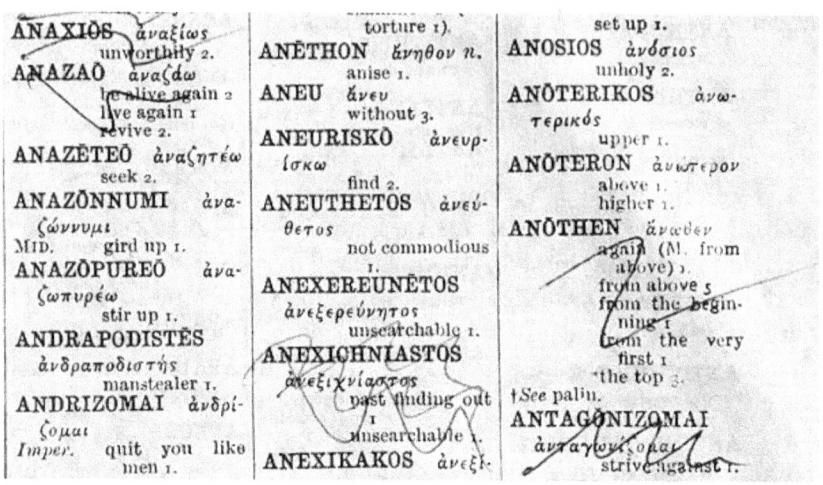

From the Lexicon, we learn that anōthen is translated **again** once, **from above** 5 times, **from the beginning** once, **from the very first** once, and **the top** 3 times. This makes 11 usages, while e-sword gave us 14. Yes, you guessed it, all these works of men are flawed. They're not God-breathed so you will have to learn to work with what is available. Young's is excellent for tracking words and finding them in your bible so you can mark them. Youngs has served me well, though now I tend to use e-sword for most of my research. Next, jot down the different ways anōthen is used and go and look them up.

Here we learn that anōthen is used as **from above** five times in John and James, so it is a simple task to look them up and mark them in your bible. I use an Oxford wide margin, which gives me plenty of space around the text for my notes. I believe the Oxford wide margin is now published

Walking *by* the Spirit

by RL Allan under licence to Oxford, but it's still available. Sure, it's over £100, so what? People pay that to watch a two hour rock concert. How much does your car cost you a month to run? And you tell me £100 is too much to spend on a decent working bible that will last you your whole life? If you love rock concerts more than you love God, perhaps it's time to reevaluate what's important.

The circled numbers are references to my notes at the top and bottom of the pages.

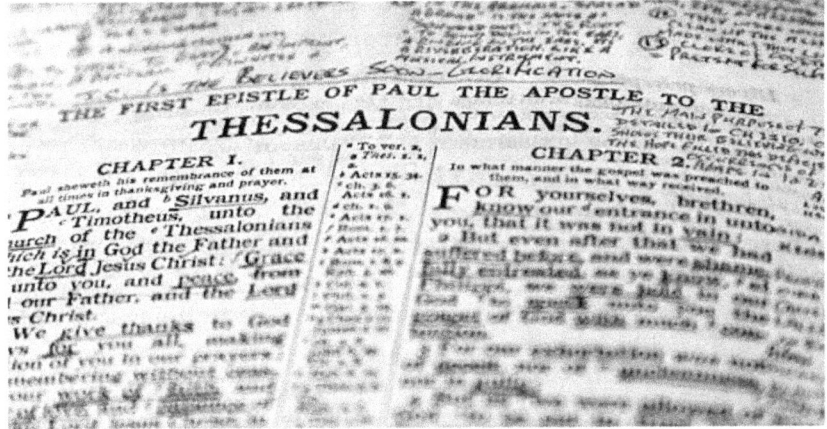

By now you will be starting to realise that just having a Young's Concordance by itself is not enough. Although an excellent tool for tracking Greek and Hebrew words, it's absolutely no help when trying to figure out what Greek and Hebrew words actually mean. Although Strongs is a much better resource for getting to grips with the meanings of Greek and Hebrew words, it still isn't adequate and you will have to use other resources to check for precise meanings. For that, Bible dictionaries are excellent tools. E-sword has an untold number of free add-ons you can download. As an example, a few of the e-sword add-ons I've installed are a Greek new testament, a Hebrew old testament, the King James with Strongs, the Derby bible, Murdock's bible, Webster's bible, and a few bible dictionaries.

There are many excellent Greek dictionaries around, as well as thousands of study resources. Anything by EW Bullinger is worth reading as long as you bear in mind that he was a trinitarian and didn't quite see through that horseshit. When it comes to Greek, he's unparalleled. His Critical Lexicon and Concordance to the English and Greek New Testament is a fabulous tool, and if you do an internet search you can even find online versions.

Once you begin to discover the treasures in the word, you might start digging into works such as EW Bullinger's Numbers in Scripture or his astonishing work Figures of Speech used in the Bible. His companion bible has more than enough research in it to keep anyone happy a lifetime. It's all out there and it's all available. There hasn't been so much of God's word available to the world since man lost the ability to read it in the stars. The word is so easy to lose and yet so difficult to find again once lost.

You already know a few Greek words from studying my class so why not go and track them through the bible? Words like plethō and pleroō, dechomai and lambanō, pneuma and hagion, dunamis, kratos, energeō, exousia, allos and heteros amongst many others you already know. How far do you want to go with God? It really depends on how far you want to go with his word. If you want to know God, you are going to have to know his word because there is no other way to learn about him. You are going to have to study the bible, read it, and memorise it daily to ensure a healthy diet so you can enjoy daily fellowship with your father.

You may think moonlit walks under the stars with a few tears in your eyes will get you close to God, but if that's how you think, I'm sorry but you're full of horseshit. Teary walks under the stars will not pull you through a major life crisis, only the word in your head and the strength and believing in your heart that grows from it can do that.

If you want to know God, you're going to have to roll up your sleeves and make his word your own, like I did. I've been faithful to study to show myself approved, and God for his part has been faithful to teach me his word just as he promised he would all those years ago sailing up the Gulf of Aqaba in the Red Sea. Put your heart into his word and he will be faithful to teach you too.

> Proverbs 2:1-5
> My son, if thou wilt receive my words, and hide my commandments with thee;
>
> So that thou incline thine ear unto wisdom, *and* apply thine heart to understanding;
>
> Yea, if thou criest after knowledge, *and* liftest up thy voice for understanding;
>
> If thou seekest her as silver, and searchest for her as *for* hid treasures;
>
> Then shalt thou understand the fear of the LORD, and find the knowledge of God.

It has taken me over 18 years to write this class and publish it, but my research really began forty years ago. In this class you're getting 40 years of study, research, and sheer hard work which you only have to read. You're beginning your spiritual journey with what has taken me a lifetime to dig out of the word. Think about that. How far do you want to go with God?

67. Peter, a very Human Man

We saw with the four crucified with Christ that all available information on any given subject isn't always recorded in every record, and that to build a full picture in our minds we have to pull all the records together. There is much in the word about Peter and we're now going to find out what kind of a man he was by pulling all the information together. First of all, let's dispel a myth about him.

> Matthew 4:18-20
> And Jesus, walking by the sea of Galilee, saw two brethren, Simon called Peter, and Andrew his brother, casting a net into the sea: for they were fishers.
>
> And he saith unto them, Follow me, and I will make you fishers of men.
>
> And they straightway left *their* nets, and followed him.

On reading this you might be tempted to think that Jesus Christ was some kind of wizard who went around hypnotising people, and that Peter was gullible and trotted off after Jesus on a whim. This is far from the truth because Peter and Jesus Christ had met many times before this event, and they were well acquainted. The first time the two men met was weeks, possibly months earlier. That record is in John.

> John 1:35-42
> Again the next day after John stood, and two of his disciples;
>
> And looking upon Jesus as he walked, he saith, Behold the Lamb of God!
>
> And the two disciples heard him speak, and they followed Jesus.

Then Jesus turned, and saw them following, and saith unto them, What seek ye? They said unto him, Rabbi, (which is to say, being interpreted, Master,) where dwellest thou?

He saith unto them, Come and see. They came and saw where he dwelt, and abode with him that day: for it was about the tenth hour.

One of the two which heard John *speak,* and followed him, was Andrew, Simon Peter's brother.

He first findeth his own brother Simon, and saith unto him, We have found the Messias, which is, being interpreted, the Christ.

And he brought him to Jesus. And when Jesus beheld him, he said, Thou art Simon the son of Jona: thou shalt be called Cephas, which is by interpretation, A stone [Greek - petros].

While we're here, John also records where Peter was born and raised.

John 1:44
Now Philip was of Bethsaida, the city of Andrew and Peter.

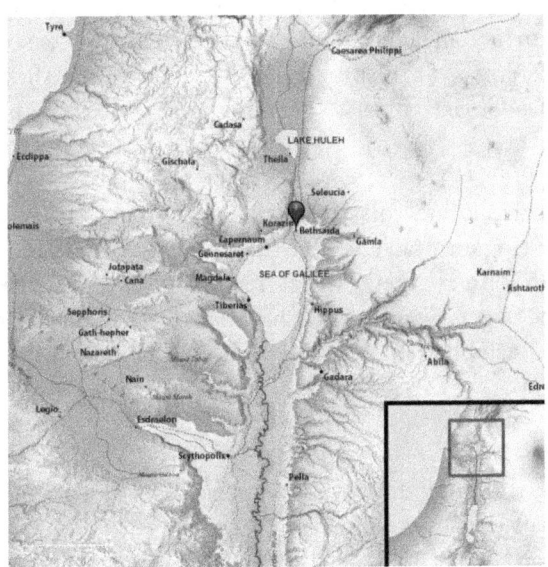

Map copyright Biblos.com, used by permission

What else can we learn about Peter's background? Well, from Matthew and Luke we learn that he was married and that he was in a business partnership with James and John, the sons of Zebedee.

> Matthew 8:14,15
> And when Jesus was come into Peter's house, he saw his wife's mother laid, and sick of a fever.
>
> And he touched her hand, and the fever left her: and she arose, and ministered unto them.

> Luke 5:9,10a
> For he [Peter] was astonished, and all that were with him, at the draught of the fishes which they had taken:
>
> And so *was* also James, and John, the sons of Zebedee, which were partners with Simon.

Now we're beginning to get a feel for the man. He was from Bethsaida on the Sea of Galilee, he had his own fishing business, and he was married. Being an Israeli he would have had a beard, and being a fisherman he would have been weather hardened and tough, a no nonsense man as fishermen tend to be. From all this we can safely assume that Peter wasn't in some kind of trance in Matthew 4 when he accepted Jesus Christ's offer to become a fisher of men and trotted off after him.

To further corroborate this truth, consider that Jesus hadn't done so much as one single miracle yet when Peter first decided to follow him. The record in John chapter 1 which records Jesus and Peter meeting for the first time was *before* Jesus' first miracle when he turned water into wine. Jesus already had a following of disciples before he performed any miracles.

> John 2:1-11
> And the third day there was a marriage in Cana of Galilee; and the mother of Jesus was there:
>
> And both Jesus was called, and his disciples, to the marriage.

And when they wanted wine, the mother of Jesus saith unto him, They have no wine.

Jesus saith unto her, Woman, what have I to do with thee? mine hour is not yet come.

His mother saith unto the servants, Whatsoever he saith unto you, do *it*.

And there were set there six waterpots of stone, after the manner of the purifying of the Jews [Judeans], containing two or three firkins apiece.

Jesus saith unto them, Fill the waterpots with water. And they filled them up to the brim.

And he saith unto them, Draw out now, and bear unto the governor of the feast. And they bare *it*.

When the ruler of the feast had tasted the water that was made wine, and knew not whence it was: (but the servants which drew the water knew;) the governor of the feast called the bridegroom,

And saith unto him, Every man at the beginning doth set forth good wine; and when men have well drunk, then that which is worse: *but* thou hast kept the good wine until now.

This beginning of miracles did Jesus in Cana of Galilee, and manifested forth his glory; and his disciples believed on him.

See, Peter had already decided to follow Jesus and become a disciple before he had actually seen any miracles. It was the teaching of the word that attracted Peter and prompted him to become a disciple, not witnessing a few miracles. What attracted you to the word? It is the word that changes people, not seeing miracles. If you want to help people, don't spend your days wishing you could perform miracles just so you can impress people, teach them the word. That's what Jesus did. The signs, miracles and wonders came later.

It wasn't seeing miracles that convinced Sergius Paulus to follow Paul and Barnabas on Crete either, it was the teaching of the word. Read it, it says he was astonished at the doctrine of the Lord, not that he was astonished at the blinding of Elymas the sorcerer.

> Acts 13:12
> Then the deputy [Sergius Paulus], when he saw what was done, believed, being astonished at the doctrine of the Lord.

So we know Peter and Jesus were acquainted before Jesus extended the invitation to follow him and become a fisher of men. Peter was in fact already a disciple, someone who was already following Jesus. The invitation to become a fisher of men therefore was an invitation to something more, it was an invitation to leadership, an invitation to do the work of the ministry full time. The word records that Peter had no problem with that. He already had enough knowledge of the word and enough experience working with Jesus to make an intelligent and informed decision. He left his nets and followed him.

When I started writing this teaching I wasn't looking for new light as I didn't think I needed any to handle this subject. Yet there's God, energising in me to will and to do of his good pleasure, teaching me the word so I can teach you. I never realised before now that Jesus' disciples followed him before they had ever seen any miracles done by him. Jesus Christ had a large following of disciples long before he ever did any miracles. What can we learn from this astonishing new perspective? Plenty. Consider this verse in Romans.

> Romans 10:17
> So then faith [believing] *cometh* by hearing, and hearing by the word of God.

Believing doesn't come by seeing miracles, it comes by hearing the word of God. That's what the word says and that's what the word means. We hear the word, it builds our believing, and as our believing grows we see the signs, miracles and wonders. See how this makes complete sense? Jesus Christ taught the word, and as believing grew in his disciples and in those around them, doors opened for him to perform signs, miracles and wonders. This doesn't happen in reverse. Signs, miracles and wonders follow believers, but how believing grows is from hearing the word of God. Think about that.

So, Andrew introduced his brother Peter to Jesus in John chapter 1. Some time after that, after much teaching, Jesus approached Peter and invited him to become a fisher of men by working full time with him as he carried out his ministry. Jesus Christ had recognised the leadership potential in Peter and invited him to work full time with him.

> Matthew 4:18-20
> And Jesus, walking by the sea of Galilee, saw two brethren, Simon called Peter, and Andrew his brother, casting a net into the sea: for they were fishers.
>
> And he saith unto them, Follow me, and I will make you fishers of men.
>
> And they straightway left *their* nets, and followed him.

Between Jesus' and Peter's first meeting and this record in Matthew, Jesus Christ had met Philip and Nathanael, performed the miracle of wine at the wedding in Capernaum, had travelled to Jerusalem for Passover and had a chat with Nicodemus, had gone out into the countryside where the word records that his disciples water baptized, he had left Judea for a while where he met the woman at the well, had returned to Galilee and performed his second miracle, and he had opened his public ministry and confronted the people in his home town of Nazareth for their unbelief. So Peter had seen and heard some amazing stuff before Jesus Christ invited him to become a fisher of men. Peter had spent enough time with Jesus and had enough knowledge of the word to make an informed and intelligent freewill decision to leave his life as a fisherman and go work full time with Jesus Christ.

Now, although Peter responded to the invitation and followed him, he later left Jesus and went back to his fishing business. A few weeks later, Jesus invited him a second time to leave his business and work full time with him doing the work of the ministry.

Luke 5:1-3
And it came to pass, that, as the people pressed upon him [Jesus Christ] to hear the word of God, he stood by the lake of Gennesaret [the Sea of Galilee],

And saw two ships standing by the lake: but the fishermen were gone out of them, and were washing *their* nets.

And he entered into one of the ships, which was Simon's, and prayed him that he would thrust out a little from the land. And he sat down, and taught the people out of the ship.

Jesus Christ was surrounded by so many people, he borrowed Peter's boat so he could teach. They anchored the boat a little offshore, Jesus and the people made themselves comfortable, and he taught them out of the boat. Peter was right there with him, listening to every word.

Luke 5:4
Now when he had left speaking, he said unto Simon, Launch out into the deep, and let down your nets for a draught.

After the teaching, it was time to repay Peter for the use of his boat. God never takes something for nothing and Peter was to be rewarded for his giving. Jesus Christ told him to let down his nets. Notice that Jesus told him to let down his *nets*, plural, all his nets. Peter had more than one net.

Luke 5:5
And Simon answering said unto him, Master, we have toiled all the night, and have taken nothing: nevertheless at thy word I will let down the net.

Will you just look at that! Peter humoured Jesus Christ. I get humoured all the time. Folks just can't seem to see the word in people because they have been conditioned by religion to think of spiritual men as some kind of weird beings with creepy eyes and halos around their heads. What do you picture when you think of Jesus Christ? Some tall white man with long hair, flowing robes and a halo around his head? Religion puts that picture into folks heads. Jesus Christ looked nothing like this creepy asshole.

If you carry images like this of Jesus around in your mind, you need to get that religious horseshit out of your life. For a start, Jesus Christ was not white, he was Semitic, he was an Israelite. He probably looked something like this.

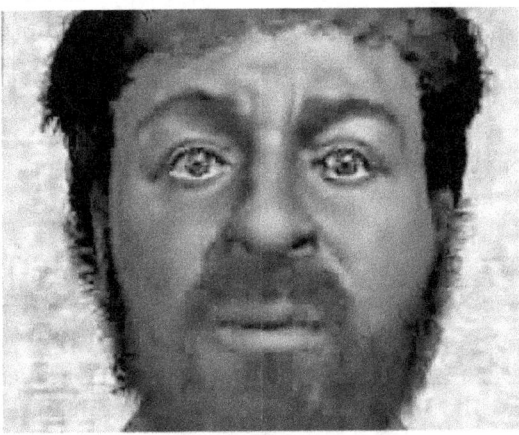

Peter just couldn't see the word in Jesus Christ, just as people today can't see the word in me. Even I have trouble seeing the word in people. We are conditioned to seeing everything through our eyes and evaluating everything with our five senses, so it's not surprising that we can't see the spiritual things going on in people. Peter was the expert on fishing and he politely put Jesus in his place. To humour him, he let down a net, one single net.

> Luke 5:5-7
> And Simon answering said unto him, Master, we have toiled all the night, and have taken nothing: nevertheless at thy word I will let down the net.
>
> And when they had this done, they inclosed a great multitude of fishes: and their net brake.
>
> And they beckoned unto *their* partners, which were in the other ship, that they should come and help them. And they came, and filled both the ships, so that they began to sink.

They caught so many fish their net broke. Can you imagine how many fish they would have caught had they put down all their nets? They caught so many fish that they had to call for help and both boats began to sink. I've caught a few salmon in my day and I know that two boats filled with fresh salmon would be worth many thousands of pounds. Do you think this had an impact on Peter? Do you think he was finally beginning to see the word in Jesus Christ?

> Luke 5:8-11
> When Simon Peter saw it, he fell down at Jesus' knees, saying, Depart from me; for I am a sinful man, O Lord.
>
> For he was astonished, and all that were with him, at the draught of the fishes which they had taken:
>
> And so *was* also James, and John, the sons of Zebedee, which were partners with Simon. And Jesus said unto Simon, Fear not; from henceforth thou shalt catch men.
>
> And when they had brought their ships to land, they forsook all, and followed him.

This fishers of men is interesting. Being an ambassador for Christ in this administration is automatic. I am an ambassador for Jesus Christ regardless of how good or how bad a job I do. However, to become a fisher of men is something that must be learned, it is an art that can be refined and practiced. At this point, Peter again made the decision to dedicate his life to the word. He left his home and fishing business and again followed Jesus Christ full time.

People don't change overnight. It doesn't happen. Peter didn't change overnight. Nor did Jesus Christ expect him to. He just kept working with him, even when he ran off back to his fishing business.

It takes time to work with people, to teach them the word, to live the word with them before they begin to see it. Raising disciples takes time. It can take years. We must love people enough to keep teaching them and showing them until they see it for themselves. You can't make anyone be a disciple, it is a decision they make for themselves. Jesus Christ saw the leadership potential in Peter and worked with him and taught him and encouraged him until he made the decision for himself. Jesus Christ didn't expect him to be perfect either, and when he ran off home to his old way of life, he filled his net with fish and gave him another chance.

At this point we had better clear something up. In this Administration of the Mystery, this Administration of Grace, we are not asked to drop everything and run off after some dude in robes wandering around the countryside teaching the bible. That was how Jesus Christ worked during the Christ Administration, but it is not how we work during this administration. God has set up family style home churches where we teach the word and raise disciples in a family setting.

Running a home church is doing the work of the ministry in this administration, and homes require money to keep them in good order and to pay the bills. Therefore we are to work so we can earn money to keep our homes comfortable. Paul worked with Aquila and Priscilla as a saddle maker in Corinth to keep money coming in as he established new home churches. Not even Paul operated the same way Jesus Christ did in the gospels. In the first century the believers had jobs and established churches in their homes. They were never asked to leave everything and run off into the wilderness.

As we're back on the subject of money, let's explore it a little further. Believers who go to a home church are to give God's money to the home church leader to steward and spend as God energises in him to will and to do of his good pleasure. Remember, it's God's money so he can spend it any way he damn well pleases. Our job is to walk by the spirit so we know how God wants his money spent. It is not unusual for God to want to contribute to the running costs of a home to keep it functional, comfortable and clean so his word can be taught in a homely environment. God's money is to be kept and used at the home church level to do the work of the ministry.

When home churches grow and homes become too small to hold everyone, or if there are so many people that some are not getting their needs met in a timely manner, then the home church splits in two and a new home church is born. The original home church leader is now not only responsible for his own home church, but also for the new church leaders as they get to grips with their responsibilities. He will know them well, most likely because he witnessed to them and taught them how to walk by the spirit, and he is still responsible to keep an eye on them, to get in there and help when they need it.

The next time these two home churches split and there are four home churches, the original home church leader may find himself so busy he might have to consider working only part time at his job so he has more time for the work of the ministry. If that's the case, then his living expenses would have to be supplemented from the money being shared between the four home churches. That's what it's there for.

As the word continues to grow, and the numbers of believers increase and multiply, it is quite likely that full time ministers will be needed to ensure the work of the ministry continues to grow unhindered and everyone has all their needs met. These ministers are not some dudes with flashy nametags sent from the headquarters of temples made with hands, they are the men and women who have built that ministry work from the ground up. It is those men and women who are entitled to be supported from God's money which is held at the home church level. They are the labourers who are worthy of their hire, not some spiritual bums stuck behind desks thousands of miles away at the headquarters of temples made with hands who have done absolutely nothing to help you move the word in your area.

If there is a need for full time ministers, then the home church leadership are to get together and figure out who and how much they are to be paid. Home churches are to be self supporting, self governing and self propagating, and everyone is to prove their own work. This is only possible if we all walk by the spirit with Christ as our head. You can't legislate this stuff because every situation is different.

Paul was working full time moving the word in Corinth, and yet God told him not to touch the money in the home churches even though he was entitled to it. Instead, God told him to ask for help from home churches in other areas. Paul walked by the spirit. See it? You just can't legislate this stuff. Man can take his rules and stupid regulations and shove them up his fucking ass. This will only work if we walk by the spirit.

> 2 Corinthians 11:8,9
> I robbed other churches, taking wages *of them*, to do you service.
>
> And when I was present with you, and wanted, I was chargeable to no man: for that which was lacking to me the brethren which came from Macedonia supplied: and in all *things* I have kept myself from being burdensome unto you, and *so* will I keep *myself.*

Home churches will continue to grow and split for as long as the home church leader who began the work is capable of overseeing things. If for some reason a leader can no longer do the work of the ministry, either because they move to other areas to begin new work as Paul did frequently, through retirement or death, or for any other reason, the existing home church leaders are then to become responsible for their own work and build the body of Christ as they are able without any interference from without. This is unbelievably important. Everyone must prove their own work and be responsible for it.

Some people will only be able or willing to handle one home church, and that's fine. However, it's unlikely they will be required to work full time doing the work of the ministry unless, of course, they have dozens of believers under their care. Some leaders will be capable of handling and overseeing hundreds of home churches, and the home churches they build up are to support them as they work full time doing what they need to do. Once they leave their position, the existing leadership take responsibility for the work they have built without any interference from without. All home churches are to be self governing, self supporting, and self propagating.

Of course, as home churches grow and the numbers of believers increase, God will give gift ministries to the church to look after the saints, for the work of the ministry and for the building up of the body of Christ. One or two of them may also be required to work full time so that everyone gets their spiritual needs met and the work of the ministry is done.

Remember, these gift ministries are the higher powers of Romans 13 and the home church leaders are to submit themselves to them and pay tribute where it's needed and take care of them from God's money. In return the home churches are taken care of spiritually. Cut off the gift ministries and you will not survive in the spiritual competition. If you're a home church leader and you think you can do it all by yourself without their help, you need to rethink how you're doing things. You are not the higher powers, the energised gift ministries are the higher powers and you are to subject yourself to them, not the other way around. The love of money is the root of all evil, so keep greed out of your life and spend God's money as he wants it spent. The following scriptures from Corinthians deal exclusively with God's money.

> 2 Corinthians 8:1-3
> Moreover, brethren, we do you to wit of the grace of God bestowed on the churches of Macedonia;
>
> How that in a great trial of affliction the abundance of their joy and their deep poverty abounded unto the riches of their liberality.
>
> For to *their* power, I bear record, yea, and beyond *their* power *they were* willing of themselves;

The believers in the first century even shared God's money between different areas as needs came up. You can't understand this unless you walk by the spirit. Notice also that Paul had absolutely no control over God's money because he was not responsible for it, the home churches were.

> 2 Corinthians 8:4-8
> Praying us with much intreaty that we would receive the gift, and *take upon us* the fellowship of the ministering to the saints.
>
> And *this they did,* not as we hoped, but first gave their own selves to the Lord, and unto us by the will of God.
>
> Insomuch that we desired Titus, that as he had begun, so he would also finish in you the same grace also.
>
> Therefore, as ye abound in every *thing, in* faith, and utterance, and knowledge, and *in* all diligence, and *in* your love to us, *see* that ye abound in this grace also.
>
> I speak not by commandment, but by occasion of the forwardness of others, and to prove the sincerity of your love.

To prove the sincerity of your love is to put your money where your mouth is. When God energises in you to do something with his money, are you going to withhold it or are you going to spend it as he wants it spent? One is walking by the senses, one is walking by the spirit. It's none of your business how God spends his money, it's your business to steward it properly and walk by the spirit.

> 2 Corinthians 8:9-12
> For ye know the grace of our Lord Jesus Christ, that, though he was rich, yet for your sakes he became poor, that ye through his poverty might be rich.
>
> And herein I give *my* advice: for this is expedient for you, who have begun before, not only to do, but also to be forward a year ago.

Now therefore perform the doing *of it;* that as *there was* a readiness to will, so *there may be* a performance also out of that which ye have.

For if there be first a willing mind, *it is* accepted according to that a man hath, *and* not according to that he hath not.

We obviously don't give until we have need ourselves, that would be ridiculous and God certainly does not expect it from us.

> 2 Corinthians 8:13-15
> For *I mean* not that other men be eased, and ye burdened:
>
> But by an equality, *that* now at this time your abundance *may be a supply* for their want, that their abundance also may be *a supply* for your want: that there may be equality:
>
> As it is written, He that *had gathered* much had nothing over; and he that *had gathered* little had no lack.

How we handle money will ultimately determine how the word will move. If we can't get our minds off ourselves and start looking after our brothers and sisters in Christ, the word will never live.

We are a family. We're supposed to look after each other and care for each other and love each other as families. We are to be living life every day in our home churches as families. We're supposed to be going out together, eating together, watching movies together as a family. If we start living life as families, the word will live.

> Acts 2:44-47
> And all that believed were together, and had all things common;
>
> And sold their possessions and goods, and parted them to all *men*, as every man had need.
>
> And they, continuing daily with one accord in the temple, and breaking bread from house to house, did eat their meat with gladness and singleness of heart,
>
> Praising God, and having favour with all the people. And the Lord added to the church daily such as should be saved.

These verses are the word of God, not the word of George. The verses don't even require any teaching, they are self-explanatory, they interpret themselves quite clearly. In our home churches, we have to start loving each other as families and we have to start living life together as families. If we only see each other once or twice a week at a stupid meeting, the word will never move in a thousand years. Might as well go to church.

It's time to start giving our lives to others and allowing others into our lives on a daily basis, living life together as families and having all things common. As others see us living life together as families, they will want to be a part of it. That's how the word moves.

> Galatians 6:10
> As we have therefore opportunity, let us do good unto all *men*, especially unto them who are of the household of faith.

To reiterate a point we've already touched on, no one is to walk into positions of responsibility in the body of Christ who has not first proven their own work. That is how man-made temples operate, but it is not how the body of Christ is to function. God gives the increase to those who are doing the planting and watering. If God gives you increase, then those people are your responsibility until they mature and can walk by the spirit for themselves. We are all to prove our own work. That's what the word says and that's what the word means.

> Galatians 6:3-5
> For if a man think himself to be something, when he is nothing, he deceiveth himself.
>
> But let every man prove his own work, and then shall he have rejoicing in himself alone, and not in another.
>
> For every man shall bear his own burden.

This is the only way to keep the wolves from God's people. The love of money is the root of all evil, and once you have an area with a few home churches established there is going to be a lot of money in God's petty cash tin. God's money isn't there to keep lazy bums and arrogant pricks who think they know everything in comfortable lifestyles at everyone else's expense. If you are a home church leader you have a responsibility to keep the wolves away from God's kids so do your job, walk by the spirit, and keep those fuckers away from your churches. If they're so spiritual, let them prove their own work by establishing their own home church.

> James 2:17,18
> Even so faith [believing], if it hath not works, is dead, being alone.
>
> Yea, a man may say, Thou hast faith [believing], and I have works: shew me thy faith [believing] without thy works, and I will shew thee my faith [believing] by my works.

If they're walking by the spirit, the increase will be there and you will see it because the word guarantees it.

> 1 Corinthians 3:5-8
> Who then is Paul, and who *is* Apollos, but ministers by whom ye believed, even as the Lord gave to every man?
>
> I have planted, Apollos watered; but God gave the increase.
>
> So then neither is he that planteth any thing, neither he that watereth; but God that giveth the increase.
>
> Now he that planteth and he that watereth are one: and every man shall receive his own reward according to his own labour.

You can't make hard and fast rules about this stuff though, you can't legislate it, you can't have written procedures, you have to be walking by the spirit to see it as every situation will be different. When we walk by the spirit, this stuff is easy. God may only give increase to those he knows will do the job, but in an emergency, he may just ask someone to step in unannounced to help out. That's what the gift ministries are for. Counsels of men don't decide these things, God decides them and gives orders to men and women walking by the spirit. That's why we make Christ our head, that's the key to understanding this.

Look, I've had it with lazy bums and spiritual hitchhikers with flashy nametags. If you're such an amazing leader, get out there and prove your own work, get a home church established and move the word. Let's see how spiritual you are. Jesus Christ proved his own work. He wasn't so high and mighty he could plant his backside behind a desk and tell everyone else to go do the work of the ministry, he was out there showing them how to do the work of the ministry. He was a leader, not a boss.

Matthew 20:25-28
But Jesus called them *unto him*, and said, Ye know that the princes of the Gentiles exercise dominion over them, and they that are great exercise authority upon them.

But it shall not be so among you: but whosoever will be great among you, let him be your minister;

And whosoever will be chief among you, let him be your servant:

Even as the Son of man came not to be ministered unto, but to minister, and to give his life a ransom for many.

Jesus Christ was this kind of leader and he moved the word. He gave his life for people and spent time with them every day. He and his apostles lived life together every day as a family. He didn't just talk about the word, he lived it. He saw in Peter leadership potential and worked with him patiently, teaching him the word and showing him how to apply it practically in his life. Peter, like all of us, was human, he wasn't perfect anymore than we are, and that's okay with God.

In Matthew 4, Jesus Christ invited Peter to follow him and he would make him a fisher of men. The word records that Peter straightway left his nets. Yet a few weeks later, Peter was back at his fishing business. Jesus came along, borrowed his boat, filled his net with fish and Peter once again left all to follow him. It's just so human. That wasn't the last time Peter would leave the work of the ministry and run off back to his old way of life either, as we shall see.

As well as his wavering nature (I couldn't resist the pun), Peter also had a habit of speaking out of turn, and Jesus Christ had to publicly sort him out on one or two occasions.

> Mark 8:31-33
> And he began to teach them, that the Son of man must suffer many things, and be rejected of the elders, and *of* the chief priests, and scribes, and be killed, and after three days rise again.
>
> And he spake that saying openly. And Peter took him, and began to rebuke him.
>
> But when he had turned about and looked on his disciples, he rebuked Peter, saying, Get thee behind me, Satan: for thou savourest not the things that be of God, but the things that be of men.

Will you look at that. Peter took a stand against Jesus Christ and tried to sort him out in front of the other disciples. If it wasn't recorded in the word, I wouldn't have believed it. Jesus Christ had to take a strong stand sometimes with Peter. He never gave up on him though, he kept working with him and kept teaching him the word.

Some folks think Jesus Christ built his church on Peter, but that's not what the word teaches at all. That's what the vatican teaches, but it's more of that dribbly religious horseshit they seem to enjoy drip feeding their people. Jesus Christ didn't build his church on Peter, he built it on himself.

Matthew 16:18
And I say also unto thee, That thou art Peter [petros], and upon this rock [petra] I will build my church; and the gates of hell [death] shall not prevail against it.

Petros refers to small grain sized bits of stone, like sand, which are blown around on the wind. Petra is a solid rock which no storm can move. Jesus Christ told Peter he was a petros, a grain sized piece of sand which was blown around with the wind. Then he told Peter that he himself, Jesus Christ was a petra, a solid mass of rock, and on himself, the petra, he would build his church and the gates of death would not be able to prevail against it.

See, it took time for Peter to get the word engrained in his soul and established in his heart. It takes time to raise disciples. That's why we must work with people in families, in home churches, where we can work with them and teach them the word. We have to give our lives to people if we ever want to see them become disciples. They have to see the word in our lives as we live the word. It's no different to raising children in earthly families. That's what it takes to raise disciples and it can take years. Each one win one is the only way to do this thing. This isn't about filling football stadiums and preaching to tens of thousands, it's about working with people one on one as parents with children.

To put this into perspective for you, Jesus Christ was perfect and he worked with twelve men as he moved the word and ministered, yet even he lost one of them, Judas Iscariot. To give you an idea of how good he was, I suggest you work with one person at a time. If you can handle two or three, great, but forget about filling football stadiums or establishing world wide ministries with thousands of people. This is about running home churches and raising disciples in families, where folks live the word together every day.

Despite his big mouth and vacillating nature, Jesus Christ had no hang ups or problems working with Peter. Towards the end of his ministry, after Peter had been with him for months, Jesus told the disciples he was going to be arrested and killed. He wanted to prepare them for what was coming because he cared about their hearts.

> Mark 14:27-31
> And Jesus saith unto them, All ye shall be offended because of me this night: for it is written, I will smite the shepherd, and the sheep shall be scattered.
>
> But after that I am risen, I will go before you into Galilee.
>
> But Peter said unto him, Although all shall be offended, yet *will* not I.
>
> And Jesus saith unto him, Verily I say unto thee, That this day, *even* in this night, before the cock crow twice, thou shalt deny me thrice.
>
> But he spake the more vehemently, If I should die with thee, I will not deny thee in any wise. Likewise also said they all.

Did Peter deny him? Oh yes, he sure did.

> Matthew 26:73-75
> And after a while came unto *him* they that stood by, and said to Peter, Surely thou also art *one* of them; for thy speech bewrayeth thee.
>
> Then began he to curse and to swear, *saying*, I know not the man. And immediately the cock crew.
>
> And Peter remembered the word of Jesus, which said unto him, Before the cock crow, thou shalt deny me thrice. And he went out, and wept bitterly.

Where was Peter after the resurrection? He was hiding behind closed doors for fear of the Judeans, for fear of the same men who had just had

Jesus Christ murdered by the Romans. He was afraid for his life. Peter was very human.

John 20:19
Then the same day at evening, being the first *day* of the week, when the doors were shut where the disciples were assembled for fear of the Jews [Judeans], came Jesus and stood in the midst, and saith unto them, Peace *be* unto you.

Some time after that, after seeing the resurrected Christ and talking to him, Peter once again chucked it all in and went back to his fishing business and his old way of life. That's Peter.

John 21:3-7
Simon Peter saith unto them, I go a fishing. They say unto him, We also go with thee. They went forth, and entered into a ship immediately; and that night they caught nothing.

But when the morning was now come, Jesus stood on the shore: but the disciples knew not that it was Jesus.

Then Jesus saith unto them, Children, have ye any meat? They answered him, No.

And he said unto them, Cast the net on the right side of the ship, and ye shall find. They cast therefore, and now they were not able to draw it for the multitude of fishes.

Therefore that disciple whom Jesus loved saith unto Peter, It is the Lord. Now when Simon Peter heard that it was the Lord, he girt *his* fisher's coat *unto him*, (for he was naked,) and did cast himself into the sea.

Once Peter knew it was Jesus Christ standing on the shore, he just chucked himself overboard. No matter what he did, he just couldn't get away from the guy. His heart must have crunched when he realised it was Jesus again. That wasn't the first time Jesus had filled his nets with fish either, was it?

John 21:8-12
And the other disciples came in a little ship; (for they were not far from land, but as it were two hundred cubits,) dragging the net with fishes.

As soon then as they were come to land, they saw a fire of coals there, and fish laid thereon, and bread.

Jesus saith unto them, Bring of the fish which ye have now caught.

Simon Peter went up, and drew the net to land full of great fishes, an hundred and fifty and three: and for all there were so many, yet was not the net broken.

Jesus saith unto them, Come *and* dine. And none of the disciples durst ask him, Who art thou? knowing that it was the Lord.

Look at how Jesus Christ dealt with Peter and the others after they'd run off to make a few bucks and get on with their old ways of life. He didn't lecture them, he found them by the seaside after a long night of catching nothing and made them breakfast.

John 21:13-15
Jesus then cometh, and taketh bread, and giveth them, and fish likewise.

This is now the third time that Jesus shewed himself to his disciples, after that he was risen from the dead.

So when they had dined, Jesus saith to Simon Peter, Simon, *son* of Jonas, lovest thou me more than these? He saith unto him, Yea, Lord; thou knowest that I love thee. He saith unto him, Feed my lambs [male lambs].

Once they were all seated, Jesus Christ eventually brought things back to the word and confronted Peter. He asked Peter if he loved his old way of life and his fishing business more than he loved the work of the ministry. When Peter told him the word was first, Jesus Christ told him to feed his male lambs. He then pressed him again, a second time.

John 21:16
He saith to him again the second time, Simon, *son* of Jonas, lovest thou me? He saith unto him, Yea, Lord; thou knowest that I love thee. He saith unto him, Feed my sheep [female lambs].

He then pressed him again, a third time.

John 21:17
He saith unto him the third time, Simon, *son* of Jonas, lovest thou me? Peter was grieved because he said unto him the third time, Lovest thou me? And he said unto him, Lord, thou knowest all things; thou knowest that I love thee. Jesus saith unto him, Feed my sheep [adult sheep].

Did Peter eventually respond and give his life to the word? Oh yes. Just look at the man he became in the book of Acts. Where would we be today without Peter's life and ministry? The time Jesus Christ spent teaching him, confronting him and bringing him back to the word when he needed it was time well spent. The time we spend with people, teaching them, confronting them and bringing them back to the word when it's needed is also time well spent.

I trust you now have a deeper appreciation of how human Peter and all the other men and women mentioned in the bible really were. They were not supermen or superwomen, they were human, just as we are. Even Jesus Christ was human. Always remember that the people we work with are human, just like Peter, just like we are. Walk by the spirit and raise disciples with patience and love, despite their being human. Work with them in home church families as earthly parents do with their children until they can walk by the spirit on their own two feet and believe God for themselves. Even then we're still family and we always look out for each other.

68. The British Olympic Opening Ceremony

Hailed as a triumphant celebration of everything British, the opening olympic ceremony was televised around the world to billions. I watched it too, but I had to watch it until almost the end to figure out what it was all about spiritually.

As we know, the god of this world moves the courses of the world through religious secret societies who practice witchcraft. The most obvious symbol of their religion is the pyramid with the all seeing eye. Well, check these images. Notice anything?

Need a clue? Okay, here's a clue. See the pyramids and eyes now?

And here's one from the BBC olympics website, showcasing the illuminating of the stadium from eyes within the pyramids, as well as being displayed in the most prominent spot on the BBC website.

The London 2012 Olympic opening ceremony was nothing more than a huge witchcraft ritual to the god of this world. The olympic torch, which was carried around almost the entire British Isles, symbolised the fire of witchcraft. The culmination was the all seeing eye flaring up as the torches came together and were raised in the midst of the pyramids. Everyone there was part of a huge witchcraft ceremony worshipping the god of this world, and most didn't even know it.

Well, here's something to think about. The olympic torch never came to Sutherland in the Highlands of Scotland where this class was being written.

69. The Making of a Patriarch

How the god of this world destroys the effectiveness of energised ministries of men and women of God and transforms the word they stood for into religious horseshit is quite something to understand. As a present day example, let's consider how Dr Victor Paul Wierwille's ministry of the Way International, one of the most powerful ministries of all time was compromised after his death and transformed into just another religious temple made with hands.

It is an interesting phenomenon that men and women in religions and churches around the world think they are right, that they are in what they believe to be the only true household of God. Quite how the devil instils this lie into people is really quite brilliant. The vatican believes it is the only true church on earth. Muslims believe they are the only true followers of God on earth. Buddhists believe they have found the true way to God. Jehovah's witnesses, a particularly insipid brand of religion, believe they are the only true way to God. Mormons believe they are the only true church of God on earth. The Way International believes it is the only true household of God and instils that lie into its followers. Before we start, remember that God does not dwell in, he does not live in, he does not frequent temples made with hands. Religions and manmade ministries are all broken cisterns and any word they once held eventually leaks out of them. If God doesn't live in them, how can they be a source of living waters?

> Jeremiah 2:13
> For my people have committed two evils; they have forsaken me the fountain of living waters, and hewed them out cisterns, broken cisterns, that can hold no water.

The living waters in Jeremiah refer to God, who is the fountain of living waters. People just seem to feel a need to hew out for themselves cisterns. A cistern is something man makes to hold water. If our supply is

God, a living fountain, there is no requirement for a cistern as a fountain has an endless supply. Men hew out cisterns because they do not believe God will supply all their need. Consequently, they turn their backs on the fountain and hew out for themselves cisterns - they build churches, ministries, and organisations to contain their religion. They put their trust in the work of their own hands rather than in God.

As we have clearly seen, the biblical definition of the word ekklēsia, the word church, when used of the church of God is used exclusively in reference to people called out from among both Judeans and Gentiles. It cannot be used to mean a church building, a religion, a ministry, or any ecclesiastical structure of any kind. No church or ministry or religion can claim to be the church of God, the household of God, because ekklēsia cannot be used in that context.

The Roman Catholic church is not the church of God. Its people may be part of the church of God if they are born again, but the Roman Catholic church itself is just another temple made with hands. The Mormons, the Jehovahs, the Anglicans, the Baptists, the Pentecostals, the Episcopalians, and all the other churches and religions around the world are not the church of God. The people within may be part of that church if they are born again, but those religions are all just temples made with hands. The Way International is not the church of God. The people within may be part of that church, but the ministry itself is just another temple made with hands. Men have built them all and God does not dwell in temples made with hands.

So how does the god of this world transform energised ministries, like the ministries of Martin Luther, John Wesley and Dr Wierwille for example, into powerless, ineffective religious cisterns which do nothing but churn out worthless ceremonies every week? He accomplishes it by constructing temples made with hands over their graves.

In the 1300's, Dr Wierwille's family lived in Vierville-sur-mer in northern France. The Viervilles were Huguenots who stood against the religious horseshit dribbling out of Rome. After the Reformation, the Viervilles fled to Germany to escape persecution from the murderous jesuits. While in Germany, the family changed their name to Wierwille. Johann Heinrich Wierwille, Dr Wierwille's great grandfather, arrived in

America with his family in 1839 and settled in the New Knoxville area of Ohio.

Victor Paul was born to Ernst and Emma Wierwille on December 31, 1916, the youngest of seven children. Growing up he rode motorcycles and played basketball. In June 1941, Dr Wierwille was ordained as a minister in the Evangelical and Reformed church and accepted a call to serve in their church in Payne, Ohio. In June 1944, believing he had taken his congregation as far as they wanted to go, he and his family moved to the church in Van Wert, Ohio, moving from a congregation of one hundred and twenty members to just sixteen. It was during his time in Van Wert that Dr Wierwille left his denomination and founded the Way Ministry because he had seen that the greatness of God's power lay in the holy spirit field and not in religious nonsense. In 1953, he began teaching his classes on Power for Abundant Living. He had learned how to energise the gift of holy spirit by speaking in tongues and he wanted to teach it to the world. In the early 1980's, Dr Wierwille's ministry was active on every continent in over 120 countries around the world.

Was Dr Wierwille a patriarch? In the old testament, before the day of Pentecost, holy spirit was not generally and freely available to man, therefore men needed special leaders with holy spirit upon them, someone they could go to for answers from God, someone who could lead them. Since the day of Pentecost, every born again believer has holy spirit, every born again believer has access directly to God, and every born again believer can walk by the spirit with Christ as their head. In this administration, we do not need patriarchs or priests because we have someone far better, the Lord Jesus Christ who is head over all things to the church. We can all go directly to God ourselves through the gift of holy spirit, that Christ in us, without having to go through men.

However, there *is* a need for leadership to teach new believers how to walk by the spirit for themselves, to undershepherd them until they can walk on their own two feet in the spiritual competition. As this is best done in families, God has set up a leadership system in this Age of Grace that is based on family relationships rather than the leadership and patriarchal systems of previous administrations. Everyone in the family of God has spirit, it's just that some are more mature and know more about spiritual matters, and they are to oversee and look after the younger children until they mature. This can only be achieved in a family setting, which is why God wants his word living in home churches. Dr Wierwille was not a patriarch, he was faithful to raise disciples and he established home churches all over the world.

Dr Wierwille always publicly stated that the highest positions available in his ministry were the home church leaders, and his Way Corps leadership training programme was set up to train home church leaders. When the word moved over the world from the Way while Dr Wierwille was still alive, it was moved by home church leaders who held meetings in their homes. Those leaders walked by the spirit and God energised in them to will and to do of his good pleasure. Christ was their head and the word moved. Dr Wierwille's entire ministry was based on the church in the home and he left the home church leadership alone to do their job. The Way International's sole purpose was to support the home church leaders as they moved the word and raised disciples in their homes.

After Dr Wierwille's death, the purpose of the Way Corps changed from training home church leadership to training a ministry hierarchy. The scriptures used to force that legislation through were taken from the time the Patriarchal Administration was transitioning to the Law Administration, a time when people had no spirit, a time when people needed a patriarch. That was the moment when the Way International became just another temple made with hands run by a patriarch. Dr Wierwille was not a patriarch because he did not attempt to control his leadership, he taught them to walk by the spirit and trusted them to move the word in their areas. The man who came after him was solely intent on taking control of everything, claiming that God was giving him all the revelation for the entire Way International. Well, we now know from scripture that God no longer honours such patriarchal systems and that he refuses to attend any such temples made with hands.

All the leadership of the Way International at that time who left the ministry also set themselves up as patriarchs in their own little man-made temples. One man even used the tithe money that still went to him to build a new church. Everyone wanted to be the big boss and if they didn't get the job, most of them left and hewed them out broken cisterns of their own. The patriarchal system is over. If you want to be a leader and do something for God, establish a church in your home that is self governing, self propagating and self supporting, walk by the spirit, move the word, and show others how to do the same. To be fair, I think perhaps Chris Geer may have seen some of this stuff, but he was wrong to call Dr Wierwille a patriarch. All his book The Passing of a Patriarch accomplished was to divert attention away from Craig Martindale who was busily setting himself up as one.

We have all been given grace according to the measure of the gift of Christ. So, did you get any more spirit than me? No, you did not. So what makes you think you know better than I do how I should live my life? You live your own fucking life. Everyone wants to be a patriarch these days, the big boss. Did I get anymore spirit than you? No, I did not. We all got the same amount, we each were given grace according to the measure of the gift of Christ, which is the gift of holy spirit, that Christ in us. No one gets any more spirit than anyone else and no one gets any less spirit than anyone else. There is only one measure of the gift of Christ, and we all get the same measure, the same amount. You have spirit just as I do, so what right then do I have to try to run your life for you? I have no right whatsoever. I have no interest in running your life for you. You take responsibility for your own life and prove your own work and then shall you have rejoicing in yourself and not in another.

> Galatians 6:3,4
> For if a man think himself to be something, when he is nothing, he deceiveth himself.
>
> But let every man prove his own work, and then shall he have rejoicing in himself alone, and not in another.

The Age of Grace is not a patriarchal administration. We all have the spirit in full measure, and so we all have a responsibility to learn to walk by that spirit with Christ as our head and not men. That's why God no longer dwells in temples made with hands. Trying to run a religious organisation, where a handful of men and women make all the decisions for everyone else is spiritual horseshit in this Age of Grace.

God knows everything, you don't, and I don't care how intelligent and educated and right you think you are. You cannot do God's job for him.

What makes you think you can handle spiritual matters 4000 miles away by telephone? You don't know the first fucking thing about what's going on in that area, but the home church leaders over there do. If you're so spiritual, get back out into real life and show us how to run a home church. If you want to be an example, go and show us how to move the word, run a church in your home and raise disciples who walk by the spirit.

We don't need any more patriarchs or priests, we need people to run churches in their homes, to teach, to walk by the spirit and minister, to raise disciples in families. Dr Wierwille would have dismantled the Way International and committed the word to his worldwide ministry of home church leaders before his death had he seen the depth of the truth that God dwelleth not in temples made with hands. Paul didn't see it either, which is why he deserted the Gentiles and ran off to Jerusalem in Acts 21 to try and save the 'ministry'. What a waste of time that was. He should have stayed with his people. This is God's will in the Age of Grace. There are no more excuses.

Dr Wierwille's ministry was to take the word over the world. He fulfilled that calling, he accomplished that work before his death. His ministry, his calling from God was to take the word over the world, not to construct a man-made temple. The Way International was his ministry, his means of taking the word over the world. When that goal was accomplished, the Way International had fulfilled its purpose. Dr Wierwille was not a patriarch, he was simply a man big enough to oversee a world wide ministry built by his own work.

Anyone who has Christ in them is part of the church of God, the ekklēsia, the called out of God. And I don't give a shit what the Way International or the vatican claim to the contrary. By definition and by scripture, ecclesiastical and religious structures built by men which claim to be the church of God are liars. God dwelleth not in temples made with hands. Today, we don't need any ministry running our lives for us because we have Christ in us and we can walk by the spirit. Following the direction of a council of men is turning your back on God and hewing out a man-made cistern. It is putting your trust in men. It is walking by the senses.

People, if you want to be a disciple learn to read your bible and study this class, speak in tongues much and learn to walk by the spirit with

Christ as your head. Get out of those churches and ministries you attend, those man-made broken cisterns. Don't be afraid, for you can do all things through Christ who strengthens you. That strength doesn't come by mindlessly following a board of directors, a council of men, it comes from the Christ in you.

Dr Wierwille taught that churches in the home should be self governing, self propagating, and self supporting. He learned that from the work of Henry Venn, one of the shapers and movers of the nineteenth-century missionary movement who taught God's word in meetings at his home. Both Henry Venn and Dr Wierwille were right. God's plan for his people in the Age of Grace is to teach and minister in their homes. To be successful, each home church is to be self governing, self propagating, and self supporting. What Dr Wierwille and Henry Venn meant by self governing was that each home church was to conduct its affairs from within, not allow itself to be governed by outside councils of men. Self governing by definition requires breaking away from the restraints and control of central governing councils of men. When Dr Wierwille stated that home churches should be self governing, that is what he meant. In other words, each home church is the headquarters of the move of God's word in that area.

Since Dr Wierwille's death, I've not heard much from the lectern in the auditorium at the headquarters of the Way International about home churches being self governing, self propagating and self supporting. The Way International no longer teaches Dr Wierwille's classes and conveniently ignores sections of his teachings which don't support their patriarchal system. When the word moved over the world, the word moved from churches in people's homes, and the entire Way ministry was geared up to support the home church leaders in their efforts to get that word over the world. Since Dr Wierwille's death, the Way International has been restructured to support a patriarch surrounded by a central governing body of men. The Way International no longer teaches its people to walk by the spirit, rather it teaches them to submit themselves to a structure of leadership who walk by counsels of men. Ladies and gentlemen, that is walking by the senses and having confidence in the flesh. That is how the devil constructs temples made with hands over the graves of energised ministers.

Philippians 3:3
For we are the circumcision, which worship God in the spirit, and rejoice in Christ Jesus, and have no confidence in the flesh.

So you think you have the word over there in Ohio, do you? You've already forgotten the basic fundamental truths of the Mystery that Dr Wierwille taught regarding the church of God and the body of Christ. As Dr Wierwille so prophetically stated, it is the truths of the mystery that are the first to be lost and the last to be regained. You are not the body of Christ nor are you the household of God, and I can prove that from scripture. In fact, I now consider you one of the most dangerous brands of religion on the planet, for indeed, you did have the word but you chose to honour men rather than God, you put your own needs above the needs of God's people, and when Dr Wierwille died you blindly followed a patriarch and constructed a temple over his grave.

God gave to us, to each one of us, the ministry of reconciliation. That means it's our job to do the work of the ministry, not yours. The church of God is not some man-made temple you call the Way International, any more than it is the Roman Catholic church, or the Church of Jesus Christ of latter day saints (whatever that garbage is supposed to mean), or any other church or denomination on earth.

The Way International is not the ministry of reconciliation, it is a man-made temple. God did not give the ministry of reconciliation to the Way International. God did not give the ministry of reconciliation to Dr Wierwille. God gave the ministry of reconciliation to all of us, those of us who have the gift of holy spirit and are part of the church of God. Dr Wierwille sure made full proof of his ministry and God energised in him to move the word over the world, and God blessed his ministry, that's for sure, but God didn't just give the ministry to Dr Wierwille, that's the point.

Dr Wierwille was not a patriarch, he was simply a man big enough to oversee a worldwide ministry, but all those who came after him were indeed patriarchs, attempting to do Christ's job for him by being the head over all things to what they call the church.

Okay, perhaps you didn't know any better. However, you know now. So what is it going to be? Is all that tithe money you steal from God's people more important to you? The money shared by God's people should be used by the home church leaders to move the word in their areas. It most definitely should not be sent to the headquarters of a temple made with hands to keep a council of men in comfortable lifestyles. The word says the love of money is the root of all evil, and that must include how the god of this world constructs temples made with hands over the graves of energised ministers like Dr Wierwille.

Instead of establishing the Way International as a temple made with hands and transferring leadership of his work to others, Dr Wierwille should have released the word to the home church leaders around the world and dismantled the Way International before his death. Had the home church leaders at that time been given responsibility to oversee their areas without any interference from without, the word would have lived on. Each of us is to take responsibility for those God entrusts to our care, not relinquish that care to others. When you can no longer take care of God's people, either through retirement or death, or for any other reason, those you have raised into leadership positions are then to assume responsibility for their own work, those God entrusted to them, without any interference from without.

We are all to prove our own work, not go stealing work from others to hide our impotence and make ourselves feel important. If you want to be a leader, go and move the word and show us how it's done, never mind trying to steal my work from me. That's how this thing moves. We all have Christ in us, so we all have the ability to do this. God even committed to us his word, so we can move this ministry and learn to walk with Christ as our head.

Dr Wierwille taught that every home church should be self governing, self propagating, and self supporting, that the highest positions in his ministry were the home church leadership, and his Way Corps was designed and set up to teach disciples how to be good home church leaders. There is no higher position available in the body of Christ. All those man-made temples out there may not like what I'm teaching, but I really don't give a fuck. All I care about is that the word lives. If you want to be a leader, then set your sights on learning to walk by the spirit and running a church in your home with Christ as your head.

70. Christ in You, the Hope of Glory

The apostle Paul is an intriguing character. The more you get to know him, the more you will learn to love the guy. We have a lot to thank him for too. Without his epistles, where would we be today?

The first time we meet the man is at Stephen's murder. The Sanhedrin had hired criminals to lay false legal complaints against Stephen so they could summon him before their council. Rather than try to wriggle out of their net, Stephen confronted those bastards to their faces. He called them stiff necked and uncircumcised in heart and ears. Blinded by rage, the Sanhedrin had him stoned to death.

> Acts 7:54-60
> When they [the Sanhedrin] heard these things, they were cut to the heart, and they gnashed on him with *their* teeth.
>
> But he [Stephen], being full of the Holy Ghost [holy spirit], looked up stedfastly into heaven, and saw the glory of God, and Jesus standing on the right hand of God,
>
> And said, Behold, I see the heavens opened, and the Son of man standing on the right hand of God.
>
> Then they cried out with a loud voice, and stopped their ears, and ran upon him with one accord,
>
> And cast *him* out of the city, and stoned *him:* and the witnesses laid down their clothes at a young man's feet, whose name was Saul.
>
> And they stoned Stephen, calling upon *God,* and saying, Lord Jesus, receive my spirit.

And he kneeled down, and cried with a loud voice, Lord, lay not this sin to their charge. And when he had said this, he fell asleep [he died].

Paul and Saul are the same man. Paul was his Greek name, while Saul was his Hebrew name. The witnesses laying their clothes at Paul's feet is a reference to his authority at Stephen's stoning. It is likely that Paul was the man in charge of his illegal execution and murder. So here is our first encounter with Paul. Before he was born again, Paul was a murderer of God's children.

Acts 9:1,2
And Saul [Paul], yet breathing out threatenings and slaughter against the disciples of the Lord, went unto the high priest,

And desired of him letters to Damascus to the synagogues, that if he found any of this way, whether they were men or women, he might bring them bound unto Jerusalem.

Paul was a religious dragon, a man who thought nothing of torturing and murdering God's children, a man who actively sought open doors to persecute them and kill them. Religious men are the cruellest and most vicious cunts on the face of the earth. They may hide their nature behind trite little slogans of world peace, but in reality the passion of their hearts is the extermination of God's people and the eradication of the accurate knowledge of the bible from the face of the earth. This is where the apostle Paul came from. His worldly credentials are worth noting.

Philippians 3:4
Though I [Paul] might also have confidence in the flesh. If any other man thinketh that he hath whereof he might trust in the flesh, I more:

Paul states that he had more reasons to have confidence in the flesh than any other human being on the planet at that time. That is quite a statement, yet God told him to write it by revelation so it is the truth.

Walking *by* the Spirit

Philippians 3:5-7
Circumcised the eighth day, of the stock of Israel, *of* the tribe of Benjamin, an Hebrew of the Hebrews; as touching the law, a Pharisee;

Concerning zeal, persecuting the church; touching the righteousness which is in the law, blameless.

But what things were gain to me, those I counted loss for Christ.

Paul had everything the world could offer. He had education, background, and family, a man who had been brought up as a Pharisee. Here he was on the road to Damascus, breathing out threatenings and slaughter against the church of God. Did he think he was right? Did he believe he was doing God's will? Unquestionably, and therein lies the paradox of religion - they all think they're so right and yet they're all so wrong. Religion is a disease that blinds men's eyes, deafens their ears, and hardens their hearts. That's why God refuses to dwell in them.

Acts 9:3,4
And as he journeyed, he came near Damascus: and suddenly there **shined round about** him [periastraptō] a light from heaven:

And he fell to the earth, and heard a voice saying unto him, Saul, Saul, why persecutest thou me?

I've always been taught that this appearance of Jesus Christ on the road to Damascus was so brilliant that it blinded Paul. I've had a few problems with this for years. Now bear with me here and just stop for a minute and track with me. Does the bible actually state that God or Jesus Christ blinded Paul? No it doesn't. It says there shined a light around him that came from heaven, and then he heard a voice. The two events are not axiomatically one and the same.

In which of Jesus' post resurrection appearances does he ever float around in a blinding flash of light? Most of the appearances I read have him standing on the ground like a normal human being. And why would Jesus, or God for that matter want to blind the man anyway? If God did indeed blind him, then why did Jesus Christ send Ananias over to give him his sight back? If God wanted him blind, surely Jesus Christ would have left him blind.

Shined round about is translated from the Greek word periastraptō. Peri means round about. Astrapē is translated 8 times as lightning and once as bright shining. There are no other Greek words translated lightning in the bible. Astrapē means lightning.

> Matthew 24:27
> For as the lightning [astrapē] cometh out of the east, and shineth even unto the west; so shall also the coming of the Son of man be.

Astrapē comes from the Greek word astraptō, which is only used twice in the new testament where it is translated as lighten and shine. Periastraptō is also only used twice, here and later when Paul was recounting the incident to Agrippa.

> Acts 26:13,14
> At midday, O king, I saw in the way a light from heaven, above the brightness of the sun, **shining round about** me [periastraptō] and them which journeyed with me.
>
> And when we were all fallen to the earth, I heard a voice speaking unto me, and saying in the Hebrew tongue, Saul, Saul, why persecutest thou me? *it is* hard for thee to kick against the pricks.

This concurs with the record in Acts 9. This brilliant flashing lightning cracked down from the sky and hit the earth all around him. The word then says that he and the men with him all fell to the earth, and then, *then* he heard the voice speaking to him. In other words, there was a time gap between the lightning and the voice. The flash of light and the hearing of the voice did not happen simultaneously, and there is no way anyone can categorically state that these two events were one and the same, that the voice and the lightning were the same event. To do so is private interpretation.

Periastraptō could, I suppose, be translated here as a bright light that flashed around him like lightning, inferring that it could have been a spiritual phenomenon of some kind, but I don't see any similes being used here.

Acts 9:3
And as he journeyed, he came near Damascus: and suddenly there **shined round about** [periastraptō] him a light from heaven:

Unlike the tongues like as of fire in Acts 2, which uses the figure simile to let us know it wasn't literally fire, I believe the absence of the simile here indicates this was in fact a lightning strike. It says it came from heaven. Well, heaven means any place above earth, so it came from the sky. The point is, it didn't come from just above his head or emanate from some shining white robed, long haired weirdo white man prick with creepy eyes and a fucking halo around his head, it came down from the sky in a flash of lightning.

Where am I going with this? Well, I believe this lightning strike was the devil trying to kill Paul before Jesus Christ could witness to him. The lightning strike blinded him and Jesus Christ had to send Ananias to minister to him to give him his sight back. What use would a blind Paul have been to anyone? I don't think God blinded him, I think the devil did. Do your own research, study this thing, check out periastraptō for yourself, see if these things are so.

Acts 9:3,4
And as he journeyed, he came near Damascus: and suddenly there shined round about him [periastraptō] a light from heaven:

And he fell to the earth, and heard a voice saying unto him, Saul, Saul, why persecutest thou me?

I think we all conclude that God did this to Paul because he was such a bad dude, and we still have it in the back of our minds that God punishes us for being evil. It just isn't so.

Ezekiel 18:23
Have I any pleasure at all that the wicked should die? saith the Lord GOD: *and* not that he should return from his ways, and live?

If you ever doubt the truth of Ezekiel 18:23, take a look at the life of Paul. I don't care who you are or what you've done, if God could forgive Paul, forgiving you will not be a problem for him.

Psalm 103:10
He hath not dealt with us after our sins; nor rewarded us according to our iniquities.

Perhaps you and I might like to think Paul deserved a good kicking for being such a bastard, and perhaps he did deserve to be struck by lightning, but weren't we all guilty of death before we were born again? Did God strike you with lightning to get your attention just before you were born again? I don't think so.

Do you blind people and do horrible things to them just before you teach them the word to get them born again? Hardly, so why then do we just naturally assume Jesus Christ did something to Paul that we wouldn't dream of doing to anyone in our wildest imaginations? Sure, Elymas the Sorcerer was blinded, but that was so Paul could teach the word to Sergius Paulus. Paul didn't blind Sergius Paulus to get his attention before speaking the word to him, did he? I do not believe God or Jesus Christ blinded Paul, I believe the devil tried to kill him with a lightning strike just before he got born again. I believe it was Jesus Christ's intervention that actually saved his life. How do I know Paul got born again? Read the next verse.

Acts 9:5
And he said, Who art thou, Lord? And the Lord said, I am Jesus whom thou persecutest: *it is* hard for thee to kick against the pricks.

How do you get born again? If you don't know, go and memorise this verse.

Romans 10:9
That if thou shalt confess with thy mouth the Lord Jesus, and shalt believe in thine heart that God hath raised him from the dead, thou shalt be saved.

Paul called Jesus Christ Lord, and he obviously knew he'd been raised from the dead because he was speaking to him, so it was at that moment Paul was born again. I believe that's why the devil tried to kill him just moments earlier. Imagine Paul's shock on realising just who he was talking to.

Acts 9:6-11
And he trembling and astonished said, Lord, what wilt thou have me to do? And the Lord *said* unto him, Arise, and go into the city, and it shall be told thee what thou must do.

And the men which journeyed with him stood speechless, hearing a voice, but seeing no man.

And Saul arose from the earth; and when his eyes were opened, he saw no man: but they led him by the hand, and brought *him* into Damascus.

And he was three days without sight, and neither did eat nor drink.

And there was a certain disciple at Damascus, named Ananias; and to him said the Lord in a vision, Ananias. And he said, Behold, I *am here*, Lord.

And the Lord *said* unto him, Arise, and go into the street which is called Straight, and enquire in the house of Judas for *one* called Saul, of Tarsus: for, behold, he prayeth,

At this stage, because I just got the green light, it is time to introduce what is probably the most important key to walking by the spirit, but a key which has been completely lost since the first century. We've all heard that Christ is our head a thousand times but the truth of it just has not registered. Most people think the devil's greatest work is putting things into our heads, but that's not the case at all, his greatest work is keeping things out. He doesn't educate, he blinds.

2 Corinthians 4:4
In whom the god of this world hath blinded the minds of them which believe not, lest the light of the glorious gospel of Christ, who is the image of God, should shine unto them.

Christ is our head, right? That's foundational and rudimentary, but have you ever noticed who Ananias was talking to here? Was it God? It says the Lord spoke to him in a vision. Well, who is our Lord? God is not our Lord, Jesus Christ is our Lord, so this was Jesus Christ talking to

Ananias, not God. Christ is head over all things to the church and it is Christ in us. Christ is also the mediator between God and man. What do you think that all means?

> Colossians 1:27
> To whom God would make known what *is* the riches of the glory of this mystery among the Gentiles; which is Christ in you, the hope of glory:

> Ephesians 1:22,23
> And hath put all *things* under his feet, and gave him *to be* the head over all *things* to the church,

Which is his body, the fulness of him that filleth all in all.

> 1 Timothy 2:5
> For *there is* one God, and one mediator between God and men, the man Christ Jesus;

The point is, Jesus Christ isn't just sitting up there watching everything, he has a job to do, he has a responsibility to carry out. His job isn't the ministry of reconciliation, that's our job, his job is being head over all things to the church. He is our Lord, our boss, he is the one who gives the commands, he is our head. How Jesus Christ is head over all things to the church is through the Christ in us, the gift of holy spirit. As we walk by the spirit rather than by the senses, then Christ is our head and we're taking our orders from him. Christ's head is God, so God gives the orders to Christ who passes them on to us through the Christ in us. God teaches the Christ in us, and Christ teaches our mind.

> 1 Corinthians 11:3
> But I would have you know, that the head of every man is Christ; and the head of the woman *is* the man; and the head of Christ *is* God.

> Ephesians 5:23
> For the husband is the head of the wife, even as Christ is the head of the church: and he is the saviour of the body.

Listen, God is not our Lord, Jesus Christ is our Lord. God is not Jesus Christ anymore than Jesus Christ is God. It was Jesus Christ talking to Ananias, just as it had been Jesus Christ talking to Paul. Jesus Christ's job is to oversee the church of God, that's his responsibility. God gave him that responsibility when he made him head over all things to the church. Just as God will not speak the word to anyone because that is our job, God will not direct the church because that is Jesus Christ's job. Jesus Christ is our head, our Lord, the head over all things to the church. How we make Christ our head is by walking by the spirit, by learning to listen to the Christ in us, by operating and energising the gift of holy spirit. When we walk by the spirit with Christ as our head, then Christ is head over all things to the church. When we teach others to walk by the spirit with Christ as their head, we are edifying, building up the body of Christ.

Listen to the instruction Jesus Christ gave to Ananias.

> Acts 9:12-14
> And hath seen in a vision a man named Ananias coming in, and putting *his* hand on him, that he might receive his sight.
>
> Then Ananias answered, Lord, I have heard by many of this man, how much evil he hath done to thy saints at Jerusalem:
>
> And here he hath authority from the chief priests to bind all that call on thy name.

It's exciting to realise that Ananias knew it was Jesus Christ he was speaking to, not God. He was not astonished by that either, or speechless with wonder, it was expected, it was normal. The first century church knew that Christ was their head, that Christ was their Lord, their boss, their CEO, the head over all things to the church. Ananias knew Jesus Christ was his Lord, and that it was him he was talking to.

People who call God their Lord are blind leaders of the blind and they are all in the ditch. With Christ as our head, who needs counsels of men? Christ is my head, my Lord, not some counsel of men at the headquarters of a man-made ministry. I take my orders from Jesus Christ. How I get those orders is through the Christ in me, the gift of holy spirit. We can only walk by the spirit when we make Christ our head. Jesus Christ didn't go and speak to Ananias' home church leader first, did he? Jesus Christ didn't go and speak to his branch or country coordinator first, did he?

If God had instituted a leadership structure of men for this administration, then Jesus Christ would have had to go through Ananias' leadership, who would have passed the information down the chain of command. That was how things were done in the old testament, but it is not how things are done in this administration. Jesus Christ didn't go to Ananias' country coordinator or home church leader, or the men at the top of some ministry or other, he went directly to Ananias because he is the Lord, our boss and he can give orders to anyone he fucking well likes, even if it's just a disciple who isn't even a home church leader. Get your head around this because if the word is to live we must walk away from temples made with hands and their crappy leadership structures of men who walk by their senses.

As a little morsel for you to think about here, ask yourself, why did Paul get the revelation to write the epistles to the Romans, Corinthians, Galatians, Ephesians, Philippians, Colossians, and Thessalonians? Why didn't Peter get the revelation? Or John? Or any of the other apostles? Was it because Paul was the big boss, the leader, the patriarch, the president, the head of the first century church? No, a thousand times no, it was because the home churches Paul wrote to were his responsibility because he had built those churches from the ground up. The believers he wrote to were his responsibility. If Peter had started the work in Corinth, Peter would have had the revelation to write to them, but he didn't build the work there, Paul did. That's why God worked with him. God will work with you too with those he has given you to raise as disciples. We are all to prove our own work.

If your home church leader doesn't like you walking by the spirit and confronts you for not checking things through him when you do things or handle situations, tell him to go fuck himself. What Christ tells you to do is none of his fucking business. His job is to run his home church, not run our lives for us thinking God gives him all the revelation for everyone. It's time to make Christ our head folks and disentangle ourselves from the senses, fleshly, worldly walks of men. If your home church leader is walking by the spirit, he should be delighted he has men and women around him who do the same.

Ananias understandably had a problem with his assignment. Look at Jesus Christ's response to him.

> Acts 9:15-17
> But the Lord said unto him, Go thy way: for he is a chosen vessel unto me, to bear my name before the Gentiles, and kings, and the children of Israel:
>
> For I will shew him how great things he must suffer [endure] for my name's sake.
>
> And Ananias went his way, and entered into the house; and putting his hands on him said, Brother Saul, the Lord, *even* Jesus, that appeared unto thee in the way as thou camest, hath sent me, that thou mightest receive thy sight, and be filled with the Holy Ghost [holy spirit].

Can it be any clearer? It was Jesus Christ who talked to Ananias and sent him to see Paul. It wasn't God. It's right there in the word. Read verse 17 again.

> Acts 9:17
> And Ananias went his way, and entered into the house; and putting his hands on him said, Brother Saul, the Lord, *even* Jesus, that appeared unto thee in the way as thou camest, hath sent me, that thou mightest receive thy sight, and be filled with the Holy Ghost [holy spirit].

Ananias walked by the spirit and Jesus Christ told him to go see Paul and minister to him. That's genuine outreach. It would have been madness for him or any other believer to go see Paul unless it had been by revelation.

Can't you see how this is so different to how temples made with hands do things? They hold leadership meetings at their headquarters and discuss outreach strategies and formulate plans, thinking they are getting revelation from God when in fact they're walking by the counsel and will of men. Those orders are then passed down through the chain of command to the country coordinators and their leadership until it reaches the home church leaders, who then tell their people they are going out knocking doors to annoy people. That's walking by the senses, walking by the flesh, walking by the will and counsel of men, and the love of money is their motivation because all they're thinking about is generating more tithe money. We do not walk by the flesh but by the spirit, that Christ in us, just as Ananias did. If you want to see genuine outreach, learn to walk by the spirit with Christ as your head.

Acts 9:17
And Ananias went his way, and entered into the house; and putting his hands on him said, Brother Saul, the Lord, *even* Jesus, that appeared unto thee in the way as thou camest, hath sent me, that thou mightest receive thy sight, and be filled [plethō] with the Holy Ghost [holy spirit].

Will you just look at the accuracy of the word here. The word filled is plethō, filled to overflowing, not pleroō, filled to capacity. Paul was filled to capacity with holy spirit, pleroō, when he was born again outside the gates of Damascus. Ananias ministered to him so he would overflow with holy spirit, plethō. It was at this point Paul spoke in tongues.

Acts 9:18-26
And immediately there fell from his eyes as it had been scales: and he received sight forthwith, and arose, and was baptized.

And when he had received meat, he was strengthened. Then was Saul certain days with the disciples which were at Damascus.

And straightway he preached Christ in the synagogues, that he is the Son of God.

But all that heard *him* were amazed, and said; Is not this he that destroyed them which called on this name in Jerusalem, and came hither for that intent, that he might bring them bound unto the chief priests?

Walking *by* the Spirit

But Saul increased the more in strength, and confounded the Jews [Judeans] which dwelt at Damascus, proving that this is very Christ.

And after that many days were fulfilled, the Jews [Judeans] took counsel to kill him:

But their laying await was known of Saul. And they watched the gates day and night to kill him.

Then the disciples took him by night, and let *him* down by the wall in a basket.

And when Saul was come to Jerusalem, he assayed [attempted] to join himself to the disciples: but they were all afraid of him, and believed not that he was a disciple.

If you had been in Jerusalem, you'd have been terrified of Paul too. Those disciples had friends and family who had been imprisoned, tortured, and murdered by that bastard, and he wanted to go to their home church meetings? Damn right they didn't trust him.

Acts 9:27-29
But Barnabas took him, and brought *him* to the apostles, and declared unto them how he had seen the Lord in the way, and that he had spoken to him, and how he had preached boldly at Damascus in the name of Jesus.

And he was with them coming in and going out at Jerusalem.

And he spake boldly in the name of the Lord Jesus, and disputed against the Grecians: but they went about to slay him.

Throughout his ministry, Paul's background caused him major personal problems which he had to overcome. He would have been going to home church meetings and looking into the eyes of people he had persecuted. He would have been teaching the bible to friends and relatives of people he'd had tortured and murdered, like Stephen and many others including women. The first century believers also had major personal problems they had to overcome, like forgiving him so they could hear the word he was teaching. They all had to keep their heads in the word and put the past behind them.

> Philippians 3:13,14
> Brethren, I count not myself to have apprehended: but *this* one thing *I do*, forgetting those things which are behind, and reaching forth unto those things which are before,
>
> I press toward the mark for the prize of the high calling of God in Christ Jesus.

Paul never forgot his past, he just put it behind him. Like Paul, we have pasts too that need to be put behind us. We can never forget the past, but we can refuse to live there. Whenever something from my past makes me cringe inside, I immediately replace those thoughts by bringing my mind back to the word. I think of Paul and what he put behind him and that makes it easy for me.

The same is true of our thoughts about other believers. We can never forget what they've done either, but we can refuse to harbour such thoughts and instead think the word of them. The church has to learn to put the past behind. No matter what we have done or what anyone else may have done, we must put the past behind us.

Even after we're born again and we're moving together with the things of God, we're all going to do things and say things we are going to regret. After we've dealt with things, we must learn to put the past behind and forgive ourselves and others. We can't forget, but we can refuse to live in the past by bringing our minds back to the word.

The following verses in Colossians were written by Paul, but do we believe them? This is from the all truth, the word addressed to the church of God, the scriptures that apply to us in this Administration of Grace. If you want to be a disciple, these scriptures have to be a reality in your life.

> Colossians 3:8-13
> But now ye also put off all these; anger, wrath, malice, blasphemy, filthy communication out of your mouth.

Lie not one to another, seeing that ye have put off the old man with his deeds;

And have put on the new *man*, which is renewed in knowledge after the image of him that created him:

Where there is neither Greek nor Jew [Judean], circumcision nor uncircumcision, Barbarian, Scythian, bond *nor* free: but Christ *is* all, and in all.

Put on therefore, as the elect of God, holy and beloved, bowels of mercies, kindness, humbleness of mind, meekness, longsuffering;

Forbearing one another, and forgiving one another, if any man have a quarrel against any: even as Christ forgave you, so also *do* ye.

If all you do is bitch and complain and think evil about your brothers and sisters in Christ who walk by the spirit, as some believers did with Paul in the first Century, and as many do with me, you are not a disciple and I don't give a fuck how religious and righteous you think you are. If you're a disciple, you think the word and you control your thoughts. This is not open to debate.

2 Corinthians 10:5
Casting down imaginations, and every high thing that exalteth itself against the knowledge of God, and bringing into captivity every thought to the obedience of Christ;

The word states that we are to bring every thought captive to the obedience of Christ. Do you know what that means? This isn't saying we submit to a ministry structure of leadership, it is saying we submit to the obedience of Christ. The gift of holy spirit is the Christ in us, so this means totally the opposite of what most man-made ministries teach. How we bring every thought captive to the obedience of Christ is to walk by the spirit with the Christ in us as our head. We don't walk by the counsel of men and put our confidence in the flesh, we go to God and energise the gift of holy spirit, the Christ in us. That's what Paul and the first century believers did and that's why the word moved. They lived the word, not as some monstrous worldwide ministry with a structure of leadership headed by a patriarch, but in beautiful, loving home church families which were self governing, self supporting, and self propagating.

With this understanding of Paul's background, reading the book of Acts and the epistles will add new depth to your understanding of how the believers lived and moved the word. Think about the constant and persistent mental problems Paul would have had while living and working with believers who had friends and relatives he would have had tortured and murdered. Think about the constant and persistent condemnation he would have had to deal with. Heck, what have we ever done that was as bad as Paul? If Paul can do this thing, really, any of us can.

> 1 Corinthians 15:9
> For I am the least of the apostles, that am not meet to be called an apostle, because I persecuted the church of God.

When Paul was arrested in Jerusalem, he was given an opportunity to say a few words to the rioting mob who had just tried to kill him. Read his words carefully and weigh them in your mind. Look at his heart.

> Acts 22:3
> I am verily a man *which am* a Jew [Judean], born in Tarsus, *a city* in Cilicia, yet brought up in this city at the feet of Gamaliel, *and* taught according to the perfect manner of the law of the fathers, and was zealous toward God, as ye all are this day.

To be brought up at the feet of Gamaliel is a reference to his education and background. Today folks might say they have a Harvard education, or an Oxford or Cambridge education. Paul had a PhD from the most renowned educational institution on earth at that time, he had been brought up at the feet of Gamaliel. He used this to get their attention, to let them know he was one of them. He really did try to be all things to all men.

> Acts 22:4-18
> And I persecuted this way unto the death, binding and delivering into prisons both men and women.

As also the high priest doth bear me witness, and all the estate of the elders: from whom also I received letters unto the brethren, and went to Damascus, to bring them which were there bound unto Jerusalem, for to be punished.

And it came to pass, that, as I made my journey, and was come nigh unto Damascus about noon, suddenly there shone from heaven a great light round about me.

And I fell unto the ground, and heard a voice saying unto me, Saul, Saul, why persecutest thou me?

And I answered, Who art thou, Lord? And he said unto me, I am Jesus of Nazareth, whom thou persecutest.

And they that were with me saw indeed the light, and were afraid; but they heard not the voice of him that spake to me.

And I said, What shall I do, Lord? And the Lord said unto me, Arise, and go into Damascus; and there it shall be told thee of all things which are appointed for thee to do.

And when I could not see for the glory of that light, being led by the hand of them that were with me, I came into Damascus.

And one Ananias, a devout man according to the law, having a good report of all the Jews [Judeans] which dwelt *there*,

Came unto me, and stood, and said unto me, Brother Saul, receive thy sight. And the same hour I looked up upon him.

And he said, The God of our fathers hath chosen thee, that thou shouldest know his will, and see that Just One, and shouldest hear the voice of his mouth.

For thou shalt be his witness unto all men of what thou hast seen and heard.

> And now why tarriest thou? arise, and be baptized, and wash away thy sins, calling on the name of the Lord.
>
> And it came to pass, that, when I was come again to Jerusalem, even while I prayed in the temple, I was in a trance [I saw a vision];
>
> And saw him [Jesus Christ] saying unto me, Make haste, and get thee quickly out of Jerusalem: for they will not receive thy testimony concerning me.

Paul here received revelation and just look at who he was talking to. It wasn't God giving him this information, it was the Lord Jesus Christ. What do you think the word means when it says Christ is our head? That's who we take our orders from. He is our boss, our Lord, the head over all things to the church.

> Acts 22:19-21
> And I said, Lord, they know that I imprisoned and beat in every synagogue them that believed on thee:
>
> And when the blood of thy martyr Stephen was shed, I also was standing by, and consenting unto his death, and kept the raiment of them that slew him.
>
> And he said unto me, Depart: for I will send thee far hence unto the Gentiles.

Paul, like all of us, had a past to forget. We must learn to put the past behind, reach forth unto those things which are before, and press toward the mark for the prize of the high calling of God in Christ Jesus.

> 1 Timothy 1:12-15
> And I thank Christ Jesus our Lord, who hath enabled me, for that he counted me faithful, putting me into the ministry;
>
> Who was before a blasphemer, and a persecutor, and injurious: but I obtained mercy, because I did *it* ignorantly in unbelief.

> And the grace of our Lord was exceeding abundant with faith and love which is in Christ Jesus.
>
> This *is* a faithful saying, and worthy of all acceptation, that Christ Jesus came into the world to save sinners; of whom I am chief.

Like Paul, God doesn't care what you did yesterday, only about what you want to do today. I know I harp on about the jesuits and all their evil, but really, Paul was one of them, or their equivalent in that day. He changed and God was right there for him, and he will be right there for you too, even if you're a jesuit. I don't care who you are, or what you've done, or what god you serve, come on over and enjoy the light. God has always been there for me, just as he was always there for Paul, and he will be there for you too. There is always a need for another Paul.

This is perhaps the most important class session I've ever written and has some new light that hasn't been known since the first century. Actually, most important isn't quite accurate as every session is important. I guess what I'm trying to say is that every session of the class has been leading up to this. This teaching could very well change the world as we know it because now you know that it is Christ in you, the hope of glory.

71. Distinctions

Now we understand that Jesus Christ is our Lord, that Christ is head over all things to the church, and that it is Christ in us, we need to clarify a few distinctions between him and God. Jesus Christ's role is as head over all things to the church, he runs the ministry, he is the president of the body of Christ. His elevated position however, does not make him our father, we don't pray to him, he does not meet our needs, he does not bring deliverance, and he does not heal us. Let's take a stroll through the book of Acts to see some of this.

> Acts 1:1-5
> The former treatise have I made, O Theophilus, of all that Jesus began both to do and teach,
>
> Until the day in which he was taken up, after that he through the Holy Ghost [holy spirit] had given commandments unto the apostles whom he had chosen:
>
> To whom also he shewed himself alive after his passion by many infallible proofs, being seen of them forty days, and speaking of the things pertaining to the kingdom of God:
>
> And, being assembled together with *them*, commanded them that they should not depart from Jerusalem, but wait for the promise of the Father, which, *saith he*, ye have heard of me.
>
> For John truly baptized with water; but ye shall be baptized with the Holy Ghost [holy spirit] not many days hence.

Who gave the orders to the apostles here? God or Jesus Christ? Jesus Christ did. There is absolutely no possible way anyone could claim God was giving this information to the apostles. Jesus Christ is head over all things to the church and here we see him carrying out his responsibilities by giving instructions to the apostles. These were the preparations for the launch of the Administration of Grace in the days leading up to Pentecost, so this is basically the first occurrence of Jesus Christ being head over all things to the church. It is Jesus Christ giving the orders to the apostles, not God. First occurrence sets the standard, the precedent for this administration. Jesus Christ is our Lord just as he was the apostles' lord. He gives the orders regarding all things concerning the church of God because he is the head of it.

On the day of Pentecost, Jesus Christ did not send the promise of the Father, God did. Jesus Christ is not God and God is not Jesus Christ, they both have their responsibilities and we need to understand the distinctions between them. God is our father and supplies all our need, while Jesus Christ is responsible for all things concerning the church.

> Acts 1:6,7
> When they therefore were come together, they asked of him, saying, Lord, wilt thou at this time restore again the kingdom to Israel?
>
> And he said unto them, It is not for you to know the times or the seasons, which the Father hath put in his own power.

That was an interesting question the apostles asked. Note that they didn't ask if God was going to restore the kingdom to Israel at that time, they asked if he was going to do it. The apostles knew beyond question that Jesus Christ was their Lord, their boss, their commander in chief, their CEO, their head, the man whom they took their orders from regarding all things concerning the church.

> Acts 1:8
> But ye shall receive power, after that the Holy Ghost [holy spirit] is come upon you: and ye shall be witnesses unto me both in Jerusalem, and in all Judaea, and in Samaria, and unto the uttermost part of the earth.

According to Acts 1:8 we are not witnesses for God, we are witnesses for the Lord Jesus Christ. At that time it wasn't available for anyone to be a witness for the Lord Jesus Christ, because the holy spirit had not yet been given. It logically follows then that witnessing is not teaching the bible because the apostles were already doing that.

Preaching and teaching is not witnessing. Knocking doors and annoying people is not witnessing. Being a witness of the Lord Jesus Christ can only be done after receiving into manifestation the gift of holy spirit, by manifesting the Christ in you. As you manifest the Christ in you, you are a witness of the Lord Jesus Christ. Knocking doors and annoying people isn't witnessing, it's just being an asshole (unless you've had revelation of course, when it would be appropriate).

> Acts 5:32
> And we are his witnesses of these things; and *so is* also the Holy Ghost [holy spirit], whom God hath given to them that obey him.

Manifesting the gift of holy spirit is witnessing to these things. Of course, the apostles having lived and worked with Jesus Christ were also eye witnesses of him. None of us have ever met Jesus Christ personally or spent time with him, so we can't be witnesses in that sense, we can only be witnesses by manifesting the Christ in us.

The believers in the first century were called Christians because they were always manifesting the gift of holy spirit and talking about the Christ in them. They were known, somewhat derogatively, as the Christ-ins, hence Christians. It is Christ in you the hope of glory. If you want to witness to the Lord Jesus Christ, then you are going to have to demonstrate God's power to people, which is most easily done by speaking in tongues.

> 1 Corinthians 14:22a
> Wherefore tongues are for a sign, not to them that believe, but to them that believe not:

This doesn't mean you walk down the street speaking in tongues out loud to everyone you meet, it means you demonstrate God's power as you have opportunity. If you walk by the spirit, this will all fall into place and make sense. Let's head back to the day of the ascension.

Acts 1:9-11
And when he had spoken these things, while they beheld, he [Jesus Christ] was taken up; and a cloud received him out of their sight.

And while they looked stedfastly toward heaven as he went up, behold, two men stood by them in white apparel;

Which also said, Ye men of Galilee, why stand ye gazing up into heaven? this same Jesus, which is taken up from you into heaven, shall so come in like manner as ye have seen him go into heaven.

Jesus Christ may have gone up into the sky, but he is still our Lord, he is still the head over all things to the church to this day.

Jesus Christ is very real, he is up there, he is doing his job by carrying out his responsibilities. Why didn't God appear to Paul on the road to Damascus? I'll tell you why, because it wasn't his responsibility. Jesus Christ had a chat with him because it concerned the church, it was part of his responsibilities as head over all things to the church. It certainly wouldn't have been very wise for a believer like you or me to approach Paul outside Damascus with a bible and invite him to a home church meeting now, would it?

Note another important distinction here too, in that Jesus Christ did not teach Paul anything, he sent Ananias to do that. Why? The ministry of reconciliation is not Jesus Christ's responsibility, it's ours. If someone wants to learn the word, they have to come to us or we have to go to them. God isn't going to teach them and nor is Jesus Christ. It's not their job, and nor is it the angels' job either. God gave the ministry of reconciliation to us, it's our responsibility.

There is a fabulous little truth buried here when it comes to home churches being self governing in that God honours responsibility. When God gives someone a responsibility, it is theirs and theirs alone. He does not interfere, and neither does Christ, so I can assure you that neither of them would give revelation to any counsels of men to interfere in your affairs.

Sure, if you're off the word and need confrontation you may find a prophet in your face, or if you've been hurt by the world and need patch-ing up you may find a pastor knocking at your door, but they will be there because they walk by the spirit, not because a council of men sent them. And another thing, they will only be there to do a specific job, they will not be there to tell you how to run your home church because that's your job. The gift ministries are there for the mending of the saints, the work of the ministry, and the edifying of the body of Christ. If someone with a gift ministry is also a home church leader, they have two very different responsibilities in the body of Christ. Distinctions folks, we need to be clear on who is responsible to do what.

When God gives you someone to raise as a disciple, he expects you to do your job. Those people are your responsibility, that's why God gave them to you. If you start a home church, that church is your responsibility and any revelation regarding it will be given to you because it's your responsibility. If God gives you a gift ministry, that is a special gift to the church and you are responsible to stir up that gift and use it to look after God's kids. God honours responsibility and there is to be no interference from any outside man-made structures of leadership. Christ is our head, not men, and that's why God refuses to dwell in temples made with hands.

Not many days later on the day of Pentecost, Peter had this to say after they had received the gift of holy spirit and manifested it to the people in the temple by speaking in tongues.

> Acts 2:32,33,36
> This Jesus hath God raised up, whereof we all are witnesses.
>
> Therefore being by the right hand of God exalted, and having received of the Father the promise of the Holy Ghost [holy spirit], he hath shed forth this, which ye now see and hear.
>
> Therefore let all the house of Israel know assuredly, that God hath made that same Jesus, whom ye have crucified, both Lord and Christ.

Who made Jesus Christ our Lord? God did, therefore we are to submit to Jesus Christ as our Lord, our boss, the head over all things to the church. That is what God expects of us. The word of God is the will of God, remember?

Acts 2:37,38
Now when they heard *this*, they were pricked in their heart, and said unto Peter and to the rest of the apostles, Men *and* brethren, what shall we do?

Then Peter said unto them, Repent, and be baptized every one of you in the name of Jesus Christ for the remission of sins, and ye shall receive [lambanō] the gift of the Holy Ghost.

How we are born again isn't by confessing God as anything, it is by confessing Jesus Christ as our Lord and believing God raised him from the dead. Being baptized in the name of Jesus Christ is to receive the gift of holy spirit, at which time we are spiritually washed and receive the righteousness of God. To lambanō the gift of holy spirit is to manifest the power of God, which starts with speaking in tongues. Moving on, Acts 3 has some intriguing and important information.

Acts 3:1-5
Now Peter and John went up together into the temple at the hour of prayer, *being* the ninth *hour*.

And a certain man lame from his mother's womb was carried, whom they laid daily at the gate of the temple which is called Beautiful, to ask alms of them that entered into the temple;

Who seeing Peter and John about to go into the temple asked an alms.

And Peter, fastening his eyes upon him with John, said, Look on us.

And he gave heed unto them, expecting to receive [lambanō] something of them.

That cripple was expecting to lambanō something, to receive something into manifestation. The use of lambanō indicates he wasn't just looking for money. It couldn't have been money he was looking for as folks didn't take their wallets and purses to the temple. The man was looking for healing. Peter was obviously given the green light and energised the Christ in him.

> Acts 3:6
> Then Peter said, Silver and gold have I none; but such as I have give I thee: In the name of Jesus Christ of Nazareth rise up and walk.

Why didn't Peter heal him in the name of God? Don't just skim over this, stop and think about it. We say Jesus Christ is our Lord, but do we really believe it?

> Acts 3:7-9
> And he took him by the right hand, and lifted *him* up: and immediately his feet and ankle bones received strength.
>
> And he leaping up stood, and walked, and entered with them into the temple, walking, and leaping, and praising God.
>
> And all the people saw him walking and praising God:

The man was healed in the name of Jesus Christ, but notice that God got all the glory. This is so important to recognise. Peter didn't get the glory, and Jesus Christ didn't get the glory, God did. There are some clearly defined distinctions here. We operate the gift of holy spirit by our own freedom of will and manifest the power of God, Jesus Christ is our Lord, the head over all things to the church, and we do everything in his name, yet it is always God who gets the glory. We don't look for praise from men, and we certainly don't worship Jesus Christ even though he is our Lord.

> Colossians 1:18,19
> And he [Jesus Christ] is the head of the body, the church: who is the beginning, the firstborn from the dead; that in all *things* he might have the preeminence.
>
> For it pleased *the Father* that in him should all fulness dwell;

Jesus Christ is the preeminent one, the head of the body, our Lord, the head over all things to the church. We must keep the distinctions between God and Jesus Christ clear in our minds if the word is to live.

Here's something for you to think about. What if Jesus Christ's torture, crucifixion and death was him showing us what we have to do to get born again? Can you imagine that? Jesus Christ was beaten for two days until he was no longer recognisable as a human being, then he was dragged up a hill and nailed to a tree where he hung for six hours before dying. Would it have been unreasonable for God to demand we go through the same in order to redeem ourselves? What if that had been the only legal way to pull it off and Jesus Christ died to show us what we had to do?

Thankfully we don't have to give our lives as dead sacrifices, we are to be living sacrifices.

> Romans 12:1,2
> I beseech you therefore, brethren, by the mercies of God, that ye present your bodies a living sacrifice, holy, acceptable unto God, *which is* your reasonable service.
>
> And be not conformed to this world: but be ye transformed by the renewing of your mind, that ye may prove what *is* that good, and acceptable, and perfect, will of God.

I'm rather thankful Jesus Christ went through all that for me so I don't have to. Aren't you? Well, speaking in tongues is giving thanks well. We are to be living sacrifices by renewing our minds so we can demonstrate God's power and prove the good, acceptable and perfect will of God. Look at Philippians.

> Philippians 2:9-11
> Wherefore God also hath highly exalted him [Jesus Christ], and given him a name which is above every name:
>
> That at the name of Jesus every knee should bow, of *things* in heaven, and *things* in earth, and *things* under the earth;
>
> And *that* every tongue should confess that Jesus Christ *is* Lord, to the glory of God the Father.

We are to confess that Jesus Christ is our Lord, which is to the glory of God the father. Those who confess that God is their Lord are full of horseshit. We are to believe the word, and the word says that Jesus Christ is our Lord, that God has given him a name which is above every name, that he is the preeminent one, the head over all things to the church.

After Peter had healed the cripple, he had an opportunity to teach, and there is much we can learn from it.

> Acts 3:22
> For Moses truly said unto the fathers, A prophet shall the Lord your God raise up unto you of your brethren, like unto me; him shall ye hear in all things whatsoever he shall say unto you.

Moses foretold that God would raise up a prophet, referring to Jesus Christ, that we are to hear in all things he says unto us. Either this is the word of God or it isn't. Either this is the truth, or lets just forget the whole thing. Jesus Christ is our Lord, our boss, our head, and it is him we take our orders from. We are to listen to the Christ in us. To follow men in temples made with hands is to walk away from God's word. It is hewing out broken cisterns to contain our religion. It is turning your back on the living God because it is putting your trust in the work of men's hands, it is putting your trust in the flesh.

Immediately following Peter's teaching in the temple after he healed the lame man, the Sanhedrin sent men to arrest the apostles and throw them in prison. The next day they were dragged before their council and interrogated. The Sanhedrin demanded to know by whose authority they had healed the cripple, which they obviously considered to be a crime. The god of this world expends a great deal of time, money, and resources in making people sick, diseased and crippled, and he doesn't like them being healed. To him, it is a criminal offence. Well, what do you expect from the world? Here's Peter's response to those religious creatures.

> Acts 4:8-10
> Then Peter, filled [plethō] with the Holy Ghost [holy spirit], said unto them, Ye rulers of the people, and elders of Israel,
>
> If we this day be examined of the good deed done to the impotent man, by what means he is made whole;

> Be it known unto you all, and to all the people of Israel, that by the name of Jesus Christ of Nazareth, whom ye crucified, whom God raised from the dead, *even* by him doth this man stand here before you whole.

The use of plethō in verse 8 indicates that Peter energised the gift of holy spirit, the Christ in him. These words came from the Christ in him. We are to hear Christ in all things, remember? How do you think Christ talks to us? Through television? Through Facebook?

> Acts 4:11-14
> This is the stone which was set at nought of you builders, which is become the head of the corner.
>
> Neither is there salvation in any other: for there is none other name under heaven given among men, whereby we must be saved [made whole].
>
> Now when they saw the boldness of Peter and John, and perceived that they were unlearned and ignorant men, they marvelled; and they took knowledge of them, that they had been with Jesus.
>
> And beholding the man which was healed standing with them, they could say nothing against it.

When we walk by the spirit with Christ as our head, then and only then will we be super conquerors.

After this confrontation with the religious leaders, Peter and the others returned to the believers and told them what happened. The account gives us more extremely important information.

> Acts 4:23-31
> And being let go, they went to their own company, and reported all that the chief priests and elders had said unto them.
>
> And when they heard that, they lifted up their voice to God with one accord, and said, Lord, thou *art* God, [God, thou art the

creator] which hast made heaven, and earth, and the sea, and all that in them is:

Who by the mouth of thy servant David hast said, Why did the heathen rage, and the people imagine vain things?

The kings of the earth stood up, and the rulers were gathered together against the ~~Lord~~ [Jehovah - God], and against his Christ.

For of a truth against thy holy child Jesus, whom thou hast anointed, both Herod, and Pontius Pilate, with the Gentiles, and the people of Israel, were gathered together,

For to do whatsoever thy hand and thy counsel determined before to be done.

And now, ~~Lord,~~ [God] behold their threatenings: and grant unto thy servants, that with all boldness they may speak thy word,

By stretching forth thine hand to heal; and that signs and wonders may be done by the name of thy holy child Jesus.

And when they had prayed, the place was shaken where they were assembled together; and they were all filled with the Holy Ghost [holy spirit], and they spake the word of God with boldness.

Who did Peter and the others pray to? God or Jesus Christ? They prayed to God. There are distinctions here between God and Jesus Christ that we must keep clear in our minds. Jesus Christ is our Lord, the head over all things to the church, but he is not God. Jesus Christ does not supply our need or answer our prayers, that's God's job. We pray to God.

Philippians 4:6
Be careful [full of care, worried, anxious] for nothing; but in every thing by prayer and supplication with thanksgiving let your requests be made known unto God.

God is our father, and it is God we pray to and it is God who supplies all our need. Jesus Christ is our Lord, the head over all things to the church. We must keep these distinctions clear in our minds.

> Philippians 4:19
> But my God shall supply all your need according to his riches in glory by Christ Jesus.

Ephesians also has important information in this regards.

> Ephesians 5:22
> Wives, submit yourselves unto your own husbands, as unto the Lord.

Women are to submit themselves to their own husbands as if he was the Lord Jesus Christ. Ephesians doesn't say women should submit themselves to their husbands as if he was God. Christ is our Lord, our head, our boss, and that's the relationship a husband has with his wife. He isn't her God, he's simply the boss of that relationship, the one responsible for its direction, the one with the authority to lead.

> Ephesians 5:23
> For the husband is the head of the wife, even as Christ is the head of the church: and he is the saviour of the body.

The leadership structure in the body of Christ, the church of God, is Christ to us as individuals. When a woman marries, that changes to Christ to her husband to her. This is the leadership structure for the Age of Grace, the Administration of the Mystery. It is not Christ to the president of some man-made ministry, to a board of directors, to your country leader, to your home church leader, then to you. See it? We all walk with Christ as our head. Anything else is a broken cistern.

> Colossians 3:23
> And whatsoever ye do, do *it* heartily, as to the Lord, and not unto men;

Read that again and think about it, Selah. Who is our Lord? God or Jesus Christ? Get it clear in your mind. In this case, we don't have to guess about it, because the next verse spells it out.

> Colossians 3:24
> Knowing that of the Lord ye shall receive the reward of the inheritance: for ye serve the Lord Christ.

If we think we do absolutely everything heartily only to God, we're not rightly dividing the bible. In fact, we're not even reading it correctly. God made Christ our Lord and it's him we serve heartily in all matters relating to the church of God. Think of it in terms of your earthly job. You leave home and go to work where you submit yourself to your boss. You work heartily for him and do whatever he tells you and in return you get paid. God is our father, and we live with him in fellowship, but when we go to work to do the things of the ministry, Jesus Christ is our boss. We work heartily to him because he's the one with the responsibility to run the church.

When reading the book of Acts, keep it clear in your mind who our Lord is. For example, who was giving the orders in Antioch here?

> Acts 13:1,2
> Now there were in the church that was at Antioch certain prophets and teachers; as Barnabas, and Simeon that was called Niger, and Lucius of Cyrene, and Manaen, which had been brought up with Herod the tetrarch, and Saul.
>
> As they ministered to the Lord, and fasted, the Holy Ghost [holy spirit] said, Separate me Barnabas and Saul for the work whereunto I have called them.

Whose work do we do? To whom do we work heartily? Who is our Lord? Making Jesus Christ our Lord is not worshipping Jesus Christ as God, it is doing the word. He is our Lord because God made him our Lord.

A cautionary note is needed here. As we saw earlier in the class, the word Lord has been criminally tampered with and there are many forgeries in the bible where God is called our Lord when he is no such thing. Reading the context will usually make it easy to see when the word is referring to God or if it's referring to Jesus Christ.

> Acts 16:6-10
> Now when they had gone throughout Phrygia and the region of Galatia, and were forbidden of the Holy Ghost [holy spirit] to preach the word in Asia,
>
> After they were come to Mysia, they assayed to go into Bithynia: but the Spirit suffered them not.
>
> And they passing by Mysia came down to Troas.
>
> And a vision appeared to Paul in the night; There stood a man of Macedonia, and prayed him, saying, Come over into Macedonia, and help us.
>
> And after he had seen the vision, immediately we endeavoured to go into Macedonia, assuredly gathering that the Lord had called us for to preach the gospel unto them.

It says the Lord called him. Is this referring to God or Jesus Christ? Well, who is our Lord, who is head over all things to the church? As this situation is without doubt concerning the church of God, this has to be Jesus Christ giving this information because it would have been his responsibility. Try these next two verses for yourself.

> Acts 18:9,10
> Then spake the Lord to Paul in the night by a vision, Be not afraid, but speak, and hold not thy peace:
>
> For I am with thee, and no man shall set on thee to hurt thee: for I have much people in this city.

It's not difficult, is it? That was Jesus Christ talking to Paul. What about healing? Who does the healing when we operate manifestations?

> Acts 19:11,12
> And God wrought special miracles by the hands of Paul:
>
> So that from his body were brought unto the sick handkerchiefs or aprons, and the diseases departed from them, and the evil spirits went out of them.

See, God does all the healing, not Jesus Christ. We minister to people and heal them in the name of Jesus Christ. It is the authority in the name of Jesus Christ our Lord that backs off the devil spirit realm, but it is God who answers our prayers and heals us.

Who tried to stop Paul from going to Jerusalem? God or Jesus Christ? Read it and see for yourself.

> Acts 21:11
> And when he [Agabus] was come unto us, he took Paul's girdle, and bound his own hands and feet, and said, Thus saith the Holy Ghost [holy spirit - usage 2, the gift of holy spirit], So shall the Jews [Judeans] at Jerusalem bind the man that owneth this girdle, and shall deliver *him* into the hands of the Gentiles.

Who tied to stop Paul from going to Jerusalem? I know we've always been taught it was God, but God is not our Lord and the church of God is Jesus Christ's responsibility, not God's. This situation of Paul going to Jerusalem lies clearly within Jesus Christ's responsibilities. Paul even tells us later that it was Jesus Christ.

> Acts 22:17-21
> And it came to pass, that, when I was come again to Jerusalem, even while I prayed in the temple, I was in a trance [saw a vision];
>
> And saw him [Jesus Christ] saying unto me, Make haste, and get thee quickly out of Jerusalem: for they will not receive thy testimony concerning me.
>
> And I said, Lord, they know that I imprisoned and beat in every synagogue them that believed on thee:
>
> And when the blood of thy martyr Stephen was shed, I also was standing by, and consenting unto his death, and kept the raiment of them that slew him.
>
> And he said unto me, Depart: for I will send thee far hence unto the Gentiles.

See, it was Jesus Christ who tried to stop Paul from going to Jerusalem, not God. It was also Jesus Christ who later appeared to Paul while he was in prison.

> Acts 23:11
> And the night following the Lord stood by him, and said, Be of good cheer, Paul: for as thou hast testified of me in Jerusalem, so must thou bear witness also at Rome.

To close, let's look at one more astonishing record, where Paul is about to be shipwrecked on his way to Rome. They were in a storm so severe, the crew had chucked the cargo overboard and had given up all hope. However, Paul received revelation that they would all get to shore safely. Who gave that revelation to Paul? God or Jesus Christ? Before answering, think responsibility.

> Acts 27:23-25
> For there stood by me this night the angel of God, whose I am, and whom I serve,
>
> Saying, Fear not, Paul; thou must be brought before Caesar: and, lo, God hath given thee all them that sail with thee.
>
> Wherefore, sirs, be of good cheer: for I believe God, that it shall be even as it was told me.

In this case, God sent an angel and the revelation came directly from God, not Jesus Christ. Why? The situation was God's responsibility to sort out. Delivering us from situations like this is God's responsibility not Jesus Christ's, and I find it rather intriguing that this revelation didn't come from the Christ in him, it came from an angel sent by God. Jesus Christ is our Lord, but he does not answer our prayers, meet our needs or bring deliverance and healing. Jesus Christ's responsibilities are limited to being head over all things to the church.

Keep these distinctions clear and teach them so these truths will live. This is new light that has not been known since the first century and we must teach it so it will never be lost again.

72. The Manifestation of Believing

Next to speaking in tongues, the most beneficial manifestation to me personally throughout my life has been the manifestation of believing.

The manifestation of believing differs from human believing in that it is a spiritual reality. Sometimes it can be difficult to distinguish between the two, but as long as you remember that human believing is a law built into the fabric of life which every human being on earth can tap into whether they have the spirit of God or not, and that the manifestation of believing is energising the power of God and as such is only available to those who operate the gift of holy spirit, you will have no difficulty distinguishing between the two.

One way I like to compare the two is with waves on an ocean. Every time the wind blows, there are waves. The stronger the wind blows, the higher the waves. To me, this is like every day human believing. The stronger the believing, the bigger the waves, but no matter how big the waves, it's all natural, it is all part of normal human believing. However, something far more powerful can stir the oceans producing tsunamis, huge tidal waves with terrible destructive power.

I like to think of the manifestation of believing as a tsunami of believing that wrecks the works of the devil. With your human believing you can stir up waves, but nothing like that which you can stir up with the manifestation of believing. The manifestation raises tsunamis that cause catastrophic damage to the works of the devil and totally wrecks his purposes and agendas. No amount of regular human believing could ever destroy the works of the devil like the manifestation of believing. The profit to us is that when the devil's works are destroyed, we enjoy peace to get on with our more abundant lives.

With this in mind, let's revisit Moses and the parting of the Red Sea. We know that by the power of God the sea levels dropped until the underwater land bridge at Nuweiba broke the surface, enabling the children of Israel to cross safely. There is one important detail in that account which I've so far deliberately not touched on, and that was the part Moses played. Let's read the record again to familiarise ourselves with what happened.

> Exodus 14:5-7
> And it was told the king of Egypt that the people fled: and the heart of Pharaoh and of his servants was turned against the people, and they said, Why have we done this, that we have let Israel go from serving us?
>
> And he made ready his chariot, and took his people with him:
>
> And he took six hundred chosen chariots, and all the chariots of Egypt, and captains over every one of them.

It's difficult to comprehend the arrogance in the heart of that Pharaoh. Who the fuck did he think he was? There is no doubt he was born of the seed of the serpent, that he was a child of the devil, because his head was so far up his ass his emotions were totally out of his control.

This might be a good time to touch on the seed of the serpent again, because just as teaching is required before anyone can walk by the spirit and serve God, teaching is required before anyone can walk in witchcraft and serve Lucifer.

Whenever and wherever a person commits their lives knowingly and willingly to the service of lucifer, at that moment they are born again of the seed of the serpent. There is one exception to this of course, in that if someone is born again of God's seed, he cannot also be born of the seed of the serpent even if he commits his life in service to the god of this world. You can't have two fathers, so it is impossible to be born of the seed of the serpent if you are already born again of God's seed.

Seed is permanent and cannot be removed, which is why those who are born of the seed of the serpent commit a crime which the bible calls unforgiveable. It's unforgiveable because the seed with which they are impregnated is permanent. Consider the words Jesus Christ spoke to the religious leaders of his day and time.

John 8:37-44
I know that ye [the religious leaders] are Abraham's seed; but ye seek to kill me, because my word hath no place in you.

I speak that which I have seen with my Father: and ye do that which ye have seen with your father.

They answered and said unto him, Abraham is our father. Jesus saith unto them, If ye were Abraham's children, ye would do the works of Abraham.

But now ye seek to kill me, a man that hath told you the truth, which I have heard of God: this did not Abraham.

Ye do the deeds of your father. Then said they to him, We be not born of fornication; we have one Father, *even* God.

Jesus said unto them, If God were your Father, ye would love me: for I proceeded forth and came from God; neither came I of myself, but he sent me.

Why do ye not understand my speech? *Even* because ye cannot hear my word.

Ye are of *your* father the devil, and the lusts of your father ye will do. He was a murderer from the beginning, and abode not in the truth, because there is no truth in him. When he speaketh a lie, he speaketh of his own: for he is a liar, and the father of it.

Just as there were men and women born of the seed of the serpent in Jesus Christ's day, so there are men and women born of the seed of the serpent in our day. How they are trained is in secret societies and religious orders. When a 32nd degree freemason goes for his initiation to the 33rd degree, he is asked to state to whom he gives his life in service. He answers that he serves lucifer. Whenever and wherever anyone by his freedom of will stands up and declares that he serves lucifer, at that moment he commits the unforgiveable sin and is born of the seed of the serpent (unless he is already born again, of course). Freemasonry is the devil's maternity ward and kindergarten where he breeds his offspring.

Once they reach that 33rd degree and have committed their lives to lucifer, doors open into other secret societies where they are then further educated in the ways of the world. This Pharaoh was one of these men.

> Exodus 14:10
> And when Pharaoh drew nigh, the children of Israel lifted up their eyes, and, behold, the Egyptians marched after them; and they were sore afraid: and the children of Israel cried out unto the LORD.

Good lesson here. If we're ever attacked by the world, we must go to God for our answers. When stuff comes up, we go to God. That's how you walk by the spirit. Moses went to God and received the following revelation.

> Exodus 14:13,14
> And Moses said unto the people, Fear ye not, stand still, and see the salvation of the LORD, which he will shew to you to day: for the Egyptians whom ye have seen to day, ye shall see them again no more for ever.
>
> The LORD shall fight for you, and ye shall hold your peace.

Then God, again by revelation, told Moses what to do. When Moses carried out the instruction, that was when the manifestation of believing went into operation.

> Exodus 14:15,16,21
> And the LORD said unto Moses, Wherefore criest thou unto me? speak unto the children of Israel, that they go forward:
>
> But lift thou up thy rod, and stretch out thine hand over the sea, and divide it: and the children of Israel shall go on dry *ground* through the midst of the sea.
>
> And Moses stretched out his hand over the sea; and the LORD caused the sea to go *back* by a strong east wind all that night, and made the sea dry *land,* and the waters were divided.

I think too many of us skim over these verses without stopping to think about Moses and his part in all this. You see, without believing, God can't do anything. To see the power of God in our lives we must energise holy spirit, and to do that we must believe. Without believing, nothing happens. If Moses had cowered in fear that day instead of believing God, they would have been taken by Pharaoh.

What exactly did Moses do then? Well, he did exactly what God told him to do. He held up his rod and stretched out his hand over the sea. Do you think that was easy? There is another record in the old testament when Moses was told to hold up his hands.

Exodus 17:8-13
Then came Amalek, and fought with Israel in Rephidim.

And Moses said unto Joshua, Choose us out men, and go out, fight with Amalek: to morrow I will stand on the top of the hill with the rod of God in mine hand.

So Joshua did as Moses had said to him, and fought with Amalek: and Moses, Aaron, and Hur went up to the top of the hill.

And it came to pass, when Moses held up his hand, that Israel prevailed: and when he let down his hand, Amalek prevailed.

But Moses' hands *were* heavy; and they took a stone, and put *it* under him, and he sat thereon; and Aaron and Hur stayed up his hands, the one on the one side, and the other on the other side; and his hands were steady until the going down of the sun.

And Joshua discomfited Amalek and his people with the edge of the sword.

See this? As long as Moses held up his arms, the power of God was manifested. When Moses could no longer hold up his arms because they were tired, the power of God no longer manifested itself. If we want to see the power of God, we must carry out the instruction we are given by revelation to the letter. If we don't carry out the word, we won't see the power of God. Thankfully, Aaron and Hur were there to help him and they sat Moses down and took an arm each and held it up for him. That's not cheating, that's believers helping each other to do the word.

Back on the shores of the Red Sea, Moses was told to hold up his rod and stretch his arm out over the sea. As long as he stretched out his arm over the sea, the wind and the waves gradually lowered the sea level until the underwater land bridge between Nuweiba and Saudi Arabia broke the surface.

What if Moses had not kept his arm stretched out over the sea all night? I think you're getting the picture. You see, the manifestation of believing is something we do, not something God does. Moses kept his arm stretched out all night. He kept his mind riveted to the sea and stayed his thoughts on seeing the sea part. It took all night. I find it difficult to keep my thoughts stayed on something for more than a few minutes sometimes. Distractions are plenty. As Moses kept his mind stayed on the word and kept his arm stretched out over the sea, the power of God was manifested. Have you ever tried holding out an arm all night? I'll bet most of us would struggle to stretch out an arm and hold a staff for 10 minutes. Try it and see. Moses had to do it all night. Who knows, maybe he rested the base of the rod on a big rock or something, but the point is he kept his arm stretched out. Yes, it was God's power that parted the Red Sea, but it was Moses operating the manifestation of believing that made it possible.

> Exodus 14:22-31
> And the children of Israel went into the midst of the sea upon the dry *ground:* and the waters *were* a wall unto them on their right hand, and on their left.
>
> And the Egyptians pursued, and went in after them to the midst of the sea, *even* all Pharaoh's horses, his chariots, and his horsemen.
>
> And it came to pass, that in the morning watch the LORD looked unto the host of the Egyptians through the pillar of fire and of the cloud, and troubled the host of the Egyptians,
>
> And took off their chariot wheels, that they drave them heavily: so that the Egyptians said, Let us flee from the face of Israel; for the LORD fighteth for them against the Egyptians.

And the LORD said unto Moses, Stretch out thine hand over the sea, that the waters may come again upon the Egyptians, upon their chariots, and upon their horsemen.

And Moses stretched forth his hand over the sea, and the sea returned to his strength when the morning appeared; and the Egyptians fled against it; and the LORD overthrew the Egyptians in the midst of the sea.

And the waters returned, and covered the chariots, and the horsemen, *and* all the host of Pharaoh that came into the sea after them; there remained not so much as one of them.

But the children of Israel walked upon dry *land* in the midst of the sea; and the waters *were* a wall unto them on their right hand, and on their left.

Thus the LORD saved Israel that day out of the hand of the Egyptians; and Israel saw the Egyptians dead upon the sea shore.

And Israel saw that great work which the LORD did upon the Egyptians: and the people feared the LORD, and believed the LORD, and his servant Moses.

Until now I've always had a problem picturing the difference between the law of believing and the manifestation of believing. I've never really had anything tangible in my mind, an image that clearly illustrated the difference between them until I began working on this chapter. When I was shown the tsunami picture compared with waves whipped up by the wind, it certainly made an impact. However, at first I argued and explained that I thought it might perhaps put negative imagery into folk's minds regarding manifestations. I was then shown that the only reason we have revelation and power manifestations is because there is a devil. If there was no devil, there would be no need for them. They are only there so we can destroy the works of the devil, therefore the tsunami imagery is appropriate.

Acts 10:38
How God anointed Jesus of Nazareth with the Holy Ghost [holy spirit] and with power: who went about doing good, and healing all that were oppressed of the devil; for God was with him.

1 John 3:8b
For this purpose the Son of God was manifested, that he might destroy the works of the devil.

The manifestation of believing creates spiritual tidal waves, tsunamis of believing that wrecks the devil's works, and I think the crossing of the Red Sea is the perfect example of that. When the waters returned it says the Egyptians fled against it. As that tsunami thundered against the land bridge, they turned their chariots north and drove their horses away from the destruction bearing down on them. That tsunami totally wrecked Pharaoh's army and killed every last one of them. The manifestation of believing delivers people who are oppressed of the devil and it destroys his works.

To establish this we will consider another record where God parted water so his people could cross. When Joshua and the Israelites were on the banks of the River Jordan on the verge of crossing into the promised land, the Jordan was in full spate and was overflowing its banks. Not only that, all the bridges had been demolished to prevent God's people from crossing. Joshua had been at the Red Sea with Moses. He knew from experience that parting an ocean wasn't a problem for God, but what about a turbulent river in full flood?

Before we get into the bible and look at this, just for the record, I've never understood what happened that day by the River Jordan. This has always puzzled me. How did God dry up a flooded river so they could cross? It wasn't until yesterday morning while out walking along the shore pondering where to go next after Moses that I understood how God did it. How do you like that for timing?

Joshua 3:1
And Joshua rose early in the morning; and they removed from Shittim, and came to Jordan, he and all the children of Israel, and lodged there before they passed over.

These people had been wandering around in the wilderness for 40 years. The only men still alive who had crossed the Red Sea with Moses were Joshua and Caleb. All the other men had died because of unbelief. This multitude was the children who were now grown. Moses was dead and Joshua was leading God's people. God had promised Joshua that he would be with him as he had been with Moses.

Joshua 1:1-5
Now after the death of Moses the servant of the LORD it came to pass, that the LORD spake unto Joshua the son of Nun, Moses' minister, saying,

Moses my servant is dead; now therefore arise, go over this Jordan, thou, and all this people, unto the land which I do give to them, *even* to the children of Israel.

Every place that the sole of your foot shall tread upon, that have I given unto you, as I said unto Moses.

From the wilderness and this Lebanon even unto the great river, the river Euphrates, all the land of the Hittites, and unto the great sea toward the going down of the sun, shall be your coast.

There shall not any man be able to stand before thee all the days of thy life: as I was with Moses, *so* I will be with thee: I will not fail thee, nor forsake thee.

So there was Joshua on the banks of the Jordan looking across the flooded river at the promised land. I have absolutely no doubt whatsoever that Joshua was continually running the events of the crossing of the Red Sea through his mind the entire time he was looking at that river. With the Red Sea, a strong wind coupled with an ebbing tide had lowered the sea level until the underwater land bridge from Nuweiba had broken the surface. There was no way a wind was going to do much against a swollen river, and I'm pretty sure Joshua had no idea how God was going to pull it off. However, God told him they would cross and he believed him. Joshua had old testament holy spirit given to him before Moses' death, and he put the manifestation of believing into operation.

> Joshua 3:2-4
> And it came to pass after three days, that the officers went through the host;
>
> And they commanded the people, saying, When ye see the ark of the covenant of the LORD your God, and the priests the Levites bearing it, then ye shall remove from your place, and go after it.
>
> Yet there shall be a space between you and it, about two thousand cubits by measure: come not near unto it, that ye may know the way by which ye must go: for ye have not passed *this* way heretofore.

Again, note the specific instruction given that had to be carried out in order to see the power of God come to pass. This is so important, unbelievably important. We absolutely must carry out the instruction implicitly in every detail if we are to see the power of God come to pass. The Levites were to hoist up the ark of the covenant and walk to the Jordan until their feet were in the water. The people were to rise up and follow them leaving a space between them and the priests. If any of these conditions were not met, the power of God would not have manifested itself. When operating the manifestation of believing we absolutely must carry out every detail of any instruction we are given by revelation or it will not work.

> Joshua 3:5-13
> And Joshua said unto the people, Sanctify yourselves: for to morrow the LORD will do wonders among you.
>
> And Joshua spake unto the priests, saying, Take up the ark of the covenant, and pass over before the people. And they took up the ark of the covenant, and went before the people.
>
> And the LORD said unto Joshua, This day will I begin to magnify thee in the sight of all Israel, that they may know that, as I was with Moses, *so* I will be with thee.
>
> And thou shalt command the priests that bear the ark of the covenant, saying, When ye are come to the brink of the water of Jordan, ye shall stand still in Jordan.

And Joshua said unto the children of Israel, Come hither, and hear the words of the LORD your God.

And Joshua said, Hereby ye shall know that the living God *is* among you, and *that* he will without fail drive out from before you the Canaanites, and the Hittites, and the Hivites, and the Perizzites, and the Girgashites, and the Amorites, and the Jebusites.

Behold, the ark of the covenant of the Lord of all the earth passeth over before you into Jordan.

Now therefore take you twelve men out of the tribes of Israel, out of every tribe a man.

And it shall come to pass, as soon as the soles of the feet of the priests that bear the ark of the LORD, the Lord of all the earth, shall rest in the waters of Jordan, *that* the waters of Jordan shall be cut off *from* the waters that come down from above; and they shall stand upon an heap.

There are a few details here, but what are they actually saying? The bible states that as soon as the feet of the priests stepped into the Jordan, the waters in front of them would be cut off from the waters flowing from upstream, and that the waters upstream would stand on a heap. In other words, water upstream would be cut off from the water downstream. What does that mean? Here are a few other translations of the verse.

American Standard Version
And it shall come to pass, when the soles of the feet of the priests that bear the ark of Jehovah, the Lord of all the earth, shall rest in the waters of the Jordan, that the waters of the Jordan shall be cut off, even the waters that come down from above; and they shall stand in one heap.

Brenton
And it shall come to pass, when the feet of the priests that bear the ark of the covenant of the Lord of the whole earth rest in the water of Jordan, the water of Jordan below shall fail, and the water coming down from above shall stop.

God's Word
The priests who carry the ark of the LORD, the Lord of the whole earth, will stand in the water of the Jordan. Then the water flowing from upstream will stop and stand up like a dam.

Lexham English Bible
When the soles of the feet of the priests carrying the ark of Yahweh, Lord of all the earth, rest in the waters of the Jordan, the waters of the Jordan will be cut off upstream, and they will stand *still in* one heap.

After reading these various translations, we can safely conclude that the waters upstream were cut off by some kind of dam, in this case most likely a landslide that temporarily blocked the river. If we keep reading, we will get more information.

Joshua 3:14-17
And it came to pass, when the people removed from their tents, to pass over Jordan, and the priests bearing the ark of the covenant before the people;

And as they that bare the ark were come unto Jordan, and the feet of the priests that bare the ark were dipped in the brim of the water, (for Jordan overfloweth all his banks all the time of harvest,)

That the waters which came down from above stood *and* rose up upon an heap very far from the city Adam, that *is* beside Zaretan: and those that came down toward the sea of the plain, *even* the salt sea, failed, *and* were cut off: and the people passed over right against Jericho.

And the priests that bare the ark of the covenant of the LORD stood firm on dry ground in the midst of Jordan, and all the Israelites passed over on dry ground, until all the people were passed clean over Jordan.

Here are a few more translations of verse 16.

American Standard Version
that the waters which came down from above stood, and rose up in one heap, a great way off, at Adam, the city that is beside Zarethan;

and those that went down toward the sea of the Arabah, even the Salt Sea, were wholly cut off: and the people passed over right against Jericho.

Darby
the waters which flowed down from above stood *and* rose up in a heap, very far, by Adam, the city that is beside Zaretan; and those that flowed down towards the sea of the plain, the salt sea, were completely cut off. And the people went over opposite to Jericho.

Contemporary English Version
the river stopped flowing, and the water started piling up at the town of Adam near Zarethan. No water flowed toward the Dead Sea, and the priests stood in the middle of the dry riverbed near Jericho while everyone else crossed over.

New Living Translation
the water above that point began backing up a great distance away at a town called Adam, which is near Zarethan. And the water below that point flowed on to the Dead Sea until the riverbed was dry. Then all the people crossed over near the town of Jericho.

By reading these verses, it isn't too difficult to realise what happened. The Jordan was in full flood, and overflowed its banks. Upstream there was a landslide that blocked the river. The waters flowing downstream gradually dried up as the waters behind the dam created a temporary lake. When the river dried up, the Israelites crossed. When the last of them were on the other side, the waters behind the dam breached the landslide and the waters of the river once again overflowed the banks.

Joshua 4:15-18
And the LORD spake unto Joshua, saying,

Command the priests that bear the ark of the testimony, that they come up out of Jordan.

Joshua therefore commanded the priests, saying, Come ye up out of Jordan.

And it came to pass, when the priests that bare the ark of the covenant of the LORD were come up out of the midst of Jordan, *and* the soles of the priests' feet were lifted up unto the dry land, that the waters of Jordan returned unto their place, and flowed over all his banks, as *they did* before.

Most agree that the City of Adam was sited near the Damieh Ford, close to the mouth of the River Jabbok, which is quite a few miles north of Jericho. There the Jordan is narrow and flows through gorges where landslides have been known to block the river.

After reading all this you might be tempted to think that it wasn't really the power of God after all then. I mean, there was a landslide, the river was blocked, the river dried up, the children of Israel crossed, the dam upstream burst, and the river overflowed its banks again. Just because God does not break the laws of nature does not mean this was not the power of God.

Same with the parting of the Red Sea. It was all perfectly natural. As to the power of God, well, what about the timing? As soon as the feet of the priests entered the River Jordan the water level began to drop. They didn't know a landslide had blocked the river miles upstream, they just stepped into the river and it dried up. Same at Nuweiba. As soon as Moses stretched out his arm, the waters began to recede. Look at the timing. God had Moses and his people in the right place at the right time. When they'd crossed, the returning waters hit the land bridge as a tsunami and wrecked the Egyptian army. Look at the timing and tell me it wasn't the power of God.

I've seen stuff like this hundreds of times throughout my life, perhaps not on the same scale as Moses and Joshua, but the same principles hold true. I was staying at a Holiday Inn where Dr Wierwille was teaching, and I was sharing a room with a guy from Northern Ireland. There was only one key between us so we discussed things and we both agreed that the only way things would work would be if we always left the key at reception. If either of us needed into the room, the key would be available.

About 20 minutes before the evening teaching, I went to reception to get the key so I could get changed and grab my bible. No key. Went up to the room, it was locked. Went back to reception, no key. Went back to the room, it was still locked. That's people for you. I checked my watch. I had to get into my room right then or I was going to miss the teaching. I had words with God and asked him to open the door in the name of Jesus Christ. As soon as my hand grabbed the door handle, a voice behind me asked if I was locked out. It was one of the hotel staff and she had a key in her hand and let me in. The power of God? He didn't break any laws of nature to get me into my room, but look at the timing.

I regularly use the manifestation of believing to bring good weather to dark skies. I picture blue skies and sunshine, speak in tongues, sometimes for hours, and the sun always comes through when I choose to believe.

The manifestation of believing is available to us. We can bring the impossible to pass by operating the manifestation of believing. It was impossible for God's people to cross the Red Sea, it was impossible for God's people to cross the River Jordan, it was impossible for me to get into that hotel room without breaking down the door, and it is impossible to turn dark skies blue. As we believe, we see the power of God and the impossible comes to pass.

Mark 11:23
For verily I say unto you, That whosoever shall say unto this mountain, Be thou removed, and be thou cast into the sea; and shall not doubt in his heart, but shall believe that those things which he saith shall come to pass; he shall have whatsoever he saith.

As Paul states in Hebrews, we could write forever on this subject.

Hebrews 11:17-34
By faith [the manifestation of believing] Abraham, when he was tried, offered up Isaac: and he that had received the promises offered up his only begotten *son*,

Of whom it was said, That in Isaac shall thy seed be called:

Accounting that God *was* able to raise *him* up, even from the dead; from whence also he received him in a figure.

By faith [the manifestation of believing] Isaac blessed Jacob and Esau concerning things to come.

By faith [the manifestation of believing] Jacob, when he was a dying, blessed both the sons of Joseph; and worshipped, *leaning* upon the top of his staff.

By faith [the manifestation of believing] Joseph, when he died, made mention of the departing of the children of Israel; and gave commandment concerning his bones.

By faith [the manifestation of believing] Moses, when he was born, was hid three months of his parents, because they saw *he was* a proper child; and they were not afraid of the king's commandment.

By faith [the manifestation of believing] Moses, when he was come to years, refused to be called the son of Pharaoh's daughter;

Choosing rather to suffer affliction with the people of God, than to enjoy the pleasures of sin for a season;

Esteeming the reproach of Christ greater riches than the treasures in Egypt: for he had respect unto the recompence of the reward.

By faith [the manifestation of believing] he forsook Egypt, not fearing the wrath of the king: for he endured, as seeing him who is invisible.

Through faith [the manifestation of believing] he kept the passover, and the sprinkling of blood, lest he that destroyed the firstborn should touch them.

By faith [the manifestation of believing] they passed through the Red sea as by dry *land:* which the Egyptians assaying to do were drowned.

By faith [the manifestation of believing] the walls of Jericho fell down, after they were compassed about seven days.

By faith [the manifestation of believing] the harlot Rahab perished not with them that believed not, when she had received the spies with peace.

And what shall I more say? for the time would fail me to tell of Gedeon, and *of* Barak, and *of* Samson, and *of* Jephthae; *of* David also, and Samuel, and *of* the prophets:

Who through faith [the manifestation of believing] subdued kingdoms, wrought righteousness, obtained promises, stopped the mouths of lions,

Quenched the violence of fire, escaped the edge of the sword, out of weakness were made strong, waxed valiant in fight, turned to flight the armies of the aliens.

At the beginning I wrote that next to speaking in tongues, the most beneficial manifestation to me personally throughout my life has been the manifestation of believing. While reading through the final draft I realised why. Check these usages of heteros, which means another or other when only two are involved, and allos, which means another or other when more than two are involved.

1 Corinthians 12:7-10
But the manifestation of the Spirit is given to every man to profit withal.

For to one is given by the Spirit the word of wisdom; to another [allos] the word of knowledge by the same Spirit;

To another [heteros] faith [the manifestation of believing] by the same Spirit; to another [allos] the gifts of healing by the same Spirit;

To another [allos] the working of miracles; to another [allos] prophecy; to another [allos] discerning of spirits; to another [heteros] *divers* kinds of tongues; to another [allos] the interpretation of tongues:

This is remarkable and it's something I didn't know when I first made the statement regarding speaking in tongues and the manifestation of believing being the two most beneficial manifestations to me throughout my life. Now I see that the word documents this by these usages of allos and heteros. Heteros being another when only two are involved ties the manifestation of believing and speaking in tongues together, while allos ties all the others together. Speaking in tongues and the manifestation of believing are different to all the other manifestations in that they are for our own personal use, while all the rest are there to help others. How do you like that for biblical accuracy?

It has taken me over eighteen years to bring Walking by the Spirit to publication. That whole time God worked within me to will and to do of his good pleasure, showing me many things by revelation which I've had to believe to get down into printed words in book form. All that revelation wasn't just for me, it was for you, although I get to profit from it as well. If God had known I wouldn't teach it, he wouldn't have given it to me, that's the point. This was all for you.

I was born again one starry night while sailing up the Gulf of Aqaba on a cargo ship when I was a young navigating cadet. God spoke to me that night and told me that if I'd receive his words, that if I would incline my ear to knowledge, apply my heart to wisdom, and search for his word as if it were hidden treasure, that he would teach me his word and I would find the knowledge of God. I did search, and I'm still searching over 40 years later, and God has kept his promise.

It was only very recently I realised that God spoke to me at the very spot where Moses parted the Red Sea. My ministry is to lead God's people once again out of slavery by leading them out of the world's churches, ministries, and religions, and by showing them how to run home churches where they can teach others how to walk by the spirit and worship God in spirit and in truth.

It has been a long road, but the truth is now out there, truths that have not been known since the first century. The ocean of religion has parted, there is a way to escape for anyone anywhere in the world, to anyone who has an internet connection, by PC, laptop, tablet or phone. How long it will remain open I don't know. The pope is already making moves to clamp down on the internet by passing international laws restricting freedom of speech by banning anyone from speaking up against the vatican and what he calls the mother church. To the pope I say this: you can do whatever you want with the ungodly and unbelieving, they're yours dude, but you will let God's people go. Bear in mind what happened to Pharaoh and his army when he refused to let God's people go.

My brothers and sisters in Christ, it is time to walk away from the pope and the Roman Catholic church. It is time to walk away from the Baptist Church. It is time to walk away from the Jehovah's Witnesses. It is time to walk away from the Salvation Army. It is time to walk away from the Muslim religion. It is time to walk away from Buddha. It is time to walk away from the Protestant religion. It is time to walk away from the Way International. It is time to walk away from freemasonry. It is time to walk away from the Presbyterians, the Pentecostals, the Mormons, Judaism and the Hindu religion. It is time to walk away from every church, ministry and religion on the planet and once again walk in the freedom wherewith Christ has made us free. The way is open, all you have to do is walk to freedom. God has parted the Red Sea for you through my life and believing, the way to escape their slavery is right before you. All you have to do is walk away and cross into the promised land of the Age of Grace.

Walking by the spirit rather than by the counsel of men, making Christ your head rather than following men, and having churches in your homes rather than giving your lives to temples made with hands is the way of life and freedom in our day and time.

73. 1 Corinthians 14

In the last chapter we saw that two of the manifestations were distinctly different to the others in that speaking in tongues and the manifestation of believing are there for our own personal use and profit, while the rest are there so we can help others. We learned that from those usages of allos and heteros.

> 1 Corinthians 12:7-10
> But the manifestation of the Spirit is given to every man to profit withal.
>
> For to one [profit] is given by the Spirit the word of wisdom; to another [allos] the word of knowledge by the same Spirit;
>
> To another [heteros] faith [believing] by the same Spirit; to another [allos] the gifts of healing by the same Spirit;
>
> To another [allos] the working of miracles; to another [allos] prophecy; to another [allos] discerning of spirits; to another [heteros] divers kinds of tongues; to another [allos] the interpretation of tongues:

Now this might come as a bit of a surprise and a shock, it certainly was for me when I first saw it, but the revelation manifestations are not there for our own personal use and profit. You might want to sit down and read that a couple of times to let it sink in. The revelation manifestations are not there for our own personal use and profit. Interpretation of tongues, prophecy, word of knowledge, word of wisdom, discerning of spirits, miracles and healing are not there for our own personal use and profit, they are there so we can help others. There's quite a bit of new light coming in the next few chapters, so track with me and take the time to study the bible to see if these things are so.

1 Corinthians 13 clearly falls within the context of the spiritual matters of 1 Corinthians 12:1, so the love of God is a spiritual matter and as such has nothing whatsoever to do with emotion or intellect.

> 1 Corinthians 12:1
> Now concerning spiritual [pneumatikos - spiritual matters] ~~gifts,~~ brethren, I would not have you ignorant.

As renewing your mind is a human ability it can't therefore lead you to the love of God. The renewed mind is the key to unlocking spiritual matters, but it is not a spiritual matter in and of itself. The bible is the instruction manual on how to walk by the spirit. Reading the manual and doing what it says is the key to walking by the spirit. Unless we walk by the spirit, reading the manual is a waste of time. If we study the bible every day for the rest of our lives and develop our human abilities to become the most personable people on earth, but never walk by the spirit with Christ as our head we will never get to the love of God. That's why chapter 13 is sandwiched in a parenthesis between chapters 12 and 14.

As chapter 13 is a parenthesis, we can basically read from the end of chapter 12 to the first verse of chapter 14 without losing the flow of the narrative. Huh? I'm not going to teach chapter 13? Listen up you 1 Corinthians 13 fans, are you aware that the entire chapter is a parenthetical insertion into the context of chapters 12 and 14? It isn't even part of the immediate context. You can't stick chapter 13 on a pedestal and praise it to the skies while ignoring chapters 12 and 14 and stand approved before God as a workman rightly dividing the word of truth. If you don't live chapters 12 and 14, your definition of the love of God is horseshit.

If we live chapters 12 and 14, then yes, chapter 13 takes on beautiful depth and meaning, and the parenthetical figure of speech highlighting the entire chapter for special emphasis can be enjoyed. Those who worship chapter 13 while ignoring chapters 12 and 14 can be likened to people who daydream about living with the love of God but never do what it takes to get there. The love of God is a spiritual matter that grows from what we do with the gift of holy spirit. Read from chapter 12 to chapter 14 and see how the word flows.

1 Corinthians 12:31, 14:1
But covet earnestly the best gifts: and yet shew I unto you a more excellent way.

Follow after charity [agapē - the love of God], and desire spiritual *gifts*, [pneumatikos - spiritual matters] but rather that ye may prophesy.

The context of chapter 14 is still **in the church** from chapter 12. Not only that, but if you read the flow of the context, walking with the love of God is something that grows and develops from operating the manifestations. We follow after, we earnestly pursue the love of God by desiring spiritual matters as they relate to helping others in the church. This ties in beautifully with Galatians where the fruit of the spirit is listed. Note that this is fruit of the spirit, not fruit of the good works of man. If you don't walk by the spirit, you will never cultivate this fruit and you will never walk in the love of God.

Galatians 5:22,23
But the fruit of the Spirit is love, joy, peace, longsuffering, gentleness, goodness, faith,

Meekness, temperance: against such there is no law.

If you want to walk with the love of God and manifest this kind of fruit, look for opportunities to manifest the gift of holy spirit. Get serious about living chapters 12 and 14 or you'll never experience chapter 13 in your life. These spiritual qualities are not human qualities we can develop by renewing our minds or doing any other works of the flesh.

1 Corinthians 14:1
Follow after [diōkō] charity, and desire spiritual *gifts*, [pneumatikos - spiritual matters] but rather that ye may prophesy.

This really is quite a verse. Diōkō is more usually translated as to persecute, and it means to earnestly pursue. We are to earnestly pursue the love of God. How we earnestly pursue the love of God isn't by ignoring chapters 12 and 14, it's by doing our best to live them. It's like getting out of debt. Unless you earnestly pursue that goal by refusing to go further into debt, refusing to buy on impulse, keeping to a rigid budget, living within your means and controlling your expenses, you will never get there. If you want out of debt, you have to do what's required. Sure, God will help you, but don't expect all your problems to be waved away by magic. If you do the word and fight to get out of debt with commitment and faithfulness, you will get there and God will help you if you do things his way. What do you think being a super conqueror means? Daydreaming and all your problems magic away? If you get serious about living chapters 12 and 14, you will eventually experience what it is to live with the love of God. If you don't give of your life in service to others by manifesting the gift of holy spirit with commitment and faithfulness you won't ever experience the love of God. If you want to walk with the love of God and enjoy fruit of the spirit in your life, this is how you get there.

1 Corinthians 14:1-3
Follow after charity, and desire spiritual *gifts*, but rather that ye may prophesy.

For he that speaketh in an ~~unknown~~ tongue speaketh not unto men, but unto God: for no man understandeth ~~him;~~ howbeit in the spirit he speaketh mysteries.

But he that prophesieth speaketh unto men *to* edification, and exhortation, and comfort.

We've already established that the context here is in the church, and that none of these scriptures can be taken out of that context. Keeping this in mind it's easy to make sense of this. In the church our perspective changes from operating manifestations for our own personal use and profit to operating manifestations that help others. When we go to a church meeting where believers are gathered we are to seek to edify and build them up with the manifestations of tongues with interpretation and prophecy. When we speak in tongues we edify ourselves, but when we manifest tongues with interpretation and prophecy we speak words of edification, exhortation, and comfort which builds up the church.

When you speak in tongues, you're not speaking to men you're speaking to God. You have no idea what you're saying, you're speaking mysteries, divine secrets with God. When you energise the manifestation of prophecy in a church meeting, you're speaking in your own language or in the language of the believer's present so everyone there understands what you're saying.

Prophecy, as well as interpretation of tongues, will always edify, exhort and comfort the church. The manifestations are given for profit, and the profit arising from prophecy and interpretation of tongues is that we are edified, exhorted and comforted. This means of course that there will never be reproof or correction in any interpretation of tongues or manifestation of prophecy.

At this point, let's consider the profit of the manifestations. The uses of allos and heteros define who the manifestations profit, either ourselves or others. However, there is an amazing distinction here. For example, when we speak in tongues, we are edified spiritually, no one else is, but others do profit from that as we grow spiritually and become more effective ministers. Speaking in tongues is for our own use, but the profit is actually shared in the church in different ways. When we speak in tongues and interpret or prophesy, it is for the edifying of the church. Well, it just so happens that the person speaking is also part of the church and those words edify, exhort and comfort their minds as well. The profit is actually shared!

The distinction here is that the *primary* profit of each manifestation is tied closely together with to whom each manifestation is for. See the distinction here? The usages of allos and heteros therefore are quite unique in that they define there is a *primary* profit for each manifestation together with an emphasis on who they are for.

> 1 Corinthians 12:7-10
> But the manifestation of the Spirit is given to every man to profit withal.
>
> For to one is given by the Spirit the word of wisdom; to another [allos] the word of knowledge by the same Spirit;
>
> To another [heteros] faith [believing] by the same Spirit; to another [allos] the gifts of healing by the same Spirit;

To another [allos] the working of miracles; to another [allos] prophecy; to another [allos] discerning of spirits; to another [heteros] divers kinds of tongues; to another [allos] the interpretation of tongues:

In verses 8-10 God isn't just telling us there is a profit for this and a profit for that, he's showing us *who* each manifestation is primarily profitable to by those usages of allos and heteros. To illustrate, consider the record of Tabitha being raised from the dead by Peter.

Acts 9:36-42
Now there was at Joppa a certain disciple named Tabitha, which by interpretation is called Dorcas: this woman was full of good works and almsdeeds which she did.

And it came to pass in those days, that she was sick, and died: whom when they had washed, they laid *her* in an upper chamber.

And forasmuch as Lydda was nigh to Joppa, and the disciples had heard that Peter was there, they sent unto him two men, desiring *him* that he would not delay to come to them.

Then Peter arose and went with them. When he was come, they brought him into the upper chamber: and all the widows stood by him weeping, and shewing the coats and garments which Dorcas made, while she was with them.

But Peter put them all forth, and kneeled down, and prayed; and turning *him* to the body said, Tabitha, arise. And she opened her eyes: and when she saw Peter, she sat up.

And he gave her *his* hand, and lifted her up, and when he had called the saints and widows, presented her alive.

And it was known throughout all Joppa; and many believed in the Lord.

The manifestations Peter operated here were not for his own profit, they were for Tabitha's. However, did anyone else profit from it? Sure, the word says many believed in the Lord, that's profit isn't it? Peter and the other disciples would have profited from Tabitha's life after she was raised from the dead don't you think? The usages of allos and heteros only refer to the *primary* profit of each manifestation, so we can safely conclude that God's real intent wasn't just to string together a list of differing profits, but so we would know that speaking in tongues and believing were for our own personal use and profit while interpretation of tongues, prophecy, the revelation manifestations, miracles and healing are only there to be used to help others. So the revelation manifestations are not there for our own personal use.

By the way, while we're here, the manifestation of prophecy is different to the gift ministry of a prophet. A man or woman with the gift ministry of a prophet may be given information about future events by revelation, like Agabus in the book of Acts.

> Acts 21:10,11
> And as we tarried *there* many days, there came down from Judaea a certain prophet, named Agabus.
>
> And when he was come unto us, he took Paul's girdle, and bound his own hands and feet, and said, Thus saith the Holy Ghost, So shall the Jews at Jerusalem bind the man that owneth this girdle, and shall deliver *him* into the hands of the Gentiles.

The gift ministry of a prophet has absolutely nothing to do with the manifestation of prophecy. Every born again believer can operate the manifestation of prophecy because we all have the gift of holy spirit, but the gift ministry of a prophet is a special extra gift to the church. Of course, a man with the gift ministry of a prophet would obviously be able to operate the manifestation of prophecy as well. We are dealing here with the manifestation of prophecy, not the gift ministry of a prophet. The manifestation of prophecy will always, without exception, provide edification, exhortation and comfort. I can assure you that is very different to what a prophet usually delivers when he's energising his gift ministry.

> 1 Corinthians 14:3
> But he that prophesieth speaketh unto men *to* edification, and exhortation, and comfort.

Edification means to build up, exhortation means to encourage, and comfort means just that, to speak kindly. The words spoken while interpreting tongues and prophesying in the church will always fall clearly within these boundaries. This is an example of a possible interpretation of tongues or a prophecy as could be spoken in a home church meeting.

> I am your God, your father, and I love you. My heart is written in the words of my word, so study them, be diligent to search out my heart for you for then you will truly understand my love for you. Walk fearlessly, knowing that I am with you and will never leave you or forsake you.

> 1 Corinthians 14:4
> He that speaketh in an *unknown* tongue edifieth himself; but he that prophesieth edifieth the church.

Here we clearly see differences in profit between speaking in tongues and prophecy. Speaking in tongues edifies the person doing the speaking, while prophecy edifies those listening in a church meeting. Speaking in tongues is how we build ourselves up spiritually. When we get to a church meeting with other believers we are to think more in terms of building them up. That's exactly what Paul says in the next verse.

> 1 Corinthians 14:5
> I would that ye all spake with tongues, but rather that ye prophesied: for greater *is* he that prophesieth than he that speaketh with tongues, except he interpret, that the church may receive edifying.

Interpretation and prophecy are only greater than speaking in tongues when we are in the church. This makes complete sense because speaking in tongues is for our own personal use, while interpretation of tongues and prophecy are to be used to profit the church. We are to speak in tongues much in our private lives, but when we get together as a church we are to prefer tongues with interpretation and prophecy so others can be edified and built up in their minds with words they can understand, words of edification, exhortation and comfort.

> 1 Corinthians 14:6
> Now, brethren, if I come unto you speaking with tongues, what shall I profit you, except I shall speak to you either by revelation, or by knowledge, or by prophesying, or by doctrine?

The logic here is that if we simply just speak in tongues out loud at a church meeting, what good is it to anyone? All they hear are words that mean absolutely nothing to them. If we want to help people, they have to understand what we're saying.

> 1 Corinthians 14:7-9
> And even things without life giving sound, whether pipe or harp, except they give a distinction in the sounds, how shall it be known what is piped or harped?
>
> For if the trumpet give an uncertain sound, who shall prepare himself to the battle?
>
> So likewise ye, except ye utter by the tongue words easy to be understood, how shall it be known what is spoken? for ye shall speak into the air.

Unless we speak in the language of the people present our words will be meaningless.

> 1 Corinthians 14:10,11
> There are, it may be, so many kinds of voices in the world, and none of them *is* without signification.
>
> Therefore if I know not the meaning of the voice, I shall be unto him that speaketh a barbarian, and he that speaketh *shall be* a barbarian unto me.

If we go to our church meetings and we all speak in tongues out loud to each other it would just be a noise. We would be as well grunting like animals for all the good it would do for the church.

> 1 Corinthians 14:12
> Even so ye, forasmuch as ye are zealous of spiritual [pneuma - spirit] *gifts*, seek that ye may excel to the edifying of the church.

I think the reason pneuma was translated spiritual here was so they could insert the word gifts into the text. Scratch it out, it's a forgery. We're zealous to energise the gift of holy spirit which includes all nine manifestations. People in the world are zealous for television, for computers, for music, for education, for politics, for cars, for relationships, for clothes, for family, for books, for movies and a million other things, but we are to be zealous to energise and manifest holy spirit. When we meet with other believers in a church meeting, we should be excited about having an opportunity to edify them by way of manifestations. That is, after all, how we develop fruit of the spirit and grow into walking with the love of God.

> 1 Corinthians 14:13
> Wherefore let him that speaketh in an *unknown* tongue pray that he may interpret.

To pray here is in the essence of we are to believe for God to inspire us to interpret tongues at the meeting. If there are forty people there, God isn't going to inspire everyone to prophecy or give an interpretation, so we are to quietly speak in tongues and believe and pray for that open door. Inside we should be champing at the bit for God to inspire us to manifest at church meetings. That's being zealous of spirit and seeking to excel to the edifying of the church.

This brings up an intriguing aspect of how we are to conduct our church meetings when it comes to manifestations. The word clearly states here that we are to be zealous for and to pray that we get an opportunity to interpret tongues and prophesy at our church meetings, right? How does God answer that prayer? By telling your home church leader to pick you? No, that's not how walking by the spirit works in this administration. God does not dwell in temples made with hands, we are all to walk by the spirit. Christ is our head, not men. If God wants you to speak in tongues and interpret at a church meeting, he will tell you through the Christ in you, not through your home church leader. That's why we are to pray that we may interpret.

> 1 Corinthians 11:3
> But I would have you know, that the head of every man is Christ; and the head of the woman *is* the man [her husband]; and the head of Christ *is* God.

It's God in Christ in you, and Christ is our head. That's how we walk by the spirit. The Christ in us is the gift of holy spirit. God communicates to the Christ in us, and the Christ in us communicates with our minds. Where does man come into that? Man does not determine who manifests, Christ does because Christ is our head. Do home church leaders pick people to receive revelation? Do home church leaders pick people to perform miracles? Men picking people to manifest is just ridiculous. Christ is our head.

Manifestations should be operated by those inspired by God, not those instructed to by men. We don't pick people to manifest prior to a home church meeting, we make it available to manifest and those who are inspired speak. Anything else is a religious ceremony and it will profit you nothing. As soon as men start dictating who does what in home church meetings when it comes to manifestations, Christ is not our head and we are following men.

I know this from experience. When I used to run a home church for a temple made with hands, I didn't get revelation on who to pick to manifest, I picked people out of my own head, sometimes days in advance. That's not how we do things in the church, not if Christ is our head. If our home church leader is responsible for who manifests, what is the point of praying that we may interpret? Why not just go ask the home church leader if you can do it at the next meeting? See, these verses only make sense if we're walking by the spirit. Christ has to be our head, not men.

> 1 Corinthians 14:14
> For if I pray in an *unknown* tongue, my spirit prayeth, but my understanding [nous - my entire mind] is unfruitful.

When we speak in tongues, it is that spirit of Christ in us that is praying and we're edified when we do it, but our understanding is unfruitful, which means our minds get nothing out of it. The Greek word nous is our entire minds. Our minds get absolutely nothing out of speaking in tongues. That's right, speaking in tongues edifies our spirit, how we build up our minds is with faithful study of God's word and by hearing words of edification by way of manifestations at church meetings. Speaking in tongues will do absolutely nothing for your mind because your entire mind is unfruitful, it gets nothing out of it. If you want a strong mind, you need to put the word in there and believe it.

> 1 Corinthians 14:15
> What is it then? I will pray with the spirit, and I will pray with the understanding also: I will sing with the spirit, and I will sing with the understanding also.

Singing with the spirit is a lot of fun, and it's a great way to build yourself up through the day.

> Ephesians 5:18,19
> And be not drunk with wine, wherein is excess; but be filled with the Spirit;
>
> Speaking to yourselves in psalms and hymns and spiritual songs, singing and making melody in your heart to the Lord;

Making melody in our hearts with spiritual songs is singing in tongues.

> 1 Corinthians 14:16,17
> Else when thou shalt bless with the spirit, how shall he that occupieth the room of the unlearned say Amen at thy giving of thanks, seeing he understandeth not what thou sayest?
>
> For thou verily givest thanks well, but the other is not edified.

Paul has made his argument well and clearly explains why interpretation of tongues and prophecy are profitable in our church meetings while speaking in tongues is not. Speaking in tongues is giving thanks well and it's profitable to you, but no one else in the meeting gets anything out of it because our minds get nothing from speaking in tongues. This doesn't mean speaking in tongues isn't important, or is less important than interpretation of tongues or prophecy, it simply means it's not directly profitable to the church. It's for our own personal use and profit.

1 Corinthians 14:18,19
I thank my God, I speak with tongues more than ye all:

Yet in the church I had rather speak five words with my understanding, that *by my voice* I might teach others also, than ten thousand words in an ~~unknown~~ tongue.

There's nothing difficult about this. Paul isn't saying here that speaking in tongues isn't important, he's saying that when he's **in the church** he'd rather interpret tongues and prophecy so that others benefit.

When you're not with other believers, the manifestations you can operate for your own profit are speaking in tongues and believing. As interpretation of tongues and prophecy are not for our own personal use, it logically follows then that we are not to ever attempt to manifest them on our own to ourselves. If we do, the words we speak will not be coming from God they will be coming from our own heads. Those manifestations are not for us, they're to be used in church meetings to edify, exhort and comfort the church.

1 Corinthians 14:20-22
Brethren, be not children in understanding: howbeit in malice be ye children, but in understanding be men.

In the law it is written, With *men of* other tongues and other lips will I speak unto this people; and yet for all that will they not hear me, saith the Lord.

Wherefore tongues are for a sign, not to them that believe, but to them that believe not: but prophesying *serveth* not for them that believe not, but for them which believe.

Speaking in tongues is a demonstration of God's power to those who have no understanding of spiritual matters. Hearing men and women speaking languages they don't know and then giving the interpretation is going to get their attention. If there are no new people at your home church, prophecy would be just fine. There wouldn't really be a need for speaking in tongues as it is the interpretation that carries the edification, exhortation, and comfort. Speaking in tongues with interpretation serves more as a sign to new people that you're manifesting the power of God.

> 1 Corinthians 14:23
> If therefore the whole church be come together into one place, and all speak with tongues, and there come in *those that are* unlearned, or unbelievers, will they not say that ye are mad?

If we speak in tongues out loud without giving any interpretations and someone new is there, they might think we were lunatics speaking gibberish. It's appropriate to speak in tongues together without interpretation in controlled sessions for practice and to teach people how to do it, but not if someone new has just walked in off the street. Chances are they'd walk right back out again, so use your head when operating manifestations during meetings. Everything must be done decently and in order, for edifying.

> 1 Corinthians 14:24-27
> But if all prophesy, and there come in one that believeth not, or *one* unlearned, he is convinced of all, he is judged of all:
>
> And thus are the secrets of his heart made manifest; and so falling down on *his* face he will worship God, and report that God is in you of a truth.
>
> How is it then, brethren? when ye come together, every one of you hath a psalm, hath a doctrine, hath a tongue, hath a revelation, hath an interpretation. Let all things be done unto edifying.
>
> If any man speak in an *unknown* tongue, *let it be* by two, or at the most *by* three, and *that* by course; and let one interpret.

At church meetings, two or three people speak in tongues and interpret. Similarly with the manifestation of prophecy. By course means one after the other, decently and in order, not all at the same time, which would not be by course and would be out of order.

Here we have a standard within which the manifestations are profitable. From these verses we can see that between two and six people manifest at a church meeting, with two or three people speaking in tongues and interpreting and between two and three people giving prophecy. Remember, we're not talking about preparing a ceremony in advance and selecting a few individuals out of our own heads to manifest, as home church leaders we simply make it available and those inspired to manifest get their opportunity to excel to the edifying of the church. Rather than ask specific people to speak in tongues and interpret or prophesy, make it available and then shut up and enjoy seeing and hearing people inspired by God speak messages that edify, exhort and comfort.

Let one interpret means the one who did the speaking in tongues does the interpretation, not someone else. If someone speaks in tongues, and then someone else gives what they call the interpretation, all they're doing is energising the manifestation of prophecy. Those who do that should read the next verse, because the non interpreter is obviously the person who would be doing the speaking in tongues.

> 1 Corinthians 14:27
> But if there be no interpreter, let him keep silence in the church; and let him speak to himself, and to God.

By the way, this establishes the truth that we do not select beforehand those who are to manifest at a church meeting. Choosing people beforehand and picking on them in a meeting introduces fear into believers, especially new people. Don't think it doesn't happen either. I've met young believers who practiced messages before a meeting and memorised them because they were terrified of being asked to manifest. Even as a mature believer, there were days I really just did not want to manifest and dreaded being asked because I was not in the right frame of mind. So instead of going to church meetings and believing to be inspired by God to manifest, folks go there worried about whether or not they're going to be picked on to do it? How is that edifying to the church? It also encourages ego as folks who are picked the most are often tempted to think they're really spiritual or something.

If we did things God's way, things like this wouldn't happen. Only those who believe and who desire to do so should be operating manifestations at church meetings. You don't know who those people are, but God does and he certainly isn't going to tell you the day before who to pick off the top of your head. That's walking by the senses, and it turns what should be inspiring and edifying messages from God into dry ceremonial horseshit. If people don't want to manifest at a church meeting, that's fine according to the word. Read verse 27 again.

> 1 Corinthians 14:27
> But if there be no interpreter, let him keep silence in the church; and let him speak to himself, and to God.

Believers who don't have the confidence to interpret tongues or prophecy are to speak in tongues quietly to themselves, and that's okay with God, it's no big deal. You speak in tongues to yourself by speaking quietly in your head. In the meantime, keep studying the word and strive towards excelling in the church by building your believing to get there. There's no fear or coercion or ego in this if it's done according to the word. You home church leaders, stop picking on people to manifest. It breeds fear in young believers and ego in those with flashy nametags.

Are you struggling with this new light? I did at first until I realised how loving it is. Haven't you had enough of ceremonial horseshit yet? Don't you want to walk with Christ as your head instead of men? Don't pick people to manifest, let those who are seeking to excel, those who are praying and believing, those who are zealously desiring spiritual matters and who want to walk in the love of God interpret tongues and prophesy. Let's make Christ our head again and start walking by the spirit and strip all that broken cistern horseshit out of our lives and out of our home churches.

By the same token, if you're at a church meeting and God inspires you to speak up, don't hold back in fear, open your mouth and speak, get that Christ in you energised with believing. The home church leader will call on folks to manifest and make it available, so if you're inspired, get in there and edify the church.

Verses 29-36 deal specifically with the gift ministries of a prophet and how they are to be properly conducted at home church meetings. The prophets take their turn, and their wives are not to interrupt them during the meetings. Paul then concludes this whole section dealing with how we conduct our affairs within the church.

> 1 Corinthians 14:37
> If any man think himself to be a prophet, or spiritual, let him acknowledge that the things that I write unto you are the commandments of the Lord.

Everything Paul wrote in chapters 12 and 14 are commandments. If you want to know what the will of God is in our day and time, you've just read some of it.

> 1 Corinthians 14:38
> But if any man be ignorant, let him be ignorant.

A couple of things here before we close. First of all, the same mechanics of speech are involved when you interpret tongues and prophesy as when you speak in tongues. The only difference is that the words you speak are in your own language. You don't make the words up, you just speak the interpretation of the tongue or the prophecy and the words will be there. If you can speak in tongues, you can interpret just as easily. If you can speak in tongues you can prophesy just as easily because it's coming from the same Christ in you as the tongues came from. You don't make up the words as you go along, you simply speak and the words will be there. As you speak words forth, the rest will follow just as they do when you speak in tongues.

Secondly, when it comes to interpretation of tongues, the interpretation will be approximately the same length as the speaking in tongues because that's how language works. It doesn't matter in which language I say, *it's a lovely day*, the length of the sentence will always be about the same. It wouldn't take a minute to say *it's a lovely day* in *any* language.

If someone speaks five sentences in tongues, the interpretation should be five sentences as well, not two or ten, with me? If someone speaks in tongues for a minute and then interprets for ten seconds, they are not manifesting accurately. If someone speaks in tongues for ten seconds and then interprets for a minute, they're not manifesting accurately. As you speak in tongues in a church meeting, be conscious of how long you're speaking for and aim to give an interpretation of about the same length, don't cut it short and don't go on repeating yourself over and over.

How you accomplish this is up to you. How I do it is by counting on my fingers how many sentences I've said in a tongue so I have an idea when I'm done with the interpretation. I don't get it right every time, no one does, but on the odd occasion when I do cut an interpretation short or go over I always know and make sure I don't do it again.

You can also cut short prophecy or go over and beyond the message. Don't worry about it though, it's all part of the learning. This isn't about being perfect and being judged by men, it's about children learning to walk by the spirit and growing in the love of God. It's no big deal. How many young children do you know get up on their feet and walk perfectly the first time they try it without falling down? It doesn't happen. If you cut a message short, just smile and enjoy it anyway, at least you're learning and growing. If you go over with a message, you'll find you just keep repeating yourself anyway, saying the same thing over and over again. Learn and grow.

When you learn by experience, you'll eventually get it right just about every time. You mature believers, quit frowning at the kids as they're learning. Do you frown and scold toddlers with reproof and correction when they fall over as they're learning to walk? How cold and religious is that? Come on folks, let's get back to loving people again and walking with the love of God.

> 1 Corinthians 14:38
> But if any man be ignorant, let him be ignorant.

74. The Revelation Manifestations

The revelation manifestations of word of knowledge, word of wisdom and discerning of spirits are not for our own personal use and profit, they are only there so we can help others. This means of course that we cannot operate revelation manifestations for our own personal profit, benefit and gain. I know I'm repeating myself here, but you might have to read this a few times before the truth of it starts to hit you. You see, for decades I've wondered why God has never given me revelation regarding personal matters.

Let me illustrate. I read a book once about Dr Victor Paul Wierwille's brother Harry, who owned a furniture rental business. The book said that Harry used the revelation manifestations to make money through his business. When he had a quiet morning or afternoon, he would drive around town and God would give him revelation if he drove by a house and they were thinking of renting furniture. He would stop, knock the door, introduce himself, and hand them a business card. He made fortunes by receiving revelation like this. Terrific hey?

I was in sales and sales management for twelve years, and not once in all that time did God ever give me revelation so I could make money. Not once, yet he gave revelation to Harry. You have no idea how much this has been in the back of my mind through the years. Did God not want to talk to me or something? Was Harry some kind of special person? Whenever these thoughts came up in my mind, although I didn't understand it, I always countered them with scriptures that clearly state that God is no respecter of persons, and that I had the same amount of holy spirit that Harry did.

Is God a respecter of persons? No, he isn't. Do any of us have any more spirit than anyone else in the body of Christ? No, absolutely not. Harry had no more spirit than you and me, and I have no more spirit than anyone else and nor do you. We all have the same measure of the gift of Christ. So what's the answer? Why did God give Harry revelation that made him money in his business but never gave me any? I never understood this until I began work on this chapter, and I'm still in a bit of a daze as it's sinking in.

The key to understanding this is realising that revelation manifestations are not there for our own personal use and profit, they are not for our own personal benefit and gain, they are only there so we can help others. You see, every year Harry would empty his bank account leaving just $1 and give the entire proceeds of his business to his brother Victor to help him with his ministry work. Dr Wierwille mentioned a few times that he didn't know how he would have moved the word without his brother's financial support. Harry received revelation to make money because it wasn't for his own personal profit, it was to profit us as Dr Wierwille moved his ministry.

In all my years in sales, the revelation I dreamed about receiving was only to make me money. That's why the revelation was never there. Hey, if God always supplies all my need, what do I need revelation to make money for?

> Philippians 4:19
> But my God shall supply all your need according to his riches in glory by Christ Jesus.

Harry was operating revelation manifestations to help his brother move the word, I was trying to operate revelation manifestations to make me more money. My need was supplied, but I wanted more. I remember driving around in a lovely new Vauxhall Cavalier, yet all the time wishing I had a Mercedes. A couple of years later I was driving around in a gorgeous black Mercedes 190e, with lowered suspension, alloys and a rear spoiler. Was I thankful? No, I then drove around wishing I had an Aston Martin. All my need was supplied abundantly, but instead of being thankful, I always wanted more. Revelation manifestations are not there to satiate greed.

One thing I now have clear in my mind since looking around in this new light is that walking by the spirit and receiving revelation are two very different things. Walking by the spirit and operating any of the 9 manifestations for that matter are very different things. Sit down and think about that for a minute. Walking by the spirit and operating revelation manifestations are not the same thing.

Walking by the spirit doesn't mean you are operating manifestations all the time. Similarly, you don't have to be operating manifestations to be walking by the spirit. Manifestations are there to help us when we're walking by the spirit. Do you need to walk by the spirit to speak in tongues? No, that's absurd. The distinction is if you're walking by the spirit God may very well give you revelation to speak in tongues for situations which require perfect prayer. He does that for me by making me feel a little sick inside. Listen carefully, stop and read this a few times until you see it - the manifestations of holy spirit are spiritual tools to help us when we're walking by the spirit.

This new light becomes even more intriguing when you stop to think that the bible was given by revelation.

> Galatians 1:11,12
> But I [Paul] certify you, brethren, that the gospel which was preached of me is not after man.
>
> For I neither received it of man, neither was I taught *it*, but by the revelation of Jesus Christ.

If you want to receive revelation, there's a bible full of it you can read. The entire bible is revelation. It wasn't given to anyone for their own personal use, it was given to them for us. That's why walking by the spirit begins with reading the bible, believing it and then living it. If you live by the principles of the bible when rightly divided and applied, you are walking by revelation because the word, the bible is revelation. Note also that this revelation to Paul came through the Christ in him. Paul operated the manifestations of revelation to receive the all truth which fulfilled the word of God.

> Colossians 1:25-27
> Whereof I am made a minister, according to the dispensation [administration] of God which is given to me for you, to fulfil the word of God;

> *Even* the mystery which hath been hid from ages and from generations, but now is made manifest to his saints:
>
> To whom God would make known what *is* the riches of the glory of this mystery among the Gentiles; which is Christ in you, the hope of glory:

Do we need revelation from God to know that it's Christ in us the hope of glory? No, that revelation was given to Paul and it's written in the bible for us. We also don't need revelation to know that the mystery was hidden in God and was kept secret so the devil wouldn't know of his plans because that's written in the bible as well.

> 1 Corinthians 2:7,8
> But we speak the wisdom of God in a mystery, ~~even~~ the hidden ~~wisdom,~~ which God ordained before the world unto our glory:
>
> Which none of the princes of this world knew: for had they known *it,* they would not have crucified the Lord of glory.

The same is also true regarding homosexuality and everything else the bible addresses because it is all God-breathed, it was all given by revelation. The bible has to be our standard for truth, not the United Nations, the television, man-made churches or our newspapers.

> 2 Timothy 3:16,17
> All scripture *is* **given by inspiration of God** [God-breathed], and *is* profitable for doctrine, for reproof, for correction, for instruction in righteousness:
>
> That the man of God may be perfect, throughly furnished unto all good works.

The point is, if we're born again, if we're studying our bibles faithfully and doing our best to live it, as well as being tuned in to the Christ in us, then we're walking by the spirit. The revelation manifestations are there as extra tools to help us in situations where the bible does not have the information we need in order to help someone. Operating manifestations is part of walking by the spirit, not the other way round. You have to be walking by the spirit to be in a position to receive revelation.

Let's take this a step further. If you want revelation, then you're going to have to put yourself into situations where you need it. If you want revelation you're going to have to look for people to help. Isn't that *exactly* what we learned in the last chapter?

> 1 Corinthians 14:1
> Follow after [diōkō, earnestly pursue] charity [agapē, the love of God], and desire [zēloō, earnestly desire] spiritual [pneumatikos, spiritual matters] *gifts*, but rather that ye may prophesy.

Sure when we're in the church we're to prefer tongues with interpretation and prophecy to speaking in tongues as they are manifestations that build up the church, but what about when we're not at church? What about all the time we're not actually at a church meeting, which would be the majority of our time? We are to earnestly pursue the love of God by earnestly desiring open doors to teach the word and minister the spirit, which is to operate manifestations to help people. Jesus Christ exemplified this as he was always looking for ways to help people. You earnestly pursue the love of God by seeking opportunity to deliver people from oppression by dismantling the works of the devil. This doesn't mean wandering around among unbelievers all the time, it means looking for ways to help believers who you should be living life as a family with every day. If new people are being added to the church on a regular basis, there will be plenty of opportunities to help!

> 1 John 3:8b,16
> For this purpose the Son of God was manifested, that he might destroy the works of the devil.
>
> Hereby perceive we the love *of God*, because he [Jesus Christ] laid down his life for us: and we ought to lay down *our* lives for the brethren.

> Acts 10:38
> How God anointed Jesus of Nazareth with the Holy Ghost [holy spirit] and with power: who went about doing good, and healing all that were oppressed of the devil; for God was with him.

Jesus Christ was given the full measure of the spirit available at that time, and it was so he could go around doing good by healing all that were oppressed of the devil. Well, do we have holy spirit? Yes, and we can do greater works than Jesus Christ did.

> John 14:12
> Verily, verily, I say unto you, He that believeth on me, the works that I do shall he do also; and greater *works* than these shall he do; because I go unto my Father.

The manifestations are there so we can help others. We have speaking in tongues and believing for our own personal use, interpretation of tongues and prophecy when we are in the church, but the revelation manifestations, as well as healing and miracles are there for us to use to help others in our everyday lives. The question is, are we looking for, are we earnestly pursuing, are we earnestly desiring and looking for ways to help people? The manifestations are there for us to use. God does not make you speak in tongues and God will not make you receive revelation either. Just as it is you who does the speaking in tongues, it is you who operates the revelation manifestations of word of knowledge, word of wisdom, and discerning of spirits. Are you putting yourself into situations where you need these manifestations so you can help people? If you do, they will be there. If you're working with people and running a home church, you'll receive more revelation than you know what to do with.

Now, we can't just barge into situations recklessly and attempt to force manifestations into operation.

> Proverbs 26:17
> He that passeth by, and meddleth with strife belonging not to him, is like one that taketh a dog by the ears.

Putting yourself into situations where you can operate manifestations to help people begins with walking by the spirit. Earnestly desiring and earnestly pursuing does not mean barging in recklessly where you're not wanted. We need to have the open door. If people need healing, they will have to believe for it. You can't heal someone who isn't believing. Which of the manifestations are for our own personal use and profit? One of them is believing!

If you're walking by the spirit and looking for ways to help, that's when the doors will open and then the revelation manifestations will come into operation for you. Consider this record of Jesus Christ with the woman at the well.

> John 4:5-8
> Then cometh he [Jesus] to a city of Samaria, which is called Sychar, near to the parcel of ground that Jacob gave to his son Joseph.
>
> Now Jacob's well was there. Jesus therefore, being wearied with *his* journey, sat thus on the well: *and* it was about the sixth hour.
>
> There cometh a woman of Samaria to draw water: Jesus saith unto her, Give me to drink.
>
> (For his disciples were gone away unto the city to buy meat.)

Did Jesus Christ need revelation to talk to this woman? No, you don't need revelation to begin a conversation with someone. If you're at your lunch break at work, do you need revelation to begin conversations with people? If you're out walking along the beach and meet someone, do you need revelation to start a conversation with them? If you go to the pub and sit down next to folks, do you need revelation to start talking to them? If you go to your photography or guitar or running club, do you need revelation to chat with people? No, that's silly. Jesus Christ was thirsty so he asked the woman for a drink. Do you need revelation to go to the shop and buy a drink if you're thirsty?

> John 4:9
> Then saith the woman of Samaria unto him, How is it that thou, being a Jew [Judean], askest drink of me, which am a woman of Samaria? for the Jews [Judeans] have no dealings with the Samaritans.

The woman responded with a sincere spiritual question, and it got Jesus Christ's attention. He then continued the conversation to see if she was looking for genuine spiritual answers.

John 4:10-15
Jesus answered and said unto her, If thou knewest the gift of God, and who it is that saith to thee, Give me to drink; thou wouldest have asked of him, and he would have given thee living water.

The woman saith unto him, Sir, thou hast nothing to draw with, and the well is deep: from whence then hast thou that living water?

Art thou greater than our father Jacob, which gave us the well, and drank thereof himself, and his children, and his cattle?

Jesus answered and said unto her, Whosoever drinketh of this water shall thirst again:

But whosoever drinketh of the water that I shall give him shall never thirst; but the water that I shall give him shall be in him a well of water springing up into everlasting life.

The woman saith unto him, Sir, give me this water, that I thirst not, neither come hither to draw.

The woman was indeed spiritually hungry and looking for answers, so Jesus Christ then operated the revelation manifestations to see if there was a way to get her attention so he could help her. He was earnestly pursuing the love of God by earnestly desiring to operate manifestations so he could help her.

John 4:16-19
Jesus saith unto her, Go, call thy husband, and come hither.

The woman answered and said, I have no husband. Jesus said unto her, Thou hast well said, I have no husband:

For thou hast had five husbands; and he whom thou now hast is not thy husband: in that saidst thou truly.

The woman saith unto him, Sir, I perceive that thou art a prophet.

In this case, there was indeed revelation, and it did get her attention. She then opened her heart to him.

> John 4:20,21
> Our fathers worshipped in this mountain; and ye say, that in Jerusalem is the place where men ought to worship.
>
> Jesus saith unto her, Woman, believe me, the hour cometh, when ye shall neither in this mountain, nor yet at Jerusalem, worship the Father.

If this had been the 21st Century, the conversation may very well have gone something like this:

Our fathers worshipped in the Catholic church; others say that we should join the Mormons or the Way International, or join the Salvation Army, or go to the Methodist Church, or join the muslims, or go to a synagogue, or join the Jehovahs witnesses, or the Anglican church, or the Baptist church, or the Presbyterians, or the church of Scotland in order to worship God.

Jesus saith unto her, Woman, believe me, the hour cometh, when it will not be available to worship God in any of those shithole places.

The conversation continued.

> John 4:22-26
> Ye worship ye know not what: we know what we worship: for salvation is of the Jews [Judeans].
>
> But the hour cometh, and now is, when the true worshippers shall worship the Father in spirit and in truth: for the Father seeketh such to worship him.
>
> God *is* a Spirit: and they that worship him must worship *him* in spirit and in truth.
>
> The woman saith unto him, I know that Messias cometh, which is called Christ: when he is come, he will tell us all things.

Jesus saith unto her, I that speak unto thee am *he*.

What do you think her heart did when she realised she was talking to the messiah, the son of God? I have absolutely no doubts whatsoever that this woman was later born again when the gift of holy spirit was first made available. Was Jesus Christ operating manifestations when he struck up a conversation with the woman? No, he wasn't. Was he walking by the spirit? Yes, he was. It was walking by the spirit and earnestly pursuing opportunities to help people that opened the door to the manifestations. The manifestations are tools to help us walk by the spirit.

Before taking this further, we need to look at a few examples of the revelation manifestations being operated in the book of Acts to determine if there are any common traits they share which will help us understand them.

When Paul learned a better way on the road to Damascus and he was blinded, Ananias received revelation to go and minister healing to Paul. How did Ananias receive this revelation?

> Acts 9:9-12
> And he [Paul] was three days without sight, and neither did eat nor drink.
>
> And there was a certain disciple at Damascus, named Ananias; and to him said the Lord in a vision, Ananias. And he said, Behold, I *am here*, Lord.
>
> And the Lord *said* unto him, Arise, and go into the street which is called Straight, and enquire in the house of Judas for *one* called Saul, of Tarsus: for, behold, he prayeth,
>
> And hath seen in a vision a man named Ananias coming in, and putting *his* hand on him, that he might receive his sight.

Ananias received revelation by seeing a vision in his mind. A vision is either a static or a moving picture. Ananias saw a vision, he saw a moving picture, a short video in his mind with sound. Notice also that Paul had just been born again and he was already receiving revelation before he had even spoken in tongues. He was also clearly believing to be healed. As soon as people have holy spirit, it's available to energise right away.

When Peter was praying on the housetop in Joppa, he received revelation to accompany some men and go and visit Cornelius the Roman centurion. How did Peter receive that revelation?

> Acts 10:9-16
> On the morrow, as they went on their journey, and drew nigh unto the city, Peter went up upon the housetop to pray about the sixth hour:
>
> And he became very hungry, and would have eaten: but while they made ready, he fell into a trance [he saw a vision],
>
> And saw heaven opened, and a certain vessel descending unto him, as it had been a great sheet knit at the four corners, and let down to the earth:
>
> Wherein were all manner of fourfooted beasts of the earth, and wild beasts, and creeping things, and fowls of the air.
>
> And there came a voice to him, Rise, Peter; kill, and eat.
>
> But Peter said, Not so, Lord; for I have never eaten any thing that is common or unclean.
>
> And the voice *spake* unto him again the second time, What God hath cleansed, *that* call not thou common.
>
> This was done thrice: and the vessel was received up again into heaven.

Peter saw a vision, a moving picture, a video in his mind, and then he heard a voice. Ananias spoke in his vision as well and heard Jesus Christ's voice.

When Paul was looking for an open door to speak the word in Acts 16, how did the revelation to go to Macedonia come to him?

> Acts 16:6-10
> Now when they had gone throughout Phrygia and the region of Galatia, and were forbidden of the Holy Ghost [holy spirit] to preach the word in Asia,
>
> After they were come to Mysia, they assayed to go into Bithynia: but the Spirit suffered them not.
>
> And they passing by Mysia came down to Troas.
>
> And a vision appeared to Paul in the night; There stood a man of Macedonia, and prayed him, saying, Come over into Macedonia, and help us.
>
> And after he had seen the vision, immediately we endeavoured to go into Macedonia, assuredly gathering that the Lord had called us for to preach the gospel unto them.

Paul received revelation by seeing a moving picture in his mind, a man of Macedonia waving to him and asking him to come and help him. Paul saw a vision and heard a voice. How did he know it was a man of Macedonia? If you saw a man in a kilt waving to you, you would know it was a Scotsman, right? Paul knew from the man's clothing where he was from because in those days folks wore traditional cultural clothing, they didn't all dress up in stupid suits. He may even have recognised the man's accent.

How did Paul receive revelation to stay in Corinth in Acts 18 when he was so used to travelling around?

> Acts 18:9-11
> Then spake the Lord to Paul in the night by a vision, Be not afraid, but speak, and hold not thy peace:
>
> For I am with thee, and no man shall set on thee to hurt thee: for I have much people in this city.
>
> And he continued *there* a year and six months, teaching the word of God among them.

Paul saw a vision, a moving picture in his mind, and heard Jesus Christ speaking to him. There is definitely a pattern emerging here, wouldn't you say? We can safely assume then that the revelation manifestations of word of knowledge, word of wisdom and discerning of spirits involve our senses. We will either see a static or moving picture, hear something, taste something, feel something, or smell something. That is how the revelation manifestations work. When you think about it, that makes sense because the word revelation actually means to reveal and all we have to learn with is our five senses. Revelation is God giving us information by way of the Christ in us to one or more of our five senses so we can help people.

Now, when we're walking by the spirit, often we just know things right? We perceive things, we just know we have to do something, or go somewhere or whatever. This perceptiveness is not us operating the revelation manifestations, it's part of walking by the spirit. They are not the same thing.

> Act 14:8-10
> And there sat a certain man at Lystra, impotent in his feet, being a cripple from his mother's womb, who never had walked:
>
> The same heard Paul speak: who stedfastly beholding him, and perceiving that he had faith to be healed,
>
> Said with a loud voice, Stand upright on thy feet. And he leaped and walked.

It says Paul perceived. He just knew the man was believing to be healed. Perception is also a human quality, an innate human ability. Here's an account of a Scribe perceiving information when they were trying to catch Jesus Christ out in words so they could incriminate him.

> Mark 12:28
> And one of the scribes came, and having heard them reasoning together, and perceiving that he had answered them well, asked him, Which is the first commandment of all?

This kind of perception is a perception in the mind, it isn't a moving picture, and nor do you hear anything. This kind of perception is not the revelation manifestations. Natural man can hone his perceptive skills and develop what they term peripheral vision. Well, so can we, only to a much greater degree. As we walk by the spirit and speak in tongues, our spiritual perceptiveness will grow and develop.

> Hebrews 5:13,14
> For every one that useth milk *is* unskilful in the word of righteousness: for he is a babe.
>
> But strong meat belongeth to them that are of full age, *even* those who by reason of use have their senses exercised to discern both good and evil.

This perception grows as we grow spiritually, but it isn't revelation. This is part of walking by the spirit with Christ as our head. As we walk by the spirit, tuned in to the Christ in us, then doors will open for us to energise the manifestations of holy spirit to help people. The manifestations are tools to help us as we walk by the spirit.

Keeping these truths in mind, it's easy to see and understand now how Ananias received revelation to go and see Paul in Damascus. The revelation was not for his own profit, it was for Paul's. Peter received revelation to go with the men sent by Cornelius so the word would go to the Gentiles. When Paul was in Asia looking for open doors to speak the word, the revelation was to go into Macedonia. That revelation wasn't for himself, for his own profit, was it? When it comes to revelation, the first thing we must look for is the profit. Who is it for? If the profit would be primarily for us, the revelation manifestations simply will not work. If we're looking to profit ourselves by operating the gift of holy spirit, we have speaking in tongues and believing.

Back in Lystra, Paul perceived the man was believing to be healed.

> Acts 14:8-10
> And there sat a certain man at Lystra, impotent in his feet, being a cripple from his mother's womb, who never had walked:
>
> The same heard Paul speak: who stedfastly beholding him, and perceiving that he had faith [believing] to be healed,

Said with a loud voice, Stand upright on thy feet. And he leaped and walked.

There were a number of manifestations working together that day in Lystra, word of knowledge, word of wisdom, discerning of spirits, and gifts of healing. We can also safely assume Paul was speaking in tongues. First, Paul perceived the man was believing for healing. There's a manifestation right there on the man's part. Paul then got the green light to minister to him. That would have been word of knowledge. How Paul got that go sign we don't know, but it may very well have been compassion. In this case there was no devil spirit to remove, so discerning of spirits wasn't applicable, and the word of wisdom was to simply tell the man in a loud voice to stand up on his feet. When the man carried out that instruction, he stood up and received the healing.

How God communicates with you by revelation is personal. He will communicate with you on your level, in language you understand by way of your five senses. The most common instances seem to be pictures we see and sounds we hear, but he may reveal information in other ways, such as by smell, taste or touch. I often feel compassion inside which is my green light to get involved in a situation to help people. I feel sick inside when I need to speak in tongues and pray perfectly for something or someone. When a job is done, for example if I'm ministering or writing a chapter of this class, he lets me know by flushing me inside with a deep peace that goes right through my whole body.

When I was having problems regarding teaching on the bride of Christ and the body of Christ in chapter 63 because I knew I didn't understand it, he showed me a picture in my mind through the Christ in me. That's revelation. I've probably read as much on the bride and body of Christ as anyone, and the information I needed to fully understand the figures of speech just was not available. I needed new light because there was no more I could do. I had done my best, I'd studied everything worth reading and waded through a sea of horseshit that wasn't, and that information was not available. The revelation wasn't primarily for my benefit either, it was for yours, although I do profit from it as well. See how this all works? It's easy hey.

All this revelation God has given me in this class isn't for me either, it's for you. The revelation manifestations are not there for my own personal profit, they're there so I can help others. God knew I would teach it, which is the only reason he's given it to me. If this information was available somewhere else in the world, I wouldn't be receiving revelation either because God would expect me to go to wherever his word was and study it. The word I'm teaching regarding God not dwelling in temples made with hands is just not available anywhere else in the world. This also means that if anyone in the world wants the truth I teach, they will have to come here to get it, God isn't going to give them revelation when it's already available.

By the way, the revelation manifestations being there to help others and not being for our own personal use obviously includes discerning of spirits. You will only ever receive revelation regarding the presence of devil spirits if it would help someone, perhaps so you could then receive word of knowledge and word of wisdom on whether you could cast them out or not. Always remember, devil spirits are powerful so never underestimate them. Respect them for what they are. It's the power of God that brings deliverance from devil spirits, not anything we do with our five senses.

This brings up another interesting point we might as well touch on. I've been getting quite a bit of revelation writing this class, but do you know something? For years and years, I got none at all. That's right, nothing, not one jot or tittle by way of revelation came to me regarding new light in the word until I started working this class. Why? Well, because revelation isn't for my own profit and I wasn't writing any classes. Besides, there was plenty available that I didn't know and God expected me to study my ass off so I could rightly divide his word.

> 2 Timothy 2:15
> Study to shew thyself approved unto God, a workman that needeth not to be ashamed, rightly dividing the word of truth.

That study began with Dr Wierwille's ministry, and for over 30 years I studied everything his ministry had to offer. It was only many years after his death and after his ministry had been transformed into a horseshit temple where men walked by their senses rather than by the spirit of Christ, when there was no more they could teach me and there was nowhere else to go, that God began giving me revelation so I could write this class.

Listen, I love you, but don't expect God to give you revelation regarding new light in his word if you've not studied this class and learned all you can from it. Study all that's available and make the word your own, and then God can touch your heart in special personal ways when you're studying and reading and show you amazing perspectives you perhaps hadn't thought of before. When he shows you stuff that touches your heart like that, be sure to teach it at the very next home church you go to because chances are it will be new light to someone there. Remember, Christ is our head, not men, so you have a right and a duty to teach at your home church what God is touching your heart with. Your home church leader should make it available to teach, and if there are a few of you bubbling over with stuff God has shown you in his word, open your mouth and get in there and teach when you have an opportunity. This is how we keep our home churches fresh and alive in the present truth.

Another thing that has helped me understand how revelation works is by spending God's money. He always, without exception, gives me revelation when he wants me to spend his money, but he never gives me revelation when I'm spending my own. When God wants me to spend his money, I know because I get that peaceful feeling inside. It's God's way of giving me a green light. A few times I've thought of good ways I thought God should spend his money, I've gone to him but the peaceful feeling wasn't there so I didn't spend the money.

When it comes to my own money, there's never any revelation. Why? I don't need it, that's why. It's my money, I have a brain, I have a budget, and God isn't going to interfere with that. My money is my responsibility. When I need something for myself, I don't need revelation, I need to do my homework and budget for it. When I'm sure I know what I'm buying and the money is in my budget, I find a supplier and make the purchase. Revelation isn't needed for that. If I make mistakes and have to live with something that doesn't do the job properly, that isn't God's fault, it's mine for not doing all my homework before spending the money.

This brings us to another intriguing point. As the revelation manifestations are not there for our own use, would we therefore require revelation to operate the manifestation of believing? No, we wouldn't. Do you need revelation to speak in tongues? No, that's just plain silly. Unless God needs me to speak in tongues for specific situations I don't know anything about, which comes by way of a sick feeling inside, I don't need revelation to speak in tongues. When I do get revelation to speak in tongues, it is always for someone else's profit.

Believing is also there for our own personal use, it's ours to energise just like speaking in tongues. That's why I don't need revelation to believe for good weather when I need it. If I speak in tongues, picture blue skies, and keep my mind stayed on blue skies and continue to speak in tongues, the sun comes through. If I lose my concentration and stop speaking in tongues, I don't get the results. Same with problem solving, no matter what it is. God has shown me through Christ on literally thousands of occasions how to solve problems at work, with computers, with cars, with personal health issues, and a thousand other things. That information came because I was walking by the spirit and I was believing, it didn't come by revelation. We have speaking in tongues and believing at our disposal for our own personal use. If we don't operate them though, nothing will happen.

Would there be any exceptions regarding revelation when operating the manifestation of believing? Yes, if other people are involved who would profit from our believing, as in Moses parting the Red Sea. In that situation Moses needed revelation on what exactly to believe for so they could all escape. If God's people are involved, God may very well give you revelation on what to believe for so you all profit. The distinctions between the manifestations may be subtle but they are not difficult to understand if you simply keep an eye on the profit.

Learning to see the profit when manifesting holy spirit is important, and not just for determining when we can and when we can't energise certain manifestations, but also in distinguishing between the genuine and the counterfeit. Learning to see spiritual profit will help us as we walk by the spirit.

It's not difficult to walk by the spirit, it just requires walking away from temples made with hands run by men who walk by their senses and who make everything so damn complicated and burdensome. Revelation is not walking by the counsel and will of men, it's walking in fellowship with God through the Christ in us. Revelation doesn't come from a telephone, it comes from the Christ in you.

And there's my peaceful feeling inside, God's way of letting me know by revelation that I've done my job and this chapter is ready to prepare for publishing. Let's have some fun and raise a few tsunamis of believing and get out there and help people.

75. Miracles

The manifestation of miracles is extraordinary. I think the best way to define exactly what a miracle is would be to look at a few examples, and what better place to begin than with Jesus' first recorded miracle? Remember, the manifestation of miracles is only there so we can help people. Have a read through the record and then I'll point out what a miracle actually is.

John 2:1-11
And the third day there was a marriage in Cana of Galilee; and the mother of Jesus was there:

And both Jesus was called, and his disciples, to the marriage.

And when they wanted wine, the mother of Jesus saith unto him, They have no wine.

Jesus saith unto her, Woman, what have I to do with thee? mine hour is not yet come.

His mother saith unto the servants, Whatsoever he saith unto you, do *it*.

And there were set there six waterpots of stone, after the manner of the purifying of the Jews [Judeans], containing two or three firkins apiece.

Jesus saith unto them, Fill the waterpots with water. And they filled them up to the brim.

And he saith unto them, Draw out now, and bear unto the governor of the feast. And they bare *it*.

> When the ruler of the feast had tasted the water that was made wine, and knew not whence it was: (but the servants which drew the water knew;) the governor of the feast called the bridegroom,
>
> And saith unto him, Every man at the beginning doth set forth good wine; and when men have well drunk, then that which is worse: *but* thou hast kept the good wine until now.
>
> This beginning of miracles did Jesus in Cana of Galilee, and manifested forth his glory; and his disciples believed on him.

Jesus Christ's first miracle was to turn water into wine. How do you turn water into wine? There is only one way it can be done. There must have been a change in the water at the molecular level. There was a restructuring of the molecules. That's what a miracle is, atoms and molecules are changed or added. This might sound like a big deal, but remember, this is the power of God we're talking about.

When Jesus Christ fed the multitudes they are referred to as miracles.

> Matthew 14:13,14
> When Jesus heard *of it*, he departed thence by ship into a desert place apart: and when the people had heard *thereof,* they followed him on foot out of the cities.
>
> And Jesus went forth, and saw a great multitude, and was moved with compassion toward them, and he healed their sick.

Here we see compassion, the revelation green light to help people. In this case it came by way of compassion that welled up inside him.

> Matthew 14:15-21
> And when it was evening, his disciples came to him, saying, This is a desert place, and the time is now past; send the multitude away, that they may go into the villages, and buy themselves victuals.
>
> But Jesus said unto them, They need not depart; give ye them to eat.

And they say unto him, We have here but five loaves, and two fishes.

He said, Bring them hither to me.

And he commanded the multitude to sit down on the grass, and took the five loaves, and the two fishes, and looking up to heaven, he blessed, and brake, and gave the loaves to *his* disciples, and the disciples to the multitude.

And they did all eat, and were filled: and they took up of the fragments that remained twelve baskets full.

And they that had eaten were about five thousand men, beside women and children.

How do you feed 5000 men, plus women and children with five loaves and two fish? It's impossible, but that was all that was available. As Jesus Christ broke the bread and the fish, God replaced the food at the molecular level so it never ran out. When everyone was fed, they gathered up what was left and filled twelve baskets. Miracles involve change at the molecular level. Miracles don't contradict nature, it's simply a changing or an adding of atoms and molecules where needed to bring deliverance. Later on, Jesus Christ fed another multitude, this time of four thousand men, plus women and children.

Mark 8:1-3
In those days the multitude being very great, and having nothing to eat, Jesus called his disciples *unto him*, and saith unto them,

I have compassion on the multitude, because they have now been with me three days, and have nothing to eat:

And if I send them away fasting to their own houses, they will faint by the way: for divers [many] of them came from far.

There's compassion again, the green light revelation to help people. There were thousands of men, women and children there, many a long way from home and they had no food. To just leave them would have risked many of them collapsing with hunger as they walked home.

Mark 8:4-9
And his disciples answered him, From whence can a man satisfy these *men* with bread here in the wilderness?

And he asked them, How many loaves have ye? And they said, Seven.

And he commanded the people to sit down on the ground: and he took the seven loaves, and gave thanks, and brake, and gave to his disciples to set before *them;* and they did set *them* before the people.

And they had a few small fishes: and he blessed, and commanded to set them also before *them*.

So they did eat, and were filled: and they took up of the broken *meat* that was left seven baskets.

And they that had eaten were about four thousand: and he sent them away.

Here is the same account in Matthew.

Matthew 15:36-38
And he took the seven loaves and the fishes, and gave thanks, and brake *them,* and gave to his disciples, and the disciples to the multitude.

And they did all eat, and were filled: and they took up of the broken *meat* that was left seven baskets full.

And they that did eat were four thousand men, beside women and children.

In this case, when they gathered what was left over they filled seven baskets. I'm sure Jesus and the disciples enjoyed a good meal out of it as well, so they also profited from the miracle.

The raising of Lazarus from the dead is referred to as a miracle.

John 12:1,2,9-11,17,18
Then Jesus six days before the passover came to Bethany, where Lazarus was which had been dead, whom he raised from the dead.

There they made him a supper; and Martha served: but Lazarus was one of them that sat at the table with him.

Much people of the Jews [Judeans] therefore knew that he was there: and they came not for Jesus' sake only, but that they might see Lazarus also, whom he had raised from the dead.

But the chief priests consulted that they might put Lazarus also to death;

Because that by reason of him many of the Jews [Judeans] went away, and believed on Jesus.

The people therefore that was with him when he called Lazarus out of his grave, and raised him from the dead, bare record.

For this cause the people also met him, for that they heard that he had done this miracle.

Why would Lazarus being raised from the dead be a miracle rather than a healing? Well, Lazarus had been dead for four days. He was actually decomposing and stinking when Jesus Christ walked into the tomb. Quite a bit of molecular reconstruction would have been needed to restore Lazarus' body to a habitable state. I don't think Lazarus would have been too happy had be simply been raised from the dead into a decomposing body. His body required restoration at the molecular level and decomposed atoms and molecules would have had to be replaced. That's why it was a miracle. We can also see this in Acts.

Acts 3:1,2
Now Peter and John went up together into the temple at the hour of prayer, *being* the ninth *hour*.

> And a certain man lame from his mother's womb was carried, whom they laid daily at the gate of the temple which is called Beautiful, to ask alms of them that entered into the temple;

This man had been lame from birth, and we learn later that he was over 40 years old. He had never walked, not even as an infant. He couldn't walk because he was missing feet and ankle bones from his birth. He was deformed.

> Acts 3:3-8
> Who seeing Peter and John about to go into the temple asked an alms.
>
> And Peter, fastening his eyes upon him with John, said, Look on us.
>
> And he gave heed unto them, expecting to receive [lambanō] something of them [he was believing].
>
> Then Peter said, Silver and gold have I none; but such as I have give I thee: In the name of Jesus Christ of Nazareth rise up and walk.
>
> And he took him by the right hand, and lifted *him* up: and immediately his feet and ankle bones received strength.
>
> And he leaping up stood, and walked, and entered with them into the temple, walking, and leaping, and praising God.

As Peter took his hand and the man made the effort to get to his feet, God got involved at the molecular level and gave him the bones and other parts he needed so he could walk. As he had never walked in his life before, his muscles would have also required molecular help so he would have had the strength to get to his feet.

For their efforts, Peter and John were arrested and thrown in jail. The following day they were brought before a council of top religious men and interrogated.

> Acts 4:5-7
> And it came to pass on the morrow, that their rulers, and elders, and scribes,

And Annas the high priest, and Caiaphas, and John, and Alexander, and as many as were of the kindred of the high priest, were gathered together at Jerusalem.

And when they had set them in the midst, they asked, By what power, or by what name, have ye done this?

Peter and John were treated as criminals for that miracle of healing. The devil considers healing people he has crippled as a crime. These religious leaders were on side with the devil, not the true God, as are most religious leaders in our day and time.

Acts 4:8-22
Then Peter, filled with the Holy Ghost [holy spirit], said unto them, Ye rulers of the people, and elders of Israel,

If we this day be examined of the good deed done to the impotent man, by what means he is made whole;

Be it known unto you all, and to all the people of Israel, that by the name of Jesus Christ of Nazareth, whom ye crucified, whom God raised from the dead, *even* by him doth this man stand here before you whole.

This is the stone which was set at nought of you builders, which is become the head of the corner.

Neither is there salvation in any other: for there is none other name under heaven given among men, whereby we must be saved [made whole].

Now when they saw the boldness of Peter and John, and perceived that they were unlearned and ignorant men, they marvelled; and they took knowledge of them, that they had been with Jesus.

And beholding the man which was healed standing with them, they could say nothing against it.

But when they had commanded them to go aside out of the council, they conferred among themselves,

Saying, What shall we do to these men? for that indeed a notable miracle hath been done by them *is* manifest to all them that dwell in Jerusalem; and we cannot deny *it*.

But that it spread no further among the people, let us straitly threaten them, that they speak henceforth to no man in this name.

And they called them, and commanded them not to speak at all nor teach in the name of Jesus.

But Peter and John answered and said unto them, Whether it be right in the sight of God to hearken unto you more than unto God, judge ye.

For we cannot but speak the things which we have seen and heard.

So when they had further threatened them, they let them go, finding nothing how they might punish them, because of the people: for all *men* glorified God for that which was done.

For the man was above forty years old, on whom this miracle of healing was shewed.

Now we begin to get a feel for the distinctions and differences between the manifestations. This particular healing is referred to as a miracle, but not all healings are miracles. Only healings where changes at the molecular level are required are referred to as miracles. Sometimes when ministering healing, we will be required to perform miracles as well if body parts are deformed, eaten away or missing.

John 4:46-54
So Jesus came again into Cana of Galilee, where he made the water wine. And there was a certain nobleman, whose son was sick at Capernaum.

When he heard that Jesus was come out of Judaea into Galilee, he went unto him, and besought him that he would come down, and heal his son: for he was at the point of death.

Then said Jesus unto him, Except ye see signs and wonders, ye will not believe.

The nobleman saith unto him, Sir, come down ere my child die

Jesus saith unto him, Go thy way; thy son liveth. And the man believed the word that Jesus had spoken unto him, and he went his way.

And as he was now going down, his servants met him, and told *him*, saying, Thy son liveth.

Then enquired he of them the hour when he began to amend. And they said unto him, Yesterday at the seventh hour the fever left him.

So the father knew that *it was* at the same hour, in the which Jesus said unto him, Thy son liveth: and himself believed, and his whole house.

This *is* again the second miracle *that* Jesus did, when he was come out of Judaea into Galilee.

The word records that this was Jesus' second miracle. Both miracles recorded so far required molecular reconstruction. What's even more remarkable about this miracle is that Jesus Christ didn't even go and see the boy, so revelation manifestations were obviously in operation as well. We can see that the man's believing was also a requirement. Believing is always required for healing.

John 6:1,2
After these things Jesus went over the sea of Galilee, which is *the sea of* Tiberias.

And a great multitude followed him, because they saw his miracles which he did on them that were diseased.

The accuracy of the word is astonishing. It says he performed miracles on those which were diseased. It doesn't say he performed miracles on those which needed healing. Diseases like leprosy eat away at parts of the human body, so to heal them Jesus would also necessarily have had to perform miracles to put the molecules back which the diseases had eaten away.

It's important to understand that not all healings are miracles. It's only perhaps a small point, but we really should be more careful with how we use the word miracle. Jesus Christ filled Peter's nets with fish on a number of occasions and almost everyone refers to these records as miracles. No they weren't. There was no molecular reconstruction required to fill Peter's nets with fish. None of the records are referred to as miracles in the bible and it's important that we understand why. How can you help people with the manifestation of miracles if you don't understand what a miracle is?

The manifestation of gifts of healing and the manifestation of miracles are two very different manifestations used for two very different things. Sometimes you have to operate both together, sometimes you don't. If all healings were miracles there would be no need for two separate manifestations. Not all healings are miracles, but the two are often closely related in healing situations.

The word records that Paul performed 'special' miracles.

> Acts 19:11,12
> And God wrought special miracles by the hands of Paul:
>
> So that from his body were brought unto the sick handkerchiefs or aprons, and the diseases departed from them, and the evil spirits went out of them.

When Paul was at Ephesus, he was so busy and there were so many people believing to be healed that he simply couldn't get round to see everyone. Does that put God out of business? Not at all. He gave Paul revelation to send hankies to those who were diseased and believing to be healed. It is intriguing that the word specifically mentions those who were diseased in the context of this being special miracles.

Many times diseases are caused by devil spirits that lodge in the body and eat away at it. There isn't much point in performing miracles and restoring diseased bodies to health if you don't remove the devil spirit causing it. So here we see healing, miracles and the revelation manifestations of word of knowledge, word of wisdom and discerning of spirits all working together to help people.

Even in the old testament we can see that miracles required molecular reconstruction.

> Exodus 7:8-12
> And the LORD spake unto Moses and unto Aaron, saying,
>
> When Pharaoh shall speak unto you, saying, Shew a miracle for you: then thou shalt say unto Aaron, Take thy rod, and cast *it* before Pharaoh, *and* it shall become a serpent.
>
> And Moses and Aaron went in unto Pharaoh, and they did so as the LORD had commanded: and Aaron cast down his rod before Pharaoh, and before his servants, and it became a serpent.
>
> Then Pharaoh also called the wise men and the sorcerers: now the magicians of Egypt, they also did in like manner with their enchantments.
>
> For they cast down every man his rod, and they became serpents: but Aaron's rod swallowed up their rods.

Here we can also see that those who operate witchcraft can get devil spirits to work at the molecular level and change matter. They do it all the time. Devil spirits can make things disappear, go through walls and reappear in the next room. All they're doing is deconstructing matter at the molecular level, transporting it through walls above the speed of light, and then reconstructing it back to its original form. How do you think magicians pull off some of their tricks?

Surely if devil spirits can break down and reconstruct matter at the molecular level so they can steal, kill and destroy, God has a right to reconstruct matter at the molecular level to help people.

If you get involved in healing situations where people need help with the power of God and they are believing, the revelation will be there and you will know which manifestations you need to operate to bring the deliverance. In these situations compassion welling up inside you, or any other way God communicates with you will be your green light to get involved. God will give you all the information you need so you can help them. The more you operate the manifestations to help people, the more the fruit of the spirit will be evident in your life. This is how we grow into walking with the love of God.

Galatians 5:22,23
But the fruit of the Spirit is love, joy, peace, longsuffering, gentleness, goodness, faith,

Meekness, temperance: against such there is no law.

If you want this kind of fruit in your life and if you want to walk with the love of God, then start looking for ways to help people. The more you get in there and help, the more you will earnestly desire and pursue open doors to help more people. The more people you help, the more you will see the manifestations in your life. The more you operate the manifestations to help people, the more fruit of the spirit you will enjoy and the more you will walk with the love of God.

Helping people with the manifestations of holy spirit is a walk with a learning curve. How do children learn to walk? They get up, take a step, and fall down. However, they get right back up on their feet and try again. They may fall down dozens of times before they learn to toddle around the room. Eventually though they'll be running all over the place having the time of their lives. The key is just to get up and walk. The only thing that can stop us is fear. Look for open doors to help people in your home churches and get in there. Sure you're going to fall down a few times, so what? If you're faithful it won't be long before you're running through life with the manifestations flowing from you like living waters.

When I first started studying the bible, I used to scratch my head and wonder how on earth I could become like Paul, Peter or Jesus Christ when it comes to manifesting holy spirit. I scratch my head no longer. It is no more difficult than earnestly desiring and pursuing opportunities to help people, and when the doors open we get in there and put the manifestations into operation. The more we practice, the better we get at it, and the more we walk with the love of God in the renewed mind in manifestation. How simple is that?

76. Healing

To understand the manifestation of gifts of healing, and when it's appropriate to use it, there are a number of important points we need to consider. First of all, let's make it absolutely clear that God wants us to enjoy good health. He says so in his word, and God is not a man that he should lie.

> 3 John 2
> Beloved, I wish above all things that thou mayest prosper and be in health, even as thy soul prospereth.

This is God's will for us. God, our father, wishes above all things that we prosper and be in health. He's on our side, he's ready, willing and able to fight for us and help us to overcome anything.

> Jeremiah 32:27
> Behold, I *am* the LORD, the God of all flesh: is there any thing too hard for me?

Secondly, good health isn't magic. God gave us our bodies and they're our responsibility. If we don't look after them properly, for example by eating and drinking shit, and we never exercise, sooner or later we're going to run into serious health issues. That isn't God's fault, that's our fault. We have a responsibility to look after our bodies. If we don't, we won't get the best out of them. In many cases where people have health issues, a simple change of diet and some exercise is all that's needed. If folks don't look after their bodies and they become ill, there isn't much God can do about it. In those cases, simply confronting the person to sort out their diet and do some exercise will usually fix them if they listen.

Thirdly, even if we are eating properly and exercising adequately, we must understand that none of us are exempt from life. Being a believer and knowing the word and living it doesn't mean we're automatically immune to health problems. Even if we look after our bodies with a perfect diet and a perfect daily exercise schedule, although that lowers the risks considerably and helps us get better much more quickly when we are ill, we may still have to deal with health issues from time to time. The difference is that once we know the word, once we understand how to walk by the spirit and energise manifestations of holy spirit, once we know how to believe and refuse to fear, we have the ability to overcome serious health issues and be victorious. This isn't make-believe, this is the truth. The question is, do we believe it?

> Romans 8:35-37
> Who shall separate us from the love of Christ? *shall* tribulation, or distress, or persecution, or famine, or nakedness, or peril, or sword?
>
> As it is written, For thy sake we are killed all the day long; we are accounted as sheep for the slaughter.
>
> Nay, in all these things we are more than conquerors through him that loved us.

These verses absolutely do not say that as believers we will not have to face tribulation, distress, persecution, famine, nakedness, peril and sword. The verses clearly state that if we do face such challenges we are more than conquerors through him that loved us. As believers we may have to face tribulation, distress, persecution, famine, nakedness, peril and sword, but we can be victorious over them. The more abundant life isn't about avoiding challenging situations, it's about having the strength to overcome them and soundly defeat them no matter what life throws at us. Think about that.

Many religious people have the notion that if you're a believer nothing bad should ever happen to you. The rest of them walk around thinking God makes them sick and kills them. They are good people, no doubt about it, but church strips them of common sense when it comes to spiritual matters. Does your church, ministry, or religion teach you how to speak in tongues and manifest the power of God? If not, what's the point in going there? I know people who have gone to church every week for sixty years and still don't speak in tongues. No flowing of living waters indicates a broken cistern.

There are many records in the bible where disciples had bad things happen to them without cause, men and women who were righteous and had done nothing wrong and yet they had serious issues to contend with. Take Job for example. Not only did he lose his children and his business empire, he was probably one of the sickest men the earth has ever seen. Yet he prevailed, he got through it.

We have to learn to deal with life and not be afraid of it. Believing the word makes us more than conquerors, it gives us the strength to prevail. Instead of being afraid of challenges when they come up or crying our eyes out, we take the challenges on and defeat them. If you're someone who cries your eyes out and feels sorry for yourself when life attacks, man, get some bible into your fucking head.

Dorcas was a disciple who lived during the book of Acts. She was a disciple, full of good works, yet she fell sick and died. She wasn't evil, she hadn't done anything to deserve being sick. She wasn't out of fellowship with God, she hadn't committed any crimes, yet she fell sick and died. The god of this world is just good at what he does, which is stealing, killing and destroying. The disciples got together, discussed it, sent for Peter, and he got the green light to raise her from the dead.

> Acts 9:36-40
> Now there was at Joppa a certain disciple named Tabitha, which by interpretation is called Dorcas: this woman was full of good works and almsdeeds which she did.
>
> And it came to pass in those days, that she was sick, and died: whom when they had washed, they laid *her* in an upper chamber.
>
> And forasmuch as Lydda was nigh to Joppa, and the disciples had heard that Peter was there, they sent unto him two men, desiring *him* that he would not delay to come to them.
>
> Then Peter arose and went with them. When he was come, they brought him into the upper chamber: and all the widows stood by

> him weeping, and shewing the coats and garments which Dorcas made, while she was with them.
>
> But Peter put them all forth, and kneeled down, and prayed; and turning *him* to the body said, Tabitha, arise. And she opened her eyes: and when she saw Peter, she sat up.

Peter put them all forth. He did what he'd seen Jesus Christ do a few times, get rid of unbelief by asking people to leave. This is an excellent key to walking by the spirit. If those widows had believed Peter was going to raise her from the dead, they wouldn't have been crying their eyes out. Get rid of any unbelief around you before you minister.

> Acts 9:41
> And he gave her *his* hand, and lifted her up, and when he had called the saints and widows, presented her alive.

Dorcas was a disciple, yet she wasn't magically protected from life's challenges, was she? Neither are we. If we were protected by magic, God wouldn't have had to write Romans 8:35-37 for us, because there would have been no need for us to be super conquerors because we would never face challenges that needed defeating. The promises to us as believers is that if we get hit by illness or other major challenges, we can get through them, we can defeat them and we can be victorious over them. Was Dorcas victorious? Certainly. Don't you think she would have been thankful when she sat up and saw Peter and realised she'd been raised from the dead?

I've been sick and at the point of death on more than one occasion. In September 2015, while working on this class, I had serious health issues to deal with. During an afternoon in September, I was so breathless I had to call the doctor. When he arrived, he immediately put me on emergency oxygen and called for paramedics. When they arrived, they called for a coastguard helicopter and strapped me into a stretcher. Before I knew it, I was whisked off to intensive care at Raigmore hospital in Inverness. When we arrived, I can remember a doctor leaning over me and telling me I was going to be put on life support for a few days and would be heavily sedated.

When I regained consciousness, I was in a terrible state. I had blood clots on both lungs and couldn't breathe without oxygen. To make matters worse, I also had pneumonia. As if that wasn't enough, I was bleeding internally and over the next few days I required two blood transfusions. Have you ever spewed up a pint of blood? It isn't very pleasant, but I'll tell you something, I was not afraid of it. When I was on the coastguard helicopter, I was not afraid. When I was wheeled into intensive care, I was not afraid. At no time did I ever fear for my life. Not once did I ever fear death. In fact, I had to gently reprimand one or two nurses for looking at me as if I was already a corpse. I learned later, one or two of them didn't think I was going to make it.

That's not the only time I've faced death either, but each time I've been more than a conqueror because I chose to believe the word and I refused to fear. Just because we're believers and God is our father doesn't mean we will never have to face challenges in life. Even men of God are not exempt from life. The prophet Ahijah went blind, but the manifestations still energised for him. Just because he was blind didn't mean he was out of fellowship. God still loved the dude and still spoke to him.

> 1 Kings 14:1-5
> At that time Abijah the son of Jeroboam fell sick.
>
> And Jeroboam said to his wife, Arise, I pray thee, and disguise thyself, that thou be not known to be the wife of Jeroboam; and get thee to Shiloh: behold, there *is* Ahijah the prophet, which told me that *I should be* king over this people.
>
> And take with thee ten loaves, and cracknels, and a cruse of honey, and go to him: he shall tell thee what shall become of the child.
>
> And Jeroboam's wife did so, and arose, and went to Shiloh, and came to the house of Ahijah. But Ahijah could not see; for his eyes were set by reason of his age.
>
> And the LORD said unto Ahijah, Behold, the wife of Jeroboam cometh to ask a thing of thee for her son; for he is sick: thus and thus shalt thou say unto her: for it shall be, when she cometh in, that she shall feign herself *to be* another *woman*.

Even men of God in this administration in the bible were not exempt from life. What about Epaphroditus? He was a man of God, a disciple. He wasn't evil, he hadn't done anything wrong. The word says he was a companion in labour to Paul, a fellowsoldier, and he ministered to Paul's wants, yet he was so sick he was at the point of death. He obviously refused to fear though, claimed the promises of God and fought for his life because he recovered. He was more than a conqueror over his sickness.

> Philippians 2:25-27
> Yet I supposed it necessary to send to you Epaphroditus, my brother, and companion in labour, and fellowsoldier, but your messenger, and he that ministered to my wants.
>
> For he longed after you all, and was full of heaviness, because that ye had heard that he had been sick.
>
> For indeed he was sick nigh unto death: but God had mercy on him; and not on him only, but on me also, lest I should have sorrow upon sorrow.

Not even Paul was exempt from life. While sitting around a fire warming himself on Malta after being shipwrecked, an extremely poisonous snake latched onto his hand and bit him.

> Acts 28:3-6
> And when Paul had gathered a bundle of sticks, and laid *them* on the fire, there came a viper out of the heat, and fastened on his hand.
>
> And when the barbarians saw the *venomous* beast hang on his hand, they said among themselves, No doubt this man is a murderer, whom, though he hath escaped the sea, yet vengeance suffereth not to live.
>
> And he shook off the beast into the fire, and felt no harm.
>
> Howbeit they looked when he should have swollen, or fallen down dead suddenly: but after they had looked a great while, and saw no harm come to him, they changed their minds, and said that he was a god.

If a poisonous snake bit you suddenly like that, where would your thoughts go? Most christians who go to church would think God was killing them because they were sinners or because their time was up. Most believers who think they know the word would likely think they were out of fellowship, condemn themselves and wait for death. Disciples like Paul however, are afraid of nothing.

Paul wasn't afraid of that snake. He shook it off into the fire and believed God for deliverance. He was a super conqueror who feared nothing. What do you think being a super conqueror means? Nothing bad ever happens to us? If nothing bad ever happened to us, there would be no need to be super conquerors and Romans 8:31 and 39 would be a waste of time memorising.

> Romans 8:31,39
> What shall we then say to these things? If God *be* for us, who *can be* against us?
>
> Nay, in all these things we are more than conquerors through him that loved us.

If you think that just because you're a disciple, you won't ever have to face things like peril, famine, and sword, you're living in a dream world. Life isn't like that. Lucifer is the god of this world and when it comes to the spiritual competition, he's industrious, diligent, and tireless in his efforts to destroy the word. The more abundant life isn't about avoiding spiritual attack, it's about being able to overcome, to be victorious, to be a super conqueror despite any attacks.

I'll tell you something else too, while we're here. For every challenge you face, there are probably dozens of challenges God has saved you from that you don't even know about. When I was a part of Dr Wierwille's ministry there were hundreds of believers in Mexico City. In September 1985, Mexico City was hit by an earthquake that destroyed much property and over 5000 people lost their lives. A week later we heard a report that not one believer had been killed and no believer's property had been damaged. God is doing his job, we just need to learn how to do ours.

There are dozens of records in the bible where men and women of God had to deal with serious life issues. Being a believer is not an escape from life, it's the solution for dealing with it. Even Adam and Eve had to deal with life when one of their sons murdered their other son. Joseph was sold into slavery in Egypt by his own brothers, the men who gave birth to the tribes of Israel. When David and his men returned to Ziklag in 1 Samuel 30, they found it burned to the ground, their possessions stolen, and their wives and children taken captive. David didn't blame God for his problems, he went to God to find the solutions he needed to deal with it.

> 1 Samuel 30:1-19
> And it came to pass, when David and his men were come to Ziklag on the third day, that the Amalekites had invaded the south, and Ziklag, and smitten Ziklag, and burned it with fire;
>
> And had taken the women captives, that *were* therein: they slew not any, either great or small, but carried *them* away, and went on their way.
>
> So David and his men came to the city, and, behold, *it was* burned with fire; and their wives, and their sons, and their daughters, were taken captives.
>
> Then David and the people that *were* with him lifted up their voice and wept, until they had no more power to weep.
>
> And David's two wives were taken captives, Ahinoam the Jezreelitess, and Abigail the wife of Nabal the Carmelite.
>
> And David was greatly distressed; for the people spake of stoning him, because the soul of all the people was grieved, every man for his sons and for his daughters: but David encouraged himself in the LORD his God.
>
> And David said to Abiathar the priest, Ahimelech's son, I pray thee, bring me hither the ephod. And Abiathar brought thither the ephod to David.

And David enquired at the LORD, saying, Shall I pursue after this troop? shall I overtake them? And he answered him, Pursue: for thou shalt surely overtake *them*, and without fail recover *all*.

So David went, he and the six hundred men that *were* with him, and came to the brook Besor, where those that were left behind stayed.

But David pursued, he and four hundred men: for two hundred abode behind, which were so faint that they could not go over the brook Besor.

And they found an Egyptian in the field, and brought him to David, and gave him bread, and he did eat; and they made him drink water;

And they gave him a piece of a cake of figs, and two clusters of raisins: and when he had eaten, his spirit came again to him: for he had eaten no bread, nor drunk *any* water, three days and three nights.

And David said unto him, To whom *belongest* thou? and whence *art* thou? And he said, I *am* a young man of Egypt, servant to an Amalekite; and my master left me, because three days agone I fell sick.

We made an invasion *upon* the south of the Cherethites, and upon *the coast* which *belongeth* to Judah, and upon the south of Caleb; and we burned Ziklag with fire.

And David said to him, Canst thou bring me down to this company? And he said, Swear unto me by God, that thou wilt neither kill me, nor deliver me into the hands of my master, and I will bring thee down to this company.

And when he had brought him down, behold, *they were* spread abroad upon all the earth, eating and drinking, and dancing, because of all the great spoil that they had taken out of the land of the Philistines, and out of the land of Judah.

> And David smote them from the twilight even unto the evening of the next day: and there escaped not a man of them, save four hundred young men, which rode upon camels, and fled.
>
> And David recovered all that the Amalekites had carried away: and David rescued his two wives.
>
> And there was nothing lacking to them, neither small nor great, neither sons nor daughters, neither spoil, nor any *thing* that they had taken to them: David recovered all.

The god of this world is going to attack occasionally, so we have to make our minds up. Are we going to believe the word or not? Are we going to live without fear and believe God for deliverance when we need it? Are we going to be disciples? Are we going to be super conquerors? If so, we must get our heads into the word every day. We must memorise scriptures so we have them in our heads and we don't have to run home for our concordances when we need them. There is no point playing around with the word. God does his job, that's for sure, the question is are we doing ours? This isn't simply a case of going to a stupid religious meeting once a week and sitting through a boring shit ceremony, this is life. If you want to live with this kind of strength, get serious about living the word and believing it.

> Hebrews 11:6
> But without faith [believing] *it is* impossible to please *him:* for he that cometh to God must believe that he is, and *that* he is a rewarder of them that diligently seek him.

How do we learn to believe? Simple, we keep our heads in the word, in the scriptures. It is something we discipline into our lives. If we don't get serious about living the word and being in it every day, we won't prevail over anything.

> Romans 10:17
> So then faith [believing] *cometh* by hearing, and hearing by the word of God.

Next, we must understand the authority we have to use the name of Jesus Christ. Without the authority in the name of Jesus Christ, we would be powerless.

> Philippians 2:5
> Let this mind [let these thoughts] be in you, which was [were] also in Christ Jesus:

What thoughts did Jesus Christ have? He thought the word. If we're going to think his thoughts, we're going to have to know the word because the word was what he thought. This isn't a game, this is a matter of the way of life or the way of death. People get serious about environmentalism, their careers, their relationships, politics, their hobbies and their pursuits, but as disciples we must get serious about studying the word, making it our own and believing it.

> 2 Corinthians 10:5
> Casting down imaginations, and every high thing that exalteth itself against the knowledge of God, and bringing into captivity every thought to the obedience of Christ;

How are we obedient to Christ? Does Christ come down from heaven and talk to us? No, it's a reference to the Christ in us, the gift of holy spirit. How we're obedient to Christ is to walk by that spirit. Christ is the head of the body, not men.

> Philippians 2:6
> Who [Christ], being in the form of God, thought it not robbery to be equal with God:

This verse does not state that Jesus Christ was God. Being equal with something logically implies that you're not one and the same thing with that something. An object cannot be equal with itself. And that's all I'm going to say about it. If you read this and think Jesus Christ is God, please go to chapter 1 and start this class from the beginning.

> Philippians 2:7-9
> But made himself of no reputation, and took upon him the form of a servant, and was made in the likeness of men:

And being found in fashion as a man, he humbled himself, and became obedient unto death, even the death of the cross.

Wherefore God also hath highly exalted him, and given him a name which is above every name:

Is Jesus Christ's name above every name or not? This is something we must become convinced about. God exalted Jesus Christ when he raised him from the dead, and it is God who gave him a name which is above every name. His name is above the pope's name, it is above Buddha's name, it is above any king or queen's name, it is above Muhammad's name, it is above any politician's name, it is above every name. When Lucifer was the angel of light and was full of wisdom and beauty, and was perfect in all his ways, his name was above every name. Jesus Christ's name is now even above Lucifer's name. That's why we can cast out devil spirits in Jesus Christ's name.

Philippians 2:10,11
That at the name of Jesus every knee should bow, of *things* in heaven, and *things* in earth, and *things* under the earth;

And *that* every tongue should confess that Jesus Christ *is* Lord, to the glory of God the Father.

There is power and authority in the name of Jesus Christ. That power and authority is of such magnitude that devil spirits have no choice but to respect it when spoken with believing.

Acts 16:16-18
And it came to pass, as we went to prayer, a certain damsel possessed with a spirit of divination met us, which brought her masters much gain by soothsaying:

The same followed Paul and us, and cried, saying, These men are the servants of the most high God, which shew unto us the way of salvation.

And this did she many days. But Paul, being grieved, turned and said to the spirit, I command thee in the name of Jesus Christ to come out of her. And he came out the same hour.

Just as Paul could use the name of Jesus Christ to cast out devils and deliver people, so can we. As children of the living God we have the authority to use the name of Jesus Christ. Others, however, do not.

> Acts 19:13,14
> Then certain of the vagabond Jews [Judeans], exorcists, took upon them to call over them which had evil spirits the name of the Lord Jesus, saying, We adjure you by Jesus whom Paul preacheth.
>
> And there were seven sons of *one* Sceva, a Jew [Judean], *and* chief of the priests, which did so.

Just look at who these exorcists were, the sons of the chief priest in Ephesus. You will not find God in temples made with hands, but you will find plenty of religious men operating devil spirits. These exorcists had been so impressed by the power Paul energised in the name of Jesus Christ that they thought they would try to use Jesus Christ's name as well.

> Acts 19:15
> And the evil spirit answered and said, Jesus I know, and Paul I know; but who are ye?

That devil spirit knew Jesus and it knew Paul, but it didn't recognise those men. The spirit knew they did not have the authority to use that name.

> Acts 19:16
> And the man in whom the evil spirit was leaped on them, and overcame them, and prevailed against them, so that they fled out of that house naked and wounded.

That man who was possessed took on those seven sons of Sceva, ripped off their robes, and beat them up so badly they ran away naked and wounded. Unlike those religious exorcists, we have the authority to use the name of Jesus Christ.

Ephesians 5:20
Giving thanks always for all things unto God and the Father in the name of our Lord Jesus Christ;

Colossians 3:17
And whatsoever ye do in word or deed, *do* all in the name of the Lord Jesus, giving thanks to God and the Father by him.

The first healing recorded in the Grace Administration is when Peter healed the lame man. As this is the first occurrence of healing in this administration, as well as the first recorded miracle, it sets the standard for the Age of Grace, it sets an example for us to follow.

Acts 3:1-6
Now Peter and John went up together into the temple at the hour of prayer, *being* the ninth *hour.*

And a certain man lame from his mother's womb was carried, whom they laid daily at the gate of the temple which is called Beautiful, to ask alms of them that entered into the temple;

Who seeing Peter and John about to go into the temple asked an alms.

And Peter, fastening his eyes upon him with John, said, Look on us.

And he gave heed unto them, expecting to receive something of them.

Then Peter said, Silver and gold have I none; but such as I have give I thee: In the name of Jesus Christ of Nazareth rise up and walk.

Peter used the name of Jesus Christ. Can we use the name of Jesus Christ when we minister healing? Of course we can, that's why God had this recorded in Acts. This is the first recorded miracle and healing in this administration and God had it recorded so we could learn from it. When Peter and John were arrested and dragged before the Sanhedrin, look at their response.

Acts 4:6,7
And Annas the high priest, and Caiaphas, and John, and Alexander, and as many as were of the kindred of the high priest, were gathered together at Jerusalem.

And when they had set them in the midst, they asked, By what power, or by what name, have ye done this?

It's intriguing to note that the Sanhedrin recognised that some power or some name was behind the healing. They recognised that. Things like this don't just happen in life unless there is a power or a name behind it. Even in spiritualism this is true, which is why the Sanhedrin understood this. They didn't know which particular power or name Peter had used, which is why they demanded Peter tell them.

Acts 4:8-10,22
Then Peter, filled with the Holy Ghost [holy spirit], said unto them, Ye rulers of the people, and elders of Israel,

If we this day be examined of the good deed done to the impotent man, by what means he is made whole;

Be it known unto you all, and to all the people of Israel, that by the name of Jesus Christ of Nazareth, whom ye crucified, whom God raised from the dead, *even* by him doth this man stand here before you whole.

For the man was above forty years old, on whom this miracle of healing was shewed.

The man had been made whole, and this is the scripture that tells us he had bones missing from his feet and ankles, which was why a miracle was required as well as healing. Those bones had to be replaced. Before his healing, he was not whole, there were bits and pieces of him missing. Those missing bits and pieces were put into his feet and ankles when Peter ministered to him, which is why this was a miracle of healing. When the missing bones were replaced, he was made whole. Look at how accurate the word of God is. You just cannot break the word.

One more point we need to understand is that many times just teaching the bible will deliver people without us having to do anything else. The word is that powerful. I was set free and delivered from all sorts of garbage when I was first taught the word, not least of which was being a drunkard. No one ministered to me, in fact no one even confronted me. I heard the word, decided to clean up my life, and I beat the drink. The word healed me because I believed it and took appropriate action. I quit drinking. It didn't happen overnight, but that's all part of being human. God loved me and looked after me while I fought for my life. I was victorious, a super conqueror.

Communion plays a large part in enjoying good health. As you might expect, it isn't a religious ceremony so there is no need for makeshift little alters, robes, candles, or any other ceremonial horseshit. Neither is it a time for boozing and having parties. Some of the believers in Corinth became sick and died for abusing communion. The word says in Peter that we were healed by his stripes. Jesus Christ's death paid for our salvation, but it was his beatings that paid for our health. Communion is simply recognising and appreciating what Jesus Christ went through for us. You do that in your heart, not with any ceremonial garbage. The bread represents his broken body, and the wine represents the blood he shed for us. When you take the bread and sip the wine, do it in recognition of what Christ accomplished for us, and do it as a church as often as you feel it's appropriate.

Playing music and singing from a heart of believing can heal people. I know of people who had been dumb for years suddenly bursting into song while listening to live music and live singing. I know of people who had dementia suddenly recognising people around them while listening to live music and singing.

> 1 Samuel 16:23
> And it came to pass, when the *evil* spirit from God was upon Saul, that David took an harp, and played with his hand: so Saul was refreshed, and was well, and the evil spirit departed from him.

Walk by the spirit and this will all make sense. Don't attempt to do God's job for him and try to force manifestations into operation just because you see a need. Our job is to earnestly desire and earnestly pursue opportunities to minister and help people, but we must wait for the green lights. Christ is our head, and the head of Christ is God. We just need to be ready to move when the green lights come on.

There are four distinct and different types of healing mentioned in the bible, so we will quickly look at them now. Understanding them will help us to be more effective ministers.

To be made whole means to have parts replaced. Consider this record of the ten lepers Jesus Christ healed. The details are astonishing.

> Luke 17:12-14
> And as he entered into a certain village, there met him ten men that were lepers, which stood afar off:
>
> And they lifted up *their* voices, and said, Jesus, Master, have mercy on us.
>
> And when he saw *them*, he said unto them, Go shew yourselves unto the priests. And it came to pass, that, as they went, they were cleansed.

Jesus Christ told the ten lepers what to do, and as they carried out his instruction they were all cleansed of their leprosy, they were all healed. None of them had leprosy any longer, they were clean. All ten of them were clean.

> Luke 17:15-19
> And one of them, when he saw that he was healed, turned back, and with a loud voice glorified God,
>
> And fell down on *his* face at his feet, giving him thanks: and he was a Samaritan.
>
> And Jesus answering said, Were there not ten cleansed? but where *are* the nine?
>
> There are not found that returned to give glory to God, save this stranger.

> And he said unto him, Arise, go thy way: thy faith [believing] hath made thee whole.

This leper, this Samaritan leper, had been cleansed, but here he was also made whole. The other nine lepers were cleansed of their leprosy, but were not made whole. What does that mean? Well, leprosy eats away at the human body. This one leper was made whole, his body was restored to its original condition before he caught leprosy. The other nine were healed, cleansed, but they were not made whole, they still had body parts eaten away which they would have had to live with despite being cleansed of their leprosy. They were not made whole. How do you like that for biblical accuracy?

Another type of healing is referred to as a restoration. This is illustrated beautifully in Mark with the man who had the withered hand. It was his arm that was withered, probably up to the elbow or beyond.

> Mark 3:1,2
> And he [Jesus] entered again into the synagogue; and there was a man there which had a withered hand.
>
> And they [the religious leaders] watched him, whether he would heal him on the sabbath day; that they might accuse him.

Don't you find it intriguing that church leaders don't like their people being healed? Church leaders seem to enjoy having a sick congregation. They even teach that it's God who is making them sick. Full of dead men's bones springs to mind. Indeed, aren't most churches built in the middle of graveyards and don't you have to walk over dead men's bones to get into them? If you've reached this stage of my class and you still go to church, it's time to make your mind up where you stand. If you lie down with dogs, you're going to catch fleas. The word says so.

> 1 Corinthians 15:33
> Be not deceived: evil communications [associations] corrupt good manners [good ethics, good morals, good life habits, good believing].

Look, I don't really give a fuck about all your stupid excuses about why you still go to church meetings and associate yourself with all your old religious mates. Sure, they smile inanely and make nice cups of tea, but you have to look beyond the physical to the spiritual. It all boils down to whether or not you believe God's word. I don't care if they read the bible, claim they are christians, and go to fucking church every week. Muslims do that, Hindus do that. Religious people all over the world do that. It means nothing. Do they speak in tongues and energise the power of God? Do they walk by the spirit with Christ as their head? If not, you had better disassociate yourself from them or you're going to be corrupted, you're going to catch spiritual fleas and be talked out of the word. If you want to be a disciple, you do things God's way. If they won't hear the word from you, leave, separate yourself, that's the word.

2 Corinthians 6:14-18
Be ye not unequally yoked together with unbelievers: for what fellowship hath righteousness with unrighteousness? and what communion hath light with darkness?

And what concord hath Christ with Belial? or what part hath he that believeth with an infidel?

And what agreement hath the temple of God with idols? for ye are the temple of the living God; as God hath said, I will dwell in them, and walk in *them;* and I will be their God, and they shall be my people.

Wherefore come out from among them, and be ye separate, saith the Lord, and touch not the unclean *thing;* and I will receive you,

And will be a Father unto you, and ye shall be my sons and daughters, saith the Lord Almighty.

The world's churches and religions and ministries worship the god of this world, the devil in their meetings. They are dangerous places, dry broken cisterns with no fountain of living waters, full of dead men's bones, run by scorpions and vipers, so get out of them and quit giving them your money. Back to the man with the withered arm.

Mark 3:3-6
And he saith unto the man which had the withered hand, Stand forth.

And he [Jesus] saith unto them [the religious leaders], Is it lawful to do good on the sabbath days, or to do evil? to save life, or to kill? But they held their peace.

And when he had looked round about on them with anger, being grieved for the hardness of their hearts, he saith unto the man, Stretch forth thine hand. And he stretched *it* out: and his hand was restored whole as the other.

And the Pharisees went forth, and straightway took counsel with the Herodians against him, how they might destroy him.

The man had a withered arm and it was restored, so at first glance it would appear to be a miracle. However, this was not a miracle, it was a restoration healing. No parts of his arm were missing and had to be replaced. No bones were missing, no muscles were missing, no nerves were missing, no veins were missing, no skin was missing, no flesh of any kind was missing. His arm had withered up, but it was all still there, like a dried up prune. That's why the manifestation of miracles wasn't needed. This was a restoration healing where his arm was restored to its original state before it withered. No body parts were missing, nothing needed to be replaced, so this was not a miracle. The accuracy of the word is stunning.

A restoration implies that there is no cause to remove and no devil spirit to cast out. If someone has had health at one time but been robbed of it, all they need is a restoration. By the way, this could mean a gradual progression of recovery which may take some time. Not all healings are instantaneous.

When Paul was blinded outside Damascus, he only needed his sight to be restored. He'd had sight and had just been robbed of it, so he needed his sight restored. There was no cause to remove, no parts to replace, no disease to remove, no health issues to cure, no devil spirits to cast out, he just needed his eyesight restored.

Acts 9:17-19
And Ananias went his way, and entered into the house; and putting his hands on him said, Brother Saul, the Lord, *even* Jesus, that appeared unto thee in the way as thou camest, hath sent me, that thou mightest receive thy sight, and be filled with the Holy Ghost [holy spirit].

And immediately there fell from his eyes as it had been scales: and he received sight forthwith, and arose, and was baptized.

And when he had received meat, he was strengthened. Then was Saul certain days with the disciples which were at Damascus.

Another healing is referred to as a cure, but a cure requires removing a cause. Sometimes ill health is due to there being something in the body that must be removed, such as cancer. Curing someone sets them free from whatever it was causing the sickness. Remember the epileptic deaf and dumb boy? We met his father earlier in the class. That boy's problems were caused by a devil spirit. All Jesus Christ had to do was remove the cause, which in that situation required casting out the devil spirit. Once the cause was removed, the boy was cured. He wasn't made whole, he wasn't restored, it wasn't a miracle, nothing needed to be replaced, he was cured.

Mark 9:20-23
And they brought him unto him: and when he saw him, straightway the spirit tare him; and he fell on the ground, and wallowed foaming.

And he asked his father, How long is it ago since this came unto him? And he said, Of a child.

And ofttimes it hath cast him into the fire, and into the waters, to destroy him: but if thou canst do any thing, have compassion on us, and help us.

Jesus said unto him, If thou canst believe, all things *are* possible to him that believeth.

And here we see that believing is always required for healing. We can't manifest healing to ourselves, but there is another manifestation we can operate for our own profit, right? Sure, the manifestation of believing. It is ours to operate for our own profit. If we are ill and we believe to be healed, the door will open for someone to help us.

> Mark 9:24-27
> And straightway the father of the child cried out, and said with tears, Lord, I believe; help thou mine unbelief.
>
> When Jesus saw that the people came running together, he rebuked the foul spirit, saying unto him, *Thou* dumb and deaf spirit, I charge thee, come out of him, and enter no more into him.
>
> And *the spirit* cried, and rent him sore, and came out of him: and he was as one dead; insomuch that many said, He is dead.
>
> But Jesus took him by the hand, and lifted him up; and he arose.

If the word says Jesus Christ cured people, then we know causes were removed, which included casting out devils. In order to cure people, he would have needed to energise discerning of spirits, as well as word of knowledge and word of wisdom.

> Luke 7:21
> And in that same hour he cured many of *their* infirmities and plagues, and of evil spirits; and unto many *that were* blind he gave sight.

The manifestation of word of knowledge gives you information on what you need to do, while the manifestation of word of wisdom tells you how to do it. Discerning of spirits simply gives you information on whether or not someone is possessed with devil spirits, and if you can cast them out. Possession doesn't just mean someone has mental problems, it could be a health issue. Devil spirits can lodge in the body and pump poisons into it. Remove the cause, and that person is cured.

The revelation manifestations are required before energising the power manifestations of miracles and healing, and occasionally, if others are involved, believing. Here is an excellent record which illustrates how the manifestations of holy spirit work together.

> John 5:1-6
> After this there was a feast of the Jews [Judeans]; and Jesus went up to Jerusalem.
>
> Now there is at Jerusalem by the sheep *market* a pool, which is called in the Hebrew tongue Bethesda, having five porches.
>
> In these lay a great multitude of impotent folk, of blind, halt, withered, waiting for the moving of the water.
>
> For an angel went down at a certain season into the pool, and troubled the water: whosoever then first after the troubling of the water stepped in was made whole of whatsoever disease he had.
>
> And a certain man was there, which had an infirmity thirty and eight years.
>
> When Jesus saw him lie, and knew that he had been now a long time *in that case*, he saith unto him, Wilt thou be made whole?

First of all, Jesus Christ had to be walking by the spirit to be in the right place at the right time down by the pool. When he was by the poolside, how do you think he found the one man in that entire multitude who was believing to be healed? Luck? No, revelation manifestations. He walked by the spirit to be at the poolside, and then God showed him by revelation the dude who was believing for healing. Note Jesus Christ's earnest desire to help people and how he pursued that desire everywhere he went.

> John 5:7
> The impotent man answered him, Sir, I have no man, when the water is troubled, to put me into the pool: but while I am coming, another steppeth down before me.

Jesus Christ then put the revelation and power manifestations to work. To understand the problem, he needed word of knowledge and word of wisdom. If a cause needed to be removed, he would have required discerning of spirits. Once he had energised the manifestations and knew what to do, he spoke a few words.

> John 5:8-11
> Jesus saith unto him, Rise, take up thy bed, and walk.
>
> And immediately the man was made whole, and took up his bed, and walked: and on the same day was the sabbath.
>
> The Jews [Judeans] therefore said unto him that was cured, It is the sabbath day: it is not lawful for thee to carry *thy* bed.
>
> He answered them, He that made me whole, the same said unto me, Take up thy bed, and walk.

Here we see that the man was cured, so we know Jesus Christ had to remove a cause. The word also tells us he was made whole so something was put back that was missing. Jesus Christ by way of the revelation manifestations identified a cause that needed to be removed and he also energised manifestations to make the man whole.

When we minister to believers who need healing, we may have to minister to a number of problems before they're completely delivered. There may be a cause to remove, and once it's removed, we may have to minister to the person to replace body parts that may have been destroyed or eaten away by disease. There may even be poisons left behind which need ministering to.

At the other end of the scale, perhaps all someone needs is confrontation to get their diet and exercise sorted out. The key is to walk by the spirit. When we get into a ministering situation, we put the revelation manifestations into operation and God gives us the information we need to deliver that person by way of the Christ in us. Some healings are quite involved and may require several problems to be ministered to, while others can be very simple affairs where we just need to speak a few words and the person is completely delivered.

If a person is ill because of bad personal habits of diet and lack of exercise, God may simply tell you to confront them. If they heed the reproof and start eating properly and exercising faithfully, they will gradually get better. That would be a restoration to health which may take some time. The point is, you walked by the spirit, carried out God's instructions, the person heeded the reproof and therefore got the deliverance.

If we remove a cause by revelation, there may not be anymore revelation. In that case, we would leave the person alone so they can recover by themselves. The body will heal itself once a cause has been removed, and that may take some time.

If we walk by the spirit, this will all make sense. You can't mandate how to minister healing because every situation is different. When Jesus Christ spat on the ground and made clay to put on a blind man's eyes, does that mean that's what we do every time we minister to a blind man? No, that's absurd, that's nonsense, we walk by the spirit because every situation is different. You can't legislate this stuff. That's how doctrines of men are born.

When I ministered to that woman lying by the side of the road late at night, the guidance was to first get someone who was with me to phone the emergency services. I then knelt down and felt for a pulse. There was no pulse, not in her wrists, not in her arms, and not in her neck. I couldn't find a pulse. While I held her hand, I prayed for her in the name of Jesus Christ. After I'd prayed, I checked for a pulse again and felt a faint clicking in her wrists. It was weak, but it was a pulse. By that time, the person with me had a paramedic on the phone and started relaying instructions. I was to lay her on her back, lift her chin and tilt her head back. I'd been taught coma position and clear airways so I questioned the instruction. The person with me then practically commanded me to carry out the instruction to the letter and I recognised the authority in her voice. God was at work. When I carried out the instruction, the woman convulsed three or four times and then opened her eyes. I checked her pulse again and it was banging away like a bass drum. The key is to walk by the spirit.

If God gives you information on a cause to remove, and you remove it and there is no further revelation, your job is done even if the person still has all the symptoms of illness. Once a cause has been removed, the nature of the human body is to heal itself. Healings are not always instantaneous.

Walking by the spirit is the key to understanding all this. The more you look for open doors to get in and help people, the more you desire and pursue opportunities to energise the gift of holy spirit and help people, the more proficient you will become with the manifestations. It's a learning and growing process. If a child never attempts to walk and never practices it, they will never walk. The key to learning to walk is to fall down a few times. Those who persevere with it and are not afraid of falling down learn to walk.

Another thing, we're not talking about ministering to unbelievers here. The vast majority of healings will occur in our home churches, among people who are doing their best to live the word. Home churches that are growing and thriving and which have new people constantly coming through the doors are where we should be earnestly desiring and pursuing opportunities to help people who are looking for and believing for deliverance.

The fourth and final healing mentioned in the bible is a reconciliation, where parts are stuck back on which have come off. To reconcile simply means to bring back together that which has been severed or cut off.

> John 18:10,11
> Then Simon Peter having a sword drew it, and smote the high priest's servant, and cut off his right ear. The servant's name was Malchus.
>
> Then said Jesus unto Peter, Put up thy sword into the sheath: the cup which my Father hath given me, shall I not drink it?
>
> Luke 22:50,51
> And one of them smote the servant of the high priest, and cut off his right ear.
>
> And Jesus answered and said, Suffer ye thus far. And he touched his ear, and healed him.

Jesus Christ picked the ear up off the ground and stuck it back on. That's a reconciliation. Obviously Jesus Christ must have energised the revelation manifestations first to see if it was available. Perhaps he felt compassion inside to help the man and that was his green light. As he put the ear in place, it sewed itself to the man's head perfectly and all the bleeding would have stopped.

So there are the four types of healing illustrated in the bible - to make whole, to restore, to cure, and to reconcile. Not a lot to remember, but it's all important information.

Here are a few other things to consider. When Paul healed Publius after being shipwrecked on his way to Rome, the word says he prayed, then laid his hands on him and healed him. Praying is everything in ministering situations. The first thing Peter did when he was alone with Dorcas was he prayed. The first thing Elijah did when he was alone with the widow woman's dead boy in 1 Kings 17 was he prayed. The first thing I did with that woman by the side of the road was pray for her. In this Age of Grace we pray in the name of Jesus Christ. We have the authority to use the name of Jesus Christ.

> Acts 28:7,8
> In the same quarters were possessions of the chief man of the island, whose name was Publius; who received us, and lodged us three days courteously.
>
> And it came to pass, that the father of Publius lay sick of a fever and of a bloody flux: to whom Paul entered in, and prayed, and laid his hands on him, and healed him.

By the way, don't lay hands on people unless you've had revelation. There are very few healings mentioned in the bible where hands were laid on people. The laying on of hands has become a religious ritual, a mindless ceremony, and it's dangerous. Lay your hands on someone like that possessed man in Ephesus and you may find yourself running out of the house naked and wounded. Always, always walk by the spirit and never do things mindlessly by following men and their stupid fucking doctrines.

One final thing. Just as the manifestations of prophecy, interpretation of tongues, word of knowledge, word of wisdom, discerning of spirits and miracles are not for our own use and we can only energise them to help others, so it is with gifts of healing. In other words, we can't manifest healing to ourselves. The manifestations we have for our own use are speaking in tongues and believing. We can't heal ourselves using the manifestation of healing. When I was in intensive care, I asked God for help and the guidance was to ask a believer to come down and minister to me. When she arrived, we pulled the curtain around the bed for privacy and she then prayed and ministered to me in the name of Jesus Christ. When she was done, she told me I would regain my health and that I would walk out of that hospital. And that's exactly what happened. It wasn't instantaneous, but my health was restored.

Now that's what I call a deep peaceful feeling. It was so powerful it brought tears to my eyes. This class is finished.

77. The Way of Life Today

Moses was raised in the royal courts of Egypt as the son of Pharaoh. As the son of the most powerful man on earth, Moses understood the ways of the world. When he wrote by revelation the warnings in Deuteronomy and set before God's people the way of life and the way of death, he understood from his education and upbringing how the world operated. He perhaps didn't explain all the intricate details of precisely *how* the god of this world moved the courses of the world at that time, but he understood religion, he understood politics, he understood mysticism, he understood witchcraft, and he understood how secret societies manipulate and control people on behalf of their god. Nothing much has changed since then except fashion.

When Moses grew to be a man, he looked around at everything the world had to offer and compared it to what God had to offer. Then he made a choice, he made a decision.

> Hebrews 11:24-26
> By faith [believing] Moses, when he was come to years, refused to be called the son of Pharaoh's daughter;
>
> Choosing rather to suffer affliction with the people of God, than to enjoy the pleasures of sin for a season;
>
> Esteeming the reproach of Christ greater riches than the treasures in Egypt: for he had respect unto the recompence of the reward.

We too have a choice to make. God went to a lot of effort to have his word written for us so we can understand spiritual matters. God is the same yesterday, today and forever, he changes not. He wants all men to be made whole and to come to the knowledge of the truth. He wishes above all things that we prosper and be in health. He really does want to open the windows of heaven for us. To this end he took the time to warn us in his word about the god of this world, and had Moses spell out the consequences for going the world's way.

Good examples to check as regards doing things the devil's way and doing things God's way are Eve and Jesus Christ, so we will revisit a few scriptures, but this time look at them from a different perspective.

After God formed, made, and created Adam and Eve they lived in a perfect world. Six times in Genesis chapter 1 God calls what he made *good*, and once he calls it *very good*. If God calls something *good* six times and then crowns it with a seventh usage of *very good*, you can be sure the earth was in good shape.

> Genesis 1:28
> And God blessed them [Adam and Eve], and God said unto them, Be fruitful, and multiply, and replenish the earth, and subdue it: and have dominion over the fish of the sea, and over the fowl of the air, and over every living thing that moveth upon the earth.

Adam and Eve lived on a perfect earth, in fellowship with God. They had dominion and authority over the earth and everything on it. They were the Lords of the earth, the gods of this world. Now, put yourself in the devil's shoes. You want to take the world from man, but what on earth do you tempt a woman with who has everything? We talk about those who have everything, but really, Adam and Eve are the only humans to ever have had *everything*.

The devil as the serpent knows how to seduce. He has been doing it a long time and he knows his job. He took Eve down because he offered her something more than the world which she already had. It was the offer of secret knowledge from the gods that overwhelmed her. She said so herself. The promise of secret knowledge from the gods completely seduced her. The serpent knows how to seduce human beings. He has been watching us a long time and he knows how we work.

> Genesis 3:4,5
> And the serpent said unto the woman, Ye shall not surely die:

For God doth know that in the day ye eat thereof, then your eyes shall be opened, and ye shall be as gods, knowing good and evil.

Genesis 3:13
And the LORD God said unto the woman, What *is* this *that* thou hast done? And the woman said, The serpent beguiled me, and I did eat.

Eve had everything. She was married to the Lord of the earth. The entire planet was theirs. What higher position, what higher prestige, what higher power could anyone aspire to? Only the promise of secret knowledge from the gods, to know what the gods knew, could have touched her emotions with such intensity as to cloud her judgement so completely that she turned her back on the word of God and reached out for the serpent's lies. Eve lusted after the secret knowledge of good and evil the devil had tempted her with. She wanted it and she was going to have it.

2 Peter 1:4
Whereby are given unto us exceeding great and precious promises: that by these ye might be partakers of the divine nature, having escaped the corruption that is in the world through lust.

Oh yes, Eve experienced secret knowledge. She experienced guilt and condemnation, she experienced fear, she experienced unworthiness, and she experienced loss. That was the secret knowledge of good and evil for which she lost everything. After taking her husband down with her, they hid themselves from the presence of God.

Genesis 3:8
And they heard the voice of the LORD God walking in the garden in the cool of the day: and Adam and his wife hid themselves from the presence of the LORD God amongst the trees of the garden.

In our day and time, secret spiritual knowledge from the gods filtered down through the jesuits, freemasonry and witchcraft will corrupt and destroy anyone who dabbles in it. Lucifer's will is simply to steal, to kill, and to destroy. This secret knowledge may carry the promise of illumination, and those who envelop themselves in its shrouds of mysteries may think themselves philanthropists bringing peace on earth, but like Eve, they will lose everything, including that which they think they have.

In contrast to Eve, Jesus Christ was not fooled, nor was he seduced. He defeated the devil with three easy to memorise scriptures. Do not underestimate the power of the written and spoken word.

Luke 4:3,4
And the devil said unto him, If thou be the Son of God, command this stone that it be made bread.

And Jesus answered him, saying, It is written, That man shall not live by bread alone, but by every word of God.

Luke 4:5-8
And the devil, taking him up into an high mountain, shewed unto him all the kingdoms of the world in a moment of time.

And the devil said unto him, All this power will I give thee, and the glory of them: for that is delivered unto me; and to whomsoever I will I give it.

If thou therefore wilt worship me, all shall be thine.

And Jesus answered and said unto him, Get thee behind me, Satan: for it is written, Thou shalt worship the Lord thy God, and him only shalt thou serve.

Luke 4:9-12
And he brought him to Jerusalem, and set him on a pinnacle of the temple, and said unto him, If thou be the Son of God, cast thyself down from hence:

For it is written, He shall give his angels charge over thee, to keep thee:

And in *their* hands they shall bear thee up, lest at any time thou dash thy foot against a stone.

> And Jesus answering said unto him, It is said, Thou shalt not tempt the Lord thy God.

Perhaps you think Jesus Christ just sauntered into this confrontation, flashed a few peace signs at the devil, and laughed things over when the confrontation was over. Well, think again. Jesus Christ had fasted for forty days and forty nights just prior to this confrontation. He was hungry. The first temptation was about food. The devil knows our weaknesses and always goes for them.

Have you ever gone without food for a few days? The aroma of freshly prepared food can be overpowering. Try not eating for forty days and see if fresh food appeals to you. Jesus Christ's senses would have been overwhelmed, but he kept the word in mind and refused to allow his senses to break him.

The second temptation was unbelievable in scope and power. The presidency of a one-world government? I will bet Jesus Christ was tempted to take that one. He was offered back what Adam had lost – the authority and dominion of the entire earth. Do you think that was easy to resist? We break the word on paltry little things like going into debt for new computers, clothes, and cars. Jesus Christ was offered the whole world and he turned it down. Do you think that was easy?

The third temptation was perhaps the most deadly because it was so subtle. The devil went for his trust in God and enticed him to jump to see if his father really cared for him and really was there for him. The devil even quoted accurate scripture, albeit out of context. Think that one through sometime.

Do you think all this had an effect on Jesus Christ? I know it did. That confrontation was so exhausting, angels had to minister to him when the devil left. It says so in Matthew.

> Matthew 4:11
> Then the devil leaveth him, and, behold, angels came and ministered unto him.

So don't go thinking Jesus Christ had it easy. He just didn't break on the word. How does this apply to us today? Well, like Jesus Christ, we have to know the word and live it. For example, what does the word say about going into debt?

> Romans 13:8
> Owe no man any thing, but to love one another: for he that loveth another hath fulfilled the law.

The word is clear here, owe no man anything means owe no man anything. That is what the word says. It isn't a difficult scripture to memorise, in fact, it only takes a few seconds. Do we bring this scripture to mind and clearly enunciate the words in our hearts when tempted to go into debt? If we don't keep the word in mind, we will not be able to stand against the serpent when he dangles his deceitful credit cards with their empty promises of fulfilment in our faces.

I was once in debt over my head, and I know all the arguments. So, you need a new car. The only problem is you can't afford it. You don't have the money. Your credit card smiles disarmingly at you. All you have to do is flash it and the car is yours. That is how the devil works through the senses realm to bring people down. What does the word say?

> Philippians 4:19
> But my God shall supply all your need according to his riches in glory by Christ Jesus.

Are you going to do things God's way and trust him to meet your need, or are you going to do things the world's way? Can you defeat such overwhelming emotions with the word when you really want something badly but don't have the money? You will never do it with a head filled with television.

Never mind the smiling faces on your televisions offering everything you will ever need if you simply flash your credit cards. Stay out of debt. Save up. If you don't have the money, do without. Rent if you can't afford to buy a home. If you want to own a home, that is okay with God, just don't break his word to do it. He is big enough to supply your need.

Buy a second hand car with the deposit you were going to put down on the new car. Forget what the neighbours think.

Are you aware that credit cards are in fact debt cards? You don't go into credit when you use them, you go into debt. Don't use them unless you have the money to pay off the full amounts immediately.

Own everything you have. That is the way of life. Going into debt to buy stuff you don't have the money for is insane, it is the way of death. That includes mortgages. That includes business loans. That includes whole countries going into debt. Have you any idea how much misery is out there in the world because people are in debt? Doing things God's way is a lot more fun. Living debt free and owning everything you have is amazing. It's the way of life.

If you are in debt, God will help you get out of debt if you want him to. Staying out of debt is easy if you live within your budget, which means your outgoings are less than your income every month. If you can't afford something, save up for it or do without. Make a decision to do things God's way, do your best to get out of debt, and he will show you how to get there.

If you are listening and follow his guidance, you will get out of debt. It doesn't matter if you're a single person, a married person, a tradesman, business owner, prime minister, king, queen or president, God can and will make a way out of debt for you and your countries if you make up your mind to do things according to his word. It is not so hard to live on the way of life, just keep your emotions under control and do what the word says.

Let's move onto witchcraft, which is perhaps a little more subtle than you might realise. Witchcraft includes things like horoscopes, tarot cards, fortune telling, palm reading, séances, ouija boards, astrology, divination, astral projection, hypnosis, lucky charms, guardian angels, drugs and a thousand other things. Yes, hypnosis is part of it. If you are not in control of yourself, what is? Don't open your mind to spirit possession. If you have been involved in witchcraft, apologise to God and move on. God is faithful to forgive and forget. He's great that way.

Psalm 103:11,12
For as the heaven is high above the earth, *so* great is his mercy toward them that fear him [reverence and respect him].

As far as the east is from the west, *so* far hath he removed our transgressions from us.

Television and Hollywood promote witchcraft. Julie Andrews, a lesbian, opened the floodgates to my generation with the movie Mary Poppins. Children all over the world were entranced and a new generation of witches was groomed. Television programmes like Bewitched continued the devil's education of our children. These days, it's Harry Potter luring our kids into the devil's dark world. Why don't you teach your children the truth and drag them away from those damnable televisions programming them for witchcraft and homosexuality?

The United Nations promotes witchcraft. The United Nations grants legal protection to those who practice witchcraft. The United Nations prosecutes anyone who infringes the human rights of those who practice witchcraft. I don't give a fuck what the United Nations mandates. The UN stands in direct opposition to God's word on everything. This verse sums them up very nicely.

Isaiah 5:20
Woe unto them that call evil good, and good evil; that put darkness for light, and light for darkness; that put bitter for sweet, and sweet for bitter!

Never mind the United Nations, what are *you* going to do? Are you going to walk the way of life or the way of death? Which path do you want to take? If you lust after your tarot card readings, your fortune tellers, your horoscopes, your psychics, and your astrology, you need to change direction. There are no grey areas in witchcraft. Contrary to what Hollywood promotes, there are no good and bad witches and good and bad wizards, they all operate devil spirit power. Witchcraft will absolutely destroy you. If you play with spiritual fire, you will get burned and be taken down like Eve.

> Deuteronomy 18:10-12
> There shall not be found among you *any one* that maketh his son or his daughter to pass through the fire, [walk on hot coals] *or* that useth divination, [tarot cards and other forms of fortune telling] *or* an observer of times, [horoscopes and astrology] or an enchanter, [hypnosis, snake charming and other forms of enchantment] or a witch,
>
> Or a charmer, or a consulter with familiar spirits [calling up devil spirits which impersonate dead people at séances], or a wizard, or a necromancer.
>
> For all that do these things *are* an abomination unto the LORD: and because of these abominations the LORD thy God doth drive them out from before thee.

If you choose to ignore God and practice witchcraft, your life will be stolen from you despite how much money you make from it. Do you want blue skies in your heart, or the world's misery, slavery and death? The choice is yours. Both are available. You determine which path you walk.

Homosexuality has already been handled previously in great depth. Just to recap, here is the way of life.

> Leviticus 20:13
> If a man also lie with mankind, as he lieth with a woman, both of them have committed an abomination: they shall surely be put to death; their blood *shall be* upon them.

This is God's word, not my word. I didn't write the bible. Flooding your countries with homosexuals and lesbians is the way of death. God told Moses to execute homosexuals. What then do you suppose God thinks about religions who ordain them as ministers, or countries who elect them as presidents? The pope may try to cover the vatican's tracks, but if you want a definitive answer as to why there has been an explosion in homosexuality in our western cultures these last few decades, you need look no further than the jesuits. Celibacy among priests breeds homosexual predators.

1 Timothy 4:1-3
Now the Spirit speaketh expressly, that in the latter times some shall depart from the faith, giving heed to seducing spirits, and doctrines of devils;

Speaking lies in hypocrisy; having their conscience seared with a hot iron;

Forbidding to marry, *and commanding* to abstain from meats, which God hath created to be received with thanksgiving of them which believe and know the truth.

Forbidding to marry is a doctrine of devils. It is a seductive doctrine of the god of this world. If you shack up young men for years in religious dungeons away from women with predatory homosexual peers they will become homosexuals. The vatican knows this, and actively cultivates homosexuality within their priesthood. They then send these monsters around the world to bugger your little boys up the ass. The world explosion in homosexuality in recent decades was systematically implemented to destroy you. At the time of writing, President Obama has appointed over 250 openly gay and lesbian *professionals* to his administration, more than all previous US presidents combined. He obviously loves homosexuality. Whose side do you think he is on? Which god do you suppose he worships?

Psalm 12:8
The wicked walk on every side, when the vilest men are exalted.

If you want answers, come back to God and his word. Turn your nose up at God and continue down the way of death regarding homosexuality, and your civilisations will become extinct. You will become the Sodoms and Gomorrahs of the new world order.

World terrorism. Now there is a subject. World terrorism is breathtaking in scope and monstrous in execution. However, to put it into perspective, I believe terrorism could be stamped out all over the world in less than a week. God has the answers. The United Nations has nothing. It is the United Nations which recruits, trains, houses, feeds, pays and foments terrorism all over the planet in their quest for what they call world peace. They, along with the thousands of subversive criminal human rights organisations who operate within their framework are the heart of world terrorism. The International Red Cross is the modern Ho Chi Minh trail that keeps the world's terror organisations supplied and operating through what they glibly term humanitarian aid. And guess what? God's people, christians, are so fucking stupid they donate their money to the world's charities.

Robert Mugabe rose to power as a terrorist leader in Zimbabwe, then called Rhodesia. The United Nations trained and financed him and his communist army. The International Red Cross supplied his medical needs. His rag tag band of communist murderers had worldwide public support only because of effusive television reports lauding the moral high ground of human rights. Power to the black man, cried Mugabe, as they murdered the white farmers and stole their farms. In just a few years, Mugabe turned a food exporting country into a famine-ridden cesspit of poverty and crime run by gangsters. That is what the United Nations does behind its banners of solidarity and human rights.

United Nations refugee camps are nothing more than terrorist training camps. The Israeli's know that. There is no such thing as a terrorist problem. The only problem is that we have turned our backs on God and look to the world for our answers. There are no answers in the world, only lies, treachery, misery, and death.

Oh and don't go blaming terrorists for all the world's ills either, that isn't the case at all. For the most part they are good men doing what they believe is right. I've met IRA terrorists who have given up their ways and become great men of God. The apostle Paul was a terrorist who persecuted and murdered God's children in the 1st Century before he learned a better way on the road to Damascus. Anyone can change and God will be there for them when they do. God doesn't wish evil against evil men, but rather that they change and come back to him, and he *will* be there for them, no matter what they have done.

> Ezekiel 18:21-23
> But if the wicked will turn from all his sins that he hath committed, and keep all my statutes, and do that which is lawful and right, he shall surely live, he shall not die.

All his transgressions that he hath committed, they shall not be mentioned unto him: in his righteousness that he hath done he shall live.

Have I any pleasure at all that the wicked should die? saith the Lord GOD: *and* not that he should return from his ways, and live?

Amazingly enough, this even includes jesuits. Jesus Christ had some notable successes among the religious leaders. Joseph of Arimathaea was a Pharisee, for example. Nicodemus was another. And what about the apostle Paul, one of the most committed and murderous religious nuts on the planet? Where would we be today without his change of heart after Jesus Christ had words with him on the road to Damascus?

Most terrorists believe that what they are doing is right, and that they are doing the will of God. They don't know they are serving the wrong god. They don't know that the devil is using them, and they certainly don't understand his nature or they wouldn't do his bidding. Any god who demands worship at the point of a gun really doesn't have a lot going for him. Sure, at one time Lucifer was full of wisdom and beauty, perfect in all his ways. That was then, this is now. There is another God you can choose, a God who is dependable and trustworthy, one who isn't afraid to commit himself to a written standard that he guarantees to honour and fulfil.

Remember Manasseh, Hezekiah's son? How much more evil can a man be? Yet he gave up his witchcraft, and God was right there for him. Give up your witchcrafts, and like Manasseh, you will be forgiven and protected. All God has for us will be yours.

2 Chronicles 33:9-16
So Manasseh made Judah and the inhabitants of Jerusalem to err, *and* to do worse than the heathen, whom the LORD had destroyed before the children of Israel.

And the LORD spake to Manasseh, and to his people: but they would not hearken.

Wherefore the LORD brought upon them the captains of the host of the king of Assyria, which took Manasseh among the thorns, and bound him with fetters, and carried him to Babylon.

And when he was in affliction, he besought the LORD his God, and humbled himself greatly before the God of his fathers,

And prayed unto him: and he was intreated of him, and heard his supplication, and brought him again to Jerusalem into his kingdom. Then Manasseh knew that the LORD he *was* God.

Now after this he built a wall without the city of David, on the west side of Gihon, in the valley, even to the entering in at the fish gate, and compassed about Ophel, and raised it up a very great height, and put captains of war in all the fenced cities of Judah.

And he took away the strange gods, and the idol out of the house of the LORD, and all the altars that he had built in the mount of the house of the LORD, and in Jerusalem, and cast *them* out of the city.

And he repaired the altar of the LORD, and sacrificed thereon peace offerings and thank offerings, and commanded Judah to serve the LORD God of Israel.

Freemasons for the most part are good men, at least initially. They really do believe that they are all working together for a better world. The earth is overcrowded they are taught, and in danger of being destroyed unless billions of the world's population are exterminated. They really do believe that mass genocide is the only way to save the planet. The vatican teaches them that. The United Nations teaches them that. The communists teach them that. Freemasonry teaches them that. They all work together to further one world governance on behalf of the vatican, whose real aim is nothing more lofty than simply the extermination of all those who don't worship their god Lucifer.

The secret knowledge offered to new initiates into freemasonry does not illuminate them, it corrupts them. As masons move up the circles, they are gradually corrupted to the point they will commit criminal acts under the illusion they are doing good. It begins with little things, like human resources managers lying to ensure masons get promoted, while those who work hard and deserve the promotions are not.

If you give control to masons in politics, law and business, you are giving control to the jesuits who will infiltrate and control your media, your businesses, your schools, your military, your police, your judicial systems, and your governments. From that position of strength, they will orchestrate your destruction.

If you are a freemason, your duty is not to your order or to your lodge, it is to God and his word. Don't sell us out to the jesuits. If you're not a freemason, don't join them. Don't be seduced by the *secret* knowledge they offer. Sure, they'll bribe you with good jobs, property, money and power, but how long will that last? It is as fleeting and transient as the grass in your garden.

Don't be fooled by Hollywood either. Hollywood may portray terrorism as heroic and noble in films such as The Last Samurai, but strip the glitz and glamour from the movie and all you see is a drunken bum who sold out his country. Did you know that the Samurai were homosexuals? It was part of their initiation rites. They were even rumoured to eat human flesh. And you want to swallow Hollywood?

I'm Scottish and Mel Gibson's brilliantly directed movie Braveheart really does touch the heart of Scotland. But it is twisted. William Wallace was an emissary of the pope, and his commission was to take the throne from England. The vatican used the Scottish people. Do you think Scotland won its freedom in 1314 at Bannockburn? All that did was drive the Scottish people deeper into the Dark Ages. It wasn't until a real hero came along, Martin Luther, that the world again saw light in the Reformation and emerged from the Dark Ages.

The same is true about Bonnie Prince Charlie, another Roman Catholic undercover agent who used the Scottish people in an attempt to take the throne from England. Culloden is a bloody vatican stain on Scottish soil, and I would not be surprised if the so-called prince was a jesuit. I believe he died of syphilis in France, an alcoholic. Some hero.

The god of this world will infiltrate every facet of social fabric if he is permitted. Be wary of human rights and animal rights groups, for freemasons control them all. Take the Royal Society for the Protection of Birds, for example. The RSPB is staffed by wonderful people who love birds, and there is nothing wrong with that, but why does the RSPB keep introducing birds of prey into Scotland, birds which were either extinct in this country or which are not indigenous? Birds of prey eat other birds, birds that are becoming extinct because they are being eaten to death by birds introduced by the RSPB. What is going on?

Small birds eat ticks and other pests. Since small birds were driven almost to extinction in the countryside by sparrow hawks and other birds of prey, tick numbers have exploded in Scotland. Red Grouse numbers have plummeted as there are so many ticks infesting their chicks that they are dying in their nests. Gaming Estates in Scotland are struggling to survive because their game birds are being driven to extinction. Gamekeepers and farmers poison birds of prey because they are harmful to the environment, yet they are being prosecuted by the RSPB and taken to court for it. The RSPB is destroying Scotland, yet we send money to them and permit them into our primary schools to terrify our children by demonising gamekeepers?

Gamekeepers have been managing the land for centuries. It's in their genes. Activists are young fools fresh out of school with heads full of propaganda. Yet we listen to fools with loud mouths rather than listen to gamekeepers when it comes to land management?

The RSPB recently expressed public alarm at a review of habitat and bird protection laws in the UK, which they claimed would harm vital protections for wildlife. George Osborne, however, was simply looking out for Britain's best interests, and told MPs he wanted to make sure that EU rules on things like habitats were not putting ridiculous extra costs on firms doing business, and that he was worried about the impact of these EU rules on UK firms and warned against pricing British business out of the world economy. Don't you see it? The RSPB aren't interested in birds, they are only interested in using birds to destroy you. This is another example of economic warfare, another example of how the god of this world steals, kills, and destroys.

High tax rates are another example. President Calvin Coolidge (1872-1933) had this to say regarding business and commerce:

I want the people of America to be able to work less for the government and more for themselves. I want them to have the rewards of their own industry. This is the chief meaning of freedom. Until we can re-establish a condition under which the earnings of the people can be kept by the people, we are bound to suffer a very severe and distinct curtailment of our liberty.

Regarding rights in the workplace and trade unions, consider these words from the Protocols of Zion, purportedly penned by Jews but in reality entirely the work of the jesuits.

All people are chained down to heavy toil by poverty more firmly than ever. They were chained by slavery and serfdom; from these, one way and another, they might free themselves. These could be settled with, but from want they will never get away. We have included in the constitution such rights as to the masses appear fictitious and not actual rights. All these so-called 'Peoples Rights' can exist only in idea, an idea which can never be realised in practical life.

What is it to the proletariat labourer, bowed double over his heavy toil, crushed by his lot in life, if talkers get the right to babble, if journalists get the right to scribble any nonsense side by side with good stuff, once the proletariat has no other profit out of the constitution save only those pitiful crumbs which we fling them from our table in return for their voting in favour of what we dictate, in favour of the men we place in power, the servants of our agentur... Republican rights for a poor man are no more than a bitter piece of irony, for the necessity he is under of toiling almost all day gives him no present use of them, but the other hand robs him of all guarantee of regular and certain earnings by making him dependent on strikes by his comrades or lockouts by his masters.

The people, under our guidance, have annihilated the aristocracy, who were their one and only defence and foster-mother for the sake of their own advantage which is inseparably bound up with the well-being of the people. Nowadays, with the destruction of the aristocracy, the people have fallen into the grips of merciless money-grinding scoundrels who have laid a pitiless and cruel yoke upon the necks of the workers.

Walking *by* the Spirit

We appear on the scene as alleged saviours of the worker from this oppression when we propose to him to enter the ranks of our fighting forces – Socialists, Anarchists, Communists – to whom we always give support in accordance with an alleged brotherly rule (of the solidarity of all humanity) of our social masonry. The aristocracy, which enjoyed by law the labour of the workers, was interested in seeing that the workers were well fed, healthy, and strong. We are interested in just the opposite – in the diminution, the killing out of the goyim. Our power is in the chronic shortness of food and physical weakness of the worker because by all that this implies he is made the slave of our will, and he will not find in his own authorities either strength or energy to set against our will. Hunger creates the right of capital to rule the worker more surely than it was given to the aristocracy by the legal authority of kings.

By want and the envy and hatred which it engenders we shall move the mobs and with their hands we shall wipe out all those who hinder us on our way.

You may think the stock markets of the world keep you prosperous, but you are mistaken. All the stock markets do is steal the profits made by workers and hand them to gangsters, communists and masons. If you want a strong country, you need a strong middle class, and you can only do that if you quit gambling on the stock markets and instead give those profits to the people who earned them. It wouldn't be hard to change things. Why not just stop buying from the cunts who are trying to exterminate you instead of making them rich? It's not hard to see them. Just look for the pyramids with the eyes and don't do business with them. You'd be surprised where they show up.

Do you think social security, government welfare, keeps you safe? The word states that if a man does not work he should not eat.

> 2 Thessalonians 3:10
> For even when we were with you, this we commanded you, that if any would not work, neither should he eat.

This is in essence talking about men who do not *want* to work, who actively avoid it, those who leech off the efforts of others. There is nothing wrong with being out of work, or being between jobs, and God will surely meet all your need, as he promises.

> Philippians 4:19
> But my God shall supply all your need according to his riches in glory by Christ Jesus.

All work is honourable and God will honour those who work and who actively seek work. However, if people do not want to work, if people prefer to sit on bar stools every day, their life paid for by others, the word says they should not eat. This is actually a good thing. Not giving money to bums, drunks and deadbeats would help our communities and it would help our countries. You cannot legislate the poor into prosperity by legislating the wealthy out of it. What one receives without working for, another person must work for without receiving. The government cannot give anything to anyone without first stealing it from someone else. You cannot multiply wealth by dividing it.

If you think welfare is good, then consider this – I believe it is in Germany (now that prostitution has been legalised) that young women on welfare are being sent to brothels and told if they turn down the work their welfare will be cut. This is the way of the world. The jesuits have absolutely no compunction whatsoever about forcing your daughters, sisters, and mothers into prostitution. They will do it through your own governments and your own courts. This is the way of the world, but there is a better way available.

As I said before, I never understood evil until I began to understand the jesuits. They may conceal their treachery and hatreds beneath a veil of religious piety, feeding us lies about world peace and of a need to save the planet, but the truth is they are the most vicious, cruel, and heartless bastards on earth.

France's General Lafayette warned:

It is my opinion that if the liberties of this country, the United States of America, are destroyed, it will be by the subtlety of the Roman Catholic Jesuit priests, for they are the most crafty, dangerous enemies of civil and religious liberty. They have instigated most of the wars of Europe.

After Napoleon was exiled to St Helena, he had this to say regarding his jesuit masters:

The Jesuits are a military organization, not a religious order. Their chief is a general of an army, not the mere father abbot of a monastery. And the aim of this organization is: power. Power in its most despotic exercise. Absolute power, universal power, power to control the world by the volition of a single man. Jesuitism is the most absolute of despotisms: and at the same time the greatest and most enormous of abuses.

The general of the Jesuits insists on being master, sovereign, over the sovereign. Wherever the Jesuits are admitted they will be masters, cost what it may. Their society is by nature dictatorial, and therefore it is the irreconcilable enemy of all constituted authority. Every act, every crime, however atrocious, is a meritorious work if committed for the interest of the Society of the Jesuits, or by the order of the general.

In this context, it is worth repeating what Abraham Lincoln stated regarding them:

The Protestants of both the North and South would surely unite to exterminate the priests and the Jesuits, if they could learn how the priests, the nuns, and the monks, which daily land on our shores, under the pretext of preaching their religion... are nothing else but the emissaries of the Pope, of Napoleon III, and the other despots of Europe, to undermine our institutions, alienate the hearts of our people from our Constitution, and our laws, destroy our schools, and prepare a reign of anarchy here as they have done in Ireland, in Mexico, in Spain, and wherever there are any people who want to be free.

In 1816, John Adams wrote to President Jefferson regarding them:

Shall we not have regular swarms of them here, in as many disguises as only a king of the gypsies can assume, dressed as painters, publishers, writers, and schoolmasters? If ever there was a body of men who merited eternal damnation on Earth and in Hell it is this Society of Loyola's.

Elizabeth the First banished the jesuits from the British Empire. If any were ever caught within her borders, they were to be drawn and quartered. After the issuing of a Papal Bull, Elizabeth viewed the vatican as a major threat. When jesuits began to arrive in England, with catholic troops literally just a few hours sailing away, England went on the offensive. In 1585, an Act of Parliament ordered that all jesuits and catholics priests should be driven from the kingdom. Reports from spies in Spain about the impending Armada only made a campaign against the vatican more vigorous. When the Armada came, the vast bulk of the population rallied around Elizabeth. The defeat of the Spanish Armada is one of the most famous events in British history. It was arguably Queen Elizabeth's finest hour. Consequently, the impact of the jesuits, who were considered the main threat to British freedom, was broken.

In 1605, the jesuits hatched the Gunpowder plot to blow up the Houses of Parliament in another attempt to take the country. Catesby and Fawkes were most likely jesuits themselves. Again, they failed. We should return to celebrating Guy Fawkes night every November the 5th, and once again enjoy burning effigies of jesuit priests on our bonfires.

When Napoleon was defeated at the battle of Waterloo, the jesuits sent runners to Rothschild in London with orders to proclaim defeat. On hearing the news, the stock market crashed as everyone rushed to dump their useless British currency. Rothschild even sold a few shares to fuel the collapse, and then immediately bought up all the shares in the United Kingdom for pennies. When news arrived the following day of victory, share prices soared and the vatican owned Great Britain. Those cunts swindled you out of your country. You have the right to legally take back from them everything they have stolen from you.

The jesuits are not a religious order, they are a military unit. They will take control wherever they are permitted to operate, and they will use whatever methods suit their purposes, legal or otherwise. Whatever the jesuits can do to destroy our cultures, our economies, our countries, our families, our health, and our children, they will do. They are the worm tongues of Tolkien's Lord of the Rings.

They outlaw the death penalty under a banner of human rights and flood our streets with rapists and paedophiles. They force us to hand over our orphaned children to homosexual and lesbian couples to adopt so they can gang rape them in the privacy of their own homes. They promote adultery to destroy our families. They sexually confuse our children and turn the homosexuals and lesbians loose on them. Our morals and ethics are broken down through their control of our televisions, newspapers, schools, and universities. They dismantle our trade laws so they can siphon off our wealth. They destroy our farming, fishing, and agriculture so they can poison us with their dog foods. They dismantle our immigration laws, and flood our countries with bums and deadbeats from trashed backward countries so they can come here and trash ours.

To the jesuits we are but rats to be exterminated. How we are exterminated matters not to them, and if they can make the vatican rich in the process so much the better. The jesuits break our laws with impunity. Exterminating rats, after all, isn't a crime, and it explains how they can do such atrocious things and walk away. It is the jesuits who control the Knights of Malta, the Mafia, and the other drug running criminal gangs, like the IRA, PIRA, ETA, the CIA, the United Nations, and MI5. The CIA wasn't created to protect the American people, it was created to spy on them so they could be destroyed. The CIA has an office at the vatican and answers directly to the pope, not the American president. In the words of an ex-CIA agent who was involved in the MkII Ultra programme:

I was trained as a federal officer. I don't believe what we are looking at is earthly, but demonic. These people want to wipe Christianity off of the Earth. I have seen their consciences die within their eyes.

And that, ladies and gentlemen, sums up the god of this world's true intentions – to wipe christianity and the knowledge of the bible off the face of the earth. That is the true motivational force and power behind the jesuits, communism, masonry, and one world governance.

You know, I love catholics, I really do. A few centuries ago, before the Reformation, all christians were catholics. There were no other christian groups, other than a handful of underground movements. Today, all christians have their roots in catholicism. It took a catholic man of God, Martin Luther and the catholics of his day to bring us the freedoms we have. That freedom was bought at great expense in catholic blood. The jesuits are quite happy to murder their own people should it serve their purpose.

From the time of the first pope in 606AD to the present, it has been estimated that more than fifty million people have been murdered by the vatican for the crime of heresy, an average of more than forty thousand religious murders every year.

The vatican has not changed. It still believes every person on earth should bow to the pope (or the black pope, the jesuit general, who is the real power behind that cult), and they are committed to exterminating anyone who will not. That is the power behind one world governance, including the United Nations, freemasonry, communism, and world terrorism. If you are looking for the anti-Christ, he is not in America, he is not in Israel, he is not an Arab, he is in Vatican City, and it is from Vatican City that the world is corrupted.

We owe a great deal to the catholic men and women who gave their blood during the Reformation so we could enjoy the freedoms we have today. Never forget that. Our fight is not against flesh and blood, but against spiritual wickedness from on high.

To sum the class up then, the change from the walk of the senses to the spiritual walk requires a renewing, a retraining of the mind. This first involves changing our thoughts to line up with the word. Instead of thinking homosexuality is normal and healthy, we think it a crime worthy of death. As we hold the word in mind, eventually homosexuality will become naturally abhorrent to us and make us shudder with revulsion. Instead of being drunkards, we quit drinking and clean up our lives. Rather than smoke dope or take drugs, we spend our time in the word and learn to walk by the spirit. We replace television and the internet as sources of education with the bible. Comparing what we've been taught as freemasons and communists with the truths of God's word, we acknowledge where we've been missing the mark, apologise to God and instead rely on the bible as our only standard for truth, our only centre of reference for what is right and what is wrong.

Once a man or woman has come the place where they believe God's word rather than the inane babblings of the world, they will speak in tongues faithfully and take their first steps into walking by the spirit.

If they are faithful, eventually they will begin helping others. They will share the word when they have opportunity to give people a chance to know the truth for themselves. When one or two respond and begin to ask questions, that is usually the time a home church is born in a new area.

The next phase of a growing believer's life is to begin to earnestly desire and earnestly pursue opportunities to help people by energising the manifestations of holy spirit. When new folks come to a home church, they will look for doors to open so they can minister and help people. As they remain faithful, they will develop fruit of the spirit, they will become disciples, and they will go on to become effective ministers for the Lord Jesus Christ, walking with the love of God.

When disciples live the word, people see the deliverance and power in their lives and want it for themselves. Home churches then grow until they have to split and new home churches are born. This is how the word moves.

In conclusion then, we have choices to make. Do we walk the way of life or the way of death? Discipleship requires discipline. It isn't difficult or burdensome, but it does require faithful daily application. God is always there, and he will always be there for us.

These promises in Proverbs are just as true for anyone today as they have been for me. Put the work into the word and you will find the knowledge of God.

> Proverbs 2:1-5
> My son, if thou wilt receive my words, and hide my commandments with thee;
>
> So that thou incline thine ear unto wisdom, *and* apply thine heart to understanding;
>
> Yea, if thou criest after knowledge, *and* liftest up thy voice for understanding;
>
> If thou seekest her as silver, and searchest for her as *for* hid treasures;
>
> Then shalt thou understand the fear of the LORD, and find the knowledge of God.

The way of life starts with a decision, just as studying to be a doctor or a plumber starts with a decision. It does not happen overnight, but it doesn't have to take a lifetime either. Nothing has changed with either God's will or the devil's will since Moses wrote the book of Deuteronomy all those centuries ago. Those same truths apply today so choose which way you are going to walk. It is your decision. As for me and my house, we will serve God.

> Deuteronomy 30:19
> I call heaven and earth to record this day against you, *that* I have set before you life and death, blessing and cursing: therefore choose life, that both thou and thy seed may live:

> Psalm 33:12
> Blessed *is* the nation whose God *is* the LORD; *and* the people *whom* he hath chosen for his own inheritance.

The benefits for living God's way and walking by the spirit are very much worth your effort. Don't be afraid of the world, manifest the power of God, walk by the spirit and truly you shall be more than conquerors through him that loved us. It is time to hold our heads up and walk as children of the living God.

>1 John 4:4
>Ye are of God, little children, and have overcome them: because greater is he that is in you, than he that is in the world.

Appendix – Uses of Pneuma

When considering the usages of pneuma (spirit) and hagion (holy) in the new testament, we need to consider a few things. First of all, according to the majority of the Greek texts and the Aramaic Peshitta text, eleven scriptures with the word pneuma in them should have it deleted, and three scriptures should have it added.

We must also consider the article *the*. In English, the article *the* affects the sense of a sentence. In the Aramaic language – which most scholars believe was the original language of the written bible while Greek was a translation from it – there is no article *the*. As there is such a huge difference between holy spirit and the Holy Spirit, we must carefully check the context to determine whether or not the article *the* should or should not be included.

Uses of pneuma can generally be categorised, and for this work I will categorise them thus:

Usage 1 – God, who is Holy Spirit.

Usage 2 – the gift of holy spirit or the gift of holy spirit in manifestation.

Usage 3 – old testament spirit.

Usage 4 – devil spirits.

Usage 5 – angels.

Usage 6 – used figuratively, such as for the soul of man.

Usage 7 – Christ in his resurrected body or a reference to the one we receive at the return.

Matthew 1:18 usage 1
Now the birth of Jesus Christ was on this wise: When as his mother Mary was espoused to Joseph, before they came together, she was found with child of [ek – by, out from] the Holy Ghost [pneuma].

Matthew 1:20 usage 1
But while he thought on these things, behold, the angel of the Lord appeared unto him in a dream, saying, Joseph, thou son of David, fear not to take unto thee Mary thy wife: for that which is conceived in her is of the Holy Ghost [pneuma].

Matthew 3:11 usage 2
I [John the Baptist] indeed baptize you with water unto repentance: but he that cometh after me is mightier than I, whose shoes I am not worthy to bear: he shall baptize you with the Holy Ghost [pneuma], and *with* fire:

This baptism with pneuma hagion and fire is a prophecy referring to the new birth and the receiving of the gift of holy spirit.

Matthew 3:16 usage 3
And Jesus, when he was baptized, went up straightway out of the water: and, lo, the heavens were opened unto him, and he saw the Spirit [pneuma] of God descending like a dove, and lighting upon him:

The pneuma of God is the spirit from God. Some Greek texts omit the article the before pneuma. This isn't referring to the gift of holy spirit which came on the day of Pentecost as that wasn't yet available so this is referring to old testament spirit.

Matthew 4:1 usage 3
Then was Jesus led up of the Spirit [pneuma] into the wilderness to be tempted of the devil.

Matthew 5:3 usage 6
Blessed *are* the poor in spirit [pneuma]: for theirs is the kingdom of heaven.

This is a figure of speech referring to people within themselves, within their own minds.

Matthew 8:16 usage 4
When the even was come, they brought unto him many that were possessed with devils: and he cast out the spirits [pneumata] with *his* word, and healed all that were sick:

Matthew 10:1 usage 4
And when he had called unto *him* his twelve disciples, he gave them power *against* unclean spirits [pneumata], to cast them out, and to heal all manner of sickness and all manner of disease.

Matthew 10:20 usage 3
For it is not ye that speak, but the Spirit [pneuma] of your Father which speaketh in you.

Matthew 12:18 usage 3
Behold my servant, whom I have chosen; my beloved, in whom my soul is well pleased: I will put my spirit [pneuma] upon him, and he shall shew judgment to the Gentiles.

Matthew 12:28 usage 3
But if I cast out devils by the Spirit [pneuma] of God, then the kingdom of God is come unto you.

Matthew 12:31 usage 1
Wherefore I say unto you, All manner of sin and blasphemy shall be forgiven unto men: but the blasphemy *against* the ~~Holy~~ Ghost [pneuma] shall not be forgiven unto men.

Mathew 12:32 usage 1
And whosoever speaketh a word against the Son of man, it shall be forgiven him: but whosoever speaketh against the Holy Ghost [pneuma], it shall not be forgiven him, neither in this world, neither in the *world* to come.

Matthew 12:43 usage 4
When the unclean spirit [pneuma] is gone out of a man, he walketh through dry places, seeking rest, and findeth none.

Matthew 12:45 usage 4
Then goeth he, and taketh with himself seven other spirits [pneumata] more wicked than himself, and they enter in and dwell there: and the last *state* of that man is worse than the first. Even so shall it be also unto this wicked generation.

Matthew 14:26 deleted
And when the disciples saw him walking on the sea, they were troubled, saying, It is a spirit [phantasma]; and they cried out for fear.

Spirit is to be deleted here as the Aramaic uses phantasma. Pneuma should therefore be replaced with phantasma, an apparition or phantom.

Matthew 22:43 usage 3
He saith unto them, How then doth David in spirit [pneuma] call him Lord, saying,

Matthew 26:41 usage 6
Watch and pray, that ye enter not into temptation: the spirit [pneuma] indeed *is* willing, but the flesh *is* weak.

Matthew 27:50 usage 6
Jesus, when he had cried again with a loud voice, yielded up the ghost [pneuma].

Pneuma is used figuratively to mean he died.

Matthew 28:19 deleted
Go ye therefore, and teach all nations, baptizing them in the [my] name ~~of the Father, and of the Son, and of the Holy Ghost~~:

If Jesus Christ had issued this command to his disciples just prior to his ascension, why didn't his disciples ever carry it out? Not once anywhere in the book of Acts did his disciples ever baptise anyone in the name of the father, son and holy ghost. Rather, they exclusively baptised in the name of Jesus Christ.

Acts 2:38
Then Peter said unto them, Repent, and be baptized every one of you in the name of Jesus Christ for the remission of sins, and ye shall receive the gift of the Holy Ghost.

Acts 8:16
(For as yet he was fallen upon none of them: only they were baptized in the name of the Lord Jesus.)

Acts 10:48
And he commanded them to be baptized in the name of the Lord. Then prayed they him to tarry certain days.

Acts 19:5
When they heard this, they were baptized in the name of the Lord Jesus.

Further, Eusebius, who died in 340 AD, quoted Matthew 28:19 eighteen times from manuscripts in existence at the time and he never once used the forged words, he always quoted Matthew 28:19 as 'baptising them in my name'. Pneuma must be deleted as all the evidence points to a vatican forgery sometime after the Council of Nicaea.

Mark 1:8 usage 2
I indeed have baptized you with water: but he shall baptize you with the Holy Ghost [pneuma].

Mark 1:10 usage 3
And straightway coming up out of the water, he saw the heavens opened, and the Spirit [pneuma] like a dove descending upon him:

Mark 1:12 usage 3
And immediately the Spirit [pneuma] driveth him into the wilderness.

Mark 1:23 usage 4
And there was in their synagogue a man with an unclean spirit [pneuma]; and he cried out,

Mark 1:26 usage 4
And when the unclean spirit [pneuma] had torn him, and cried with a loud voice, he came out of him.

Mark 1:27 usage 4
And they were all amazed, insomuch that they questioned among themselves, saying, What thing is this? what new doctrine *is* this? for with authority commandeth he even the unclean spirits [pneumata], and they do obey him.

Mark 2:8 usage 3
And immediately when Jesus perceived in his spirit [pneuma] that they so reasoned within themselves, he said unto them, Why reason ye these things in your hearts?

Mark 3:11 usage 4
And unclean spirits [pneumata], when they saw him, fell down before him, and cried, saying, Thou art the Son of God.

Mark 3:29 usage 1
But he that shall blaspheme against the Holy Ghost [pneuma] hath never forgiveness, but is in danger of eternal damnation:

Mark 3:30 usage 4
Because they said, He hath an unclean spirit [pneuma].

Mark 5:2 usage 4
And when he was come out of the ship, immediately there met him out of the tombs a man with an unclean spirit [pneuma],

Mark 5:8 usage 4
For he said unto him, Come out of the man, *thou* unclean spirit [pneuma].

Mark 5:13 usage 4
And forthwith Jesus gave them leave. And the unclean spirits [pneumata] went out, and entered into the swine: and the herd ran violently down a steep place into the sea, (they were about two thousand;) and were choked in the sea.

Mark 6:7 usage 4
And he called *unto him* the twelve, and began to send them forth by two and two; and gave them power over unclean spirits [pneumata];

Mark 6:49 deleted
But when they saw him walking upon the sea, they supposed it had been a spirit [phantasma], and cried out:

Pneuma should be replaced with phantasma, an apparition or phantom.

Mark 7:25 usage 4
For a *certain* woman, whose young daughter had an unclean spirit [pneuma], heard of him, and came and fell at his feet:

Mark 8:12 usage 3
And he sighed deeply in his spirit [pneuma], and saith, Why doth this generation seek after a sign? verily I say unto you, There shall no sign be given unto this generation.

Jesus Christ could not have stated that no sign would be given to that generation unless he had received that information by revelation from God. So this is old testament spirit in operation.

Mark 9:17 usage 4
And one of the multitude answered and said, Master, I have brought unto thee my son, which hath a dumb spirit [pneuma];

Mark 9:20 usage 4
And they brought him unto him: and when he saw him, straightway the spirit [pneuma] tare him; and he fell on the ground, and wallowed foaming.

Mark 9:25 usage 4, usage 4
When Jesus saw that the people came running together, he rebuked the foul spirit [pneuma], saying unto him, *Thou* dumb and deaf spirit [pneuma], I charge thee, come out of him, and enter no more into him.

Mark 12:36 usage 3
For David himself said by the Holy Ghost [pneuma], The LORD said to my Lord, Sit thou on my right hand, till I make thine enemies thy footstool.

Mark 13:11 usage 3
But when they shall lead *you*, and deliver you up, take no thought beforehand what ye shall speak, neither do ye premeditate: but whatsoever shall be given you in that hour, that speak ye: for it is not ye that speak, but the Holy Ghost [pneuma].

Mark 14:38 usage 6
Watch ye and pray, lest ye enter into temptation. The spirit [pneuma] truly *is* ready, but the flesh *is* weak.

Luke 1:15 usage 3
For he shall be great in the sight of the Lord, and shall drink neither wine nor strong drink; and he shall be filled with the Holy Ghost [pneuma], even from his mother's womb.

Luke 1:17 usage 6
And he shall go before him in the spirit [pneuma] and power of Elias, to turn the hearts of the fathers to the children, and the disobedient to the wisdom of the just; to make ready a people prepared for the Lord.

This is a figurative reference to the old testament spirit John would manifest.

Luke 1:35 usage 1
And the angel answered and said unto her, The Holy Ghost [pneuma] shall come upon thee, and the power of the Highest shall overshadow thee: therefore also that holy thing which shall be born of thee shall be called the Son of God.

Luke 1:41 usage 3
And it came to pass, that, when Elisabeth heard the salutation of Mary, the babe leaped in her womb; and Elisabeth was filled with the Holy Ghost [pneuma]:

Luke 1:47 usage 3
And my spirit [pneuma] hath rejoiced in God my Saviour.

Mary was obviously manifesting old testament spirit here.

Luke 1:67 usage 3
And his father Zacharias was filled with the Holy Ghost [pneuma], and prophesied, saying,

Luke 1:80 usage 6
And the child grew, and waxed strong in spirit [pneuma], and was in the deserts till the day of his shewing unto Israel.

John was born with old testament spirit, which was tailor made and custom built for the job for which it was intended, so this is figurative. See Luke 2:40.

Luke 2:25 usage 3
And, behold, there was a man in Jerusalem, whose name *was* Simeon; and the same man *was* just and devout, waiting for the consolation of Israel: and the Holy Ghost [pneuma] was upon him.

Luke 2:26 usage 3
And it was revealed unto him by the Holy Ghost [pneuma], that he should not see death, before he had seen the Lord's Christ.

Luke 2:27 usage 3
And he came by the Spirit [pneuma] into the temple: and when the parents brought in the child Jesus, to do for him after the custom of the law,

Luke 2:40 usage 6
And the child grew, and waxed strong in spirit [pneuma], filled with wisdom: and the grace of God was upon him.

Most Greek texts omit spirit, but the Aramaic includes it. As Jesus Christ did not receive old testament spirit until he was 30 years old, if left in then this must be a figurative reference similar to Luke 1:80.

Luke 3:16 usage 2
John answered, saying unto *them* all, I indeed baptize you with water; but one mightier than I cometh, the latchet of whose shoes I am not worthy to unloose: he shall baptize you with the Holy Ghost [pneuma] and with fire:

Luke 3:22 usage 3
And the Holy Ghost [pneuma] descended in a bodily shape like a dove upon him, and a voice came from heaven, which said, Thou art my beloved Son; in thee I am well pleased.

Luke 4:1 usage 3, usage 3
And Jesus being full of the Holy Ghost [pneuma] returned from Jordan, and was led by the Spirit [pneuma] into the wilderness,

Luke 4:14 usage 3
And Jesus returned in the power of the Spirit [pneuma] into Galilee: and there went out a fame of him through all the region round about.

Luke 4:18 usage 3
The Spirit [pneuma] of the Lord *is* upon me, because he hath anointed me to preach the gospel to the poor; he hath sent me to heal the brokenhearted, to preach deliverance to the captives, and recovering of sight to the blind, to set at liberty them that are bruised,

Luke 4:33 usage 4
And in the synagogue there was a man, which had a spirit [pneuma] of an unclean devil, and cried out with a loud voice,

Luke 4:36 usage 4
And they were all amazed, and spake among themselves, saying, What a word *is* this! for with authority and power he commandeth the unclean spirits [pneumata], and they come out.

Luke 6:18 usage 4
And they that were vexed with unclean spirits [pneumata]: and they were healed.

Luke 7:21 usage 4
And in that same hour he cured many of *their* infirmities and plagues, and of evil spirits [pneumata]; and unto many *that were* blind he gave sight.

Luke 8:2 usage 4
And certain women, which had been healed of evil spirits [pneumata] and infirmities, Mary called Magdalene, out of whom went seven devils,

Luke 8:29 usage 4
(For he had commanded the unclean spirit [pneuma] to come out of the man. For oftentimes it had caught him: and he was kept bound with chains and in fetters; and he brake the bands, and was driven of the devil into the wilderness.)

Luke 8:55 usage 6
And her spirit [pneuma] came again, and she arose straightway: and he commanded to give her meat.

Luke 9:39 usage 4
And, lo, a spirit [pneuma] taketh him, and he suddenly crieth out; and it teareth him that he foameth again, and bruising him hardly departeth from him.

Luke 9:42 usage 4
And as he was yet a coming, the devil threw him down, and tare *him*. And Jesus rebuked the unclean spirit [pneuma], and healed the child, and delivered him again to his father.

Luke 9:55,56 deleted
But he turned, and rebuked them, ~~and said, Ye know not what manner of spirit ye are of.~~

~~For the Son of man is not come to destroy men's lives, but to save *them*~~. And they went to another village.

According to the majority of Greek texts, verses 55 and 56 should be deleted as indicated.

Luke 10:20 usage 4
Notwithstanding in this rejoice not, that the spirits [pneumata] are subject unto you; but rather rejoice, because your names are written in heaven.

Luke 10:21 usage 3
In that hour Jesus rejoiced in spirit [pneuma], and said, I thank thee, O Father, Lord of heaven and earth, that thou hast hid these things from the wise and prudent, and hast revealed them unto babes: even so, Father; for so it seemed good in thy sight.

Some Greek texts add *hagion* and the preposition *by*. The Aramaic reads *by holy spirit*.

Luke 11:13 usage 3
If ye then, being evil, know how to give good gifts unto your children: how much more shall *your* heavenly Father give the Holy Spirit [pneuma] to them that ask him?

If this were prophetically referring to the coming gift of holy spirit, it would be usage 2, but it appears Jesus Christ was telling these people this spirit he referred to was already available.

Luke 11:24 usage 4
When the unclean spirit [pneuma] is gone out of a man, he walketh through dry places, seeking rest; and finding none, he saith, I will return unto my house whence I came out.

Luke 11:26 usage 4
Then goeth he, and taketh *to him* seven other spirits [pneumata] more wicked than himself; and they enter in, and dwell there: and the last *state* of that man is worse than the first.

Luke 12:10 usage 1
And whosoever shall speak a word against the Son of man, it shall be forgiven him: but unto him that blasphemeth against the Holy Ghost [pneuma] it shall not be forgiven.

Luke 12:12 usage 3
For the Holy Ghost [pneuma] shall teach you in the same hour what ye ought to say.

God teaches his spirit within you and your spirit teaches your mind.

Luke 13:11 usage 4
And, behold, there was a woman which had a spirit [pneuma] of infirmity eighteen years, and was bowed together, and could in no wise lift up *herself.*

Luke 23:46 usage 6
And when Jesus had cried with a loud voice, he said, Father, into thy hands I commend my spirit [pneuma]: and having said thus, he gave up the ghost.

Luke 24:37 usage 4
But they were terrified and affrighted, and supposed that they had seen a spirit [pneuma].

Luke 24:39 usage 4
Behold my hands and my feet, that it is I myself: handle me, and see; for a spirit [pneuma] hath not flesh and bones, as ye see me have.

John 1:32 usage 3
And John bare record, saying, I saw the Spirit [pneuma] descending from heaven like a dove, and it abode upon him.

John 1:33 usage 3, usage 2
And I knew him not: but he that sent me to baptize with water, the same said unto me, Upon whom thou shalt see the Spirit [pneuma] descending, and remaining on him, the same is he which baptizeth with the Holy Ghost [pneuma].

John 3:5 usage 6
Jesus answered, Verily, verily, I say unto thee, Except a man be born of water and *of* the Spirit [pneuma], he cannot enter into the kingdom of God.

This is a figurative usage, hendiadys meaning spiritual water, referring to the coming gift of holy spirit.

> John 3:6 usage 1, usage 2
> That which is born of the flesh is flesh; and that which is born of the Spirit [pneuma] is spirit [pneuma].
>
> John 3:8 usage 1, usage 1
> The wind [pneuma] bloweth where it listeth, and thou hearest the sound thereof, but canst not tell whence it cometh, and whither it goeth: so is every one that is born of the Spirit [pneuma].

This is the only scripture where pneuma is translated wind.

> John 3:34 usage 3
> For he whom God hath sent speaketh the words of God: for God giveth not the Spirit [pneuma] by measure *unto him*.
>
> John 4:23 usage 6
> But the hour cometh, and now is, when the true worshippers shall worship the Father in spirit [pneuma] and in truth: for the Father seeketh such to worship him.

Hendiadys – in spiritual truth.

> John 4:24 usage 1, usage 6
> God *is* a Spirit [pneuma]: and they that worship him must worship *him* in spirit [pneuma] and in truth.

Hendiadys – in spiritual truth.

> John 6:63 usage 3, usage 6
> It is the spirit [pneuma] that quickeneth; the flesh profiteth nothing: the words that I speak unto you, *they* are spirit [pneuma], and *they* are life.

Metonymy – his words were spiritual life.

John 7:39 usage 2, usage 2
(But this spake he of the Spirit [pneuma], which they that believe on him should receive: for the Holy Ghost [pneuma] was not yet *given;* because that Jesus was not yet glorified.)

Obviously referring to the coming gift of holy spirit that came on the day of Pentecost.

John 11:33 usage 3
When Jesus therefore saw her weeping, and the Jews also weeping which came with her, he groaned in the spirit [pneuma], and was troubled,

Jesus was walking by the spirit here. The spirit communicates to us in ways we would understand, like having compassion well up inside being a green light to minister.

John 13:21 usage 3
When Jesus had thus said, he was troubled in spirit [pneuma], and testified, and said, Verily, verily, I say unto you, that one of you shall betray me.

Jesus could not have known this except by revelation.

John 14:17 usage 2
Even the Spirit [pneuma] of truth; whom the world cannot receive, because it seeth him not, neither knoweth him: but ye know him; for he dwelleth with you, and shall be in you.

John 14:26 usage 2
But the Comforter, *which is* the Holy Ghost [pneuma], whom the Father will send in my name, he shall teach you all things, and bring all things to your remembrance, whatsoever I have said unto you.

John 15:26 usage 2
But when the Comforter is come, whom I will send unto you from the Father, *even* the Spirit [pneuma] of truth, which proceedeth from the Father, he shall testify of me:

John 16:13 usage 2
Howbeit when he, the Spirit [pneuma] of truth, is come, he will guide you into all truth: for he shall not speak of himself; but whatsoever he shall hear, *that* shall he speak: and he will shew you things to come.

John 19:30 usage 6
When Jesus therefore had received the vinegar, he said, It is finished: and he bowed his head, and gave up the ghost [pneuma].

John 20:22 usage 2
And when he had said this, he breathed on *them*, and saith unto them, Receive ye the Holy Ghost [pneuma]:

Acts 1:2 usage 3
Until the day in which he was taken up, after that he through the Holy Ghost [pneuma] had given commandments unto the apostles whom he had chosen:

Acts 1:5 usage 2
For John truly baptized with water; but ye shall be baptized with the Holy Ghost [pneuma] not many days hence.

Acts 1:8 usage 2
But ye shall receive power, after that the Holy Ghost [pneuma] is come upon you: and ye shall be witnesses unto me both in Jerusalem, and in all Judaea, and in Samaria, and unto the uttermost part of the earth.

Acts 1:16 usage 3
Men *and* brethren, this scripture must needs have been fulfilled, which the Holy Ghost [pneuma] by the mouth of David spake before concerning Judas, which was guide to them that took Jesus.

Acts 2:4 usage 2, usage 1
And they were all filled with the Holy Ghost [pneuma], and began to speak with other tongues, as the Spirit [pneuma] gave them utterance.

Acts 2:17 usage 3
And it shall come to pass in the last days, saith God, I will pour out of my Spirit [pneuma] upon all flesh: and your sons and your daughters shall prophesy, and your young men shall see visions, and your old men shall dream dreams:

This is a quote from Joel of a prophecy which is still future, so this cannot be referring to the gift of holy spirit. This will be old testament spirit which will again be available to people in the next administration.

Acts 2:18 usage 3
And on my servants and on my handmaidens I will pour out in those days of my Spirit [pneuma]; and they shall prophesy:

Acts 2:33 usage 2
Therefore being by the right hand of God exalted, and having received of the Father the promise of the Holy Ghost [pneuma], he hath shed forth this, which ye now see and hear.

Acts 2:38 usage 2 or 1
Then Peter said unto them, Repent, and be baptized every one of you in the name of Jesus Christ for the remission of sins, and ye shall receive the gift of the Holy Ghost [pneuma].

If this is the gift of God, it is usage 2, if it is the gift from God, it is usage 1.

Acts 4:8 usage 2
Then Peter, filled with the Holy Ghost [pneuma], said unto them, Ye rulers of the people, and elders of Israel,

Acts 4:25 usage 3 (added)
Who by *pneuma hagion* by the mouth of thy servant David hast said, Why did the heathen rage, and the people imagine vain things?

According to the Greek texts and the Aramaic, pneuma hagion is to be added here.

Acts 4:31 usage 2
And when they had prayed, the place was shaken where they were assembled together; and they were all filled with the Holy Ghost [pneuma], and they spake the word of God with boldness.

Acts 5:3 usage 1
But Peter said, Ananias, why hath Satan filled thine heart to lie to the Holy Ghost [pneuma], and to keep back *part* of the price of the land?

Acts 5:9 usage 2
Then Peter said unto her, How is it that ye have agreed together to tempt the Spirit [pneuma] of the Lord? behold, the feet of them which have buried thy husband *are* at the door, and shall carry thee out.

Christ is our Lord, not God, so the spirit of the Lord is the Christ in us.

Acts 5:16 usage 4
There came also a multitude *out* of the cities round about unto Jerusalem, bringing sick folks, and them which were vexed with unclean spirits [pneumata]: and they were healed every one.

Acts 5:32 usage 2
And we are his witnesses of these things; and *so is* also the Holy Ghost [pneuma], whom God hath given to them that obey him.

Acts 6:3 usage 2 and usage 6
Wherefore, brethren, look ye out among you seven men of honest report, full of the Holy Ghost [pneuma] and wisdom, whom we may appoint over this business.

Hendiadys – spiritual wisdom, referring to believers adept at manifesting word of wisdom.

Acts 6:5 usage 2
And the saying pleased the whole multitude: and they chose Stephen, a man full of faith and of the Holy Ghost [pneuma], and Philip, and Prochorus, and Nicanor, and Timon, and Parmenas, and Nicolas a proselyte of Antioch:

Acts 6:10 usage 2
And they were not able to resist the wisdom and the spirit [pneuma] by which he spake.

Acts 7:51 usage 1
Ye stiffnecked and uncircumcised in heart and ears, ye do always resist the Holy Ghost [pneuma]: as your fathers *did*, so *do* ye.

Acts 7:55 usage 2
But he, being full of the Holy Ghost [pneuma], looked up stedfastly into heaven, and saw the glory of God, and Jesus standing on the right hand of God,

Acts 7:59 usage 6
And they stoned Stephen, calling upon *God*, and saying, Lord Jesus, receive my spirit [pneuma].

Acts 8:7 usage 4
For unclean spirits [pneumata], crying with loud voice, came out of many that were possessed *with them:* and many taken with palsies, and that were lame, were healed.

Acts 8:15 usage 2
Who, when they were come down, prayed for them, that they might receive the Holy Ghost [pneuma]:

Acts 8:17 usage 2
Then laid they *their* hands on them, and they received the Holy Ghost [pneuma].

Acts 8:18 usage 2
And when Simon saw that through laying on of the apostles' hands the Holy Ghost [pneuma] was given, he offered them money,

Acts 8:19 usage 2
Saying, Give me also this power, that on whomsoever I lay hands, he may receive the Holy Ghost [pneuma].

Acts 8:29 usage 2
Then the Spirit [pneuma] said unto Philip, Go near, and join thyself to this chariot.

Acts 8:39 usage 2
And when they were come up out of the water, the Spirit [pneuma] of the Lord caught away Philip, that the eunuch saw him no more: and he went on his way rejoicing.

Jesus Christ is our Lord and being head over all things to the church this would have been his responsibility. As it is Christ in us the hope of glory, this is referring to that Christ in us.

Acts 9:17 usage 2
And Ananias went his way, and entered into the house; and putting his hands on him said, Brother Saul, the Lord, *even* Jesus, that appeared unto thee in the way as thou camest, hath sent me, that thou mightest receive thy sight, and be filled with the Holy Ghost [pneuma].

Acts 9:31 usage 2
Then had the churches rest throughout all Judaea and Galilee and Samaria, and were edified; and walking in the fear of the Lord, and in the comfort of the Holy Ghost [pneuma], were multiplied.

Acts 10:19 usage 2
While Peter thought on the vision, the Spirit [pneuma] said unto him, Behold, three men seek thee.

Acts 10:38 usage 3 and usage 6
How God anointed Jesus of Nazareth with the Holy Ghost [pneuma] and with power: who went about doing good, and healing all that were oppressed of the devil; for God was with him.

Hendiadys – spiritual power.

Acts 10:44 usage 2
While Peter yet spake these words, the Holy Ghost [pneuma] fell on all them which heard the word.

Acts 10:45 usage 2
And they of the circumcision which believed were astonished, as many as came with Peter, because that on the Gentiles also was poured out the gift of the Holy Ghost [pneuma].

Acts 10:47 usage 2
Can any man forbid water, that these should not be baptized, which have received the Holy Ghost [pneuma] as well as we?

Acts 11:12 usage 2
And the Spirit [pneuma] bade me go with them, nothing doubting. Moreover these six brethren accompanied me, and we entered into the man's house:

Acts 11:15 usage 2
And as I began to speak, the Holy Ghost [pneuma] fell on them, as on us at the beginning.

Acts 11:16 usage 2
Then remembered I the word of the Lord, how that he said, John indeed baptized with water; but ye shall be baptized with the Holy Ghost [pneuma].

Acts 11:24 usage 2
For he was a good man, and full of the Holy Ghost [pneuma] and of faith: and much people was added unto the Lord.

Acts 11:28 usage 2
And there stood up one of them named Agabus, and signified by the Spirit [pneuma] that there should be great dearth throughout all the world: which came to pass in the days of Claudius Caesar.

Acts 13:2 usage 2
As they ministered to the Lord, and fasted, the Holy Ghost [pneuma] said, Separate me Barnabas and Saul for the work whereunto I have called them.

Acts 13:4 usage 2
So they, being sent forth by the Holy Ghost [pneuma], departed unto Seleucia; and from thence they sailed to Cyprus.

Acts 13:9 usage 2
Then Saul, (who also *is called* Paul,) filled with the Holy Ghost [pneuma], set his eyes on him,

Acts 13:52 usage 2
And the disciples were filled with joy, and with the Holy Ghost [pneuma].

Acts 15:8 usage 2
And God, which knoweth the hearts, bare them witness, giving them the Holy Ghost [pneuma], even as *he did* unto us;

Acts 15:28 usage 2
For it seemed good to the Holy Ghost [pneuma], and to us, to lay upon you no greater burden than these necessary things;

Acts 16:6 usage 2
Now when they had gone throughout Phrygia and the region of Galatia, and were forbidden of the Holy Ghost [pneuma] to preach the word in Asia,

Acts 16:7 usage 2
After they were come to Mysia, they assayed to go into Bithynia: but the Spirit [pneuma] suffered them not.

Acts 16:16 usage 4
And it came to pass, as we went to prayer, a certain damsel possessed with a spirit [pneuma] of divination met us, which brought her masters much gain by soothsaying:

Acts 16:18 usage 4
And this did she many days. But Paul, being grieved, turned and said to the spirit [pneuma], I command thee in the name of Jesus Christ to come out of her. And he came out the same hour.

Acts 17:16 usage 2
Now while Paul waited for them at Athens, his spirit [pneuma] was stirred in him, when he saw the city wholly given to idolatry.

Acts 18:5 deleted
And when Silas and Timotheus were come from Macedonia, Paul was pressed in the ~~spirit~~, and testified to the Jews *that* Jesus *was* Christ.

The Aramaic and all the Greek texts except Stephens omit pneuma, and read Paul was engrossed in the word. The Darby bible translates the verse thus:

Acts 18:5
And when both Silas and Timotheus came down from Macedonia, Paul was pressed in respect of the word, testifying to the Jews that Jesus was the Christ.

Acts 18:25 usage 6
This man was instructed in the way of the Lord; and being fervent in the spirit [pneuma], he spake and taught diligently the things of the Lord, knowing only the baptism of John.

... being fervent spiritually...

Acts 19:2 usage 2, usage 2
He said unto them, Have ye received the Holy Ghost [pneuma] since ye believed? And they said unto him, We have not so much as heard whether there be any Holy Ghost [pneuma].

Acts 19:6 usage 2
And when Paul had laid *his* hands upon them, the Holy Ghost [pneuma] came on them; and they spake with tongues, and prophesied.

Acts 19:12 usage 4
So that from his body were brought unto the sick handkerchiefs or aprons, and the diseases departed from them, and the evil spirits [pneumata] went out of them.

Acts 19:13 usage 4
Then certain of the vagabond Jews, exorcists, took upon them to call over them which had evil spirits [pneumata] the name of the Lord Jesus, saying, We adjure you by Jesus whom Paul preacheth.

Acts 19:15 usage 4
And the evil spirit [pneuma] answered and said, Jesus I know, and Paul I know; but who are ye?

Acts 19:16 usage 4
And the man in whom the evil spirit [pneuma] was leaped on them, and overcame them, and prevailed against them, so that they fled out of that house naked and wounded.

Acts 19:21 usage 6
After these things were ended, Paul purposed in the spirit [pneuma], when he had passed through Macedonia and Achaia, to go to Jerusalem, saying, After I have been there, I must also see Rome.

Aramaic uses reyana for mind and not rucha for spirit. If pneuma is left, it must be regarded as figurative usage for his mind because God certainly did not want Paul going to Jerusalem.

Acts 20:22 usage 2
And now, behold, I go bound in the spirit [pneuma] unto Jerusalem, not knowing the things that shall befall me there:

Acts20:23 usage 2
Save that the Holy Ghost [pneuma] witnesseth in every city, saying that bonds and afflictions abide me.

Acts 20:28 usage 2
Take heed therefore unto yourselves, and to all the flock, over the which the Holy Ghost [pneuma] hath made you overseers, to feed the church of God, which he hath purchased with his own blood.

The pronoun he in which he hath purchased can be tracked back through the verse to be associated with the holy spirit. As this holy spirit purchased the church of God with his own blood, it must refer to Christ. The holy spirit is Christ in us. As Christ is head over all things to the church, selecting overseers would be his responsibility. This must be referring to the Christ in us.

Acts 21:4 usage 2
And finding disciples, we tarried there seven days: who said to Paul through the Spirit [pneuma], that he should not go up to Jerusalem.

Acts 21:11 usage 2
And when he was come unto us, he took Paul's girdle, and bound his own hands and feet, and said, Thus saith the Holy Ghost [pneuma], So shall the Jews at Jerusalem bind the man that owneth this girdle, and shall deliver *him* into the hands of the Gentiles.

Acts 23:8 usage 2 and 3
For the Sadducees say that there is no resurrection, neither angel, nor spirit [pneuma]: but the Pharisees confess both.

This can't be referring to angles because angels are already listed, so it must be referring to both old testament and grace administration holy spirit.

Acts 23:9 usage 2 or 3.
And there arose a great cry: and the scribes *that were* of the Pharisees' part arose, and strove, saying, We find no evil in this man: but if a spirit [pneuma] or an angel hath spoken to him, let us not fight against God.

The Pharisees didn't understand spiritual matters, so this is a general reference to any spirit available to man, but they certainly wouldn't have inferred a devil spirit.

Acts 28:25 usage 1
And when they agreed not among themselves, they departed, after that Paul had spoken one word, Well spake the Holy Ghost [pneuma] by Esaias the prophet unto our fathers,

Christ wasn't around in Isaiah's time, he wasn't head over all things to the church then, and there was no gift of holy spirit, so this must be referring to God.

Romans 1:4 usage 1
And declared *to be* the Son of God with power, according to the spirit [pneuma] of holiness, by the resurrection from the dead:

Romans 1:9 usage 6
For God is my witness, whom I serve with my spirit [pneuma] in the gospel of his Son, that without ceasing I make mention of you always in my prayers;

Romans 2:29 usage 2
But he *is* a Jew, which is one inwardly; and circumcision *is that* of the heart, in the spirit [pneuma], *and* not in the letter; whose praise *is* not of men, but of God.

This usage of spirit contrasts the Christ in us with the law administration.

Romans 5:5 usage 2
And hope maketh not ashamed; because the love of God is shed abroad in our hearts by the Holy Ghost [pneuma] which is given unto us.

Romans 7:6 usage 2
But now we are delivered from the law, that being dead wherein we were held; that we should serve in newness of spirit [pneuma], and not *in* the oldness of the letter.

This usage of spirit contrasts the Christ in us with the law administration.

Romans 8:1 deleted
There is therefore now no condemnation to them which are in Christ Jesus, ~~who walk not after the flesh, but after the Spirit.~~

The balance of the verse from Christ Jesus is omitted. Spirit is also omitted in the Aramaic.

Romans 8:2 usage 2
For the law of the Spirit [pneuma] of life in Christ Jesus hath made me free from the law of sin and death.

This usage of spirit contrasts the Christ in us with the law administration.

> Romans 8:4 usage 2
> That the righteousness of the law might be fulfilled in us, who walk not after the flesh, but after the Spirit [pneuma].
>
> Romans 8:5 usage 2, usage 2
> For they that are after the flesh do mind the things of the flesh; but they that are after the Spirit [pneuma] the things of the Spirit [pneuma].
>
> Romans 8:6 usage 2
> For to be carnally minded *is* death; but to be spiritually [pneuma] minded *is* life and peace.

To mind the things of the spirit, as verse 5.

> Romans 8:9 usage 2, usage 2, usage 2
> But ye are not in the flesh, but in the Spirit [pneuma], if so be that the Spirit [pneuma] of God dwell in you. Now if any man have not the Spirit [pneuma] of Christ, he is none of his.
>
> Romans 8:10 usage 2
> And if Christ *be* in you, the body *is* dead because of sin; but the Spirit [pneuma] *is* life because of righteousness.
>
> Romans 8:11 usage 2, usage 2
> But if the Spirit [pneuma] of him that raised up Jesus from the dead dwell in you, he that raised up Christ from the dead shall also quicken your mortal bodies by his Spirit [pneuma] that dwelleth in you.
>
> Romans 8:13 usage 2
> For if ye live after the flesh, ye shall die: but if ye through the Spirit [pneuma] do mortify the deeds of the body, ye shall live.

How you mortify the deeds of the body is by walking by the spirit, not by renewing your mind. Without using it to walk by the spirit, renewing the mind is just a work of the flesh, a five senses ability, and there is nothing spiritual about it.

Romans 8:14 usage 2
For as many as are led by the Spirit [pneuma] of God, they are the sons of God.

Romans 8:15 usage 4, usage 2
For ye have not received the spirit [pneuma] of bondage again to fear; but ye have received the Spirit [pneuma] of adoption, whereby we cry, Abba, Father.

Romans 8:16 usage 1, usage 2
The Spirit [pneuma] itself beareth witness with our spirit [pneuma], that we are the children of God:

Romans 8:23 usage 2
And not only *they*, but ourselves also, which have the firstfruits of the Spirit [pneuma], even we ourselves groan within ourselves, waiting for the adoption, *to wit*, the redemption of our body.

Christ is the first fruits, and it is Christ in us, and Christ is the head over all things to the church.

Romans 8:26 usage 2, usage 2
Likewise the Spirit [pneuma] also helpeth our infirmities: for we know not what we should pray for as we ought: but the Spirit [pneuma] itself maketh intercession for us with groanings which cannot be uttered.

Romans 8:27 usage 2
And he that searcheth the hearts knoweth what *is* the mind of the Spirit [pneuma], because he [it] maketh intercession for the saints according to *the will of* God.

He that searches the hearts is God, and God knows the mind of our spirit which makes intercession for us, as stated in verse 26, therefore, it must be the same usage as verse 26.

Romans 9:1 usage 2
I say the truth in Christ, I lie not, my conscience also bearing me witness in the Holy Ghost [pneuma],

Romans 11:8 usage 4
(According as it is written, God hath given them the spirit [pneuma] of slumber, eyes that they should not see, and ears that they should not hear;) unto this day.

Romans 12:11 usage 2
Not slothful in business; fervent in spirit [pneuma]; serving the Lord;

Spiritually fervent by manifesting holy spirit and walking by the spirit, for that is how you serve the Lord who is the head over all things to the church.

Romans14:17 usage 2
For the kingdom of God is not meat and drink; but righteousness, and peace, and joy in the Holy Ghost [pneuma].

Romans 15:13 usage 2
Now the God of hope fill you with all joy and peace in believing, that ye may abound in hope, through the power of the Holy Ghost [pneuma].

Romans 15:16 usage 2
That I should be the minister of Jesus Christ to the Gentiles, ministering the gospel of God, that the offering up of the Gentiles might be acceptable, being sanctified by the Holy Ghost [pneuma].

It is God who sanctifies us, yes, but it is by having the gift of holy spirit that we are sanctified, set apart, hence usage 2.

Romans 15:19 usage 2
Through mighty signs and wonders, by the power of the Spirit [pneuma] of God; so that from Jerusalem, and round about unto Illyricum, I have fully preached the gospel of Christ.

Romans 15:30 usage 2
Now I beseech you, brethren, for the Lord Jesus Christ's sake, and for the love of the Spirit [pneuma], that ye strive together with me in *your* prayers to God for me;

Walking *by* the Spirit

The Lord Jesus Christ is head over all things to the church, and it is Christ in us. It is our love for the Lord and our love to walk by the spirit with him as our head that this is referring to.

1 Corinthians 2:4 usage 2
And my speech and my preaching *was* not with enticing words of man's wisdom, but in demonstration of the Spirit [pneuma] and of power:

Hendiadys is also employed – spiritual power.

1 Corinthians 2:10 usage 2, usage 2
But God hath revealed *them* unto us by his Spirit [pneuma]: for the Spirit [pneuma] searcheth all things, yea, the deep things of God.

1 Corinthians 2:11 usage 6, usage 2
For what man knoweth the things of a man, save the spirit [pneuma] of man which is in him? even so the things of God knoweth no man, but the Spirit [pneuma] of God.

1 Corinthians 2:12 usage 4, usage 2
Now we have received, not the spirit [pneuma] of the world, but the spirit [pneuma] which is of God; that we might know the things that are freely given to us of God.

1 Corinthians 2:13 usage 2
Which things also we speak, not in the words which man's wisdom teacheth, but which the Holy Ghost [pneuma] teacheth; comparing spiritual things with spiritual.

Holy (hagion) is omitted in all Greek texts except Stephens, and also in the Aramaic.

1 Corinthians 2:14 usage 2
But the natural man receiveth not the things of the Spirit [pneuma] of God: for they are foolishness unto him: neither can he know *them*, because they are spiritually discerned.

Natural man who is not born again cannot receive anything of the gift of holy spirit because he does not have it. However, natural man can receive things from God like healing, as well as the gift of holy spirit itself in the new birth, so this must be referring to his gift.

> 1 Corinthians 3:16 usage 2
> Know ye not that ye are the temple of God, and *that* the Spirit [pneuma] of God dwelleth in you?

> 1 Corinthians 4:21 usage 6
> What will ye? shall I come unto you with a rod, or in love, and *in* the spirit [pneuma] of meekness?

> 1 Corinthians 5:3 usage 2
> For I verily, as absent in body, but present in spirit [pneuma], have judged already, as though I were present, *concerning* him that hath so done this deed,

> 1 Corinthians 5:4 usage 2
> In the name of our Lord Jesus Christ, when ye are gathered together, and my spirit [pneuma], with the power of our Lord Jesus Christ,

This has to be the same usage as verse 3.

> 1 Corinthians 5:5 usage 2
> To deliver such an one unto Satan for the destruction of the flesh, that the spirit [pneuma] may be saved in the day of the Lord Jesus.

> 1 Corinthians 6:11 usage 2
> And such were some of you: but ye are washed, but ye are sanctified, but ye are justified in the name of the Lord Jesus, and by the Spirit [pneuma] of our God.

It is the gift of holy spirit that sanctifies us, sets us apart, and which justifies us, so this is usage 2.

> 1 Corinthians 6:17 usage 2
> But he that is joined unto the Lord is one spirit [pneuma].

1 Corinthians 6:19 usage 2
What? know ye not that your body is the temple of the Holy Ghost [pneuma] *which is* in you, which ye have of God, and ye are not your own?

1 Corinthians 6:20 omitted
For ye are bought with a price: therefore glorify God in your body, ~~and in your spirit [pneuma], which are God's~~.

All Greek texts except Stephens omit the word pneuma. It is in the Aramaic.

1 Corinthians 7:34 usage 6
There is difference *also* between a wife and a virgin. The unmarried woman careth for the things of the Lord, that she may be holy both in body and in spirit [pneuma]: but she that is married careth for the things of the world, how she may please *her* husband.

1 Corinthians 7:40 usage 2
But she is happier if she so abide, after my judgment: and I think also that I have the Spirit [pneuma] of God.

1 Corinthians 12:3 usage 2, usage 2
Wherefore I give you to understand, that no man speaking by the Spirit [pneuma] of God calleth Jesus accursed: and *that* no man can say that Jesus is the Lord, but by the Holy Ghost [pneuma].

1 Corinthians 12:4 usage 1
Now there are diversities of gifts, but the same Spirit [pneuma].

1 Corinthians 12:7 usage 2
But the manifestation of the Spirit [pneuma] is given to every man to profit withal.

1 Corinthians 12:8 usage 2, usage 2
For to one is given by the Spirit [pneuma] the word of wisdom; to another the word of knowledge by the same Spirit [pneuma];

The immediate context is the profit of the manifestation of the gift of holy spirit.

1 Corinthians 12:9 usage 2, usage 2
To another faith by the same Spirit [pneuma]; to another the gifts of healing by the same Spirit [pneuma];

1 Corinthians 12:10 usage 2,4 and 5
To another the working of miracles; to another prophecy; to another discerning of spirits [pneumata]; to another *divers* kinds of tongues; to another the interpretation of tongues:

It is discerning of any kind of spirit.

1 Corinthians 12:11 usage 2
But all these worketh that one and the selfsame Spirit [pneuma], dividing to every man severally as he will.

All the profits of the manifestation come to us by energising the gift of holy spirit.

1 Corinthians 12:13 usage 2, usage 2
For by one Spirit [pneuma] are we all baptized into one body, whether *we be* Jews or Gentiles, whether *we be* bond or free; and have been all made to drink into one Spirit [pneuma].

1 Corinthians 14:2 usage 2
For he that speaketh in an *unknown* tongue speaketh not unto men, but unto God: for no man understandeth *him;* howbeit in the spirit [pneuma] he speaketh mysteries.

1 Corinthians 14:12 usage 2
Even so ye, forasmuch as ye are zealous of spiritual [pneumata] *gifts* seek that ye may excel to the edifying of the church.

How you edify believers in a home church meeting is by being zealous of things of the spirit, the gift of holy spirit in manifestation.

1 Corinthians 14:14 usage 2
For if I pray in an *unknown* tongue, my spirit [pneuma] prayeth, but my understanding is unfruitful.

1 Corinthians 14:15 usage 2, usage 2
What is it then? I will pray with the spirit [pneuma], and I will pray with the understanding also: I will sing with the spirit [pneuma], and I will sing with the understanding also.

1 Corinthians 14:16 usage 2
Else when thou shalt bless with the spirit [pneuma], how shall he that occupieth the room of the unlearned say Amen at thy giving of thanks, seeing he understandeth not what thou sayest?

1 Corinthians 14:32 usage 2
And the spirits [pneumata] of the prophets are subject to the prophets.

1 Corinthians 15:45 usage 7
And so it is written, The first man Adam was made a living soul; the last Adam *was made* a quickening spirit [pneuma].

1 Corinthians 16:18 usage 6
For they have refreshed my spirit [pneuma] and yours: therefore acknowledge ye them that are such.

2 Corinthians 1:22 usage 2
Who hath also sealed us, and given the earnest of the Spirit [pneuma] in our hearts.

2 Corinthians 2:13 usage 2
I had no rest in my spirit [pneuma], because I found not Titus my brother: but taking my leave of them, I went from thence into Macedonia.

It was the spirit energising within Paul. God energises that spirit within us to give us information. This is a good example of it. Paul could very well have felt peace inside at not finding Titus there, which would have been the spirit giving him different directions.

2 Corinthians 3:3 usage 2
Forasmuch as ye are manifestly declared to be the epistle of Christ ministered by us, written not with ink, but with the Spirit [pneuma]

of the living God; not in tables of stone, but in fleshy tables of the heart.

It is the walking by the spirit within us that declares us to be epistles of Christ.

2 Corinthians 3:6 usage 2, usage 2
Who also hath made us able ministers of the new testament; not of the letter, but of the spirit [pneuma]: for the letter killeth, but the spirit [pneuma] giveth life.

2 Corinthians 3:8 usage 2
How shall not the ministration of the spirit [pneuma] be rather glorious?

2 Corinthians 3:17 usage 2. usage 2
Now the Lord is that Spirit [pneuma]: and where the Spirit [pneuma] of the Lord *is,* there *is* liberty.

Jesus Christ is our Lord, and he is the head over all things to the church.

2 Corinthians 3:18 usage 2
But we all, with open face beholding as in a glass the glory of the Lord, are changed into the same image from glory to glory, *even* as by the Spirit [pneuma] of the Lord.

2 Corinthians 4:13 usage 2
We having the same spirit [pneuma] of faith, according as it is written, I believed, and therefore have I spoken; we also believe, and therefore speak;

2 Corinthians 5:5 usage 2
Now he that hath wrought us for the selfsame thing *is* God, who also hath given unto us the earnest of the Spirit [pneuma].

2 Corinthians 6:6 usage 2
By pureness, by knowledge, by longsuffering, by kindness, by the Holy Ghost [pneuma], by love unfeigned,

2 Corinthians 7:1 usage 6
Having therefore these promises, dearly beloved, let us cleanse ourselves from all filthiness of the flesh and spirit [pneuma], perfecting holiness in the fear of God.

Synecdoche. We cannot corrupt the gift of holy spirit.

2 Corinthians 7:13 usage 6
Therefore we were comforted in your comfort: yea, and exceedingly the more joyed we for the joy of Titus, because his spirit [pneuma] was refreshed by you all.

2 Corinthians 11:4 usage 4
For if he that cometh preacheth another Jesus, whom we have not preached, or *if* ye receive another spirit [pneuma], which ye have not received, or another gospel, which ye have not accepted, ye might well bear with *him.*

2 Corinthians 12:18 usage 2
I desired Titus, and with *him* I sent a brother. Did Titus make a gain of you? walked we not in the same spirit [pneuma]? *walked we* not in the same steps?

If we all walk by the spirit with Christ as our head, we walk together in the same mind, in the same spirit.

2 Corinthians 13:14 usage 2
The grace of the Lord Jesus Christ, and the love of God, and the communion of the Holy Ghost [pneuma], *be* with you all. Amen.

Galatians 3:2 usage 2
This only would I learn of you, Received ye the Spirit [pneuma] by the works of the law, or by the hearing of faith?

Galatians 3:3 usage 2
Are ye so foolish? having begun in the Spirit [pneuma], are ye now made perfect by the flesh?

Galatians 3:5 usage 2
He therefore that ministereth to you the Spirit [pneuma], and worketh miracles among you, *doeth he it* by the works of the law, or by the hearing of faith?

Galatians 3:14 usage 2
That the blessing of Abraham might come on the Gentiles through Jesus Christ; that we might receive the promise of the Spirit [pneuma] through faith.

Galatians 4:6 usage 2
And because ye are sons, God hath sent forth the Spirit [pneuma] of his Son into your hearts, crying, Abba, Father.

Galatians 4:29 usage 1
But as then he that was born after the flesh persecuted him *that was born* after the Spirit [pneuma], even so *it is* now.

Ishmael was born because Abraham walked by the senses, but Isaac was born because he walked by the spirit of God which was upon him and because of what God did for Sarah.

Galatians 5:5 usage 2
For we through the Spirit [pneuma] wait for the hope of righteousness by faith.

Galatians 5:16 usage 2
This I say then, Walk in the Spirit [pneuma], and ye shall not fulfil the lust of the flesh.

Galatians 5:17 usage 2, usage 2
For the flesh lusteth against the Spirit [pneuma], and the Spirit [pneuma] against the flesh: and these are contrary the one to the other: so that ye cannot do the things that ye would.

Galatians 5:18 usage 2
But if ye be led of the Spirit [pneuma], ye are not under the law.

Galatians 5:22 usage 2
But the fruit of the Spirit [pneuma] is love, joy, peace, longsuffering, gentleness, goodness, faith,

Galatians 5:25 usage 2, usage 2
If we live in the Spirit [pneuma], let us also walk in the Spirit [pneuma].

Galatians 6:1 usage 2
Brethren, if a man be overtaken in a fault, ye which are spiritual, restore such an one in the spirit [pneuma] of meekness; considering thyself, lest thou also be tempted.

How you restore someone is by being spiritual and walking by the spirit. It isn't a five senses ability.

Galatians 6:8 usage 2, usage 1
For he that soweth to his flesh shall of the flesh reap corruption; but he that soweth to the Spirit [pneuma] shall of the Spirit [pneuma] reap life everlasting.

Galatians 6:18 usage 2
Brethren, the grace of our Lord Jesus Christ *be* with your spirit [pneuma]. Amen.

Nothing spiritual has anything to do with the five senses. It is because of the gift of holy spirit that we have the grace of our Lord Jesus Christ.

Ephesians 1:13 usage 2
In whom ye also *trusted*, after that ye heard the word of truth, the gospel of your salvation: in whom also after that ye believed, ye were sealed with that holy Spirit [pneuma] of promise,

Ephesians 1:17 usage 2
That the God of our Lord Jesus Christ, the Father of glory, may give unto you the spirit [pneuma] of wisdom and revelation in the knowledge of him:

Spiritual wisdom refers to the manifestation of word of wisdom, which is a manifestation of the gift of holy spirit.

> Ephesians 2:2 usage 4
> Wherein in time past ye walked according to the course of this world, according to the prince of the power of the air, the spirit [pneuma] that now worketh in the children of disobedience:
>
> Ephesians 2:18 usage 2
> For through him we both have access by one Spirit [pneuma] unto the Father.
>
> Ephesians 2:22 usage 2
> In whom ye also are builded together for an habitation of God through the Spirit [pneuma].
>
> Ephesians 3:5 usage 2
> Which in other ages was not made known unto the sons of men, as it is now revealed unto his holy apostles and prophets by the Spirit [pneuma];
>
> Ephesians 3:16 usage 2
> That he would grant you, according to the riches of his glory, to be strengthened with might by his Spirit [pneuma] in the inner man;
>
> Ephesians 4:3 usage 2
> Endeavouring to keep the unity of the Spirit [pneuma] in the bond of peace.

Keeping the unity of spirit has nothing whatsoever to do with the five senses, it is exclusively a spiritual quality only those who walk by the spirit with Christ as their head can accomplish. This has absolutely nothing whatsoever to do with getting along with everyone in a temple made with hands.

> Eph 4:4 usage 2
> *There is* one body, and one Spirit [pneuma], even as ye are called in one hope of your calling;

Ephesians 4:23 usage 6
And be renewed in the spirit [pneuma] of your mind;

Ephesians 4:30 usage 2
And grieve not the holy Spirit [pneuma] of God, whereby ye are sealed unto the day of redemption.

We are sealed unto the day of redemption because of the gift of holy spirit.

Ephesians 5:9 deleted
(For the fruit of the ~~Spirit~~ light *is* in all goodness and righteousness and truth;)

Ephesians 5:18 usage 2
And be not drunk with wine, wherein is excess; but be filled with the Spirit [pneuma];

Ephesians 6:17 usage 1
And take the helmet of salvation, and the sword of the Spirit [pneuma], which is the word of God:

Ephesians 6:18 usage 2
Praying always with all prayer and supplication in the Spirit [pneuma], and watching thereunto with all perseverance and supplication for all saints;

Philippians 1:19 usage 2
For I know that this shall turn to my salvation through your prayer, and the supply of the Spirit [pneuma] of Jesus Christ,

Philippians 1:27 usage 2
Only let your conversation be as it becometh the gospel of Christ: that whether I come and see you, or else be absent, I may hear of your affairs, that ye stand fast in one spirit [pneuma], with one mind striving together for the faith of the gospel;

Keeping the unity of spirit has nothing whatsoever to do with the five senses, it is exclusively a spiritual quality only those who walk by the spirit with

Christ as their head can accomplish. This has absolutely nothing whatsoever to do with getting along with everyone in a temple made with hands.

> Philippians 2:1 usage 2
> If *there be* therefore any consolation in Christ, if any comfort of love, if any fellowship of the Spirit [pneuma], if any bowels and mercies,
>
> Philippians 3:3 usage 2
> For we are the circumcision, which worship God in the spirit [pneuma], and rejoice in Christ Jesus, and have no confidence in the flesh.
>
> Philippians 4:23 added usage 2
> The grace of our Lord Jesus Christ *be* with your spirit [pneuma] Amen.

The grace of our Lord Jesus Christ can only be with us through the gift of holy spirit.

> Colossians 1:8 usage 2
> Who also declared unto us your love in the Spirit [pneuma].

This agapē love is a spiritual quality that only comes by energising the gift of holy spirit.

> Colossians 2:5 usage 2
> For though I be absent in the flesh, yet am I with you in the spirit [pneuma], joying and beholding your order, and the stedfastness of your faith in Christ.
>
> 1 Thessalonians 1:5 usage 2
> For our gospel came not unto you in word only, but also in power, and in the Holy Ghost [pneuma], and in much assurance; as ye know what manner of men we were among you for your sake.
>
> 1 Thessalonians 1:6 usage 2
> And ye became followers of us, and of the Lord, having received the word in much affliction, with joy of the Holy Ghost [pneuma]:

1 Thessalonians 4:8 usage 2
He therefore that despiseth, despiseth not man, but God, who hath also given unto us his holy Spirit [pneuma].

1 Thessalonians 5:19 usage 2
Quench not the Spirit [pneuma].

1 Thessalonians 5:23 usage 2
And the very God of peace sanctify you wholly; and *I pray God* your whole spirit [pneuma] and soul and body be preserved blameless unto the coming of our Lord Jesus Christ.

2 Thessalonians 2:2 usage 4
That ye be not soon shaken in mind, or be troubled, neither by spirit [pneuma], nor by word, nor by letter as from us, as that the day of Christ is at hand.

2 Thessalonians 2:8 usage 6
And then shall that Wicked be revealed, whom the Lord shall consume with the spirit [pneuma] of his mouth, and shall destroy with the brightness of his coming:

An idiom for *breath of our Lord Jesus Christ*.

2 Thessalonians 2:13 usage 2
But we are bound to give thanks alway to God for you, brethren beloved of the Lord, because God hath from the beginning chosen you to salvation through sanctification of the Spirit [pneuma] and belief of the truth:

1 Timothy 3:16 usage 3
And without controversy great is the mystery of godliness: ~~God~~ (which) was manifest in the flesh, justified in the Spirit [pneuma], seen of angels, preached unto the Gentiles, believed on in the world, received up into glory.

The word God is a pagan trinitarian forgery.

1 Timothy 4:1 usage 2, usage 4
Now the Spirit [pneuma] speaketh expressly, that in the latter times some shall depart from the faith, giving heed to seducing spirits [pneumata], and doctrines of devils;

Paul received this revelation through the gift of holy spirit, so it is usage 2. God teaches his spirit within you, which is that Christ in you, and your spirit teaches your mind.

1 Timothy 4:12 deleted
Let no man despise thy youth; but be thou an example of the believers, in word, in conversation, in charity, ~~in spirit~~, in faith, in purity.

Omitted in all critical Greek texts except Stephens, and also omitted in the Aramaic.

2 Timothy 1:7 usage 4
For God hath not given us the spirit [pneuma] of fear; but of power, and of love, and of a sound mind.

2 Timothy 1:14 usage 2
That good thing which was committed unto thee keep by the Holy Ghost [pneuma] which dwelleth in us.

2 Timothy 4:22 usage 2
The Lord Jesus Christ *be* with thy spirit [pneuma]. Grace *be* with you. Amen.

Titus 3:5 usage 2
Not by works of righteousness which we have done, but according to his mercy he saved us, by the washing of regeneration, and renewing of the Holy Ghost [pneuma];

Philemon 25 usage 2
The grace of our Lord Jesus Christ *be* with your spirit [pneuma]. Amen.

Hebrews 1:7 usage 5
And of the angels he saith, Who maketh his angels spirits [pneumata], and his ministers a flame of fire.

Hebrews 1:14 usage 5
Are they not all ministering spirits [pneumata], sent forth to minister for them who shall be heirs of salvation?

Hebrews 2:4 usage 3
God also bearing *them* witness, both with signs and wonders, and with divers miracles, and gifts of the Holy Ghost [pneuma], according to his own will?

Hebrews 1:1 begins the context informing us that God spoke in times past to the old testament believers through their prophets, referring to old testament spirit. The context hasn't changed to the gift of holy spirit since then. Paul is addressing Hebrews, those zealous for law, and is using their understanding of the old testament to teach.

Hebrews 3:7 usage 3
Wherefore (as the Holy Ghost [pneuma] saith, To day if ye will hear his voice,

Referring to prophesies given to men with old testament spirit.

Hebrews 4:12 usage 2 and 3
For the word of God *is* quick, and powerful, and sharper than any twoedged sword, piercing even to the dividing asunder of soul and spirit [pneuma], and of the joints and marrow, and *is* a discerner of the thoughts and intents of the heart.

Hebrews 6:4 usage 2
For *it is* impossible for those who were once enlightened, and have tasted of the heavenly gift, and were made partakers of the Holy Ghost [pneuma],

Hebrews 9:8 usage 1
The Holy Ghost [pneuma] this signifying, that the way into the holiest of all was not yet made manifest, while as the first tabernacle was yet standing:

Hebrews 9:14 usage 3
How much more shall the blood of Christ, who through the eternal Spirit [pneuma] offered himself without spot to God, purge your conscience from dead works to serve the living God?

It was acting on revelation given to the spirit upon him that Christ offered himself to God. If it were usage 1 it would read, who through God offered himself to God, *which doesn't make much sense.*

Hebrews 10:15 usage 2
Whereof the Holy Ghost [pneuma] also is a witness to us: for after that he had said before,

Hebrews 10:29 usage 2
Of how much sorer punishment, suppose ye, shall he be thought worthy, who hath trodden under foot the Son of God, and hath counted the blood of the covenant, wherewith he was sanctified, an unholy thing, and hath done despite unto the Spirit [pneuma] of grace?

The spirit we receive by grace is the gift of holy spirit.

Hebrews 12:9 usage 2
Furthermore we have had fathers of our flesh which corrected *us*, and we gave *them* reverence: shall we not much rather be in subjection unto the Father of spirits [pneumata], and live?

Hebrews 12:23 usage 2
To the general assembly and church of the firstborn, which are written in heaven, and to God the Judge of all, and to the spirits [pneumata] of just men made perfect,

James 2:26 usage 2
For as the body without the spirit [pneuma] is dead, so faith without works is dead also.

Body with soul is dead according to the word, so this is referring to the gift of holy spirit which makes us alive. It also follows then that these works refer

Walking *by* the Spirit

to demonstrating God's power by energising that gift of holy spirit, not any works of the flesh.

James 4:5 usage 6
Do ye think that the scripture saith in vain, The spirit [pneuma] that dwelleth in us lusteth to envy?

1 Peter 1:2 usage 2
Elect according to the foreknowledge of God the Father, through sanctification of the Spirit [pneuma], unto obedience and sprinkling of the blood of Jesus Christ: Grace unto you, and peace, be multiplied.

1 Peter 1:11 usage 3
Searching what, or what manner of time the Spirit [pneuma] of Christ which was in them did signify, when it testified beforehand the sufferings of Christ, and the glory that should follow.

1 Peter 1:12 usage 2
Unto whom it was revealed, that not unto themselves, but unto us they did minister the things, which are now reported unto you by them that have preached the gospel unto you with the Holy Ghost [pneuma] sent down from heaven; which things the angels desire to look into.

1 Peter 1:22 deleted
Seeing ye have purified your souls in obeying the truth ~~through the Spirit~~ unto unfeigned love of the brethren, *see that ye* love one another with a pure heart fervently:

Omitted in all critical Greek texts except Stephens, and also omitted in the Aramaic.

1 Peter 3:4 usage 2
But *let it be* the hidden man of the heart, in that which is not corruptible, *even the ornament* of a meek and quiet spirit [pneuma], which is in the sight of God of great price.

Hendiadys – spiritual peace is a fruit of the spirit.

1 Peter 3:18 usage 7
For Christ also hath once suffered for sins, the just for the unjust, that he might bring us to God, being put to death in the flesh, but quickened by the Spirit [pneuma]:

1 Peter 3:19 usage 4
By which also he went and preached unto the spirits [pneumata] in prison;

1 Peter 4:6 usage 7
For for this cause was the gospel preached also to them that are dead, that they might be judged according to men in the flesh, but live according to God in the spirit [pneuma].

1 Peter 4:14 usage 2
If ye be reproached for the name of Christ, happy *are ye;* for the spirit [pneuma] of glory and of God resteth upon you: on their part he is evil spoken of, but on your part he is glorified.

Hendiadys employed. It isn't God who rests on us, it is the gift of holy spirit he gave us that rests on us.

2 Peter 1:21 usage 3
For the prophecy came not in old time by the will of man: but holy men of God spake *as they were* moved by the Holy Ghost [pneuma].

1 John 3:24 usage 2
And he that keepeth his commandments dwelleth in him, and he in him. And hereby we know that he abideth in us, by the Spirit [pneuma] which he hath given us.

1 John 4:1 usage 2 and 4, usage 2 and 4
Beloved, believe not every spirit [pneuma], but try the spirits [pneumata] whether they are of God: because many false prophets are gone out into the world.

1 John 4:2 usage 2, usage 2
Hereby know ye the Spirit [pneuma] of God: Every spirit [pneuma] that confesseth that Jesus Christ is come in the flesh is of God:

1 John 4:3 usage 4
And every spirit [pneuma] that confesseth not that Jesus Christ is come in the flesh is not of God: and this is that *spirit* of antichrist, whereof ye have heard that it should come; and even now already is it in the world.

1 John 4:6 usage 2, usage 4
We are of God: he that knoweth God heareth us; he that is not of God heareth not us. Hereby know we the spirit [pneuma] of truth, and the spirit [pneuma] of error.

1 John 4:13 usage 2
Hereby know we that we dwell in him, and he in us, because he hath given us of his Spirit [pneuma].

1 John 5:6 usage 2, usage 2
This is he that came by water and blood, *even* Jesus Christ; not by water only, but by water and blood. And it is the Spirit [pneuma] that beareth witness, because the Spirit [pneuma] is truth.

When we demonstrate God's power, we demonstrate truth.

1 John 5:7,8 Omitted, usage 2
For there are three that bear record ~~in heaven, the Father, the Word, and the Holy Ghost: and these three are one.~~

~~And there are three that bear witness in earth,~~ the Spirit [pneuma], and the water, and the blood: and these three agree in one.

According to all critical Greek texts except Stephens, the text is to be amended as shown. The inserted words are a trinitarian forgery.

Jude 19 usage 2
These be they who separate themselves, sensual, having not the Spirit [pneuma].

Jude 20 usage 2
But ye, beloved, building up yourselves on your most holy faith, praying in the Holy Ghost [pneuma],

Revelation 1:4 usage 7
John to the seven churches which are in Asia: Grace *be* unto you, and peace, from him which is, and which was, and which is to come; and from the seven Spirits [pneumata] which are before his throne;

Revelation 1:10 usage 2
I was in the Spirit [pneuma] on the Lord's day, and heard behind me a great voice, as of a trumpet,

Revelation 2:7 usage 2
He that hath an ear, let him hear what the Spirit [pneuma] saith unto the churches; To him that overcometh will I give to eat of the tree of life, which is in the midst of the paradise of God.

Revelation 2:11 usage 2
He that hath an ear, let him hear what the Spirit [pneuma] saith unto the churches; He that overcometh shall not be hurt of the second death.

Revelation 2:17 usage 2
He that hath an ear, let him hear what the Spirit [pneuma] saith unto the churches; To him that overcometh will I give to eat of the hidden manna, and will give him a white stone, and in the stone a new name written, which no man knoweth saving he that receiveth *it*.

Revelation 2:29 usage 2
He that hath an ear, let him hear what the Spirit [pneuma] saith unto the churches.

Revelation 3:1 usage 7
And unto the angel of the church in Sardis write; These things saith he that hath the seven Spirits [pneumata] of God, and the seven stars; I know thy works, that thou hast a name that thou livest, and art dead.

Revelation 3:6 usage 2
He that hath an ear, let him hear what the Spirit [pneuma] saith unto the churches.

Revelation 3:13 usage 2
He that hath an ear, let him hear what the Spirit [pneuma] saith unto the churches.

Revelation 3:22 usage 2
He that hath an ear, let him hear what the Spirit [pneuma] saith unto the churches.

Revelation 4:2 usage 2
And immediately I was in the spirit [pneuma]: and, behold, a throne was set in heaven, and *one* sat on the throne.

Revelation 4:5 usage 7
And out of the throne proceeded lightnings and thunderings and voices: and *there were* seven lamps of fire burning before the throne, which are the seven Spirits [pneumata] of God.

Revelation 5:6 usage 7
And I beheld, and, lo, in the midst of the throne and of the four beasts, and in the midst of the elders, stood a Lamb as it had been slain, having seven horns and seven eyes, which are the seven Spirits [pneumata] of God sent forth into all the earth.

Revelation 11:11 usage 3
And after three days and an half the Spirit [pneuma] of life from God entered into them, and they stood upon their feet; and great fear fell upon them which saw them.

After the return of Jesus Christ to gather his saints, the old testament principles will again become the standards for life, and the same spirit from the old testament will once again be available.

Revelation 13:15 usage 4
And he had power to give life [pneuma] unto the image of the beast, that the image of the beast should both speak, and cause that as many as would not worship the image of the beast should be killed.

Revelation 14:13 usage 1
And I heard a voice from heaven saying unto me, Write, Blessed *are* the dead which die in the Lord from henceforth: Yea, saith the Spirit [pneuma], that they may rest from their labours; and their works do follow them.

Revelation 16:13 usage 4
And I saw three unclean spirits [pneumata] like frogs *come* out of the mouth of the dragon, and out of the mouth of the beast, and out of the mouth of the false prophet.

Revelation 17:3 usage 2
So he carried me away in the spirit [pneuma] into the wilderness: and I saw a woman sit upon a scarlet coloured beast, full of names of blasphemy, having seven heads and ten horns.

Revelation 18:2 usage 4
And he cried mightily with a strong voice, saying, Babylon the great is fallen, is fallen, and is become the habitation of devils, and the hold of every foul spirit [pneuma], and a cage of every unclean and hateful bird.

Revelation 19:10 usage 3
And I fell at his feet to worship him. And he said unto me, See *thou do it* not: I am thy fellowservant, and of thy brethren that have the testimony of Jesus: worship God: for the testimony of Jesus is the spirit [pneuma] of prophecy.

Revelation 21:10 usage 2
And he carried me away in the spirit [pneuma] to a great and high mountain, and shewed me that great city, the holy Jerusalem, descending out of heaven from God,

Revelation 22:6 usage 2 (added)
And he said unto me, These sayings *are* faithful and true: and the Lord God of the [pneumata of the] holy prophets sent his angel to shew unto his servants the things which must shortly be done.

Revelation 22:17 usage 1
And the Spirit [pneuma] and the bride say, Come. And let him that heareth say, Come. And let him that is athirst come. And whosoever will, let him take the water of life freely.

www.ingramcontent.com/pod-product-compliance
Lightning Source LLC
Chambersburg PA
CBHW071326080526
44587CB00017B/2746